POLITICAL THEORY

(PRINCIPLES OF POLITICAL SCIENCE)

For Graduation Courses and also useful for Competitive Examinations

V D MAHAJAN

MA (Hons.), LLB, PhD

Formerly Professor

History and Political Science

Punjab University, Lahore

and

Faculty of Law

University of Delhi

S Chand And Company Limited

(ISO 9001 Certified Company)

S Chand And Company Limited
(ISO 9001 Certified Company)
Head Office: D-92, Sector–2, Noida – 201301, U.P. (India), Ph. 91-120-4682700
Registered Office: A-27, 2nd Floor, Mohan Co-operative Industrial Estate, New Delhi – 110 044, Phone: 011-49731800
www.**schandpublishing.com**; e-mail: **info@schandpublishing.com**

Marketing Offices:

Chennai	:	Ph: 23632120; chennai@schandpublishing.com
Guwahati	:	Ph: 2738811, 2735640; guwahati@schandpublishing.com
Hyderabad	:	Ph: 40186018; hyderabad@schandpublishing.com
Jalandhar	:	Ph: 4645630; jalandhar@schandpublishing.com
Kolkata	:	Ph: 23357458, 23353914; kolkata@schandpublishing.com
Lucknow	:	Ph: 4003633; lucknow@schandpublishing.com
Mumbai	:	Ph: 25000297; mumbai@schandpublishing.com
Patna	:	Ph: 2260011; patna@schandpublishing.com

First Edition 1988
Reprints 1992, 95, 97, 99, 2000, 2001, 2003, 2005, 2006, 2008, 2009, 2010, 2012
Fifth Revised Edition 2013
Reprints 2014, 2015, 2016, 2021, 2022 (Twice), 2024 (Twice)

Reprint 2025

ISBN: 978-81-219-0369-1 **Product Code:** H5POL41PLSC10ENAE13O

PRINTED IN INDIA

By Vikas Publishing House Private Limited, Plot 20/4, Site-IV, Industrial Area Sahibabad, Ghaziabad – 201 010 and Published by S Chand And Company Limited, A-27, 2nd Floor, Mohan Co-operative Industrial Estate, New Delhi – 110 044.

Preface to the Fifth Revised Edition

The courses on Political Theory have been revised and made more comprehensive by a number of Indian Universities. This edition incorporates all the new themes and necessary corrections. Revised Edition is published in bigger size with new get-up. It is hoped that this edition will be even more useful to both the students who are preparing for various University exam or competitive exam.

Author

Preface to the Fourth Edition

It gives me great pleasure to place in the hands of the readers the new edition of the book on Political Theory. Not only the name of the book has been changed from "Principles of Political Science" to "Political Theory", the contents of the book have also been changed. A large number of chapters in this edition are new. The first chapter on "Political Theory", the second chapter on "Approaches to Political Analysis", the third chapter on "Methodology of Political Science", the fifth chapter on "The Nature and Scope of Political Science", the sixth chapter on "Politics and Society", the eighth chapter on "The Political System", the ninth chapter on "Political Culture and Political Socialisation", the tenth chapter on "Power, Authority and Legitimacy", the eleventh chapter on "Political Modernisation and Political Development", the nineteenth chapter on "Property", the twentieth chapter on "Justice", the thirty-third chapter on "Liberal Theory of the Nature and Functions of the State", the thirty-fourth chapter on "Marxian Theory of the Nature and Functions of the State", the forty-second chapter on "Democracy", the forty-third chapter on "Nationalism and Internationalism" and forty-fourth chapter on "Imperialism" are absolutely new. Many of the other chapters such as the twelfth chapter on "Origin of the State", the sixteenth chapter on "Rights and Duties" etc. have been re-written and new facts added.

This new edition contains a comprehensive study of the subject, with the latest thinking by the political scientists of the world today.

It is hoped that the book will be liked by all those for whom it is meant.

Dr. VIDYA DHAR MAHAJAN

CONTENTS

CHAPTER

Political Theory

For a long time, the necessity of political theory was hotly debated. The argument was that theory is an abstraction and hence its study is a waste of time without much utility. However, this view has changed. The view of Catlin is that the maturity and advancement of a subject is to be judged from the soundness and abstraction of that subject. David Easton has laid stress on the study of political theory. As a matter of fact, he was the person who drew the attention of political scientists in that direction. His contention was that a subject can advance only when its theory and research is regularly conducted. Moreover, changes in theory help in analytical study of the subject. Sub-disciplines in a discipline are created and developed only with the help of a good and sound theory. Political theory alone can get for political science an independent status. Political theory is responsible for producing and bringing out facts. Facts do not speak themselves unless some values are added to them.

Learning Objectives

- Definition of Political Theory
- Normative and Empirical Theory
- Empirical Political Theory
- Contemporary Political Theory
- Advantages of Political Theory
- Decline of Political Theory
- Political Philosophy
- Political Ideology
- End of Ideology
- Suggested Readings

Definition of Political Theory

The view of Catlin is that the word theory is like a blank cheque whose value is its utility and the way in which it is put into practice. Arnold Brecht has defined theory as a proposal which is expressed in terms of some data and supports some idea. Sometimes, the word theory is used as a synonym for speculation, idea or conjectures and therefore political theory is political speculation or philosophizing about political and governmental activity. We sometimes use the word theory to designate a conjecture about causal relationships or about the most effective means of promoting a given end. Thomas P. Jenkin writes, "A theory about anything is an abstracted generalisation. As such, it is primarily and initially a matter of mind rather than matter of fact. Such intellectualisations are not facts, no matter how closely they are related to or guided by facts."

Andrew Hecker writes in his "Political Theory" that theory has broadly two meanings. One of the meanings can be closely associated with traditional political approach, while the other with modern. In this traditional sense, he means history of political ideas, while in the modern sense this reference is to modern political behaviour and its scientific study. In one form or the other, the theorist plays the role of a philosopher and a scientist because in this theory he is bound to assign some place to facts and values, as both are complementary to each other. The view of Alex N. Dragnich and John C. Wahlk is that political theory includes philosophy, art and politics. Some thinkers are of the view that science and theory have no close relationship. It is not essential that every theory must be scientifically correct. Likewise, it is not necessary that every scientific analysis must have theoretical background or base. A factual research without scientific base can be scientific.

Some political scientists consider political theory as a field within political science just as they consider comparative government, public administration and international politics as its other sub-divisions. However, Vernon Van Dyke objects to that classification in these words: "The practice has an objectionable aspect in that it seems to suggest that books and courses in other sub-divisions go beyond their proper limits if any theory is included. If theory is taken to be synonymous with thought, this attitude becomes disastrous for the other sub-divisions". According to Catlin, politics can be divided into two parts, practice and theory. The view of Arnold Brecht is that science is inter-subjectivity transmissible knowledge and can be interpreted to have broad and narrow aspects. In the broad sense, science includes reasoning, intuition, self-evidence, religious revelations etc. In the narrow sense, science includes scientific methods, practical reasoning etc. In order to give political science the status of science, he takes into consideration only the narrow aspect and on that basis tries to build up the super-structure of political theory.

Political theory is concerned with two different types of knowledge. In the first place, it is concerned with political belief-systems of a general and comprehensive sort. Those belief-systems may be called ideologies. Secondly, it is concerned with political philosophy which is thought about political thought.

Karl Popper refers to theory as an interpretation or a "crystallization of a point of view." He believes that numerous complex sets of conditions produce political events. The political theorists may come forward with different types of explanations on the basis of specific approaches and at different levels of generalisation. Description and explanation are selective activities. A random choice of the data may be unsatisfactory and the alternative to it is "the adoption of either a point of view or an interpretation."

The theories in politics can be expressed at low, high or middle ranges of generality. V.V. Dyke compares a theoretical system to a tree whose outermost small branches represent the data or the facts with which we start.

Political theory is not merely an expression of the existing knowledge about politics. It may also direct the way to the acquiring of new knowledge. Scientific theory is a series of inter-related concepts and conceptual schemes arising from observation and experiment and fruitful of further experiments and observations. The test of a theory is its fruitfulness, its ability to suggest a policy which can provide guidelines in real life. Explanation is closely related to prediction. If theory is the consummation of explanation, it should be helpful in prediction. Given a theory, we should be able to make deductions from it concerning future events. We make predictions and advance theories in order to contribute to the rationality of decision-making. V.V. Dyke writes, "The scholarly purpose of theorizing may simply be to express knowledge and to help in enhancing it. The social purpose is to provide a basis for more reliable predictions on the basis of which rational choices can be made."

Prof. Frank Thakurdas writes that unlike political thought, political theory is the speculation of a single individual who is attempting to offer a theoretical explanation of political reality, namely, the phenomenon of the state. Every theory by its very nature is an explanation built upon a certain hypothesis which may or may not be valid and which is always open to criticism. What we know as the history of political theories (Sabine or Dunning) and a host of others who chose to engage in this difficult exercise, is nothing more than a summary of attempts made by thinkers from Plato to Oakeshott to unravel to us the mysteries of man's political life. The specific theories are so many models of explanation which may or may not convince us but to which we are not obliged to lend a ready intellectual acceptance of any of them as the final and true explanation. One explanation is as perfect or imperfect as another and as we have no universal criteria to judge, we are not in a position to pass a final judgment as to which one is most acceptable or most valued. We are also not obliged to accept any one of them as sheer consideration of the source from which it might have emanated however great that source may be.

Unlike political thought which is general and has no fixed form, political theory expresses itself through a treatise, e.g., Plato's Republic, Hobbes' Leviathan and Rousseau's Social Contract and many others are such treatises. Another attribute of this specific form is that it is discipline-based which means that a specific political theory propounded reflects the discipline of the writer. The phenomenon which theorists attempt to explain remains the same, viz., the phenomenon of the state in which and by which we live political life. However, the starting point of the theoretician is determined by his individual discipline. If the writer is a historian, his approach will be strictly historical like that of Sir John Seeley. If he is a sociologist, his approach will be entirely dominated by sociological principles like MacIver. If he is a jurist like John Austin, the theoretical explanation will be purely in juridical terms. We have the geo-political approach of writers like Hausofer and Mackinder, the biological approach of Herbert Spencer, the psychological approach of writers like Graham Wallas and Ginsberg or the theological approach of the Christian Fathers like St. Augustine and St. Thomas or thinkers like Plato, Hegel and Kant. That, in turn, may be entirely based on the metaphysics of Plato and Hegel or the ethical principles of Kant and Green. The result is that we are confronted by a variety of political theories, each distinguished by the discipline on which it is based. (Essays in Political Theory, pp. 5-6).

Normative and Empirical Theory

An important distinction is made between two types of political theories viz., normative or prescriptive and empirical or descriptive theories. The normative theory, in a general way, suggests the mode by which an imperfect political or social order could be made perfect. The thinker is expressing himself in the imperative mood and is primarily concerned with political values which are to be implemented in order to achieve harmony, stability and unity in our common political life. Much of the writings of the Idealist School from Plato to Bosanquet fall in this category. The same is the case with Hobbes and Locke. The thinker assumes the role of a reformer suggesting the path which might help mankind to overcome numerous obstacles which hinder the organised community from achieving peace and harmony. Plato's Republic, Rousseau's Social Contract and other great works are typical examples of a normative type of theorising.

In the normative approach, there is *a priori* commitment to certain ideals or values like liberty or social justice and speculation about the type of the state which can achieve those ideals. Normative theory implies "systematic thinking about the purposes of government". It is a kind of "practical philosophy as it relates to government." Normative theory begins by postulating or laying down certain self-evident truths or assumptions from which it proceeds to deduce or draw various inferences or conclusions. Plato postulated four natural classes of men and rule by a philosopher king. To Dante and Aquinas, the monarch was the image of the divine ruler of the universe. Rousseau began by postulating a general will which is not the actual or empirically observable majority will but the will of each individual as it ought to be. Hegel postulated a dialectical process which viewed the history of nations as the movement of ideas.

The normative approach starts with certain basic postulates, ideals or assumptions or values from which other postulates are deduced. It chooses not to concern itself with what was and is but prefers to contemplate on what ought to be. The normative approach focuses attention on ethical questions or values viz., the good order of society, the ends of the state etc. It is prescriptive and value-loaded.

Early political philosophers tended to build theory, but they had in mind contributions to ideal models rather than process models. They concentrated on describing the various parts of the model in terms of what it ought to be like rather than contenting themselves with trying to diagram what actually happened in the development, modification and carrying out of public policy. The ideal models were often built on systems of logic and were little constrained by existing observable factors. To the Greeks, politics was all that was concerned with the good life in a well-organised self-sufficient community. They did not limit their study to the formal structure of the state. Their society was less differentiated than ours. Law, customs, religion etc. were not as distinct as they are today. Their conception of politics included certain basic ideas: It called attention to the phenomenon of authority. The place of ethics in political life was essential to the Greek conception of politics which was the study of political values and the means of achieving them. The Greek view of politics as a field was extraordinarily a broad one. Plato and Aristotle conceived of the political art as involving almost every discipline in what we now call social sciences. The Greek view of politics was heavily and curiously culture-bound.

This conception of politics set the tone in a broad sense for centuries of political writing. This traditional way of using the phrase political theory—also called value theory—has been distinguished from causal theory. The former is what we usually think of as political theory. The latter is theory in the scientific sense of the term. Causal theory would be the body of laws or generalisations, established by scientific technique and with scientific vigour concerning political activity. Traditional political theorists do not show an interest in causal theory. They hold and propagate an image of theory "as narrowly engaged in and committed to the quest for an understanding of the way others have viewed it. Analysis of the moral rather than of the strictly empirical world has stood at the peak of theory's hierarchy of priorities."

George Kateb refers to four main characteristics of traditional political theory. (1) All the books, fragments or essays included within the corpus of political theory have a moral purpose. (2) Political theorists are interested in whole systems of politics. Their work seeks to provide the lineaments of a complete doctrine of government. They are not content with being partial. They are inclusive. (3) Political theory is sometimes called political philosophy. This is the quality of being philosophical. (4) There is the quality of being general. The political theorist does not let the problems facing him and his society exhaust his interest. His "writings are meant to be useful for future generations, not merely to endure as curiosities of thought...What defines political theory is an approach to political life that is moral (or normative) in intent, inclusive in scope, philosophical in procedure and general in relevance". (Political Theory, Its Nature and Uses. pp. 2-5).

Empirical Political Theory

The empirical or descriptive theory is primarily concerned with things like state structure, political process etc. as they are. The argument is that political institutions and political behaviour have to be described with as much scientific accuracy as possible. This type of study may be based upon observation or may refer to some universal constant attribute of human nature. A third variety of this may concern itself with purely external behaviour of the individual. The behaviouralists are obsessed by the fact that the quantitative assessment of individual behaviour, be he a voter or a legislator or a judge or administrator, might enable us to discover some general principles which may be valid in similar situations elsewhere. This approach precludes the incorporation of any value judgement in the study of institutional political life. The behaviouralists first want to explore a new kind of data which had not hitherto been attended to. They want to study politics by focussing attention on the individual and group behaviour and also what goes on in the political process and within political institutions. They advocate a new method. They insist upon survey researches and the application of statistics to the data observed and other field work exercises. They have invented many new interpretative categories largely borrowed from social sciences, particularly sociology and even to a certain extent from natural sciences. These concepts like elite, role, influence, decision-making, policy-making, systems, subsystems, structures and functioning of structures, political culture etc. have passed into the political literature of our times. These concepts are the essence of contemporary empirical political theory and are related to the type of question which the theorist has in mind. The neo-empiricists are concerned in drawing generalisations from the data collected and also constructing models through which the interpretation of political process can be made with scientific accuracy. All this is done with a view to establish a science of politics, to infuse a new spirit in the study of the subject and to make the approach realistic, scientific and precise.

It is worthy of notice that from Plato to the nineteenth century, the generally accepted approach to politics was the normative approach. However, in the early twentieth century men like Max Weber, Graham Wallas and Arthur Bentley gave an empirical dimension to the study of politics. Graham Wallas brought realism to politics by emphasizing the psychological dimension through his book "Human Nature in Politics" published in 1908. Max Weber contributed to the development of empiricism by a study of bureaucracy and by his separation of "what is to be done" (questions of ought) from the analysis of "what is happening" (questions of is). Bentley contributed to the new style of thought by elaborating the sociological dimension of politics and exploring "group politics" through his book "*Process of Government*" published in 1908. Since the 1940s, empiricism has come into its own with the rise of logical positivism, systems analysis and behaviouralism. The logical positivists insist on strict "physicalist" or behavioural methods, on the elimination of metaphysical terms and on the verifiability principle. They denounce unverifiable propositions and sentences as non-scientific and meaningless. By 1936, the growth of logical positivism seriously challenged the view that there can be any "objective truths" in political theory. The logical positivist position seriously affected political theory because many assertions in political theory are neither true by definitions nor they can be verified experimentally. Political principles are matters of individual preference. The implication of the positivist position is that political inquiry provides no basis for choice among ultimate values. If Liberals, Communists and others choose different values, the positivist can react emotionally but he cannot demonstrate that one set is to be preferred, over others except in terms of a still more ultimate set of values which in turn is simply postulated. However, philosophers today do not accept the logical positivist view that political values are meaningless and political evaluation cannot be rational but only subjective and preferential. Modern writers are paying attention to such problems as how value judgements are justified and how reasons are adduced in support of value judgements. Rationalist philosophers today give more importance to right reason as a source of knowledge than to verification by observation.

Systems analysis seeks to provide a value-free analysis of politics. A system is "any collection of real objects that interact in some way with one another." As Robert Dahl puts it, political system means "any persistent pattern of human relationships that involves, to a significant extent, power rule or authority". Systems can be of two types. One is organic or physiological (David Easton) and the other is structure and functions (Gabriel Almond).

Contemporary Political Theory

The object of contemporary political theory is to understand politics in the most comprehensive fashion possible, to discover the general pattern and order in political facts, to explain those facts adequately and to construct rules of political action based on that analysis. Contemporary political theory focuses research on actualities, that is, on the disclosure of facts and their relationships, basing its findings on painstaking observation and measurement. It favours the development of new language and new concepts in establishing intellectual links among its several sub-fields. Its exponents are largely responsible for the development and use of such concepts as power, political system, political socialisation and the like. These concepts cross traditional lines and their pursuit is essential to the attainment of what they believe should be the major goal of political theory: the building of a body of an empirical and enduring theory about political life. Whereas the classical political theory referred to moral or philosophical prescription and was interchangeable with political philosophy, contemporary political theory means a systematic, empirical and causal explanation of certain phenomena. Modern political theory is considered as "the master discipline whereby the science of politics is to be unified, systematized and empirical investigation oriented and guided." It is concerned as much with the analysis and investigation of ends as with the analysis and selection of means. It is much broader than the field of political methodology and analysis. Viewed in this way, political theory is neither prescriptive nor oriented towards an action. It is explanatory and oriented towards understanding. It is the tool of the seeker rather than the doer. It does not imply a set of facts, but is a process by which sense is made out of facts by relating and ordering them. The main concern of contemporary political theorists is to end political theory as an exercise in intellectual history and replace it by a search for the development of general principles which give meaning and life to political science.

Contemporary political theory is intended to offer an explanation of what politics is all about, a general understanding of the political world. It is becoming a discipline which can weigh the findings of statisticians, psychologists, historians and all the rest of the researchers and tie together, cross reference and contemplate to the end that meaning and significance may be obtained from the huge mass of data. It represents in political science what in other fields, such as economics or sociology, has been called general as against partial theory. David Easton writes, "In this function lies the truly creative and most rewarding potential of general theory, one that we can expect will assert itself increasingly in political science as theoretical inquiry acquires a deeper sense of security and a greater appetite for innovative boldness."(Varieties of Political Theory, p. 2).

Modern political theory is growing and developing. Political scientists do not care much for traditionalism. Political facts and happenings which might be available in any social science, are now seriously studied and given proper thought. Political theory now includes the study of circumstances and environments, individual and family.

Modern political theory is realistic. It puts emphasis on the inter-disciplinary approach. Objectivity has considerably increased in its study. Modern political theory has very liberally borrowed not only from social sciences but also from natural sciences. Scientific value relativism is closely linked and connected by which the researcher does not attach his values while reaching conclusions. Values do not influence the course of his study. In his behaviour, there is intellectual neutrality and integrity. He also tries to keep away from hyper-factualism. Modern political theorists establish close relationship between theory and research. Political theory is based on hard facts which are the product of research. The theory-building process has been considerably delinked from historical approach.

Modern political theorists are conscious of the autonomy of their discipline. Political scientists like David Easton, Catlin and Dahl have tried to make political theory as independent as possibly they can. They want to bring coherence between political theory and conclusions.

Modern political theorists want to see and develop political science as an important link in other disciplines so that it can give an important direction to different subjects. They want to have expertise in different fields and are quite conscious of autonomy. For that purpose, they have developed General Systems theory and systems approach. As such, all political scientists have recognised the value of political theory.

Modern political theory is still in formulative stages. At the present stage, it cannot be said how much time it will take to reach its maturity. However, this does not mean that development and advancement of political theory is impossible. All that can be said is that at this stage it is difficult to set any time-limit about its full advancement. Dimensions have already been fixed but values to be attached and solution of the problems, has yet to be done. The view of Michael Hass is that political theory is focussing its attention towards decision-making, political development and conflicts and integration.

Advantages of Political Theory

There are many advantages of political theory. It is most essential in making political science a discipline. The unity, maturity, predictibility and scientific character of the subject is dependent on it.

No subject can develop or grow without theory. Theory provides a framework of study and a direction towards research and collection of facts and data. It helps in deciding what is to be accepted and what is to be rejected. Like a compass, it gives proper direction. It is a very useful gauge in finding out the stage of maturity of the subject. It helps in giving scientific explanation. It is only with the help of theory that new fields can be discovered and new ideas developed which help political scientists to predict and anticipate about the happenings and the way things were likely to shape themselves in the future. A sound political theory is bound to provide a satisfactory understanding of all the important political problems. The view of Lenin was that without a revolutionary theory, there could not be a revolutionary agitation. Stalin also believed that theory alone could provide confidence and direction to Communism. Political theory is needed by the public to know about a form of government and the legitimacy of the rulers. The elite usually remain in power with the help of theory, whether they are otherwise educated or not. It is with the help of theory that such destructive tendencies which lead us towards war and help in the growth of individualism and nationalism in its extreme form, can be checked. In the absence of a good theory, natural and technical resources dominate the man and destroy him. Political theory helps in finding out what is being done to establish values and what political alternatives are being developed. It helps in establishing a balance between facts, happenings and human values.

According to David Easton, a political theory fulfils a number of functions. (1) It makes it possible for us to identify the significant political variables and describe their mutual relations. Without first taking up an analytical scheme, it is difficult to do so. However, if we have a theoretical framework to guide us, we can make our research meaningful and arrange our facts with a view to helping us to reach generalisation. (2) The existence and wide acceptance by workers in the field of a theoretical framework makes it possible for the results of the various researches to be compared, with the help of which one may not only be able to verify conclusions drawn by the earlier researcher, but also to point out the areas of research in which more empirical work is needed. (3) The existence of a theoretical framework, or a relatively consistent body of concepts, also helps in making our research more reliable. One may not claim at this stage that a theoretical framework can also help us in making predictions, but if facts can be collected in the light of a theoretical framework, if researches carried out by various researchers at different times and places can be compared in the light of that framework, and if reliable conclusions can be drawn, we can certainly reach a point where predictions may be successfully made.

Decline of Political Theory

It is generally claimed that the decline of normative political theory set in with the advance of science in the modern world and the revolutionary achievements of science and technology. Scientific discoveries contradicted the presumptions of natural law philosophers and philosophical-absolutists that there is a fixed fundamental order, an absolute reality which exists independently of human knowledge and experience and the function of knowledge is to reflect passively this objective reality.

David Easton has mentioned four main factors responsible for the decline of value-oriented political theory. (1) The first factor is historicism by which he means undue emphasis on historical studies or merely trying to understand the factual conditions. The contention of Easton is that throughout the nineteenth and twentieth centuries, modern writers did not use "the history of values" to stimulate new thinking or new values and that explains why since Karl Marx and J.S. Mill there have been no outstanding political philosophers.

(2) Two other movements of that period also contributed to the decline of normative political theory. Those are moral relativism and scienticism. Moral relativism is a movement that began with Hume but is best expressed by Max Weber and Conite. It emphasized the need for social scientists to be neutral between different values and treat them as mere expressions of individual or group

preferences based on the life experience of the individual or group. As values are not capable of being transplanted from one age or group to another, they cannot be treated as universal. If there are no universal values, there can be no universal theory.

(3) Another cause for the decline of political theory was "the craze for science". Political scientists and behaviouralists advocate the importance of studying what is actual behaviour and claimed it to be more important than the study of what ought to be. The view of Easton is that political scientists confused social theory with science and came to believe that the purpose of theory is merely to describe and analyse what is. They ignored the fact that the purpose of theory is to go beyond science and to provide justification to create commitment.

(4) Easton also attributes decline of normative theory to hyper-factualism, the obsession with facts, their mere collection and enumeration. Since the 1920s the main interest of political theorists shifted to the development of new techniques for the collection of data and for understanding voting behaviour, public opinion and legislative leadership. Easton describes this phase as "one of theoretical malnutrition and surfeit of facts."

Nothing can be more windy and empty, more dry and frigid and barren than such librications upon sovereignty as we find in John Austin and other writers. In his earlier works, Lord Bryce tried to lay emphasis on the fact that the study of facts was essential for scientific values, but later on, in his writings theory became subordinate to the accumulation of facts. On the whole, Bryce was satisfied in restricting himself to crude empiricism. That tendency changed when political scientists made an attempt to search researchable problems. New techniques for data collection were adopted and better sophisticated techniques were developed for a proper understanding of such problems as voting behaviour, public opinion etc. However, there was no theoretical orientation to their studies. There was no comprehensive view of politics to their studies and largely they confined themselves to the study of particular-problems. Easton writes, "Theory without facts may be a well piloted ship with an unsound keel. But pre-occupation with fact-gathering syphons away energy from seeing the facts in their theoretical significance and then the ultimate value of factual research itself may be lost."

Alfred Cobban believed that political theory is positively on the decline. In the past, an interaction had been going on in the West between ideas and institutions and both were inter-changeable, but in our own times such an interaction has ceased to exist. He does not agree with the view that a gap or stagnancy which had come in political theory in our times is not alarming because such gaps have been occurring in the past also. He is alarmed by the increasing influence of bureaucracy in the state and society on the one hand and military machine on the other and the influence which these two factors are bound to exert on political thinking. Although democracy is the dominant political idea in the West, yet there is no political theorist on democracy today. No attempt has been made by political theorists to recast democracy to suit the changing conditions. The result is that democracy has ceased to be a living political idea. This is evident from the fact that in the last century, Nationalism, Fascism, Nazism and Communism threw a serious challenge to democracy. To quote Cobban, "Coins can remain a valid currency even when they are worn quite smooth. Political ideas need periodical recoining if they are to retain their value."

The view of Cobban is that both bureaucracy and military organisations and machines are external conditions which have given a serious setback to political theory. If the argument is that external conditions are not responsible for the decline of political theory, internal conditions can be held responsible for that. That means that there is something wrong with the nature of political thinking itself. His own view is that there is something definitely wrong with thinking in political theory. An important reason is the lack of purpose among the political scientists. The contention of Cobban is that important political thinkers in the past like Plato, Aristotle, Burke, J.S. Mill, Bentham, Hobbes, Locke, Rousseau etc. wrote with a purpose. They were practical in their approach and wanted to change the political behaviour of their times. They supported or condemned the existing institutions and systems but never ignored contemporary facts of political life. They were men of purpose and passion. They preached and defended what they considered as morally right. The change in the contemporary political thinkers is due to the influence of the historical approach and scientific attitude. A historian has no other standard of values except success or power. This dependence on history has indentified political science with crude Machiavellianism. What was left by historians has been destroyed by scientists. Science may give us a magnificent technical equipment for going somewhere, but it cannot tell us where we have to go. It does not give us a sense of direction or a feeling of purpose which it is the responsibility of theory alone to give.

Germino is also of the view that political theory is on the decline. Partly that is due to positivism but an important cause for the decline is ideology or political doctrines. According to Germino, political theory has been for quite some time under the influence of intellectual forces and political movement and also craze for science. Germino has given important causes for the decline of political theory during the last about 150 years. According to him, one major and important cause of the decline was the ideological reductionism of Tracy, Comte and Karl Marx.

Isaiah Berlin and Seymour Martin Lipset attribute the decline of normative political theory to the triumph of the democratic social revolution in the West. Political philosophy thrives "only in a world where ends collide." However, democracy today is a universally accepted goal. To quote Lipset, "The age old search for the good society has been terminated, for we have got it now." On account of the triumph of the democratic ideal and the near universal consensus regarding the liberal democratic state, the age of debate about the ends of political theory is over. There is no theory because there are no arguments relating to ends. The arguments about means to achieve the end being scientific and empirical in character, those can be settled by observation and experimentation.

Generally those who speak of the decline of political theory have in their minds the philosophical political theory which is derived from general beliefs about the nature of reality, or ideological political theory which is not based on philosophical deduction but on "moral reflection, on elaborating and advocating conceptions of the good life and of describing the forms of social action and organisation necessary for their advancement." It is conceded that there is a decline in philosophical political theory and we hardly come across any attempt to derive political theory from ultimate principles. However, this does not mean that there is a real decline in political theory. What has actually happened is that political theory has been delinked from philosophy and "is instead being linked with empirical social inquiry." We no longer say men are created equal by God or are born equal, but simply relate equality to social needs. In that sense, political theory has not declined. What has happened is that it has undergone a transformation.

As regards the decline of ideological political theory, those who hold this view generally claim that today social change does not take place through ideological motivation, but is brought about by a process of bargaining and compromise. Robert Dahl and Schumpeter refer to this method of change as "incrementalism" which means change by increments or gradual change or piecemeal engineering. The view of Dahl is that democracy is not a rule by majority but a rule by minorities and the making of decisions is not the majestic march of great majorities but the steady appeasement of relatively small groups. However, it is contended that ideological theory has not declined or the age of ideology has passed. Writers like Berlin and Lipset say, "If classical political theory has died, perhaps it has been killed by the triumph of democracy." These writers overlook the fact that they have already assumed an ideological infra-structure of modern liberal democracy. They also overlook the fact that even incremental change through bargaining takes place only in an ideological context of liberal democracy which believes in bargaining and compromise. The view of Partridge is that it is not possible to dismiss ideological politics as an obsolete and irrational method of social change. Ideological political theory has not been replaced by incrementalism. The fact is that incrementalism is possible only because of the ideology of liberal democracy. On account of the rise of behaviouralism, ideology has gone below the level of general political controversy instead of being on the surface.

The conclusion is that normative political theory is not dying and cannot die. All that has happened is that political theory is delinked with philosophy and is instead being linked with empirical social enquiry which often takes place in a given ideological context. If we understand its function correctly, political theory can never die. The function of theory is to justify, produce commitment and clarify concepts and those things are necessary even today. We may not derive universal principles like equality from belief in God, but that does not mean that they have become invalid or superfluous. John Plamenatz rightly points out that every man needs some philosophy which gives order to life and helps him to find his bearings and normative political theory tries to meet that need. It provides man with a coherent system of values and indicates what should be done to live in conformity with them. It produces a hierarchy of principles (values) and tries to explain how men should use them to make their choices. Normative political theory provides man with a practical philosophy which can help him to go through life.

Political Philosophy

The term political philosophy signifies the logical analysis of thought about politics expressed either by political activists or critics and interpreters of the political process. By logical analysis we mean an attempt to indicate the constituent elements of the subject being investigated and also verification of the hypotheses of the political actors and interpreters about it. Arnold Brecht uses the term theory to denote philosophy in the above sense. A.R.M. Munay prefers to use the term philosophy for ideologies and belief systems. These terms are often used interchangeable.

Unlike political theory and political ideology, political philosophy has a wider purpose and deeper concern about man's political life. It deals with the nature and purpose of the state, the rights and duties of the people who inhabit it, the place of the individual in relation to the state and the ideal it ought to achieve. It also deals with the nature of political obligation, political disobedience, justice, equality and liberty.

Like a political theorist, the political philosopher seeks an explanation or offers one for the complex phenomenon of the state but his focus of attention is the enduring elements of political life and he endeavours to suggest how best the purposes of political life are to be realised. He is a seeker after truth and for knowledge based on truth. He is not concerned with a particular issue or problems that confront state and require immediate solution. He wants an enduring solution of the complexities of man's political life. He travels beyond the frontiers of a particular country or region. His recommendations are for all people and for all climes and may command universal significance transcending the immediate historical context which influences philosophy. The philosophy of all great political philosophers is their personal vision of the complexities of political life in their search for an ideal society of their way of thinking, they delve deep into the realm of imagination and create the web of an ideal model which may be different from the realities of life.

There is a distinction between a political philosopher and a political theorist. While every political theorist is not a political philosopher, every political philosopher is a political theorist. David Easton is not a political philosopher but a great political theorist. Political philosophy belongs to the category of normative political theory. The political philosopher is not concerned with giving an explanation of the collective phenomenon called the state. There are certain issues of man's political life which are perennial which will be always there as long as men choose to lead an organised life together and which may or may not be affected by the type of economic system he may choose to live by.

Political Ideology

In the words of Mark N. Hagopian, political ideology is "a programmatic and theatrical application of some grandiose philosophical system which arouses men to political action and may provide strategic guidance for that action." (Regimes, Movements and Ideologies, p. 390). Political ideologies are political ideas presented in a systematic and coherent pattern to achieve specific political goals through definite action programmes. Those are methodically formulated and are often related to a grand philosophical system. Their focus is basically on the distribution of political power which might mean both defence or change of the existing political structures and relationships. The main structural elements of ideology are its linkage with a grand philosophical system, its programme contents derived from its philosophy, its strategy of achieving the programmatic goal and the coverage of its following. Ideologies are not the values and attitudes of political culture. Fundamentally, they are "programmes for action and instruments of evaluation." Functionally, political ideologies seek to motivate people to action. Four important functions of ideologies are to evaluate distribution and exercise of political power and the working of political institutions, to rouse people to action and to mobilise political movements, to provide distinct language or vocabulary to facilitate the process of examination of political regimes and to "provide some mental organisation for the frequent confusion of political life."

The relationship of ideology to the political system depends on the nature of that political system and the nature of the ideology. For example, socialist regimes have based themselves on Marxism which apparently looks a more coherent, well-elaborated philosophical system that appeals to many minds as scientific. Liberalism is a very loosely formulated set of ideas expressed by many philosophers and scattered over numerous writings. Ideologies often assume the role of a saviour when societies are in crisis. At that time, people look around for ideas which can help them to understand the present reality and hold promise of a better future. Certain ideologies appeal to the public mind at certain periods. Ideologies differ in respect of their organisation of thought. Marxism is better organised than others. Classification of ideologies may be also made on the basis of their linkage with the political system. One can then build up a topology of ideologies with reactionary and conservative ideologies at one end and radical and revolutionary ideologies at another. The reformist ideology can hold a middle position. According to Alan R. Ball, most of the contemporary ideologies are "mainly the consequences of reactions to the French Revolution of 1789 and the Industrial Revolutions that dominated the nineteenth century." (Modern Politics and Government, p. 255). Ideologies have not remained constant. They change societies and are also affected by social change. New political realities have to be accommodated with the passage of time. Shifts in ideological positions are known to have caused splits in the ranks. The pro-changers are denounced as revisionists or reactionaries while those who cling to the original ideological position are considered the old faithfuls.

There is a distinction between political ideology and political philosophy. While all political ideology is political philosophy, all political philosophy may not have the attributes of political ideology. In the twentieth century, many ideologies are competing for man's loyalty and allegiance, for instance, Fascism, Nazism, Communism, Liberalism and Maoism. What is peculiar about political ideology is its dogmatic character. The ideologist compels us to believe that in his ideology lies the salvation of the country and it is the only pattern of organised living worth adoption, a kind of perfect political model. While the political philosophy of a thinker is open to criticism, scrutiny and analysis, the ideologue with his firm dogmatic manner is averse to any criticism or doubt regarding the truth which he thinks is embodied in the brand of ideology he is advocating. All ideologies are by nature averse to any sort of criticism or doubt regarding their validity. According to Marx, all political philosophy, whether it be that of Plato or Hobbes or Hegel, reflects a distinct ideology which the thinker is giving expression to. We cannot think of a political philosophy as something which is pure, free from any kind of partisan bias whether it is for or in defence of the *status quo* or is advocating change. However, ideologies demand complete intellectual acceptance and emotional allegiance from those who choose to follow them. That generates a kind of fanaticism and blind faith for which any sacrifice on the part of the individual is not too great. The lessons of Germany and Italy do not need repetition.

The view of C.B. Macpherson is that the revolutions and ideologies likely to be most important in the second half of the twentieth century are those of the under-developed countries. He has given his own notion of ideology which is in a neutral sense. According to him, liberalism, conservatism, democracy, Marxism, Populism, Nkrumaism, Pan-Africanism and various nationalisms are all ideologies. Ideologies contain elements of explanation of fact and of history, justification of demands and faith or belief in the ultimate truth or Tightness of their cause. They are less precise and systematic than political theories or political philosophies. They are necessary to any effective political movement or revolution because they perform the triple function of simplifying, demanding and justifying.

Bernard Crick, Aron, Popper and Camus identify ideology with totalitarian government. Western democracies are non-ideological because they are pluralistic. Soviet Russia and Nazi Germany should be called ideological states because they are ruled by a monolithic party machine.

Edward Shils suggests articles of faith of an ideological politician. Politics should be conducted from the standpoint of a coherent and comprehensive set of beliefs which must override every other consideration. Supreme importance is attached to one group or class. The nation, the ethnic group or the proletariat and the leader of the party is regarded as the supreme embodiment of virtue. Ideological politics spreads beyond the political sphere and includes religion, philosophical thought and even sexual and family life. The ideologue shuns the central institutional system of the prevailing society, feels no affinity with such institutions and thinks that membership in a parliamentary body or the acceptance of public office involves only an opportunity to destroy and overthrow the system rather than to work within it and improve it. Ideological politics is the politics of "Friend-Foe", "We-They" or "Who-Whom". Those who are not on the side of the ideological politician are considered to be against him.

End of Ideology

The ideological controversy between Marxism and liberal capitalism assumed a new form during the post-War era when some social scientists in the Western countries started advocating the end of ideology theory. The other terms used were "de-ideological" and "The twilight of the era of ideology." The end of ideology theory seeks fresh ways and means of defending the theory and ideology of liberal capitalism which is threatened by the general crisis of the capitalist system and the growth of the world revolutionary process.

The cold war character of the end of ideology theme is apparent from the fact that it was first discussed at a seminar organised by the Congress for Cultural Freedom, an association of Western intellectuals, in Milan (Italy) in September, 1955. The main issues discussed at that Congress were how the future of freedom in Western societies could be secured and what methods should be adopted to maintain free and open society. Most of the participants endorsed the view that there should not be any ideological conflicts in the free society. They maintained that there should be an ideological accord in society and ideological conflicts should be replaced by consensus on ideological matters.

Subsequent to that Congress, many other conferences of Western "Ideologues" took place and the theory was favourably discussed. Daniel Bell is the most powerful exponent of the theory of "end of ideology". He wrote his book "The End of Ideology: Why Exhaustion of Political Ideas in the Fifties." S.M. Lipset wrote his book "Political Man — The Social Basis of Politics." According to Bell and Lipset, the ideological issues dividing the left and right have been reduced to a little less or a little more economic planning and state control. It did not really matter in terms of actual policies whether a Labour Party or a Conservative Party was at the moment running a particular government. Raymond Aron developed the theme of end of ideology in his book "The Opium of the Intellectuals". To him, the end of ideology meant an abatement of revolutionary passion, a democratic-liberal consensus, eradication of a mythical consciousness and the end of Marxist influence on wide sections of the people, but mainly the intelligentsia.

From 1945 to 1955, there was a cold war between liberal and Marxist ideologies. Due to the cold war, the power and influence of the socialist ideology increased. It was during that period that the end of ideology theory developed. It emphasized the fact that the aim of both capitalism and socialism is to establish an industrial society. Both are two different ways to achieve the same aim. There is no fundamental difference between the economic structures of capitalist and socialist states as the state plays a dominant role in both the societies. Moreover, the nature of capitalism has changed and the contemporary Western societies are "post-capitalist societies". The socio-economic and political problems of industrial societies are the same. The technological and scientific developments have virtually wiped off the differences between the two societies. In Western societies, the working class has socio-economic and political rights and there is no exploitation of the working class in those societies. The capitalists and workers are equal partners in all affairs, including profits in industries. Class conflict is over and class harmony is an established fact in Western societies. The state belongs to the whole of the community and is devoted to welfare functions for the weaker sections of society. Through progressive taxation, it is redistributing incomes. Instead of unplanned and free enterprise economy, there is now regulated and planned mixed economy in Western societies. An overall supervision of the economy by the state is a well-accepted economic principle. The problems of both Western and socialist industrial societies are not economic or ideological, but purely and simply technological, scientific and administrative. In the industrial societies, the approach should be technical, rather than ideological. The main issue in industrial society is not that of social revolution but "social engineering".

A number of thinkers known as "new philosophers" has emerged in France and they also support the theory of "end of ideology". Their main view is that Marxist ideology has come to an end. M.L. Bris has written a book namely, "God is Dead, Marx is Dead and I am Not Feeling Too Well Myself." The new philosophers have criticised both liberalism and Marxism.

The theory is being supported on many grounds. The ideological differences between the different parties in the developed Western societies have vanished. The two major political parties in the United States and Britain do not have any ideological conflict and hence ideology has become meaningless in politics. The working class in the developed Western countries has adopted the bourgeois norms, values and life-styles and it has become bourgeoisified and does not believe in ideological conflicts. The idea of peaceful co-existence advocated by the Soviet Union implies mutual tolerance of liberalism and Marxism. The objectives of socialism have been partially fulfilled in the liberal societies and those have not been fully fulfilled in socialist societies as they have become bureaucratic societies and not classless societies. Both liberalism and Marxism have changed. Liberalism has changed in the radical direction and Marxism in the bureaucratic direction. The result of this change is that both the ideologies of liberalism and Marxism have lost their original positions.

The exponents of the "end of ideology" theory maintain that though ideologies have lost their importance in the developed industrial societies, they still have importance in the under-developed and developing countries of the Third World. Ideology is important in those countries on account of their socio-economic and political problems. To quote Lipset, in the countries of the Third World, "there is still a need for intense political controversy and ideology."

There are many critics of this theory. They point out that in a class-divided society, the economically dominant class may support the "end of ideology" theory, but the economically weaker and exploited working class wants a revolutionary change and hence is badly in need of an ideology. Without an ideology of its own, the working class cannot carry on its struggle for its improvement. For the working class, the end of ideology would mean the end of revolution, and the end of way to liberation. It will mean an everlasting bondage of the capitalistic industrial society. There is a great difference in the socio-economic systems and relations of production in the socialist and capitalist countries. In capitalist countries, the people have not received the benefits of industrialisation in a fair manner. Social and economic inequalities have become greater. Class division has become sharper. Hence, there cannot be any ideological accord. Hence, the end of ideology theory is wrong. It is incorrect to say that class struggle has come to an end in Western societies. There is the need of a revolutionary ideology.

One may say that the classical liberal ideology has come to an end but it is not correct that all ideologies have ended. The end of ideology theory is also an ideology and it has been advanced to maintain the status quo. It is opposed to all change. This theory will not end the crisis of capitalism. So long as society is class divided and class struggle is going on, there will be ideological conflicts. The end of ideology theory is irrational, anti-revolutionary and reactionary in nature. It is a thinly veiled form of bureaugeois ideology. It expresses the need of the ruling class in a liberal capitalist society to find ways of denying historical inevitability and the necessity of restructuring the social and economic system on socialist lines. The theory serves an ideological alternative to Marxist theory. The theory consists of a number of notions which are often fragmentary, unclear and contradictory. Ideology today is more important and a sharper instrument of class struggle than previously. No wonder, the Marxists are the severest critics of this theory. Even non-Marxist writers like Henri Aiken have criticised this theory.

SUGGESTED READINGS

Aron, R. : *The Opium of the Intellectuals,* 1955.

Ball, Alan R. : *Modern Politics and Government,* Macmillan, 1973.

Bell, D. : *The End of Ideology.*

Brecht, Arnold : *Political Theory,* Bombay, 1965.

Brick, Bernard : *In Defence of Politics.*

Catlin, George F.G. : *The Science and Method of Politics,* New York, 1927.

Cox, Richard H. (Ed.) : *Ideology. Politics and Political Theory.*

Dahl, Robert A. : *A Preface to Democratic Theory,* Chicago, 1967.

Doctor, Adi H. : *Issues in Political Theory,* Sterling Publishers, New Delhi, 1985.

Drucker. H.M. : *The Political Uses of Ideology.*

Dyke, V.V. : *Political Science — A Philosophical Analysis.*

Easton, David : *The Political System—An Inquiry into the State of Political Science,* New York, 1971.

Easton, David (Ed.) : *Varieties of Political Theory,* 1966.

Easton, David : *A Systems Analysis of Political Life.*

Galbraith, J.K. : *The New Industrial State,* London, 1967.

Gould, J.A. and Thursby, V.V : *Contemporary Political Thought,* New York, 1967.

Guild, Nelson P. and Palmer, K.T. : *Introduction in Politics,* New York, 1968.

Hacker, Andrew : *Political Theory,* New York, 1961.

Hagopian, Mark N. : *Regimes, Movements and Ideologies,* Longman, New York. 1978.

Jenkin, Thomas P : *The Study of Political Theory.*

Kateb, George : *Political Theory: Its Nature and Uses,* New York, 1968.

Lipset, S.M. : *Political Man.*

Mayo, H.B. : *An Introduction to Democratic Theory.*

Miller, J.D.B. : *The Nature of Politics.*

Moskvichov, L.N. : *The End of Ideology: Illusions and Reality.*

Qulnton, Anthony (Ed.) : *Political Philosophy.*

Roucek, Joseph S. : *Introduction to Political Science,* New York, 1954.

Schumpeter, Joseph A. : *Capitalism, Socialism and Democracy,* New York, 1950.

Swingewood : *Marx and Modern Social Theory.*

Thakurdas, Frank : *Essays in Political Theory,* Gitanjali Publishing House, New Delhi, 1982.

Waxman, C.I. (Ed.) : *The End of Ideology Debate,* New York, 1968.

Zeitlin, I.M. : *Ideology and Development of Sociological Theory.*

CHAPTER

Approaches to Political Analysis

Political problems have been subjected to different kinds of analysis from time to time. Various explanatory methods have been followed to increase our understanding of the things political. What we call approaches to political analysis are a variety of orientations to looking at the world of politics. An approach provides a framework for explanation and prediction.

Approaches to political analysis have been classified into traditional and modern approaches. Philosophical, historical and institutional modes of analysis are often associated with traditional thinking. Modern political analysis is supposed to be value-free, empirical and behavioural. However, this classification is a very crude one. The reason is that the modes of analysis which are now called modern often had their roots in traditional political thinking. Moreover, there is a degree of continuity in political analysis, both substantively and methodologically. In addition to traditional and modern approaches, there is also the Marxist approach to politics.

Learning Objectives

- Traditional Approaches
- Philosophical Approach
- Historical-Evolutionary Approach
- Institutional Approach
- Legal Approach
- Criticism of the Traditional Approaches
- Modern Approaches
- Behaviouralism
- Meaning and Definition of Behaviouralism
- Salient Characteristics of Behaviouralism
- Criticism of Behaviouralism
- Advantages of Behavioural Approach
- Behaviouralism Versus Traditionalism
- Post-Behaviouralism
- Systems Approach
- Structural-Functional Approach
- Input Functions
- Output Functions
- Communication Theory Approach
- Group Approach
- Decision-Making Approach
- Conflict Approach
- Public Choice Approach
- Political Economy Approach
- The Game Theory
- Inter-disciplinary Approach
- The Marxist Approach
- Khun's Paradigms
- Suggested Readings

TRADITIONAL APPROACHES

The traditional view of politics deals with the study of state and government in their various aspects. It includes a study of the organisation and activities of the state and principles and ideas which underlie political organisations and activities. It considers the problem of adjusting political authority to individual liberty, the relations among men which are controlled by the state and the relations of man with the state. It also deals with the distribution of governing power among the various agencies by which the actions of the state are determined, expressed and exercised and the problems of international life.

Till the outbreak of the behavioural revolution after the World War II, the study of politics was mainly dominated by the traditional approach. The traditional approach is an amalgam of views on the nature and functions of the state in human society expressed generally in philosophical and ethical terms. From the days of Plato and Aristotle, the great issues of politics revolved round the organisation and operations of the state and its relationship with society. The great issues raised and debated in traditional thought related to citizenship, the organisation and use of authority, the functions of the state and the legitimate fear of the state etc. Traditional thinking was characterised by a normative orientation. The questions of value were debated. No distinction was made between political and ethical questions. Political thinkers were concerned with "what should be the size of the state", "what is an ideal state" etc. Concepts like freedom and order were debated and were considered as desirable things. Writers like Locke and Rousseau gave their own views and preferences about human nature or state of nature. There was philosophical orientation in their thinking. They took keen interest in the description and classification of constitutions. Formal aspects of government such as the constitution, the election laws and organs of government were the objects of study. Emphasis was put on laws, rules and regulations which determine the structure and processes of governmental institutions. Traditional political thought made significant contribution to our understanding of government and politics. Even now, much of political thinking and governmental researches continue to have the traditionalist orientation.

Traditional approach can be sub-divided into philosophical, institutional, historical-evolutionary and legal approaches.

Philosophical Approach

As regards the philosophical approach, it is the oldest approach to the study of politics. According to Von Dyke, the word "philosophical" refers to thought about thought. A philosophical analysis is an effort to clarify thought about the nature of the subject and ends and means in studying it. The philosophical approach includes all the aspects of the activities of man. To quote Stephen Wasby, "For centuries the interest in the actual political activities of man was principally derived from a desire to find out why he did not live up to the ideal postulated in Natural Law or to postulate Utopias such as Plato's Republic, Harrington's Oceana, Hobbes' Leviathan and Butler's Erewhon. Other writers like Locke in his *Treatise on Civil Government* postulated the existence of state of nature which if not Utopias in the sense of what the writer preferred, were clearly intended to show an ideal in the sense of an abstract state of affairs portraying "pure" human nature.

Leo Strauss was the main advocate of the philosophical approach. According to him, "Philosophy is the quest for wisdom and political philosophy is the attempt truly to know about the nature of political things and the right or the good political order." For him, "values are an indispensable part of political philosophy and cannot be excluded from the study of politics". A political scientist must possess the knowledge of good life and good society. Political philosophy is an attempt to know both the nature of political things and the right or good political order. It is an attempt to replace opinion about the nature of political things by knowledge of the nature of political things. The view of S.P. Verma is that "political philosophy in this comprehensive form has been cultivated since its beginning almost without any interruption till very recently when the behaviouralists started raising disputes about its subject-matter, methods as well as functions and challenging its very possibility."

The view of Von Dyke is that the word philosophy has also been used in some other senses. "It may denote to arrive at truth sought, may be normative, descriptive and prescriptive. The object of philosophical inquiry is to establish standards of the good, the right and the just and to appraise or prescribe political constitutions and practices in the light of standards". According to Wasby, political philosophy is also a study of political ideologies. Political scholars like Hobhouse, Laski and Barker had their own conceptions of political theory. Many other scholars formulated or reformulated abstract theories based on religion, natural law etc. They had their own conceptions of political theory relating to rights, liberty, equality, justice, political obligation etc. Robert Lane writes in "Political Ideology" that political ideologies embrace a programme for the defence or reform of important social institutions and are normative in tone and content. The study of ideologies is not restricted to the study of ideas alone but also includes their impact and inter-relationship between ideas and political activity.

Leo Strauss was critical of the distinction which was being made between political philosophy and political science. According to him, originally, political philosophy was identical with political science and it was the all-embracing study of human affairs. Now we find it cut into pieces which behave as if they were parts of a worm. There could not be a non-philosophical political science or a non-scientific political philosophy. Strauss was also critical of both historicism and social science positivism advocated by Sabine and Catlin respectively. He laid stress on the philosophical approach to study politics.

Historical-Evolutionary Approach

Another traditional approach was the historical-evolutionary approach. It was one of the most important approaches to the study of political science. That approach is represented by Sabine in his book "A History of Political Theory". According to him, Political science includes all those subjects which have been discussed in the writings of important political philosophers like Plato, Aristotle, Hobbes, Locke, Rousseau, Bentham, J.S. Mill, T.H. Green, Kant, Hegel, Karl Marx, Lenin etc. Political theory includes factual statements about the postures of affairs that gave rise to it, statement of what may be roughly called "a causal nature" and statement that something ought to happen or is ripe and desirable thing to have happened. Political theories constitute three basic elements: the factual, the causal and the evaluative. Political thinkers do not deal merely with their age but with all ages. As such, they can study the history of ideas and institutions. Sibley says that a full comprehension of "political phenomena" would embrace an understanding of the way in which men in all ages and cultures have actually formulated and implemented public policy as well as the goals which they achieved, thought they were achieving, or thought they ought to achieve." For example, Plato and Aristotle throw light on the political structure, organisation, problems, assumptions and objects of contemporary political institutions. To quote Sibley, "If Greek city states are significant examples of ways in which men have been organised politically, then the classical political theorists certainly give us important clues as to their development and functioning. Platonism had a great impact on the late eighteenth and early nineteenth century thinkers—on Hegel, Rousseau and the Idealists. Among the modern writers who have been deeply influenced by Plato are H.G. Wells, R.H.S. Crossman, Warner Fite, Karl Popper and many others." The study of the old political theories is important not only from the point of view of their role in a particular period of history but also from the point of view of the contribution they have made to the political behaviour of society as a whole throughout history. History focuses not only on the past but also has a pronounced and general tendency to use chronology as an ordering device.

The historical approach also leads to synthetic and dynamic results. Fredrich W. Watkins writes, "By studying political thought as an integral part of a total historic context, it sets ideologies in meaningful relationship to all the other political and social forces operating at a given time and place. By placing these events in a moving stream of historical development, it provides the basis for an estimation of the possibilities of future change."

The evolutionary approach also deals with the historical growth of political institutions. It pays more attention to facts than the historians generally do Ancient Law (1861) and Early History of Institutions (1874) of Sir Henry Maine, Introduction to Political Science (1896) of Sir John Seeley, The State and the Nation (1919) of Edward Jenks, Political Institutions (1938) of E.M. Sail and The Modern State of R.M. MacIver all bear the impact of the historical approach.

Institutional Approach

The institutional approach is an old approach to the study of political science. Wasby writes, "While its roots extend back in time to Aristotle's description and classification of the constitutions of Greek city states, its place in the study of politics comes after the philosophical approach and it is still either the pre-dominant approach to contemporary study of politics or of equal rank with the much newer behavioural approach." Again, "The emphasis of the institutional or structural approach is almost exclusively on the formal aspects of government and politics." In this approach, political thinkers restrict the study of political science to political institutions. In that study, they include state, government, executive, legislature, judiciary, political parties etc. Somit and Tanenhaus describe the institutional approach as "a routine description and pedestrian analysis of formal political structures and processes, based on the more readily accessible official sources and records. Attention ranges from constitutions and other basic documents on which government is supposed to rest through the structure of legislatures, courts and executive branches, to the rules by which political parties are run, registration and election laws and the intricacies of different forms of municipal government."

The view of Almond and Powell is that the institutional approach is concerned with the study of the central governmental institutions and their legal aspects and opinions. Von Dyke writes, "The study of politics is the study of state or of government or related institutions. Those who define politics in this way are likely to ask questions calling for an examination of one or another aspect of institutional activity. Those taking an institutional interpretation have little difficulty in identifying the institutions with which they are concerned. A government for example as a whole is an institution and no doubt the name can also be properly applied to many of the agencies and the sub-divisions of the government, for example, the Congress in the USA." The institutionalists emphasise the study of institutions and structures, constitutions and basic documents, rules and regulations and various other similar things. Thus, politics is the study of the formal aspects (structures and institutions) of political activity. The institutional approach has been very popular in many European countries.

Legal Approach

As regards the legal approach, political thought tended to become increasingly subjective in the late nineteenth and early twentieth centuries. Almond and Powell point out that "the study of foreign governments during these decades continued largely all along formalistic lines. Perhaps it would be more accurate to say that there was some real intellectual deterioration in this field of study. For, historically, comparative government and political theory had been closely connected." That was due to three reasons. The people were led to believe that democracy would be successful everywhere and all that they could do was to study the constitutional framework of important democracies like that of the United Kingdom and the United States. If facts were to be studied, that they could do by studying constitutional and legal facts. That led to the study of the formal, legal and institutional structures of different countries. The constitutional or legal position of the King of England, his cabinet, the House of Commons, the House of Lords etc. were examined in detail. The view was that the formal institutions were more important than the individuals.

It is worthy of notice that the institutional and the legal approaches in politics are complementary and not contradictory. They are closely related to each other.

Criticism of the Traditional Approaches

Roy C. Macridis points out certain drawbacks in the traditional approaches to political science. This approach focussed analysis on the formal institutions of government to the detriment of a sophisticated awareness of the informal arrangements of society and their role in the formation of decisions and the exercise of power. This approach proved to be relatively intensive to the non-political determinants of political bases of governmental institutions. Comparison was made in terms of the formal constitutional aspects of the Western systems, *i.e.*, Parliaments, chief executives, civil services, administrative law etc. which are not necessarily the most fruitful concept for a truly comparative study. Except for some studies of proportional representation, legislation and electoral systems, the field was insensitive to hypothesis and verification. Even in the purely descriptive approach to the political systems, it was relatively insersitive to the methods of cultural anthropology, in which descriptions are fruitfully made in terms of general concepts or integrating hypotheses. This description in traditional political science did not readily tend itself to the testing of hypothesis, to the compilation of significant data regarding a single political phenomenon or a class of such phenomena in a large number of societies.

In spite of the shortcomings of the traditional approach to the study of political science, its influence is still continuing. There are a number of influential contemporary political thinkers such as Michael, Oakeshott, Hannah Arendt, Bertrand Jouvenel, Leo Strauss and Eric Voegelin who continue to defend and uphold the traditional classical political theory. Even the modern or behavioural political scientists feel the need of studying the role of political institutions in the study of politics.

MODERN APPROACHES

Partly as a reaction against the traditional approaches and partly in search of more scientific knowledge about politics, political scientists have in recent times suggested a variety of approaches. The first breakthrough came with the emergence of the behavioural movement in political science.

Behaviouralism

The behavioural movement in the field of politics owes its origin to the intellectual developments in philosophy and psychology in the present century. The writings of Pavlov in Russia and John B. Watson in the United States who wrote extensively on behavioural psychology and the writings in the field of philosophy by logical positivists influenced the behaviouralists in political science. The new trend witnessed its manifestation in the writings of political scientists who received inspiration from the essential nature of the behaviouralist movement. The period just preceding the World War I and falling between the two World Wars witnessed the increasing use of empirical and quantitative methods. In the early 1900's, studies to investigate voting behaviour, party identification and attitudes and opinions were also undertaken. The political behaviour approach became prominent in the 1920s. The prominent writers in the field included Graham Wallas of England and Arthur Bentley of the United States. The view of Graham Wallas was that politics without the study of psychology of the individual is meaningless. Bentley advocated the significance of the role of the groups. He advocated the study of the individual as a member of the groups.

The behavioural revolution received patronage mainly from the American political scientists although many European thinkers, psychologists, philosophers and social theorists also made substantial contributions in that field. Charles E. Merriam of the Chicago University is rightly called the intellectual father of the behavioural movement. He along with a group of political scientists began to develop methods of research derived from the methodology of psychology, sociology, economics and mathematics. In his Presidential address to the American Political Science Association in 1925. Merriam observed, "Some day, we may take another angle of approach than the formal as other sciences do, and begin to look at political behaviour as one of the essential objects of inquiry." The pioneering contribution of Merriam was enriched by the leading lights of the Chicago School as it is popularly known. They included V.O. Key, David B. Truman, Herbert Simon and Gabriel Almond. They began to emphasize strongly the behavioural approach to political science. George E. Catlin of the University of Cornell also contributed to this movement. A large number of European scholars shifted to the United States in the 1920s. They had the benefit of studying the messages of psychologists like Freud and sociologists like Max Weber. The result was that political scientists gradually moved closer to the methodology followed in psychology and sociology.

The behavioural movement gained momentum in the years preceding the World War II. The American political scientists began to use the quantitative data and statistical tables following the lead given by Stuart Rice and Harold Gosnell. In 1928, Franck Kent wrote the book, "Political Behaviour". However, he confined the use of this term only to news correspondents who should report the things which actually happened and not the way they are supposed to happen. Herbert Tingston wrote in 1937 the book entitled "Political Behaviour—Studies in Election Statistics". Despite the use of sophisticated techniques, the influence of the traditional methodology was found in those writings. Harold Lasswell's contribution was noteworthy. His content-analysis and psycho-analytical theory were some of the notable contributions to the behavioural movement. Developments in techniques of survey design, sampling, interviewing, questionnaire design and personality measurement during the 1930s and 1940s further strengthened the movement. The political scientists were more interested in the field of comparative government and political behaviour than public law and political theory.

The behavioural approach became the order of the day after the World War II. The behaviouralists made significant contributions to political science during that period. A number of writers like Gabriel A. Almond, Robert A. Dahl, David Easton, Harold Lasswell and Karl Deutsch evolved a large number of theoretical frameworks and research designs. They tried to build up empirical or causal theory. In the early fifties, the systems approach, the decision-making theory and the focus on communication became popular among the American political scientists. It is also contended that behaviouralism became very prominent in the United States after the World War II in order to counter the spread of Communism. It was realised that under the political and ideological impact of the Soviet Union, the nature and character of the political system of several East European countries experienced a change from landed aristocracy to socialist democracy. That was the reason why political scientists, especially from the United States, needed new approaches and new techniques of research which they borrowed from other disciplines. There was also a change in the methodology of analysing political phenomena in Britain and elsewhere though it was not so extensive as in the United States. The works of Myron Weiner, Sidney Verba, G.B. Powell and David Apter made a substantial contribution to the behavioural revolution.

Meaning and Definition of Behaviouralism

The behavioural approach was a protest movement within political science because the political scientists in the United States were thoroughly dissatisfied with the achievements of the traditional study of political science. They believed that the traditional approaches totally neglected the political phenomena. In their view, the abstract study of political institutions such as the state and government was not adequate and additional methods could be developed which may yield better results. Hence, they advocated a careful study of the political phenomena which could be done through the behavioural method. Behaviouralism emphasises scientific, objective and value-free study of political phenomena as conditioned by the environment, particularly the behaviour of the individuals involved in that phenomena.

According to Robert A. Dahl, behaviouralism is "a protest movement within political science associated with a number of political scientists mainly Americans" who shared "a strong sense of dissatisfaction with the achievements of conventional political science, particularly through historical, philosophical and the descriptive institutional approaches" and "a belief that additional methods and approaches either existed or could be developed that would help political science with empirical propositions and theories of a systematic sort, tested by closer, more direct and more vigorously controlled observations of political events." It is a movement for "bringing political studies into closer affiliation with theories, methods, findings and outlooks in modern psychology, sociology, anthropology and economics and is an attempt to make the empirical component of political science more scientific." Behavioural approach "is an attempt to improve our understanding of points by seeking to explain the empirical aspects of political life by means of methods, theories and criteria of proof that are acceptable according to canons and assumptions of modern political science."

The view of Heinz Eulou is that "modern behavioural science is eminently concerned not only with the acts of man but also with his cognitive, effective and evaluative process. Behaviour in political field refers not simply to directly or indirectly observable political action but also to those perceptual motivational and attitudinal components of behaviour which made for man's political identification, demands and his system of political benefits, values and goals."

David B. Truman writes, "Roughly defined, the term political behaviour comprehends those actions and interactions of men and groups which are involved in the process of governing." According to Truman, research in behavioural political science must be systematic and primary emphasis should be put on empirical methods. Systematic research involves a precise statement of hypothesis and a rigorous rendering of evidence. While political science should be ready to learn from other social sciences, there should not be indiscriminate borrowing.

David Easton observes that "the behavioural researcher wishes to look at the participants in the political system as individuals who have the emotions, prejudices and pre-dispositions of human beings as we know them in our daily lives." Again, "Behavioural research seeks to elevate the actual human being to the centre of attention. Its premise is that the traditionalists have been reifying institutions virtually looking at them as entities apart from their component individuals."

Vernon Van Dyke says, "The term political behaviour in its lexical meaning denotes all human political activity. In this sense, the study of political behaviour is the study of politics, and not the study of a sub-division or aspect of politics."

Prof. R.N. Gilchrist writes, "The peculiarities of this new approach are that "(*a*) the unit (behaviour of persons) firstly is subjected to a theoretical and empirical analysis rather than a simple study of structures, institutions and ideologies; and (*b*) this approach is carried on within the framework of other disciplines, namely psychology, sociology and cultural anthropology. This inter-disciplinary approach focuses concern with the individual behaviour which is part of the total ethos."

The names of some of the important behavioural political scientists are Max Weber, Arthur Bentley, Graham Wallas, Robert A. Dahl, David Easton and Heinz Eulau. They describe the traditional approach as descriptive empiricism. Scholars like Lord Bryce are criticised for giving brute facts. They advocate the use of precision techniques for observing, tabulating and measuring data. Statistical and mathematical formulations are also used if necessary. They also employ interview-cum-survey techniques. They are also interested in the study of comparative government, local government, international relations, constitutional law and public administration by behavioural techniques.

The behavioural approach is different from the historical, legal or other approaches only in its orientation and not in objectives. It is pragmatic, catholic and eclectic. It is based on positivism and induction. It puts emphasis on the study of the behaviour of individuals and groups and not abstract principles. "Political behaviour is assumed to be a function of personality, social organisation and society." According to the behaviouralists, "Political institutions are behaviour systems of action" which have no existence apart from individuals.

The basic elements of political behaviour are "leadership, political groupings, public opinion, representation, party organisation and the use of economic, psychological and coercive pressures in politics all of which occur very generally, on all levels of government, in all political institutions and in pursuit of all kinds of goals." The political behaviouralists give great importance to the study of leadership as the influence of the leader is paramount in every community, association, group, lobby and political party.

According to Leslie Lipson, "The behavioural method records the details of what men do, seeking to explain why they do.. Politics is defined as a decision-making process. The political scientist examines the persons who make the decisions, how they make them and why. The passions that permeate the subject he considers with clinical detachment of a doctor and charts with dispassionate neutrality."

Behaviouralism is a sort of a protest movement against the inadequacies of conventional political science. It has shifted its emphasis from the ideal state, government and political institutions to the day to day problems of the people and new methods of study and research have been developed for that purpose. Behaviouralism has made the individual as the centre of attention in the study of political phenomena. It lays emphasis on the special importance of a scientific outlook and objectivity. It stands for value-free science of politics. Some scholars consider behaviouralism as nothing but a methodological revolution in political science. The behaviouralists advocate the techniques of observation, interviews, survey, research, case studies, data collection, statistical analysis, quantification etc They draw frequently from natural sciences such as Mathematics, Statistics, Physics, Biology etc. The political behaviour of an individual is a part of total social behaviour of all the individuals and hence the necessity of studying all those aspects. Eulau Writes, "As man's political behaviour is only one of his total behaviour as a social being, political behaviour analysis must be inter-disciplinary. It cannot neglect the wider context in which political action occurs. It is bound, therefore, to consider the possible effects of social, cultural and personal factors on political behaviour."

Salient Characteristics of Behaviouralism

David Easton has given certain salient characteristics of behaviouralism. Those are regularities, verifications, techniques, quantifications, values, systematization, pure science and integration.

(1) *Regularities.* As regards regularities, there are certain discernible uniformities in political behaviour which can be expressed in generalisations or theories in order to explain and predict political phenomena. Political behaviour is more or less similar in certain respects under given cirumstances. The task of the researcher is to find out the existence of regularities. That will help to explain and predict the political phenomena and ultimately make political science a truly scientific discipline with explanatory and predictive value. Political science may not be comparable to Physics and Chemistry in regard to the exactness of its results but it can be compared with astronomy or biology.

(2) *Verification.* The behaviouralists do not accept anything as guaranteed as the traditionalists did. They do not believe in abstract theories. They insist on verifying and testing everything. What cannot be verified or tested is merely dogmatic and not scientific.

(3) *Techniques.* The behaviouralists put emphasis on the mechanisms that facilitate acquisition and interpretation of data for making an objective analysis. They put emphasis on the use of those research tools and methods which can generate valid, reliable and comparative data. A researcher must make use of sophisticated tools like sample surveys, mathematical models, simulation, multi-variate analysis etc. They insist on neutralising the effects of personal judgement and values of the researcher concerned in planning, executing and assessing his own research. Rigorous means should be employed for observing, recording and analysing data.

(4) *Quantification.* The researcher must not only collect the data but also measure and quantify the same. Quantification and measurement are absolutely essential. To quote David Easton, "Precision in the recording of data and the statement of their findings requires tables, graphs and curves are drawn in behavioural research."

(5) *Values.* Behaviouralists believe in separating facts from values. In order to be valid, scientific inquiry must be free from ethical or moral orientations. In order to be objective, scientific inquiry must be value-free. Political science is a scientific study of politics in its functional aspect and has nothing to do with moral or ethical questions.

(6) *Systematization.* The behaviouralists believe that research in political science must be systematic. It must be theory-oriented and theory-directed. Theory and research should form part of a closely inter-related, coherent and orderly body of knowledge. Theory should be of causal nature. It should consist of analysis, explanation and prediction and not speculation and introspection. "Research, untutored by the theory may prove trivial and theory, unsupported by data, futile."

(7) *Pure Science.* The behaviouralists insist on what they call "pure science" approach. Research should be of a pure type. It should be perfectly verifiable by evidence. It may or may not be applicable to a specific social problem.

(8) *Integration.* The behaviouralists advocate inter-disciplinary approach. They do not treat political science as a separate and distinct discipline. According to them, political science is one of the social sciences and hence should be integrated with other social sciences like psychology, sociology and economics. Political behaviour can be studied only by understanding how other social, economic and cultural factors influence it.

Kirkpatrick has given the following main characteristics of behavioural analysis in political science :—

(1) Behavioural analysis rejects political institutions as the basic unit for research and identifies the behaviour of individuals in political situations as the basic unit of analysis.

(2) It identifies 'social sciences' as behavioural sciences and emphasises the unity of political science with the social sciences so defined.

(3) It advocates the utilisation and development of more precise techniques of observing, classifying and measuring data and urges the use of statistical or quantitative formulations wherever possible.

(4) It defines the construction of systematic, empirical theory as the goal of political science.

Heinz Eulou also refers to four characteristics of behaviouralism. According to him, behaviouralism concentrates on the theoretical and empirical analysis of the behaviour of persons and social groups and not on the origin of the state, functions of the government and political institutions. It tries to integrate theory and research in relation to social psychology, sociology and cultural anthropology. It emphasises the inter-dependence of theory and research. It tries to develop rigorous empirical research methodology and applies it to political problems arising out of the behaviour of individuals.

Criticism of Behaviouralism

The Behavioural approach has been criticised on many grounds. It is pointed out that in their craze for a pure science of politics, the behaviouralists have committed serious errors. Wasby criticises behaviouralists on the ground that they attach too much importance to techniques and methods and not to the subject. They select only those topics for research in which better techniques are available and ignore the rest even if those are more important than the topics on which they conduct their researches.

Political phenomena cannot be subjected in any rigorous study because those are very complicated. It is very difficult to study human behaviour, whether individual or group behaviour. Political phenomena are the result of an interplay of a number of variables and historical contingencies and hence difficult to generalise them. Human beings behave differently under similar circumstances and are motivated by different reasons.

Value-neutrality position is untenable. Researchers have their value preferences which inevitably influence their researches.

An over-emphasis on the inter-dependence of political phenomena and other aspects of individual behaviour may prove dangerous because that would result in an undesirable loss of identity, integrity and autonomy of political science.

The quantification of political phenomena is an unattainable goal and only very trivial questions can be measured. Most of the phenomena in politics are by nature unquantifiable and immeasurable. The observability of political phenomena is very much limited and hence for a comprehensive understanding of political phenomena one has to go beyond observable behaviour.

It is not possible to apply methodology of the natural sciences to the study of human behaviour. Controlled experiments are of limited value in political analysis. The objects of study — human beings — are not passive and they are not fully understandable through the study of apparent and observable behaviour.

Leo Strauss writes about behaviouralism, "The break with the commonsense understanding of political things compels the new political science to abandon the criteria of relevance that are inherent in political understanding. Hence, the new political science lacks orientation regarding political things; it has no protection whatever, except by surreptitious recourse to commonsense, against losing itself in the study of irrelevancies."

Sibley observes, "We are not questioning the proposition that behaviouralism in its several forms has an important contribution to make in the study of political things. We do question, however, whether the behavioural approach is adequate in itself for an understanding of politics."

Wasby says, "The fact that almost all early studies of voting behaviour took place in the United States or within single communities or states made it easy for researchers to forget the possible effects of institutional environment on electoral activity."

Bertrand Jouvenel write, "The instability of behaviour is a great difficulty for political provision. We know, of course, that a man's behaviour is variable but in no realm it is as variable as in the political field."

Joyce Mitchel writes, "The behaviouralist is engaged in great numbers game literally and figuratively. In the former stance, he seems to believe that nothing is meaningful unless it has been reduced to statistics or equations. In the figurative sense, he is common for he confounds the innocent especially businessman, with his special form of magic and numbo jumbo."

The behavioural approach seems to be indifferent to moral values in its over-enthusiasm to make political science absolutely positive and empirical. Leslie Lipson refers to the danger of relying on facts alone without making any reference to moral values in these words, "The amassing of details concerning how men behave is a dead weight of intellectual slumber unless it suggests how men ought to behave. The factual data of politics must be judged and appraised by moral criteria." Likewise, Peter Odegard observes, "In general, contemporary behaviouralists eschew concepts of what *ought* to be or even of what *could* be were people of a mind to have it so. To be scientific, they seem to say, one must be neutral among values and indifferent to the outcome of the great game of politics. It is this posture, as much as anything, that accounts for the failure of the behavioural frame of reference to give new life and new direction to political science."

The behaviouralists lower the status of political science as an independent social science. Some even fear that the subject of political science as an autonomous social science may die. The subject becomes a satellite of sociology and the emphasis of study is shifted from governments to political parties, voting behaviour, public opinion etc.

Advantages of Behavioural Approach

In spite of criticism, behaviouralism has made its own contribution to political science. The achievements of the movement can be seen in the theory-building and techniques of research. There has been a refinement of tools and techniques of research in the fields of content-analysis, case-analysis, interviewing and observation and statistics. In the light of the general systems approach, a number of new approaches in the field of political science have been evolved such as structural-functionalism and input-output analysis. The behaviouralists also make use of new approaches like decision-making approach, the game theory, the field model etc.

The behaviouralists have shown that it is possible to conduct studies in political science in a more scientific and realistic manner. Peter H. Odegard writes, "Because behaviouralist subordinates imagination to observation and metaphysical abstractions to observed realities, he has carried political science another step in the direction of becoming what Auguste Comte hoped it might some day be a positive science." (Political Power and Social Change, p. 54).

The behaviouralists have thrown much light on important matters like "the quality of political participation, the intensity of political preference or the individual's orientation to political action." Problems of leadership, voting pattern, role of parties, lobbies and pressure groups and political attitude, prejudices and preferences have been investigated by the behaviouralists. The result is that we now have a lot of useful scientific and analytical data in individual and group behaviour. Peter Odegard observes, "The development of improved procedures for sampling, interviewing and observing populations and for the coding and analysis of data, have added new dimensions of nearly every aspect of political science. New data-processing equipment has speeded up the accumulation of knowledge concerning political behaviour by a factor not easily estimated." (Ibid).

The acceptance of the behavioural approach by many political scientists and rejection by a few has created useful controversy and thought provocation. Political science is a dynamic discipline and it has been made more so by the behaviouralists. Peter Merkl writes, "The more recent wave of methodological innovation in political science, the behavioural approach had been beating on the ramparts of the established methods of political science for the last decade and a half and has now been generally accepted and integrated into the discipline. There is hardly a doubt that the conflict and challenge to accept new ideas brought about the waves of innovation of great benefit to the development of the discipline." (Political Continuity and Change, p. 22).

Behaviouralism Versus Traditionalism

Behaviouralism started as a protest movement against the traditional approach and the traditionalists find fault with the behavioural approach. They criticise each other and the outcome is a synthesis of the two.

The behaviouralists criticise the traditionalists on many grounds. They point out that the traditionalists concentrate mainly on theory. They are "idle spectators about human nature, novel gazers and essayists." The traditional approaches are not relevant to the current and contemporary issues. The traditionalists take into account only bigger issues of a general nature and ignore the small problems which actually trouble society. The traditionalists are regarded as primarily interested in recording the uniqueness of the world, values and not in the construction of a scientific body empirically verified propositions. Their search for 'meaning', 'insight', 'essence' is regarded as old-fashioned and primitive. The traditionalists use literary and metaphorical language to prove their thesis but that is against empirical and scientific conclusions. The historical approach among the traditionalists excludes the study of society and concentrates only on the origin and development of the state, government and political institutions and hence they do not do full justice to political science. The philosophical approach of the traditionalists is based on ideal speculations and ignores the actual political phenomena. The traditionalists ignore the political behaviour of individuals and the sociological environments which usually condition political phenomena. The institutionalists among the traditionalists concentrate on the origin and growth of political institutions, but they ignore the fact that institutions are actually run by individuals and their working is moulded by their behaviour. The traditionalists concentrate on national institutions and ignore the study of international institutions and problems.

The traditionalists also criticise the behaviouralists on many grounds. They point out that the behaviouralists take only a mechanical view of man and ignore human values and norms. They concentrate their attention on petty problems and group behaviour and not only ignore the bigger issues of the world but also do not pay any attention to basic ideas and values. They attach too much importance to techniques and do not bother about results. Instead of studying the problems facing the Third World, they have chosen only those subjects for research for which better techniques are available in the United States. The behaviouralists give attention only to statistics and not to ideals. The study of politics can never be value-free as advocated by the behaviouralists. Politics cannot be separated from value. The analytical method followed by the behaviouralists is defective because they consider American institutions to be the best in the world. The behaviouralists are biased in favour of democracy and the *status quo.* They advocate American interests and not universal interests. As a results of too much dependence of the behaviouralists upon other social sciences, political science has lost its identity.

Post-Behaviouralism

For a time, the behavioural movement created a crisis within the discipline of political science and it almost divided the political scientists into two warring camps of behaviouralists and traditionalists. However, there was a realisation among the political scientists that the subject-matter of political science was so complex that it was futile to think of its systematic and orderly study with the help of one single approach. A behaviouralist must concede that the study of man in the societal context was a far more complex pursuit than the study of objects in the natural sciences. David Easton who himself at one time was an ardent supporter of behaviouralism, made a serious attack on the research techniques of the behaviouralists. In his Presidential address to the annual Convention of the American Political Science Association held in 1969, David Easton declared that "he felt dissatisfied with the political research and teaching made under the impact of behaviouralism. The behavioural approach was trying to convert the study of politics into a discipline based on the methodology of natural sciences. Mathematics was making its way in political science to the extent that it began to look more of Mathematics than a science related to the realities of social life. In their efforts at research and application of scientific methods, the behaviouralists have gone far away from the realities of social behaviour. In this way, political science again lost touch with the current and contemporary world."

There was general dissatisfaction with the achievements of behaviouralists as they had failed to solve any practical problems of the world. Hence, post-behaviouralism arose as a protest movement against behaviouralism. The post-behaviouralists complain that the behaviouralists had not taken into account serious social maladies and the growing danger of a nuclear and thermo-nuclear war. It was contended that it was no use to develop highly technical and sophisticated research tools if the political scientists were not able to understand contemporary social and political problems.

The post-behaviouralists opposed the efforts of the behaviouralists to make political science a value-free science. David Easton maintained that the role of the intellectuals had been and must be to protect human values and the behaviouralists should concentrate on it. Dwight Waldo wrote, "Political scientists should be more concerned with values, with issues of justice, freedom, equality with political activity. In a period of stress, turmoil and gross inequalities, it is irresponsible to carry on as usual any academic detachment. At minimum, political scientists need to be concerned with issues of public policy and political reform." It was contended by the post-behaviouralists that political science must be relevant to society and it must deliberate over basic issues of society such as justice, liberty, equality, democracy etc.

Post-behaviouralism is both a movement and an intellectual tendency. The post-behavioralists are not confined to any particular section or society. Its followers can be found among all the sections of society. Although the post-behaviouralists prefer behavioural approach, they want to link their methods of research in making such theories which may be able to solve the present and future problems of society. David Easton points out that the post-behavioural revolution is future-oriented. It does not seek to return to some golden age of political research or to conserve or even to destroy a particular methodological approach.

David Easton has stated seven major characteristics of post-behaviouralism and described them as "The Credo of Relevance" or a "distillation of the maximal image." According to David Easton, substance must have precedence over technique. It is good to have sophisticated tools for investigation but we must not forget the purpose for which those tools were applied. Research was not worthwhile unless it was relevant and meaningful for solving the social problems of contemporary society. The view of the behaviouralists was that it was better to be wrong than vague, but the view of the post-behaviouralists is that it is better to be vague than non-relevantly precise.

The view of the post-behaviouralists is that political science should put emphasis on social change and not social preservation as the behaviouralists were doing. The behaviouralists had lost touch with the brute realities of politics and post-behaviouralism arose to find out a solution of the ills of society and mankind.

According to Austin Ramney, the post-behaviouralists put emphasis on substance instead of on method. They emphasize relevance and press for radical social change. The new revolution of post-behaviouralism is not anti-behaviouralism.

David Easton is dissatisfied with the attitude of the behaviouralists in putting emphasis on metholodogy and not on the problems and ills of society. To quote him, "Must we be committed eternally to an unchanging image of the discipline, behavioural or otherwise? Is it not incumbent on us to take account of changing conditions and to be ready and willing to reconsider old images and modify them to the extent deemed necessary?"

Post-behaviouralism is a reform movement. According to David Easton, the political scientist should "take the initiative by calling for the establishment of a federation of social scientists. The tasks of such a federation would be to identify the major issues of the day, clarify objectives, evaluate action taken by others, study and propose alternative means and press those rigorously in the political sphere."

The post-behaviouralists stand for action-oriented research relevant to social conditions. David Easton writes, "The battlecries of post-behaviouralism are relevance and action, its objects of criticism are the disciplines, the professions and the universities. It appears to be a specific and important episode in the history of our discipline, if not in all of the social sciences."

Post-behaviouralism is future-oriented. It seeks to propel political science in new directions. It adds but does not deny its past heritage. It is a genuine revolution and not a reaction. It is a reform and not a counter-revolution. The post-behaviouralists accept the achievements of the behaviouralists but seek to push political science farther and forward in the new direction. Research in political science must relate to the study of the relevant social and political problems.

The post-behaviouralist revolution is a timely warning against the overplay of scientism by the behaviouralists. It draws the attention of the political scientists to the more urgent social and political problems.

Post-behaviouralism is a clear attack against the obsession or craze for "scientific research". The view of the post-behaviouralists is that the bifurcation of political theory into normative and empirical directions and giving importance to the latter at the expense of the former has resulted in creating anomalies in the conceptual structure of political science. Research should not be unnecessarily loaded with the rigours of a scientific formulation. The post-behaviouralists focus their attention on applied research in order to tackle urgent social problems.

Systems Approach

The systems approach is one of the new approaches developed as a reaction against the traditional approach to politics. It is an attempt to describe the relationship of political activity to other aspects of social life. It does not pre-judge the relative merits of various types of political arrangements devised by various societies. It attempts to relate political science to other social sciences like sociology, economics, psychology and anthropology. It is emphasized that political life should be seen as a system or a set of systems of interaction.

The central proposition of the systems approach is that all social, including political, phenomena are inter-related and they affect each other. It is assumed that it is not possible to understand one part of society in isolation from the other parts which affect its operation. The systems approach covers all types of political systems. In its broadest sense, the term system denotes any set of inter-related elements. If a human being is viewed as a system, all the active elements of the body would be included as parts of the system, including the circulatory and respiratory systems. The circulatory and respiratory systems could also be considered as sub-systems. Like biological, mechanical, educational and other systems, a political system has also to be analysed from the point of view of its functions. The systems approach is one of the several alternatives which could be used in the study of politics. This approach views politics as the activities and structures of a system. Within a particular system, demands and conditions are imposed upon or presented to political leaders by the members of a society. The decision-makers make general policy decisions and supervise how they are enforced. The consequences are also evaluated. Throughout this mechanism, communication takes place between the different parts of the entire system.

There are two characteristics of a system. It is composed of separate units that interact in order to perform certain functions. The removal of any unit directly affects others. There is a degree of inter-relationship between the units. The system consists of mutually constraining or conditioning units. A system is marked by differentiation. This means the existence of distinct units and integration. There is interaction of the units in order to perform functions. The term function refers to the purpose, goal or job of the system. A function is the result or consequence of the activity of a system. The system operates within an environment of some sort from which it is distinguishable. A major condition of a system is that somehow or other the energy which keeps the system together, must be maintained. This is necessary to ensure that the system is not to be run down or merged with the environment. Within the system, energy is exchanged between the units in such a manner that if one unit is affected, all other units are affected in varying degrees. Energy is also lost in the process of maintaining the system as an entity within its environment and that must be regained somehow.

A political system allows the legal authority to use force. It possesses legitimate and heavy sanctions and rightful power to punish. A political system includes not only governmental institutions such as legislatures, executives, courts and administrative agencies but also all structures in their political aspect. Among them are included organisations like political parties, interest groups and media of communications, traditional structures such as kinship ties, caste groupings and anomic phenomena such as associations, riots and demonstrations. The political system includes interaction between all the formal and informal institutions. The process of interaction is divided into three phases — input, conversion and output.

David Easton classifies input functions into two types of demands and supports. Demands are classified into allocation of goods and services such as demand for more wages and fixation of working hours, opening of educational institutions, provision of recreational facilities, roads and transportation, participation in the political systems such as the right to vote, to hold office, to petition government bodies and officials, to organise political associations such as pressure groups and political parties. Demands also include the regulation of behaviour such as provision of public safety, control over markets and rules pertaining to marriage, health and sanitation and communication and information.

Examples of supports which the people get in the political system are material support, attention paid to government communications and manifestation of respect to public authorities, symbols and ceremonials, obedience to laws and regulations and participatory support such as voting, political discussion and other forms of political activity.

The manner and mechanism through which political system converts inputs and responds to the process in the environment is called the conversion process. The political system has more control over output than over inputs. The flow of decisions coming out of the political system can to some extent be regulated, channelled and organised by the operation of the procedures which are imposed on the polity by governmental structures. The conversion mechanism turns inputs into outputs after some process of selection, limitation or re-arrangement. The conversion process operates dynamically because the selection takes place over a period of time and not merely among the inputs which are fed into the system at a given moment. The process of conversion depends upon the capability of the political system for extraction of resources, regulation and control over individuals and goods, distribution of resources and its capacity for development.

The outputs of the political system consist of authoritative decisions. Those decisions are either application or interpretation of rules. They affect the environments of the political system. The outputs are rules, regulations, actions, laws etc. which are authoritative vis-a-vis the environment. Outputs may help to maintain support for the political system. A political system maintains itself partly through its own regulatory mechanism and partly through the support which it can generate in society. However, the main test for its effectiveness is what it does in society. The outputs of a political system are decisions and actions of the authorities. The outputs "not only help to influence events in the broad society of which the system is a part, but also in doing so, they help to determine such succeeding round of inputs that finds its way into the political system." This process is called a feedback loop. Outputs, flowing through the feedback loop are primarily a means generating specific support. The feedback is a dynamic process through which information about the performance of the system is communicated back to it. This affects the subsequent behaviour of the system.

David Easton was the first political scientist to have introduced the system model for the analysis of politics. Talcott Parsons applied systems analysis in the field of sociology. David Easton is often called Talcott Parsons of politics.

David Easton's systems analysis is in many ways a pioneering effort to systematize ideas about political life. This approach provides a general framework for a scientific and empirical study of all political systems. On account of a high level of abstraction in the systems analysis, the realities of political life may not always be neatly placed in the system model. However, this has been acclaimed as an important device for the study and analysis of politics. There are some difficulties in defining authoritativeness, especially when in many developing countries formal decisions of government are not allowed to be challenged. It may not be correct to say that the system allocates values almost exclusively. The normal state functions of defence, external relations and currency and finance cannot be easily placed in the allocative model of David Easton. In spite of this, the system model marks an improvement on earlier approaches to political analysis. It has great explanatory value when applied to the analysis of functioning political systems.

Structural-Functional Approach

Few concepts in the history of modern social sciences have created as much discussion as those of structures and functions and the type of analysis associated with them. The structural-functional approach has come to politics as an offshoot of the systems analysis.

Functionalism as an approach dates back to the days of Aristotle. However, Monstesquieu gave it a proper shape by propounding the theory of separation of powers. The old theory of functional analysis of the structures of government was based upon the theory of separation of government into three organs, but in modern times, various new factors such as adult suffrage, political parties and changes in communication media have brought a number of new functions. In its modern form, the stress on functionalism is derived from anthropological and sociological theories of Malinowski and Radcliff-brown. It was adopted by Talcott Parsons and Marion Levy and it became a major framework of analysis in sociological discussion. Since the 1930's, this mode of analysis has been gaining acceptance in political science, particularly in the field of comparative politics.

In this approach, the foci of attention are the structures and functions. Structures are patterned behaviour and they need not be formalised and located in concrete institutions. Functions are the relevant consequences of activity and relevance is traced to the system of which the activity generating unit is an integral component. In structural-functional analysis, one identifies the important structures and then seeks to discover their functions.

Gabriel Almond defines the political system as a special system of interaction that exists universally in all societies performing the functions of integration and adaptation by means of employment or threat of employment, of more or less legitimate physical compulsion. "Legitimate force is the thread that runs through the inputs and outputs of the political system, giving it its special quality and salience and its coherence as a system." The political systems, in structural-functional analysis, are systemic wholes that influence and are influenced by their environments. Their characteristic features are comprehensiveness, inter-dependence and the existence of boundaries. The basic units of structural-functional analysis are "roles", not individuals. The interactions that characterise a political system take place between the roles which individuals come to occupy. Political systems are "open systems" in the sense that they engage in transactions with systems outside their boundaries and are influenced by those transactions.

The view of Almond is that all political systems must perform a set of tasks for the sake of survival and equilibration. This can be called the functional requirements of the systems. Those functions can be performed by different kinds of political structures in different political systems. Those can even be performed by structures which are not formally regarded as political.

Input Functions

According to Almond, all political systems must perform two sets of basic functions viz., the input functions and output functions. The input functions are political socialisation and recruitment, interest-articulation, interest-aggregation and political communication. Political socialization is the learning process by which people acquire political beliefs, values and attitudes. It is the process by which individuals come to share a common 'orientation' towards a political system. All political systems tend to perpetuate their cultures and structures through the process of socialization at different stages of human development. The political recruitment function begins where the general political socialisation function ends. It recruits members of the society out of the religious communities, classes, ethnic communities etc. They are inducted into specialised roles of the political system and are trained in the appropriate skills. As regards interest-articulation, every system has some kind of articulating interest, claims and demands for political action. The interest-articulation function involves the formulation of demands and their transmission from society at large to the political system. This function is performed by a number of structures viz., institutional interest groups, non-association interest groups, anomic interest groups and associational interest groups. As regards interest aggregation, it may be done by means of the formulation of general policies in which interests are combined, accommodated or otherwise taken account of. The functions of articulation and aggregation overlap. In the authoritarian and primitive political systems, the three functions of articulation, aggregation and rule-making may not be easily differentiated. However, this can be done in modern Western systems. The aggregate functions may be performed within all the sub-systems of the political system. The aggregate functions are performed by legislative bodies, political executives, bureaucracies, media of communication, party systems, interest groups etc. In modern democratic political systems, political parties play a prominent role and provide durable links between elites and masses. As regards political communication, all functions in the political system are performed by means of communication. The agents of political socialization perform their functions through communication. Legislators enact laws on the basis of information communicated to them and by communicating with one another and with other elements of the political system. The bureaucrats receive and analyse the information. The political communication function is the crucial boundary-maintenance function, as all political functions are performed by means of communication. Autonomy in the media of communication makes possible a free flow of information from society to polity and inside the polity from one political structure to another political structure. It also facilitates the feed-back from output to input again. The performance of the communication function in different political systems may be compared according to the structures performing it.

Output Functions

Almond makes a three-fold classification of governmental output functions which are associated with policy-making and implementation. The three authoritative governmental functions are rule-making, rule-application and rule-adjudication. Rule-making processes are present in some form or other in all political systems. Rules must be made in certain ways and by specific institutions and with certain limitations. The problem of identifying rule-making structures in political system is one of specifying the whole set of agencies and institutions involved in the process, determining the kind of things they do, the way they do them and how they interact to produce general rules. This approach is too abstract to explain meaningfully the myriad processes and institutions that are irrelevant politically. It suffers from the "fallacy of functional teleology." This refers to the tendency to trace out and explain the origins of a pattern of action in terms of its being a functional necessity for the survival of the system. A specific structural arrangement may fulfil an important function but that does not adequately explain its origin or existence. It is just possible that there exist a number of alternative forms that could have played the same role. Hence, it is wrong to ascribe indispensability to a particular pattern of action. The functionalists defeat the very purpose of their approach by misapplying their tools of empirical investigation while studying the political systems of the countries of the Third World. It is pointed out that these sophisticated tools of empirical investigation are not applicable to the study of economically poor and backward countries. There are many indigenous problems of religion, caste, poverty, linguism, chauvinism, sub-nationalism etc. in the developing countries which have not been taken into consideration by the structural-functional approach. The tools of analysis of the functionalists are conceptually and theoretically neat and good but those are of little use in terms of the realities of the situation.

The view of Jean Blondel is that Almond's approach leads, to certain difficulties. It does not tell us about the aims of the participants. It must depend on what we accept as a function and it is difficult to achieve complete objectivity. This approach is primarily culture-bound and modelled on the Western political system.

The seven-function approach of Almond has been criticised by Leonard Binder. He points out that Almond has simply generalised the broad classes of political activity found in the Western political systems. His analysis does not tell us much about the nature of the political system. The idea of functionalism derived from sociology and anthropology does not fit well with the idea of system.

Communication Theory Approach

The pioneer of the communication theory was Robert Weiner, a mathematician. He used the term cybernetics which is fundamentally a body of theory and technique for the study of probabilities in different but analogous universes such as certain types of machines, animals, individual human beings, societies and nation states and the way in which message transactions function to control such universes. According to Weiner, "The process of receiving and using information is the process of our adjusting to the contingencies of the outer environment of our living effectively with that environment." Cybernetics as formulated by Weiner is a theory of information, self-regulating systems and the physiology of the nervous system. Cybernetic analysis is concerned with ways in which certain kinds of apparatus are maintained through devices by which the entropy of a system is counter acted by returning some of its output into input. This theory was applied to political science by Karl Deutsch.

According to Deutsch, the political system is a "network of communication channels" which have processes and mechanisms for acquiring, collecting, transmitting, selecting and storing information. They are essentially self-regulating or self-controlling systems. Control and regulation imply that the relevant information has to be directed towards or away from particular communication channels. To quote Deutsch, "Essentially control involves the transmission of messages and the understanding of control processes is a branch of communications engineering, not of power engineering." Government is a form of administration of communication channels. His suggestion is "to look upon government somewhat less as problem of power and somewhat more as a problem of steering; and steering is decisively a matter of communication".

According to Deutsch, power as physical force is not a decisive element in the definition of politics. In a society, the enforcement of decisions relies not merely on the threat of force. Over a period of time, the members of a society come to habitually comply with the authoritative decisions. In a political system, 'information precedes compulsion'. To quote Deutsch, "The inner source of political power — the relatively coherent and stable structure of memories, habits and values — depends on existing facilities for social communication, both from the past to the present and between contemporaries."

The communication theory starts with the presumption that the government is a decision-making system. The decisions taken by the government are based on certain information flows. The effectiveness of the information of the receiver depends on this that at least some parts of the receiving system must be in highly unstable equilibrium so that even a small amount of energy carrying the signal must be sufficient to start off a much larger process of change. The information can be measured and counted and the performance of the communication channels in transmitting or distorting communication can be evaluated in quantitative terms. According to Deutsch, "Information could conceivably be .measured in an extremely crude way in terms of the percentage of image points transmitted or lost in a line screen of a given fineness or in teems of number of outstanding details transmitted." Again, "The information approach offers an independent way of measuring basic cohesion, however, crudely, and that it can do so independently from the current political sympathies of the participants. Such sympathies or conflicts might show up sharply in the execution of controversial commands."

According to Deutsch, there are four factors of analysis in communication theory and those are lead, lag, gain and load. *Load* is the indicator of the total amount of information in the possession of a system at any point of time. *Lag* signifies the amount of delay between receiving reports on the consequences of decisions and the action taken on the information received. *Gain* refers to the manner in which the system reacts to the information received by it. *Lead* stands for the ability of the system to respond to predictions about the future consequences of actions and decisions.

The view of Deutsch is that as compared with traditional analysis, the feedback is more important because it is with the help of this system that it becomes easy to find out the lead on the political decision-making system of the state and also upon the decision system of particular international groups, political organisations and social classes. The system helps in finding out the response a government or party to a new challenge and the time which the policy-makers usually take in dealing with a situation. It can be found with its help how much time is taken for arriving at new decisions and how delay occurs in consultation. It can also be found out how much time is taken in communicating decision to those who are ultimately responsible for execution and how much time they usually take in re-adjustment. The view of Deutsch is that gain helps in finding out how quickly bureaucracies, interest groups, political organisations and citizens respond with major recommitment of their resources. It helps in finding out "to what extent do authoritarian regimes have an advantage in enforcing a massive response to new policies, once they have been adopted ? To what extent can democracy have a high rate of gain ?" With the help of lead, it becomes easy to find out the capability of a government to predict and anticipate new problems effectively and the rate at which the governments attempt to improve their rate of lead by setting up efficient intelligence organisations and other devices. It becomes easy to find out the effect of free public discussions upon predictive efficiency of political decision system and also "what is the relationship of the institutions, organisations or practices that produce forecasts to those that control their selection, evaluation and acceptance for action?"

The view of Deutsch is that a political system which is based on a correct understanding of the communication approach, is in a position to change its goals deliberately and intentionally. Goals can never be static and social and political leaders always change the goals. A political system goes through the process of innovation, growth and self-transformation. "Governments or political organisations whose rates of lag, gain and lead were sufficiently adjusted to each other for dealing with moderate rates of change in their environments, may find themselves unable to control their behaviour effectively in times of rapid changes that may put an excessive load upon their decision-making system."

The communication theory has both its critics as well as those who realise the importance of the approach. The view of O.R. Young is that the communication theory is responsible for giving a powerful thrust towards the efforts to operationalise hypotheses. This theory has also helped in undertaking quantitative analysis of the problems facing political scientists. However, critics maintain that this theory lays more stress on decision-making as a process and not the consequences of the decisions made. It is more concerned with the flow rather than with the substance of the decision or information itself. The theory provides excellent tools for studying the incoming information, but the study of politics is a very complicated affair and those tools need to be used further. The communication approach can provide us information and tools to find out where power is located, but the study of power itself is very baffling and the communication theory does not help in its study in any manner. There are differences between power and influence and the communication theory does not provide any help in studying the behaviour of various elites handling the power. This theory can be of some help to the political system in bringing about revolutionary changes, but in so far as those changes, the concept does not go very far. It will be rather impossible to study revolutionary changes with the help of this theory. The theory is very much mechanistic in nature and has tried to give engineering orientation to human behaviour. From the study of this approach, it appears as if an attempt has been made to transfer something bodily from the sphere of engineering to that of social sciences. This is not proper so far as the study of human behaviour is concerned. It is said that due to rapidly advancing sophisticated devices, differences have been increasingly breaking down, but that is not correct in so far as the question of engineering model for the study of human behaviour is concerned. Deutsch, while expounding his approach, has laid more stress on processes than on outcomes and consequences. It is true that the importance and significance of processes cannot be under-estimated but consequences and outcomes are always more important than the processes. In this approach, quantity occupies a more important and significant place than quality, but in the study of political science, quality is always more important than quantity. Everywhere models are built to simplify the phenomenon, but in this approach the model built by Deutsch has become more complex and complicated and the result is that the model has made the whole concept confusing and difficult to understand. In the communication theory, many terms have been taken from engineering, but those have not been used in the manner in which they should have been used. They have been used rather carelessly and not in the strict technical sense. That has created confusion and the result is that the meanings which were intended to be communicated have not been communicated. The application of cybernetics in the study of social problems and political systems is not a success.

The conclusion is that the whole approach is only suggestive. It has its own difficulties when applied to the study of political problems and systems.

Group Approach

Group theory is gradually assuming more and more significance in political science. It starts with the presumption that the group is a basic unit of political analysis. In this theory, political behaviour is defined in terms of group interaction. Group approach is not new to political science. However, Arthur Bentley has made a very significant contribution to this theory. He looks upon group approach as a tool of investigation. According to him, all phenomena of government are basically phenomena of groups pressing one another.

The group approach considers group as the basis for the study of politics. The approach proceeds on the basis that political behaviour can best be defined in terms of group inter-action. The whole approach concentrates on describing political life in terms of groups to which the people belong as formal members. The group approach was not studied seriously in the beginning but gradually its importance and significance were realised. The pioneers of the group approach were Arthur Bentley and David Truman.

Essentially, this approach seeks to interpret government policy in terms of pulls and pressures of different groups in the society. It is presumed that plurality of interests resides in the society. In their effort to achieve specific goals, the groups interact among themselves and influence the formal decision-making processes. The disposition of groups in a society is advanced as the major explanation for the nature of political outcomes in that society. Charles Hagan writes, "Values are authoritatively allocated in society through the process of the conflict of groups."

Critics point out certain defects in the group theory. The exponents and supporters of the group theory have failed to provide any satisfactory definition of the term "group" which could form the basis of further discussion and that creates its own problems. Even Bentley did not touch such important problems as the relation of man with the group, extent and intensiveness of concentration in a group and what number of people should constitute a group. Bentley has also not given a clear definition of the term "interest". There are very many interests in each group and each individual has his own interests to follow. As these interests are unlimited in number, we are faced with the problems of having innumerable groups which are bound to create problems, rather than solving them. Neither Bentley nor Truman has been able to define clearly as to what kind of interest inspires a group of individuals to come closer and near to each other. The advocates of group theory have failed to provide the basis of motivation in group theory. Bentley has talked about equilibrium but he has failed to define the term. The group theorists have used the term access. They have directed this term towards decision-making but failed to give clarification in this regard. They have not clarified the forum where the struggle is going on and at what stage it is presumed that it has come to an end and equilibrium has been achieved. The view of the group theorists is that in the decision-making process, there is no place for reason, knowledge and intelligence but this view is not accepted. Group theorists are criticised for reducing everything to group. They underestimate the value and importance of the individual and even of the society as a whole. They give no place to individual in the interpretation of politics. Group theory leaves out a great deal to individual behaviour. It also omits problems like those of individual leadership, sources of attitude, opinions and significance of role and status which can be understood only in terms of individual behaviour in the group. The group theorists have also failed to take into consideration intangible influences on individual behaviour. They have failed to explain even if equilibrium is once achieved, how the same can be maintained. The group theorists have failed to explain who sets the goals. It is true that it is the fundamental duty of groups to achieve goals but it is not explained how those goals are formulated, articulated and adopted by various groups. Group theorists ignore broad institutional settings in which groups and governments act and function. This approach insists only on group interaction but ignores effective aspects of institutions in a political situation. The theory leads one to the conclusion that government agencies frame policies primarily to satisfy group interests and not national interests. The group theory is useless in the case of developing societies which are prone to totalitarianism. Group theory presumes a certain level of systematic attainment which is lacking in developing societies.

Decision-Making Approach

Decision-making theory or approach was developed and popularised by writers like Richard Synder and Charles Lindblom. It focuses attention on the processes of public decision-making. A political action has the character of a decision taken by some actors in a specific situation through a particular process. Political action can be understood by referring to the person who took the decision and the inter-active processes by following which the decision was reached. While following the decision-making approach, the political scientist has to encounter a complex set of social-psychological and institutional processes. Hence, this approach has to draw on several concepts developed in sociology, social psychology and psychology.

It is true that the decision-making approach has been criticised but its importance cannot be under-estimated. Credit goes to Synder for stirring widespread thought among political scientists, especially those in the field of international politics and foreign policy. He made a bold attempt from abstractions towards investigation of empirical choices. James N. Roseneu writes, "The coherence and thoughtfulness of Synder's formulation serve to crystallize the ferment and to provide guidance, or at least legitimacy for those who had become disenchanted with a world composed of abstract states and with a mystical quest for single cause explanations of objective reality." Another impact of this approach was that scholars viewed the process with care and attention. The students of foreign policy "spoke less of compelling realities and more of conflicting alternatives, less of the formalities of diplomacy and more of dilemmas of the diplomats, less of the demands of situations and more of their limits and opportunities, less of the primacy of international affairs and more of the, competition between domestic and foreign policy goals." James N. Rosenu concludes, "The decision-making approach, in other words, had been absorbed into the practice of foreign policy analysis. The habits it challenged have been largely abandoned and the new ones it proposed have become so fully incorporated into the working assumptions of practitioners that they no longer need to be explicated or the original formulation from which they came cited."

Conflict Approach

The view of many political scientists is that conflict is the essence of politics. Conflict is the outcome of exchanges between individuals or groups. In a political system characterised by scarcity of values, conflict takes the form of a competition for the attainment of goods or values which are to be allocated within the system. In a situation of scarcity, competition is intense and frequent. A conflict process is an on going contest between two or more groups each seeking certain rewards or values which are in short supply. Conflicts are not always bad. As a social phenomenon, those should be understood in the larger context of social stability and change. Lewis Coser has described the functionality of social conflicts. The Marxian view is that class struggle acts as the propeller of history.

There are two kinds of conflicts viz., a cleavage conflict and an overlapping conflict. A cleavage conflict refers to a pattern in which groups and nations are divided in the same way again and again over different kinds of conflict issues. If a group continues to lose in the contests, it may resort to violent means to redistribute the gains and losses in the political system. An overlapping conflict divides groups and nations in different ways depending upon the nature of specific conflict issues. There are no permanent winners and losers and regular friends and regular enemies.

The conflict theory is concerned with linking conflicts and individuals to the political system Conflict is studied with reference to risks and strategies, pay-offs and preferences, coalition forming rules and decision rules terminating conflicts.

As politics is associated with conflict situations, the conflict theory appeals to political scientists. However, there are many assumptions and pitfalls in this theory and its explanatory strength should not be taken on mere face values.

Public Choice Approach

Public choice approach is growing in importance in the field of public administration. It is concerned with the nature of public goods and services and their allocative processes. It deals with the relationships between the formal decision-making structures and human propensities for individual and collective action. Governmental structures and processes can be evaluated with the help of this approach. The multiplicity of governments in a large metropolitan area is explained by this approach.

Political Economy Approach

The political economy approach is being applied more and more to both political and administrative analysis on account of its comprehensiveness and explanatory strength.

The Game Theory

The game theory is one of those theories which is used in political science for the study of international problems and also the problems connected with such intricate matters as diplomacy. According to the exponents of this theory, as in the games of chess, poker and bridge, there are also parties to the game in politics. Those parties can be both individuals and institutions. Each party is most interested to win the game. The parties have different choices before them and each party to the game is supposed to have perfect knowledge of the choices. No player can be independent in his choice because he has to take into consideration the choice of the other party. The parties to the game can be two or more. In words of Martin Shubik, "Games theory is a mathematical method for the study of some aspects of conscious decision-making institutions involving the possibilities of conflict and/or cooperation. It deals with process in which the individual decision unit has only partial control over the strategic factors affecting its environments. The decision unit may be individual, a firm, a government or any formal or informal institution."

The game theory is based on the expectations of others. A diplomat will like to judge the behaviour of the other, a candidate in the election that of the voters, a bureaucrat that of his counterpart in finalising deals and negotiations and a commander on the battlefront that of his opponent. The theory believes that each party to the game is wise and it is a game of wits which is played in international politics. There are certain rules of the game which are usually observed and those can be written as well as informal understandings, but well-defined and explicit. Each party to the game has a clear understanding of them.

There are certain important characteristics of the game theory. It is believed that every participant in the game is selfish and all parties use their maximum intelligence and wisdom for gaining their ends and objectives. They have different choices. While making a final choice, they take into consideration the utility of the choice. The player may be an individual, group or institution and each will behave rationally and reasonably. Every individual will always try to take his maximum interests into consideration and struggle to achieve them. He first decides his gains and advantages and then takes any other step. The parties to the game always try to be efficient.

The game theory has certain concepts. One basic concept is that each player to the game has certain set of resources which help him in combating his opponents with whom he is engaged in the game. Those resources are used only on the basis of certain well-established understandings. Those rules in politics are laid down by those who are powerful enough to apply them. Any threat to the rules of the game can result in the change depending upon the resources of the players. The outcome is the relationship between the players and the objectives they wish to achieve. The outcome can be either winning or loss or draw of the game. Another concept of the theory is strategy. According to Martin Shubik, "A strategy may be viewed as a book of instructions which a player could give to a delegate telling him what to do under all contingencies. It is a general plan of action worked out in complete detail." Again, "In politics and other human affairs individuals rarely, if ever, are in a position to plan in the detail indicated by a strategy. When a General uses a strategy, he counts for the major contingencies leaving much of the final details to be delegated to his subordinates." It is believed in the game theory that the player has knowledge of the game and is aware of the strategies available to him. He wants to maximise his pay-offs. As the player is rational, he can design strategies which cover all possible eventualities and contingencies.

The game theory has been put to maximum use in the international field because in diplomacy, the parties to the game use their maximum knowledge and wisdom. Diplomats and politicians feel that the whole world is a big game and the universe is a system. Morton Kaplan, William H. Riker and Thomas C. Shelling are among those who have tried to put the game theory into use.

The game theory has been subjected to *criticism*. Martin Shubik is of the view that "the essence of the game is that it involves decision-makers with goals and objectives whose fates are intertwined. They have some control but the control is partial. Each group or individual faces a cross purposes optimisation problem. His plans must be adjusted not only to suit his own desires and abilities, but also to those of others. The view of Arthur Lee Burns is that this approach does not give any basic information about international power politics and hence it is useless. This theory also does not deal with such important problems as population, scientific inventions, technical researches and philosophical contemporary trends. It is better and easy to understand politics with the help of cultural and sociological stresses and strains rather than the game theory. This theory is based on the mental understanding and development of players. It is believed that instead of laying stress on the facts of life and international politics, it lays stress on terminologies which are of no use. The game theory can provide only outlines but it does not lead to any conclusions. The theory does not help us to come to any conclusion regarding the priorities of a nation in international politics. According to this theory, wars are not serious in international politics. The exponents of this theory under-estimate the value and significance of important affairs. The theory has failed to discuss or give due place to the cold war in international politics. It proceeds on the assumption that the decision-makers are perfectly moral and rational. The theory is not at all interested in the ethics of man. It is concerned with ultimate outcomes and not with intermediary processes. Motives and attitudes are kept out of consideration.

In spite of all these defects, the game theory has also its utility. It has helped in the understanding of the intricate problems of international politics. After the World War II, it has helped in understanding significantly international politics between the two power *blocs.* With the help of this theory, it is comparatively easy to understand and analyse the working of NATO, SEATO and Warsaw Pact and the role of neutral nations in international politics on the one hand and their mutual relationship on the other. If one international happening is analysed with the help of this theory, it becomes easy to understand and analyse happenings of another international event. With the help of this theory, it becomes possible to find a solution to international problems and predict about international events. Martin Shubik writes, "Given a sufficient understanding of both political science and formal game theory, its uses are many though not necessarily all of spectacular import." Again, "In the study of bureaucratic process, they help in investigating communication, information and centralisation or decentralisation of decision-making. In the study of bargaining and negotiation, they help to explore the meanings of concepts such as threat. They also raise questions concerning the meaning of social and political stability." Again, "It helps to answer questions, how far one can go with formal rational models of political man. In helping to set the limits and to provide an understanding why they exist game theory serves to point out how it connects naturally with other methods in the behavioural sciences."

Inter-disciplinary Approach

During the last few decades, a new approach has developed in the study of social sciences. That is known as inter-disciplinary approach. According to this approach, researchers and students of one specialised social science should work in coordination with the researchers and students of other specialised social sciences. As society is a totality, its various aspects are inter-connected and inter-dependent. That totality cannot be studied by separating one aspect from the rest. There is the necessity of cross-fertilization. According to David Easton, specialisation in social sciences "has stimulated a movement towards a re-integration of our compartmentalised knowledge which should go a long way towards remedying these defects."

All social sciences have a common body of theory or general theory and the paths of different social sciences cross and run parallel at some points. Although each discipline is busy in formulating its own boundaries, scope, methods and concepts, the urge for mutual cooperation and exchange is there because it is not possible to study any specific discipline without mutual exchange with other disciplines. This approach is known as inter-disciplinary approach in social sciences. When politics is studied by adopting methods and concepts from other social sciences, it may be called inter-disciplinary study of politics.

The inter-disciplinary approach gives a broader perspective and enables us to understand problems more thoroughly and more fruitfully. The study of politics as a social process provides ample scope for an inter-disciplinary approach. That implies (1) making use of the findings, theories and models of other social sciences in understanding a political phenomenon, (2) Verification of the theories and findings of political science from the data and theories of other social sciences and (3) developing a broader perspective about political life. However, the expanding scope of our study should be purposeful and well-conceived. While interpreting the sphere of other social sciences, we should not deviate from our main focus. Any reference to the problems of economics, sociology, anthropology or psychology should be made with the definite object of understanding the problems of politics and not at random. If we study the psychology of crowd behaviour in a given situation, we should undertake those studies only to analyse their impact on politics and not to understand those problems for their own sake.

The inter-disciplinary approach treats society as a totality whose various aspects are closely inter-related. Political science undertakes the study of the political aspect of society for which the data provided by other social sciences are relevant and useful. Interest of the political scientists in political socialization and political culture has inspired them to draw heavily from the data of psychology and sociology. Their interest in political development has increased their reliance on the data provided by sociology and economics. Their interest in political communication has brought them nearer to social psychology.

The inter-disciplinary approach has also encouraged political scientists to make an abundant use of the theories and models evolved by the other social sciences. For example, the elite theory was first systematically developed by Pareto Mosca and Michels in the field of sociology. It was then applied to the analysis of political institutions, leadership and good behaviour and also for giving new interpretations of democracy. The Marxian concept of "base super-structure" (that politics, culture, morals, ideas and institutions in any society are shaped by the prevailing mode of material production) was first evolved in the field of economics and sociology and then adopted as a tool of political analysis. Some contemporary approaches to the study of politics originated in other social sciences. The concept of the political system of David Easton is derived from the concept of the social system originally developed in the field of sociology. The structural-functional approach was originally developed in the field of cultural anthropology by Malinowski and Radcliffe-Brown, then adopted in sociology by Talcott Parsons and subsequently introduced in political science by Almond and Powell. The model of the problem-solving approach of Harold Lasswell was derived from psychology. Understanding of politics as a process of bargaining is based on the theories of competition originally evolved in the field of economics. Schumpeter and Anthony Downs have used the model of the open market from economics to analyse democratic politics.

The use of theories and models of the other social sciences in political science is very common. History is used as a rich store-house of data for understanding and interpreting political phenomena and a comparative study of political institutions. When history gives us not only an account of events but also cause and effect relationship of historical development, this knowledge can be used for understanding the course of politics in a given situation. Political science is today deeply concerned with the socio-economic foundations of political phenomena and that material is available from history on account of a change in the approach to the study of history in recent times. A study of history today is not confined to the great acts of kings and princes, their battles, victories, expansion and consolidation of empires, defeats, disintegration and downfall. Due consideration is being given to the study of social, economic and political conditions. Theories of political science can be verified from historical data and that can give them precision.

Likewise, political science can derive useful help from economics. Political theory today is primarily concerned with the conflicting demands of various groups and classes within a community or between different nations in the international sphere and a study of economics can be useful for this purpose. No political system can sustain itself unless it shows its ability to cope with the conflicting demands by evolving a suitable equilibrium, harmony or reconciliation and that requires a deeper study of the economic forces which is available from a study of economics. The welfare state has to take care of the economic security of citizens by providing them full employment, a reasonable standard of living, nutrition and health and a Study of economics is useful. The politics of the developing countries cannot be studied without due consideration of the requirements of their economic development. The object of political power is mainly to serve economic interests. Political behaviour is dependent on economic conditions and motives.

Likewise, a study of sociology is useful in political science. Contemporary students and researchers in politics have borrowed research techniques and survey methods from sociology. The main problems of sociology like social equilibrium, cooperation, social engineering, problems of social control, process of social change etc. have been adopted by politics. During the nineteenth century, traditional political theory tried to analyse the origin and evolution of the state and other institutions from sociological studies. Writers like Sir Henry Maine, L.H. Morgan and J.J. Bachhofen have emphasized the sociological evolution of the state and political institutions. Morgan elaborated the theory of political evolution on the basis of sociological studies. In his masterpiece, "The Origin of the Family, Private Property and the State", Dr. Engels gave a scientific, sociological evolution of the state. Bentley gave a beautiful sociological conception of the process of government. His contention was that the essential process of government is the adjustment of the conflicts between the interest groups. Likewise, sociological studies of political parties and many other political institutions have been carried out. Prof. Maclver has analysed the nature of the state from the point of view of a sociologist in his book "The Modern State". The theory of plural elites, nature and evolution of political elite was founded on sociological basis. Behaviouralism has tremendously influenced studies in political science. Political scientists have imported from sociology concepts like political socialization, political culture, political system, political development, political recruitment and political communication and approaches like structural-functional and systems approach etc. A study of political behaviour is less a political and more a sociological study. Political behaviour is influenced by sociological factors. It is desirable to see political socialisation process and political culture in a society. Behaviouralism emphasizes an inter-disciplinary study of politics and sociology. The view of Sartori is that politics has got socialised and society has got politicised in modern times.

The supporters of the contemporary inter-disciplinary approach strongly recommend sociological and psychological consideration in the study of politics. Studies in voting behaviour, bureaucracy, behaviour of political leaders etc. are based on inter-disciplinary study of politics and sociology.

The famous sociologist like Max Weber, Robert Michels, Pareto and Durkheim turned to political analysis as a part of their sociological inquiry. Bentley was trained as a sociologist in Europe but ultimately he became a major intellectual force in political science. Franklin Giddings encouraged his students to undertake empirical studies of voting behaviour. The application of various concepts and methods of sociology to the study of political behaviour and institutions has given rise to "Political Sociology". The practitioners of political sociology seek to explain political behaviour.

Politics involves taking public decisions and that requires a study of the social motivations of the relevant groups. An inquiry into value-orientations, attitudes, habits, beliefs and prejudices of the people becomes necessary to know the possible response and chances of success of any social measure and sociology is helpful for that purpose.

Likewise, a study of psychology is useful to political science. An inquiry into the formation of attitudes has inspired psychologists to examine political values and behaviour. The growth of totalitarian political movements in the 1930's and 1940's aroused interest in the study of authoritarian personality. Similar orientations influenced the work of Harold Lasswell and his disciples in their study of the influence of psychological factors on the appeal of extremist movements. Social psychology is helpful to understand the formation and expression of public opinion, patterns of leadership including charismatic leadership, impact of propaganda and the role of mass communication, including political culture.

Lasswell has emphasized the need of considering psychological factors in the study of politics. His contention is that every political process and movement has psychological causes. His suggestion is that political deviancies like revolution, anarchy, violence, conflict, dictatorship and war should be studied on psychological basis. Many studies of public opinion indicate the relation between mass mind, democracy and dictatorship. Mass movements are regarded as psychological disorders. Voices of violent dissent are classified as mental disorders.

Lasswell analysed the cause of social conflict in psychological tensions and maintained that behind every struggle there is a "castration complex". He gave the idea of preventive politics on psychological basis. Instead of recommending change in society and social environment, Lasswell has suggested that the human brain should be influenced in such a way that it adjusts within the existing social framework. The whole logic of psychological studies in politics rests on the principle that social and political conflicts can be avoided and consensus arrived at by psychological treatment. The use of psychological methods has been suggested for manipulating human mind. The emergence of the behavioural psychology also emphasizes the utility of psychology to politics. Psychological methods are used to influence the masses.

Inter-disciplinary approach, although of recent origin, has assumed special importance in modern times. It does not merge all social sciences into a single master science. However, it is insisted that the results of our inquiry in any sphere should be based on and verified from the findings of all relevant social sciences. Political science should not only make use of the data, theories and models of other social sciences, but should also make a suitable contribution to the study of other social sciences.

The Marxist Approach

The Marxist approach to politics takes into consideration the writings of not only Marx, Engels and Lenin but also of a galaxy of writers like Rosa Luxemburg, Trotsky, Gramsci and others. Marxist approach to politics can be understood if we understand the concept of politics embedded in the whole structure of Marxist thought.

According to Marx, the individual is individual-in-society. He has no meaning without society. All societies in history have been class societies. The contending classes from "free man and slave, patrician and plebian, lord and serf, guildmaster and journeyman" to the bourgeoisie and the proletariat have "stood in constant opposition to one another." All class societies are marked by domination and conflict which are based on specific, concrete features of their mode of production. There has always been an attempt on the part of the dominant classes to maintain and extend their domination of society. Politics can be understood only if we understand the nature of the conflict in society. Politics is concerned with the, "specific articulation of class struggle". The political life processes are considered a part of the "super-structure" standing on the economic structure of society. "The mode of production of material life conditions the social, political and intellectual life-process in general". Polities, economics, culture and ideology are all inseparably intertwined. The forces of production at a particular stage of historical development are matched by definite relations of production that characterise the society.

The real nature of politics has to be understood from "the hidden basis of the entire social structure". Politics is a very determined and conditioned activity and that gives it a derivative, subsidiary and epiphenomenal character.

Alan R. Ball writes about the economic approach, "The essence of the approach is the view of the political process as a process of change; the vote, for example, is a type of money that can be exchanged for something else. Politics is a market place. Politics is concerned with the allocation of resources, the optimising of social welfare and thus choices within the political process are concerned with government finance, budgets, types of taxes and the effects of these choices on political structures."

The view of Dr. L.S. Rathore is that the Marxist approach may not be the infallible method of studying politics, but it could surely be a great improvement upon the existing scientific theories if conjoined with systematic study of history and philosophy. The most remarkable thing about Marxism is that "despite being scientific, it is suffused with humanism; it is the social womb of a new man." (Political Science in Transition, edited by J.S. Bains and R.B. Jain).

Kuhn's Paradigms

The use of paradigms in the field of physical sciences by Thomas Kuhn has recently interested political scientists. According to him, the history of science has been characterised by a succession of distinct thought styles or paradigms and those have a considerable influence on the kinds of problems scientists select for investigation. According to him, there are a number of phases through which a science tends to pass. The first phase is the pre-paradigmatic phase in which no single theoretical approach or school predominates, although a number of such schools or approaches compete for recognition. That is followed by the paradigmatic phase in which the scientific community adheres to a dominant paradigm. The third phase is called "the crisis phase" which comes when the dominant paradigm is subject to challenge and revision and new paradigms may evolve, old ones revived, giving rise to competition among a variety of perspectives. The fourth phase is called "the phase of scientific revolution" and that occurs when the scientific community makes a significant shift to different paradigms. Thus, a paradigm is a scientific community's perspective of the world, its set of beliefs and commitments.

Political scientists have debated the existence or non-existence of paradigms in political science and they have come to the conclusion that there are certain major paradigms in political science. The first is the Greek philosophers' paradigm of the state as an organism. Plato and Aristotle describe the state as an organism which was subject to development and degeneration. Political science was considered similar to medicine and the statesman was compared to the physician. Justice, like health, was a condition of the system as a whole. Then came the Romans who cast their approach in terms of jurisprudence rather than medicine with a natural law as a ideological principle towards which all constitutions must strive. Then came Christendom with its emphasis on natural laws as the principle of a heavenly political order. With the Renaissance came a new paradigm: the secularising attitude insisting that people be taken as they are rather than as they ought to be. Today we have conceptualizations of politics in terms of Cybernetics, Systems, Structural-Functionalism, Rational Choice etc.

It is worthy of notice that the different approaches are not always exclusive and self-contained explanations of politics. The decision-making and conflict approaches are closely interlinked. The models offered by Easton and Deutsch have much in common. The plurality of approaches shows the complexity of the problem. They demonstrate the need for drawing upon different disciplines to explain political phenomena. Sometimes one and sometimes many approaches have to be applied at the same time. They are all important in their own ways.

SUGGESTED READINGS

Almond, G.A. and J.S. Coleman (Eds.) : *The Politics of the Developing Areas, Princeton University Press, 1960.*

Almond, G.A. and Powell, G.B. : *Comparative Politics—A Developmental* Approach.

Bains, J.S. and Jain, R.B. (Eds.) : *Political Science in Transition,* Gitanjali Prakashan, New Delhi, 1981.

Ball, Allan R. : *Modern Politics and Government,* 1971.

Bersleson and Steiner : *Human Behaviour: An Inventory of Scientific Findings,* Harcourt Brace, New York, 1964.

Brick, Bernard : *In Defence of Politics,* London.

Butler, D.E. : *The Study of Political Behaviour,* 1958.

Care, W.J. and Dyson, J.W. (Eds.) : *The Making of Decisions,* New York, 1964.

Charlesworth, C.J. (Ed.) : *Contemporary Political Analysis,* Free Press, New York, 1968.

Chilcote, Ronald H. : *Theories of Comparative Politics: Search for a Paradigm,* Westview Press, Colorado, 1981.

Dahl, Robert A. : *A Preface to Democratic Theory,* Phoenix Books, University of Chicago Press, Chicago, 1967.

Dahl, Robert A. : *Modern Political Analysis,* Prentice-Hall, 1963.

Deutsch, Karl W. : *The Nerves of Government,* Free Press, 1953.

Doctor, Adi H. : *Issues in Political Theory,* Sterling Publishers, New Delhi, 1985.

Dyke, Vernon Van : *Political Science: A Philosophical Analysis,* Stanford University Press, California, 1960.

Easton, David : *The Political System—An Inquiry Into the State of Political Science,* Alfred A. Knopf, New York, 1971.

Easton, David : *A Frame- Work for Political Analysis.*

Eulau, Heinz : *The Behavioural Persuasion in Politics,* Random House, New York, 1964.

Eulau Heinz, Eldersweld, *Sammual J. and Janowitz,* Morris (Eds.) : *Political Behaviour: A Reader in Theory of Research,* Amerind Publishing Co., New Delhi, 1972.

Gould, J.A. and Thursby, V.V. : *Contemporary Political Thought.* Holt, Rinehard and Winston, Inc., New York, 1967.

Greenstein, Fred I. and Polsby, Nelson W. (Eds.) : *Handbook of Political Science: Political Science, Scope and Theory,* Vol. I, Massachusetts.

Haas, Michael and Kariel, Henry S. (Eds.) : *Approaches to the Study of Political Science,* Chandler Publishing Co., Scranton, 1970.

Kuhn, Thomas : *The Structure of Scientific Revolution,* University of Chicago Press, Chicago, 1962.

Lasswell, Harold : *The Future of Political Science,* New York, 1963.

Lipset, Seymour Martin : *Political Man and the Social Bases of Politics,* Arnold Heinemann (India), New Delhi, 1973.

Lipset, S.M. (Ed.) : *Politics and the Social Sciences.*

Lipson, L. : *The Great Issues of Politics,* Bombay, 1967.

Mannheim, K. : *Ideology and Utopia,* London, 1936.

Mayo, H.B. : *An Introduction to Democratic Theory,* Sterling Publishers, New Delhi, 1967.

Miliband, Ralph : *Marxism and Politics,* Oxford University Press, 1978.

Miller, J.D.B. : *The Nature of Politics,* Penguin Books, Great Britain, 1967.

Polsby, Nelson W. and Greenstein, Fred I. (Eds.) : *Handbook of Political Science. Government Institutions and Processes,* Vol 5, Addison-Wesby Publishing Co., Massachusetts.

Quinton, Anthony (Ed.) : *Political Philosophy,* Oxford University Press, 1967.

Ranney, Austin (Ed.) : *Essays on the Behavioural Study of Politics,* University of Illinois Press, Urbana, 1962.

Schumpeter, Joseph A. : *Capitalism, Socialism and Democracy,* 1950

Seliger, M. : *Ideology and Politics,* London, 1976.

Sills, D.I.(Ed.) : *International Encyclopaedia of Social Sciences,* Macmillan and Free Press, 1968.

Smith, Barbara Leigh : *Political Research Methods: Foundations and Techniques,* Boston, 1976.

Storing, Herbert J. (Ed.) : *Essays on the Scientific Study of Politics,* New York, 1962.

Strauss, Leo : *Essays on Scientific Study of Politics,* edited by H.J. Strong, New York, 1962.

Vickers, Geoffrey : *Value Systems and Social Process,* 1968.

Wasby, Stephen L. : *Political Science—The Discipline and Its Dimensions, An Introduction,* Scientific Book Agency, Calcutta, 1972.

Wiseman, H.V. : *Political Systems.*

Young, Oran R. : *Systems of Political Science,* Prentice-Hall, 1968.

Young, Roland (Ed.) : *Approaches to the Study of Politics, North-Western University Press,* 1958.

CHAPTER

Methodology of Political Science

Learning Objectives

- Experimental Method
- Observational Method
- The Historical Method
- Advantages
- Disadvantages
- The Comparative Method
- The Philosophical Method
- Statistical or Quantitative Method
- Biological Method
- Psychological Method
- Juridical Method
- Method of Analogy
- Sociological Method
- Conclusion
- Suggested Readings

The natural sciences like Chemistry and Physics have developed a number of mechanical apparatuses for studying the phenomena concerning themselves. Political science does not possess such instruments for carrying on a systematic study of the goals, institutions and processes of the state. Hence, the adoption of a proper method or methods is of great importance in political studies. It was rightly said that "what the microscope is to biology or the telescope to astronomy, a scientific method is to social sciences." While studying any political phenomenon, the method adopted should be clearly studied so that the conclusions arrived at can be examined and verified. As the scope of political science has widened, the importance of methodology also has increased in modern times. Arnold Brecht writes, "It is not saying too much that ours has become the methodological century in the social sciences." (Political Theory, p. 5).

It may look strange but it is a fact that political scientists gave very serious thought to methodology only as late as the nineteenth century. Auguste Comte suggested three principal methods of investigation viz., observation, experiment and comparison. The view of Bluntschli was that only philosophical and historical methods were required for investigation and correct conclusions. J.S. Mill recognised four methods: the chemical or experimental method, the geometrical or abstract method, the physical or concrete method and the historical method. Mill considered the first two methods false and put all the emphasis on deductive and historical methods. The view of Lord Bryce was that the observational, experimental, historical and comparative methods were the only correct and proper methods to give satisfactory result. Deslandres recognises six methods viz., the sociological method, the comparative method, the dogmatic method, the juridical method, the method of good sense and the historical method. Some recent writers have emphasized the importance of sociological, biological, psychological and statistical methods of investigation. In Britain, the following seven methods are in use: historical method, juridical method, philosophical method, institutional method, analytical method, observational method and sociological method. The Marxist dialectical method is followed in Communist countries. The basic principle of Marxist dialectical method lies in postulating the examination of problems in their integrity, that is, in examining phenomena in their interdependence and mutual relations. In order "to attain knowledge of political reality, the Marxist dialectical method makes use of sociology which is built on a consistent material basis and resorts, in turn, to an analysis of the social process in terms of the property relations which exist in any given society."

It is clear that from above that even now it is difficult to point out clearly and precisely the methods and prejudices of studying political science. The picture of methodology is blurred and the methods and prejudices adopted are far from scientific clarity and systematisation. Charles Eisenmann writes, "The writers proceed implicitly no doubt from a notion of method that is neither very reliable nor very accurate. Many writings on the method of political science base themselves on the wider and more popular notion which suffers from the fact that it is of a heterogeneous nature."

When the political scientists gave their first serious thought to methodology in the nineteenth century, they copied the methods of researchers in the natural sciences. David Easton observes, "For two thousand years after Aristotle, the first scientific scholar in the West to treat facts seriously, few great socialist thinkers turned to empirical research. When they finally did feel the need to examine the behaviour of men more closely, the method of physical sciences stood as a model." (The Political System (1951), p. 7). There was a sort of a craze for a thoroughly scientific investigation and the methods of Physics and Chemistry were adopted by political scientists. Superficial resemblances were struck between physical phenomena, ignoring the tremendous work done in laboratories in natural sciences. The result was that political scientists were disillusioned. The two World Wars created doubts in the minds of political scientists regarding the value of scientific methods. It was realised that political science could not be put on par with the value-free natural sciences as the former has to deal with human beings and not with inanimate substances. The craze for cent percent scientific investigation in political science gradually diminished. It was realised that moral and spiritual values were necessary for the very survival of mankind and could not be ignored while conducting researches in political science. It was realised that value-free political science is impossible.

Though all political scientists agree about the goal of political science, there is no unanimity about the methods and approaches to be followed to reach the end. M. Salvadori writes, "As far as methodology in political science is concerned, experts want to speak of a variety of methods: philosophical, dialectical, juridical, sociological, psychological, economic and normative methods, methods of liberty and of the natural sciences, experimental, integral and statistical methods etc. The outstanding feature of this terminology is perhaps its ambiguity. Clearly specialists use the word method in a great variety of meanings." (Contemporary Political Science (1950), pp. 3-4). Alan R. Ball says, "There is a marked lack of agreement in what constitutes the best approach to the study of politics. The bewildering array of titles of degree courses in Britain at present illustrates some of the confusion: names such as Government, Political Institutions, Political Science are umbrellas protecting the various specialisms of Public Administration, Political Theory, Political Philosophy, Comparative Government and International Politics." (Modern Politics and Government (1971), p. 3).

The UNESCO launched in 1948 the project "Methods in Political Science" under the guidance of Dr. William Ebenstein. Writers from various countries contributed fifty essays which were published in the book form under the title of "Contemporary Political Science." This book also shows no unanimity regarding, the method to be followed in political science.

Many political thinkers in recent years had shown their preference for the empirical — scientific methods and approaches vis-a-vis the traditional normative methods and approaches. The new trend is to draw a sharp line of distinction between fact and value. More and more emphasis is put on experience and observation. However, all political thinkers are not prepared to accept the principle that political science should be value-free.

In recent times, there is fresh thinking on the methodology of political science and special contributions have been made by such authorities as Max Weber, John Dewey, Felix Kaufmann, Leo Strauss, Eric Voegelin and Karl Popper.

EXPERIMENTAL METHOD

Experimental method is regarded as the most popular and the best-suited method for natural sciences. This method is generally adopted while dealing with natural and physical sciences. However, there are writers who believe that this method is not suitable for political science. Physical phenomena basically differ from social phenomena. Dr. Garner writes, "Social facts never occur at regular intervals as the manifestation of general laws, but rather as the actions of individuals or groups. The facts of natural sciences are susceptible of evaluation; they are governed by uniform and invariable laws, each particle of matter is identical with every other of its own kind. An atom of carbon or a molecule of carbolic acid is not different from any other atom or molecule, but the units of the social organism may differ infinitely from one another." Political science deals with man and the laws, constitutions and political institutions. As his nature goes on changing, the laws framed by him and the constitution and political institutions made and supported by him are bound to undergo changes with the changing conditions. Physics and Chemistry and other natural sciences deal with matter which remains the same. Human tendencies which affect social and political life to a very great extent cannot be measured with the help of any artificial apparatus. We cannot observe the same degree of objectivity in our experiments of political science as we observe in Physics and Chemistry. Experiments in political science are not so objective because the angle of our vision and our view-points indirectly influence us.

Sir George C. Lewis remarks, "We cannot treat the body politic as corpus vile and vary its circumstances at our pleasure for the sake only of ascertaining abstract truth. We cannot do in politics what the experimenter does in Chemistry. We cannot try how the substance is affected by change in temperature, by dissolution in liquids, by combination with other chemical agents and the like. We cannot take a portion of the community in our hands as the King Brobdignag took Gulliver, view it in different aspects and place it in different positions in order to solve social problems and satisfy our speculative curiosity." (Methods of Observation and Reasoning in Politics, Vol. I, pp. 164-165).

A similar view is expressed by Lord Bryce in these words, "The phenomena with which the chemist deals are and always have been identical; they can be weighed and measured, whereas human phenomena can only be described. We can measure temperature, humidity and the force of wind but we cannot determine how hot were the passions of a mob. We may say that in political crisis the opinion of a cabinet will have weight but we cannot say how much will it be. Opinions, emotions and other factors which influence politics are not capable of computations." Again, "Experiments can be tried in Physics over and over again till a conclusive result is reached, but that which we call an experiment in politics can never be repeated because conditions can never be exactly reproduced, as Heraclitus says that one cannot step twice into the same river. Prediction in Physics may be certain, in politics it can at best be no more than probable." (Modern Democracies, Vol. I, p. 14).

The view of Vaughan is that "Political experimentation in the sense in which it applied to the study of Physics or Chemistry is impossible since the power of isolating each individual process of enquiry which is the essence of such experimentation, does not exist."

However, Prof. Merriam does not altogether rule out the possibility of experimentation in politics. According to him, "Certainly the state has more material available for such observation than any other institution. The army, the schools, the public personnel and an array of public institutions are directly under its management and may be utilised for purposes of experiment if so desired." (New Aspects of Politics, pp. 55 and 227). Comte points out that every political change is a sort of experiment. Every new law passed by the government, every new policy adopted by the nation and every political change that has been made in the political structure of the country is a sort of experiment. When the government of a country passes a new law and if the public opinion accepts the new law, it is believed that the new political experiment tried by the government is a success. If the public does not recognise the new law passed by the government, the experiment is regarded as a failure.

All laws, policies and political systems are instituted within a necessary framework of experiments and by studying such experiments the political scientist is able to reach positive conclusions. It is his task to take note of the political events and innovations that constantly go about him and to make deductions from them. Governments are ever trying experiments on the community. History is experimentation on a vast scale. In the modern world, we make conscious political experiments in the light of past experience, when and where circumstances permit. The laboratory of political science also consists of the sovereign and independent states into which the world is divided. Prof. Harold Laski writes, "We deal with tendencies; we can predict on the basis of experience. But our predictions are limited by the necessity of recognising that the facts are not within our control. We can influence and attempt and hope; the certainty and precision of the chemist or even the physiologist can never be ours."

In modern times, Western democratic institutions are sought to be planted on the soil of a number of underdeveloped countries in Africa and Asia. Those institutions can be considered as experiments in the sense that their validity is being tested and examined. The results of such experimentation would prove their competence or otherwise to cope with the peculiar problem-situations in the under-developed countries.

The grant of responsible self-government to Canada was based on the Durham Report of 1839 and the same experiment was carried out in Australia, New Zealand, South Africa and India.

On the basis of the Report of the States Reorganisation Commission, Bombay was created a bilingual state in 1956 and Maharashtra and Gujarat were included in that bilingual state. However, the experiment was a failure. There was a strong demand for the division of the new state into two separate states on the basis of language, written and spoken in those states. Prime Minister Jawaharlal Nehru refused to divide the state into two separate states. The result was riots. Dr. C.D. Deshmukh, the then Finance Minister of India, tendered his resignation under protest. After his resignation, the situation further deteriorated and ultimately the State of Bombay had to be divided into two separate States of Maharashtra and Gujarat.

Dyarchy was experimented in the provinces under the Government of India Act, 1919 but as its working was found to be defective, the same was discarded in the provinces under the Government of India Act, 1935.

The experiment of prohibition was made in India after her independence in 1947. The Government of India appointed the Tek Chand Committee to recommend a uniform policy based upon a rational evaluation of such an experiment. The experiment proved to be a failure and had to be given up. Prime Minister Morarji Desai tried to introduce prohibition but he was warned by a large number of people that it might lead to a great loss of revenue and increase in corruption.

The experiment of separating the judiciary from the executive has been tried in India after independence and the same has yielded favourable results.

In British India, the experiment of communal electorates proved to be disastrous and the same was avoided when the new Constitution of India was made after her independence.

The experiment of adult franchise in free India has proved to be a success as proved by the many general elections held after 1950 for the Lok Sabha and State Assemblies.

The experiment of three-tier Panchayati Raj has failed miserably in several parts of India owing to the indifference of the people and other factors.

Experiments like the Compulsory Deposit Scheme, economic planning and family planning have also been tried with different results.

The experiment of a democratic government was tried in Germany under the Weimar Constitution of 1919 but the same failed and Hitler established his dictatorship in 1933. However, democratic institutions have again been set-up in West Germany after the World War II. A democratic government was set-up in Japan after her defeat in the second World War in 1945.

The Community Development Project or Rural Integrated Development Programmes, Adult Education and other new experiments have been unsuccessful to a very great extent. The three-language formula, in spite of its good intentions, has not succeeded.

The British Constitution is considered to be the mother of Constitutions and The British Parliament the mother of Parliaments. This means that other countries have borrowed from Britain what she was the first to experiment with.

Such experiments will continue to be made in every country. Dr. Garner rightly says that "the enactment of every new law, the establishment of every new policy is experimental in the sense that it is regarded merely as provisional or tentative until the results have proved its fitness to become permanent." (Political Science and Government, p. 19).

OBSERVATIONAL METHOD

The older generations of political scientists discounted the observational method and based their theories on *a priori* assumptions. They drew their specific conclusions from premises presumed to be infallible. It was only during the Renaissance and particularly as a result of new discoveries that the search for reality prompted political thinkers to observe, collect and analyse facts about the actual workings of governments and their institutions.

The method of observation was first adopted by Plato and Aristotle. Plato visited a large number of countries and closely studied their social, economic and political conditions and then propounded certain principles of political science. Likewise, Aristotle visited several countries with a view to widening his mental horizon and adding to his knowledge. Montesquieu came to England, studied its Constitution and felt impressed by it. He then propounded the theory of separation of powers.

President Lowell declares that "Politics is an observational and not an experimental science". The method of observation is the true method of investigation. A library is a laboratory of political science only in a limited sense. For the most part, books are no more original sources for the "physiology of politics" than they are for geology or astronomy. "The main laboratory for the actual working of political institutions is not a library but the outside world of political life. There the phenomena must be sought and observed at first hand."

Lord Bryce also was an advocate of the observational method. In order to attain precision and exactitude, he actually visited countries like the United States, Canada, Switzerland, Australia and New Zealand. He observed the actual operation of their political institutions at close range, collected valuable first-hand data and finally reached certain profound conclusions on the working of those political institutions. His "American Commonwealth" and "Modern Democracies" are the rich products showing his range and depth of observation. He repeatedly insisted that observation must not be superficial but profound, based on factual information and free from subjective distortions. According to Bryce, while adopting this method, a political investigator "must not confine his observation to a single country; the field must be enlarged to include the phenomena of all countries; the fundamentals of human nature are the same everywhere but political habits and temperaments vary in different countries. He must be aware of superficial resemblances and deadly analogies; he must avoid generalisations not based on facts; he must be critical of his sources of information and must disengage personal or accidental causes from general causes." According to Bryce, the first desideratum is to know the fact. Then, "make sure of it. Get it perfectly clear. Polish it till it sparkles and shines like a gem. Then connect it with other facts. Examine it in its relations to them, for in that lies its worth and its significance. It is of little use alone. So make it a diamond in the necklace, a stone, perhaps a corner-stone in your building."

The observational method can be followed successfully only by competent and critical minds. The observer must be a trained person. He must be well-equipped mentally and in other respects.

A scholar directly observing political institutions should have a thorough knowledge of the past, their origin and development. Experience shows that very few political scientists possess the requisite calibre to follow the method of observation. David Easton writes, "Relatively few political scientists have the opportunity to participate extensively in high level politics at the national and state capitals, a slightly broader group eddy round the scholars." (The Political System (1959), p. 49).

The method of observation was very popular during the nineteenth century. Comte, Spencer and Marx were the triumvirate who dominated the century.

The main advantage of the method of observation is that it is practical and realistic. The material collected by the researcher can be verified and its veracity can be ascertained. The researcher writes down what he observes and studies and not what is imaginary and speculative. Another merit of this method is precision, provided the researcher is well-informed and truly competent. The political scientist following this method must be in living touch with facts and free from the charge of being abstract and doctrinaire.

However, the method of observation must be used with caution. When the facts are very many and often conflicting, only a man with a trained eye and mature judgment can arrive at sound conclusions. There is the danger of seeing the things that one wants to see and leaving out those things of which one chooses to be oblivious. There is also the danger of missing the wood for the trees. Not only facts have to be collected, but a penetrating and understanding mind is required to interpret them in the right manner and make them real and living. There is always the danger that the researcher may mislead others by his inadequate study and incorrect observation. He may overlook important facts but include facts and comments of minor importance. He may not make an objective and detached approach and his writings after his faulty observation may be coloured by bias and pre-conceived notions.

Direct observation of political institutions is not adequate and complete unless it is combined with a historical knowledge of their origin and development. The present is a continuation of the past and the historical thread of continuity must always be in the reference of a political observer. Moreover, what is important in political science is not a cursory glance but a sustained observation of the recurrence of the same phenomena. As the political phenomena continue to change, observation of such recurrences is seldom possible. This puts a definite limit to the application of the observational method.

Another defect of the method of observation is that it does not deal with moral and ethical values and badly requires the prop of the philosophical method.

THE HISTORICAL METHOD

In the words of Sir Frederick Pollock, "The historical method seeks an explanation of what institutions are and are tending to be, more in the knowledge of what they have been and how they came to be what they are, than in the analysis of them as they stand." The view of Gilchrist is that "the source of experiments of political science is history, they rest on observations and experience. Every change in the form of government, every law passed, every war is an experiment in political science." Prof. Laski says that the study of political science "must be an effort to modify the results of experience in the history of states." Again, "What it is and why it is, it is by reason of its history. Its becoming is the clue of its being and it is from that being that we must wrest its secret."

Dr. Garner calls the historical method a particular form of comparative method. According to him, "It brings in review the great political movements of the past, traces the organic development of the national life, enquiries into the growth of political ideas from their inception to their realisation in objective institutions, discovers the moral idea as revealed in history and thereby points out the way of progress." Again, "None can deny the fact that political institutions can be better analysed and understood only through the knowledge of the past, that is how they have developed, or become what they are and to what extent they responded to the purposes for which they were originally destined."

History serves as the best kind of laboratory for political science. It is the store-house of incidents pertaining to human life. It keeps in secret the record of the progress and downfall of human civilisations and cultures. The origin of every political institution can be traced in the pages of history. If we want to learn about the origin and development of a political institution, we must seek the help of history. The present is the gift of the past. That is the reason why we seek the help of history when we study the origin, development and the present nature of such political institutions as the state and the government.

In his book "Nationality and Government", Zimmern writes, "It is contact with the past which equips man and communities for the tasks of the present, and the more bewildering the present, the greater the accumulation of material goods and material cares, the greater the need for inspiration and refreshment from the past."

The historical method is as old as Aristotle who maintained that to understand anything we must study its beginning and development. Montesquieu, Savigny, Sir John Seeley, Sir Henry Maine, Freeman and Laski are some of the eminent exponents of the historical method. Karl Marx found it an exclusive method. He explained the origin of the capitalist society in history and gave it the name of materialistic conception of history. Sir Ivor Jennings and J.B. Mackintosh wrote on the cabinet system of government with reference to the history of England during the nineteenth century. The study of political parties in Britain was conducted by Prof. Sammuel Beer by using the historical method. According to W.A. Dunning, political theory is a historical record of the conditions and effects of political ideas. The view of David Easton is that in the hands of Dunning, "the study of political science is virtually converted into the history of factual ideas and theories." C.H. McLlwain, the author of "The Growth of Political Thought in the West" and W.H. Sabine, author of "A History of Political Theory", have given great importance to the historical method.

Sidgwick and other followers of the philosophical school give a secondary importance to the historical method for two reasons. Their contention is that the historical method serves no useful purpose in solving our present and future needs as it refers only to the experience of what the political institutions had been. Every age has its own problems and every problem requires a solution relative to the time in which it occurs. Moreover, history is a mere narration of events and is not concerned with the goodness or badness of those events. Goodness or badness is determined only by ethical or philosophical standards and hence the philosophical method must precede the historical method.

While using the historical method, we must take certain precautions. We should guard against superficial resemblances and parallels. We should not let the present and the future be determined solely by the past. The historical method should not become a synonym for hide bound conservatism. Because a thing has been thus and so in the past, it does not follow that it should be thus and so in the present. We should avoid the temptation to make history support our preconceived notions. We should be altogether objective or scientific in our outlook. We should remember that the oft-quoted saying that history repeats itself is only a half-truth. The other half-truth is that history never repeats itself. Historical conditions never exactly reproduce themselves.

Advantages

There are certain advantages of the historical method. It is indispensable for a student of political science. It is through this method that he comes to know how and why certain political ideas and institutions originated and developed. The origin and growth of liberalism, nationalism and democracy cannot be understood without the use of the historical method. It is history which tells us why the Greek city-states were ultimately destroyed, why the ancient Roman Republic failed and on its ashes an Empire was built. History explains the gradual growth of political institutions. By adopting the historical method, students of political science can take advantage of the great contributions made by Plato, Aristotle, Machiavelli, Bodin, Hobbes, Locke, Montesquieu, Hegel, J.S. Mill, Karl Marx and others. The historical method enables us to arrive at certain generalisations on the basis of facts garnered from history. It assists in subjecting the generalisations to a process of continuous verification. It helps us to test the validity of excogitated ideas against concrete historical facts. It gives us a sense of history, a historical perspective. It teaches us that events are not isolated occurrences. They are terms in an infinite series. Sir John Seeley writes, "We must think, reason, generalise, define and distinguish; we must also collect, authenticate and investigate. If we neglect the first process, we shall accumulate facts to little purpose, because we shall have no test by which to distinguish facts which are important from those which are unimportant; and, of course, if we neglect the second process our reasoning, will be baseless and we shall but weave scholastic cobwebs."

Disadvantages

There are certain disadvantages also of the historical method. History only mentions what happened in the past without advising what ought to be done to political institutions. History being inductive does not deal with values. The deficiency has to be removed by a study of ethics and philosophy. History does not explain the advantages and disadvantages of political institutions. Historical material may be misused for supporting *a priori* or pre-conceived notions and we have to guard against that. This method may not be of much value to a dynamic or rapidly changing society. Some of the changes that take place with the passage of time may be revolutionary. In the historical method, superficial resemblances, though fascinating, may mislead a study of political science. Lord Bryce points out that the historical investigator is exposed to emotional influences and he very often contuses "the personal or accidental factors with the general cause at work." Ernest Barker has criticised the historical method in these words, "The state is concerned less with the historical, processes than with the fundamental realities — essence, purposes and value — which transcend the category of time." The view of David Easton is that the historical approach degenerates into historicism which means that researchers mix up their own values with history. They try to uphold their own values on the basis of historical evidence. That has been done by Dunning, Sabine and McLlwain.

THE COMPARATIVE METHOD

In the words of Vernon Dyke, "The comparative method consists of identifying similarities and differences. The process is pervasive in political inquiry as in all inquiry. Finding that various phenomena are similar enough we may group them together and give them a label which means that the comparative method enters into the process of concept formation. By the same token, the identification of comparisons and contrast is basic to classification". (Political Science: A Political Analysis (1960), p. 164). According to Dr. Garner, the comparative method aims at the study "of existing politics or those which have existed in the past, to assemble a definite body of material from which the investigator, by selection, comparison and elimination may discover the ideal types and progressive forces of political history". Prof. Gunner Heckscher points out that "comparative studies are the core of any study of foreign governments. They are of pedagogical importance, especially if we are to gain a reasonably realistic and relativistic view of our government." Again, "If we regard our field of study as mainly descriptive, comparisons are required to help us refine our tools of description. If we have hopes of establishing a general theory on an inductive basis, we do so only through comparison. If we attempt to test specific hypotheses, this is possible only if we bring in a sufficient number of examples, to be investigated by the comparative method".

The very essence of this method lies in comparing different historical facts and political events with a view to finding the causes responsible for them. Similar events may occur under different political conditions or vice versa. Prof. Gilchrist has given the example of Revolutions which, according to him, have taken place at all times and under various conditions. By the use of the comparative method we may try to know what is common and seek to find out common causes and consequences. We may take the example of the Russian Revolution of 1917. Political thinkers compare it to the Great Rebellion and the French Revolution. They not only try to explain what had happened but also point out the general principles which may serve as a guide for the future.

Many great scholars have used the comparative method in ancient and modern times. Aristotle was the pioneer in this field. He studied as many as 150 constitutions for his detailed comparative research and succeeded in deducing certain general principles. After a comparative study, he was able to give the features of tyranny, oligarchy and democracy. In modern times, the comparative method has found favour with many political scientists of high repute. We may refer to the comparative study made in the eighteenth century by Montesquieu, the author of "Spirit of Laws" (1748). De Tocqueville, Laboulaye, J.S. Mill and Lord Bryce have also followed this method.

J.S. Mill refers to three forms of comparative method. He regards the single factor difference as the "most perfect". By this method, two states which are identical in all respects except one, are taken for comparison to find out the results of single point difference. There may be perfect similarity between two states regarding natural resources, system of law, ethnic conditions and other factors, but economically one may be highly advanced while the other may be backward. This great contrast in the economic sphere may be explained by the single point difference concerning tariffs. One of them may have *laissez faire.* Likewise, two states may resemble each other in several respects and may look identical, but there may be a difference in the standard of living. The difference may be due to planning on a vast scale in one country and the absence of planning in the other. (2) The second form of comparative method may be indirect difference between two countries. Two states may be taken up for comparative study by finding out the presence of one factor in one country and its absence in the other. One state may have a protective trade system and other Laissez faire. (3) By the method of agreement, two states having many differences may be made the subject of comparative study, but there may be two points of agreement between them. The common thing between them may be restrictive trade policy and the prosperity may be attributed to restrictive trade in both cases.

Two other methods of comparative study are the *method of residues* and the *method of concomitant variations.* The scholar using the method of residues first of all takes into consideration the whole picture of political phenomena concerning two or more states marked out for comparative study. From the whole phenomena, he finds those positions which can be linked by cause and effect and the remaining portion of residue is taken up for further study which leads him to say that it is the product of the causes other than those discovered at the first instance. The researcher using the method of concomitant variations tries to establish cause and effect connection between two phenomena. He may find that whenever one phenomenon changes in a certain manner, another phenomenon changes in another way.

Lord Bryce compared the working of democracy in various countries like England, the United States, France, Australia, New Zealand etc. and came to his conclusions with regard to the relative merits and demerits of democracy. About the comparative method, he wrote: "That which entitles it to be called scientific is that it reaches general conclusions by tracing similar results to similar causes, eliminating those disturbing influences which, present in one country and absent in another, make the results in the examined cases different in some points while similar in others. When by this method of comparison the differences between the working of democratic government in one country and another have been noted, the local and special conditions, physical or social or economic, will be examined so as to determine whether it is in them that the source of these differences is to be found. If not in them, then we must turn to the institutions and try to discover which of those that exist in popular governments have worked best...When allowance has been made for the different conditions under which each acts, it will be possible to pronounce upon the balance of considerations, which form offers the best prospect of success. After the differences, between one popular government and another, have been accounted for, the points of similarity which remain will be what one may call democratic human nature, viz., the normal or permanent habits and tendencies of citizens in a democracy and of a democratic community as a whole."

When the present Constitution of India was to be framed, Sir B.N. Rau, the Constitutional Adviser to the Government of India, was deputed to visit various countries with a view to studying the working of their political institutions. He not only submitted his report but also a book containing the constitutions of the various countries was compiled for the guidance of the members of the Constituent Assembly.

G.A. Almond and Powell in their book "Comparative Politics: A Developmental Approach" (1966) have expressed dissatisfaction at the manner in which a study of comparative government has been made till recent years. They have raised three points of criticism. The approach to comparative government is marked by parochialism as it is confined to the European area only. The study of foreign governments is configurative as it illuminated the peculiar characteristics of individual political systems. It is marked by formalism as it deals with legal norms, rules, political ideas and ideologies rather than performance, interaction and behaviour.

As a result of the work of David Easton, G.A. Almond and D. Apter, the discipline of comparative politics has been reoriented by the influence of structure-function analysis. According to Easton, a solution to the problem of comparing governments can be found by examining political life in terms of a system receiving certain inputs from the society. All governments process inputs and transform them into outputs. General comparisons can be made and they amount to a detailed examination of the content of both sides of the operation. Taking Easton's analysis as the starting point, Almond looks for the functions which can be included among the inputs and outputs of all political systems. Looking at the conversion process which takes place within the political system, Easton shows that six such functions can be separated. First, on the input side, demands are formulated (or articulated) and combined (or aggregated). Second, on the output side, rules as formulated (rule-making), applied (rule-application) and adjudicated in individual cases (rule-adjudication). These various activities are communicated within the system and outside. According to Almond, "Apart from converting inputs into outputs, the system has also to be defined in terms of its ability to maintain and adapt itself (through a process of political socialisation) and in terms of the character of its achievements (capability)." Almond's analysis is known as structural-functionalism. The yardstick with which political systems are measured consists of the functions which are performed by the political system and the units which are being compared are the various structures which compose individual political systems. According to Almond, once the functions of a political system are defined operationally and the structures are categorised with precision, it becomes possible to write an equation of each political system which shows how much of which function is fulfilled by a particular structure.

The comparative method can be used only under certain conditions. The states under study should be contemporary. They should have a common historical basis with common political and social institutions. For example, Britain and India cannot be put on par as they do not satisfy the necessary conditions.

The researcher following the comparative method studies the historical facts, political conditions and events and tries to examine whether there are resemblances and differences. He makes a comparative study of political events and institutions in different countries at different times. He may find striking resemblance between the backgrounds to the origin and growth of democratic institutions in two countries. A comparison may enable him to know the conditions which favoured the growth of those institutions and he may be able to draw his own inferences. Likewise, he may study why democratic governments established at the same time in two different countries did not work satisfactorily. The comparative method can help us to find out why political development was relatively smooth in the United States after the American War of Independence and why the French Revolution was followed by Reign of Terror and the emergence of Napoleon as a dictator in France.

It has rightly been said that the comparative method must be used with great care. Dr. Garner has warned against the danger of the comparative method. According to him, the danger of this method "lies in the liability to error" to which it is susceptible in practice since in the effort to discover general principles, the diversity of conditions and circumstances such as differences of temperament and genius of the people, economic and social conditions, moral and legal standards, political training and experience are apt to be ignored or minimized". A comparison of the United States and India with regard to democracy is not of much use. Herbert Spencer's comparison is another glaring example of the wrong use of this method. He compared the state to a living organism and arrived at absurd conclusions. While considering a living organism, he tried to establish an analogy between functions of the state and those of a living organism. Barker rightly points out that one must not forget that metaphor is not an argument and a parallel between a state and an individual is not an explanation of their relation.

The view of Prof. Gilchrist is that in the comparative method, the ordinary process of inductive logic must be followed. That implies the method of simple agreement, the method of single difference, the double method of agreement or the joint method of agreement and difference, the method of residues and the method of concomitant (accompanying) variations. Those methods, applicable in natural sciences like Chemistry, are equally applicable in political science though the results are not so accurate.

The fact must not be ignored that there is a limited practicability of transferring the fruits of political ingenuity from one country to another. While trying to find out the general principles underlying the political institutions, we must take into account the differences in the social, moral, intellectual, temperamental, political and economic conditions of the countries or the communities concerned. A comparison between India and Pakistan is advantageous because there are similar conditions in both countries. The parliamentary system of government as in practice in Britain cannot work in the same way in India or Pakistan on account of the temperament and genius of the people belonging to both countries, their economic and social conditions, their moral and legal standards and their political training and experience in administration. The comparative method succeeds only when due prominence is given to the human element, their manners, customs, habits and environments. Otherwise, there is the danger of meaningless comparison of "empty form and ossified rituals". The view of Prof. Merriam is that political science "can be truly scientific only to the degree in which it contributes to the creation of a science of man." The growing importance of sociology in the comparative method must not be ignored. One of the great contributions of contemporary political science is "that it is proving...to the great contributions of contemporary political science is "that it is proving...to the extent to which cooperation with sociology is possible as well as indispensable to political science in general and especially to comparative studies."

It is worthy of notice that the study of comparative governments has grown in recent years and has become a major branch of study "with scholars working on detailed problems and theorists attempting grand syntheses." The potentiality of the comparative method must not be ignored. It is one of the most rewarding and stimulating parts of political science.

THE PHILOSOPHICAL METHOD

Some of the advocates of the philosophical method are Plato, Rousseau, Hegel, Bradley, Bosanquet, Kant, J.S. Mill and Sidgwick. The philosophical method is speculative and deductive in nature. We begin with certain assumptions and determine institutions which can best realise them. According to Prof. Gilchrist, the philosophical method "starts from some abstract original ideas as to the nature of the state, its aims, its functions and its future. It then attempts to harmonise its theories with the actual facts of history." Abstract ideas and concepts are taken as the starting point and an effort is made to substantiate those ideas with reference to the facts of history. This method combines and relates ideas with facts.

Robert E. Murphy refers to two aims of the philosophical approach to the study of political science. In the first place, the political philosopher is engaged in the study of right concerning the nature, meaning and measure of truth within such topics as law the state, freedom, power, consent and authority. He is interested in finding solutions to trans-national, moral-political problems. He is interested in finding answers to the relation between law and morality and how good life can be realised through the state. Another aim of the political philosopher is empirical. Owing to the philosopher's training in logic, epistemology and semantics, collection of facts by the political scientists becomes more correct and precise.

The philosophical method suffers from certain limitations. The user of this method sometimes forgets the facts and allows his imagination to run riot. He deduces theories which have little or no foundation in historical facts. As this method aims at discovering what the state ought to be, the ends and purpose of the state are drawn from philosophical angle. Plato, in his Republic and Sir Thomas More in Utopia conceived of an ideal state which has no or little foundation on the basis of historical facts and does not bear any relationship to human nature and reality of this earth. This type of state is the reality of imaginary world. Likewise, Karl Marx judged everything in terms of the economic factor. He based his political ideology on the theory of economic interpretation of history. The result is that the philosophical method degenerates into what Bluntschli calls an ideology which pays little or no attention to facts. The leaders of the French Revolution and their followers preached the doctrines of liberty, equality and fraternity. The result was that thousands of persons were killed due to violence during the Reign of Terror which came in the wake of the French Revolution. The Soviet Union, China and many other Communist countries became the victims of the theory of economic interpretation of history, class-war and surplus value propounded by Karl Marx.

Critics of the philosophical method point out certain defects in this method. The political philosopher formulates a large number of principles which cannot be substantiated. Conclusions are drawn upon maxims which cannot be verified. Political philosophers are not able to reach a universally accepted definition of philosophy. Philosophical principles may be of great value from the theoretical point of view but it may be almost impossible to translate some of them into practice. There is a wide gap between the soaring idealism of the political philosopher and the hard realities of the imperfect world. The views expressed in the Republic of Plato are too idealistic to be followed in the world of political affairs. Plato himself realised that nowhere in the world there could be a state answering the description of the ideal state depicted in his Republic. The same can be said about the Utopia of Sir Thomas More. The same applies to the Ram Rajya of Mahatma Gandhi. There is a tendency in the philosophical method to establish certain conclusions on non-verifiable and self-evident axioms. The result is that political analysis is exposed to the danger of lapsing into speculative phantasies divorced from realities.

The philosophical method takes into account bigger areas and ignores the smaller ones. It ignores the role that sociological environments and behaviour of the individuals play in conditioning a political phenomenon. The actual actors in all political phenomena are the individuals whose behaviour is in turn formed by his psychological make-up and the sociological environments.

The philosophical method has also certain advantages. It helps in distinguishing good Trom bad. It helps in value-laden study which eventually helps in evaluating a theory. Leo Strauss writes, "Values cannot be excluded from the study of politics. A theory is regarded good or bad only from the angle of its value. Generally speaking, it is impossible to understand thought or action or work without evaluating it."

The view of Sail is that the philosophical method "is a good antidote to pedestrianism. Philosophic argument develops the intelligence; it imparts resourcefulness and elasticity of mind." (Political Institutions—A Preface, p.5) Observation and comparison have great value in political analysis, but an obsession with the living realities must not cloud our vision of the ideal. The reason is that much of what happens in politics is as much a product of empirical investigation as an enthusiasm for an ideal

The political philosopher deserves credit for laying down great principles for whose realisation the state is supposed to exist. In this age of science and materialism, the philosophical method is of great value. While science must be given due importance, great principles, human values and ethical considerations also must be given a proper place. The philosophical method guides the investigation properly and prevents political scientists from getting lost in the world of mere facts and experiments.

However, the fact remains that the political scientist must make a very cautious use of the philosophical/deductive method to a limited extent only. He must see to it that he is not led into the clouds of empty speculation and idealism which have no bearing in actual life.

STATISTICAL OR QUANTITATIVE METHOD

This is one of the most modern and most useful methods for dealing with political phenomena and hence it is very popular these days. This method is particularly applied to the study of political parties, public opinion, comparative governments and international relations. The view of David Thomson is that "until some such statistical and sociological technique is applied to international relations, the science of studying international relations will make little further progress in method." This method has been employed by Tarde, Le Bon, Graham Wallas, Lord Bryce, Lowell, Water Lippmann, Stuart Rice, Louis Bean, H.D. Anderson, P.F. Davidson and H.F. Gosnell. The view of D. Waldo is that '*Public Opinion and Popular Government* by Lowell and *Public Opinion* by Lippmann "did much to delineate the field in terms meaningful to American political science." The subject of public opinion has become a field for specialisation in many universities. This method has been used in such fields as voting motivation, occupational mobility, occupational trends on a national and local basis, concentration of economic power along with its effect on political power etc. In some countries, Gallup Polls or public opinion polls are held to find out the trends in public opinion. "If skillfully framed and conducted, such polls have shown themselves in Britain as in America to be capable of a high degree of accuracy. A week before the 1945 elections, the News Chronicle Gallup Poll showed within 1% accuracy the results of the General Election."

In order to be apprised of the exact situation and to know the exact position of its population, the government collects the data of majority and minority groups of the people. That data plays a decisive role at the time of general elections. Every, political party collects the data of the people of the various races, religions and castes inhabiting different constituencies and on that basis, it makes a guess as to how many people would vote for it. The government collects data, about the economic condition of the people and on that basis arrives at the conclusion whether there has been any increase in the national income or not. The opposition parties criticise the government only on the basis of that data.

Before preparing the Five-Year Plan and deciding national policies, the government collects data of production, distribution, consumption, import and export of various items and on that basis, it deals with the present situation.

H. Dewey Anderson and Percy E. Davidson have applied the statistical method to voting motivation, occupational mobility as it affects state-governmental operations, occupational trends upon a national and local basis and concentration trends upon a national and local basis and concentration of economic power and its effect on political power.

However, the statistical method must be used with great care. We must be careful in the collection and use of the statistics. There is the possibility of the data supplied not being exact. Wrong decision may be taken on the basis of wrong data. Lowell rightly says that "statistics, like real pies are good if you know the person who made them and are sure of the ingredients" as "by themselves they are strangely likely to mislead, because unless the subject is understood in all its bearings, some element can easily be left out of account which wholly falsifies the result." Statistics may be manipulated to suit the interests of a political party. Those may be distorted for electoral gains and political manoeuvring. In spite of this, it cannot be denied that a knowledge of statistical principles and sampling method is useful to the students of political science.

BIOLOGICAL METHOD

The advocates of this method regard the state as an organism and point out the similarities between the structure and development of the state and those of a living organism. The state organs and functions are studied by employing terminology and procedure similar to those in biological science. Auguste Comte, Herbert Spencer, Gumplowicz, Schaiffle, Durkheim, De Greef, Fouillee, Worms, Letourneau, Lilienfeld and Novicov are some of the writers who have made notable contributions to the study of organised society from the biological point of view.

Like many other methods, an important drawback of the biological method is that it rests mainly upon analogy instead of real similarity in essentials. It also applies biological laws to the development of the state as if the state was not different from an organism. The resemblance between the state and human organism is merely superficial. The laws of growth and change which govern one cannot be applied to the growth and development of the other. Nothing is gained by putting emphasis on analogy. Prof. Giddings writes. "The attempts to construct a science of society by means of biological analogies has been abandoned by all serious investigators of social phenomena."

The weakness of the biological method makes serious thinkers cast doubts upon the very status of this method. Some writers do not even regard this as a method, but only as a point of view.

PSYCHOLOGICAL METHOD

This is one of the most modern methods of dealing with political phenomena. This method has been recently employed by many writers to explain political phenomena through psychological laws. While making laws, the state pays due regard to the possible reaction of the public. It also gives due consideration to public reaction to the legislation to be passed by the government.

Many writers in the past including Plato, Aristotle, Machiavelli and Hobbes dealt with human nature in their writings, but they did not study human nature in a systematic manner. That has been done only in recent times. Modern writers like Lowell and Lasswell have tried to build up political theory on the basis of human psychology. *Psychopathology and Politics* (1930) by Lasswell shows how he used medical psychology with the help of eminent doctors to study political behaviour. Individual psychology and motives as well as group psychology and motives are studied in relation to political activities.

The importance of this method in dealing with elections, public opinion and political parties is great, but this method on its own cannot cover much distance in the study of political science. This method has to be employed alongwith other methods.

JURIDICAL METHOD

The most favourite method of studying political phenomena among German political writers is the juridical method which aims at determining the contents of the rules of public law and drawing therefrom conclusions to which they lead. This method is favoured by the analytical jurists. It regards the state as a legal personality or a juridical person and considers political science as a science of legal norms. It regards organised society not as a social or political phenomenon, but a purely juridical regime, and ensemble of public law, rights and obligations founded on a system of pure logic and reason.

This method was used by John Austin and many other eminent jurists who made valuable contributions to the study of political science. The development of the legal concepts of sovereignty, state law, international law, constitutional law and administrative law is a distinct achievement of the jurists. However, this method highly restricts the field of study of political science. It considers only the legal principles although political processes are at work far beyond the legal frontiers. This method puts too much emphasis on legalism and formalism, Extra-legal factors are either belittled or totally ignored. If this method is followed, the study of political science can neither be complete nor correct.

METHOD OF ANALOGY

This method was used by Herbert Spencer who compared the state to an organism. His view was that both the state and an organism possess the sustaining, distributary and regulating system and both exhibit the same process of development. From that, he came to the conclusion that the state was an organism.

It is true that the method of analogy serves a useful purpose, but it must not be forgotten that analogy is no proof. A thing may look like another but it cannot be equated with the other. The difficulty "of its application in political science is all the more marked because of the vast number of circumstances surrounding any given instance."

SOCIOLOGICAL METHOD

This method regards the state chiefly as a social organism, which has the qualities of the individuals forming it. Like the life of the individual, the life of the state is studied by the application of the theory of evolution. This method explains the origin, growth, structure and activities of the state in terms of the physical and psychical causes working together in a process of evolution.

This method is becoming very popular these days and that has led to the birth of a new subject known as political sociology.

Conclusion

Leslie Lipson writes that Plato, Aristotle and Machiavelli represent three points of view in politics. Plato projects his imagination into the future and portrays a picture of an ideal state. For that reason, his method is called idealistic. Aristotle is more scientific and realistic. He relies upon the wisdom of experience and bases his conclusions upon an analysis of what he saw around him. His method is called scientific and realistic. The pre-occupation of Machiavelli was "with the techniques that will lead to the desired goal." Questions of right and wrong do not enter his calculations.

A careful student of political science combines the historical and philosophical methods. He tests and corrects his deductive principles by the actual facts of human experience and interprets the facts of life in the light of abstract or *a priori* principles. While his feet stand four square on solid facts, his head soars high into the skies. He tries to combine realism with idealism. He does not like that realism which does not look beyond his nose or that idealism which loses itself in the clouds. He follows the footsteps of men like Aristotle and Burke who combine in their writings the historical and philosophical methods.

However, many American writers put too much emphasis on methods, techniques and skills, almost to the exclusion of first principles and value-judgements. Dr. Macpherson points out that in Britain there is much "less emphasis on purely empirical research and more inclination to examine political institutions and processes from the point of view of the purpose they serve and the purpose they ought to serve." Political scientists in Britain are not worried about new techniques. There is among them an appreciation of value-judgements and a perceptible mistrust of purely empirical research. Even in the United States, writers like Prof. J.H. Hallowell are of the view that "The social sciences are not so much in need of new research techniques as some suppose, but of convictions based upon rational principles."

In modern times, great reliance is placed on the inductive method. That is due to the fact that in an age of science and reason, "the spirit and method of all true science is inductive and pragmatic, not deductive and dogmatic. It is also positive, that is, it rejects all *a priori* arguments, purely abstract ideas and absolute standards, and builds conclusions upon the accumulated experience of the past as modified by the changing conditions and circumstances of the present." Instead of following only one method, different inductive methods should be followed according to the problem to be studied. A student of political science must take advantage of the fruits of the historical, observational, experimental and comparative methods and also study the subject from the sociological, juridical and psychological angles. It is only then that facts and ideas can be understood and appreciated properly. A political scientist must refrain from making a fetish of only one of two methods at the cost of others.

There is also the necessity of taking into consideration the philosophical, values. The philosopher should guide the politician and statesman as human values cannot be ignored in the name of scientific reasoning and precision. Today the world is more in need of moral values as never before as the power-crazy politicians forget human values and moral standards. Ethical principles have to be given a respectable place in the study of political science. The champions of positivism, empiricism and behaviouralism should not ignore the methods which rely on values.

The correct method to be followed in political science is called evaluative analysis. Theory and description should be studied together. Things should be studied not only in theory but also in practice. While studying the working of the Parliament of India, we have to find out how the people have been voting, how its members have been behaving, what efficiency they have shown in their work and the spirit of sacrifice which governs their lives. We have to study the effect of the introduction of universal suffrage on election results and the quality of legislation passed by Parliament.

A political philosopher cannot work in a vacuum. He has to take into consideration the actual political institutions of a country. Dr. Finer writes, "Since political achievement is for man and through man, political achievement is through institutions which are nothing but man acting more or less deliberately in a fairly durable concert for the attainment of a considered complex of ends." A political philosopher is concerned not only with an end but also with the ways and means. Plato started with the ideal of justice and to achieve that he had to provide for institutions under which alone justice could be achieved Hobbes was terribly afraid of lawlessness and he gave his theory of social contract to achieve the object of security. His conclusion was that monarchy was the most suitable and orderly kind of government. Locke was in search of happiness and for that purpose he advocated government by consent. Dunning writes, "The happiness and security of the individual figure, not as essential to the perpetuity of a government, but as the end for which alone government is ever called into existence."

While studying political science, we have to take into consideration human nature because the state exists for man and not vice versa. We have to study his psychology to find out where lies his interest. Till recently, it was believed that man is a rational being, but that view has been challenged by Graham Wallas in his book *Human Nature in Politics.* His view is that man is not rational in his behaviour. To quote him, "If indeed a man were followed through one ordinary day without his knowing it by a cinematographic camera and photographer and if all his acts and sayings were produced before him next day, he would be astonished to know how few of them were the result of a deliberate search for the means attaining ends." We may agree or not with Graham Wallas, but the importance of psychology in the study of political science cannot be denied or minimised. Moreover, no institution of the government is eternal and perfect. It must change for the better or for the worse. Dr. Finer says, "Institutions are nothing but useful or useless habits: they were acquired for a purpose and purpose changes. The world of political reality is not the printed world of books or of statutes or of administrative rules and orders. The cut and dried is not political." We have to study the changing institutions and their effect on the government and the people.

The view of Prof. Gilchrist is that political science as a science "is more difficult than the natural sciences. The difficulty in the application of the methods arises out of the innumerable elements, undefined and undefinable, which occur in any science of man. Much patience in comparing details, much care in applying inductive methods, much mental balance in making judgements, all these are necessary in political science. It is a science which taxes the scientific mind to the utmost and its conclusions no less than the discoveries of Chemistry vitally affect the daily lives of the inhabitants of the globe."(Principles of Political Science, p. 11)

Scholars are not satisfied with the progress of research in political science. David Easton writes, "We might attribute part of the cause of the inching pace of political research of relative lack of concern for questions on methodology, the logic behind the scientific procedures which political scientists often say they are using." (The Political System (1959), p.48)

SUGGESTED READINGS

Almond, G.A. and Powell, G.B. : *Comparative Politics, A Developmental Approach.*

Asirvatham, Eddy : *Political Theory,* 1984.

Ball, Alan R. : *Modern Politics and Government,* 1971.

Barker, Ernest : *The Study of Political Science and Its Relation to Cognate Studies.*

Brecht, Arnold : *Political Theory.*

Bryce, James : *Modern Democracies,* 1921.

Catlin, G.E.G. : *A Study of Principles of Politics.*

Catlin, G.E.G. : *The Science and Method of Politics,* 1927.

Deutsch, Karl W. : *Politics and Government.*

Dyke, Vernon Van : *Political Science: A Political Analysis,* 1960.

Easton, David : *The Political System,* 1951.

Eisenmann, Charles : *Contemporary Political Science,* 1950.

Finer, H. : *Theory and Practice of Modern Government.*

Garner, J.W. : *Political Science and Government,* 1955.

Gettell, R.G. : *Political Science.*

Giddings : *Principles of Sociology.*

Gilchrist, R.N. : *Principles of Political Science.*

Greaves, H.R.C. : *The Foundations of Political Theory.*

Hacker, Andrew : *The Study of Politics: The Western Traditional and American Origins.*

Heckscher, Gunnar : *The Study of Government and Politics.*

Laski, H.J. : *The Danger of Being a Gentleman and Other Essays.*

Lasswell, H.D. : *The Future of Political Science.*

Leacock, Stephen : *Elements of Political Science.*

Lewis, G.C. : *Methods of Observation and Reasoning in Politics.*

Lipson, L. : *The Great Issues of Politics.*

Merkl, Peter H. : *Political Continuity and Change,* 1967.

Merriam : *New Aspects of Politics.*

Oakshott, Michael : *Rationalism in Politics.*

Parsons, Talcott : *The Social System.*

Pennock, J. Ronald and David G. Smith : *Political Science, An Introduction.*

Pollock, F. : *An Introduction to the History of the Science of Politics.*

Popper, Karl : *Conjectures and Refutations.*

Sail : *Political Institutions—A Preface.*

Sidgwick, H. : *Elements of Politics.*

Waldo, Dwight : *Political Science in the United States of America.*

Wallas, Graham : *Human Nature in Politics,* 1920.

Wilson, F.G. : *The Elements of Modern Politics.*

Wiseman, H. Victor (Ed.) : *Political Science: An Outline for the Intending Student of Government, Politics and Political Science.*

Zimmern : *Nationality and Government.*

4

CHAPTER

Political Science and Its Relation to Allied Sciences

Learning Objectives

- Political Science and History
- Political Science and Economics
- Political Science and Ethics
- Points of Distinction Between Political Science and Ethics
- Political Science and Sociology
- Differences
- Political Science and Psychology
- Political Science and Biology
- Political Science and Anthropology
- Political Science and Jurisprudence
- Political Science and Public Administration
- Political Science and Statistics
- Political Science and Geography
- Suggested Readings

Human knowledge can be divided into two broad categories viz., natural sciences and social sciences. While natural sciences deal with the physical world, social sciences deal with human beings, their collective social life, social behaviour, organisations and activities. Man is a social animal and he lives in society. There are many dimensions of his social life; economic, political, psychological, historical, sociological etc. Many problems are the common concern of all the social sciences which view them from their own standpoint. Politics is a social science which is concerned with the political aspect of social man and its subject-matter is political institutions, processes, activities, behaviour etc. It is related to other social sciences such as history, economics, sociology, psychology, ethics etc.

In recent times, a new approach has developed in the study of social sciences known as the inter-disciplinary approach which means that researchers and students of one specialised social science should work in coordination with the researchers and students of other specialised social sciences. It is contended that many social sciences cannot be objectively studied because society is a totality whose various aspects are inter-connected and inter-dependent. That totality cannot be studied by separating one aspect from the rest and hence the need for cross-fertilization in the social sciences. The view of Easton is that specialisation in social sciences "has stimulated a movement towards an integration of our compartmentalised knowledge which should go a long way towards remedying these defects."

All social sciences have a common body of theory or general theory and the paths of different social sciences cross and run parallel at some points. In spite of the fact that each social science is busy in formulating its own boundaries, scope, methods and concepts, the urge for mutual cooperation and exchange is there because it is not possible to study any specific social science without mutual exchange with other disciplines. This approach is known us inter-disciplinary study in social sciences. When political science is studied by adopting methods and concepts from other social sciences like history, economics, sociology, psychology etc., it can be called inter-disciplinary study of political science. Various subdivisions of political science like political sociology, political psychology, political economy etc. have emerged on that basis. The factors which have given rise to inter-disciplinary study are the development of new methods in the study of political science, complexity of the social organisation and the subject-matter of politics, increase in the scope of political science and inadequacy of political science as a self-contained independent discipline. This approach has been favoured by both the Liberal writers and the Marxists. The only difference is that while the Liberals put emphasis on psychology, sociology and anthropology, the Marxists put emphasis on economic factors and historical analysis.

POLITICAL SCIENCE AND HISTORY

History is a study of man, human society, associations and the state and gives information about the rise, development and fall of the state and other human associations. It deals with changes in history and their causes. The cause and effect relationship of social phenomena can be understood by scientific understanding of history. History is not merely concerned with past happenings, contingencies and events. It also enriches our knowledge about the processes through which changes have taken place in society. History gives a scientific understanding of the past which enlightens human understanding by giving legitimate generalisation, laws of social development and change, processes of change etc. E.H. Carr writes, "Scientists, social scientists and historians are all engaged in different branches of the same study, the study of man and his environment, of the effects of man on his environment and of his environment on man. The object of the study is the same: to increase man's understanding of and mastery over his environment." (What is History? p. 80).

The relation between political science and history is very intimate. The view of Sir John Seeley is that "History without political science has no fruit and political science without history has no root." Again, "History without political science is a study incomplete, truncated, as on the other hand, political science without history is hollow and baseless." Again, "Politics are vulgar when not liberalised by history and history fades into mere literature when it loses sight of its relation to politics." His view is that ultimately political science and history will become identical with each other.

According to Lord Acton, "The science of politics is the one science that is deposited by the stream of history like the grains of gold in the sands of a river." Burns writes, "So conceived, history will be made something more than the luxury of a scholar. It will be the inspiration of honest politicians; it will be real basis for criticism of the present and modification of the future. It will be then recognised to be what it really is—the biography of ideals." (Political Ideals, p. 27). Lipson observes, "With its chronological treatment, history offers to the students of politics a sense of growth and development and thus affords insight into the processes of social changes." (The Great Issues of Politics, pp. 78-80). Garner says, "To fully comprehend political science in its fundamental relations, we must study it historically and to interpret history in its true significance, we must study that politically."(Political Science and Government, p. 30).

The view of Lord Bryce is that "Political Science stands mid-way between history and politics, between the past and the present. It has drawn its material from the one; it has to apply them to the other." Dr. Lencock says that some history "is part of political science, the circle of their contents overlapping an area enclosed by each." Prof. Freeman says that history is past politics and politics is present history. Burgess writes that if history and politics are separated, one becomes a cripple if not a corpse, the other a will-of-the-wisp.

According to Prof. Willoughby, "History gives us the third dimension of political science." It provides us with the raw material of political science. It serves as the best kind of laboratory for political scientists. Prof. Gilchrist writes, "In the treatise of political science, we must trace the history of various institutions, not for the sake of history but to enable us to form conclusions of our science. In so much as history not merely records events but analyses causes and points out tendencies, it overlaps political science. Political science, however, goes further. It uses historical facts to discover general laws and principles; it selects, analyses and systematises the facts of history in order to extract the permanent principles of political life. Political science further is Ideological, that is to say, it deals with the state as it ought to be, whereas history deals with what it has been." (Political Science, p. 12). Soltau says, "History is really the past tense of a subject of which political science is the present."

History deals with past events, movements, revolutions, national movements etc. and gives information about the origin and development of political institutions and thought. When various issues and concepts are discussed in political science, generally their historical development is also taken into account. Without an understanding of the past and the knowledge between clause and effect of various events, the present cannot be understood and no line of action for the future can be decided. There is continuity and change in political processes and history gives a record of those processes. By studying history, the students of political science can find out meaningful patterns and information which guides them in understanding the present and outlining the future. Present politics has its roots in the past and history is the key to the roots of politics. It is like an X-ray film which helps in the diagnosis of the evils of present politics. Without historical foundations, politics becomes merely speculative. History is not only a guide-line. It is the laboratory of political science. As experimentation in politics is very costly, it is better that we should learn from the mistakes and experiences of others and that is possible only if we study history. The origin and nature of the state and other institutions can be understood by analysing history. Liberalism accepts the historical theory of the origin of the state. The Marxist view is that the state originated with class division and class struggle in society. History gives information about class struggles, revolutions and political movements which help us in formulating our own theory of revolution or the theory of bringing about a change. History is a searchlight for political research. It is a light-house for political action.

Politics is not merely a beggar at the doors of history. It has also influenced history. Political ideas, thoughts, leaders and motives have contributed in shaping human history. However, politics is not the most important factor in history. Economic factors have also contributed towards the shaping of history. Without understanding political concepts such as democracy, liberty, equality etc. and political ideologies like Marxism and Fascism, it is not possible even to understand the historical process. Political revolutions have contributed in making the history of societies. The development of behaviouralism in contemporary politics brought about a separation between history and political science. The emphasis is shifted to a realistic factual analysis, planning, cooperation and equilibrium to solve political problems. The result was that political science drifted away from history and ethics and came closer to psychology, sociology and economics. Traditional descriptions and historical methods of the study of political science are out of tune. The view of Charles Merriam is that the work of historians is irrelevant to the study of contemporary politics and emphasis has to be put on sociological, psychological and economic factors while analysing human life.

There are certain differences between political science and history. History is wider in scope than political science. History is concerned not only with political institutions but also with art, religion, culture, society, sciences etc. Political science has nothing to do with those subjects. History is concerned mainly with the past but political science is concerned not only with the present but also with the future. History is mainly descriptive but political science is both normative and descriptive. History gives the events in the chronological order but politics is concerned with the analysis of those events and tries to find out the cause and effect relationship of historical events.

Gunner Heckshcr points out that the problems facing the students of political science are not the same as those of the historians. For certain purposes, history does not provide us the data which we need. A historian studying the political institutions of France, will describe the origin, development and ideological and institutional factors of the French multi-party system. A student of comparative politics would ask whether the conditions for the existence of a multiple party system are institutional, social, sectional or ideological. He would also compare the French party system with similar systems in other countries. He may find that similar conditions in the United States had not produced a multi-party system. It is not correct to say that we should "use history but not as historians do," for the historians are in principle interested in all aspects of data and developments, including our own, but not excluding a number of others. (The Study of Comparative Government and Politics, pp. 55-56).

Political Science and Economics

The relation between political science and economics is very intimate. As a matter of fact, economics started its early career as political economy. When the Greek philosophers used the concept of political economy, they meant that economics is a part of politics and the state. Adam Smith, the father of modern economics, named his book as "Wealth of Nationals." He conceded that economics is a science to enrich people and the state. Writers like Machiavelli, Locke, Bentham, James Mill and J.S. Mill discussed political and economic affairs together. The modern state is regarded as a welfare state whose main functions are economic. Karl Marx regarded politics as a part of political economy. Instead of accepting economics as a part of politics, his contention was that politics is merely an aspect of economics. The economic basis of society or sub-structure is also the basis of politics which in turn forms a part of the superstructure of the economic sub-structure of society. According to Marx, it is the economic factor alone which determines the entire history of a country. To quote him, "It is not the consciousness of man which determines the material conditions of life but it is material conditions of life which determine their consciousness." Politics has its roots in the material conditions of human life. The view of Sabine is that "the most important part of Marx's social philosophy was the theory that the system of economic production is the foundation on which the institutional and ideological super-structure of society is based." Dr. Engels writes, "The ultimate causes of all social changes and political revolutions are to be sought not in the minds of men, in their increasing insight into eternal truth and justice but in changes in the mode of production and exchange. They are to be sought not in the philosophy but in the economics of the period concerned."

The political conditions of a country are greatly affected by its economic conditions. Political ideologies are also influenced to a large extent by economic conditions. Political policies are generally influenced by the system of production and distribution. Stable and solid economy provides for a strong and efficient administration of a country.

The cause of all revolutions in the world has been primarily economic. Economic exploitation and injustice give birth to political movements. The exploitation of India by Britain gave birth to the nationalist movement in the country. Every political slogan has a smell of economic reform. Political ideologies like Liberalism, Socialism, Communism, Imperialism and Fascism have all economic basis. The hunger for economic exploitation is the cause of war. The political behaviour of man and associations is influenced by economic factors. Economic factors have contributed to the origin and development of the state. Political structure is closely associated with economic structure. The main functions of a modern welfare state are economic. There are economic motives behind political laws and policies. Political ideals like liberty, equality, rights, social justice and democracy etc. can be evaluated only on an economic basis. The subject-matter of both is the social man and the objective is human welfare.

According to Robins, "Economics is the science which studies human behaviour as a relationship between ends and scarce means which have alternative uses." Alfred Marshall writes, "Economics is study of man in ordinary business of life; it enquires how he gets his income and how he uses it. Thus, it is on one side a study of wealth and on the other and more important side, a part of study of man." The ideal of the welfare state is bringing closer both economics and political science. The main object of both is to enhance the well-being of the people and that is possible only when political and economic activities of the people go together. Poverty and unemployment are economic problems but they have a very close relationship with the policies of the government. At present, the government is trying to improve the economic condition of the people. It is the government which performs such economic activities as industrialisation, protection of infant industries, tariff laws, rate of economic growth, restrictions on internal and external trade etc. Every state tries to improve economic conditions of the people. It is rightly said that "political equality without economic equality is a myth." Gettell writes, "Since the Industrial Revolution, the relation of politics to economics has been very close. Mercantilist theories of the state control, individualistic theories of Laissez faire, the recent theories of governmental relation or of state control and of state planned economy represent the cycle of change in modern society." The extensive nationalisation of industry in Great Britain and the establishment of the Communist states in Russia and China are examples of the close relation between politics and economics.

There is no doubt that politics influences the economic system. Changes in government, political instability, war etc. influence the economic system profoundly. The state decides and defines all the economic policies and regulates the economy. Economic planning is one of the important functions of the modern state. The state plays an important role in production, distribution, price control, currency, trade, employer-employee relationship, budget, banking, export and import etc. The view of Prof. Galbraith is that the modern state is an "Industrial State."

The basis of many political issues agitations turns out to he economic. Likewise economic problems have political roots. When OPEC resorted to a hike in the prices of oil mainly with a view to forcing the Arab solution to the Arab-Israel political problem, that decision had far-reaching consequences on the economic and political systems of various developed and developing countries. It cannot be denied that political and economic power go together. Those who have political power ultimately come to possess economic power. That is so not only in a democracy, but also under dictatorship. In a democracy, when a political party comes to power, it tries to bring on the statute book such legislation as is in the interests of those who support it. The Labour Party in England is bound to pass those laws which are in the interests of its supporters. The same applies to the Conservative Party in England and the Indian National Congress in India. However, that does not mean that the party in power can bring about changes in the economic field without meeting any opposition from the vested interests who are adversely affected. The New Deal of Roosevelt was severely condemned by his opponents. What is true of democracy is also true of dictatorship. The only difference is that while under a democracy, changes are brought about by constitutional and peaceful methods, those are brought about by a revolution under dictatorship. The Bolshevists in Russia captured the machinery of the government in 1917. Before that, the economic resources of the country were in the hands of the privileged classes and the masses lived a life of misery and degradation. After the capture of political power in 1917, the machinery of the state was used by the Communists to improve the lot of the workers.

If it is true that economic power ultimately goes into the hands of those who wield political power, it is also true that those who possess economic power also capture political power in the long run. Experience shows that even if political power is transferred to the masses and wealth is allowed to be concentrated in the hands of a few, it is those few who continue to manage the government. The reason is that the poor masses are always ready and willing to sell their votes and that gives an opportunity to the rich. However, the masses who possess political power learn by degrees to vote for their own colleagues and thereby return them to the legislature and control the government. There is a potential danger which cannot be ignored. That danger is that those who possess the economic power manage to set aside the democratic institutions with a view to averting the doom which might follow as a result of the working of the government in favour of the poor. The experience of Spain shows how the nobility, the Church and the army in Spain joined hands under the leadership of General Franco to overthrow the Republican Government which attempted to enact legislation in favour of the working classes. In similar circumstances, Mussolini came to power in Italy in 1922. The dread of the Bolshevists frightened the industrial and propertied classes in Italy and they supported the Black Shirt Movement of Mussolini. The imperialist policy, aiming at the exploitation of the backward or weaker nations, is backed by the capitalist states. That shows that economic and political forces act together. Most of the problems which have to be faced in the imperialistic civilisation of our times, can be attributed to economic causes. A realistic student of political science is as much concerned with the problems of consumption, production, exchange, distribution and public finance, as that of economics. That is due to the fact that the economic problems have their repercussions in the political field also. The worldwide depression started in the Wall Street in the United States but it had its repercussions all over the world. The successful tackling of the economic problems strengthens the hands of the party in power. It was on account of the success of the New Deal that Roosevelt was elected President of the United States four times. There may be a split in the party in power on some economic issue which may lead to the fall of the ministry. Sir Robert Peel repealed the Corn Laws in 1846 and that led to the fall of his ministry resulting in the ruin of his political career.

Elections have become very costly. The candidates and the political parties to which they belong, have to collect huge amounts for election purposes. The result is that those who pay the money really control the whole show. The advent of Hitler lo power was facilitated by the help which was given to him by German industrialists like Hugenberg and Thyssen. Similar things have happened in other countries.

War is also caused by factors which are largely economic. The clash of conflicting interests forces nations to fight against one another. The view of some writers is that war cannot be abolished so long as the capitalist society exists in the present form.

The political institutions of a country are largely conditioned by the economic development of that country. The system of government which meets the needs of an agricultural country, cannot suit a highly industrialised country. The institutions of the Greek city states can find no place in modern society. The constitution of a country expresses the needs of its people. Law, to be law, must suit the requirements of the people. A system of government which caters to the needs of the people at one stage of economic development, cannot satisfy the people in another stage of growth. The needs of a society are determined largely by its economic environments and since it is the function of the government to cater to those needs, it follows that political science has very much to do with economics.

The government of a country is affected by its population which may be mainly urban or rural. The reason is that in the case of their concentration at one place, there are greater chances for the people to organise themselves and present a united front and thereby put an effective check on the power of the government. The Parisian Revolutions of 1830, 1848 and 1870 in France illustrate this point. However, that is not so in a country where most of the people live in villages. The reason is that it is very difficult to organise the villagers who are scattered. The means of transport and communication present formidable difficulties. The problems of finance have also to be overcome. Moreover, the people who live in villages are temperamentally conservative and radically different from those who live in cities.

The relation between political science and economics is so very intimate that sometimes the Departments of Political Science and Economics are combined together as in the case of the London School of Economics and Political Science and the Canadian School of Economics and Political Science.

However, there are differences between political science and economics. There is a difference in the approach of economics and political science. The study of economics is descriptive while that of political science is mainly normative. Ivor Brown points out that economics deals mainly with commodities and politics is concerned with human beings. Economics concentrates more on the study of prices and political science on the study of moral values. There is also a difference in the method of studying political science and economics. The method of studying economics is more scientific and empirical as compared to political science. The results drawn in the case of economics are more accurate than that of political science. Mathematical and statistical methods are applied in the study of economics but that is not possible in the case of political science. However, after the behavioural revolution in the study of political science, political scientists have also started the use of mathematical and statistical methods. The study of political science now includes statistical formulas, graphs, models etc. Efforts are being made to scientise the knowledge of political science. However, the conclusions drawn in political science are not so accurate and correct as in the case of economics. Political science deals with moral values but economics deals with the fixation of prices of the different commodities. While economics is basically a one assumption science *i.e.*, how to maximise satisfaction, political science has innumerable issues to resolve, though the main issue there also is the greatest good of the greatest number. Politics is concerned mainly with the political life of man which includes political views, activities, associations etc. Economics is concerned mainly with the material life of man which includes the system of production, production relations, price, value etc. Political science deals with power in society and economics is concerned with the economic system and wealth. According to Marxism, the economic system constitutes the sub-structure or base and political system is a part of the super-structure.

Political Science and Ethics

Political science is the science of political order and ethics is the science of moral order and both of them have to deal with questions of right and wrong. The relation between the two is so near that Plato regarded political science a sub-division of ethics and the function of the state was to produce virtuous people. Plato's Republic is as much a study in ethics as in political science. The view of Aristotle was that a good citizen is possible in a good state and a bad state makes bad citizens. While the state comes into existence for the sake of mere life, it continues to exist for the sake of good life. Good life is the end of the state and all political problems revolve around it. What is morally wrong cannot be politically right. There cannot be a good state where wrong ethical ideals prevail. The view of Kant was : "True politics cannot take a single step forward unless it has first done homage to morals." The view of Lord Acton was: "The great question is to discover not what governments prescribe, but what they ought to prescribe." According to Mahatma Gandhi, "There are no politics devoid of religion." He insisted on the spiritualisation of politics.

Ivor Brown writes, "Politics is but ethics writ large. Ethical theory is incomplete without political theory because man is an associated creature and cannot live fully in isolation; political theory is idle without ethical theory because its study and its results depend fundamentally on our scheme of moral values, our conceptions of right and wrong."

Both political science and ethics are social sciences and the aims of both are the same. Both of them aim at doing good to man and promoting common welfare. The state was organised for maintaining law and order and peace and for promoting the welfare of the people. Ethics deals with laws of morality and recommends the code of conduct. Prof. Gilchrist writes, "Ethics is a study of human motives, an analysis of intentions, of desires and of the moral end and this moral end is the ultimate justification of political science. Both the sciences are ideological and in their deals they must be in agreement, but the main body of material is distinct." Ideal cannot be divorced from ethical ideal. We cannot conceive of a perfect state where wrong ethical principles prevail. The ethical and political ideals in this case coincide. The view of Catlin is that from ethics the statesman can learn which courses among several are desirable and from political science we may learn which among several may be feasible. According to Gettell, "The proper form and functions of government must be determined in the last analysis on the basis of the ethical compromise that secures the greatest good to the individual and at the same time promotes the greatest common welfare." Stephen L. Wasby writes, "Because values are crucial to politics and are its motivating and lubricating force, they are crucial to the study of politics. Without them, politics might be simpler to study but would not exist as we know it." (Political Science — The Discipline and Its Dimensions, p. 26).

Politics cannot be divorced from ethics. The political man cannot be divorced from the ethical man. No government can do anything which is against the fundamentals of the moral standards of the people. If a state decides to do things which are against the morality of the people, it cannot expect obedience from them. It is suicidal for a government to force things on the people against their conscience. Experience shows that whenever governments want to pass new laws, they take into consideration the public opinion on that matter. No law is passed if it is opposed by the public. Even if it is passed, there is no guarantee that it will be enforced. Although the Government of India wanted to pass the Hindu Code Bill, it failed to do so on account of opposition from the people. Even the meaningless superstitions of the people cannot be brushed aside. It is true that legislation passed by the government can influence the morality of the people indirectly, but it cannot do so directly. Morality cannot be enforced by the state. However, the moral standards of those in power go a long way in influencing the moral standards of the people.

Writers like Machiavelli and Kautilya did not attach importance to morality in the field of politics. The view of Machiavelli was that a prince should know how to play the fox and the lion. To quote Machiavelli, "A prudent ruler ought not to keep faith when doing so would be against his interest and when the reasons which made him bind himself no longer exist. If men were all good, this precept would not be a good one; but as they are bad and would not observe their faith with you, so you are not bound to keep faith with them." Hobbes followed Machiavelli in his arguments and reasonings. The view of Kautilya is that the principles of morality should not be taken into consideration in politics. The politician should care more for the security of the state than for the rules of morality. There should be no hesitation to murder any prince or send a Vish-Kanya to kill him.

The modern view with regard to the relation between political science and ethics is rather conflicting. The concept of scientific relativism creates an unbridgeable gulf between political science and ethics and the very validity of the relationship between political science and ethics is questioned. Their contention is that the introduction of value-judgments in political analysis impedes scientific objectivity and makes any enquiry into its processes speculative. Stuart Rice blames the social scientists for having set their task as the creation of a science of moral ends which is a contradiction in terms. He stands for a clear distinction between political science and philosophy. Karl Llewellyn emphasizes the separation of the realms of "is" and "ought" and the inability of political science to teach us where to go. Regarding values, he observes, "As we move into these value-judgements, we desert entirely the solid sphere of objective observation, of possible agreement among all normal trained observers and enter into the airy sphere of individual ideals and subjectivity." In order to prove a value, one must refer to another more general value and in the last analysis "the end which is sought must be posited or assumed, it cannot be arrived at by scientific procedure."

Prof. R.M. MacIver supports Stuart Rice and writes, "Science itself tells us nothing, just nothing about the way we should act, and the ends we should seek." In 1936, Harold D. Laswell brought out his book "Politics; Who Gets, What, When and How" which was a thesis on the scientific method and value-relativism. In his book "Power and Society", he made political science "a value-free science" and defined it as "an empirical discipline, as the study of the shaping and sharing of power" and "a political act as one performed in power perspectives." Power, rule, authority or political influence became the central organising idea of the subject of political science and its scope was riveted upon it. Laswell tried to make politics a "value-free science". To quote him, "The study of politics is the study of influence and the influential". According to these writers, the introduction of value-judgments in political analysis would impede scientific objectivity.

"However, this view has been contested by eminent writers like Jacques Maritam, Eric Voegelin and Alfred Weber. Jacques Maritam calls for a reinclusion of metaphysics in the realm of political science. According to him, metaphysics wrongly ousted from science by the scientific method is science in the ampler sense. In his famous book "The New Science of Politics", Eric Voegelin pleads for a reorientation of political science through a resuscitation of the efforts of the ancient Greek and Medieval Christian philosophers to provide "the theoretical orientation of man in his world, the great instrument for man's understanding of his own position in the universe." He refutes the argument that science alone can apply the scientific method. The opinion of Alfred Weber is that all scientific activity is "entirely tied to values."

In a paper submitted to the UNESCO project "Methods in Political Science", Thomas I. Cook wrote, "I urge, finally, that the most glaring need of the social sciences today is to relate ethical concepts, in their general outline long discovered and scientifically verified, at once to the methods and results of modern sociological investigation, to determine the proper sphere of the methods; to winnow and relate in systems, the results. I add here that in political science this need is specially obvious." The view of Cook was that the approach mentioned by him was the only one which promised an effectively unified system of social sciences "within which political science may receive a definable place, fulfil an intelligent role, possess clear scope and function and consequently develop appropriate methods and relevant special techniques."

Points of Distinction Between Political Science and Ethics

The intimate relation between political science and ethics should not blind us to the important points of distinction between the two. The subject-matter of politics is the political behaviour of man but ethics is concerned with his ethical behaviour. Political science is normative, practical and descriptive but ethics is mainly normative and theoretical Political science is concerned with "is" and "ought", but ethics is primarily concerned with "ought." Political science is concerned with man as a citizen but ethics deals with man as a moral being. Political science is concerned primarily with the external aspect of man but ethics is concerned with the inner development of human beings. The scope of political science is limited in comparison to that of ethics. Politics is concerned with ends but ethics is concerned with both means and ends. Ethical considerations vary from individual to individual and those are governed by the myriad changing situations. No code of laws can ever encompass the whole orbit of morality. The area of morality is larger than that of law. Formal law receives its strength and sustenance from social morality. Political science seeks to make a compromise between considerations of ethics and expediency. Drinking wine may be contrary to the moral convictions of the bulk of the people of India but considerations of expediency may prevent the government from pursuing a policy of total prohibition on the ground that it involves a huge waste of revenues. However, ethics prescribes absolute standards of right and wrong and is blind to considerations of expediency.

Political science and ethics must not be confused and must be kept separate not because the study of ethics is not valuable to give taste and sanity to the ends which the individual seeks through political means or because the student of political science can do away with the study of facts of morality, but because the maintenance of a close alliance between ethics and political science diminishes the value of each discipline by confusing the requirements and conclusions of the two. A very intimate alliance between political science and ethics is dangerous. Through association with ethics, some amount of subjectivity tends to creep into political analysis which may be destructive of the scientific objectivity of the latter. While noting the danger lying in the intrusion of ethical theory into the treatment of politics, Catlin observes, "The result is an unwillingness to reach a dispassionate judgment on the facts so far as the evidence goes apart from their bearing on human values which is a grave hindrance to the development of the social sciences and is prejudicial to disinterestedness in thought." (The Science and Method of Politics, p. 297).

Political Science and Sociology

Sociology is the science of society. "It is the science of men in their associated process." It deals with social development in general and describes social life in all its phases. According to Ogburn, "Sociology is a body of learning about society. It is description of ways to make society better. It is social ethics, a social philosophy." In the words of Ward, "Sociology is the science of society or of social phenomena." Sociology is the root of all social sciences. It is a general and comprehensive science which studies all the aspects of collective human life or the life of man in society. It possesses an all-inclusive character and studies all the aspects and fundamentals of society. Comte, the father of sociology, emphasized the fact that all aspects of society should be studied under one social science, namely sociology. He was opposed to the division of the study of society into several social sciences. He regarded sociology to be the study of social structures, organisations, their inter-actions, their origin and evolution.

No two social sciences are so closely related as political science and sociology though the relationship is more akin to that between a mother and a daughter than that between two sisters. The view of Dr. Garner is that political science and sociology are so intimately connected that the "political is embedded in the social and if Political Science remains distinct from sociology, it will be because the breadth of the field calls for the specialist and not because there are any well-defined boundaries marking if off from sociology." They are mutually contributory. A political scientist must be a sociologist and a sociologist must be a political scientist. Giddings makes an illuminating observation, "To teach the theory of the state to men who have not learned the first principles of sociology, is like astronomy or Thermodynamics to men who have not learned the Newtonian laws of motion." (Principles of Sociology, p. 37). Political organisations and processes are influenced by social circumstances. Politics in influenced by social stratification and various non-political issues tell upon politics. Politics and the state interfere in all the aspects of society. Social forces and customs which become disruptive are controlled by politics. Politics can play a major role in influencing public opinion against the evils in the existing social system. All the issues of society are connected with politics in one way or the other. The state, as an institution, towers above all other associations and coordinates their activities. Politics paves the way for a peaceful social change in society. It tries to maintain social integrity, cooperation and equilibrium. In a country where differences exist in various classes, the state alone can maintain functional unity and order. It coordinates all activities and relations and maintains conditions under which the people can live a perfect and self-sufficing life. Barnes writes, "The state is the final arbiter or umpire of the social process, controlling and directing the conflicts and struggles of lesser social groups and interests. Without control and direction by the state, anarchy and chaos would result."

Contemporary studies of political science have borrowed methods, research techniques and survey methods from sociology. The main problems of sociology have been adopted by political science. During the nineteenth century, traditional political theory tried to analyse the origin and evolution of the state and other institutions from sociological studies. Sir Henry Maine, J.J. Bachhofen and L.H. Morgan emphasized the sociological evolution of the state and political institutions. In his book "The Origin of the Family, Private Property and the State", Dr. Engels gave a scientific sociological evolution of the state. Important contributions were made by Bentley in "The Process of Government", by Truman in "The Government Process", by V.O. Key in "Political Parties and Pressure Groups", by David Easton in "Political System" and by R.M. MacIver in "The Modern State" and "Webb of Government". The new concepts of renowned sociologists like Robert K. Meiton, Talcott Parsons and Merrium Levygr greatly influenced the writings of political scientists like David Easton, G.A. Almond, G.B. Powell and David Apter. The emergence of behaviouralism in political studies imported from sociology concepts like political socialisation, political culture, political system, political development, political recruitment, political communication etc. and approaches like structural-functional system approach and various orientations and methods. S.M. Lipset writes, "No sociologist can conceive of a study of society that does not include the political system as a major part of the analysis. And many political scientists, particularly in recent years, have argued sometimes with others in their own field, that it is impossible to study political processes except as special cases of more, general sociological and psychological relationships." Increasing collaboration between sociology and political science will in future help political science to formulate sounder genralisations about political facts." (Principles of Sociology, p. 37).

A branch of sociology which is intimately connected with socio-political aspects is known as political sociology about which Lewis Coser writes, "One may say that political science has tended to concentrate on the visible part of the political ice-berg whereas political sociology has paid greater attention to the submerged portions." (Political Sociology, p. 5). Among the sociological works of great political significance" we may mention some of them like Gunnar Myrdal's "An American Dilemma" (1940), Schapera's "Government and Politics in Tribal Societies" and Ruth Benedict's "The Chrysanthemum and the Sword".

Political sociology takes the concept of political system, first developed by David Easton, and seeks to examine it in sociological terms on the basic assumption that the political system of a country is "integrally related to its social system." A system implies the inter-dependence of parts which means that when the properties of one component in a system change, all other components and the system as a whole are affected. When the rings of an automobile wear away, the motor car burns oil, the functioning of the other parts of the machine or system deteriorates and the power of the vehicle declines. In the political system, the emergence of mass political parties or the media of mass communications, like the press, the radio and television, have changed the performance of structures of the system and the general capabilities of the system in its domestic and foreign environments. Almond and Powell write, "When one variable in a system changes in magnitude or in quality, others are subjected to strains and are transformed; the system changes its pattern of performance, or the unruly component is disciplined by regulatory mechanism." (The Comparative Politics: A Developmental Approach, pp. 17-18).

About the sociological approach to political science, Sartori observes, "Political sociology is only born when the sociological and political approaches are combined at the point of intersection. If the sociology of politics deals with non-political reasons, while the people act the way they do in political life, then political sociology should include also the political reasons why people act the way they do. A real political sociology is then a cross-disciplinary breakthrough, seeking enlarged models which reintroduced as variables the 'givens' of each component source."

The present sociological impact on the study of political science can be traced back to Max Weber (1864-1920) whose ideas influenced areas such as administrative theory and political analysis. The study of social anthropology has contributed in a large measure towards the enrichment of certain areas of politics. For example, the study of culture was taken over by political scientists and political culture today constitutes an important part of the comparative method of the study of political system. Talcott Parsons applies the concept of culture to the study of social systems and presented the famous fourfold functional analysis of the social systems. Functional analysis has enabled the social scientists to understand the nature of functional problems of social systems. Those four functions are pattern maintenance meaning thereby the maintenance of symbols, codes, values, normative systems etc. functions which make the individual a part of the social system such as voting in general elections, adaptation and adjustment of various sub-systems in society and goal attainment. The goals of polity may be more production, social justice, effective leadership etc.

In addition to the above functional analysis, Parsons provided us with a set of pattern-variables which help us in the study of inter-action between various subsystems and comparison of qualitatively different social systems. These pattern-variables have been used by a number of political scientists, notably S.M. Lipset, in their studies of political systems. Importance of non-governmental factors for the explanation of political reality has been underlined by Francis G. Castles. A study of government in isolation from all other elements of social structure is like Hamlet without the Prince of Denmark.

Differences

Although political science and sociology are intimately connected, there are certain differences between the two. Giddings rightly says that the province of political science is not co-extensive with "the investigations of society but that the lines of demarcation can be drawn." Sociology is concerned with man in all his relations and in all forms of human associations, but political science is concerned only with the political aspects of man. Political science has a narrower field than sociology.

Political life of man began much after his social life and hence it is rightly said that sociology is prior to political science.

Sociology deals both with organised and unorganised communities and the conscious and unconscious activities of man, but political science is concerned with man only in a politically organised society.

Political science is concerned with the past, present and future political organisations of mankind but sociology is concerned with social institutions which exist or had existed in the past.

Sociology is the science of society but political science is the science of the state.

Sociology studies man as a social being and as a political organisation is a special kind of social organisation but political science is a more specialised science than sociology.

Sociology is mainly concerned with the historical growth of the political community, but political science assumes such a community as existent.

Sociology deals with the development any working of all the organs of social control but political science deals only with the states and the problems connected with them.

Sociology takes the individual as the unit of study, but political science takes the state as the unit for investigation.

Political science is concerned with norms while sociology is merely descriptive.

The distinction between political science and sociology has been described by Ernest Barker in these words: "Political theory only deals with political associations, united by a constitution and living under a government; sociology deals with all associations. Political theory assumes as a datum that man is a political being, it does not explain, as sociology seeks to do, how he came to be a political being". (Political Thought in England, p. 138).

Political Science and Psychology

Psychology is the science of Psyche. It is "the positive science of behaviour". According to Ward, "Psychology is the science of individual experiences." Woodworth writes, "Psychology is the science of the activities of the individual in relation to the environments." It is the "science of social consciousness and deals with the rational and irrational aspects of human life." Psychology is the science of mental attitudes and human behaviour, consciousness, experience, motives etc. It studies human behaviour in various social conditions and social relationships. It studies sentiments, emotions and instincts of man. It seeks to determine how far human conduct is rational or instinctive or traditional. Political science which deals with the political relationship of human beings, cannot ignore the psychological effects. The state and its political institutions are the products of the human mind and can best be studied in terms of the mind. Theories about political conduct which are not grounded in an adequate psychology are apt to be defective. This has been shown in some of the contributions which modern social psychology has made to political science. To quote Ernest Barker, "The application of the psychological clue to the riddles of human activity has indeed become the fashion of the day. If our forefathers thought biologically, we think psychologically". Gabriel Tarde, Le Bon, MacDougall, Graham Wallas and Baldwin are some of the important writers who have given psychological explanations of almost all the political problems. They ascribe the unity of the state to psychological factors. Political traditions and institutions are influenced by the human mind. In his book "Physics and Politics", Bagehot has explained the successful working of the constitutional system of government in Britain in terms of the psychology and genius of the people of that country. The view of Le Bon is that only that government is stable which is in harmony with the mental constitution of the race. Graham Wallas observes, "Politics is only in a slight degree the product of conscious reason; it is largely a matter of sub-conscious processes of habit and instinct, suggestion and imitation." Lord Bryce writes, "Politics has its roots in psychology, the study (in their actuality) of the mental habits and volitional proclivities of mankind."

The psychological approach to the problems of political science is very valuable. Political science has been much under the sway of philosophy divorced from the realities of human nature. It is necessary "to reinvigorate our minds from the wells of direct observation". We cannot go very far in our study of political science unless we know and appreciate the way in which human beings behave as individuals and members of society under different influences.

Public opinion is the basis of all the governments and propaganda helps in forming that opinion. Propaganda operates in all fields of human activity. Modern governments do not rule by naked physical power. Ideological power is used to control and rule the masses. Psychological manipulation of the masses is the safest and best form of political manipulation. No political system can satisfy the demands and expectations of all the people and hence it has to use psychological methods to ensure the maximum consensus in society. Knowledge of mass psychology is the key to political success. Modern governments use the ideological weapons of brain-wash. Frustration and aggression are regarded as psychological maladies with psychological solutions. The mass media such as newspapers, the radio, television, cinema etc. are used to create a sound psychological basis of the state. In order to capture political power, political parties coin attractive slogans and a psychological study of the masses is important for that purpose. The slogans of "Garibi Hatao" proved better than "Indira Hatao" in 1971. Likewise, the slogans of "Democracy or Dictatorship" proved more effective than "Stability and Socialism" in 1977. In 1980, the slogans of "Elect the Government That Works" won a majority for Indira Gandhi. Psychological methods, opinion polls, attitude studies etc. are gaining stronghold in politics.

Lasswell has emphasized the need of considering psychological factors in the study of political science. His view is that every political process and movement has psychological causes. According to him, political deviances like "revolution", anarchy, violence, conflict, dictatorship and war should be studied on psychological basis. Many studies of public opinion indicate the relationship between the mass mind and democracy and dictatorship. Mass movements are considered as psychological disorders which help the establishment of dictatorship by posing a danger to the stability of the system. Lasswell has analysed the cause of social conflict in psychological tensions. His view is that behind every struggle there is a "castration complex".

While taking the help of psychology in the study of political science, we should not go to extremes. Ernest Barker has pointed out the limitations of the psychological method. According to him, the psychologist does and cannot deal in terms of value. Values belong to the moralists. Psychology deals with things as they are and ethics with things as they ought to be. Therefore, political theory should look to ethics rather than to psychology for constructive help. Psychology seeks to explain civilised life in terms of savage instinct — the higher by the lower. This does not seem to be the correct evolutionary method. The right procedure is to explain the lower by the higher. Man explains the monkey and not monkey the man. It is illogical to explain civilised life by the conditions of life in pre-historic times. Habit and instinct, suggestion and imitation exist, but they exist in connection with intelligence. Because a thing is primitive, it does not mean that it is final.

In spite of these limitations, study of psychology, particularly of social psychology, is of great help to the student of political science. It shows him how men in general are not moved as much by ideas and ideals, by theories and the logic of facts as by their pre-conceived notions, habits and dispositions and their fears and prejudices. Man is more sub-rational and irrational than rational.

There is a difference between political science and psychology. While psychology is more concerned with human behaviour and its description, political science is more concerned with ideals and values of human behaviour. Psychology is a study of attitudes, motives and instincts of man, but political science is mainly concerned with organisations and institutions of society. Psychology studies human activities and behaviour, but political science is concerned more with human relations in society. Psychology does not concern itself with moral values. It does not say anything about what the state and its institutions ought to be. Psychology is concerned with mental acts which must be considered in relation to the observable individual mind, but political science is concerned with the impulsive or willed relations of social beings. Psychology deals with the inward nature of man, but political science deals with the outward behaviour of man. Psychology deals with the instincts of man and does not deal with their practical shape whereas political science studies only the practical performance.

Political Science and Biology

Biology deals with animal life and its evolution. There are two views about the relationship between political science and biology. One view is that the state is an organism. The other view is that the state is like an organism. There is no substance in the view that the state is an organism, but the state in its unity is like an organism. Some eminent writers have tried to convert political science into a biological science by treating its central theme, the state, as "a phase of development from associations formed among animals of a species included in the subject-matter of natural history". According to them, the state possesses the characteristics of a biological organism. In its growth and operations, it is supposed to follow the laws governing the organic bodies. In the writings of Herbert Spencer, political science became biology. He tried to explain the structure and life of the state in biological terms. He pointed out in detail the similarities and differences between the state and an organism. He referred to the sustaining, distributary and regulating systems in the state and the organism. The state is like a biological organism in all its essentials. It is the product of an evolution and is subject to the laws of birth, growth and decay. In an organism, there is mutual dependence of the parts. There is a similar relation between the individuals who constitute the state and the state itself.

It is rightly pointed out that the analogy between the state and an organism should not be taken to extremes. Lord Acton rightly says that if that is not done we may come to grief to which analogies, metaphors and parallelisms generally lead to.

Political Science and Anthropology

According to the definition of anthropology as given in the Encyclopaedia of Social Sciences, anthropology deals with man as a social being. It deals with the racial division of man, his physical character, his geographic division, his environmental and social relations and his cultural development. It studies mankind in relation to physical, social and cultural development.

Political science gleans a wealth of material from the store-house of anthropology. The latter records a succession of diverse type of social systems which constitute an invaluable aid to comparative analysis in politics. As the roots of many of our contemporary customs and institutions lie in the distant past, anthropology enriches political analysis by furnishing a full account of the past. Anthropological data are of great importance while studying the formation of the national character. Some Germans created the myth of Nordic or Aryan Race with a view to making it "serviceable to consolidating the German nation and to strengthening its will to expand", but modern anthropologists do not subscribe to that theory.

Previously, anthropology was regarded as implying wholly or mainly to primitive society, but its scope is now widening and it includes all types of society. This has resulted in the development of Social anthropology. W.A. Robson writes, "A knowledge of social anthropology is essential for the study or practice of colonial administration: and it is necessary also for several other special topics of political science such as area studies, colour and racial conflicts, international organisations for assisting under-developed countries, immigration and emigration."

A large number of countries in Asia and Africa became independent after World War II. They started their careers with democratic institutions but in many of those countries authoritarian regimes came into existence. We can solve this riddle by resorting to the data supplied by political anthropology. It is rightly contended that the traditional elements, attitudes, values, patterns of behaviour and leadership weigh very heavily in those countries as compared with the advanced countries of Western Europe. Lord Bryce has rightly said that there are institutions which "like plants, flourish only on their hillside and under their own sunshine."

The view of Lasswell is that the links between social anthropology and political science have become closer in recent times "as whirlwind modernisation added to the turbulence of politics in Asia, Africa, South America and many heretofore-isolated island communities." According to him, in future years, "the data of anthropology will be highly pertinent to the consideration of various problems that are likely to grow into large dimensions."

Political Science and Jurisprudence

Jurisprudence is defined as the science of law. Political science is defined as the science of state and government which are controlled and regulated through law. The state creates the super-structure in which laws are framed and the government administers and enforces law. The result is that both political science and jurisprudence influence each other. The laws of Communist countries are different from the laws of democratic countries. The governments of the two systems are different and they make different types of laws. That indicates the intimate relation between political science and jurisprudence. Jurisprudence is called a sub-division of political science as it is the state which creates and maintains the conditions of law. Jurisprudence is treated as a separate study because of the vastness of its scope and its specialised study of law. Law is concerned with classes of persons and classes of situations in general, and often hypothetical terms. Law may establish fictions which may have no bearing on actual life. The approach of a lawyer is normative but that of a student of political science is both normative and descriptive.

Every state develops its own constitutional law and every political philosophy embraces or implies a jurisprudence. From a social point of view, laws must be influenced by their environments. The contents of laws depend upon the structure of society. The laws in a community of large land-owners will be different from the laws in a country of peasant-proprietors. Likewise, the laws governing private property and conditions of labour will be different in capitalist and Communist countries. The constitutional law of a democratic state will be different from the constitutional law of a dictatorship.

The legal system has to keep pace with the changing pattern of a community. Law regulates social relations and when those relations change, law must change accordingly. The capital-labour relation which existed in England about hundred years ago, has undergone a radical change under the impact of growing democratization and organisation of trade unionism. English law has taken, cognizance of that fact and changed along collectivist lines. A social ideal primarily deduced from prevalent social relation is sought to be embodied in the legal code of a society.

It is worthy of notice that lawyers in India have made a great contribution to the development of political institutions and the freedom movement in the country. A study of law in some of its phases is necessary to a student of constitutions and public administration. The primary function of legislators is law-making and that requires acquaintance with the intricacies of law. Such concepts as fundamental rights and directive principles of state policy impinge as much on law as on ethics and politics.

Gunner Heckscher writes that in many countries, political science is still regarded as a part of legal studies and comparative government as a part of the study of comparative law to be pursued by scholars with a legal training. For a study of the role of the judiciary in the government, legal knowledge is indispensable. The role of the legal system as a whole is a factor of primary importance for a study of political institutions. A comparison between the approaches of law and politics is highly illustrative. To the jurists, constitutional and political practices are of interest in so far as they form a part of or at least influence the legal system. To a study of comparative law, the legal system is important in so far as it forms the basis of certain influences on political developments. A study of law may explain differences of political structure and, development which otherwise may seem extremely puzzling to us. Other important examples of this are found in comparative administration. Such things as the justiciability of civil service, the legal means of safeguarding the rights of citizens etc. "are fundamental to the understanding of how administration works. In themselves, they are almost unintelligible except in the context of the legal system as a whole (The Study of Comparative Government and Politics, pp. 56-7).

Political Science and Public Administration

Public administration deals with the administrative activities of the government. The term public administration was used in the nineteenth century in two senses. In a broader sense, public administration referred to the work involved in the actual conduct of the affairs of the government. In a narrow sense, it referred to the operations of the administrative branch only, with the function of enforcing the policy as distinct from the function of determining the policy. The function of deciding the policy was with the political branch of the government and the function of enforcing it was with the administrative branch. This distinction between the two branches of government led public administration to be considered as a separate study. Goodnow wrote, "The fact is that there is a large part of administration which is unconnected with politics, which should be relieved very largely, if not altogether, from the control of political bodies. It is unconnected with politics because it embraces fields of semi-scientific, quasi-judicial and quasi-business or commercial activities—work which has little, if any, influence on the expression of the true state will."

However, this view is not accepted today. L.D. White writes about the purpose arid scope of public administration in these words, "The immediate objective of the art of administration is the most efficient utilisation of resources at the disposal of officials and employees. In their broader context, the ends of administration are the ultimate objects of the state itself—the maintenance of peace and order, the progressive achievement of justice, the instruction of the young, protection against disease and insecurity, the adjustment and compromise of conflicting groups and interests—in short, the attainment of the good life. "(Introduction to the Study of Public Administration, p. 3). This shows that the ends of both political science and public administration are the same and hence it is not desirable to demarcate in clear-cut terms the functions of government. It is true that there are two phases in the process. One phase is legislation and the second phase is administration. However, they are merged together and are not distinguishable at certain points. The distinction between administrative functions and the policy determining functions is not clear. The whole process of government and administration is one of decision-making. Administration today is not merely the execution of a policy. It also reacts upon policy and actively participates in the making of the policy.

Previously, the Department of Public Administration used to be a part of the Department of Political Science in certain universities in India, but there is a tendency to make public administration as a separate and independent department.

Political Science and Statistics

Statistics deals with numerical facts and figures. A statistician collects and classifies numerical facts in a systematic manner. The data collected by him is helpful to the politicians and administrators.

Historically, statistics and politics have been closely related. Two seventeenth century roots of modern statistics are "political arithmetic" and "university statistics". "Political arithmetic" was introduced in England by William Petty and "university statistics" was founded by Hermann Conring, a German professor. "Both were concerned with the political problems of their day—state-building and state-preservation—and both were concerned with achieving empirical foundations for their political ideas."

Statistics is concerned with the systematic and methodical collection, analysis and presentation of numerical data. The study of government involves empirical investigations of various kinds concerning political processes, political institutions, activities and outputs of government and their impact on the citizens. Data analysis is necessary for all the purposes. The main contribution of statistics to politics is to facilitate causal data analysis to increase political understanding and there are various well-developed statistical methods and models which are being used more and more in political analysis to introduce scientific rigour and to produce better explanations to political phenomena. Dr. Garner explains the relation between statistics and politics in these words: "Statistics, it has been said, contributes to the study of political and social institutions somewhat as microscopy contributes to pathology."

The importance of the study of statistics is being felt more and more in modern times. This is due to the fact that with the passage of time, more and more facts and figures are available on whose basis laws can be passed to tackle the problems facing society. Beatrice Webb writes, "I had learnt the relation between personal observation and statistics....though I never acquired the statistical instrument because I had not the requisite arithmetic. I became aware that every conclusion derived from observation or experiment had to be qualified as well as verified by the relevant statistics".

There are writers who maintain that statistics is a branch of political science but that is not correct. Statistics is a separate field of investigation in itself. Modern governments rely upon statistics to solve their problems. There can be no successful legislation without a study of the relevant statistics. F.G. Wilson observes, "While statistical result does not provide an ethic or a norm to be embodied in policy, once the policy has been supported by rational conclusions as to what men desire of political society, statistics is invaluable in attaining the result."

However, there is a saying that in a society where statisticians thrive, liberty and individuality are likely to be emasculated. Statistical data are often manipulated by the state to serve narrow and partisan interests. Instead of revealing the truth, data analysis is done in such a way that truth does not actually come out. Lowell has given in the following words the warning that we should be very careful while making use of statistics for purposes of legislation: "Statistics, like real pies are good if you know the person who made them and are sure of the ingredients." Again, "By themselves they are strangely likely to mislead, because unless the subject is understood in all its bearings, some element can easily be left out of account which wholly falsifies the result." There are three kinds of lies and it is the last which is difficult to counteract.

Political Science and Geography

"Geo" means earth and "Graphy" means description and hence geography is the description of the earth. It is the science of "the earth's surface, form, physical features, natural and political divisions, climate, production, population etc." It deals with the climate, insularity, the character of the soil, the mountains, plains, rivers and outlets upon the sea and topography. A political investigator studies geography with a view to knowing the influence of the geographical conditions and physical environments on political science.

Since the days of Aristotle it has been the favourite theme of a number of writers that the character of the soil, climatic conditions, topography etc. are the guiding factors of state policy. The view of Aristotle was that without geography neither political nor strategical wisdom can go far. Bodin dealt with the relationship of political science and geography. Rousseau tried to establish a relationship between climatic conditions and form of government. He argued that warm climates are conductive to despotism, cold climates to barbarism and moderate climates to a good polity. Montesquieu emphasized the influence of physical environments on the forms of government and liberty of the people. In his book "History of Civilisation", Buckle attributed the character of human inhabitants of a society completely to geographical and climatic conditions. To quote him, "The actions of men, and therefore of societies, are determined by reciprocal inter-action between the mind and external phenomena." Buckle repudiated the generally accepted view that the free will of man determines the action of the individual and society. Lord Bryce writes, "In any country, physical conditions and inherited institutions so affect the political institutions of a nation as to give its government a distinctive character." There is an obvious reference to Britain and Switzerland.

In recent years, Bluntschli, Treitschke, Ritter, Ratzel, Reclus, McKinder, Huntingdon and others have emphasized the influence of physical or geographical factors upon individual character, political institutions and the policies of the government. Keltic, Repley, Geddess, Semple and James Russel Smith have also emphasized the importance of geological factors. In his book "Nature and Man in America", Prof. Shaler has emphasized the importance of the English Channel in the history of England. According to him, "The independent political development of England for the last thousand years has been in large part due to the measure of protection afforded by the British Channel." Philip II of Spain, Napoleon Bonaparte and Hitler could not conquer England on account of the barrier of the English Channel. German writers have asserted that the geographical position of Germany, situated as it was in the centre of Europe without having natural boundaries on several of its frontiers, made it necessary for her to become a strong military power. Prof. Hintze of the University of Berlin, writes, "This position is the decisive factor in our political geography, nor would it be difficult to trace much of our peculiar political character to the same source." Again, "Our historic-political destiny lies in our geographical position." The view of Prof. Seligman is that the so-called Anglo-Saxon individualism is largely the product of climatic conditions. He believes that the whole theory of individualism "was a natural result of the economic and at bottom, of the climatic conditions of a new environment."

In modern times, a lot of attention has been given by a number of writers to the influence of geographical factors on political institutions. Their researches and writings have contributed to give political geography a name, Geo-politics. Geopolitics deals with "the application of political and economic geography to the external problems of states, notably problems of national power, frontiers and possibilities for expansion." As territory is an essential feature of a state, geopolitical factors influence political activities and national politics. An island nation can readily become a naval power and a nation with rich natural resources can become more powerful in world politics. The nation controlling the Suez Canal or the Panama Canal becomes extremely important to other nations. A good illustration of the importance of geo-politics is the way in which Canada and the United States have harnessed the waters of the river St. Lawrence for the material benefit of both the countries. As a result of it, ocean-going steamers can now go right upto Chicago, more than 1400 kilometers away from the Atlantic Sea border. The Atlantic Ocean and the Pacific Ocean and the Himalayas are not the insuperable barriers which they once might have been.

Geographical location is an important factor in moulding the destiny of a state. It affects not only its political institutions but also its national and international policy. However, geography today is a much less important factor in moulding social and political institutions than it was in earlier times.

It is clear from above that political science is related to a number of other disciplines. For a proper understanding of the political phenomena, one has to rely upon a number of sister disciplines such as history, economics, sociology etc. The new trend towards systems analysis of political life reflects the need for broad-based understanding of politics. All social sciences have branched out for the sake of specialisation.

The view of Prof. Heckscher is that the place of political science in relation to other cultural and specially social sciences is not altogether easy to determine. The unity of sciences is becoming increasingly evident and the delimitations are appearing as somewhat futile. Particularly as our work develops, the borderline fields grow increasingly important. (The Study of Comparative Government and Politics, p. 25).

SUGGESTED READINGS

Almond and Powell : *The Comparative Politics: A Developmental Approach.*

Barker, Ernest : *The Study of Political Science and Its Relation to Cognate Studies.*

Barker, Ernest : *Political Thought in England* (1848-1914).

Barnes, H.E. : *Sociology and Political Theory. Bluntschli: Theory of the State.*

Brecht, Arnold : *Political Theory.*

Bryce, James : *Modern Democracies,* 1921.

Burns: Political Ideals.

Burns : *Sociology and Political Theory.*

Catlin : *The Science and Method of Politics.*

Catlin : *A Study of Principles of Politics.*

Garner : *Political Science and Government.*

Giddings : *Principles of Sociology.*

Graham Wallas : *Human Nature in Politics.*

Heckscher, Gunnar : *The Study of Comparative Government and Politics.*

Joad, C.E.M. : *Guide to the Philosophy of Morals and Politics.*

Kaplan, Abraham : *Power and Society.*

Laski, Harold J. : *An Introduction to Politics.*

Lasswell and Kaplan : *Power and Society.*

Lasswell, H.D. : *The Future of Political Science.*

Leacock, S. : *Elements of Political Science.*

Lerner, C.D. : *The Passing of Traditional Society.*

Lipset, S.H. : *Political Man.*

Lipset, S.M. (Ed.) : *Politics and the Social Sciences, New Delhi,* 1972.
Lipson : *The Great Issues of Politics.*
Oakshott, Michael : *Rationalism in Politics.*
Pemiock, Ronald and Smith : *Political Science.*
Popper, K.R. : *Conjectures and Reflections.*
Popper, K.R. : *The Open Society and Its Enemies.*
Rice, Stuart : *Quantitative Methods in Politics.*
Robson, W.A. : *The University Teaching of Social Sciences: Political Science (UNESCO).*
Ross : *Foundations of Sociology.*
Seeley, J.R. : *Introduction to Political Science.*
Seligman : *Principles of Economics.*
Shaler : *Nature and Man in America.*
Sidgwick, H. : *Elements of Politics.*
Strausz-hupe, Robert : *Geopolitics: The Struggle for Space and Power.*
White, L.D. : *Introduction to the Study of Public Administration.*
Willoughby : *The Nature of the State.*

CHAPTER

The Nature and Scope of Political Science

Learning Objectives

- Meaning and definition of Politics
- Traditional View
- Modern View
- Power View of Politics
- Political Power
- Economic Power
- Ideological Power
- Criticism of Power View of Politics
- Liberal View of Politics
- MacIver
- Laski (1893-1950)
- The Marxist View of Politics
- Political Science and Politics
- Scope of Political Science
- Is Political Science a Science ?
- Arguments Against
- Arguments in favour
- Is Political Science an Art ?
- Utility of the Study of Political Science
- Suggested Readings

Politics exists everywhere. It is all-pervading and as old as human beings. Politics prevails in every sphere of life. Whether one likes or not, virtually no one is completely beyond the reach of some kind of political system. A citizen encounters politics in the government of the country, town, school, church, political party, civic association, trade union, club and a host of other organisations. Politics has always been created by human beings. They gave birth to empires, nations, wars, revolutions, symbols, institutions, constitutions etc. The view of Heinz Eulan is that the notion of politics does not come from heaven. It does not come from Oak trees. It is not a gift of any angel. It is a human venture centred in man and created by man.

Political science is a social science and like its sister subjects revolves round man and his social environment. Being one of the oldest social sciences, its nature and scope of study have undergone several changes over the centuries. Political science first began with the Greeks. Although Greece was a small country in. Europe, it was a land of enlightenment and knowledge in ancient times. Almost all branches of knowledge originated in Greece. It is often said that "excepting the blind forces of nature, nothing moves in this World which is not Greek in its origin." According to Robert A. Dahl, politics "has thrived in all cultures that have inherited the enormous legacy of that ancient people, few in number yet great in influence, the Greeks of pre-Christian era. Like many other arts and sciences, political analysis achieved an extraordinary degree of sophistication among the Greeks some twentyfive centuries ago under the tutelage of Socrates, Plato and Aristotle. Since their time ever age in Western Civilisation has furnished a few great students of politics who have tried to answer certain fundamental question."

In Greece, political science was treated as the science of the city state. The term "politics" is derived from Polis which in Greek language meant the city state. In those days, each city was an independent state, a principality in its own right. Politics as the science of the city state emerged as an instrument to serve as a moral guide to the ruling section of the society for the realisation of good life in all its aspects and to adjust the mutual relationships within society. Apart from the state, it included the study of such social groups as the family. In ancient Greece, political science covered the social and political organisation and functioning of the city without making any distinction between the local and national politics. It was considered as a master science which was broad enough to cover all those activities which paved the way for good life in society.

Aristotle is rightly regarded as "the father of political science" on account of his far-reaching and permanent contribution in the field of politics. Frederick Pollock writes, "There was political speculation before him, but it was he who first brought to bear on political phenomena the patient analysis and unbiased research which are the proper marks and virtues of scientific inquiry. The science of politics, like so much else of our knowledge and endeavours to know, begins with Aristotle."

In his famous book *Politics*, Aristotle wrote, "Man is by nature a political animal and he who by nature and not by mere accident is without state, is either above humanity or below it." Again, "He who is unable to live in society or who has no need because he is sufficient for himself, must be either a beast or God." It is undoubtedly true that man is a social and political animal. He cannot live without society or state. By nature, he desires to live in society and follow the rules and regulations of the state. By leading a lone life, he cannot develop his faculties in the best possible manner. Civilisation and culture cannot progress unless human beings are safe and secure and that is possible only in a well-governed state. Without a state, there will be anarchy. A well-governed state is a must for the progress of man.

The advantages of living in a state are obvious to every person. However, certain persons while living in a state may not participate in political life. Robert A. Dahl observes, "An individual is unlikely to get involved in politics if he places a low valuation on the rewards to be gained from political involvement relative to the rewards expected from other kinds of human activity. For many people, political activity is a good deal gratifying than other outlets—family, friends, recreation and the like. For many, political involvement yields far less affection, income, security, respect, excitement and other values than working at one's job, watching television, reading, fishing, playing with the children, attending a football game or assembling a new hi-fi set. For many, the rewards of other activities are more immediate and concrete." Whether a person takes more or less interest in politics, there is no doubt that the destiny of man is linked with the state and government.

Meaning and definition of Politics

The word "politics" has different interpretations. From Plato to Easton, it has been interpreted in different ways. Scholars differ greatly on the definition of the subject. That is natural because as Stanley Hoffman remarks, "How could one agree once and for all upon the definition of a field whose scope is in constant flux, indeed a field whose fluctuation is one of its principal characteristics?" Politics cannot be defined in any generally acceptable way. Different political scientists have defined the term politics/political science in different ways. We can discuss the same under two heads—traditional and modern.

Traditional View

According to traditional political scientists, politics deals mainly with the study of state or government or related institutions. According to Gettell, "Political Science deals with the associations of human beings that form political units, with the organisation of their governments and with the activities of these governments in making and administering law in carrying on inter-state relations." Bluntschli defines political science as "the science which is concerned with the state, which endeavours to understand and comprehend the state in its fundamental conditions, in its essential nature, its various forms of manifestation, its development." According to Sir John Seeley, "Political Science investigates the phenomena of government as Political Economy deals with wealth, Biology with life, Algebra with principles and Geometry with space and magnitude." The view of Paul Janet is that "political science is that part of social science which treats of the foundations of the state and principles of government." According to Prof. Laski, "The study of Politics concerns itself with the life of man in relation to organised states".

According to Dr. Garner, political science begins and ends with the state. The view of Prof. Fairlie is that political science deals "with the life of man as organised under government and law, in what is known as the state. It includes a study of the organisation and the activities of states, and of the principles and ideals which underlie political organisation and activities. It considers the problems of adjusting political authority to individual liberty, the relations of men which are controlled by the state and the relations of men to the state. It also deals with the distribution of governing power among the several agencies by which the actions of the state are determined, expressed and exercised, and with the problem of international life." Treitschke treats politics as both an art and a science. He describes the problem of political science in these words: "First, it should aim to determine from a consideration of the actual world of state the fundamental idea of the state; second, it should consider historically what the people have chosen, what they have created and what they have attained in political life and how; and, third, through this means, it should determine historical laws and moral imperatives. As such, it is applied history."

According to Gareis, "Political science deals with the origin, development, purpose and all political problems of the state." Lord Acton says, "Political science is concerned with the state and with conditions essential for its development." According to Dr. Leacock, "Political science deals with government." It is clear from the above definitions that according to the traditional view, the main subject of the study of political science is the state and government.

Modern View

Political science as the study of the state and government and its relationship with the individual remained valid for a very long time until the dawn of the twentieth century which saw fresh ground being covered by political scientists led by George Catlin, Charles Merriam, Almond, Powell, G. Bingham and others. This was the time when other social sciences began to flourish on their own, whereas political science which was described as the master science by Aristotle remained confined to the study of the government and its institutions with a heavy thrust on the legal aspects. Sociologists like Max Weber in an attempt to distinguish political science from other social sciences made a departure and pointed out that the central idea of the subject must be power. After all, the state was the repository of power. The point was well taken up and a host of writers in the United States began to give attention to and focus on the study of power. The earlier attempts to emphasize were recalled. Machiavelli and Hobbes were quoted effectively. Hobbes had said, "There is a general inclination of all mankind, a perpetual and restless desire of power after power, that ceaseth only in death." It was contended that politics all along had been and continued to be power politics—be it slavery in ancient times, supremacy of the church and the state in medieval ages, or the expansion of franchise in the modern era—all were manifestations of a struggle in which individuals or nations promoted from power through influence or control over group action. Care was taken to emphasize that in the context of power fellowship, power neither meant physical nor mechanical power but the ability to induce, involve and determine the actions of individuals by yet another set of individuals. At times, that resulted in the use of force, but often it meant a competition to hunt for political power.

A host of new definitions based on this premise came up. Harold D. Lasswell brought the concept of politics down to earth as is revealed from the title of his book: "*Politics: Who Gets What, When and How*". In his other book co-authored with Abraham Kaplan, "Power and Society", Lasswell defined "political science, as an empirical (resting on trial or experience) discipline, (as) the study of shaping and sharing of power" and a political act "as" one performed in power perspective. According to Robson, "Political science centres on the struggle to gain and retain power, to exercise power or influence over others or to resist that exercise." Max Weber observes, "Politics is the struggle for power or the influencing of those in power." According to Wasby, "To some politics involves power, authority and influence." In his book "Modern Political Analysis", Robert A. Dahl ,writes, "Power, influence and authority are commonplace words that ordinary men share with political practitioners and political theorists. One hears of power to govern, the power of the purse, political power, spiritual power, economic power, national power, judicial power, presidential power, black power, student power, state power."

According to Shaw and Pierce, politics is the struggle for power to make authoritative decisions for the whole society. V.O. Key says that politics as power consists fundamentally of relationship of subordination, dominance and submission to the governors and the governed. The study of politics is the study of these relations. In the words of Catlin, politics as a theoretical study is concerned with the relations of man in association and competition, submission and control, in so far as they seek not the production and consumption of some art but to have their ways with their fellows. What they seek in their political negotiations is power.

According to J.H. price, "Politics has been defined as the study of the general principles on which government can be carried on successfully; in other words, the study of the exercise of power." Allan R. Ball says that the concept of political power "is a key concept in the study of politics, for if politics is the resolution of conflict, the distribution of power within a political community determines how the conflict is to be resolved and whether the resolution is to be effectively observed by all parties." In the study of political science, we focus our attention on power, its location, how it is exercised or misused, how the ruled react to its exercise etc. "The stuff of politics is power—who governs and how, the reciprocal relationships of authority and obligation between the governors and the governed as well as between different sets of governors and among the governed themselves. The product of political inter-action is more than a series of particular policies like foreign aid or civil rights; it is a way of life."

As the power view of politics was found to be defective and inadequate, attempts were made to modify it by an appeal to the legitimacy of the government. It was said that only legitimate power would become the basis for the acceptance of the government by the bulk of the people. David Easton assigned a moral function to the exercise of power by asking for the authoritative allocation of values for the society. The important word in the phrase "authoritative allocation of values" is authoritative, but many politically important decisions "are made outside the government structure; only those made within the structure can be considered authoritative. The word suggests an air of finality and conveys the idea that once decisions are made, they will stick...The idea of legitimacy or correctness also seems to be suggested by authoritative. While many people, including some of those operating in violation of the law, have political power, only policies coming from a certain source or sources or which have been determined in a certain way *e.g.*, through due process, are accepted as proper."

Another important element in the study of politics is controversy and conflict. Stephen Wasby writes, "Where there is politics, there is controversy; where there are issues, there is politics. Where no controversy exists, where no issues are being debated, politics does not exist." Vermon Von Dyke observes, "Politics consists of struggle among actors pursuing conflicting desires on public issues." The view of Dimock is that the term politics is used in a special sense to describe personal competition, manipulation and intrigue. Sir Ernest Bell writes that politics is the art of looking for trouble, finding it whether it exists or not. According to Ranney, politics in all societies involves conflict which is some form of struggle among human beings to achieve different goals and to satisfy opposing interests. A basic, though perhaps painful, first step towards understanding the government of man is to face the fact and political conflict is not an unfortunate aberration from the norm of perfect cooperation and harmony. It arises from the very nature of life itself. Quincy Wright is of the opinion that politics exists only when ends or means are controversial. Conflict is basic to politics. Controversy and conflict are not limited to the activities of political institutions but also include other groups and individuals whether political or not.

The study of politics also includes the element of consensus and general arrangements of society. Bernard Crick says that politics implies creative, reconciliation of interests, persuasion, acceptance of rules etc; rigidity to build bridges over inter-personal relationships, not only to allocate but to reconciliate. Edward Banfield defines politics as "the activity (negotiations, arguments, discussion, application of force, persuasion etc.) by which an issue is agitated and settled." Eric Rowers writes that politics is the activity which occurs in an ordered community—a way in which disagreements are resolved and translated into policies. Such authoritative decisions reflect the divergence of beliefs, interests and influences within the community. Agreement is necessary for conflict to occur.

According to another view, politics is concerned with man. Heinz Eulan points out that the notion of politics does not come from heaven. It is certainly a human venture, centred in man and created by man. In his book "*Great Issues of Politics*", Leslie Lipson writes that everything can be found in politics that is contained in man himself (ambition, will, love, passion, hatred, memory, learning, calculation and logical thought). Stephen Wasby says that politics is what political scientists do from 9 to 5. According to Prof. Laski, the study of politics concerns itself with the life of man in relation to organised state. It deals with human beings in organised society.

Another view is that politics is concerned with internationalism. The study of internationalism is necessary for establishing world peace and to have the modern welfare state. Garrison comments, "Our country is the world, our countrymen are all mankind, we love this land of our nationality as we love all other lands."

Thus, the study of politics includes the study of power, influence and authority, authoritative allocation of values, conflicts, controversy and cooperation, group involvement, process of decision-making, political institutions, internationalism etc.

Almond, Powell and other modern American writers have studied political science by sociological, anthropological and psychological methods and criticised the traditional theory of political science on grounds of parochialism and formalism. Their contention is that the political theorists in the past concentrated mainly on the state, government, institutions and their legal norms, rules and regulations or on political ideas and ideologies. They did not concern themselves with the performance of, institutions, their inter-action and political behaviour of man. Therefore, modern American political scientists concentrate their attention upon such basic principles as the search for more comprehensive scope, search for realism, for precision and for intellectual order. The American writers have discarded the traditional concept of state and substituted it by political system. They used the word functions instead of powers because the latter is a legal term. They preferred the use of the word "role" in place of "offices". They used the word structure in place of institutions. The word public opinion has been substituted by them with political culture and political socialisation. The justification given is: "we are not simply adding terms to a new vocabulary, but rather are in the process of developing or adapting a new one; this is not only a matter of conceptual vocabulary; it is an intimation of a major step forward in the nature of political science as science."

The growth of behaviouralism has also influenced the nature of political science. Political scientists put emphasis on the study of human behaviour on which rests the policy-making and policy-implementing functions of the government. The result is that political science has gone a long way to become a part of social sciences. It studies the state (through the government), the citizens and the community at large who are all engaged in the pursuit of certain values to uphold general elections.

To many political thinkers, politics denotes freedom. "Politics is a pre-occupation of free men and its existence is a test of freedom". Politics is an agglomeration of various ideologies, various shades of opinion. Bernard Crick writes, "Politics is conservative—it preserves the minimum benefits of established order; politics is liberal—it is compounded of particular liberties and requires tolerance; politics is socialist—it provides conditions for deliberate social change by which groups can come to feel that they have an equitable stake in the prosperity and survival of the community". Politics is "realistic good", "moral activity", "free activity", "civilising", "inventive and flexible", "enjoyable and human", "open-minded" and "inventive and sceptical".

Power View of Politics

There are three main views about politics and those are the power view, the liberal view and the Marxian view. Among them, power view of politics has become prominent during this century.

Although power is an important concept in politics, it is difficult to define it. To quote Parsons, "Unfortunately, the concept of power is not a settled one in the social sciences, either in political science or sociology". However, power has been defined by Wiseman "as the ability to get one's wishes carried out despite opposition". Guild and Palmer write, "By power we mean the ability to affect or to control the decisions, policies, values or fortunes of others." Friedrich says, "Power is not primarily a thing, a possession, but rather a relation". Hoogerwerf defines power as the "possibility to influence the behaviour of others in accordance with the actors' own purposes". David Easton says that power is "a relationship in which one group of persons is able to determine the actions of another in the direction of the former's own ends". According to Russell, power is the production of intended effects. It is ability to cause things to happen.

There are certain *characteristics of power.* It is a rational concept. It is relational as well as relative. No man is weak or powerful in a void. He is weak in relation to some and strong in relation to others. Thus, power is an aggregate of inter-actions among certain actors. Power is bilateral as well as rational. According to Lasswell and Kaplan, even those whose acts are affected also participate in decision-making. By conformity to or disregard of the policy they help to determine whether it is or it is not in fact a decision. Power is situational. The exercise of power depends upon the position/roles of the persons concerned. All American Presidents may have the same power but their exercise of the power varied from person to person and time to time. It is not possible to identify those who wield real power. The most powerful people in a community may be those who remain behind the scenes, or control the atmosphere and the issues raised rather than those who openly participate in settling issues actually raised. Like the concept of love, the concept of power cannot be subjected to rational discussion. To a large extent, it is personal. Being a personal experience, it is subjective. Power is neutral. It can be used for the good of society or to harm it. In many cases, power can be assessed only after it has been actually used. That reduces the predictive value of the concept. Power is a method by which resistance is reduced but it is not the only method to reduce resistance. Another method suggested by Etjzioni is consensus formation. Power is generally viewed in a negative sense. It has closer relationship with conflict than with cooperation. The relation between power and ethics is generally weak. The ethics of power depends upon the purpose which is achieved by the use of power and the manner in which goals are set and attained. The power enjoyed by a person can be stretched by communications backed by his power.

There are certain *laws of power.* It invariably fills any vacuum in human organisation. People in general prefer order as compared to chaos which a power vacuum generally implies. The instinct for power is present in all human beings to a lesser or greater degree. Power is invariably personal. It is both gained and exercised by an individual. It is not correct that power is exercised by classes and elites. It is exercised by some persons in certain classes and elites. Power comes to an end through death, resignation, abdication, revolution, foreign conquest etc. Power is invariably based on a system of ideas or philosophy. Power which has no such basis is short-lived. Power is exercised through and depends on institutions. It is organised within the boundaries of certain institutions. Some of the political institutions which enable the exercise of power in Britain are monarchy, Parliament and the Cabinet. Power is invariably confronted with and acts in the presence of a field of responsibility. Democratic power has a definite area of responsibility. Even the exercise of dictatorial power is not totally devoid of responsibility.

Political Power

Political power is concerned with the maintenance of law and order and justice in society. It is generally held that it is an independent supra society power which is used to maintain peace and security and to serve the common interests of society. Political power belongs to the state and various state apparatuses. It is exercised not only by the state but also by smaller political associations and groups within it, by socio-political organisations extending beyond state boundaries and also those groups which have no inherent political function. However, state power towers above the powers exercised by other institutions and groups. Political power is not always coercive power. Power to control or influence, pressurise or persuade those who are at the helm of political affairs also forms a part of political power.

It is generally said that the people are the fountain-head of all political power in modern liberal democracies. The pluralist view is that political power in a liberal society is diffused among many interest groups, associations and organisations competing with each other for power. It is the groups which enjoy political power. The Elitist view is that in a democratic society, political power resides in the pluralist elite. Every society is ruled by a minority (elite) which has necessary qualities for political leadership. It possesses political power which is divided into the military, police, bureaucratic, political, economic, religious and other elites. Political power in a society is not centralised. It is divided into plural elites and it is there to serve the interests of all.

The Marxist view is that political power is a strong, organised and unified power of the economically dominant class. It is not divided among various plural elites but generally resides in one particular class of society.

Economic Power

Economic power means the ownership of the means of production. Those who have economic power also enjoy political power. Etzioni calls economic power the utilitarian assets which include economic possessions, technical and administrative capabilities, manpower etc. He calls economic power utilitarian because it includes administrative and technical assets. A powerful man is not necessarily wealthy and vice versa a wealthy man is not necessarily powerful. In spite of that, wealth is an important source of power and influence in society. The Marxist view is that the control over the means of production gives rise to political power and social prestige.

There is an inter-action between economic power and political power. Both of them do not merge. A politician controls the state but economic power is controlled by business magnates and technocrats. When both economic and political power is combined in one person, the results are not desirable. In his book, "The Modern State", Prof. MacIver writes, "Economic power has many weapons and political power has few. Political power must fight in the open; economic power has the advantage of secrecy. Economic power, once established, has a single and definite aim; political power is composite and easily divided. Economic power can scarcely be corrupted because what it seeks is only for itself, because also there are scarcely any means of corruption but its own. "The view of C. Wright Mills is that the real power in the United States is exercised by the power elite consisting of persons who control large business organisations.

In a liberal democracy, those who possess economic power exercise their influence on politics in many ways. Their pressure groups are stronger, more organised and more vocal. The unions of the workers are not strong. The unions of the peasants are much weaker. The organisations of the consumers are practically absent. The results are obvious. The major newspapers in India are owned by a handful of big business houses and they carry on propaganda in their favour. The capitalists give a lot of financial help to political parties and thereby influence the decisions of the government and that influence may be against the interests of the masses.

Ideological Power

Ideology may be defined as "a systematic set of arguments and beliefs used to justify an existing or desired social order." Political ideology involves not only a set of beliefs, but is also action-oriented. It puts forward a cause for which the people are prepared not only to fight but also to make sacrifices. To quote Alan Ball, "Individuals are prepared to fight for causes, often realistically hopeless causes, or to undergo ill treatment and torture in the belief that some political values are superior to others." Political ideology can be used to give legitimacy to the ruling classes and help them to remain in power. Through ideology, the people are made to believe that the existing government or the social or economic system is in their best interest and they should be prepared to make sacrifices for maintaining the same. Ideology is not based on reason and hence if an ideology is accepted by the people, they get ready to make sacrifices even if what they are doing is against their own interest. Ideological power represents the manipulative power of the dominant class which controls the thinking and emotions of the people. Ideology can be used to create an illusion of consent even if that consent is detrimental to their real interests. The ruling class creates an ideological atmosphere in which its power looks legitimate and an impression is created that political power is based on their consent. Ideological power converts dissent into consent to some extent.

There is every possibility that the ideological power of the ruling class may be challenged by the ideological power of the other classes, including the workers, peasants etc. In that case, there is always the danger of confrontation between the two which may lead to chaos.

Ideological influences have assumed much greater importance these days on account of the modern communication media which can be used successfully for the propagation of myths and ideologies. In such a situation, propaganda is presented as information and the people "are receivers, not transmitters".

Criticism of Power View of Politics

Power view of politics has been criticised on many grounds. The Liberals attacked the power view on the ground that politics is a process in society by which conflicts are resolved, common interests are served and an equilibrium is maintained in society. Power is the enemy of rights and liberties. Power may be one aspect in the study of politics but politics should mainly be concerned with social welfare. Power can neither be the sole subject for politics nor the basis of state. Laski writes, "Power is not conferred upon men for the sake of power but to enable them to achieve ends which win happiness for each of us." Power can never be the end of politics. It is merely a means to serve the people. Politics is a welfare activity for the good of society. It cannot be simply a struggle for gaining power. MacIver writes, "Force always disrupts unless it is made subservient to common will...Within a society it is only the clumsy and the stupid who seek to attain their ends by force... Coercive power is a criterion of the state, but not its essence." The view of Oakeshott is that "the words politics and political in relation to a modern European state do not belong to the vocabularies either of authority or of power."

Power view of politics is also criticised on normative basis. Politics is concerned with violence and by making power the subject and object of the study of politics, politics becomes valueless and value-free. When politics becomes merely a power struggle, political and social principles decline. David Easton says, "Where a social philosopher has adopted the idea of power as central to his thinking, as in the case of Machiavelli or Hobbes, it has usually seemed to imply abusive coercion on behalf of the coercer. Where political life seemed to be reduced to a mere struggle for power, all the noble aims which the philosophers have depicted as the matrix of life seemed to crumble."

Power view of politics is also criticised by Marxism. The view of the Marxists is that all power, whether political, economic or ideological, is concentrated in the hands of the ruling class and is connected with private property. Ultimately, power is class power. Power cannot be diffused. It cannot be exercised in the interests of the whole community. There is unity in political, economic and ideological power and it is class power.

We may conclude by saying that while power is an important concept in politics, it cannot be the sole basis of politics. Power is only a means and not the end of politics. It is not correct to say that politics is nothing but a study of power. Power can never be the sole factor in political process.

Liberal View of Politics

Liberalism emerged at the time of the Renaissance and Reformation in response to an age characterised by the absolutist state, established religion and a society encrusted with restrictive customs and authoritarian ways. The Liberals advocated freedom of conscience, individual liberty and a check on the power of the state and they succeeded to a very great extent. The liberal view is that politics must promote individual and common well-being. John Locke believed that the state exists for the people and not the people for the state. The view of Bentham was that the state is a group of persons organised for the promotion and maintenance of individual and group happiness or pleasure. The end of the state is the pursuit of maximum happiness or pleasure and avoidance of pain. J.S. Mill advocated liberty. His view was that there should be no state interference in the self-regarding actions of man.

The liberal view of politics is that man as an individual is the centre of the study of politics. Each individual becomes a member of society to further his own interests. Different individuals seek their interests as members of different groups. There are many groups in society which seek to protect the interests of their members against the conflicting interests of the competing groups. Each group is conscious of its particular interests and actively pursues them to secure the authoritative allocation of values in its favour. As that allocation is made by the state, the Liberals regard politics as a state activity. According to liberal view, politics is a group activity and also state activity.

The liberal view is that although different groups have conflicting interests, there are also common interests to which the interests of the competing groups can be reconciled. Politics is essentially an instrument of conflict-resolution. It aims at securing order and justice in society. J.D.B. Miller writes, "Politics is about policy, first and foremost; and policy is a matter of either the desire for change or the desire to protect something against change. Politics, then, is about disagreement or conflict; and political activity is that which is intended to bring about or resist change, in the face of possible resistance." Again, "Politics is, in a sense, the application of government to social situations which will not settle themselves. The aim of those who practise politics is often to secure agreement over what is to be done, to pacify quarrels and to strive for reconciliation and compromise." Miller further says that politics is concerned with conflict and disagreement. If there were general agreements, we would not need politics. The origin of politics lies in social diversity. Politics will continue because diversity is not going to stop.

About the liberal view of politics, Duverger says, "Ever since men have been reflecting on politics, they have oscillated between two diametrically opposed interpretations. According to one, politics is conflict, a struggle in which power allows those who possess it to ensure their hold on society and to profit by it. According to the other views, politics is an effort to bring about the rule of order and justice in which power guarantees the general interests and common good against the pressure of private interests. Organised power in any society is always and at all times both the instrument by which certain groups dominate others, as instruments used in the interest of the rulers and to the disadvantage of the ruled, and also a means of ensuring a particular social order or achieving some integration of the individual into the collectivity for the general interest. The two elements always co-exist.

According to the liberal view, politics is a dimension of the social process. It is a human activity to resolve social conflicts, maintain law and order, serve the general interest, facilitate the peaceful change in society and contribute to the social, economic and ethical development of human beings and protect their rights and liberties.

According to the liberal view, behind the conflicting interests of the various groups, there is a common interest or common good and it is the business of the state to achieve that. The conflicts among the people have to be resolved and a policy that will ensure better conditions for workers and higher produce for employers, a reasonable price for producers and consumers, suppliers and customers has to be evolved. The end is the concept of the welfare state.

MacIver

In this connection, a reference may be made to the views of MacIver and Laski. According to MacIver, society has a thousand manifestations—political, religious, philanthropic, literary, intellectual etc. and a social scientist should consider society as a system with many component parts. It was not proper for him to select one aspect and to present it as the determinant of all other aspects. MacIver did not agree with Marx and Spengler who held the view that one single factor determines the entire social system. Moreover, MacIver's view was that society as an institution has existed at all stages of the evolution of man. Society may change but it does not die. To quote MacIver, "As a flame is communicated from coal to coal, so is the life of society communicated, in conscious and unconscious ways, from person to person. It is communicated, not transferred. The inheritance of society, like that of life itself, is not a gift which one relinquishes when another receives it. And it is so communicated, so communicable, because it is no sense outside its members but lives only in them, is their nature or being a fact. Society is neither prior nor posterior to its members, for the term 'person' and the term 'social person' are at every stage of life identical in connotation. When persons enter into any social relation, it is their respective attitudes towards one another which constitute the relation."

According to MacIver, the relation between the individual and society is two-way relationship. To quote him, "The ant and the bee give themselves upto their society, but because they have little to give, all their social sacrifice avails them little. The hermit gives nothing to his society and therefore a country of hermits, were they never so great and wise, would also attain to nothing. But in a true society, the factors, the strength of individuality and the strength of sociality work together and indeed they never can be really independent of one another. For as each of us makes his society, so does our society make each of us." Again, "A society of persons is not a person" and "a groove of trees is not a tree, nor a colony of animals itself an animal."

As regards the relation between society and state, the view of MacIver was that society was there before the state began and hence to identify the social with the political is to be guilty of the grossest of all confusions which completely bars any understanding of either society or the state. MacIver criticised the social contract theory and the organic theory of the state. According to him, the social contract theory "rests upon the false assumption that human beings are, or could become, human beings outside of or apart from society. It implies that men are individuals before they enter into society and that they establish a social order to protect their property or their rights or their lives. Likewise, the organic view of society is also wrong because we do not belong to "society as the leaves belong to the tree or the cells to the body. Indeed society can have little meaning unless individuals themselves are real."

MacIver also criticised Rousseau, Hegel and Bosanquet for identifying the state with society. To quote MacIver, "The state stands for an area of common good not for the whole of common good" and "the political interest is determinate and has limits, the social has none." According to MacIver, the state is the institution of institutions but society is not an institution at all. It is a life continuous and progressive, the creator of institutions however supreme." The state commands a certain amount of influence over the individuals. The state itself depends on the character and temperament of the people who make the state. To quote MacIver, "The political aspect of the social system is a manifestation of the society; the society expresses itself in many forms and has a multitudinous spontaneous activity which is largely determined by the political order." The society is rooted in our nature and the state is one of its expressions. If man is a political animal, it is because he is a social animal.

MacIver differs from the liberal view in certain respects. According to him, the state represents an area of common good and not the whole of common good. Moreover, the contract may be the basis of the state but not of society. State and society are not identical. Human beings can exist only in society and not otherwise.

Laski (1893-1950)

Prof. Laski believed in the uniqueness of the individual. To quote him, "I am not a part of a great symphony in which I realise myself only as an incident in the motif of the whole. I am unique. I am separate. I am myself." Later on, he changed his view. The new view was that although there was need for the authority of the state, the rights of individuals regarding privacy, mode of thought and expression should be preserved from violation. "Private liberty is thus that aspect of which the substance is mainly personal to a man's self. It is the opportunity to be fully himself in the private relations of life. It is the chance practically to avail himself of the safeguards evolved for maintenance of those relations." The view of Laski was that the state is not identical with the social order. Men are not only members of the state but also of many other voluntary associations who make demands on the state. Hence society is federal in character. It has general and specific functions. Activities of the general nature belong to the state and those of specific nature belong to voluntary organisations and the state is only marginally concerned with those activities.

According to Laski, the state is only one of the many organisations in the social order which compete for man's loyalty and obedience. Society is plural in structure. Each organisation represents a facet of human activity. Laski placed politics in a dominant regulatory position in the social order.

The Marxist View of Politics

According to Marx, political institutions and activities are an outgrowth of the prevailing economic system, especially the mode of production. All social relations, including the political ones, are shaped by the prevailing economic relations in society. The conflicting economic interests are the motive force behind all politics. The clash of economic interests is the fundamental issue of social conflict. Other issues are superficial and their resolution cannot end the conflict. If economic issues are solved, all other issues automatically disappear and if the economic issues are evaded, the settlement of other issues is futile.

According to Marx, politics is an instrument of class domination. Conflicts arise in society as the system of production is not organised on a rational basis which means the highest advancement of technology in order to get maximum production and the social ownership of the means of production and distribution. Production is to be undertaken not for private profit but for the benefit of society.

The emergence of private property has divided society into two classes—the haves and have-nots, the masters and servants, the exploiters and the exploited and their interests are irreconcilable. Politics serves the interests of the dominant class.

The division of society into antagonistic classes gives rise to class-conflict or class-struggle. All politics is the result of class struggle. This class conflict cannot be resolved by politics. As a matter of fact, politics is used by the dominant class to suppress the conflict. So long as society is divided into two classes, state and politics will continue to be used as the tools of the dominant class for the suppression of the dependent class. This state of affairs will continue till a classless society is established. The end of class conflict will mark the end of politics itself.

Ralph Miliband writes, "The Marxist approach to conflict is different. It is not a matter of problems to be solved but a state of domination and subjection to be ended by a total transformation of the conditions which give rise to it. No doubt conflict may be attenuated, but only because the ruling class is able by one means or another—coercion, concessions or persuasion—to prevent the subordinate classes from seeking emancipation. Ultimately, stability is not a matter of reason but of force. The antagonists are irreconcilable and the notion of genuine harmony is a deception or a delusion, at least in relation to class societies." (Marxism and Politics, p. 17).

The Marxist view is that human nature is constantly changing. It is a part of an overall dialectical development. A man is a rational being and he possesses conscious power of rational self-direction. Human nature, which is rational, is changing for the better. The average man will rise to the heights of an Aristotle etc. The behaviour of man is shaped by the means of production. "As individuals express their life, so they are. What they are, therefore, coincides with their production, both with what they produce and with how they produce. The nature of individuals depends on the material conditions determining their production."

The fate of man is determined by the way he makes his living. If he can change the modes of production, he can also change himself. Economic factors are the most important for the process of social change.

According to Marx, the forces of production form the basis of society. Other things such as legal relations, forms of government, art and philosophy etc. are built on the structure of productive forces and thus form the super-structure. To quote Marx, "The totality of these relations of production constitutes the economic structure of society the real foundation on which legal and political super-structures arise and to which definite forms of social consciousness correspond."

According to the Marxists, politics is a form of class struggle. The state arises out of class struggle. It is an instrument of class rule. It is an instrument of the ruling class. The sole purpose is to protect private property. The conflict between classes is the core of capitalist politics.

Marxism supports revolutionary politics. Before revolution, politics is important because it is necessary for the working class to capture the power in the state. Revolution settles the political issue of state power once for all in favour of the working class. State and politics are the only means to end classes and establish a classless society. Politics has an important place in the social process in class struggle and it always has a class character. After revolution, politics will be unimportant and will be used only in establishing a classless society. In a classless society, politics and state will wither away.

Politics is the study of class divisions, class struggle and class relations in society. It is only a dimension of social process. In a classless society, politics also will decline. Politics cannot end the class struggle as the interests of different classes are so antagonistic that they cannot be reconciled or harmonised. There cannot be any common interest for all the classes. Only revolutionary politics is the correct politics.

There are fundamental *differences between the liberal and Marxian view of politics*. The liberal view is that politics is there to resolve conflicts, maintain order, peace and justice, to serve the common good of the whole society, to help the development of human personality and safeguard the rights and liberties of individuals. According to the Marxian view, politics is a reflection of class struggle. Politics cannot resolve the conflict but it is used by the owners of the means of production for safeguarding their interests/Class struggle in society is fundamental. In a class-divided society, class struggle will never end. Class struggle, and not class harmony, is the key notion in Marx.

Liberalism takes the individualistic view of society and politics, but Marxism takes the class view. Politics can be understood scientifically on the basis of class and class relations. The interests of the individuals of different classes may reconcile or individuals of one class may move to another class, but that does not change the position of classes. Marxism supports the conflict-model instead of the consensus model in politics. Politics cannot resolve the class conflict as it is inherent in the class system, incapable of solution within that system.

Political Science and Politics

Very often, the two terms political science and politics are used one for the other. Aristotle, the father of political science, used the term "politics" and not political science. There are writers like Jellinek, Sidgwick and Holtzendorff who prefer politics to political science. Prof. Laski named his monumental work as "The Grammar of Politics" and not "Grammar of Political Science." Wilson has also written a book called "Principles of Politics." There are many Universities in India which use the term politics and not political science for their Departments and examinations.

During the nineteenth century, the term politics was divided into two parts, theoretical and applied. In the theoretical part, was included the study of the fundamental characteristics of state. There was no reference to its activities or the means by which its ends could be achieved. The applied part embraced the study of the actual working of the government.

Sir Frederick Pollock classified politics into two parts, theoretical politics and applied politics. According to him, theoretical politics is concerned with the theory of the state, theory of government, theory of legislation and the theory of the state as an artificial person. The theory of the state is concerned with the origin of the state, the classification of forms of government and sovereignty. The theory of government is concerned with the forms of institutions, executive departments and the province and limits of positive law. The theory of legislation deals with the objects of legislation, philosophy of law or general jurisprudence, the methods and sanction of law, interpretation and administration of law and the mechanics of law-making. The theory of the state as an artificial person is concerned with the relations of one state with another and bodies of men and also international law. Applied politics deals with the state, government, laws and legislation and the state personified. It is concerned with the existing forms of government, constitutional law and usage, parliamentary system, army, navy, police, currency, budget and trade, legislative procedure, courts of justice and their machinery, judicial precedents and authority, diplomacy, peace and war, conferences, treaties and conventions and international agreements.

Sir Ernest Benn defines politics as "the art of looking for trouble, finding it whether it exists or not, diagnosing it wrongly and applying the wrong remedy."

Prof. R.N. Gilchrist writes, "Politics nowadays refers to the current problems of government which as often as not are more economic in character than political in the scientific sense. When we speak of a man as interested in politics, we mean that he is interested in the current problems of the day, in tariff questions, in labour questions, in the relation of the executive to the legislature, in any question, in fact, which requires or is supposed to require the attention of the law-makers of the country." (Principles of Political Science, p. 2).

A line of distinction has to be drawn between politics and political science as also between a politician and a political scientist. In ordinary parlance, by politics we mean current politics or the day to day problems of government. Peter H. Merkl writes, "In the broadest sense of the word, politics is a process at work and continuously, in the smallest groups as well as among the great powers on the international level. Everyday the newspapers carry considerable news about it, because the public wants to know what is going on in politics." The man who takes interest in current politics and participates actively in political affairs and government is called a politician. According to Webster's Unified Dictionary and Encyclopaedia, a politician is "one skilled in government or actively engaged in some branch of it; a person closely affiliated with a political party." The Random House Dictionary gives the following meanings of the term politician: a person who is active in party politics, a seeker or holder of public office who is more concerned about winning favour or retaining power than about maintaining principles, a person who holds political office, a person skilled in political government or administration (statesman), an expert in politics or political government, or a person who seeks to gain power or advancement within an organisation in ways that are generally disapproved.

A politician need not be a political scientist who takes keen interest in the study of political principles and governmental organisation and is an expert in the subject. A politician may have a superficial knowledge of political science. Well read statesmen and administrators may have a deep knowledge of political affairs. They may be well-informed political scientists and seasoned politicians. A political scientist may not become an active politician. All of his activities may be restricted to the realm of reading, writing and discussing about his subject.

As a result of the recent advancement made in the discipline of political science, politics has acquired a new meaning. It is regarded as a political activity which is widespread. According to Bertrand de Jouvenal, political activity is the urge in the human person to control and dominate and direct the wills of other individuals which may assume many forms, but is manifest wherever men enter into group life. Political activity expresses itself through innumerable associations and political parties, each offering its own programme for the solution of various problems facing the country and thereby seeking to control the power of the state by manning the government. Politics is a struggle for power on all levels. The rule of leadership is inherent in the game of politics.

Modern politics has a preference for particular and limited scale of studies of a restrictly empirical character, an aspiration towards precision and objectivity. It is a study of the political systems in their relation to social structure. It says nothing as to how the state and its institutions emerged and the process of their development.

SCOPE OF POLITICAL SCIENCE

There is no unanimity among scholars regarding the scope of political science. There is lack of precision in the definitions and meanings of political science and that creates confusion regarding the precise boundaries of the subject. Vernon Van Dyke observed thus in December 1965, "In these terms no one would contend that the scope of political science is fixed very sharply and that any boundaries are sacrosanct. We have somewhat different conceptions of the subject of our inquiries variously describing it as politics or government or the policy process or the political system; and each label carries with it some probable implications for the probable scope of the subject. Moreover, we pursue various approaches and methods and again the choices that we make are inter-related with the selection of questions and data and so affect scope." According to Willoughby, political science has to deal with three great topics: State, Government and Law. The fundamental problems of political science are an investigation of the nature and origin of the state as the highest political agency for the realisation of the common ends of society and the formulation of fundamental principles of state life, an enquiry into the nature, history and forms of political institutions and a deduction therefrom, so far as possible, of the laws of political growth and development.

The view of Prof. Goodnow is that political science divides itself into three distinct parts: the expression of the state will, the content of the state will as expressed and the execution of the state will. The first division includes political theory and the network of extra legal customs and extra legal organisations which influence the political system of a country. The second division is concerned with law and the third deals with the ascertainment and application of the correct principles of administration.

Gettel writes that political science deals with a historical survey of the origin of the state, tracing the beginnings of political life as they emerge from earlier social forms. It also deals with the development of the state as it evolved from simple to complex. It is concerned not only with the evolution of the state but also with the development of political ideas and theories. Political science must analyse the fundamental nature of the state, its organisation, its relation to individuals and other states. It must describe modern states as they actually exist and must compare and classify their governments. Political science deals, to a certain degree, with what the state ought to be, with the ultimate ends of the state and with the proper functions of its government. "It is thus a historical investigation of what the state has been and analytical study of what the state is and a politico-ethical discussion of what the state should be." Its leading sub-divisions are historical political science dealing with the origin and development of political forms, political theory dealing with the fundamental concept of the state, descriptive political science dealing with analysis and description of existing political forms and applied political science.

At the UNESCO Conference held in September 1948, distinguished political scientists from the various parts of the world marked out the subject-matter of political science which included (1) Political Theory, (2) Political Institutions, (3) Political Dynamics, and (4) International Relations. Under the first category, the history of political theory and political ideas is studied. The second covers a study of the constitution, national government, regional and local government, public administration, economic and social functions of government and comparative political institutions. The third topic studies political parties, groups and associations, participation of the citizen in the government and administration, public opinion etc. The fourth topic deals with international relations. This demarcation delimits the scope of Political Science within the bounds of four zones.

As the importance of political science is increasing day by day, its scope is also increasing and becoming wider. In spite of this difficulty, we may discuss the scope of political science as the study of the state and government, a study of political theory, a study of political institutions, a study of political dynamics, a study of adjustment of the individual with the state, a study of international law and international relations, study of the concept of power etc.

(1) Study of State and Government

Political science is the science of state and government. It conducts a scientific study of both the state and government. It deals with the nature and formation of the state and tries to understand various forms and functions of the government. Scholars like Bluntschli, Garris and others believe that the scope of political science is restricted to the study of the state alone. Scholars like Dr. Leacock attach more importance to the study of the government than that of the state. The view of Dr. Leacock is that political science deals only with the government. A similar view is expressed by Karl W. Deutsch in these words: "Because politics is making of decision by public means, it is primarily concerned with government, that is with the direction and self-direction of large communities of the people." The term state does not occur in his definition of political science. The view of Laski, Gilchrist and Gettell is that the scope of political science includes a study of both the state and government. According to Bluntschli, political science is a science which is concerned with the state, endeavours to understand and comprehend the state in its essential nature, various forms, manifestations and developments. Janet writes, "It is that part of social science which treats of the foundations of the state and the principles of the government."

According to Aristotle, "The state originated in the bare needs of life and is continued in existence for the sake of good life". The view of Burke is that the state "is to be looked upon with reverence because it is not a partnership in things subservient only to the gross animal existence of a perishable nature. It is partnership in all science, a partnership in all art, a partnership in every virtue and in all perfection. As the ends of such a partnership cannot be obtained in many generations, it becomes a partnership not only between those who are living, but between those who are living, those who are dead and those who are to be born."

Though the state includes government as one of the essential elements, it is necessary to employ the term government also as governmental machinery has to be brought into a focus in the study. As a matter of fact, about half of the study is devoted to political institutions or governmental machinery. Regarding the scope of political science, Dr. Garner writes, "All the opinions quoted above are in substantial agreement on the essential point, namely, that the phenomena of the state in its varied aspects and relationships, as distinct from the family, the tribe, the nation and from all private associations or groups, though not unconnected with them, constitute the subject of political science."

Political science makes a thorough investigation into the origin of the state from the tribal state to nation state. It deals with the history of the state to know how people organised themselves for law and order in the remote past. It also deals with elements of state, sovereignty and law, ends and functions of state, sphere of state activity, the rights and obligations of the individual, political institutions, forms of government, branches and departments of government, elections, political parties, public opinion and its agencies, local bodies, international bodies etc. Political science deals not only with the state as it actually is but also with what it ought to be. It lays down norms to which the state should conform. It studies the state "as it is, as it has been and as it ought to be". Applying ethical and other norms, the political scientist tries to give shape to a state in which the primary aim of achieving human welfare can be realised. He also tries to peep into the future and speculates about the nature of the future state.

(2) Study of Political Theory

Political theory is a major branch of political science. On the basis of the political ideas or thoughts of political thinkers, political theory formulates definitions of concepts like democracy, liberty, equality, grounds of political obligation etc. A student of political science must start his lessons with political theory which explains the rudimentary concepts of political science.

Speculations of political philosophers and other ideologies are put together in one volume which is given the title of political theory. The underlying assumption is that other parts of political science on governmental organisation, political parties and pressure groups, international relations etc. are distinct from political theory. The danger of viewing political theory in this way is that a special meaning is attached to the word theory which rules out the possibility of the existence of any theory in other parts of political science. "The practice has an objectionable aspect in that it seems to suggest that all statements expressing theory belong to the subdivision labelled political theory; and conversely, it seems to suggest that books and courses in other sub-divisions go beyond their proper limits if any theory is included. The theory is taken to be synonymous with thought, this attitude becomes disastrous for the other sub-divisions."

(3) Study of Political Institutions

The study of political institutions includes a study of constitutions and comparative governments. It deals with the nature of different political institutions, including government, explains their merits and demerits, their structure and working and arrives at different conclusions on comparative basis. The study of public administration and local government may be included under this heading. However, the study of public administration has become an independent subject in recent times. There are many types of political institutions in a country or in a society and the institution of the state controls all of them. These institutions are useful to the nation and have their utility in society. That is why we study these institutions alongwith the state.

(4) Study of Political Dynamics

The study of political dynamics has become important in the twentieth century. It means the current forces at work in government and politics. It covers a wide range and includes the study of political parties, public opinion, pressure groups, lobbies etc. A scientific study of the working of these political dynamics helps to explain the political behaviour of individuals and groups. The study in this field is often done in collaboration with other social sciences like sociology, anthropology and psychology. The study of political parties has become important in modern times. New conditions and experience make the people wiser and in the light of new knowledge, they can improve the machinery of the state. Human nature is not static but dynamic. "To understand the functioning of government, it is necessary for political science to work outward from the nucleus of the study of government and to take into consideration social, psychological and economic-factors." Many changes often take place. The principles of governance change from time to time. The state today is not what it was one thousand years ago. These changes have to be studied in political science.

(5) Study of Adjustment of Individual with the State

In political science, we have to study the nature of the relationship between the individual and the state. It is interesting to examine how man adjusts himself within society. Man is the root of politics. The process of adjustment of man with society is an important aspect of political science. The state guarantees certain rights and liberties to its citizens and also imposes certain reasonable restrictions on them. If maximum state intervention leads to loss of liberty, the complete absence of state intervention results in anarchy. It is a difficult problem to adjust or reconcile the authority of the state with individual liberty. Political science has to probe into this difficult and complicated problem.

(6) Study of International Relations and International Law

The scope of political science includes a study of international relations. It covers a wide range and includes diplomacy, international politics, international law, international organisations like the United Nations etc. On account of scientific inventions and discoveries, cooperation and contact among the different nations of the world have become easier and the whole world turns to be a family. Human society today is viewed from world perspective. The idea of World Government in the distant future is being advocated. The study of international relations has also become an independent subject in modern times. The study of political science also includes a study of international law. The states are the subjects of international law. International law is defined as a body of general principles and specific rules which are ordinarily binding upon the member states. The states are the subjects of international law which has assumed greater importance in modern times.

(7) Study of National and International Problems and Political Study of Man

Political science is intimately related to the English word "Politics" which itself has been derived from the Greek word "Polis". It stands for city state. The view of Burgess is that the modern demands of land extension, representative government and national unity have made political science not only the science of political independence but that of state sovereignty also. To quote Laski, "The study of political science concerns itself with the life of man in relation to organised states."

Political science enquires into the working of the legislature, the civil service and the judiciary. The conduct of diplomacy is also within its scope. The same is the case with the political ethics of a polity. It also deals with the purposes, ends and limits of political obligation. As the chief concern of political science is to help people to live in harmony, it takes up political problems and offers solutions based upon particular situations reflecting on the capacity of a political system and the attainment of its goals. As a branch of social sciences, it provides for the overall framework for the evaluation of political phenomenon.

In recent times, there has been an "intellectual revolution" in the thoughts and ideas of the American political scientists and the innovations introduced by them have greatly influenced the nature and subject-matter of political science. The traditional approach is criticised on the ground of parochialism and formalism. The traditional approach was primarily concerned with institutions and their legal norms, rules and regulations, or political ideas and ideologies rather than performance, interaction and behaviour. The modern political analysis, guided by sociological, anthropological and psychological methods and theories, rests upon four basic principles viz., the search for more comprehensive scope, search for realism, search for precision and search for intellectual order. The object is to free political science from value-judgements or quasi-ethical or philosophical judgments. The modern political scientists seek to develop a kind of empirically oriented and value-free political science and bring it at par with natural sciences.

For a long time, political science was mainly concerned with the legislature, executive and the judiciary. As the study of political science advanced, the scope was extended to an analysis of political parties, bureaucracies, interest groups and other groups. This has been supplemented by how political communications work through the press, radio, television, discussions or meetings and how demands emerge and are formulated through interest groups and political parties and their impact on the policies of the government. The emphasis is on procedures and institutions through which authoritative decisions are made and the outcome of those decisions in the form of rule-making, rule-application and rule-adjudication.

The behaviouralists concentrate on the behaviour of individuals and groups within political institutions. They deal with the actual processes of politics.

Modern political scientists under behavioural and systems approach have widened the scope of political science to cover many more aspects like political socialisation, political culture, political development and informal structures like pressure groups etc.

The process of specialisation in various aspects of political science, changes in methodology, particularly behavioural and inter-disciplinary, have brought about a radical change in the scope of political science. Political decisions are not made in a vacuum or due only to the personal idiosyncrasies of political actors. Economic factors, the social structure and stratification systems influence both the content and mode of making political decisions. We have to take into consideration political orientations of the members of society, how they see the political system itself, how they react to it emotionally and how they evaluate it morally. The process of political socialisation is also important. Prof. Frank Thakurdas writes that the analytical-cum-empirical method "has definitely enlarged the field of our inquiry as it has cleared up the rust in which many helpful distinctions within the framework of political studies lay obscured. It is not that the traditional boundaries have been obliterated; they may merely have been extended and given a sharpness and depth hitherto unknown".

IS POLITICAL SCIENCE A SCIENCE?

Arguments Against

The question is whether political science is a science or not. There are many who do not favour calling political science a science. According to Buckle, in the present state of knowledge, politics, far from being a science, is one of the most backward of all arts. There is no agreement regarding the method of study of political science and the conclusions arrived at by various political scientists. There is no continuity in the development of political science. It deals with man and political institutions which have been changing from time to time. It is not possible to have political experiments in the same way as we have in the case of other sciences. On these grounds, Buckle rejects the claim of political science to be called a science.

A similar view was held by Auguste Comte. The grounds given by him in support of his view were that the writers of political science differed regarding its methods and conclusions. There was no continuity in its development. It failed to supply material out of which hypotheses could be built up.

The view of Amos is that practical statesmen "immersed in actual business and oppressed by the ever-recurring presence of new emergencies almost resent the notion of applying the comprehensive principles of science. The result is that politics floats in the public mind either as a mere field for ingenious chicane or as a boundless waste for the evolution of scholastic phantasy." Prof. Henry J. Ford says that the "idea of determining state policy upon scientific principles has no place in practical politics."

According to Prof. Ernest Barker, "Each professor of political science is apt to feel about the other professors, if not about himself, that they argue from questionable axioms, by a still more questionable process of logic, to conclusions that are almost unquestionably wrong. The layman, even more sceptical, is inclined to adopt towards political science the attitude of Mrs. Prig to Mrs. Harris so often mentioned by Mrs. Gamp: "I don't believe there's so sick a subject."

The view of Prof. F.W. Maitland is that "When I see a good set of examination questions headed by the words 'Political Science', I regret not the questions but the title."

Burke wrote, "There is no science of politics any more than there is a science of aesthetics—for the lines of politics are not like the lines of mathematics. No lines can be laid down for civil or political wisdom. They are a matter incapable of exact, definition."

J.S. Mill wrote in 1843, "It is accordingly but of yesterday that the concept of a political science has existed anywhere but in the mind of, here and there, an isolated thinker, generally very ill-prepared of the realisation."

Many reasons are given in support of the contention that political science cannot claim the status of a science. One reason is that there are controversies over definition, terminology and methods of political science. Among the political scientists, there is no general agreement regarding the definition, scope, terminology, methods and principles of the subject. Different methods and approaches are open to students to conduct investigation in political science instead of a universally accepted single method or set of methods. Likewise, political principles are not universally accepted, and applied. The principles regarding rights and obligations of the individual are not fully accepted by all political thinkers. The same is the case regarding the sphere of the activities of the state. The meanings of different words and expressions have created sharp controversies among political scientists. Terms like imperialism, democracy, communism, socialism, liberalism and nationalism do not have uniform definitions. They have been interpreted and defined in many ways. The terms in political science convey different meanings. R.G. Gettell writes, "The terms of political science are often used carelessly in ordinary speech, are given double meanings and are frequently distorted deliberately by being given a favourable or unfavourable connotation or partisan and national purposes."

The principles of political science have been vague and imprecise and have created multifarious controversies. Universally accepted rigorous methods of scientific investigation, observation and experimentation cannot be followed. It is impossible to obtain correct results in a science. Natural sciences employ a uniform technical vocabulary or jargon. A formula in Physics or Chemistry is universally accepted. It is clear and accurate and there is no scope for any doubt about its veracity or precision. However, that is not the case with the state and government. Political theories or principles cannot be put on par with the principle of Archimedes, the laws of gravitation or the theory of relativity. Certain meanings of democracy have been accepted by many, but not by all. While many thinkers regard democracy as the best form of government, some scholars point out the fact that democracy is government by the ignorant and incompetent people. Likewise, it cannot be said definitely whether state should be mono-national or poly-national and whether legislatures should be unicameral or bicameral.

Another difficulty with political science is that it is not possible to have laboratory experiments in political science. The political researcher has to deal with human beings, while the researcher in

Physics and Chemistry experiments with inanimate substances. All human beings are not like one another. Even the same human being does not behave in the same manner at all times. Political activity cannot be given a made-to-order shape. The emotions and actions of man cannot be controlled. Atmospheric pressure and temperature can be measured but the intensity of political reactions and forces cannot be measured. Political principles cannot be weighed in a laboratory by the scales of precision or tested with litmus paper. A political scientist has no mechanical aids at his disposal. He cannot duplicate laboratory experiments as is the case in Chemistry or Physics. Political conditions cannot be artificially created as human beings cannot be treated as lifeless tools. Identical social conditions cannot be reproduced for experimentation at the will of a political scientist or a politician or a government. No government can command that a nation will react favourably to a particular policy. No government can calculate the intensity of resentment which may be created as a result of an enactment. Prohibition has been a failure in India as the government could not control the behaviour of men and women.

"One chemical element is exactly the same all the world over; any variation in its composition can be tested and explained." Graham Wallas points out that metallurgy became a science when man could actually take two pieces of copper ore unlike in shape and appearance and chemical constitution and extract from them two pieces of copper so nearly alike that they would give the same results when treated in the same way. A student of political science does not possess similar control over his material. He cannot create an artificial uniformity in man. "He cannot after twenty generations of education or breeding render even two human beings sufficiently like each other for him to prophesy that in approach to certainty that they will behave alike under like circumstances."

This is how a teacher of medicine put it to his students: "There are two words in medicine which you never use. They are 'Always' and 'Never'." The same cannot be said of political science. Lord Bryce compared political science to a relatively undeveloped and inexact natural science like meteorology, somewhat in the same way as Prof. Marshall compared economics to the science of tides.

Prof. G.N. Gilchrist writes, "In political science it is difficult to find uniform and unvarying laws. The material is constantly varying. Actions and reactions take place in various and- often unforeseen ways." However, the descriptive and classificatory approaches employed by the political scientists can yield approximately correct results. David Easton writes, "Political research has still to penetrate to the hard core of political power in society. In spite of the intensive research activity of the last 75 years, only limited knowledge can as yet be offered on the fundamental distribution of powers among the basic social aggregates. But the energies of the discipline as a whole have not been given to developing consistent and integrated research in order that it might identify the major variables affecting power relations and the significant kinds of data to be observed."

While there is objectivity in the study of physical sciences, it is lacking while studying problems relating to state and government. While dealing with political questions, a completely impartial attitude may not be possible even in the case of the best thinker. The attitude of thinkers of various countries towards political problems may not be detached. Indian political problems are viewed differently by different thinkers and politicians as they may be guided by economic and imperialist prejudices. Problems of nationalism and minorities are frequently approached in a subjective, passionate and prejudiced manner. Racial, religious, economic and other considerations weigh much in the study of political questions. Political disabilities of the coloured people and backward countries may not be examined objectively. Political verdicts may be passed without considering the merits of a case.

Arguments in favour

However, if by the term science we mean a systematised body of knowledge, political science can certainly be called a science. Dr. Finer rightly says that "we can become the prophets of the probables if not the seers of the certain". "The phenomena of the state present a certain connection or sequence which is the result of fixed laws, though less immutable, to be sure, than those of the physical world, that these phenomena form proper subject of scientific investigation, and that the laws and the principles deducible therefrom are susceptible of application to the solution of concrete problems of the state." It is true that students of political science do not have laboratories in which they can test their theories like other scientists, but it cannot be denied that there are certain political experiments from which the political scientists can benefit. It is well-known that Aristotle based his "Politics" on his study of the working of 158 constitutions. Likewise, Lord Bryce compared the working of democracy in various countries and then came to his conclusions with regard to the relative merits and demerits of democracy. Sir B.N. Rau, the Constitutional Adviser to the Government of India, visited many countries and placed the results of his comparative study of the various constitutions before the members of the Constituent Assembly for their guidance while framing the Constitution of India. The political scientists can benefit from their study of the Russian Revolution of 1917. Lord Durham laid down certain principles for the development of self-government in Canada. As those principles were found to be useful, those were applied to other colonies also. The bicameral experiment of Britain has encouraged many countries to adopt the same. The same can be said about the working of the two-party system, proportional representation and direct democracy. Dyarchy was introduced in the provinces of India under the Government of India Act, 1919. As it did not work successfully, the same was abolished by the Government of India Act, 1935. The new experiment of provincial autonomy was made under the Government of India Act, 1935 and that too did not work harmoniously. It has been found by experience that democracy is a better form of government than others. It is more permanent than most other forms of government and helps more in promoting the welfare of the common people. Monarchy, dictatorship, aristocracy, oligarchy and other forms of government have been experimented in different parts of the world in ancient, medieval and modern times, but none of them proved successful.

It is true that there is no consensus of opinion among experts regarding the methods, principles and conclusions of political science, but the fault is not with the subject. Political science is a dynamic study of a living subject-matter which is to be translated in terms of living human activity. Unlike other natural sciences, political science does not deal with a static subject-matter. It deals with man and his institutions. As man is dynamic, the same is true of the institutions created by him. The nature of man changes with the changing conditions and hence institutions are bound to adjust themselves with the changing needs of human life in accordance with the changing circumstances of time.

While German scholars have adopted the analytical method to give political science the character of a science, Holtzendorff defends the claim of political science to be ranked as a science. To quote him, "With the enormous growth of knowledge, it is impossible to deny that the sum total of all the experiences, phenomena and knowledge respecting the state may be brought together under the collective title of political science." The same is the view of Von Mohl, Bluntschli, Retzenhofer, Treitschke, Liber, Burgess and Willoughby. Dr. Garner is also willing to recognise the scientific nature of political science. According to him, "Science is a knowledge relating to a particular subject acquired by a systematic observation, experience or study which have been coordinated, systematised and classified." According to Pearson, the function of science is "the classification of facts, the recognition of their sequence and relative significance. "Thomson believes that science includes "all knowledge communicable and verifiable which is reached by methodical observation and experiment and which admits of concise, consistent and connected formulation."

The view of Lord Bryce is that political science is a science, although it is undeveloped and incomplete. To quote him, "Politics is a science in the sense that there is constancy and uniformity in the tendencies of human nature, which enables us to regard the acts of men at one time as due to the same causes which have governed their acts at previous times."

Prof. R.N. Gilchrist believes that general laws can be deduced from given material and those are useful in the actual problems of the government. To quote him, "While we may agree that the exactness of natural sciences is impossible of attainment in the social science, nevertheless social problems can be treated with the same scientific methods as Chemistry and Physics. These results indeed may not be so accurate or so easily tested, but as we shall see the various subjects with which we deal, present a systematised mass of material which is capable of being treated by ordinary scientific methods. We shall see that general laws can be deduced from given material and these laws are useful in actual problems of government." Again, "To say that the only real sciences are those which have exact results with dogmatic proof of experiments is to deny the possibility of ethics, political economy, political science, sociology, metaphysics being sciences."

Huxley writes, "Whether there is a political science depends on whether any rational principles can be found to regulate the form of constitutions, the determination of the sphere of the state which makes a complete and systematized branch of knowledge, clearly formulated and understood in their mutual relations."

The conclusion of Sir Frederick Pollock is that there is a science of politics in the same sense and to the same or about the same extent as there is a science of morals. "Those who deny the existence of a political science, if they mean that there is no body of rules or laws from which a Prime Minister may infallibly learn how to command a majority in Parliament, would be right as to the fact, but would betray a rather inadequate notion of what science is." Political science has a scientific character because the scientific method is applicable to its phenomena. The development of psychology, a critical use of history and the application of the inductive method will enhance the claim of political science to be considered a science.

Is Political Science an Art ?

By art we generally mean "practical application of knowledge for the achievement of a particular end." A scientist may possess a thorough knowledge of the chemical composition, nature and characteristics of colours, but when an artist applies that knowledge of colours in painting a picture, it is an art. The knowledge of colours is applied to produce a painting.

Political science is a body of systematized knowledge about the state. The question arises whether that knowledge can be applied in actual practice and the answer is in the affirmative. When drafting a constitution, the knowledge of political science is applied. In administering the day to day affairs of a state, knowledge of political science is necessary. The same is the case with formulating foreign policies and conducting diplomatic relations with foreign states. Political science does not merely accumulate theoretical knowledge, but the same is applied by statesmen, diplomats and administrators to achieve their respective ends in their day to day functions. Hence, political science can be called an art.

However, political science is primarily a science as it is a body of systematised knowledge. It can also be called an art because its knowledge is not of mere theoretical importance. It is of practical value also. Hence Gettell and Bluntschli are of the view that political science bears the character of art also. Like other arts, it deals with the various aspects of life and tells us how and in what way we should lead our lives. It also tells us how we can become better citizens and what our rights and duties are. The view of Buckle is that political science is the most backward of all arts.

The conclusion is that political science can be called both a science and an art.

Utility of the Study of Political Science

The study of political science is of great value and with its help people can know how and why the state was organised in the past and why its continuation is justified. Political science makes people conscious of their rights and obligations. People who are mentally equipped with the knowledge of political science are an asset to the state. The lessons of political science are useful. Intelligent citizens can play a useful part in social and political affairs. Others also can take advantage of the knowledge in political science. While there exists a high level of political consciousness in Britain and the United States, the same is lacking in underdeveloped and politically backward countries. Standards in politics, administration and statesmanship cannot be high on account of the low level of political research, lack of sound knowledge of political science and absence of good political traditions and conventions. Statesmen, leaders and administrators in backward countries do not discharge their duties honestly and efficiently on account of the absence of public criticism. If the electorate is well-informed and has a sound knowledge of political science, it becomes vigilant and does not allow the government to rule arbitrarily. If the citizens have a high level of political consciousness, they are an asset to the government. They can give cooperation to the government. This is particularly so in times of grave national emergency or foreign invasion.

Knowledge of political science has become indispensable in modern times because now everyone is directly or indirectly concerned with politics. Robert A. Dahl writes, "A citizen encounters politics in the government of a country, town, school, church, business firm, trade union, club, political party, civic association and a host of organisations. Politics is one of the unavoidable facts of human existence. Everyone is involved in some fashion at some time in some kind of political system." Those administrators and statesmen who have knowledge of political science, are aware of the principles which should guide them and hence they can avoid the pitfalls. In order to understand the affairs of the world, it is desirable to know the affairs of one's own country, the working of various institutions, the nature and conduct of the government and the postures and policies of political parties and various other matters. The knowledge of political science is of great value to "constitution-makers, legislators, executives and judges who need models or norms that can be applied to immediate situations."

The knowledge of political science enriches one's mind and widens one's intellectual horizon. Those who specialise in various fields of political science conduct researches to discover hitherto unknown principles underlying political phenomena and make a rich contribution to the realm of knowledge. If the ultimate philosophy of human life is to enrich knowledge, political science makes a major contribution to the storehouse of knowledge.

Every man must know his rights and duties and a study of politics makes him aware of his rights and responsibilities. In order to be a good citizen, one must know the government, its objectives and its basis. A study of politics helps in this matter. A man without an ideology is less than a man and the absence of ideology gives birth to amoral, normless and opportunist behaviour. A study of politics makes him aware of the different ideologies in society. Without understanding politics and participating in revolutionary politics, it is not possible to change society. In order to live as a fully developed man, a study of politics is a necessity. The object of knowledge about society is not only to understand it but also to change it. In politics, all activities are either to bring a change or to resist a change and a knowledge of politics is essential for both.

Political science is said to be a science of statesmanship and leadership. That is the reason why the recruits to the Indian Foreign Service and the Indian Administrative Service are required to undergo a course in political science at the National Academy of Administration at Mussoorie.

Political science teaches the lesson of cooperation, adjustment and toleration. Society cannot progress without cooperation and adjustment. The absence of toleration leads to anarchy. Politics teaches the principles of toleration and coexistence. It preaches the gospel of "live and let live".

A modern man without knowledge of political science is imperfect. It is said that "a people that neglect politics cannot be happy." Again, "Whoever you are, or want to be, you may not be interested in politics, but politics is interested in you." Hence it is suggested that the study of political science should be made compulsory in all democratic countries. George Bernard Shaw wrote, "Political science is the science by which alone civilisation can be saved."

SUGGESTED READINGS

Amos : *The Science of Politics.*
Apter, David E. : *Introduction to Political Analysis.*
Avineri, S. : *The Social and Political Thought of Karl Marx,* London, 1968.
Barbrook, Alec : *Patterns of Political Behaviour.*
Barry, B.(ed.) : *Power and Political Theory,* London, 1976.
Beetham, D. : *Max Weber and the Theory of Modern Politics,* London, 1974.
Benfield, E.C. : *Political Influence,* 1961.
Bentley, A.F. : *The Process of Government,* Chicago, 1908.
Berle, A.A. : *Power*, New York, 1967.
Berle, A.A. : *The Twentieth Century Capitalist Revolution,* New York, 1954.
Berman, Marshall : *The Politics of Authenticity.*
Blondel, Jean : *An Introduction to Comparative Government.*
Buckle : *History of Civilisation.*
Catlin, G.E.G. : *Systematic Politics,* London, 1962.
Cornforth, M. : *The Open Philosophy and the Open Society,* London, 1968.
Crick, Bernard : *In Defence of Politics.*
Curtis, Michael : *Comparative Government and Politics.*
Dahl, R.A. : *Who Governs?,* 1961.
Dahl, Robert A. : *Modern Political Analysis.*
Dunner, Joseph (Ed.) : *Dictionary of Political Science.*
Duverger, Maurice : *The Idea of Politics,* London, 1966.
Duverger, Maurice : *The Study of Politics,* London, 1972.
Dyke, Vernon Van : *Political Science: A Philosophical Analysis,* London, 1960.
Easton, David : *The Political System: An Inquiry into the State of Political Science,* 1953.
Engels, F. : *The Origin of the Family, Private Property and the State.*
Friedman, M. : *Capitalism and Freedom,* Chicago, 1962.
Friedrich, C.J. : *Man and his Government,* New York, 1963.
Galbraith, J.K. : *American Capitalism,* 1956.
Galbraith, J.K. : *The New Industrial State,* 1967.
Garner, J.W. : *Introduction to Political Science.*
Garner, J.W. : *Political Science and Government.*
Gettell, R.G. : *Political Theory.*
Gilchrist, R.N. : *Principles of Political Science.*
Gould and Thursby : *Contemporary Political Thought,* New York. 1969.
Gouvenal B. de : *On Power,* 1949.

Greenstein, Polsby, Nelson : *Political Science: Scope and Theory, Handbook of Political Science, Vol. I.*, 1975.

Hacker, A. : *Political Theory, Philosophy, Ideology, Science, New York,* The Macmillan Co., 1961.

Hallowell : *Main Currents in Modern Political Thought.*

Heeger, Gerald A. : *The Politics of Under-Development,* Macmillan, 1974.

Hoogerwerf : *Political Science, Concepts and Problems,* 1972.

Hunter, F. : *Community Power Structure,* 1953.

Jouvenal, B.de : *The Pure Theory of Politics,* Cambridge, 1963.

Key, V.O. : *Politics, Parties and Pressure Groups,* New York, 1965.

Klegg, S. : *Power Rule and Domination,* London, 1975.

Laski, H.J. : *Liberty in the Modern State,* London, 1948.

Laski, H.J. : *A Grammar of Politics.*

Laski, H.J. : *An Introduction to Politics.*

Lasswell, H.D. : *Politics: Who Gets What, When and How,* New York, 1936.

Lasswell and Kaplan : *Power and Society,* 1950.

Latham : *The Group Basis of Politics,* New York, 1952.

Lefevre, H. : *The Sociology of Marx,* Penguin, 1968.

Lipset, S.M. : *Political Man,* 1963.

Lipset, S.M. : *Politics and the Social Sciences,* New York, 1969.

Lipson, L. : *The Great Issues of Politics,* Bombay, 1967.

Loewenstein, K. : *Political Power and the Government Process,* 1967.

Lucas, J.R. : *The Principles of Politics.*

MacIver, R.M. : *The Modern State,* London, 1926.

Macpherson, C.B. : *The Political Theory of Possessive Individualism,* London, 1962.

Macpherson, C.B. : *Democratic Theory,* Oxford, 1973.

Maitland, F.W. : *Collected Papers.*

Merki, Peter H. : *Political Continuity and Change.*

Meniam, C.E. : *Political Powers: Its Composition and Incidence,* 1934.

Miliband, R. : *Marxism and Politics,* London, 1977.

Miller, J.D.B. : *The Nature of Politics,* London, 1962.

Morgenthau, Hans J. : *Scientific Man v. Power Politics,* 1946.

Mosca, G. : *The Ruling Class,* 1939.

Pareto, V. : *The Mind and Society,* 1935.

Pollock, Frederick : *An Introduction to the History of the Science of Politics, London,* 1918.

Poulantzas : *Fascism and Dictatorship,* 1974.

Pye L. and S. Verba : *Political Culture and Political Development,* Princeton, 1965.

Ranney, Austin : *Governing: A Brief Introduction to Political Science.*

Rieselbach and Balch : *Psychology and Politics: An Introductory Reader.*

Roberts, G.K. : *A Dictionary of Political Analysis.*

Robson, W.R. : *The University Teaching of Social Science: Political* Science (UNESCO Report), 1954)

Runciman, W.G. : *Political Science and Political Theory,* Cambridge University Press, 1965.

Russell, Bertrand : *Power: A New Social Analysis,* 1938.

Sidgwick, H. : *The Elements of Politics.*

Soltau, R.H. : *An Introduction to Politics, London,* Longmans, 1951.

Spencer : *The Man versus The State.*

Strachey, J. : *Contemporary Capitalism,* 1961.

Swingewood, A. : *Marx and,Modern Social Theory,* London, 1975.

Truman, D. : *The Governmental Process,* New York, 1967.

Wasby, S.L. : *Political Science—The Discipline and Its Dimensions,* Calcutta, 1972.

Wiseman, H.V. : Political Systems: Some Sociological Approaches.

Wolin, S.S. : *Politics and Vision, London,* 1960.

CHAPTER

Politics and Society

In the words of MacIver and Charles Page, "Society is a system of usages and procedures, of authority and mutual aid, of many groupings and divisions, of controls and human behaviour and of liberties. This ever-changing complex system we call society. It is the web of social relationships. And it is always changing." (Society, p. 5).

Learning Objectives

- Society and State
- Society and Individual
- Social Organisations
- Family
- Characteristics
- Functions
- The State and Family
- Clan
- Tribe
- Community
- Community and Association
- Association
- Classification of Associations
- Suggested Readings

Men are social beings and they express their nature by creating and re-creating an organisation which guides and controls their behaviour in myriad ways. This organisation is called society. It liberates and limits the activities of man. It sets up standards for them to follow and maintain. Whatever the imperfections and tyrannies it has exhibited in human history, society is a necessary condition of every fulfilment of life.

Society is not limited to human beings. There are animal societies of many degrees. The remarkable social organisations of the insects, such as the ant, the bee and the hornet are well-known. It is contended that wherever there is life, there is society because life means heredity and can arise only out of and in the presence of another life. There may be society between animals of different species, as between a man and a horse or dog, or between sheep and their shepherd dog. However, our concern is with society among human species.

It is often said that the family, in some form, was the first society. It is certainly true that the sex relationship is a primary and essential type of social relationship. This relationship involves both likeness and difference in the beings whom it relates.

Society depends on difference as well as on likeness. If people were all exactly alike, their social relationships would be as limited as those of the ant or bee. There would be little give and take, little reciprocity. They would contribute very little to one another. In society, each member seeks something and gives something. This is fundamentally the case however exploitative or parasitical or unjust the social system may be. A tyrannical father of a family plays a give-and-take role within the family system.

The division of labour in society is cooperation before it is division. It is because people have like wants that they associate in the performance of unlike functions. A similar wish for profit may lead men to the formation of a business partnership. The common desire for shared affection and home is often the basis for the creation of families.

Man is a social animal. He is dependent on society for protection, comfort, nurture, education, equipment, opportunity and the multitude of definite services which society provides. He is dependent on society for the content of his thoughts, his dreams, his aspirations, even many of his maladies of mind and body. His birth in society brings with it the absolute need of society itself. No wonder, solitary confinement is considered as one of the,most fearful of all punishments.

F.H. Giddings writes that "society exists among those who resemble one another in some degree, in body and mind, and who are near enough or intelligent enough to appreciate the fact." Society rests on "consciousness of mankind". Talcott Parsons, another sociologist, says, "The arrangement encompassing the most inclusive and continuous relationships in terms of which man pursued his fulfilment and survival is called society."

Society and State

Writers like Plato and Aristotle did not make any distinction between state and society. That was partly due to the peculiar circumstances prevailing in the Greek city states which were small in area and compact in population. Their problems were simple and they could consider the city as an all-embracing organisation covering the whole of the life of man. Their attitude was: "She is ours and we are hers". The Greek city was the state, the church and the school, all in one. The Greek theory was one of omnicompetent "society-state".

Like the Greeks, the Idealists like Hegel did not make any distinction between state and society. However, the relation of state and society has been correctly described by Barker in these words: "They overlap, they blend, they borrow from one another. But roughly, we may say that the area of the one is voluntary cooperation, its energy that of goodwill, its method that of elasticity; while the area of the other is rather that of mechanical action, its energy is force and its method is rigidity."

According to MacIver, "There are social forms like the family or the church or the club which owe neither their origin nor their inspiration to the state; and social forces like custom or competition which the state may protect or modify, but certainly does not create; and social motives like friendship or jealousy which establish relationship too intimate and personal to be controlled by the great engine of the state." Again, "The state is a structure not coeval and co-extensive with society, but built within it as a determinate order for the attainment of specific ends."

The scope of society is much wider than that of the state. The state deals only with the political aspect of the life of man while society is concerned with the whole of his life. It is concerned with the religious, moral, physical and social aspects of his life. There is no aspect of his life with which society is not concerned. However, experience shows that it is neither desirable nor practicable to give all that control to the state.

State refers to a definite territory. There can be no state without a territory, but that is not the case with society which does not refer to any territorial area. The Red Cross Society has its branches all over the world. The same is the case with the Y.M.C.A. and Y.W.C.A. The state is territorially integrated, but society is not limited by any kind of territory. Government is essential for a state but not for society. One of the essentials of state is that it must have a government as the state cannot act otherwise. It merely acts through the machinery of government. However, it is not necessary for society to have any government. It is possible to think of such a society. As a matter of fact, first came society and then came the government. Society is prior to the state. Even before the state came into existence, there was some sort of social organisation. MacIver writes, "In the earliest phases among hunters, fishers, root-diggers and fruit-gatherers, there have been social groups which knew nothing and almost nothing of the state. Today, there remain simple people, such as certain groups of Eskimos, which have ho recognizable political organisation." (The Modern State, p. 5).

The state is sovereign and can force its members to obey its laws, but that is not the case with society which can merely persuade its members to obey its rules and regulations. The importance of the state to society is brought out by Barker in these words: "Society is held together by the state: and if it were not thus held together, it could not exist." MacIver compares society to many planks which comprise a wooden barrel and the state to the iron band which goes around them holding them together in their proper places.

Barker points out that the state and society differ from each other with regard to their purpose or function, organisation, structure and method. As regards the purpose, the state is a legal association which acts for the single legal purpose of making and enforcing a permanent system of law and order, but society acts for a variety of purposes other than the legal purpose. To quote Barker, "The state exists for one great but single purpose; society exists for a number of purposes, some great and some small, but all, in their aggregate, deep as well as broad." As regards organisation and structure, the state is a single organisation but society has many organisations within itself. As regards method, the state employs the method of coercion or compulsion, but society that of persuasion.

Society is instinctive to man. It is spontaneous in its growth and development. To quote MacIver, "Wherever living beings enter into or maintain willed relations with one another, there society exists." Society is prior to the state and also wider than the state. It is a complex of all economic, cultural, religious, educational and political associations. Society precedes the state just as it precedes the family, the Church, the corporation, the political party. It unites all these as a tree unites its branches. The state is one of these associations and it has become the most important of all because it controls and coordinates the various aspects of social life. The state is definitely territorial while society is not. The structure of society is elastic while that of the state is rigid. Society appeals and persuades while the state uses force. Society acts through conventions and moral rules and social pressures, while the state uses force to punish those who violate the laws. The purposes of society are very many while that of the state is only one.

In totalitarian states governed by dictators like Hitler and Mussolini, the distinction between society and state was not recognised. In a totalitarian state, all aspects of human life are brought under the control of the government and the individual has no freedom. However, in a democratic state, the individual is guaranteed certain basic rights for the enjoyment of liberty and distinction between society and state is necessarily maintained.

Society and Individual

In the words of Aristotle, "Man is a social animal. He who lives without society is either a beast or a God." Man is born in society, lives in society and dies in society. Man is a gregarious animal. He possesses an inborn quality for social life which is a necessity for him. Without society, he cannot live "good life".

There are many reasons why man is essentially a social creature. The human child is born helpless. For many years, he depends on his parents and others for sustenance and growth. His prolonged dependence compels him to live in society.

The human child is endowed with many latent capacities which can be developed only in society. When he comes into contact with other fellow beings, he learns to speak, to think, to enquire etc. "The self can come into being only in society with the give-and-take of group life."

The mind of a child is like a clean slate and anything can be written on it. The child can be given any shape. Children learn to adjust themselves to different situations, customs and institutions of society.

Economic dependence compels man to live in society. He cannot produce himself all he needs. He has to depend on others for the satisfaction of his wants.

Society is the store-house of knowledge and while living in society the individual gets an opportunity to share that knowledge. The wisdom of mankind is handed over from generation to generation in society.

Isolation from society is a punishment. It results in the decay of human personality. That is the reason why human beings want to live in society.

As regards the relation between society and individuals, there can be no ideal relationship. It has been changing from time to time according to different circumstances. However, society is a congregation of individuals who are its component pans. Without the presence of one, the other cannot exist; There is no anti-thesis between society and individual.

A question is raised whether society is greater than the individual or the vice versa. The view of the socialists is that society is greater than the individuals. Society is an end in itself. It represents the highest good of the individual who should adjust himself to society. The view of the individualistists is that society exists for the individual. The object of society is to promote individual happiness. Society cannot exist without individuals. It is like an instrument to achieve human happiness. It is a means to an end which is human welfare. In case of conflict between society and individual, individual cannot sacrifice himself. J.S. Mill goes to the extent of saying that "the entire world has no right to silence a fool."

It is contended that the ideal relation between society and individual is one of reciprocity not antagonism. There should be a harmonious relationship between society and individual. Herbert Spencer compares the relationship between society and individual with the relationship of body with its parts. Human body cannot exist without its parts and likewise parts cannot live without the body. Society without individuals is meaningless.

Social Organisations

Social organisations grow out of social situations which are the products of the interaction between environments and individual responses. Individuals adjust their behaviour to environment through social organisations. Prof. Lapiere writes, "Social organisation consists of all the ways by which men live and work together, more specially of all the programmed, ordered and coordinated relations of the members of the society." Through social organisations, collective behaviour is more effective. These organisations coordinate the various interests of individuals and their energies. Prof. C.M. Case writes, "Social organisation is not so much a state or a condition as a complex process which constantly renews itself, and, in progressive societies, renovates itself to higher and more inclusive level, coordinating larger and larger numbers, with reference to more numerous interests, and upon the basis of more equitable and socially efficient principles."

The view of Herskovits is that social organisations are customarily studied under two broad heads: those which grow out of kinship and those which are the result of free association of individuals. Kinship structures include the family and its extension into broader relationship groupings such as the clan and tribe. One is concerned with the institutionalised ways in which human groups are organised through community or associations.

Family

The family is by far the most important primary group in society. Historically, it has been transformed from a more or less self-contained unity into a definite and limited organisation of minimum size. It continues to serve as a total community for the lives born within it. More profoundly than any other organisation, it exists only as a process. We can understand it only through a study of its changes, the changes it has undergone in human history and the changes within it.

According to MacIver and Charles Page, "The family is a group defined by a sex relationship sufficiently precise and enduring to provide for the procreation and upbringing of children." It may include collateral or subsidiary relationship, but it is constituted by the living together of mates, forming with their children a distinctive unity. This unity has certain common characteristics and those are a mating relationship, a form of marriage, a system of nomenclature, involving also a mode of reckoning descent, some economic provision shared by its members for the satisfaction of their needs associated with child bearing and child rearing and a common habitation, home or household. The mating relation may be life-long or of shorter duration. It may take the institutional form of monogamy in which the family consists of one husband and one wife. It may be polygamous where one man marries more than one woman or vice-versa. Polygamous family may be further classified as polygynous and polyandrous. Polygynous family consists of one husband and more than one wife. Polyandrous family is that where there is only one wife but more than one husband. Monogamous family is common these days. Polyandrous family exists among Todas of Nilgris and among the Tibetans. Polygonous family is found in Muslim states. It was also found in China and India.

When a mate for marriage is selected from outside the social group (family, caste, sub-caste etc.), it may be called exogamous family. When a bride or a bridegroom is chosen from the social group itself, it is called an endogamous family.

A family can be matrilineal or patrilineal on the basis of the manner in which descent is determined. When the children of a family take up the family name of the mother, it is called matrilineal family. Such a family is found in the Nair community in the State of Kerala. When the children of the family take up the family name of the father, the family is called patrilineal. If after his marriage, a husband is bound by the custom to live with his wife in her home, it is called matrilocal family. If the wife comes to stay with her husband in his house, it is called patrilocal family. If the mother becomes the head of the family and looks after property, home management etc., it is called matriarchal family. Such a family is common among the Khasi tribes. If father acts as the head of the family, it is called patriarchal family. When a family consists of members who have been united together on the basis of common blood-relation, the form of family is called consanguine. It is commonly found in Indian villages. A family in a Western country means husband, wife and their unmarried children. Such families are called conjugal or single families.

Characteristics

There are certain **distinctive features** of the family organisation. Family is the most nearly universal of all social forms. It is found in all societies, at all stages of social development and exists far below the human level. Almost every human being is or has been a member of some family.

Another feature is its emotional basis. It is based on a complex of the most profound impulses of our organic nature, those of mating, procreation, maternal devotion and parental care. Secondary emotions vary from romantic love to the pride of race, from the affection of mates to the desire for the economic security of a home and from the jealousy of personal possession to the yearning for perpetuity.

Family is the earliest social environment of all the higher forms of life, including man and the profoundest formative influence in the awakening lives of which it is a source. It moulds the character of the individual by the impression both of organic and mental habits. Family influence in infancy has tremendous influence on the individual.

Another feature of the family is its limited size. Family is the smallest in scale of all the formalised organisations that make up the social structure.

The family occupies the nuclear position in the social structure. Frequently, the whole social structure is built of family units.

The family makes more continuous and greater demands on its members than any other association. In times of crisis, men may work and fight and die for their country, but their toil for their families is for the whole life. The family leads men and women to perform for others than themselves the most exacting tasks and to undertake the heaviest responsibilities. The life of the family is deeply rooted in the basic impulses which lead men into the increasing responsibilities of the family and sustain them in the fulfilment of their tasks.

Family is guarded both by social taboos and legal regulations which rigidly prescribe its form. The marriage contract is more strictly defended than other contracts. The partners are not free to decide its terms or change them by mutual agreement. While the form of marriage contract is different in different types of society, in each there is a prevailing form zealously insisted upon. In modern society, the family is one of the few associations which the consenting parties may freely enter but may not, even by mutual consent, freely leave or dissolve.

While the institution of the family is permanent and universal, the family as an association is the most temporary and the most transitional of all important organisations within society.

Functions

Every family is required to perform certain functions. Biological and emotional functions are the essential functions of family. These functions are performed by all families throughout the world. Biologically, family caters to the sexual needs of husband and wife. It provides stable satisfaction of sexual needs. Another function is that of procreation. Family legalises procreation which otherwise would be chaotic. The emotional function of the family is to provide love, affection and sympathy to its members. It satisfies psychological or emotional needs of men and women.

Another function of the family is the nurture of the children. Not only the children are to be produced, they have also to be looked after. In the absence of family, no one can successfully look after the upbringing of the children. Orphanages or nurseries are not a substitute. If a child is deprived of parental care, his overall development is defective. It is not sufficient merely to provide for food and clothing. The right type of emotional training can be imparted only between the father's cares and mother's kisses. Family also serves as a recreational centre.

A family also performs certain economic functions. A family is an economic unit and its members learn how to earn as a whole and spend as a whole. Children learn the professional knowledge of their parents in the family. Family has played a dominant role among agricultural and rural societies. Even today it provides for collective effort and income. It ensures against widowhood, unemployment and old age.

A family also performs certain educational functions. The influence of the family training of the children is significant. The habits, languages, manners, ideas and other qualities are moulded by parental influences. President Abraham Lincoln used to say, "Whatever I am and whatever I hope to be, I owe to my mother."

Family is the primary school of citizenship. Qualities of a good citizen like obedience, cooperation, law-abidingness, self-sacrifice and tolerance are learnt within the family. We obey our parents and their commands. That creates the spirit of obedience and law-abidingness. Family is the "cradle of civil virtues "which are necessary for good citizens.

The State and Family

The state exercises over the family more strict control than it generally exercises over any other partnership or association. It does not leave the form of the contract to the will of its members. They cannot prescribe for themselves its conditions or duration. It fixes a minimum age of marriage. It determines degrees of relationship within which people must not marry. It treats certain violations of the contract (for example, bigamy) as criminal offences. It defines the economic and other responsibilities of the husband towards his wife and of the parents towards their children. It treats the property of the partners as not individual but family possession. The state has regulated the family on various grounds. Sociologically considered, some of the reasons given are of doubtful validity.

In many countries, the state has exercised control over the family on religious grounds which are not approved now. Experience shows that there are certain matters which the state is competent to control and others over which its control fails. As social conditions change, the character of state control also changes. Sometimes, adultery was a crime but now it is not considered that way. The state performs a regulative function. The prevention of controllable conditions that are clearly a threat to the welfare of society becomes a definite obligation of the state.

Clan

Clan is another form of social group. The members of a clan are supposed to be the descendants of a common ancestor. They usually bear a common surname. They do not live under a single roof like the members of a family. Clans are usually found among the primitive people. A clan has a chieftain who acts as its head. Its members become associated through common social or religious ceremonies.

An important characteristic of a clan is exogamy. Its members do not marry a person belonging to the same clan as they are the descendants of a common ancestor. The unity of the clan is often symbolised by totems which are worshipped by the members.

The view of Sir Henry Maine is that "clans are expanding families tracing their descent to the eldest male member of the original family". Its chief characteristics are blood relationship, common religion, common language or common residence.

Clans perform very useful functions in society. They regulate marriages and fix totems for various groups. They provide a forum for social and economic cooperation. They shape the customs and usages of the group. They maintain unity among their members. The clan chief is the symbol of authority. The members of the clan are under his control and they obey his commands.

Tribe

A tribe is described as "a social group of a simple kind, the members of which speak a common dialect, have a single government and act together for such common purpose as warfare". Tribes are formed as a result of clashes among clans in which the weaker clans are subordinated by the stronger clans. The members of a tribe may or may not belong to a single ancestor. They may not have totems. According to Dr. William, "Tribe is a rudimentary political organisation which manages the lives of the group of clans on their consent." Prof. MacIver defines a tribe as "a race with common bond of interests having consciousness of kind," Every tribe has a chief whom its members obey. A tribe has a common military organisation. It has a dialect of its own. The members of a tribe speak the same language.

Community

According to MacIver and Page, community is "the term we apply to a pioneer settlement, a village, a city, a tribe or a nation. Wherever the members of any group, small or large, live together in such a way that they share, not this or that particular interest, but the basic conditions of a common life, we call that group a community. The mark of a community is that one's life may be lived wholly within it. One cannot live wholly within a business organisation or a church; one can live wholly within a tribe or a city. The basic criterion of community, then, is that all of one's social relationships may be found within it." (Society, pp. 8-9).

Some communities are all-inclusive and independent of others, but modern communities are much less self-contained because economic and political interdependence is a major characteristic of modern communities. No civilised community has walls around it to cut it completely off from a larger one. Communities exist within greater communities: the town within a region, the region within a nation and the nation within the world community.

A community is an area of social living marked by some degree of social coherence. The bases of community are *locality* and *community sentiment.* A community always occupies some territory. Even a nomad community, a band of gypsies, has a local habitation, though it is changing. At every moment, its members occupy together a definite place on the surface of the earth. Most communities are settled and they derive from the conditions of their locality a strong bond of solidarity. To some extent, this local bond has weakened in modern times.

Every community requires not only a locality but also a community sentiment. There must be an awareness of sharing a way of life as well as the common earth.

The wholly self-contained community belongs to the primitive world. In the modern world, the nearest approach to community is to be found in the huge nation community included within the frontiers of a single state. Modern civilisation has broken down the self-containedness of communities, whether great or small. These forces are partly technological such as the improvement of the means of communication and transportation, partly economic and partly cultural. We are approaching a stage where no completely self-contained community can be found on any large scale unless we extend the limits of community to include the whole earth.

We have both small and big communities and we need both of them. The great community brings us opportunity, stability, economy, the constant stimulus of a richer, more varied culture. By living in a small community, we have the nearer, more intimate satisfaction. The larger community provides peace and protection, patriotism and sometimes war, automobiles and the radio. The smaller community provides friends and friendship, gossip and face to face rivalry, local pride and abode. Both are necessary for full life.

Community and Association

An association is a group organised for the pursuit of an interest or group of interests in common. An association is not a community but an organisation within a community. A community is more than any specific organisation that arises within it. We can compare the business of the church or the club with the village or city or nation. With respect to the business of church or club, we can ask such questions as why they exist and what they stand for. We can answer in terms of the particular interests around which they are organised. If we ask why communities exist, we can expect no such definite answer. Another difference between community and association is revealed by considering the interest aspect of association because an association is organised for particular purposes, for the pursuit of specific interests, we belong to it only by virtue of these interests. We belong to an athletic club for physical recreation or sport, to a business for livelihood or profits, to a social club for fellowship. Membership in an association has a limited significance. The interests of an association may be wider than or different from those officially professed. We belong to associations only by virtue of some specific interest that we possess. The result is that there can be a multitude of associations within the same community and the individual may belong to many associations.

Associations may become communities, at least temporarily. There are the examples of seventeenth century trading company outposts which became communities in every respect, or of military units compelled to create their own communities when isolated for a period of time. There are borderline cases between community and association such as monasteries, convents and prisons. The two major social organisations which are on the borderline between associations and communities are the family and the state.

In some of its forms, the family has many of the attributes of a community. In these cases, people toil, play and even worship almost wholly within the orbit of the family. It circumscribes largely or even wholly the lives of its members. However, in modern society, the family becomes definitely an association.

The state is frequently confused with the community. In reality, the state is one form of social organisation, not the whole community in all its aspects. We distinguish the state from the church, the political from religious organisation. The confusion of community and state is increased by the usage of the same term to indicate either.

The state is an agency of peculiarly wide range, but nevertheless an agency. The state may assume at times absolutist or totalitarian form, claiming to control every aspect of human life. Even if this claim is fully realised, the state does not become the community, but an association controlling the community.

Association

An association has been defined as "a group of people united for a specific purpose or a limited number of purposes." MacIver defines an association "as a group organised for the pursuit of interest or group of interests in common." An association may be a family, a club, a school etc. In all these cases, the social groups have a special goal to attain. The goal of school is to impart education. A family exists to provide sexual, economic and emotional needs of man.

As associations are means or agencies through which their members seek to realise their similar or shared interests. Such social organisations act, not merely through leaders, but through officials or representatives as agencies. Officials may control the organisation so that the interests of the majority are subordinated to their own. The control may reside even in the members. Whichever the case, an association normally acts through agents who are responsible to the association. This fact gives the association a distinctive character and a peculiar legal status.

An association actually has no interests that are not the interests of some or all of its members. It has methods of operation peculiar to it as an association. It may own property which is not simply an aggregation of individual properties. It may own funds which the members cannot at pleasure distribute among themselves. It possesses rights and obligations, powers and liabilities which members cannot exercise as individuals. A public utility, a trade union, a political party, a club, a church has certain duties and certain privileges. In this sense, an association has a corporate character. When legal recognition is given to the conditions, duties and privileges of an association, it becomes a corporation in the eye of law.

An association establishes a specifically defined and limited relationship between its members. They become members by virtue of particular attributes or qualifications corresponding to the particular purposes for which it is organised. They profess a trade or cultivate an art or pursue some kind of knowledge or run some kind of business and in so doing find it desirable or advantageous to join others. Practically all associations rise in this way.

The formation and maintenance of associations can be explained in terms of interests and not attitudes. Attitudes encourage or discourage the process of organising, but they do not create organisations. Associations develop as means or modes of attaining interests. An association is likely to be formed wherever people recognise a like, complementary, or common interest sufficiently enduring and sufficiently distinct to be capable of more effective promotion through collective action, provided their differences outside the field of this interest are not so strong as to prevent the partial agreement involved in its formation. This principle holds for the formation of a family, a business firm, a church, a club, a professional society and even a political state.

A heterogeneous specialised community offers more opportunity for the creation of organised groups than is the case with a simple or primitive community. In the former case, particular, interests can be distinguished from the general interests and the very fact of specialisation makes necessary the organisation of interests. The constant changes that occur in a specialised community precipitate conditions favourable to the emergence of new groups. Usually, the initiative, enthusiasm and energy of one or a small number of persons prepare the ground for organisation. The leaders play up the desirability of organisation and seek to establish attitudes in the potential members favourable to its formation. Often some precipitant, some crisis or unusual conjuncture of events stimulate the leaders to action. In order to organise an interest, it must first be presented as such and then in its organised form, it must somehow be brought into harmony with the other interests of the members.

Classification of Associations

Associations are many in number and it is difficult to classify them. However, we can have a broad classification and the names of some of them are kinship associations, religious associations, cultural associations, recreational associations, philanthropic associations, economic associations, vocational associations and political associations.

Kinship associations are based on blood relationship. The members of a kinship association claim to belong to a common ancestor. Family is a kinship association. Tribes and clans are said to be such associations.

As regards religious associations, people believing in a particular religion may form a religious association. As there are many religions, there can be many religious associations. The aim of every religious association is to develop its own religious interests. The Roman Catholics have their separate associations. The Muslims have their separate associations. The Arya Samajists have their separate religious associations. The Sikhs have their own separate associations. Some religious associations go even beyond the territory of a state.

Cultural association is formed to promote intellectual and cultural activities of man. They help to enrich social life. People in cultural associations discuss and express their opinion about art, literature, science, philosophy and other branches of knowledge. Schools, colleges, dramatic clubs and learned societies can be included in this category.

Recreational associations are formed to provide refreshment and relaxation to their members. They help in fresh thinking and creative activities. Examples of recreational associations are a music club, a sports club etc.

Philanthropic associations are set up to promote charity and sympathy for the unprivileged. The aim of such associations is to render selfless service to mankind. Examples of philanthropic associations are the Red Cross Society, the Bharat Sewak Samaj, Ramakrishna Mission etc.

Economic associations are those which are engaged mainly in economic procedures, the procedures of competing and bargaining in the production, distribution and exchange of goods and services. The typical economic association is a competitive private enterprise, engaged primarily in "making money". It can be a one-man store or a vast corporation. An economic association is a unit in a large system of private enterprises. Its focus is the market, the place of exchange and the economic order.

The distinction between an economic association and apolitical association is not so much a distinction between spheres of activity as between methods of action. Economic interests are not the exclusive field of economic associations. Every other kind of organisation has economic interests. Many economic activities depend on the concerted activity of public and private agencies.

Economic associations are typically devoted to the acquisition of wealth, to money making or at least to the provision of the means of living, without reference to the uses to which these means are subsequently applied. The economic means are their end result. Thc disposal of those means is beyond their concern.

Occupational or vocational associations have grown numerous and powerful with functional specialisation and inter-dependence of modern society. They fall under various types. We may distinguish those that are based on the performance of a specific function. This category includes trade unions, organisations of producers, dealers or traders in any particular line, organisations of school teachers, civil servants, doctors, lawyers, scientists, artists etc. The people of a particular vocation combine into an association because by their combination they can force their demand and get their grievances remedied. Vocational associations protect the cause of their respective vocations.

There are a few associations which are political in nature. Political parties are the best examples of a political association. The state is also a political association. It is called "an association of associations". It controls the activities of other associations. The United Nations may be called a political association as it aims at the maintenance of international peace.

SUGGESTED READINGS

Bogardus, E.S. : *Leaders and Leadership.*

Breckenridge, S.P. : *The Family and the State*, Chicago, 1934.

Burgess, E.W. and Locke, H.J. : *The Family*, New York, 1945.

Cooley, C.E. : *Human Nature and the Social Order*, New York, 1922.

Dewey, J. : *Human Nature and Conduct*, New York, 1930.

Faris, E. : *The Nature of Human Nature*, New York, 1937.

Fishman, N. : *Marriage: This Business of Living Together*, New York, 1946.

Folsom, J.K. : *The Family and Democratic Society*, New York, 1943.

Goodsell, W. : *A History of Marriage and the Family*, New York, 1934.

Miller, E.T. : *Social Relations and Structures.*

Howard, G.E. : *History of Matrimonial Institutions*, Chicago, 1904.

MacIver, R.M. : *Community*, London, 1917.

MacIver, R.M. : *The Modern State*, Oxford, 1926.

MacIver, R.M. : *Elements of Social Science*, London, 1921.

MacIver, R.M. : *The Web of Government*, New York, 1947.

MacIver, R.M. : *Society.: A Textbook of Sociology*, New York, 1937.

MacIver, R.M. and Page, Charles : *Society*, London, 1949.

Mead, G.H. : *Mind, Self and Society*, Chicago, 1934.

Sorokin, P.A. : *Society, Culture and Personality.*

Tead, O. : *The Art of Leadership*, New York, 1935.

Waller, W.W. : *The Family*, New York, 1938.

Warner, W.L. and Lunt, P.S. : *The Social Life of a Modern Community.*

Zimmerman, C.C. : Family and Civilisation, New York, 1947.

CHAPTER

The State

Learning Objectives

- Significance
- Meaning of the State
- Essential Elements of the State
- Population
- Territory
- Government
- Sovereignty
- State and Government
- State and Society
- State and Associations
- Institution
- Nation
- Nation and State
- Nationality
- Factors which Promote Feelings of Nationality
- Common Residence
- Common Race
- Common Language
- Common Religion
- Common Political Aspirations
- Common Historical Tradition
- Common Interests
- Common Government
- Right of Self-Determination
- Doctrine of Nation-State
- Arguments in Favour
- Criticism
- Changing Notions of the State
- Ethical Notion of the State
- Legal Notion of the State
- Church-State Notion
- Notion of National Sovereign State
- State as a Necessary Evil

Significance

The concept of the state has figured as the central theme of traditional political theory. The view of Gettel is that political science is "the science of the state". Dr. Garner says that "political science begins and ends with the state." The significance of the concept of the state has been changing. The behaviouralists go to the extent of suggesting that the concept of the state should be given up altogether. Their contention is that this concept does not help in understanding political reality or the political process because the term state refers to a formal concept while real politics transcends the formal organisation of the state. The state is usually conceived in terms of the ends of the state which drags us to the realm of moral philosophy which is away from real politics. The concept of the state postulates a particular type of organisation which excludes top organisations of certain society and introduces the idea of pre-state and stateless societies. This leads to the assumption that political organisation is not a universal phenomenon. The traditional view of the state is not political but legal. When we consider the state from a political angle, this meaning becomes useless and the state becomes invisible and abstract. The state is a social institution which evolves according to socio-economic conditions of society. The state is only an aspect of the whole social system and law is only an aspect of the state system. One aspect cannot be taken as the whole. If the state is an institution for resolving conflicts and establishing unity in society, the political nature of the state cannot be expressed by its juristic definition. The state is not merely an institution but it is a political system or an activity and process. It cannot be understood in isolation from the historical nature of the state. Benn and Peters observe, "Now the state is not a thing but a system of rules, procedures and roles operated by individuals."

About the state, David Easton writes, "One person sees the state as the embodiment of the moral spirit, its concrete expression; another as the instrument of exploitation used by one class against others. One author defines it as simply an aspect of society, distinguishable from it only analytically; another, as simply a synonym for government; and still another as a separate and unique association among a large number of other associations such as the church, trade unions and similar voluntary groups." (Political System—An Inquiry into the state of Political Science, p. 108). The conclusion of David Easton is that the word state ought to be abandoned entirely.

It is worthy of notice that the distaste for the term state is confined only to some exponents of the liberal political theory, particularly some American political scientists. However, the Marxists continue to use the term state as a form of political organisations. They use the terms pre-state society, stateless society, slave-owning state, feudal state, capitalist state, socialist/communist state. In spite of certain objections and suspicions, the concept of the state has not become entirely redundant for the study of political science.

Meaning of the State

The concept of the state is comparatively modern and owes its origin to Machiavelli who expressed this idea as the power which has authority over men. However, there is no accepted definition of the state and it has been differently defined by various writers from time to time. According to Aristotle, "The state is a union of families and villages having for its end perfect and self-sufficient life." The view of Thrasymachus is that "the state is no more than the rule of the stronger." Cicero defined the state as "a numerous society united by commonsense of right and natural participation in advantages." According to Bodin, "The state is an association of families and their common possessions governed by the supreme power and by reason." Bluntschli says, "The state is the politically organised national person of definite territory." Holland observes, "The state is a numerous assemblage of human beings, generally occupying a certain territory amongst whom the will of the majority, or of an ascertainable class or persons, is by the strength of such a majority or class, made to prevail against any of the number who oppose it."

The view of Willoughby is that "the state exists whenever there can be discovered in any community of men a supreme authority exercising control ever the social action of individuals and groups of individuals and itself subject to no such regulations." Burgess writes, "The state is a particular portion of mankind viewed as an organised unit."

According to Prof. Sidgwick, the state is "a political society or community, *i.e.*, a body of human beings deriving its corporate unity from the fact that its members acknowledge permanent obedience to the same government which represents the society in any transactions that it may carry on as a body with other political societies." Phillimore defines the state as "a people, permanently occupying a fixed territory, bound together by common laws, habits and customs into one body politic, exercising through the medium of an organised government, independent sovereignty and control over all persons and things within its boundaries, capable of making war and peace and of entering into all international relations with the communities of the globe."

According to Hall, "The marks of an independent state are that the community constituting it is permanently established for a political end, that it possesses a defined territory and that it is independent of external control."

Bluntschli writes, "The state is a combination or association of persons in the form of government and governed, on a definite territory, united together into a moral organised masculine personality, or more shortly, the state is the politically organised people of a definite country." Oppenheim says that a state exists "when a people is settled in a country under its own sovereign government. "The view of Dr. Finer is that the essence of the state lies in its monopoly of coercive power. To quote him, "This, then is the state; and its supreme power and monopoly of coercion (which it can devolve in many ways on its own terms) is sovereignty." The sovereign is "legally supreme over any individual or group" and possesses "supreme coercive power."

The view of Woodrow Wilson is that the state is "a person organised for law within a definite territory". Burns says that the state is "that political organisation which is not subordinate to any other and which generally unites men of the same race and language." According to Duguit, the state is "a human society in which there exists a political differentiation, that is, differentiation between the governed and the governors." The Supreme Court of the United States has defined the state as "a political community of free citizens, occupying a territory of defined boundaries and organised under a government sanctioned and limited by a written constitution and established by the consent of the governed."

Bakunin writes, "The state is not society; it is only a historical form of it, as brutal as it is abstract. It is born historically in all countries of the marriage of violence, rapine, pillage, in a word, war and conquest, that the gods successively created by the theological fantasy of nations. It has been from its origin and it remains still at present, the divine sanction of brutal force and triumphant in inequality. The state is authority; it is force; it is the ostentation and infatuation of force; it does not insinuate itself; it does not seek to convert. Even when it commands what is good, it hinders and spoils it just because it commands it. Liberty, morality and the human dignity of man consists precisely in this that he does good not because it is commanded, but because he conceives it, wills it and loves it."

According to MacIver, "The state is an association which, acting through law as promulgated by a government endowed to this end with coercive power, maintains within a community territorially demarcated the universal external conditions of social order." Harry Alpert says that the important contribution of MacIver to political theory is his view of the state as an agency of human purpose. According to him, the essential attributes of the state are association, law, government, coercive power, a community territorially demarcated and the regulation of the external conditions of the social order. The state is an instrumentality within a more inclusive unity. It cannot exist without society. Being a creature of society, the state reflects its value system.

In his book "An Introduction to Politics", Prof. Laski writes about the state, "Whereas all other associations are voluntary in character and can bind the individual only as he chooses membership of them, once he is a resident of some given state, legally he has no choice but to obey its commands. The state, so to say, is the crowning point of the modern social edifice, and it is in its supremacy over all other forms of social grouping that its special nature is to be found" (p. 9). Laski further observes, "The state is a territorial society divided into government and subjects claiming, within its allotted physical area, supremacy over all other institutions".

F.M. Watkins writes that the state is a geographically delimited segment of human society united by common obedience to a single sovereign. It is both a normative and a descriptive concept.

According to Morton H. Fried, the state is identified at one extreme with one or more highly specific features such as organised police power, defined spatial boundaries or formal judiciary, and at the other end the state is regarded simply as the institutional aspect of political interaction and the state being co-terminus with society vanishes in universal.

Dillon, Leiden and Steward define the state as a community or society politically organised under one independent government within a definite territory. The two dimensions of the state are society of community and government.

Max Weber sought to evolve a sociological definition of the state. He wrote, "Sociologically, the state cannot be defined in terms of its ends. Ultimately, one can define the modern state sociologically only in terms of the specific *means* peculiar to it, as to every political association, namely, the use of physical force." From that standpoint, Max Weber arrived at the following definition of the state: "A state is a human community that (successfully) claims the monopoly of the legitimate use of physical force within a given territory".

Geoffrey K. Roberts defines the state as "a territorial area in which a population is governed by a set of political authorities and which successfully claims the compliance of the citizenry for its laws and is able to secure such compliance by its monopolistic control of legitimate force." (A Dictionary of Political Analysis, p. 203).

G.D.H. Cole says that state "is the whole community of its members regarded as the organised social unit."

According to Dr. Garner, "State as a concept of political science and public law, is a community of persons more or less numerous, permanently occupying a definite portion of territory, independent or nearly so, of external control and possessing an organised government to which the great body of inhabitants render habitual obedience."

Prof. Gilchrist writes, "The state is a concept of political science and a moral reality which exists where a number of people living on a definite territory, are unified under a government which in internal matters is the organ for expressing their sovereignty and in external matters is independent of other governments."

The Marxist view is that the state arose as a result of the division of society into antagonistic classes for the purpose of curbing the exploited majority in the interest of the exploiting minority. The state is the political organisation of the ruling class which uses it for the purpose of suppressing the resistance of its class enemies. It is an organisation for the maintenance of the rule of one class over the other classes. To achieve this the state possesses such instruments of power as an army, the courts, a police force etc."

Gabriel Almond uses the term *Political system instead of the state.* According to him, the political system "is that system of interactions to be found in all independent societies which perform the functions of integration and adaptation (both internally and vis-a-vis other societies) by means of the employment or threat of employment of more or less legitimate political physical compulsion." The political system is the legitimate order-maintaining or transforming system in the society. Robert Dahl says, "The political system made up of the residents of the territorial area and government of the area is a state." (Modern Political Analysis, p. 12).

Critics point out certain *shortcomings in the definitions given above.* They point out that Aristotle's definition of the state is incomplete. Although there are four essential elements of the modern state, he did not include two essential elements viz., territory and sovereignty. Indirectly, he gave a hint to political organisation and population. Cicero's definition does not include three essential elements of the state viz., territory, government and sovereignty. Bodin's definition of the state does not mention two essential elements of the state viz., territory and sovereignty as it refers only to population and government. The definition of Holland refers to territory and population but does not include government and sovereignty. The definition of Burgess deals with population and political organisation but omits territory and sovereignty The definition given by Bluntschli deals only with territory and politically organised people but omits sovereignty. The definition of Phillimore seems to be complete because it deals with all the four essential elements of the modern state. The definition of Woodrow

Wilson deals with population and territory and gives indirect hints to peaceful political organisations but omits sovereignty. The definition of Laski deals with almost all the four essential elements of the state, but refers to internal sovereignty and not external sovereignty. Hall's definition deals with territory, population and sovereignty and indirectly refers to the other elements of the state. MacIver refers to territory, government and internal sovereignty but omits external sovereignty. Among all the definitions of the state given above, those given by Dr. Garner and Gilchrist seem to be complete and satisfactory. They deal with population, territory, government and sovereignty.

ESSENTIAL ELEMENTS OF THE STATE

Population

The essential elements of a modern state are population, territory, government and sovereignty. As regards population, it is the most important element of the state. Obviously, there can be no state without people. There cannot be a state of animals and birds. While the necessity of population as an essential element of a state is recognised, there is no unanimity with regard to its size. The view of Plato was that an ideal state should have a population of 5040. Aristotle considered 100,000 too many. His view was that the population of a state should be neither too small nor too large. It should be large enough to be self-sufficing and small enough to be well-governed. The view of Rousseau was that 10000 was an ideal number. There are states like the Soviet Union, China, India and the United States which are big and there are states like Monaco and San Marino which are very small. The old view that the population of the state should be small does not find favour in modern times. It is realised that the strength of a state depends not only on other factors but also on population. A state having a very small population is always in danger of being liquidated. Although population is not the criterion of the greatness of a state, there can be no state without population.

While considering the population of a state, we have to study not only the number but also the quality of the people inhabiting the state. The view of Aristotle was that a good citizen makes a good state and a bad citizen a bad state. A good citizen is intelligent and disciplined. He is also healthy. He will not allow religious or other considerations to stand in the way of his duties towards the state.

While the size of the population of a state cannot be fixed, it is better if the people are self-sufficient to meet all their necessary requirements. In any case, economic self-sufficiency is essential for the stability of a state.

The population of a state need not belong to a single race, religion, language or culture. It is not necessary that every state must have a homogeneous population. The modern state claims to reconcile the interests of various groups of citizens.

Modern states vary greatly in respect of population. Dr. Garner writes, "The nearest approach to a safe rule is to say that population must be sufficient to provide a governing body and a number of persons to be governed and, of course, sufficient to support a state organisation."

Territory

When we refer to the territory of a state, we mean thereby not only the land domain over which the jurisdiction of the state extends but also rivers and lakes, the sea upto the limit of its territorial waters and the air space above it. The domain of the state is terrestrial, fluvial, maritime and aerial.

There are writers who do not consider territory to be an essential element of the state. Duguit writes, "The word state designates the rulers...or else the society itself in which the differentiation between rulers and ruled exists and in which for that very reason, a public power exists." Duguit maintains that there is differentiation between the rulers and the ruled "in almost all human societies, large or small, primitive or civilised." His conclusion is that "territory is not an indispensable element in the formation of a state". A similar view was put forward by Sir John Seeley. According to him, if a society is held together by the principle of government, it constitutes a state. W.W. Willoughby says, "The state itself then is neither the people, the Government, the Magistracy, nor the Constitution. Nor is it indeed the territory over which its authority extends. It is the given community of given individuals, viewed in a certain aspect, namely, as a political unit". However, such views do not find favour these days. It is realised that there will be a lot of difficulty in the conduct of international relations if there is no fixed territory of the state and hence a fixed territory is considered to be a condition precedent for the existence of a state. Even Duguit admits that in practice there can be no state without a fixed territory.

If the people continue to move from one place to another without having any fixed territory for their residence, there is no state. The gypsies and nomads who wander from one place to another, cannot be said to constitute a state. The territory aspect of a state is very important. However, it is difficult to decide the size of an ideal state. States like Israel possess a very small territory. The state of San Marino has an area of 38 Sq. miles only. The Vatican City under the Pope covers 108 acres only in the heart of Rome. States like the Soviet Union, China and the United States have large territories.

Rousseau was in favour of a small state. To quote him, "The more the social bond is extended, the more it is weakened." A small state was considered to be stronger than a big state. According to De Tocqueville, "The history of the world offers no instance of a great nation retaining the form of a republican government for a long series of years. It may be advanced with confidence that the existence of a great Republic will always be exposed to far greater dangers than that of a small one. All the passions which are most fatal to republican institutions spread with an increasing territory, while the virtues which maintain their dignity do not augment in the same proportion." J.S. Mill writes, "There is a limit to the extent of country which can be advantageously governed or even whose government can be conveniently superintended from a single centre. There are vast countries so governed: but they, or at least their distant provinces, are in general deplorably ill-administered, and it is only when the inhabitants are almost savages that they cannot manage their affairs better separately". Auguste Comte defended the system of small states. His contention was that the law of evolution showed that the progress of human societies was away from large states and towards small ones. The great empires of the past had all dissolved under the operation of this law and in their place a succession of small states had been established. The view of Barthelemy was that the contribution of small states to humanity was the most notable. We owe to Rome the strongest juridical conceptions. The immortal monuments of art and architecture were born in small countries like Athens, Florence, Holland and England. The England of Shakespeare was not bigger than Sweden of today. The petty states of Germany gave the world Beethoven, Bach, Goethe, Schiller and Kant. The greatest sculptor of the world was born in a small Italian state. The greatest painter was a Dutchman. Norway has given us Ibsen and Belgium has given us Maeterlinck and Verhaeren. Buell points out that it is the small nations that have produced Demosthenes, Dante and Machiavelli and Denmark, another small state has won seven Nobel prizes. Lord Bryce points out that it was in small states that democracy first arose. It was from them that theories of its first prophets and apostles were first derived. It was in them that the working of the real will of the people could best be studied.

The old view is being given up. The modern trend is towards states having large territories. Experience shows that it is not possible for small states to maintain their existence and independence. They always stand in danger of being annexed by a stronger neighbour. The view of Treitschke was that the state was power and it was a sin for the state to be small. The resources of small states were not sufficient to maintain their existence. Big territorial states have become possible on account of better means of communication and transport. The size of the territory of a state also depends upon its climate, geographical configuration and the policy of its rulers. Extremes of climate are not conducive to the growth of the territory of a state. A hilly state is bound to be comparatively small while big states are possible on the plains. Sometimes, the ambitions of the rulers add to the size of a state.

Lord Action maintains that "the small states have a tendency to isolate and shut off their inhabitants, to narrow the horizon of their views and to dwarf in some degree the proportions of their ideas. Public opinion cannot maintain its liberty and purity in such small dimensions, and the currents that come from larger communities sweep over a contracted territory.... These states, like the minuter communities of the Middle Ages, serve a purpose, by constituting partitions and securities of self-government in the larger states but they are impediments to the progress of society which depends on the mixture of races under the same government."

The view of Aristotle was that the territory of a state should neither be very small nor very large. To quote him, "To the size of states, there is a limit as there is to other things, plants, animals, implements; for none of these retain their natural power when they are too large or too small, but they either wholly lose their nature or are spoiled. For example, a ship which is only a span long will not be a ship at all, nor a ship a quarter of a mile long; yet there may be a ship of a certain size, either too large or too small, which will still be a ship, but bad for sailing. In like manner, a state when composed of too few is not as a state ought to be self-sufficing; when of too many, though self-sufficing in all more necessaries, it is a nation and not a state, being almost incapable of constitutional government."

Territory symbolises the sphere of sovereignty of the state. It provides for mutual resources for the sustenance of the population of the state. Territory produces a sense of security and immense opportunities for a fuller life for its residents. It is an object of sentimental attachment. People love and worship their motherland. They are prepared to make supreme sacrifices for its protection.

Government

Another essential element of the state is government. According to Garner, the "government is the agency or machinery through which common policies are determined and by which common affairs are regulated and common interests promoted." If the state represents an abstract concept, the government is its concrete form. The authority of the state is exercised by government. Functions of the state are performed by the government. Laws of the state are made, declared and enforced by the government. Justice is dispensed by the judicial organs of the government. The government is responsible for the maintenance of law and order and the provision of common services like defence, issue of currency, foreign relations, roads, bridges and even transport, communications, water, electricity, health and education etc. and it is entitled to levy taxes for the provision of such services. Without government, there is chaos. There is no common organisation, no common aims and common interests. According to Giddings, the government is "the chief progressive organisation of civil society". There can be no state without a government. The organisation of the government may be simple and its functions may be few, but its necessity cannot be denied.

No particular type of government is essential. It may vary in kind and complexity. It is the only political organisation which makes an attempt to see whether the essential relationship between command and obedience has been well established. The government functions through its three agencies viz., the executive, the legislature and the judiciary. The executive rules over the country and enforces the laws. The legislature passes the laws which are interpreted by the judiciary. Those who violate laws are punished by the government. If two governments are formed in a .country, that country is divided into two states.

No particular type of government can be recommended as essential. It varies from country to country. Democracy may be popular in India, the United States, Canada, England, France, Italy, West Germany or Japan. The dictatorship of the Communist parties is popular in the Soviet Union, China, East Germany, Poland and Hungary. Monarchy is popular in Nepal, Saudi Arabia, Britain, Sweden and Denmark. Even in countries where democracy is popular, the types of government differ. There is parliamentary government in some countries and presidential in others. The conclusion is that no particular type of government can be recommended as an essential element for the existence of a modern state.

Sovereignty

Another essential element of the state is sovereignty. Without sovereignty, there can be no state in the legal sense. It is sovereignty which distinguishes the state from other organisations. Without sovereignty, there is every possibility of the forces of lawlessness sweeping away the whole of society. It is only the sovereign who can keep all the sections of society in their proper places. It is the final authority in the state.

It is by virtue of its sovereignty that the state declares its laws and decisions and issues commands which are binding on all citizens. By virtue of its sovereignty, a state deals independently with other states. Commands of the state are treated as superior to those of any other association or institution because sovereignty is the sole preserve of the state. Max Weber writes, "The right to use physical force is ascribed to another institutions or to individuals only to the extent to which the state permits it. The state is considered the sole source of the right to use violence." Other associations are either voluntary or based on custom or necessity. The right to use legitimate coercion in its own right is exclusive to state. A state continues to exist so long as it is armed with sovereignty. If the state loses its sovereignty on account of internal revolt or external aggression, there is anarchy and disappearance of the state as such. Some writers regard "international recognition" as an essential element of the state. That implies the recognition of the sovereignty of the state over a given territory and population by other states. International recognition is the outcome of the sovereignty of the state and not a condition of its existence. International recognition is only incidental to the sovereignty of the state and not a fundamental element of the state itself.

Internal sovereignty means that the state is supreme in all its internal matters. It exercises its supremacy over all the institutions and people of the state. No other state can be permitted to exercise its authority over the institutions and people of the state. In a federal government, power is divided between the Centre and the units, but sovereignty does not suffer in that case. In such a government, power is divided between the Centre and the units in accordance with the constitution. In this way, the government runs smoothly and sovereignty remains an indispensable element of the state.

A reference may be made to *some other aspects of the state.* Every state is more or less permanent and continues. Governments may change but a state continues. All states are equal legally and politically. The equality of states is an accepted principle of international law. However, small states cannot be expected to play an important part where big states are concerned. In the eye of international law, only that political community can be called a state which is independent and capable of fulfilling its international obligations. The small state of San Marino is not recognised as an international personality.

Although Punjab and Rajasthan are called states under the new Constitution of India, those are not states at all in the technical sense. The same is true of the fifty states of the United States of America. However, Pakistan is a state and has all the essential elements of a state. The United Nations Organisation is not a state, although it is an international organisation of which very many states are members. It has no territory of its own. It does not exercise any sovereign power or authority is the world or in any part of the world. The various states who are its members, accept its authority voluntarily.

State and Government

The two terms state and government are often used interchangeably as if there is no difference between them. The Stuart kings in England did not make any differentiation between the state and government. That was done to justify their absolute authority. Louis XIV, Emperor of France, used to say: "I am the state". Political philosophers like Hobbes employed the two terms as if they were identical in meaning. Political thinkers like Laski and Cole also find little or no difference between the state and government. According to Laski, "For the state is for the purposes of practical administration, the government". Cole is of the view that the state "is nothing more or less than the political machinery of government in a community." However, the identification of the state and government misses an important fact. "While the government is a body of some citizens, the state consists of all the citizens, however inactive and inarticulate their will may be in the governance of the country." Prof. W.W. Willoughby writes, "By the term government is designated the organisation of the state—the machinery through which its purposes are formulated and executed." The government is only one of the four essential elements of the state. It is true that the state cannot exist without a government, but however organised and established the government may be, it cannot attain the status of statehood. The government is only an agency of the state through which the collective will is formulated, expressed and executed. R.M. MacIver writes, "When we speak of the state, we mean the organisation of which government is the administrative organ. A state has a constitution, a code of laws, a way of setting up its government, body of citizens. When we think of this whole structure, we think of the state." The view of the Supreme Court of the United States is that "the state itself is an ideal person, intangible, invisible, immutable. Government is an agent, within the sphere of its agency of perfect representative but outside of that is a lawless usurpation." Woodrow Wilson says that the state "is juristically wholly organised in its government and can only speak through the government". Dr. Garner says, "Government is the agency or machinery through which the collective will of the people or state may be formulated, expressed and executed." Laski also says about government, "It exists to carry out the purposes of the state. It is not itself the supreme coercive power. It is simply the mechanism of administration which gives effect to the purpose of that power." Government is an agent to carry out the purposes of the state. It formulates the collective will of the public, expresses it and executes it. It is concrete while the state is abstract. The state operates through the government. That is why the government in a democracy is regarded as servant and the state as master.

The four essential elements of the state are population, territory, government and sovereignty. Although the government is the most essential element because the state cannot operate without government, government is merely a part of the state and cannot be the whole.

The state possesses sovereignty but the government does not. There is no state without sovereignty, but the government does not possess sovereignty as in a democracy public is regarded as a source of all power. The Constitution of India provides that the people of this country are the main source of sovereignty.

The state is permanent but not the government. Governments keep on changing from time to time but the state continues. A conservative government in England may be replaced by a labour government but that does not in any way affect the existence of the state. It is possible to classify governments according to the form of administration but states cannot be classified. We often talk of parliamentary or presidential government but not of a parliamentary state.

The government is concrete and definite. It has a physical existence. It is something which can be seen with eyes. However, the state is abstract and vague. We cannot see the state. If we have to see the state, we can see the government because it is through the machinery of the government that the state acts. Territory is an essential element of the state but not of the government. Likewise, sovereignty is an essential characteristic of the state but not of the government.

Every individual within a state is a member of that state. As a matter of fact, he is born a member of that state. Membership of the state is compulsory. However, that is not the case with the government. Only a small number of persons are members of the government. Individuals can have rights against the government but not against the state as such. The relation between the state and government is one of master and agent. The state is the original authority which possesses all the powers in a country. Its powers are absolute and unlimited. The state delegates some of its powers to the government and thus the latter comes to have those powers. The powers of the government are defined and can be taken away from it by the state. Every individual has to be loyal to the state but it is not necessary for him to be loyal to the government in power. He has the right to criticise acts of omission and commission of the government. He can adopt all those peaceful measures by which the party in power can be replaced by another party.

Whenever there is a change in government, it is not necessary that there should be violence. The experience of Great Britain and the United States shows that when one party is defeated and resigns, the other party comes in. There is no bloodshed with the change of government. However, when there is change in the state, there is violence and bloodshed. When Palestine was divided and the state of Israel came into existence, there was a lot of violence. The same happened in India in 1947 at the time of partition.

The state is uniform throughout but the governments are of many kinds. Every state has four essential elements of population, territory, government and sovereignty. However, governments are of various kinds. There is parliamentary government in England, India, France, Italy, West Germany etc. and presidential government in the United States. There are Communist governments in the Soviet Union, China, East Germany, Poland, Hungary, Bulgaria etc. There is monarchy in Nepal and Saudi Arabia. There are military governments in many countries.

The state represents a wider and more stable entity than government. R.M. MacIver writes, "When we speak of the state we mean the organisation of which government is the administrative organ. Every social organisation must have a focus of administration, an agency by which its policies are given specific character and translated into action. But the organisation is greater than the organ. In this sense the state is greater and more inclusive than government. A state has a constitution, a code of laws, a way of setting up its government, a body of citizens. When we think of this whole structure, we think of the state." (The Web of Government, p. 24). So long as a state maintains its identity and independence, governments may be formed and dissolved according to the procedure laid down in the Constitution without affecting the character of the state. However, a state itself may lose its identity when it is suppressed and conquered by a foreign power..

The state serves as a symbol of the unity of the people. The image of the state inspires unity among the people and provides them with an identity as a nation. It arouses national pride and a spirit of sacrifice among the people. However, the government represents only a working arrangement to arry out the functions of the state. The government commands our obedience but the state commands our loyalty. Whether the government is good or bad, efficient or inefficient, the state continues to be a symbol of national greatness.

The idealist theory did not make any distinction between state and government. Hegel praised the nation-state as the march of God on earth and demanded that the people should obey the authority of the state without complaining against it. The liberal-democratic theory treats the state as a product of the will of society, an instrument of conflict-resolution and demands that the government should be responsible to the people and act according to their wishes. The Marxist theory attributes the imperfections of the government to the state itself. So long as society is divided into dominant and dependent classes, any government is bound to serve as an instrument of class exploitation.

The difference between the state and government can be explained by referring to a limited company. The Directors of a company keep on changing year after year but their change does not imply a change in the company itself. Likewise, the change of a government does not imply a change in state.

State and Society

Society is defined as a "collection of individuals held together by certain enduring relationships in pursuance of common ends." On the other hand, the state is defined as "a particular portion of society politically organised for the protection and promotion of its common interests." The state is a part of society. It is necessarily a political organisation but society is not so.

Society regulates all forms of social conduct but state can regulate only the external relationships of the people. The state derives its strength mainly from law but society from traditions, customs and conventions.

The state possesses the power of coercion. If a person violates the law of the state, he is punished according to law. However, society does not enjoy the power of coercion. There may be no physical punishment even if the rules of society are violated. The only basis of the authority of society is social customs, conventions and morality. The weapon used by society is persuasion and not coercion.

The state is a territorial organisation. Its territory is well-defined. However, society is not limited to any geographical area. The Jews, the Christians, the Muslims and the Hindus are spread all over the world. There is no territorial limitation on society. Moreover, even within a state, there may be different societies. Society may be narrower or broader than the state. There may be a society without a state.

The membership of a state is compulsory while the membership of a society may be voluntary.

Society has a wider scope than state. The aim of society is to develop all aspects of human life, but the state is concerned mainly with the political relations of man. According to Barker, "The state exists for one great but single purpose, society exists for a number of purposes, some great and some small, but all in their aggregate, deep as well as broad." MacIver observes, "The state is a structure, not co-eval and co-extensive with society, but built within it as a determinate order for the attainment of specific end."

Society came into existence prior to the state. From the very beginning, man has lived in society. Society began with the birth of man on earth. Society is natural and instinctive to man because he cannot live in isolation. Aristotle rightly says that man is a social animal by nature and necessity. However, the state is the creation of will and reason. It is man's political consciousness which brought the state in society.

State is sovereign but society is not. Without sovereignty, there can be no state. State has the supreme power to command and nobody can challenge its authority. Society does not possess any sovereign power and cannot punish those who disobey its rules. Society can put only moral pressure.

Organisation is essential for state but not for society. Without organisation, a state cannot have a proper government. Society may not have the government. It includes in its purview organised as well as unorganised communities.

State controls only the external activities of man whereas society controls both internal and external activities. State has to act through law which can regulate only the external actions of man. It cannot control his thoughts. Society is concerned both with internal and external activities of man. MacIver writes, "It is perfectly obvious if we only look at the facts of the case that there are special forms like the family or the church or the club which owe neither their origin nor their inspiration to the state and social forces like custom or competition which state may protect or modify but certainly does not create and social motives like friendship and jealousy, which establish relationship too intimate and personal to be controlled by the great engine of the state." Society is natural and instinctive to man but the state is the creation of man's will.

The rules and laws of the state are clear and definite as those are enacted by the legislature, but the rules and principles of society are based on customs, traditions and conventions of the people and hence are not clear and definite.

It is clear from above that the state and society are two different terms. According to Laski, "The state may set the keynote of the social order, but it is not identical with it". However, both state and society are closely associated. Both of them work for the welfare of the people. They are connected and inter-dependent. Social conduct must conform to the way of life prescribed by the laws of the state, but the state must not trespass into the sphere not assigned to it. Barker concludes, "State and society have the same moral purpose. They blend and borrow from each other."

State and Associations

According to MacIver, an association is "a group of persons or members who are associated and organised into a unity of will for common end." Cole defines an association as "any group of persons pursuing a common purpose or system or aggregation of purposes by a course of cooperative action extending beyond a single act, and for this purpose agreeing together upon certain methods of procedure and laying down, in however rudimentary a form, rules for common action." Barker writes, "We see society less as a number of individuals leading a common life, we see it more as an association of individuals already united in various groups, each with its common life, in a further and higher group, for a further and higher common purpose." Thus, an association is a group of individuals who are associated and organised into a unity of will for a common end.

There are various types of associations, *e.g.*, political, social, economic, religious, cultural etc. and the state is also called by some scholars an association. Both state and association work for the welfare of the people. They come into existence to promote public interests. Both are organised and have their own constitutions. Both have their own budget, treasury and property. Some associations get grant-in-aid from the state also. Both state and various associations in society represent the human nature.

In spite of these similarities, there are differences between the state on the one hand and associations on the other. The state is sovereign but associations are not. Sovereignty is an attribute of the state and not of an association. Every state possesses supreme power and all individuals and associations are under the overall control of the state. No one can challenge the authority of the state. However, associations do not have sovereignty. It is not compulsory for any member of an association to obey the association and he is free to leave it. On the other hand, no one can disobey the state. According to Lipson, "The state has a monopoly, there is no choice but to submit or die".

The state is permanent but associations are temporary. Generally, an association is formed for a specific purpose and when that is achieved, the association may be dissolved. If the members of an association do not take interest in its affairs, that association may be dissolved or otherwise cease to exist.

The state is superior to other associations. It is the highest association in society. All other associations which fall within its area, are under its control. The state possesses supreme power over all individuals and associations. It has the right to intervene in the affairs of the various associations. It can issue orders and regulate the affairs of associations.

A fixed territory is essential for a state. There cannot be a state without a territory, but that is not so for an association which can function in any part of the country or the world. The examples are the Ramakrishna Mission, the Rotary Club, recreation clubs etc.

The membership of a state is compulsory but not of an association. Every individual living within a state is its member and one can leave a state only under certain special circumstances. However, the membership of an association is not compulsory. It is always voluntary.

The scope of the state is wider than that of an association. According to MacIver, "The state is essentially an order-creating organisation. It exists to establish order, not of course merely for the sake of order, but for the sake of all the potentialities of the life which require that basis of order." The state is concerned with the all-round development of the individual. It covers almost every aspect of his life. However, the scope of an association is limited to some particular object.

Man can become a member of only one state but he can be a member of many associations. He cannot be a citizen of both India and Pakistan at the same time. He has to give up the citizenship of one state to acquire the citizenship of another state. However, a man can become a member of many associations at the same time. He can be a member of many political, social, economic, religious and cultural associations at the same time, but he can be a member of only one state at one time.

The state can ban any association on the ground that its activities are against national interests or spread ill-will or hatred among the citizens. State can also create an association which promotes the well-being of the people. However, no association can create a state.

An association looks after the well-being of its members only but the state looks after the well-being of all the people within its territory.

State is national in character generally but the area of an association can be local, national and also international. The Red Cross Society is an international association. The branches of the Communist Party are in all parts of the world. The Akali Dal, DMK, ADMK etc. are regional associations. Political parties like the Indian National Congress are national parties.

It is clear from above that the state is superior to all other associations which exist within its territorial jurisdiction. The state is a sovereign body and can interfere in the working of any association. Prof. Barker writes, "The state, as a general and all-embracing institution of life, must necessarily adjust the relations of associations to itself, to other associations and to their own members."

Institution

Lieber defines an institution as a "system or body of usages, laws or regulations of extensive and recurring operation containing within itself an organism by which it affects its own independent action, continuance and generally its own further development." Institutions depend upon general acceptance and recognition by the members of a community. They get the backing of custom or tradition, but may or may not be sanctioned by law. The term institution is sometimes used to indicate not only ideas and usages, but actual human groups like army, navy, church and state. In a sense, an institution can also be regarded as an instrument or structure or frame-work of an association. G.D.H. Cole writes, "An idea is not an institution merely because it is widely or generally held or accepted. It is an institution only if, in addition to being so accepted, it is embodies in some external form of social structure or communal custom, either in an association or in some actual form of social behaviour." MacIver and Page observe, "It is sometimes the practice to refer to anything which is socially established as an institution. This broad usage is illustrated, for example, by H.E. Barnes' comprehensive study in which he describes social institutions as the social structure and machinery through which human society organises, directs and executes the multifarious activities required to satisfy human needs. According to this understanding, the family and the state no less than marriage and government, are institutions.

Institutions are a means to serve ends and not ends in themselves. An institution may be good or bad. Slavery as an institution is a curse but family as an institution is good and necessary.

No association can work without an institution which is the framework of the association. It is the instrument "through which common interests are realised, the mechanism on which is based the success or failure of an association." If a University is an association, the various colleges and faculties attached to it are the institutions. Institutions "represent the objective manifestation as against an association which is both subjective and objective. In one word, they represent the structural or organised side of social life or as we call it the social constitution. "The government is the institution of a political association, the state. It is through the mechanism of the state that the state fulfils its purpose."

It is contended that an institution is not always a mere framework. It is as living as any association. A political party is an association. Likewise, Parliament is an institution. The people who comprise they may comc or go but the institution goes on. Monarchy is an institution in England and it goes on in spite of the incumbent changing from time to time.

There can be one-man institution such as the President of India or the United States and the King or Queen in England. An institution may consist of a large number of persons such as the Parliament of India or the Cabinet or Ministry. A political party has millions as its members. Some institutions have limited goals while others have comprehensive ones. While the loyalty of the members to one institution may be active, it may not be so in the case of another institution. Andrew Hacker writes, "Politics cannot function without institutions and an understanding of politics requires an awareness of how they operate."

Nation

The term nation is derived from the Latin word "Natio" which means "born". A nation is a people descended from a common stock. It means a people brought together by the ties of blood relationship. According to Burgess, a nation is a "population of an ethnic unity inhabiting a territory of a geographic unity." By ethnic unity is meant a population having a common language and a common consciousness of rights and wrongs. Dr. Leacock writes, "The term nation, though often loosely used, is properly to be thought of as having a racial or ethnographical significance." It is a body of people united by common descent and language. The view of Barker is that a nation is a body of persons inhabiting a definite territory and united together by the fact of living together on a common land. They may come from a number of races but by living together, they develop certain things in common. The first is a common "capital of thoughts and feelings acquired and transmitted in the course of a common history; a common capital or tradition which includes as a rule a common language, a common religion (which may however assume a number of different forms), and a common culture variously expressed in art and architecture, in literature, in social habits and otherwise." There also arises a common will to live together in the future. The ties which bind the people to make them a nation are psychological and spiritual. There are common feelings to live together.

Lord Bryce defines a nation thus: "A nation is a nationality which has organised itself into a political body, either independent or desiring to be independent." The view of Prof. Hayes is that "a nationality by acquiring unity and sovereign independence becomes a nation." Ramsay Murr writes," A nation is a body of people who feet themselves to be naturally linked together by certain affinities which are so strong and real for them that they can live happily together, are dissatisfied when disunited and cannot tolerate subjection to peoples who do not share these ties." Dr. Garner says, "A nation is a culturally homogeneous social group which is at once conscious and tenacious of its unity of psychic life and expression." Zimmern defines a nation as "a body of people united by a corporate sentiment of peculiar intimacy, intensity and dignity, related to a definite home-country." Again, "If a people feels itself to be a nation, it is a nation." Burgess defines a nation as "a population of an ethnic unity, inhabiting a territory of geographic unity." By ethnic unity is meant "a population having a common language and literature, a common tradition or history, a common custom and a common consciousness of rights and wrongs." The view of Pradier-Foder is that "Affinity of race, community of language, of habits, of customs and religion, are the elements which constitute the nation." Bluntschli says that a nation "is a union of masses of men bound together, especially by language and customs, in a common civilisation which gives them a sense of unity and distinction from all the foreigners, quite apart from the bond of the state." Dr. R.N. Gilchrist writes, "Nation is a state plus something else: the state looked at from a certain point of view, viz., that of the unity of the people organised in one state."

E.H. Carr says, "The term nation has been used to denote a human group with the following characteristics:

(*a*) The idea of a common government whether as a reality in the present or past, or as an aspiration of the future.

(*b*) A certain size and closeness of contact between all its individual members.

(*c*) A more or less defined territory.

(*d*) Certain characteristics (of which the most frequent is language) clearly distinguishing the nation from other nations and non-national groups.

(*e*) Certain interests common to the individual members.

(*f*) A certain degree of common feeling or will, associated with a picture of the nation in the minds of the individual members."

Race and nation are two entirely distinct terms. We cannot vouch for the purity of blood. Claims to purity of blood seem to be somewhat fantastic. The population of the United States consists of either many races or mixed blood. Nation as such has no racial significance. What makes a group of people a nation is not necessarily a community of race, language or religion, but the sentiment of common consciousness or like-mindedness. The people of Switzerland do not speak a common language. They do not profess a common religion. In spite of that, they are a nation. Both France and Spain have a Basque population but the Basques do not form a nation. Though the Welsh and Breton Celts have a common racial and linguistic inheritance, they are not a nation. It is true that the two-nation theory of Jinnah was responsible for the division of India into India and Pakistan on the ground of religion, but in spite of the fact that East Pakistan and West Pakistan had a common religion of Islam, the people of East Pakistan revolted and set up a new state of Bangladesh in 1971.

We may come to the conclusion that it is an element of feeling which makes a nation, although many factors may help in creating that feeling.

Nation and State

The theory of "one nation, one state" became popular after the World War I and many new states were created on the principle of self-determination. The terms nation and state began to be used as synonyms. We find countries being described as nations although the proper word would have been states. The Constitution of the Republic of Argentina refers to "Argentine Nation." The name of the United Nations is a misnomer as it is an organisation of sovereign states and not nations. It is desirable that we should not identify nation with the state as the two terms are distinct.

The essential elements of the state are population, territory, government and sovereignty. Wherever these are present, there is a state. It is not necessary that the people living within that state must have a feeling of oneness. The state of Austria-Hungary before 1914 had many nationalities within its borders and hence there was no feeling of unity among its subjects. However, the term nation refers to a feeling of unity among the people.

A nation is based on the peculiar ways of thinking, feeling and living of the people. That is not so in the case of a state which is merely a recognised way of civilised existence.

It is necessary for a state to be independent. There can be no state without sovereignty. In the case of a nation, it is not essential that the people concerned must be independent. It is enough if they are determined to have an independent government of their own, even if that is in the future.

The state is external and its character is manifested by the institutions through which it expresses itself, but a nation is concerned with the inner feelings of the people which are not external.

Zimmern writes, "Nationality, like religion, is subjective, statehood is political; nationality is a condition of mind, statehood is a condition in law; nationality is a spiritual possession, statehood is an enforceable obligation; nationality is a way of feeling, thinking and living; statehood is a condition inseparable from all civilised ways of living."

The nation is ethnic and is not limited to one state alone. It may include more than one state. The German nation includes East Germany, West Germany, Austria and Switzerland (because German-speaking people live there). Generally it is believed that a nation is limited to a state.

The view of Prof. R.N. Gilchrist is that the term nation in near in meaning to state. It has a broader significance. It is the state plus nationality. When we speak of the British nation, we mean the British people organised is one state and acting spontaneously as a unity.

The view of T.H. Green is that "the nation underlies the state" and the state is "the nation organised in a certain way." The members of a nation "in their corporate or associate action are animated by certain passions arising out of their corporate or associate action." There are many states in the world to which the principle of "one nation, one state" does not apply. There are many nationalities in the Soviet Union and the problem has been solved by the Soviet leaders by giving linguistic and cultural autonomy to those nationalities. Switzerland has "developed a democratic nationalism similar to the one nation in England and the United States, a nationalism made secure and strong by its insistence on individual liberty and on respect for diversity." Although there are many nationalities in the Union of South Africa, its government follows a policy of apartheid against which there is so much agitation.

Nationality

In the words of Lord Bryce, "A nationality is a population held together by certain ties as, for example, language and literature, ideas, customs and traditions, in such a way as to feel itself a coherent unity distinct from other populations similarly held together by like ties of their own." J.S. Mill writes, "A portion of mankind may be said to constitute a nationality if they are united among themselves by common sympathies which do not exist between them and any others — which make them cooperate with each other more willingly than with other people, desire to be under the same government and desire that it should be government by themselves or a portion of themselves exclusively." According to Holland Rose, nationality is "an instinct and cannot be exactly defined. It is a spiritual conception, unconquerable and indestructible. "Hayes defines nationality as "a group of people who speak either the same language or closely related dialects, who cherish common historical traditions and thus constitute a distinct cultural society...A nationality, by acquiring political unity and sovereign independence, becomes a nation, or to avoid the use of the troublesome word nation, establishes a national state." Laveleye writes, "A nation is a group of men united under the same sovereignty, while a nationality is a group of men united by identity of origin, race, language, or by community of traditions, history and interests." Durkhein says, "Nationality is a group of which the members.. wish to live under the same laws and form a state." The view of Le Fur is that a nationality is before all a state *en germe.* Buck writes, "Contrary to a popular impression that nationality is something fixed and capable of exact definition, it has come to be recognised that it is rather a product of historical development and that all attempts to formulate a series of universally applicable pre-requisites break down. Nationality is something subjective, an active sentiment of unity within a fairly extensive group, a sentiment based upon real but diverse factors, political, geographical, physical and social, any or all of which may be present in this or that case, but no one of which must be present in all cases."

A nationality may exist without political unity. There may be many nationalities within a state. A nation is not necessarily a state although there is the view that there should be a separate state for every separate nationality. If a nationality becomes politically organised, it becomes a national state. A national state is always based on nationality, but a nationality can exist without a national state.

According to Burgess, "Nationality is a distinct socio-ethnic group within the state and ordinarily constituting minority of the total population." Prof. R.N. Gilchrist defines nationality as a spiritual sentiment or principle arising among a number of people usually of the same race, resident on the same territory, sharing a common language, the same religion, similar history and traditions, common interests with common political associations and common ideals of political unity.

Although the terms nation and nationality have been employed by political thinkers and political scientists, there is only a slight difference between the two. The two terms have been derived from the common Latin word "natio" which commonly can notes the idea of birth or race. In modern English usage, distinct meanings have been given to these two words. A nation is politically organised and an independent state but nationality is not. Nationality possesses cultural unity but it is not as politically organised as the nation. It is not an independent state as a nation is. Gilchrist says that "a nation is very near to state plus nationality." Burgess and Gumplowicz do not believe that the difference between nation and nationality is one of political unity. According to them, they differ from each other because the size of their population is different. According to them, the Scotch and Welsh in Great Britain, the Dutch in South Africa, the French in America, the Poles in Austria and Germany enjoyed their own nationalities for a long period of time but could not organise their independent state as they never wanted to do so. If they wanted to do so, they could have been successful in organising their nation.

FACTORS WHICH PROMOTE FEELINGS OF NATIONALITY

There are many factors which promote the growth of the sentiment of nationality. Sometimes one factor plays an important part in one country and sometimes another factor plays an important part in another country. Very often, the existence of many factors in a country at the same time helps the growth of the sentiment of nationality.

Common Residence

Most of the writers of political science regard geographical unity or common residence on a fixed territory as one of the basic elements of nationality. Living together at one place promotes national feelings. Likewise, people living in different places are more likely to be disunited. Geographical unity helps the people to make progress while disunity hinders national advancement. The two wings of Pakistan created in 1947 could not remain together and in 1971, the people of East Pakistan revolted and ultimately the new State of Bangladesh came into existence. The people who inhabit a common territory for a long time naturally cherish common traditions and culture and start loving their Motherland. They are found willing to make sacrifices for their country. The love for the Motherland is a factor which helps in promoting feelings of nationality. The uniformity of culture and civilisation forms the basis of nationality and those are created by common residence. However, if a particular race fails to safeguard its freedom by living on a common territory, it is desirable for that race to leave that place and reside at some other place to keep its nationality intact. Centuries ago the Jews ran away from their Motherland, Palestine, when they were attacked by the Arabs. They dispersed themselves in various parts of Europe and the world and maintained their separate feeling of nationality. At the same time, they continued their struggle for the Motherland and ultimately they succeeded in having in 1948 a new state of Israel. Likewise, Poland was partitioned in the last quarter of the eighteenth century and the Poles came under the control of Russia and Austria-Hungary. They continued their struggle for more than a century and ultimately the new state of Poland was created after the World War I. Similarly, the Slavs were residing under different states of Europe. They continued to fight for their unity and ultimately the new state of Yugoslavia was created after the World War I.

There is a close intimacy between nationality and the country in which the people live. Many countries are named after their nationality or race. France was named after the French, Germany after the Germans, Poland after the Poles, Denmark after the Danes, Sweden after the Swedes, Afghanistan after Afghans and Turkey after the Turks.

It is common experience that the people who live together at one place for a long time come to have common ideas and ideals. They start thinking in the same way. They come to possess common aspirations. Their ways of living and thinking are affected by common residence. The example of the United States shows how people from different parts of Europe went there during the nineteenth century and even earlier. On account of their common residence, they acquired a new sentiment of nationality. In spite of their different origins, they have the common fueling of being the citizens of the United States.

Common Race

Common race is also a great unifying force. Blood relationship brings the people together. Blood is always thicker than water. People having common ancestors are unconsciously brought together.

There is an inner force that unites their hearts and forces them to come to the help of one another. Thus, a common race is helpful for the growth of the sentiment of nationality. However, this does not mean that if there are many races in a country, the sentiment of nationality cannot grow there. The people of the United States have common nationality in spite of the fact that they belong to different races. The same is the case with Canada which is inhabited by the French and the English. Dr. Garner says, "The community of race and community of language are undoubtedly the most important of these elements but it is necessary to recognise that neither is absolutely essential. The science of ethnology has revealed the difficulty of drawing the links which separate one race from another, since many existing races are mixed in character, that is why they have no common origin, but have been formed by a fusion of various races." There is a mixture of various races in the United States, Canada and Switzerland. If racial unity had been the only basis of nationality, there would have been no nationality in Britain, the United States, Canada or Switzerland. Prof. R.N. Gilchrist observes, "The racial bond of nationality, however, need not be so exact as the science of races demands. Belief in a common origin either real or fictitious is a bond of nationality." Again, "Race-unity is one of the strongest bonds not because of the ethnological signification of race, but because it implies the further unities of common race, common tradition and common culture." Expedience shows that different nationalities have come into existence in spite of the lack of racial unity. It is better for nationality that the people belong to the same race, but that is not essential. The people forget the diversity of their race while living together in a particular territory. This is amply proved by the example of the United States.

Common Language

A common language is a great unifying force. The people speaking the same language have more chances of understanding one another and acting together. One of the bonds which linked the various colonies and Dominions of Great Britain was that of the English language. The people sharing a common language also share a common culture and literature. The diversity of language separates and divides the people in the same way as rivers, mountains and oceans separated one country from the other in the past. The view of Ramsay Murr is that "there is nothing that will give unity to divergent races as the use of common language and in very many cases unity of language and community of ideas which it brings, have Proved the main binding force in a nation." Ernest Barker finds "the closest affinities between nation and language. Language is not the collection of mere words. Each word is charged with associations that touch feelings and evoke thoughts. You cannot share their feelings and thoughts unless you can unlock their associations by having the key of language. You cannot enter the heart or the mind of a nation unless you know its speech. Conversely, once you have learned that speech, you find that with it and by it you imbibe a deep and pervasive spiritual thing, a manifestation of the mind of God, its chief bond of union being language." Prof. R.N. Gilchrist writes, "Community of interests or ideals is no bond of unity unless they can be understood and language is the vehicle of understanding. Cultural unity separates a particular group of people from the rest of the world and develops in them the sentiment of nationality." Prof. Laski says, "Nationality implies the sense of a special unity which marks off those who share in it from the rest of mankind. The unity is the outcome of a common history, of victories and traditions created by corporate effort. There grows up sense of kinship which binds men into oneness. They recognise their likeness and emphasize their differences from other men. Their social heritage becomes distinctively their own as a man lends his own particular character to his use. They come to have an art, a literature recognisably distinct from that of other nations. England could have produced Shakespeare and Dickens, so we admit that there are qualities in Voltaire and Kant from which they typify the nationalism of France and Germany." It is clear from this that language and culture play a decisive role in building the sentiment of nationality. However, experience shows that there can be a feeling of nationality in spite of differences in language. In the case of Switzerland, the people speak three different languages and still they have one nationality. The same is the case with Canada where the Frenchmen speak French and the Englishmen the English language. Still the people of Canada have one nationality. Many examples can be quoted from various parts of the world in support of this proposition.

Common Religion

Religion also is a great unifying force. Particularly in the past, religion acted as a great cementing force. The people professing the same religion were attracted towards one another and they all felt that they could come together under one banner. They were prepared to make all sorts of sacrifices for the sake of their religion. Islam united the Arabs into one nation. It was this national unity which enabled the Arabs to conquer vast territories from the Indus to Spain. During the Middle Ages, the Crusades were fought between the Muslims and Christians in Palestine. The peopie who were killed in the war became martyrs. The impact of religion on the political movements of the Sikhs and Marathas in Indian history is well known. The cry of Pakistan brought most of the Muslims together in India and they were ready to make all kinds of sacrifices. The demand for Pakistan was based on the two-nation theory which in its turn, was based on two religions, Islam and Hinduism. The Congress of Vienna united Belgium and Holland together into one state in 1815 but the union failed in 1831 because the people of Belgium were Roman Catholics and those of Holland were Protestants. They refused to live together and Belgium revolted and ultimately got separated. The national movement in Ireland was weak on account of the differences between the Protestants and Catholics of Ireland. When Britain decided to quit Ireland, the Protestants of Ulster refused to join the independent state of Ireland and referred to maintain their link with Britain.

The view of Dr. Garner is that "community of religion was once regarded as a mark of nationality and in earlier times it played an important part in the process of national consolidation." A similar view is held by Prof. Gilchrist. However, religion does not play an important part in advanced countries although it does play a vital part in a backward country like India where people can be infuriated in the name of religion and they start thinking differently from the rest of their countrymen and thereby weaken or destroy the unity of the country.

Common Political Aspirations

Common political aspirations play a prominent part in promoting feelings of nationality. In such a case, a common nationality grows in spite of differences of language, caste, creed and culture. The people living under foreign yoke develop a sentiment of nationality. They come together and organise themselves to fight for their freedom. It was this factor which promoted feelings of nationality in India, Africa and Asia. The people of these countries forgot their difference and fought for their independence. Common political aspirations are visible in all the national movements. National feelings were in evidence in India in 1857. The same was the case when India was attacked by China in 1962 and by Pakistan in 1965 and 1971. National feelings grew in Germany, Austria-Hungary and Italy against Napoleon who had conquered their countries. Likewise, there was the national sentiment in Greece, Rumania and Bulgaria to drive out the Turks from their territories. Dr. Garner writes, "Independent political union is the natural fruit of nationality where the population is sufficiently numerous and capable of maintaining a separate state existence and conversely political union has sometimes been the means of creating genuine nationality out of heterogeneous race elements as for example Switzerland."

Common Historical Tradition

A common historical tradition also helps the growth of the sentiment of nationality. The view of Ramsay Murr is that a common historical factor is "the one indispensable factor" in promoting the feelings of nationality. To quote him, a common historical tradition embraces "a memory of sufferings endured and victories won in common, expressed in song and legends, in the dear names of personalities that seem to embody in themselves the character and ideals in the nation, in the names also of sacred places wherein the national memory is enshrined....Here is the source of that paradox of nationality, that it is only intensified by sufferings, like the giant Antaeus in the Greek fable, rises with redoubled strength every time it is beaten down into the bosom of its mother earth. Heroic achievements, agonies heroically endured, these are the sublime food by which the spirit of nationhood is nourished; from these are born the sacred and imperishable traditions that make the soul of nations."

J.S. Mill referred to the causes which generate the sentiment of nationality in these words; "Sometime it is the effect of identity of race and descent. Community of language and community of religion greatly contribute to it. Geographical limits are one of its causes. But the strongest of all is identity of political antecedent; the possession of national history and pleasure and regret connected with the same incidents in the past. None of these circumstances, however, are either indispensable or necessarily sufficient by themselves." He further pointed out that the national feeling is proportionately weakened by the failure of any of the causes which contributed to it.

According to Prof. Laski, "That unity is the outcome of a common history, of victories won and traditions created by a corporate effort. There grows up a sense of kinship which binds them into oneness. They recognise their likenesses and emphasize their differences from other men. Their social heritage becomes distinctively their own, as a man lends its own particular character to its house. They come to have an art, a literature, recognizably distinct from that of other nations. So England only could have produced Shakespear and Dickens. So we admit that there are qualities in Voltaire and Kant from which they typify the nationalism of France and Germany."

Common Interests

In the words of Prof. R.N. Gilchrist, "Common interests are rather aids towards strengthening union than fundamental agents of union. They have had their importance in conjunction with other elements more than by themselves. They have played their part in nationalities such as the Dutch and Belgian, but were they sole determinants, Holland and Belgium probably did not exist at all. They were obvious considerations in the Anglo-Scottish union in 1707, but they are discounted in Northern America where the material interests of the United States and Canada are very much the same. With the cooperation of other agents, we see it working in the British dominions where distinct colonial nationalities in the Australians, South Africans etc. are visibly developing. It was the Zollverein (Customs Union) which strengthened the national bonds in Germany and ultimately led to the unification of the country under the Hohenzollerns. The Union of England and Scotland of 1707 was successful on account of the common interests between the English and the Scotts. The religious differences between the people of Belgium and Holland resulted in the independence of Belgium in 1831. It is clear from above that common interests are conducive to the development of the feelings of nationality.

Common Government

The very fact that the people are under one government brings them together. They are all governed by the same system of laws and they all suffer or gain in the same way on account of the working of those laws. A common government is a great unifying force. The sentiment of Indian nationality was created by the British conquest of India and also by the common government for all the people of India which lasted for more than a century. People belonging to different races and nationalities settled in the United States and as they lived under a common administration for a long period of time, they forgot their original nationalities and started calling themselves Americans instead of German Americans, French Americans or English Americans. The same applies to the French, Italians and Germans living in Switzerland and having a common administration.

However, none of these factors is either indispensable or adequate. In the words of Spengler, "Nations are neither linguistic nor political nor biological, but spiritual unities." The feeling of nationality is the product of the community of interests and ideals. It comes into existence when social consciousness cuts across the different social sub-divisions. It applies to all men and women, whether rich or poor, high or low. Nationality is never fixed. It is constantly evolving. However, it is not altogether a natural phenomenon. It is "a product of the growth of social and intellectual factors at a certain stage of history."

RIGHT OF SELF-DETERMINATION

Doctrine of Nation-State

The growth of nationalism demands that every nation must have an independent state of its own. The domination of one nation over another is considered "politically inexpedient and morally wrong". States having many nationalities within their boundaries have been criticised as 'monstrous hybrids". Towards the middle of the last century, it was accepted as a political principle that each nationality had a natural right to free itself from the control of a foreign government and shape its own destiny. To quote Prof. Hayes, "It would redraw the political map of Europe — and of the World — so that disjointed parts of the same nationality would be knit together in a common polity and supra-national empires would be broken up into their constituent national parts. It would make nationalities rather than states the units of international relationship and law." Eminent authorities like J.S. Mill, Lord Bryce and President Woodrow Wilson came out as the champions of self-determination for the subject nationalities. J.S. Mill wrote, "There is a prima facie case for uniting all the members of nationality under the same government, and a government, to themselves apart. This is merely saying that the question of government ought to be decided by the governed. Free institutions are next to impossible in a country made up of different nationalities." Again, "It is in general a necessary condition of free institutions that the boundaries of governments should coincide in the main with those of nationalities." Again, "Where the sentiment of nationality exists in any force, there is a prima facie case for uniting all the members of the nationality under the same government and giving a government to themselves apart. This is merely saying that the question of government ought to be decided by the governed. One hardly knows what any division of the human race should be free to do, if not to determine with which of the various collective bodies of human beings they choose to associate themselves. Free institutions are next to impossible in a country made up of different nationalities. Among a people without fellow feeling, especially if they read and speak different languages, the united public opinion necessary to the working of representative government cannot exist."

During and immediately after the World War I, President Wilson advocated and defended the principle of self-determination. While introducing his famous Fourteen Points in January 1918, President Wilson said, "An evident principle runs through all the programme I have outlined. It is the principle of justice to all peoples and nationalities and their right to live on equal terms of liberty and safety with one another, whether they be strong or weak." In his Address to the American Congress, he declared, "Peoples and provinces are not to be bartered about from sovereignty to sovereignty as if they were more chattels and pawns in the game. Peoples may now be dominated and governed only by their own consent. Self-determination is not a mere phrase. It is an imperative principle of action which statesmen will henceforth ignore at their peril." The underlying idea in these statements was that each nationality should have a state of its own. It involved the *principle of "one nation, one state"*.

Arguments in Favour

Those who advocated the principle of self-determination maintained that if a human group possesses a distinct culture and a peculiar way of living, it should have a separate state of its own for their preservation and promotion. The state was to act as a boundary wall guarding a culture against the blizzard of alien influences. The political independence of the people provides a suitable climate for the blossoming of its unique culture. The creative production in art, literature, philosophy and science was characteristic of Athens, Florence and Greek city states.

Another argument given in support of the principle of self-determination was that the peculiarity of a national culture entitles a nationality to distinct laws and political institutions. The structure of the state was to vary in accordance with the variation of its culture content.

The principle of self-determination of nationalities is in conformity with democratic theory. As a nationality seeks to determine its own political destiny, it implies a government by the people. Public opinion flourishes best in a mono-national state. According to Lord Bryce, the principle of self-determination symbolises the struggle of the nationalities for the realisation of liberalism and democracy. Prof. MacIver writes, "It has prepared the way for our modern democracies since the demand for self-government expands into the demand that the nation really governs itself." President Wilson supported the principle of self-determination on grounds of justice and liberty.

The advocates of self-determination point out that in practice the co-existence of different nationalities within a single state leads to conflicts of interests. The Balkan people under the Turkish rule revolted from time to time. The Czechs and Slovaks revolted against the rule of Austria-Hungary. The underlying hostility between divergent groups is bound to create an explosive situation under which peace and prosperity are not possible.

Those who believe in the old maxim that variety is the spice of life also support the principle of self-determination. The principle is a suitable reply to any possible drive for the standardisation of human type. Burns writes, "If each nation is to develop its own characteristics then each nation is valuable to every other not as a rival of exactly the same kind but as a contrast; and humanity at large is benefited by the preservation of so many distinct types."

Criticism

The principle of self-determination of nationalities has also its critics. Gumplowicz is of the view that there is no historical or sociological justification for the belief that a mono-national state is stronger than a poly-national state. The view of Bluntschli is that a state may gain "in breadth and variety by the inclusion of foreign elements which serve to establish and keep open communication with the civilisation of other peoples." Such an admixture may serve as an alloy to give strength and currency to the nobler metal. The view of Francis II, Emperor of Austria-Hungary, was: "My people are strangers to one another and yet it is for the better. They never have the same ills at the same time. In France when there is epidemic of fever, you all have it the same day. I have Hungarians in Italy and Italians in Hungary. Each watches his neighbour; they never understand one another and in fact detest one another. Their antipathies, however, conduce to order and their mutual hate to the general peace."

Lord Acton was of the view that the concept of mono-national states was more absurd and more criminal than the theory of socialism. To quote him, "There is no principle of change, no phase of political speculation conceivable, more comprehensive, more subversive or more arbitrary than this. It is a confutation of democracy because it sets limits to the exercise of the popular will and substitutes for it a higher principle." Again, "The combination of different nations in one state is a necessary condition of civilised life as the combination of man in society. Inferior races are raised by living in political union with races intellectually superior. Exhausted and decaying nations are revived by the contact of a younger vitality. Nations in which the elements of organisation and the capacity for government have keen lost, either through the demoralizing influence of despotism, or through the disintegrating action of democracy are restored and educated anew under the discipline of a stronger and less corrupted race. This fertilizing and regenerating process can only be obtained by living under one government. It is in the cauldron of the state that the fusion takes place by which the vigour, the knowledge, and the capacity of one portion of mankind may be communicated to another. Where political and national boundaries coincide, society ceases to advance, and nations relapse into a condition corresponding to that of men who renounce intercourse with their fellow men...The coexistence of several nations under the same state is a test as well as the best security of its freedom. It is also one of the chief instruments of civilisation; and as such it is in the natural and providential order and indicates a state of greater advancement than the national unity which is the ideal of modern liberalism."

There is no historical or sociological justification for the view that a mono-national state could ensure a greater degree of strength and popular freedom. Although Switzerland does not possess an ethnically homogeneous population, she is not lacking in vigour and freedom.

There is no necessary connection between nationalism and democracy. Free institutions and democracy have worked successfully in Switzerland and the United States although their population is heterogeneous in character. Nationalism in Germany was anti-democratic. Bismarck brought about the unification of Germany through sheer force. Field writes, "When the Saarlanders voted to rejoin Germany in 1935, they were deliberately putting themselves under dictatorial rule in obedience to their national feelings." (Political Theory, p. 247).

Critics also point out that the principle of self-determination would disrupt many existing states and a large number of small states will come into existence. At the Lausanne Peace Conference held in 1923, Lord Curzon observed, "The right of self-determination is like a two-edged sword and can be admitted only with reservation." The Peace Settlement of 1919-20 added a large number of states in Europe. There were 20 states in 1914 and in 1924, the number had risen to 26. There has been a similar increase in the number of states in Asia and Africa, particularly after the World War II. The principle of self-determination has also added to the number of international conflicts. That is partly due to the increase in the number of states in the world. Moreover, as many of the new states are economically weak, they have to depend upon the Big Powers for their support and existence. Prof. Laski points out that the nation states in their zeal for political independence enter into "a competition in the armament of power which acts so as to jeopardise the maintenance of peace, to provoke an atmosphere of nervous hostility and to induce the smaller states into alliance with powerful neighbours so that they may win security by that multiplied strength. So organised, the distribution of nation-states resembles nothing so much as a power-magazine which, as in 1914, a single chance spark may suffice to provoke into conflagration." (A Grammar of Politics, pp. 224-25). The view of Morgenthau is that the adoption of the principle of "collective security" in a world community consisting of a multiplicity of nation-state has created an explosive situation. There is always the danger of collective warfare.

The right of self-determination is opposed to qualities of truthfulness, friendliness etc. These qualities are twisted and misinterpreted by the nationalists to serve their purpose. The nationalists adopt double-standards. Inside his group, a nationalist is a Mr. Jekyll and outside his group a Mr. Hyde. If nationalists in a country succeed in establishing their nation state, they are intolerant towards those who differ from them. The nationalists of Hungary denied to the Slavs and Rumanians the rights which they claimed for themselves. Likewise, the Poles after 1919 ruthlessly suppressed the nationalist movements among the Ruthenians and Ukrainians.

The nationalists display pride and arrogance in their dealings. They have an aggressive spirit. Even if a fragment of their nations are found to live outside the boundary of their nation state, the new nation state indulges in intervention and commits military aggression on grounds of irredentism or get a secure frontier or an outlet to the sea. This is what was done by Hitler in Austria and Czechoslovakia. A similar policy was followed by Mussolini. The view of Prof. Hayes is that it is doubtful if "the recasting of political geography on national lines has actually promoted either humanity or justice and whether nationalism is a reliable harbinger of a quieter and better world in the immediate future." (Essays in Nationalism, p. 137).

The principle of self-determination has its own weakness. It is true that the nationalists are able to create a nation state but that may not have enough economic resources to cater to the material welfare of its people. If there is a gain, there is also a loss.

In order to make themselves self-sufficient, the nation-states follow a policy of "economic nationalism". That leads to tariffs, trade barriers, discriminatory practices, state trading and a restriction of foreign immigration.

If the principle of self-determination is taken to extremes it can be a stumbling block to the development of internationalism. Bertrand Russell writes, "It should be generally admitted that anything so internationally important as the Suez Canal or the Panama Canada should be under an international authority. The claim that those who happen to live on its banks should have the right to inflict enormous damage upon those who live elsewhere is one in which there is no justice. One might as well claim that two people who live opposite each other in Fifth Avenue should have the right to put a wall across the street." (Fact and Fiction, p. 119).

Critics point out that the modern world has become inter-dependent and unified but the principle of self-determination encourages the forces of division and not unity. That is not a happy development. Joad writes, "On the one side—the side of technology, economics and commonsense—is a manifest drive to unity; and on the other—the side of politics, pugnacity and reaction—are the nation-states that impede and obstruct it."

On the whole, it may be said that while the principle of self-determination is of great political significance and the people who are under a foreign government, should have the right to win their independence, the principle should not be taken to extremes. The problems "of multinational states can be reasonably tackled through the adoption of a federal scheme under which the cultural diversities of different nationalities may be protected and promoted so that they do not have any complaint.

CHANGING NOTIONS OF THE STATE

In the words of Prof. MacIver, "The state has no finality, can have no perfected form. The state is an instrument of social man". (The Modern State, p. vii). The state has existed from times immemorial. The Greek city states were the first form of states. City-states were tribal states and cannot be termed as states. They were city communities. After the Greek city-states, the Roman Empire arose but it was defeated by Teutonic conquerors who established feudal states in Europe. Feudal states were changed into Church states which were neither sovereign nor powerful. Out of the womb of feudal order emerged the modern notion of national states which gave law and order and justice to the people.

Prof. MacIver has referred to different notions of the state such as class organisation, power system, legal institution, mutual insurance agency, unnecessary evil, necessary evil, the organisation of the whole community, the march of God on earth, the very basis of life, welfare system, power system etc. These views emphasize one or the other notion of the state. The state is an association of society which has served in different ways at various stages of historical development. As society has changed from time to time, the state has also changed and the views about the state have also changed. To quote MacIver, "The state is an agency of human purpose and its character changes as it is directed more to the interests of this or that class within the community, as it serves more this or that set of aims, as its area or purpose narrows or widens" (The Modern State, p. 423). The state is an agency of society. It has not remained static and its notion has changed from time to time in course of history. The various notions of the state are the ethical notion, legal notion of the state, the church-state notion, notion of the nation state, state as a man-made institution or machine, the state as a necessary evil or an unnecessary evil, the totalitarian notion of the state, pluralist notion of the state, the Marxist notion of the state as a class instrument, the state as a welfare system, the state as organism etc.

Ethical Notion of the State

The ethical notion of the state was propounded by Plato and Aristotle. According to them, the state is the first and most important condition of virtuous life. It is the highest moral order. It is the supreme all-comprehensive, all-powerful and all-embracing institution. It inculcates humanity in the being. The view of Aristotle was that the state was prior to man because it is by virtue of the state that a person becomes man. The Greek philosophers made no distinction between the state and society. The state was an end in itself because self-perfection and self-fulfilment could be achieved only through the state. State was the highest morality. It was necessary for intellectual, moral and material development. The state had a majestic real personality of its own which was superior and independent of individual. The view of Aristotle was that the state was a natural institution rather than a man-made institution. Citizenship was limited. It "was a function, almost a profession. The life of the citizen was the life of the city. His good was, in ideal, wholly identified with that of the commonwealth. "The life of the citizens was very active. To use Burke's phrase, it was "a partnership in all science, a partnership in all art, a partnership in every virtue and in all perfection."

The ethical notion of the state was not confined to the Greek philosophers alone. Many idealists and non-idealist political philosophers like Rousseau, Kant, Hegel, T.H. Green, Bradley and Bosanquet supported the idealist conception of the state as an ethical institution. According to Kant, the authority of the state came from God and obedience to its authority was a sacred duty even though its authority was illegitimate. Obedience was due because the state realised a holy and divine idea. It was the duty of the citizen to obey and serve the state. Kant put more emphasis on the performance of duty than on the use of authority. Man gave consideration to his own interest and ignored the claims of society. The state forced or compelled him to give due consideration to the claims of others.

According to Hegel (1770-1831), the state is the reality of ethical spirit. It is an entity above and apart from the people who compose it. It is a new personality. "It is in the General Will and in the personality of the state that will and personality of each individual are made to transcend themselves." "It is man in his fullness and perfection of development". It has the personality of its own and the real will which is the general will and not the sum total of individual wills. The state is an entity having a personality of its own and a real will of its own. Divorced from the state, the individual has no significant role to play. The state is the supreme ethical institution. It is the march of God on earth. Whatever is done by the state is always justified. The state is above the level of morality. It is not a means but an end. It is the main source of human freedom, morality and personality. The state does not commit any wrong because it represents the general will. It acts representatively. The state is the divine idea as it exists on earth. It is the divine will as the present spirit unfolding itself to the actual shape and organisation of the world. Dr. Garner writes, "Thus, the state, to Hegel, is a God state, incapable of wrong, infallible, omnipotent and entitled to every sacrifice and devotion which it has a right to demand; it elevates and ennobles the individual whose tendency is to become selfish and self-centred and carries him back into the life of universal substance."

T.H. Green (1836-82) emphasized the moral value and majesty of the state. According to him, the state is the source and creator of individual rights. If the individual challenges the authority, the burden of proof is on him to show that the state is wrong. Green regarded the state as a natural plus moral institution. The state was needed for the moral development of man. It was the main source of individual rights. Freedom could be achieved only within the state. The state could make man free by granting him a few rights. Sanction of rights of the individual was essential for the perfection of morality. It was the function of the state to guarantee the enjoyment of those rights. The state represents the general will. The real function of the state is to hinder hindrances to good life. The state aims at providing a better standard of living.

According to Bosanquet (1848-1924), the state is the supreme moral institution as it brings about all other institutions. The state is essential for providing a good standard of living to the people.

According to him, art, morality and religion are outside the scope of the state and the state should not interfere with them.

According to Bradley (1846-1924), the individual depends on society for the development of his personality. His progress is possible only in society and not without it. The prevailing social conditions enable an individual to occupy his definite place in society. He regarded the state as a moral organism and the individual was completely under the authority of the state. Divorced from society, an individual could not have any right and it was his duty to obey the state.

The ethical notion of the state is criticised on many grounds. It places the state over and above the individual, groups, associations and the people. The state is regarded as an end in itself and not a means for the moral and intellectual development of man. Such a view may have been correct in the Greek period but in modern times, it has provided a foundation for the totalitarian notion of the state. The organic theory is also based on this view.

R.H. Soltau criticises this notion of the state in these words, "As a rule this noble ideal was vitiated by the belief that the good citizen had to conform to one single pattern laid down for him so that it was not always easy to distinguish between Plato's ideal of the good and just man and the later totalitarian ideas of the standardised citizen. It is certainly unfair to Plato to couple his name with that of modern dictators from whose aims and methods he would have recoiled with horror, but it cannot be denied that his philosophy seems to imply that only in the state can man really be himself, and it is only a step from this to the conclusion that the state must be an end in itself, irrespective of any other function or purpose". (An Introduction to Politics, p. 45).

Legal Notion of the State

The Roman Empire gave birth to the legal notion of the state which was viewed as the highest law-making power. Laws were applicable to both the governors and the governed. The Roman Empire gave birth to Roman law which is the basis of the legal systems of the world even today. Successful Roman commanders, Marius, Sulla, Caesar, Augustus etc. established bureaucratic and despotic empires with concentration of authority, uniformity of law, sovereign organisation, limited participation of citizens or citizenship without participation in political affairs etc. All democratic institutions were made powerless. The Roman Empire nursed political ideals like unity, order, law, discipline, strength, cosmopolitanism etc. The Romans gave to posterity a universal code of law. They were practical, skilful and ambitious. They were concerned more with the art of government than with the ends and purposes of the state. Their political problems were administrative and legal and not ethical. Both Polybius and Cicero concentrated themselves on the art of governing and law-making.

The legal notion of the state which had disappeared after the downfall of the Roman Empire, emerged again in the modern period. Bodin, Hobbes, Bentham and Austin are the chief exponents of the legal notion of the state. They interpret the state as entirely a legal construction. The state was formed for making, interpreting and enforcing law. It creates laws and norms in order to regulate human behaviour. If law is violated, the state has coercive power at its command which it can impose upon its recalcitrant members. The state protects the legal rights of individuals. It is the only organisation which can give validity to laws.

The legal notion of the state is still prevailing in one form or the other. The state is a law-making power. Laws are the command of the sovereign. Law has coercive power known as the sovereignty of the state. With the law-making power in the hands of the state, there emerged universal laws in national states. Positive laws made by the state overshadowed natural law, moral laws, divine laws, social customs and traditions. The legal notion of the state regarded the state as a unrestricted supreme power for making laws and it was the duty of every citizen to obey them. The state becomes an institution above society and law, the master of law and maintainer of justice and order.

The legal notion regards the state as a legal person having a distinct personality and will of its own. As a legal person, the state expresses itself through words and acts and creates and possesses rights which are quite distinct from those of the people constituting it. Its claims are superior to those of any other single body, group or association. They legally override all other claims. As a legal personality, the state can sue and can be sued. Gettell writes, "States own property, direct economic enterprises, appear as plaintiffs in civil and criminal cases and permit themselves to be sued in the courts in certain matters". (Political Science, p. 110). The state regulates, coordinates and harmonises the activities of the various members of society. It is the supreme social organisation, the culminating source of legal decisions and the *cul-de-sac* of all enforcement.

The view that the state has a personality of its own was advocated by a group of German writes, notably Stahl, Stein, Gerber, Lasson, Gierke, Treitschke, Rehm, Bluntschli, Jellinek etc. Gierke attributed personality not only to the state but to other institutions also. Maitland also supported the views of Gierke. Bluntschli regarded the state as a person *par excellence* in the sense of public law, having a legal will of its own distinct from the sum of wills of the individuals composing the state and a capacity for expressing its will in words and acts and as the creator and possessor of rights. Its personality is not merely a juristic function or metaphor but a reality. The interests of the state may differ from the interests of an individual because the state is permanent and the individual is temporary. The state pays attention to the interests of the people not only in the present, but it thinks about the future of man also.

The juridical theory regarding the nature of the state has been severely criticised by Duguit and Le Fur. According to Duguit, "The notion rests upon a metaphysical, *a priori* conception and upon old scholastic concepts which have no value". Moreover, it is unscientific. The only significance of this theory is that it enables us to follow the nature of the state easily. It regards the state as a legal personality. There is no doubt that the state possesses the qualities of an individual. It can own property, purchase land and dispose of its property. It reserves the right to file a suit against others and likewise others can also file a suit against the state. The state chalks out its plans and operates accordingly. Hence it can be said that the state has a personality of its own.

However, critics point out that the legal notion of the state does not conform to the facts of daily life. It is true that the state coordinates the activities of individuals and has coercive power at its command. However, it is not absolute and there are many practical limitations on the exercise of political power by the state. The sovereign has to consider the rights of other states without which it would be involved in a series of confrontations with them. The cost of those clashes today is prohibitive. Today some sort of an international community is emerging, setting its own ethical and moral norms and patterns which place moral limitations on the behaviour and activities of the states.

Moreover, law is not the totality of politics and political processes. The legal notion of the state emphasizes only the legal dimension of the state, politics and other political concepts. With this notion of the state, it is difficult to understand the political system. With this notion of the state, democracy as a political system cannot be understood. Sovereignty, rights, liberty, justice and equality cannot be understood politically with the legalistic outlook. Law can help us in understanding social realities but it is not the only basis of politics and political process. Purely legal notion of the state makes the study of politics narrow. Social circumstances cannot be understood on a legal basis alone. The state is a social institution serving the interests of society by performing certain functions and the legal notion of the state makes it an abstract institution whose duty is to make laws.

Church-State Notion

When the Roman Empire was declining in the fourth century A.D., it compromised with Christianity. A partnership began between the Roman Empire and the Church which created peace and order in society for some time. In the fifth century, the Roman Empire was attacked by the Teutonic people and destroyed. A new system called the feudal system was born. Instead of a centralised authority of the Roman Empire, many political authorities emerged and unity was replaced by diversity. A large number of feudal lords came into existence. Under feudalism, political authority went with land and the relation of the individual with land determined his rights and duties. In this way, political authority was decentralised in the feudal system. The concept of sovereign state was missing in the medieval period because there was an hierarchy of political power based on the ownership of land. There was no centralised law. Customs and traditions dominated society. There was neither unity nor liberty in such a society. Inequalities by birth were well recognised.

In the medieval period, the Church mustered a good deal of power, wealth and prestige. The power of the Church went on increasing and it started interfering with temporal affairs. The Pope as the Head of the Church began to claim superiority over all kings and princes and virtually became the state. The view of St. Augustine was that the King should be under the power of the Church. There were bitter conflicts between the church and the state. Feudalism was the weakness of the kings and the Church found an ally in it.

The claims of the Church for supremacy led to conflicts between the Church and the state. The Church began to limit the authority of the states and interfered in their internal affairs. Pope Glasius gave the theory of two swords. God gave one sword to the Pope to conduct spiritual affairs and another sword to the king to run temporal affairs. However, this view was not acceptable to the Church which claimed that God had given both the swords to the Pope and he for his own convenience handed over the temporal sword to the king. It meant that the king was not directly under God but was under the Pope who alone had the sole agency to conduct all the affairs from God. The result of this conflict was that one Emperor, barefooted in the snow, did humble penance for three days and nights before his spiritual master. However, ultimately the kings were victorious and the Eagle (sign of the king) swallowed the Cross (the sign of the Church). In this way, modern national sovereign secular states came into existence in Europe.

Critics point out that the church-state was a very weak state as it had no sovereign power. That led to conflicts and chaos. Religion dominated all aspects of social life and that hindered the development of scientific thinking.

Notion of National Sovereign State

The national sovereign state came into existence after the Middle Ages. The power of the Church was curbed and brought under the authority of the state. The feudal lords were humbled and the ruler became all-powerful. All authority came to be centred in the hands of the king. A large number of national sovereign states came into existence in Europe such as England, France etc. The state and the king were understood as one. Louis XIV, the Emperor of France, is said to have declared with pride, "I am the state". The king represented the state and he exercised all the powers of the state. He personified the state.

State as a Necessary Evil

The individualists considered the state as a necessary evil. According to them, the state is an evil but it is rendered necessary on account of the selfishness and rapacity of man. If each individual is left to himself, he will seek his own self-aggrandisement at the expense of others and there will be no law and order and peace. The result is that the state becomes a concession to human weakness. Adam Smith, Bentham and Herbert Spencer supported this view.

Critics point out that the state is not a negative institution. It is not an evil which must be put up with. The state is capable of performing many positive functions for the welfare of society at large.

Anarchist View of the State as Unnecessary Evil

The anarchist view is that the state is an evil but a day will come when it will become unnecessary. They rely upon the changeability of human nature. With the increasing moral development of man, the state will become less and less necessary and eventually wither away. The extreme anarchists are of the view that the state is an unmitigated evil and the sooner we get rid of it, the better for the moral growth of man.

According to the anarchists, the state is an instrument of oppression. A healthy society does not require an unhealthy institution like the state. They believe in a stateless society. They believe in destroying the state and placing the society under the control of self-governing associations. The prominent anarchists who support this view are Proudhon, Bakunin, Kropotkin, Stirner etc.

Critics of the anarchist view point out that state is a necessity and without it, equilibrium cannot be maintained in society. The consequences of abolishing the state will be disastrous.

Totalitarian Notion of State

Philosophers like Hegel and Nietzsche, writers like Bernhardi and Treitschke and dictators like Mussolini and Hitler support the totalitarian notion of the state. Their view is that the state must have absolute powers and individuals have no right against the state. The state can do no wrong. It cannot be opposed by any individual, group or association. The whole of the life of an individual is within the jurisdiction of the state. There is no part of his life which he can call his own. If he lives, he lives for the state. If he dies, he dies for the state. To quote Mussolini, "All within the state, none outside the state, none against the state". He put the following motto before his countrymen: "To believe, to obey, to fight".

Critics rightly point out that such a view of the state is highly undesirable. It is undemocratic and does not leave any scope for individual rights and freedom. It denies the worth and dignity of human personality. It leads to a system in which the individual becomes a cog in the wheel of the state machine. All dictatorships are founded on such a view of the state.

Pluralist Notion of State

According to the Pluralist view of the state, the state is to be reduced to the position of equality with other permanent groups like the family, the church, the trade union, the social club etc. which cater to our various needs. The various permanent groups within society have a definite and distinct place to fill in the life of man and hence they should have as large a degree of internal autonomy as possible.

The Pluralists oppose the absolute sovereignty of the state and stand for decentralisation of political power. They do not consider the state in any way superior to other associations which perform their due functions in society. The important advocates of this view are MacIver and Laski.

Critics point out that even if other organisations have to be given a lot of internal autonomy, there is the necessity of a superior organisation to adjust their relationships and to keep them in their proper places. That organisation is the state.

Power Notion of State

Some writers interpret the state as a power system. Machiavelli was the forerunner of this point of view. The same view was upheld by many German writers like Treitschke.

The advocates of this view interpret the state exclusively in terms of might. They make power their chief aim and subordinate to it the personal freedom and cultural development of their members. When individuals come into contact with each other, conflicts and contradictions arise in society. The necessity of power arises to resolve them and maintain peace and harmony in society. Power arises spontaneously to cope with the demands of the individuals and society. It is not correct to say that the state curbs and restricts the freedom of individuals. As a matter of fact, freedom in society is born out of the rules made and enforced by it. Without those rules, life would become intolerable and personal security would be endangered. By keeping in check the anti-social forces and reconciling the conflicting claims of the people, the power of the state helps society to attain a state of near-perfect equilibrium.

The power view of the state is not accepted by many writers. They do not deny that force is an essential part of the state, but they point out that force is not the foundation of the state. T.H. Green emphasized this point of view in these words, "Will, not force, is the basis of the state". Prof. MacIver writes, "Coercive power is only the criterion of state and not its essence". Power relationship is not one-way relationship. Naked power or brute power can never justify a state. It is only when power is transformed into an authority that it becomes a pillar for the state. Power becomes authority when it is well organised, regularised and used for social ends. The rational transition is from force to power and from power to authority. Many writers of the behaviouralist school prefer to discuss the state in terms of power relations.

State as Welfare System

The contemporary liberal view of the state is that of a welfare state. The main supporters of this view are T.H. Green, MacIver, Laski and the American writers who have evolved the idea of political system. The state is not merely an abstract legal institution. It is an active system operating in society. It includes all policies and activities concerning authority, institutions influencing the authority, political behaviour and functions of the political system. The state as a political system has certain functions, activities and processes in the whole social system. It is not merely a static legal institution having population, definite territory, government and sovereignty. It performs the functions of maintaining stability and equilibrium, policy-making and serving the common welfare functions in society.

The welfare state performs positive functions besides maintaining law and order. It promotes human welfare. The state is required not only to achieve socio-economic goals but also to act as an instrument of socio-economic change which will ultimately pave the way to the promotion of the greatest happiness of the largest number. The welfare state has become a social service organisation. It acts as a father, a nurse, a manager and an industrial entrepreneur. The state is required to regulate the working conditions of workers, spread education, run social services and eradicate social evils. It has to promote the health of the people. The welfare state performs a number of social services. The Beveridge Report on Social Insurance (1942) wants the state to provide unemployment and disability benefits, retirement pensions, maternity benefit, dependant allowance, industrial pensions etc. The New Deal legislation of President Rossevelt aimed at the promotion of human welfare. The National Health Act and the National Assistance of Children Act are among the pillars supporting the struggle of welfare state in the United Kingdom. Similar legislation has been enacted not only in the Soviet Union and other European countries but also in India.

However, the role of the state in the context of change and development is looked upon with suspicion and fear. It is felt that in the process of social and economic transformation, the state will be controlled by the economically dominant elite who will not allow basic and structural changes to be brought about which are opposed to their basic interests. It is contended that instead of being an instrument of socio-economic change, the state has been responsible for maintaining the *status quo.*

State as Mutual Insurance Society

The view of some writers is that the state is a mutual insurance society for purposes of mutual protection. Herbert Spencer was a staunch advocate of this theory. He considered the state as a "joint stock protection company for mutual assurance".

Vocational or Missionic Notion of State

Another notion of the state is called vocational or missionic notion. Some states claim to represent a certain type of civilisation. They believe that they have a mission in the world. Ancient Israel is an instance. The same is true of the Communists of the Soviet Union. The revolutionaries of the French Revolution also believed in such a mission. H.R. Soltau writes, "Unfortunately, the cultural mission is often accompanied by a belief in the use of force for its extension and vocational or missionic states have often used their soldiers as their chief missionaries". (An Introduction to Politics, pp. 44-5). The view of Bosanquet is that "the state has no determinate function in a larger community, but is itself the supreme community, the guardian of a whole world". Again, "The moral relations pre-suppose an organised life, but such life is only within the state and not in the relations between the state and other communities". (Ibid., p. 45).

Organic View of State *(Organic Theory of the State)*

The organic or organismic theory of the state represents the earliest thinking about the state although it has received some new interpretations in recent times. This theory compares the state with an organism or a living body and the individuals with its organs. According to Prof. Wayper, the idea of state as an organism means, firstly, a close relationship of parts to the whole, secondly that the organism develops from within and lastly that the organism is an end in its own self or in the organism produced by it. As the existence and worth of the organs depends on the existence of the organism, likewise the existence and worth of individuals depend on the existence of the state. Different organs are fit to perform different functions within the organism and some of them are naturally superior to others. Likewise, different groups and classes in society, are naturally fit to perform different functions. Some of them are destined to enjoy a superior position than others in the interests of the entire society.

The idea of the state as an organism was hit upon by the Greeks. Plato compared the state to a man of great stature. He pointed out the resemblance between the functions of the state and those of an individual. He based his three-fold classification of society, the rulers, warriors and working classes, upon three faculties of the human soul: wisdom, greed and appetite. To him, the state was like the capital letter (A) and the individual was like the smaller letter (a). While the state was the macrocosm, the individual was the microcosm.

The view of Aristotle was that the state comes into existence for the sake of life and continues for the sake of good life. The existence of the state is essential for the existence of man. Man by nature is a political animal. He who lives without the state is either a beast or a God.

Hobbes compared the state to the great Leviathan "which is but an artificial man, though of greater strength and stature than the natural". He compared the sovereignty of the state to the soul of man and the magistrates to the joints. He found an analogy between the weakness of the state and certain human diseases such as boils, scabs, pleurisy etc.

Rousseau compared the body politic to a human body both of which possess the motive powers of force and will. The former was the heart of the state and the latter its brain.

The view of the state as a natural institution was challenged by the scientific revolution of the seventeenth century which advanced the mechanistic theory of the state, but towards the end of the eighteenth century and throughout the nineteenth century men became dissatisfied with the mechanistic theory which looked upon individuals as so many related atoms. The result was a renewed interest in the organic theory of the state. With the development of nationalism during that period, the state was described as the embodiment of the nation and an object of worship.

Fichte was the first to point out clearly the inter-dependence of society and individual. His view was that the individuals had no meaning without society. To quote him, "In the organic body, each part constantly maintains the whole and is in maintaining the whole thereby itself maintained; just so stands the citizen in relation to the state".

The view of Bluntschli was that the state is the very image of human organism. Each has its member parts, its organs, its functions and its life processes. The state is masculine in character while the church is feminine. According to him, the state is "no mere artificial, lifeless machine" but a living spiritual organic being. As an oil painting is something more than a mere aggregation of drops of oil, as a statue is something more than a combination of marble particles, as a man is something more than a mere quantity of cells and blood corpuscles, so the nation is something more than a mere collection of external regulations. "The state is a union of mind and will; it is the community in action.

The modern theory of evolution gave a new impetus to likening the state with biological phenomena. The organic theory received a new fillip from the contributions of the biological school of political theory which flourished in the nineteenth century. The pioneers of this school likened the development of political institutions with the growth of living beings towards higher forms of life as characterised by the increasing differentiation of parts. To quote Wayper, "They spoke of the tissues of the state, of its systems of nutrition and circulation, of organs within it fulfilling specifically the functions of brain, nerves, fibres, heart, muscles, even stomach and nose."

The view of Herbert Spencer was that the state was a natural organism which did not differ much from a biological organism. Both of them began as germs and had to undergo many changes in the course of development. Both of them were simple to begin with and both of them became complex later on. The lower type of animal was all stomach, respiratory surface or limbs. Likewise, the primitive society was all warrior, hunter, hut-builder and tool-maker. When the organism became complicated, the division of labour followed. Different organs began to perform different functions and they were mutually dependent on one another. There was a sustaining system consisting of alimentation in the animal organism and production in the social organism. There was the transport system in society and the circulatory apparatus in the animal organism. There was the government and the army in the state and there was the regulatory system in the animal organism. However, Spencer felt that the analogy between society and state was not complete. He pointed out two exceptions. While there was "nerve sensorium" in the organism, there was no such thing in a state. If an organ of the body was injured, the general health of the individual was affected. If one individual was injured, the others did not seem to bother about him. They continued their merry-making. Another difference was that while the relation of the organism and the organs was concrete, the relation between man and man was discrete. Each individual could grow independently of the action of other individuals.

Schaffle emphasised the anatomical, physiological, biological and psychological resemblances between society and the individual. His contention was that society was an organism "whose protoplasm or unit is man, the state or government in the one corresponding to the brain in the other."

Comte described human society as the highest stage in organic evolution, "embodying the completest development of that natural harmony or organisation and action." According to Worms, "The anatomy, physiology and pathology of society possess striking similarities to the structure, function and pathology of living beings." The view of Gumplowicz was that there is complete identity between the state and an organism. The organic nature of the state is a literal fact and not merely a matter of analogy.

The view of the exponents of the biological school is that the state possesses all the three characteristics of an organism and hence should be regarded as organic in nature. They recognise an intrinsic relation between man and state. As an organism is the real source of life and energy for its parts, the state is also the spring of good life for its citizens. The view of some writers is that the state makes an appeal to the rational nature of man and they praise the state as a "moral organism", "super-organism" and an "organism of organisms". Some of them glorify it as a "real person" or "super-person". As the individual organs of an organism such as hands, teeth or feet can have no real interests of their own apart from the interests of the organism itself, the interests of the individuals cannot be distinguished from those of the state. Individuals can have rights within the state but not against the state. True freedom of the individual lies on obedience to the laws of the state.

Merits

Undoubtedly, the organic theory of the nature of the state rendered a great service in one way. It emphasized the intimate relationship between the state and individuals. It emphasized the fact that the state "is not the hasty product of a day but the well-ripened fruit of wise delay." As a leaf cannot live separate from a tree, likewise an individual cannot live independent of the state. By putting emphasis on the state, this theory facilitated the unification of New states.

The view of Prof. Gettell is that the organic theory has a certain value in emphasising the unity of the state, the inter-dependence of the individuals composing it and the gradual and continuous evolution of its historical growth. In this respect, it was a useful antidote to the eighteenth century theory that viewed the state as a mechanical and artificial creation of man which could be re-made at his pleasure, regardless of history and tradition. This theory emphasises the interdependence of citizens and political institutions. It puts emphasis on the unity of social life and the intricate inter-relations of all its parts. It points out that society is something more than an aggregate of individuals. The members are dependent on the whole and the whole is conditioned by the parts.

Criticism

The organic theory has also its defects. Its exponents started by saying that the state is like an organism but ended by saying that the state is an organism itself. Writers like Bluntschli went to the extent of saying that the state is masculine and church is feminine. However, analogy is not proof. Even if it is conceded that the state is like an organism, it cannot be said that the state is an organism in itself. Barker writes, "The state is not an organism, but it is like an organism; it is not an organism because it has no physical structure." To suggest a parallel between two things is not to determine the relation between them. The more we labour the parallel, the more we ate liable to forget to determine the relation. Criticising Herbert Spencer who faced the problem but instead of solving it hid his head in the sands of metaphor, Barker observes, "Spencer is the classical instance of the labour and the forgetting. In the second place, if you seek to establish a parallel, it is necessary to be clear about the true terms of the parallel. If you compare two organisms, you must be clear about both. Spencer is clear about the individual organism which is obviously physical, he is by no means equally clear about the social organism."

Individuals are not like cells in a state. Every individual has a separate and independent existence of his own. He has his own thoughts, feelings and actions. Individuals are like islands that dot the vast sea of humanity. However, the cells of an organism are not free and isolated. There is no independent life of a cell, which lives for the whole. If a cell is separated from the organism, it dies. However, individuals can continue to exist even if they are separated from the state.

A living cell cannot be a part of two distinct organisms at the same time, but an individual can join as many associations as he pleases. If we compare the state to an animal organism on the ground that "its roads and its railways and soon, perhaps, its balloons correspond to our arteries and our veins, we shall experience the feeling that it is a defiance of all commonsense." (Le Fur).

The state was not born like an organism, it changes rather than grows. It has no old age or death. Although growth, decline and death are inseparable from the life of an organism, they are not necessary for the life of a state.

The view of Dr. Leacock is that this theory does not give us any criterion of conduct. To quote him, "The organic theory, in telling us that our institutions grow and are not made, hardly offers a practical guide to political conduct." It can lead to inactive fatalism.

Hobhouse points out that "to speak of society as if it were a physical organism is a piece of mysticism, if, indeed, it is not quite meaningless." However, he maintains that "the life of society and the life of an individual do resemble each other in certain respects and the term 'organic' is as justly applicable to the one as to the other, for an organism is a whole, consisting of interdependent parts. Each part lives and functions, and grows by subserving the life of the whole. It sustains the rest and is sustained by them and through mutual support comes a common development."

The view of Dr. Garner is that the organic theory "is not only fanciful and absurd but even mischievous, and would not merit notice were it not relied upon by some respectable writers as the justification of an important theory concerning the relation of the state to the individual members composing it...The organic theory, in the sense in which it is understood by many writers, rests on mere analogy, and we should do well to heed Lord Acton's warning about analogies, metaphors and parallelism lest we come to grief." (Political Science and Government, pp. 203-204).

The organic theory of the state is full of dangers. "Some of these biological comparisons are ingenious and well stated; to many writers they have proved fascinating and seductive, to others they have constituted the basis of an argument for a theory of the state which would sacrifice individual to society." If there is some truth in it, there is also a lot of untruth in it.

The comparison between society and an organism is superficial. There is no similarity between the cells of an organism and the individuals who compose society. Cells have no independent life of their own. They are mechanical pieces of matter. Each is fixed in its place and has no power of thought or will. It exists solely to support and perpetuate the life of the whole. On the other hand, individuals are independent, intellectual and moral human beings. They do not act like a machine.

The state has grown from similarity and simplicity to dissimilarity and complexity. It is not subject to the same process of birth, growth and decay as an organism. An animal organism comes into existence by the union of two organisms. That is not true of the birth of the state. The process of its growth is also not similar. Organisms grow from within and through internal adaptation. They grow unconsciously, independent of volition, entirely dependent on its environment and the natural laws of the biological world. However, the machinery of the state and its laws change to adjust themselves to the altered needs and requirements of the people. This change is brought about as a result of volition and conscious efforts of its members.

In this theory, man is completely overshadowed by the state. His personality is not only subordinated but submerged in the personality of the state. Man is treated "no more than a conduit pipe for the divine energy, as a passive creature for whom things must be done, not as a being who finds fulfilment in positive activity."

The organic theory, in its actual working, subjects man to the authority of state officials who may be as imperfect as their subjects, if not more. At times, state officials may take decisions according to their narrow and selfish interests. Disastrous decisions may be taken on account of the whim or lack of vision on, the part of the decision-makers. If the authority of the state is considered beyond challenge and if citizens are required to sacrifice everything in the name of the state, those decisions may destroy the state itself. That is proved by the fall of Hitler and Mussolini in Germany and Italy.

The organic theory gives a distorted view of freedom. According to this theory, man can have no rights against the state. He has merely to obey the commands of the state.

This theory ignores the distinction between state and society. Prof. MacIver rightly points out that if we do not make a distinction between society and state, we are on the dangerous road to totalitarianism. The state can demand complete surrender from the people. That makes the government the complete master of man. To quote MacIver, "This is the road Rousseau opened up when he spoke of 'forcing man to be free'. That is the road Fichte and Hegel prepared, making them the forerunners of the ruinous and finally nihilistic doctrine of Fascists and Nazis. This is the road that under the signs of liberty and unity, invites men to concentration camp and the death of the creative spirit. "(The Web of Government, p 306).

The organic theory is essentially undemocratic. As toes cannot dictate to the brain, there is no question of representation of the ordinary people to the seat of authority. Wisdom and authority become the monopoly of the chosen few and the masses are alienated from the process of decision-making.

The organic theory has been exploited by different writers to support their own points of view. The individualists point out to the discrete relationship between one individual and another and maintain that the state should not exercise any control over individuals. On the other hand, the idealists think that the whole of the life of an individual should be merged into that of the state and the individual should have absolutely no liberty.

The organic theory throws little light on the practical questions facing the state. It is neither a satisfactory explanation of the nature of the state nor a trustworthy guide to state activity.

The conclusion of Jellinek is in these words, "We had better reject the theory in toto lest the danger from the larger amount of falsity in the analogy should outweigh the good in the little truth it contains."

State as Man-made Institution

The origin of this view can be traced to ancient times. Epicurus, the Greek philosopher, was of the view that the state is not a divine inspiration guiding the footsteps of men into Eternal Truth. It was merely a device of his own making for the convenience of his social life. The Romans made a distinction between *Nomos* and *Lex.* Nomos represented Internal Truth which was only to be discovered. Lex signified the body of law created by man himself. The state obviously belonged to the realm of Lex and was the creation of man. Some Christian thinkers of medieval Europe distinguished between Divine Will which represented justice from civil society which was treated as artificial.

The idea of the state as an artificial device is to be found throughout the history of political thought. However, the view that the state was created by man was given in a systematic manner during the seventeenth and eighteenth centuries. Scientific discoveries changed the views of the people regarding nature, reason and artifice. The invention of new machines captured the imagination of the people. The result was that like a machine the state came to be considered as a creation of man himself, a product of will and artifice.

The main exponents of this view were Hobbes, Locke and Bentham. According to Hobbes, there existed a state of nature prior to the civil society in which the life of man was solitary, poor, nasty, brutish and short. The condition of the people in the state of nature was so bad that they were prepared to pay any price to get out of it. Hence, they decided to enter into a perpetual and irrevocable contract to form a civil society and thus the state came into existence. The machinery of the state was created by the people themselves for their good. According to Locke, the people were equal and free in the state of nature. They had rights to life, liberty and property. In view of the insecurity and need for an authority to protect those rights, they created the state for their good. The view of Bentham was that the state was an artificial creation which aimed at the promotion of the happiness or pleasure of the people.

According to the mechanistic view of the state, the state is not a natural institution but a social institution created by the people. The state is not the whole of society but only a special organisation of society. Society is a natural growth but the state was created for the survival and advancement of civilisation.

According to this theory, man as the creator of the state must be more real than the state. Like a machine, the state exists for its maker. The state is not an end in itself. Like a machine, it is only a means to an end. This theory gave rise to the doctrine of individualism which made the state a servant of the individual. It curtailed the regulatory powers of the state over social and economic matters.

This theory refutes the organic view that the state represents Superior Reason or Eternal Truth. At the most, the state can have a superior will but not superior reason. The state is a manifestation of the will of the people who have created it. According to this view the state does not embody the interests of all the people. It merely tries to harmonise and regulate the varying and conflicting interests of the people within society.

This theory has been responsible for laying the foundations of modern institutions. It has transformed itself according to the changing needs of time. It regards the individual as real and makes the state subservient to him. The state can justify its existence by working for the good of the people who live within its jurisdiction. This theory makes a distinction between state and society. It gives a choice to individuals to resist the state on the ground of conscience. While the organic theory advocates complete subordination of the individual to the state, this theory lays foundations for constitutional government under which a check can be put on the power of the state. This theory facilitates the development of democratic institutions. It believes in the wisdom of individuals and gives them equality of political rights. As the state is the product of the will of the people, this theory stands for government by consent. It gives equal weightage to all citizens without discrimination of any kind. It has laid the foundations of the welfare state. It secures social justice for the people.

Class View of the State

This theory is associated with Marxism. According to it, the state is neither a natural institution nor an ethical institution. It treats the state as an artificial device. The state is not the will of the people or an instrument for the reconciliation of the varying and conflicting interests of the people. The state comes into existence when society is divided into two classes, one owning the means of production and the other without them. Society is divided into two classes after the emergence of private property and not earlier.

According to this theory, society is divided into dominant and dependent classes. The dominant class controls political power and the state is the embodiment of that power. It is subordinate to economic power. The state does not originate in the will of the people. It does not stand for the benefit of all. It is an instrument devised by the dominant class for its own benefit. It is imposed on society to serve the interests of the dominant class. The state has not existed from eternity. It is a product of the conscious effort of the dominant class which acquires the means of production and political power. The state is not a natural institution.

There is a clear distinction between the state and society. They did not come into existence together. While society is a natural institution, the state is an artificial institution. Man by nature is a social animal but not a political animal. Society is a natural institution as it is necessary for the production of those goods which are necessary for the survival of man. The forms of production at any given stage of social development determine the pattern of social relations. There was no private property at the beginning of society. When the hunting, fishing and food-gathering economy was transformed into an agricultural economy, there came into existence what is known as surplus production which was cornered by the class owning the means of production. The structure of society is always determined by the prevalent form of production. The hand-mill gave the feudal lord. The steam mill gave the industrial capitalist. The attitude and outlook of society was determined by the material conditions of life. The state is an instrument of the dominant class whatever the form of government. The dominant class uses the machinery of the state for oppression and exploitation. The state does not rest on moral foundations. It does not harmonise the conflicting interests of the people. The state is a device for the suppression of the class conflict.

The view of Karl Marx, Engels and Lenin was that the machinery of the state was used by the dominant class for the suppression of class conflict. It maintains order in society. It uses its ideological power to create an illusion of consent of the governed.

The state is the embodiment of social injustice but the object is to establish a classless and stateless society through a revolution by the workers. The proletariat would take away the property of the capitalists and socialize the major means of production. The state still remained an instrument of class exploitation. The dictatorship of the proletariat will be used to suppress the bourgeoisie and socialize the major means of production. The state would still continue as an instrument of class exploitation. When the proletariat succeeds in suppressing the bourgeoisie, a classless society will come into existence and the state will wither away.

The great merit of this theory lies in the fact that it emphasizes the role of economic forces in shaping history. This theory traces the roots of social injustice in the conditions created by the social system itself. The poverty of the masses is due to their oppression and exploitation by property-owners. This can change only when a classless and stateless society is established with the help of the dictatorship of the proletariat.

The critics of this theory point out that there is no rigid division of society into two classes, the dominant class and the dependent class. Under the capitalist system, the size of the middle class is actually increasing and power has actually shifted from the hands of the capitalists to the managerial class which controls production. The capitalism of today is different from the capitalism of the nineteenth century on which Marx based his philosophy. Modern Capitalism has been given a humane face through the welfare activities of the state. There are no signs of the withering away of the state in the Soviet Union and Communist China as predicted by Marx. The class theory of the state is now being revised to suit the changed conditions. As there is no rigid class division in society today, it is desirable to look for "structures of domination" and "forms of domination" and attack them with a view to establishing social justice, freedom and equality.

SUGGESTED READINGS

Acton, Lord : *History of Freedom and Other Essays.*

Almond, G.A. and J.S. Coleman (Ed.) : *The Politics of Developing Areas,* Princeton, 1960.

Asirvathan, E. : *Political Theory.*

Barker, Ernest : *Political Thought in England from Spencer to Today.*

Barker, Ernest : *Principles of Social and Political Theory.*

Blackburn, R. (Ed.) : *Ideology in Social Sciences,* Fontana, 1972.

Bluntschli : *Theory of the State.*

Burgess : *Political Science and Constitutional Law.*

Burke : *Reflections on the Revolution in France.*

Chang, S.H.M. : *The Marxian Theory of the State,* New York, 1965.

Cole, G.D.H. : *Social Theory.*

Cole, G.D.H. : *Self-Government in Industry.*

Cole, G.D.H. : *Fundamentals of Political Science, Progress Publishers,* Moscow, 1975.

Dahl, Robert A. : *Modern Political Analysis.*

Dillon, C.H., C. Leiden and P.D. Stewarts : *Introduction to Political Analysis.*

Easton, David : *Political System—An Inquiry into the State of Political Science.*

Field, G.C. : *Political Theory.*

Finer, Herman : *The Theory and Practice of Modern Government.*

Garner, J.W. : *Political Science and Government.*

Gerth, H.H. and C. Wright Mills (Ed.) : *From Max Weber.*

Gettell, R.G. : *Political Science,* Calcutta, 1950.

Gettel, R.G. : *Problems of Political Evolution.*

Gilchrist, R.N. : *Principles of Political Science.*

Gooch, G.P. : *Nationalism.*

Hayes, C.J.H. : *Essays on Nationalism.*

Hegel, G.W.F. : *Philosophy of History.*

Holland : *Elements of Jurisprudence*

Hunt, Richard N. : *Political Ideas of Marx and Engels.*

Jenks, E. : *The State and the Nation.*

Kohn, Hans : *The Idea of Nationalism.*

Laski, Harold J. : *An Introduction to Politics.*

Laski, Harold J. : *The State in Theory and Practice.*

Laski, Harold J. : *A Grammar of Politics.*

Leacock : *Elements of Political Science.*

Lipson : *The Great Issues of Politics.*

MacIver, R.M. : *The Modern State.*

MacIver, R.M. : *Society: Its Structure and Changes.*

MacIver, R.M. : *The Web of Government.*

MacIver, R.M. and C.H. Page : *Society: An Introductory Analysis.*

Mackenzie, W.J.M. : *Politics and Social Sciences,* Penguin, 1967.

Maritain : *Man and the State.*

McMurtry, John : *The Structure of Marx's World View,* Princeton, 1978.

Mehta, Vrajendra : *A Theory of Politics.*

Miliband : *The State in Capitalist Society,* London, 1973.

Miliband : *Marxism and Politics,* Oxford, 1977.

Mill, J.S. : *Representative Government.*

Morgenthau : *Politics Among Nations.*

Pennock, J.D. and D.G. Smith : *Political Science.*

Poulantzas, N. : *Political Power and the Social Class,* 1972.

Roberts, Geoffrey K. : *A Dictionary of Political Analysis.*

Russell, Bertrand : *Fact and Fiction.*

Shafer, Boyd C. : *Nationalism, Myth and Reality.*

Shills, D.L. (Ed.) : *International Encyclopaedia of Social Sciences,* Vol. 12, 1964.

Sidgwick, H. : *The Elements of Politics.*

Soltau, R.H. : *An Introduction to Politics.*

Treitschke, H.V. : *Politics.*

Vyshinsky, A.Y. : *The Law of the Soviet State.*

Waper, C.L. : *Political Thought.*

Watkins, Frederick : *International Encyclopaedia of the Social Sciences.*

Willoughby, W.W. : *The Nature of the State.*

Wilson, W. : *The State.*

Wiseman, H.V. : *Political Systems*, London, 1966.

Zimmern, A.E. : *Nationality and Government.*

CHAPTER

The Political System

The political scientists in the United States prefer to use the term *political system* to the term *state* on the ground that it is a vaule-free power system operating in the whole of the social system with its set boundaries, goals, processes etc. Their contention is that the sphere of politics is much wider than that of the state. David Easton maintains that the use of the term state "succeeds in substituting one unknown for another; for the unknown political science, we now have the unknown of the state." Again, "If we were to use the concept of the state with its most widely adopted meaning today, we would find that it has a number of obvious shortcomings for an understanding of the political system. It describes the properties not of all political phenomena but of only certain kinds, excluding, for example, the study of pre-state societies, it stands over-shadowed as a tool of analysis by its social utility as a myth, and it constitutes at best a poor formal definition." Mackenzie observes, "If we are to regard politics as a permanent feature of human society, we must not pin it to the study of states, a temporary and changing type of social organisation. It is wrong to say that political science is about states, to define states ostensively and to leave it at that."

David Easton points out certain difficulties in using the term *state*. It does not help us in understanding all political situations. The political system of the period before the sixteenth century when the concept of the state came to be frequently used, cannot be understood with the concept of state. The concept of state is not sufficient for social analysis because this has been used mainly as a social myth. The view of David Easton is that the state emerged as a historical entity in particular circumstances and it has lost validity for an analysis of present day politics. G.A. Almond holds similar views. To quote him, "Instead of the concept of the state, limited as it is by legal and institutional meaning, we prefer political system".

Learning Objectives

- Political
- System
- Definition of Political System
- David Easton
- Almond
- Characteristics of the Political System
- Problems or Challenges to Political System
- Functions of Political System: Input Functions
- Political Socialisation
- A Political recruitment
- Interest articulation
- Interest Aggregation
- Political Communication
- Output Functions
- David Easton on Political System
- Equilibrium Analysis
- Inputs
- Conversion Process
- Outputs
- The Feed-back
- Political System and Social System
- Political System and Economic System
- Suggested Readings

Political

Before we discuss the meaning and nature of the concept of political system, it is desirable to explain the words "political" and "system". The word political mainly refers to power or authority. According to Marion Levy, political allocation can be defined "as the distribution of power over and responsibility for the actions of the various members of the concrete structure concerned, involving on the one hand coercive sanctions, of which force is the extreme form in one direction and, on the other, accountability to the members and in terms of the structure concerned, or to the members of other concrete structures." The word political refers to power, influence, control or authority, use or threat of use of physical force etc. The inter-actions which are involved in the struggle for power, are generally political.

System

The word 'system' has been used and defined differently by different writers belonging to different disciplines. The Concise Oxford Dictionary defines it as (1) a complex whole set of connected things or parts, organised body of material or immaterial things; (2) method, organisation, considered principles of procedure. Ludwig Von Bertallanfy describes it as a set of elements standing in inter-action. Hall and Pagan define it as "a set of objects together with relations between the objects and between their attitudes." Morton A. Kaplan writes, "A brief and non-technical description of the object of system analysis would include the study of a set of inter-related variables as distinguished from the environment of the set, and of the ways in which the set is maintained under the impact of environmental disturbances." According to Collin Cherry, a system "is a whole which is compounded of many parts—an ensemble of attitudes." According to Almond, a system is characterised by comprehensiveness, inter-dependence and existence of boundaries. Thus, a system consists of a set of elements or objects composing a whole, their interactions and the regular pattern of interaction, their interdependence, comprehensiveness, existence of boundaries, structures and functions performed by structures.

Definition of Political System

Max Weber says that "a political system is a human community that successfully claims the monopoly of the legitimate use of physical force within a given territory."

David Easton

According to David Easton, "Political system is that system of interaction in any society through which binding and authoritative allocations of value are made and implemented." Political system is a part of the whole social system in the same way in which political process is a dimension of the whole social process. The whole of political life is included in the political system which for the sake of simplification of political analysis is artificially set apart from the whole of the social system because it is difficult to ascertain what is political. However, all kinds of activities involved in the formulation and execution of social policy constitutes the political system. There are three aspects of the political system: policy, authority and society. Policy is concerned with who will get what. In the study of policy, Easton includes legal and executive policies and also their formulation and execution which require many actions activities. Thus, the first aspect of the study of the political system is the making and execution of policies. Policies must have the backing of authority in order to be the subject-matter of political system. Political system is not concerned with all the policies in society but only with those policies which are made for the whole society. It is not concerned with those policies which are made by a group for a group. Policies must have a general character. According to Easton, political system is concerned with policy-making, policy-execution, authority and the role of all those in society in general. The study of political system is the study of an activity, a process rather than the study of an institution like the state.

Almond

Before giving his own definition of the term political system, Gabriel Almond criticises the existing definitions. He criticises the definition of Max Weber on the ground that it appears to be a definition of the state rather than of the political system because it ignores the functional aspect of the political system. Then he takes up the definition of Lasswell and Kaplan who regard "Shaping and sharing of power as the main concern of political system with the help of threatened or actual use of severe deprivation for non-conformity". According to Almond, the term severe deprivation has not been made clear by Lasswell and Kaplan and hence no distinction can be made between the political system and other social systems. Almond takes the definition of David Eastern and condemns it on the ground that authoritativeness does not clearly differentiate political system from other systems like church or business firm.

After rejecting the above definitions, Almond gives his own meaning of the political system as "that system of interaction to be found in all independent societies which perform the function of integration and adaptation (both internally and vis-a-vis other societies) by means of employment, or threat of employment, of more or less legitimate, order-maintaining system in the society. We use the term 'more or less' to modify legitimacy because we do not want to exclude from our definition political systems like the totalitarian ones where the degree of legitimacy may be very much in doubt, revolutionary systems where the use of legitimacy may be in process of change, or non-Western systems in which there may be more than one legitimacy system in operation."

There things emerge out of Almond's definition of the political system. (1) A political system is a concrete whole influencing and, in turn, influenced by the environments, it is held in fact by the legitimate force in the last analysis holding it together. (2) Interactions take place not between individuals but between roles that they play. (3) the political system is an open system engaged in a continuous communication with entities and systems outside its own boundaries. Almond's definition of the political system is characterised by comprehensiveness, interdependence and existence of boundaries. A system is comprehensive in the sense that it includes all the interactions-inputs as well as outputs. Inter-dependence means that the various sub-sets of the political system are so closely connected with each other that a change in one sub-set produces a change in all the other sub-sets. In other words, parts or sub-sets of the political system have validity only in terms of the working of the entire system. Almond defines boundary as the "point where one political system ends and the other political system begins."

According to H.V. Wiseman, "Any political system involves political structures, political roles performed by actors or agents, patterns of interaction between actors, whether individuals or collectivities, and a political process." Again, "A political system is the legitimate, order-maintaining or transforming system within society."

Robert A. Dahl defines political system as "any persistent pattern of human relationships that involves to a significant extent power, rule or authority."

According to Almond and Powell, "Political system includes not only governmental institutions such as legislatures, courts and administrative agencies, but all structures, in their political aspects. Among these are traditional structures such as kinship ties and caste groupings; and anomic phenomena such as association, riots and demonstrations, as well as formal organisations like parties, interest groups and media of communication." Again, "A political system is made of the increasing roles of nationals, subjects as the case may be with the legislator, bureaucrats and judges. The same individuals who perform roles in the political system, perform roles in other social systems such as the economic, the religious community, the family and voluntary associations. As individuals expose themselves to political communication, form interest groups, vote or pay taxes, they shift from non-political to political roles. One might say that on election day as citizens leave their farms, plants and offices to go to the polling places, they are crossing the boundary from the economy to the politics."

The concept of political system has been criticised on many grounds. It is contended that political system is studied by dissociating it from its historical development on a purely empirical, structural-functional basis, but it can be studied meaningfully only with due consideration of its historical evolution. It is also pointed out that though the political system is regarded as an aspect of the whole social system, it is assumed that it can be temporarily set apart from the whole social system for political research. This is highly objectionable as social and political systems are not related in a formal way. Political system is an inseparable part of the whole social system. The boundaries of the political system cannot be ascertained because it is intermingled with the whole of the social system. In order to see the political aspect to society, one has to take into account both historical development of society and ideology which are rejected by the American political scientists. It is further contended that while it is assumed that political system has some boundaries, it is difficult to fix them as the state is penetrating all aspects of the social system in modern times. Moreover, the American political scientists use very difficult terminology and new concepts such as political culture, political socialisation, interest-articulation, interest-aggregation, modernisation, political development etc. These concepts have a very specific and technical meaning. The use of these difficult terms makes the subject complicated and difficult for the people to understand it. The result will be that the people in general will be discouraged from studying politics and also from participating in politics. Moreover, the political system of the state can be understood only on an historical basis and not otherwise.

Characteristics of the Political System

There are many characteristics of the political system. (1) One characteristic is that it allows the legal authority to use force. Easton refers to "authoritative allocation of values". Dahl refers to power, rule and authority. These definitions show that legal authority can use force to compel anybody to obey its orders. It possesses legitimate and rightful power to punish. Max Weber rightly says that the legitimate use of force is a distinct feature of the political system. It gives it a special quality and importance and its unity as a system.

(2) Another characteristic of political system is interactions. According to Almond, political system is that system of interaction which is to be found in all independent societies which perform the functions of integration and adaptation by means of the employment or threat of employment of legitimate physical compulsion. The political system includes not only governmental institutions such as legislatures, executives, courts and administrative agencies but also all structures in their political aspect. Among them are included organisations like political parties, interest-groups and media of communication, traditional structures such as kinship ties, caste groupings and anomic phenomena such as associations, riots and demonstrations. The political system includes interaction between all the formal and informal institutions. The process of interaction is divided into three phases inputs, conversion and output.

(3) Another characteristic of the political system is the inter-dependence of parts. This means that when the properties of one component in a system change, all other components and the system as a whole are affected. Moreover, the emergence of trade unions and pressure groups affects the working of political parties, the electoral press, the legislature, the bureaucracy and the judicial system.

(4) Another characteristic of political system is its comprehensiveness. The political system includes all interactions whether those are from formal or informal institutions. It includes the interaction of regionalism, religious upheavals, inflation, party politics, tactics of pressure groups and social changes brought about by modernization.

(5) Another characteristic of the political system is the change of boundary. The political system consists of the interacting roles of nationals, subjects, voters, legislators, bureaucrats and judges.

When individuals form interest-groups, vote or pay taxes, they change their role from non-political to political ones. Great fluctuations in the boundaries of political system take place during the war-time.

(6) The political system lives in environment and outside and beyond that political system, there are other systems or environments. The environment of a political system may be intra-societal as well as extra-societal. A political system is always subject to challenges from its environment. From the environment come energy to activate a system and information with regard to which this system uses this energy. As a political system lives in environment, it is open to influences from it.

(7) Every political system continues to persist even in the face of stresses. It is not necessarily defenceless in the face of disturbances to which it may be subjected. This means that the political system will continue to exist or persist. However, this does not mean that there will be no change of any kind whatever in it. Every political system undergoes changes and a degree of change determines the persistence or failure of the system. A political system receives challenges as well as support from society. It is expected to deal with challenges in such a way that it can maintain itself with the help or support it receives or can manipulate. The political system is a complex cyclical operation. It has its own dynamism. It has a purpose of its own and tries to move towards that. At every stage it may have to face problems of stress and maintenance. Every political system has its own regulatory mechanism.

(8) Apart from being a system in itself, the political system consists of subsystems which are involved in the decision-making process. There are several internal political systems of groups and organisations.

(9) Almond refers to certain characteristics of a political system. Political systems exist everywhere. There is the universality of political system. Every political system performs the same functions though there may be differences in different political systems and their structures. Every political system has some structures. Every political system is mixed in the sense of culture because the system can be more advanced or less advanced. Every political system is multi-functional and performs a number of functions irrespective of the degree of specialisation.

Problems or Challenges to Political System

Almond and Powell refer to four types of problems which a political system faces in the process of political development. Those are the problem of state-building, nation-building, participation and distribution.

(1) As regards the *problem of state-building*, it arises out of external threat or internal threat within the society challenging the very existence of a political system. State-building occurs when the political elites create new structures and organisations designed to penetrate the society in order to regulate behaviour in it and draw a large volume of resources from it. State-building is commonly associated with a significant increase in regulative and extractive capabilities of the political system.

(2) The *problem of nation-building* puts emphasis on the cultural aspect of political development. It involves the process whereby people transfer their commitment and loyalty from smaller tribes, villages or petty principalities to the larger central political system. What is involved is primarily a matter of differentiation of the new roles, structures and sub-systems which penetrate the countryside.

(3) The *problem of participation* is concerned with the increase in the demand of participation in the decision-making process of the political system by various groups in the society.

(4) The *problem of distribution* occurs when there is a rapid increase in the volume and intensity of demands which the political system cannot control or fails to effect the proper distribution of resources among different elements of the population. These four main problems occur in the development of a political system.

Functions of Political System: Input Functions

A political system performs two types of functions viz., input functions and output functions. David Easton classifies *input functions* into two types: *demands and supports*. Almond and Powell classify demands into (1) allocation of goods and services such as demands for more wages and fixation of working hours, opening of educational institutions, provision of recreational facilities, roads and transport; (2) participation in the political system such as the right to vote, to hold office, to petition government bodies and officials and to organise political associations such as pressure groups and political parties; (3) regulation of behaviour such as provision for public safety, control over markets and rules pertaining to marriage, health and sanitation, and (4) communication and information such as demand for affirmation of norms, display of majesty and power of the political system in time of threat or on ceremonial occasions.

Examples of support are: (1) material support such as the payment of taxes or other levies and rendering services as labour on public works or military services; (2) attention paid to government communications and manifestation of respect to public authority, symbols and ceremonials; (3) obedience to laws and regulations and (4) participatory support such as voting, political discussion and other forms or political activity.

According to Gabriel Almond, the input functions are political socialisation and recruitment, interest articulation or selection, interest aggregation and political communications and output functions are rule-making, rule-application and rule-adjudication. The input functions are performed by non-governmental sub-systems by the society and the general environment and the output functions are performed by the government. Though the input functions can be from the general environment, it must pass through a process of conversion into output functions. Inputs and outputs are feed-back to each other.

Political Socialisation

According to Almond, political socialisation is the process of induction into the political culture which leads to the development of a set of attitudes among the members of the system. The process of political socialisation brings change in the patterns of political culture. Political socialisation can be either manifest or latent. It is manifest when it involves the explicit communication of information, values or feelings towards political objects. The civics course in public high schools exemplifies manifest political socialisation. Latent political socialisation is the transmission of non-political attitudes which affect attitudes towards analogous roles and objects in the political system. Such latent political socialisation may occur with particular force in early experience. Latent political socialisation involves many of the most fundamental characteristics of the general culture which may in turn have great effect on the political sphere.

A Political recruitment

Political recruitment is concerned with the recruitment of citizens into the specialised role of the political system. Every political system, whether developed or under-developed, Western or non-Western, has to perform the function of political socialisation and political recruitment. Citizens are recruited into specialised roles of the political system. They are trained in appropriate skills and given political values, expectations and effects. The main concern is to recruit citizen to enable them to play their special role.

Interest articulation

Interest articulation is concerned with the formulation and expression of interest claims and demands for political action. Almond writes, "The process by which individuals and groups make demands upon the political decision-makers, we call interest articulation. It is the first functional step in the political conversion process." As it occurs at the boundary of the political system, the structures which perform the function and the style of their performance determine the character of the boundary between policy and society. Almond refers to four main types of interest articulation structures which are institutional interest groups, non-associational interest groups, anomic interest groups and associational groups. The institutional interest groups include legislatures, political executives, bureaucrats, armies, churches etc. Non-associational interest groups include kinship and lineage groups, ethnic, regional, religious, status and class groups. They often perform the articulation function intermittently and informally. Anomic interest groups are concerned with spontaneous breakthrough into the political system from society riots, demonstrations and the like. Although anomic interest groups articulate interest, they may end up by transferring power (recruitment), changing the Constitution (rule-making) and freeing political prisoners (rule-application). The associational groups include specialised structures like trade unions, businessmen's organisation, professional associations, civic associations, educational associations etc. They are formed to represent explicitly demands and channelling them to the other political structures, parties, legislatures, bureaucrats etc. Interest articulation is important because it marks the boundary between society and the political system. If groups within society do not find open channels to express their interests and needs, those demands are likely to remain unsatisfied. They may erupt in violence or may require suppression by the elite. It is through interest articulation that the conflicts inherent in the political culture and social structure become evident. The manner of expression either intensifies the conflict or reconciles or mitigates it.

Interest Aggregation

The function of converting demands into general policy alternatives is called interest aggregation. It is achieved either by the formulation of general policies in which interests which have been articulated may be combined, accommodated and compromised or by the recruitment of political personnel who are more or less committed to a particular pattern or policy. Political parties constitute the main instrument of interest aggregation. Pressure groups and parties in developed modern systems have distinctive and regulative functions, the first for articulation and the second for aggregation. In some systems, the aggregation function may be performed by the legislature, the bureaucracy, the media of communications, the interest groups specially of the general or civic type and also by political parties.

Political Communication

All functions are performed by means of communication. Almond compares political communication with the circulation of blood which he describes as the medium through which other functions in the political system are performed. To quote him, "It is not the blood but what it contains that nourishes the system. The blood is the neutral medium carrying claims, protests and demands through the veins to the heart, and from the heart through the arteries flow the outputs of rules, regulations and adjudications in response to the claims and demands." They determine the flow of information between society and the political system. According to Almond, "In modern systems, some media of communication have developed a vocational ethic of neutral or adjective communication and performs functions separately from the other political systems in the homogeneous political cultures and autonomous and differentiated structures of interest articulation and aggregation have to the greatest extent developed autonomous and differentiated media of communication." Political communication is the crucial boundary maintenance function. "Autonomy is the media which makes for free flow of information from society to polity and from one political structure to another as well as an open feed-back from output to input again. It can communicate the articulation of interest emanating from political parties, legislatures and bureaucracies which themselves can correct the actions of interest groups." On the basis of various media communications, one can compare the political systems of different countries.

OUTPUT FUNCTIONS

(1) Rule making

The output functions are rule-making, rule-application and rule-adjudication. (1) *Rule-making* was previously known as legislation. The new name is preferred because it refers to a specialised structure and explicit process as legislation. Rule-making goes on in every type of government whether it is democracy, dictatorship or monarchy. It is exercised by the legislature or Parliament in a democracy.

According to Almond, the problem of identifying the rule-making structures in political system is one of specifying the whole set of agencies and institutions involved in the process, determining the kind of things they do, the way they do them and how they interact to produce general rules. Almond writes, "The rules must be made in certain ways and by specific institutions and with certain kinds of limitations."

(2) Rule-application

By *Rule-application function* we mean the enforcement of rules made by the rule-making authority in one form or the other. In modern times, rules are executed by officials who require a very high degree of administrative capacity. The role of bureaucracy has considerably increased. Max Weber says that bureaucratization is the very essence of the political modernisation process. The view of Karl Friedrich is that bureaucracy is the core of modern government. Gabriel Almond writes, "In the modern era, most legislation is of a very general kind; in order that it may be effectively enforced, administrative officials must work out regulations or regulatory codes elaborating the policy which has been adopted by the political branches of the government. Usually, the extent to which a general policy is carried out is dependent upon the interpretations which bureaucrats give to it." Again, "In the absence of such a central, directing policy-making agency, the trend towards inertia and decentralisation appears to be inevitable, for in the nature of the case the bureaucratic monster is a technical instrumental monster." The presence of differentiated and well-developed structures for rule-application greatly expand the capability of apolitical system to manipulate its environment.

(3) Rule adjudication

Rule-adjudication was previously known as judicial function. It is the duty of the judiciary to interpret the laws and punish the guilty. It also resolves the conflicts between the government and citizens and among the citizens themselves. Rule-adjudication function involves the process of making authoritative decisions whether or not rule has been transgressed in a given case. The process of adjudication requires a certain set of settled or presumed rules which are applied to conflict situations in society.

Many have criticised Almond's view of the functions of the political system. According to Meehan, "Almond has not produced a theory, of course, nor even a well-articulated classification scheme. The taxonomy is incomplete and ambiguous."

In his later book entitled "*Comparative Politics: A Developmental Approach*". Almond has modified his previous model and given a new list of functions to be performed by every type of political system. Those are the capability functions, conversion functions and communication functions. The capability functions are the extractive capability, the regulative capability, the distributive capability, symbolic capability and responsive capability. The conversion functions of a political system are interest articulation and interest aggregation. The communication functions are socialisation and recruitment.

The *extractive capability* of a political system is its capability to extract taxes and obedience from the people. It extracts material and human resources from domestic and international environments.

It extracts those resources which are essential for the performance of the political system of a nation. The extraction of service from population depends upon the size of the population, its skills and its motivation. If a nation depends on single material resource such as oil or agriculture, it is difficult for it to maintain a suitable extractive capability.

By the *regulative capability* we mean how far the political system is capable of regulating law and order. For this purpose, legitimate coercion has to be employed. Consumers have to be protected from monopoly pricing in foodgrains and businessmen from unfair practices. There is a limit to the regulatory powers of a political system. In many cases, regulations are enforced according to some procedure which protects the individual so long as he remains within the boundary of law.

The *distributive capability* refers to the distribution of goods and services in society. "It is activity of the political system as dispenser or distributor of benefits among individuals and groups."

Symbolic capability means whether the political system is in a position to get love for its symbols like the national flag, the national anthem, the Constitution etc. Symbolic output includes affirmation of values by elites, display of flags and statements of policy and intent by political leaders.

The *responsive capability* refers to the response of the people to the cause of the political system. The political system is responsible for considering what individuals and groups are demanding. A political demand for certain needs may be met by the political system in the form of a response which not only provides certain immediate benefits, but also institutionalizes the responsiveness of the system in that area.

David Easton on Political System

Before David Easton, political scientists studied only isolated political institutions or areas. That did not lead to a useful study because environments around them were totally ignored. Easton found political system the most suitable unit through which all the political processes and forces could be analysed. He was primarily concerned with showing the relationship between a system and the environment in which it was located. His view was that the political system was constantly receiving from other systems a stream of events and influences that shaped the conditions under which its members acted. Easton put emphasis on the adaptive character of the political system. The view of Easton was that political systems accumulate large repertories of mechanisms by which they try to cope with their environments and thereby regulate their own behaviour, transform their internal structure and even remodel their basic goals.

Equilibrium Analysis

David Easton did not approve of the idea of equilibrium analysis employed by the sociologists. He pointed out two major defects in that view. It attaches too much importance to equilibrium. It does not attach importance to the processes or problems formulated by the processors. The system may have some other goals than that of reaching one or any other point of equilibrium. To quote Easton, "A system need not react to disturbances just by oscillating in the neighbourhood of a prior point of equilibrium or by shifting to a new one. It may cope with the disturbances by seeking to change its environment so that the changes between its environment and itself are no longer stressful; it may seek to insulate itself against any further influences from the environment, or the members of the system may even fundamentally transform their own relationships and modify their own goals and practices so as to improve their chances of handling the inputs from the environment. In these and other ways, a system has thc capacity for creative and constructive regulation of disturbance." Political scientist must concentrate on processing and concerting a variety of influences which flow from the environment into the political system and on the ways in which systems respond to these influences together with the typical notes of response through which systems manage to sustain them.

In spite of his criticism, Easton has given the concept of systematic persistence the central place of his analysis. He has concerned himself mainly with the source of stress and modes of regulating it.

Inputs

The inputs are the pressures of all kinds which are exercised on the system. There are two types of inputs into the political system and those are demands and supports. They are received by the system from the society. A demand is "an expression of opinion that an authoritative allocation with regard to particular subject-matter should or should not be made by those responsible for doing so. Demands are the motive power for the working of a political system. The sources of those demands may be traced to a wide range—from the general public to small groups. They may vary from virtual commands to timid requests. Their means of expression may vary from voting to rioting. Demands may vary in sources, forms and means of expression but they are indications of desires that certain decisions must be made by the political decision-makers. The people make demands upon the political system. A political system has its own way of reacting to those demands.

As regards *support*, no political system can last long without the support of the society. This support may take many forms. It may take the form of obeying or accepting the decisions of the political system. The public may decide that the decisions of the political system are legitimate. A political system receives considerable support from the environment. The support is both overt and covert. Overt supports are forms of action which are clearly and manifestly supported. Covert supports are attitudes and sentiments towards the political system. Support may be for a specific political object or an all-out support to the political community, the regime, or the political authorities holding power at any given time. The political system can adapt itself to the support stress in several ways. That includes change in structures, change in the system of representation, party system etc. Political support declines if the political system fails to deliver the goods. If a substantial number of people are dissatisfied with the achievements of the political system for a substantial length of time, that may result in withdrawal of their support, either partially or completely.

Conversion Process

The manner and mechanism through which a political system converts inputs and responds to the process in the environment is called the conversion process. The conversion mechanism turns inputs into outputs after some process of selection, limitation or rearrangement. The conversion process operates dynamically because the selection can take place over a period of time. The process of conversion depends when the capability of the political system for extraction of resources, regulation and control over individuals and goods, distribution of resources and its capacity for development.

Outputs

The outputs of the political system consist of authoritative decision which are either application or interpretation of rules. Those decisions affect the environment of the political system. Outputs may help to maintain support for the political system. The political system maintains itself partly through its own regulatory mechanism and partly through the support which it can generate in the society.

The Feed-back

Feed-back is a dynamic process through which information about the performance of the system is communicated back to it. That affects the subsequent behaviour of the system. Information is essential to the authorities who take the decision. It is conducive to the persistence of the system. Through feed-back loop, the system may take advantage of adjusting its future behaviour. Without information about what is happening in the system, the authorities have to operate in the dark. The feed-back loop has a number of parts, worthy of detailed investigation. It consists of production of outputs by the authorities, a response by the members of the society to these outputs, the communication of information about the response to the authorities and possible action by the authorities. This is a cyclic process. According to Easton, outputs are not the terminal points. They feedback into the system which in turn shapes the subsequent behaviour. Thus, the feedback has a profound influence on the capacity of the system to persist and to cope with the stress.

David Easton has illustrated his concept of the political system with the help of the following diagram. His view is that the political system, functioning with the general social environment largely consists of the input and output structures and conversion process. One must study all those aspects analytically to understand a political system.

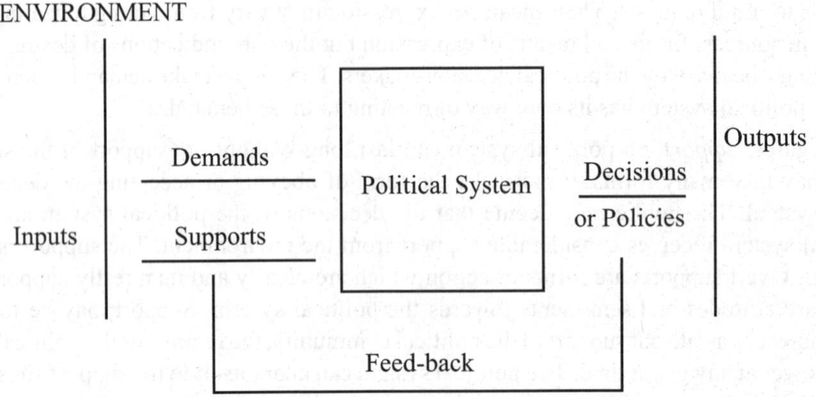

Political System and Social System

There is a very close relationship between political system and social system. Political system cannot exist without the social system. It is a sub-system of the social system. The social system is a broad concept which includes all the subsystems like the political system, economic system and others. It covers all aspects of human life. It influences all other sub-systems. Political system is influenced to a large extent by the social system. Ratzenhofer writes, "The state in its early stages was more of a social-political institution. The political is embedded in social and if political science remains distinct from sociology, it will be because the cause of the field calls for specialised and not because there are any well-defined boundaries marking it off from sociology. The political system of a country depends upon its social system. The social environment determines the nature of politics.

Various social elements affect the political system. The culture of the society determines the nature of the political system to a large extent. It is true in the case of a democratic society. The political system operates within a certain framework. Through a study of culture, it is possible to locate the special attitudes and propensities. The cultural factors make positive contribution for determining the nature of a political system. Economic factors also play their part to determine the nature of a political system. The main function of the political system today is to improve the economic condition of the people. It must utilise the natural resources properly and allocate them among the competitive groups and individuals impartially. Geographical factors also influence the political system of a country. If the geographical conditions are not proper, they can create a problem for political system. Geography influences the political institutions of a country. The view of Treitschke is that direct democracy in Switzerland is due to the fact that, that country is mountainous. The strength of German army is due to the geographical conditions of the country. Demography deals with the distribution of social characteristics in the population including vital statistics, in order to find out patterns of those characteristics and their explanation. Demographic variables like education, income, occupation and population movements affect the functioning of a political system. Social and psychological factors also exercise their influence on the political system. The social values of a society influence its political system.

Likewise, the political system of a country influences its social system. The social system is reformed by the political system.

There are certain differences between the political system and social system. There is a difference of antiquity between them. The social system is prior to the political system and creates the political system. They also differ in the matter of scope. The scope of the social system is wider than that of the political system. Social system includes all aspects of human life but political system is mainly concerned with politics. Social system regulates all aspects of human relations, whether those are organised or unorganised, conscious or unconscious. The political system is concerned only with the political relations. It is mainly concerned with power. The view of David Easton is that the major function of the political system is the authoritative allocation of values with threat or actual use of severe deprivations to make this allocation binding on all. Power is not an attribute of the social system. It cannot compel its members to follow its rules.

Political System and Economic System

There is a close relation between the two. In ancient society, no distinction was made between the two and the economic system was not independent of the political system but a part of it. Even now they are closely related and influence each other. If the economic system of a country is not sound, it has its adverse effect on the political system. Both are inter-dependent.

Karl Marx has laid great emphasis on the economic system. According to him, politics has its roots in the material conditions of life. The system of economic production is the foundation on which the institutional and ideological superstructure of society is built. Political policies are generally influenced by the system of production and distribution. Likewise, the political system influences the economic system. The political system looks after the economic problems of the people. Both are complementary to each other.

There are certain differences between the two. The scope of the political system is much wider than the economic system which is mainly concerned with production and distribution and has not much concern with political, cultural or social activities. There is also a difference in their approach. The economic system deals mainly with commodities and the political system with human beings. The political system is mainly concerned with the element of power, but power is not an attribute of the economic system. The political system deals with political values and the economic system with the fixation of prices of the different commodities. The political system is a set of interactions but the economic system is a set of institutions. Nowadays, the economic system is regulated by the political system everywhere.

SUGGESTED READINGS

Almond, G. and J.S. Coleman (Eds.) : *The Politics of the Developing Areas, Princeton University Press, 1960*

Almond, G.A. and G.B. Powell : *Comparative Politics: A Developmental Approach.*

Chang, S.H.M. : *The Marxian Theory of the State, New York, 1965.*

Charlesworth, C.J. : *Contemporary Political Analysis, New York, 1968.*

Dahl, Robert A. : *A Preface to Democratic Theory, Chicago, 1967.*

Dahl, R.A. : *Modern Political Analysis, Prentic-Hall, 1963.*

Easton, David : *The Political System — An Inquiry into the State of Political Science, New York, 1971.*

Easton, David : *A Systems Analysis of Political Life, New York, 1965.*

Kaplan, Morton A : *Systems and Process in International Relations, New York. 1957.*

Kuhn, Thomas : *The Structure of Scientific Revolution, Chicago, 1962.*

Mackenzie, W.J.M. : *Political and Social Sciences, Penguin, 1967.*

Miller, James G. : *Living Systems, New York, 1978.*

Poulantzas, N. : *Political Power and Social Class, 1972.*

Singer, J. David : *A General Systems Taxonomy for Political Science, New York, 1971.*

Strauss, Leo : *Essays on Scientific Study of Politico, New York, 1962.*

Wiseman, H.V. : *Political Systems, London, 1966.*

9

CHAPTER

Political Culture and Political Socialization

The most significant development of the post-World War II period was the rise of a new approach to the study of political science which gave birth to a large number of new concepts like the political system, political culture, political socialisation, power, authority, influence, legitimacy, political modernisation and political development etc. To know the working of any political system, it is necessary to know the political culture of that nation. Political culture is the sum total of the beliefs, attitudes, values and behaviour of the people towards a political system.

The concept of political culture tries to integrate psychology and sociology to make it possible to apply it to dynamic political analysis, psychological methods and sociological techniques for computing attitudes in mass societies. A study of political culture enables us to understand the political ideals and standards of behaviour people have set for themselves in a polity. It constitutes an important link between the behaviour of individuals and political events. Wars, election campaigns, laws, acts of government officials etc. affect the behaviour of individuals and groups and their behaviour is also influenced by their own reaction to events which are interpreted according to attitudes, beliefs and values. Political culture does not include formal or informal political institutions, governments, political parties, pressure groups, lobbies etc. Sidney Verba writes, "It refers not to what is happening in the world of politics, but what people believe about these happenings. And these beliefs can be of several kinds: they can be empirical beliefs about what the actual state of political life is; they can be beliefs as to the goals or values that ought to be pursued in political life; and these beliefs may have an important expressive or emotional dimension."

Learning Objectives

- Definition of Political Culture
- Political Culture and Sub-Culture
- Political Culture and Change
- Dimensions of Political Culture
- Factors which Mould Political Culture
- Different Kinds of Political Culture
- Mixed Political Culture
- Civic political Culture
- Secular Political Culture
- Ideological Political Culture
- Homogeneous Political Culture
- Fragmented Political Culture
- Determinants of Political Culture
- Measurement of Political Culture
- Political Culture and Symbols
- Usefulness of Study of Political Cultures
- Drawback in Theory of Political Culture
- Political Socialisation
- Definition and Meaning of Political Socialisation
- Aims of Political Socialisation
- Types of Political Socialisation
- Process of Political Socialisation
- Agents of Political Socialisation
- Importance of Political Socialisation
- Suggested Readings

Definition of Political Culture

The concept of political culture owes its origin to Gabriel A. Almond's observation that every political system is embedded in a particular pattern of orientation to political actions. Political culture, like culture in general, is learned behaviour. In a certain political community, it stands for the pattern of individual attitudes and orientation towards politics of that community among the members of polity. Political behaviour is not a random phenomenon. Every individual citizen learns and steadily internalizes within his personality the knowledge and feelings about the on-going politics in his community. Lucian Pye writes, "The notion of political culture assumes that the attitudes, sentiments and cognitions that inform and govern political behaviour in any society are not just random congeries but represent coherent pattern which fit together and are mutually reinforcing. In spite of the great potentialities for diversity in political orientations, in any particular community there is a limited and distinct political culture which gives meaning, predictability and form to the political process."

According to Eric Rowe, "A political culture is a pattern of individual values, beliefs and emotional attitudes." Ray Macridis says, "Political culture means commonly shared goals and commonly accepted rules." Jalcott Parson writes, "Political culture is concerned with orientation towards political objectives." Dennis Kavanagh observes, "For our purpose we may regard the political culture as a shorthand expression to denote emotional and attitudinal environment within which the political system operates. It is the particular pattern of orientations in which according to Gabriel Almond, every political system is embedded.......Orientations are pre-dispositions to political action and are determined by such factors as traditions, historical memories, motives, norms, emotions and symbols." According to Almond and Powell, "Political culture consists of attitudes, beliefs, values and skills which are current in an entire population as well as those special propensities and patterns which may be found within separate parts of that population." Political culture "refers not to what is happening in the world of politics but what people believe about these happenings."

According to Lucian Pye and Sydney Verba, "Political culture is a recent term which seeks to make explicit and systematic much of the understanding associated with long standing concepts as political ideology, national ethos and spirit, national political psychology and fundamental values of a people." Rose and Dogan define the concept of political culture as "a convenient shorthand way of referring to the values, beliefs and emotions that give meaning to political life. In analysing political culture, one can conveniently distinguish outlooks towards the national community, towards specific political institutions and offices, towards particular incumbents of such offices and towards the policy outputs of the system or government. The sum of individual beliefs, values and emotions constitutes the political culture of a country. While analytically separate from the total culture which includes attitudes towards such things as family relations and economic activity, the political culture tends to be affected by general social norms." Beer and Ulam write, "Certain aspects of the general culture of a society are especially concerned with how government ought to be conducted and what it shall try to do. This sector of culture we call political culture." Samuel Beer writes, "The components of political culture are values, beliefs and emotional attitudes about how government ought to be conducted and about what it should do."

According to Davies and Lewis, "The concept of political culture is an attempt to find one rubric to include what in the past have been variously described as attitudes to politics, political values, ideologies, national character and culture ethos... Political cultures are measured in terms of orientation to political action which refers to the knowledge the individual has of political objects, events, actions and issues; whether or not he invests them with any emotional and significance; how he evaluates them and whether he is sufficiently stirred to action by them. Political culture is thus the pattern of orientations to political actions within any given society."

Heinz Eulau refers to political behaviour or groups and individuals. To quote him, "Political culture refers to the patterns that can be inferred from the political behaviour of groups as well as the beliefs, guiding principles, purposes and values that the individuals in a group, whatever its size, hold in common." In studying political culture, efforts are made to use behavioural form of analysis for dealing with political ideology, legitimacy, sovereignty, nationhood and the rule of law.

The International Encyclopaedia of Social Sciences defines political culture in these words: "Political culture is the set of attitudes, beliefs and sentiments which give order and meaning to a political process and which provide the underlying assumptions and rules that govern behaviour in a political system. It encompasses both the political ideals and the operating norms of a polity. Political culture is thus the manifestation in aggregate forms of the psychological and subjective dimensions of politics."

Political culture is only a part of the general culture. It includes only the set of political beliefs held by an individual and those beliefs are only a part of the totality of his beliefs. The view of Dennis Kavanagh is that political culture may be regarded as sub-culture influenced by the general culture.

Political Culture and Sub-Culture

According to Alan R. Ball, "In stable societies, the political culture is homogeneous, but where differences between one group and others are marked, there is said to exist a political sub-culture. Political sub-culture is not a distinct set of attitudes, beliefs and values, but a set of attitudes, some of which are in common with other sub-cultures." Austin Ranney observes, "No nation's political culture is evenly diffused among all its social strata and political groups. Its components are found in varying strength in different segments of the population, and some segments may hold views shared little or not at all by others. When the views of a particular segment vary significantly in content or intensity from those of the nation as a whole, the segment is said to have its own distinctive political sub-cult me." In India, we find a number of political sub-cultures. The culture of the elite is different from that of the masses. The Blacks or Negroes in the United States constitute a political sub-culture. The political culture of the officers in France is different from that of the politicians.

Political Culture and Change

The political culture of a nation is never static and continues to change with the passage of time. Cultural change is not a process or goal unique to new states only. Several societies possessing well-established national identities are beset by the problem of cultural transformation.

Dimensions of Political Culture

According to Almond and Powell, the concept of political culture involves three components of individual orientations: cognitive orientations, effective orientations and evaluative orientations. Cognitive orientations mean knowledge of and belief about the political system, its role, its objects and officials, its inputs and outputs. Effective orientations mean feelings of attachment, involvement, rejection and the like about the political system, its personnel and performance and about other political objects. Evaluative orientations mean judgments and opinions about political objects which usually involve applying value standards to political objects and events.

The view of Robert Dahl is that there can be five types of orientations in a political culture: Orientation of problem solving means how people think about their natural problems and how they face them. Orientation to collective action means whether people have the tendency to work collectively in a political system or not. Orientation to political system means the attitude of the people towards their political system and whether they like it or not. Orientation to other people means whether the people have faith in others or not. Self-orientation means whether the people are in a position of making original proposals or they are just moved by the opinions of others.

Factors which Mould Political Culture

According to Lucian Pye, "Political culture is shaped by the general historical experiences of a country as also by the private personal experiences of the individuals. It is because the individuals first became the members of society and then of the polity. Political culture is gradually built on the cumulative orientations of the people towards their political processes. Each generation inherits attitudes and beliefs towards politics partly from the earlier generation and partly it is formulated as a reaction to the on-going politics. In other words, political culture is a product of the learning process and the actual experiences of the people." Political culture can be found only in men's minds, in the pattern of action, feeling and reflection which they have internalised and made part of their very existence. It is true that we cannot deny the importance of political events such as elections, party competition during the elections, role of pressure groups, group behaviour, changing social basis of the elite, governmental performance, stability of government and working of political institutions. The political culture studies the interaction between the beliefs, the political events and the governmental structure. If the Constitution of a country is not according to its political culture, it has to be changed. The Weimar Constitution of Germany of 1919 failed because it did not coincide with the political culture of that country. Political culture not only affects the Constitution but also political ideologies. The Fascism of Italy was different from that of Germany and Spain. Likewise, the Communism of the Soviet Union is different from that of China. According to Almond, every political system is embedded in a particular pattern of orientation to political action. Political culture provides controlling guidelines for effective political action. It provides the underlying assumptions and rules that govern behaviour in the political system. It encompasses both the political ideals and the operating norms of a polity. Political culture is thus the manifestation in the aggregate form of the psychological and subjective dimension of politics. Political culture is to the political system what culture is to the social system.

Different Kinds of Political Culture

According to Alan R. Ball, political culture can be classified "according to whether members of a society take an active role in the political process and expect benefits from governmental activity or whether there is a passive relationship in which individuals know very little about government activity and do not expect to share in the decision-making process."

Almond and Powell have classified political culture in three ways: parochial political culture, subject political culture and participant "political culture. (1) By *parochial political culture* we mean those people who have little or no awareness of their political system. Such individuals are found in every society. Their number is more in a traditional society or in a backward society. According to Davies and Lewis, the parochial political culture "exists in simple traditional societies in which there is very little specialisation and where actors fulfil a combination of political, economic and religious rules simultaneously." The view of Almond and Verba is that "a parochial orientation involves the comparative absence of expectations of change initiated by the political system. The parochial expects nothing from the political system." The political cultures of the states in Central Africa are mainly parochial.

(2) According to Almond and Verba, *subject political culture* exists where "one finds a high frequency of orientations to the differentiated political system and to its outputs, but very little to its inputs or the self as a political actor. The relationship is passive. When there are democratic (input) structures, the effective and normative reaction may be against them, as for example with the French Royalists." Those citizens who are not aware of numerous government roles are called political subjects. Such individuals may have no specific knowledge of the ways in which they can influence the political system and have no understanding of the infrastructure of society. Their image of themselves as initiators of demands remains diffused and undeveloped, perhaps limited to some

vague notions of seeing the local chief or family head if problems arise. These individuals can be called political subjects.

(3) *Participant political culture exists* in highly developed societies where the people take an active part in political life. In the words of Almond and Powell, "The members of the society tend to be explicitly oriented to the system as a whole and to both the political and administrative structures; in other words, to both input and output aspects of the political system. Individual members of the participant polity may be favourably or unfavourably oriented towards an activist role of the self in the polity, though their feelings and evaluations of such a role may vary from acceptance to rejection." Political participants are those individuals who are aware of the structure and process of their political system and are engaged in making demands from the political system and are involved in the making of decisions. The political participants develop a set of specific attitudes towards the political structure such as parties and interest groups and towards the roles they can play in these structures.

Mixed Political Culture

Individuals with parochial and subject political culture may be found in predominantly participant political cultures. A single individual may combine in himself all the three aspects. The mixture of types will have a profound influence upon the ability of the nation to support a democratic system. Almond and Verba refer to three types of systematically mixed political cultures: parochial-subject political culture, subject-participant political culture and participant-parochial political culture. In most of the societies, these varieties of political culture are found in the mixed form.

Civic political Culture

In addition to the above-mentioned political cultures, there are some other types of political culture. Civic political culture exists in a society in which decision-making powers are vested in a particular elite and the people do not participate directly. They express their sentiments only through their representatives who are responsible to them. Such a type of political culture exists in a democratic society.

Secular Political Culture

This type of political culture exists where the people are secular, rational and analytical. Secular culture is one where traditional orientations and attitudes give way to more dynamic decision-making processes involving gathering of information, evaluation of information, laying out of alternative course of action, selection of course of action from among possible courses and means whereby one tests whether or not a given course of action is producing the intended consequences.

Ideological Political Culture

This type of political culture exists in a society where one particular ideology is encouraged and the people are not free to accept the ideology of their liking. They are compelled to abide by a particular ideology. Such is the case in the Soviet Union and Communist China.

Homogeneous Political Culture

This type of political culture exists where the people hold similar views about political objectives and the means for their attainment. The leaders of the different political parties have the same ideology. Such a thing exists in the United States and England.

Fragmented Political Culture

This type of political culture exists in a country where the people do not hold similar views about political objectives and the means for their attainment. Such a thing exists in a country where there are many political parties. This type of political culture is to be found in France and Italy.

Determinants of Political Culture

Political continuity, colonial domination, geography, ethnic differences, religious differences and socio-economic structure play an important part in developing political cultures. Political continuity plays an important part in the development of political culture. The political culture of Britain has been influenced by political continuity in that country. If there had been no political continuity for a long time, there was no scope for the development of the particular political culture in that country. Unlike Britain, the political structure in France was shaken by the French Revolution of 1789 and the events that followed. A similar thing happened in Russia as a result of the Revolution of 1917.

Political culture is also affected by colonial domination and imperialist control. The political culture of India has been influenced by the British rule in India for about two centuries. Likewise, the political culture in Africa, Indonesia, China and Sri Lanka has been influenced by foreign domination. A particular type of colonial domination has its own effect. We have the example of Congo where the Belgian authorities created a particular type of political culture different from that created by British domination in other countries. The geographical factor also moulds the political culture of a country. The insular position of England created a political culture different from that of the countries on the Continent. Likewise, the United States has developed a political culture different from that of England and other European countries.

Ethnic differences also mould the political culture of a country. If there had been no racial differences in Africa, the political culture of the countries in that region would have been different. However, racial differences can be removed by mutual understanding and tolerance. Religious homogeneity or differences have their effect on the political culture of a country. The religious differences in India aye affected its political culture. Those differences led to the partition of 1947. The same religious differences mould the political culture of India even now. The Sikhs in the Punjab are an outstanding example.

The political culture of a country is also influenced by its socio-economic structure. These differences explain the differences of political cultures of the countries.

Measurement of Political Culture

The political culture of a community can be measured to ascertain the general run of orientation towards politics in that country. There are many difficulties and limitations. The primary tools of measurement are the public opinion and attitudes survey. Individual cases can be studied through interviews and other techniques. Writings and public speeches offer clues to the understanding of a political culture.

Political Culture and Symbols

Certain symbols are associated with political attitudes, emotions, beliefs and values of the people in a country. Those are of great importance to all as they create a sense of loyalty, obedience and oneness among them. The head of the state may symbolise the emotions, values and beliefs of the people. Thus, the King or Queen of Britain or the President of the United States may symbolise national pride, hopes and aspirations of the people. A great national leader with a charisma may serve as a great national symbol. Such was the case of Mahatma Gandhi in India and President De Gaulle in France. The national flags like the Union Jack of Britain, the Stars and Stripes of the United States and the Tricolour flag of India serve as symbols of the nation. Certain ceremonies like the coronation ceremony in Britain or oath-taking ceremony of the Presidents of the United States and India are important from a national point of view. Party symbols have also their effect. Party symbols like the Hammer and Sickle in the Soviet Union and the Swastika in Nazi Germany had their influence on political culture.

Portraits of great political leaders serve as great national symbols. Examples are the portraits of Mahatma Gandhi in India, John Kennedy in the United States, Lenin in the Soviet Union, Mao Tse-tung in China, Kemal Pasha in Turkey and Nasser in Egypt. Great historical events also have their own effect. Example are the Dandi March of Mahatma Gandhi in 1930 in connection with the Salt Satyagraha, the Russian Revolution of 1917, the Jallianwala Bagh tragedy of 1919 etc.

Usefulness of Study of Political Cultures

A scholar of political culture brings together in his study the whole political system and individual psychology. Political culture enables him to know the connection between private socialisation processes and the working of public institutions. He comes to know the dynamics of continuity and changes taking place in the political system.

A study of political culture enables us to understand the connection between social and economic factors on the one hand and political developments on the other. It tells us a lot about the non-political dimensions of life and helps us to realise the impact of those dimensions on the political behaviour of man.

A study of political culture helps us to understand the process of political socialisation and how political culture is transmitted from one generation to another.

A study of political culture enables us to understand how laws and the Constitution are observed by individuals and groups. With different political cultures and political ideologies, the people in two political systems observe and evaluate laws and the Constitution differently. A Constitution may fail in one country on account of the political culture of that country and likewise it may succeed in another country on account of its different political culture. The political cultures of India on the one hand and the United States and Britain on the other are different and hence federalism has succeeded in the United States but not so well in India. Likewise, parliamentary system functions smoothly in Britain and not so smoothly in India.

A study of political culture helps us to understand the attitude of citizens to the political system. It enables us to understand why particular types of demands are made, how those are expressed and how there is a response to them. Our ability to describe and analyse the inter-actions between the political system and its culture is increased.

A study of political culture enables us to understand why similar phenomena in various countries do not produce similar results. That explains why the labour movement is aggressive in France and not in England.

A study of political culture may provide us with a valuable conceptual tool by means of which we can bridge the micro-macro gap of political theory. It helps us to locate the special aptitudes and propensities for political behaviour among different parts of the population.

The political culture approach has made political science a more complete social science through its insistence on a combined micro-macro approach. It has encouraged political scientists to take up the study of social and cultural factors which were responsible for giving a political culture of a country its broad shape. It helps us to combine the study of the rational factors which shape the actions of individuals to a large extent with the more latent, irrational determinants of behaviour which could be subjected to empirical research. Political culture helps us to understand why different political societies inevitably move in different directions of political development or find themselves suffering from socio-economic and political constraints which force them to move towards political decay.

Drawback in Theory of Political Culture

The theory of political culture is very attractive and is used by many political scientists to explain many things which it is not capable of doing so. Dennis Kavanagh writes, "It has been used to cover so many disparate phenomena that it is easily used as a residual factor." The theory gives sweeping explanations of diverse political behaviour. It is used to supply the missing links.

There is a tendency to de-emphasize the influence of political variables with reference to the performance of government. Critics also point out that it is not possible to give a full picture of the political culture of a system as the people do not have clear political opinions or attitudes. Political researchers dealing with political culture may give a picture of political beliefs and attitudes in a country and make certain forecasts about political performance, but their actual performance may be different from their expectations. Basic concepts about political culture are not fully worked out and hence it is difficult to test satisfactorily and completely the theories given by the advocates of political culture. The theory of political culture is hardly better than a new label for old ideas. It is too early for the advocates of political culture to claim so many virtues for their theory. The view of Davies and Lewis is that the concept of political culture is an attempt to find one rubric to include what in the past have been variously described as attitudes to politics, political values, ideologies, national character, cultural ethos etc. None of these terms is sufficiently broad to provide a basis for classifying political system and each one of them is relevant to the study of comparative politics. However, it cannot be denied that the concept of political culture has made significant contribution to the development of political science.

Political Socialisation

Political socialisation is one of the major concepts of modern political science. It is important for the understanding of political stability of a country. The term socialisation has been defined in a number of ways. According to Gillin and Gillin, "By the term socialisation we mean process by which individual develops into a functioning member of the group according to its standards conforming to the modes, observing its traditions and adjusting himself to the social situations he meets, sufficient will to command the tolerance, if not admiration of his fellows." Ogburns writes, "Socialisation is the process by which the individual learns to conform to the norms of the group." According to MacIver, "It is the process by which social beings establish wider and profounder relationships with one another, in which they become more bound up with and more dependent on one another, in which they develop the sense of their obligation to and responsibility for others and build up the complex structure of nearer and wider association." Bogardus says, "Socialisation is the process of working together or developing group responsibility of being guided by the welfare needs of others." The view of Cooley is that socialisation is "a social process through which an individual develops his own self by learning the norms and by knowing about his own self from others."

Definition and Meaning of Political Socialisation

According to Almond and Powell, "Political socialisation is the process by which political cultures are maintained and changed." Individuals are inducted into the political culture and orientations towards political object are formed through the process of political socialisation. Socialisation is a continuous process. From his childhood an individual is exposed to various life experiences and learning situations which keep on moulding his ideas about politics.

Easton and Dennis defined political socialisation as "those development process by which persons acquire political orientation and pattern of behaviour." The view of Austin Ranney is that "political socialisation generally means socialisation of masses, the process by which ordinary people develop their attitudes toward their political system." Roberta Siegel says that political socialisation" is the gradual learning of the norms, attitudes and behaviour acceptable to the on-going political systems." Allan R. Ball defines political socialisation as establishment and development of attitudes to beliefs about the political system. Dennis Kavanagh writes, "Political socialisation is the term used to describe the process whereby the individual learns and develops orientations to politics." Stephen L. Wasby says that the subject-matter of political socialisation is the process by which people acquire political values not simply during active political participation but also the period before they engage in an explicitly political activity. Political socialisation covers all political teaching, whether formal or informal, whether deliberate or unplanned, at every stage of the cycle of life including not only explicitly political learning which affects political behaviour, but also the learning of politically irrelevant social attitudes. It is a learning process by which individuals are trained to become well-functioning members of a political community.

According to Rush, "Political socialisation is a process by which an individual becomes acquainted with the political systems which determine his reaction to political phenomenon."

Aims of Political Socialisation

The main aim of political socialisation is the transmission of political values from one generation to another. Political socialisation shapes and transmits a nation's political culture. It maintains, transforms and sometimes creates the political culture of a people. It maintains a political culture by successfully transmitting it from an old generation to a new one. Political socialisation introduces values, norms and orientations in the minds of the individuals so that they develop trust in their political system and leave their imprints on the minds of their successors. Sometimes, a country which has just won its independence may try to find a new political system for itself and create a new political culture for itself and maintain the same. Such a process of maintaining, transforming and creating a political culture is going on in all those countries of Asia and Africa which have won their independence recently. The process of political socialisation goes on throughout the life of the individual. Political beliefs and attitudes developed in youth may change in old age on account of contact with new education, changing social environment, new experiences in life and performance of every political party.

Types of Political Socialisation

According to Almond and Powell, political socialisation is of two types, manifest and latent. Political socialisation is in its manifest or direct form when "it involves the explicit communication of information, values of feelings towards political objects." Examples of manifest political socialisation are the teaching of civics in the United states or India or the compulsory study of Marxism-Leninism in the Soviet Union. Latent political socialisation is "the transmission of non-political attitudes which affect attitudes towards analogous roles and objects in the political system." Such orientation affects his attitudes towards political leaders and his fellow citizens.

Process of Political Socialisation

The process of political socialisation generally operates in a casual or quiet manner without the people being aware of it. A child who is born is not a socialised creature. He becomes socialised as a result of a learning process. Such learning is not limited to the acquisition of appropriate knowledge about society norms but requires that the individual so makes these norms his own, internalises them, that to him they appear to be right, just and moral. The view of Allan R. Ball is that political socialisation is not a process confined to childhood but continues throughout life. It begins with childhood, continues in adolescence and adulthood and ends with the death of man in his old age. Almond and Powell say that the process of socialisation goes on continuously throughout the life of an individual. Frank and Elizabeth Estana write, "The process of political socialisation starts from the time when the child becomes aware of a wide environment, feels increasingly perceptive in response to particular situations and comes to have an outlook that becomes increasingly coherent and total where before it was fragmented and limited. It is at this stage that the general attitude of the children towards authority, obedience, resistance, cooperation, aggression etc. is created. What a child gets from the family is developed in the school."

Easton and Dennis refer to four stages in the process of political socialisation at the childhood stage. Those are recognition of authority through particular individuals such as parents, policemen and President of the country, distinction between public and private property, recognition of impersonal political institutions like the national legislature, judiciary and voting behaviour and distinction between political institutions and persons engaged in the activities associated with those institutions. Rush and Altnoft write, "The knowledge, values and attitudes acquired during the childhood and adolescence will be measured against the experience of adult life; to suggest otherwise is to suggest a static political behaviour. If the process of adult socialisation tends to reinforce those of childhood and adolescence, the degree of change may be limited to that of increasing conservatism with age; but where conflict occurs, then radical changes in political behaviour may result. Such conflicts may have its roots in early socialisation, but it may also be attributable to the experience of later socialisation."

Sometimes the process of socialisation may be discontinued. It may be due to migration from one country to another or from the village to the city or vice versa. Migration from village to city results in discontinuity because their early socialisation does not help them. The problems to be faced by them in the cities are different. The nature of political socialisation in countries having dictatorships is different from those which have a democratic form of government.

Agents of Political Socialisation

Political socialisation is the process by which the values, beliefs and emotions of a political culture are passed on to succeeding generations. The process starts at an early age and continues throughout life. The main agents of political socialisation are the family, the school, peer groups, employment experiences, mass media, government and party agencies, religious institutions and symbols.

(1) The first and foremost agent of socialisation is the *family.* This primary organisation has an authority, structure and a decision-making process. The influences of childhood have a decisive impact on his orientation towards authority and obedience in other spheres including the political sphere. In the family, mother, father, brothers and sisters exercise their influence over the child. Almond and Verba observe, "An early experience in participation in decision-making can increase the child's sense of political competence, provide him with skill for political interactions and thus enhances the probability of his active participation in the political system when he becomes an adult."

(2) The *educational institutions* exercise the strongest possible influence upon the child. Children getting education in a particular institution may develop a particular kind of frame of mind. The selection of courses in the schools assumes great importance. Alien R. Barec says that "the educational system has important effects on the process of socialisation. The values imparted by school and universities may not be the result of direct political indoctrination, but are nonetheless important." Almond and Verba point out that the more extensive an individual's education, the more likely he is to be aware of the impact of government to follow politics, to have more political information, to possess a wider range of opinions on political matters, to engage in political discussions with a wider range of people, to feel a greater ability to influence political affairs, to be a member of political organisations and express confidence in his social environments and exhibit feeling of trust.

(3) The *peer group* is a group of people approximately of the same age, sharing similar problems. The view of Austin Ranney is that "in addition to parents and teachers, most of the people spend a great deal of their lives in the company of peer groups of people outside their families, who are

approximately of the same age and share similar status, problems and concerns." James S. Coleman writes that in developed societies like the United States and Sweden, the socialising influence of parents and teachers begins to wane in early adolescence and from then onwards, peer groups become increasingly important influences on political attitudes and behaviour.

(4) Another agent of socialisation is the *employment experiences.* Political orientations are shaped through participation in unions, collective bargaining, demonstrations and other forms of decision-making. Informal groups of employees exert influence on the attitude of their members towards political objects and events.

(5) Another agent is the *mass media.* Radio, television, newspapers and other forms of mass media provide information about political happenings. The manipulation of media is often resorted to in different countries to influence and change the political orientation of citizens. Austin Ranney writes, "In all nations with technologically mass communications, the media play a direct role in shaping the basic orientations as well as the specific opinions of most people." By reading newspaper reports, by listening to radio talks and seeing television films, people develop taste as well as distaste for certain norms and values. Lucian Pye observes, "Socialisation through the mass media is best short run technique available and it is crucial to modernisation."

(6) Individual orientation to politics is often conditioned by direct contact with the political system. His relationship with *political parties and pressure groups and influential political leaders* determine his attitudes towards politics. Almond and. Powell write, "No matter how positive the view of political system which has been influenced by family and school, when a citizen is ignored by his party, cheated by his police, starved in the bread line and finally conscripted into the army, his views on the political realm are likely to be altered. Direct formal and informal relationships with specific elites in the political system are inevitably a powerful force in shaping orientations of individuals to the system." Political parties are also important agents of political socialisation. Through political propaganda, electioneering, presenting their views in written and spoken language, by recruiting people and by articulating and aggregating their political interests, political parties become direct agents of political socialisation.

(7) *Religious institutions* also play an important role in political socialisation. The effect of the Church on political attitudes "is less apparent when reinforces other socialising agencies, but the role of Roman Catholicism in many European countries, liberal democratic and totalitarian, offers illustrations of its conflict with both state and education, and is possibly a vital factor in the political behaviour of women in some countries." Religious institutions have played and are playing an important role among the Sikhs in India in general and Punjab in particular. The same can be said of the Muslims in India.

(8) *Symbols* also play an effective role in political socialisation. The observation of birth days or martyrdom days of national heroes like Mahatma Gandhi, Bhagat Singh, Subhash Chandra Bose, Lala Lajpat Rai etc. inculcates a new spirit among the youths and they begin to work for the nation.

Importance of Political Socialisation

Political socialisation helps in a comparative study of the political system. Political culture depends largely on political socialisation. From political socialisation, we can know when particular qualities and elements of a political culture grew. It also helps us to understand who the leaders of a particular country are, what qualities they possess and how they are involved in politics in different countries. A study of political socialisation is essential to the understanding of political stability and development.

SUGGESTED READINGS

Almond, G.A. and G.B. Powall	:	*Comparative Politics: A Developmental Approach.* New Delhi-1972.
Ball, Alan	:	*Modem Politics and Government, Macmillan,* 1971.
Eulau, Heinz	:	*The Behavioural Persuasion in Politics, Random House,* 1963.
Hyman, Herbert H.	:	*Political Socialisation, Amerind Publishing Company,* New Delhi, 1972.
Kavanagh, Dennis	:	*Political Culture, Macmillan,* 1972.
Pye, Lucian W. and	:	*Political Culture and Political Development, Princeton University*
Sindey Verba (Eds.)		*Press*, 1965.
Pye, Lucian	:	*Politics, Personality and Nation-buildings,* New Delhi, 1962.

CHAPTER

Power, Authority and Legitimacy

In the words of Robert A. Dahl, "Power, influence and authority are commonplace words that ordinary people share with political practitioners and political theorists. One hears of power to govern, the power of purse, political power, spiritual power, economic power, national power, judicial power, Presidential power, black power, student power, state power."

Power is central to the study of politics. Politics is nothing but struggle for power. We cannot separate power from the study of politics. All states possess power which is the most important and essential element of the state. No state system can work in the absence of power. The view of Robert A. Dahl is that power is synonymous with politics. Harold Lasswell says that politics gives an answer to the question: "Who gets what, when and how?". Wasby observes that the concepts of power and influence are central to the study of politics.

Power is the key concept because if politics is the resolution of conflict, it is the distribution of power within a community that determines how the conflict is to be resolved and whether the resolution is to be effectively observed by all parties.

Political power is not evenly distributed. It is usually concentrated in the hands of a few who may be called "the power elite." In both the liberal Western democracies and the Communist states, we have the power elite.

Some scholars have defined politics itself in terms of power struggle. Their contention is that political relationships are mainly power relationships. However, this view is not accepted by the normative theorists who maintain that it is not easy to accept the concept of power as a key concept. They consider authority as the key concept. The moral philosophers are dissatisfied with the power concept. They point out that man is motivated not only by power considerations, but there are other urges and

Learning Objectives

- Meaning of Power
- Difference Between Power and Force
- Difference Between Political and Military Power
- Development of the Concept of Power
- Characteristics of Power
- Sources of Power
- Kinds of Power
- Forms of Power
- Methods of Exercising Power
- Measurement of Political Power
- Authority
- Concept of Authority
- Sources of Authority
- Characteristics of Authority
- Basis of Authority
- Authority and Power
- Authority and Freedom
- Structure of Authority
- Legitimacy
- Basis of Legitimacy
- Types of Legitimacy
- Suggested Readings

drives in him which lead him to accommodate others and resolve differences. Man is not exclusively a power-hungry animal who always seeks to control the actions and behaviour of others. Power is a means to an end for which power is sought and that is more important. To understand politics as essentially a power struggle has dangerous normative implications. It stresses the importance of brute force and justifies the existence of a system based on power. That is why it is difficult to accept power as the key concept in politics. Authority, and not power, is the key concept and the state, though enjoying power, ought to be based on authority.

Meaning of Power

There is no agreement among scholars regarding the meaning of the term "Power." James G. March writes that power is a disappointing concept. It is not easy to define power because it is a complex term. Many definitions of power have been attempted. According to Herbert Goldhamer and Edward Shills, "Power is ability to influence the behaviour of others in accordance with one's own ends." Hans Margenthau defines politics as a struggle for power, as a psychological relation between those who exercise it and those over whom it is exercised. It gives the formal control of certain actions of the latter. To quote him, "By power we mean the power of man over the minds and actions of other men." Power is a possession but not in a tangible form like money. MacIver writes, "By the possession of power we mean the capacity to centralise, regulate or direct the behaviour of persons or things." According to Samuel Beer, "One person exercises power over another when he intentionally acts in such a manner as to affect in a predictable way actions of others." Lasswell and Kaplan define power as participation in the making of decisions. Erich Kaufman says, "The essence of the state is Machtentfaltung (development, increase and display of power)". Karl Baker writes, "The simple fact is that politics is inseparable from power. States and government exist to exert power. In each country and in the world at large, there is either a balance of power, and an unstable balance of power, or no balance of power at all. But there is always power. Political power exists in the world and will be used by those who have it." M.G. Smith says that "power is the ability to act effectively over people and things using means ranging from persuasion to coercion". In the words of George Schwarzenburger, "Power is capacity to impose one's will over another by reliance on effective sanctions in case of non-compliance." Robert A. Dahl defines power "as a special case of influence involving losses for non-compliance. If A confronts B with the prospects of shifting his behaviour, A is attempting to exercise power over B."

David Easton defines power as the "relationship in which one person or a group is able to determine the actions of another in the direction of the former's own ends." Power is the capacity of an actor to affect the actions of others in accordance with his own intentions. It implies a relationship. It is something one can use against somebody else. It is also a possession. It is something that one has and which one may choose to use or not to use. Hobbes has used the term power in the sense of something possessed, the present means to obtain some apparent "future good". He speaks of every man in the state of nature being afraid of the power of every other man. The weak man fears the physically strong. The strong man fears the scheming intellect of the weak. Today, when a man is elected to an office, he receives certain stipulated powers which he regards as his personal possession. The two aspects of power, power as a possession and power as a relationship are in one sense mutually inter-dependent. The skilful use of power as a possession can enable the user to make many more do his bidding. On becoming Prime Minister, every leader of the majority party in a parliamentary democracy holds certain stipulated powers as a possession, although some Prime Ministers used their possession more skillfully than others and thereby increased their total power.

Power is invariably used to produce certain desired effects. Bertrand Russell refers to power as "the production of intended effects." One can produce intended effects either by persuasion or influence or by force and domination. Persuasion can be honest and technical when scientific reasons are given for changing one's view. It can also be fraudulent and propagandistic when facts are distorted or deliberately certain events are played down in order to convince a person. In the case of power as domination, there is manifestly a conflict situation. As power includes at one end of the pole influence and at the other end domination, Partridge calls it "the most inclusive term".

Power is compared with a scale at one end of which is influence and at the other end domination. A number of situations involving the exercise of power are arranged along this scale.

There are three dimensions of power viz., the range of power, the zone of acceptance and the intensity of power. The range of power has reference to the number of persons the power-wielder can influence or induce to follow. The zone of acceptance refers to those matters of areas or zones within which the power-wielder exercises power. A government may be able to exercise great power when the people obey it but not so if they oppose. Scholars have tried to use this concept of zone of acceptance in describing the distribution of social and political power. Even within a given zone of power, there will be a limit to the amount of influence or domination that a power-wielder may be able to exercise. A commander in the army may be able to induce or compel his troops to endure hardships and sufferings to a certain limit and not beyond that on account of the danger of revolt. This is called the intensity of power.

Power relationships do not follow the "zero-sum game". An increase in the power of one man does not necessarily mean a decrease in the power of another. During the World War II, the British Government increased its powers but that does not mean that British citizens who conferred that power, lost their power.

Difference Between Power and Force

The view of Robert Bierstedt is that "force is manifest power. Force means the reduction or limitation or closure of even total elimination of alternatives to the social action of one person or group by another person or group". When a man surrenders his money to a dacoit in order to save his life, the dacoit has achieved his objective by merely a threat of force without using it. When the dacoit has to resort to actual force in order to snatch the money and other belongings, he has used force. The actual manifestation of power is force. Force is power in action or force is power exercised.

Difference Between Political and Military Power

There is a lot of difference between political power and military power. The basis of political power is psychological influence, leadership and its will power. Political power includes the power of money, arms and ammunition and influence regarding votes. In democratic countries, power is gained through elections in which money and other methods are frequently used. Military power plays a secondary role as compared with political power because military authorities have to obey the President of India and the Prime Minister of India. When one country attacks another country, the military power of both the sides comes into action and force is used.

Development of the Concept of Power

The concept of power is very old. It can be traced to the time of Aristotle. The view of Montesquieu was that power was the central point for the study of political science. Almost all political scientists have used the term power in their writings.

Characteristics of Power

There are certain characteristics of power. Power is the capacity to influence the behaviour of others. An individual or a nation wields power to the extent he is capable of changing others behaviour according to his wish. Power is the capacity of an individual to get things done from others according to his desires.

According to Frederick, "Power is a certain kind of human relationship. For the use of power, the presence of an actor or subject and some other individuals is essential so that the actor can influence "other individuals according to his capacity and wish. Power does not exist in vacuum. Power can be exercised only in relation to others. This establishes a kind of relationship.

Power is situational. It depends on situation, circumstances and position. A teacher may exercise power on his student while he is in college but not after he has left the college. Likewise, an officer may use power and authority on his subordinates, but they may not accept his power when he retires. Hence, power depends upon the situation, circumstances and position.

Power depends on its use. The President of India has powers but he does not use them as he is merely a constitutional head. The President of the United States has vast powers and he actually uses them.

Power must be backed by sanction. If the capacity of a person to get work done from others is devoid of coercion, that capacity or ability cannot be called power. Robert A. Dahl writes, "Whoever can visit penalties like these on people, is bound to be important in any society. Indeed, the state is distinguished from other political systems only to the extent that it successfully upholds the claim to the exclusive right to determine the conditions under which certain kinds of severe penalties, those involving serious physical pain, constraint, punishment or death, may be legitimately employed." Political power must be exercised for the attainment of some purpose or goal. If it is used without any goal or purpose, it is ineffective and useless. Karl Deutsch writes," Power cannot accomplish more than a succession of random impacts on the environment unless there is some relatively fixed goal or purpose. There are some decisions by which the application of power can be guided or directed. The guidance is indispensable for the sustained effectiveness of any system that applies power to its environment and any such system must receive this guidance from its memories, its past decision, its will or somewhat move generally from its character."

In the opinion of Lasswell and Kaplan, power is always relational. It is not the property of one single individual. At least two actors are required, one who exercises the power and the other upon whom the power is exercised. "Power is an interpersonal relationship. Those who hold power, are empowered. They depend upon and continue only so long as there are continuing streams of empowering responses." It is useless to talk about the power of an individual or of a nation unless they, by establishing relations with other individuals and nations, affect their behaviour.

Another characteristic of power is that it is not absolute but relative only. If an individual has power, it is essential that there should be someone who is prepared to accept its use as well. Power depends upon time. Power-relation changes with the changing circumstances.

Power has two aspects, actual and potential. There is the actual power of a person and a community and also the potential power of a person and a community. By actual power we mean that power which a person or community actually uses. Potential power is that power which a person or community can exercise although the same may not be actually exercised.

Sources of Power

There are many sources of power. The major source of power is knowledge which helps us to move from darkness to light. It helps us in investigating, learning thinking and development of mind and soul. The capacity for leadership comes through knowledge. Hence, knowledge is an important source of power.

Another source of power is organisation. It is a great power in itself. When people work together, their power and strength increases. Likewise, when a person enjoys the support of the leader of an organisation, his power increases. Political parties are organised to capture power and exercise the same.

Another source of power is the status of an individual. Economic status helps a person to attain power. A rich man can put pressure even on the highest officials and ministers and get things done in his own way. Dahl rightly says that an individual with better resources will capture more power than others. The status of a person in the religious field is also a source of power as the followers of that religion support him.

Another source of power is the skill of an individual. A tactful person can get more powers than others.

Another source of power is faith or belief. Power cannot be based on repression or brute force. It is necessary to win over the faith of the people also. A government enjoying public faith is more powerful than others.

Another source of power is authority. Authority means legitimate power. When a person occupies a political or legal post legitimately, his power increases automatically. Authority not only adds to power but also makes it effective. When a person becomes a minister and gets the authority of a minister, he becomes more powerful than others.

Another source of power is the mass media like newspapers, radio and television. The owners and editors of newspapers can easily influence others and are admittedly powerful.

Another source of power is the personality of a person. That personality may be due to his wisdom, courage, oratory, organisational ability and capacity to take quick and proper decisions. A leader who possesses a charismatic personality is more powerful than others.

Kinds of Power

Power may be legitimate or illegitimate. Legitimate power is that which is used according to the laws, Constitution or the accepted traditions of the people. It may be constitutional, traditional, or charismatic. *Constitutional power* is derived from the Constitution of the country. Traditional power is based on customs and traditions of a country. Charismatic power is based on the personal qualities of an individual.

Illegitimate power is that which is exercised not according to laws, Constitution or the accepted traditions or customs of the people. It is based on force or repression.

Power may be direct or indirect. When a person himself uses his power, it is called direct power. When he gets it used by others or by subordinates, it is called indirect power. Power which is exercised openly or explicitly is called manifest power. The police and the army are examples of manifest power. The power which cannot be exercised openly or clearly is called latent power such as the power of the people. When a person uses his power over others who do not have any power on him, it is called unilateral power. When both sides use power for each other, it is called bilateral power. When power is centralised at one place, it is called centralised power. When it is divided at different places, it is called decentralised power. Power is decentralised in a federation. It is centralised in a unitary government. National power is always exercised by the state. It may be psychological power, economic power or military power.

Forms of Power

Crespigny classifies power relationship into six categories viz., coercive, inductive, reactional, impedimental, attrahent and persuasive power relationships. A *coercive relationship* exists between A and B when A gets B to do what he wants by threatening to make things unpleasant for B if he does not comply. Basically, coercive relationship implies conflict and deprivation. Over a period of time, it may come to generate voluntary behaviour.

An *inductive power* relationship exists when A gets B to do what he wants by providing him something attractive, by offering a kind of award. By granting additional release of newsprint, the government may induce a newspaper not to publish a critical review.

In a *reactional power* relationship, A exerts power over B or B does what A wants, not because of inducement or constraint but because B hopes or expects that A will help him if he complies or will harm him if he does not comply. The power relationship between superiors and their subordinates is usually reactional because subordinates believe that they may prosper or win promotion by complying with the wishes of the superiors.

In the case of *impedimental power,* A gets B to comply with his wishes by putting impediments or obstacles in the attainment of his goal. A minister may prevent a contractor from doing his building work by withdrawing the "no-objection" certificate.

A power relationship in which A exercises power over B because the latter loves or is impressed or attracted by his personality and desires to imitate or obey him, is called *Attrahent power.* No conflict or tension is involved as power is willingly conceded by B to A. The power of a charismatic leader is generally of this kind.

Persuasive power is that power which may be exercised by A over B and which is based on rational or non-rational arguments. There is no conflict or tension in this power relationship.

There is a *legitimate power* relationship when A affects the actions of B because B regards him entitled to do so. Legitimate power must be exercised by a person authorised by a set of rules to do certain things or issue certain commands. A exercises legitimate power over B only when B feels that the action of A is just and he is authorised to act by a set or system of rules.

Methods of Exercising Power

Power may be exercised in different ways. *Persuasion* is the most effective and widely used method of exercising power. Most of the work of international organisations consists of the efforts of the various delegates to persuade one another. Another method of exercising power is by offering *rewards.* Rewards may be psychological, material, economic or political. A diplomat may change the policy of his country to win the appreciation of a fellow diplomat from another country. Rewards may be in the shape of military aid, weapons, troops and training facilities. Rewards may be in the form of loans or gifts. Punishment is another method of exercising power. Rewards and punishments are closely related. Another method of exercising power is the *use of force.* Punishment is threatened as a preventive measure but when it is actually carried out, it becomes the use of force.

Measurement of Political Power

It is a difficult thing to measure political power. One important reason is the universal tendency to present power relationship in the garb of morality. During the period between the two World Wars, it was believed in certain quarters that with the establishment of the League of Nations, power has been eliminated from international relations. That impression was created because the big Powers spoke in moral terms of peace and security. It was not realised that the big Powers were speaking in those terms because that enabled them to maintain their superior position. A power pursuit was presented in moral terms. However, an attempt can be made to measure political power by asking such relevant questions: how many times has A effected change in the behaviour of B? Did B change dramatically or was he almost at the position that A desired? Was the change in B's behaviour relatively permanent or temporary? Did A have similar success in the behaviour of C,D,E, etc. as he had with B?

One way to measure power is to rely on the judgment of the people. Many observers can be asked to judge the power of certain people.

AUTHORITY

Concept of Authority

The word authority is derived from the old Roman notion of "Auctor" or "Auctoritas" which generally meant counsel or advice. It was the Roman custom to get the Senate made up of "men of reason" and "Elders with experience" to approve or reject the decisions of the popular assembly. According to Carl Friedrich, an authority is the embodiment of reason and depends on "the capacity of reasoned elaboration. The man who possesses authority has the capacity for reasoned elaboration." Authority regulates behaviour mainly by speech and words, not force. Authority is inevitable in any society. Men are "rule-following animals." They talk and regulate their own behaviour and that of others by means of speech and framing rules. The term authority is essential to indicate the people who are considered to have the right to make pronouncements or announce decisions. Authority has a double implication. It implies not only that someone with the capacity to reasoned elaboration has the right to issue regulations and make final pronouncements. It also implies that someone has the right to receive obedience. The view of Peters is that the concept of authority is "incompatible with science and morality." This is due to the fact that science proceeds by its own logic while morality depends on inner conviction. In both cases, authority is out of place.

According to MacIver, "Authority is often defined as being power, the power to command obedience." Jouvenel is of the view that "authority is ability of man to get his proposals accepted." Herbert A. Simon defines authority as "the power to make decision which guides the actions of another. It is relationship between individuals, one superior and the other subordinate. The superior frames and transmits decisions with expectations that they will be accepted by subordinates. The subordinates accept such decisions and his conduct is determined by them." Robert A. Dahl writes, "A commands B and B feels A has perfect right to do so and which he has a complete obligation to obey. Power of this kind is often said to be legitimate. But when B feels A has absolutely no right to ask him to obey, which he has no obligation to obey, and which perhaps he actually has no obligation to resist. Power of this kind is often said to be illegitimate. Legitimate power is often called "authority". An important element of authority is legitimacy.

Sources of Authority

According to Max Weber, there are three types of sources of political authority: traditional, charismatic and legal-rational. When the right to rule emerges from a continuous use of political power based on customs and traditions, it is called traditional authority. When the right to rule springs from the great qualities of head and heart of the political leader, it is called charismatic authority. When the right to rule emerges from constitutional rules, it is called legal-rational authority.

Characteristics of Authority

There are certain characteristics of the concept of authority. The most important is *legitimacy.* It is legitimacy which determines the effectiveness of authority. Legitimacy is very essential for authority.

Another important characteristic of authority is dominance. Authority is the capacity of the individual to command others. An individual or group which possesses authority, exercises dominance over others. Authority is the command of senior officials given to their subordinates which is accepted by them.

Another characteristic of authority is that it is informal. It lacks those characteristics which are the main characteristics of power. Frederick writes, "Authority is not a power, but something that accompanies power."

Another characteristic of authority is reason. Frederick writes, "The man who has authority possesses something that I would describe as the capacity for reasoned elaboration, for giving convincing reasons for what he does or proposes to have other to do." The basis of authority is reason. We accept authority because it is based on logic.

Another characteristic of authority is responsibility or accountability. The individual or the group which possesses authority is also answerable to some higher authority. In a democracy, responsibility or accountability is an important characteristic of authority.

When authority is claimed to be derived from God, it is called authority based on divine right. James I of England and Louis XIV of France considered themselves as the representatives of God and maintained that they got their authority directly from God. Such a view is not acceptable today. Another kind of authority is based on brute force. Generally, dictators possess this type of authority but it is never permanent.

Another kind of authority is based on ancestral heritage. This type of authority exists under a monarchical system.

Another kind of authority is that of the elite. It is possessed by a small group of individuals on the basis of their knowledge, money or personality.

When a person or a group derives its power from the Constitution of the country, it is called constitutional authority.

Traditional authority is that which is based on ancient customs or traditions or conventions.

Rational-legal authority is that which is used in accordance with the laws of the land. Such a kind of authority exists only in a democracy.

When the right to rule springs from the great qualities of the leader, it is called charismatic authority. Max Weber says, "Charismatic authority rests on the devotion to the specific and exceptional sanctity, heroism or exemplary character of an individual person."

Religious authority is possessed by those individuals who occupy a high position of authority in some religious sect or religion.

Authority may be *dejure* or *defacto.* De jure authority pre-supposes a system of rules which determine who shall be the actors, that is, who shall be those who with reasoned elaboration, shall take decisions, make pronouncements, issue commands and perform certain acts. Dejure authority is exercised through speech and word and enjoys the right to receive obedience. While de jure authority is concerned with a prior set of rules that determine who shall be the author, *de facto* authority has reference to the man whose word, in fact, goes as law (and is obeyed) in these spheres. Normally, dejure and de facto authorities go hand in hand. The Parliament of England has both de jure and de facto authority.

In addition to dejure and de facto authorities, there is also an *intermediate kind of authority.* This authority is held by a man not according to any system of rules but because "he is special sort of person". Such an authority rests on the devotion of the people to the personal characteristics of the man, his heroism, or special or unusual abilities. Max Weber calls this kind of authority charismatic and considers continuing success as the necessary condition for the maintenance of this kind of authority. Scientists and economists are considered authorities although they have not been put in authority by any set of rules, but because of their training, study and competence. Peters writes that intermediate authority implies "a self-generating system of entitlement which is confined to specific spheres of pronouncement and decision."

Basis of Authority

There was a time when the only sanction behind authority was sheer physical force. Religion also was another basis. The view of the exponents of the social contract theory was that a social contract provided a basis for state authority. In the nineteenth century, democracy was the most important force. Political thinkers refer to the principle of consent as something necessary for the use of state authority. The state which is based on the consent of the people has no need to make use of its coercive power as the people are loyal spontaneously. The success of a government depends upon the cooperation which it can evoke from the people. When the aims and objectives of the state are identical with those of the people, the latter whole-heartedly obey and support the state and the use of coercion is the minimum.

A reference may made to the *sanctions of authority.* There may be social sanctions of authority. Society expects individuals to be obedient in certain social situations. Individuals also accept authority on account of fear of society. There is also psychological sanction when the juniors accept the authority of seniors. Another sanction of authority is purpose. For the proper functioning of an organisation, its employees accept the authority of their elders. Authority is accepted by individuals for the achievement of some goal or object. Sometimes, the people accept authority if it brings money or status for them.

Authority and Power

Some scholars regard authority as a species of power. For example, Weldon defines authority as "power exercised with the general approval of the people concerned." There are scholars who use the two terms interchangeably. As a matter of fact, the term authority was not conceptually analysed satisfactorily by scholars. Machiavelli and Hobbes devoted considerable space in analysing how power was used to regulate human life but said practically nothing about authority.

Normative theories reject the attempt to analyse authority in terms of power. R.S. Peters writes, "But, my claim is that power usually has meaning by contrast with authority rather than as a generic term of which authority is a species. The concept of authority is necessary to bring out the ways in which behaviour is regulated without recourse to power, that is, force, incentive and propaganda." C.J. Friedrich observes, "Authority is not a kind of power for something that accompanies it."

Power and authority are both ways of regulating social behaviour and conduct. The man with authority does this by virtue of his "capacity for reasoned elaboration", his capacity for giving convincing reasons for what he does or wants others to do. On the other hand, power is the way of regulating social conduct or behaviour by means other than reasoned elaboration, by means such as force, propaganda, enticement, fear of putting obstacles in the way, even love etc.

Both authority and power may increase or decrease, but for different reasons. We speak of decline in authority with age. Authority may decline owing to hastiness, emotionalism and favouritism in the exercise of authority. In contrast, the loss of power is due to the loss of wealth, military force, threat or strife. There is no system of rules authorising the actor to act or make pronouncements and there is no obligation to render obedience. However, there is an intimate connection between power and authority. So long as the rule or system is generally respected by most people, there is exercise of authority. However, with reference to the few who do not respect the system or rules, authority may also be a source of power. The exercise of authority will always imply the exercise of power, not in relation to the majority who accept it but in relation to those who do not. The Government of India exercises authority as most of the Indians accept to be governed by the Constitution of India. However, if a handful of extremists or secessionists choose not to accept them and flout the Constitution, the Government of India exercises authority as well as power in relation to them. Every government based on authority must have sufficient power to maintain its authority against the few who reject it, against those who choose to bring about change in violation of the accepted rules or by force overthrow it. A government with authority but without power, may easily be overthrown by a handful of armed rebels. The bulk of the people concede authority to the government to maintain law and order and realise other goals. Authority must be effective to attain its purpose or it will not be respected. Power always goes with authority but every instance of the exercise of power is not an expression of authority.

Authority in the state can decline or disappear. It happens when a government having authority does not possess enough military strength or force to suppress an armed revolt or a challenge from a determined minority. The government itself may lose the capacity of ruling by reasoned elaboration and thereby forfeit the right to receive obedience. From the point of view of normative theory, it is more meaningful to speak of the rise and decline of authority in the state than the rise and decline of power.

Authority is always legitimate whereas power can be legitimate as well as illegitimate. In the words of Lasswell, "Power becomes authority when it is legalised. Capacity to issue orders is power, whereas authority is that point where the decisions are taken." Power is generally based on force, whereas authority is based on consent. Authority is more democratic than power. It is always legitimate and based on popular support. Authority is the ability of a man to get his proposals accepted but power is the capacity of man to change the behaviour of others.

Authority and Freedom

Authority and freedom are not opposed to each other. As a matter of fact, freedom finds authority as something indispensable because without authority there will be anarchy. Authority has to be exercised in a legitimate way for a good social purpose, for maintaining peace, order and harmony and for solving the multifarious problems of the people. Trouble arises when authority is misused for purposes other than those promoting the happiness and welfare of the people. A dictator makes his authority repulsive to the people and his authority can never be reconciled with freedom. The misuse of authority destroys freedom.

Structure of Authority

The term structure of authority refers to the widely accepted fixed and regular channels, institutions and set procedures by which authority is exercised. The structure of authority varies from state to state depending upon such factors as the size of the country, the size of its population, its traditions, social requirements and expectations. Changes in these factors result in changes in the structure of authority. As the traditions and expectations of the community change or are modified by the historical process and the requirements to the situation, the structure of authority tends to become outdated. The structure of authority must respond to those factors by making necessary adjustments because an outdated structure can be a serious threat to the survival of authority itself.

There are two basic features of the structure of authority which cannot be tampered with. One is that the structure of authority must provide a two-way traffic-from top to bottom and from the base upwards. The decisions and pronouncements of the government must be clearly formulated and effectively communicated downwards to the masses. Secondly, the structure of the authority in the state must be plural. No single individual or association can speak for all the rest. Modern societies are complicated and plural and hence the structure of authority has to reflect this plurality.

LEGITIMACY

The term "legitimacy"' is derived from the Latin word "Legtimus" which means lawful. However, in modern times, the term has a different meaning. According to S.M. Lipset, "Legitimacy involves the capacity of the system to engender and maintain the belief that existing political institutions are most appropriate for the society." Dahl writes, "According to one use of the term, a government is said to be legitimate if the people to whom its orders are directed believe that the structure, procedure, acts, decisions, policies, officials or leaders of the government possess the quality of righteousness, propriety or moral goodness and should be accepted because of this quality irrespective of the specified content of the particular act in question." Though different political systems can acquire legitimacy, democracies are more in need of it than others. Jean Blondel observes, "Legitimacy can be defined as the extent to which the population accepts naturally, without questioning, the organisation to which it belongs." The broader the area of agreement or acceptance, the more legitimate is the organisation. Legitimacy is concerned not only with the political system but also with the group that exists in a society. G.K. Robert opines, "Legitimacy is that principle which indicates the acceptance on the part of the public of the occupancy of a political office by a particular person, or the exercise of power by a person or group, either generally or in some specific instance, on the grounds that occupancy or exercise of powers is in accordance with some generally accepted principles and procedures of enforcement of authority." J.C. Piano and R.E. Riggs write, "Legitimacy means the quality of being justified or willingly accepted by subordinates that converts the exercise of political power into rightful authority. Legitimacy reflects an underlying consensus that endows the leadership and the state with authority and that offers respect and acceptance for individual leaders, institutions and behaviour norms." Legitimacy means the capacity to produce and maintain a belief that the existing political system is the most appropriate for the society and the people must regard it as sacred and worthy of respect and obey it unhesitatingly. As regards the extent of legitimacy, Jean Blondel writes, "There are, in fact, two ways in which one can talk about the extent of legitimacy or a dimension of legitimacy. One relates to a number of persons, who support the political system or group, the greater this percentage, the more legitimate the political system or group would seem to be; the other relates to the intensity of the system, members of the political system or group may be very passive, almost neutral, or else intensely opposed or intensely in favour. When these two aspects are linked, it becomes conceivable to measure the legitimacy of a group or political system by considering its weighted support minus the weighted rejection. If the figures were near zero or even negative, the group would have no legitimacy and would be in considerable danger of not maintaining itself."

Basis of Legitimacy

Max Weber refers to certain grounds of legitimacy. Legitimacy may be based on the rational ground resting in a belief in the legality of patterns of normative rules and the right of those elevated to authority under those rules to issue commands. The traditional basis of legitimacy rests on an established belief in the sanctity of immemorial traditions and legitimacy of the status of those exercising authority under them. The charismatic basis of legitimacy rests on devotion to the specific and exceptional sanctity, heroism or exemplary character of an individual person and the normative patterns or orders revealed or ordained by him. Dahl refers to three kinds of the basis of legitimacy viz., personal choice, competence and economy.

Types of Legitimacy

There are two types of legitimacy: legitimacy towards authority or authorities and legitimacy towards regime. David Easton refers to three types of legitimacy viz., ideological legitimacy, structural legitimacy and personal legitimacy. Ideological legitimacy is based on the moral convictions about the validity of the regime and incumbents of authority. Structural legitimacy is based on an independent belief in the validity of the structure and norms and the incumbents of the authority. Personal legitimacy is based on the belief in the validity of the incumbents of authority roles to the authority roles themselves. The belief in the validity of authorities is based on their personal qualities. When the source of legitimacy is the ideology prevailing in the society, it is called ideological legitimacy. The principles which motivate the members of a system to accept their authorities as legitimate also contribute to the validation of structures and norms of the regime. Legitimacy also flows from the personal qualities and worth of the authorities rather than their position in the system. There are leaders who are able to build up a belief in their legitimacy.

SUGGESTED READINGS

Ball. A.R. : Modern Politics and Government. Macmillan Press. London. 1975.

Benn and Peters : Social Principles and the Democratic State. S. Chand & Co.. Delhi. 1970

Crespigny and Weretheimer (Eds.) : Contemporary Political Theory. New York. 1975.

Friedrich, C.J. : An Introduction to Political Theory. Bombay, 1967.

Friedrich. C.J. : Tradition and Authority. Macmillan. London, 1972.

Friedrich. C.J. : Philosophy of law in the Historical perspective, Chicago. 1969.

Lasswell. H.D. : Politics, who gets what ? when ? How ?, New York, 1958.

Mills. C. Wright : The Power Elites, Oxford University Press. 1959.

Quinton. Anthony : Political Philosophy. Oxford University Press, 1928.

Weldon. T.D. : Vocabulary of Politics, Penguin Books, London 1953.

CHAPTER

Political Modernisation and Political Development

Learning Objectives

- Basic Characteristics of Modernisation
- Agents of Modernisation
- Factors which help Modernisation
- Political Development
- The Concept
- Difference Between Political Development and Political Modernisation
- Factors Leading to Political Development
- Problem of State-building
- Problem of Nation-building
- Problem of Participation
- Problem of Distribution
- Crises in Political Development
- Criticism of Modernisation and Development
- Merits
- Suggested Readings

In the words, of Eisenstadt, modernisation "is the process of change towards those types of social, economic and political systems that have developed in Western Europe and North America from the seventeenth century to the nineteenth and then have spread to other European countries and in the nineteenth and twentieth centuries to South American, Asian and African countries." According to R.E. Ward, a modern society is characterised "by its far-reaching ability to control or influence the physical and social circumstances of its environment and by a value system which is fundamentally optimistic about the desirability and consequences of this ability." Rustow identifies a modern society with a "rapidly widening control over nature through closer cooperation among men." Modernisation has been defined by Welch as "a process based upon the rational utilisation of resources and aimed at the establishment of rational society." Benjamin Schwartz describes political modernisation as "the systematic, sustained and powerful application of human energies to the rational control of man's physical and social environment for various human purposes." According to Davies and Lewis, modernisation stands for the transformation of the political culture in response to the changes in social and physical environments. Sinai writes that a modern society is "a society based on advanced technology and the spirit of science, on a rational view of life, a secular approach to social relations, a feeling for justice in public affairs and above all else, on the acceptance in the political realm of the belief that the prime unit of the polity should be the nation state".

Political modernisation is regarded as a result of "social mobilisation" and "economic development." Karl Deutsch defines social mobilisation as "a process by which major clusters of old social, economic and psychological commitments are eroded or broken and people become available for new patterns of socialisation and behaviour." Economic development means "growth in the total economic activity and output of society and could be measured in terms of per capita Gross National Product, level of industrialisation and level of individual welfare." According to Huntington, political modernisation contains three more elements in addition to economic development and social mobilisation. Those three elements are rationalisation of authority, differentiation of structure and expansion of political participation.

Modernisation is a process which means a change in all fields, whether social, cultural, psychological, economic or political. Though it is mainly an economic concept, it puts emphasis on social mobilisation which means an overwhelming change in a large population of those countries which are moving from their traditional way of life to the modern way of life. When an ancient society steeped in ignorance and poverty, old and outdated beliefs and superstitions and mainly dependent on sluggish agriculture begins to discard them and moves forward to a new way of life and adopts the path of social transformation, urbanisation, industrialisation, mechanisation, new technology and increasing literacy, we can say that it is marching towards modernisation.

Basic Characteristics of Modernisation

The most important characteristics of modernisation are the application of technology and mechanisation, industrialisation, urbanisation, rise in national income and per capita income, increase in literacy, political participation, development of mass-media techniques, social mobility and cultivation of national identity.

(1) As regards the *application of technology and mechanisation,* the people give up their old ways of living, old methods of agriculture and travelling. Previously, the majority of the people in India lived in villages in Kuccha houses and cultivated their lands through ploughs and travelled by means of bullock-carts. As a result of modernisation, the people now live in well-built houses, cultivate their fields with the help of tractors and use other modern methods of agriculture. The people prefer to travel by buses, trains and aeroplanes. In other words, the people use modern methods of technology and mechanisation.

(2) As a result of *industrialisation*, the people give up their traditional, rural and agricultural economy. New factories and mills start coming up with the latest techniques.

(3) As regards *urbanisation*, the people living in villages migrate in large numbers to the new centres in the cities in the hope that they would go back to their villages after earning enough of money. As it is not convenient for the villagers to come daily to the cities on account of distances, the people living in villages continue to migrate from villages to cities and settle there permanently. That creates many problems in the cities such as those of sanitation, means of communication, transport etc.

(4) Agriculture alone cannot *increase national income and per capita income.* The same has to be supplemented by industrial growth and income from it.

(5) Another feature of modernisation is that all possible efforts are made by the government and the people to wipe out *illiteracy* from the country. Avenues of higher education are also made available to every person in all fields.

(6) Modernisation also brings *political mobilisation.* The people who are educated and have enough of per capita income, can afford to take part in the affairs of the country. Every voter reads newspapers and votes for the party which can deliver the goods. Political participation is made possible in a democracy through political parties, interest groups and various other organisations.

(7) Modernisation helps the *development of mass-media techniques* such as newspapers, broadcasting, movies, roads, rails and air services. Through these facilities, citizens become enlightened and well-informed and take an active part in the politics of the country.

(8) When modernisation takes place, the people start migrating from villages to the cities in search of better amenities and avenues for future progress. This brings *social mobility.* The people in

cities become members of various organisations and they rally round their leaders who are expected to protect their interests.

(9) Modernisation helps the cultivation of *national identity.* The people begin to give up their narrow loyalties and parochial considerations of caste, colour, sex or creed. Their interests are identified with those of the nation.

It is not necessary that modernisation must result in the discarding of all traditional values and cultural or political heritage. In spite of their modernisation, the British, continued to be conservative and they retained the old institutions like kingship and the House of Lords.

Agents of Modernisation

There are many agents of modernisation. (1) An important agent of modernisation was *colonialism.* The colonialists build roads, railways, telegraph and telephone services, banking system, processing plants etc. To begin with, they do these things in order to strengthen their hold over their colonies. When a country becomes free, these very means are utilised to bring about further modernisation.

(2) The *elite* have also played an important part in the modernisation of the country. The colonialists set up schools and colleges to give education in their language and literature so that the people of the colonies may give up their cultural heritage and ignore their history and literature. However, when the natives come back home, they find the existing conditions most unsatisfactory and they start agitation for reform.

(3) In certain backward countries, *military leaders* take advantage of the situation and capture power. Having done so, they take keen interest in modernisation. This was done when Kamal Ataturk captured power in Turkey and modernised it. Field Marshal Ayub Khan did the same and president Zial-ul-Haq is doing the same now. General Ershad is also modernising his country after having captured political power.

(4) *Political parties* are also agents of modernisation. They develop a spirit of patriotism and secular outlook among the people.

(5) After having captured power, the military authorities curb the disintegrating tendencies with a strong hand and launch the country on the path of progress. Thus, the military modernises the country. This has happened not only in Turkey, Egypt and Pakistan but also in many other countries.

(6) *Bureaucracy* plays an important role in modernising the country as it is through this that all development programmes are implemented.

Factors which help Modernisation

There are many factors which help the process of modernisation. The development of science and technology plays a major role in the process of modernisation. A mad race is going on in the world for the development of science and technology. Only that country is considered to be civilised which develops science and technology.

Industrial development is essential for modernisation. It is this realisation which induced Prime Minister Jawaharlal Nehru to set up various factories in different parts of the country. The same was the object of the Five-Year Plans. A factory for making railway coaches was set up at Perampur (in Tamil Nadu). Nehru also set up the Chitranjan Locomotive Works in West Bengal. He also established Bhopal Heavy Electricals.

Democracy is considered to be the best means to modernise a country. That was so in England, the United States, West Germany and France. However, the Communists regard this political democracy as the rule of the bourgeoisie. The Commusist countries themselves have modernised themselves to a great extent and they compare favourably with the industrialised countries of the West.

POLITICAL DEVELOPMENT

The Concept

The history of the concept of political development can be traced back to the period after the World War II and the liberation of many Asian and African countries. Dozens of American political scientists wrote on this concept and different models of political development. Important among them are Lucian Pye, Colman, Wriggins, Leonard Binder, Myron Weiner, David Apter, Lerner, Huntington, Riggis, Turner, Holt, etc.

Lucian Pye is the pioneer among the writers who analysed the concept of development in depth and kept on evolving his ideas on the subject and left an abiding impression on the entire literature of political development. In his books, "Aspects of Political Development", "Political Culture and Political Development" and "Communication and Political Development", he evolved the key elements of political development. He acknowledges the relevance of social, economic, administrative, political and cultural variables in shaping political development. He has traced the science of political development at three different levels; with respect to population as a whole, with respect to governmental and general systemic performance and with respect to organisation of policy.

Before giving his own interpretation of the term political development, Pye discusses the various definitions of political development given by other writers and accepts some parts of them and rejects the other parts of those definitions. There are economists who are of the view that political development should be taken as a result of economic development. Politics and social conditions can also play decisive role in impeding or facilitating economic growth. Pye criticises this view on the ground that this concept of political development is a negative one. Such a concept of political development does not focus on a common set of theoretical considerations. Problems of political development vary according to the specific economic problems of each country. In most of the under-developed countries, the people are anxious about political development independent of their economic growth. To link political development solely to economic events ignores much that is of dramatic importance in the developing countries.

There are certain writers who are of the view that the process of political development relates only to countries of industrialisation. According to Pye, this view ignores the role of several other factors like forces which threaten the vested interests of many segments of society.

Many writers like Coleman, Deutsch and Lipset are of the view that political development means a study of the developed Western countries and their ways which the developing countries are trying to follow. This means that the advanced Western and modern countries are the pace-setters of political development. Pye does not accept this view.

Some writers identify political development with the politics of nationalism within the context of social and political institutions a modern state possesses. The view of Pye is that while nationalism is necessary, it is not a sufficient condition to ensure political development.

Writers like Max Weber and Talcott Parsons are of the view that political development is intricately linked up with the legal and administrative order of the community. Pye says that this view of political development overlooks entirely the problems of citizenship training and popular participation.

Some writers link up political development with mass mobilisation and participation. The view of Pye is that although the process of mass participation is a legitimate part of political development, it is fraught with dangers of either sterile emotionalism or corrupting demagoguery.

Another view is that political development is integrally connected with the building of democracy and the inculcation of values of a democratic order in the minds of the people. Pye points out that such a concept would exclude the cases of those countries where democracy is non-existent. Democracy is a value-laden term while development is more value-neutral.

Another view is that stability is legitimately linked with the concept of development. According to Pye, this view leaves unanswered how much order is necessary or desirable and for what purpose change should be directed. The maintenance of order, however desirable or essential, stands second to getting things done.

The view of Coleman, Almond and Talcott Parsons is that the concept of political development can be evaluated in terms of the level or degree of absolute power which the system is able to mobilise. The view of Pye is that this explanation is applicable to democracy and not to other political systems.

Political development is only one aspect of a multi-dimensional process of social change. It is not independent of social and economic factors.

The above discussion shows that there is a great degree of confusion regarding the definition of political development. Pye tries to resolve this confusion by identifying factors which are common to all the views mentioned above.

The meaning of political development given by Pye has three characteristics—equality, capacity and differentiation. The degree of development of a country can be determined with the help of these characteristics.

(1) The first characteristic is a general spirit or attitude towards *equality*. The subject of political development involves mass participation and popular involvement in political activities. Participation may be either democratic or a form of totalitarian mobilisation, but the key consideration is that subjects will become active citizens and at least the pretence of popular rule is necessary. Equality also means that laws should apply to all and be more or less impersonal in their operation. This means the development of a codified legal system and explicit legal procedures. Equality also means that recruitment to political office should reflect achievement standards of performance.

(2) *Capacity* is closely associated with governmental performance and the conditions which affect that performance. Developed systems are presumed to be able to do a lot more than the less developed systems can. Capacity also means effectiveness and efficiency in the execution of public policy. Concern with efficiency and effectiveness leads to universally recognised standards of performance.

(3) An important theme running through much of the discussion on political development is that of *differentiation* and *specialisation*. Differentiation is not fragmentation and isolation of the different parts of the political system but specialisation based on an ultimate sense of integration.

According to Pye, in recognising the three dimensions of equality, capacity and differentiation, we do not suggest that they necessarily fit easily together. Historically, tendency has usually been that there are acute tensions between the demand for equality, requirements for capacity and the process of greater differentiation. A pressure for greater equality can challenge the capacity of the system and differentiation can reduce equality by stressing the importance of quality and specialised knowledge.

G.A. Almond refers to political development as "the acquisition of new capability, in the sense of a specialised role, structure and differentiated orientation which together give a political system the range of problems." Hagan regards political development as the "growth of institutions and practices that allow a political system to deal with its own fundamental problems more effectively in the short run, while working towards more responsiveness of the regime to popular demand in the long run." The view of Alfred Diamont is that "political development is not a process which aims at achieving a particular political condition, but one which creates an institutional frame-work for solving an ever-widening range of social problems."

Difference Between Political Development and Political Modernisation

(1) Political development implies movement forward to some goal or preferred political order and is thus value-oriented, but modernisation is open-ended and value-free.

(2) The term political development carries the notion that it is a movement towards some higher order, but political modernisation is a natural concept which provides both the possibilities of development as well as decay.

(3) Political modernisation is a narrow term and political development is a broad term. The concept of political development submerges the concept of political modernisation.

(4) Political modernisation emphasises the spread of secular world culture and democratisation of political institutions, but political development emphasizes the overall socio-economic development.

C. H. Dodd writes, "Certainly, modernisation does not seem to be so vague as development when the latter is used to denote little more than a process of change. Nor does it seem to call for quite the same precision in the description of the desired end as when development is used with some object in mind. We feel more comfortable while asserting that the society is modernising than in claiming that it is developing. Modernisation also seems more open-ended. If we describe USA as modernised, we can more easily accommodate the notion of future change than if we say it is developed. Modernisation implies the existence of traditional order to be changed. Properly speaking, modernisation is the effect of the new on the old, not the eradication of the old and its substitution by the new. Modernisation does not necessarily result in modernity. Hence the definition of modernisation given above is to make or become more modernised, not mere modern." Again, "The whole problem of distinction between political development and political modernisation is full of ambiguity and theoretical difficulties."

Factors Leading to Political Development

Usually, broad changes occurring in the political realm are regarded as subordinate to the general process of industrialisation, urbanisation, spread of education and literacy, increasing exposure of the mass media and the expansion of secular culture. These factors are said to account for a variety of political development such as the growth of modern bureaucracies, development of a sense of nationhood, advent of political parties, expansion of popular political participation, increased capacity of the political system to mobilise resources for the accomplishment of its ends in the most modern politics and decline in the missionary fervour of the political movement.

According to Almond and Powel, the events which lead to political development come from the international environment, from the domestic society or from political elites within the political system itself. Events like wars of aggression bring about conditions of change in the political system. Events taking place within the system may also have the same effect. Development results when the existing structure and culture of the political system are unable to cope with the problem or challenge which confronts it without further structural differentiation and cultural secularisation.

According to the same authors, there are four types of problems or challenges to political development viz., penetration and integration or state-building, loyalty and commitment or nation building, pressure from various interest groups in the society for taking part in the decision-making process or participation and pressure from domestic society to employ the coercive power of the political system to redistribute income, wealth, opportunity and honour or the problem of distribution.

Problem of State-building

This problem arises when there is a threat to the survival of the political system from international environment or from society in the form of revolutionary pressure, challenging the stability or the survival of the political system. It may result from the development among the political elite of new goals such as national expansion or the creation of an extravagant court life. Almond and Powell write, "State-building occurs when the political elite creates new structures and organisations designed to penetrate the society in order to regulate behaviour in it, and draw a larger volume of resources from it. State-building is commonly associated with significant increases in the regulative and extractive capabilities of the political system, with the development of a centralised and penetrative bureaucracy related to the increase in these capabilities, and with the development of attitudes of obedience and compliance in the population which are associated with the emergence of such a bureaucracy."

Problem of Nation-building

National-building puts emphasis on the fact that one should give up narrow loyalties such as loyalty to the tribal chief, family, caste, ethnic group, religion, region etc. and concentrate on his loyalty to the nation. One should owe allegiance to the state in preference to narrow loyalties. State-building and nation-building may go together. However, in many cases the problem of state-building may go together. However, in many cases the problem of state-building has been solved and not the problem of nation-building. The problem of nation-building or national integration has not been solved in India on account of the attitude of the various minorities who put emphasis on their separate interests. There are examples in which the elite never sought to create a common national culture of loyalty and commitment and were content to develop a centralised and penetrative bureaucracy.

Problem of Participation

Whenever a society develops politically, there is an increasing demand from the public for a share in the decision-making process. These demands are generally put forward through such political structures as political parties, pressure groups, factions, cliques and various organisations. The government has to respond to these demands. Political participation implies the development of the requisite political infra-structure and the responsive attitude and bargaining skill of the elite.

Problem of Distribution

Increased political participation leads to the demand that the values, benefits and national income should be distributed equally among all the sections of society, irrespective of caste, colour, sex and creed. Equal opportunities should be given to all and merit alone should be the criterion for selection to the high posts.

According to Almond and Powell, there are at least five major factors which must be considered while discussing political development. Those are the nature of the problems confronting the political system, resources of the system effect of other social systems, functioning pattern of the system and response of the political elites.

It cannot be denied that the stability of a system depends very much upon the *types of problems faced* by it. Much of the stability and success of the gradual development of the political systems of the United States and Britain can be attributed to their relative isolation during long periods of their formative history. The political system of Italy and Germany were subjected to many diverse and intense pressures simultaneously. Demands for unification, participation and welfare appeared suddenly. The people demand participation, national unity, economic betterment and law and order simultaneously and immediately.

A second factor is the *resources* the system can draw upon under various circumstances. Support and demand can fluctuate. The people of France had to give up their Fourth Republic in 1958 and they replaced it with the Fifth Republic under the leadership of De Gaulle.

Development in other social systems may also affect political development. The extent to which the political system is loaded or overloaded will vary according to the capabilities of other social systems in the domestic society and the international system. When an economy develops new capabilities, the loading of the political system with demand for welfare may be reduced, thereby affecting political development. A religious system may develop regulative capabilities, reducing the flow of innovative demands on the political system. The international political system may develop a regulative or a distributive capability which reduces the pressure on the domestic political systems. The existence or development of capabilities in other social systems may affect the magnitude of the challenges confronting political systems, keep the flow at an incremental and low intensity level and avoid some of the disruptive consequences of cumulative pressures.

A political system can withstand demands and submit fluctuations better than others. A system with a developed and differentiated bureaucracy can accommodate demands for new regulations and services much more readily than a less differentiated system. Law and order can be maintained much easily if an organised army or police force is available. Some systems are geared for change and adaptation, while others are not.

Another factor is the response of the political elites to political system challenges. Such responses cannot be predicted. Some responses may lead to accommodation of new demands without changes in the political system or with minor level of such change. Some other responses may lead to disaster. The elites may misjudge the seriousness and intensity of input fluctuations.

Crises in Political Development

There are certain well-accepted factors which play a dominant role in bringing about political development in a political system. The factors promoting political development may also serve the cause of crises in political development if they are not properly bandied. Lucian Pye refers to six types of crises in political development viz., the identity crisis, legitimacy crisis, penetration crisis, participation crisis, integration crisis and distribution crisis.

(1) When people in political system fail to achieve a common sense of identity, they face the *identity crisis.* Such a problem has been faced by many states which have become newly independent on account of the sharp tribal, linguistic, ethnic and cultural differences.

(2) The *legitimacy crisis* arises when negotiations fail to reach an agreement on certain fundamental questions with those whom they govern. An authoritarian regime which governs against the wishes of the people is likely to face legitimacy crisis. The only remedy for the government is to legitimatise its authority by ascertaining the wishes of the people.

(3) The penetration problem is that of building up the effectiveness of the formal institutions by government and of establishing confidence and rapport between rulers and subjects. The *penetration crisis* can be overcome by making the institutions of the government more efficient and effective.

(4) *Participation crisis* occurs when there is uncertainty over the appropriate rate of expansion and when the influx of new participants creates serious strains on the existing institutions. The participation crisis arises out of the emergence of interest groups and the formation of a party system. The appearance of a participation crisis does not necessarily signal pressures for democratic processes. In a totalitarian state, the participation crisis can be organised to provide the basis for manipulated mass organisations and demonstration politics.

(5) The *integration crisis* covers the problems of relating popular politics to governmental performance. The problem of integration deals with the extent to which the entire polity is organised as a system of interacting relationships, first among the offices and agencies of government and then among the various groups and interests seeking to make demands upon the system and in the relationship between officials and articulating citizens.

(6) The *distribution crisis* refers to the questions about how governmental powers are to be used to influence the distribution of goods, services and valucs throughout society. In some cases, the government directly intervenes in the distribution of wealth. In other cases, it strengthens the opportunities and potentialities of the disadvantaged groups.

Criticism of Modernisation and Development

The concepts of political development and political modernisation have been criticised on many grounds. It is contended that there is the absence of any coherent political model of development process. The analysis is often left at the point where extra-political factors have set the stage for political change. Political change itself has been dealt with more with the time-honoured tools of historians than those of political scientists. The political scientists dealing with the phenomenon of political change have confined themselves to mere generalities and have "floundered in abstractions of limited utility" or have been content to rely on the ground of historical description.

The concept of political development implies goals or ideals to be achieved by traditional societies. The ideal society is American or Western democracy to which the traditional societies of Asia, Africa or Latin America must look for as an ideal. However, the American system is not fit for the Third World. Moreover, Western democracies are not ideal goals. They have many defects and they are torn apart by internal contradictions.

The concept of political modernisation hardly says anything about the Communist or socialist countries of the Soviet Union, China etc. Those tools are not suitable for the study of socialist countries. Hence those concepts are one-sided, distorted and politically motivated.

Political modernisation is nothing but Westernisation in general and Americanisation in particular. The Americans wish that the people of Asia, Africa and Latin America should follow their models. They are including neo-colonialism to safeguard their interests of imperial exploitation.

On account of their ambiguity, these tools cannot be used to study the political phenomenon of the Third World.

Merits

While the defects are a few, the merits are many. (1) The management of political systems. Once we have identified the stage of development of a particular development is gradual, purposeful and ordered manner of bringing about political change. (2) It is a useful tool for description, explanation and classification of political change is an important issue in the contemporary politics and political political system, its comparison with other systems becomes easier. (3) A study of the development of the political system at different periods of time can reveal the strength and weakness of the ideology to which that system subscribed at a certain point of time. We can compare characteristics associated with democratic systems at different levels of development. (4) A study of the stage of political development would reveal other features of the polity such as sub-system autonomy, structural role differentiation and cultural secularisation. (5) A study of the development indicators and time series would lead to the development of a new discipline which is given the name of *polimetrics* by Almond. The measurement of political performance is a difficult task but it is hoped that soon political systems would be judged by their "liberty" score, welfare score and other ethical scores.

Karl Von Vonys writes, "The most salient feature of the study of political development is its relevance. It is relevant first of all to the evolution of our discipline. The last decades saw revolution in methodology. Beyond its academic and scientific significance, the study of political development is also relevant to a crucial problem of our time: the instability of political system." Again, "It would be outright tragic if the fruits of development theory would present the Asian and African masses with a choice between frustration and chaos on one hand and total submission on the other." Almond and Powell observe, "The world of politics has never waited, for the observer to finish his quiet contemplation. In the present century, political development seems to be proceeding at an ever accelerating rate, overwhelming our comparative snap-shots by making them obsolete before we finish our books and articles. It is increasingly obvious that the study of politics must be a dynamic system — and process analysis and not a static and structural one."

SUGGESTED READINGS

Almond and Coleman	:	The Politics of the Developing Areas.
Almond and Powell	:	Comparative Politics: A Developmental Approach.
Beer, Samuel H.	:	Patterns of Government.
Blondel	:	An Introduction to Comparative Government.
Bluhm, William T.	:	The Theories of the Political System.
Deutsch, Karl	:	The Nerves of Government.
Easton, David	:	A Systems Analysis of Political Life.
Hages, E.	:	On the Theory of Social Change.
Hyman, Herbert	:	Political Socialisation, 1959.
Lapalombara J. (Ed.)	:	Bureaucracy and Political Development.
McClell and. D.	:	The Achieving Society.
Merkl, P.H.	:	Comparative Politics.
Merton. R.K.	:	Social Theory and Social Structure.
Netti. J.P.	:	Political Mobilisation: A Sociological Analysis of Methods and Concepts.
Pye. Lucian	:	Aspects of Political Development.
Pye. Lucian	:	Political Culture and Political Development.
Pye. Lucian	:	Communication and Political Development.
Wiseman	:	Political Systems.

CHAPTER 12

Origin of the State

Dr. Garner rightly says that the origin of the state is a matter of speculation and controversial discussion. Ever since political philosophers began to philosophise, there has been a difference of opinion among them. The social contract theory which tried to explain the origin of the state by means of a contract, does not hold the field today. Likewise, the theory of the divine origin of the state stands discredited. The idea of revelation and the creation of state by God does not find favour in this century of science and experimentation. Nobody is prepared to go to the extent of saying that God created the state and kings are his servants and as his agents on earth are responsible not to the people but to Almighty God. The theory of force which ascribed the creation of the state to brute force has been discredited. It is contended that although force is a necessary factor in the creation and maintenance of the state, it is not and cannot be the only factor in the creation of the state. It is the evolutionary theory which is generally accepted in modern times.

Prof. R.N. Gilchrist writes, "Of the circumstances surrounding the dawn of political consciousness, we know little or nothing from history. Where history fails, we must resort to speculation. (Principles of Political Science, p. 48). J.W. Burgess observes, "The state is a gradual and continuous development of human society out of a grossly imperfect beginning through crude but improving forms of manifestation towards a perfect and universal organisation of mankind." The origin of the state is shrouded in mystery. How the state came into existence is still an enigma. Political scientists and historians only imagine the various factors which might have contributed and were responsible for the origin of the state. Most of the theories are only imaginary. Nowhere in history it has been recorded when the state actually came into existence.

Learning Objectives

- Social Contract Theory
- Thomas Hobbes (1588-1679)
- State of Nature
- The Social Contract
- Criticism of Views of Hobbes
- Value of His Theory
- John Locke (1632-1704)
- Locke's Concept of Human Nature
- State of Nature
- Social Contract
- Governmental Contract
- Criticism of Locke
- Values of his Theory
- Comparison of Views of Hobbes and Locke
- J.J. Rousseau (1712-1778)
- State of Nature
- Social Contract
- Law
- State and Government
- General Will
- Criticism of Rousseau
- Value of Rousseau's Theory
- Comparison of Hobbes, Locke and Rousseau
- Decline of the Theory of Social Contract
- Criticism of Social Contract Theory
- Value of the Theory
- Theory of Divine Origin
- Criticism

SOCIAL CONTRACT THEORY

The social contract theory is not only the most ancient but also the most famous of all the theories regarding the origin of the state. This theory influenced and practically dominated political thought for centuries. As long as this theory was not completely demolished, there was not much scope for any other theory.

The substance of this theory is that the state is the result of an agreement entered into by men who originally had no governmental organisation. The advocates of this theory divided the history of the world into two periods. In the first period, there was no government and no law. The people lived in a state of nature. After some time, they decided to set up a state. That they did by means of a contract. Thus the state was born and the state of nature was ended. The views of the various philosophers with regard to the state of nature and the terms of the contract differ. The state of nature was either too idyllic to last long or too inconvenient and unbearable for man to put up with. Hence men in the primitive state abandoned it and set up a political society through the instrumentality of a covenant. As a result of the covenant, each man lost his natural liberty in part or in whole and in its place he obtained the security and protection of the state. The contract was entered in different ways by its advocates. According to some, it was responsible for the institution of civil society alone, while others regarded it as resulting in the institution of a particular government. The contracting parties of the original contract were the individuals themselves emerging from the state of nature agreeing with one another and with all. The parties to the government contract were the people in their corporate capacity on the one hand and an agent or ruler on the other. Some regard it as actual historical fact while others consider it as a historical fiction.

The social contract theory can be traced as far back as the Greeks. In his book, *The Crito*, Plato shows Socrates awaiting the execution of his sentence even though he considered the same to be unjust. The reason given was that he would not like to break his covenant with the state by escaping from prison into exile. Likewise, in his *Republic*, it is stated that legislation and contracts between man and man originated in a compact of mutual abstinence from injustice.

The idea of contract was prominent in Roman law. A kind of contract is noticeable in feudalism. In Kautilya's Arthasastra, there is a reference to the creation of the state. The people agreed to give one-sixth of grains grown by them and one-tenth of their merchandise to the King and the latter agreed to take upon himself the responsibility of maintaining the safety and security of his subjects.

During the eleventh century A.D., Menegold developed the idea that a King could be deposed if he violated the agreement on the basis of which he was chosen. The view of Thomas Aquinas was that by his oath at his coronation, a king was supposed to have made a pact with his people to promote a happy and virtuous life and if he failed to fulfil his implied pact with his people, he ceased to deserve the right to expect that the pact would be kept by the people. Similar views were expressed by Mornay in *The Grounds of Rights Against Tyrants* (1579), by Buch in *On The Sovereign Power Among the Scots* and by Mariana in *On Kingship and Education of a King* (*1599*). In *The Laws of Ecclesiastical Polity,* Hooker stated that in the state of nature, men were subject only to the law of nature, but in course of time, they realised that there was no way but "growing into composition and agreement amongst themselves, by ordaining some kind of Government public and by yielding themselves subject thereunto." Althsuius used the idea of an original social contract in constructing his political system. In 1620, the Pilgrim Fathers entered into the following covenant: "We do solemnly and mutually, in the presence of God and of one another, covenant and combine ourselves together into a civil body politic for our better ordering and preservation." In his *Tenure of Kings and Magistrates,* Milton contended that men were born free and wrong sprang up through Adam's sin. In order to avoid their destruction, men "agreed by common league to bind each other from mutual injury and jointly to defend themselves against any that gave disturbance or opposition to such agreement." Again, "The power of kings and magistrates is nothing else, but what is only derivative, transferred and committed to them in trust from the people, to the common good of them all, in whom the power yet remains fundamentally and cannot be taken from them, without a violation of their natural birth-right". In the writings of Hobbes., Locke and Rousseau, the theory of social contract received systematic and wide treatment.

THOMAS HOBBES (1588-1679)

Hobbes was once a tutor to King Charles II of England. Hewasbornin 1588 at the time of the invasion of the Spanish Armada and he lived during the stirring times of the Great Rebellion and the Commonwealth. He saw the Civil War in England and was immensely affected by it. His conclusion was that the salvation of the country lay in having a ruler having absolute power as he alone could save England from anarchy and maintain law and order. He justified the rule of the Stuart Kings and defended their absolute powers. His views are to be found in his book "The Leviathan" which was published in 1651.

State of Nature

Hobbes has given a vivid picture of the people in the state of nature and how the same was ended by means of a social contract. According to him, the people in the state of nature were selfish and self-seeking. Their actions were dictated by self-interest. The motive of gain and the wish to satisfy appetite and desires was the motive behind all human action. Man, by nature, was anything but social animal. He found "nothing but grief in the company of his fellows". All men were equal, self-seeking and rapacious. The state of nature was a state of war, war of each against all. It was a state of continual fear. There was the constant danger of violent death. The life of man was solitary, poor, nasty, brutish and short. There was fear, distrust and suspicion among the people. That was clear from the fact that men locked their doors from within at night. Housewives locked their chests even from their own children and human beings went out armed. According to Hobbes, "We find three principles of quarrel — first competition, secondly diffidence, thirdly glory. The first maketh man invade for gain, the second for safety, the third for reputation." Again, "During the time men live without common power to keep them all in awe, they are in that condition, there is no place for industry, no culture, no navigation, no commodious building, no society." In the state of nature, there was no law, no justice and no property as these are the creation of the state. There was no distinction between right and wrong, no notion of justice and injustice and no distinction between good and bad. There was only force and fraud. Might was the only right. The only slogan was: "Kill whom you can, take what you can".

According to Hobbes, man undoubtedly wanted peace but his fear of others, his anxiety to retain what he already had and never-ending desire for acquiring more, led him to continuous conflict with his neighbours. Only considerations of his private interest could move him. Even if he knew that his private interests could best be served by cooperation with his friends, he was helpless. Later on, man's reason discovered the truth that peace was definitely more useful than war and the fear of violent death brought "man's passion into line with his reason."

Hobbes believed that in the state of nature certain laws governed the conduct of human-beings and he called them the laws of nature. The laws of nature were laws of prudence and expediency. Those laws demand that everybody should aim at and strive to secure peace. Men, in concert with others, should willingly give up their natural rights. They should assiduously keep their contracts. They should show gratitude or return beneficence for beneficence.

The Social Contract

The state of nature was ended by the people by entering into a covenant. Every man said to every other man: "I authorise and give up my right of governing myself to this man or this assembly of men on this condition that thou give up thy right to him and authorise all his actions in like manner. This done, the multitude so united in one person is called a Commonwealth. This is the generation of that great Leviathan or rather (to speak more reverently) of that Mortal God to which we owe under the Immortal God, our peace and defence." It was in this way that the state came into existence.

The sovereign was not a party to the contract. The people authorised and gave up the right of governing themselves to the sovereign who came into being as a result of the contract. They could not break the contract because it was based on the sentiment of fear. They entered into the contract for protecting their lives and safeguarding their interests. If they broke the contract and acted according to their will, they would degenerate into a primitive state and their lives would be in peril. As they had authorised the sovereign and offered him all their rights and had not reserved to themselves the right to break the ties of the contract, the question of breaking the ties of contract did not arise. As all persons had willingly entered into the contract, none had any right to break the terms of the contract. If any particular person did so, the sovereign could award him capital punishment and his action was justified. Hobbes deprived the people of their right to revolt against the sovereign even if his authority became arbitrary and despotic. To quote him, "Whatsoever the sovereign doth is unpunishable by the subject." Sovereignty cannot be divided. The sovereign has the authority to impart justice and deal with mutual disputes. He is the main source of law and his commands are laws. The contract is both social and political. It establishes the society and government at the same time. The contract is binding on the whole community as a perpetual bond. If the sovereign loses his power and the country is conquered by another person, the subjects of the first authority become the subjects of the conqueror. Hobbes allowed the individual to disobey the commands of the sovereign only when his life was in peril. The contract is eternally binding because to break the terms of the contract is to slip back into the insecure conditions of the state of nature from which the people had contracted to escape.

Sovereignty was inalienable and indivisible. The sovereign was the judge of what was necessary for the peace and defence of his subjects. Sovereignty could be in one person or in an assembly of persons, although Hobbes preferred monarchy. Law was the command of the sovereign. The sovereign was all-powerful. He had the power to declare war and conclude peace. He could choose his counsellors, ministers, magistrates and officers, both in times of peace and war. Sovereignty was indivisible, inseparable and incommunicable. Gettell writes, "Bodin limited sovereignty by divine law, natural law and the law of nations. Hobbes made sovereignty all-powerful and unlimited. His theory of sovereignty resulted in absolutism." He created an all-powerful sovereign on account of his belief that without such a sovereign power, law, order, peace and security could not be maintained in society. The obligation of the subjects to the sovereign lasted as long as the sovereign was in a position to protect them. They had the right to shift their allegiance when the sovereign was no longer in a position to protect them.

All men had agreed to renounce their rights but the sovereign had renounced nothing. He was not a party to the contract. The people had abandoned the state of nature, but the sovereign continued to be in the state of nature and did not abandon it. He possessed the unlimited right of nature. Although the sovereign derived his authority from the people, he was under no obligation to them. His subjects had a right to do only those things which were not prohibited by him. There was no limit to his powers.

Neither the Constitution nor any fundamental right could bind the sovereign. The sovereign could do no wrong. He could do no injury to his subjects because whatever he did was by the authority of his subjects. The sovereign had been authorised to do whatever seemed to him to be for the good of the people. The sovereign could not be punished by his subjects under any circumstances because to punish the sovereign for actions authorised by the subjects, was unjust and cruel. Every act of disobedience by the subject was unjust. The people killed by the sovereign for attempting to resist his authority committed suicide. A covenant with God could not be the basis for disregarding the authority of the sovereign. Without the knowledge of the sovereign, no contract could be made with God. Without the consent of the sovereign, there could be no other agreement. An agreement to recognise a new sovereign without the permission of the former was unjust because it was a violation of the pact by which his will was recognised. The breach of the original contract by the sovereign could not be a ground for disregarding his authority as he was not a party to the contract. The contract was social contract between individuals to give up their natural rights and vest them in the sovereign. The sovereign gave up nothing and retained all his natural rights and powers. The sovereign could do no injustice to his subjects as injustice means violation of the covenant. The sovereign had the power to control opinions and doctrines. According to Hobbes, the freedom of expression was the greatest source of evil. To govern men effectively, their opinions must be controlled first. The sovereign had unrestricted power over the property of individuals. He had the right to determine all controversies between the subjects. He was the fountain of justice. He had the power to make war and conclude peace. He had the right to command the army and levy and collect taxes. He was the sole source of all civil authority, all honours and all wealth. Law was the command of the sovereign and he alone had the power to interpret it. The sovereign was supreme both in spiritual and temporal matters. The Church could not claim any authority against the King. It was not divinely ordained and not independent of the sovereign. It obtained legal status by a gift of the sovereign and its claim to supernatural authority was baseless. The powers of the sovereign were incommunicable and inseparable.

Hobbes was opposed to the division of powers or mixed government. His view was that there would have been no civil war in England if the view that sovereignty was divided between the King, Lords and the Commons had not gained ground in England. Hobbes advised his sovereign not to allow the growth of groups and institutions that intervened between him and the individuals. Although the sovereign possessed unlimited and indivisible powers, the government was to interfere as little as possible in the day to day life of individuals. It was to permit them whatever did riot tend to disturb peace.

Hobbes formulated a new doctrine of liberty. He did not give the individual any right against the state. According to him, liberty had a double meaning, one for the sovereign and another for the subjects. The sovereign had the liberty to do anything but the individual, by his original contract, had set up another will to supersede his own. He could do only that which was not prohibited by law and not surrendered at the time of contract. Without injustice, the individual could refuse to kill himself. He could resist an assault on him. He could refuse to accuse himself of that offence which would involve his loss of life or honour. Under certain circumstances, he could even refuse to serve in the army.

Criticism of Views of Hobbes

Hobbes has been criticised for his anti-clericalism, secularism and contempt for universities. He was condemned on account of his view that theology was a branch of politics. Bently attributed the decay of morals to him. Dr. La Chaverel called him an atheistical monster. The clergy detested him. The Royalists disliked his theory because they recognised the state as a divine institution and according to them, it was shameful to the king to say that the state was the outcome of a social contract. Lord Clarendon, a Royalist, burnt Hobbes' book *The Leviathan* to ashes and declared, "I never saw any book which contains so much sedition, treason and impiety."

Hobbes is criticised for drawing a very dark picture of the state of nature and then evolving civil society through a social contract. In the state of nature, no contracts were possible as there was no sovereign to enforce them, but the social contract itself was made in the state of nature. The sovereign resulted from but did not co-exist with the social contract.

The view of Hobbes is that collective social action is impossible without the state but the ending of the state of nature and the foundation of the state by the surrender of natural rights was itself a collective social action preceding the state.

The sovereign of Hobbes was representative of the people. There was no guarantee that he would represent them, *i.e.*, follow the public opinion and look after public welfare. Locke ridicules the social contract of Hobbes in these words: "When men, quitting the state of nature, entered into society, they agreed that all of them but one should be under the restraint of laws, but that he should still retain all the liberty of the state of nature, increased with power and made licentious by impunity. This is to think that men are so foolish that they care to avoid what mischief may be done by them by polecats and foxes, but are content, nay, think it safety, to be devoured by lions."

The views of Hobbes are based on unsound foundations. His state of nature was a state of war of all against all in which "cardinal virtues are force and fraud." The man in the state of nature was anti-social. Such a man could not enter "a state not of war, but of peace, a state in which force and fraud are deliberately set aside, a state which is founded upon ideas of right and justice and in which acts of wrong and injustice are put under the double ban of public disapproval and of positive prohibition." Such a natural man could not become suddenly a cringing slave. Hobbes did not realise that man has always possessed gregarious instincts. He is not all force and fraud. Even primitive people have their code of morality, Savages have their customs which are as effective as law in a civilised society.

Hobbes used his concept of the law of nature as it suited him. Sometimes that law represented a brute instinct and sometimes a normal idea. Hobbes was neither a utilitarian nor purely an idealist. With him, the self-interest of an individual before the social contract was suddenly changed into his duty towards his sovereign after contract. The difficulty with Hobbes was that he ignored all tendencies and forces which bring people together and over-emphasized selfishness and mutual fear which separated them. He did not admit that men by nature were sympathetic, generous, altruistic and gregarious and had a sense of social obligations to their fellow beings. The cynical view of human nature of Hobbes was unsound. He did not realise that the unit of primitive life was not an individual but the family or a group. Man in the state of nature was neither a moral nor a political animal and such a person could not be expected to enter into an agreement by which he irrevocably and unconditionally surrendered all his natural rights. The view of Hobbes was that the only alternative to the absolutism of a single individual sovereign was anarchy, but this view is not supported by the history of the Middle Ages when power was divided between the state and the Church and the King and his feudal vassals. It is not correct to say that wherever there is not absolute sovereign, there is anarchy.

Hoobes did not realise that there were other factors besides the fear of law and punishment which kept men from relapsing into anarchy and those were commonsense, reason, conviction and public opinion. Even wolves act together because of herd instinct. Even the beasts do not hurt or kill their own species.

According to Hobbes, the function of the state was merely a negative one. Its sole duty was the preservation of life and maintenance of order. The Leviathan of Hobbes was essentially a policeman. "This state is a necessary evil, an instrument to defend men against their savage instincts, not to achieve a free and progressive civilisation." Such a view is not accepted today. We believe in a welfare state.

The state of Hobbes was authoritarian and not totalitarian. It was based on contractual obligation. It was not anti-individualistic because the sovereign had to "deliver the goods" to the individual by protecting him.

Hobbes' explanation of the social contract is illogical and irrational. There is absolutely no historical evidence to show that the state emerged at a particular period of history by a natural and deliberate agreement. The social contract is impossible because the history of primitive societies has shown conclusively that man moved from status to contract. The view of Hobbes was that man moved from contract to status.

The theory of Hobbes is legally not sound. In law, a contract is always made between two parties. It cannot be unilateral or one-sided. Hobbes did not make the sovereign a party to the contract but its beneficiary. His contract is perpetual and irrevocable. In jurisprudence, a contract is always revocable under certain conditions.

Hobbes' theory of sovereignty has been criticised. Vaughan rejects it as "pernicious and impossible". It is pernicious because it leads to despotism. It gives the subjects no defence against oppressive and tyrannical rule of a despot and reduces the whole herd to slavery. The sole bond of union between the members of the Leviathan is a common terror, the fear of relapsing into the state of nature. His theory opens the floodgates to absolutism and lays the foundation of authoritarian state. Dr. G.P. Gooch writes, "Leviathan is the policeman, not an instructor. His state is a necessary evil, an instrument to defend men against savage instincts, not to achieve a free and progressive civilisation (Political Thought in England, p. 33).

Hobbes' theory explains only the concept of legal sovereignty and does not recognise the theory of political sovereignty. The political sovereign is at the back of legal sovereign and superior to it. The king is not completely independent of the people who retain ultimately the right to change and replace him if he fails to perform the functions assigned to him. Changing the ruler does not imply relapsing into the state of nature.

Hobbes failed to distinguish between state and government. According to him, a successful revolution in a society disintegrates it and means a return to the anarchy of the state of nature. This is not a correct view. The dissolution of a particular government does not mean the dissolution of the state. It also does not amount to the abolition of civil society. Willoughby points out that the cardinal fault of Hobbes was his utter failure to distinguish between state and government. The state is sovereign and not the government which enjoys only that authority which is delegated to it by the state. Hence, the change of government does not involve the death of the state.

According to Laski, Hobbes' legal view of rights is insufficient for political philosophy. It fails to distinguish between the rights recognised by the state and the rights which require recognition as the indispensable conditions for the development of individual personality. The very concept of rights emanates from the moral personality of man. The legal sanction for them is only provided by the state.

Value of His Theory

In spite of his shortcomings, it must be conceded that Hobbes was the first to present a scientific and logical system of political philosophy. The view of Dr. Dunning was that Hobbes was the first Englishman to present a system of political philosophy that could stand among the great systems of history. His work "placed him at once in the front rank of political thinkers and his theory became, from the moment of its appearance, the centre of animated controversy and enormous influence throughout Western Europe." Dr. Sabine says that "Hobbes was probably the greatest writer on political philosophy that the English-speaking people have produced." Oakeshott considers "Leviathan" the greatest, perhaps the sole, masterpiece of political philosophy in the English language. According to Wayper, "Hobbes is no liberal or democrat; but he is an individualist not because he believes in the sanctity of an individual man but because for him the world is and must always be made of individuals." He made the state a Leviathan, but reduced it to a utility, good for what it does. The power of the state is justified because it contributes to the security of individual human beings.

According to Ivor Brown, Hobbes was the first great philosopher of discipline. He made it very clear that law and order was most essential for the smooth running of the state. In the absence of discipline, the progress of culture and civilisation would be hampered. Law and order could be maintained only by the use of power.

By making a clear distinction between natural and civil laws, Hobbes "laid the foundation for that system of Analytical Jurisprudence that was afterwards elaborated by Bentham and Austin."

From the moment of its appearance, the work of Hobbes became the centre of animated controversy and had an enormous influence throughout Western Europe. Bacon paid his tribute to Hobbes in these words: "Truth emerges more easily from error than from confusion."

The greatest contribution of Hobbes to political thought was his theory of sovereignty. He gave to the concept of sovereignty the shape and content which it holds today. He saw more clearly than anybody before him that the idea of sovereignty lay at the very root of any theory of the state. His view that law is the command of the sovereign and no law can be recognised which cannot be enforced by punishment was adopted by Austin and forms the basis of the latter's system of jurisprudence. The Austinian theory of sovereignty is substantially the Hobbesian theory of sovereign power. While Machiavelli had separated politic from religion and morals, Hobbes not only kept up the separation but subordinated religion and morals to politics. Bodin had limited his sovereignty by divine laws, natural laws and law of nations, but the sovereignty of Hobbes was unlimited and indivisible. However, Hobbes was an individualist in so far as he believed in the natural equality of man.

Hobbes was not the spiritual father of totalitarianism, Fascism or Communism. Government is set up by a covenant that transfers all power and authority to the sovereign. There can be no contract without consent. This contractual foundation is an anathema to totalitarianism. According to the Nazis, the state originated in the spirit of the people and was not a deliberate creation. The Fascists attacked the contractual theory of the state. The Communists reject the theory of social contract because state is not the product of a rational compact. It is the result of violence and exploitation. The state of Hobbes was individualistic. It is not guided by the longing of the citizens for happiness but by a collective purpose which is the promotion of the glory of the master race in Germany, the revival of the Roman Empire in Italy and the victory of the proletariat in Soviet Russia. Hobbes was authoritarian but not totalitarian. He stood for equality before law so that the rich and the poor may be equal before it. Totalitarianism is based on inequality before law. Hobbes believed in the theory of *Laissez-faire.* In a totalitarian state, economy is rigidly controlled and planned. Hobbes gave freedom in bringing up children which is opposed to the regimentation and drilling of children in totalitarian states. According to Hobbes, the sovereign may be one man or an assembly of men but totalitarianism puts emphasis on the principle of leadership. The sovereign of Hobbes was the supreme administrator and law-giver and not a top rabble-rouser propagandist or snowman. Hobbes did not glorify war but the totalitarian states glorify war. The Communists believe in the inevitability of war between classes and the liquidation of the bourgeoisie by violent means. The sovereign of Hobbes insisted on outward conformity of the subjects to law. They were bound to obey the law but not bound to believe in it. Hobbes was not prepared to destroy man for the sake of truth, but the totalitarians are always ready to destroy man for the sake of truth. The state of Hobbes did not completely swallow the individual. The civil society was set up for the preservation and protection of the life of man, not his annihilation. The individuals have certain inalienable rights, in the state which is not true of totalitarian states.

John Locke (1632-1704)

John Locke was an ardent advocate of constitutional monarchy and an opponent of absolute monarch in England. He expressed his views in his book entitled *Two Treatises On Civil Government* which was published in 1689. In that book, Locke tried to justify the Glorious Revolution of 1688 and the deposition of James II. His contention was that Parliament reserved to itself the right to dethrone the King if he disobeyed the commands and overlooked or ignored the claims of the public will. He justified the deposition of James II and supported the coronation of King William III and Queen Mary. Locke sought to "establish the throne of our great Restorer, our present King William, and make good his title in the consent of the people." The words "in the consent of the people" (form the keynote of Locke's theory. According to Locke, civil power is based upon consent.

The historical background of both Hobbes and Locke is similar. Hobbes, impressed by the miseries of the Great Rebellion, argued on the basis of the social contract for a system of absolute monarchy. Locke, on the same basis, tried to justify the deposition of James II and establishment of constitutional government. Like Hobbes, Locke also begins his essay with a description of the state of nature. However, his views are different from those of Hobbes.

Locke's Concept of Human Nature

Locke considered human beings as pretty decent fellows, far removed from quarrelsome, competitive, and selfish creatures of Hobbes. Locke believed that desire is the main string of all human acts and a feeling of pleasure comes when desire is satisfied. The object of all human action is the acquisition of pleasure and avoidance of pain. Locke believed in the goodness of human nature. According to him, men are basically decent, orderly and society-loving, capable of ruling themselves. They are rational and social. Rationality is a pervasive characteristic of man. Macpherson writes, "We are accustomed to think that Locke held man to be essentially rational and social. Rational, in that they could live together by the Jaw of nature which is reason, or which at least (though not imprinted on the mind) is knowable by reason, without the help of revelation. Social, in that they could live by the laws of nature without the imposition of rules by a sovereign". According to Locke, the individual can live in a moral way even without the state. Man by nature is endowed with the light of reason which he calls the "spark of divine nature." This spark enables man to discern and follow the law of nature which is behind all things. The state of nature could not be a state of war. It was one of peace, goodwill, mutual assistance and preservation.

State of Nature

While the state of nature of Hobbes was both pre-social and pre-political, that of Locke was only pre-political. According to Locke, people lived in society in the state of nature. They were social and had rights and liberties. The state of nature was not one of universal war but one of inconvenience. The reason was that there was the standing want of an established and known law. The law of nature was given individual interpretation by every individual. There was the lack of a "known and indifferent judge" who could give an authoritative interpretation of the law of nature. Life was inconvenient because each individual had to interpret the law of nature for himself and had also to enforce it without the help of any other authority.

According to Locke, the state of nature was a state of equality and freedom. The individual was endowed with sound natural rights. To quote him, "The state of nature has a law of nature to govern it which obliges every one; and reason, which is that law, teaches all mankind who will but consult it, that being all equal and independent, no one ought to harm another in his life, health, liberty, or possessions. "Barker writes, "Locke's state of nature, with his regime of recognised rights, is already a political society."

In the state of nature, people experienced certain inconveniences. There was no clear definition of the law of nature. There was no common and independent arbiter having authority to decide dispute in agreement with the law of nature. There was no sufficient authority to enforce those decisions.

According to Locke, "Though this state of nature be a state of liberty, yet it is not a state of licence, that man in that state has uncontrollable liberty to dispose of person or possessions, yet he has no liberty to destroy himself or so much any creature in his possession but where some nobler use than its above preservation calls for it." Again, "Reason teaches all mankind who will to consult it, that being equal and independent, no one ought to harm another in his life, health or possession." The result was that the people obeyed the laws of nature and lived peacefully. They staked career, happiness and their whole future on their judgement of what they thought either right or wrong. Difficulties arose after some time as there were no fixed laws or any judge to interpret the laws and give justice. Everybody interpreted the law of nature in his own way. That created trouble, anarchy and disorder.

Social Contract

Locke deals with two contracts: social and governmental. Social contract leads to the formation of civil society and the governmental contract to the establishment of the government. The social contract put an end to the primitive state of nature. Society is organised for protecting human life and safeguarding its property and freedom. Man does not give up all of his rights to society but only the rights of health, liberty and possession. Anybody who disobeys is liable to be punished by society. Society transfers some of its power to a selected few persons who form the government. The ruler and the people enter into this contract.

Each individual contracted with other to unite in the social society. Man "willingly give up every one his single power of punishing to be exercised by such alone as shall be appointed to it amongst them and by such rules as the community and those authorised by them to that purpose, shall agree on." Each individual gave up his right of interpreting and enforcing the law of nature. Only that right was surrendered and not all the natural rights as in the case of Hobbes. That right was given to the community as a whole and not to a man or assembly of men as in the case of Hobbes.

Governmental Contract

After the first contract was concluded, the people in their corporate capacity entered into another contract, the governmental contract. The government was empowered by the community to legislate any agreement with the law of nature, decide disputes and enforce laws. It became a party to the contract and was bound by the terms of the contract. Sovereignty belonged to the community or the people who had an inalienable right to dismiss the government if it proved false to the trust reposed in it. Thus, Locke made the consent of the people the source of all government authority. To quote Locke, "The community perpetually retains a supreme power of saving themselves from the attempts and designs of anybody. Wherever they shall be so foolish or so wicked as to lay and carry on designs against the liberties and properties of the subject. Whenever any one shall go about to bring them to slavish condition, they will always have a right to rid themselves of those who invade this fundamental, sacred and unalterable law of self-preservation. "The governmental contract is subordinate to the social contract because the Government is "only a judiciary power" to act for certain aims and its authority is limited to achieving those ends. It is confined to the condition that it is used in the exercise of "established known laws." If the Government fails to attain those ends for which it was established and to which it agreed, the community can dismiss it and replace it. The government is like a trustee. If the Government fails to protect the life of the people and safeguard their property and liberty, the people have the right to rise in revolt and dismiss it and replace it. In this way, Locke supported limited monarchy or constitutional monarchy.

According to Gettell, the social contract of Locke was specific and unlimited and not general as in the case of Hobbes. Men surrendered only the right of enforcing the law of nature. All other rights were retained by them as before. The rulers were excluded from the social contract. The agreement was between free individuals and not between the rulers and the ruled. The rulers were merely given fiduciary power or trust to be exercised solely for the good of the community. Locke made a distinction between society and government. By one contract, the society was created and by the other the government. The sovereign power created by the contract vested in the community as a whole and not in a single man or any organ. The government must be based firmly upon the consent of the masses. To quote Locke, "Men being by nature all free, equal and independent, no one can be put out of this estate and subjected to the political power of another, without his consent." The contract is irrevocable because after having once made it, the people cannot revert back to the freedom of the state of nature. Even after the social contract, the people do not forfeit their natural right to life, liberty and property.

According to Wayper, the state of Locke exists for the people who form it They do not exist for the state. The state is based on the consent of the people. It is a constitutional state where there is rule of law. It is limited and not absolute. The dissolution of the government does not mean the dissolution of civil society. It is a tolerant state. It tolerates differences of opinion. It is a negative state which does not interfere in the lives of the people. It transforms selfish interests into public good.

Criticism of Locke

According to Willoughby, the basic defect in the writings of Locks is that he did not sufficiently distinguish between the community as simply a social aggregate and as a political body and sovereignty in its true legal sense resides in the latter and not in the former. The view of Barker is that Locke had no clear view of the nature and residence of sovereignty. He spoke of the supreme power of the people and yet he attributed supreme power to the legislature.

Sabine says that "the greatest weakness of Locke's philosophy in all its branches was that he never got back to first principles. His commonsense saved him perhaps from many dialectical quibbles, but in the end it meant that he took much for granted on inadequate analysis and combined propositions that analysis showed to be incompatible." Again, "Locke's political philosophy was an effort to combine past and present and also to find a nucleus of agreement for the reasonable men of all parties, but he did not synthesize all that he combined."

Locke's description of the state of nature is unreal and unhistorical. History does not give us any example where the state of nature was the state of equality and freedom. Locke says that people had certain rights in the state of nature but in the absence of the state, they could not have any rights. Locke put emphasis on the physical aspect of the state and not on its moral aspect. The view that the consent of the people forms the basis of the state is only partially true because force has also played a decisive role in the origin and development of the state. Hobbes has given a theory of sovereignty without recognising the existence and power of political sovereignty. Locke recognises the force of political sovereignty but does not give an adequate recognition to legal Sovereignty. He also failed to see that revolution, however desirable, is never legal.

The sovereignty of Locke is divisible. It is divided between the people and the king, but in fact it is not so. Locke tried to save the people from the tyranny of the state but overlooked the fact that if the people revolted against the state, no punishment could be given to them.

Locke protects the people from the tyranny of the state but he does not provide for the protection of the state. Even a minority of the people could denounce the laws of the state on the pretext that they were against the natural law. That could pose a danger to the state.

Critics maintain that Locke's theory is ambiguous, confused and unclear. His explanation of human nature is unreal and one-sided because man is not always . rational. The state of nature as depicted by him is also hazy. It is not clear whether it was pre-social or pre-political.

Value of his Theory

Locks occupies a very important place among the political philosophers of the modern age. According to Maxey, although there is little that is absolutely original in the political philosophy of Locke, it is nonetheless a fact that he must be ranked as one of "the few political thinkers whose work will never die." He gave the world a systematic, rational and eminently realisable philosophy of individualism, popular sovereignty and constitutional government.

Locke was the first utilitarian and he was essentially an individualist. His theory of consent and the theory of revolt are important contributions to political theory. His doctrine of natural rights constitutes his most distinctive contribution to political philosophy. Every constitutional limitation on sovereign power, every constitutional safeguard of individual liberty, every security accorded to property, every barrier against arbitrary and unlimited authority and every declaration of rights in the written Constitutions of the last two centuries was predicted by Locke.

Sabine writes, "His sincerity, his profound moral conviction, his genuine belief in liberty and in the dignity of human nature united with his moderation and good sense, made him the ideal spokesman of the middle class revolution. As a force in propagating the ideals of liberal but non-violent reform, Locke probably stands before all other writers whosoever. Even his more doubtful ideas such as separation of powers and the inevitable wisdom of majority decisions, remained a part of democratic creed." Again, "The mark of his genius was neither learning nor logic but an incomparable commonsense by which he gathered together the chief convictions, in philosophy, politics, morals and eduction,that the experience of the past had generated in the more enlightened minds of his generation. By giving to these a simple and sober, yet persuasive statement, he passed them on to the eighteenth century where they became the matrix from which grew the later philosophy both of England and the Continent."

Bentham's utilitarian philosophy is based on Locke's philosophy. The heroes who led and participated in the French Revolution were greatly influenced by the ideas of Locke. The makers of the American Constitution sought inspiration from his philosophy. His views awakened the people of Europe politically and the authority of the rulers began to be confined which gradually resulted in the dawn of democracy.

Comparison of Views of Hobbes and Locke

If we compare the views of Hobbes and Locke, we find a lot of difference between the two. The state of nature of Hobbes was a state of war. It was a war of all against all. According to Locke, the state of nature was a state of equality and freedom. The view of Hobbes was that the people in the state of nature were selfish and quarrelsome and their life was solitary, poor, nasty, brutish and short. The view of Locke was that the people in the state of nature had the right to life, liberty and property. Their life was merely inconvenient because each interpreted his rights in his own way. According to Hobbes, the people gave up all their rights to the sovereign by means of a social contract. Hobbes stood for absolute sovereignty. Locke stood for constitutional or limited government. The right to life, liberty and property were not given to the sovereign. The sovereign of Hobbes was not a party to the social contract and hence was not subjected to the conditions of the contract. In Locke's theory, the people surrendered only a few of their rights. They also reserved to themselves the right to dethrone the ruler. According to Locke, the ruler was a trustee of the people, but that was not the view of Hobbes. There was only one contract in the case of Hobbes but there were two contracts in the case of Locke. According to Hobbes, the main source of law was the ruler. According to Locke, laws were passed by the legislature. Locke made a distinction between the executive and the legislature but Hobbes did not. According to Locke, the government was based on consent and the people had the final power. There was no place for the public in the theory of Hobbes. According to Locke, the people could revolt against the ruler but that was not so in the case of Hobbes.

J.J. ROUSSEAU (1712-1778)

Rousseau was born in Geneva in 1712 but he settled down in Paris after many wanderings. He gave a theory of social contract in his books *The Social Contract and Emile.* Unlike Hobbes and

Locke, Rousseau had no axe to grind. He had no purpose to serve. He was deeply affected by the political situation in France. His views were also affected by Plato, Montesquieu, Cicero, Hobbes and Locke. His ideas were vehemently criticised and his books were burnt. He was so much disgusted and disappointed that he committed suicide in 1778. However, his greatness was recognised later on and his views had tremendous influence on the outbreak of the French Revolution in 1789.

State of Nature

According to Rousseau, the state of nature was an era of idyllic felicity. Reason did not guide the actions of individuals who were moved by their emotions. Rousseau wrote, "Man by nature never thinks and he who thinks is a corrupt creature." Every individual had unlimited liberty in the state of nature. There was no private property, no competition and no jealousy. Every individual lived the free life of a savage. He know neither right nor wrong and was away from all notions of virtue and vice. There was innocence everywhere.

According to Rousseau, "Man is born free and everywhere he is in chains." He revolted against the established canons of society and advocated the doctrine of "Back to nature."

With the passage of time, things changed in the state of nature. The increase in population and dawn of reason were mainly responsible for the change. Simplicity and happiness disappeared. The people started thinking in terms of mine and thine. In the words of Rousseau, "The first man who after enclosing a piece of ground, bethought himself to say 'this is mine', and found people simple enough to believe him, was the real founder of civil society." The arts of agriculture and metallurgy were discovered and in the application of them men had need of one another's aid. Cooperation revealed and emphasized the diversity of man's talents. The stronger man did the greater amount of work but the craftier got more of the product. Thus appeared the difference of rich and poor — the prolific source all other sources of inequality. Life became intolerable. There were wars and murders everywhere. The problem was "to find a form of association which protects with the whole common force the person and property of each associate, and in virtue of which everyone, while uniting himself to all....remains as free as before." The problem was solved through a social contract.

Social Contract

By a social contract, everyone surrendered to the community all his rights and the result was that the community became sovereign. The sovereign was absolute. However, even after the contract, the individual remained as free as he was before. To quote Rousseau, "Since each gives himself up to all, he gives himself up to no one; and as there is acquired over every associate the same right that is given up himself, there is gained the equivalent of what is lost, with greater power to preserve what is left." Law was the expression of the general will. Sovereignty could never be alienated or represented or divided. The government was not the same thing as the sovereign. The government was not a party to the contract. In the words of Rousseau, "There is only one contract in the state and this excludes every other." The government was created in this manner. First of all a law was passed by the sovereign to the effect that there will be a government and after that, the governors were appointed.

Rousseau identified sovereignty with the general will or the common interests of the community. His sovereignty was infallible, indivisible, unrepresentative and illimitable. Sovereignty was unrepresentative because it lay in the general will which could not be represented. The sovereign of Rousseau was absolute like that of Hobbes. The only difference was that while Hobbes assigned sovereignty to the head of the state; Rousseau gave it to the whole community. According to Rousseau, the sovereign people could not divest themselves of their sovereignty even if they wished so. Rousseau united the absolute sovereignty of Hobbes and the popular consent of Locke into the philosophic doctrine of popular sovereignty. Hobbes made no distinction between the sovereign and the government, but Rousseau made a distinction between the two. Rousseau ruled out a representative form of government. His belief that the people of England who had a representative form of government were not free. They were free only on the election day and after that they were enslaved. Rousseau stood for a small state where the people could meet and pass laws and had no necessity of sending their representatives to the Central Government.

Even after giving absolute powers to the sovereign, Rousseau laid down that the sovereign must rule properly. He must not do anything which is not in the interests of the people. He must ensure equality of all before law and maintain a rule of justice. He "cannot impose upon its subjects fetters that are useless to the community." Rousseau's view of sovereignty was a compromise between the constitutionalism of Locke and the absolutism of Hobbes. According to Rousseau, sovereignty lies in the general will which cannot impose any limitation on itself. It cannot have any interest apart from those of the people and therefore there is no need for any limitation on it.

According to Rousseau, just as nature gives each individual an absolute power over all his parts, likewise the social contract gives an absolute power to the body politic over all its parts. It is this power which is called sovereignty. The absolutism of the sovereign is not based on fear or compulsion but on consent. The various powers such as legislative, executive etc. are only emanations of sovereignty which is one and unified and which collectively belongs to the people. Sovereignty is the source of all laws. The separation of powers is not the division of sovereignty but the exercise of it for the sake of convenience.

According to Rousseau, the individual is free in the state because he does not surrender his rights to an outside authority but to the corporate body of which he himself is a member. Any restrictions on the liberty of individuals are self-imposed. "Obedience to a law which we prescribe to ourselves is liberty." The rights of liberty, equality and property are rights of the citizen and not the natural and inherent rights of the individual. Liberty is civil liberty and not natural liberty. Men are equal by law and not by nature. In actual practice, man alienates only such of "his powers, goods and liberty as it is for the community to control but it must be guaranteed".

Law

According to Rousseau, law is the expression of the general will. "A law is a resolution of the whole people, for the whole people, touching a matter that concerns all." Law must relate to general interest. It represents the general will. The enactments of the government are merely a corollary of the general will. Nobody in the state is above the law as everybody is a member of the sovereign body which is the source of law. The laws representing the general will cannot be unjust because nobody is unjust to himself. One is free when he is subject to laws because laws merely reflect his own will. A state is legitimate only when it is ruled by law. Laws are the sole motive power of the community "which acts and feels only through them." "The law considers the subjects collectively and their actions in the abstract; it never has for its object an individual man or particular action."

State and Government

Rousseau made a distinction between the state and government. According to him, a state denotes the community as a whole created by the social contract and manifesting itself in the supreme general will, while a Government denotes merely the individual or group of individuals that is designated by the community to carry into effect the sovereign will. The government is an intermediary between the sovereign state and the subjects. It is a subordinate agency through which the sovereign people expresses its will and realises it. No form of government is ideal. An individual can resist the government but not the state. The social contract creates not the government but the state which is sovereign. The government is created by a decree of the sovereign to serve as a means of complying with the general will. It is an agent of the sovereign who can change it. The government does not make laws but merely administers them. Rousseau's view of government is that of the executive side of a modern democracy whose power may be withdrawn or modified by the sovereign legislature. The laws represent the general will and therefore every state ruled by law, whatever its form of government, is a republic.

As regards the origin of government, the sovereign people assemble to institute the government. To begin with, they vote that a certain form of government shall be instituted and then vote that certain individuals shall be appointed to the offices thus created. The first vote expresses the general will and is law. The second vote represents a mere government decree. Between the two votes, there is a change in the character of the popular assembly. In its first form, the assembly is the sovereign and in the second form it becomes a democratic government. Thus, every form of government originates in democracy.

The sovereign of Rousseau is as absolute as that of Hobbes. His individual surrenders his person and all his fights to the community. If after the formation of civil society he enjoys his rights, it is as a citizen and not as an individual. The sovereign state can regulate those rights and even abrogate them at its will and convenience. The sovereignty of state is unlimited. No fundamental law can limit the sovereign community of the state. The state works for the good of all and there is no necessity of limiting its powers. It is the sovereign community which has absolute and unlimited powers and not the government. The sovereign of Rousseau is the people.

General Will

The concept of the general will is the crux of Rousseau's political system. It has created a revolution in the realm of political philosophy. Rousseau makes a distinction between the real will and the actual will. The actual will corresponds to the will of the individual. This will makes man self-centred who does not think of the good of others. The real will always aims at the general good. It is pure and perfect and always leads to general welfare.

Rousseau also makes a distinction between the general will and the will of all. According to him, the general will is always just and always aims at the public good, but it does not follow that the deliberations of the people are always right. There is a considerable difference between the general will and will of all. The former aims at the common interest but the latter aims at private interests and is only a sum of particular wills. If we take away from these wills the various particular interests which conflict with each other, what remains is the general will. The general will is the will of all citizens when they are willing not their own private interests but the general good. It is the voice of all for the good of all. It is the attribute of all individual citizens willing their best wills for the general good. It is a group mind being the compound of the best wills of all citizens willing the best interests of the state. It represents not a mere compromise after cancelling out pluses and minuses but represents a higher type of will of society. It represents the common conscience of the common good after proper discussion and deliberations. However, in actual practice it is difficult to distinguish between the general will and the will of all.

The will of each individual is merged into the general will which corresponds to the common interests of all the members of the community. It is the expression of what the common interests require. It is arrived at by asking each member to vote for what he believes to be the common good. Everybody is allowed to will his own will and thus the majority will is found. When the majority will is found, those who did not vote with the majority must say to themselves that they did not will the general will and hence they must will what the majority will is. It is in this way that the majority will becomes the general will by the minority willing as the majority had willed.

General will cannot be self-contradictory. It is a reasonable will. It makes for unity in diversity. It is permanent. It is not to be found in the tempest of popular feelings or in the vagaries of statement. It is always the right will. It always stands for the welfare of the whole. It is infallible. It can never be wrong. There can be no justifications for disobeying it. Whenever an individual differs from the general will, he is in the wrong because his will is merely a selfish will and not the general will. There is no coercion even when a man is made to do something which is against his will. As his real will is to be found in the general will which is manifested by the authority of the state, he is free even when he is put in jail by the government. In other words, he wills his own imprisonment.

The general will is inalienable and indivisible. It cannot be represented in any legislature. The general will cannot be delegated. The moment it is delegated, it ceases to be the general will. "The moment there is a master, there is no longer sovereign." Rousseau stood for direct democracy and popular sovereignty.

The view of Rousseau was that so long as the general will was the sovereign, the form of government did not matter. However, the state should be a small one so that all the people may be able to assemble at one place and make laws. To quote him, "The larger the state, the less the liberty."

Critics point out that the doctrine of general will is too abstract and narrow to be found in the practical world. The general will is neither general nor will. It can be determined only by a majority vote and not otherwise. The doctrine of general will may lead to state absolutism. In the name of the general will, the worst type of tyranny may be practised. It is amusing to know how a person can be made free against his own will in the name of the general will. It is no consolation for him if he is told that he is not willing the general will which is willed only by the sovereign and even when he is being made to do something which is against his conscience, he is actually being made free. The doctrine of general will is based on the idea of common interest which is difficult to define. Even the worst of the tyrants can justify their actions on the ground of common good. Even if it is assumed that the general will is always right, it is not true that the machinery of the government is never in the wrong.

In defence of the doctrine of general will, it is contended that this doctrine emphasizes the organic unity of society. "The state, indeed, has no life apart from the lives of its members, but it has or may have a longer, broader and fuller life than that of any individual or any organisation of its citizens." The doctrine of general will also emphasizes the fact that "the state exists and claims all our obedience because it is a natural extension of our personality." It also shows that the true basis of democracy is not force but the active will of the people. The view of T.H. Green that "will, not force, is the basis of the state", is also based on the principle of the general will.

Criticism of Rousseau

The idea of general will as given by Rousseau is not very clear at different places particularly when he makes a distinction between the general will and the will of all. Wayper writes, "So much vagueness about something as important as the finding of the general will is to be regretted. Rousseau who has told us so much about the general will has still not told us enough; indeed he has left us in such a position that nobody can be sure what the general will is on any particular point." History does not confirm Rousseau's description of the state of nature or the creation of a state by means of a contract. His views are unhistorical and imaginary. General will can encourage absolutism and justify tyranny. The social contract is illogical. The will of the individual is indivisible and cannot be divided into actual will and real will.

Value of Rousseau's Theory

Rousseau was the apostle of popular sovereignty. His social contract upheld the ideals of democracy. He brought into prominence the idea of consent and established once for all that the will, not force, is the basis of the state. He championed the cause of direct democracy by vesting the legislative power in the people. He immensely affected the events leading to the outbreak of the French Revolution in 1789. The Declaration of Rights of Man (1789) bears the stamp of his personality. Dr. Leacock writes, "With Rousseau the doctrine of social contract, which in the hands of Hobbes was made a weapon of defence for absolutism and with Locke a shield for constitutional limited monarchy, becomes the basis of popular sovereignty." Liberty and equality are "the sheet-anchors" of Rousseau's thought. Those are highly prized by democracies.

Rousseau's doctrine of sovereignty aimed at reconciling liberty and authority. Through Rousseau, the general welfare of the people and the general will of the community assumed great importance and became the starting point of all later theories of the state.

Rousseau's theory promoted unity and solidarity in the state. He is rightly considered as one of the creators of the modern national state. He emphasized the fact that the people are the ultimate source of all political authority and the government is merely the agent and delegate of the sovereign people.

Rousseau had a passion for democracy. His emphasis on popular sovereignty helped the cause of democracy. He made a distinction between state and government. He erected the governmental structure on the consent of the people. He assigned a moral primacy to the will of the state. In the case of a conflict between the will of the state and that of an individual, Rousseau decided in favour of the state. Rousseau did not make any distinction between state and society and thereby made possible total control of human life by the state. It is said that Rousseau's general will is Hobbes' Leviathan with its head chopped off.

His philosophy was against absolute kingship or despotic monarchy. He justified revolutions against arbitrary rule. He was the apostle of direct democracy According to Rousseau, law is the symbol of the general will and hence he refuted absolutism which was popular in his time.

Dunning writes, "Rousseau's spirit and dogmas, however disguised and transformed, are seen everywhere both in the speculative systems and in the government organisations of the stirring era that followed his death." About Rousseau, J.M. Cohen observes, "No one had as much influence as he on two centuries."

Comparison of Hobbes, Locke and Rousseau

It is said that Rousseau blended together the premises of Hobbes and conclusions of Locke. Some of his principal ideas closely resembled those of Hobbes: one single contract out of which the state emerged and to which the government was not a party, total surrender of individual rights and interests to the sovereign. However, his conclusions are different from those of Hobbes. According to Rousseau, the government was not absolute. He accepted the essentials of Locke's creed that the source of governmental authority lies in the consent of the community. Like Locke and unlike Hobbes, he believed in the surrender of individual rights not to the ruler but to the community. He made a clear distinction between state and government. In certain respects, Rousseau differed from Locke. There is reference to one contract in Rousseau as against two in Locke. Unlike Rousseau, Locke made the government a party to one of the contracts. The sovereign of Rousseau was absolute but that of Locke was limited. According to Rousseau, popular sovereignty is in perpetual operation. The view of Locke is that it is latent authority which is to be called into operation when the government violates popular trust. Unlike Locke, Rousseau lapsed into totalitarianism. In the philosophy of Rousseau, the individual has no security against the absolutism of the general will. No area of the life of the citizen was free its control.

It is said that Rousseau's voice is the voice of Locke but the hands are those of Hobbes. The points in common between Hobbes and Rousseau are: the state was the result of a contract entered into by men who originally lived in a state of nature, there was only one contract to which the government was not a party, individuals surrendered all their rights to the sovereign who became absolute. However, Rousseau did not agree with Hobbes that the government was absolute. He made the government dependent upon the people and thereby accepted the conclusions of Locke. He made the individual surrender his rights not to the ruler but to the community. He made a clear-cut distinction between the state and the government.

There were differences between Rousseau and Locke. While Rousseau advocated the complete surrender of rights to the sovereign, that was not so in the case of Locke who stood for limited sovereignty. The popular sovereignty of Rousseau is in continual exercise. According to Locke, the supremacy of the people is held in reserve and manifests itself only when the government acts contrary to the trust.

To Hobbes, the natural man was essentially selfish. He was envious. The state of nature was a gloomy state. It was a state of constant warfare. To Rousseau, the natural man was necessarily good and the state of nature was state of bliss and happiness. To Locke, the state of nature was neither too good nor one of constant warfare. It was simply inconvenient on account of the lack of an authority to enforce the rights possessed by men in the state of nature.

To Hobbes, a change in government meant the dissolution of the state and a return to the state of nature. The view of Locke was that the people had the supreme right to choose their government and also change the same if it was found unsatisfactory. According to Rousseau, the government was merely an agent or tool to execute the popular will.

Hobbes described the state of nature as pre-social and pre-political. Locke's state of nature was pre-political but not pre-social. Rousseau's man in the state of nature was a noble savage who led a life of primitive simplicity and idyllic happiness. He was independent, contented, self-sufficient, healthy, fearless and "without need of his fellows or desire to harm them." His life was regulated by instinct.

According to Hobbes, law was the command of the sovereign. Locke considered law as the expression of the will of the people, but it had to be consistent with the law of reason. According to Rousseau, law is merely the expression of the general will.

Locke gave the people the right of revolution. Hobbes also gave the people the right to transfer their allegiance from that sovereign who could not protect their lives. There was no scope for revolt in the philosophy of Rousseau.

According to Hobbes, the people surrendered all their rights except that of self-preservation. In the case of Locke, there was no surrender of rights. In the case of Rousseau, rights were surrendered to the general will of which individuals themselves were parts and hence they shared rights even after transferring them.

The view of Hobbes was that in the state of nature, everybody had the right of self-defence. There was no law in the state of nature and might was right. Everybody tried to defend himself. According to Locke, the people enjoyed their rights to life, liberty and property. According to Rousseau, man did not obey any command or law in the state of nature. He was inspired by his own instinct.

According to Hobbes, there were no natural rights. The view of Locke was that the people reserved to themselves the right to life, liberty and property. Rousseau believed that all men were equal and free in the state of nature.

Hobbes, Locke and Rousseau differ from one another regarding the causes responsible for ending the state of nature. The view of Hobbes was that the state of nature was a state of savagery and life was insecure. In order to end that state of nature, the people created the state. The view of Locke was that the state of nature was peaceful but there was no government or judge to maintain law and order and interpret the laws. The people ended the state of nature in order to get their rights protected by the state. The view of Rousseau was that although things were ideal to begin with in the state of nature, trouble arose on account of various reasons and thus the people ended the state of nature.

Hobbes believed in absolute sovereignty wielded by one person or a group of persons. Generally, by sovereign he meant the king. Locke believed in limited monarchy. The king was trustee of the people. Rousseau regarded the general will as the sovereign.

The view of Hobbes was that an individual could enjoy only those rights which were given to him by the sovereign and he enjoyed his liberty to the extent to which it was granted to him by the sovereign. According to Rousseau, an individual remained as free after the contract as he was in the state of nature.

Decline of the Theory of Social Contract

The theory of social contract began to decline after Rousseau. The view of Sir Henry Maine was that nothing could be more worthless than an account of the origin of the state as given by Hobbes. Bluntschli characterised it as "in the highest degree dangerous, since it makes the state and its institutions the product of individual caprice." Bentham condemned the social contract theory in these words: "It bid adieu to the original contract and left it to those to amuse themselves with this rattle who think they needed it."

Another cause of the decline of the theory was that the attitude of the thinkers changed and they adopted the historical method. The approach of philosophers like Montesquieu and Burke adversely affected the social contract theory. Montesquieu's book, *The Spirit of Laws* (*1748*), indicated the beginning of the new historical and positive attitude of writers. Speculative attitude gave place to pragmatic attitude. Darwin's theory of evolution influenced the different branches of study and political science was one of them. The result was that the study of the state and government was made in the light of the principle of evolution.

The rise of new theories also resulted in the decline of the social contract theory. While the defects in the social contract theory were criticised, the same ideas of the theory were given a place in new theories. The theory of political sovereignty as developed in modern times was nothing but an elaboration of the ideas of Locke. The modern form of referendum is merely a modified version of Rousseau's concept of popular sovereignty. The evolutionary theory of the state and the Marxian theory of the nature of the state sounded the death-knell of the social contract theory.

Criticism of Social Contract Theory

The social contract theory has been subjected to serious criticism. Sir Frederick Pollock described it as "one of the most successful and fatal political impostures." Bentham criticised it as a "rattle" for amusement. T.H. Green dismissed as a mere "fiction". Sir Henry Maine described it as "worthless" as an explanation of the origin of the state. Paine criticised the concept of contract because it is eternally binding and hence a dead weight on the wheel of progress. "Every age and generation must be as free to act for itself in all cases as the age and generations which preceded it."

Dr. Garner says that the social contract theory fails to explain the origin of the state. As an explanation of the origin of the state, it is now entirely discredited like various other political doctrines and no reputable philosopher or political writer could be found to defend it. (*Political Science and Government, p. 207*). According to Kranenburg, the theory of social contract "employs too much deductive and too little inductive reasoning."

(1) The social contract theory is *unhistorical.* It is merely a fiction. History does not give us any example of persons who had absolutely no idea of a state and one day created a state by means of a contract. Referring to the Pilgrim Fathers who went to North America in the Mayflower in 1620, Prof. Ritchie writes, "When Carlyle objects that Jean Jacques could not fix the date of the social contract, it would be at least a probable retort to say that the date was eleventh of November 1620". However, this example is not an appropriate one. The Pilgrim Fathers migrated from England where there was already a state and were not absolutely ignorant of the idea of a state. They merely set up in North America what they already knew in England. Moreover, they expressly declared that they were "loyal subjects" of an existing sovereign.

The social contract theory assumes that primitive man was a free man and could enter into voluntary agreement with other free men. This is not borne out by researches into early times. Early law was more communal than individual and the individual had no importance. The family was the unit and property was held in common. Law took the form of customs and the individual had his prescribed place in society. Under these circumstances, the free contracting of individuals with one another to set up a state, is an absurdity. Gettell writes about primitive society. "The family was the unit, property was held in common. Custom formed law and each man was born into his status in society." (*Introduction to Political Science, p. 86*). Sir Henry Maine says, "Contract is not the beginning but the end of society".

(2) The social contract theory is also attacked on *legal grounds.* It is contended that a legally sound contract implies the prior existence of some authority and its sanction before the contract is entered into. In the case of social contract theory, there was neither the authority nor the sanction before the contract was concluded. It was the social contract which created the authority. There could be no sanction because there was no state. T.H. Green writes, "The covenant by which a civil power is for the time constituted cannot be a valid covenant. The men making it are not in a position to make a valid covenant at all."

The basic requirement of a contract is the existence of two or more parties. In the case of Hobbes, the sovereign was not a party to the contract and hence not bound. Moreover, every contract lapses after the death of one of the contracting parties. It cannot be made legally binding on future generations, heirs or descendants of the original parties to the contract. Bentham writes, "I am bound to obey not because my great grandfather may be regarded as having made a bargain which he did not really make with the great grandfather of George III, but simply because rebellion does more harm than good".

If the original contract has no legal meaning and is invalid, all subsequent contracts based upon it are equally invalid and the rights derived from it have no legal foundation.

(3) The social contract theory is also criticised *on philosophical grounds.* The theory assumes that the relation between the individual and the state is a voluntary one. This is not correct. We are members of a state in the same way in which we are members of a family. The state is not an artificial creation of man and its membership is not voluntary. If the state were a voluntary organisation like a company or firm, individuals would be at liberty to join it or leave it at will. The obligations of citizens to the state are not contractual at all. Edmund Burke writes, "The state ought not to be considered as nothing better than a partnership agreement in a trade of pepper and coffee, calico or tobacco, or some other such low concern, to be taken up for a little temporary interest and to be dissolved by the fancy of the parties. It is to be looked on with reverence. It is a partnership in all science, a partnership in all art, a partnership in every virtue and in all perfection. As the ends of such a partnership cannot be obtained in many generations, it becomes a partnership not only between those who are living but between those who are dead and those who are to be born."

The entire concept of the state of nature and the laws of nature is unsound. It assumes that whatever preceded the institution of the state is "natural" and whatever followed it is artificial. There is no warrant for dividing history into two parts. Civilisation is as natural today as barbarism was in the past. Man is a part of nature and the state is the highest expression of his nature The state is a growth and not a manufacture.

The social contract theory assumes that natural rights and natural liberty existed in the state of nature. This assumption is illogical and fallacious. Liberty cannot exist in the state of nature as law is the condition of liberty. The state of nature being pre-political and even pre-social, it was subject to no civil law. Rights also arise in a society and every right implies a corresponding duty. If there was no society, there could not be any rights. Hence, no right existed before the state arose.

There can be no rights without a consciousness of the common interest on the part of members of a society and common consciousness was conspicuous by its absence in the state of nature. Green writes, "Without a common consciousness, there might be certain powers on the part of which they allow the exercise, nor any claim to such recognition; and without this recognition or claim to recognition there can be no right." The social contract theory makes the state purely the handiwork of man, an artificial contrivance. However, the state is neither the handiwork of man, nor the creation of God, nor the result of force. It is the product of growth and evolution and many factors have contributed to its development. It is not correct to say that the supposed state of nature alone was natural and civil society is artificial.

The social contract theory implies a false notion of rights. T.H. Green says, "The real flaw in the theory of contract is not that it is unhistorical, but that it implies the possibility of rights and obligations independently of society." According to any sound view of rights, the basis of rights is social recognition.

The view of Hobbes is that man by nature is unsocial and the only feeling which he has in the company of others is one of unhappiness. This is not correct. Man is social both by nature and necessity. Rousseau's view is that man by nature never thinks and he who thinks is a corrupt creature. All the activities of individuals are dictated by instinct. Experience shows that this view of human nature is absolutely incorrect. Human beings are rational creatures.

More than one exponent of the theory has stated that men were equal in the state of nature, but it is more appropriate to agree with Von Haller, the German Jurist, that inequality rather than equality, is natural.

The social contract theory is criticised as "mechanical, *a priori* and juristic theory." The idea of contract is a juristic proposition. The state is reduced to the position of a machine or an instrument which exists to serve definite purposes. The ideas of state of nature and even contract are *a priori* ideas which were accepted without reasoning.

Carre de Mallberg says that the state is not the result of a conventional arrangement between individuals but of forced submission to social exigencies which they are powerless to elude. The view of Le Fur is that "the state, like the family, is necessary to society and like it is not the result of a contract but rather of the force of things." Esmein says that the theory is unsustainable because it sacrifices the right of the individual, as it involves an alienation of himself and his rights for the benefit of the community and because it makes the right of the individual rest upon a primitive and absolute independence resulting from a state of nature, which with the social contract are historical hypotheses contrary to the facts of history and of sociology. Duguit has rejected the social contract theory on the ground that it assumes that the idea of contract could be present in the minds of men in the so-called state of nature. This is an impossible assumption because men who are not already living in society cannot have any notion of contractual relationship and obligations.

The social contract theory is criticised as bad history, bad law and bad philosophy. Historically it is erroneous because there is no evidence to prove either the existence of the state of nature or the creation of a state through contract. It is bad law because it makes contract binding on the succeeding generations. It is bad philosophy because it looks upon the state as an artificial contrivance and not a natural process and growth.

Value of the Theory

In spite of its many shortcomings, the theory of social contract is important in many ways. The theory served as an antidote to absolute monarchy. The Glorious Revolution of 1688 stood for the principle of constitutional monarchy. Rousseau's idea of popular sovereignty was partly responsible for the French Revolution. Nobody bothered whether the state really originated in a contract or not but millions were powerfully stirred by the idea that the people were the ultimate sovereign and the state was an expression of the popular will.

The theory of social contract preached the idea that "will, not force, is the basis of the state." The idea of consent lies behind this theory and that was of immense importance in the evolution of democratic government.

Hobbes gave the concept of legal sovereignty which ultimately led to Austin's theory of sovereignty. Locke gave the idea of political sovereignty and supported the cause of limited monarchy. Rousseau advocated popular sovereignty with enormous influence on the future of history.

The view of Dr. Garner is that the social contract theory "served a useful purpose in its day by providing a weapon for combating irresponsible rulers and a justification for resistance to tyranny. Out of it, there developed the doctrine that kings derived their authority from the people, were responsible to them and could be deposed for breaking the pact which they were assumed to have entered into at the time of their coronation." (*Political Science and Government, p. 210*).

The ideas of Rousseau "appealed to the Americans and these are traceable in almost every American Constitution drawn up at that time." In their Declaration of Independence of 1776, the Americans declared that all men are born equal and have equal rights. In 1789, the National Assembly of France issued Declaration of the Rights of Men and Citizens in which it recognised that sovereignty belongs to the people who possess certain rights which no government can or should take away. The idea of equal political rights can be traced back to the theory of Rousseau. It is rightly said that "That English Revolution of 1688 was cradled in contract."

By combining political authority with what Willoughby calls "a predicated individual right to free self-determination of action", the contractualists laid down the foundation of democracy.

The theory of separation of powers as bulwark of political liberty, was indistinctly present in the philosophy of Locke and the same was developed by Montesquieu.

Rousseau's ideas awakened politically the slave races and they revolted and struggled against the despotism of foreign rulers.

MacIver writes, "Historically, the contract theory swept out of the way the endless deductive arguments based on subjective interpretations of scriptures and refounded the state on its true foundation, the will of man and the common purpose which inspires that will to institutional life."

We may conclude with the following words of Kant, "It is unnecessary to pre-suppose the contract as a historical fact; it is, however, practical reality. It ought to bind every legislator by the conditions that he shall enact such laws as might have arisen from the united will of a whole people and it will be likewise binding upon every subject in so far as he will be a citizen so that he shall regard the law as if he had consented to it of his own free will."

Theory of Divine Origin

The theory of divine origin is the oldest theory regarding the origin of the state. According to it, "The state is established and governed by God Himself or by some superhuman power. God may rule the state directly or indirectly through some ruler who is regarded as the agent of God." According to the Mahabharat, there was anarchy in the beginning of the world and the people prayed to God to come to their rescue. They offered the following prayer: "Without a chief, O Lord, we are perishing. Give us a chief whom we shall worship and who will protect us." It was under these circumstances that God appointed Manu to rule over the people. According to the Jews, "The king is treated as owing responsibility to God alone for his acts." There are many references in the Old Testament where it is stated that God selects, appoints, dismisses and even slays rulers. The Greeks and the Romans regarded the state as indirectly divine. According to the Bible, "Let every soul he subject unto the higher powers. For there is no power but of God; the powers that be are ordained of God. Whosoever therefore resisteth power resisteth the ordinance of God's and they that resisteth shall receive to themselves damnation." Jesus Christ observed thus: "Render unto Caesar the things that are Caesar's."

The teachings of the Old Testament and the Church Fathers influenced the Mediaeval writers in the controversy between the church on the one hand and the Empire on the other. While some "writers used the theory of divine origin to establish the supremacy of the Church over the state, the others used it to support the supremacy of the state over the Church. The Protestant Reformation gave a new impetus to the theory of divine origin. It was stated in the Augsburg Confession of 1530 that "all authority, government, law and order in the world have been created and established by God Himself." Sir Robert Filmer stated in his *Patriarcha* in 1681 that Adam was the first king and "present kings are, or are to be reputed, next heir to him". Pope Gregory ascribed the authority of land to God. Bousset advocated the theory of divine origin to support the despotism of Louis XIV.

The theory of divine origin was used to support the theory of the divine right of kings. James I, King of England, supported the theory of divine right of kings in his book, *The Law of Free Monarchies.* His view was that kings were kings because God had made them kings and consequently they were responsible to God alone. They were not responsible to the people for their acts of omission and commission because they were merely the agents of God and if they committed any mistake, God alone was responsible for it and not they themselves. To quote James I, "A king can never be monstrously vicious. Even if a king is wicked, it means God has sent him as a punishment for people's sins and it is unlawful to shake off the burden which God has laid upon them. Patience, earnest prayer and amendment of their lives are the only lawful means to move God to relieve them of that heavy curse." Again, "A bad king will be judged by God but he must not be judged by his subjects or by any human agency for enforcing the law, such as the estates or the courts." The law resided ultimately "in the breast of the kings." "Kings are breathing images of God upon earth. As it is atheism and blasphemy to dispute what God can do, so it is presumption and high contempt in a subject to dispute what a king can do or to say that a king cannot do this or that. The state of monarchy is the supremest thing upon earth; for kings are not only God's lieutenants upon earth and sit upon God's throne, but even by God Himself they are called gods. Kings are justly called gods; for they exercise a manner of resemblance of divine power upon earth."

According to Prof. G.P. Gooch, there were certain features of the theory of divine right of kings. Those were: monarchy is divinely ordained; hereditary right is indefensible; kings are accountable to God alone and resistance to a lawful king is sin.

The theory of divine origin was popular for a long time but later on it began to decline on account of many factors. The theory of social contract, with its emphasis on consent, was a great setback to the theory of divine origin. It was maintained that the state was created by individuals by means of a contract and not by God. The separation of the Church from the state was also partly responsible for the decline of the theory. Religion began to lose its hold on the people and consequently the people refused to believe that everything was to be attributed to God and the state was also created by God. The ideas of evolution which became popular during the 19th century also discredited altogether the theory of divine origin. The growth of democratic ideas gave a setback to the theory because the theory of divine origin supported the ideas of absolute monarchy.

Criticism

The theory of divine origin has been criticised on many grounds. According to Gilchrist, "To say that God selects this or that man as ruler is contrary to experience and commonsense." God cannot be expected to do such worldly things for human beings.

We all believe in the theory of evolution. Everything in the world has grown up by slow degrees and consequently the same must have been the case with state. It is too much to believe that one day God thought of creating the state and created one.

The theory is dangerous because it justifies the unlimited and arbitrary power of the kings. The rulers must be held responsible for their actions. They cannot be allowed to put forward the excuse that they are merely the agents of God and consequently are not responsible for their actions. There can be no liberty of the individual under such circumstances. According to Bluntschli, a statesmen may "tempt God and shirk his own responsibility."

The theory puts emphasis on revelation and not reason. In modern times, we attribute everything to reason and no wonder the theory of divine origin is not accepted today.

The state is the creation of man. He has created it out of necessity. If we attribute the origin of the state to God, we do not render any service to man. We minimise and even ignore his capacity for organisation. Man must be given his due.

The theory of divine origin of the state advocates only a monarchical form of government. However, the monarchical form of government is practically disappearing from the world. No wonder, the theory of divine origin also does net find its supporters in modern times.

Although the theory has many defects and is no longer accepted today, it cannot be denied that it had its utility. At a time when man was emerging from semi-civilized conditions and was not accustomed to obey any regular authority, this theory served as a bulwark against anarchy. It did a lot to strengthen the respect of man for person, property and government. This theory indirectly emphasises the moral basis of political order. Even an absolute ruler owes a moral responsibility to God for whatever he does. Gettell has rightly pointed out that this theory taught men to obey when they were not yet ready to govern themselves. According to Gilchrist, "To regard the state as the work of God is to give it a high moral status, to make it something which the citizen may revere and support, something which he may regard as the perfection of human life."

Theory of Force

According to the theory of force, the state was created by force. The state is the result of the subjugation of the weaker by the stronger. It can also be said that "war beget the king." History tells us that great empires were created by generals and war lords.

Hume says, "It is probable that the first ascendancy of one man over multitudes began during a state of war, where the superiority of courage and of genius discovers itself most visibly, where unanimity and concert are most requisite, and where the pernicious effects of disorder are most sensibly felt. The long continuance of that state, an incident common among savage tribes, inured the people to submission."

Oppenheimer has traced the origin of the state through various stages and has advocated the theory of force as the origin of the state. In his *History of Politics*, F. Jenks observes thus: "Historically speaking, there is not the slightest difficulty in proving that all political communities of the modern type owe their existence to successful warfare." According to him, with the increase of population and the consequent pressure on the means of subsistence, the methods of warfare were improved and fighting became the work of specialists. A state was founded when a great leader, with the help of soldiers, was able to establish his authority over a certain territory. Later on, he extended his authority over the neighbouring areas. It was in this way that the state came into existence. In the case of Scandinavia a large number of tribes were gradually consolidated and the states of Norway. Denmark and Sweden came into existence. Jenks also refers to the creation of the state of Lombarby by the same process.

The theory of force has been advocated from time to time by different institutions and individuals to serve their own ends. It was advocated by the Church during Middle Ages with a view to prove its own superiority over the state. It was pointed out that while the Church was the Kingdom of God on earth, the state was the outcome of aggression and bloodshed. Pope Gregory VII wrote in A.D. 1080: "Which of us is ignorant that kings and lords have had their origin in those who, ignorant of God, by arrogance, rapine, perfidy, slaughter, by every crime (with the devil agitating as the prince of the world) have contrived to rule over their fellowmen with blind cupidity and intolerable presumption."

The individualists relied upon this theory to show that there were certain fields in which the state should not interfere. Their view was that the state was an evil, although a necessary one and hence it was but proper that the state should leave the individual alone. The individualists relied upon the principle of the survival of the fittest and argued that it is only the strong who survive and the weak go to the wall. The view of Karl Marx was that the state was based on force and when the classless society was established, it will wither away. Marx maintained that the existing system of industrial organisation was backed by force. "A part of the community has succeeded in defrauding their fellows of the just reward of their labour."

The theory of force was advocated by the German writes. Treitschke maintained that "the state is the public power of all offence and defence, the first task of which is the making of war and the administration of justice." It was during war that differences among the people disappeared and the qualities of patriotism and idealism came to the fore. "The appeal to arms will be valid until the end of history". The grandeur of history lies in the perpetual conflict of nations" and "the appeal to arms will be valid until the end of history". The view of Bernhardi was that might is "the supreme right and the dispute as to what is right is decided by the arbitrament of war. War gives a biologically just decision, since its decisions rest on the very nature of things." Nietzsche advocated the theory of the superman who could compel others to act in fulfilment of his will. He glorified the masterly virtues of men. His view was that a truly moral man "has no place for the vulgar and slavish virtues of humility, self-sacrifice, pity, gentleness." Both Hitler and Mussolini emphasised the importance of force and glorified war. They advocated "a creed of dominance by intimidation, militancy in international relations and forcible suppression of political dissent in domestic government."

The importance of force was emphasised during the 19th century by many writers. Herbert Spencer put forward the principle of survival of the fittest. It was no business of the state to come to the rescue of the weak. The view of Herbert Spencer was that "the Government is the offspring of evil, bearing about it the marks of its parentage." Sir Henry Maine emphasised "the beneficent private war which makes one man strive to climb on the shoulders of another and remain there through the law of the survival of the fittest."

Criticism

The theory of force as the origin of the state is criticised on many grounds. It is pointed out that this theory is anti-democratic as it ignores the general will of the people. The view of T.H. Green was that will, not force, is the basis of the state. It is impossible to maintain a state with the help of force. It is created and maintained by the willingness of the people to obey the authority of the state. To quote Green, "It is not coercive power as such but coercive power exercised according to law, written or unwritten, for the maintenance of the existing rights of the citizens from external and internal invasions that makes a state." Again, "Might without right can at best be temporary; might with right is a permanent basis for the state." Kant says, "Even a population of devils would find it to their advantage to establish a coerce state by general consent."

It is not denied that force must have played its part in the creation of the state. However, it is too much to say that force was the only factor which created the state. The theory of force "makes prominent one element which is indispensable to the state, namely, force."

This theory does not put the right emphasis on the part played by cooperation in society. The fact is that people are social by nature and it is this fact that brings them together and helps them to create a state.

The theory of force is considered to be against the principles of international law which aim at maintaining peace and security in the world and eliminating both force and war.

The theory justifies despotism. It is opposed to the idea of freedom. It is foo much to believe that the state is created and maintained by sheer force and the spiritual and moral values have absolutely no place in life.

The Patriarchal Theory

According to the patriarchal theory, the state is the enlargement of the family. To begin with, the family consisted of man, his wife and their children. The father was the head of the family and he exercised complete control over all the members of the family. With the marriage of the children, new families came into existence. However, the authority of the father continued over all the members of the families. Thus came into existence a patriarchal family. In course of time, the patriarchal family developed into a clan. When the clan expanded, a tribe came into existence. Dr. Leacock has described the process in these worlds: "First a household, then a patriarchal family, next a tribe of persons of kindred descent and finally a nation—so emerges the social series erected on this basis."

The view of Aristotle was that the society of many families "is called a village, and a village is most naturally composed of the descendants of one family, the children and the children's children for which reason, states were originally governed by kings, as the barbarian states now are, which are composed of those who had before submitted to kingly Government; for every family is governed by the elder, as are the branches thereof, on account of their relation thereto....and when many villages so entirely join themselves together as in every respect to form but one society, that society is a state and contains in itself, if I may so speak, the end and perfection of Government."

However, the strongest advocate of the patriarchal theory is Sir Henry Maine (1822-1888). He propounded this theory in his books entitled *Ancient Law* (1861) and *Early History of Institutions* (1875). To quote him, "The elementary group is the family, connected by common subjection to the highest male ascendant. The aggregation of families forms the gens or House. The aggregation of Houses makes the Tribe. The aggregation of Tribes constitutes the Commonwealth." According to Maine, the state is an extension of the family, the head of the state being father and the people his children. Maine has given the examples of the Patriarchs of the Old Testament, the "Brotherhoods" of Athens, *patria potestas* in Rome and the family system in India in support of his theory. Among the Hebrews, the eldest male parent was absolutely supreme and he exercised almost despotic powers over his dependants. He held the possession of the family in a representative manner and not proprietary manner. The Athenians had their brotherhoods and families. In Rome, the *Patria potestas* "gave the head of the household almost unlimited authority over its members." Sidgwick points out that over his wife, children and their descendants, they exercised so much power that the individual member had no "separate juridical existence at all. This complete control within the family carried with it a correspondingly extensive responsibility." In the case of India, a large number of members are included in a single household under the joint family system.

The patriarchal theory rests on certain fundamental assumptions. The patriarchal family was based on permanent marriages and kin relationships. Permanent marriage was the rule, whether monogamy or polygamy. The head of the family was the basis of all authority and he had full control over his children and their houses etc. He controlled not only the business affairs of the group but also its religion and conduct. The state is a collection of persons descended from the progenitor of the original family. Descent was traced only through males and from the same ancestor.

The patriarchal theory has also been supported by Duguit. According to him, the father "is the natural chief, the governor of the little state of which the members of the family are the governed. The ancient city was merely a union of families in which political power belonged to the father."

Professor R.M. MacIver says, "In the family, the primary social unit, there are always present the curbs and controls that constitute the essence of government......which is the continuation by the more inclusive society of a process of regulation that is highly developed within the family. The same necessities that create the family create also regulation....He is the Government in miniature, and already government of a quite elaborate character.

Criticism

Modern researches have show that the patriarchal family was not universal. McLennan points out that the matriarchal family came first and the patriarchal family came later on. It is later on that polyandry developed into a monogamous family and the matriarchal family into the patriarchal state.

According to Jenks, the process by which families that expand into clans and clans into tribes, is not what has been given by Sir Henry Maine but the actual position was quite the opposite of it. The tribe was the earliest and the primary group. Then came the clan and finally came the family. Jenks has given examples from Australia and the Malay Archipelago to support this contention. Critics also point out that patriarchal family did not exist continuously. There were matriarchal families also in certain countries.

The patriarchal theory does not give an adequate explanation of the origin of the state. It merely gives us an idea about the beginning of early society.

Sir J.G. Frazer has observed this in *The Golden Bough:* "He who investigates the history of institutions should constantly bear in mind the extreme complexity of the causes which have built up the fabric of human society and should be on his guard against a subtle danger incidental to all science the tendency to simplify unduly the infinite variety of phenomena by fixing our attention on a few of them to the exclusion of the rest."

The Matriarchal Theory

Another theory about the origin of the state is the matriarchal theory. The chief advocates of this theory are McLennan, Morgan and Jenks. McLennan gave his views in *Primitive Society* (1865), Morgan in *Studies in Ancient Society* (1877), and Jenks in *A History of Politics* (1900). The view of these writers is that the primitive group had no common male head. Kinship among them could be traced only through women and not through men. There was neither monogamy nor polygamy. The earliest form of marriage was polyandry, one woman having several husbands. The relations of husband and wife did not exist. Promiscuity of sexual relation prevailed and kinship could be traced through females only and not males. "Maternity is a fact, paternity an opinion." According to Jenks, "The tribe, instead of the family, is the primary group; in time it breaks into clans; these turn into households and ultimately into individual members."

Jenks has supported the matriarchal theory by a reference to the primitive society in Australia. He says: "The real social unit of the Australians is not the tribe but the totem group. The totem group is, primarily, a body of persons distinguished by the sign of some natural object, such as an animal or tree, who may not intermarry with one another. The Australian may not marry within his totem. 'Snake may not marry snake. Emu may not marry Emu.' That is the first rule of savage social organisation. Of its origin we have no knowledge; but there can be no doubt that its object was to prevent the marriage of near relations....The other side of the rule is equally startling. The savage will not marry within his totem, but he must marry into another totem specially fixed for him. More than this, he not only marries into the specified totem but he marries the whole of the women of that totem in his own generation."

The fundamental features of a matriarchal society were transient marriage relationship, tracing of kinship through females, established maternal authority and the succession of women alone to property and power.

The view of J.J. Bachofen is that in primitive society, descent was traced through the mother and property also passed in the female line. Women also "played a conspicuous, in fact, dominant role in body politic."

According to MacIver, "The woman here is regarded as the agent of transmission, not the active wielder or even the participant of power." It was at a later stage that the mother's right gave place to patriarchal society "through the adoption of settled pastoral and agricultural habits in place of the purely wandering or hunting life of primitive man."

It cannot be denied that the matriarchal family had existed in the world and even Sir Henry Maine had to admit later on the importance of the evidence collected by McLennan about the matriarchal family. Even today, polyandry exists in certain parts of India, *e.g.*, Kangra, Lahaul Spiti, Kinnaur and Renuka, in Tehri Garhwal and Uttar Kashi districts in Uttar Pradesh, etc. However, it cannot be maintained that matriarchal family was universal or the earliest form of society. Moreover, other forces, in addition to the matriarchal family, must have helped the growth of the state. The matriarchal theory is more sociological than political. It seeks to explain the origin of the family and not that of the state.

Dr. Leacock observes thus about the patriarchal and matriarchal theories of the state: "No single form of the primitive family or group can be asserted. Here the matriarchal relationship and there a patriarchal regime, is found to have been the rule, either of which may perhaps be displaced by the other. Indeed, one has to admit the fact that there is no such thing as a beginning of human society. All that can be asserted is that in the course of time, the monogamic family tended to become the dominant form, though even until today it has not altogether supplanted other forms of organisation."

Evolutionary or Historical Theory

The evolutionary theory regarding the origin of the state was neither created by God nor by force. It was not the outcome of a social or political contract. It has grown gradually and many factors have played their part in its evolution.

According to Dr. Garner, "The state is neither the handiwork of God, nor the result of superior physical force, nor the creation of convention or a contract, nor a mere expansion of family." It is an institution of natural growth. "The state is a growth and evolution and not an artificial product." According to Professor Burgess, "The proposition that the state is a product of history means that it is gradual and continuous development of the human society out of a grossly imperfect beginning through crude but improving forms of manifestation towards a perfect and universal organisation of mankind." Again, "It is futile to seek to discover just one cause which will explain the origin of all states. The states must have come into existence owing to a variety of causes, some operating in one place and some in other places. Whatever it is, the state is not the deliberate creation of man any more than language is a conscious convention. Political consciousness must have taken a very long time to develop and the primitive state must have grown along with the development of this consciousness." According to Dr. Leacock, the state is "the result of a gradual process running throughout all the known history of man and receding into the remote and unknown past." Just as speech has evolved from the uncouth gibbering of animals, so the government had its origin in remote and rudimentary beginnings in pre-historic society.

Kinship

Many factors have played their part in the evolution of the state and kinship is the most important among them. It is admitted by all that the family was the unit of society at the beginning. The blood relationship brought the members of the family together and they all accepted the authority of the head of the family. With the passage of time, the family expanded and clans came into existence. With the expansion of clans, tribes came into existence and ultimately the state came into existence.

While it is admitted that kinship played an important part in bringing the people together, there is a difference of opinion among scholars regarding the nature of kinship. According to the exponents of the patriarchal theory, the father was the head of the family and he continued to be the head even when the family expanded and the clan, the tribe and the state came into existence. The eldest male member was absolutely supreme in his household. "His dominion extends to life and death and is unqualified over his children and their houses as over his slaves; indeed, the relations of sonship and serfdom appear to differ in little beyond the higher capacity which the child in blood possesses of becoming one day the head of a family himself. The flocks and herds of the children are the flocks and herds of the father and the possessions of the parent which he holds in a representative rather than in a proprietary character, are equally divided at his death among the descendants in the first degree, the eldest son sometimes receiving a double share under the name of birth-right, but more generally endowed with no hereditary advantage beyond an honorary precedence." (Maine). According to the matriarchal theory, previous to the patriarchal family, men were living in hordes or packs in which the usual relationship of husband and wife did not exist and the relationship could be traced through women and not men. According to Jenks, "As far as there is any recognition of blood relationship at all, it is through women and not through men."

It is to be observed that the patriarchal society differed from modern society in many ways. It was personal and not territorial. Membership was based upon kinship and not on locality. It was exclusive and there was no desire to have more members. It was non-competitive and its life was based on custom. The ideas of change or progress were not welcome. It was communal but not necessarily communistic. Interdependence and independence was the idea of patriarchal society.

After considering the evolution of society, one cannot help coming to the conclusion that neither the patriarchal family nor the matriarchal family was universal. At some places, one kind of kinship was prevalent and at other places another kind of kinship was to be found. To quote Tarde, "Of all these endless controversies in reference to relationship and marriage, what seems to me most evident is that the primitive family has assumed various forms, here monogamic, there polygamic, elsewhere polyandric, sometimes exogamic, sometimes endogamic, often more authoritative, sometimes less so than it has become later."

According to Professor MacIver, the magic of names "reinforced the sense of kinship, as the course of generations enlarged the group. The blood bond of sonship changed imperceptibly into the social bond of the wider brotherhood. The authority of the father passes into the power of the chief. Once more under the aegis of kinship new forms arise which transcend it. Kinship creates society and society at length creates the state."

Religion

Another factor which brought the people together in ancient society was religion. The people who were bound by the bonds of blood were also brought together by the bonds of religion. The worship of a common ancestor and common gods created a sense of social solidarity. The priest or the magician was considered to have mastery over the forces of nature and this fact created awe among the people and thus they were willing to obey the orders of such a person. It was in this way that religion paved the way for the evolution of the state.

According to Gettell, kinship and religion were simply two aspects of the same thing. Common worship was more important than kinship in making the people obey some authority.

According to Frazer, the first form of tribal government was the gerontocracy or council of old men representing the various families constituting the tribe. Their control over the tribe was complete. Out of this council emerged the magician, "a resolute and ambitious man, a clever and unscrupulous man who pretended to have extraordinary powers of divination and sorcery. The fertility of the soil, rain or drought, the success or failure of crops seemed to depend more upon his incantations and rituals than upon human efforts. His influence, especially among an agricultural people, assumed enormous proportions. The magician eventually made himself priest-king."

Even now, religion plays an important part in various parts of the world. The newly created state of Pakistan is an Islamic state. Likewise, religion plays an important part in the states of the Middle-East.

Property and Defence

The institution of property and the necessity of defence facilitated the creation of the state. Prof. Laski rightly points out that "The basic factor in any given society is the way it earns its living; all social relations are built upon provision for those primary material appetites without satisfying which life cannot endure. And an analysis of society will always reveal the close connection between its institutions and culture and the method of satisfying material appetites. As these methods change, so also will the institutions and culture of the society change......Changes in the methods of economic production appear to be the most vital factor in the making of changes in all other social patterns we know. For changes in those methods determine the changes of social relationships; and these, in their turn, are subtly interwoven with all the cultural habits of men."

These are three economic stages through which primitive peoples have passed: the huntsman stage, the herdsman or pastoral stage and the husbandman or agricultural stage. The huntsman led a miserable life. He just managed to live on. He had no property except his crude weapons and tools. It was a stage of savagery. First of all, he kept domestic animals as pets but later on he realised that he could gain more by keeping them on a permanent basis and deriving from them the maximum advantage. The result was that the huntsman became a herdsman and flocks and herds became his wealth. Other forms of property such as domestic utensils, weapons, improved clothings, etc., appeared. The patriarch exercised absolute control over the family and its property. When the family expanded into the gens and the tribe, the ground was prepared for tribal government. The institution of property brought many complications in its wake. There arose property disputes and the necessity to settle them. That brought forth the necessity of social control. The tribesman accepted the authority of the Council of Elders and the Chieftain. Organised military force was also necessary to check the raids from the neighbouring tribes. The necessity of common action against foreign aggression added to the solidarity of the tribe and increased the authority of the tribal organisation. Gettell says that the saying that "War beget the King" is "at least a half truth, since military activity was a powerful force, both in creating the need for authority and law and in replacing family organisations by systems purely political." There arose the necessity for individual leadership and some of the members of the Council of Elders gave the lead and became chiefs. Slowly and slowly, the office of the chieftain became hereditary. In due course of time, the Herdsmen began to settle on a particular territory and became husbandmen. "By trial and error or by the imitation of some neighbouring agriculturists, the methods of tillage are improved and their potentialities realised." When the herdsmen settled on a particular territory, the state began and agriculture also developed.

Political Consciousness

Political consciousness among the people also brought them together. "Just as the forces of nature operated long before the discovery of the law of gravitation, political organisation really rested on the community of minds, unconscious, dimly conscious or fully conscious of certain moral ends present throughout the whole course of development." When primitive people gave up hunting and wandering habits and took to pastoral and agricultural life, many changes took place. Population began to multiply. Contacts increased and wealth began to accumulate. The idea of property captured the minds of the people. All this required some organisation which could give them order and protection. Such a need was felt in the minds of a few natural leaders in the beginning and later on the idea spread among the people. It is under these circumstances that they got ready to give their whole-hearted support to the state.

The economic interests must have helped the origin and growth of state. Man cannot produce single-handed all that he needs. Thus, many professions must have come into existence in primitive society. Later on, it must have been realized that even the professional classes required the help and cooperation of one another. There was felt the necessity of a common authority and in course of time, the state came into existence. According to Professor Laski, "The basic factor in any given society is the way it earns its living; all social relations are built upon provision for those primary material appetites without satisfying which life cannot endure. And an analysis of society will always reveal the close connection between its institutions and culture and the method of satisfying material appetites. As these methods change, so also will the institutions and culture of the society change. Changes in the methods of economic production appear to be the most vital factor in the making of changes in all other social patterns we know. For changes in those methods determine the changes of social relationships; and these, in their turn, are subtly interwoven with all the cultural habits of man."

Force

Force also played its part in the evolution of the state. People with stronger military power were able to establish their hold over those who were weak from the military point of view. It was the use of physical force that was responsible for the growth of kingdoms and empires. Even today we find the states growing as a result of war and conquest. According to Oppenheimer, "The cause of the genesis of all states is the contact between bottom-lands and prairies." The view of Professor MacIver is that the emergence of the state "is not due to the force, although, in process of expansion, force undoubtedly played a part."

It is the natural instinct of man to live in society and this social instinct must have been partly responsible for the creation of the state. Man is a gregarious animal and he wants to live in the company of others. This fact itself must have been an important factor which helped the growth of the state.

It follows that many factors helped the growth of the state. No single factor alone was responsible for its origin. Sometimes all and sometimes many of them helped the process by which uncivilized society was transformed into a state.

Marxist Theory of the Origin of the State

The Marxist theory of the origin of the state is to be found in the writings and views of the revolutionaries, philosophers and thinkers like Karl Marx, Dr. Engels, Lenin, Stalin, Mao, Gramsci and Lukas.

According to the Marxist theory, the state neither originates in the will of society nor it is maintained for the benefit of all sections of society. Society and state are essentially different. Society is a natural institution but the state is not. Henri Lefebvre writes, "Marx maintains that the essence of man is not political but social. Man is not a political animal. The social forces that blindly seek a way out of their conflicts become subject to political power, the state" (*The Sociology of Marx, p. 123*). The state does not come into existence for the fulfilment of a moral purpose. It does not emanate from the will of the people. It originates in conflict and operates as an instrument of domination.

According to Marx, the forces of production constitute the basis of all social relationships. They belong to the sub-structure while religion, morals, social customs and politics belong to the super-structure. Like other super-structures of society, the state rests upon economic conditions. Karl Marx wrote thus in Critique of Political Economy, "Legal relations as well as form of state are rooted in the material conditions of life." Elaborating the relation between the real foundation and the super-structure, Marx observed. "In the social production which men carry on, they enter into definite relations that are indispensable and independent of their will; these relations of production correspond to a definite state of development of their material powers of production. The sum total of these relations of production constitutes the economic structure of society – the real foundation on which rise legal and political super-structures and to which correspond definite forms of social consciousness. The mode of production in material life determines the general character of the social, political and spiritual processes of life." Hence, the origin of the state should be traced in the material conditions of production prevailing at different historical stages. As soon as mankind emerge from the stage of primitive communism, at every stage of history a particular class assumes ownership and control of the means of production and becomes the dominant class in all the spheres of social life. This class exploits the rest of society which is subjected to its domination. The dominant class alone has freedom and in order to preserve it, it creates an executive by the use of which it hopes to maintain its position. Thus the state comes into existence.

Views of Dr Engels

In his original version of Communist Manifesto published in 1848, Marx had stated, "The history of all hitherto existing society is the history of class struggles." That did not indicate whether there had been, prior to recorded history, any societies where class struggle was not known. When the Communist Manifesto was originally published, the history of society before the historical ages, was little known. Later anthropological researches, particularly those of Lewis H. Morgan, revealed the existence of some primitive communities and tribes that had no idea of state. On the basis of those findings, Dr. Engels came to the conclusion that the dissolution of those primeval communities was responsible for the division of society into antagonistic classes, accompanied by the emergence of the state. In his famous book "The Origin of the Family, Private Property and the State" published in 1884, Engles wrote, "The state is, therefore, by no means a power forced on society from without; just as little is it the reality of the ethical idea, 'the image and reality of reason' as Hegel maintains. Rather, it is a product of society at a certain stage of development; it is the admission that this society has become entangled in an insoluble contradiction with itself, that it is cleft into irreconcilable antagonisms which it is powerless to dispel. But in order that these antagonisms, classes with conflicting economic interests, might not consume themselves and society in sterile struggle, a power seemingly standing above became necessary for the purpose of moderating the conflict, of keeping it within the bounds of order and this power, arisen out of society, but placing itself above it, and increasingly alienating itself from it, is the state."

Engels further wrote that the state "is as a rule, the state of the most powerful, economically dominant class which, through the medium of the state, becomes also the politically dominant class, and thus acquires now means of holding down and exploiting the oppressed class. Thus, the State of antiquity was above all the State of the slave owners for the purpose of holding down the slaves, as the feudal state was the organ of the nobility for holding down the peasants, serfs and bondsmen and the modern representative state is an instrument of exploitation of wage labour by capital." Thus, the state has originated with the origin of classes and class struggle in society and is merely an instrument of exploitation in the hands of the dominant class. With the help of the state, the ruling classes maintain their power over economically poor classes Engles wrote, "The state is an organisation of the possessing class for its protection against non-possessing class." The state has not originated because of social contract or because of the will of all the people, but has originated because of class division and class struggle in society. If the state has originated only with the origin of classes, it follows that before the division of society into classes, there was a when society was stateless. To quote Engles, "The state, the, has not existed from all *eternity.* There have been societies that did without it, that had no conception of the state and state power. At the certain stage of economic development which was necessarily bound up with the cleavage of society into classes, the state became a necessity, owing to this cleavage". It follows that if society becomes classless, the state will not be necessary and it will wither away automatically. Engels wrote, "We are now rapidly approaching a stage in the development of production at which the existence of these classes not only will have ceased to be a necessity, but will become a positive hindrance to production. They will fall as inevitably as they arose at on earlier stage. Along with them the state will inevitably fall. The society that will organise production on the basis of a free and equal association of producers will put the whole machinery of state where it will then belong, into the Museum of Antiquities, by the side of the spinning wheel and the bronze axes".

While MacIver and other liberal writers are of the view that the state emerged due to certain changes in man's consciousness, Engels gives primary importance to material factors such as production and re-production. Engels writes, "According to the materialistic conception, the determining factor in history is, in the last resort, the production and reproduction of immediate life. But this itself is of a twofold character. On the one hand, the production of the means of subsistence, of food, clothing and shelter and the tools requisite, therefore; on the other, the production of human beings themselves, the propagation of the species. The social institutions under which men of a definite historical epoch and of a definite country live are conditioned by both kinds of production: by the stage of development of labour, on the one hand, and of the family, on the other. The less the development of labour, and the more limited its volume of production and, therefore, the wealth of society, the more preponderatingly does the social order appear to be dominated by ties of sex. However, within this structure of society based on ties of sex, the productivity of labour develops more and more; with it private property and exchange, differences in wealth, the possibility of utilizing the labour power and others, and thereby the basis of class antagonisms: new social elements, which strive in the course of generations to adapt the old structure of society to the new conditions, until, finally, the incompatibility of the two leads to a complete revolution. The old society based on sex groups bursts asunder in the collision of the newly developed social classes; in its place a new society appears, constituted in a state, the lower units of which are no longer sex groups but territorial groups, a society in which the family system is entirely dominated by the property system, and in which the class antagonisms and class struggles, which make up the content of all hitherto written history, now freely develop."

According to Engels, the state in ancient Greece represented the purest, most classical form of evolution from the tribal *Polls.* There the state arose directly and mainly out of the class struggles that developed within the Greek Communes. In Rome, the tribal, gentile society became an exclusive aristocratic group amidst a large group of common people standing outside of it, having only duties but no rights. Later the victory of the Commoners broke up the gentile constitution and created a state which absorbed both the classes. Finally, among the Germanic barbarian invaders of the Roman Empire, the state emerged as a direct result of the conquest of large foreign territories which the gentile constitution had no means of ruling.

The gentile constitution had no coercive power except public opinion. A society arose which split up into masters and slaves, the exploiting rich and the exploited poor. That society could not reconcile class antagonisms and could only exist either in a state of continuous, open struggle of these classes against one another or under the rule of a third power which apparently stood above the classes, suppressed their open conflict allowing the class struggle to take place in the economic sphere within the bounds of law. Engels writes, "The gentile constitution had outlived its usefulness. It had burst asunder by the division of labour and by its result the division of society into classes. Its place was taken by the state."

According to Engels, the state comes into existence for the protection of private property. The state of economic development which coincided with the division of society into antagonistic classes and the consequent emergence of the state is characterized by the beginning of private property. When the means of production were not well developed the amount of production was just enough for survival. There was no private property and there was no state. When surplus production became possible, private property came into existence and society was divided into two classes — the haves and the have-nots, dominant and dependent, masters and slaves, exploiters and exploited — and the machinery of the state was created by the dominant class with the primary purpose of protecting its private property.

Since the emergence of private property is accompanied by the division of society into mutually antagonistic classes and formation of the state, the state is essentially a product of class conflict. The state arises when a tiny class of property-owners creates an organisation in order to preserve its superior status and property. The state enables the dominant class to impose law and order on society in order to keep the class-conflict in check.

Characteristic features of the state

Engels has identified four important characteristics which attend the birth of the state. In the first place the state divides its subjects according to territory. Citizens are allowed to exercise their public rights and duties wherever they reside, irrespective of gens and tribe. To quote Engels, "This organisation of citizens according to locality is a feature common to all states. That is why it seems natural to us; but long and arduous struggles were needed before it could replace, in Athens and Rome, the old organisation according to gentiles."

The second distinctive feature of the emergence of the state is the establishment of public power which no longer directly coincides with the population organising itself as an armed force. This public power exists in every state. Public power grows stronger in proportion as class antagonisms within the state become more acute and adjacent states become larger and more populous.

In order to maintain public power, contributions are recovered from citizens in the form of taxes which were absolutely unknown in gentile society. As civilization advances, these taxes become inadequate and the state makes drafts on the future, contracts loans and raises public debts.

Armed with public power and the right to levy taxes, the public officials stand above society. Being the vehicle of power, respect for them must be enforced by means of exceptional laws by virtue of which they enjoy special sanctity and inviolability.

In the state, the authority of the rulers as well as the bureaucracy is maintained by the use of naked force, while in tribal society it flowed from genuine respect for the tribal chief.

The views of Engels can be summarised in this manner. The state has not existed from the beginning. There were stateless societies in history. The state is not a natural institution. It has not been created by a social contract by the whole of society. It has emerged at a specific stage of the historic development of society torn by class division and class struggle. State is not something above society or super-imposed on it. It has not been made by God or any divine power. It is not the image and reality of reason as maintained by Hegel. It is not the product of a contract among the people but the product of specific historical circumstances. The state is merely an instrument of the dominant economic class and is used to maintain its rule. The state does not belong to the whole society. It is instrumental in the exploitation of the economically poor classes. It tries to keep the class struggle in society within bounds. It tries to act as shock-absorber, but it cannot end the class struggle. The state may seem sometimes a supra-class by its functions, but in the final analysis it safeguards the interests of the owning classes only. By virtue of the state, the powerful economic class becomes the most powerful political class also in spite of its being in minority. The state in the ancient period was the state of slave-owners. In the medieval period, it was feudal state, an organ of nobility. The modern representative state is an instrument of the bourgeois class. With the change in the economic system or mode of production and with the abolition of private property when society will become classless, the state will automatically "wither away."

While explaining the views of Engels on the subject, Plamenatz questions the validity of some of his assumptions. His contention is that the increasing division of labour does not of itself divide society into classes; at least not unless we so define or use the word class that differences of occupation are differences of class. Though tinkers and tailors have different occupations, they do not belong to different classes in the Marxian sense of class. Engels does not see that the need (for state) would be there even if there were no classes in the Marxian sense. He sees the need and takes it for granted that the classes create the need. The truth is that Engels is not using the word class in the same sense as when he speaks of class exploitation or calls feudal lords or capitalists a class. An increased division of labour gives rise to groups with divergent interests leading to disputes which cannot be settled by the old methods and therefore the groups are called irreconcilable. New methods of settling disputes are used by a new type of authority, the state, whose function is said to keep the peace between irreconcilable groups. If peace can be kept by these new methods between groups, it cannot be said that they are irreconcilable.

Views of Lenin (1870-1924)

The views of Lenin are very much similar to those of Engels. In his work, "The State and Revolution", Lenin has supported the views expressed by Engels. Lenin writes, "The state is a product and manifestation of the irreconcilability of class antagonisms. The state arises where, when and in so far as class antagonisms objectively cannot be reconciled. And, conversely, the existence of state proves that the class antagonisms are irreconcilable". (Selected Works, P. 266)

According to Lenin, the state is the product of class conflict. To quote him, "According to Marx, the state is an organ of class rule, an organ for the oppression of one class by another; it is the creation of order which legalises and perpetuates this oppression by moderating the conflict between the classes". (Selected Works, pp. 266-67).

Lenin did not accept the view that the state emerged to bring unity, peace and order in society. To quote him, "The state is an organ of the rule of a definite class which cannot be reconciled with its antipode (the class opposite to it)."

Lenin made an important contribution by explaining the origin of a socialist state. He explained the theory and practice of revolutions and the nature of a working class state. He wrote about the withering away of the state and gave a strong reply to the anarchists who supported the theory of abrupt overthrow of the state. Lenin wrote, "According to Marx, the state withers away – as distinct from the anarchist doctrine of the abolition of the state."

The views of Lenin can be summarised in this manner. The bourgeois state can only be abolished by a socialist revolution under the leadership of an organised working class who will capture the state power forcibly. To quote Lenin, "Revolution alone can abolish the bourgeois state. The suppression of the bourgeois state by the proletarian state is impossible without a violent revolution." After capturing the state power, the working class will destroy the bourgeois state machinery and a working class state will be established. The task of the working class state will be to build a socialist economy and to abolish private property so that a classless and stateless society may come into being. With the establishment of a classless society, the state will automatically "wither away". The bourgeois state will be abolished by creating a socialist state through a revolution and the socialist state will also wither away. Lenin writes, "According to Engels the bourgeois state does not wither away, but is abolished by the proletariat in the course of the revolution. What withers away after the revolution is the proletarian state or semi state.

Views of Gramsci (1891-1937)

Antonio Gramsci was perhaps the most interesting and suggestive thinker since Marx. According to him, states come into being through the struggle of three kinds of social forces-social forces which provide leadership, social forces against whom struggle is waged and some auxiliaries or allied forces which give active or passive consent to the leaders. To quote Gramsci, "Numerous principles of historical research can be established by examining the innovatory forces which led the national Risorgimento in Italy. These forces took power and united in the modern Italian state in the struggle against specific other forces. In order to become a state, they had to subordinate or eliminate the former and win the active or passive assent of the latter."

Gramsci maintains that the state has originated on account of domination and hegemony. To quote him, "The supremacy of a social group manifests itself in two ways, as domination and as intellectual and moral leadership. A social group dominates antagonistic groups which it tends to liquidate or to subjugate perhaps even by armed force: it leads kindred and allied groups. A social group can and indeed must, already exercise leadership before winning governmental power. It subsequently becomes dominant when it exercises power." According to Gramsci, state originates when some class gets the active or passive support of some other allies and suppresses some enemies.

Gramsci regarded the state as an instrument of the ruling classes. "The historical unity of the ruling classes is realised in the state and their history is essentially the history of states and of groups of states." He does not regard state merely as an instrument of force or coercion, but maintains that state is based On both hegemony and domination.

According to Gramsci, the bourgeois state only serves the interests of one class and not of the whole community. The state has not originated merely because of naked force or oppression. State uses naked power only as the last resort. In order to bring about a revolution, it is necessary to break down the hegemony and ideological basis of the slate. With the destruction of the ideological base of the state, the possibilities of its destruction increase.

Criticism of the Theory

Marxist theory of the origin of the state has been criticised on various grounds. (1) The Marxian theory of class struggle is not convincing. State is not the product of class antagonisms. It is a growth and not a make. Hunt writes, "Marx's thesis that all conflict among men arises from the class struggle, albeit of undoubted practical value as calculated to convince the masses that their misfortunes are attributed to the capitalist system and will disappear with the victory of the proletariats, is nonetheless facacious."

(2) The prophecy of Karl Marx that with the division of society into two classes of the bourgeoisie and the proletariat all other classes will disappear, has not come out to be true. His prophecy that the state will wither away after the establishment of classless society has been proved to be wrong.

(3) The Marxian theory preaches violence. To Marx, a change in the state can be brought about only through class struggle. William Ebenstein writes, "If Marx had accorded the political factor its due weight, if he had fully grasped the importance of the Reform Act in England and of the Jacksonian Revolution in the United States, he might have realised that socialism, too, might be accomplished without violence in countries that possessed democratic traditions strong enough to absorb far-reaching social and economic changes without resorting to civil war. A recognition of the cultural and political factors in the equation of social change would have amounted, however, to a virtual abandonment of the central position of Marx that history is the history of class wars and that ruling classes defend their position to the bitter ends."

(4) The Marxian theory of the origin of the state regards economic factor as the most important factor in the formation of the state. It ignores the importance of other factors.

(5) The Marxists have denounced the state as the instrument of exploitation. According to them, the state always looks to the interests of the capitalists and exploits others. This is not correct. The modern state has become a welfare state and it protects the interests of all the people.

(6) Prof. MacIver and Plamenatz do not accept the Marxist theory regarding the origin and nature of the state as propounded by Engels and Lenin. They reject the concept of primitive communism as a correct description of the pre-political tribal society. Prof. MacIver does not agree with Engels that matriarchal societies actually implied any greater authority of women over men. There was no common ownership of the means of production. There was only the common use of consumable articles. Neither communism and common ownership nor matriarchal authority can be accepted as adequate concepts to describe the nature of the tribal and clan systems out of which the state evolved. They also point out that the division of labour does not necessarily create antagonistic classes in the Marxian sense. That only creates numerous occupations which need not be hostile to each other.

(7) Plamenatz contends that Engels does not realise that the state will still be required even if there were no antagonistic classes. The state will be required to settle non-antagonistic disputes between different occupational groups which arise in society.

(8) The view of Plamenatz is that the real class structures arise after the state has already come into existence. The antagonistic classes of slave-owners and slaves, of feudal lords and serfs, of capitalists and wage labourers emerge when the state has already come into existence. The social classes are post-state phenomenon. The class struggles have followed the creation of the state instead of preceding it.

(9) Critics point out that Marx and Engels ignore the element of consent in the evolution of the state and the role of the state in promoting the common good. The state could have functioned as an instrument of class domination in ancient or feudal society or even under early capitalistic system. With the arrival of political democracy based on universal suffrage, the state has become an institution to promote the collective well-being of all social groups. The modern democratic state cannot be described as an instrument of class domination.

(10) Critics also point out that the state is not an organ of class rule in a liberal democracy. It exists for the conciliation of divergent socio-economic interests.

SUGGESTED READINGS

Bluntschli, J.K. : *Theory of the State, Oxford University Press,* London, 1901.

Boas, Franz : *The Mind of Primitive Man,* New York, 1911.

Brown, Ivor : *English Political Theory,* London, 1920.

Chang, Sherman, H.M. : *The Marxist Theory of the State.*

Davidson, W.L. : *Political Thought in England from Bentham to Mill,* New York, 1920.

Dealey, J.A. : *The Development of the State.*

Dunning, W.A. : *History of Political Theories, Macmillan,* New York, 1905, 1920.

Engels, F. : *The Origin of the Family, Private Property and the State,* Moscow, 1952.

Figgis, J.N. : *The Divine Right of Kings, Cambridge University Press,* London, 1914.

Ford, H.J. : *The Natural History of the State, Princeton,* 1915.

Fraser, J.G. : *The Golden Bough,* 1922.

Garner, J.W. : *Political Science and Government,* New York, 1928.

Garner, J.W. : *Introduction to Political Science.*

Gettell, R.G. : *Introduction to Political Science.*

Gettell, R.G. : *Problems of Political Evolution.*

Gettell, R.G. : *Political Science,* Calcutta, 1950.

Gierke, O. : *Political Theory of the Middle Ages,* London, 1900.

Gilchrist, R.N. : *Principles of Political Science,* New York.

Gooch, G.P. : *Political Thought in England from Bacon to Halifax,* London, 1911.

Gooch, G.P. : *English Democratic Ideas in the Seventeenth Century,* London, 1898.

Graham, Wallas : *English Political Philosophy from Hobbes to Maine,* London, 1914.

Hartland, E.S. : *Primitive Society,* London, 1921.

Hoare and Mathews : Antonio Gramsci, Selections from Political Writings (1910-20), London, 1977.

Hoare and Smith (Ed.) : *Sleet ions from the Prison Notebooks of Antonio Gramsci,* London, 1971.

Laski, H.J. : *Political Thought in England from Locke to Bentham,* New York, 1920.

Leacock, S. : *Elements of Political Evolution.*

Leacock, S. : *Elements of Political Science.*

Lenin, V.T. : *The State and Revolution,* 1917.

Lichtheim, George : *Marxism: An Historical and Critical Study.*

Lowie, R.H. : *The Origin of the State,* New York, 1927.

Lowie, R.H. : *Primitive Society,* New York, 1920.

MacIver, R.M. : *The Web of Government.*

MacIver, R.M. : *The Modern State.*

Maine, Henry : *Ancient Law,* New York, 1890.

Maine, Henry : *Early History of Institutions,* New York, 1875.

Marx : *The Poverty of Philosophy,* 1847.

Marx and Engels : *The Communist Manifesto.*

Marx and Engels : *Anti-Duhring.*

McLennan, J.F. : *The Patriarchal Theory,* London, 1885.

Morgan, L.H. : Ancient Society, New York, 1907.

Morris, C.R. and Morris, M. : *History of Political Ideas,* New York, 1924.

Murray, R.H. : *History of Political Science from Plato to the Present,* Cambridge, 1926.

Murrary, R.H. : *English Social and Political Thinkers of the Nineteenth Century,* Cambridge, 1929.

Paul, W. : *The State, Its Origin and Functions, Glasgow,* 1918.

Plamenatz, John : *Man and Society.*

Pollock, Frederick : *History of the Science of Politics.* London, 1910.

Randhir Singh : *Reason, Revolution and Political Theory,* New Delhi, 1967.

Rivers, W.H.R. : *Kinship and Social Organisation,* London, 1914.

Rockow, L. : *Contemporary Political Thought in England,* London, 1925.

Sabine, G.H. : *History of Political Theory,* New York, 1937.

Seeley, J.R. : *Introduction to Political Science,* London, 1908.

Soltau, R.H. : *An Introduction to Politics.*

Vaughan, C.E. : *Studies in the History of Political Philosophy,* New York, 1925.

Willoughby, W.W. : *The Ethical Basis of Political Authority.*

Willoughby, W.W. : *The Nature of the State.*

CHAPTER

Evolution of the State

In the words of Gettell, the state did not have a single origin or a regular or continuous evolution. Various forms of states have arisen at different times and places as a result of causes by no means uniform. These states had widely different histories and worked out governmental organisations far from similar. At first glance, it seems difficult to follow the evolution of the state but if attention is directed chiefly to those states that occupied the leading positions in the world of their day and contributed most to the development of later political forms and ideas, a fairly uniform course of development can be found. In broad outline, the state evolved through the tribal state, the Oriental Empire, the Greek city states, the Roman World Empire, the feudal state and the national state. The periods of time during which each of these forms predominated show wide variation and within the general type, important changes in government took place. Moreover, earlier forms usually survived in some parts of the world long after later types had arisen elsewhere. There have also been tendencies to revive earlier forms.

Learning Objectives

The Tribal State

Tribal organisation was the earliest stage of state organisation. Family was the first political unit. The elements that constitute the state or the government were present in the tribe. The head of the tribe or a selected few persons wielded authority and they were obeyed. The head of the tribe dictated and his dictates were obeyed by the members of the tribe. He who disobeyed was punished by the head. Punishment was decided according to the customs and traditions of the tribe. The head of the tribe reserved the right to give capital punishment to the person who disobeyed him. There was no written law and matters were decided according to customs and traditions. Wars were waged among the tribes. When the head or the leader of a powerful tribe conquered other weak tribes, he became the leader of the defeated tribe and the latter became his subjects. In this way, most of the tribes attained the stature of state. Towns and cities sprang up. Customs and traditions gave place to written laws. Taxes were levied in place of giving of gifts by the members of the tribe to their head. In some tribes, the authority of the chief was despotic while in some others, it was strictly limited by a democratic public opinion or assemblies of warriors. In some, authority was transmitted by heredity or some accepted rule of succession. In others, the rulers were chosen freely by the members of the tribe. Sometimes, the tribal organisation was permanent and sometimes temporary. In some cases, a number of tribes combined into a loose confederation. The tribal form of organisation existed in some parts of the earth through the entire period of recorded history.

The Oriental Empire

By and by, tribes settled in places where their basic needs and necessities were fulfilled. They settled in those places where they could get food to eat, water to drink and pastures for their cattle. They settled in places where the climate was neither too cold nor too hot. Gradually, tribes reached the stature of the state. Tribal centres became small kingdoms in course of time. Gradually, small kingdoms flowered into big empires which were ruled on the basis of wealth and military power. Big empires were established in the valley of the rivers Indus and the Ganges in India, in the valley of Huang Hoangho and Yang Tse-Kiang in China, the Euphrates and Tigris in Mesopotamia and the Nile in Egypt. It is also likely that the earliest states rose in the Plateaus of Mexico and Peru in South America.

The Oriental Empires were neither strongly centralised nor closely knit together. They were "at best a loose congeries of semi-independent states in which the imperial sceptre shifts not only from dynasty to dynasty but also from city to city." They were based on wealth and military force. They were not properly organised. Everything depended upon the personality and character of the Emperor and his favourite courtiers. On account of lack of cohesion, slow communication, conspiracies of the regional commanders and Provincial Governors against the central authority and the court intrigues, there was no stability in those days. Conquests were often followed by repeated revolts and countries had to be reconquered again and again. Soltau writes, "Expansion by annexation; then disruption and reconstitution, either from within or by conquest from the outside were the normal process that marked those early empires." (*An Introduction to Politics, p. 60*).

Greek City States

The next stage was the Greek city states which are considered to be the first communities who gave conscious thought to politics. They were organised on the basis of clans and tribes, each clan and tribe occupying a separate valley or island. Those valleys and islands became the centres of political life of the Greeks. The Greek city was a state in the modern sense of the term. Each city state was proud of its independence. The Greeks refused to merge their cities into one big state. Each city state was small in size and population. The Greek view was that a small state was the best as the same could be governed well. The Greeks believed in direct democracy in which the citizens could actively participate in the affairs of the state. Every citizen was normally a soldier, a judge and a member of the governing assembly. He performed his duties personally and not through deputies or representatives. To borrow the language of Burke, the Greek city state was "a partnership in all science, a partnership in all art, a partnership in every virtue and in all perfection." The Greek city was at the same time a state, a church and a school and embraced the whole life of man. The Greeks did not make any distinction between state and society.

The assertion of too much of independence by each city state ultimately respited in their doom. City states were so small that they were no match for any strong state and that explains their disappearance from the scene of history. The Greeks not only lacked discipline but also the spirit of compromise and tolerance. They wasted their time and energy in faction fights between the rich and the poor, the nobles and the commons and the friends of Athens and the friends of Sparta. They also lacked humanity. They believed in liberty for themselves and denied the same to others. They not only maintained plenty of slaves but also defended the institution of slavery which was considered as natural without which civilised life was impossible. They failed to realise that there could be no democracy where there was slavery. A democratic society cannot be divided into free people and slaves. Slavery is the very negation of democracy. The Greeks never felt a common political consciousness uniting them all into a single political whole. Frequent wars destroyed the power of the leading cities.

The Roman Empire

The Roman State passed through three different periods. The first period was that of the monarchic state and that lasted from about 753 B.C. to 510 B.C. During that period, the king was not only the head of the state but also the chief priest of the community. On the death of a king, the sovereignty of the state reverted to the Council of Elders which appointed a temporary king who in turn nominated another Elder who actually named the new king subject to the approval of the people. "The vote of the people was ratified by the approval of the gods as given in the ceremony of inauguration." The king was required to consult the Council of Elders and follow their advice. All cases involving capital punishment had to be submitted to the people for their approval. During this period, the nobles known as the Patricians shared political power with a monarch, but that was not the case with the Plebians who enjoyed no political rights.

Monarchy in Rome was succeeded by a Republic under which civil and military power were in the hands of two Consuls who were elected annually. The Patricians controlled the administration and the Plebians did not figure anywhere. There was a struggle between the two classes for the control of political power. Ultimately, both of them got equal political and civil rights. During this period, Rome started annexing the neighbouring territories. By 90 B.C., almost all the people were granted full citizenship. MacIver writes, "From early times the Romans had the wit to distinguish between civil rights–rights of equality before the law and political rights–rights of membership in the sovereign body." Some citizens of Italy were given civil rights but not political rights.

The Republic gave way to the Roman Empire which at one time extended over Austria, Germany, France, Spain, England, the Balkans, Greece, Asia Minor and the whole of the Mediterranean coast and its hinterland. The Empire was divided into Provinces, each under a Proconsul who had full powers in civil and political matters. The Emperor was all-powerful and popular assemblies stopped functioning. For a time, the Emperor was worshipped as God. While Christianity was accepted as state religion, the theory of the divine origin of the state was interpreted to mean that the Emperor was the agent of the will of God on earth. Rome put before the world the ideals of unity, order, universal law and cosmopolitanism. Less importance was given to the ideas of liberty and equality. The law of nations developed during this period. It was a great step forward widening the notions of law-givers and statesmen. The Romans also applied the Greek notion of the law of nature, to their legal system.

In due course of time, the Roman Empire began to decay and the causes responsible for it were "the sacrifice of individual liberty for the sake of securing unity, the soulless efficiency which characterised her administration, the moral depravity of the upper classes, devastating pestilence, the unsound economic basis of the Empire, failure to make rules for the succession of Emperors, religious disintegration and the invasion of barbarian hordes." The weakness in the Roman system was that "it remained too Roman, too centralised, too much dominated by the desires and interests of Rome, too dependent on the personality of the Emperor of the day." Gettell writes, "Greece developed democracy without unity, Rome secured unity without democracy."

The Feudal State

After the downfall of the Roman Empire, there was a long period of confusion. The barbarians who overthrew the Roman Empire were still living in the tribal stage and when they came into contact with the Roman political institutions, there was a conflict between the two and out of that conflict arose feudalism as a compromise. It was feudalism which gave to the people of Europe comparative peace and protection and preserved the machinery of the state. Feudalism marked the transition from Roman imperialism to the national state.

After the fall of the Roman Empire, its vast territories fell into the hands of powerful nobles. Each of those nobles created a community of his own around him by a process of "sub-infeudation" of land. The supreme lord gave his land to tenants-in-chief who in their turn gave the same to tenants. An hierarchy was built upon the basis of land-holding. The rigid system of classes was set up and the state was swallowed up in the community. As the loyalty of each class was in the first instance to the class immediately above it, the idea of a sovereign power reigning supreme in a given territory was not possible during the feudal period. Custom took the place of the uniform law of the Romans. Real political progress was not possible so long as feudal ideas prevailed. The Church occupied a very privileged position. It had its own organisation on the Roman imperial model. During the Middle Ages, the Church was able to control the state and itself became a powerful temporal authority, possessing a lot of landed property and other wealth. Dr. Figgis says, "In the Middle Ages, the Church was not a state; it was the state; the state or rather the civil authority (for a separate society was not recognised) was merely the police department of the Church." However, from the beginning of the 14th century, the Papacy fell on evil days and lost all its prestige.

Feudalism was only "a temporary scaffolding or framework of order." It gave to the people of Europe some order but such a state of affairs was not conducive to human progress and no wonder feudalism declined in course of time. The Renaissance and the Reformation accelerated its pace. The Tudor kings took advantage of the situation and established a centralised authority. The example of England was followed by France, Spain and Portugal.

The Nation-State

Feudalism was succeeded by national states, each one of which was based on the bonds of nationality strengthened by the natural boundaries. The nation states began their career as absolute monarchies. All the great Reformers asked their followers to obey the state and taught "that the powers that be are ordained of God." Their view was that political authority came ultimately from the will of God and the rulers to whom obedience was due ruled by divine right. The general tendency of the Reformation was to strengthen the hold of the monarchic principle in monarchic lands and that of aristocracy in aristocratic lands. "In both, the effect was to strengthen absolutism in the political sovereign."

The next stage in the development of the nation state was the conflict between the king and the people. It is true that royal absolutism was necessary to weld the people together and to bring order and unity out of feudal disorder and disunity, but once that object was achieved, there was no justification for continuing that state of affairs. The people demanded their rights and privileges and ultimately were successful in depriving the king of all his powers. The democratic movement worked so satisfactorily that till recently, the democratic national state came to be regarded as the final stage in the evolution of the state. Bentham hoped to better "this wicked world by covering it over with Republics."

The modern state is a nation-state and it has become the basic pattern in the world. New nation-states keep on coming into existence from time to time. Each nation-state puts emphasis on ethnic and geographic unity. It does everything to preserve its integrity and its natural frontiers and keep its people together.

Colonial Empires

During the 19th century, there came into existence many colonial empires. Great Britain was the leader in this respect and she had her colonies all over the world. There was regular scramble for power in Africa and various states were able to establish their hold over various parts of Africa. France was able to set up a big colonial empire in Africa. She also had her colonies in other parts of the world. The Dutch colonial empire was big one. However, in recent times, there was lot of agitation against the foreign colonies and many of the colonial powers gave up their hold over their erstwhile colonies. The Communist movement played an important role in this matter.

Important changes took place within the British Empire and the commonwealth of Nations. The autonomy and independence of the Dominions was formally recognised in the Statute of Westminster.

Separate representation was given to Canada, Australia, New Zealand, the Union of South Africa and India at the Peace Conference in 1919. They also became members of the League of Nations. India got her independence in 1947. Pakistan also became independent in the same year. The Irish Free State was set up in 1922. Burma was separated from India in 1937 and was given independence in January 1948. Ceylon became a Dominion in 1948. In 1963, the Federation of Malaysia was created. In 1960, the Gold Coast became a Republic under the new name of Ghana. In 1965, Ghana became an independent member of the Commonwealth of Nations. In 1963, Nigeria became a Republic. In 1964, the State of Zambia came into existence in place of North Rhodesia. Southern Rhodesia became independent in April 1980 under the new name of Zimbabwe. In 1964, the new State of Malawi came into existence in place of Nyasaland. In December 1962, Tanganyika became a sovereign state within the Commonwealth of Nations. In 1964, Zanzibar and Pemba merged with Tanganyika to form the new State of Tanzania. In October 1962, Uganda became an independent state. In December 1963, Kenya became independent. In 1956, Britain recognised the independence of Sudan. In 1961, Union of South Africa became a Republic. In 1948, Britain withdrew from Palestine and the Jewish State of Israel came into existence. Iraq became independent in 1932. Congo became independent in 1960. In 1956, Morocco and Tunisia became independent. Algeria became independent in 1962. Mali became independent in 1960. In 1949, Indonesia became independent. Angola became independent in 1975.

World Federation

If our fathers thought nationally, we think internationally. The history of the last century shown that nationalism in actual practice leads to rivalry, competition and even war. Factors such as scientific discoveries of recent years, better facilities for travel and international intercourse among the people of the world, international trade on a large scale and the nature of the world problems have resulted in the "shrinkage of the world." The narrow ideas of patriotism and national sovereignty tend to break down. It appears that the only way out of the present difficulty is a world federation in which each state maintains its individuality but joins others in solving problems common to all. The view of Prof. Harold Laski was that in other than purely domestic matters, settlement in terms of common rules for all nations was becoming necessary. He also maintained that the sovereignty of the state was in the process of disappearance in international affairs as that had served its purpose. To quote him, "What the individual today requires is not the concept of imperialism but the concept of federalism." In his well-known book entitled "Union Now", C.A. Streit advocates a federal union of the existing democracies of the world. His view is that the doctrine of absolute sovereignty is not suited to modern conditions. The new organisation is to regulate only the external relations of its members, leaving them alone so far as their domestic affairs are concerned. In the Federal Union, there were to be common citizenship, common currency, common postage, common tariff and common defence.

It is true that the establishment of some sort of a world federation can help the nations of the world to solve their problems to some extent. However, it is not possible to set up such a world federal union unless and until the nations of the world change their present political and economic attitudes. Judging from the actions of the present states, it is too much to believe that they will adjust themselves so easily in the near future. Experience shows that wherever the interests of one state conflict with those of another, no state is prepared to surrender its claims to avoid war. Human beings even today are selfish and it is difficult to expect that they will change overnight and work in harmony in the higher interests of the world as a whole.

From a study of the evolution of the state, Gettell has come to certain conclusions. According to him, the evolution of the state has been from the simple to the complex. Government has become complex and complicated, with interdependence of its various organs. The functions of the organs of the government differ but there is a fundamental unity underlying them all. The authority of the state has become more definite and regular. There has been the growth of political consciousness among the people. State authority is being based on a rational and stable foundation. The size of the state has become bigger and the area of each state has become larger, along with increased population. The improvements in the means of transport and communication have helped this process. The increasing respect of man for law and order has helped the state. The authority of the state in certain respects has increased while in others it has decreased. In all civilised states the state does not try to control religion. It is realised that it is harmful for the state to try to regulate religion and morality. It is also recognised that the state should not interfere with the domestic life of the people. However, there is more and more demand for state interference in such matters as education, sanitation, public health, prevention and punishment of crime, works of public utility and many other things which the individuals cannot do efficiently and which the state must take over for public welfare. In course of time, a compromise has been arrived at between the sovereignty of the state and the liberty of the individual. "By the principles of local self-government and representation, an organisation which secures unity in common affairs without sacrificing individual liberty is made possible and democracy over large areas is at last secured." It is true that no two modern states are agreed as to what is the proper adjustment between sovereignty and liberty and as to how best to secure it, but the problem has to be faced by the statesmen of every country.

SUGGESTED READINGS

Brett, G.S. : *The Government of Man*, London, 1913.
Carter, G.M. : *Independence for* Africa, 1960.
Cassirer, E. : *The Myth of the State.*
Cowan, A.R. : *Master-Clues in World History*, New York, 1914.
Cowen, Zelman : The British Commonwealth of Nations in a Changing World, 1964.
Dealey, J.A. : *The Development of the State.* New York, 1909.
De Grazia, S. : *The Political Community.*
Derley, J.A. : *The Development of the State.*
Emerson, R. : *From Empire to Nation, Calcutta*, 1960.
Fowler, W.W. : *The City-State of the Greeks and Romans.*
Fowler, J.G. : *The Golden Bough*, 1922.
Garner, J.W. : *Introduction to Political Science.*
Garner, J.W. : *Political Science and Government.*
Gettell, R.G. : *Problems of Political Evolution.*
Gettell, R.G. : *Introduction to Political Science.*
Gettell, R.G. : *Political Science*, Calcutta, 1950.
Hatch, J. : A History of Post-War Africa.
Jenks, E. : The State and the Nation, New York, 1919.
Jenks, E. : *History of Politics*, London, 1900.
Lipson, L. : *The Great Issues of Politics*, 1965.
Lowrie, R.H. : *Origin of the State.*
Lowrie, R.H. : *Primitive Society*, 1920.
MacIver, R.M. : *The Web of Government.*
MacIver, R.M. : *The Modern State*, London, 1976.

Marx, M.	:	*Foreign Governments.*
Openheimer, F.	:	*The State*, 1914.
Palmer, Leslie H.	:	*Indonesia and the Dutch*, 1962.
Robertson, J.M.	:	*The Evolution of States*, New York, 1913.
Sidgwick, H.	:	*The Development of European Polity.*
Soltau, R.H.	:	*An Introduction to Politics*, 1951.
Strachey, John	:	*The End of Empire*, 1960.
Streit, C.A.	:	*Union Now.*
Wallerstein, I.	:	*The Road to Independence: Ghana and the Ivory Coast*, 1964.
Watson, J.	:	*The State in Peace and War.*
Wehl, D.	:	*The Birth of Indonesia*, 1948.

14 CHAPTER

Sovereignty

Learning Objectives

- Definition of Sovereignty
- Characteristics of Sovereignty
- Kinds of Sovereignty
- Titular Sovereignty
- De facto and de jure Sovereign
- Legal and Political Sovereignty
- Popular Sovereignty
- National Sovereignty
- Austin's Theory of Sovereignty
- Pluralist Theory of Sovereignty
- Factors Responsible for Rise of Pluralism
- Principles of Pluralism
- Exponents of Pluralist Theory
- Gierke and Maitland
- Durkheim
- Boncour
- Figgis
- Cole
- Barker
- Webbs
- Lindsay
- Duguit
- Krabbe
- Follett
- Laski (1894-1950)
- Criticism of monistic theory of Sovereignty
- Robert M. MacIver (b. 1882)
- Criticism of Pluralist Theory of Sovereignty
- Merits of Pluralistic Theory
- Suggested Readings

The concept of sovereignty is the basis of modern political science. It underlies the validity of all laws and also determines all international relations. Sovereignty is one of the most essential elements of the state as there can be no state without it. The term sovereignty is derived from the word "superanus" which means supremacy or superior power.

Although the term "sovereignty" is a modern one, the idea goes back to the time of Aristotle who referred to the "supreme power" of the state. This idea was also known to the Roman jurists and the civilians throughout the Middle Ages. Jenks points out that the heads of Cambridge colleges were designated sovereigns in fifteenth century law reports. The modern terms "sovereign" and "sovereignty" were first used by French jurists such as Beaumanoir and Loyseau in the fifteenth century. To quote Beaumanoir, "The king is sovereign above all and we name him when we speak of the sovereignty which belongs to him."

Bodin claims to be the first modern writer to give the idea of sovereignty. He discussed at length his idea of sovereignty in his *Six Books on the Republic.* The prevailing chaos in France at that time demanded the exposition of a philosophy which would give all powers into the hands of an authority whom everybody would obey. The civil war in France had practically ruined the country. It was against this background that Bodin defined sovereignty as supreme power over citizens and subjects unrestrained by law. He emphasized the perpetual nature of sovereignty. His view was that a sovereign could not be a sovereign for a few years. He had no objection to a life-tenure for a sovereign. Although the sovereign was bound by the covenant into which he entered himself, a wise sovereign would not bind himself by such promises. The sovereign was bound by the law of God. Sovereignty could be in one person or a body of persons.

Hobbes gave his theory of sovereignty in *The Leviathan.* The sovereign was created by means of a social contract. He was not a party to the contract and there was no limitation on his authority, which was absolute. Sovereignty was indivisible. The sovereign was the source of all authority. The only occasion when an individual could disobey the sovereign was when the sovereign wanted to kill him or was not in a position to protect him. Sovereignty could be in one person or a body of persons.

The sovereign of Locke also was created by a social contract. However, he did not possess unlimited powers. His function was merely to interpret and enforce the rights which the people had in the state of nature. The people had the right to revolt against the sovereign if he did not fulfil the duties which were given to him by the people. To quote Locke, "There can be but one supreme power which is the legislative, to which all the rest are and must be subordinate, yet the legislative being only a fiduciary power for certain ends, there remains still in the people a supreme power to remove or alter the legislative, when they find the legislative act contrary to the trust reposed in them."

The sovereign of Rousseau was the general will which was created by means of a social contract by which all the individuals gave up all the rights which they possessed in the state of nature to the sovereign. Rousseau stood for the sovereignty of the people or what is known as popular sovereignty. His sovereign was absolute, indivisible, infallible and inalienable.

Hegel made the theory of sovereignty philosophical and metaphysical. His view was that the state was perfected rationality, the eternal and necessary essence of spirit, and an absolute fixed end in itself. The rights of the state were unlimited. The state was the supreme community and was the source of morality and all civilized existence. The people had no right to revolt against the state, whose authority was supreme in every way.

According to Bentham, the sovereign possessed absolute powers. Austin gave a classic definition of sovereignty. His view was that the sovereign was a determinate person or a body of persons. Neither the general will nor the people taken together were the sovereign. The power of the sovereign was legally unlimited. It was absolute and indivisible. Law was the command of the sovereign.

In recent times, the old idea of sovereignty has been attacked by writers known as the pluralists. The names of some of them are Gierke, Maitland, Dr. Figgis, Duguit, Cole, Laski and MacIver. These writers emphasize the fact that sovereignty is not absolute and authority is shared by the state with other associations and groups which are joined by individuals for the satisfaction of their different needs.

At present there is hopeless confusion regarding the subject of sovereignty. That is partly due to the differences of views regarding the nature of the state as it is and what some people would like the same to be. The German writers like Hegel praised the state of the skies and advocated an ideal state where sovereignty is absolute. Similar views were advocated by the Nazis and the Fascists. Some writers busy themselves with the abstract nature of sovereignty and in the words of Lord Bryce, their barren discussions drag us through a "dusty desert of words rather than of substance." Some writers have an ulterior motive "to get a speculative basis for practical propaganda." There is confusion between legal theory and political practice. Legal sovereignty vests in some definite persons or body of persons and the sovereign has the power to enforce obedience to its will. However, it has been difficult to locate legal sovereignty in actual practice and the same varies from country to country. While in Britain, the Parliament is sovereign and no court there can challenge it, the same cannot be said about the American Congress where the Constitution is supreme and not the Congress. In a totalitarian state, sovereignty is with the executive and the legislature and the judiciary are subordinate to it. Hitler used the Reichstag merely as a rubber stamp. It is true that the legal sovereign must ultimately bow before the political sovereign but again there is confusion as to where political sovereignty actually lies. There is a confusion between actual authority and its source. In the words of Soltau, "It is one thing to say that all authority comes from the people and another to say that the people actually govern." It goes without saying that the people cannot govern themselves and they have to be governed by a few in whom authority rests. It is on account of these difficulties and confusion that Prof. Laski suggested that the whole concept of sovereignty be dropped altogether. However, it is pointed out that it is not possible to do so. It is partly due to the fact that it is a useful concept. We can understand the character of any system of government from the fact as to where sovereignty is actually located and how the same is exercised in actual practice. Moreover, merely because there is some confusion regarding the subject of sovereignty, the same cannot be dropped altogether.

Definition of Sovereignty

The term "sovereignty" has been variously defined by different writers. Grotius defined it as "the supreme political power vested in him whose acts are not subject to any other and whose will cannot be overridden." Jellinek defined it as "that characteristic of the state in virtue of which it cannot be legally bound except by its own will or limited by any other power than itself." Duguit says that sovereignty is the "commanding power of the state; it is the will of the nation organised in the state; it is the right to give unconditional orders to all individuals in the territory of the state." Burgess describes sovereignty as "original, absolute, unlimited power over the individual subjects and over all associations of subjects." It is "the underived and independent power to command and compel obedience." Willoughby defines sovereignty as "the supreme will of the state." The view of Carre de Malberg is that sovereignty is not a "power" but rather a "quality". Pollock says that "sovereignty is that power which is neither temporary nor delegated, nor subject to particular rules which it cannot alter, nor answerable to any other power on earth."

According to Karanenburg, it is the nature of the state "to impose its own will unconditionally on others; for such is the definition of ruling and it is of the essence of the state that it should rule." Le Fur says: "The expression 'external sovereignty' is only an abbreviated expression for designating the totality of rights by which internal sovereignty manifests itself *vis-a-vis* foreign states."

About sovereignty, Giddings observes: "In all the dictionaries, there is no other word that has more disastrously been conjured with by the metaphysical juggler.....Jurists and political theorists, losing sight of concrete fact, gave their minds to abstractions. And sovereignty became for political science a thing that never was on sea or land." D.F. Russell defines sovereignty as "the strongest power and supreme authority within a state, which is unlimited by law or anything else, since otherwise it would be neither strongest nor supreme." Soltau describes sovereignty as the exercise of "final legal coercive power by the state."

According to Laski, the sovereign is "legally supreme over any individual or group." It possesses "supreme coercive power." Jenks defines sovereignty as "an authority which, in the last resort, controls absolutely and beyond appeal the actions of every individual member of the community."

Characteristics of Sovereignty

There are many characteristics of sovereignty. *Sovereignty is absolute and unlimited.* This means that neither within the state nor outside it is there any power which is superior to the sovereign. There is no authority outside the state to which a sovereign is obedient or dependent. It is up to the sweet will of the sovereign to obey any authority outside the state or not. Even if a sovereign enters into a treaty, it is not bound to obey it. The sovereign is not bound by the rules of international law. Experience shows that sovereigns repudiated their obligations under international law whenever they found them to be inconvenient. As regards the authority of the sovereign within the state itself, it is absolute. There is absolutely no rival. The sovereign can make any law it pleases. It can change even the Constitution itself. The ordinary laws are made, amended and repealed by the sovereign. Neither the law's of nature nor divine law act as a limitation on the authority of the sovereign.

Critics point out that absolute sovereignty is neither possible nor desirable. The sovereign acts through law and law can regulate and control only the external actions of the individuals. It is also not desirable to give absolute power to any person or body of persons because "all power corrupts and absolute power corrupts absolutely." Bluntschli says: "There is no such thing as absolute independence;

even the state as a whole is not almighty, for it is limited externally by the rights of other states and internally by its own nature, and the rights of its individual members." Professor Dicey referred to two limitations on sovereignty. The external limit is due to the possibility that the citizens may disobey or resist the laws. The internal limit lies in the very nature of the sovereign power. There are certain things which the sovereign will not do on account of its very nature.

Another characteristic of sovereignty is its *universality or all comprehensiveness.* The sovereign is supreme over the persons, associations, and things within the state. No persons or body of persons can claim exemption as a matter of right. The only apparent exception to the universality of sovereignty is the extra-territorial sovereignty of diplomatic representatives in certain countries. On this point, Gilchrist says: "An embassy in a country belongs to the country which it represents, the members of the embassy being subject to the law of their own country. This, however, is only a matter of international courtesy and is no real exception. Any state in virtue of its sovereignty could deny the privileges so granted."

Sovereignty is also *inalienable.* It cannot be transferred. The obvious reason is that if the sovereign transfers its supreme powers, it no longer remains the sovereign. Lieber, an American writer, says: "Sovereignty can no more be alienated than a tree can alienate its right to sprout, or a man can transfer his life or personality without self-destruction." The abdication of a monarch or sovereign does not mean the alienation of sovereignty. "It is merely a change in the form of Government by the resignation of his position by a titular sovereign." The view of Rousseau was that power could be transferred but not will. Sovereignty was the essence of the personality of the state, and to alienate that was equivalent to suicide. A few writers adopt the contrary view. Prof Ritchie says that the doctrine of inalienability is belied by the facts of history.

Sovereignty is *permanent* in the same way as the state itself is permanent. So long as the state lasts, sovereignty also lasts. The two cannot be separated from each other. The death of a king or President does not mean the cessation of sovereignty. "It is only a personal change in the Government, not a break in the continuity of the state."

Sovereignty is *indivisible.* The reason is that if sovereignty is divided, there arises the possibility of two or more sovereigns. Jellinek rightly says that the idea of a "divided, fragmented, diminished, limited, relative sovereignty" is the very negation of sovereignty. Gettell says : "If sovereignty is not absolute, no state exists; if sovereignty is divided, more than one state exists." Sovereignty "is an entire thing: to divide it is to destroy it. It is the supreme power in a state and we might just as well speak of half a triangle as of half of a sovereignty." Calhoun says, "There is no difficulty in understanding how powers appertaining to sovereignty may be divided and the exercise of one portion be delegated to one set of agents and another portion to another, or how sovereignty may be vested in one man, in a few or in many. But how sovereignty itself, the supreme power, can be divided, it is impossible to conceive." Treitschke says: "A state where sovereignty is divided would be impossible; only political dilettanti like Cicero would dally with such eclectic fooleries." Curtis says: "It is manifest that there cannot be two supreme powers in the same community if both are to operate on the same objects. But there is nothing in the nature of political sovereignty to prevent its *powers* from being distributed among different agents for different purposes."

There has been a lot of controversy regarding the effect of the division of powers on sovereignty in a federal state. It is contended that on account of the division of powers, there is a division of sovereignty also. Both the federal government and the units are sovereign in their own spheres. There is no authority in the state which can do whatever it pleases. The authority of both, the units and the federal government, is limited by each other. However, it is pointed out that the idea of divided sovereignty arises from the failure to distinguish between state and governments. The division of powers or the delegation of powers by one part to another does not affect the idea of undivided sovereignty.

KINDS OF SOVEREIGNTY

Titular Sovereignty

There are different kinds of sovereignty in the world: Sometimes, a distinction is made between *titular sovereignty* and actual sovereignty. A titular sovereign is one who is sovereign only in name and not in fact. Although outwardly the power is vested in one person, the real power is enjoyed by another. The king of England is the titular head and he does not enjoy any real power. Actual powers are enjoyed by King-in-Parliament. Lowell says, "According to the early theory of the Constitution, the ministers were the counsellors of the King. It was for them to advise and for him to decide. Now parts are almost reversed. The King is consulted but the ministers decide." In case of India, the President of India is the titular sovereign and the real power lies in the hands of the cabinet. An absolute sovereign is all-powerful. He is the source of all law and authority. However, it is difficult to find such a King today. Even the Shah of Iran cannot be said to be an absolute monarch. In the past absolute monarchs were common and they did what they pleased. The name of Louis XIV can be quoted as an example of an absolute monarch.

De facto and de jure Sovereign

A distinction is also to be made between "de facto" sovereign and "de jure" sovereign. The term "de facto" means something which does not exist in the eye of law. A "de jure" sovereign is one who is considered to be sovereign in the eye of law, although he may not be so in actual practice. The de facto sovereign is one who possesses the actual power. When Mussolini came to power in Italy in 1922, de facto power passed into his hands although Victor Emmanuel was the de jure sovereign. Likewise, Cromwell was the de facto sovereign to begin with, although his authority was recognised by law later on. After the overthrow of Chiang Kai-shek in 1949, the Communists became the de facto sovereign of China. Experience shows that generally the de facto sovereign becomes the de jure sovereign in the long run.

Lord Bryce has described the relation between de facto sovereign and de jure sovereign in these words: "When sovereignty de jure attains its maximum of quiescence, sovereignty de facto is usually also steady, and is, so to speak, hidden behind it. When sovereignty de jure is uncertain, sovereignty do facto tends to be disturbed. When sovereignty de facto is stable, sovereignty de jure, though it may have been lost for a time, reappears, and ultimately becomes stable. When sovereignty de facto is disturbed, sovereignty de jure is threatened. Or, more shortly, the slighter are the oscillations of each needle, the more do they tends to come together in that coincidental quiescence which is an index to the perfect order, though not otherwise to the excellence, of a Government.

Legal and Political Sovereignty

According to Ritchie, "The legal sovereign is the lawyer's sovereign qua lawyer, the sovereign beyond which lawyers and courts refuse to look." It is determinate and definite. It may vest in one person or a body of persons. It is definitely organised, precise and recognised by law. It alone declares in legal terms the will of the state. Law is a command of the sovereign and he who violates it is liable to be punished. Rights emanate from the legal sovereign who is absolute, illimitable and supreme. The King-in-Parliament is the legal sovereign in England.

The political sovereign is the sum total of the influences in a State which lie behind the law. Dicey says: "That body is politically sovereign the will of which is ultimately obeyed by the citizens of the state". In England, this sovereign is the electorate, which in the long run can always enforce its will. The judges "know nothing about any will of the people except in so far as that will is expressed in an Act of Parliament and (they) would never suffer the validity of a statute to be questioned on the ground of its having been passed or being kept alive in opposition to the wishes of the electors."

Sidgwick attempted to illustrate the nature of political sovereignty by giving certain examples. To quote him, "Suppose that a monarch habitually obeys a priest, not for fear of extra-mundane penalties threatened by the latter, but from fear of finding it difficult to obtain obedience from his subjects if they believe him to be a special object of God's anger – we shall agree that he no longer completely possesses supreme political power. And if the influence of the priesthood over the monarch's subjects were so strong that the bulk of them unquestionably obey a direction of the chief priest to cease obeying the monarch, and if, therefore, the chief priest's directions were habitually obeyed by monarch, it would hardly be denied that the priest had become really, if not nominally, the political superior of the monarch." (*The Elements of Politics,* pp. 627-28)

In the case of direct democracy, there is no distinction between legal sovereign and political sovereign. The people themselves are both the political sovereign and legal sovereign. It is only in the case of indirect democracy that the distinction between political and legal sovereign becomes clear. While King-in-Parliament is the legal sovereign in England, it is the electorate which is the political sovereign. The ideal of democracy is to see that the legal sovereign does what the political sovereign desires. It is the duty of the legal sovereign to do all that lies in its powers to come up to the expectations of the political sovereign.

Prof. Gilchrist has brought out the relation between political and legal sovereign in these words : "In other words, the political sovereign lies behind, and conditions and thus limits the legal sovereign though, legally speaking, the legal sovereign is omnipotent. The political sovereign in the state is the influence in the state which, formulated in a legal way and passed by the legal law-making body, ultimately becomes the law of the state. The political sovereign manifests itself by voting, by the press, by speeches, and in many other ways not easy to describe or define. It is, however, not organised, and it can only become effective when organised. The organisation of political sovereignty leads to legal sovereignty. The two are aspects of the one sovereignty of the State. They constantly react on each other."

Leacock says, "Following upon this line of argument we might well expect to find that the legal and political sovereign would but rarely coincide. In one State the priesthood, in another the military or landed classes, in another the personal entourage of the king or the predominant influence of the metropolis, might supply the real motive power that controls the public administration."

Lord Bryce writes, "To an ordinary layman, the sovereign is that person or body of persons which can make his or their will prevail in the state, who is acknowledged to stand at the top, who can get his own way and make others go his. For the lawyer, however, a more definite conception is required. To him the sovereign is no other person or body than he or they to whose directions the law attributes legal force, the person or body in whom resides as of right the ultimate power of laying down general rules. This person or body is the legal sovereign and represents the juristic conception."

A lot of confusion arises when we attempt an exact definition of political sovereignty. It is vague and indeterminate, and cannot be located with exactness. It is for this reason that some writers prefer to confine sovereignty to its legal meaning and give up the concept of political sovereignty altogether. Gettell says: "Any attempt...to find a 'political sovereign' at the back of the legal sovereign destroys the value of the entire concept and reduces sovereignty to a mere catalogue of influences." Dr. Leacock also says: "The moment one passes from the dry certainty of the Austinian conception of legality, all is confusion."

It is suggested by some writers the there is no justification for making a distinction between legal and political sovereignty, as that involves the division of sovereignty which is not possible. The reply to that criticism is that when we make a distinction between political and legal sovereignty, we do not thereby divide sovereignty. It merely shows that the same sovereign manifests itself in two different ways. We may conclude by saying that the distinction between legal and political sovereignty is real and the relation between them is also intimate.

Popular Sovereignty

The doctrine of popular sovereignty implies that the supreme power in the state rests with the people. It is they alone who decide as to how the administrative machinery of a country has to be worked. This theory was put forward by the anti-monarchical writers of the sixteenth and seventeenth centuries as a counterblast to the despotic power claimed by the monarchs at that time. Writers like Marsiglio of Padua, William of Ockam, George Buchanan, Thomas Barclay, Francis Hotman, Boucher, Saurez, Bellarmin, Althusius and others attacked the exercise of unlimited powers by the kings and advocated the assumption and exercise of that power by the people as a whole. Rousseau also advocated the sovereignty of the people. He took pains to show that sovereignty rests with the general will, which is the will common to all the people. His view was that the people were the repository of all the powers in the state, and the government was merely a servant who carried out the will of the state. In the American Declaration of Independence, Jefferson stated that governments derive their just powers from the consent of the governed. Lord Bryce says that the idea of popular sovereignty is "the basis and watchword of democracy."

The doctrine of popular sovereignty was popularised in the nineteenth century by the writings of Professor Ritchie. According to him, "Sovereignty, in the last resort, is a matter of force and depends upon the ability to secure or to compel obedience, hence the power that in case of a struggle would have the strength to command obedience is the sovereign."

The theory of popular sovereignty appeals to the man in the street, and no wonder it has served as the battle-cry on many occasions in the history of many countries. In spite of its fascination, it is difficult to say what popular sovereignty actually implies. It is not possible to know where that popular sovereignty lies. The people, who are supposed to possess that sovereignty, are not determinate and it is to be seen how popular sovereignty can be given effect to. The concept of the general will is a confusing one. We have no means to find out the general will of the people. The general will cannot be the will of all the people as the masses have no definite will of their own. Sometimes, they hold many views which contradict one another. The result is that it becomes difficult to realize in actual practice the general will, except in a very general way.

Professor Gettell says that the theory of popular sovereignty is a contradiction in terms and does not stand the test of logic. "The state is a people organised by means of Government which makes and enforces law." If the word "people" implies all the people living in a state, we have the state resolved into its atoms, and supreme power ascribed to the unorganised mass or the majority of the individuals. If, however, by the people we refer to them as united and politically organised, we have only repeated the proposition, that sovereignty is a necessary ingredient of the state: for people politically organised is the state.

The exercise of the right of voting is no criterion of popular sovereignty. It has been found that in modern states, not more than 30% of the people vote. The result is that the legislature represents only a minority view. Even out of these 30%, the party that carries on the government does not and cannot represent more than 16%. It is the will of their leaders that has to be carried out, and the electors are not free to act in any way they please.

The doctrine of popular sovereignty takes it for granted that superior physical force rests with the people. However, that is not the case in actual practice. In modern warfare, with its mechanised armed forces, a handful of soldiers can put down the revolt of thousands or people. Hence, numerical majority does not necessarily imply superiority in physical force. If it is contended that sovereignty rests with the strongest group of persons who are trained to act together, sovereignty rests with the group of persons who are habitually obeyed.

All that can be said about the doctrine of popular sovereignty is that the government of a country should be carried on according to the public opinion prevailing in that country. There should not be unnecessary use of force by the state. "The highest ideal of statesmanship is to render the actual exercise of such force as seldom necessary as possible, and the extent to which this aim is attained, will depend largely upon the degree in which state action corresponds with the desire of public opinion or the general will."

The doctrine of popular sovereignty contains many valuable ideas. The government exists not for its own good but for the good of the people. If the wishes of the people are ignored, there is always the possibility of a revolution. Proper means must be provided for the expression of public opinion. The government should be held responsible to the people through frequent elections, local bodies and the devices of direct legislation such as referendum, initiative and recall. The Government should not act arbitrarily and help the establishment of the rule of law in the country.

National Sovereignty

The idea of national sovereignty was given by the leaders of the French Revolution. It was stated in the declaration of the Rights of Man that "all sovereignty resides essentially in the nation." This theory of sovereignty became "one of the intangible dogmas like the articles of a revealed religion and it forms today assuredly a positive principle of our political law" (Duguit). The same writer says: "Now it is not difficult to demonstrate that it is null and that the pretended dogma of national sovereignty is a gratuitous hypothesis and, moreover, a useless postulate." It is false because it implies that the nation possesses a personality and a will distinct from the persons and wills of the individuals who compose it. Malberg points out that the idea of national sovereignty is considered in France to be "one of the fundamental principles of public law and of the organisation of the public powers." But he also says that tire theory was invented for the negative purpose of denying the absolute authority of the monarch. It was also intended to mean that sovereignty in France was not divided into some 40 million fragments as suggested by Rousseau, each individual exercising a portion of it, but actually resided in the collectivity as a whole viewed as a corporate person.

Austin's Theory of Sovereignty

In his *Province of Jurisprudence Determined* (1832), Austin defined sovereignty thus: "If a determinate human superior not in the habit of obedience to a like superior receives habitual obedience from the bulk of a given society, that determinate superior is sovereign in that society and that society (including the superior) is a society political and independent." "Furthermore," he continued, "every positive law or every law simply and strictly so called, is set, directly or circuitously, by a sovereign person or body to a member of the independent political society wherein that person or body is sovereign or supreme."

Professor Laski says that there are three implications of the definition of sovereignty as given by Austin. The state is a legal order in which there is a determinate authority acting as the ultimate source of power. Its authority is unlimited. It may act unwisely or dishonestly but there is no limit on the exercise of its power. From the legal point of view, the character of the action is immaterial. If the order comes from the sovereign, that order is lawful. Command is the essence of the law. Law is in the form of "You must do certain things" or "You must not do other things" and failure in either direction would be punished.

On a general view of the theory, it appears that there is nothing very objectionable in it, but when we analyse it, it is full of many shortcomings.

Sir Henry Maine was very critical of the Austinian theory of sovereignty. His view was that sovereignty did not reside in a determinate human superior. To quote him, "A despot with a disturbed brain is the sole conceivable example of such sovereignty." Sir Henry emphasized the existence of "vast mass of influences, which we may call for shortness moral, that perpetually shapes, limits or forbids the actual direction of the forces by its sovereign." Referring to Maharaja Ranjit Singh of the Punjab, Sir Henry pointed out that the Maharaja "could have commanded anything; the smallest disobedience to his command would have been followed by death or mutilation". In spite of this, the Maharaja never "once in all his life issued a command which Austin could call a law. The rules which regulated the life of his subjects were derived from their immemorial usages and these rules were administered by domestic tribunals in families or village communities." The conclusion of Sir Henry was that even a Maharaja like Ranjit Singh could not issue a command which was opposed to the customs, usages and religious beliefs of the people. This was so not only in the East but also in the West. According to him, in the world of Western civilisation, no sovereign could disregard "the entire history of the community, the mass of its historic antecedents, which in each community determines how the sovereign shall exercise or forbear from exercising, his irresistible coercive power".

Austin says that the sovereign is possessed of unlimited powers. However, experience tells us that there is no power on earth which can wield unlimited powers. The reason is that the state or the sovereign acts through law, which can regulate only the external actions of human beings. It is helpless to regulate their internal actions. Whatever the government might do, it cannot control the morality of the people, the beliefs of the people, their religion or the public opinion. It is clear that the state has a limit imposed on its sovereign power in so much as it cannot control the internal lives of the people. Hence, it cannot be said that the sovereign possesses unlimited powers.

Bluntschli says that "the state as a whole is not almighty, for it is limited externally by the rights of other states and internally by its own nature and by the rights of its individual members." Leslie Stephen says that sovereignty is limited both from within and without: "from within because the legislature is the product of a certain social condition and determined by whatever determines society, and from without because the power of imposing law is dependent upon the instinct of subordination which is itself limited. If a legislature decided that all blue-eyed babies should be murdered, the preservation of blue-eyed babies would be illegal; but legislatures must go mad before they could pass such a law and subjects be idiotic before they could submit to it." The same writer says: "As there is in nature no such thing as a perfect circle or a completely rigid body, or a mechanical system in which there is no friction or a state of society in which men act simply with a view to gain, so there is in nature no such thing as an absolute sovereign."

Professor Laski has also criticised the theory of unlimited sovereignty on many grounds. He points out that "no sovereign has anywhere possessed unlimited power and the attempt to exert it has always resulted in the establishment of safeguards." He rightly points out that even the British Parliament does not enjoy absolute powers in actual practice. Legally, the King-in-Parliament may outrage public opinion, but practically it can do so only on the implied condition that it ceases, as a consequence, to be the King-in-Parliament. Referring to the interests of other associations within the state, he points out that those associations are, in their spheres, not less sovereign than the state itself. He comes to the conclusion that "the conception that authority not merely is, but ought to be limited, is fundamental to political philosophy." Laski further points out that the interests of humanity also demand a limited sovereignty. To quote him, "Externally surely, the concept of an absolute and independent sovereign state which demands an unqualified allegiance to Government from its members and enforces that allegiance by the power at its command, is incompatible with the interests of humanity. Our problem is not to reconcile the interests of humanity with the interest of England; our problem is so to act that the policy of England naturally implies the well-being of humanity."

It is also pointed out that "legally an autocratic Tsar may shoot down his subjects before the Winter Palace at Petrograd; but morally it is condemnation that we utter... There is, therefore, a vast difference between what Dean Pound has admirably called 'Law in books' and 'Law in action."

It cannot be denied that it is not only impossible to exercise unlimited powers, but it is also undesirable to give unlimited powers to any body. History tells us that whenever any king or queen was given unlimited powers over the people, the people could not grow. Their lives were insecure and their property was unsafe. They could not enjoy their liberty. As a matter of fact, the whims of one man prevailed and there was no certainty about anything. Moreover, unlimited sovereignty or the exercise of unlimited power not only destroys those over whom that power is exercised, but also destroys ultimately the wielders of unlimited power. The reason is that as a result of the persecutions at the hands of the autocrat, grievances of the people multiply and ultimately they revolt against him and pull him down.

It is also difficult to find the unlimited sovereign in the United States of America. The powers of the Congress are carefully defined and the residuary powers are with the states. The Constitution can be amended by a two-thirds majority of the Congress and three-fourths of the States. Even the amendment of the Constitution is limited by the provision that no state shall, without its own consent, be deprived of its equal representation in the Senate. Prof. Laski says: "In the theoretical sense, therefore, the United States of America have no sovereign organ, for the Judges of the Supreme Court, being overridden by the constitutional amendment, are a court of reference." It is said that the discovery of sovereignty in a federal state is practically an impossible adventure. However, Prof. Laski points out that this difficulty is not confined to the federal states alone. It is doubtful whether in the Austinian sense, Belgium can be called a sovereign state at all. The Constitution guarantees certain rights to every citizen regarding his religion, property, right of assembly, etc. It is true that all these rights can be altered by amending the Constitution, but before the Constitution can be altered, the decision of one Assembly has to be ratified by a new one, re-chosen by the electorate for that purpose. There is no guarantee that the new Assembly will, in a sitting at which two-thirds of the members are present and two-thirds of them vote for the change, ratify the constitutional alteration. There is also no guarantee that the new Assembly will have the same complexion as the old one and it might prove impossible to alter the Constitution. Against this background, says Laski, either Belgium is not a sovereign state in its internal affairs, or its sovereignty resides in the electorate. Laski points out that the electorate is an indeterminate body but the view of Austin is that sovereignty must be determinate and unlimited. Both these things do not apply to Belgium. Laski says that the testimony of Sir Henry Maine is sufficient to show that from the historical point of view, "the Austinian theory is artificial to the point of absurdity."

Austin says that the sovereign must be a determinate authority. He also tells us that the King-in-Parliament is the sovereign in England. This determinate authority can do anything and everything. The view of Austin is that a determinate authority is to be found in every sovereign state. However, a critical study of the problem shows that he did not base his conclusions on a wide basis. He does not seem to have used the inductive method which takes into consideration the practice of the various countries. We find that the attempt to discover a determinate human authority in every state which commands others but does not obey anybody, fails. In the case of the United States, one fails to find a determinate sovereign who is possessed of unlimited power. Neither the President nor the Congress nor the Governors of the States nor the Supreme Court can be said to posses sovereign power. Each of these functionaries possesses limited powers. One might say that sovereignty in the United States lies in two-thirds of the Congress and three-fourths of the States. It is true that if a two-thirds majority of the Congress agrees to any measure and if that measure ratified by three-fourths of the State legislatures, that measure becomes law, but it cannot be said that such a sovereign is a determinate sovereign. It is clear that it is difficult to find a body which is not only determinate but also sovereign. The same difficulty is faced if we attempt to discover a determinate human superior in any Oriental country, where custom plays a very important part. As public opinion in modern times is becoming more and more effective, the forces which affect and determine a sovereign power seem to be very many and it becomes difficult to say where the determinate sovereign is. One may agree with Laski that the real rulers of the society are undiscoverable. The view of Austin may apply to the British Constitution but it does not apply to others.

According to Austin, Sovereign is indivisible. All power must be centred in the hands of one person called the sovereign. The reason given is that if authority is divided, it is not possible to say that one controls the whole because each controls only a part. Hence, it is contended that it is necessary that all sovereign power must reside in one hand. Such a view might have been right before the experiment of a federal state was made, but it is a characteristic of federal State that powers must be divided between the federal government and its units. Each is supreme in its own sphere. Neither can be said to be supreme over the other. Hence, the idea of divided sovereignty has to be accepted.

Gilchrist points out that Austin says variously that (1) Parliament is sovereign, (2) the King and Peers and Electors are sovereign, (3) the electorate is sovereign when Parliament is dissolved, and (4) the Commons have powers free from trust, and are trustees.

Austin says that law is essentially a command of the sovereign. It appears to Laski that to think of law as simply a command is, even for the jurist, to strain definition to the verge of decency. While the law is the same for all, both for the legislators and the subjects, the case is different with a command. A command separates the giver from one who obeys the command. The man who gives the command himself does not obey it. The characteristic of law is that it is obeyed not only by the people for whom it is made but also by the legislators who make it. Law is universal and uniform for all, but command is not. Laski points out that the element of command does not enter in all enabling statutes. When the Lord Chancellor of England is directed to sell the presentation to benefices of which he has the advowson, the statute is undoubtedly a law, but the element of command is very indirectly present. The Lord Chancellor is not directed to do anything. Unless he takes certain action, there is no obligation of any kind. When a Franchise Act gives the right of vote to women, it is not fair to interpret it as a command. No obligation is imposed unless we regard the duty of the registration officer to accept women as voters as an obligation. Laski also points out that it is difficult to see how the exercise of delegated authority can be interpreted as a command. A royal warrant regulates the pensions and pay of the army. It is a command emanating from a qualified authority but the Secretary of State for War cannot be compelled to obey it.

It is also pointed out that an adequate view of law must take into account the historical and sociological aspects of it. The essence of the historical approach to law can be expressed in these words: "Law grows as the people grow, develops with the people. Law is the result of a varying, progressive, slow and lengthy formation by society, rather than of the arbitrary will of law-giver." Such was the view of Sir Henry Maine. The sociological view is illustrated by Duguit and Krabbe. According to Duguit, social solidarity is the foundation of law. The view of Krabbe is that law springs from men's sense of right. It has rightly been pointed out that the conception of a legal sovereign as the authority creating law is not adequate, as the content of law is never actually "created."

About Austin's view of law and sovereignty, Buckland says: "This, at first sight, looks like circular reasoning. Law is law since it is made by the sovereign. The sovereign is sovereign because he makes the law." As it is put, the statement is undoubtedly circular. Law is defined in terms of the sovereign and the sovereign is defined in terms of the law. However, Austin did not do so. He defined law in terms of the sovereign, but he defined the sovereign as the body that receives the habitual obedience of the bulk of a given society and that was obviously not circular. We should also not accuse Buckland of having misrepresented Austin because what he said was that superficially Austin's arguments looked circular. Buckland himself observed thus: "But, this is not circular reasoning; it is not reasoning at all. It is definition. Sovereign and law have much the same relation as centre and circumference."

We may conclude with the following statement of Laski in *Grammar of Politics:* "It would be of lasting benefit to political science if the whole concept of sovereignty were surrendered."

PLURALIST THEORY OF SOVEREIGNTY

The pluralist Theory of sovereignty was a reaction against the legal, monistic, absolutist Austinian theory of sovereignty and the theory of Fascist absolute state supported by idealist philosophers like

Hegel and supporters of power view of politics like Nietzsche, Treitschke and Bernhardi. It was an attack against those who regarded the state as the highest and supreme power in society. It was an attack on the absolutism of the state and unlimited sovereignty. It demanded that the sovereignty of the state should be limited, divided and controlled. It was a movement of labour, economic, religious and professional associations and unions for the fulfilment of their rights against the state. It demanded that the individuals must be saved from the absolute and unlimited power of the state. Sovereignty should not belong to the state alone but should be divided among the various associations in society. Unlike the anarchists who demanded that the state be abolished, the pluralists demanded that the state be continued to exist but its powers must be limited.

Factors Responsible for Rise of Pluralism

Pluralism was a reaction against the absolute conception of the state as held by Hegel in the nineteenth century and as it influenced the idealists, militarists and Fascists. Hegel raised the state to mystical heights. He regarded the state as the march of God on earth. The state possessed not only supreme legal authority but also supreme moral authority.

During the nineteenth century itself, the Idealists, particularly Marx and Engels, emphasized the fact that the economic interests of the dominant class exclusively determined the policy of the state. The rise of capitalism combined with the theory of absolute state posed a real threat to individual freedom. In the twentieth century, there was an all-round development of social sciences which promoted new theories regarding the nature of the state. Modern psychology exploded the myth of the personality of the state which had been used to exalt the authority of the state. Modern sociology proved that law was the product of the prevailing social conditions and not a command of the sovereign. There was realisation that the state was a partial manifestation of the social nature of man with a well-defined sphere of its activity. It could not be considered as an all-comprehensive institution which encompassed all aspects of the social life of man. That gave rise to the pluralist theory of the sovereignty of the state. The pluralist theory tried to redefine the nature of the state as one of the many associations of human beings operating in society to safeguard the various interests of individuals. The role which the state was to play in the new situation was to be different from its previous role. It was to act as an arbiter over the conflicting claims of the various associations. It was to act as a coordinator and not dictator. It was to compete with other human associations to establish its claim to the allegiance of the people to it on the ground of its contribution to the good of society as a whole.

During the World War I, the state demanded from its citizens everything, including their dear and near ones, even their own lives, to protect itself. The people made sacrifices for the state. The question raised was whether the state was logically entitled to make such enormous demands on the people as was done during the World War. There were conscientious objectors who maintained that their conscience urged them to oppose bloody wars as a means of settling human disputes. The policy of war was determined by men in power who could not claim infallibility and it could not be denied that a little folly on their part could lead to war which brought in its wake untold sufferings to citizens of all the states involved in the war. This made the people think that a check should be put on the absolute authority of the state which gave an opportunity to those holding power to declare wars and the result was the pluralist theory.

Prof. Laski refers to two important factors which prompted the pluralist attack on sovereignty of the state. One factor was that the state claimed legal omnipotence and allegiance of its citizens on the ground that it represented the total interests of the society within its territorial jurisdiction. The pluralists pointed out that legal omnipotence was a purely formal concept, often invalid in fact. However majestic and powerful the state may be, it was in fact only one of the many associations in society. Experience showed that there were always limits to powers which were set by the relations between the purpose the state sought to fulfil and the judgment made by men of that purpose. The pluralist view was based on the realisation that the claim of the state to pre-eminence always meant, in fact, the sovereignty of a government composed of fallible men whose intentions alone were not a sufficient justification for so vast a claim. They went into the making of pluralism as historic analysis derived from the conflict between the churches and the state, between trade unions and the state, between, as in the case of the conscientious objector to military service, the individual and the state.

The rise of federal state and the consequent division of powers under the Constitution was a big blow to the indivisible, absolute and determinate sovereign. Those who most powerfully shaped the theory of sovereignty–Bodin, Hobbes, Rousseau, Bentham and Austin — with the exception of Austin, wrote before the nature of a federal state was fully explored.

The notion of an independent sovereign state in the international field proved to be fatal for the well-being of humanity. Although limitations on state sovereignty under international law are largely self-imposed for the good of humanity, yet the fact that there are limitations supports the point made by the pluralist that the sovereignty of the state must be limited and controlled.

Guild Socialists like G.D.H. Cole advocated functional representation on the basis of "one interest, one vote." That underlined the importance of functional associations within the community. This was also the view stressed by the pluralists.

If the Austinian view of sovereignty is applied to the working of the present day state, its machinery would get highly overloaded. Hence, the pluralist argument for greater degree of decentralisation was in consonance with the requirements of the changed times. The change in the nature of the functions of the state also strengthened the pluralist view. Previously, the state performed merely police functions but that view was replaced by the social welfare view of the functions of the state. If the state was to perform very many functions, it was desirable that a check must be put on the exercise of its authority.

T.H. Green, the English idealist philosopher, made a distinction between the spheres of law and morality and contended that political obligations could be enforced but not moral duties. Therefore, the state had a limited sphere which could not be identified with the whole of society.

A noticeable feature of modern society is the growth of voluntary associations of all kinds, whether cultural, economic, political, religious, ethnic or regional associations. Those associations or groups satisfied the numerous needs of individuals. It was realised that those groups were instinctive to man and were legal entities with a life of their own. Gierke and Maitland thought that each group possesses a real personality and a will. To quote Gierke, "The state should accept the common point of view that permanent associations have rights and duties as groups, whether or not the state has accepted them as corporations." Dr. Figgis wrote that human society is not a "sand heap of individuals" related only through the state but an "ascending hierarchy of groups." He criticised the traditional view of sovereignty "a venerable superstition."

The growth of representative institutions and political parties, the introduction of adult suffrage and elections, the spread of education and diversification of trade and industry, and an increased awareness of socio-economic injustices brought about significant changes in the pattern of social existence. It became clear that the allegiance which some of the groups commanded from their members was of a higher order. Apart from citizens' loyalty to the state, other loyalties which these groups evoked, became a regular and forceful feature of social reality.

Principles of Pluralism

Pluralism was a reaction against the monistic view of state sovereignty. According to K.C. Hsiao, "A monistic state is one which possesses, or which should possess, a single source of authority that is theoretically comprehensive and unlimited in its exercise. This unitary and absolute power is sovereignty, and the theory which affirms the existence of such sovereignty in the state is designated by the pluralists as monism." Monism regards sovereignty as the absolute, indivisible and supreme power of the state. The pluralist state is intended to be the antithesis of the monistic state. Hsiao observes, "The pluralistic state is simply a state in which there exists no single source of authority that is all-competent and comprehensive, namely, sovereignty, no unified system of law, no centralised organ of administration, no generalisation of political will. On the contrary, it is a multiplicity in its essence and manifestation, it is divisible into parts and should be divided." (Political Pluralism, p. 8). Pluralist sovereignty is limited and divided sovereignty. It is not all-comprehensive, absolute and indivisible. The state is merely an association of society for common welfare like any other association. Society is not unity but unity in diversity. As man owes allegiance to other organisations and associations, his total allegiance is not and cannot be towards the state. Law is not the command of the sovereign as it is based on moral and natural rules, customs, traditions etc. The external sovereignty of the state is restricted by international law.

The pluralists emphasized the sociological character of the state. They recognised the role of several associations in society formed by men in pursuance of their multifarious interests. Some of those associations existed even prior to the origin of the state itself. Some of them exist independent of the state. They are neither created, nor sponsored, nor maintained, nor even regulated by the state. The state is but one of those associations, standing side by side with them and not above them. Such associations include the church and other religious organisations, trade unions, cooperative societies and chambers of commerce and voluntary associations devoted to education, cultural and scientific pursuits. All these associations have a social value of their own. They satisfy some needs and other worthwhile pursuits. Peter H. Merkl writes, "Every group within this vast plurality of varied group activities could devote its whole life to the pursuit of its own major interest in the manner suggested by the inner rationale of its particular activity and by its own preference. There would be no outside agency to tell the farmer what to grow, or the steel mills what to charge for their product, or the communal groups how to live, or the teacher what to teach. Everyone engaged in a meaningful activity could savor the inherent meaning of his activity to the fullest degree and could derive the deep satisfaction of doing a job well and of exercising to the fullest his creative ability and good judgement." (Political Continuity and Change, p. 65)

According to the pluralists, the state is not above the various associations existing in the society. As a matter of fact, it cannot be conceived as distinct from those associations. It itself is an association of associations. As an association coordinates the activities of its members, the state also coordinates the activities of the other associations in society. It resolves the conflicting claims of those associations. It harmonises and compromises those interests for the higher interests of society. The pluralist theory does not seek to abolish the state. It merely seeks to curtail or limit the absolute authority of the state.

The pluralists maintain that the claim of the state to superior authority cannot be taken for granted. The state enjoys a privileged position in the sense that its jurisdiction is compulsory over all individuals and associations within the state. Unlike other associations, it possesses coercive powers by which it can punish those who ignore or defy its command. However, this does not automatically establish the superior authority of the state but imposes a higher moral responsibility on the state. The state, must justify the exercise of its special powers. It must fulfil its function of harmonising the interests of all associations operating in society. Some of those associations may be more organised and more vocal than others and some of them may be weak and not organised. It is the duty of the state to see that the interests of all are given due weight. The state must show that it is not dominated by any special interest or vested interest while exercising its authority. It must justify the confidence reposed in it. To quote Benn and Peters, "The state must not be allowed to fall into the hands of men concerned only for the interest of a limited group. It must be sensitive to all without succumbing to any one or any limited coalition of interests." (*Social Principles and the Democratic State,* p.276).

The pluralists do not accept the state as a Leviathan as was imagined by Hobbes. They repudiate the monopoly of state on the allegiance of all individuals. They demand that the state must justify its claim to allegiance on moral grounds. The management and control of society must be shared by various associations in proportion to their contribution to the common good. The pluralists stand for the decentralisation of authority so that all authority is not centralised in the hands of the state.

The monistic theory of sovereignty regards society as a unified whole in which there is complete unity with no place for diversity. There is only one interest of the whole society which can be served by a single sovereign power of the state. The pluralists object to this view of society and maintain that there is diversity rather than unity in society. Even if there is unity, it is unity in diversity. According to MacIver, in a social organisation, there are communities like country, city, village, nation and tribe. There are associations like family, church, party, class and business firms. There are institutions like inheritance, baptism, the party machine, class distinctions and the market. Laski says, "Society as a complex whole is pluralistic." Lipson writes, "Not only is society a pluralistic union of groups but the ways in which every human being associated are also plural." Society is divided into groups, communities, associations etc. and it is not unity but unity in diversity. Every association and community has real personality of its own". Society is federal rather than unitary.

All those writers who cherish the ideals and ideas of democracy like pluralism because the monolithic power of the state can suppress the initiative and freedom, of the individual which is very dear to liberal democrats. The democrats support pluralism for the sake of human rights. One of the objects of limiting the sovereignty of the state by dividing it among various association is to strengthen the rights of the people and different social associations. Pluralism has liberal democratic values which favour the conversion of the absolutist state into a limited welfare state. Pluralism suspects the principles of representation and maintains that elected representatives cannot represent the total interests of man and man in society should participate in decision-making through various associations. The pluralists recognise the state as a servant of the people and not as a super-imposed power. The sphere of state should decrease and that of man should increase. The pluralists give importance to consultation and discussion in the decision-making process and decry arbitrary decisions. They regard territorial representation as insufficient.

The dictum, "Law is the command of the sovereign", is opposed by the pluralists. Laski writes, "It is impossible to make the legal theory of sovereignty valid for political philosophy." MacIver observes, "Law is the very antithesis of command." Law is something higher and more extensive than the state. MacIver observes, "The state is both the child and the parent of law." Duguit, Krabbe and Holland criticise the theory of legal sovereignty. Law is necessary for social welfare. It has positive use for society. It is because of social utility that law is generally obeyed by the people. The view of Duguit is that the basis of law-making is not command but "social solidarity." The people obey laws not because they are afraid of the sovereign power of the state but because they find that laws are good for them and society and for social security. The basis of law is not the power of the sovereign but morality, the sense of right, customs, traditions, social utility etc. It is not the state which is above law. It is more accurate to say that it is the law which is above the state.

The argument that society cannot pull on without sovereign power is met by the pluralists by the historical example of Medieval Europe. At that time, power was divided among various centres and state sovereignty in the present sense was missing. The state had neither internal sovereignty nor external, as the feudal order shared internal sovereignty and the Holy Roman Empire restricted the external sovereignty of the state. Feudal localised economy restricted the centralisation of the economic power.

The pluralists make a distinction between the state and society. According to them, it is not correct to contend that there is "nothing above state, nothing beyond it and nothing beside it." The various groups in society make important contributions. MacIver writes, "The state is a structure not coeval and co-extensive with society, but built within it as a determinate order for attainment of specific ends."

According to the pluralists, the authority of the sate is neither sovereign nor absolute, but a limited one. The existence of many associations limits the authority of the state.

Gettel has summed up the pluralistic view in these words: "The pluralistic theory of sovereignty, in general, insists on democracy and has a strong tinge of individualism. It has, however, not so much the rights of separate individuals that are aimed at, but the rights of various associations and groups which represent the real interests of man. Pluralism lays great stress on function, and believes that the natural organisations and communities within the state should manage their own affairs. It opposes a centralized, all-powerful state, and urges a division of power along the lines of functional democracy. It rejects the psychology of the general will and the conception of absolute sovereignty as based on a formal and metaphysical rationalism that does not correspond with actual and changing political reality. In this respect it allies itself to a certain extent with the anti-intellectualism that characterizes social psychology and the new economics." Again, "The pluralists are impressed with the complexity of modern social organization and with the importance of numerous associations, non-political in nature. They argue that some of these associations represent the interests of their members more truly than does the state, and receive from them more perfect obedience. They deny that the state is a unique organisation; they hold that other associations are equally real and natural. They argue that such associations are for their purposes as sovereign as the state is for its purpose. They emphasize the inability of the state to enforce its will in practice against the opposition of certain groups within it. They deny that the possession of force by the state gives it any superior right. They insist upon the equal right of all groups that command the allegiance of their members and perform valuable functions in society. Hence, sovereignty is possessed by many associations. It is not an indivisible unit; the state is not supreme or unlimited."

EXPONENTS OF PLURALIST THEORY

Gierke and Maitland

The doctrine of political pluralism was developed by a number of social and political thinkers in different countries. Otto von Gierke, a German writer and F.W. Maitland, an English legal historian, enunciated the theory of the real personality of groups. According to them, these groups in society possess a real personality and will. They play a distinctive role in the process of law-making. Although the state plays a principal role in this sphere, it is not exclusive. Law is not made by the state alone and several social groups make their own contributions to that process. Those social groups have certain privileges and obligations independent of any formal sanction from the state.

Durkheim

Emile Durkheim, a sociologist, pleaded that professional groups should be re-established both as the bases for political representation and sources of economic regulation. He advocated the regulation of state economy by vocational groups on the ground that state as a general scheme of life is not adequately fitted to undertake the specialised tasks of economic control. To quote him, "We have at present no clear principles and no clear juridical sanctions through which to determine relations between employers and employees, between competing employers, employees and the public."

Boncour

The view of J. Paul Boncour is that professional associations are natural and spontaneous. In course of time, they grow in size and their laws tend to acquire an obligatory character. The law of the state recognises the free right of associations, grants privileges to them and thus makes them sovereign rather than voluntary associations.

Figgis

The doctrine of the "real personality" of groups was advocated by J.N. Figgis in relation to the Church. According to him, the Church did not exist by an act of grace on the part of the state, but had "powers of self-development like a person." Its corporate personality is neither granted nor withheld by the state but has simply to be recognised. Human society is not a "sand-heap of individuals related only through the state, but an ascending hierarchy of groups." The traditional doctrine of sovereignty is "a venerable superstition." The general trend of his thought is that there are different spheres of action in which different groups should function exclusively.

Cole

G.D.H. Cole pleads for the formation of consumers' groups and producers' groups which are to be given co-sovereign status. He goes to the extent of saying that national producers' guilds should be given legislative authority besides administrative powers. He also speaks of consumers' parliament and producers' parliament.

Barker

Ernest Barker rejects the concept of the real personality of groups but he admits that the permanent groups within society existed prior to the state and each of them has a corporate character and functions of its own. To quote him, "We see the state less as an association of individuals in a common life; we see it more as an association of individuals, already united in various groups for a further and more embracing common purpose." The state should adjust the relations of associations to itself, to other associations and to their own members in order to maintain the integrity of its own scheme, to preserve the equality of associations before law and to protect individuals from the possible tyranny of the groups. He views the state as an association of associations, a community of communities and an agency for harmonising the interests of the groups and individuals.

Webbs

Sidney and Beatrice Webb envisage a "social parliament" and a "political parliament," the former to represent individuals as members in a "social democracy" and the latter to represent them in the capacity of citizens in a "political democracy."

Lindsay

A.D. Lindsay accepts the theory of the real personality of the associations of human beings. According to him, the state is only one of the numerous associations each of which possesses a corporate personality of its own. Many other associations, being smaller than the state, are more homogeneous and represent a closer community of interests. If they are permitted to act autonomously, they are likely to attract the deeper loyalties of their members and prove themselves to be more effective agencies of social coordination than the state itself. Each one of these associations should be given greater authority and initiative and they should also be allowed to make laws for themselves. Lindsay stands for breaking the monopoly of the state in law-making. He advocates the decentralisation of legislative powers to the various associations in society.

According to Lindsay, the state can have control over the corporations within it only if, and in so far as, the citizens are prepared to give it such powers. The state has no personality of its own. The idea of a group mind, a group will or a group personality in reference to corporations is an absurdity. While other associations have a voluntary and selective membership, the state has a compulsive and comprehensive membership.

Duguit

According to Leon Duguit, laws are not an expression of the command of an absolute sovereign. They are the conditions of social solidarity, that is, interdependence of man in society. Laws embody those fundamental rules which sustain the social life of man. They are obligatory not because they are the commands of a "determinate human superior" but because their observance is crucial to the functioning of human society. Laws exist even before the origin of the state itself. They are not a product of the state. The state itself is an instrument of securing social solidarity. Public service and not sovereignty, is the essential characteristic of the state. Duguit does not believe in the theory of absolute sovereignty. He makes the state responsible to society.

Krabbe

The view of Hugo Krabbe is that law and political sovereignty were distinct entities in the eighteenth century but gradually became amalgamated. He wants to separate them once again. According to him, the only sovereignty is the sovereignty of law. Law is independent of and superior to the state. It does not arise of social solidarity as contended by Duguit, but is the outcome of the sense of right of the majority of the community constituting the state. Law is subjective and spiritual in origin. Power is not an essential feature of the state. The characteristic mark of the state is that it is a legal community. "The state is nothing except a legal community... a portion of mankind having its own independent body of legal relations. Hence the state performs no function whatever except to impute legal value to certain interests."

Krabbe carries his idea of law into the realm of international relations. According to him, the sense of right should extend to international affairs also and to the extent progress is made in that direction, the legal activity of the existing state should contract. Krabbe believes that the present states will become provinces of one super-national state, but before that happens, the "international community must pass through the phase of the idea of sovereignty."

The view of Krabbe is that owing to the rise of important economic associations like labour unions, the state can no longer pretend to be one all-powerful agency of social life. His conclusion is that "the notion of sovereignty must be expunged from political theory."

Follett

Miss M.P. Follett in her book "The New State", shows distinct pluralistic tendencies but does not take an extreme view. The state is treated as a unifying agency which acts upon the individual not through the various groups to which he belongs, but also directly. To quote her, "The state cannot be composed of groups because no group nor any number of groups can contain the whole of me and the ideal state demands the whole of me. My citizenship is something bigger than my membership in the vocational groups. We want the whole man in politics. The ideal unified state is not all-absorptive. It is all-inclusive. The true state must gather up every interest within itself. It must take our many loyalties and find how it can make them one. The home of my soul is in the state."

Miss Follett regards the pluralist theory as a "prophecy of the future" because it recognises the importance of associations and sees society as an association of many smaller associations.

Laski (1894-1950)

Prof. Harold J. Laski was one of the most eloquent and forceful exponents of the pluralist theory of sovereignty. The view W.Y. Elliot is that in his writings, we probably have the best statement of the pluralistic doctrine. In the formulation of his views, he was greatly influenced by Gierke, Maitland, Figgis and Ernest Barker and also by the anti-statist and anti-idealist currents in political thought.

Laski was a prolific writer and his views on pluralism lie scattered in a number of his works: *A Grammar of Politics, An Introduction to Politics, Studies in Law and Politics, The Foundations of Sovereignty, Authority in the Modern State, The State in Theory and Practice, Reflections on the Revolution of Our Time, Crisis in the Theory of State etc.* Laski was not consistent in his views about the nature of sovereignty. He went on adjusting his pluralist position between liberalism and Marxism and ultimately combined liberalism and socialism. In his scheme of the reorganisation of the state on the basis of democratization of power, he comes out as a pluralist. In the 1920s, Laski criticised very strongly the theory of state sovereignty and expressed the view that the theory would pass like the theory of the divine right of kings which was once very prominent. He thought of sovereignty as nothing more than a legal fiction and a barren concept. However, in the 1930s, he began to evolve a balanced view of pluralism. He conceded the importance of sovereignty as an essential element of state power, but he considered the state as an agency for regulating class-relations in society.

Criticism of monistic theory of Sovereignty

Laski started his exposition of the pluralist theory by way of his criticism of the Austinian theory of sovereignty, according to which there is a single source of power in all societies which enjoys absolute, all-comprehensive and unlimited power. According to Laski, the doctrine of absolute sovereignty is a "legal fiction" and a "barren concept". A theory of sovereignty has three aspects. It needs a historical analysis. It is a theory of law. It is a theory of political organisation. All the three aspects were examined by Laski in detail and finally rejected as inadequate explanations of the exercise of sovereign power. The view of Laski was that the monistic theory of sovereignty is "historically untrue", "legally untenable" and "politically unsound". Laski's view was that a time will come when state sovereignty will be as much discredited as the divine right theory of the king. Laski's attack on state sovereignty was biting and relentless. His view was that the state should be shorn off its absolute sovereignty and demoted from a superior status to a coordinate status with other associations. Laski went to the extent of saying that the legal theory of sovereignty could not be made valid for political philosophy and it would be for the good of society if the whole concept of sovereignty was surrendered.

Laski *challenged the moral validity of the doctrine* which attributed sovereignty to the state. To quote him, "The only state to which I owe allegiance is the state in which I discover moral adequacy; and if a given state fails to satisfy that condition, I must, to be consistent with my own moral nature, attempt experiment. Our first duty is to be true to our conscience."

Laski criticised the theory of state sovereignty *on pragmatic grounds also.* He pointed out that the pragmatic test of truth lies in its workability. A doctrine is true if its usefulness or workability can be proved in the given circumstances. The theory of state sovereignty fulfilled a pragmatic need in the past in securing the independence of the secular state from Papal dominance. It unified the political allegiance of the people to a common sovereign and produced united nations out of warring religious factions. However, the theory of sovereignty has lost its pragmatic validity in modern times, particularly in view of the growing challenge of powerful groups from within and some kind of international organisation from without.

Laski pointed out that a *historical analysis of the state repudiates the idea of absolute sovereignty.* He accepted Sir Henry Maine's criticism of Austin and pointed out how custom and tradition substantially limit the exercise of sovereign power. Those were not legal checks imposed by some determinate human superior. They did not operate with the express or tacit consent of the sovereign himself. The deference which even omnipotent monarchs had to show to customs was a political need, a dictate of prudence and expediency. Besides those limitations in the internal sphere, sovereignty is also subject to limitations in the external sphere. Laski found the claims of absolute sovereignty incompatible with the interests of humanity. He wrote, "In a creative civilisation what is important is not the historical accident of separate states, but the scientific fact of world-interdependence. The real unit of allegiance is the world. The real obligation of obedience is to the total interests of our fellowmen." (A Grammar of Politics, p. 94).

Laski pointed out that even the *idea of absolute sovereignty was not workable.* To quote him, "Everyone knows that to regard the King-in-Parliament as a sovereign body in the Austinian sense is absurd. No Parliament would dare to disfranchise the Roman Catholics or to prohibit the existence of trade unions. If it made the attempt, it would cease to be a Parliament. That is to say that in practice legally unlimited power turns,out to be power exercised under conditions fairly well-known to each generation."

Laski also pointed out that the *emergence of federal politics* shows the limitations and inadequacy of Austin's concept of sovereignty. It is not possible to find out the determinate human superior as the political sovereign in the United States. To quote him, "The Congress is a limited body the powers of which are carefully defined; the separate states are similarly confined within the four corners of the Constitution; and even the amendment of the Constitution is limited by the exception that no state shall, without its own consent, be deprived of its equal suffrage in the Senate. In the theoretical sense, therefore, the United States has no sovereign organ; for the judges of the Supreme Court, being overridden by constitutional amendment, are clearly only a penultimate court of reference. A peculiar historical experience has therefore devised the means of building a state from which the conception of sovereignty is absent." (The Foundations of Sovereignty, p. 49)

Laski put a lot of emphasis on the *position of groups and associations.* According to him, the state is only one among various other groups and associations which are as important to the individual as the state is. Man's social nature finds expression in numerous groups or associations pursuing various ends–religious, social, economic, professional, political and recreational. The state is one of those groups and no one of them is superior to the other. Laski pleaded for complete autonomy for all the groups and associations. To quote Laski, "We do not proceed from the state to the parts of the state on the ground that the state is more fundamentally unified than its parts, but we, on the contrary, admit that parts are as real and as self-sufficient as the whole." (The Problem of Sovereignty, p. 9)

Groups and associations arise naturally and spontaneously. They act independently of state control. They compete with the state for man's loyalty and obedience. They have as much right to exist and grow as the state itself. Laski conceded that the state is a primary and the most important association and in so far as it deals with law and order and coordinates the activities of other groups and associations, it is different from them and hence could claim to be the first among equals. However, it could not claim to be the sole repository of power or focus of loyalty.

Laski admitted that the state differs from every other association in that it is an association in which membership is compulsory. It is essentially territorial in nature. It controls the level at which men are to live as men. In administrative terms, it is a government whose activities are shaped by the common needs of its members. To satisfy those common needs, it must control other associations to the degree that secures from them the service such needs require. The claim of the state to the allegiance of individuals rests on the efficient performance of its functions. The state should perform its coordination function, but it has no right to omnipotence. The power of the state should become coordinative instead of being hierarchical and authority should become federal instead of being absolute and indivisible. *Laski's plea to make authority federal is* the cornerstone of his pluralist doctrine.

Laski made a *distinction between the state and government* to demonstrate the inadequacy of the theory of absolute and unlimited sovereignty. He pointed out that in actual practice, the so-called sovereign powers of the state are claimed by the government which is a body of persons issuing orders and enforcing obedience thereto. In the exercise of those powers, the government can never be allowed to become absolute and irresponsible. Laski emphasised the fact that the government is but an agent of the state. "It exists to carry out the purpose of the state. It is not itself the supreme coercive power; it is simply the mechanism of administration which gives effect to the purpose of that power. It is not, we are told, sovereign in the sense in which the state is sovereign, its competence is defined by such authority as the state may choose to confer upon it; and if it oversteps that authority, it may, where such provision exists, be called to account." (The State in Theory and Practice, p.23)

Laski pointed out the *dangers of conferring absolute powers on the government.* Every government is composed of fallible men who may deliberately exploit their authority for their own selfish purposes. They may mistake the private interests of a few for the well-being of the whole community. They may be ignorant of the position confronting them or incompetent to handle them. Hence the state must not be given absolute powers.

Laski was deeply concerned about the undemocratic control of industry and politics by the economic overlords in society. He pointed out that in modern society, the large industrial corporations are controlled by directors who are remarkable for their skill in financial manipulation, who are also masters of their shareholders and consumers and who are in a position to hold even the state to ransom. Their power is as massive in volume as it is largely irresponsible in operation. Their power must be subordinated to the interests of the community or those interests will not be protected. That can be done only if the vital instruments of production are owned and controlled by the community. *There must be democratization and decontrol of power* and that is not possible if the power of the sovereign is absolute and unlimited.

The view of Laski was that sovereignty is not monistic, but pluralistic. It is not absolute but constitutional and responsible. Authority is not unitary but federal. The state can act only as a coordinating authority. It cannot claim for itself the supreme or superior position. It is one of the many associations which play an important part in the life of man. Groups and associations should be completely autonomous.

Robert M. MacIver (b. 1882)

MacIver was a sociologist and he viewed everything from that standpoint. He analysed society, the state, human associations and relationships, social organisations together with their functioning and mutual relationships. His political ideas are based on his sociological frame of mind. His view was that none of the aspects of social life could be separated from others and the political aspect of social life must be studied by associating it with other aspects of human life. He studied the relation of man with community, of community with other communities, of communities with the state, of the state with society and of one society with an other society.

After a deep analysis, MacIver came to the conclusion that the plurality of social life is a fact of modern society. He believed that different groups or associations perform very important and vital functions. These interests were often highly personal and could best be served through individual initiative, leaving the state to deal with general functions. The views of MacIver are to be found in his two outstanding works: The Modern Stale (1926) and The Web of Government (1947).

Prof. MacIver *criticised the monistic theory of absolute sovereignty* of the state in these words, "The sovereignty of the state is no simple final power, as free and unconditioned over human life as the will of an over-ruling God might be supposed to be. It is the exercise rather of a function, limited by and dependent on the prevailing conception of what that function should be, and no less limited by and dependent on the kind and degree of organisation established for its exercise. It is the attribute of an association and is no more absolute than the association itself."

MacIver pointed out that the theory of the state had been dominated for long by the legalistic conception of sovereignty, but the state is nothing but an association like any other association in society and the law of the state is only a form of social regulation. To quote him, "The legalistic doctrine is formal. Legally, the state is unlimited, but it is no more absolute on that account than, say, the church, because it is the source of ecclesiastical law, or the Royal and Ancient Club, because it alone prescribes the laws of golf. We merely insist that political law is but one form of social regulation. "The state is one of the organs of community, and we must reconcile with this cardinal fact both its great services and its greater claims."

According to MacIver, because of the complexity of social organisation in modern times, the old concept of unlimited sovereignty does not hold good. In the modern industrialised plural society, sovereignty is relative as well as limited. To quote him, "The great difference between the political thought of our times and that of the past is the definite assertion of the limited and relative character of sovereignty. In other ages, men have protested against absolute power, appealing on moral grounds. The newer doctrine arose out of the social developments of the nineteenth century. The complexity of social organisation which the industrial age had brought overthrew the simple anti-thesis of the individual and the state. The real powers exercised by the numerous and often vast associations of the new age confounded the idea of a single, all-comprehensive authority."

The basis of the authority of the state cannot be different from that of other associations or corporations. The state derives its authority from the will of the majority of the people, not in its own rights. A corporation is recognised by law and has certain rights and obligations. A state is similar to other corporations in that sense. It is recognised by law and has its definite rights and obligations. The state does not create the corporations but only regulates their legal character. It cannot either make or unmake them. The great associations are as native to the soil of society as the state itself. The state can scarcely even decide whether it will or will not recognise them. The state does not regulate the internal affairs of other corporations. It does not and cannot determine their purposes or their lives. It does not treat them as its own agencies or instruments. It comes into the picture only when the interests of one group encroach upon another. It acts only to resolve the conflicting interests of various associations in society. It cannot impose its own will on human associations for the protection of a common interest. Even if it claims to be the protector of the common interests, it cannot demand superior authority on that account. Other associations may cater to less extensive interests of man but they may attract their deeper loyalties because they are more intimate and more closely bound with the traditions and beliefs of groups. To quote MacIver, "On this account, the doctrine of absolute sovereignty, if actually practised in the states of today with all their diversities of culture, would be fatal to the harmony of social life."

MacIver also condemned the "power element" inherent in the monistic theory of sovereignty. To quote him, "The legalistic doctrine speaks in terms of power and not of service. But power is only an instrument of service. No one ever regards the service of the state as unlimited, and therefore the conception of unlimited sovereignty is dangerously false. To attribute power to government beyond the limit of its capacity for service is the grave error on which all tyranny is based."

The main points of criticism of the monistic theory by MacIver are that it is legal and formal. It is untrue in social form. As other associations and communities also make laws like the state, the state cannot be considered to be superior to other associations on that ground. The monistic theory considers the state as an organ of power but the state is an instrument of service and power is given to it merely to serve society. As the state does not perform all the services to society, it cannot be given all powers. Associations do not owe their origin and existence to the state and the state merely regulates and controls their external relations. The authority of the state should be limited and divided among the various associations in society.

MacIver makes a *distinction between the state and society* and criticises the view which identifies the state with society. To quote him, "To identify the social with the political is to be guilty of the grossest of all confusions, which completely bars any understanding of either society or the state." Again, "There are social forms like the family or the churches or the club, which owe neither their origin nor their inspiration to the state; and social forces like custom or the competition which the state may protect or modify but certainly does not create; and social motives like friendship or jealousy which establish a relationship too intimate and personal to be controlled by the great engine of the state."

MacIver points out that the state is smaller than society. It is within society and its structure is different from that of society. State is for society, to serve society by maintaining external law and order. Society is prior to the state. There were societies without the state. The state originated at a certain point of social development to serve and fulfil some of the interests of society. The scope of the state is limited as compared to that of society. The existence of society is independent of the state and society is above the state. Society is an open organisation and the state is a closed hierarchical structure. The state cannot fully control an open organisation like society. The state is only an association of society like the family or the church. The state is merely a group of individuals which is highly organised and works for definite objects.

MacIver *criticises the Austinian view of law as a command of the* sovereign. To quote him, "The Austinian idea that law is the command of political superior to political inferiors, is particularly misleading, since it conceals and even denies two of the attributes which law everywhere exhibits, its universality and its formality." Again, "Law is the very antithesis of command, for command separates the giver and the receivers, separates their status always and sometimes their interest as well. But law unites, for it applies no less to the legislator than to those for whom he has authority to legislate. Law is permanent and fundamental as compared with command."

As regards the relation of law with the state, MacIver writes, "The state is both the child and the parent of law." This means that the states the child of constitutional law which lays down the guidelines for the functioning of the state or government and limits its authority. The state is the parent of ordinary law which is enacted by the state. Ordinary laws are made by the state not in the form of command or an expression of its authority, but oh behalf of society at large as its servant. The right of compulsion is given to the state as an organ of society. The state may have an unlimited power to make laws but if it makes anti-social laws, those will not be obeyed and there will be a danger to the survival of the state itself.

From the political viewpoint, the state does not possess unlimited law-making power. The law-making power of the state is not absolute. It enacts laws to give certainty and legality to customs and traditions. To quote MacIver, "In the great book of the law, the state merely writes new sentences and here and there scratches out an old one. Much of the book was never written by the state at all." Again, "The authority of law is greater than the authority of the state. At any moment the state is more an official guardian than the maker of the law." Again, "In the last resort, obedience to law rests on the will to obey, supported as it is by all the sentiments and traditions of citizenship. Government applies the compulsion of law against individuals and minorities, but government would be powerless to do so, unless in the last resort they willed the law." Laws are not obeyed out of fear of the rod of the policeman or the guns of the army but because they have some social utility and the people want to obey them. The root of obedience to law is not coercion but the will to obey.

MacIver gives three arguments against the doctrine of sovereignty. The concept of general will as formulated by Rousseau and Green is sometimes invoked as the basis of sovereignty, but it is difficult to discover the existence of the general will in the state. There are many persons in the state who differ from the prevalent will in the state. The states in the past included vast numbers of aliens and slaves apart from the citizens whose will could not be reconciled with the so-called will of the state. The state appears as an upholder of custom and loyalty to the state is derived from man's regard for custom and not for the state itself. Even in a democratic state, it is difficult to locate the ultimate sovereign. There is no homogeneous will of the people. The majority and minority opinions exist simultaneously. One government is replaced by another and the will goes on changing. Power in the state is always exercised by a political government. The stability of the authority of the government depends on its legitimacy.

Law cannot be regarded as an expression of the will of the state. The state does not create law. It existed even prior to the state. The state merely grasps it and gives it a definite expression in the form of its statutes. The state only codifies laws or modifies its form. It cannot make or remake it. To quote MacIver, "The state can no more reconstitute at any time the law as a whole than a man can remake his body." The authority of law is greater than the authority of the state.

The state can use force and coercion to secure respect for law but that does not make the state absolutely sovereign. The state is justified in using force in view of the universal nature of the service it performs. Its laws apply to all within its territory and all have to obey law whether they like it or not. Force is a function and not power. It is an instrument of service and not an engine of domination. It is not the essence but only the criterion of the state. MacIver believes in the service conception of the state and not power conception.

The state is an order-creating organisation. Its business is to maintain order. Law must have the backing and approval of the community. Order is not for the sake of order but for the sake of society. There is no such thing as peace of the desert or order in a military regiment. Such a view does not appeal to the rational and progressive mind of MacIver.

MacIver believed in the concept of a limited state, a state whose business is carried on according to the fundamental rules made for the state by the general will of the community. MacIver does not believe in the concept of an authoritarian and omnipotent state. As the service rendered by the state is limited, hence its powers must be limited. The state should not try to do everything because it is not capable of doing so. It can serve only a limited end and purpose. The state is not a partnership in all arts, a partnership in all science and a partnership in every virtue and in all perfections as contended by Burke. The state is not a mystical unity.

According to MacIver, the function of the state is to respect personality and maintain order. The former is negative while the latter is positive. State interferes and state regulation is a clumsy intrusion in those things which are related to human personality and whose worth and quality are determined by the spontaneous urge of the personality.

The state stands for the common interests of all individuals and associations but not for the whole of the common interest. The function of the state is merely to give a form of unity to the whole system of social relationship.

According to MacIver, the basis of sovereignty is justice, order and security, not power. MacIver criticises the power view of politics as given by Hobbes, Bentham, Austin, Merriam, Lasswell and Kaplan. He is willing to give power to the state provided it is lawful power. Power is neither the basis of the state nor its essence. It is only one aspect of sovereignty which is a minor aspect. To quote MacIver, "It is true that there is no state where there is no overruling force. But the exercise of force does not make a state, or a pirate ship or mutinous army would be a state." The basis of sovereignty and state is not power. MacIver associates power with the functions of the state. Power is given to the state to perform certain functions. As the states does not perform all the functions, it cannot be given all the powers. To quote him, "Power should be relative to function." Again, "None ever regards the service of the state as unlimited and therefore the conception of unlimited sovereignty is dangerously false."

Criticism of Pluralist Theory of Sovereignty

The pluralist theory of sovereignty has been attacked on many grounds. Critics maintain that without the establishment of a classless society, sovereignty can neither be divided nor be limited. In order to limit the sovereignty of the state, pluralism must aim at a classless society. The sovereignty of state can be limited or finished by breaking the class structure of society and that is possible only through a socialist revolution for which the pluralists are not ready.

The need for unity in diversity is accepted by all, including the pluralists, but the pluralists assume that unity in society can be established by the state without any sovereign power. This view is not correct. If the sovereign state is not there and sovereignty is divided among various associations, the state cannot maintain unity and order in society. It is basically wrong to assume that unity can be established in society even without the sovereign state.

The pluralists demand independence for different kinds of associations. That is not possible without a superior power being given to the state. The division of sovereignty among associations is not only impossible but also improper. The pluralist view will lead to political anarchy and social instability. Sovereignty is unified power and by dividing it, there will be neither unity nor diversity. There will be disorder everywhere. Two or more than two equal powers cannot co-exist peacefully in a society. In order to avoid social conflict, unified power must be given to the state.

The pluralists demand independence for economic organisations from the state and they assume that the economic system can remain aloof from the state. Experience shows that such a thing is not possible. The Marxist view is that the political system is a part of the super-structure which is based on the economic sub-structure. Even the Liberals consider it impossible to separate economic affairs from political affairs.

The pluralists limit the sovereignty of the state in the interests of the rights of individuals and other associations in society. However, in order to maintain the rights of individuals and associations, the state must have sovereign power. The interests of individuals and associations will conflict and the state will be helpless if it does not possess sovereign power. A non-sovereign state will result in political anarchy.

The pluralist theory of sovereignty is not a practical one. It is not clear how with divided sovereignty coordination and equilibrium can be maintained in the political system. It is a mistake to regard the division of powers or the separation of powers or administrative decentralisation as division of sovereignty.

The pluralists want to establish legal authority on the principles of social solidarity or the sense of right by separating it from political authority, but those principles are indefinite, ambiguous and a weak basis of law. Certainty is the most essential feature of law and that will get lost in the jungle of pluralistic laws, meaning different things to different people. The existence of a legal system presupposes the existence of legal sovereignty. Laws should be definite and that is possible only if there is legal sovereignty of the state. Moreover, obedience to laws cannot be ensured without the use of force in exceptional cases. The state must have sovereign power both to make laws and to punish those who do not obey the laws.

The pluralists demand that external sovereignty of the state must be restricted in the interest of humanity, peace and security. That is possible only if capitalism and imperialism are ended. However, the pluralists do not talk of finishing capitalism and imperialism.

The historical basis of pluralism is the feudal economic order and non-sovereign state of Medieval Europe. However, modern national sovereign states have emerged to satisfy the political requirements of modern times. The political system of feudalism cannot be imposed on the modern states as every political system develops according to the requirements of the socio-economic system.

Critics point out that when interest-groups become the centre of individual loyalty, there is a danger that some groups may become unduly powerful and they may dictate unjust terms on society on account of their power. The unions of those performing essential services such as mechanics, engineers, doctors, dispensers, drivers and even sweepers may exert undue pressure on authorities because they can disrupt normal social life while others may not be able to press their just and genuine demands. Moreover, some categories of persons such as traders and workers are usually more organised and vocal than consumers etc. Under the circumstances, the responsibility of protecting the common interests will devolve on the state. The state has to act not only as an agency for harmonising the conflicting claims of different interest groups but also to protect the interests of those who are not able to organise themselves and articulate their genuine interests. The state will not be able to perform its duties if it is like any other organisation and not a dominant organisation.

The pluralist theory is based on wrong assumptions. It is wrong to assume that the various associations run along parallel lines and there is no overlapping of functions. The fact is that life cannot be divided into watertight compartments, allowing various associations to control various aspects of life. As society is constituted, there is always a clash of interests and conflict of loyalties. The result is that if there is no final legal authority in society, the various groups or associations are bound to clash with one another and thereby create an atmosphere in which human progress becomes impossible. Even if the conception of co-sovereignty of the political Parliament and economic Parliament is accepted, things are not going to improve because we cannot avoid conflict where the same is inherent. The interests of the producers and consumers are never identical.

The concept of sovereignty which is adopted by the pluralists is something which is not advocated by the exponents of sovereignty. With the exception of Hegel, the other advocates of sovereignty did not assign omnipotence to the state. They all admitted that in actual practice, the authority of the state is limited in many ways. Bodin, Hobbes, Rousseau and Austin did not claim that "to criticise or challenge, to destroy or resist, state authority is necessarily immoral, unethical, irrational, antisocial or even impracticable. What is contended by them is that the state does not accept a rival. It is not responsible or subordinate to another authority. "In brief, the state, as an organisation for law within any given territory, is superior to all other social groups within such territory." Dr. A.D. Lindsay admits that the state is unique in so far as it possesses coercive authority and is also comprehensive in its membership, but he maintains that this unique feature of the state is not enough to constitute a sovereign state. Critic; point out that such an attitude is not logical.

The pluralists are not clear regarding their goal. Various writers have expressed different opinions on the subject. While Gierke and Maitland recognise the real personality of groups, they did not challenge the final legal authority of the state. Dr. Figgis held the view that the state was to perform the function of coordination and adjustment. Barker expressed himself in these words: "We see the state invited to retreat before the guild, the national groups, the church, yet whatever rights such groups may claim to gain the state will still remain as a necessary adjusting force; it is even possible that if groups are destined to gain new ground, the state, will also gain, perhaps even more than it loses, because it will be forced to deal with ever graver and ever weightier problems of adjustment." Cole changed his mind many a time with regard to the position of the state. To start with, he put the state on the same footing as other guilds. The state was to possess and exercise powers appropriate to its function. While the guilds were to regulate the conditions of production, the state was to control the means of production and regulate prices and distribution of income. The state was also to perform such functions as the defence of the country, control of marriage and divorce, education of children, care of defective and dependent persons and prevention and punishment of crime. Cole was also in favour of the creation of a "Democratic Supreme Court of International Equity" which was to act as the final court of appeal. The state was to exercise powers of coercion. However, he changed his mind later on and relegated the state to an insignificant position. He advocated the delegation of all functions to the guilds. His view was that the state can be allowed to wither away and ultimately disappear altogether, "either after a frontal attack or by atrophy following upon dispossession of its vital powers."

It is not clear what exactly the pluralists want to achieve. If their intention is merely to give recognition to various associations and also to give them a large measure of autonomy in their work, the demand is so reasonable and legitimate that no advocate of state sovereignty will refuse to accept it. Hence "it seems neither necessary nor useful to abandon the doctrine of state sovereignty in order either to resist perversions of the doctrine or to promote the adoption of proposals for greater diversification and decentralisation in the organisation for the initiation and execution of state policy." There is no fundamental conflict between true sovereignty and true functionalism. If the state accepts the position of associations and gives them a lot of autonomy in their work, the present conflict may disappear.

Society cannot be harmoniously organised in a peaceful manner without the authority of the state. It is wrong to presume that all associations are the species of the same genus. The state occupies a unique position. This is true whether we accept it or not. Dr. Garner writes, "State renders important service in keeping within proper limits the classes and struggles between competing groups and performing the role of a referee or umpire and adjusting or reconciling their conflicting interests." Conflicts among the various associations will not be automatically adjusted by a process of give and take and the state has to be retained for maintaining peace and order and adjusting and coordinating the interests of the various associations. In order to avoid the anarchy of associations and to save society from collapse and dissolution, the authority of the state has to be maintained.

Pluralism is anti-patriotic. It is the doctrine of revolution and internationalism. Whatever may be said against loyalty to the state, it cannot be denied that patriotism is still the most potent force in civic life. The two World Wars have proved that patriotism transcends local, professional and sectional interests.

The pluralist view is full of dangers. If the individual conscience is to determine the authority of group opinion, any subversive group can claim a right to function and what is true of the larger groups, is also true of smaller groups. If a large trade union is to have powers independent of the state, a similar claim can be put forward on behalf of a village debating society or any criminal organisation.

Any theory which seeks to put voluntary groups or associations "on the same level with the state, which maintains that there is no essential difference between them and the state, which suggests that the individual may have two or more allegiances or loyalties, one to the state and one or more to the groups to which he is attached and that the former is not necessarily superior to the latter, which would throw overboard the principle of the sovereignty of the state and parcel out its power and functions between the state and a multitude of other associations, cannot stand the test of criticism. It would mean a return in large measure to the semi-anarchy of the Middle Ages when sovereignty was divided amongst various contending rulers or bodies, the church, the state, the feudal lords, clans, guilds etc. The vision of a working class organisation building up for itself an economic state governed by the workers and for the workers, within the political state, but virtually independent of the state for the regulation of economic life, is a dangerous fantasy. If the theory be put into practice, it would, in all probability, lead to innumerable conflicts of jurisdiction: the authority of the state, confronted as it would be by competing and rival associations would shrivel up, and its power to maintain order and security would be materially impaired. The very recognition of the autonomy demanded by the pluralists for the other associations would only intensify the need of a superior power, such as the state, to protect society against the consequences of the inevitable conflict between them as well as protect their own members against the possible, tyranny and oppression of their governing bodies. One of the most important services which the state renders, in fact, is keeping within proper limits the classes and struggles between competing groups and performing the role of a sort of a referee or umpire in adjusting or reconciling their conflicting interests."

Merits of Pluralistic Theory

In spite of the criticism, it cannot be denied that the pluralist theory of sovereignty was a welcome reaction against the glorification of state authority. It emphasized the dangers involved in the deification of the state. It was a timely protest against the rigid and dogmatic legalism of the Austinian theory of sovereignty. The pluralists point out the growing importance of the non-political groups, the danger of over-interference on the part of the state with the proper functions of groups or associations and the desirability of not only recognising them but also giving them a large measure of autonomy in their work.

Pluralism was a healthy, humanistic and democratic reaction against absolutism. It was the call of the time against absolute sovereignty. It was a revolt based on the ideas of liberty and liberalism against Austinian theory of sovereignty and the Hegelian view of the state. When the voice of anarchism and syndicalism against the greatness of the state was colling down, pluralism raised its voice to keep the state merely as a human association to serve the general interests of society as a whole. It had no desire to kill the state. It wanted to keep the state alive after taking away its soul, sovereignty and here lies the weakness of the theory.

Miss Follett has tried to summarise the chief contributions of pluralism. According to her, the pluralists pricked the bubble of the right of the state to supremacy. They recognised the value of the group in political life. They pleaded for a revivification of local life. They asserted that the interests of the state are not always identical with the interests of its parts. It marked the beginning of the disappearance of the people as a mere crowd. They stand for federalism and restoration of local life.

Gettell describes the contribution of the pluralists in these words : "Their emphasis on the fact that states, in spite of legal omnipotence, should be subject to moral restraints is a desirable reaction against the idealization of the state and the doctrine that state is an end in itself, free from all moral restraint. The pluralists also make a timely protest against the rigid and dogmatic legalism of the Austinian theory of sovereignty." Again, "The pluralists emphasize the necessity of studying the actual facts of political life in a rapidly changing social system. In this connection, they point out the growing importance of non-political groups, the danger of over-interference by the State with the proper functions of such groups and the desirability of giving to such groups greater legal recognition in the political system."

The view of Gunner Heckscher is that the pluralist approach is definitely a general theory. It was formerly regarded as a mere curiosity but now it is becoming more and more widely accepted by political scientists all over the world. This is an important change in the basic assumptions of political science and in particular of comparative government. It is largely because of this change that some of the earlier characteristics of political science are being criticised today. Pluralism leads us to recognise that fact that what we have to study is not the government alone but politics, including a great number of factors which are disregarded. Many of those factors are not only the political parties but also more or less organised groups of an seemingly non-political or at least predominantly non-political type — practically on the whole everything which tends to influence public opinion. The pluralist has to draw much more on economics and sociology than the institutionalist. (Study of Comparative Government and Politics, p. 34).

Merriam and Barnes have shown that in spite of attacks of the pluralists, the theory of state sovereignty has not been given up. The view of Rockow is that pluralist criticism is becoming more and more a general theory of the social structure of the state than an attack on the state as a coordinating agency. Sabine writes, "For my own part then I must reserve the right to be a monist when I can and a pluralist when I must."

In spite of these contributions, political pluralism has not been able to have a solid base so far as its attack on sovereignty is concerned. It can be termed as a misfired shot on state sovereignty. It is impracticable so far as politics is concerned, anarchic as a social theory, unscientific as an economic theory and ambiguous as a legal theory.

SUGGESTED READINGS

Adams, May	: *The Modern State.*
Austin, J.	: *Lectures on Jurisprudence.*
Barker, E.	: *Political Thought in England from Spencer to Today.*
Bliss, P.	: *On Sovereignty.*
Brown, W.J.	: *The Austinian Theory of Law.*

Bryce, J. : *Studies in History and Jurisprudence, Vol. II.*

Burgess, J. W. : *Political Science and Comparative Constitutional Law.*

Cohen, H.E. : *Recent Theories of Sovereignty.*

Coker, R.W. : *Recent Political Thought.*

Deaey, J.Q. : *The State and Government.*

Deane, H.A. : *The Political Ideas of Harold J. Laski.*

Duguit, Leon : *Law in the Modern State.*

Elliot, W.Y. : *The Pragmatic Revolt in Politics,* 1928

Figgis, J.N. : *Churches in the Modern State, New York,* 1914.

Follett, M.P. : *The New State,* 1918.

Garner, J.W. : *Political Science and Government.*

Hocking, W.E. : *Man and the State.*

Hsiao, K.C. : *Political Pluralism, A Study in Contemporary Political Theory,* London, 1927.

James, W. : *The Pluralistic Universe,* New York, 1909.

Krabbe, Hugo : *The Modern Idea of the State.*

Laski, H.J. : *Authority in the Modern State.*

Laski, H.J. : *A Grammar of Politics,* London, 1925.

Laski, H.J. : *Studies in the Problem of Sovereignty,* New Haven, 1917.

Laski, H.J. : *The Foundation of Sovereignty,* 1921.

Lipson : *The Great Issues of Politics,* Bombay, 1967.

Mabbott, J.D. : *The State and the Citizen,* London, 1948.

MacIver, R.M. : *The Modern State,* London, 1926.

MacIver, R.M. : *The Web of Government,* 1947.

Mahajan, V.D. : *Recent Political Thought.*

Maine, Sir Henry : *Lectures on the Early History of Institutions,* 1914.

Maritain, J. : *Man and the State.*

Martin, Kingsley : *Harold Laski.*

Mattern, J. : *Concepts of State, Sovereignty and International Law.*

Maxey, C.C. : *Political Philosophies.*

Merkl, Peter, H. : *Political Continuity and Change.*

Merriam, C.E. : *History of the Theory of Sovereignty Since Rousseau.*

Merriam, C.E. and H.E. Barnes : *A History of Political Theories—Recent Times.*

Pollock, F. : *History of the Science of Politics.*

Rockow, L. : *Contemporary Political Thought in England.*

Roucek, J.S. and Others : *Introduction to Political Science.*

Ward, P.W. : *Sovereignty. A Study of Contemporary Political Notions.*

Webb, Sidney and Beatrice : *History of Unionism and Industrial Democracy, London, 1902.*

Willoughby, W.W. : *The Nature of the State.*

CHAPTER

Citizenship

Learning Objectives

- Meaning of Citizenship
- Legal and Moral Aspects of Citizenship
- Distinction between Citizen and Alien
- Citizen and National
- Citizen and Voter
- Citizen and Subject
- Methos of acquiring citizenship
- Naturalisation
- Loss of Citizenship
- Citizenship in a Federal State
- Qualities of a Good Citizen
- Hindrances to Good Citizenship
- How to remove hindrances to good citizenship
- Suggested Readings

Meaning of Citizenship

The word 'citizen' literally means resident of a city who enjoys certain privileges of such residence. The word is derived from the Latin word "Civics". In Civics, the world has a wider meaning. By a citizen, we mean a member of a state who enjoys all rights and privileges granted by it and also discharges his duties and obligations towards the state and other associations within it.

The notion of citizenship was a narrow one in ancient times and it has changed in course of time. According to Aristotle, "He who has the power to take part in the deliberative or judicial administration is said by us to be a citizen of that state." (Politics translated by Jowett, p. 202). Aristotle did not include the majority of the people in the category of citizens on the ground that they did not have the necessary ability and leisure to exercise properly the rights of citizens. His idea of citizenship was purely aristocratic.

In the days of feudalism also, citizenship was confined to the privileged few and the ignorant many who formed the bulk of the population, were excluded from it. Naturally, political leadership, high offices and high places of honour were monopolised by the privileged class.

Through a historical process, the Greek city states have evolved into the nation-states of today. Modern states are large-sized and political privileges are possessed by all. The result is that the people cannot directly participate in the administration of the state. What constitutes citizenship today is not direct participation in administration but allegiance to the state in which a citizen resides and enjoys political privileges. Allegiance means the respect of the citizen for the basic ideals of the state and defend it in the hour of its crisis. If a citizen is entitled to all civic and political rights, he has also duties to discharge towards the state. In order to perform his functions properly, a citizen must be equipped with adequate mental and moral faculties. In a broad sense, a citizen may be defined as one who owes allegiance to the state in which he resides. He has full share of civil and political privileges and makes an intelligent contribution to the flow of social richness.

The success of democracy depends on good citizenship. Democracy stands for equality of human beings. The absence of such equality is opposed to the true spirit of citizenship. A totalitarian or a dictatorial state demands from its citizens unquestioning submission, suppressing thereby the freedom of thought, speech and action of its citizens. In such a state, citizenship is a misnomer.

Two important elements in the idea of modern citizenship are liberty and membership of the state. A good citizen is a free citizen and he enjoys certain rights and liberties. The right of the membership of the state includes the right to share in the Government, formulate laws and pay taxes. There is no distinction between the ruler and the ruled and the ruler and a subject. Modern citizenship is broad, comprehensive and all-inclusive. It includes within its ambit not only men but also women, not only city-dwellers but also villagers. It does not tolerate any principle which subjects any class of people to slavery or serfdom. It includes all those who permanently reside in a country and owe permanent allegiance to the state.

Legal and Moral Aspects of Citizenship

Legally, a citizen is a person who owes allegiance to the state and receives in return the protection of the state, both at home and abroad. He has a status in the eye of law. He is provided with opportunities for the legitimate enjoyment of his freedom, property and political rights.

While it is easy to define the legal aspect of citizenship, it is difficult to define its moral aspect. Citizenship implies a sense of responsibility in the citizen to fulfil all his obligations to the state and the various social groups of which he is a member. It recognises the value of self-discipline and self-control. A citizen should not be too selfish. His personal motives should not stand in the way of common good. He must not forget that he is not only a member of a family, but also a member of a village or a town in which he lives or a member of the occupation which gives him his livelihood. He must not forget that he is also a member of his country and humanity at large and his function is to give and take. He can receive all that is necessary to equip himself as a citizen but he must be ready at the same time to give back to the community all that can promote general happiness and common well-being. There are three main characteristics of citizenship and those are allegiance to the state, enjoyment of civil and political rights and the desire to promote general happiness and common well-being.

Distinction between Citizen and Alien

The residents of a state are broadly classified into citizens and aliens. Citizens own their allegiance to the state in which they reside, but aliens owe allegiance to some other state. For example, the Englishmen residing in India owe their allegiance to England and not to India. Secondly, the citizens of a state enjoy all civil and political privileges of that state, but aliens are denied the political privileges. They do not share in the full life of the state in which they reside. However, both citizens and aliens are bound to obey the ordinary laws of the state in which they reside.

An alien may be expelled from the state for misconduct but a citizen cannot be expelled from his own state. The state looks after the interests of its citizens even if they go abroad, but that is not so in the case of aliens. An alien does not always have full freedom to acquire or sell landed property.

Citizen and National

There is a distinction between a citizen and a national. A citizen is a member of the state who enjoys full civil and political rights. A national is a citizen without full political rights. A national owes allegiance to the state and is subject to the control of the state both at home and abroad, but has no voting right. Minors, criminals, insolvents etc. who do not possess the right to vote, are regarded as the nationals of the state. The bulk of the population of a modem state consists of nationals and citizens.

Citizen and Voter

There is a distinction between a citizen and a voter. A voter is a person who has the right to cast his vote at the time of election. However, there may be citizens who are not voters.

Citizen and Subject

There is a distinction between a citizen and a subject. A citizen is one who enjoys full civil and political rights while a subject is one who is not entitled to any political rights. Generally, the word subject is used for the members of a state where a monarchical form of Government prevails. It has been used in history to describe the relation between the absolute king and those whom he ruled. However, this distinction has lost its practical importance with the growth of the democratic states.

Methods of acquiring citizenship

Citizens are of two types, viz. *natural citizens* and *naturalised citizens.* Natural citizens are citizens by birth. Naturalised citizens are citizens by adoption. A naturalised citizen is an alien who for certain reasons decides to give up his original citizenship to become the citizen of another state by fulfilling the conditions laid down by that state.

There are two principles by which citizenship by birth can be acquired. One is called *Jus Sanguinis* (rule of blood relation) and the other *Jus Soli (rule* of the place of birth). According to the principle of Jus Sanguinis, the citizenship of a child follows his parents or any of them, irrespective of the place of birth. States like France, Italy and Germany follow this principle. The result is that the child of a French parent becomes a French citizen even if he is born outside France.

According to the principle of Jus Soli, the place of birth is the guiding consideration in conferring citizenship. The children of a citizen born abroad become aliens and the children of alien parents born within the territory of the state become its citizens.

States like India, England and the United States follow a mixed principle. Children born of alien parents on their territory are as good natural citizens as the children born of citizens at home or abroad. Of the two principles, the Jus Sanguinis appears to be more logical. It is natural that a child should become the citizen of the parent state. To establish citizenship on the basis of Jus Soli is somewhat illogical because the place of birth in most cases is fixed by accident. An Indian mother while staying in England for some time, may give birth to a child and he become the citizen of England. This does not seem to be logical.

The actual practice of conferring citizenship also depends upon treaty, agreements and other provisions. England and the United States apply the principle of Jus Sanguinis to their own citizens and the principle of Jus Soli to aliens. The result is that children born of American parents are American citizens and children born of alien parents in the United States are also American citizens. This leads to the problem of what is known as "double nationality". In the above case, the child has double nationality. He is not only the citizen of the United States but also of the state to which his parents belong. The child is allowed to choose either citizenship after attaining adulthood.

Naturalisation

Naturalisation is an important method of acquiring citizenship. A foreigner becomes a citizen of another state on fulfilling certain conditions. A foreign lady marrying a citizen of a particular state may become, as a matter of right, a naturalised citizen of that state. The laws of some states allow the naturalisation of a foreigner on his appointment as a public servant. In some states, an alien becomes a citizen just by long residence. In Mexico, an alien who purchases real property is allowed to acquire citizenship. If a state or a part of a state is conquered by another state, the inhabitants of the conquered territory get the citizenship of the conquering state.

In all states, a foreigner who applies for citizenship has to pass through certain formalities. The state granting citizenship may lay down certain conditions. One of them is usually residence for a specified period without break. In England, the period is five years.

Some states put certain restrictions on the acquisition of citizenship. This was a device to check the influx of undesirable foreigners belonging to a different culture, religion, race or colour. In Australia, people who are non-white, are not made citizens. The policy of restrictions often results in international friction and racial animosity.

Naturalisation may be complete or partial. When a foreigner receives the full share of rights and privileges in the state of his adoption, his naturalisation is called complete. In England, there is no discrimination against naturalised citizens in respect of privileges. They enjoy the same rights as natural citizens. In the United States, the naturalised citizens are denied certain privilege which are granted only to natural citizens. For example, a naturalised citizen is debarred by law from becoming the President of the United States. This is a case of partial naturalisation.

Loss of Citizenship

Just as citizenship can be acquired, it can also be lost. In some states, the acceptance of some employment under an alien Government or desertion from military service results in loss of citizenship. A woman marrying a foreigner acquires the citizenship of her husband and loses her won citizenship. There is a rule in some states that the acceptance of foreign decorations or titles will lead to the loss of citizenship. Long continued absence from the home state also results in loss of citizenship. When a person is expelled from a state for objectionable activities or when he is dismissed from the service of the state on other grounds, he may be deprived of his citizenship. A person may renounce his citizenship and take up the citizenship of another state by naturalisation. This is known as expatriation. In the past, the privilege of changing citizenship was denied in most cases but today most of the states accept the right of a citizen to resign one citizenship to take up another.

Citizenship in a Federal State

In a federal state, there are two sets of governments, viz., national and local. The result is that a citizen in a federal state owes a double allegiance. He has to obey the laws made by the national Government and the local Government. Dual polity leads to dual citizenship. In Switzerland, a citizen is primarily a citizen of a Canton and he automatically becomes a citizen of the Swiss Federal Republic. In the United States, a person is the citizen of a state in which he is born and resides. He is also a citizen of the United States. An African is a citizen of the state in which he resides and also a citizen of the federation. In India there is only one citizenship and that is the citizenship of India. Nobody is the citizen of the state in which he is born or resides.

Qualities of a Good Citizen

The view of Voltaire was that a people will get the kind of government it deserves. Good citizenship and good states are co-relative terms. It is the virtues of good citizens that make the state good. Likewise, it is the soundness of political system that makes the citizens good. Democracy is accepted as an ideal political system and a good citizen is defined as one who faithfully lives up to the necessary conditions of a democratic state. Democracy implies the sovereignty of the people and the quality of the citizens determines the quality of actual democracy.

Burns refers to "two characteristics in the conduct and outlook of all men; first, a sturdy independence and secondly, an imaginative sympathy". In order to be successful, democracy must involve the reciprocity of freedom and responsibility and the inseparability of the state and citizens. In the words of Prof. Laski, the essence of good citizenship is "the contribution of one's instructed judgement to the public good." (A Grammar of politics, p. 113). The people must actively share in the democratic vision and work towards its fulfilment.

According to Lord Bryce, "A good citizen is one who possesses the following three qualities, namely, intelligence, self-control and conscience." By intelligence is meant a strong commonsense and the capacity to understand properly the interests of the community to which he belongs. A good citizen must possess self-control. He must know how to subordinate his private interests to the general interests of the society. Selfishness stands in the way of good citizenship.

Another quality of good citizenship is conscience or devotion to duty. Conscience creates a sense of responsibility and service towards the community. A good citizen is expected to discharge his duties honestly and diligently. He should always be ready and willing to render every kind of service to the community. He should exercise the right of vote honestly and take active interest in the affairs of the state.

Hindrances to Good Citizenship

According to Lord Bryce, the hindrances to good citizenship are indolence, private self-interest and party spirit. These defects in the citizens stand in the way of the full realisation of the ideal of good citizenship.

(1) *Indolence* or lack of consciousness is the mortal enemy of democracy. If citizens are indifferent to their rights and duties and are too much pre-occupied with their private safety and security, that would result in the long run in the downfall of democracy. The indolent citizen is everywhere the founder and perpetuator of dictatorship. Prof. Laski writes, "The state is built so certainly upon the character of men that they can only mould it to their desire by consistent devotion to its activities. If men are indifferent or careless, if they are satisfied to withdraw from the arena, not the most ingenious mechanism can ultimately prevent abuse of power". (A Grammar of Politics, p. 171)

(2) Men are usually guided by *self-interest.* If while doing so, an individual shirks his public responsibility or ignores general welfare, his attitude is a positive hindrance to good citizenship. No democracy can survive for long if the industrialists are motivated by private profit alone, if the officials indulge in corruption and bribery and the ruling party is busy all the time in the loaves and fishes of office. Prof. MacIver writes, "Any group whatever, if armed with the requisite power, destroys the reciprocity of interests that democracy postulates. Every group, if it is not restrained from so doing, puts its interests above the interest of the whole. Every monopoly of power destroys the participant unity of all groups that democracy pledges." (The Web of Government, p. 221).

(3) It is true that party system is necessary for the working of democracy but the citizens of a democracy must not work in *a party spirit* and must keep before themselves the national interest. However, in actual practice, the political parties deviate from the national interest and further the interests of particular groups. The members of a political party do no hesitate to adopt fair or foul means to win elections. Everything is subordinated to the interests of the party. Allegiance to the party blinds its members to their allegiance to the whole nation. The result is that politics is reduced to what Prof. MacIver calls "the jockeying of organised groups for relative advantage". The situation that encourages insincerity, falsehood and selfishness is a positive hindrance to democracy and good citizenship.

(4) Another obstacle to good citizenship is *poverty.* A poverty-stricken citizen is indifferent towards life and its problems. He is not in a position to take an active part in the management of the affairs of the state. He is frightened by the nightmare of hunger. Poverty often drives citizens towards anti-social activities such as theft, cheating, murder etc. It follows that unless every citizen possesses a basic economic minimum, he cannot be a good citizen. It becomes the duty of the state to provide every citizen a reasonably decent standard of living.

(5) Another hindrance to good citizenship is *ignorance.* If we expect a citizen to make his full contribution to public good, he should be educated and well-informed. An ignorant person cannot make a distinction between right and wrong. Narrow-mindedness based on evil customs and institutions obstructs the right judgement of citizens and makes them unfit to cooperate in the achievement of the goal of common good of the whole community. Burke is said to have observed, "Education is the best defence of citizenship".

(6) Among other hindrances to good citizenship are the *defects of the electoral system,* the *corruption of the organs of public opinion* and the *vast size of contemporary states.* Sometimes, on account of the inherent defects in the electoral machinery, large sections of the people go unrepresented. Those persons cannot take interest in the affairs of the state. The organs of public opinion like the newspapers may distort truth and misinform the public. In such a situation, an intelligent evaluation of the issues of the day becomes impossible.

(7) Another hindrance to good citizenship is the *vast size of the modern state.* The result is that the modern citizen finds little opportunity to take direct part in the process of the Government. The problems of modern Government are highly technical and complex and an ordinary citizen finds himself helpless. The anarchic conditions of unplanned economy lead to increasing isolation and powerlessness of the individual in modern industrial society. This hinders the spontaneous integration of the citizen with the political community.

How to remove hindrances to good citizenship

According to Lord Bryce, the hindrances to good citizenship can be removed by administrative and moral means. To quote him, "The remedies that may be applied to any defects in the working of Governments are some of them Mechanical, some of them Ethical. By Mechanical remedies I understand those which consist in improving the structure or the customs and working devices of Government, *i.e.,* the laws and the institutions or political methods, by Ethical those which affect the character and spirit of the people." (*The Hindrances to Good Citizenship,* p. 106).

(1) *Administrative or mechanical remedies* are those which seek to remove the hindrances to good citizenship by introducing changes in political and social institutions. Structural changes are many. There should be constitutional reforms. The grant of fundamental rights, extension of franchise, more frequent elections, introduction of referendum, initiative, recall etc. can make citizens conscious of their rights and induce them to take more interest in public affairs. In countries like Belgium and Switzerland, the system of compulsory voting has been adopted to force the people to take part in the affairs of the state. It is suggested that the adoption of the system of proportional representation would secure the representation of all sections of the people and ensure public interest in public affairs. The problem of corruption and immoral and anti-social activities is sought to be met by appropriate administrative measures.

(2) As regards *moral or ethical remedies,* steps should be taken for the spiritual upliftment and mental elevation of the citizens so that they take an active interest in public affairs. J.S. Mill writes, "Thus a people may prefer a free Government, but if, for indolence, or carelessness, or cowardice or want of public spirit, they are unequal to the exertions necessary for preserving it; if they will not fight for it when it is directly attacked, if they can be deluded by the artifices used to cheat them out of it; if by momentary discouragement or temporary panic, or a fit of enthusiasm for an individual they can be induced to lay their liberties at the feet even of a great man, or trust him with powers which enable him to subvert their institutions; in all these cases they are more or less unfit for liberty; and though it may be for their good to have it even for a short time, they are unlikely long to enjoy it." (Representative Government, p. 149). The danger to good citizenship arises from the mental attitude of the citizens and the remedy lies in increasing dissemination of education with a view to inculcating in the citizens the moral virtues of courage, honesty, tolerance and a spirit of accommodation. In

the words of Mannheim, that must be supplemented by "political mass education of the citizenry to heighten understanding of antidemocratic threats, their sources and techniques". (Freedom, Power and Democratic Planning, p. 119).

(3) Another suggestion is that there should be comprehensive planning for introducing elements of stability and justice in the community. There should be planning from the top and it should be combined with active participation from below. There should be a large number of functional and territorial autonomous organisations which will integrate the citizen with the community.

SUGGESTED READINGS

Bryce : *The Hindrances to Good Citizenship.*

Fromn, Erich : *The Fear of Freedom.*

Laski, Harold, J. : *A Grammar of Politics.*

MacIver : *The Web of Government.*

Mannheim : *Freedom, Power and Democratic Planning.*

Mill, J.S. : *Representative Government.*

16

CHAPTER

Rights and Duties

Rights

Every state is known by the rights it maintains. Experience shows that unless the citizens of a state are guaranteed a certain number of right, it is not possible for them to live a full life. Without them, find themselves handicapped in many ways. They can grow only if they are guaranteed those minimum conditions of existence which have been found to be necessary by actual experience. Laski says: "Rights are those conditions of social life without which no man can be his best self." Dr. Beni Prasad observes: "Rights are nothing more and nothing less than those social conditions which are necessary or favourable to the development of personality. Rights are in their essence, aspects of social life." Srinivas Sastri says: "In its essence, a right is an arrangement, rule or practice sanctioned by law of the community and conducive to the highest moral good of the citizen." Green says that a right is a power claimed and recognized as contributory to common good. The view of Holland is that right is man's capacity of influencing the acts of another by means of the opinion and force of society.

Learning Objectives

- Rights
- Characteristics of Rights
- Classification of Rights : Natural Rights
- Moral Rights
- Legal Rights
- Fundamental Rights
- Various Theories of Rights
- Theory of Natural Rights
- The Legal Theory of Rights
- Historical Theory of Rights
- The Idealist Theory of Rights
- Social Walfare Theory of Rights
- Laski's Theory of Rights
- The Marxist Theory of Rights
- How to safeguard Rights
- Duties of citizens
- Suggested Readings

Hobhouse says that rights are "what we may expect from others and others from us and all genuine rights are conditions of social welfare. Thus, the rights any one may claim are partly those which are essential to every man in order to be a rational human person, and partly those which are necessary for the fulfilment of the function that society expects from him. They are conditioned by, correlative to, his social responsibilities." Bosanquet says, "We have a right to the means that are necessary to the development of our lives in the direction of the highest good of the community of which we are a pan." Rights are recognised and sanctioned by society. There can be no rights outside society.

Characteristics of Rights

There are certain characteristics of rights which are being demanded by the people everywhere in the world. Rights do not mean the grant of some historic conditions possessed in the child-hood of man and lost in the course of time. There is no golden age to which we can return. It is foolish for the people of the twentieth century to insist upon the enjoyment of the rights which the people of the Gupta Period of Indian history enjoyed. It need not be emphasized that as the needs of human beings go on changing with time, the contents of the rights must go on changing. The rights must correspond to the needs of the people. Since the needs of the people are recognised by the law of the land they become precise and capable of enforcement.

The rights are not absolute. If circumstances demand that certain restrictions must be put on the enjoyment of certain rights so that the higher interests of the society as a whole may be secured, that has to be done. That is why the fundamental rights guaranteed by the Indian Constitution have been restricted in many ways. Article 19 says that all citizens shall have the right of freedom of speech and expression, the right to assemble peaceably and without arms, the right to form associations or unions, the right to move freely throughout the territory of India, the right to reside and settle in any part of the territory of India, the right to acquire, hold and dispose of property and the right to practise any profession or to carry on any occupation, trade or business. However, the right of freedom of speech and expression does not affect the operation of any existing law or prevent the state from making any law which imposes reasonable restrictions on the exercise of this right in the interests of the security of the state, friendly relations with foreign states, public order, decency or morality, or in relation to contempt of court, defamation or incitement to an offence. The right to assemble peaceably and without arms does not affect the operation of any existing law in so far as it imposes reasonable restrictions on the exercise of this right in the interest of public order. As regards the right to form associations or unions, it does not affect the operation of any existing law in so far as it imposes reasonable restriction in the interest of public order or morality. As regards the right to move freely throughout the territory of India, this right does not affect the operation of any existing law in so far as it imposes reasonable restrictions either in the interests of the general public or for the protection of the interests of any scheduled tribe. The same applies to the passing of new laws by any state on the same subject. As regards the right of practise any profession or to carry on any occupation, trade or business, it does not affect the operation of any existing law in so far as it imposes reasonable restrictions in the interest of the general public. Likewise, a state can pass a new law with the same object. This right does not affect the operation of any existing law in so far as it relates to professional or technical qualifications necessary for practising any profession or carrying on any occupation, trade or business. The same applies to the other rights guaranteed by the Constitution. Even in religious matters, restrictions can be imposed by the state in the interest of society as a whole. Even the right to property is not absolute. It can be taken away by the state for a public purpose and courts cannot go into the question of the adequacy of the compensation given to the owners of property.

The state exists to maintain all those conditions which are necessary for the full growth, of human beings and as such it seems idle to think of individuals having rights against the state. However, this does not mean that an individual has no right against any particular government. If the officials of the government violate the provisions of law, an individual must have a remedy against them. Likewise, if an officer acts arbitrarily, the aggrieved party must have a remedy in the form of a right to move the court. The same can be done if an executive or legislative action is ultra vires. The right against the government has been conceded in many cases in modern times. Formerly, no government employee could file a suit against the government for the realisation of the arrears of his salary but the Supreme Court of India has guaranteed this right. In a recent judgement (1966) the Supreme Court of India has held that the government cannot take up the plea that a particular law does not apply to it as it has not agreed to submit to it. Article 311 of the Constitution of India gives certain rights to civil servants in the case of dismissal, etc. Likewise, Articles 14 and 16 of the Constitution can be resorted to challenge the action, of the government.

Rights are co-relative with functions. The number of rights possessed by an individual must correspond to the contribution which he makes to society. The governor of a state is entitled to have more rights than his peon because his contribution is definitely greater than that of his peon. The rights possessed by a professor must be more than those possessed by a coolie. The same applies to the rights possessed by a lawyer and his clerk. The reason is that neither a governor, nor a professor nor a lawyer can perform the duties given to him unless he is provided with adequate means for their performance. It must not be forgotten that the contribution to be made by the individual must be personal or it is no contribution at all. I do not contribute by being the child of my parents. I may discharge my duty to the state by being a brick-layer or an artist or a mathematician. Whatever form my contribution may take, it is essential that it must be personal. He who does not perform functions cannot enjoy rights, any more than he who does not work, has right to his food.

The question is what rights the state has over the individual. The view of Dr. Bosanquet is: "The state is the guardian of the whole moral world and not a factor within an organized moral world." This view is not accepted today. It is contended that the state is only a factor in the lives of the citizens. The state acts through law and law can regulate only the external actions of the individuals and that points to the limited scope of the sphere of the state. If the state is going to perform only a few functions and not many, its authority cannot be all-comprehensive. The measure of authority to be given to the state or enjoyed by it must correspond to the functions of the state. In the life of an individual, the state is merely an association. It is not the association of associations. It has no right of life and death over other associations or individuals. It merely regulates their activities to some extent. As the whole of the life of man is not to be regulated or influenced by the state, this points to the limited rights of the state.

Rights imply duties. Rights and duties go together. One cannot exist without the other. If I have a right, the enjoyment of my right implies a duty on the part of others. Rights are real only to the extent to which they have been accepted by others as an obligation. As my right implies a duty on others, the larger the number of rights I enjoy, the greater must be the number of duties imposed on others and vice versa. I have my rights against the state, society and individuals, and hence I owe my duties to them all.

L.T. Hobhouse says, "Rights and duties, then, are conditions of social welfare, or as we define such welfare, of a life of harmony to this welfare every member of the community stands in a double relation. He has his share in it. This is the sum of his rights. He has to contribute his share. That is the sum of his duty." "Rights without duties are like men without shadows: they only exist in fairy tales."

Dr. Beni Prasad says: "Rights and duties are interdependent. They are two aspects of the same thing. If one looks at them from one's standard, they are rights. If one looks at them from the standard of others, they are duties. Both are social and both are, in substance, conditions of right living to be secured to all members of society. It is futile to consider whether rights are prior to duties or vice versa. They are counterpart of each other. If every-one insisted on his right himself, but denied is duties towards others, there would soon be no right left for any one."

The right of an individual implies his duty to exercise his right in a proper way. The object of rights is not to satisfy the whims and caprices of individuals. Rights are intended to serve some moral purpose. An individual should exercise his rights in such a way that society is not adversely affected. If that is not done by any individual, the very object of the right is forfeited. To take one example, my right to speak imposes a duty on others not to interfere with it. But I must use my right in such a way that the higher interests of society as a whole do not thereby suffer. I have no right to preach violence among the people.

Classification of Rights : Natural Rights

Rights are divided into three categories: natural rights, moral rights and legal rights. Legal rights are further subdivided into three parts: civil rights, political rights and economic rights. As regards natural rights, it is not possible to define them as different meanings have been given to them by different writers at different times. In ancient times, they implied the fundamental rights based on rationalism and universal divine law. The Jus Gentium of the Romans was based on natural rights. According to writers like Hobbes and Locke, natural rights were those which were enjoyed by the individuals in the state of nature. However, these writers differed on the question of the contents of those rights. According to Rousseau, natural rights were the ideal rights and they existed before the state came into existence. The old view with regard to natural rights is not accepted today. The only sense in which the theory of natural rights is accepted is that these are considered to be natural and essential for the individuals whether they are actually recognized or not. There are certain rights which must be recognized and guaranteed to every individual. No state can be considered to be civilized unless it guarantees these rights. Green says: "In these days, the doctrine of natural rights can be accepted only in one way. Rights are natural in the sense that they are necessary for the moral development of man in the present stage of society. They represent an attainable ideal which the state seeks to achieve." Gilchrist says: "Rights arise, therefore, from individuals as members of society and from the recognition that, for society, there is an ultimate good which may be reached by the development of the powers inherent in every individual. The consciousness of the common interests turns powers into rights: and the only proper sense in which we can speak of natural rights is as rights necessary to the ethical development of man as man."

Moral Rights

"Moral rights" are those rights which are recognised by the moral sense of the people. Their existence is due to custom, long usage and the force of public opinion. There is no sanction of the state to enforce them. While no legal action can be taken against those who violate moral rights, the force of public opinion is so strong that it is difficult for an individual to violate them. A wife has a moral right to be kindly treated by her husband. If she is not so treated, she cannot go to a court of law for the enforcement of her right but public opinion condemns such an attitude on the part of her husband.

Legal Rights

According to Dr. Leacock, a 'legal right' is "a privilege or immunity enjoyed by a citizen against any of his fellow citizens, granted by the sovereign power of the state and upheld by that state." Legal rights are recognised by the state and the police and the courts ensure their enforcement. Legal rights are embodied in the law of the country.

There are three kinds of legal rights: civil rights, political rights and economic rights. Civil rights are those rights without which civilised life is not possible. According to Dr. Beni Prasad, "A civil right is pre-eminently one which its possessor can enforce or at least ought to be able to enforce, by the help of social agencies against all who seek to violate it." A well-organised state must protect the civil rights of the people. Political rights enable citizens to have control over the administration of the country. Gettell says, "Political rights are possessed by those persons whom the state permits to share in the legal expression and administration of its sovereign powers." Civil rights find their guarantee in political rights but political rights have no significance without civil rights. Each state decides who shall enjoy political rights and the extent of those rights. All states exclude minors, criminals and lunatics from the right to vote. Only a few deny this right to women. The age of adults enjoying political rights varies from country to country. Aliens do not enjoy political rights. Gettell says that the problem of the state "in creating political rights is to secure an organisation in which legal sovereignty will coincide as nearly as possible with political sovereignty, in which as many persons as possible may possess political rights as nearly equal as possible without destroying the efficiency of government, and in general public opinion may be made into law without tyrannizing over those who hold different opinions." (*Introduction to Political Science*, p. 154).

(*a*) Civil Rights

The importance of civil rights cannot be overemphasized and every civilized state has to guarantee these rights. The most important civil right is the "right to life". It is the fundamental of all rights. Other rights are meaningless without this right. In order to safeguard this right, many states punish attempts at suicide and impose the maximum penalty of capital punishment on those who attempt to kill others. Every life is valuable from the point of view of the general welfare. Therefore, to take one's life or that of another is to eliminate "an individuality which has rights as well as duties." The view of St. Thomas Aquinas was that suicide is an offence to oneself, an offence to the community as well as an offence to God Himself. At the most, suicide can be excused but it can never be approved.

There is a demand from various quarters that the penalty of death for murders should be abolished. It is pointed out that the death penalty is merely a survival of the law of retaliation and it must not be allowed to continue in modern times. Judges are likely to make mistakes and there is a possibility of innocent persons sometimes being sent to the gallows. There is no such danger if the penalty is one of imprisonment for a long period. Great jurists like Beccaria and Bentham have advocated the abolition of death penalty. To quote Bentham, "By disusing the death penalty as a punishment, you will prevent it as a crime." The death penalty has actually been abolished in countries like Denmark, Holland, Belgium, Norway and Sweden. From the experience of these countries, it is found that situation has not deteriorated and the same can be expected if the death penalty is abolished in other countries. Experience shows that although the death penalty has been in existence for centuries, the number of murders has not gone down. Those who commit murders do not care for the consequences. Murders are committed owing to certain circumstances and it is desirable that instead of hanging people, an attempt should be made to reform them and also to remove the circumstances which were responsible for those acts. It is instructive to refer in this connection to the book entitled, *Capital Punishment in the Twentieth Century* by E. Roy Calvert. His view is that where the death penalty has been abolished, there has been a decrease in murders.

Included in the right to life is the right to self-defence. Such a right is recognised by the Indian Penal Code. If a person is in imminent danger of being murdered by another person, he has the right to murder him in self-defence. The extent to which a person can go while exercising his right of self-defence depends upon the nature of the danger facing him. The right of self-defence must not be exceeded.

Another right is the right to personal safety and freedom. Blackstone describes this right as a person's legal and uninterrupted enjoyment of his life, his limbs, his body and his health. It also means "the power of locomotion, of changing one's situation or removing one's person to whatever place one's own inclination may direct, without imprisonment or restraint, except by due course of law." A person must not be assaulted, wounded or imprisoned except by the due process of the law. He has a right not to receive injury from any dangerous substance or animal kept by another. A person who is unlawfully imprisoned can move the court to issue a writ *of habeas corpus* and thereby get himself released. A person who is injured by the careless act of another can claim compensation for damages.

Every individual must have the right to family life. This means that he should have the full liberty to marry wherever he pleases. However the sanctity of marriage has to be maintained. Both the husband and wife must be faithful to each other and there should be provision for divorce in case of infidelity by any party. Parents must have control over their children and children can claim that they must be supported by their parents during their minority. They must also have the right of inheritance to the property of their parents. The right of privacy of life must be guaranteed, Prof. R.N. Gilchrist says, "The family state is a condition of the good life, but whereas in property, the right is exercised in a thing, in the family state it is exercised over a person or persons, which implies that the individual exercising family rights must recognise that the good of others is permanently and indefeasibly bound up with his own good." (*Principles of Political Science,* p. 150).

Every individual must have the right to freedom of speech and expression. Without such a right, it is impossible for citizens to make their best contribution to the society and state. They cannot grow unless and until they are allowed to give expression to their views either by speaking or by writing in the press. It is not possible to develop a healthy public opinion in the country unless the freedom of speech and expression are guaranteed to individuals. Dr. Beni Prasad says: "Free discussion leads to the detection of errors and falsehood, paves the way for the discovery of truth, stimulates the mind and enriches personality. Freedom of expression thus ranks among the indispensable conditions of personal development and social good."

Freedom of speech is a valuable right and the successful working of democracy is not possible without such a right. Democracy is a Government by criticism, clash of ideas and the conflict of opinions and out of these emerges the truth. The criticism of the Government creates an enlightened public opinion. It is one of the ways to get grievances of the people redressed. Euripides says:

"This is true liberty, when free-born men.
Having to advise the public, may speak free,"

About the significance of freedom of expression, Prof. Laski says, "To allow a man to say what he thinks is to give his personality the only ultimate channel of full expression and his citizenship the only means of moral adequacy. To act otherwise is to favour those who support the *status quo*, and thus either drive the activities of men underground and therefore dangerous channel, or to suppress experience not less entitled than any other to interpret publicly its meaning." Laski goes to the extent of saying that a citizen has the right "to preach the complete inadequacy of the social order. He may demand its overthrow by armed revolution." Again, "It is no answer to this view to urge that it is coronation of disorder. If views which imply violence have a sufficient hold upon the state to disturb its foundations, there is something radically wrong with the habits of the state." Prof. Laski does not mind the prevalence of anarchy or chaos in the country and he prefers these to injustice and tyranny which are unworthy of human existence. The view of Laski is an extreme one and very often restrictions are imposed on such a right. Article 19 of the Constitution of India illustrates some of those limitations.

In the right of freedom of speech and expression is included the freedom of the press. A free press is essential for the successful working of democracy. It not only gives news and views but also helps in creating an enlightened public opinion. However, press should not be controlled either by the Government or by the moneyed people. It is rightly said that "democracy is a Government by talk, but when money talks, democracy degenerates into plutocracy." Milton says, "Give me the liberty to know, to utter and to argue freely, according to conscience above all liberties."

However, the right to the freedom of speech and expression does not imply the right to scandalise others. One cannot talk indiscriminately against the character of another person. The aggrieved party can start judicial proceeding against the wrong-doer and thereby get him punished. Likewise, the state cannot allow any person to make speeches or write articles or books asking the people to overthrow the government by the use of force. But this does not mean that the people do not have the right to criticise the actions of the government and demand a change. However, all the that has to be done by peaceful means. Similarly, when a case is *subsidise*, no comments are allowed to be made about it as that interferes with the course of justice.

The right to freedom of public meeting and association must be guaranteed to the people. Man is a social animal and he can live his full life only in association with others. Life has become complicated and it is difficult for individuals to safeguard their interests single-handed. No wonder, it is considered necessary that people should be allowed to form associations for the realisation of their common objective. Unity is strength and it is only these associations which can fight for the rights and interests of their members. That is the reason why the number of trade unions is increasing in every part of the world. Laski says that, voluntary associations give the individual "a feeling that he has found himself, a power of self-recognition that is an invaluable factor in the achievement of personal harmony. What, without them, is a chaotic world, becomes a world ordered by the opportunity to do with others who share an experience akin to his own." While the associations are entitled to do all that lies in their power to safeguard the interests of their members, they have no right to incite people to violence or adopt tactics which undermine the authority of the state or endanger its very existence.

Likewise, the people should be allowed to meet in public and thereby ventilate their grievances. The police should not be allowed to interfere with these meetings unnecessarily. Unless the speakers preach violence and there is an immediate danger of the breach of peace, public meetings should not be interfered with. Democracy is not possible unless the people are given the freedom to meet in public and discuss matters which concern them intimately.

Every citizen has the right to education. According to Antiphon, the Sophist, "First of all things, I place education." It is education which makes a man a good citizen. Dr. Beni Prassad says: "Education is the foremost right and its promotion is the foremost duty of all members of society. It is a part of the right to education to place full opportunities of continued education within reach of all young people. It may take any of thy numerous forms of technical education or of what is called liberal education, according to one's aptitude and inclination." However, the right to education does not imply the right to identical intellectual training for all citizens. What it implies is that every individual must be given that minimum of education which is essential for the performance of his duties. Every citizen is entitled to demand elementary education and it is only when this much has been guaranteed to every individual that provision can be made for higher education for others.

Laski syas: "In the long run, power belongs to those who can formulate and grasp ideas." They alone can do this who have received education. An uneducated person goes "through life a stunted being whose impulses have never been ordered by reason into creative experiment."

All citizens must be guaranteed freedom of religion and conscience. There must not be any interference in their religious beliefs. They should be allowed to worship in any way they please provided that is not against morality or public health. The state should be impartial in religious matters. It should not favour any particular religion. This has been provided for in Articles 25 to 28 of the Indian Constitution. Article 25 says that all persons are equally entitled to freedom of conscience and the right freely to profess, practise and propagate religion. Article 26 says that every religious denomination or any section thereof shall have the right to establish and maintain institutions for religious and charitable purposes, to manage its own affairs in matters of religion, to own and acquire movable and immovable property and to administer such property in accordance with law. Article 27 provides that no person shall be compelled to pay any taxes, the proceeds of which are specifically appropriated in payment of expenses for the promotion or maintenance of any particular religion or religious denomination. Article 28 provides that no religious instruction shall be provided in any educational institution wholly maintained out of state funds. No person attending any educational institution recognised by the state or receiving aid out of state funds shall be required to take part in any religious instruction that may be imparted in such institution or to attend any religious worship that may be conducted in such institution or in any premises attached thereto unless such person or, if such person is a minor, his guardian, has given his consent thereto. The Indian Constitution embodies the ideal of a secular state.

Every individual has a right to reputation. Holland says: "A man has a right, as against the world, to his good name; that is to say, he has a right that the respect, so far as it is well-founded, which others feel for him shall not be diminished." A defamatory statement is punishable by law if it can be proved that the statement in question was made in public, that it was untrue and was not of public importance. However, "statements in the course of judicial proceeding ..fair reports of trials, legislative debates or public meetings, fair comments on public men and fair criticisms of literary and artistic production are privileged."

Every individual must have the right to property. He should be allowed to keep to himself his earnings. Experience shows that the right to property and the growth of civilization have gone hand in hand. If a person is always worried about his immediate needs he cannot be expected to put in his very best. "The right to own private property has been given to man by nature, or rather by the Creator Himself, both in order that individuals may be able to provide for their own needs and those of their families, and also that by means of it the goods which the Creator has destined for the whole human race may truly serve this purpose."

Hobson says: "From the earliest times, the existence and sense of property, the exclusive acquisition and use of material objects that are scarce and desirable, have been important factors in the life of man. Such ownership of property has been desired and striven for, partly for pleasurable consumption, partly as a means to further acquisition of consumable goods, but also for power over beings and for the prestige that attaches to ownership and power." Many theories have been put forward to explain the origin of property and its justification.

According to the natural law theory, property is based on the principle of natural reason derived from the nature of things. Property was acquired by occupation of an ownerless object and as a result of individual labour. Grotius, Pufendorf, Locke and Blackstone are the great supporters of the theory. According to Grotius, all things originally were without an owner and whosoever captured them or occupied them, became their owners. According to Pufendorf, originally, all things belonged to the people as a whole. There was no individual ownership. By means of an agreement or a pact private ownership was established. According to Blackstone, "By the law of nature and reason, he who first began to use a thing acquired therein a kind of transient property that lasted so long as he was using it and no longer; or to speak with greater precision, the right of possession continued for the same time only that the act of possession lasted. But when mankind increased in number, craft and ambition, it became necessary to entertain conceptions of more permanent dominion and to appropriate to individuals, not the immediate use only but the very substance of the thing to be used. The theory of occupancy is the ground and foundation of all property or of holding those things in severalty by which the law of nature, unqualified by that of society, were common to all mankind."

The metaphysical theory was propounded by writers like Kant and Hegel. Kant says: "A thing is rightfully mine when I am so connected with it that anyone who uses it without my consent does me an injury. But to justify the law of property, we must go beyond cases of possession where there is an actual physical relation to the object and interference therewith is an aggression upon personality." According to Hegel, property is the objective manifestation of the free personality of an individual. To quote him, "Property makes objective my personal individual will." Property is the object on which a person has the liberty to direct his will.

According to historical theory, private property had a slow and steady growth. It has grown out of the collective group or joint property. There were many stages in the growth of individual property. The first stage was that of natural possession which existed independently of the law of the state. The second stage was the juristic possession. Juristic possession was a conception both of fact and law. The last stage of development was that of ownership. It is purely a legal conception a person having control and enjoyment of the thing owned by him. According to Sir Henry Maine, "Private property in the shape in which we know it was chiefly formed by the gradual disentanglement of the separate rights of individuals from the blended rights of the community." Again, "For many years past, there has been sufficient evidence to warrant the assertion that the oldest discoverable forms of property in land were forms of collective property and to justify the conjecture that private property had grown through a series of changes, out of collective property or ownership in common." Again, "Property originally belonged not to individuals, not even to isolated families, but to larger societies composed on the patriarchal model." It was later on that family property disintegrated and individual rights of property came into existence. According to Dean Roscoe Pound, the earliest form of property was group property. It was later on that families were partitioned and individual property came into existence.

Spencer was the propounder of the positive theory. He based his theory on the fundamental law of equal freedom. Property is the result of individual labour. No man has a moral right to property which he has not acquired by his personal effort.

According to the psychological theory, property came into existence on account of the acquisitive instinct of man. Every individual desires to own things and that brings into existence property. According to Bentham, "Property is nothing more than the basis of a certain expectation of deriving hereafter certain advantages by a thing by reason of the relation in which we stand towards it. There is no image, no visible lineament which can portray the relation that constitutes property. It belongs not to physics but to metaphysics. It is altogether a conception of mind." Again, "To hold the object in one's hand, to keep it, to manufacture it, to work it up into something else, to make use of it, all or any of these physical circumstances failed to assist in conveying the idea of property. A piece of cloth actually in the Indies may belong to me, but the coat which I have, too, may not belong to me. The very food which has mingled with my body may be the property of another to whom I must account for the price. The conception of property consists in a fixed and settled expectation; in the persuasion of my capacity to derive from the object, hereafter, certain advantages of a character dependent upon the nature of the case." According to Dean Pound, "Moreover, whatever we do, we must take account of the instinct of acquisitiveness and of individual claims grounded thereon."

According to the sociological theory, property should not be considered in terms of private rights but should be considered in terms of social functions. Property is an institution which secures a maximum of interests and satisfies the maximum of wants. According to Jenks, "The unrestricted right to use, neglect or misuse his property can no longer be granted to any individual and the rights of the property should be conformable to rules of equity and reason." According to Laski, "Property is a social fact like any other and it is the character of social facts to alter. It has assumed the most varied aspects and it is capable of yet further changes."

"Property and law were from together and would die together. Before the laws, property did not exist; take away the laws and property will be no more. That which in a state of nature is no more than a thread becomes, when society is constituted, a veritable cable."

According to Rousseau, "It was to convert possession into property and usurpation into a right that law and state were founded. The first man who enclosed a piece of land and said, 'This is mine,' was the real founder of civil society." Again, "The law of property is the systematic expression of the degree and forms of control, use and enjoyment of things by persons that are recognised and protected by law." Thus, property was the creation of the state.

The trend of legislation in recent times shows that the right to property is not so sacrosanct as it used to be before. The spread of communistic and socialistic ideas has revolutionised the modern conception of property. No wonder, even if individuals are deprived of their property by the law of the state, that is not considered extraordinary.

Another right is concerned with the general advantages of social life. By that is meant the right of a person to the unmolested pursuit of the occupation by which he gains his living, the free use of public roads, parks and libraries, the use of the posts, telegraphs and railways on payment, the right to the use of public dispensaries and hospitals and the right to avail of those communal advantages which are provided by the modern welfare state.

Every individual has the right to be provided with judicial safeguards which guarantee him his liberty. This means that justice should be done to every individual without fear or favour. Justice must not be harder upon the poor than upon the rich. Whether one is a government official or a rich person, one must not be given any privileged position before the law. The law must be the same for everyone and it must not make any distinction between the rich and the poor.

Citizens should be given the freedom of contract. All valid contracts must be respected and enforced by the state. It is well known that where there is no sanctity of contracts, there can be no progress in commerce, agriculture, industry etc. However, the state can declare illegal those transactions which are considered to be against the interests of society.

(*b*) Political Rights

The citizens must be given an opportunity to take part in the affairs of the state. No democratic government is possible without the active participation and cooperation of the citizens. The future of a country is doomed if political rights are denied to individuals. Political rights include the right to vote, the right to become members of legislatures, the right to become ministers, presidents, etc., and the right to resist the unjust actions of the state.

All citizens must have the "right to vote." The right should be given in the case of elections to local bodies, state legislations and the central legislature. It is the right of voting which enables the individuals to decide who should be given the authority to rule over them for the next few years. If they find that the persons whom they elected last time have not done their work conscientiously, they can remove them at the time of the next general elections. The greatest emphasis has to be put on the right of vote. It is this right which makes the people feel that they are the ultimate sovereign in the country. They have the authority to change their rulers. That is why it is insisted that there should be a provision for elections at certain definite intervals so that the people may have the chance to decide whether they want the old administration to continue or whether they want to change it. The introduction of the system of secret ballot enables the people to speak out their minds without any fear. Adult suffrage must be the ideal and no adult should be deprived of the right to vote on the ground of sex or any other disqualification.

The right to vote alone is not sufficient. The people must also have the right to become members of legislatures. It is well known that in the beginning of the nineteenth century, the Catholics of Ireland were given the right to vote but they were not given the right to sit in the British Parliament. The result was that they could not send to Parliament the persons whom they trusted. If the voters are forced to send to the legislature persons in whom they have no faith, the right of voting becomes meaningless. As members of the legislature, they have ample opportunities to watch and criticize the acts of omission and commission of the government. The fear of its condemnation on the floor of the house has healthy effect on the activities of the government. In countries having a parliamentary form of government, the ministers are chosen from the members of the legislature and that adds to the importance of the right of getting elected to legislatures.

The citizens should have the right to become ministers, presidents, etc. There should be no legal bar to the election of an individual as the President of India, Prime Minister of India or a minister of a state. However, certain restrictions can be imposed with regard to the age of the individual.

Every individual should have the right to resist the unjust actions of the state. He must have the right to challenge the law of the state if he considers it to be unjust and oppressive. A conscientious objector must have the right to maintain that he cannot obey a particular law of the state because it is against his conscience. However, this right should be used with caution and the people should remember that the greatest good of the greatest number demands that they should ordinarily obey the laws of the state and think of defying them only under exceptional circumstances.

Another valuable right is the right to petition. Every citizen must be given the right to send petitions either individually or collectively, to the competent authority for the redress of his or her grievances. The authority may be the executive or the legislature. In a democratic set-up, the people are the ultimate sovereign and there is no reason why they should not have the right to bring to the notice of the authorities concerned their legitimate grievances. It is also the duty of the authorities concerned to redress their grievances. No Government worth its name can afford to ignore the people who are ultimately going to decide their fate at the time of the next election. A classical example of the right to petition is the Grand Remonstrance in the history of England. The system of initiative which prevails in countries like Switzerland gives an opportunity to the people even to initiate legislation embodying their needs and aspirations.

The people also must have the right to criticise the Government. Then alone a Government can be rightly called a democratic Government. To quote Sir Stafford Cripps, "Democracy is a system of Government in which every adult citizen is equally free to express his views and desires upon all subjects in whatever way he wishes and to influence the majority of his fellow citizens to decide according to those views and to influence those desires." Prof. Laski says, "A society that is able to discuss does not need to fight and the greater the capacity to maintain interest in discussion, the less danger there is of an inability to effect the compromises that maintain social peace." John Stuart Mill also put emphasis on the importance of free and frank criticism of the policies of the Government and its day-to-day working. The right of criticism exists only in a democracy and such a thing is unheard of in a totalitarian state.

Another right is the right to get his rights enforced. It is obvious that unless and until there is a machinery to enforce the rights which the citizens claim or which are given to them by the law of the country, those rights have no meaning. Article 32 of the Constitution of India guarantees to every Indian citizen the right to move the Supreme Court of India for the enforcement of his fundamental rights. Similar powers are given to the High Courts of India under Article 226 of the Constitution. These rights can be enforced by the courts by issuing directions, orders or writs, including writs in the nature of Habeas Corpus, Mandamus, Prohibition, Quo Warranto and Certiorari. By these writs and directions, the illegal orders of the administration can be set aside. Courts can also declare laws illegal and invalid if they conflict with the fundamental rights or are otherwise against the Constitution. However, these rights are not available when a proclamation of emergency is made in the country but those rights are restored as soon as the proclamation of emergency is revoked.

(*c*) Economic Rights

It is only in recent times that the importance of economic rights has been recognised. It is felt that without these rights political and civil rights have no meaning. Life has no meaning for a person whose very existence is precarious. Economic rights are three in number: the right to work, the right to adequate wages and the right to reasonable hours of work. The importance of the "right to work" lies in the fact that it is only when a person has been given some work that he gets an opportunity to show his worth. The personality of an individual finds expression in his work. However, this does not mean that a citizen has a right to any particular kind of work. An ex-Prime Minister cannot insist that he must be given the work of a Prime Minister. The same applies to workers. The right to work merely means the right to be occupied in producing a part of those goods and commodities which are useful for society.

Every citizen must have the right to adequate wages. This does not mean that he has the right to equal wages. Such a proposition is impossible and impracticable. What this right means is that all those who work must be given sufficient wages to maintain themselves. No person should be allowed to starve when he has made his contribution to the best of his ability. The wages of a worker must be sufficient to enable him to live reasonably well. He should not have any worry regarding the support of his children.

Every citizen has right to reasonable hours of work. This means that no individual should be made to work for long hours as was the case during the nineteenth century in England and other countries as well. What is required is that every individual should be asked to put in that amount of work which does not exhaust him completely, and thereby make him unfit to fulfil his duties as a citizen. He must have some leisure to look after himself and take an interest in the affairs of his locality, the country and the world. It is rightly stated that leisure helps the individual to discover the land of the mind which is "the key to the intellectual heritage of the race."

Fundamental Rights

It is becoming common to incorporate what are considered to be fundamental rights of individuals in the Constitution of a country. Such rights are to be found in the Constitutions of India, the United States, Ireland, etc. The fundamental rights are inherent rights because they mean life itself. If a citizen is to live and not merely exist, these rights must be recognised as sacred and inviolable and fundamental to the state itself. The object of the state is to enable the people to have full lives and if the fundamental rights are denied, a full life is not possible. Any country where these rights are not honoured is described by the lovers of liberty as a "prison house." The fundamental rights are given in Part III of the Indian Constitution and they relate to the right to equality, the right to freedom, the right against exploitation, the right to freedom of religion, cultural and educational rights, the right to property and the right to constitutional remedies.

It is the sacred duty of the courts to guarantee the fundamental rights of the people and the judges consider it as a privilege to perform this nightly important job. The judges of the Supreme Court of India can take pride in the fact that they have performed their duty admirably even at the cost of personal sacrifice and inconvenience in certain cases. Mr. Justice Mathews of the Supreme Court of America observed thus in Hurtado vs. People of California: "The limitations imposed by constitutional law upon the actions of the Government, both state and national, are essential to the preservation of public and private rights notwithstanding the representative character of our political institutions. The enforcement of these limitations by judicial process is the device of self-governing communities to protect the rights of individuals and minorities, as well against the power of numbers, as against the violence of public agents transcending the limits of public authority, even when acting in the name of wielding the force of government." President Taft of America declared that the constitutional safeguards "are the self-imposed restraints of a whole people upon a majority of them to secure sober action and a respect of the rights of the minority... In order to maintain the rights of the minority and the individual and to preserve our constitutional balance, we must have judges with courage to decide against the majority when justice and law require." Regarding the fundamental rights, Prof. Laski says, "Bills of Rights are quite undoubtedly a check upon a possible excess of the Government of the day. They warn us that certain popular powers have had to be fought for, or may have to be fought for again... It (Bill of Rights) acts as a rallying point in the state for all who care deeply for the ideal of freedom." Experience shows that such fundamental rights are necessary for safeguarding the rights of the minorities.

Critics point out certain defects in the inclusion of fundamental rights in a constitution. A constitution is framed at one time and naturally the fundamental rights included in it must represent the prevailing ideas at that time. With the passage of time, the values of life change and consequently there must be a change in the fundamental rights as well. If those rights are embodied in a written constitution, it is difficult to amend them without amending the constitution which is not an easy job. The result is that the fundamental rights included in a written constitution may not serve the needs of the people of the coming generations. Moreover, there is the defect in the manner in which the courts decide their cases regarding fundamental rights. Sometimes they decide with a majority of 5 to 4 as in America or 6 to 5 or 7 to 6 as in the case of India. In spite of these shortcomings, the inclusion of fundamental rights in a constitution has been found to be of great value for safeguarding the rights of the people.

VARIOUS THEORIES OF RIGHTS

The concept of rights emerged in the modern times during the period of the Renaissance and Reformation and is associated with the theory of individualism. The Renaissance "was the greatest progressive revolution that mankind had so far experienced, a time which called for giants and produced giants – giants in power or thought, passion and character, in universality and learning". The demand for rights arose on account of the evergence of a new socio-economic and political order and it was the need of the then progressive capitalist class. Various theories of rights emerged during the different phases of the development of rights. The main theories are the theory of natural rights, legal theory of rights, historical theory of rights, social welfare theory of rights, idealist theory of rights, Laski's theory of rights and Marxist theory of rights.

Theory of Natural Rights

The theory of natural rights was very popular during the seventeenth and eighteenth centuries. This theory treated the rights of man as "self-evident truth". Those rights were not granted by the state but came from the very nature of man. The theory of natural rights is based on the liberal theory of the origin of the state from social contract. Certain rights were enjoyed by man in the state of nature, before the formation of civil society itself and those were the natural rights of man and those must be respected and protected by the state. John Locke was the strongest supporter of the theory of natural rights. His theory of social contract which established a limited constitutional government, his theory of political power as a trust in the hands of the rulers, his theory of revolution against the government which violates the trust by attacking the natural rights of man, all flow from his theory of natural rights. The view of Locke was that men were born free and came into the world with certain natural rights. Among the natural rights, Locke considers the right to life, liberty and property as the most important. Those natural rights flow from the strong desire of man for preserving his life and being. Locke gave prime importance to the right to property.

Paine (1737-1809) enunciated in his book "Rights of Man" (1791), the theory of natural rights on teleological basis. He rejected the doctrine of the social contract as it was "eternally binding and hence a clog on the wheel of progress". His view was that every generation should be free to think and act for itself. The rights to liberty, property, security and resistance to oppression derived their sanction from the natural rights "pre-existing in the individual".

The theory of natural rights of T.H. Green also invoked the teleological basis of rights. His view was that the rights of man do not emanate from a transcendental law but came from the moral character of man himself. Impelled by his moral consciousness, each individual tends to seek ideal objects. When the individuals form a state, they agree to recognise the claims of each other to pursue their ideal objects. Rights depend on recognition which depends upon the moral consciousness of the community and not the state. Green was concerned not with legal rights but with ideal rights.

The theory of natural rights inspired the American and French Revolutions. The American Declaration of Independence (1776) was in these words: "We hold these truths to be self-evident, that all men are created equal, that they are endowed by their Creator with certain inalienable Rights, that among these are Life, Liberty and pursuit of Happiness. That to secure these rights, Government are instituted among Men, deriving their just powers from the consent of the governed. That whenever any Form of Government becomes destructive of these ends, it is the Right of the People to alter or to abolish it, and to institute new Government, laying its foundation on such principles and organizing its powers in such form, as to them shall seem most likely to affect their Safety and Happiness".

The French Declaration of the Rights of Man and of the Citizen (1789) expressed similar ideas. Men are born and remain free and equal in rights. Social distinctions can be based only upon public utility. The aim of every political association is the preservation of natural and imprescriptible rights of man. Those rights are liberty, property, security and resistance to oppression.

The Virginian Constitution declares: "That all men are by nature equally free and independent, and have certain inherent rights, of which, when they enter into a state of society, they cannot by any compact deprive or divest their posterity; namely, the enjoyment of life and liberty, with the means of acquiring and possessing property, and pursuing, and obtaining happiness and safety."

In spite of the historical significance of the theory of natural rights, there is a lot of criticism. Critics point out that it is very difficult, if not impossible, to define the term natural. Ritchie has written a whole volume on natural rights and he has brought out clearly the various senses in which the term has been used. Some of the meanings assigned to the term are the whole universe, or the non-human part of the universe, or the ideal, the original, the normal or the average. As the terms nature and natural are indefinite and are used rather loosely, we are not surprised to find that among the supporters of the theory of natural rights, there is an ambiguity as to what these rights mean. There is no official or complete or generally agreed upon list of natural rights. Some justify slavery as natural and others condemn it as being unnatural and artificial. Some assert that men and women by nature are equal but others deny it. Some hold that men are naturally good, but others believe that by nature they are wicked. Some regard private property as a natural right, but others deny it completely and recommend social ownership of property.

Hocking says that it is natural for human beings to be artificial. Wearing clothes which was artificial at one time is natural today. If natural means the whole process of nature, the civilised condition is just as natural as the savage or barbarous condition. There is no reason in equating natural with primitive. In order to be natural Diogenes lived in tub but we live in houses. The civil state is as natural as a pre-civil state.

Another criticism is that natural rights conflict with one another. The French Revolution declared liberty, equality and fraternity to be the absolute rights of men. They are supposed to be self-evident truths. However, when we apply them in practice, we are faced with endless difficulties. In no rational system there can be a place for absolute liberty because in a regime of absolute liberty, we soon get inequality. If we start with absolute equality, liberty soon vanishes. If property belongs to all as is assumed by the supporters of the theory of natural rights, we must know what that right implies. If it implies private property, the question arises whether it includes the right to dispose of one's property as one wills. The right to do exactly what one wills to do with one's own property, may cause harm to society.

Another defect in this theory is that it assumes that we can have rights and obligations independent of society, but that is not correct. We have rights only as members of society. Apart from society, we may have powers but not rights. Rights arise from the fact that man is a social being. Dr. Bosanquet writes, "A right is a claim recognised by society and enforced by the state".

According to the theory of natural rights, the state and social institutions in general are artificial. They have robbed man of certain inherent rights which belonged to him in a state of nature. The logical conclusion to which the theory of natural rights leads is extreme individualism. This theory can be used both by the anarchists and conservatives. The defect in the theory is that it assumes that we can have rights and obligations independent of society. That is wholly incorrect. We have rights only as members of society and not otherwise. Rights antecedent to society are meaningless as there can be no right without a co-relative duty.

The supporters of this theory are hostile to the state and maintain that rights are pre-political. The legal theory of rights shows that without the protection of laws, enforcement by courts and guarantee by the constitution, rights are futile. Rights cannot be enjoyed in a vacuum. There must be some authority to protect and enforce them.

Most of the advocates of natural rights do not accept the logical relationship between rights and duties. The fact is that without duties, there cannot be any rights.

In spite of its shortcomings, the theory of natural rights played an important role against the absolutism represented by kings, the Papacy and feudalism. It was a dynamic battle-cry of the rising middle class against the static socio-economic and political order of the seventeenth and eighteenth centuries. This theory gave rise to many valuable democratic principles like the doctrine of consent, power as trust, limited government and the right of resistance against the government. Although the theory of natural rights has been rejected in our times, its spirit still exerts considerable influence.

The Legal Theory of Rights

According to this theory, all rights of men depend on the state for their existence. There can be no right in the proper sense of the term unless it is so recognised by the state. There are no absolute rights. There are no rights inherent in the nature of man as such. Rights are relative to the law of the land and they vary with time and space. Rights have no substance until they are guaranteed by the state. There were no rights prior to the sate and they came into existence with the state itself. It is the state which declares the law and thereby guarantees and enforces rights. There can be no rights beyond the legal frame-work provided by the state. As law may change from time to time, the substance of rights will also change. There can be no fixed rights in any society, no to speak of eternal or universal rights.

Hobbes was the first to propound the legal theory of rights. He established the relation between rights and authority and maintained that without authority, there could be no rights at all. This theory was fully developed by Bentham, Austin, Ritchie and Salmond. Bentham was the greatest champion of the legal theory of rights. He rejected the theory of natural rights as unreal and ill-founded. In his "Principles of Legislation (1789)", Bentham writes, "Rights, properly so-called, are the creatures of law properly so called; real laws, give birth to real rights. Natural rights are the creatures of natural law; they are a metaphor which derives its origin from another metaphor...What there is natural in man is means – faculties. But to call these means, these faculties, natural rights is again to put language in opposition to itself. For rights are established to insure the exercise of means and faculties. The right is the guarantee; the faculty is the thing guaranteed. How can we understand each other with a language which confounds under the same term things so different?"

The view of Bentham was that natural rights were an invention of fanatics who were dogmatic and unintelligible and without reason. To quote him, "Instead of examining laws by their effects, instead of judging them as good or as bad, they considered them in relation to these pretended natural rights; that is to say, they substitute for reasoning of experience the chimeras of their own imagination."

According to Bentham, "Rights are the fruits of law and of the law alone. There are no rights without law – no rights contrary to law — no rights anterior to the law". Rights are not natural. They are in the form of demands from society and individuals living in society, which get recognition through the laws.

Barker writes, "Law contains rights and indeed is right. Law and rights are simply two aspects of something which is essentially one". Ritchie observes, "Legal right is the claim of an individual upon others recognised by the state." The rights are the demands of an individent against society and the other individuals living in society. Those rights must get recognition through the law of the state. Without that recognition by laws and protection of the state, rights have no existence of their own.

The legal theory of rights entrusts three functions to the state with regard to rights. The first function is to determine the rights. The second function is to define the scope of rights. The third function is to remove hindrances which come in the way of the fulfilment of rights. However, this theory does not maintain that rights are the creation of the state and depend upon the state. It simply maintains that rights are no rights without proper recognition and protection by the state.

Prof. Laski has criticised the legal theory of rights in these words, "So purely legalistic a view has nothing to contribute to an adequate political philosophy. A legal theory of rights will tell us what in fact the character of a State is; it will not tell us, save by the judgment we express upon some particular State, whether the rights there recognized are the rights which need recognition" (*A Grammar of Politics,* p. 91).

The legal theory of rights takes account of the factual position only. It takes note of what rights are legally recognised and guaranteed in a particular state. Political philosophy would like to inquire what rights must be guaranteed by the state according to the community's concept of justice. Political theory is interested to know what rights of man are essential for the fulfilment of the social purpose or human personality.

The view of Spencer is that the state does not create rights. It exists in order to maintain rights. N. Wilde writes, "The law does not create our rights, but only recognises them and protects them. The rights themselves exist whether they are thus legalised or not. They are enforced because they are rights and not rights because they are enforced."

What makes a claim a right is not the fact that it is recognised by law, but that it is morally justifiable. A typical right should combine legal and moral recognition. To say that the state is the sole creator of rights is to make it absolute which is not desirable. Technically, the sovereignty of the state is supreme, but there are certain practical limitations imposed upon it by customs, traditions, history and morality. Law is often determined by the customary rules of the community. In very many cases, justice follows customs. Hence, to argue that all rights are derived from law is a simplification.

Another defect with the legal theory of rights is that it does not cover the whole scope of rights. Whether rights are derived from history, customs or laws, they all require a moral basis. The legal theory of rights does not enable us to decide whether the rights that are recognised are rights which ought to be recognised.

In spite of its shortcomings, the legal theory of rights cannot be dismissed lightly. We are not prepared to go to the extent of saying that rights are possible apart from the state. Claims which are essential for the moral development of man but which are violated or ignored by the state, can at best be only potential rights. They are the raw material or ground of rights. The are not full-fledged rights. In a democratic country, all rights should win legal recognition. A right should have both a legal and a moral aspect. According to T.H. Green, a right has both a legal and moral reference.

Historical Theory of Rights

According to this theory, rights are a product of long historical evolution of society and are based on traditions and customs. With the change in time and circumstances, rights also change. Rights are the crystallisation of customs and traditions. This theory originated in the eighteenth century conservative political thought. Its upholders defended evolutionary changes and condemned revolutionary changes. At best, they supported a revolution inspired by the established order of society.

An emphatic assertion of this theory is to be found in the writings of Edmund, Burke (1729-1797) who is considered to be the greatest champion of the historical theory of rights. According to him, political institutions form a vast and complicated system of prescriptive rights and customary observations. Those practices grow out of the past and adapt themselves with the present without any break in the continuity. The tradition of the constitution and the society at large ought to be the objects of reverence similar to religion because it forms the repository of collective wisdom and intelligence of a particular civilisation. Burke criticised the French Revolution as being an injudicious exercise in the direction of a struggle for liberty, equality and fraternity but praised the Glorious Revolution of 1688 as a re-assertion of the centuries-old rights of the Englishmen. The supporters of the historical theory of rights were Savigny (1779-1861), Sir Henry Maine (1822-1888), Ranke and Burgess. Those writers were jurists who raised their voice of protest against the natural law theorists and the positive law school represented by Bentham and Austin.

According to this theory, rights are the result of historical evolution. While in modern state, rights are recognised and supported by law, in ancient times, rights were based on custom and usage. In course of ages, human beings evolved certain usages, traditions and customs for the common good and those became the basis of rights of individuals.

This theory is correct to the extent that several rights arose as a result of historical evolution. When the state was evolved, human beings must have had some certain customs and traditions which provided a basis for the written law of the state. However, it cannot be accepted that all rights are the result of well-established customs. Only some rights are the result of historical evolution. Certain rights are created by law and they do not have history as a source of their origin. All products of history are not regarded as rights or continued as rights. Slavery was a recognised institution in Greece, but today no state supports slavery as a right. Likewise, the customs of Sati, Devdasi and untouchability are not recognised as rights today as those were based on injustice and oppression. The state had to ban those customs in order to ensure that rights became the vehicles of justice and not of tyranny. Hocking writes, "History cannot be ignored, but history cannot be relied on alone". (*Law and Rights,* p.7).

The Idealist Theory of Rights

According to the Idealist or personality theory of rights, human beings need congenial external conditions for the development of their personalities and those conditions are created by the state. The theory links rights with the moral development of man and looks at rights essentially from the ethical point of view. Without these conditions, it is not possible for the individual to live and realise his full stature. These opportunities are rights to be enjoyed by the individual in society. Those rights are to be understood in a social context. Rights are linked with the individual good and the common good of all.

Moderate idealists like Kant and Green speak not in terms of the growth of individual personality alone, but also in terms of the common good. Conditions for the ethical and moral development of man are created by the state. According to Green, human consciousness postulates liberty, liberty involves rights and rights demand the state. According to Bosanquet, rights are the conditions for the realisation of the end of the state. They are the claims recognised by the state. The view of Krause, Henrici and Wilde is that without rights man cannot become his best self.

The idealist theory looks at rights from a highly moral point of view. Rights are rooted in the mind of man, They are powers granted to him by the community so that he alongwith others may realise a common good of which his good is an intrinsic part. According to Wilde, a right "is a freedom of action possessed by a man by virtue of his occupying a certain place and fulfilling a certain function in a social order." (*The Ethical Basis of the State,* p. 12).

Critics point out that there are certain defects in the theory. It is vague and objective standards cannot be applied. Just as the greatest happiness of the greatest number as expounded by the Utilitarians cannot be measured, the conditions supposed to be aiming at the moral perfection of the individual cannot be assessed. Extreme idealists do great harm to the liberty of the individual by asking him to obey the state implicitly. The idealist view is too abstract to be easily understood by an average man. The idea of moral development is abstract and it is difficult for the state to judge the conditions which are conducive to the best possible development of the personality of the individuals. The very idea of personality is subjective and no generally acceptable list of rights can be drawn on the basis of this theory. This theory sacrifices social good for the sake of individual good. The view of Dr. Asirvatham is that the idealist theory of rights "furnishes a safe test of rights which can be applied at all times, and herein it is superior to the legal, historical and social welfare theories. The one absolute right of all human beings is the right of personality". (*Political Theory,* pp. 175-76)

Social Welfare Theory of Rights

According to this theory, rights are created by society and they aim at realising social welfare. The conditions which make the individual and society happy are rights and those should have precedence over customs, usages, traditions and natural rights. This theory looks at rights solely through the angle of social welfare.

The main contention of this theory is that the rights of individuals are limited by social welfare. No individual can be given rights against the welfare of society. Rights are not given to anti-social individuals. They are always restricted in the interests of society. Individuals are given rights so that they may contribute to the common good. An individual who does not perform his social functions, cannot claim any right. This theory emphasises social character of rights. It is based on the demands of social justice and values of social welfare. The great protagonists of this theory are Roscoe Pound, Chafee and Laski.

Critics point out certain shortcomings in this theory. The maxim of social welfare is highly ambiguous. In actual practice, it may mean different things to different persons. If carried to extreme, the point of individual welfare may be lost as it seeks to sacrifice individual good at the altar of social welfare. N. Wilde is of the view that if rights are created by the consideration of social expediency, the individual is without an appeal and is helplessly dependent upon its arbitrary will.

In the name of social welfare, governments are arming themselves with excessive powers which result in the erosion of the rights of the individual. Social welfare can be made convenient excuse for trampling upon the rights of the individual. In the name of social welfare, the Parliament and State Legislatures in India have passed many laws eroding the fundamental rights of the individual.

However, the essential merit of this theory lies in its linking up the idealistic version of rights with its utilitarian counter-part and thereby makes it a commendable affair so far as the liberal political theory is concerned. Rights are not only related to the essential condition of social welfare, they are also given a dynamic character.

Laski's Theory of Rights

Laski's theory of rights is given in a number of his works such as "Liberty in the Modern State", "The Dilemma or Our times", "Reflections on the Revolution of Our Time", "Democracy in Crisis", "The State in Theory and Practice" and "A Grammar of Politics". Laski refuses to accept the historical theory, the legal theory and the theory of natural rights. He does not accept the view that rights are a power to satisfy the personal desires of an individual. Rights are those conditions of social life without which no man can seek, in general, to be at his best. Laski takes a dynamic view of rights which means that rights change with time and circumstances. Rights are given to the individual. "We build rights upon individual personality because ultimately the welfare of the community is built upon the happiness of the individuals". Again, "Any social order which fails consistently to recognise the claims of personality is built upon a foundation of sand".

Laski correlates the rights with duties and functions. No individual can have any right without performing his duties and functions in society. If an individual has a right to life, it is also his duty that he should not take the life of an other. If we have a right to education, there is a corresponding duty that we must educate and enlighten others and contribute to the well-being of society. "I should realise that the rights I have are given to me because I am performing some given duties. He that will not perform functions cannot enjoy right any more than he who will not work ought to enjoy bread." Rights are correlative with functions and function is implicit in rights. Rights are based on the principle of give and take. One cannot enjoy rights while forgetting one's duties. Laski was critical both of liberal capitalist social system and socialist societies for the denial of personal and political rights, especially the right to criticise. Laski denounced Fascist states for denying rights and equalities. Laski was a champion of equality. He had firm faith in the equality of rights. By their very nature, rights must be equal. Rights are valuable to all members of the state. Rights at a minimum basis are identical.

According to Laski, "Every state is known by the rights that it maintains... They are not rights merely by reason of the authority from which they emanate.. The state, briefly, does not create, but recognises, rights and its character will be apparent from the rights that, at any given period, secure recognition." Rights are not at the mercy of the state. The state is merely the servant of rights and not their master. Rights are prior to the state and it has merely to recognise and serve them. The moral basis of the authority of the state is the protection of rights by it. The state exists to make possible the achievement of rights. Rights are the claims of the citizen upon the state. The state must give those conditions to citizens in which they may develop their personality. The state must provide meaning to the rights by removing hindrances in the realisation of those rights by citizens. It citizens have a right to life, the state must provide security to life by maintaining law and order and peace. It citizens have a right to equality, the state must remove socio-economic and political inequalities.

Laski was seriously concerned with the satisfaction of the material needs of the people. He was ahead of T.H. Green in dealing with the maladies of the capitalist system. His view was that rights are not concessions by the state. They are superior to the state because they provide for a standard to judge the state itself. Rights are not historical in the sense that they have at some time won their recognition. They are historical in the sense that they are demanded by a society at a certain level of its development. Rights are not natural in the sense that they can be compiled into a permanent and unchanging catalogue. They are natural in the sense that they must demand their recognition according to the level of development of society. The contents of rights change with time and place.

The moral basis of rights postulates equal treatment of all citizens in the matter of securing their rights. The state must postulate the equal claims of its citizens to the benefits which accrue from the exercise of power. Laski was in favour of a differentiation of rights according to functions provided the elementary needs of each individual were satisfied. Laski drew a distinction between the state and the community. A person may have rights against the state but not against the community. The moral authority of the state to claim allegiance is based on its devotion to common good and its recognition of the claims of personality.

According to Laski, rights are not the creature of law but the ideal objects of law itself. To quote Laski, "A State...exists, it exerts authority, it claims allegiance, in order that those citizens may realize in their lives the best of which they are capable. To that end they have rights....Obviously, therefore, rights are not the creatures of law, but its condition precedent. They are that which law is seeking to realize. Institutions are, then, bad or good in proportion as they fail or succeed in the promotion of the purpose of rights."

According to Laski, rights are not the creature of law but the ideal objects of law itself. To quote him, "State....exists, it exerts authority, it claims allegiance, in order that those citizens may realize in their lives the best of which they are capable. To that end they have rights....Obviously, therefore, rights are not the creatures of law, but its conditions precedent. They are that which law is seeking to realize. Institutions are, then, bad or good in proportion as they fail or succeed in the promotion of the purpose of rights."

As rights are erected on moral foundations, they are accompanied by duties. To quote Laski, "The possession of rights does not mean the possession of claims that are empty of all duties...Our rights are not independent of society, but inherent in it. To provide for me the conditions which enable me to be my best self is to oblige me at the same time to seek to be my best self. To protect me against attack from others is to imply that I myself will desist from attacking others". Rights are correlated with duties or function. A man is entitled to rights to enable him to make his contribution to the social good.

As the rights of man are subservient to common good, it is his duty to contribute to the common good in the exercise of his rights. To quote Laski, "Men must learn to subordinate their self-interest to the common welfare. The privileges of some must give way before the rights of all." Where a society is divided into privileged and unprivileged classes, there can be no rights and duties.

Laski has recommended the recognition of certain rights. According to him, the right to work is the most important as it is associated with his idea of social functions and rights of the individual. To quote Laski, "The citizen has a right to work....To leave him without access to the means of existence is to deprive him of that which makes possible the realisation of personality." Those who are unemployed must be paid unemployment allowance by the state.

Every individual must be paid adequate wages so that he may have a minimum standard of living without which creative citizenship is impossible. Laski did not stand for equality of incomes. To quote him, "The right to an adequate wage does not imply equality of income; but it does imply that there must be sufficiency for all before there is superfluity for some". The view of Laski was that with an enormous increase in production and abundance in society, the minimum claims of everybody could be easily satisfied. The only difficulty was the profit-oriented nature of the industrial system. Laski recommended that the state must controlled industrial system. To quote him, "Either the state must control the industrial power in the interest of its citizens, or industrial power will control the state in the interests of its possessors". The wages of the workers must not be left to the mercy of free contract. The state must make laws like the Minimum Wages Act.

Every individual must have the right to reasonable hours of work as leisure is very important for recreational activities. An individual should not be asked to work for more than eight hours a day.

Every worker must be given a right to participate in the management of the affairs of his establishment.

Every citizen has the right to such education as will fit him for the task of citizenship. Education makes a man worthy of taking part in the social and political affairs of the state. A citizen who lacks education, is bound to be the slave of others.

Every individual must have the right to political power. He must have an opportunity to share in political power. This right includes the right to vote as well as the right to be chosen for political office.

The right to freedom of speech and expression must be given to every individual. Every individual must have the right to criticise the government. To quote Laski, "A Government can always learn more from the criticism of its opponents than from the eulogy of its supporters". This right is beneficial not only to individuals but also to the government. This right demands that the government should not have the powers of censorship. Even in the time of war, the right to freedom of speech cannot be taken away. To quote Laski, "Freedom of speech is a right that war does not mitigate."

Laski insisted that every individual must have the right to freedom of association and public meeting. He should have the right to form an association with like-minded persons and also have a right to public meetings.

Laski stood for a limited right to property. The right to property must be subordinated to the maintenance of common welfare. This right loses its moral justification the moment it becomes an instrument of power over others. Laski evolved a synthesis of individual rights with common welfare.

In order to safeguard the above-mentioned rights, he suggested the rule of law, separation of powers, independence of the judiciary, written constitution and limited government. However, he felt that those safeguards were not sufficient in the changed circumstances of the twentieth century. His recommendation was that the state must be a decentralised state. The Central Government must be surrounded with the "bodies it is compelled to consult". The state should not be given any "authority to intervene in the internal life of other associations".

Laski's theory of rights takes into consideration three essential aspects: the interests of the individual, the interests of the various groups through which his personality finds expression and the interests of the community. The individuals cannot be allowed to define their own rights by conflict. The state can resolve their conflicts and regulate the behaviour of individuals and groups by common rules.

Laski attempted a fusion of the liberal-individualist, liberal-pluralist and liberal-socialist theories. He tried to fit liberty and equality in a common scheme. His view was that the existing liberal capitalist system could somehow be remodelled to secure the ends of social justice. He presented elaborate plans for the de-centralisation and democratization of power.

The Marxist Theory of Rights

The approach of Marx, Engels and Lenin towards the question of rights was dialectical. They welcomed the existence of civil and political rights in the contemporary bourgeois-democratic state because they represented an advance from the condition of man in a state based on slavery or feudalism. The prevailing rights enabled the working class to organise themselves and raise their demands for their betterment in a legal manner. Marx also felt that in a class-divided society, though rights were granted in general terms, only the members of the ruling class could take advantage of them. The result was that the existing rights were the special privileges of the ruling class.

As the Editor of the Rheinixhe Zeitung, Marx wrote many articles defending the freedom of the press but criticised the law of censorship imposed by the state. He pointed out that under censorship, only the underground writings were free and the people became accustomed to regard what was lawless as tree, freedom as lawless and what was lawful as unfree. According to Marx, censorship killed the very spirit of freedom and rights and hence he advocated a press law which guaranteed freedom of expression and made the press answerable only for libel and that also only after publication.

Marx recognised the fact that the main advantage of the civil liberties would go to the capitalist who had a lot of money to publish newspapers and control the press. In spite of that he felt that spokesmen of the proletariat like him also could use the freedom of the press to advocate communist ideas which promoted the class struggle of the workers. Engels had similar views about political rights such as the right to vote. Though the capitalists benefited most under bourgeois democracy, yet universal suffrage was also a demand of the working class. He praised the Chartist movement for demanding manhood suffrage in England.

Marx pointed out that the French Republic set up after the February Revolution of 1848 proclaimed the rights of men and declared them to be absolute rights. However, in the marginal note in the constitution, it was mentioned that those rights could be limited by the needs of public security or security of the state or by laws which were intended to bring about harmony between different types of rights.

According to the Marxist theory, the rights guaranteed by a liberal constitution really safeguarded the interests of the bourgeois class. The most important right guaranteed was the right to acquire and accumulate unlimited property. The majority of the people who were wage workers were denied the right to work and gainful employment. The rights of the proletariat could be protected only by a socialist constitution. The view of Marx was that the Paris Commune was the first example of a workers' state. It was based on full civil liberty for the toiling masses. Elections were held on the basis of universal adult suffrage. It also recognised the right to vote. Lenin also proclaimed the rights of the proletariat in the first Soviet Constitution.

The Marxist theory does not accept the atomised and alienated view of man as a possessive individual or a creature concerned only with his self-respect. Marxism believes in the self-creative nature of man. It views man "as a self-creating being: that is to say, a being who develops the capacities peculiar to his species as he lives and works with his fellows, and who in this process acquires his ideas of the world and of himself." Marx believes in man's unique powers of self-fulfilment.

The Marxist view of rights is that those are not enjoyed by man as an alienated being. Those are enjoyed by people as a part and parcel of society. Rights are granted by society which also creates the conditions for their fulfilment. Rights have a social character. In order to be real, the conditions of their realisation must be provided by society. Man is a social creature and his essence is the totality of social relations. Rights are not given to individuals but to social man. For Marxism, an isolated individual is a mere fiction. Marxism rejects social atomism. In a Marxist society, the free development of each is the condition for the free development of all. In a Marxist society, rights are not acquired, but only the conditions for self-fulfilment are needed. There is no exploitation in such a society.

The Marxist view that each will get according to his contribution, shows that rights and duties are closely associated with each other. One who does not contribute anything, will not get anything. One who does not work will not get bread. Duties are the social responsibilities of man. Marx stipulated no rights without duties and no duties without rights.

Marxism associated rights with classes. Rights emerge in specific historical circumstances on account of class struggle and in a class-divided society. Rights cannot be viewed in isolation from the economic system of a given society. If there are two classes in a society — capitalists and working class—then rights will have meaning only for one class and for the other class these will be a mere illusion. If ownership of the means of production is in the hands of the capitalist class, rights also belong to that class. In a society based on economic inequality, equality may be a cherished dream but it will be missing in reality. The right of equality has to be sacrificed for the necessity of survival. The purchaser of one's labour also purchases the right to equality of the seller.

When the socialist system was established in the USSR in 1917 under Lenin, he took care to secure the social and economic rights of the citizens substantially. The latest Soviet Constitution of 1977 has substantially enlarged those rights. The citizens of the Soviet Union are guaranteed equality before law and equal rights in all fields of economic, political, social and cultural life. They are entitled to the right to work which implies guaranteed employment and pay in accordance with the quantity and quality of work. They have the right to rest and leisure, the right to health protection and social security, including the right to maintenance in old age, in sickness and in the event of complete or partial disability or loss of the bread winner. They have the right to housing, right to education, right to enjoy cultural' freedoms — freedom of scientific, technical and artistic work in accordance with the aims of building communism. They are entitled to freedom of speech, of the press and of assembly, meetings, street processions and demonstrations, in accordance with the interests of the people and in order to strengthen and develop the socialist system. They have the right to associate in public organisations in accordance with the aims of building communism. They also have the right to profess or not to profess any religion and to conduct any religious worship etc.

The critics of the Soviet system strongly criticise the suppression of opinion and protest. The new rights granted to the citizens are merely conditional so that communism reigns supreme.

How to safeguard Rights

There is a difference of opinion regarding the best method of guaranteeing rights to individuals. The view of one school of thought is that the easiest method of protecting the rights is to embody them in a written constitution. Since they are a part of the constitution and the constitution is going to be enforced, the rights are also automatically enforced. So long as a constitution remains operative, rights also remain safe. The courts, while punishing those who violate the constitution, incidentally safeguard the rights of the people also. However, experience does not support this view. It has been found that the embodiment of rights in a written constitution is no guarantee that rights will remain secure even in times of national emergency and periods of storm and streets.

Laski rightly says: "Rights are not merely, or even greatly a matter of the written record. Musty parchments will doubtless give them greater sanctity; they will not ensure their realization." The first amendment of the American Constitution legally secures freedom of speech and right of peaceful assembly. The fourth Amendment guarantees to the citizens that their houses will not be searched except upon a warrant of probable cause. The eighth Amendment protects them against the tyranny of excessive bail. But in spite of all these provisions, in one hysterical week, the action of the American executive rendered all these amendments worthless. A study of the "deportations delirium" will give one an idea as to how the liberty of the American people was encroached upon during World War I. The fifteenth Amendment of the American Constitution gave political equality to all coloured citizens of the south but this was never applied by the executive or the courts. The example of France shows that the maintenance of rights is much more a question of habits and traditions than the formality of a written enactment. It is well known that Dr. Preuss, the author of the Weimar Constitution of 1919, collected together and put into the German Constitution a long list of the rights which seemed to be desirable to him for enjoyment by all and sundry. However, the working of the administrative machinery in Germany under Hitler shows that the mere embodiment of rights in the constitution is no guarantee that they will be protected. During the supremacy of Hitler, the German Government was able to ride roughshod over the liberties of the individuals.

The view of Locke and Montesquieu was that the liberty of the people could be secured only if there was separation of powers. Experience shows that the mere separation of the three departments of the government, *viz.*, the legislature, the executive and the judiciary, is not enough for the safeguarding of rights. The rights of the people have been safeguarded even in some countries where there is no separation of powers. This does not mean that the independence of the judiciary does not help a lot in safeguarding the rights of the individuals.

Probably, stronger and more effective public opinion is a better safeguard for the guaranteeing of rights than any other method. If the people are awakened to the importance of rights which have either been given to them or which have been wrested from the government by them, they will not tolerate their infringement by any authority, however great it may be. The people will always be vigilant about their rights. They will not tolerate the least infringement. Lord Bryce was not wrong when he said that eternal vigilance is the price of liberty. If the people cherish their rights and are prepared to go to the length of even fighting against the authority which attempts to invade them, rights are bound to be protected. The history of England corroborates this point of view. The people of England did not hesitate to execute a king like Charles I or turn out a king like James II or Richard II or Edward II when they found that they were invading their rights. The speeches made by Pym and Hampden on the eve of the Civil War in the time of Charles I show the spirit which is necessary to protect the rights of the people. No wonder, it is maintained that the best guarantee for safeguarding the rights of the people is a strong public opinion.

Prof. Laski tells us that three are three general conditions which facilitate the task of guaranteeing rights to the people. The first condition is that the state must be a decentralized one. In such a state, the people are bound to take more interest in those problems which affect them intimately. As the authority functions before their eyes, any infringement of any law is noticed by the people and they come to take more interest in the affairs of the state. As people come to learn to take to task the local authority for the neglect of its local duties, they also cultivate the habit of questioning the authority of the state whenever it violates the laws of the country. A sense of responsibility can be created among the people through the exercise of power. The concentration of all power at one place is bound to create a sense of irresponsibility. The second general condition is that the central government should be surrounded by consultative bodies. To every department should be attached a group of experts of the line whose duty is to advise the department regarding the problems facing it. The object is to enable the consultative bodies to put forward their own points of view for consideration. The state should also refrain from interfering, in the internal lives of the people and the associations which they join. The associations must be allowed full opportunity to chalk out their own programmes and act accordingly. For example, if a trade union chooses to devote its funds to maintain its members in the legislatures, it is no business of the state to interfere. The state should not intervene so long as an association does not openly advocate the use of force for its overthrow.

Duties of Citizens

People have been clamouring for rights, They have led revolutions to get then, recognised if they found it impossible to attain them through peaceful means. It is only in recent times that emphasis has been put on the duties of citizens. It is realised that unless and until the people are prepared to perform their duties, it is idle for them to expect any rights from society. The Soviet Constitution of 1936 specifically lays down certain duties which the citizens of that country have to perform. It is stated there that it is the duty of every citizen to abide by the state Constitution, to observe the laws, to maintain labour discipline, to perform public duties honestly and to respect the rules of socialist intercourse. It is the duty of every citizen to safeguard and fortify public, socialist property. To defend the country is the sacred duty of the citizen. Treason to the Motherland is punishable with all the severity of law. Work is not only a duty but a matter of honour for all able-bodied persons. The Constitution expressly says that he who does not work shall not eat.

The following are the duties which citizens in general are required to perform in modern society. Every citizen owes a duty to himself to maintain good health. It cannot be denied that without physical fitness, he cannot make his full contribution to society. A sickly person is a burden to society. There is every likelihood of his ignoring all those duties which he must perform in the interest of his family, locality and the country. The importance of a sound mind in a sound body must be emphasised. If every individual is fit physically, mentally and morally, society is bound to achieve a lot.

Every citizen owes certain duties to the members of his family. If he is a married man, he must look after his wife and children. He must give his children the very best education. He must aim at making them ideal citizens of whom be himself and his country can be proud. That citizen is a criminal who indulges in the luxury of having children but ignores their proper training. It is the duty of society to look down upon such a person and make him realise that he is an object of contempt and not respect.

Every citizen owes certain duties to his neighbours. He must not hate them but love them. He must be always willing to extend his hand of cooperation to them. He must try to share their worries and joys. His relations with his neighbours can add to his happiness.

A good citizen must not be contented with his own progress, the progress of his family and that of his immediate neighbours. He must look to the welfare of the locality in which he lives. A person who cannot love the people of the state in which he was born and brought up and in which he has the privilege to live, cannot be expected to love the people of his country living in far off states. However, love for the locality must not go to such an extent that the interests of the country as a whole are sacrificed. In the ultimate analysis, the country must come first. It must not be forgotten that if the country goes down, there is no hope for the prosperity of any individual, family, state or province.

Every individual owes certain duties towards the state. He owes his allegiance to the state in which he lives and that allegiance must be paramount. It is true that an individual owes certain duties towards his family, religion, province and certain associations, but his duty towards the state stands above all other duties. Whenever there is a conflict of loyalties, the state must be given the first place. It is the neglect of this principle in India which has been responsible for our humiliations in the past and if we neglect it in the future, we are bound to come to grief. Under the circumstances, it is the duty of every citizen to put the state first in the order of loyalties.

It is the duty of every citizen to obey the laws of the country. Every effort should be made to inculcate the habit of law-abidingness. Everybody should consider it his duty to obey the laws of the country. This does not mean that we cannot criticise any law of the country. The sovereignty of India rests with the people of India and consequently they have the right to demand a change in a particular law. They can agitate for this in a constitutional manner. However, so long as the law remains on the statute book, it is the duty of all citizens to obey it. The officers of the government must not take pleasure in humiliating and dishonouring people when they are trying to disobey an unjust law. Every effort should be made to remove the sting from the law so that it may become convenient for the people to obey it.

All citizens must pay taxes to the state according to their capacity. A democratic government is the most expensive form of government, and no wonder, there is need for a lot of money to run the machinery of the government in such a way as to add to the good of society as a whole. If the people want to have the pleasure of having a government of their own, they must also bear the duty of paying more taxes.

Every good citizen must be public-spirited. He must be happy and proud to help every member of his country to the best of his ability and capacity. It is only by the spirit of self-sacrifice that nations grow. One must subordinate one's interests to those of others and do all that lies in one's power to promote the welfare of society. We require in this country lakhs of public spirited boys and girls and men and women who think and dream in terms of India and who are prepared to sacrifice their all for their country.

Every citizen owes a duty to make an honest exercise of his right to vote. He should vote only for that person who is going to work for the good of society and not for his personal and selfish ends. It must be remembered that the successful working of democracy depends upon the honest exercise of the right of vote by every individual. A country is bound to be doomed where the voters are dishonest and corrupt. If a voter accepts money at the time of voting, he should realise that by doing so, he is not only digging his own grave and that of his family but also mortgaging the future of his country. Democracy works well only if the people are wide awake and realise that, by making an intelligent use of their vote, they can set up a system of government which can bring about the happiness and strength of the country and the people at large. To quote Root, "Of course, voting is a fundamental and essential part of the qualified citizen's duty to the government of his country. A man who does not think it worthwhile to exercise his right to vote for public offices and on such public questions as are submitted to the voters is strangely ignorant of the real basis of all the prosperity that he has or hopes for and the real duty which rests upon him as a man of elementary morals."

A good citizen owes a duty to help the public officials in the performance of their duties. It is provided in the Code of Criminal Procedure in India that it is the duty of every individual to bring to the notice of authorities any information which be may have regarding the commission or any attempt to commit certain offences. The cooperation of the people can be sought to disperse unlawful assemblies. If the people refuse to help the police, no offender can be convicted as there will be no evidence to prove his guilt.

It is the duty of every citizen to resist injustice from every quarter. All the unjust acts of the state and individuals must be resisted. It is only then that we can hope to have good administration. There cannot be a good society unless the people are prepared to resist evil.

All citizens must develop a spirit of toleration towards one another. They should love not only those who agree with them but also those who differ from them. We must learn to tolerate the different views of others. Progress of society is possible only in an atmosphere of goodwill and that can be created only by a spirit of toleration among the people. More and more emphasis should be put on this quality in our country because we have practically forgotten the spirit of toleration during the course of centuries. Without such a spirit, we cannot have a prosperous India.

Every citizen owes a duty to his country to work hard. Idlers and parasites must be condemned. Under the Soviet Constitution of 1936, it is the duty of every citizen to work. It is rightly emphasized that he who does not work shall not eat.

It is the duty of every citizen to serve on die various local bodies in his country. Even if that involves a waste of time and money, the duty must be performed happily and willingly. The central government cannot be expected to look to every detail of every locality and it is the local bodies who can be expected to look after local needs on account of their local knowledge and local interest. It must not be forgotten that democracy can work successfully only if the people have their training in the art of administration by serving on the local bodies for some years. It is time that the leaders of our country realise the imnortance of this simple truth and thereby strengthen the foundation of democracy in India.

SUGGESTED READINGS

Alien, G.K. : *Democracy and the Individual.*

Barker, E. : *Principles of Social and Political Theory,* London, 1951.

Barker, E. : *Reflections on Government.*

Bentham : *Principles of Legislation.*

Benn, S.I. and R.S. Peters : *Social Principles and the Democratic State,* London, 1959.

Bosanquet, B. : *The Philosophical Theory of the State.*

Burns, C.D. : *Political Ideals.*

Calvert, E. Roy : *Capital Punishment in the Twentieth Century.*

Carlyle, A.G. : *Political Liberty.*

Carver, T.N. : *Essays in Social Justice.*

Catlin, G.E.G. : *A Study of the Principles of Politics.*

Cranston, Maurice : *Human Rights Today.*

Deane, H.A. : *The Political Ideas of Harold Laski.*

Dickinson, G.L. : *Justice and Liberty.*

Dunham, B. : *Man against Myth,* New York, 1947.

Fellman, D. : *The Limits of Freedom.*

Gettell, R.G. : *Introduction to Political Science.*

Gettell, R.G. : *Political Science.*

Gilchrist, R N : *Principles of Political Science.*

Green, T.H. : *Lectures on Principles of Political Obligation,* London, 1895.

Hegel, G.W.F. : *Philosophy of Right.*

Hersch, Jeanne (Ed.) : *Birthright of Man.*

Hobhouse, L.T. : *The Elements of Social Justice.*

Hocking, W.E. : *Law and Rights.*

Hunt, Richard N. : *The Political Ideas of Marx and Engels.*

Joad, C.E.M. : *Liberty Today.*

Joad. C.E.M. : *Guide to the Philosophy of Morals and Politics.*

Laski, H.J. : *A Grammar of Politics,* London, 1925.

Laski, H.J. : *The Dangers of Obedience and Other Essays.*

Laski, H.J. : *Liberty in the Modern State.*

Laski, H.J. : *The Dilemma of Our Time.*

Laski, H.J. : *Reflections on the Revolution of Our Time.*

Laski, H.J. : *Democracy in Crisis.*

Laski, H.J. : *The State in Theory and Practice.*

Leacock, S. : *The Unsolved Riddle of Social Justice.*

Lipson : *The Great Issues of Politics.*

Locke, John : *Two Treatises of Government.*

Lord, A.R. : *Principles of Politics.*

MacIver, R.M. : *The Web of Government,* 1961.

MacIwain, C.H. : *Constitutionalism: Ancient and Modern.*

Macpherson, C.B. : *Democratic Theory,* Oxford, 1973.

Macpherson, C.B. : *The Political Theory of Possessive Individualism.*

Maxey, C.C. : *Political Philosophies.*

Medvedev, R.A. : *On Socialist Democracy,* London, 1975.

Melden, A.I. : *Rights and Right Conduct,* Oxford, 1959.

Paine, Tom : *Rights of Man.*

Panikkar, K.M. : *The State and the Citizen,* 1960.

Pickles, Dorothy M. : *Introduction to Politics.*

Plamenatz, J. : *Man and Society,* London, 1963.

Pound, R. : *The Development of Constitutional Guarantees of Liberty.*

Quinton, A. (Ed.) : *Political Philosophy,* 1967.

Ranney, Austin : Governing: A Brief Introduction to Political Science.

Ritchie, D.G. : Natural Rights, London, 1952.

Sidgwick, H. : *Elements of Politics.*

Spencer, H. : *Justice.*

Wilde, N. : *The Ethical Basis of the State.*

Willoughby, W.W. : *Social Justice.*

CHAPTER

Liberty

Definition and Meaning of Liberty

In the words of Caudwell, "Liberty is a concept about whose nature men have quarrelled perhaps more than about any other". The term liberty has meant different things to different people. It is derived from the Latin word *Liber* which means free. It is not merely a philosophical or legal concept. It is a product of historical circumstances and its meaning can be made clear by looking at its development in the Western political thought. Liberty is not merely an idea, or ideal, or slogan, or an emotion, but it is a fundamental concept without which man is hardly a man. It is concerned with the quality of human life. Freedom for man is not merely an empty claim but a basic necessity.

In the words of R.N. Gilchrist, "Everyone has a vague notion of liberty of some kind and a desire for it, but among ten people using the word, perhaps no two will be able to say exactly what they mean, or, if they do say it, will agree with each other in their definition", (*Principles of Politican Science*, (*1961*), p. 119).

Dr. S. Leacock wrote thus in his "Elements of Political Science" (1932): "Let us begin by observing that such terms as liberty, freedom and free are used in a variety of senses and great latitude of connotation. The term liberty is used also as a vague generality to stand for something evidently desirable, and yet so simple in its nature as to need no further definition. It is freely assumed that everyone ought to have complete liberty and that every violation of liberty is an injustice without the need being felt for any special inquiry into the meaning of liberty itself." (p. 69)

The dictionary meanings of the term liberty show the varied uses to which the term is put. According to the Chambers' Twentieth Century Dictionary (1961), liberty is "freedom from constraint, captivity or tyranny; freedom

Learning Objectives

- Definition and Meaning of Liberty
- Development of Concept of Liberty
- Renaissance
- Milton
- Utilitarians
- Kant
- Green
- J.S. Mill
- Barker
- Laski
- Marxian view
- Negative and Positive Liberty
- Negative Liberty
- Sir Isaiah Berlin
- Friedman
- Criticism
- Concept of Positive Liberty
- Laski
- Macpherson
- Comparison of Negative and Positive Liberty
- Scope of Liberty
- Liberty and Authority
- Liberty and Law
- Kinds of Liberty
- Personal or Civil Liberty
- Political Liberty or Public Liberty

to do as one pleases; the unrestrained enjoyment of natural rights; power of free choice, privilege: permission, free range: leisure, disposal: the bounds within which certain privileges are enjoyed; (often in pl.) a limited area outside a prison in which prisoners are allowed to live: presumptions or undue freedom: speech or action violating ordinary civility." (p. 614)

It is stated in the Columbia Encyclopaedia (1956), that liberty is "a word used to describe various types of individual freedom such as religious liberty, political liberty, freedom of speech, right of self-defence and the like." (p. 1129)

R.H. Soltau writes, "We are unable to make a satisfactory distinction between the terms freedom and liberty; the only difference is that one is English, the other Latin; and we cannot follow Mr. Carritt when in his *Morals and Politics* he defines as 'unconstraints from human action, especially from socially organised and legally constraint, and liberty as a 'voice in deciding among claims to unconstraint between ourselves and others', (*An Introduction to Politics* (1959), p. 127).

Prof. Ramsay Muir expressed himself in these words, "By liberty I mean the secure enjoyment by individuals and by natural and spontaneous groups of individuals such as a nation, church, trade union, of the power to think their own thoughts and to express and act upon them, using their own gifts in their own way under the shelter of the law, provided they do not impair the corresponding rights of others."

Massimo Salvobadori defines liberty in these words, "Liberty is free choice, each individual's own decision concerning his own course of action; it belongs to himself, not to the external world that surrounds him" (*Liberal Democracy* (1957), p. 21).

According to Seeley, "Liberty is the opposite of over-government". Burns observes, "Liberty means liberty to grow to one's natural height, to develop one's abilities." According to Gettell, "Liberty is the positive power of doing and enjoying those things which are worthy of enjoyment and work". G.D.H. Cole observes that "Liberty is the freedom of the individual to express without external hindrances to personality". McKechnie says, "Freedom is not the absence of all restraints but rather the substitution of rational ones for irrational". According to Bakunin, "Liberty of man consists solely in this that he obeys the laws of nature, because he has himself recognised them as such and not because they have been imposed upon him externally by any foreign will whatsoever, human or divine, collective or individual".

Laski defines liberty as "the absence of restraint upon the existence of those social conditions which in modern civilisation are the necessary guarantees of individual happiness". Again, "Liberty is the eager maintenance of that atmosphere in which men have opportunity to be their best selves". Again, "Liberty may be defined as the affirmation by an individual or group of his or its own essence". It needs three factors: harmonious balance of personality, absence of restraint and organisational opportunities for the exercise of a continuous initiative.

DEVELOPMENT OF CONCEPT OF LIBERTY

The concept of liberty has developed mainly in modern times and is closely associated with the philosophy of individualism. In the ancient and medieval periods, the concept of liberty in the present form was missing. However, it does not mean that they had no such idea. Greek thinkers, Socrates and

Plato, refused to accept the notion of individual liberty against society or the state. Socrates refused to run away from the prison and readily drank the hemlock because he believed that freedom lies in the obedience to the laws of the state or society. For Greek statesman Pericles, “Freedom meant advancement and political activity for full citizen”. Liberty involved participation in the affairs of the state or society. The Greek philosophers of Stoicism maintained that availability of conditions of the development of human personality was liberty. However, the Greeks did not know the concept of liberty as we understand it today. They did not differentiate between state and society, state and government and thought in terms of life partnership with the state. They did not have any rights as such against the state. Individual liberty as the product of rights enjoyed in modern times, did not exist.

During the medieval period, there was no idea of liberty of the individual as such. Human liberty was a prisoner of faith in God. In those days, the ideas of salvation and freedom of soul were prominent. The Reformation emphasized the freedom of conscience.

Renaissance

As a result of the Renaissance, a multi-dimensional demand for liberty was made. Religious liberty was demanded against the Church and the Papacy. Economic liberty of free contract and free market was demanded against the feudal economic order. Political liberty was demanded against the monarchs. The demand for liberty was raised against the then existing religious, economic, social and moral order. The absence of restraints was regarded as a pre-condition for individual liberty. Regarding this demand for liberty during the seventeenth and eighteenth centuries, Laski writes, “The individual became the antithesis of the state and liberty itself became a principle of anarchy rather than a body of claims to be read in the context of the social process”. This was a negative concept of liberty.

Milton

The case for freedom of speech was eloquently stated by John Milton in his *Areopagitica* in 1644. Milton’s view was that given free communication, truth would prevail over false food. In his *Social Contract*, Rousseau was faced with a paradox: “By what inconceivable art has a means been found of making men free by making them subject?” His problem was that human beings must be made citizens before they could be made men, but to make them citizens government must give them liberty under the law, among other things. Man became free by obeying the General Will. On account of his fascination for Greek direct democracy, Rousseau felt that the only free government would be under direct democracy in which citizens could participate directly.

Utilitarians

The Utilitarians like Bentham considered the government as a necessary evil. For them, liberty was not an end in itself but a valuable means to happiness. If people were left alone, they would naturally seek happiness. Thus, the law of the state was nothing but a restriction on the liberty of the individual. There was greater scope for individual liberty if very few restrictions were imposed by law and there was less interference by the government.

Kant

This view of freedom as absence of restraint and the ability to do what one wished was attacked by Kant (1724-1804). His view was that a man who was free in the above mentioned sense was only a slave of his lower self. A man became really free when he subjected himself to the dictates of universal reason and when he did what he ought to do. This idea was further emphasized by Hegel. According to him, freedom must be understood as a social phenomenon. It was gift of the social, legal and ethical institutions of the community. It could not be equated with self-will. Freedom consisted in reconciling one’s rights with duties imposed by the community. One could not exist without the other. Law took away liberty only when it was not based on reason. Men were free when there was harmony between subjective values and imposed norms (law of the state). Man was rational and self-conscious creature and he could get freedom only in the state.

Green

T.H. Green described Bentham's idea of freedom as a negative one. He viewed liberty as a positive power or capacity of doing or enjoying something worth doing or enjoying. It was not only a legal but an actual possibility. It was both social and individual conception. The quality of liberty enjoyed by the people depended upon the moral quality of society and the persons who constituted that society. It was the duty of the government to remove obstacles which stood in the way of the moral development of people.

J.S. Mill

The view of Prof. Sabine is that J.S. Mill's Essay "On Liberty" (1859) "is one of the classical defences of freedom in the English language". Mill divided the different spheres of human action into two parts : self-regarding and others-regarding actions. The individual was free with regard to self-regarding actions but was subject to the control of the government as regards others – regarding actions. To quote Mill, "*Over himself, over his own body and mind, the individual is sovereign*". The interference of the state in the liberty of an individual was justified only to prevent harm to others.

Barker

Prof. Ernest Barker has given a new interpretation of the concept of liberty. According to him, "It is the greatest common measure of liberty which is possible for all, as determined and defined by the need of each to enjoy similar and equal liberty with others and by the need of all to enjoy the specific liberty of realising specific capacities." Liberty in the state is plural. It is civil, political and economic. It is a complex notion. Many battles have been fought under the banner of liberty. The broad conclusions of Barker are that liberty is one of the principles of justice and one of the procedural rules on which the state and its law must act. In the actual application of that principle and rule, justice and law have both the difficult task not only of reconciling the liberty of one man with that of others, but also of reconciling the different liberties or forms of liberty with one another.

Laski

The view of Laski is that liberty is the product of rights. Without rights, there cannot be any liberty. Without rights, men are the subjects of law unrelated to the needs of personality. Laski rejected the view that liberty means the absence of restraint. He did not accept Mill's attempt to define the limits of state interference. Man did not live and act away from society. Human conduct was social conduct. Whatever we did, affected others. Therefore, we could not do without restraints. Historically speaking, freedoms were opportunities necessary for the development of personality. Those opportunities were in the context of the state. The view of Laski was that liberty was never real unless the government was called to account. Laski classified liberty into there parts: private, political and economic. By private liberty he meant the opportunity to exercise freedom of choice in those areas of life where the results of his efforts mainly affected him in that isolation by which he was always surrounded. Private liberty was personal to a man's self. Political liberty was the power to be active in the affairs of the state. In order to make political liberty real, there should be a fair level of public education and provision for an honest and straight-forward supply of news. According to Laski, three conditions were necessary to safeguard liberty. Freedom could never exist in the presence of special privilege. All persons should have equal access to power. There cannot be liberty where the rights of some depend upon the pleasure of others. The incidence of state action should be unbiased.

Marxian view

The latest development in the field of liberty is the Marxian view of liberty which differs fundamentally from the liberal view of liberty. It puts emphasis on the liberty of the working class. It does not believe in liberty under a capitalist system.

NEGATIVE AND POSITIVE LIBERTY

Negative Liberty

In a formal sense, liberty is defined as the "absence of restraint". This view of liberty treats liberty as a claim of the individual on the state. The state should not impose any restraint or impose minimum restraints on the actions of the individual. This view is called the negative view of liberty. It was prominent during the seventeenth and eighteenth centuries in Europe. It was advocated by the middle class which demanded a free market society against the mercantile policies of the state. A demand was made that the state should not interfere in the economic activities of the individual. It was contended that in such an atmosphere the interaction between the self-interest of each individual would result in the promotion of the good of the society as a whole. The advocates of this view of liberty regarded society as an aggregate of atomized, alienated individuals who were joined together by a bond of mechanical unity. Liberty consisted in the freedom of trade, freedom of enterprise, freedom of contract and a free competition of the market forces of supply and demand. The state was considered as a necessary evil which was required only to maintain liberty by protecting the person and property of individuals from onslaughts from others and not to interfere with their natural liberty. Thinkers like Hobbes, Locke, De Tocqueville, Jefferson, Burke, Paine, Adam Smith, Bentham, Spencer and J.S. Mill supported this view of liberty. In recent years, writers like Sir Isaiah Berlin and M. Friedman have supported this view.

The beauty of J.S. Mill lies in his support for the negative concept of liberty together with support for the positive view of the state. Mill maintained that there was the possibility of the tyranny of the majority resulting in the denial of liberty to the minorities. Hence, the liberty of the individual was also to be protected against the interference of democratic states. Mill was afraid of the restraints of both the democratic state and society on the liberty of the individual.

Mill started with the assumption that there were two spheres of action of the individual viz., self-regarding and others-regarding. As regards self-regarding actions, every individual must have the liberty to do whatever he pleases. Neither the state nor the society or any other member could interfere with that sphere of individual action. The society and state could interfere with those actions of the individuals which affected the society. To quote Mill, "The only purpose for which power can be rightfully exercised over any member of a civilised community, against his will, is to prevent harm to others. His own good, either physical or moral, is not a sufficient warrant. The only part of the conduct of any one for which he is amenable to society is that which concerns others. In the part which merely concerns himself, his independence is of right, absolute. Over himself, over his own body and mind, the individual is sovereign".

Mill included most of the actions of the individual in the personal sphere and pleaded for non-interference of the state in that sphere. His contention was that if the state and society interfered with the personal sphere of man, he will lose the opportunity of choice which was fundamental for the development of his personality and there was also the danger of tyranny, either of majority or minority or a dictator. The most important liberties of the individual described by Mill were liberty of thought and expression, belief, faith and worship and liberty of forming associations having any trade or profession. The state should not interfere with those liberties on any ground so long as those did not harm similar liberties of others and did not become a social nuisance. Mill considered liberty of thought and discussion as a fundamental liberty which could not be suppressed even by the best government. According to him, the peculiar evil of silencing the expression of opinion was that it robbed the human race. If the opinion was right, the human race was deprived of an opportunity of exchanging error for truth. If the opinion was wrong, the society lost the clearer perception and livelier impression of truth produced by its collision with error. Even if an opinion was wrong, it should be allowed to be expressed and it should be countered with a correct opinion. There must be a free play of opinions, a free market, free exchange of opinions in the process of which truth will come out. Truth cannot defend itself by suppressing the wrong, but can do so only by fighting with wrong. An individual can make progress only in an atmosphere of free play of opinions. If the state and society can suppress any wrong opinion, they can also suppress right opinions. Hence, Mill strongly pleaded for non-interference with the liberty of thought and discussion and other personal liberties of individuals. His general position is that all "restraint is an evil.. leaving people to themselves is always better than controlling them." "The only freedom which deserves the name is that of pursuing our own good in our own way, so long as we do not attempt to deprive others of theirs, or impede their efforts to obtain it. Each is the proper guardian of his own health, whether bodily or mental and spiritual. Mankind are greater gainers by suffering each other to lives as seems good to themselves, than by compelling each to live as seems good to the rest."

The view of Mill was that the state and society could control the individual and his action if those were harmful to the society or other members. If the liberty of one individual became a nuisance to other individuals, the other individuals could not enjoy their own liberty. An individual had the liberty to move his hand in any direction but his liberty ended where the nose of another individual began. Mill supported state interference in those spheres of individual actions which were harmful to others.

The views of Mill have been criticised on many grounds. Ernest Barker points out that Mill separated the inseparable. The conduct of any man is a single whole and there can be nothing in it that concerns himself only and not others. Whatever he is and whatever he does, affects others and therefore concerns others.

Another defect pointed out by Barker is that Mill failed to separate the separable. We cannot separate two different compartments of individual conduct, but we can separate the sphere of society from that of the state. The state acts by the method of compulsory enforcement but society acts by the method of free cooperation.

Patrick Devlin points out that harm to individual directly is harm to society indirectly, *e.g.*, sexual immorality. Moreover, a society is a moral community which is held together by a shared morality. Anything which tends to destroy or harm it weakens the bonds of society and thereby harms it.

It is also pointed out that if the individual needs the community for the development of himself, his freedom is meaningless without others in society. Society is a continuous partnership. To quote Edmund Burke, "As the ends of such a partnership cannot be obtained in many generations, it becomes a partnership not only between those who are living, but between those who are living, those who are dead and those who are to be born".

Critics also point out two other difficulties in the views of Mill. No line of demarcation can be drawn between the interests of an individual and those of the society. Being an individualist, Mill accepts the liberal assumption of the individual as an isolated being, but logically no social theory can be built upon this view of man and society. At the practical level, it is difficult to demarcate the personal and social sphere of man. The other difficulty is a moral one. Even in their own spheres, individuals cannot be given the liberty to harm themselves. The view of Mill was that only the individual knows what his interest is and he must be totally free in his own sphere. Hence, a man is free to smoke, drink, gamble, take drugs, read pornographic literature and commit suicide because these are his personal matters. This is really a dangerous situation and it makes the position of Mill very weak. Hence, Barker calls Mill a "prophet of empty liberty".

However, the importance of Mill lies in his contention that social and political progress depends largely on the originality and energy of the individual and his free choice. Personal liberty is of supreme importance for developing the individual in all the completeness of his being and every encouragement should be given to him to assert himself in his own peculiar way. Without that, Mill thought that general progress of the society was not possible. He objected to state education as it may lead to brain-wash or kill originality by moulding people to be exactly like one another. He was right in pointing out that democracy may transform itself into the tyranny of the majority over the minority.

Sir Isaiah Berlin

Of the contemporary writers, Sir Isaiah Berlin is an advocate of negative liberty. He has cleverly used the terms negative liberty and positive liberty in his book "Two Concepts of Liberty" (1958) to show that the state can only secure negative liberty to the individual and positive liberty does not come within the purview of the state. According to Berlin, negative liberty consists in not being prevented from choosing one's course of action and positive liberty treats the individual as his own master. In both cases, liberty implies an absence of restraint. Political liberty belongs to the sphere of negative liberty. It simply demands that an individual is not prevented from attaining his goal by other human beings. Positive liberty belongs to the sphere of man's own capacities. If a man is too poor to afford something on which there is no legal ban, he cannot complain that he has been deprived of political liberty. The capacity or incapacity to fulfil one's desires belongs to man himself and the state is not concerned with that. The view of C.B. Macpherson is that Berlin's concept of negative liberty is "at bottom a mechanical, inertial concept of freedom which is fully appropriate only to a complete market society". (*Democratic Theory*, p. 95). In asserting positive liberty as the desire of the individual to be his own master, to be self-directed, to be moved by his own conscious purpose, Berlin saves the individual from the authoritarian claims of the idealist theory and makes his contribution to the liberal-individualist theory. His concept of positive liberty does not correspond to positive liberalism's concept of positive liberty.

Friedman

M. Friedman is also a supporter of negative liberty. He finds a necessary connection between liberty and capitalism. His view is that without capitalism there cannot be freedom in society. According to him, political freedom means "the absence of coercion of a man by his fellow men". Friedman supports a negative, state and negative liberty and maintains that all the social welfare functions of the state and regulation of the economy by it are improper. Competitive capitalism is a necessary condition of political freedom. He considers socialism as the main enemy of personal initiative and political freedom. He attacks the positive state and positive view of liberty as state interference in economic affairs is harmful to the economic liberty of individuals.

There are certain main points of negative liberty. Liberty is a negative thing. It is the absence of restraint. An individual is rational and he knows what is in his interest. Each individual should be given personal liberty with regard to his personal affairs and neither the state nor society should interfere with it. Among personal liberties, the liberty of thought and discussion, of association and assembly are the most important. There is no conflict between personal interest and social interest. By serving his personal interest, an individual also serves the social interest personal liberty is a pre-condition for social progress. The state cannot take away personal liberty. It can only regulate it for social welfare. The interference of the state in the personal life of the individual should be the minimum.

Criticism

The critics of negative liberty point out that this view of liberty is founded on the assumption of an atomised and alienated individual and society is viewed as a market society, composed of atomised, self-seeking individuals, where equilibrium can be maintained through personal liberties of individuals, free contract and free exchange. This view of the individual and society is not correct. It has been found by experience that state action is necessary to save the liberty of individuals from interference by other individuals. Social interest is of greater importance than personal liberty which can be harmful to society. It is difficult to draw the border-line between individual liberty and social interest and even the supporters of negative liberty admit the necessity of state interference in matters concerning social interest. Private property and free contract lead to enslavement and exploitation of the propertyless people. The concept of negative liberty is unsound because it gives asocial liberty to an asocial man. The social basis of personal liberty is missing. This type of liberty can be enjoyed only by the rich.

Concept of Positive Liberty

It is true that the concept of negative liberty played an important historical role. It released the forces of production which were blocked by the feudal system. However, by the middle of the nineteenth century, the capitalist system supported by negative liberty resulted in the miserable condition of the workers and consumers. There came into existence enormous disparities of wealth and power. There was oppression, exploitation and injustice in society. The result was that humanist writers, Socialists, Marxists and positive liberals came forward to demand a new definition of liberty. They put forward the thesis that a policy of non-intervention by the state was not compatible with liberty as a universal principle. The liberty of the employer to hire and fire workers at his will made a mockery of the freedom of contract. The workers were made to live a life of abject poverty. It was demanded that the benefit of liberty should go not only to the rich people but also to the workers. The result was that the negative view of liberty gave way to positive liberty.

The concept of positive liberty developed during the later half of the nineteenth century. A discussion of this view is to be found in the writings of Kant, Hegel, Green, Bosanquet, Barker and Laski. Kant (1724-1804) maintained that there are higher and lower selves in an individual and freedom comes when an individual subjects himself to the dictates of universal reason. The free play of emotions and satisfaction of brute desires could not satisfy the higher self and liberty was concerned with the higher self. Green associated personal liberty with society, morality, rights and the state. According to him, human consciousness needs liberty, liberty needs rights and rights need the state. Green sought to establish the positive role of the state in creating conditions under which men could effectively exercise their moral freedom. He viewed liberty as a positive power or capacity of doing or enjoying something worth doing or enjoying. The Government should remove obstacles that stand in the way of the moral development of the people.

J.S. Mill gave signs of transition from negative to positive liberty. He indicated a sphere where intervention by the state could be vindicated in the common interest. He pleaded for the limitation of the right of inheritance. He insisted that the state must provide for education.

If negative liberty consists in the absence of restraint, positive liberty consists in extending the opportunity to the individual to pursue his happiness where he is obstructed for want of means or capacity due to the prevailing socio-economic conditions. S.I. Benn and R.S. Peters write, "If education is expensive and the parents are poor, it makes a mockery of freedom to say that one is free to educate one's children merely because there is no law or custom against it. Choice may be formally unlimited; there can be no freedom unless it is also effectively unlimited. To remove any hindrance to people doing what they want to do thus counts as an extension of freedom." (Social Principles and the Democratic State, p. 212). Again, "To provide a cripple with an artificial leg, an ignorant man with education, an unemployed man with a job, all count as positive extensions of freedom. Legal compulsions are then a small price to pay for positive freedoms of this sort; for we yield a little only to receive back more. And the absolute goodness of freedom remains intact." (Ibid).

If negative liberty denotes that the state shall abstain from imposing unreasonable restraints on the individual, positive liberty signifies the removal of constraints which are the product of the social set-up and which are capable of being removed by making the necessary changes in the social set-up. If a man is faced with the lack of capacity in the fulfilment of his desire, he will not make it a political issue unless his incapacity is due to socio-economic conditions which can be removed by changing the socio-economic conditions. If a man cannot fly like an eagle or swim like a whale, he cannot make it a political issue as his incapacity is not due to socio-economic conditions, but if he does not get a job, or adequate wages or quality goods at a reasonable price or essential supplies and services or an opportunity for education, he can demand a political solution of those problems as those conditions can be changed by changes in social policy. Men do not complain that the black races should be converted into white as they know that, that condition cannot be altered. However, when society discriminates between white and black races and denies certain privileges to the black although the same are enjoyed by the white people, the resentment by the black people is justified as it is due to social injustice which can be set right by making necessary changes in social policy. Positive liberty implies the removal of only such constraints and provision of only such opportunities which can be accomplished through alteration of socio-economic conditions. D.D. Raphael writes, "A man who is locked up in prison is not at liberty, because he is restrained by the action of other persons. And we may speak of freedom from want, or of freeing mankind from the scourge of cancer, when we mean that the impediments to which we refer, although not imposed by human action are, capable (we hope) of being removed by human action. But we should not say that a man is unfree because he is restrained by a natural impediment which cannot be removed by human action." (Problems of Political Philosophy, pp. 315-16).

Positive liberty is not the absence of restraint. It is the provision of those socio-economic and political conditions without which liberty cannot be realised. The object of liberty is the development of man as a social being. Liberty cannot be realised without proper opportunities and social conditions. Rights are necessary for liberty. They are related to justice, morality and equality. The liberties of an individual must correspond with social welfare. It is the duty of the state to create positive conditions for the realisation of liberty. The state cannot limit the liberties of some individuals. The state is not an enemy of personal liberty. Liberty is a social requirement of social man. It is not given to asocial or anti-social beings.

Laski

The most comprehensive discussion on positive liberty can be found in the writings of Laski who gave importance to the relationship of individual liberty with society. Personal liberty cannot be enjoyed in isolation from society. However, this does not mean that liberty should be left at the mercy of the state. Liberty is never real unless the government can be called to account. Although Laski supports positive liberty, he was suspicious of governments and did not surrender liberty to the state. He differs from the idealist view of liberty which lies in obedience to the laws of the state. He associates liberty with opportunities for the development of personality. The positive character of liberty is emphasized by Laski who maintains that liberty is concerned with availability of those opportunities which are necessary for the development of the personality of man.

Laski refers to three kinds of liberties which are essential to the development of human personality. Those are private, political and economic liberty. Private liberty is an opportunity to be fully himself in the private relations of life. Political liberty means the power to be active in the affairs of state. Two conditions are necessary for real political liberty and those are education and the provision of an honest and straightforward supply of news. Economic liberty means security and opportunity to find reasonable significance in the earning of one's daily bread. Laski pleads for democracy in industry.

According to Laski, certain things are necessary for the realisation of positive liberty. One of them is the absence of special privileges. Freedom cannot "exist in the presence of special privileges".

Special privilege is incompatible with freedom because the latter quality belongs to all alike in their character as human beings. Liberty is possible only when equality is there. It can only be enjoyed in the presence of rights. The rights of some must not depend upon the pleasure of others. The government must be responsible. It is only a responsible government which can create those socio-economic and political conditions which are necessary for the realisation of liberty.

Macpherson

In recent years, Macpherson has put forward a forceful case for positive liberty which he prefers to call as "developmental liberty". According to him, liberty means availability of means of life and labour to each member of the society. He suggests that the capitalist mode of production based on private property, should be replaced by some other system. Liberty is not negative liberty because the liberty of one individual can destroy the liberty of another individual. Macpherson gives importance to the social dimensions of liberty.

The issue of positive liberty is closely associated with the economic structure of society. Only that economic system can give positive liberty which is free from exploitation. Gerassi writes, "Freedom is not the right to say or do anything you want that does not infringe on the freedom of others. Freedom means having the material and psychological power to say or do that thing. Freedom is the real possibility of being relevant, of being meaningful, of being total. No man who is poor, when the other is rich, is free. No man who does not exert control, equal to all other men, over his courts, police, government or army, is free. No country which is financially or geopolitically dependent on another is free. To talk about freedom of the press when only the rich control the media, to herald free enterprise when health (hospitals, doctors, medicine etc.) cost money, to cherish free courts when lawyers, bail, appeal etc. require wealth — in general to hail a society as free when money is the means by which one buys one's free choice — is a travesty".

The concept of positive libertv has been misused by the idealist thinkers and they have left liberty at the mercy of the state. Macpherson writes, "This is the idealist road (or slippery slope) which ends in coercion: the individual is forced to be free. There is no doubt that the concept of positive liberty has been taken to these conclusions and, so perverted, has been used to deny the very freedom for human self-development that it began by invoking." The contribution of the concept of positive liberty lies in its recognition of the socio-economic and political dimensions of liberty.

Comparison of Negative and Positive Liberty

Both the views of negative and positive liberty have been given by liberal thinkers and they are associated with the problem of the relationship between liberty and authority. The negative view of liberty was given when the liberal thinkers were suspicious of the authority of the absolutist state. The positive view of liberty was given when the state power was firmly in the hands of the middle classes and when the negative concept of liberty was challenged by the working classes. Negative liberty gave more weight to the personal aspect of man and considered liberty necessary for the personality of an individual. The view of positive liberty is based on the socio-economic and political conditions of society. Negative liberty emphasizes the absence of restraint by the state. Positive liberty emphasizes the positive conditions which are necessary for the realisation of liberty. Negative liberty regards the state as an enemy of personal liberty. The concept of positive liberty asks the state to create those positive conditions which are necessary for the realisation of liberty. Negative liberty emphasises the personal and political aspects of liberty. Positive liberty emphaises the social and economic aspects of liberty. Negative liberty is based on the market concept of society. Positive liberty emphasises the social aspect of man. Negative liberty is not associated with rights, equality, morality and justice. Positive liberty regards liberty, equality and justice as mutually related.

Scope of Liberty

The problem of liberty involves the adjustment of claims between the individual and society. The state comes into the picture as it has to regulate that relationship. If the claim of the individual is stretched to an extreme in utter disregard of the interests of society, liberty becomes license. If more and more restrictions are put on the individual by the state, that results in the loss of liberty. Hence, It is necessary to fix the proper frontier between liberty and authority.

Liberty is good but to be free to do undesirable things is to enjoy not liberty but license which is bad. Such a condition is not desirable for the maintenance of social order. It is also not conducive to the maintenance of liberty itself. The liberty of one man becomes a constraint on another or his oppression. The liberty of the strong results in the suppression of the weak. The liberty of a thief to take away the property of another person becomes a threat to the security of everybody. The liberty of a driver to drive the car at any speed endangers the lives and liberties of all others who use the road. Such a situation cannot be allowed in a civil society as it is bound to result in chaos. If liberty is to be liberty for all, restraints have to be put on the liberty of all. Liberty of every individual has to be regulated in such a way that he does not use his liberty to destroy the liberty of others. L.T. Hobhouse writes, "The uncharted freedom of one would be the conditional servitude of all but one and conversely a freedom to be enjoyed by all must impose some restraint upon all". (*Elements of Social Justice*, p.59). Ernest Barker observes, "The need of liberty for each is necessarily qualified and conditioned by the need of liberty for all..The liberty of the owner of capital to determine the conditions of work in the factory which he owns is a relative liberty which must be adjusted to the liberty of the worker to do his work under such conditions as leave him still a free agent and give him also a share in the determination of the conditions of work. Because the liberty of each is thus relative to that of others, and has to be adjusted to that of others, it must always be regulated; and indeed it would not exist unless it were regulated". (*Principles of Social and Political Theory*, p. 145.)

Liberty and Authority

If liberty is to be enjoyed by all, that liberty has to be limited. The liberty of one cannot be allowed to become an obstruction in the liberty of another. Liberty is demanded for man as a rational being and it is intended to be exercised to pursue rational objects or ideal objects. If that is done, every individual has his liberty and happiness. The good of an individual becomes an integral part of the good of the society. This is possible only in a perfect state. However, as individuals are not perfect, it becomes necessary to regulate liberty to safeguard liberty itself. Ernest Barker writes, "Liberty within the state is thus a relative and regulated liberty: it is the greatest common measure of liberty which is possible for all, as determined and defined (1) by the need of each to enjoy similar and equal liberty with others, and (2) by the need of all to enjoy the specific liberty of realising specific capacities", (*Principles of Social and Political Theory*, pp. 145-46). Again, "A relative and regulated liberty actually operative and enjoyed, is liberty greater in amount than absolute liberty could ever be — if indeed such liberty could ever exist, or ever amount to anything more than nothing at all". (*Ibid.*, p. 146).

The liberty of an individual can be regulated only by the authority of the state. However, if the authority of the state is absolute or unlimited, then also there is no liberty. There is a conflict between liberty and absolute authority. If absolute liberty is denied to the individual as no individual is perfect, no state can be given absolute authority as no state on earth is perfect. D.D. Raphael refers to the conflict between liberty and authority in these words, "Most political theorists recognize that individual liberty and State authority conflict with each other, and that a balance has to be struck between them and the values they represent. Some, like Hobbes, are prepared to say that liberty must be severely limited to make way for the benefits of State authority. Others, like Locke and J.S. Mill, think that State authority should be markedly limited so as to leave as much room as possible for liberty". (*Problems of Political Philosophy*, p. 136).

The state can use the methods of compulsion against the individual. However, it is found that a moral weapon is more effective and conducive to the social purposes of state authority. The authority of the state is more justified if it is backed by moral support and legitimacy instead of mere force. Legitimacy denotes the support extended by the people to the state and its law out of their moral beliefs and values. Spencer writes, "Legitimacy comes from the people. It depends on the people believing that state is necessary and that its actions are lawful and valuable to society. As long as its legitimacy is unquestioned, the state will rarely need to use force. But if the legitimacy of its use of power is widely questioned, the state is in a dangerous situation. A regime is in serious trouble if the people believe that its military is illegitimate, its police brutal, and its courts unfair. It may have power – the ability to get its orders obeyed despite widespread opposition – but it does not have authority." (*Foundations of Sociology*, p. 431).

A similar view is expressed by D.D. Raphael in these words, "The authority of the law, although it does depend on and make use of sanctions, could not be effective unless most people accepted it on moral grounds. If most people recognize a moral obligation to obey the law, they are acting from a moral motive and not under compulsion". (*Problems of Political Philosophy*, p. 136).

Liberty and authority do not contradict each other, but supplement and complement each other. To quote Locke, "Where there is no law, there is no freedom". The view of Hocking is that the greater the liberty a person desires, the greater is the authority to which he should submit himself. However, the state must act as a servant to our will and the extent to which it carries out our will faithfully, we are free and have positive liberty.

Liberty and Law

A question can be asked whether law and liberty are antithetical or friendly to each other. It is not possible to give a direct answer to this question as much depends upon the form of the government people have, the spirit of the people and other factors. In a normal form of government which is free from perversions, law helps liberty. Without law, there can be no liberty. A state can make laws by which restrictions can be put on the liberty of individuals but those are reasonable and necessary. They act as a bulwark of liberty. To quote Rousseau, "Obedience to a law which we prescribe to ourselves is liberty". According to T.H. Green, man is free when he obeys the law of which he is the author and obeys it from the impulse for self-preservation. Locke says, "Law is, in its true notion, not so much the limitation as the direction of a free and intelligent agent to his true interest...So that however it may be mistaken, the end of law is not to abolish or restrain but to preserve and enlarge freedom". Ritchie observes, "Liberty in the sense of positive opportunity for self-development is the creation of law and not something that could exist apart from the action of the state".

If good laws can be the conditions of liberty, bad and oppressive laws are obstacles and dangers to liberty because they narrow down the opportunities for the development of the personalities of individuals. That explains why laws in various states do not provide the same amount of liberty. In some states, laws provide good conditions for the enjoyment of liberty. In some states, they provide a limited amount of liberty. In some states, laws are antagonistic to liberty.

In the case of India, the Constitution of India guarantees to the citizens of India full political and civil liberty which they did not enjoy during the British rule in this country. In England, there is great harmony between law and liberty. Laws in that country are made by Parliament which consists of the representatives of the people. There are long standing healthy democratic traditions in that country and there are very few chances of a conflict between law and liberty. Moreover, Englishmen are vigilant, politically conscious and well-informed. They jealously got their liberty and can force their government to resign if it tries to ride roughshod over their liberty. The people in that country have struck a balance between sovereignty and liberty which is not to be found in developing countries where the people are not politically conscious and well-informed and vigilant about their liberty.

There are always the dangers of despotism and mob rule. R.G. Gettell writes, "The balance between sovereignty and liberty is too nicely adjusted to be easily maintained and tends always towards despotism on one hand and anarchy on the other. Constant vigilance is necessary to preserve the balance under changing conditions and modern states are not agreed as to what is proper adjustment or how it may best be secured". (*Political Science*, p. 98). In India, the people are not so politically conscious as the people in England are. There is also no strong and responsible opposition party in the country. The party in preserve treats the opposition with contempt. The continuation of the Emergency declared in October 1962 till January 1968 and the repeated extensions of the Preventive Detention Act. 1950 till the end of December 1969 restricted the liberty of the people in India. The Preventive Detention Act was replaced by much worse Maintenance of Internal Security Act. The passing of the Twenty-fourth Amendment of the Constitution enabled the Parliament to amend any provision of the Constitution of India including those dealing with fundamental rights and thereby endangered of the enjoyment of liberty in India. On 25 June 1975, Prime Minister Indira Gandhi imposed internal Emergency which continued upto 21 March 1977. The sole purpose of imposing Emergency was to keep herself in power because without that she would not have remained in power as Justice J.M.L. Sinha of the Allahabad High Court had by his judgement dated 12 June 1975 held her election to the Lok Sabha illegal. It is well-known that during the Emergency thousands of innocent persons including national leaders like Loknayak Jayaprakash Narayan, Morarji Desai, Choudhry Charan Singh, Atal Behari Vajpayee, L.K. Advani and others were imprisoned without trial. A large number of persons were tortured. The people were prevented even from moving the High Court.

Law and liberty can be friendly to each other only when the government in a country is responsive and sympathetic to the people and understands their aspirations, when the opposition is effective and criticises and warns the government from time to time, when the press makes constructive criticism of the working of the government, when the judiciary acts independently and fearlessly and when the people are vigilant, politically conscious and well-informed, and jealously guard their liberty.

The relation between law and liberty is not a static one. It has to change with the changing times. However, every effort should be made to bring about harmony between the two. Gettell writes, "Sovereignty carried to the extreme becomes tyranny and destroys liberty and liberty carried to the extreme becomes anarchy and destroys sovereignty. The efforts made by states to reach a satisfactory compromise between these two equally undesirable extremes comprise a large part of the history of politics and no permanent solution has yet been reached." (*Political Science*, p. 149)

The laws of the state secure the conditions of liberty in many ways. The penal laws of a country lay down what must be done by the individuals and prescribe the punishments for those who violate them. The civil laws guarantee those rights without which human progress is not possible. They define the rights and obligations of individuals and thereby provide a basis for human progress and growth. The laws provide the necessary conditions of life without which life will be solitary, nasty, brutish and short. Not only the constitutional laws but also the ordinary laws of a country guarantee liberty to individuals. The importance of the Habeas Corpus Act in England cannot be over-emphasized for the preservation of personal liberty. Likewise, the Chapter on Fundamental Rights in the Constitution of India goes a long way to secure liberty to the people of India. Laws which ensure old age pension or healthy conditions in factories positively help the enjoyment of liberty. The view of Popper is that no precise formula can be devised "to determine exactly the degree of freedom that can be left to the citizens without endangering that freedom whose protection is the task of the state. But that something like an approximate determination of that degree is possible is proved by experience *i.e.*, by the existence of democratic state. In fact, this process of approximate determination is one of the main tasks of legislation in democracies" (*The Open Society and Its Enemies, Vol. I*, pp. 100-11).

If there can be liberty in a democracy, there is no liberty under a dictatorship. In such a state, liberty is wept aside by arbitrary and oppressive laws. The government of a despot is neither responsive nor responsible to the public. Laws are not passed to serve the interests of the community but to help the despot in the exercise of unbridled power by him. Under a dictatorship, the people have to obey the dictator and they do not have any civil, political or economic liberty. Law is not intended to serve the interests of the people but becomes an instrument of oppression. Even if dictatorship is good, people do not have liberty. A totalitarian state exercises complete control over all aspects of the life of individuals and leaves no room for liberty. The people live in an atmosphere of fear and suspicion. Any attempt to regain liberty is ruthlessly put down by the dictator.

KINDS OF LIBERTY

Personal or Civil Liberty

There are different kinds of liberty. As regards civil liberty or personal liberty, it is liberty enjoyed by individuals in society. According to Gettell, "It includes liberty has a positive as well as a negative aspect. It imparts activity. It implies spontaneous exercise of the powers of willing and doing. A person is said to enjoy spontaneous exercise of the powers of willing and doing. A person is said to enjoy civil liberty when he has the right to life, freedom of association, freedom of speech and thought, freedom of conscience, freedom of action and movement, right improperly, equality before law etc. It is the duty of the state to punish those who violate the civil liberty of an individual.

According to Ernest Barker, Civil liberty consists in "three somewhat differently expressed articles : physical freedom from injury or threat to the life, health and movement of the body; intellectual freedom for the expression of thought and belief and practical freedom of the play of will and the exercise of choice in the general field of contractual action and relations with other persons" (*Principles of Social and Political Theory*, pp. 146-47). An individual wants to be left alone to think freely, speak freely, move freely, act freely, live freely and suffer from no coercion of any type. Civil liberty is of great value to individuals and associations in a state.

Civil liberty includes personal freedom which means the existence of conditions in which an individual can act as he pleases without any arbitrary or illegal restraint or control. According to F.A. Hayek, freedom or liberty is a "condition of man in which coercion of some by others is reduced as much as possible in society. The state in which a man is not subject to coercion by the arbitrary will of another or others is often also distinguished as individual or personal freedom". Every individual must have the maximum freedom necessary for the development of his personality. There should be a balance between the freedom of one individual and that of others.

In Britain and the United States, great importance is attached to civil liberty and there is great resentment if there is any encroachment on it. An Englishman or American does not like to be dictated by the state as to how he should live, what religion he should profess, what profession he should follow, what opinion he should have, how he should dress and how he should plan his life in general. Every Englishman is jealous of his rights as a person and he regards his home as his castle free from any outside interference. In the twentieth century, Bertrand Russell put great emphasis on the importance of personal freedom. The rise of Fascism in Italy under Mussolini and of the Nazis under Hitler was a great threat to democracy and freedom and hence President Roosevelt announced Four Freedoms in 1941. Those freedoms were freedom of speech and expression, freedom of religion, freedom from want and freedom from fear.

The recognition and protection of civil liberty is an important duty of the state. Law protects individual liberty from encroachment by others. The individual has to be protected from government action which is dangerous to civil liberty. The Bill of Rights in the United States and the fundamental rights in India protect the individual from any encroachment by the state.

Civil liberty in democratic countries is realised through the recognition of the distinction between state and government, a democratic constitution, whether written or unwritten, the actual definition of the rights of private action and the recognition of fundamental rights.

Civil liberty also includes the freedom of contract. It is generally said that the people enjoy the freedom to enter into contracts for their mutual advantage, provided no damage is caused to a third party. The difficulty arises when this freedom is exploited by a stronger party in a bargain to impose very disadvantageous terms on the weaker party. L.T. Hobhouse observes, "Freedom of contract is insufficiently defined when it is regarded as consisting solely in the absence of control. Freedom of contract implies such a substantial equality between the parties as on the whole leaves to each a real choice between concluding and rejecting the bargain. Where no such equality exists, one party acts under a degree of compulsion" (*Elements of Social Justice*, p. 75). In an extreme case, absolute freedom of contract may be used to allow a man or even to force him to sell himself to slavery and thereby deprive himself of his personal freedom in perpetuity, Hence, it is desirable that freedom of contract should operate under reasonable limitations.

Political Liberty or Public Liberty

According to Blackstone, political liberty means the power of curbing government. However, according to Ernest Barker, political liberty is "a liberty not of curbing government, but of constituting and controlling; constituting it by a general act of choice or election in which we all freely share on the basis of universal suffrage; controlling it by a general and continuous process of discussion, in which we all freely share according to our capacities." (*Principles of Social and Political Theory*, p. 147).

An individual enjoys public or political liberty in his capacity as a citizen. As a member of the state, he has the right to constitute and control the government. Universal adult suffrage is the means through which the citizens constitute the government. The right to vote is an expression of the political liberty of the citizen. The government is controlled by citizens through meetings, processions and discussion. When an individual participates in forming and controlling the government, he enjoys his political liberty.

Political liberty includes such minimum rights as the right to vote, the right to stand for election, the right to hold public office and the right to express political views and criticise the government. In countries like Britain, the United States and India, an individual enjoys full political liberty. Political liberty should be recognised constitutionally and legally and proper conditions should be created to give it the maximum scope. The spread of education, formation of political parties and freedom of the press increase the scope of political liberty.

Economic Liberty

It has rightly been said that democracy is meaningless without economic liberty. Without adequate economic security the individual cannot develop himself. He can have no interest in life even in a democratic state. Any type of liberty is barren unless there is economic liberty. Civil liberty and political liberty mean nothing to a hungry man and these two liberties do not prevent the exploitation of the poor by the rich.

Economic liberty is a ticklish issue. It is capable of conflicting interpretations by conflicting parties, *e.g.*, employer and worker, trader and consumer, landlord and tenant. One party may interpret it as the freedom to secure maximum profit, while the other may insist on reasonable terms, reasonable price and reasonable quality. Hence, if the stronger party is not curbed to safeguard the interests of the weaker party, the principle of liberty becomes a mockery. It is in this sphere that adjustment between the claims of liberty and equality becomes most essential. R.H. Tawney writes, "Where liberty is construed realistically as implying not merely a minimum of civil and political rights, but the securities that the economically weak will not be at the mercy of economically strong, and that the control of those aspects of economic life by which all are affected will be amenable, in the last resort, to the will of all, a large measure of equality, so far from being inimical to liberty, is essential to it". (*Equality*, p. 214)

Prof. Laski writes, "By economic liberty, I mean security and the opportunity to find reasonable significance in the earning of one's daily bread. I must, that is, be free from the constant fear of unemployment and insufficiency which, perhaps more than other inadequacies, sap the whole strength of personality. I must be safeguarded against the wants of tomorrow" (*A Grammar of Politics*, p. 148). Again, "Economic liberty, therefore, implies democracy in industry. That means two things. It means that industrial government is subject to the system of rights which obtain for man as citizens, and it means that industrial direction must be of a character that makes it the rule of laws made by cooperation and not by compulsion". (*Ibid.*, p. 148).

Economic liberty can be secured by defining the economic rights of the people, by recognising the status of the worker and providing scope for the development of his personality, by guaranteeing the individual's right to work, by making provision for minimum wages, by providing adequate leisure and by shielding workers from the woes of unemployment, sickness and old age.

Economic liberty is closely connected with both civil liberty and political liberty. It can be incorporated into the articles of civil liberty as economic relations form a part of the general area of contractual action and the relation of the individual with other persons. The association of economic liberty with political liberty is borne out by the fact that in the absence of economic liberty, a citizen can hardly enjoy his right to constitute and control the government.

Intra-Liberty Quarrel

Civil liberty, political liberty and economic liberty constitute the complex character of liberty. There may be a quarrel between one form of liberty with another form of liberty. For example, economic liberty may fall out with political liberty. If liberty and law do not quarrel, liberty may quarrel with itself. If a person enjoying civil liberty publishes a political pamphlet severely criticising some of the policies of the government, the parliamentary majority acting in the name of political liberty may take punitive measure against the writer on the ground that his pamphlet is calculated to excite disaffection against the government. Here, the civil liberty of the individual Conies into conflict with the political liberty of the parliamentary majority. By virtue of civil liberty, a factory-owner may employ labourers on contract in his factory. He is in a position to dictate the terms of wages and conditions of work. In this case, there is a conflict between the civil liberty of the factory owner and the economic liberty of the labourers. A parliamentary majority, acting in the name of political liberty, may impose restrictions which are detrimental to the enjoyment of economic liberty of the labourer. In such a case, there may be a quarrel between political liberty and economic liberty.

Moral Liberty

Moral liberty implies the right of an individual to act according to his own conscience. It is not possible under a totalitarian regime because the people there are required to act according to the orders of the government and not according to the dictates of their inner conscience. The morality of the people under dictatorship is dictated by the dictator and not decided by the individuals themselves.

Moral liberty is contained in the idealistic interpretation of scholars like Plato, Aristotle, Kant, Hegel, Green, Bradley and Bosanquet. Kant described moral liberty as the "autonomy of the rational will". In the opinion of Hegel, such liberty implies that the individual should recognise and perform his duties properly. To Bradley, moral liberty is connected with individual's self-realisation that has a meaning only in the context of common good or welfare of all. Moral liberty is not concerned with the state but with one's own self. Without moral liberty, there is no free scope for the development of the personality of an individual. Moral liberty is a very important characteristic of man.

Natural Liberty

Natural liberty means complete freedom for the individual to do whatever he wants to do. Such liberty existed only in the state of nature described by Hobbes. According to him, natural liberty signifies the liberty possessed by every man to do what seems best for the preservation of his existence. Here liberty means the absence of external impediments. That power may be limited by the circumstances. The view of Rousseau also is that man enjoyed natural liberty only in the state of nature. Liberty of that type was based on the principle that might is right. Natural liberty which existed only in the state of nature, came to an end after the establishment of civil society. Natural liberty in the real sense is no liberty. It is the freedom of the jungle. It is not applicable to the life of an individual as a social being. If every individual is given absolute liberty to do whatever he wants to do, there will be confusion and chaos. Natural liberty is merely a contradiction in itself.

National Liberty

National liberty is of great importance as it provides a basis for civil, political and economic liberty. There is national liberty in a state when the people are completely free from any foreign control and have a government of their own. National liberty is possible when a state attains a full sovereign status. National liberty means freedom of nation to solve its problems according to its own will without any interference from any quarter. A nation should be free to determine its foreign policy, n has to struggle for attaining national liberty. The American colonies had to fight for their liberty and the same was done by the people of India who became independent on 15 August 1947.

The love of one's country is deep-rooted in man and patriotism, even in its narrow form, evokes feelings which cannot be easily awakened by other ideals. The ideal of national liberty has played an important part in world history. Wars of independence are still applauded by the bulk of mankind in spite of the fact that there is a growing revulsion of feeling against war as a means of settling international disputes. So long as we are governed by the concept of sovereign nation states, freedom from the control of other states is essential to the concept of national liberty.

International Liberty

The ideal of international liberty is based on the conviction that "in proportion as the world becomes free, the use of force becomes meaningless and that there is no purpose in aggression if it is not to issue in one form or another of national subjection". The ideal of international liberty implies renunciation of war, limitation on the production of armaments, abandonment of the use of force and pacific settlement of disputes. Adequate curbs should be put on the strength of military force so that it may not crush the liberties of the local people or the people of a different culture.

Safeguards of Liberty

The importance of safeguarding liberty cannot be denied and various devices have been provided to safeguard the same. (1) A democratic government is a safeguard for liberty. People can enjoy full liberty only in a democratic state. There can be no liberty under dictatorship. In a democracy, the people have the government of their own choice. All political power is in their hands and they have a complete control over the government and hence they can safeguard their rights and liberties. Democracy is the government under which every citizen has a share in the running of the administration through their representatives who are responsible to the people. If they fail to safeguard the rights and liberties of the people, they can be removed by the people. Hence, under a democratic government, it is very easy for the people to safeguard their liberty. That is not so under any other form of government.

(2) Another device which has been adopted to safeguard liberty is the inclusion of fundamental rights in the constitution of a country. Those rights are guaranteed rights. The fundamental rights are the basic laws of the country which ensure non-interference by the state in an arbitrary manner. If

fundamental rights are violated by the government or any individual, the aggrieved party can go to the court and the courts pass the proper orders. Liberty is guaranteed by the judiciary from encroachments from any quarter. In this way, the judiciary and the Constitution protect the liberty of the people. The Indian Constitution provides for fundamental rights and it is the duty of the Supreme Court of India and the High Courts to safeguard those rights.

(3) Another safeguard of liberty is the independence of the judiciary. The judiciary can protect the rights and liberties of the people only if it is independent, impartial and honest. The judiciary can act as the custodian of the fundamental rights of the people which guarantee the liberty of an individual. This is possible only if the judges are allowed to function independently and impartially. The separation of the judiciary from the executive is an essential requirement for the maintenance of the liberties of the people. The independence of the judiciary is one of the corner-stones of a democratic government and the structure of civil liberty is built upon it.

(4) The view of Montesquieu is that the system of separation of powers can safeguard the rights and liberties of the people. This theory requires that the powers of the government should be separated into three different organs and each of them should function independently. No organ should interfere in the functioning of the other two. There should be no concentration of powers in the hands of a few persons or one person or a body of persons so that they may not rule tyrannically. Each organ should check the activities of the other two organs so that the same cannot destroy the liberty of the people. To quote Montesquieu, "There are no liberties to the people if the power of judging be not separate from the legislative and executive power". The principle of separation of powers is embodied in the American Constitution. In that country, the courts have the power of judicial review of administration and legislation. In many democracies, the national legislature plays an important part in protecting civil liberties. In continental Europe, administrative courts give protection against encroachments on liberty.

(5) The view of Sir Ivor Jennings is that besides limiting the powers of the executive, it is necessary to check the powers of the legislature. A legislature does not always reflect public opinion and the majority party dominating the legislature in a parliamentary democracy may ignore altogether the interests of or work against the wishes of the minorities. Legislature may be the hand-maid of the party in power, and may trample on the rights of the minority. Sir Ivor Jennings writes, "It is, therefore, usually regarded as desirable not only that the ordinary law shall protect the right of free speech, the right of association and the right of public meeting, but also that the powers of changing the law whether by legislation or administrative regulation shall be so restricted that these rights may not be interfered with".

(6) Another safeguard for liberty is the rule of law in the country. It is true that the people of England do not have a Bill of Rights, but still they enjoy as much liberty as the people of the United States. This is due to the fact that England has the rule of law which is regarded as the key to British liberty. In Britain, power is not exercised arbitrarily but according to law and the principles of the Constitution. Prof. A.V. Dicey writes, "There is in the English Constitution an absence of those declarations or definitions of rights so dear to foreign constitutions....In England, the right to individual liberty is a part of the Constitution because it is secured by the courts, extended or confined as they are by the Habeas Corpus Acts."

(7) Another safeguard for liberty is public opinion and a free press. Healthy public opinion and a free press can do a lot to protect liberty. The press and other agencies mould the public opinion. "In the final analysis, public opinion is the ultimate sanction behind all bills and declarations of individual liberties. Courts as well as legislative assemblies, reflect (whether promptly or belatedly) the temper of the popular mind".

(8) Free and honest press plays an important role in safeguarding the liberty of the people. Newspapers give us news regarding all social, economic, political, religious, cultural etc. activities happening at different places. Different political and other problems are given in the editorials and articles. The press throws light on various current issues which help in the formation and expression of public opinion. The news published in the newspapers and other media are not always correct and impartial, the people are not well-informed about the various development in the country or outside and hence a free and honest press is essential. Prof. Laski writes, "A people without reliable news is sooner or later a people without a basis for freedom".

(9) Political parties also help to safeguard the liberty of the people. If the government interferes with the rights and liberties of the people, the parties of the Opposition condemn the same and keep a strict watch on the activities of the government. Political parties act as the "broker of ideas." They raise different issues, present facts to the people, with alternative solutions and try to analyse them. Powell writes, "The parties enable the people to hold the government in check. The constant presence of recognised opposition with a programme fairly within the limits of a possible public opinion, is a bulwark against the tyranny, not only of a despot but also of a practical political majority".

(10) According to Laski, liberty can be safeguarded only if there are no special privileges in the society. Special privileges may be based on birth or property and their existence militates against liberty. If some people in society enjoy special rights, they endanger the liberties and rights of others. If the rights of one class depend upon the rights of others, liberty cannot be maintained. Nobody should be given special rights or privileges in society.

(11) A very important safeguard for liberty is the urge for liberty among the people. The people in a state should have not only the urge for liberty but should also be vigilant to preserve it after it is secured. The love of liberty cannot be artificially thrust into the hearts of the people from outside. It should rise naturally from within. If the people do not have the urge to preserve their liberty, they are sure to lose it sooner or later. They should feel in their hearts that there is nothing as precious as liberty.

According to Lord Bryce, "Eternal vigilance is the price of liberty". The people must be so watchful that they do not tolerate any violation of liberty at any time from any quarter and also must be prepared to make sacrifices to safeguard their liberty. It is rightly said that "The secret of liberty lies in courage". Laski writes, "Liberty is never real unless the Government is called to account when it invades the rights of the people". De Tocqueville writes, "There are nations which have tirelessly pursued freedom through every kind of peril and hardship. They loved it, not for its material benefit, they regarded freedom itself as a gift so precious and so necessary that no other could console them for the loss of everything else. I attempt no analysis of that great emotion for those who cannot feel it. It enters of its own accord into the generous heart God has prepared to receive it; it fills them, it inspires them; but to the meaner minds which have never felt it, it is past finding out".

Thomas Jefferson writes, "What country can preserve its liberties if the rulers are not warned from time to time that this people preserve the spirit of resistance". Judge Learned Hand says, "Liberty lies in the hearts of men and women; when it dies there, no constitution, no law, no court can save it; no constitution, no law, no court can even do much to help it".

(12) Another safeguard for liberty is political education. The people can enjoy liberty only if they are politically educated. Political education helps them to know their rights and liberties. It makes them politically conscious. Without that education, the people will not fight for their liberties.

(13) Another safeguard for liberty is the decentralisation of power as the concentration of power is the biggest danger to liberty and leads to despotism. Laski writes, "The more widespread the distribution of power in the state, the more decentralised its character, the more likely are men to be zealous for freedom". Decentralisation helps in promoting individual liberty. According to De Tocqueville, "A nation may establish a system of free government, but without the spirit of

municipal institutions it cannot have the spirit of liberty". The view of Lord Byrce is that the local self-governing institutions are essential for promoting the liberty of the people. Thus, decentralisation of power is essential for maintaining liberty.

(14) Another safeguard for liberty is economic security. If the people are not free from economic worries, they cannot enjoy real freedom. A poor man cannot think of political liberty. Liberty has no meaning for those who are economically backward.

(15) Another safeguard for liberty is the spirit of tolerance and cooperation among the people. They should respect the views and feelings of others. There should be full cooperation between the Government and the people as without that cooperation liberty cannot be maintained.

(16) Widespread social justice is a significant pillar to the mansion of freedom. The freedom of a people is reduced to a shadow without substance if economic and social privileges become the monopoly of a select minority. Modern welfare states are undertaking measures for reducing disparities in income and wealth. The diffusion of economic power over widest area is a necessary adjunct to the fulfilment of liberty.

New Menace to Liberty

It is true that there is no liberty under a dictatorship and liberty is possible in a democratic government, but there are certain tendencies even in a democratic state which are a menace to liberty. (1) This is partly due to the fact that in the name of welfare state, governments all over the world are rapidly extending their functions and powers and that results in the tremendous growth of the power of the state which cannot be consistent with the liberty of the individual. About the present position of the state in a welfare society, K.M. Panikkar writes, "It speaks with a million voices on the radio. It overhears our conversations on the telephone. It pries into our secret thoughts by censoring our letters. It controls the water we drink, the food we eat, the lights we use, our modes of transport and in fact practically everything in our lives. It gives with one hand and takes away with the other" (*The State and the Citizen*, p. 5).

(2) As the functions of the state are increasing, more and laws have to be passed dealing with those functions. The existence of too many laws and their enforcement by the government results in the proportionate loss of individual liberty. The bureaucracy becomes all-powerful.

(3) Another danger to liberty is the tyranny of the majority. Under a democratic form of government, the ruling party may have a brute majority which may enable it to pass any law unmindful of the liberties of the people. The government based on a brute majority can trample upon the liberty of the people unless the people themselves are able to exert their pressure on the government through the press, platform and other agencies of public opinion and force it to desist from passing laws or acting in a manner which is destructive of liberty.

(4) In some countries, the government does all the thinking and tells the people what is good for them and what is not good for them. The government refuses to respond to public opinion. Leaders in those countries profess democratic principles but deny liberty to their people. When the government suppresses public opinion and takes over the function of thinking and speaking for the people, great harm is done to the cause of liberty.

Marxist Concept of Freedom

Marxism is usually denounced as a totalitarian doctrine based on the theory of economic determinism. Both determinism and totalitarianism are ideas which are incompatible with the concept of freedom. However, James J.O. Rourke does not accept this view. According to him, "The notion of freedom plays a central role in the thought of Karl Marx. His notion of freedom often figures significantly in the background which gives meaning to his more specific and immediate concerns. It is for him one of those fundamental categories which are constantly assumed, and often too obvious to be explained, For example, one can easily forget that the ultimate meaning of history is not the mere development of socio-economic forms but the progressive liberation of mankind. Similarly, the notion of freedom lurks behind the critique of religion and the whole description of the forms of alienation... the theme of the freedom of men has a pervasiveness and extent in the long development of his thought which marks it as one of those basic themes providing continuity to his work." (*The Problem of Freedom in Marxist Thought*, p. 9).

The Marxist concept of freedom is different from the liberal view of freedom. It treats freedom as relative to socio-economic conditions. The Marxist view is that freedom is not something that an individual enjoys in isolation or by "being left alone". Marxism does not accept the theory of an atomized, alienated and possessive individual being capable of enjoying freedom. Marx and Engels wrote thus in *Holy Family.* "The members of civil society are not atoms. The specific property of the atom is that it has no properties and is therefore not connected with beings outside it by any relations determined by its own natural necessity. The atom has no needs, it is self-sufficient; the world outside it is absolute vacuum, *i.e.* it is contentless, senseless, meaningless, just because the atom has all its fullness in itself. The egoistic individual in civil society may in his non-sensuous imagination and lifeless abstraction inflate himself to the size of an atom, *i.e.*, to an unrelated, self-sufficient, wantless, absolutely full, blessed being".

While rejecting the atomistic view of the individual, Marx and Engels maintained that the natural needs of man, the very conditions of his existence, brought him into a natural relation with other individuals and civil society came into existence which holds the individuals together. To quote them, "It is natural necessity, essential human properties, however alienated they may seem to be, and interest that holds the members of the civil society together; civil not political life is their real tie.... Only political superstition today imagines that social life must be held together by the state whereas in reality the state is held together by civil life."

Marxism does not accept the utilitarian view that common interest can be derived from a mechanical aggregation of the self-interest of different individuals. The Marxist view is that the common interest can be served only by creating socio-economic conditions conducive to the enjoyment of freedom within society. Those conditions involve access to the material means of satisfaction of wants and the opportunity for self-development. The key to freedom lies in a rational system of production which can provide the means of such satisfaction and development.

The Marxist view is that the capitalist system of production is not conducive to the conditions of human freedom. It is characterised by constraint or necessity. Necessity denotes the condition under which the life of man is governed by the laws of nature which exist independent of man's will. A man can acquire scientific knowledge of those laws for his own benefit, but cannot change them at his will. To quote Engels, "Necessity is blind only in so far as it is not understood. Freedom does not consist in any dream of independence from natural laws, but in the knowledge of those laws, and in the possibility this gives of systematically making them work towards definite ends." This applies both to the laws of external nature and the laws of our own nature. Engels writes, "Freedom therefore consists in the control over ourselves and over external nature, a control founded on knowledge of natural necessity; it is therefore necessarily a product of historical development. The first men who separated themselves from the animal kingdom were in all essentials as unfree as the animals themselves, but each step forward in the field of culture was a step towards freedom".

According to Engels, the capitalist system is facing crisis after crisis because "society is suffocated beneath the weight of its own productive forces and products, which it cannot use, and stands helpless, face to face with the absurd contradiction that the producers have nothing to consume, because consumers are wanting. The expansive force of the means of production bursts the bonds that the capitalist mode of production had imposed upon them. Their deliverance from these bonds is the one precondition for an unbroken, constantly-accelerated development of the productive forces, and therewith for a practically unlimited increase of production itself". The view of Engels is that only the socialization of the means of production can help society to tide over the crisis and usher in a new era of freedom. To quote him, "Man's own social organization, hitherto confronting him as a necessity imposed by nature and history, now becomes the result of his own free action. The extraneous objective forces that have hitherto governed history pass under the control of man himself. Only from that time will man himself, with full consciousness, make his own history – only from that time will the social causes set in movement by him have, in the main and in a constantly growing measure, the results intended by him. It is humanity's leap from the kingdom of necessity to the kingdom of freedom".

Marx criticised in very strong terms the capitalist system of production for its dehumanising effect and pointed out that the capitalist system deformed the productive activity of man and caused his alienation in many ways. The alienation of man in contemporary society was the result of the system of commodity production, division of labour, private ownership, market economy, monetization of the exchange and similar features of the capitalist system. Marx identified four levels of alienation: alienation from the product of the work, alienation from the work itself, alienation from one's fellow-beings and alienation from human species-life. Alienation is a radical loss of freedom because it is the negation of free genuinely human creative activity.

(1) As regards alienation from the product of work, the worker in the capitalist system of production does not own and control the products of his own labour. He does not use the wealth which he creates. He is alienated from his own product. The life which he has given to the object sets itself against him as an alien force. The worker himself becomes a commodity whose value is equal to the bare means of his subsistence. The capitalist who purchases the labour-power of the worker, is the real owner of the wealth which he creates.

(2) As regards alienation from work itself, Marx points out that the alien relationship of the worker to the product is only an expression of the alienated nature of productive activity itself. The worker who sells his labour-power produces commodities under orders from his employer. Therefore, his work is neither free nor voluntary because he does not satisfy any creative urge of his own by working in the factory owned and managed by his capitalist employer.

(3) As regards alienation from his fellow-being, the alienated work results in the alienation of the worker from other men. It results in the hostility between the employed worker and the unemployed worker at the factory gate and they face one another as alien forces. The worker sees in the manager and the proprietor alien forces profiting from his alienated work. Thus, the basis of genuine social relation is totally destroyed.

(4) The above-mentioned three aspects of man's alienation produce his alienation from his species-life. The egoistic, self-centred existence of the alienated worker alienates him from man's entire cultural heritage. According to Marx, the oppressed members of the working class are hardly aware of the artistic, scientific and other cultural achievements of the human race. They lack the capacity to understand and enjoy those beautiful gifts of human creativity. Thus, man is cut off from the history and life of his own species. By dehumanising his existence, man becomes a slave to his own alienated activity. What is true of the worker is also true of those who live on the products of alienated labour. The capitalist who rides on the backs of the proletariat also leads an alienated life because he also is not personally engaged in any creative work and is a victim of the fetishization of the commodities. In a society based on unfreedom, the slave and his master are equally unfree.

Deliverance from this bondage can be found in the realisation that society is a creation by which man attains a fuller measure of freedom which is obstructed by the peculiar conditions created by private property and those conditions exist in their worst form under the capitalist system. The remedy lies in a socialist revolution which will enable society to restore human values and inaugurate a new era of freedom. Engles writes, "By this act, the proletariat frees the means of production from the character of capital they have thus for borne, and gives their socialized character complete freedom to work itself out. Socialized production upon a predetermined plan becomes henceforth possible. The development of production makes the existence of different classes of society thenceforth an anachronism. In proportion as anarchy in social production vanishes, the political authority of the state dies out. Man, at last the master of his own form of social organization, becomes at the same time the lord over nature, this own master — free."

While the liberal view of freedom is that freedom can be secured with minor adjustments within the capitalist system, the Marxist theory postulates a transformation of capitalist system itself to secure the conditionals of freedom.

The Marxist view is that in the capitalist system, the concept of freedom has always been a symbol of individual's separation from society. The freedom of individual is a kind of private acquisition of an insular person who regards other people in the society as his rivals in the constant struggle for wealth, status and life. As Marx commented on the bourgeois ideology of freedom, "Man's right to freedom is based not on association of man with man but on the contrary, on the isolation of man from man. It is a right to this isolation, the right of the limited, secluded individual". The Marxist view puts emphasis on the need for creating new socio-economic conditions conducive to the enjoyment of freedom by all as distinguished from the limited freedom of the propertied class in the capitalist society. Therefore, freedom cannot be secured by retaining the capitalist system even after necessary readjustments. True freedom can blossom only in a new socialist classless society that would come into being after the liquidation of the capitalist state.

Marxism does not regard the absence of restraint as freedom. It also does not accept the view that personal and political freedoms are the highest ideals and other freedoms are based on them. It defines freedom by associating it with essence and purpose of man. Explaining the Marxian view of freedom, Huberman and Sweezy write, "Freedom means living life to the fullest – the economic ability to satisfy the needs of the body in regard to adequate food, clothing and shelter, plus effective opportunity to cultivate the mind, develop one's personality and assert one's individuality". Petrosyan observes, "Marx's understanding of freedom implies activity aimed at creating real conditions for the free all-round development and flowering of man's individuality". Again, freedom's "full significance is the free all-round development of all members of society". Chesnokov says, "A full man will develop only in freedom, but true freedom is uncorrectable without a free society." This issue of freedom is not seen in isolation from society. Society should be a free society which is an association of free individuals.

The Marxist view of freedom is linked up with equality. In a society based on private property, there can neither be equality nor freedom. Freedom is associated with the abolition of property and in creating a society based on social ownership of the means of production. Freedom from exploitation is a pre-condition for freedom. Freedom becomes meaningless if the majority of the population is exploited by a small minority of property-owners. The freedom of a few cannot be built on the unfreedom of the many.

Marxism regards knowledge of objective laws as the necessary conditions for freedom, but this alone is not sufficient. Freedom can only be achieved by revolutionary social activity based on the knowledge of objective laws of nature and society. Knowledge makes possible the mastery of man over nature and society, but without man's revolutionary social activity, that knowledge is useless. Petrosyan writes, "Freedom, in the sense of the laws of nature and society, only comes as a result of practical revolutionary activity based on such knowledge of the laws of historical development".

The Marxist view is that in a class-divided society, freedom will mean different things to different classes. For the owners of property, it will mean freedom of private property, profits, free contracts, exploitation and employment and dismissal of persons. For the property-less, it will mean freedom to starve, to be exploited, to be removed from job, unlimited hours of work and bad working conditions. Freedom of one class becomes the bondage of another class. Thus, freedom does not possess a universal character in a class-divided society. Freedom remains fake freedom because working class cannot make use of it. In such societies, the capitalist class maintains a vast political and ideological apparatus to secure its freedom against the revolutionary struggles of the working class. "Police, standing army and laws were all brought into being to protect the 'haves' from the 'free' desires of the have-nots. Bourgeois liberty at once gives rise to bourgeois coercion; to prisons, armies, contracts, to all the sticky and restraining apparatus of the law, to all the ideology and education centred round the sanctity of private property, to all the bourgeois commandments. The bourgeois liberty was built on a lie bound to reveal in time its contradiction."

In a class-divided society, freedom is meaningless for the working people. For them, freedom means emancipation from exploitation, starvation, poverty, excessive hours of work and social insecurity. Freedom for them will mean struggle for socialist revolution and the establishment of a classless society. It will mean struggle for the establishment of a free society in which freedom may blossom and life may become delightful. Even for the bourgeois class, freedom does not mean real freedom in a class-divided society because it is not in accordance with' man's essence, purpose and values.

The Marxist view is that freedom can be available in the free atmosphere of a free society. Free society will be a classless society in which every one will be free from the exploitation of his fellow-beings. The wall of private property will not remain between man and society and man can live in society with his true essence, purpose and values. Freedom means multi-dimensional development of social man and free society provides ample opportunities for this. Alienation between man and his nature, society and its labour will come to an end and man will not be dehumanised. Marx writes, "Communism will lead to reintegration of his personality, to man's return to himself, to his assumption of his own human essence or, in other words, to the elimination of all form of human alienation, to elimination of the contradictions between essence and existence to the all-round development of man as a person and individual."

The production will be for the general consumption of all and not for the profits of a few. The ownership of the means of production will be social. Property will not be master of man, rather man will be its master. The measure of humanity will not be money, but human values. In such a society, scarcity will be replaced by abundance, exploitation of man by man, by cooperation among men, inequality by equality and unfreedom by freedom. Mart will have enough time and money for cultural and human activities. Real freedom will begin only when the slavery of mere physical needs will end.

Criticism

The Marxist theory of freedom has been criticised by Rossiter on many grounds. Marx failed to resolve the tension between liberty and authority. He pinned his hope on the withering away of the state which has not materialised. He did not envisage that political power at one time would pose a threat to personal liberty. He underestimated the importance of formal freedoms such as laws, charters, elections etc. He made human rights dependent on the fact of human needs, a principle which hurts human dignity. With the end of distinction between public and private man, Marx passed a sentence of death upon privacy. There is too much emphasis upon economic freedom and less upon the positive and creative practice of liberty. Marx put too much emphasis on class liberty, but liberty is essentially personal. He ignored the central question of who was to hold control of effective power in personal freedom – the individual or some authority outside him. (The View from America, pp. 86-87)

Estimate

The view of Herbert Aptheker is that in contrast to the bourgeois theory of freedom, the Marxist view looks at freedom positively, "that is, while bourgeois theory of freedom focuses upon the absence of restraint upon the individual and the presence of restraint upon the government, in terms of what it may not do, the focus of Marxist theory is opposite. It tends to view freedom not so much in terms of what may not be done, but rather in terms of what can be and should be done". (The Nature of Democracy, Freedom and Revolution, p. 43). The Marxist criticism of the bourgeois theory of freedom has influenced the structure and working of the state in capitalist society. Attempts are being made to bring about institutional changes to bridge the gap between the state and the individual.

SUGGESTED READINGS

Avineri, S. : *The Social and Political Thought of Karl Marx*, Cambridge, 1971.

Barker, E. : *Principles of Social and Political Theory*, 1951.

Benn, S.I. and Peters, R.S : *Social Principles and the Democratic State*, London, 1959.

Carr, R.K. and Others : *American Democracy in Theory and Practice.*

Cornforth, M. : *Dialectical Materialism*, Calcutta, 1955.

Corry, J.A. : *Democratic Government and Politics*, 1958.

Cranston, M. : Freedom, A New Analysis, London, 1953.

Dicey, A.V. : *Introduction to the Study of the Law of the Constitution*, 1956.

Friedman, M. : *Capitalism and Freedom*, Chicago, 1962.

Gerassi, John : *Towards Revolution*, London, 1971.

Hayek, F. : *The Road to Serfdom*, Chicago, 1945.

Hayek, F. : *The Counter-Revolution of Science*, New York, 1955.

Hayek. F. : *The Constitution of Liberty*, London, 1960.

Hobhouse, L.T. : *Elements of Social Justice.*

Hodges, D.C. : *Socialist Humanism*, 1974.

Hunt, Richard N. : *Marxism and Totalitarian Democracy.*

Jennings, Ivor : *The Law and the Constitution*, 1955.

Kamenka, E. : *The Ethical Foundations of Marxism*, London, 1962.

Kerning, C.D. (Ed.) : *Marxism, Communism and Western Society*, New York, 1972.

Laski, H.J. : *A Grammar of Politics*, 1925.

Lewis, John : *Marxism and Open Mind.*

Lukacs, G. : *History and Class-Consciousness.*

Macpherson, C.B. : *Democratic Theory, Oxford*, 1973.

Martin, E.W.	:	*The Tyranny of the Majority*, 1961.
Mill, J.S.	:	*On Liberty.*
O' Rourke, James J.	:	*The Problem of Freedom in Marxist Thought.*
Petrosyan, N.	:	*Humanism: Its Philosophical, Ethical and Sociological Aspects*, Moscow, 1972.
Plamenatz, J.	:	*Karl Marx's Philosophy of Man*, Oxford, 1975.
Popper, K.	:	*The Open Society and Its Enemies*, London, 1945.
Quinton, A. (Ed.)	:	*Political Theory, Oxford University Press*, 1967.
Raphael, D.D.	:	*Problems of Political Philosophy.*
Rodee Anderson and Christol	:	*Introduction to Political Science*, 1957.
Rossiter, Clinton	:	*Marxism: The View from America.*
Salvadori, Massimo	:	*Liberal Democracy*, 1957.
Soltau, R.H.	:	*An Introduction to Politics*, 1959.
Stephen	:	*Liberty, Equality and Fraternity.*
Tawney, R.H.	:	*Equality.*

CHAPTER

Equality

Learning Objectives

- Development of the Concept of Equality
- Definition and Meaning of Equality
- Conditions Necessary for Equality
- Kinds of Equality
- Legal Equality
- Political Equality
- Social Equality
- Economic Equality
- Natural Equality
- Marxist View of Equality
- Liberty and Equality
- Suggested Readings

Development of the Concept of Equality

The problem of equality and inequality has figured in political thought since the earliest times. In Greek philosophy, two different traditions emerged. One tradition was represented by Plato and Aristotle and that supported inequality. The other tradition represented by Pericles, the Sophists, Antiphon, Lycophron, Euripides and the Stoics supported equality among men. Artistotle discovered that inequality was a cause of rebellion in many states. He defined justice as treating equals equally and unequals unequally. He insisted on recognition and maintenance of the existing inequalities in society – between master and slave, between the rich and the poor, between morally superior and morally inferior and so on. He distinguished constitutional rule from despotic rule on the basis that constitutional rule is for the good of all (equality) and despotic rule is for the good of the ruling class only (inequality). He also laid emphasis on equality between citizens of the same state. Plato classified men into men of gold, men of silver and men of iron. The Greeks were regarded superior to other races.

The Stoic philosophers (Zeno, Cicero and Seneca) gave the idea of universal brotherhood and citizenship which was based on natural law and reason and corresponds to the modern idea of equality. They opposed slavery and pleaded for natural equality among men, Euripides considered equality as man's law of nature. According to him, equality is a force which binds together friends, cities and allies. Cicero believed in a universal law of nature binding upon all men and all nations. It was error, bad habits and false opinions which prevented men from being equal. If all men are subject to the same law as fellow citizens, they must be in some sense equal.

During the medieval period, Christianity raised the voice for equality in the beginning but soon it got converted into equality before God. It was contended that in the eyes of God all were equal, but there were inequalities on earth. During that period, feudalism emerged in Europe and unequal rules of aristocracy developed. Under feudalism, social inequality was consolidated by law. During the medieval period, social inequalities got legal recognition and legal privileges available to the clergy and the nobility were accepted in society. Against those legal privileges based on birth emerged the modern concept of equality before law and equality by birth.

The Renaissance and the Reformation played an important part in weakening and shaking the existing social and political system. The emerging middle class challenged the legal, social and political privileges of the feudal order. The Glorious Revolution of 1688 in England, the American Declaration of Independence of 1776 and the French Revolution of 1789 helped the cause of equality. Brinton writes, "The powerful and recently enriched middle classes, especially in France and England, were anxious to achieve social and political equality with the nobility....Reason and faith both showed man to be identical at birth, if they were now unlike, the cause must be sought in something outside them – their environment". Equality before law and equality by birth were the main features of the demand for equality. Various thinkers of the enlightenment raised the voice for equality. In his book "Discourse on the Origin of Inequality" published in 1754, Rousseau pleaded for equality and maintained that inequalities had emerged due to the rise of private property and civilisation. Rousseau drew an important distinction between two types of inequalities found in social life: natural inequality and conventional inequality. Natural or physical inequality consists in the differences of age, health, bodily strength and qualities of mind and soul. Conventional inequality consists in the different privileges which some men enjoy to the exclusion of others such as inequalities of wealth, prestige and power. One form of inequality is not dependent upon human choice as it is ordained more or less by nature. The other form of inequality is largely man-made and it emanates from the social order more or less deliberately designed by men themselves. The French Declaration of the Rights of Man and the Citizen (1789) which was inspired by Rousseau's revolutionary ideas, recorded: "Men are born and remain free and equal in rights. Social distinctions can be based only upon public utility". The demand for economic equality was raised by Babeuf but he was killed in 1797 and the spectre of economic equality was buried with him.

In the nineteenth century, a vigorous demand for socio-economic equality was raised by the newly emerging working class. As a result of the Industrial Revolution, economic disparities had increased and the demand for economic equality and justice came from many quarters *e.g.*, the humanists, the Utopian Socialists, the Marxists and the Positive Liberals. Karl Marx associated the question of economic equality with the abolition of private property and classless society. The demand for economic equality was not only for political and legal equality but also for positive equality which implied a check on private property, a check on the exploitation of the poor by the rich and a positive role of the state with regard to the economic system of society. During the nineteenth century, the movement for political equality also became stronger and adult franchise became the battle-cry of the democrats.

The liberals did not concentrate on one kind of equality. Their main concern was for moral equality which implied the right of each man to be treated as an end and not a means, judicial equality which implied the right of each man to justice on the same terms as other men, political equality which implied the right of each man to a vote that counts no more and no less than the vote of any other man, legal equality which implies the right to be exempt from class legislation and equality of opportunity which means the right of each to exploit his own talents to their natural limits. The liberals carried on their struggle for equality through constitutional processes. The Marxists advocated revolution to abolish all class distinctions and inequalities.

The twentieth century has witnessed many revolutionary struggles for equality. National movements emerged against imperialism in Asia, Africa and Latin America. The theory of Whiteman's burden was denounced. Various movements of the black people against the white races developed and black people won their independence. Even now the struggles of the black people against the white people are going on in different parts of the world for achieving equality. Not only the blacks in South Africa but also the blacks in the United States demand equality with the whites. After the Second World War, the movement for the liberation of women demanded equality for women in all spheres of social life. The most glorious battles for economic equality were won in the Soviet Union and Communist China during the present century.

Definition and Meaning of Equality

The concept of equality is sometimes confused with words like identical, same, similar and equitable, but in political terms, equality as a concept is different from all of them and it is very difficult to define it as an abstract concept. Laski writes, "No idea is more difficult in the whole realm of political science than equality". J.F. Stephen observes, "Equality is a word so wide and vague as to be by itself almost unmeaning" (*Liberty, Equality, Fraternity*, p. 20). R.H. Tawney writes, "The word equality possesses more than one meaning". (*Equality*, p. 35).

Equality has many facets and it cannot be defined or even described at one single glance at it. Like liberty, equality is a great democratic ideal which has been understood in different ways. To some, it is nothing more than equality before law. There are others who understand equality in the widest sense possible and bring under the general heading of equality political equality, social equality, civil equality and economic equality. Giovanni Sartori rightly says that equality "has so many facets and so many implications that after we have examined it from all angles, we are left with a feeling of not having really mastered it" (*Democratic Theory*, p. 326).

The ideal of equality is fundamentally a levelling process. Harold J. Laski writes, "Equality, broadly, is a coherence of ideas each one of which needs special examination. Undoubtedly, it implies fundamentally a certain levelling process. It means that no man shall be so placed in society that he can over-reach his neighbour to the extent which constitutes a denial of the latter's citizenship. It means that my realisation of my best self must involve as its logical result the realisation by others of their best selves. It means such an ordering of social forces as will balance a share in the toil of living with a share in its gain also....Equality, therefore, means first of all the absence of special privilege....Equality means, in the second place, that adequate opportunities are laid open to all". (*A Grammar of Politics*, pp. 153-54). J.A. Corry observes, "The ideal of equality has insisted that men are politically equal, that all citizens are equally entitled to take part in political life, to exercise the franchise, to run for and hold office. It has insisted that individual shall be equal before the law, that when the general law confers rights or imposes duties, those rights and duties shall extend to all; or conversely that the law shall not confer special privileges on particular individual or groups". (*Democratic Government and Politics*,..p. 33)

Like liberty, equality is essential for social justice. There have been many movements all over the world aiming at social justice and they have paid particular attention to the achievement of equality. The Constitution of India gives a place of pride to the fundamental right of equality.

Equality is closely connected with liberty. Without liberty, people cannot have equality. Liberty is poor in its content without the, basis of equality. The struggle for liberty cannot be considered successful without abolishing the special rights and privileges of a few. Political, social, economic and other types of inequality result in injustice to millions all over the world. In an atmosphere of inequality, only a few enjoy special privileges and the rest of the people suffer and that is why there is a demand for removal of special preferences and privileges. Throughout the nineteenth century, the concept of equality stood in the background of a great variety of social movements. One of the important causes of French Revolution of 1789 was the absence of political, social and economic equality in the *Ancien regime* in France.

All men are not born equal and absolute equality can never be realised. As a matter of fact, nature has made men unequal. Some of them are endowed with great intellectual power, some with great physical strength, some with extremely handsome features and some with very rare gifts. Elton Trueblood writes, "Physically some men are three or four times as strong as others, able to perform many times as much work. Intellectually, the contrast is still greater, as may be realised when we compare an average person with a man like Sir Winston Churchill....If intellectual inequality is more marked than physical inequality, moral inequality is still more so. The contrast between self-centred and cruel persons on the one hand and the saints and heroes on the other, is really incalculable".

(*Declaration of Freedom, p.* 73). Every individual has his own points of strength and weakness peculiar to his own personality. No two individuals, even if they are twins, are exactly alike. "Factually men are not equal and the more specific the investigation, the more apparent it is that men are unequal; unequal in strength, in spirit, in grace, in thought".

It has been found that absolute equality is neither possible nor desirable. Men never had absolute equality and it will be ridiculous to expect so. Equality does not mean uniformity and difference does not mean inequality. Though there are differences between man and man, there is something which is basically common between them "in the sense of possessing beneath the observed differences some more and universal attribute of manhood by virtue of which each should by right – and can with safety be treated as the equal of every other in reference to certain functions and privileges in society". (*Government by the People by Burns and Peltason*, p. 35).

The modern concept of equality is derived from the theory of rights. Equality is a prescriptive term and not a descriptive term. We claim that men must be treated as equal, but that does not mean that they are equal in fact. We postulate that man as such is a rational being. He is endowed with the faculty of reason. All men are created equal by God. The physical, emotional and intellectual needs of all men are similar and hence they are entitled to equal rights. It is to be noticed that we do not say that all men are equal in their physical, or mental capacities, beauty and talents. Sometimes we dwell on physical attributes to press our claim. Men may differ in the colour of their skin, but they are all similar in the colour of their blood and hence they should be treated equally.

Sometimes it is argued that the idea of equality does not derive support from nature as the idea of liberty does, and hence it is not based on reason. It is stated that nature has created all things unequal, right from the Sun and the Moon, sky and earth, mountains and oceans, plants and trees, birds and animals to men and women, older and younger, stronger and weaker, wiser and stupid and hence the principle of equality does not hold good. However, this type of argument is based on a distorted concept of liberty. Freedom in society can serve as a valid rule only when it is interpreted as equal freedom for all and not otherwise. Absolute freedom results in the liberty of the strong and clever to oppress the weak and simple. If liberty is not to degenerate into license, it must be qualified by equality. R.H. Tawney writes, "If liberty means....that every individual shall be free, according to his opportunities, to indulge without limit his appetite....it is clearly incompatible, not only with economic and social, but with civil and political, equality, which also prevent the strong exporting to the full the advantages of their strength....But freedom for the pike is death for the minnows. It is possible that equality is contrasted, not with liberty, but only with a particular interpretation of it." (*Equality*, pp. 207-8). The introduction of equality is not intended to dilute the content of liberty but to make it more relevant and substantive. Equality is invoked to prevent some section of society from acquiring unlimited money, power or prestige. It is intended to restrict the element of exploitation. Equality aims at widening the base of social benefits so that the benefits are not cornered by a small and vocal minority.

Equality as a principle of correcting the unjust inequalities in society, is a modern idea. It is true that inequalities of wealth, prestige and power have always existed in society but the traditional thinkers considered the phenomena of social inequality as divinely ordained. They took social order as something not capable of change by human design or effort. However, with the dawn of the scientific age, a rational knowledge of social structures was evolved. The social thinkers of the modern age ask as to how far the existing inequalities in society are the result of social arrangement and could be altered by making corresponding changes in the social structure. New thinking paved the way for the removal of social inequalities on the ground that those were not reasonable and were also removable by human effort.

Scientific knowledge about the social structure led to the demand for social change. With the advance of scientific knowledge and technology, more and more areas of natural inequality are coming within the sphere which can be altered. We now know that health and bodily strength can be improved by proper nutrition and mental make-up can be considerably developed by proper education and training. Even physical deformities and mental handicaps can be prevented by timely care, protection and treatment. The availability of the new benefits depends upon the resources of the person concerned. The feeling emerges that a large part of humanity is being deprived of the benefits of modern civilisation on account of the inequalities which are not ordained by God. The demand for equality is always raised as a demand for social change but changes can be made only in those spheres which are not only unjust but can also be altered. Even if some people think that the burden of child-bearing on woman is unjust, nobody makes it a political issue as this inequality between the sexes is unalterable. If some persons are more beautiful, talented or energetic than others and hence enjoy more importance, that is not resented in society unless the gifted persons exploit others. As long as authority and division of labour are based on reason, inequality of status and position does not become objectionable.

Inequality becomes a ground of complaint and resentment when it is thought to be unjust. Equality demands a progressive reduction of inequalities where they are thought to be unreasonable, but this does not imply literal equalisation. Inequality in society may be functional or dysfunctional according to the prevailing idea of social justice. In ancient society, inequality between master and slave, lord and serf and capitalist and worker was regarded functional, but with the development of the socialist view of justice, this inequality was regarded unjust and dysfunctional and hence challenged. The view of Marx and Engels is that the division of society into capitalists and workers, bourgeoisie and the proletariat, and haves and have-nots involves exploitation and hence opposed to human happiness.

The ideal of equality does not contemplate that all material goods, the entire national income or all educational opportunities available in society should be equally distributed among all the members of society. What it means is that men who are different from one another in their physical and mental capacities, aptitudes and skill, talents and energies, should be given equal opportunities for the development of their personal qualities and capacities, in the shape of material goods, comforts, education, training etc. However, this does not mean the total absence of discrimination. To give the vote only to the wealthy is arbitrary as the possession of wealth has nothing to do with the capacity to vote. However, to give the right to vote to those who are capable of exercising it, is not discriminatory. The provision of different rewards for different services does not violate the principle of equality provided discrimination is made on rational grounds.

Conditions Necessary for Equality

Equality prevails in a society in which the following conditions are present :

(1) All persons are provided with adequate, not equal, opportunities for the development of their personalities.

(2) No class or caste or group is given special privileges which are denied to others.

(3) Rights are equally distributed among all.

(4) All have equal access to opportunities leading to equality.

kinds of equality

There was a time when the concept of equality was interpreted in a narrow sense, but with the widening horizon of democracy, the concept of equality has assumed new dimensions. In democratic countries, the concept of equality is understood very broadly and equality has gained entrance in many fields. All political thinkers do not classify the kinds of equality in the same way. According to Lord Bryce, there are four types of equality viz., civil equality, political equality, social equality and natural equality. Laski refers to political equality and economic equality. Barker deals with two equalities: legal and social.

Legal Equality

In the eighteenth century, the demand for legal equality was raised to abolish aristocratic legal privileges and feudal obligations. It meant equality before law and equal protection of law. Equality meant that equals before law should be treated equally by law. Law does not make distinction between the rich and the poor and in the eyes of law, they are equal. Equality before law does not mean equal laws for each and every one. The law has to make rational discrimination. Legal equality means equal laws for equals and unequal laws for unequals, but the basis of discrimination should be rational.

Legal equality does not merely mean equal laws. It also means equal opportunities to get justice from the courts. In a capitalist society, law courts are very costly and the poor cannot pay those costs. Legal equality is meaningless in the absence of equal opportunity to get justice. In liberal societies, man needs both time and money to have justice which the poor cannot afford. Legal equality is fictitious in a society where the people are not able to pay the cost of justice.

Ernest Barker has used the phrase "equality of legal personality" to explain the legal dimension of equality. Legal personality is a legal term devoid of any nontechnical implications regarding its meaning. It merely implies that the citizen is granted certain rights by law specifying the nature and extent of those rights. Hobhouse defines equality before law as equal enjoyment of certain fundamental rights and duties.

Law may apply equally and impartially to all persons who come within a certain category. The impartiality of man having social, communal or class biases, cannot be guaranteed in the application of these laws. Benn and Peters write, "Inequality in the administration of the law may arise not only from the partiality of judges and jurists, but from the defects of a different sort. If poor men are kept from the courts by the cost of a legal action; if a rich man can force a settlement on less favourable terms than a poor opponent would get in court by threatening to carry the case to appeal; if the former's case is put by more skilful – and more expensive counsel than the poor man can afford; then the formal equality in law of rich and poor is contradicted by a substantial inequality of access to justice".

The idea of legal equality emanates from moral considerations and serves as the basis of equal rights of man. Ernest Barker writes, "The principle of equality accordingly means that whatever conditions are guaranteed to me in the form of rights, shall also and in the same measure, be guaranteed to others, and that whatever rights are given to others shall also be given to me". (*Principles of Social and Political Theory*, p. 151.)

Legal equality was won after a prolonged struggle in human history. Ancient societies usually did not even entertain the idea of legal equality. Aristotle recommended differential punishments for the same offence for free men and slaves. The reason given was that the slave was less sensitive to punishment. Barker writes, "There was a long reign of legal inequality. Down to 1772 the slave was denied any legal capacity on English soil; he was not a person in the eye of the law, and he had no share in the enjoyment of rights.....Under the laws regulating the suffrage down to the year 1918 a person in receipt of poor relief was similarly condemned to an inferior degree of legal capacity by being denied the right of voting along with and on the same terms as others....Under the common law relating to property, married women down to 1870 were destitute of legal capacity for ownership;.... under the laws regulating the suffrage all women, down to 1918, were without any legal capacity for exercising a vote". (*Ibid*, pp. 152-53).

The principle of legal equality or equality before law, comprises the foundation of legal justice in modern society. J.R. Lucas writes, "Equality before the law does not guarantee equal treatment by the law but equal access to the law, and consideration only of those factors laid down by the law as relevant. Nobody is so lowly as not to have recourse to the courts, nobody is so mighty as not to have to answer to the courts; anybody can invoke the courts' aid, everybody must render them obedience; and the courts will decide disputes, after hearing arguments on both sides, fairly and impartially, without fear or favour". (*Principles of Politics*, p. 253).

Legal equality implies equal subjection of all citizens to the law and equal protection of the law for all citizens, but legal equality by itself is no guarantee for perfect justice. Equality before law can secure an equal benefit of law for all citizens when all citizens can equally afford to approach to the courts of law for the restoration of their rights or any injury suffered by them. Prof. Laski writes, "Nor must we forget the fact that wealth is a decisive factor in the power to take advantage of the opportunities the law affords its citizens to protect their rights. The ability to undertake an action in the courts, even with the provision made for legal aid to the poor, remains a grim financial question, and, on the civil side of the law, with its massive hierarchy of appeals, the advantage is solidly with the rich....as a general rule, the ablest lawyers will be at the service of those only who are able to afford them." (*State in Theory and Practice*, pp. 175-76).

As a result of lack of legal equality, an innocent poor person is not able to defend himself in a court of law, but smugglers, black-marketeers, profiteers, adulterators and other anti-social elements can engage the best lawyers to defend them. Lucas points out that "justice is not served if the case of one party is incompetently presented and that of the other is presented at its highest by the best lawyer money can buy. Hence, a great responsibility devolves on the judges who must view the cases in their proper socio-economic perspective". Lucas writes, "We rely heavily on our judges to discover the real merits of the case in spite of the differing abilities of counsel. But we rightly ensure by means of Legal Aid that equal access to the courts is at least not an empty equality, and that nobody is denied a hearing through inarticulateness or poverty". Unfortunately, judges are guided by their own social philosophy which is a product of socio-economic conditions. Usually, judges come from the upper strata of society and they apply their energies to safeguard the interests of the rich out of their conviction. Prof. Laski writes, "Our judges are recruited from the ranks of successful lawyers; and, overwhelmingly, our system makes the successful lawyer a man who has spent the major part of his life in serving the interests of property. He comes, therefore, almost unconsciously, to accept the assumptions of the economic system in being, and to adopt, without examination, the legal doctrines evolved for the protection of those interests". (*Parliamentary Government in England*, p. 372).

Political Equality

The demand for political equality was raised during the nineteenth century and it had a limited meaning viz., equal right to vote or adult franchise. Every individual should have the right to vote, right to contest elections, equal right to public services, and no distinction should be made on the basis of caste, colour, sex, religion and language. It meant "one man, one vote". In practice, the ideal of political equality has centred on universal suffrage and representative government. Each and every citizen, with the exception of insolvents and idiots, over the age of 18 years has a right to vote in England and the United States and the fact of property, tax-paying, education and sex are not taken into consideration. Adult franchise is an important step towards political equality but it is not sufficient. The right to vote was granted in the nineteenth century due to the political movements of the working class and their demand for the right to vote could not be resisted. In the twentieth century, women have won the right to vote through their movements.

The doctrine of political equality is derived from the general belief that man, as such, is a rational being, capable of political judgement irrespective of his physical and mental capacities, education and wealth etc. It also proceeds from the assumption that when equal political rights are extended to all, they will be able to give their best expression to the common good and prevail upon policy-makers to adjust public policy to the requirements of the common good. However, there are some writers who doubt the reality of genuine political equality in the modern democratic state. The view of Mosca, Pareto and Michels is that ordinary citizens, even when they have votes, have no real access to political power because, the political process results in the usurpation of power by a governing elite which is oligarchical in nature. Michels has propounded the iron law of oligarchy according to which political parties even in a democracy are controlled by a clique of self-appointed leaders. Prof. Laski also feels that political equality "is never real unless it is accompanied by virtual economic equality; political power, therefore, is bound to be the hand-maid of economic power." According to Marx, there can be no real political equality in a society based on capitalism. The bourgeois parties, supported financially and organisationally, do not allow a proletarian party to win elections, or to form a government which may change the capitalist system. The members of the working class may have equal voting rights in a formal sense, but owing to the lack of resources, they cannot send their true representatives to Parliament. The men of property have control over the mass media. Moreover, in modern times, the functioning of government has become very complex and real power is in the hands of the bureaucracy over which the people have virtually no control. The slogan of "government by experts" is replacing the slogan of "government by the people." In a class-divided society, higher government jobs are generally in the hands of the highly educated youngmen of the ruling class and if by chance some youngmen from the poor sections of society reach there, they are soon integrated into bureaucratic system of values. The bureaucracy is never impartial and always favours the economically dominant class. The elitist theory of democracy maintains that political equality is a myth and political power is always enjoyed by an elite. Lasswell and Kaplan write, "Power is never equally distributed; there is always an elite....If political equality were defined so as to exclude the existence of an elite, the concept would be vacuum". John Rees remarks, "The existence of government implies inequality because government consists of a set of arrangements whereby some individuals are authorised and have the power to control the actions of others."

Social Equality

Social Equality means that every citizen must have equality of opportunity for the development of his personality, irrespective of his social status, caste, colour, sex, race, language, education and age. There may be rational distinctions in a society with regard to occupations and professions, but the feeling of inferiority and superiority should not be attached with them. The social status or prestige of a man should not be determined by his aristocratic birth.

S.I. Benn and R.S. Peters write, "The term 'social equality' has been adopted by socialists largely to distinguish their objective from the earlier egalitarian ideals of the French Revolution. The men of 1789 sought 'equality before the law', which for them meant eliminating aristocratic legal privileges and feudal obligations. The Jacobins, and the nineteenth century Republicans on whom their mantle descended, sought 'political equality' or universal suffrage. To socialists these ends by themselves seem inadequate; they are at best ways of achieving 'real' equality – social equality. Without that, 'political equality' is an illusion". (*Social Principles and the Democratic State*, pp. 121-22).

The demand for social equality arose in the nineteenth century against the aristocratic privileges, against slavery, against the capitalists and against social inequalities on the basis of race. In the twentieth century, social equality has been demanded on the basis of sex, caste and colour.

The struggle for racial equality in countries like South Africa and racial inequalities practised in the United States are the burning issue of our times. The more civilised nations and enlightened men and women condemn the practice of racial inequality. The problem is not solved by providing constitutional and legal safeguards. It is also necessary that the myth of racial superiority should be given up.

The slogan of equality between the sexes assumed political significance during the women's struggle for equal voting rights. In recent times, women have launched movements like "Women's Lib" to fight against subtle forms of inequality in society which is said to be dominated by men. Women have proved that they are not in any way inferior to men in matters of intelligence and soundness of judgement. The biological differences between the sexes cannot justify discrimination in the sphere of voting rights, entry to the professions, educational opportunities, levels of remunerations or right to hold the highest offices in the government or industry. The feminists need not complain if the national law forbids the employment of women as coal-miners or if the municipal bye-laws do not allow women to work as Rikshaw-pullers because the admitted difference in physique between the sexes makes this distinction reasonable. However, as Benn and Peters point out, the biological difference does not justify elevating the husband into a lord and master, nor the complete sacrifice of the woman's personality to the demands of the family. The emancipation of women has expressed itself not only in law and economics, but also in changes in conventional marital relations. Many husbands now recognize that the domestic burden carried by mothers of families in previous generations was out of all proportion to the difference in function implied by the difference in sex. Their readiness to share the chores and the baby minding is a sign of a practical extension of the principle of equal consideration" (*Social Principles and Democratic State*, p. 118).

The issue of social equality is associated with the equality of opportunities. It is necessary that a new social atmosphere be created in which there is equality of opportunity for all. Nobody should be deprived of entry into any public hotel, temple, church, school and playground. Likewise, access to public wells, cinemas etc. must be open to all. There should be so much of equality of opportunity in society that even the poorest man can reach the highest rung of the ladder in society. If he is an able man, he should have the right to become President or Prime Minister or a Minister. Poverty, sex or colour should not be a bar for any able man or woman. Even if a person is not a member of the elite by birth, he may be able to enter into it on the basis of his ability.

Economic Equality

It is rightly said that political, social and legal equality have no meaning without economic equality. To quote Laski, "Political equality, therefore, is never real unless it is accompanied by virtual economic equality; political power, therefore, is bound to be the hand-maid of economic power." (*A Grammar of Politics*, p. 162). Wealth provides all kinds of opportunities to those who have it and the poor are forced to suffer from serious disadvantages. A very poor or starving man, having no economic opportunities, has absolutely no use of political or legal equality. Hence, economic equality has to be given an important place.

However, economic equality does not demand the equal distribution of wealth. What is demanded is that there should be equality regarding the primary needs of life and economic inequality can be allowed beyond that point. Absolute economic equality is not possible in the world and hence it is absurd to make such a claim. Economic equality can exist when all people have reasonable economic opportunities to develop themselves. Adequate scope for employment, reasonable wages, adequate leisure and other economic rights create economic equality.

The accumulation of private property in a few hands increases inequality. This has become particularly so as a result of the Industrial Revolution. That is why Marx and Engels asked the workers of the world revolt against the existing economic system in the world which was responsible for economic inequality. The Communists demand the abolition of private property and the nationalisation of all the means of production.

Sometimes it is said that even in a capitalist society, there can be economic equality. This can be done through high taxation and the provision of welfare services by the state. Dr. W. Friedmann writes, "Taxation is one of the most important weapons by which the State can mitigate the two objectionable aspects of unrestricted private property: first, the inequalities of wealth, and secondly, the power to use property for private profit, and without regard to community purposes....By graded taxation and surtax on high incomes, gross inequalities of wealth are evened out more easily than by the equalization of incomes or the abolition of private property....Taxation is a cheap means by which the State finances its costly social service schemes" (*Law in the Changing Society*, pp. 84-85).

The view of Dahrendorf, Raymond Aron and Lipset is that through the extension of welfare services to all the strata of society, redistribution of income and wealth through progressive taxation, increased rate of social mobility, the extension of the franchise to the working class and widespread "consumer's consciousness", the issue of class antagonism in society has vanished. This view is based on the assumption that even in class-divided society, economic equality can be achieved through piecemeal engineering or reforms. However, this view is not accepted by the Communists who point out that the state is not a bulldozer which can create equality through taxation and welfare services in a class-divided society. Brinton writes, "No social equality could be complete without economic equality, and of the latter ideal there is little trace in modern America or indeed in the modern world." An unequal distribution of wealth and power results in social disorders. Economic equality is important, not only for the poor classes, but also for social stability, peace and order.

Natural Equality

About natural equality, Plato wrote, "All men are by nature equal, made of the same earth and by one workman and however we deceive ourselves, as dear unto God as the poor peasant as the mighty prince". Similar views were expressed by Rousseau. In spite of that, human-beings are not equal and they differ from one another in many respects. Cole says, "They are radically unlike in strength and physical prowess, in mental ability and creative quality, in both capacity and willingness to serve the community and perhaps more radically of all in power of imagination". Natural liberty is more an ideal than a reality, but as Soltau writes, "The ideal must be taken as most desirable and realiseable, as a guide for immediate practice."

Marxist View of Equality

It is surprising that neither Marx nor Engels gave adequate attention to the idea of equality. Marx branded the bourgeois conception of equality as formal. He called the capitalist state a class state whose laws are in the interests of the rich only. Wherever there are classes in the Marxian sense, there must be inequality. Where there are no classes, there is no inequality.

Marx did not believe in absolute equality of human beings. He was opposed to levelling. Vyshinsky criticised the proposal regarding equality of income as "petty bourgeois wage levelling".

According to Engels, the real content of the proletarian demand for equality is the demand for the abolition of classes. Marx goes beyond the capitalist society and envisages the higher phase of communist society with the motto of "from each according to his ability, to each according to his needs". The Marxian view is that inequalities emerged with the emergence of private property and there will be no inequality after the abolition of private property. The relation between property and equality was accepted by Rousseau and many other writers. Cans writes, "Societies that have no use for private property, such as nomadic and hunting tribes, find it easy to be egalitarian, but societies that enable individuals to collect such property do not". Marxism analyses the whole issue of equality and property and associates it with the abolition of classes and establishment of a classless society. To quote Lenin, "We want to abolish classes and in this sense we are for equality".

The Marxian view is that economic equality is the most fundamental and all other equalities are based on it. The state cannot create equality in a class-divided society through welfare measures and economic policies. The social ownership of the means of production in a given society is a pre-condition for economic equality. However, Marxism does not propose to finish all inequalities. "Communist equality pre-supposes the eradication not of all distinctions between people, but only of such distinctions and such conditions as would give rise to a difference in the social position of the people".

Liberty and Equality

During the later half of the eighteenth century, the rebels of America and France raised the slogans of liberty, equality and fraternity. It was assumed by them that liberty and equality were complementary to each other. Their view was that without equality, there could be no liberty. They understood equality as the abolition of special privileges or inequalities by birth. Even during the nineteenth century, the Liberals did not find any contradiction between liberty and equality. The equal right to vote and equality before law were supported on that basis. Political and legal equality were considered as a precondition for democracy. Without equality, there could be no democracy and without democracy, there could be no liberty.

However, there was a change in the attitude of the Liberals towards the relation between liberty and equality. It was contended that liberty and equality were opposed to each other. Economic and social equality were opposed to political freedom in general and freedom of private property in particular. It was maintained that any form of interference by the state in the economic affairs for the maintenance of economic and social equality was fatal to liberty. This view was criticised by the Socialists. As a result of it, there was again a change in the attitude towards liberty and equality. The necessity of both liberty and equality was realised and the state was to maintain both liberty and equality through its public welfare measures. The matter requires further elucidation. Are liberty and equality complementary and supplementary to each other or opposed to each other? If they are opposed to each other, which of them is more important? The general view is that in Soviet Russia and Communist China, there is equality but not liberty. In the liberal democratic states, there is liberty and not equality.

The view of Lord Acton, De Tocqueville, Lecky, Stephen, Friedman and Hayek is that liberty and equality are incompatible with each other. Liberty means negative liberty or absence of any restraint, but equality needs some restraint or some levelling which is against the principle of liberty. The economic condition of man is dependent on his personal ability and not on society. The liberty of private property is natural and it cannot be restricted for the sake of equality. The powers of the state have to be increased in order to create equality in society but that threatens liberty. In the name of economic equality, many states have increased their powers and attacked the rights and liberties of the people. Equality needs a positive state, but liberty needs a negative state. It is contended that without capitalism, the power of the state cannot be checked and without this type of check, liberty is in danger. Hence, capitalism is helpful for liberty. However, equality and capitalism cannot go side by side. Liberty needs the maintenance of capitalism and equality needs its overthrow and hence both liberty and equality are opposed to each other. Without an elite, democracy will change into mobocracy and populism and liberty will have no place in such a system. The presence of an elite means inequality. Thus, equality and liberty are opposed to each other.

The names of some of the writers who hold the view that liberty and equality are compatible with each other are Laski, Barker, Gans, Arnold, Tawney, Pollard, Godwin, Hume, Maitland and Harrington. According to them, without equality, there will be special privileges and liberty is impossible in such a society. Without the satisfaction of economic needs, there can be no liberty. To quote Prof. Laski, "An interest in liberty begins when men have ceased to be overwhelmed by the problem of sheer existence; it is when they have a change of leisure....Economic sufficiency and leisure for thought, these are the primary conditions of the free man". (*Liberty in the Modern State*, pp. 16-17).

It is also contended that without equality, there will be conflict and disorder in society and there can be no liberty in such an atmosphere. Equality and liberty need a check on private property and control on unlimited profits. Barrows Dunham writes, "A group of men whose social role consists of taking profits from other people's labour can have no profound belief in equality and fraternity as desirable ideals". The economic conditions required for both liberty and equality are the same and without equality, the conditions necessary for liberty will not be there.

According to Harrington, "Equality of estates caused equality of power and equality of power is liberty". Tawney writes, "A large measure of equality, so far from being inimical to liberty, is essential to it. In conditions which impose cooperative effort, liberty is, in fact, equality in action". According to H.J. Gans, "I also think that there is no inherent conflict between liberty and equality. The society we must create should provide enough equality to permit everyone the liberty to control his or her own life as much as possible, without inflicting undue inequality on others." "If liberty means the continuous power of expansion in the human spirit, it is rarely present save in a society of equals. Where there are rich and poor, educated and uneducated, we find always masters and servants".

The view of Rousseau was that liberty could not exist without equality. To quote him, "Allow neither rich men nor beggars. These two estates which are naturally inseparable, are equally fatal to the common good; from the one come the friends of tyranny, and from the other tyrants. It is always between them that public liberty is put to auction; the one buys and the other sells".

Prof. A.F. Pollard observes, "There is only one solution of the problem of liberty. It lies in equality. The liberty of the weak depends upon the restraint of the strong; that of the poor upon the restraint of the rich. Every man should have this liberty and no more, to do unto others as he would that they should do unto him; upon that common foundation rests Liberty, Equality and Morality". (*The Evolution of Parliament*).

Democracy is based on the principle of political equality which in turn is based on economic and social equality. Without socio-economic equality, there can be no democracy and without democracy there can be no liberty.

The object of both liberty and equality is the same, which is the development of the personality of individuals. Without equality, the object of liberty cannot be realised.

The conclusion is that the principle of equality must stand side by side with the principle of liberty and the two are not opposed to each other. Elton Trueblood writes, "The paradox is that equality and freedom, which begin by being ideas in conflict and tension, turn out upon analysis, to be necessary to each other. The truth is that it is impossible to make a reasonable statement of the meaning of equality except in terms of freedom. Men are equal only because all men are intrinsically free, as nothing else in all creation is free". (*Declaration of Freedom*, p. 75).

The view of Corry and Abraham is that liberty and equality "are to be reconciled by remembering that both are subordinate means to the end of realising the potentialities of individual personality on the widest possible scale. The development of a rich variety of personalities requires a large measure of liberty and forbids all attempts to impose a dead level of social and economic equality". (*Elements of Democratic Government*, p. 34). Massimo Salvadori says, "There is an intimate connection between the two because all individual liberties are related to the basic equality of all men, and because historically the aspiration for liberty became in practice the destruction of privilege or inequality". (*Liberal Democracy*, p. 36).

In a democratic state, an individual needs both liberty and equality because equality without liberty has little value and without equality liberty cannot have a proper basis. Herbert A. Deane says, "Liberty thus implies equality; liberty and equality are not in conflict nor even separate, but are different facets of the same ideal....Indeed since they are identical, there can be no problem of how or to what extent they are or can be related; this is surely the nearest, if not the most satisfactory solution ever devised for a perennial problem in political philosophy" (*The Political Ideas of Harold J. Laski*, p. 46).

In spite of the close association of liberty and equality, it is sometimes argued that liberty is superior to equality. Liberty is primarily needed for the development of personality and equality seeks to serve the needs of liberty. The cause of liberty is more likely to unite men together than that of equality. Almost all people aspire for liberty as common possession. As equality is largely a levelling process, it may create division rather than unity if it is exclusively pressed. Equality serves under liberty as its purpose is nothing but the liberation of capacity. Ernest Barker says, "Equality, in all its forms, must always be subjected and instrumental to the free development of capacity; but if it be pressed to the length of uniformity, and if uniformity be made to thwart the free development of capacity, the subject becomes the master and the world is turned topsy-turvy". (*Principles of Social and Political Theory*, p. 157).

SUGGESTED READINGS

Acton, Lord	:	*History of Freedom.*
Barker, E.	:	*Principles of Social and Political Theory.*
Benn, S.I. and R.S. Peters	:	*Social Principles, and Democratic State.*
Bottomore, T.B.	:	*Classes in Modern Society.*
Burns and Petltason	:	*Government by the People*, 1953.
Corry, J.A.	:	*Democratic Government and Politics*, 1958.
Deane, Herbert A.	:	*The Political Ideas of Harold J. Laski*, 1955.
De Tocquevill, Alexis	:	*Democracy in America.*
Dunhan, B.	:	*Man Against Myth*, New York, 1952.
Friedman, M.	:	*Capitalism and Freedom, Chicago*, 1962.
Friedmann, W.	:	*Law in Changing Society.*
Galbraith, J.K.	:	*The Affluent Society.*
Gans, H.J.	:	*More Equality.*
Hayek, F.B.	:	*The Constitution of Liberty*, London, 1963.
Hobhouse, L.T.	:	*Elements of Social Justice.*
Lakoff, S.A.	:	*Equality in Political Philosophy, Honolulu*, 1964.
Laski, H.J.	:	*A Grammar of Politics*, 1925.
Laski, H.J.	:	*Liberty in the Modern State*, London, 1930.
Laswell, H. and A. Kaplan	:	*Power and Society*, New Haven, 1950.
Leacock, S.	:	*Our Heritage of Liberty*, London, 1942.
Lecky	:	*Democracy and Liberty.*
Lipson, L.	:	*The Great Issues of Politics*, Bombay, 1967.
Lucas, J.R.	:	*Principles of Politics.*
Miller, H.P.	:	*Rich Man; Poor Man.*
Plamenatz	:	*Man and Society.*
Pollard, A.F.	:	*Evolution of Parliament*, 1920.
Raphael, D.D.	:	*Problems of Political Philosophy.*
Rees, T.	:	*Equality*, London, 1971.
Rossister, Clinton	:	*Marxism: The View from America.*
Rousseau, J.J.	:	*Discourse on Inequality.*
Sartori, Giovanni	:	*Democratic Theory*, 1965.
Shahnazgrov, G.	:	*Socialism and Equality, Moscow.*
Stephen, J.F.	:	*Liberty, Equality, Fraternity*, 1873.
Tawney, R.H.	:	*Equality*, London, 1952.
Trueblood, Elton	:	*Declaration of Freedom.*

19

CHAPTER

Property

Learning Objectives

- Concept of Property
- Locke
- Liberal Theory of Property
- Theory of contribution to public good
- Laski's theory of Property
- Justification of Property
- Theories of Reward
- Industrial Organisation
- Marxian Theory of Property
- Suggested Readings

Concept of Property

The long history of human civilisation on its material side centres round the idea of property and ownership. From the days immemorial when semi-civilised man began to claim possession of his tools, ornaments and other personal articles, to the modern times when the thoughts and activities of the average man are concerned with such matters as income, dividend and inheritance, the concept of property has been an important factor in the evolution of civilisation. All ideologies fight their doctrinal battles around the concept of property.

Prof. MacIver makes a distinction between "property for use" and "property for power". In very early times, property was generally held for use and not for power. Private property is comparatively recent in origin and collective property was the universal order in early days. The view of MacIver is that there was private property as regards personal belongings, but there was no universal rule regarding property in land. In primitive society, land was either collective property or private property or the two notions were combined together. In either case, it was held for use and not for power. The appropriation of land gradually became exclusive and permanent with the development of agriculture. The actual evolution of property rights shows that it was not simply the "creature of the state". It had its beginnings even before the appearance of the state on the historical stage.

In the Greek world, Aristophanes suggested a scheme of community of wives and a system of common property. Plato's communism prohibited private property to the ruling class and radically altered the accepted man-woman relationship. The rulers were required to live and dine together. The scheme of communism in the Republic of Plato was applicable only to the ruling class and the other classes were left with their property and wives.

Aristotle was not opposed to the institution of private property, but he recommended its communal use. The Cynics renounced private property and family. In his *Prince*, Machiavelli pointed out the extreme love of man for property in these words: "Men sooner forget the death of their father than the loss of their patrimony". In his Republic published in 1576, Jean Bodin wrote that family was a natural unit in which the right of private property was inherent. Bodin made the right to property a natural right. The view of Hobbes was that the state was created for the security of man's property.

Locke

The view of John Locke (1632-1704) on property is one of the most prominent and distinctive features of his system of politics. According to him, the state of nature was one of "peace, goodwill, mutual assistance and preservation". The law of nature provided the state with a system of rights and obligations. The natural rights included the rights to life, liberty and property and the most important among them was the right to property. The state did not create property. It was itself created in order to protect it. Hence the Government had no right to abridge or take away the right to property without the express consent of the people. Thus, Locke made it not only a natural right but also a legal right. The government had no power even to tax the subjects without their consent. For Locke, the right to property was strictly a claim to the fruits of one's own labour. Rousseau ended with the idea of property as a legal and social matter.

The reaction to Locke's liberal ideas came from Rousseau who, though not being a communist, bitterly attacked the liberal viewpoint in his "Discourse on Inequality". He did not accept the view that property was a natural right. The view of Hegel was that property is not the creation of either state or society. It is an indispensable condition of human personality.

The view of Bentham was that the right to property is a major condition of achieving the greatest happiness. This right should be protected by law.

The possession of property by one man should not interfere with the possession of property by another man. When this condition is not fulfilled, property becomes a theft. Landed property was established by force and not by expenditure of genuine labour. The view of Green was that the state should have the power to take positive action for removing the obstacles in the way of real freedom. Green laid the intellectual foundations for the modern social welfare state.

Property is either something not made by man but occupied or inherited by somebody by chance, by force, or by tradition, such as landed property, or it is a product of the cooperative efforts of a large number of individuals, employing different talents and different amounts of labour such as buildings, machinery, vehicles and capital assets. The share of each individual in the property is not determined by the value of his contribution, but depends upon external factors such as the forces of demand ad supply and competition, the condition of previous investment due to a pre-existing ownership of property, level of technological development etc. The result is that the prevailing pattern of ownership of property does not reflect the contribution of each individual to the social good or the services rendered by him to society. It is also to be determined how far the right of an individual to property amounts to diminishing the right of another individual to his property or a share, in the property. The fundamental issue is how the right to property can be made to serve the cause of social justice instead of allowing it to remain a weapon of exploitation and injustice.

There are many purposes for which property is required. Property is required for the satisfaction of physical wants. It is also required as a guarantee of a safe future. It is also required because without it, a man gets neither social status nor any prestige. It is for this purpose that a man becomes mad to acquire more and more property. This type of property is not required for consumption but for dominating or exploiting others. This is known as private property or ownership of the means of production. This property becomes a social problem. The distinction between personal property (for consumption) and private property (for power or exploitation) is fundamental. According to Tawney, private property "may be called passive property or property for acquisition, for exploitation or for power, to distinguish it from the property which is actively used by its owner for the conduct of his profession or the upkeep of his household". (The Acquisitive Society, p. 66). Private property is not for consumption but for profit and exploitation.

Property is not a natural institution. It is man-made. It emerged at a certain stage of the development of society. It creates certain social relations among men and it should be understood with reference to those social relations. Macpherson writes, "As an institution, property is a man-made device which establishes certain relations between people". (*Democratic Theory*, p. 121).

The concept of property which now prevails in Western societies is largely an invention of the seventeenth and eighteenth centuries. In feudalism, property was both common and private. There was a limited right to property-only a right to revenue – and property was mainly land which was an immovable property and which could not be sold by feudal lord. However, with the emergence of capitalism, a new wealth–capital–emerged and it was an unlimited right to property which was mobile wealth or capital. This concept of property is the basic requirement of the capitalist market society.

Liberal Theory of Property

The liberal theory of property is based on the basic assumption that property is the reward for one's labour. The justification of private property is that it gives incentive to labour. Any individual who is capable and hard-working can accumulate property in a free market society. The hard-working and able son of even a poor man can become a rich man. Ability and labour are the personal property of man and private property which is the outcome of this, should also be a right of the individual.

Among the liberal thinkers, John Locke was the chief exponent of the theory of property as the fruit of labour. He view was supported by various liberal writers like Adam Smith, Bentham, J.S. Mill and Green. According to J.W. Gough, Locke's theory of property is one of the most prominent and distinctive features of his system of politics. The law of nature provided that state was a system of rights and obligations. The natural rights included the rights to "life, liberty and property". The greatest of those rights was the right to property. Property was an essential attribute of personality. "Everyone has property in his own person". The right to property was present not only in the state of nature but existed even prior to it. That right was not subject to the consent of any one. The state did not create property, but was itself created in order to protect property. The government had no right to abridge or take away that right without the express consent of the people. Locke made property not only a natural right but also a legal right. The government had no power even to tax the people without their consent. To quote him, "For if anyone shall claim a power to lay and levy taxes on the people, by his own authority, and without such consent by the people, he thereby invades the fundamental law of property and subverts the end of government". The property referred to by Locke was the property which was the fruit of one's own labour.

According to Macpherson, the astonishing achievement of Locke was that he based the property right on natural right and natural law and then removed all the natural law limits from the property right. Locke began with the contention that in the beginning, earth and its fruits were given by nature to mankind in common. Before their use, man must appropriate them. "Every man has a property in his own person. Thus nobody has any right to but himself. The labour of his body and the work of his hand, we may say, are properly his". "Whatever a man removes out of its natural state, he has mixed his labour with it. By mixing his labour with it, he makes it his property at least where there is enough and a good left in common for others". Locke maintains that for thus making his property, man need not take permission of any one else because it is his right to appropriate from what has been given by nature of mankind in common and it is a necessity of its self-preservation. Thus; Locke justifies the natural right to property and maintains that a man may appropriate from the earth and its fruits given by nature to mankind in common, by mixing his labour in it. As labour is the personal property of man, so whatever he appropriates from the natural common property by mixing his labour with it, also becomes his private property.

Locke imposes certain limitations on the right to private property and those are: (1) No one has a right to spoil property. (2) One must leave enough for others. (3) Private property can only be that in which man has mixed his own labour.

The limitations seem to be impressive but Locke removes those limitations one by one and makes the natural right to property an unlimited right. The introduction of money itself removes the first limitation that no man has a right to spoil property. After the introduction of money economy, man may convert his property into gold and silver which do not spoil. The second limitation that one must leave enough for others, is also removed by Locke. His own view was that "he who appropriates land to himself by his labour, does not lessen but increases the common stock of mankind". The capitalists may appropriate one million and produce goods worth ten million, leaving enough for others. The third limitation that only that things is the private property of man to which he himself has added his labour, is also removed by Locke. He maintains that labour is the personal property of man and he can sell it. The purchaser of labour becomes the master and thus the seller's labour becomes buyer's labour. "Thus the grass my horse has bit; the turfs my servant has cut; and the ore I have digged in any place where I have a right to them in common with others, become my property". Macpherson writes, "To Locke a man's labour is so unquestionably his own property that he may freely sell it for wages. The labour thus sold becomes the property of the buyer, who is then entitled to appropriate the produce of that labour". (Democratic Theory p. 215).

As regards the main points of Locke's theory of right to private property, that right is natural. It is pre-social and pre-political. The right to property is a necessary requirement for self-preservation of the life of an individual. The right to property can be purchased and sold. It is earned by labour and ability which is a personal property of man and every one is free to purchase and sell it. The purchaser of one's labour and ability becomes the legitimate owner of the product of that labour and ability. The right to private property is in the interest of society as it is the basis of the system of production. It is a necessary incentive to work.

The authors of the American and French revolutions defended the institution of private property. They looked upon it primarily as a fruit of labour.

Hegel supported Locke's view that property is not the creation of either state or society. It is an indispensable condition of human personality.

Adam Smith, Jeremy Bentham and other exponents of classical liberalism regarded the institution of private property as an essential instrument of social progress. The view of Bentham was that the right to property is a major condition of achieving the greatest happiness. That right should be protected by law. While protecting equal distribution of property, law should not be used for creating arbitrary inequalities. A balance is required to be struck between equality and security. Benn and Peters write, "Classical economic theory assumed that the sole aim of the individual entrepreneur would be to maximize profits from the use of his property. In doing so, he would use it for the greatest satisfaction of consumer demand. His interest in profit was thus both an explanation for his behaviour and a reason for leaving capital under his control since it ensured beneficial results for the community at large". (Social Principles and the Democratic State, p. 160).

To begin with, J.S. Mill made a strong plea for the security of property, but later on argued that the right to property was not absolute or sacrosanct. He went to the extent of advocating considerable restrictions on the rights of inheritance and bequest. He criticised private property in land which was the original inheritance of all mankind and pleaded for a taxation of rent. His contention was that the rapid appreciation of the value of land and its rent without any effort on the part of the landlords, justified taxation on income from land.

T.H. Green gave due importance to the right to property as an instrument for exercising moral freedom. However, if unrestricted right to property creates conditions under which some men take an unduly large share and the others are prevented from acquiring requisite property as a means of their self-realisation as in the case of landed property, that right becomes a hindrance to the exercise of freedom in society. It was for that reason that Green pleaded for the imposition of reasonable restrictions on the right to property in the interest of social good. The view of Green was that landed property was acquired by force and not by expenditure of genuine labour. The original landlords were conquerors.

L.T. Hobhouse postulated the theory of the social origin of property. He defended taxation of property as a measure for securing to society the element in wealth which was of social origin.

The view of Prof. Laski was that the right to property should be co-related to the functions performed by the owner of the property. That is to depend upon the service rendered to the state by an individual or the contribution made by him to common welfare.

Modern liberal theory, instead of conceding an absolute right to property, proceeds to investigate the ethical basis of that right and indicates the proper limits of the right to property.

Theory of contribution to public good

Another theory of property is that the right to property should be tested by the contribution of the individual to the public good or well-being. With the change of the system of production as a result of the Industrial Revolution and the concentration of capital in the hands of a few persons, there has been an increasing disassociation of property and labour. In modern conditions, property becomes a means of control over the life and labour of others. That control is keenly felt in modern industry. The capitalist system enables the employer to dictate his terms to the workers and also enables him to make huge profits which widen the disparity between the rich and the poor. The profit motive is responsible for the disregard of public needs by the employer. It is felt that the right to property should be subject to certain restrictions. It should not be used as an instrument of power over others. It must take into consideration the needs of the community. Tawney has criticised the tyranny of functionless property and advocated the subordination of property to social good. To quote Tawney, "Functionless property appears natural to those who believe that society should be organised for the acquisition of private wealth. Those, however, who hold that social unity and effective work are possible only if society is organised and wealth distributed on the basis of function, will ask of an institution not, 'what dividends does it pay'? but 'what service does it perform?"

To sum up, the right to property is justified by the Liberals on many grounds. It is necessary as an incentive to work. It is also justified on moral grounds. Property is the reward of labour and ability of man and he who has earned it by working hard, has a moral claim to it. The right to property increases such social virtues as love towards family and charity. Without property, man will feel socially insecure and impotent. There cannot be production without private property. It is a necessary requirement for the economic development of society. Private property is also justified on historical grounds as it has existed from time immemorial.

Laski's Theory of Property

Prof. Laski had definite views on the subject of property. He attempted an analysis of the existing system of property and found that the number of those in any community who own enough of property is always small. Such ownership is not necessarily related to the performance of duties or the possession of virtues. The owner of property may be a lucky descendant of a wealthy person. The ownership of property involves the control of capital which involves the power to direct the lives of workers who depend upon the capitalist system of production. The development of industry in modern times made the power of capital greater than in any previous age. The regime of private property makes the state very largely an institution dominated by the owners of private property. The people without property do not have any rights.

However, there are certain mitigating factors in the present property system. The power of combination of workers enables them to get concessions from the capitalists. Humanitarian sentiments also play their part. The result is that under the present system of property, production is carried on wastefully and without adequate plan. The commodities and services necessary for the life of the community are not so distributed as to relate to the needs of the people. We build picture palaces when we need houses. We spend on battle-ships when we require the same money for schools. Not only wrong commodities are produced, but even those which are produced are distributed without regard to urgency. Goods are produced not for use but for profit. Even if the production of a thing is harmful, it is produced because it brings profits. Natural resources are ruined and commodities are adulterated merely for the purpose of profit. For the same reason, legislators are corrupted and sources of knowledge are perverted. Laski sums up the inadequacy of the present system of property in these words: "It is psychologically inadequate because, for most, by appealing mainly to the emotion of fear, it inhibits the exercise of those qualities which enable them to live a full life. It is morally inadequate, in part because it confers rights upon those who have done nothing to earn them, in part because where such rights are related to effort, this in its turn has no proportionate relevancy to social value. It makes a part of the community parasitic upon the remainder; it deprives the rest of the opportunity to live simple lives. It is economically inadequate because it fails so to distribute the wealth it creates as to offer the necessary conditions of health and security to those who live by its processes. In the result, it has lost the allegiance of the vast majority of the people. Some regard it with hate; the majority regard it with indifference. It no longer infuses the state with that idea of purpose through which alone a state can prosper."

Justification of Property

Laski refers to the various theories which justify the existing system of property. (1) One theory is that men in general need an incentive to labour and the right to property provides such an incentive. That induces the people to work and thereby the society gains. However, Laski points out that the good of society can be achieved only if those things are produced which are useful to society and are distributed among the people in the right method. If harmful things are produced merely for making profits, society does not gain by such production. The power to acquire property may defeat more incentives than actually create them. Laski suggests that incentive to labour can be there if sufficient reward for labour and self-government in industry is provided to the workers. To quote him, "By the creation in industry of self-government, we shall build institutions through which the worker can feel that he is directly related to the centre of control." Incentive can be derived from self-government in industry and sufficient reward to the workers for the work done by them. In the factories run under the control of capitalists for their profits, the poorly paid workers do not have any incentive to work.

(2) Another justification for the existing system of property is stated to be ethical. The acquisition of property is the return made to the individual for his efforts. The inventor of a safety razor, the builder of a railway and discoverer of a patent medicine, all work hard and whatever they gain on account of their hard work, is their legitimate demand. It is true that the thing invented by a person may bring him profits, but it is not necessary that the same will be useful to society. Moreover, the amount of reward depends upon the capacity to manipulate and not the value of the service rendered to society.

(3) Another theory is that property is the nurse of virtues which are essential to society and those virtues are love of one's family, generosity, inventiveness and energy. However, Laski points out that those virtues have been present in those persons also who have never amassed property at all.

(4) Another theory is that property is the result of supplying effective demand. However, Laski does not accept that view. He argues, "There is a demand for slaves in Abyssinia, but most men will, I think, agree that response to the demand ought never to be allowed. There is a demand for obscene literature, but few would respect those who trafficked in it. There is a demand for prostitutes but the law has a definite answer to those who live by satisfying it".

(5) Another theory justifies, property on historical grounds. It is contended that progressive societies are those which are built upon the regime of private property and backward societies are, in general, those which are founded upon a collectivist basis of some kind. There is some truth in

it but it is still fallacious because, viewed in historical perspective, private property has remained a changing concept. Laski writes, "Property in slaves was valid in Greece and Rome; it is no longer valid today. In England there is great freedom of testamentary disposition; in France inheritance is regulated with much stringency". Moreover historical development throughout indicates progressive limitations imposed on the right to property. The result is that no pervasive right to property can be established on historical grounds. The growth of socialism has transformed the character of the modern state and the attitude towards private property. To quote Laski, "The State which had begun the nineteenth century in the terms of *laissez-faire* began, as the twentieth century came into view, to search for a basis upon which it could compromise with socialism. So the taxation of the modern State was built upon the assumption that assessment must be graduated by ability to pay. Its franchise was well nigh universal. It offered free education – if of a low standard to the people. It began to insure against the hazards of sickness and unemployment. It made things like the provision of houses and pensions in old age a matter of corporate concern".

Theories of Reward

Laski refers to four main theories of reward. (1) According to one theory, there is the general communist case of equality of income. Every worker must be paid the same. However, the distinctions are bound to be arbitrary. It is difficult to estimate the price of the services of a judge or a brick-layer. There is no measuring rod for that purpose. What is cheaper in one country may be dearer in another country. Moreover, every individual does not put in the same amount of work and consequently there is no justice in an equal reward for unequal effort. It is also not just to reward equally where needs are unequal. A miserly bachelor should not get the same remuneration which a father with half a dozen children is given.

(2) Another view is that remuneration should be fixed by the higgling of the market. It is the forces of demand and supply which should determine the wages of a labourer. However, such a view is inadequate because labourers are not in a position from where they can bargain on equal terms. The worker must sell his labour which is a perishable commodity. He knows that if he does not sell his labour on the terms dictated by the capitalist, his family will face starvation. Moreover, the higgling of the market is not an adequate test of wealth. It leaves about one-third of the industrial community on the verge of starvation. For them, it means poor health, undeveloped intelligence and miserable homes. There is no freedom of contract on the part of labourers on account of their lack of equality of bargaining power. The master and servant cannot be on the same footing. Moreover, great fortunes are made not because there is any genuine demand for a thing but because advertisement is so effective that many customers are persuaded to buy the same. Salesmen are able to sell things which are otherwise worthless from every point of view. The capitalists distort social needs to create a demand for their own products and thereby do positive disservice to society. The same is true of professions. "The incomes made by skilful special pleaders in the days before the reform of judicial procedure largely represented wealth secured in an effort to defeat the ends of justice". The prevailing price system is seldom related to the value of the service performed.

(3) According to another theory of reward, every individual should contribute to society according to his powers and he should be rewarded according to his needs. The view seems to be simple but there are many difficulties in its practical application. Even the problem of the needs of every individual is a difficult one. We cannot recognise all the needs of every individual. Some of those needs may be positively mischievous and harmful to society. Some of them may be absolutely unreasonable. The only needs we can recognise are those which are common to all. Needs can only mean average needs. The same difficulty is experienced when we discuss the powers of an individual to contribute to society. There is no criterion by which we can fix the working capacity of an individual. Some persons may work very hard and others in a lukewarm manner. All that the state can do is to fix a minimum which must be done by every individual but that in itself may not be considered adequate.

We have to depend mainly on the honesty of individuals with regard to the amount of work they are prepared to do.

(4) Another view of reward is that it should enable {he individual to reach out towards his best self and at the same time preserve and develop the necessary functions of society. We must reconcile the interests of the individual with those of society. We have to meet the demands of children, old persons and disabled and defective persons who cannot pay their way. No person should be permitted to get any remuneration unless he performs some work which is considered useful for society. His wages must be a return for personal effort. Once he performs work which is recognised as necessary for society, he is entitled to reward. That reward must keep him in good health, give him freedom for the development of his faculties and also enable him to build a home and pay the cost of his family.

Such a view of reward applies both to a collectivist and non-collectivist society. It is a general principle of justice. It assumes that all alike are entitled to find the means of full satisfaction and beyond those means, differences must be required by the common good of society. Such a view removes the dread of insecurity and inadequacy which pervades the lives of the individuals.

According to Laski, whenever functionless property is the controlling factor in industrial production, the abolition of its rights is the necessary path to justice. The question is how the problem is to be solved. Laski is not in favour of the confiscation of property. He points out the view of Machiavelli that men will sooner forget the death of their relatives than the confiscation of their property. Hence, he is in favour of giving compensation to the holders of property. The property is to be taken over by the state and the owners are to be given guarantees of living according to the same standard as they were living before the acquisition of their property by the state. The state is to guarantee them the same income which they were getting before the acquisition of their property. If the owner dies, there is to be a reduction in the amount of money to be given to the family. His widow is to be given so much of money which is adequate to enable her to live in the same way as she did during the life-time of her husband. When the widow dies, her allowance is to be stopped. The children of the owner are to be given the same education as would have been given to them by their father if he had not been deprived of his property. When they complete their education, the contribution of the state towards them also ceases. The children must stand on their own legs and learn to live. After the completion of their education, they have no claim to get help from the state. It was in this way that Laski tackled the problem of property.

Industrial Organisation

Laski outlines an elaborate scheme of industrial organisation according to his concept of social justice. "Industry, in fact, must be made a profession. It needs to be informed by a principle of public service. It must not be merely a body of persons who are turning out goods for profit. It must be a body of persons who perform certain functions at some standard of competent performance." Laski was in favour of a thorough transformation of the capitalist system.

He advocates the alteration of the character of owner of wealth. The owner of capital should receive a fixed dividend for the service rendered by the loan of his capital. He will no longer profit by the special ability of management, the rise in price or the special privilege of a monopoly. There should be a change in the character of control exercised over the industry. Rules for the industry are to be laid by its working force. "Once the functionless owner of capital is removed, an industry becomes an intelligible entity and rules can be drawn for its governance upon the basis of the functions performed by each element therein". More room should be made for the social element in the industrial equation. That implies socialised production of essential commodities such as electric power which are necessary for the well-being of the community but do not bring profit. All industries should be regulated by standard hours and standard rates of pay. Recruitment to industrial cadres should be based on proven competence as required in the case of entry into the Bar or medical practice. These changes are intended to convert functionless property of the capitalist system into an instrument of social good. They will also remove wide economic disparities.

Laski deals with the right to property as a part of his theory of rights. To quote him, "If property must be possessed in order that a man may be his best self, the existence of such a right is clear....! have the right to property if what I own is, broadly speaking, important for the service I perform. I have the right to own if what I own can be shown to be related to the common welfare as a condition of its maintenance". This means that the right to property should be directly related to the functions performed. There is no room for functionless property in a just society. To quote Laski, "No man... has a moral right to property except as a return for function performed. He has no right to live unless he pays for his living. He has no right to live because another has earned what suffices for his maintenance....Those whose property is the result of other men's effort are parasitic upon society. They enjoy what they have not assisted to produce".

Laski was not opposed to the institution of private property as such. He admitted that the possession of property provides for a means of harmony in the shape of security. The man of property has a stake in the country. He gets a sense of security and an opportunity to develop creative tastes for art and culture. Poverty destroys the creative impulse of man. Hence the institution of private property cannot be condemned as bad in itself. Any significant property is owned by a few people and what they possess is not related to the performance of duties by them. However, the existing capitalist system must be altered so that it can serve the cause of social justice. If the scheme of Laski is seriously put to practice, it can eliminate the capitalists. They remain merely shareholders and not in a position to harm the cause of society.

Critics of Laski's view point out that the devil of private property cannot be checked. It can only be killed. The corrupting influence of private property is so strong that it can purchase all those who may try to check it. The efforts already made to check private property have proved merely an eyewash. Laski merely suggests reforms but no sermons can change the exploitative nature of private property. Laski gives importance to class division and class conflict due to property in society but he does not accept the principle of class struggle. He has faith in the capacity of the state to reform the present system of property, but his views are impracticable, ambiguous and idealistic. He accepts the Marxian criticism of property, but rejects the Marxian remedies.

Marxian Theory of Property

The early Socialists, notably St. Simon, attacked the liberal concept of property. He declared that the Liberals were deceiving themselves with abstract fictions. However, he was not in favour of the total abolition of private property. He was in favour of a drastic reform of ownership in land and not property held as capital. His followers were opposed to property both in the form of land and capital. They felt that property inculcates habits of idleness and the rich live on the labour of others. Proudhon condemned the institution of private property in very strong terms. His view was that "Property is theft". Again, "Property is the exploitation of the weak by the strong".

Marx and Engels carried the attack on private property further by making it an integral part of their attack on capitalism and advocated the abolition of private property by means of a revolution led by the working classes.

The Marxian view is that private property has not existed from eternity. It did not exist under the early social stage. At that time, the means of production were rudimentary and held in common ownership. Production was available for common consumption. It was just sufficient for the survival of the community. Surplus production became possible after the development of the forces of production and then came into existence the institution of private property and that divided the society into antagonistic classes. Private property divides society into "haves" and "have-nots". In ancient society, this division took the form of masters and slaves. In medieval society, it took the form of lords and serfs. In modern capitalist society, it takes the form of the bourgeoisie and the proletariat. Private property is a divisive force. It is a source of conflict. It is a mode of exploitation and not cooperation. Private property in this sense denotes the means of production.

Marxism makes a distinction between two kinds of properties, personal property and private property. Personal property is the genuine fruit of an individual's labour. This property is to remain intact and is not attacked by the Marxists. Marxism does not stand for the abolition of all property but only of private property with its exploitation in all spheres of social production. Marxism is the enemy of private property which has an exploitative character and wants to establish socialist property which means social ownership of the means of production. Marxism is against the exploitation of man by man and as private property is the cause of it, it has to be abolished and replaced by socialist property. Marxism is not against personal property or reasonable property for daily use like food, house, books, kitchen chattels or cloth. Whenever the Marxist view on property is analysed, property should be understood only as private property.

Marxism does not aim at the reform of the system of private property. It demands its abolition as it considers it the enemy of society. Private property is contrary to the social interests of man. Property was created by man for himself but Marx found that instead of being its master, man had become the property of property or the slave of property. All human values were sacrificed before the God of property. Private ownership of the means of production leads to alienation of man from his labour and his product. The motive for production is profit for the capitalist and such labour does not reflect the human and creative powers of man. The worker becomes a slave. He becomes a commodity to be purchased by the capitalist. In a capitalist system, man is compelled to sell his labour power and thus he becomes dehumanised. "The worker sinks to the level of a commodity and becomes indeed the most wretched of commodities". The labourer finds no joy in his work. Whatever he produces does not belong to him. His product is independent of him, uncontrolled by him. His work becomes his enemy, a burden, a source of unhappiness for him. Toquote Marx, "The more the worker products, the less he has to consume; the more values he creates, the more value-less, the more unworthy he becomes; the better formed his product, the more deformed becomes the worker; the more civilised his object, the more barbarous becomes the worker; the more powerful labour becomes, the more powerless becomes the worker". His labour is not voluntary, but coerced. It is forced labour.

According to Marx, private property is the enemy of self-realisation of man. It is a hindrance to the development of his personality. It is the destroyer of humanity or the essence of man. It paralyses the personal life of man. It is harmful not only to the man without property but also to the owners of property. Both the exploited man and the exploiter lose their humanity.

In a society based on private property, all human values are superseded by private property which becomes the basis of honesty, gentleness, beauty, power, wisdom, humanity, right, liberty and justice. Human values are lost in the race for private property. Even if a poor man is gentle, intelligent and cultured, he is considered inferior to a rich man though he is crooked, foolish, and uncultured.

Property is for man and not man for property. However, men run after property and get alienated from nature, society and their human essence. They are converted into living corpses. The worker is reduced to the condition of an animal. The capitalist becomes an abstract money power. The essence of humanity can be restored to man only by the abolition of private property and establishment of a communist society.

Because of private property, socio-economic and political inequality in society is created. Society gets divided into classes and class struggle starts. There cannot be class harmony or cooperation in society so long as there is the institution of private property. Private property creates a wall between man and society and takes away the social essence of man. No social theory can harmonise the individual and social interest in such a society.

In a class-divided society, political power comes in the hands of those who possess economic power and there is no place for the poor people. In such a system, rights, liberty, equality and justice remain mere ideals which cannot be realised in practice.

According to Marx, human labour is reduced to a commodity under the capitalist system. The more wealth is produced by the worker, the poorer he becomes. To quote Marx, "The worker becomes an ever cheap commodity, the more commodity he creates. With the increasing value of the world of things proceeds in direct proportion the devaluation of the world of man. Labour produces not only commodities; it produces itself and the worker as a commodity – and does so in the proportion in which it produces commodities generally."

The process of alienation or self-estrangement under the capitalist system takes place at four levels. Man is alienated from his own product and from his work process. He is alienated from nature as he is deprived of the sense of creative fulfilment. He is alienated from his fellowmen on account of the competitive character of the capitalist economy and the sharp class division of society. He is alienated from himself. He is reduced to an animal existence for the fulfilment of his biological needs. His human faculties, including the taste of literature, art, music etc. evaporate.

Marxism does not believe in appealing to the conscience and humanity of the property-owners to give up their property. It gives a revolutionary message to the victims of private property for the abolition of private property through a revolution. Private property is to be replaced by socialist property. Marxism is not philosophy of reforming or controlling capitalism. It is a revolutionary message for the overthrow of private property. Private property is to be abolished by the organised revolutionary power of the working class. Socialist revolution, under the leadership of organised and class-conscious workers, is the first requirement for the abolition of private property. Marx and Engels declared thus in the Communist Manifesto, "The distinguishing feature of Communism is not the abolition of property generally, but the abolition of bourgeois property. But the modern bourgeois private property is the final and most complete expression of the system of producing and appropriating products, that is based on class antagonisms, on the exploitation of the many by the few....In this sense, theory of the Communists may be summed up in the single sentence: Abolition of private property".

Marxism stands for the replacement of private property by socialist property which will lay the foundations of a new, classless, exploitation-free society and production system. Marx did not demand the abolition of property in general but the abolition of bourgeois property only. Socialist property is different from private property. It is developmental rather than exploitative. It belongs to the whole society and not to a few. It benefits all. It produces for the consumption of all and not for the profits of a few.

The opponents of the Marxist view point out that property is the first condition for liberty. No real freedom is left with the people once the right to own property is taken away from them by the state. Property is required for mental development and psychological satisfaction. The abolition of private property poses a grave danger to the existence of family. One cannot live without the other. Private property is an incentive for hard work and achievement of excellence for various professions. If one cannot own, he would work only under compulsion. If economic power is diffused, political power is evenly distributed. There can be no social progress without property. Much of the Marxian criticism of private property has lost its force after the establishment of the welfare state.

It is suggested that there must be a change in the existing system of property but it should not be through a revolution as recommended by the Marxists. The working class, including manual as well as mental workers, should strengthen their position through organisation and capture power by getting majority of the votes and thereby dictate the policy of the state. All the major means of social production can be socialised, leaving no room for socialist ownership. A common civic minimum must be provided to all by the state. Beyond that minimum, remuneration of work should be regulated according to the value of the service rendered to society. That will maintain an incentive to work and maximization of service to society. The personal property of the individual as the fruit of his labour, the tools of his work, comfort and security and leisure for pursuing creative tastes should be fully protected to maintain freedom and incentive to acquire excellence.

SUGGESTED READINGS

Apthekar, H.	:	*Marxism and Alienation.*
Avineri. S.	:	*The Social and Political Thought of Karl Marx, Cambridge*, 1968.
Barker, Ernest	:	*Principles of Social and Political Theory.*
Barker, Ernest	:	*Greek Political Thought.*
Benn and Peters	:	*Social Principles and the Democratic State.*
Chesnokov, D.	:	*Man and Society, Moscow*, 1969.
Deane, H.	:	*The Political Ideas of Harold J. Laski.*
Ginsberg. M.	:	*On Justice in Society.*
Gough., J.W.	:	*John Locke's Political Philosophy.*
Hallowell	:	*Main Currents in Modern Political Thought.*
Hobhouse, L.T.	:	*Elements of Social Justice.*
Rolakowski, L.	:	*Main Currents of Marxism*, Oxford, 1978.
Laski., H.J.	:	*The Rise of European Liberalism*, 1936.
Laski, H.J.	:	*A Grammar of Politics*, 1925.
Macpherson, C.B.	:	*Democratic Theory, Oxford*, 1973.
Martin, Kingsley	:	*Harold Laski, A Biographical Memoir.*
Noyes, C.R.	:	*The Institution of Property*, New York, 1936.
Roueek, J.C. (Ed.)	:	*Twentieth Century Political Thought.*
Swingewood, A.	:	*Marx and the Modern Social Theory*, London, 1975.
Tawney, R.H.	:	*The Acquisitive Society*, London, 1945.
Values. J.C.	:	*Personal Property*, London, 1962.
Willoughby, W.W.	:	*Social Justice.*

CHAPTER

Justice

Meaning of Justice

Learning Objectives

- Meaning of Justice
- Development of the Concept of Justice
- Dimensions of Justice
- Legal Justice
- Political Justice
- Social Justice
- Economic Justice
- Relationship between Liberty, Equality and Justice
- Suggested Readings

The term justice suggests the quality of being just or right or reasonable. It is opposed to what is unjust or wrong or unreasonable. The words just, right and reasonable are primarily moral attributes and hence justice is primarily a concept of morality. It is an ethical concept.

As a moral concept, justice is a dynamic idea. It embodies an ideal. It symbolises perfectness. It is reflected in absolute truth, it is a dynamic idea because our relisation of that ideal is a continuous process. Our progress in that direction depends upon the development of our social consciousness. What was regarded justice some centuries ago is not regarded justice today. Slavery was justified in ancient times but not today. Likewise, serfdom was considered to be just in medieval Europe but not today. Untouchability was justified in India in the past but not today. Such examples can be multiplied. The conclusion is that our outlook towards these problems and the public opinion has been changing from time to time. That is an ample proof of the dynamic character of the idea of justice.

Development of the Concept of Justice

The earliest concept of justice in Greek thought is to be found in the writings of the early Pythagoreans. Justice was viewed by them as a square number, a number multiplied into itself. It was equated with harmony or proportion. A number is square if its parts are equal. Likewise, a state is just if it is composed of equal parts and justice is the continuation of that equality. There was to be no aggressor or loser.

Plato gave that idea a more spiritual content. The theory of the state in the Republic of Plato culminates in the concept of justice. Plato considered justice as one of the four cardinal Greek virtues. The other three virtues were wisdom, courage and temperance or self-control. The last three virtues were found in the three classes in the state. The ruling class ruled by its wisdom, the soldiers fought with courage and the producing class produced with self-control. Justice resided in the mind of every citizen. A man was just if he fulfilled the duties of his station and did not meddle with the duties of the station of another person. Justice in the individual means that reason, spirit and appetite were kept within their proper limit.

The Epicureans did not believe in any intrinsic virtues or values except happiness. Their view was that "there never was an absolute justice but only a convention made in mutual intercourse, in whatever region, from time to time, providing against the infliction or suffering of harm".

The Roman lawyers' concept of positive law as conforming to higher law was a part of perfect justice and right. According to the Digest, "Justice is a fixed and abiding disposition to give to every man his right. The precepts of the law are as follows: to live honourably, to injure no one and to give to every man his own. Jurisprudence is a knowledge of things human and divine, the science of the just and unjust". The lawyer was priest of justice, the practitioner of a true philosophy and not a pretender.

St. Augustine linked the idea of justice with religion and divinity. According to him, a just state was one in which religion was taught under law and authority. Only a Christian state could be just. Justice was another name for peace, the absence of strife and conflict and building up of a right relationship between man and God. If justice was taken away, kingdoms would become robberies.

David Hume ridiculed the concept of natural justice and liberty. He replaced those concepts by the principle of utility. Bentham declared that the principle of the greatest happiness of the greatest number was the measure of right and wrong. The basis of the state was to be found in the satisfaction of human needs instead of social contract or in universal law of justice.

Karl Marx decried the talk of social justice in a capitalist society. He criticised Socialists like Proudhon who preached social justice because they failed to realise the irrelevance of the idea of justice to the social problem. According to Marx, the concept of distributive justice in a capitalist society was irrelevant, if not dangerous. The primary concern of Marx was with the relations of production. The concept of justice in a capitalist society is based on the capitalist mode of production and the capitalist relations of production. The result is that justice has meaning for those only who own the means of production. For the working classes, this justice in form is injustice in reality. There will be justice for the working classes only when the means of production were Collectivised and the exploiters were expropriated.

According to Ernest Barker, the term justice is derived from the Latin word *Jus* which embodies the idea of joining or fitting the idea of bond or tie. To quote Barker, "Primarily, the joining or fitting implied in this root idea is that between man and man in an organised system of human relations. But we may also conceive of the just or justice as connected with and expressed in, a joining or fitting between value and value in a general sum and synthesis of values". Barker identifies three different values as necessary to an organised system of human relations. Those three values are the value of liberty, the value of equality and the value of fraternity. These values were upheld by the French Revolution and those very values are embodied in the Preamble of the Indian Constitution of 1950. Barker regarded those values as necessary to an organised system of human relationship. Justice itself is a value which represents a synthesis of different values. Barker writes, "The claims of liberty have to be adjusted to those of equality; and the claims of both have also to be adjusted to those of cooperation. From this point of view the function of justice may be said to be that of adjusting, joining or fitting the different political value. Justice is the reconciler and the synthesis of political values; it is their union in an adjusted and integrated whole".

The concept of justice is concerned with the adjustment of human relations because the values which it seeks to combine are themselves necessary to an organised system of human relations. According to Barker, there are four different sources of the idea of justice and those are religion, nature, economics and ethics. To prove that religion is the origin of justice, Barker refers to four kinds of law corresponding to the four kinds of reason enunciated by St. Thomas Acquinas. He called those laws the Eternal Law, the Natural Law, the Divine Law and Human Law. Eternal Law is identical with the reason of God. It is the plan of divine reason in created things. Divine Law is the substantial revelation of the reason of God through the medium of scriptures. It is a gift of God's grace. These three laws are behind all laws made by man. They set the standards to be followed by human beings. Human Law is the law imposed by human authority. Ultimately, it derives its value from the principles of Divine Law and Natural Law.

As regards nature as the origin of justice, the Stoics equated nature with Great and reason. The implication was that man who lived in conformity with nature shared a fragment of reason and God. That means three things. Man should be free (liberty). He should be treated as equal (equality). He should be linked to his fellow beings by the common factor or reason (fraternity).

As regards economics as the origin of justice, the Marxist view is that the origin of justice lies in the area of economics. According to Marx, the positive law of the state is imposed on its members by the authority of the class which controls the means of production. Law is determined by the economic interests of the ruling class. When private property is abolished and all the means of production are collectivised, the laws of the state reflect the wishes of the working classes. The conclusion is that the idea of justice and its content varies with the economic interests of the ruling class. When the state withers away as envisaged by the Communists, there will be justice without economic origin.

According to Barker, law is related to ethics in the sense that it seeks to secure the external conditions necessary for moral action, or the general frame-work of external order in which the moral conscience can act and determine itself most easily and most freely.

The proper source of the idea of justice is reason. However, man develops his faculty of reasoning according to the social consciousness of his age. The true meaning of justice can be determined in the light of the prevalent social consciousness or what D.D. Raphael describes as "modern consciousness". Social consciousness is an ever-growing phenomenon and we should be prepared to accept new and progressive ideas regarding justice if they are supported by reason.

DIMENSIONS OF JUSTICE

The modern concept of justice is different from the traditional concept. The traditional concept of justice put emphasis on the just man. It was primarily concerned with the virtues which enhance the moral worth of a man. It consisted in the performance of the duties attached to his status determined by the prevalent law, social customs and the mode of thought. An example of the traditional approach to the problem of justice is given by Plato's theory of justice which prescribed the duties of different citizens and required them to develop virtues befitting those duties. In order to achieve perfect harmony which symbolizes justice, reason must rule within the man as well as within the state. In a just state, the reins of government were to remain in the hands of the philosopher-kings who were supposed to be the living embodiments of reason.

The traditional view insisted on the individual conforming to a pre-conceived image of society. The modern view of justice seeks to transform society itself for the realisation of certain human values. The traditional view of justice has been replaced by the modern idea of social justice. The idea of social justice is the force behind social change. When the people find the existing social order faulty, oppressive and exploitative, they raise the demand for social justice and demand changes in the social order to achieve social justice. Social justice is the voice of the oppressed against the excesses of the social system. It is the expression of what is due to the individual from society. The main problem of social justice is to decide wisdom by which the whole universe is governed. Natural Law is the reflection of what should be given to the deprived persons through the instrumentality of social organisation. When the modern idea of justice is applied to the various aspects of social life, we get legal, political, social and economic notions of justice.

Legal Justice

Legal justice is related to the process of law-making and the judicial system of society. It demands that law should be reasonable and everyone should get justice according to law. Law is not only to be reasonable but also equal for all. The object of law is the well-being of the whole community and hence law should be equal for equals and unequal for unequals. Distinctions can be made on a rational basis. Rationality of law depends upon the social requirements of a given society and is associated with the human values of a society. A law may be reasonable in one society but unreasonable in another. That depends upon the social requirements of the two societies.

If we want rational and just laws, the law-making institutions should also be rational and just. The right to make law should be given only to the representatives of the people. It is possible that a law so passed may not be reasonable or just. The majority party in the legislature may pass anti-people, unjust and unreasonable laws and the protest of the people against those laws will be just. It is also necessary that there should be an independent and impartial judiciary which has the authority to look into the justifiability of the laws made by the legislature. There is always the possibility of a conflict between the legislature and the judiciary and the people should be the final authority to decide whether a particular law is rational or not.

Legal justice demands that every individual should be able to have impartial justice under the existing judicial system. There should be equal protection of laws. That demands that the judicial process should be simple and not very costly. It should be within the reach of the poorest of the poor. The court should be independent and impartial. The pay, service conditions and the qualification of the judges should be proper so that they can decide cases without fear or favour.

Legal justice is broadly applied in two contexts: justice according to law and law according to justice. In the first case, the validity of the law is not questioned and the focus is on the principles of administration of justice according to the prevalent law. In the second case, the substance of law itself is examined to ensure that it conforms to the requirements of justice. The view of Alf Ross is that justice consists in an efficient administration of law and it should not be tested on some imaginary moral values. The same point has been elucidated by Morris Ginsberg. He points out that the notion of a legal order implies that decisions should be made not arbitrarily but in accordance with the general rules and those general rules shall be correctly applied. Justice is conformity with the existing law. A good law is known by its efficiency in achieving justice. The problem of justice has nothing to do with the purpose of law. It is solely concerned with the efficacy of law. Justice in a totalitarian society may be distorted on account of the power given to the judges to disregard the fixed rules. Barker deals with the concept of legal justice as law according to justice and he draws a distinction between positive law and natural law. Positive law is a particular law, but natural law is a universal law which is based on what is just everywhere and at all times, for all mankind. The view of Barker is that ideally, law should have both validity and value. Law will be most effective if it conforms to the principle of justice and the authority of the state.

Of the two views of legal justice mentioned above, the view of Barker is considered to be better. Justice in the legal sense consists not only in an efficient administration of law but also demands that law itself should embody human values according to the level of development of the social consciousness. If law does not reflect the changing social values, it will stand in the way of social progress and ultimately it will have to be discarded.

Political Justice

The term political justice is sometimes applied in a comprehensive sense in which it embraces a restructuring of the entire fabric of social, economic and political relations. William Godwin used the term political justice to denote a moral principle whose object was the general good and which was invoked to evolve a genuine system of property. In his book *Political Justice*, Kirchheimer described political justice as "the search for an ideal in which all members will communicate and interact with the body politic to assume its highest perfection". A specific use of the term political justice refers to the reorientation of political institutions, political process and political rights according to the current conceptions of justice. This means the establishment of democratic institutions in the political life of the community. Those institutions represent and take care of the interests of the people. The legislatures are to be constituted on the principle of universal adult franchise. The independence of the judiciary is to be maintained. This involves the rule of law which means that the government should not be arbitrary and should act according to law. Political justice implies a full guarantee of the liberty of thought and expression, particularly the right to criticise the government and its policies. There should be complete freedom for forming associations and interest groups. The organisations should be allowed to organise peaceful protests against the wrong measures of the government and put pressure on the government.

According to the liberal view, political justice means equal right to vote and equal share in government services. In this sense, political justice is associated with political rights and equality. It also means political power which should be exercised by the representatives of the people. The ultimate source of political power is the people themselves. The demand of political justice is that political power should be based on the will of the people and public opinion should be given due regard by the rulers. Political justice is possible only in a democratic state.

The essence of political justice is political equality within the state. In a polity where political rights vary from person to person or class to class, a sense of political frustration cannot be avoided. Irrespective of the grounds of unequal political treatment, discrimination in the matters pertaining to participation in the political process, leads to conflict. Political justice does not mean absolute political equality. There is no political injustice if there are rules which apply equally to all citizens and the enjoyment of certain political rights is subject to certain conditions. The minimum age for voting rights or election to the legislature, pre-requisites of any qualification for holding certain political offices, prescription of certain fundamental duties etc. are not discriminatory. It is the duty of the state to justify the differences in treatment. Whether there is political justice in a state or not can be judged from four principles; integrity, predictability, flexibility and acceptability.

The idea of political justice and equality is explained in Article 1 of the Universal Declaration of 1948 in these words, "All human beings are born free and equal in dignity and rights. They are endowed with reason and conscience and should act towards one another in a spirit of brotherhood".

Social Justice

There is social justice in a community if there are means available for equal social opportunities for the development of personality by all the people. No person should be deprived of those social conditions which are essential for his development. The issue of social justice is associated with social equality and social rights. There can be social justice only in that society where the exploitation of man by man is absent.

Social justice is the offspring of political justice. A politically unjust society can never be socially just.

In common parlance, the term social justice is usually applied to comprehend all three aspects of justice in society. Those are social, economic and political. Out of these, the economic aspect is more important. Social justice also implies reordering of social life in such a way that the material and moral benefits of social planning are not cornered by a privileged few and are available to the masses. It also involves a logical synthesis of liberty, equality and fraternity.

Economic Justice

Economic justice is viewed from two angles. The Liberals refer to the satisfaction of economic needs of the people in society as justice. The Marxist view is that economic justice prevails only after the abolition of private property. According to the Liberals, the demands of economic justice are satisfied if certain welfare services are provided by the state and disparities of income are reduced through progressive taxation by the state. Economic justice cannot be achieved without the abolition of private property and the capitalistic system of production. During the seventeenth and eighteenth centuries, liberalism regarded free competition in a free market society as the key to economic justice.

Marx has associated economic justice with the mode of production in a society. Economic justice can be secured only in a exploitation-free socialist economic system. There can be no economic justice where people are divided as the rich and the poor, exploiters and the exploited. Marxism associates economic justice with the abolition of private property and the establishment of Communism.

Relationship between Liberty, Equality and Justice

The view of Barker is that justice is the synthesis of liberty, equality and fraternity. It is the thread which runs through all these values and makes them parts of an integrated whole. It reconciles their conflicts and contradictions. Justice is the basic idea behind liberty, equality and fraternity. It is the final goal to which liberty, equality and fraternity should conform.

It is our sense of justice which compels us that human relations should be regulated by reason. Justice recognises the dignity of the human-being. The rational nature of man clothes him with dignity. It demands that every individual should be treated as an end in itself and not a means to an end. All individuals should be treated alike and none should be superior to others. Irrespective of their differences regarding language, culture, sex, education or economic status, individuals continue to acquire excellence according to their capacities and contribution to the social good. The principle of liberty does not conform to the principle of justice until the benefit of liberty is equally extended to each individual in society. The idea of absolute liberty is a contradiction in terms. Liberty has to be qualified by the principle of equality. An unrestrained liberty of one or of a few results in the slavery of the rest. The inherent contradiction of absolute liberty can be resolved by principle of equality. Barker writes, "The need of liberty for each is necessarily qualified and conditioned by the need of liberty for all; and the liberty of A will therefore be such liberty as he can enjoy concurrently with the enjoyment of similar and equal liberty by B and C and D....Because the liberty of each is thus relative to that of others, and has to be adjusted to that of others, it must always be regulated; and indeed it would not exist unless it were regulated". (Principles of Social and Political Theory, p. 145). Any restraint on liberty can be justified on the ground that it is in the interests of justice and equality.

The principle of equality is not the final principle of justice. Equality may be defined as the absence of discrimination. It may be interpreted as equality before law, equal legal personality of each individual, equal voting right of each individual etc. However, the mere absence of discrimination in the economic sphere does not meet the requirements of justice. When society is divided into classes on the basis of private property in which one class enjoys special privileges on account of its ownership of private property, the cause of justice is not served by treating them without any discrimination. Justice demands that the unprivileged people without property should be given special protection to save them from the moneyed people. Law should make a special provision to protect the rights of the weaker sections such as the tenant against landlord, the consumer against the producer and the worker against the employer. The principle of brotherhood or fraternity should be applied to the regulation of human relations in society as a matter of right and not charity. The discrimination in favour of the weaker sections of society must be in the interests of justice and fraternity.

In the final principle of justice, we regulate human relations in society on the principle of liberty, but liberty is qualified by the principle of equality and equality is further qualified by the principle of fraternity. The principle of justice demands not merely formal liberty and equality but also a change in those social conditions which stand in the way of the enjoyment of liberty and equality by ordinary men and women.

Barker has described the relation between liberty, equality and justice in the following words: "Justice is a joining or fitting together not only of persons, but also of principles. It joins and knits together the claims of the principle of liberty with those of the principle of equality. Equality may quarrel with liberty; for if its application be pushed to the length of that is called a classless society, with absolute equality of possessions....Civil liberty may be pleaded in support of claims which run contrary to those of economic liberty; and similarly political liberty may be on occasion the enemy of either civil or economic liberty. There must therefore be some final principle transcending that of liberty, as it also transcends the principle of equality and cooperation, a principle which can balance each of these principles against the others....that final principle is justice. "(Principles of Social and Political Theory, pp. 169-70).

Liberty is the first condition of justice and bondage has always been regarded as unjust. He who attacks the liberties of the people is considered to be unjust. In the name of justice, many struggles were waged against despotic rulers and those struggles were regarded as just. The voice of protest against those who take away the liberty of others, has always been regarded as just. When the Americans revolted against the British Government in the last quarter of the eighteenth century, their revolt was considered to be just. Likewise, the struggle of the people against the *ancien regime* in France was considered to be just. The same applies to the movements for independence during the current century. Liberty is one of the highest social values and is a pre-condition for any just social order. However, the liberties of the people must be based on social justice. If they go against social justice, those have to be checked. There should be no contradiction between liberty and social justice. The liberties of the individuals are justified only if they are not opposed to social justice and morality.

The notion of equality differs from society to society and the same applies to social values. The notion of equality undergoes a change when there is a change in social values. Both Plato and Aristotle considered slavery as just but now we consider the same to be unjust. Previously, although women had no right to vote, it was not thought that any injustice was being done but now if they are not given the right to vote, that is considered to be unjust.

The struggle for equality starts when there is a feeling that the prevailing inequality is unjust and based on exploitation.

Aristotle gave the theory of distributive justice and proportionate equality. Distributive justice gives to every man his due according to his contribution to society. It is identifiable with proportionate equality. Every one should be given according to his social performance and contribution. John Rees writes, "Hence justice requires that if two persons are equal, they should have equal shares; if they are unequal, they should have unequal shares but in proportion to their inequality". The principle of distributive justice is also supported by John Rawls. In every society, while some inequalities are regarded as just, others are regarded as unjust. In a feudal society, inequality by birth was considered just. In a capitalist society, inequality on the basis of private property is regarded as just. However, in a socialist or Communist society, inequality based on birth and private property is considered to be unjust. In the current century, equal opportunities for the development of personality, equality before law, equal protection of law and equal political and economic rights are considered necessary for justice. Only those inequalities are allowed which can be justified on the basis of social justice.

The Liberals did not find any contradiction between private property and justice. Their contention was that without private property, there could be no incentive to labour. However, it is, now conceded that the right to private property can be restricted in the interests of social justice. The Marxian view is that private property and the capitalist economic system are irrational. The Marxian view of justice is that it is related to the social values of society. In a socialist society, there will be no necessity for private property and the same will be unjust. "The justice of an institution depends on the particular institution and the particular mode of production of which it is a part. All judicial forms and principles of justice are, therefore, meaningless, unless applied to a specific mode of production".

SUGGESTED READINGS

Barker, Ernest : *Principles of Social and political Theory.*

Benn and Peters : *Social Principles and the Democratic State.*

Friedrich, C.J. and J.W. Chapman (Ed.) : *Justice,* New York, 1963.

Ginsberg, Morris : *On Justice in Society.*

Laski, H.J. : *A Grammar of Politics.*

Laski, H.J. : *The State in Theory and Practice.*

MacIver, R.M. : *The Modern State.*

Raphael, D.D. : *Problems of Political Philosophy.*

Rawls John : *A Theory of Justice,* London, 1971.

Rees, : *Equality,* London, 1971.

Ross, Alf : *On Law and Justice.*

Tucker, Robert C. : *The Marxian Revolutionary Idea.*

Willoughby, W.W. : *Social Justice.*

CHAPTER

Law

Definition of Law

Learning Objectives

- Definition of Law
- Different Schools of Law
- Sources of Law
- Kinds of Law
- Law and Morality
- Distinction Between Law and Morality
- Common Ground Between Law and Morality
- Whether Law is Expression of General Will ?
- Law and Public Opinion
- International Law
- Is International Law Really Law?
- Arguments in favrour
- Sources of International Law
- History of International Law
- The League of Nations
- Work of the League
- Non-Political Work
- Causes of Failure
- The United Nations Organisation
- Its Organs
- Work of the United Nations
- Criticism of United Nations
- Suggested Readings

Law has been variously defined by many writers. Vinogradoff defines law as "a set of rules imposed and enforced by a society with regard to the distribution and exercise of power over persons and things". Blackstone says: "Law in its most general and comprehensive sense signifies a rule of action and is applied indiscriminately to all kinds of action whether animate or inanimate, rational or irrational. Thus, we say, the laws of gravitation, of optics or mechanics, as well as the laws of nature and of nations," Montesquieu says: "Laws in the widest sense of the term are necessary relations derived from the nature of things. The deity has His laws. The material world has its laws, men have their laws". According to Keeton, "A law is a rule of conduct, administered by those organs of a political society which it has ordained for that purpose and imposed in the first instance at the will of the dominating political authority in that society in pursuance of the conception of justice which is held by that dominating political authority or by those to whom it has committed the task of making such rules." Erskine says: "Law is the command of sovereign, containing a common rule of life for its subjects and obliging them to obedience". Pound defines law as "the body of principles recognised or enforced by public and regular tribunals in the administration of justice." Gray says: "The law of the state or of any organised body of men is composed of the rules which the courts—that is the judicial organs of that body—lay down for the determination of legal rights and duties." Woodrow Wilson defines law as "that portion of the established thought and habit which has gained distinct and formal recognition in the shape of uniform rules backed by the authority and power of the Government." Green defines law as "the system of rights and obligations which the state enforces". Salmond defines Jaw as "the body of principles recognised and applied by the state in the administration of justice." Holland says: "A law is a general rule of action taking cognizance only of external acts enforced by a determinate paramount authority; or briefly, law is a general rule of external action enforced by a sovereign political authority." According to Austin, Law is the command of the sovereign.

From the above definitions, it appears that there are certain characteristics of law. Law is a body of rules which may be written or unwritten but have to be obeyed all the same by the people. Law is external in the sense that it is concerned only with the external action of the individuals. It does not bother about the inner thoughts and feelings of the people. Law is universal in the sense that it applies to everybody in the country. It applies even to those who make the law and not only to those for whom it is made. Law is no respecter of individuals. It applies to all in the same way. Law is imperative in the sense that it has to be obeyed by everybody and those who violate it are punished by the state. The coercive authority of the state enforces that law. Law is not necessarily a command of the sovereign. This is clear from the fact that although customs and usages are not in the nature of a command, they are obeyed by the people and they also form a part of the law of the country. Law is essential for maintaining peace and order in the country. It is the first condition of a good social life.

Different Schools of Law

(1) There are different schools of law in the world. The advocates of the "analytical school" are John Austin, Bentham and Hobbes. Their view is that law is a command given by a superior to an inferior and enforced by material sanction. The sovereign is a determinate superior. The great merit of this school is its simplicity and consistency. It is very easy to find such a sovereign and also the law made by him. However, critics point out that neither such a sovereign nor such law is to be found in primitive society. In that society, custom reigns supreme and that cannot be reconciled with the theory of command. The reply of Austin was that what the sovereign power does not forbid, it accepts, and what it accepts, it commands. Sir Henry Maine describes it as "a mere artifice of speech" and a "mere straining of language." It is pointed out that the judges in England actually "acted for the king in Norman and Plantagenet times and that their decisions were effective only as he enforced them." Sail points out that Austin "erred in thinking of the influence of masses as negative rather than positive." It is also pointed out that the analytical school made law rigid, so it could not be adjusted to the needs of the people and the times. Getell says: "Analytical jurists tend to regard the law as static rather than progressive and they are not interested in its historical evolution. As a result, they have sometimes reached absolute conclusions without examining adequate material."

(2) Savigny and Sir Henry Maine were the great exponents of the "historical school" of law. Their view was that law was the result of a varying, progressive, slow and lengthy social process rather than of the arbitrary will of a law-giver. Law must be studied in relation to historical tendencies and events. The advocates of this school go to primitive society to explain the nature of law. The conduct of the people was governed by customary rules and they were rigidly obeyed by them "Human nature is not likely to undergo a radical change and therefore that to which we give the name of law has been and still is and will for ever continue to be custom." The weight of custom cannot be disregarded by any law-making authority. Law is self-created and self-executed. Legislation is effective only if it is reinforced by custom.

The view of Zane is that "No rule of law was ever successful or ever endured unless it received practical general acceptance among the whole body of people, for the simple reason that universal human experience has demonstrated that a rule of law not accepted by any considerable portion of the people can never be enforced....Whatever the means by which law is recognised, whether it be the legislative enactments, by decisions of courts, by rescripts of rulers, law is in fact law only when it is cheerfully accepted and gladly obeyed by the great mass of the social body. Acceptance by the community is needed to breathe life into the edict of the harshest despot... Government may superficially appear to make law as Hobbes and Austin mistakenly supposed, but it is the acceptance of the rules by society that makes laws and government." (*The Story of Law*, p. 271)

(3) Duguit, Krabbe and Laski are the exponents of the "sociological school." According to them, law is the product of social forces and it must serve the needs of society. Law must be judged by its results and it must satisfy the needs of society. According to Duguit, the sanction of law is primarily psychological "resting in each individual's awareness of the social approval or reprobation of his conduct according to its conformity or non-conformity to the fundamental social rules." Krabbe says: "Law is...the expression of one of the many judgements of value which we human beings make, by virtue of our dispositions and nature. We subject to our judgement all human conduct, indeed all reality; and we distinguish as many different kinds of value as we apply different kinds of measures. The recognition or otherwise of these values is not a matter of choice; we cannot be indifferent or not, at will; our minds react within us, whether we want them to or not, and we feel ourselves subjected, as a consequence of this reaction, to what we call the good, the beautiful and the just. The rule of law likewise is due to human reaction to the sense of justice and is not a matter of external legal authority but an internal human matter." Laski says that the source of law is the individual consenting mind. People obey law because it satisfies their desires. A good law "is a law which has, as its results, the maximum possible satisfaction of desire; and no law save a good law is, except in a formal sense, entitled to obedience as such." R.G. Gettel says, "In contrast to the analytical jurists who found the sanction of law in the command of the state, to the philosophical jurist who found its sanction in its inherent justice, and to the historical jurist who found its sanction in established habits and custom, the sociological jurist finds the sanction of law in the social needs and interests that it serves."

(4) The view of the "Marxian school of law" is that law is intimately associated with the nature of the state. It is merely the will of the dominant class elevated into a statute. In a capitalist state, law helps the capitalists to safeguard their interests. In a socialist state, law is a tool in the hands of the workers to set up a socialist society. It is true that the Marxian concept of law contains an element of truth but it does not accept other refinements connected with the state and law. Moreover, Marx uses law to destroy capitalism and bring about socialism. According to Marx, as soon as that is done, the state must "wither away". This view is obviously not correct as the state is, the very life-breath of human existence and laws are required for keeping the people together in society for growth and progress.

(5) The "philosophical school" considers law as an abstraction, based upon abstract ethical principles of justice. It is not concerned with what the law is and what it has been.

(6) The exponents of the "comparative school of law" advocate the examination and comparison of the legal systems of the past and the present with a view to arrive at certain conclusions. However, it is pointed out that comparisons may not be of much use as each country has its own system of law which has grown in the course of centuries and it cannot be substituted by another foreign law which may be against the very spirit of the nation.

A study of the different schools of law shows that no single view gives an adequate explanation of the concept of law although there is some truth in every school of jurisprudence. Law is not merely a command. It is something more. It is true that force is required to enforce the laws of the state but force alone is not enough. Law is not static. All law cannot find its origin in the customary behaviour of the people. Modern law cannot depend upon customs alone which take long to grow and the speed of the modern times cannot put up with this process. It is true that physical force at the command of the state is necessary to enforce the laws but there must be willingness on the part of the people to obey the laws. No physical force of the state can enforce a law if most of the people in the state are determined not to obey it and are ready to take the consequences.

Sources of Law

(1) According to Holland, the sources of law are custom, religion, judicial decisions, scientific commentaries, equity and legislation. As regards "custom", it is the earliest source of law. No one can say exactly when a particular custom arose but it cannot be doubted that "it originated generally in the conscious choice of the more convenient of two acts though sometimes doubtless in the accidental adoption of one of two different alternatives; the choice in either case having been either deliberately or accidentally repeated till it ripened into habit. The best illustration of the formation of such habitual courses of action is the mode in which a path is formed across a common. One man crosses the common in the direction which is suggested either by the purpose he has in view, or by mere accident. If others follow in the same track, which they are likely to do after it has once been trodden, a path is made". In primitive society, the many relations of life – of the members of the family towards one another, of earning and saving and of buying and selling – were regulated by customary rules. Their sanction was the fear of public opinion, or some kind of supernatural penalty. The force of custom was so strong that there was likelihood of a revolt if it was ignored. MacIver says: "In the great book of law, the state merely writes new sentences and here and there scratches out an old one. Much of the book was never written by the state at all, and by all of it the state itself is bound, save as it modifies the code from generation to generation. The state can no more reconstitute at any time the law as a whole than a man can remake his body".

It is true that in modern times the importance of custom is decreasing but it cannot be denied that even today it plays an important part in the legal system of many countries. In Hindu law, customs are recognised by courts and enforced.

(2) Another source of law is "religion", which admittedly played an important role in primitive society and even now occupies an important place in many countries of the world. During the Muslim Period of Indian history, the Quran was the basis of the criminal law of that country and the state of affairs continued practically till the middle of the nineteenth century. Hindu law is also based primarily on the religious books of the Hindus. Mohammedan law has its origin in the *Shariat.* Woodrow Wilson says: "The early law of Rome was little more than a body of technical religious rules, a system of means for obtaining individual rights through the proper carrying out of certain religious formulas."

Throughout the centuries, God, a god or the gods have been considered to be the source of laws. These laws ranged from the statements of basic ethical precepts to the most minute regulation of the living arrangements of a people. The belief in God-revealed law exists today primarily with respect to basic ethical concepts. Others might claim that law may come from God-guided men and still others would sever all connections between law and divinity.

Supporters of natural law are of the view that man can arrive at concepts of right and wrong through the use of his reason and intelligence. Very early natural law theories can be found in the Greek philosophers but these later merged with the divine law views of the Christian scholars. Natural law as the complete explanation of the origin of law has largely been given up but it has had it influence upon the existing law.

(3) "Judicial decisions" are also a source of law. A decision given by a judge in a case is usually followed by other judges in similar cases. In this way, judges add to the law of the country. Judge-made law has played an important part in England, the United State and India. The real law of the country is the interpretation put by the judges upon the enactments of the legislature. If a particular decision is not subsequently set aside by legislation, it is a binding precedent. Lawyers keep on quoting precedents while trying to prove their cases. The judgements of the Supreme Court of India are binding on all the people of India and the law laid, down by the separate High Courts is particularly binding on the people living within their jurisdiction.

Roscoe Pound points out the distinction between judge-made law and the law made by the legislature. The legislature makes the law for the future and hence it need not proceed on predetermined premises or along predetermined lines. It is free to proceed along the lines that seem to be the best. Judge-made law lays down a legal precept which applies to the transactions of the past as well as those of the future. The social interest in general security requires that it should not have the same freedom as the legislature.

(4) "Scientific commentaries" on the legal system of a country by reputed writers are also a source of law. The opinions of these writers do not *ipso facto* become law. They become law through recognition by courts. "The commentator, by collecting, comparing and logically arranging legal principles, customs, decisions and laws, lays down guiding principles of possible cases. He shows the omissions and deduces principles to govern them." In England, the writings of Kent, Coke, Hale, Littleton, Blackstone and Anson are held in high esteem. The same is the position of Story and Kent in the United States and of Vijnaneswara and Aparaka in India. The views of Mulla on various aspects of Indian law are also followed.

(5) Another source of law is "equity". Sir Henry Maine says that equity means "a body of rules existing by the side of the original civil law, founded on distinct principles and claiming incidentally to supersede the civil law in virtue of a superior sanctity inherent in those principles." Snell defines equity as a portion of natural justice which, although of a nature suitable for judicial enforcement, was for historical reasons not enforced by the common law courts. Salmond refers to three different senses in which the, term equity is used. It is taken to be a synonym for natural justice. It aims at giving every man his due. It implies equity among men. In another sense, equity implies natural justice as opposed to the rigid principles of law. The rigidity of law can result in injustice or where the law does not provide any remedy at all. After the passing of the Judicature Act of 1873, equity has acquired a meaning peculiar to the English system. It forms a part of the law itself.

Equity is based on what is fair and just. It supplements the law when there is no provision in law for a particular eventuality and justice is required to be done. Equity is a kind of judge-made law. However, there is one important difference. In case law, the judge interprets the existing law but in equity, he adds to the law what is missing therein and creates a new one in order to make it suitable to the changed conditions. There are many maxims of equity. Some of them are: there is no wrong without a remedy; he who seeks equity must do equity: he, who comes to equity, must come with clean hands and equity delights in equality.

(6) Another source of law is common law. It had its origins in the customs of the people of England. These customs, representing the approval of a majority of the people of a community, attained the status of law as they were applied by the courts of that early time. After a court had given legal sanction to a practice, subsequent similar cases in the same locality were decided in the same way. Customs and hence common law, varied from one community to another until legal writers attempted to bring about greater uniformity through written commentaries on law. The courts of the Anglo-American tradition continued to build on custom.

(7) Another source was civil law. Five centuries before Christ, the Twelve Tables of Rome constituted a significant codification of a single type. Later on, Roman law produced the Justinian Code at Constantinople. In the time of Napoleon Bonaparte was compiled the Napoleonic Code. The method of making the law clear by codification was accepted in most of Europeland in the Latin American States. Even though some of these codes attempted to be comprehensive statements of the law of a country, the courts found it necessary to fill in the gaps.

(8) However the most important source of law in modern times is "legislation". A large number of new laws are required every year and legislation is the only method which is considered to be adequate to meet the needs of modern society. Wilson says: "Legislation has had and is having a notable development and is now the almost exclusive means of the formulation of new laws. All means of formulating laws tend to be swallowed up in one great, deep and broadening source, *i.e.*, legislation." Gilchrist writes: "It is the chief source of law and is tending to supplant the other sources.

Customs and equity are both largely replaced by legislative acts. The codification of law tends to narrow down the field of judicial decisions as a source of law and scientific commentaries are used merely for discussions."

Oppenheim says that there are not many sources of law and the only source of law is the common consent of the community. Strictly speaking, customs, religion, adjudication, equity, etc., are not so many sources of law. Every law is based on the common consent of the community, which is variously expressed in the form of customs, religion, equity, etc. They merely mark out the different stages in the development of law.

Woodrow Wilson observes thus on the sources of law: "Custom is the earliest fountain of law but religion is a contemporary, an equally prolific, and in the same stages of national development of an almost identical source. Adjudication comes almost as authority itself, and from very antique times goes hand in hand with equity. Only legislation, the conscious and deliberate organisation of law, and scientific discussion, the development of its principles, await an advanced stage of its growth in the body politic to assert their influence in law-making".

Kinds of Law

Laws have been variously classified. Some have classified them on the basis of the agency through which they are formulated and others have classified them according to the public or private character of the persons concerned. However, reference may be made in this connection to constitutional law, public and private law, statute law, common law, ordinances, municipal law, administrative law and international law.

According to Wade and Phillips, "There is no hard and fast definition of constitutional law. In the generally accepted use of the term, it means the rule of law, including binding conventions, which regulate the structure of the principal organs of government and their relationship to each other and determine their principal functions." Dicey says: "Constitutional law, as the term is used in England, appears to include all rules which directly and indirectly affect the distribution or the exercise of the sovereign power in the state." Bouvier defines constitutional law as "the fundamental law of a state directing the principles upon which the government is founded and regulating the exercise of the sovereign powers, directing to what bodies or persons those powers shall be confided and the manner of their exercise."

In the case of countries having written constitutions, a distinction can be made between constitutional law and statutory law. While the statutory law can be passed and amended by the legislature by an ordinary majority, a special majority and a special procedure is required to change the constitutional law. The constitutional law of India is to be found in the new Constitution of India which came into force on January 26, 1950.

Holland divides laws into two categories: private and public. "In so far as the rules of conduct that authoritatively obtain in a political community are devoted to the regulation of interests between individuals as such, they create only private rights and obligations and the state appears only as their enunciator, and if need be, their enforcer." These are called private laws. "Those rules that concern either the organisation of the state and the allocation and delimitation of the powers of government or the direct relations between the state and the individual" are called public laws.

The statute law of a country is made by its legislature. The sphere and scope of statutory laws is expanding in modern times.

The common law of England was brought into existence by those travelling judges who went from place to place and gave similar decisions in every nook and corner of England. Its beginning was made in the time of Henry I, Henry II and Edward I. Common law has played a very important part in the judicial system of England. It was also introduced into India by the British Government.

Ordinances are issued by the executive for short periods with a view to meet an emergency. A large number of ordinances have been issued in India from time to time. This was particularly so during the days of the Civil Disobedience Movement during the 1930's and World War II. Ordinarily, ordinances last for six months.

Public and private law, when combined together, constitute municipal law. This law is the national law which is in force in a country and is backed by the authority of the state.

Administrative law determines the relations of the officials to the state. It is "that part of public law which fixes the organisation and determines the competence of the administrative authorities and indicates to the individual remedies for the violation of its rights. It is a characteristic feature of the French judicial system that when the officials of the state use arbitrarily the powers given to them, they are tried in the administrative courts according to the administrative law.

International law is concerned with the relations of one state with another state, both in times of peace and war.

Prof. MacIver has classified laws in the following manner:

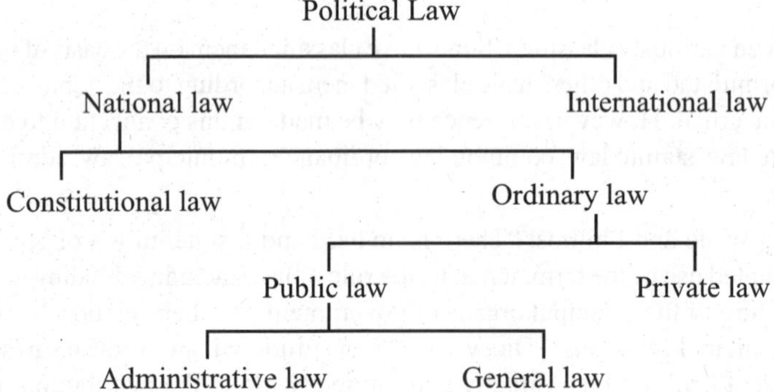

Law and Morality

Moral principles and values are not absolute. They emerge in a particular society in certain conditions. The morals of two countries can never be the same as those are conditioned not by objective standards but by subjective standards which vary from society to society and country to country. However, there are certain moral principles which are universally recognised and upheld. Truth is accepted all over the world as morally sound and anything contrary to it is positively immoral. Marriage as an institution is necessary for the regulation of sexual morality and concubinage is immoral.

Both ethics and political science are social sciences dealing with man. One is the science of morals and the other is the science of state and government. In the affairs of state and government, moral principles are absolutely essential. Political Science can never be indifferent to moral values. R.N. Gilchrist writes, "The political ideal cannot be divorced from the ethical ideal. We cannot conceive of a perfect state where wrong ethical principles prevail. The ethical and the political in this case coincide. The science of ethics is therefore prior to political science."

In a democratic state like India, the legislature has the power to make laws according to the provisions of the Constitution. However, if the legislature makes laws without taking into consideration ethical principles, the consequences would be disastrous. The people will not obey a law which is morally unsound, absurd or cruel. They will refuse to pay taxes which are without adequate moral justification. Political science is not the hand-maid of ethics but it has to respect moral principles. A judge has to keep in mind moral principles when interpreting laws and giving judgments. Even in a dictatorship, the dictator cannot afford to ignore ethical values at all times and for an indefinite period. Ethical values have to be followed not only for their own sake, but also for the sake of practical purposes. A good citizen follows scrupulously both legal and moral principles.

There is the need of moral principles even in the international field. Legally, every state is its own master and can do whatever it likes. But states in the international field are bound by moral principles for the general well-being and happiness of mankind.

In ancient times, there was ho distinction between law and morals. The Hindu jurists in ancient India did not make any distinction between law and morals. However, later on, a distinction was made in actual practice. The same was the case in Europe. In the name of the doctrine of natural rights, the Greeks formulated a theoretical moral foundation of law. Socrates gave importance to truth and morality and said that moral standards should regulate the relationship between the individual and the state. Plato established an intimate connection between politics and ethics. His view was that membership of the state is necessary for leading a good and virtuous life. In his Republic, Plato spoke of the state aiming at the establishment of justice or moral excellence. It was the duty of the state to make-its citizens moral. The Roman jurists recognised certain moral principles as the basis of law. During the Middle Ages, Christian morals were considered as the basis of law. After the Reformation in Europe, it was contended that law and morality were distinct and separate and law derives its authority not from morals but from the state. Morals had their source in religion or conscience. During the seventeenth and eighteenth centuries, the theories of natural law had moral foundation and law was linked up with morals. During the nineteenth century. John Austin maintained that law had nothing to do with morals and he defined law as a command of the sovereign. Austin was supported by many other jurists. There is a new trend in approach to law indirectly studies morals also although a distinction is made between law and morals and law alone is considered as the proper subject-matter of study.

Distinction Between Law and Morality

Law and morality differ from each other in content, sanction and definiteness. Law is chiefly concerned with the outward acts of man and not with his inner motives. It does not touch his heart or his inner springs of conscience. Law touches only a segment of human life whereas morality includes the whole of life: man's thoughts, motives and actions. Law can prescribe external acts but not morality. It is only when thoughts and motive translate themselves into action that they come within the purview of law. Falsehood, cunning, ingratitude, envy etc. are morally wrong but not legally wrong. One may be a habitual liar in his personal life, but if he does not cheat anybody or break his contract, law does not come into operation.

The sanction behind law is force. The sanction behind morality is one's own conscience, social indignation and the fear of God's wrath. The state uses the fear of legal punishment and hope of reward to do its work. Morality rests on a person's intuitive ideas of what is good and what is bad and the motive of social approbation and disapprobation. Public censure is behind morality and political punishment is behind law.

Law and morality differ in their scope and definiteness. Law is universal and is more exact, consistent and definite than morality into which enter elements of uncertainty and vagueness. In the last analysis, an individual is the best judge of what is right and what is wrong. Standards of moral judgment vary from person to person. MacIver observes, "The sphere of morality can never therefore be coincident with the sphere of political law. Morality is always individual and always in relation to the whole prevailing situation of which the political fact is never more than an aspect."

Moral duty and legal obligation do not always coincide with each other. What is morally unjustified is not necessarily legally wrong. What is prohibited by the state is not necessarily morally wrong. In India, the traffic is to the left, but in the United States and France, traffic keeps to the right of the road. Self-indulgence is morally wrong but not legally wrong. Law follows standards of convenience of expediency. While morality prescribes absolute standards of right and wrong, justice and injustice. A compromised morality is no morally.

Another difference is that while law is objective, morality is subjective. The former deals with what is permitted and what is not permitted by the law of the land. Morality is rooted in universal values as conceived and interpreted by the individual. "To turn all moral obligations into legal obligations would be to destroy morality." The state cannot dictate morality because state-directed morality is no morality at all. Morality is a matter of inner conviction and conscience and as such it does not easily lend itself to outer regulation.

Law is concerned with the external actions of individuals while morality is primarily concerned with internal actions. Law cannot regulate or control the conscience of individuals. As it is not possible for an axe to mend a pencil or for a sword to do the work of sewing although it can be done by a needle, so the machinery of the state cannot control the inner feelings of individuals. "Ethics is concerned with all the actions of individuals. It touches the rectitude of each man's life, the truth of his dealings with his own conscience, the whole substance of character and conduct, righteousness both of act and of mental habit. Law, on the other hand, is concerned with controlling the outward acts of man." MacIver writes, "Law cannot prescribe morality, it can prescribe only external conditions and therefore it should prescribe only those actions whose mere fulfilment, from whatever motive, the state adjudges to be conducive to welfare. Law does not and cannot cover all the grounds of morality. To turn all moral obligations into legal obligations would be to destroy morally. Happily, it is impossible. No code of law can envisage the myriad changing situations that determine moral obligations."

Pound says, "Law and morals have a common origin but they diverge in their development." According to Vinogradoff, "Law is clearly distinguishable from morality. The object of law is the submission of the individual to the will of the organised society while the tendency of morality is to subject the individual to the dictates of his own conscience." Pollock says, "Though much ground is common to both, the subject-matter of law and ethics is not the same. The field of legal rules of conduct does not coincide with that of moral rules and is not included in it, and the purposes for which they exist are different."

Duguit observes, "Law has its basis in social conduct. Morals go on intrinsic value of conduct. Hence it is vain to talk about law and morals. The legal criterion is not an ethical criterion." According to Korkunov, "The distinction between motels and law can be formulated very simply. Morality furnishes the criterion for the proper evaluation of our interests; law makes out the limits within which they ought to be confined."

Common Ground Between Law and Morality

There is considerable common ground between law and morality. If the people are good, the state is good and vice versa. Plato wrote, "The best state is that which is nearest in virtue to the individual. If any part of the body politic suffers, the whole body suffers." Man can develop fully his personality only within the state. It is the supreme condition of his moral life.

The state can positively promote the conditions of morality and negatively remove conditions inimical to morality. Gilchrist writes, "As a positive moral agent, the state makes good laws, *i.e.*, laws which are in accord with the best moral interests of the people. Negatively, the state must remove bad laws."

Wilson says that "law is the mirror of the moral progress of country." Sidgwick writes, "Through the general habit of observing law and the general recognition of the duty of obeying rules laid down by legitimate authority, the legislators may obtain a general obedience to rules to which current morality is indifferent or even mildly averse and then by the reaction of habitual conduct on opinions, a moral aversion to the opposite conduct may gradually grow up." This is clear from the history of law permitting the remarriage of widows among the Hindus. Although there was strong opposition against it at the beginning, it is no longer regarded as immoral to remarry a widow.

Law follows morality. It forbids what morality forbids. That is why many acts are made penal if they are condemned by morality. "Laws cannot outrun public morality, nor can public morality allow laws to be uninfluenced by it. In case of conflict between the two, however, it is morality which demands our allegiance." R.M. MacIver observes, "We regard the state as the condition of morality. The state and law continually affect both public opinion and actions; in its turn law reflects public opinion and thus acts as the index of moral progress."

Gettell writes, "Laws that attempt too soon to force new moral ideas and laws that are no longer in touch with existing ethical standards, are alike difficult to administer. There is always a mass of public opinion clamouring for legal expression and there is also a body of law becoming obsolete because it is inapplicable under existing conditions." Another writer observes, "Law does not essay to punish untruthfulness as such. It only stands with a whip for those who give overt proof of bad character in their dealings with their fellow beings." Gilchrist writes, "Though there are certain differences between the law of the state and the moral law, they are inherently connected. In the modern world, we do not make the state the supreme end as did the Greeks. We regard it as the condition of morality. The state and law continually affect both public opinion and action; in its turn law reflects public opinion and thus acts as the index of moral progress."

A study of the various legal systems shows that law and morals have had a long union with occasional desertion and judicial separation but have never been completely divorced. There are indeed many different types of relations between law and morals and there is nothing that can profitably be singled out for study as the ideal relation between them. The view of Stammler is that jurisprudence depends much upon moral ideas as just law has need of ethical doctrine for its complete realisation. Positive law and just law correspond to positive morality and rationally grounded ethics. There is no difference and if any, it is only the difference of manner in which the desire for justice presents itself. C.K. Alien observes thus on the relationship between law and morality, "Our judges have always kept their fingers delicately but firmly upon the pulse of the accepted morality of the day." Lord Mansfield says that "The law of England prohibits everything which is *contra bonos moves.*" The development of law, at all times and places, has in fact been profoundly influenced both by conventional morality and ideals of particular social groups and also by the forms of enlightened moral criticism of those people whose moral horizon has transcended the morality currently accepted.

Morals have often been considered as the end of law and many eminent jurists have defined law in terms of justice. It is contended that the aim of law is to secure justice which is very much based upon morals. In most of the languages of the world, the words used for law convey the idea of justice and morals also. In Sanskrit, the word for law is *Dharama* which also implies morals.

It is contended by some writers that even if law and morals are distinguishable, morality is in some way an integral part of law or of legal development. Morality is "secreted in the interstices" of the legal system and to that extent is inseparable from it.

The view of Lord Devlin is that there is public morality which provides the cement of any human society and law, especially criminal law, must regard it as its primary function to maintain this public morality. Whether in fact in any particular case the law should be brought into play by specific criminal sanctions, must depend upon the state of public feeling. Conduct which arouses a widespread feeling of reprobation, a mixture of interrelation, indignation and disgust, deserves to be suppressed by legal coercion in the interests of the integrity of society. The conclusion of Lord Devlin is that if vice is not suppressed, society could crumble. To quote him, "The suppression of vice is as much the law's business as the suppression of the subversive activities."

According to Prof. H.L.A. Hart, some shared morality is essential to society. If society is to survive, if any legal system is to function, then there must be rules prohibiting, for example, murder. The rules essential for a particular society may also be enforced. "For any society there is to be found a central core of rules or principles which constitutes its pervasive and distinctive style of life."

Law and morals act and react upon and mould each other. In the name of justice, equity, good faith and conscience, morals have infiltrated into the fabric of law. Moral considerations play an important part while making law, interpreting law and exercising judicial discretion. Morals act as a restraint upon the power of the legislature. No legislature will dare to make a law which is opposed to the morals of society. All human conduct and social relations cannot be regulated and governed by law alone and their many relations are left to be governed by morals and law does not interfere with them. Morals perfect the law. Paton writes, "In marriage, so long as love persists, there is little need of law to rule the relations of the husband and wife – but the solicitor comes in through the doors as love flies out of the window."

The sociological approach is very much concerned with the ends to be pursued by law. The result is that morals have become a very important subject of study for good law-making. Morals also exercise a great influence on international law. The brutalities made during the World Wars have forced the people to turn back to morals and efforts are being made to establish standards and values which must be followed by nations. If law is to remain closer to the life of the people, it cannot ignore morals.

Whether Law is Expression of General Will?

Law is sometimes characterised as the expression of the general will of the community. This view owes its origin to the concept of "general will" of Rousseau and the idea of "common conviction" of Gierke. According to this view, legislation is guided by the spirit of the life that operates as the sovereign principle within a community. According to Rousseau, law flows from the fountain of general will which is the sovereign authority. At each stage of its operation, the law of the state takes into account the will of the citizens. There is no clash of wills. There is no hostility between the authority of the state and the will of the individual.

If we accept law as an expression of the general will of a community, we have to accept all the imperfections of Rousseau's general will which pre-supposes the existence of a homogeneous community which always expresses a single unified will. Such a thing is possible only in the case of direct democracy and does not apply to contemporary society. The character of modern law cannot be explained in terms of the general will of Rousseau. There is a danger if we accept Rousseau's view that law is the expression of the general will which embodies the common interests of a community. In modern society, the authority of the state is dominated by the dominant class and law is merely the expression of the interests of the dominant class and not of the whole community. What passes for general will is merely the will of the majority. We cannot equate the will of the majority with the will of the community. We cannot invest the will of the majority with sovereign authority because that would lead to autocracy under the cover of democracy.

Rousseau's idea of the general will is accepted in modern times with an altered meaning. It is believed that democracy postulates a fundamental agreement among classes and masses. The residence of such an agreement or general will is in the society and not in the state. It is finally "transferred and translated into the state and the state's legal system." MacIver says that it is "not so much the will of the state as the will for the state, the will to maintain it." It manifests itself in patriotism, in the mood to accept majority decisions and in the readiness to abide by the legal and constitutional methods. This view of general will is different from Rousseau's general will which legislates directly and continuously.

Law and Public Opinion

There is an intimate connection between law and public opinion. Whosoever makes the law on any particular subject must take into consideration the views of the people on that point. This is so not only in the case of a democracy but also in the case of a dictatorship. In a democracy, the government has to be carried on according to the wishes of the people. All laws passed in a democracy must take into consideration the good of the people. If laws are passed which are detested by the people, there is very little chance of their being enforced. There is bound to be opposition and the whole object of law is frustrated. It is well known that there was very strong opposition to the Hindu Code Bill and consequently the Government of India had to give up its attempt to pass it although it had an overwhelming majority in the Parliament. The American Government had to withdraw the prohibition laws as there was strong opposition to them. Even a dictator has to keep in mind the fact that he should not try to enforce those laws which are disliked by the people. He knows that if he creates unnecessary opposition by trying to enforce unpopular legislation, there is the likelihood of his being overthrown. Hence, public opinion cannot be ignored by any government while passing laws.

However, it does not mean that the law must always follow public opinion. Experience shows that very often progressive ideas are opposed by the people at large and if the legislators are not prepared to look ahead, there is no possibility of progressive legislation being enacted. It is rightly pointed out that if Lord William Bentinck had taken into consideration only public opinion, the curse of Suttee would never have been abolished. If Prime Minister Nehru had not shown holdness, the agrarian reforms could not have been carried out. But this does not mean that public opinion can be completely ignored in such matters. After all, laws are meant for the people and there should be no attempt to pass those laws which are not liked by them.

Lowell says that public opinion signifies two things. Public opinion must be public and not sectional. Individual or sectional opinion is not public opinion. It does not aim at the good of all or the majority. Public opinion must really be an opinion. A mere whim or gust of popular passion cannot be called public opinion which must be stable and enduring. Public opinion must be shared as widely as possible. It does not imply unanimity. About public opinion, George William Curtis says, "It is completed by persuading the majority, by showing the reason and the advantage of the step forward, and that is accomplished by appealing to the intelligence of the majority." A true public opinion aims at the good of the people. Willoughby says, "In any community of men that which has assured the character of public opinion is the result not of the opinion of all its members but only of those persons, few or many, who are led to think and to form judgements regarding matters of general interest." In the case of true public opinion, the minority should be convinced that the majority view is for the good of all. The conviction of the minority must not arise out of fear. Likewise, if the minority opinion is inspired by the desire of public good, it is true public opinion although the majority may not share it. Only that opinion is public opinion which is in the interests of the community as a whole and is also representative.

Experience shows that there is no perfect method to find out the public opinion although we can have an idea of the same from what is published in the press or discussed at the platform. However, there is a possibility that the propaganda in the press may be manipulated by some interested parties. The true facts may be suppressed and false propaganda may be carried on. Ordinarily, it is trot possible for the average man to find out the truth.

Democracy lives and thrives upon public opinion and public opinion must be honest, forceful and vigilant.

International Law

Like municipal law operating within the territory of a state, international law as a body of recognised principles and rules, has come into being in the international community of today. It has arisen out of the necessity for peaceful adjustment of the conflicting claims of states. It deals with the rights of states and the procedure for safeguarding them. Like national law, international law is a product of evolution and has developed in response to the pressing needs of changing situations.

Several definitions of international law have been given from time to time by various writers. In the words of Wheaton, "International law, as understood among civilised nations, may be defined as consisting of those rules of conduct which reason deduces as consonant to justice, from the nature of the society existing among independent nations, with such definitions and modifications as may be established by general consent." Hall writes, "International law consists in certain rules of conduct which modern civilised states regard as binding on them in their relations with one another with a force comparable in nature and degree to that binding the conscientious persons to obey the laws of their country and which they also regard as being enforceable by appropriate means in case of infringement." Lawrence defines international law "as the rules which determine the conduct of the general body of civilised states in their mutual dealings." According to Sir Cecil Hurst, international law is "the aggregate of the rules which determine the rights which one state is entitled to claim on behalf of itself or its nationals against another state." In the words of Oppenheim, "The law of nations or international law is the name for the body of customary and conventional rules which are considered legally binding by civilised states in their intercourse with each other." According to Starke, "International law may be defined as that body of law which is composed for its greater part of the principles and rules of conduct which states feel themselves bound to observe and therefore do commonly observe in their relations with each other." Lord Russel of Killowen defines international law as "the aggregate of the rules to which the nations have agreed to confirm in their conduct towards one another." Lord Birkenhead says that international law consists of rules acknowledged by the general body of civilised independent states to be binding upon them in their mutual relations. It consists of those rules which govern sovereign states in their relations and conduct towards each other.

Previously, the scope of international law was restricted to the regulation of relations among the various states and individuals did not figure anywhere. However, international law today is concerned even with the interests of individuals and organisations operating in various parts of the world.

Is International Law Really Law?

There is a considerable divergence of opinion regarding the true nature of international law. John Austin, Willoughby and Holland regard international law as positive morality or the moral code of nations and do not concede that it is law properly so-called. According to Austin, "The law obtaining between nations is not positive law, for every positive law is set by a given sovereign to a person or persons in a state of subjection to its author." Austin defines positive law as a body of rules for human conduct set and forced by a sovereign political authority, but international law is not set or enforced by a political authority, which is sovereign over other states for the regulations of whose relations that law is intended. In international relations, all states are theoretically equal, however much they may differ in actual strength. There can be no common superior over sovereign states and in the relations between states, the notion of a positive law is excluded. According to Austin, "The law obtaining between nations is only set by a general opinion and the duties which it imposes are enforced by moral sanction." In international relations, there are no sanctions in the sense of coercion by a sovereign power as there is no such power over and above the sovereign states. There is no independent arbiter of disputed questions beyond public opinion and no tribunal exists for applying to particular cases the principles recognised by the comity of nations. In the absence of definite and compelling sanctions, the validity and obligatory force of international law is dependent on the preparedness of any particular state to accept its substance. If we accept Austin's definition of law as a command addressed to political inferiors by a sovereign superior and followed by a sanction in the event of disobedience, international law cannot be called law.

According to Holland, international law is the vanishing point of jurisprudence as it lacks any arbiter of disputed questions save public opinion. Such rules as are voluntary and though habitually observed by every state in its dealings with the rest, can be called law only by courtesy. International law differs from ordinary law in being unsupported by the authority of a state. It differs from ordinary morality as it is a rule for states and not for individuals.

According to Lord Salisbury, international law, "can be enforced by no tribunal and therefore to apply to it the phrase law is to some extent misleading." Colridge observes, "Strictly speaking, international law is an inexact expression and it is apt to mislead if its inexactness is not kept in mind. Law implies a law-giver and a tribunal capable of enforcing it and coercing its transgressor, but there is no common law-giver to sovereign states and no tribunal has the power to bind them by decrees or coerce them if they transgress. The law of nations is that collection of usages which civilised states have agreed to observe in their dealings with one another. What these usages are, whether a particular one has or has not been agreed to, must be a matter of evidence. Treaties and acts of states are but evidence of the agreement of nations and do not, in England at least, *per se* bind the tribunals."

The view of Prof. Dias is that in spite of these resemblances between international law and municipal law, there are two important differences between them which cannot be overlooked. One difference is that the subjects of international law are primarily states and the disparity in strength between them far exceeds that between individuals in society.

Those who hold the view that international law is not law, point out that it is merely a collection of principles of morality and hence is not binding on every sovereign state. While addressing the House of Lords, Lord Salisbury is stated to have observed, "I think, my Lords, we are misled in this matter by the felicity with which we use the phrase international law. International law is not in existence in the sense in which the term law is usually understood. It depends generally on the prejudices of the writers of the textbooks. It can be enforced by no tribunal and therefore to apply to it the phrase law is to some extent misleading."

Critics also contend that international law is not law because British courts do not recognise it. While giving the judgement in West Rand Central Gold Mining Co. v. The King, the British court decided not to recognise in principle international law until it was included in the municipal law.

It is also contended that international law is not law because it is not the law of any sovereign international state. There is no sovereign international state or government. Gettell writes, "If the legalistic theory be adopted that laws are always commands given and enforced by a definite political sovereign, then international law is not law since that would imply world unity and world sovereignty." The term international law involves a contradiction. If it is international, it is not law because there is no single sovereign to make or enforce it. If it is law, it is not international but the law of a world state.

International law is not law because unlike municipal law, there is no punishment of the offender if international law is violated.

Another reason why international law is not law is because there is no legislature to make international law, no judiciary to interpret it and no executive to enforce it.

The courts of international law maintain that international law is not definite as it is passing through the process of continuous development. On the other hand, municipal laws are definite and hence are laws properly so-called.

The view of Prof. Hart is that there are sufficient analogies of content, as opposed to form, to bring the rules of international law nearer to municipal law. There are rules prescribing how states ought to behave which are accepted as guiding standards as in municipal law. Appeals are made to precedent, writings and treatises as in municipal law. Rules of international law can be morally neutral and they can be changed by conscious act, *e.g.*, by treaty.

Arguments in favour

However, there are arguments in favour of the view that international law is law. It is pointed out that all laws are not the command of the sovereign. Laws are also based on the customs of the people. Sir Henry Maine and his followers maintain that there are certain laws which are based on custom. Those customs which have been in practice, are recognised by the state and they become law. The common law in England is an example. R.N. Gilchrist writes, "Law does not consist merely in the making of a definite code; it is rather the recognition of the state of principles already definitely existing among the people and the sanction of the law which in the first place is shown in the machinery of the state, really is the common agreement of the people."

It is also pointed out that although states are sovereign, they recognise international law "on account of the advantages derived from it." Chief Justice Marshall admitted that considerations of mutual benefit and advantage in practice made necessary "a relaxation of that absolute and complete jurisdiction which sovereignty is said to confer."

In the case of municipal law, the real force behind law is the public opinion. Likewise, the world public opinion is the most powerful force behind international law. It is pointed out that when Britain, France and Israel attacked Egypt in 1956, they were severely condemned in the United Nations and forced to pull out their forces from Egypt.

The allegation that international law is more violated than respected is not correct. The violation of rules is as much true of international law as of national law. Mere violation proves nothing.

The Austinian view that the states always look to their own interests and judge international law from that standpoint alone is not correct. A definite body of international rules has been formulated and administered and interpreted by the courts of arbitration and International Court of Justice. The establishment of the United Nations is the institutional expression of the idea of international legislation and sanction. In the Anglo-French operations in Egypt, definite sanctions in the form of economic pressure or armed intervention were applied. The United Nations Force helped South Korea against North Korea in 1950. The rules of international law have been normally applied by the ordinary courts of justice. This was done by Lord Parker in the case of Zamora. Legislatures of all civilised states do not make any law which goes against the rules of international law. No state will legislate supporting piracy which is prohibited by international law. The United Nations Declaration of Human Rights can be considered as the first step towards an international bill of rights. Lauterpacht writes, "As a result of the Charter of the United Nations – as well as of other changes in International Law – the individual has acquired a status and a stature which have transformed him from an object of international compassion into a subject of international rights." (International Law and Human Rights, p. 4). The trial and punishment of the political leaders of Germany by the International Military Tribunal at Nuremberg symbolises the beginning of an effective international criminal law.

The two great obstacles to the development of international law have been the theory of national sovereignty and the principle of territorial possession. In course of time, the idea of state absolutism so far as internal affairs of a government are concerned, has been successfully exploded. In respect of external relations, MacIver writes, "If public opinion further liberates itself from a tradition no longer consistent with the facts of the case, there would be no inherent difficulty in preventing the bestowal upon international law of a sanction which the most bigoted philosopher might no doubt explain away, but which he could no longer deny outright."

International law is based on logic and reasoning and is distinct from international morality. A number of cases are decided with the help of international law. Hall writes, "The doctrines of international law have been elaborated by a course of legal reasoning; in international controversies, precedents are used in a strictly legal manner; the opinions of writers are quoted and relied upon for the same purposes as those for which the opinions of writers are invoked under a system of municipal law; the conduct of states is attacked, defended and judged within the range of international law by a reference to legal considerations alone; and finally it is recognised that there is an international morality distinct from law, violation of which gives no formal ground of complaint, however odious the action of the ill-doer may be." (International Law, p. 14)

There are Prize courts in many countries and the law applied by them is international law and not municipal law.

According to Lawrence, the precepts of international law are rules whether they are laws or not. To quote him, "The rules, though like other rules they are sometimes evaded and sometimes defied, do nevertheless receive general obedience. They are no more reduced to a nullity by being sometimes broken than are the laws of the land because the habitual criminal disregards them with impunity."

According to Gray, "International law is a part of our law and must be ascertained and administered by the courts of justice of appropriate jurisdiction as often as questions of right depending upon it are duly presented for determination." Brierly writes, "The existence of some kind of international law is simply one of the inevitable consequences of this co-existence in the world of a plurality of states necessarily brought into relation with one another. The best evidence for the existence of international law is that every actual state recognises that it does exist and that it is itself under obligation to observe it." Again, "Only a very gloomy pessimist would fail to recognise that common moral and cultural standards do exist internationally, that they influence conduct between nations and that this community of sentiment, imperfect though it is, affords some basis of law."

The view of Pitt Cobbett is that international law must rank with law and not with morality. Its rules are not optional but compulsory and they rest in the last resort on force, even though that force is exerted through the irregular action of society rather than by some definite and authorised body. Jethro Brown says that international law is law in the making. It is law struggling for existence. It is struggling to make itself good.

Sir Frederick Pollock writes, "If international law were only a kind of morality, the framers of state papers concerning foreign policy would throw all their strength on moral argument. But, as a matter of fact, this is not what they do. They appeal not to the general feeling of moral writings but to precedents, to treaties and to opinions of specialists. They assume the existence among statesmen and publicists of a series of legal as distinguished from moral obligations in the affairs of nations." Again, "International law is a true branch of jurisprudence, notwithstanding what may be said about its want of sovereign power as a tribunal." Again, "International law is a body of customs and observances in an imperfectly organised society which have not fully acquired the character of law but which are on the way to become law."

According to Oppenheim, international laws is law in the true sense of the term. For hundreds of years, more and more rules have grown up for the conduct of the states with one another. Those rules are to a great extent customary rules but along with them are daily created more and more written rules by international agreements. Oppenheim admits that there is at present no Central Government above the governments of several states which could in every case secure the enforcement of the rules of international law. For that reason, compared with municipal laws and the means available for its enforcement, international law is certainly weaker of the two. A law is stronger if more guarantees are given that it can and will be enforced.

The view of Starke is that international law is weak law. It is mainly customary. The existing international legislative machinery is not comparable in efficiency to state legislative machinery. In spite of the achievements of the United Nations in re-establishing a world court under the name of International Court of Justice, there is still no universal compulsory jurisdiction for settling legal disputes between states. Many of the rules of international law can only be formulated with difficulty and are quite uncertain. It was on that account that the attempt of the International Conference of 1930 at the Hague to codify certain branches of international law failed.

About international law, Gettell writes, "While it is still an undeveloped and imperfect system of law in an imperfectly organised political world, its rules at least lie on the frontier of law and constitute a system of jurisprudence rather than a code of morals."

Sources of International Law

(1) According to the Statute of the International Court of Justice, the sources of international law are international customs, international treaties, general principles of law recognised by civilized states and judicial decisions and teachings of the most highly qualified publicists of the various countries. As regards "international custom" this is the oldest source of international law and till recently was the most important source. The rules relating to state territory, state jurisdiction, state responsibility, the doctrine of continuous voyage, the law of neutrality, and the law relating to diplomatic immunities, have been developed by custom. Pleas of international custom can be raised before the national and international tribunals and those have to be decided. In the Paquete Habana Case, the Supreme Court of the United States examined the whole material on the subject and came to the conclusion that there existed a customary rule of international law which gave immunity to small fishing vessels from belligerent action in times of war. In the Lotus Case, the Permanent Court of International Justice decided that there was no customary rule conferring exclusive jurisdiction in maritime collision cases on the country of the ship's flag as regards all incidents on the ship.

A distinction is made between an international custom and an international usage. We speak of custom when a clear and continuous habit of doing certain actions has grown up and there is a conviction that those actions are obligatory under international law. We speak of usage when a habit of doing certain actions has not yet received full legal recognition. As soon as there is a general conviction among states that a particular usage which regulated the conduct of civilized states has come to be regarded as obligatory or binding, the usage becomes a custom.

(2) "International treaties" are another important source of international law. These treaties are of two kinds: law-making treaties and treaty-contracts. Law-making treaties lay down general rules binding on the majority of states. Treaty-contracts deal with a special matter concerning two or more states exclusively. Law-making treaties are a direct source of international law but that is not the case with treaty contracts. The number of law-making treaties has grown in recent times. Hudson says that there were as many as 257 law-making treaties between 1864 and 1914. A reference to the important law-making treaties shows that they deal with Red Cross work, weights and measures, protection of industrial property, protection of submarine cables, suppression of slave trade, aerial navigation, international waterways, the pacific settlement of international disputes etc. The important examples of the law-making treaties are the Treaty of Westphalia (1648), Treaty of Paris (1815), Treaty of Versailles (1919), Declaration of Paris (1856), the Geneva Conventions of 1864, 1906, 1929 and 1949, the Kellogg-Briand Pact (1928), the Montreal Convention regarding the Straits (1936), the Charter of the United Nations (1945), the Suez Canal Convention (1888), the Covenant of the League of Nations (1919), etc.

(3) The decisions of international and national courts and the arbitral tribunals are also a source of international law. The Permanent Court of International Justice was set up in 1921 and the International Court of Justice in 1946. The judgements and advisory opinions of these courts have helped the development of international law. The decisions of the municipal courts are also a source of international law. These decisions may be treated as weighty precedents or binding authorities. The decisions of the Supreme Court of the United States in the Paquete Habana and the Scotia Cases did a lot to clarify the nature of international custom. The decisions of Lord Stowell have received universal acknowledgement as authoritative declarations of the law on blockade, contraband of war and the doctrine of continuous voyage. The decisions of the Prize Courts are also a source of international Law. Although these courts are set up by the various states, their decisions relate to questions of international law.

(4) Decisions of international arbitral tribunals such as the Permanent Court of Arbitration and the British and American Mixed Claims Tribunals are also a source of international law in the field of territorial sovereignty, neutrality, state jurisdiction, state servitudes and state responsibility. The important arbitration cases were the *North Atlantic Fisheries Case* (1910), the *Behring Sea Fisheries Arbitration* (1893), the *Alabama Claims Arbitration* (1872), and the *Pious Fund Case*, etc.

(5) Another source of international law is *the principles of law recognised by civilized states.* It is clearly stated that in the absence of any clear international custom or treaty on a point, the International Court of Justice must take into consideration the general principles of law recognised by civilized states.

(6) The Statute of the International Court of Justice directs the Court to apply the teachings of the most highly qualified publicists of the various nations as a subsidiary means for the determination of the rules of law. Some of the most important works are *War and Peace* by Grotius (1625), *Law of Nature and Nations* by Pufendorf (1672) and *Diplomatic Code of the Law of Nations* by Liebnitz. The writings of Bynkershoek, Wolff, Vattel, Kent, Wheaton, Manning, Woolsey, Westlake, Lawrence and Hall are great landmarks in the development of international law. Both lawyers and judges refer to their opinions with great respect. Kent says: "No civilized nation that does not arrogantly set all (ordinary law and justice at defiance, will venture to disregard the uniform sense of the established writers on international law." Gray says: "Where there is no treaty and no controlling executive act or judicial decision, resort must be had to the customs and usages of civilized nations, and as evidence of these, to the works of jurists and commentators who by years of labour, research and experience have made themselves peculiarly well acquainted with the subjects which they treat. Such works are resorted to by judicial tribunals, not for the speculation of their authors concerning what the law ought to be, but for trustworthy evidence of what the law really is."

(7) International comity is another source of international law. International comity means the rules of conduct required to be observed in inter-state relations on the ground of politeness, convenience and goodwill. These rules are obeyed by states, not because they are obligatory but because they embody expression of goodwill which is desirable in the mutual relations of states.

(8) International state papers, other than treaties, form a source of international law. Whenever there is any international controversy, the official jurists give their own opinion to their respective governments and their opinions are very important from the point of view of international law. The archives of the foreign affairs departments of the various countries possess a mass of valuable expert opinion on international law.

(9) The acts or declarations by statesmen and press releases or official statements by government spokesmen also constitute evidence of the usages followed by the states.

(10) Another source of international law is international legislation. This source is becoming very important in modern times. A lot has been done in this connection by the League of Nations and the United Nations. The volume of international legislation has become so great that it is really a problem to keep a correct record of it.

History of International Law

Lawrence says that the history of International law can be divided into three periods. The first period extends from the earliest times to the establishment of the universal domination of Rome under the Caesars. The distinguishing feature of this period was the belief that nations owed duties to one another if they were of the same race and not otherwise. During this period, there was constant strife among the nations. Wars were declared without any formalities. There was utmost cruelty. No mercy was shown either to the aged people or to women and children. Even the cattle were destroyed. The highly civilised Greeks despised their neighbours and considered them to be worthy of destruction. The only traces of international dealings were in Maritime trade.

The Jews had their dealings with a few foreign nations and they had their rules for the observance of treaties and respect for the ambassadors of friendly powers. The foreigners living in Jewish territory were governed by the same law as the Jews themselves. The view of Oppenheim is that the Greeks left to posterity the example that independent sovereign states can live in a community which provides a law for the international relations of the member states provided there trade existed some common interests which bound them together.

The second period extends from the beginning of the Roman Empire to the Reformation. As the Roman Empire spread over the world then known, there was no question of the international relations. The imperial idea continued even after the fall of Roman Empire. It was shaken only when the Pope and the Emperor began to claim the imperial power. The growth of the modern national states also worked in the same direction. The feudal system also helped the development of international law. It emphasized the idea of territorial state, each state having jurisdiction over citizens residing in definite territories. The spread of Christian principles taught the ideas of humanity.

The third period extends from the Reformation to the present time. During this period, the current ideas were systemised. The great havoc brought about by the Thirty Years' War (1618-1648) emphasized the necessity of international regulation. It was in this atmosphere that Hugo Grotius, the father of international law, wrote his famous book *The Laws of War and Peace in* 1625. He dealt with the grounds of a just war, the defence of self and of property, titles to property, original and acquired, the obligations of ownership, promises, contracts and oaths, treaties, obligation to repair injuries, the right of legation, punishment for wrongs done, etc. Fenwick says: "It is this analysis of the rights and duties of state, in an attempt to decide when one state has a just claim against another, that constitutes the main contribution of Grotius to the science of international law. The *de jure belliac pacis* is not merely an effort to put restraints upon the conduct of war, to which Book III of the treatise is devoted; it is an effort, guided by moral idealism and an exhaustive knowledge of the civil law, to determine specifically the rights and duties of states as to the basis of peaceful relations between them. Grotius was not the first to discuss the many particular problems that fill the pages of his great treatise, but he was the first to bring all of them together in a systematic form, and to combine in a single co-ordinated treatise the most progressive thought of the century in which he lived."

Grotius laid down fundamental principles on which the present day law of nations is founded. Those principles were two. The first principle was that states were independent, sovereign and equal. The second principle was that the force that bound the states to the observance of the rules of international law was international morality. The work of Grotius became a book of reference and guidance for kings and statesmen whenever they were faced with any question of international conduct.

After Grotius, many writers wrote on the subject of international law. The names of Bynkershoek (1673-1743) and Vattel (1714-1767) are important in this connection.

International law made a lot of progress during the 19th century. Some of the factors which contributed to this development were the further rise of powerful new states both within and outside Europe, the expansion of European civilization overseas, the modernization of world transport, the greater destructiveness of modern warfare and the influence of new inventions. There was a remarkable development of the law of war and neutrality. A large number of awards were given by international arbitral tribunals. Many law-making treaties were also made. The Declaration of Paris of 1856 embodied rules for the guidance of states when engaged in warfare at sea. The Geneva Convention of 1864 provided for the betterment of the condition of the sick and wounded in warfare on land. The Declaration of St. Petersburg of 1868 prohibited the use of explosive bullets in war. The Geneva Convention of 1906 extended to maritime warfare the provisions relating to the treatment of the sick and wounded in land warfare.

The Hague Conferences of 1899 and 1907 tried to evolve laws for the conduct of international relations. The first conference evolved a code for land warfare. The second Hague Conference adopted conventions dealing with bombardment, the laying of contact mines, rights and duties of neutrals in naval warfare, conversion of merchant ships into warships, maritime warfare, flags of truce, military hospital ships, etc.

The Permanent Court of Arbitration was established by the Hague Conferences. The Permanent Court of International Justice was set up in 1921 and it was succeeded in 1946 by the International Court of Justice. The League of Nations and the International Labour Organisation were set up after World War I and the United Nations was started after World War II.

Reference may be made to some of the important writers on international law. Manning published in 1839 his *Commentaries on the Law of Nations.* Philimore published in 1854 his *Commentaries on International Law.* Hall published his *International Law* in 1880. In 1893, Walker published his *Science of International Law.* The other English writers were Westlake and Oppenheim. In 1826, James Kent gave a systematic treatment of international law in his *Commentaries on American Law. The Elements of International Law* was published in 1826 by Wheaton. Lieber codified the laws of war and the rules with regard to the rights and duties of neutral states. Continental writers like Klubers, Bluntschli, Jellinek, Ihering and Kaufmann played their part.

Events took a very serious turn during World War I. The rules of international law regarding land and sea warfare were thrown to the winds. There were so many breaches of the rules of international law that it was reduced to a mockery. The destruction was so great that it was universally felt that something should be done to enforce the principles of international law among the nations.

The Covenant of the League of Nations was embodied in the Treaty of Versailles of 1919. The main object of the League of Nations was to maintain peace in the world. Provision was made for the principle of collective security and the enforcement of economic sanctions against the aggressors.

The Locarno Pact of 1925 strengthened the principles of the League of Nations regarding the pacific settlement of disputes and the pledges of non-aggression. The frontiers between Germany and Belgium and Germany and France were guaranteed by Great Britain and Italy. If there was any dispute, it was to be settled amicably. This pact was denounced by Germany in 1936.

The Kellogg-Briand Pact or the Paris Pact of 1928 declared the renunciation of war as an instrument of national policy. The contracting parties also agreed that "settlement or solution of all disputes or conflicts, of whatever nature and origin they may be, which may arise among them, shall never be sought except by pacific means."

On 1st July, 1929, at the invitation of the Swiss Government, representatives of 47 governments met at Geneva and adopted two conventions regarding the treatment of the sick and wounded in the battlefield and the treatment of prisoners of war. Reprisals, cruel treatment of prisoners and collective penalties for acts of individuals were prohibited. Provision was also made for the grant of immunities to medical units and persons engaged in the care of the sick and wounded. Provision was also made for the exchange of communications between the belligerents about the names of the sick, the wounded and the dead.

Reference may be made to the works of important writers on international law during this period. Many treatises were written on the Covenant of the League of Nations. Articles were written on various aspects of international law. In the U.S.A., Hyde and Stowell published their works on the principles of international law. The new editions of the works of Hall, Wheaton and Oppenheim were printed. Anzilotte, Kelsen. Roscoe Pound and others published their works on international law under the auspices of the League of Nations.

During World War II, the rules of international law were violated with impunity by the Axis Powers. However, the latter were ultimately defeated by the Allied Powers in 1945. Even during World War II, Roosevelt and Churchill issued the famous Atlantic Charter. At the Dumbarton Oaks Conference, an agreement was arrived at for the establishment of an international organization.

On 26th June, 1945, the Charter of the United Nations was signed at San Francisco. The United Nations came into existence on 24th October, 1945 when the Charter was ratified by the five original members and a majority of the other signatories. In 1946, the International Court of Justice replaced the Permanent Court of International Justice. In 1948, the Universal Declaration of Human Rights was adopted. Various other conventions regarding the position of refugees, etc., have been signed.

The prospects of the growth of international law are bright. In spite of the difficulties in its way, it is making headway. The whole world has become one in modern times and there must be a set of rules to regulate the relations of the various states with one another.

The League of Nations

The League was actually established in 1920 and its headquarters were fixed at Geneva in Switzerland. The Preamble of the Covenant of the League of Nations reads thus: "The High Contracting Parties, in order to promote international co-operation and to achieve international peace and security by the acceptance of obligations not to resort to war, by prescription of open, just and honourable relations between nations, by the firm establishment of the understanding of international law as the actual rule of conduct among governments and by the maintenance of justice and a scrupulous respect for all treaty obligations in the dealings of organized peoples with one another, agree to this Covenant of the League of Nations."

The organs of the League of Nations were the Assembly, the Council, the Secretariat and the Permanent Court of International Justice. The Assembly was the supreme body and consisted of the representatives of the various states which were the members of the League. Every Member state was given the right of one vote in the Assembly. All decisions of the Assembly were required to be unanimous. As regards the Council, it originally consisted of four permanent members and four other members elected by the Assembly. Later on, in 1926, Germany was also given a permanent seat on the Council. The number of non-permanent members continued to increase and ultimately it reached the figure of eleven. Of the Assembly and the Council, the former was certainly stronger than the latter. The Assembly acted like an international legislature and its debates were circulated all over the world. It enjoyed both dignity and respect. Most of its work was done by the various sub-committees. The Secretariat of the League of Nations was located at Geneva and the Secretary-General was the most prominent figure. He was appointed by the Council but the approval of the Assembly was essential. The staff of the Secretariat was appointed by the Secretary-General in consultation with the Council. The member states had to pay towards the expenses of the Secretariat in certain proportions. While the meetings of the Council and Assembly were held from time to time, the Secretariat continued to work throughout the year. Without it, the work of the League would have been impossible. The Permanent Court of International Justice consisted of 15 Judges and it had its headquarters at The Hague. It gave its judgments on questions involving the interpretation of international law, treaties and other mutual obligations. The judges of the court were elected for 9 years at a joint meeting of the Council and the Assembly. The International Labour Office was also attached to the League of Nations. Its object was to improve the labour conditions in the various parts of the world. Its governing body consisted of the representatives of governments, employers and workers. There were annual meetings and important decisions were arrived at on the occasion of those meetings.

The main function of the League of Nations was to avoid war and maintain peace in the world and it was required to do all that lay in its power to achieve that ideal. A check was to be put on armaments. The size of armies was to be reduced to such an extent that it was just sufficient for the maintenance of law and order and defence against foreign aggression. The members of the League were required not to go to war without exhausting all the pacific means for the settlement of disputes. The Assembly, the Council and the Permanent Court of International Justice were to help in the matter of maintaining peace. Provision was made for collective action against a state which dared to violate the provisions of the Covenant of the League of Nations. Coercive action could be taken against rebellious states. Provision was also made for the enforcement of economic sanctions against an aggressor country.

Provision was made for the mandate system under the League of Nations, The territories captured from the Central Powers and Turkey were not to be restored to them and were also not to be given to any victorious country in full sovereignty. The administration of those countries was to be given to various countries under the supervision of the League of Nations. The basis of the new policy was laid down in these words: "To those colonies and territories which as a consequence of the late War, have ceased to be under the sovereignty of the state which formerly governed them and which are inhabited by peoples not yet able to stand by themselves under the strenuous conditions of the modern world, there should be applied the principle that the well-being and development of such peoples form a sacred trust of civilization and that security for the performance of this trust should be embodied in this Covenant. The best method of giving practical effect to this principle is that the tutelage of such peoples should be entrusted to advanced nations who, by reason of their resources, their experience, or their geographical position can best undertake this responsibility and who are willing to accept it, and that tutelage should be exercised by them as Mandatory on behalf of the League. The Charter of Mandate must differ according to the state of development of the people, the geographical situation of the country, its economic conditions and other similar circumstances."

Work of the League

In twenty years, the League was called upon to examine about forty political disputes. As a rule, the cases were handled by the Council but a few were referred to the Assembly, the Council of Ambassadors, or the Permanent Court of International Justice. Some of the earlier disputes, such as that of 1923 between Italy and Greece over the murder of several Italians on Greek soil, were serious threats to world peace. Disputes such as that of 1921-22 between Finland and Soviet Russia over the treatment of the inhabitants of eastern Karelia, were of lesser importance. There were also some disputes which the League was not able to settle at all. On the whole, the League was able to assert its political mission most strongly where small nations were involved. The larger nations were more likely to regard League investigations as infringing their sovereign rights. They were also in a position to bring pressure to bear on their behalf.

(1) Aaland Islands. One of the first disputes brought to the attention of the Council of the League concerned the Aaland Islands which lie between Sweden and Finland. Both Finland and the islands once belonged to Sweden. However, they were acquired in 1809 by Russia. The latter continued to rule over them up to 1917 when the Russian Revolution took place. Finland declared her independence and it was recognised in January 1918 by Sweden without making any reservation with regard to the Aaland Islands. This was so in spite of the fact that the inhabitants of the islands were chiefly of Swedish stock and spoke the Swedish language.

The inhabitants of the islands began to agitate for union with Sweden. The Government of Sweden kept aloof from the movement but her people sympathised with the agitators. The Government of Finland sent her troops to the islands and arrested the agitators. The people of Sweden demanded of their government that help must be sent to the islanders. There was every possibility of a war. However, in June 1920, Great Britain exercised her friendly rights under the Covenant to direct the attention of the Secretary-General to the case.

A meeting of the Council was held in London and both the parties presented their cases. The matter was referred to a Committee of Jurists. After it had been settled that the League had jurisdiction in the matter, the Council gave its decision in June 1921. Finland was to have sovereignty over the islands. The Aalanders were to be guaranteed autonomy and the protection of their political rights. The rights of private properties and the use of Swedish in the schools were to be preserved. The archipelago was to be neutralized and unfortified. In April 1922, an international convention was made which guaranteed the neutrality of the islands and gave them the requisite international protection.

(2) Mosul Boundary Dispute. According to the treaty of Lausanne (1923), the frontier separating Turkey from Great Britain's mandated territory, Iraq, was to be drawn "in friendly arrangement" between Turkey and Great Britain. If no agreement was arrived at within nine months, the matter was to be referred to the League Council. Both the parties failed to agree oh a mutually acceptable boundary line as they both claimed the Mosul *villayet* which was rich in oil. The matter was referred to the League in 1924. The situation was very grave and a number of frontier incidents occurred. An emergency session of the League Council was called at Brussels. A provisional boundary line was drawn pending the final judgement. Turkey was to maintain order north of the Brussels line and Great Britain was to maintain order to the south of the Brussels line. A neutral commission of enquiry heard both the parties to the dispute and submitted its report to the League Council in September 1925. The report established the sovereignty of Turkey over the *villayet* and explained that neither Great Britain nor Iraq had a right to claim it by conquest. Certain points were referred to the Permanent Court of International Justice for its opinion. However, the dispute was not solved.

Ultimately, the League Council gave its final judgement on the subject. The Brussels line was to be the permanent boundary line between Turkey and Iraq. Great Britain was to take steps to secure extension of her control over Iraq for a further period of 25 years. The Kurdish minority in Mosul was to be guaranteed the appointment of Kurdish local officials and the use of the Kurdish language in its schools. Great Britain and Iraq accepted the award but Turkey refused to do so. As Turkey began to lean more and more on Soviet Russia, Great Britain entered into a compromise. In June 1926, a treaty was made between Turkey and Great Britain by which a small part of the *villayet* was given to Turkey. The revised boundary was recognised as definitive. Some royalties from the Mosul oil-fields were given to Turkey.

(3) Dispute between Bolivia and Paraguay. In December 1928, an armed clash took place between Bolivia and Paraguay. The matter was taken up by the League Council and a telegram was sent by it expressing its full conviction that the two States which, by signing the Covenant, had solemnly pledged themselves to seek by pacific means the solution of disputes arising between them, would have recourse to such methods as would be in conformity with their international obligations and would appear in the present circumstances to be most likely to secure the maintenance of peace and the settlement of the dispute.

Both the states agreed to accept the good offices of the Pan-American Conference on Arbitration and Conciliation. The result was that the immediate quarrel was resolved but the underlying causes of the dispute remained. Fresh trouble occurred in May, 1929. Again the representatives of the two states met at Washington to conclude a non-aggression pact. Hostilities were suspended.

Fresh trouble broke out in 1932. Efforts were made by the neighbouring states to prevent a war but all of them failed. Bloody conflict continued. The League of Nations appointed a Commission of enquiry which reported that struggle was inhuman and criminal. When attempts to restore peace failed, it was decided to put an embargo on arms shipments to Bolivia and Paraguay. Some states cooperated, while others did not. As Paraguay had the upper hand in the struggle, she refused to accept a compromise formula. Paraguay also gave notice of its resignation from the membership of the League.

The League did not take any interest in the case after March, 1935. As a result of the efforts of Argentine, Brazil, Chile, Peru, the United States, and Uruguay, the foreign ministers of Bolivia and Paraguay signed in June 1935, a protocol outlining the machinery for the negotiation of peace. It was in July, 1938 that a peace treaty was signed. Thus, the League did not succeed in the dispute between Bolivia and Paraguay.

(4) Eupen and Malmedy. In 1920 and 1921, Germany addressed to the League Council a series of protests against the giving of Eupen and Malmedy to Belgium. The League Council discussed the matter in September, 1920 and wrote to the German Government that its decision regarding the transfer of Eupen and Malmedy to Belgium was final.

(5) The Corfu Incident. In August, 1923, an Italian General, two officers and one chauffeur were murdered on Greek soil. The Italian Government demanded apologies and full reparation for the crime. As Greece refused to accept all the demands of Italy, the latter occupied the island of Corfu. In September 1923, Greece referred the matter to the League Council. It was notified by the President of the League Council that a communication had been received from the Conference of Ambassadors announcing the settlement of the dispute as a result of diplomatic negotiations undertaken by the Conference.

(6) Dispute between Great Britain and France. In 1921 there arose a dispute between France and Great Britain over the nationality decrees in Tunis and Morocco. The decrees issued by France in Tunis and Morocco provided that any person born in France or on the territory of French colonies would be a French citizen. These decrees conflicted with the British nationality laws. The British Government asked the French Government to refer the matter to arbitration but the contention of France was that it was a purely domestic affair. Ultimately, it was decided by the Permanent Court of International Justice that the matter was not purely one of domestic jurisdiction. The dispute was finally decided by mutual negotiations between the Foreign Ministers of the two countries.

(7) Dispute between Greece and Bulgaria. There was some trouble on the frontier between Greece and Bulgaria on account of the activity of Macedonian brigands. In October 1952, the commander of a Greek frontier post and one of his men were killed. By way of reprisal, a Greek army marched into Bulgaria. The latter appealed to the League. The League Council met and asked the Greek Government to withdraw its troops. The Governments of Great Britain, France and Italy were asked to send military officers to the spot to see what was happening. These measures had a deterrent effect on the Greek Government. The Greek forces were withdrawn and Greece was asked to pay compensation to Bulgaria for the violation of her territory on a scale to be fixed by a League Commission.

Non-Political Work

The League did a lot, of non-political work. A Slavery Convention met at Geneva in 1925. In 1932, it was decided to set up a Permanent Slavery Commission.

The Financial Committee of the League advised the Council on financial matters in general, on financial assistance to governments and on financial problems which could be solved by international cooperation. It helped to tackle the problems of counterfeiting, falsification of commercial documents, double taxation and the fluctuating value of gold. The Financial Committee was responsible for the issue and supervision of various League loans for Austria, Hungary, Greece, etc. A general finance conference was held in Brussels in 1920. The Economic Committee of the League did the preliminary work for the World Economic Conference of 1927 and the Monetary and Economic Conference of 1933.

In order to implement the provisions of Article 23 of the Covenant of the League, the autonomous Communications and Transit Organisation was set up in 1920. This organisation cooperated with river commissions, labour unions, railway agencies, air traffic associations, etc.

The League also set up in 1923 the Health Organisation with a Health Committee and a secretariat. It performed a lot of useful work in organising action against malaria, smallpox, leprosy, rabies, cancer, tuberculosis, syphilis, heart disease, etc. It helped researches in medicine. It helped the nations to improve national health. It organised technical conferences. It cooperated with governments in reporting epidemics and their spread. The League helped a plan to fight typhus and prevented cholera and plague from the East. It brought home from Russia 4,27,000 prisoners of war. It cooperated with China to organise relief work in the flooded areas. It helped the Greek Government to settle 15 lakhs of refugees. Dr. Nasen played an important part in the work of the settlement of refugees under the aegis of the League.

In 1922, the League appointed an International Committee on Intellectual Cooperation. In 1926 was established the International Institute of Intellectual Cooperation at Paris. It tried to coordinate "international collaboration with a view to promoting the progress of general civilisation and human knowledge and notably the development and diffusion of science, letters and arts."

The League did a lot of useful work in the field of control of traffic in dangerous drugs, peasant reforms, prohibition of traffic in women, suppression of trade in obscene literature, promotion of child welfare etc.

The International Labour Organisation and the Permanent Court of International Justice – organs of the League – also did a lot of useful work.

According to Cordell Hull, "The League of Nations has been responsible for more humanitarian and scientific endeavour than any other organisation in history."

Causes of Failure

However, the League failed in its main object of maintaining peace in the world. In spite of its efforts for two decades, the whole world was involved in a war in 1939. By that time, the machinery of the League of Nations had completely broken down. The failure of the League can be attributed to many causes. It was unfortunate that the Covenant of the League of Nations was made a part and parcel of the peace settlement. It would have been better if it had been kept separate. There were many states which considered the Treaty of Versailles as a treaty of revenge and were not prepared to ratify it. By not ratifying the treaty, they refused to be the members of the League. The absence of the great powers from the international organisation weakened it and the same was partly responsible for its ultimate failure. Japan, Germany and Italy also left the League and their defection must have weakened the League. It was felt that the League of Nations was dominated by England and France and consequently the other states began to lose their confidence in the organization. The League was intended to perform a miracle by doing the impossible task of maintaining the *status quo* in the world. That would have been possible if the Peace Settlement of 1919-20 had been based on justice and fairplay. However, as countries like Germany were completely humiliated by that settlement, there was no chance of peace. Germany was bound to defy the provisions of the Treaty of Versailles as she felt that she did not accept them voluntarily but they were imposed on her at the point of the bayonet. In such an atmosphere, any organisation would have failed to maintain peace. The rise of dictatorship in Italy, Japan and Germany also weakened the chances of success of the League. Japan was determined to acquire fresh territories and her unscrupulous patriotism threw to the winds all the principles of international law and morality. If the League was not prepared to condone her fault of conquering Manchuria, she was prepared to give up her membership of the League and that is exactly what she actually did. Likewise, as the League decided to take action against Italy on account of her aggression in Abyssinia, Italy left the League. Germany was not prepared to honour her commitments under the Treaty of Versailles with regard to her armaments and consequently she decided to leave the League of Nations. States continued to be members of the League so long as their national interests were not in any way endangered or sacrificed. They preferred to pursue and achieve their national aspirations other than to care for the strengthening and perpetuation of the international organization which was the only hope of the free world.

Small nations lost their faith in the effectiveness of the League to save them from any aggression. The principle of collective security was not applied in actual practice. If all the member states had joined hands against Japan and Italy on the question of Manchuria and Abyssinia respectively, aggression would have been checked and the prestige of the League would have risen. As each state decided to follow its own policy, the principle of collective security was weakened and thus there was nothing to check the aggressive policy of Hitler.

The League Was given an effective weapon in the form of economic sanctions. However, this weapon was not used in such a way as to produce good results. The economic sanctions against Italy were applied in a halting manner and no wonder they failed in their objective.

The League failed because it was an organization of the governmental authorities and the peoples of the various states had no say in its deliberations. There was no popular backing or enthusiasm.

Another cause of the failure of the League was that while Great Britain and France joined the League, they did not change their behaviour. Great Britain looked upon the League as a means to perpetuate the balance of power. She did not adapt the balance of power to the requirements of a new world community. France looked upon the League as a means to encircle Germany. She did not transform French security into collective security.

Likewise, statesmen in general did not face the basic economic, psychological and social problems of the world. The treatment of Germany was typical of their failure to realise the importance of such matters. Since they were dominated by a geographical-legal concept which involves thinking in terms of nations, they made no effective effort to help the internal situation in Germany. As a matter of fact, the opposite was the case. Bad treatment of Germany at disarmament conferences and the tariff policy of the United States had disastrous effects on German internal forces. The members of the League and the United States unwittingly contributed to the downfall of the Weimar Republic. That led to the rise of Hitler in Germany and this was responsible for the failure of the League.

The League of Nations demonstrated the limitations of the legal methods. The League was fairly efficient in structure and probably would have worked if there had existed a realization of a community of interests. However, the League was in advance of public opinion. Law grows out of public opinion and cannot operate in disjunction with it. In the case of the League, law proposed and public opinion disposed. According to Lincoln, "Public sentiment is everything. With public . sentiment nothing can fail, without it nothing can succeed. Consequently he who moulds public sentiment goes deeper that he who enacts statues or pronounces decision. He makes statutes and decisions possible or impossible to be executed." The League had an elaborate formal structure but it did not function adequately because its members were not aware of its community of interests. Habits of cooperation are more important than formal structure.

The League was the offspring of a marriage of two separate lines of thought. In one of these, which were developed by Mr. Taft and others in the United States, the stress was on organized forces. There was to be a "League to enforce Peace." This aspect found support at the Peace Conference in the French desire for organized security. On the other hand, the typical British attitude to the problem was extremely hesitant in its approach to the notion of enforced peace and even in its acceptance of the principle of compulsory arbitration. The British solution was rather an extension of the method of the former concert of Europe. If the 14 Points of Wilson are consulted we find that a general association of nations is projected "for the purpose of affording mutual guarantees of political independence and territorial integrity." In its proposal the word peace is not mentioned and international cooperation is restricted to one limited Object. The proposal described might well be a wide system of alliance for the forcible protection of the *status quo.* If we look at the preamble to the Covenant, the purpose placed in the forefront is "to promote international cooperation" and the preservation of peace is almost equally prominent. The League was thus from one point of view a bulwark on a territorial settlement constructed on extremely nationalised lines, and from another the instrument of the new internationalism. These two inconsistent principles were incorporated in the fabric of the League itself and no wonder it failed.

The success of the project depended upon the validity of the assumption that the whole world was now one or was capable of becoming, for major purposes, a cooperative unit. It remained questionable whether a world organized on a national basis could possibly have a sufficient, unselfish spirit of collaboration to implement the provisions of security. The conflicting exigencies of the peace settlement introduced from the first a sort of dual control in international affairs. Many of the most important issues necessarily remained under the control of the Supreme Council of the Allies and a succession of conferences between members of this body had once taken place, thus reviving in fact a concert of Europe. The same method of independent conference was inevitable in any case with which a power outside the League was concerned. There was thus from the first a danger or likelihood that this institution of diplomacy by conference would grow in popularity till the great powers succeeded in making the League itself of secondary importance.

According to Albjerg, "The League began as a post-war organization for consolidating the victors' gains while continuing to restrain the vanquished. It failed to evolve into an impartial Parliament of all nations to which any state might come and seek protection against injustice – a role which President Wilson, General Smuts, and others had anticipated for it. The victors dominated the international scene politically and economically, but failed to dominate it morally and spiritually; therefore, the League emerged neither as a universal organization in scope nor as an equitable body in action."

The League suffered from organisational defects which were probably, however, a minor rather than a major cause for its failure. Many believe that its political and non-political activities should have been separated, with the latter duties being handled by a semi-autonomous division under a governing committee composed of representatives of both member and non-member countries. Thus, the League could have continued to function effectively even during an international disturbance when the stress of a political crisis might otherwise paralyse all activities of a centralized organization. Then, too, it suffered from such handicaps as its dependence for income on the voluntary contributions of its members, the absence of an international police force to execute its decisions, and the requirement for a unanimous vote of the League Council members on major questions. Yet the Rumanian statesman Titulesu pertinently observed: "If the League has miscarried, the fault lies not in the Covenant, but in man."

Narrow nationalism was still the dominant force among the peoples of the world. France was increasingly concerned with her national security, while Great Britain considered that problem less urgent than promoting British commerce by fostering international trade. Japan, intoxicated by her emergence as a world power, wanted to consolidate her position at the expense of others, while Italy was desperate to redress her damaged national prestige even at the cost of an aggressive military adventure. Germany and Soviet Russia, smarting under the treatment of the Allies, adroitly exploited Allied differences. The United States, 'a reluctant world power', eagerly sought pre-war normalcy in diplomacy by retiring from international responsibilities. The world-wide depression of the 1930's intensified the undesirable aspects of nationalism as 'every country tried to save itself at the expense of the rest of the world'. The ruthless competition of intensely nationalistic states continued to prevail over the international cooperation of friendly nations. The result was that disarmament – one of the League's pledged objectives – was not achieved, and by 1939, armaments were greater than ever before. Actually, the League of Nations could not fulfil the dreams of its founders so long as nations thought exclusively of their own national ambitions. Each national state seemed to 'possess a provincial mind in a planetary era' and as Professor Gooch has rightly observed, "international institutions without international minds are as hollow as democracies without public spirit."

The United Nations Organisation

Before the conclusion of World War II, the United Nations Charter was signed in June 1945 at San Francisco. The Preamble of the Charter runs thus: "We, the peoples of United Nations, determined to save succeeding generations from the scourge of war, which twice in our life-time has brought untold sorrow to mankind, and to reaffirm faith in fundamental human rights, in the dignity and worth of the human person, in the equal rights of man and woman and the nations large and small and to establish conditions under which justice and respect for the obligations arising from treaties and other sources of international law can be maintained, and to promote social progress and better standards of life in larger freedom, and for these ends to practise tolerance and live together in peace with one another as good neighbours and unite our strength to maintain international peace and security and to ensure by the acceptance of principles and the institution of methods, that armed force shall not be used, save in the common interest, and to employ international machinery for the promotion of the economic and social advancement of all peoples, have resolved to combine our efforts to accomplish these aims."

The United Nations Organisation has been created for the maintenance of international peace and security, development of friendly relations among nations, achievement of international cooperation in solving international problems of economic, social or humanitarian character and the promotion and encouragement of respect for human rights and fundamental freedoms for all, without distinction of race, sex, language or religion.

There are two kinds of members of the United Nations. Some of them are original members but new members can be admitted by a certain procedure. The membership is open to all peace-loving states which accept the obligations contained in the Charter and which, in the judgement of the organisation, are able and willing to carry out their obligations. The Security Council plays the most important part in allowing or refusing admission to any state. On the recommendation of the Security Council, the membership of a state can be suspended.

Its Organs

The important organs of the United Nations are the General Assembly, the Security Council, the Economic and Social Council, the Trusteeship Council, the International Court of Justice and the Secretariat. As regards the *General Assembly*, every member-state of the United Nations is a member of this body. As a, rule, the General Assembly meets once a year but there can be a special session under certain circumstances. The General Assembly has been given powers of discussion, review, supervision and criticism of the work of the United Nations as a whole. It can discuss and recommend measures for the maintenance of international peace and security. It directs and supervises international economic and social cooperation. It supervises the working of the trusteeship system. It controls the finances of the organisation. It admits, suspends and expels members. It adopts international conventions. It initiates studies and makes recommendations for the encouragement and progressive development of international law. It appoints a large number of members of the various organs of the United Nations. It can adopt amendments to the Charter of the United Nations Organisation.

The *Security Council* meets more often than the General Assembly. It consists of 11 members, 5 of which are permanent members and the other six are elected for a two-year term by the General Assembly by a system of rotation. Regional considerations are taken into account at the time of electing the six members. Each member of the Security Council has one vote and the approval of the five permanent members is essential in every case. Thus every permanent member of the Security Council has the power of veto. According to Kelsen, "The inevitable effect of the voting procedure conferring the right of veto upon each of the permanent members must be that no decision of any importance can be taken against the will of one of the privileged states if this state is involved in the matter to which the decision refers." Again, "A permanent member of the Security Council may exercise its veto right not only in its own affairs but also in the interests of another state. Hence the members which have no such rights may be induced to secure for themselves the friendship and protection of one of the Great Powers. Since the Security Council is not bound strictly to comply with existing law, it is more important for a state, not a permanent member of the Security Council, to have a friend or a protector among those five Great Powers than to fulfil carefully its obligations under the Charter. If a state can rely upon one of the five Powers, no action can be taken against it, even in the case of open violation of the law. The veto right of the five permanent members of the Security Council may lead to a political system of more or less open clientage, that is to say, to a dismemberment of the Organisation into five groups of states each of them taking advantage of the privilege of its patron. The principle of complete unanimity does not create such a tendency." To quote another writer, "This organisation will be one for keeping small boys in order by prefects who themselves are exempt from the rules they will administer."

As regards the functions of Security Council, its primary duty is to maintain international peace and security. It has to submit annual or special reports to the General Assembly. It can submit plans to the General Assembly for the regulation of armaments of the Military Staff Committee. The Security Council has to establish regional agencies and agreements. It has to supervise and control trust territories which are put under the charge of the various states. It has to use its good offices to resolve international disputes through peaceful methods. Whenever it considers necessary, it can call upon parties to a dispute through peaceful methods. Whenever it considers necessary, it can call upon parties to a dispute to settle it by negotiation, inquiry, mediation, conciliation, arbitration, judicial settlement, action by regional agencies or under regional arrangements or other peaceful means.

The *Economic and Social Council* consists of 18 members who are elected for three years by General Assembly. However, one-third of them retire every year. Its main function is to make or initiate studies and reports with respect to international, economic, social, cultural, educational, health and other related matters. It can prepare draft conventions on these subjects and submit them to the General Assembly. It can coordinate the activities of the specialised agencies and also regulate the flow of reports from those agencies at regular intervals. It has to perform those functions which are given to it by the General Assembly and also those for which a request has been made by the member-states and the specialised agencies.

The trusteeship system is an improvement on the Mandate system provided in the Covenant of the League of Nations. The Trusteeship Council is put in charge of this work It has to consider reports submitted to it by the administering authority. It has to examine the petitions in consultation with the administering authority. It has to visit the territory under the trusteeship system to see how it is being administered. The Council can send a questionnaire to the state concerned with the object of getting information regarding the political, economic, social and educational progress of the Trust territories.

The International Court of Justice is an improvement on the Permanent Court of International Justice. It consists of 15 members who are elected by the General Assembly. It exercises two kinds of jurisdiction. It decides those cases which are the subject of dispute between two or more states. It has also been given advisory jurisdiction.

As regards the Secretariat, the Secretary-General is the chief administrative officer. He is also assisted by a large number of subordinates who have to look to details concerning the various aspects of the activities of the United Nations Organisation The headquarters of the Secretariat are in New York. The member states have to foot the bill for the maintenance of the Secretariat.

Work of the United Nations

The United Nations has done a lot of useful work in the political field. In January 1946, Iran formally charged the Soviet Union with interference in her internal affairs and asked the Security Council to investigate and effect a settlement. The Security Council asked the two Governments to settle their differences by direct negotiations. On 23 May 1946, Moscow and Tehran announced that the Soviet troops had evacuated from Iran.

After the World War II, the people of Indonesia proclaimed the Republic of Indonesia and declared their independence. Holland refused to accept her independence and there were armed clashes. The matter was brought before the Security Council which directed the parties to stop hostilities and issued cease-fire orders. It offered its good offices to settle the dispute and appointed a Good Offices Committee for that purpose. In spite of many ups and downs, the United Nations played an important part in the recognition of the independence of Indonesia.

In January 1946, the Soviet Union complained that the stationing of British troops in Greece and British interference in the internal affairs of Greece endangered peace and security in that region. The view of the Security Council was that British troops were called into Greece by her own Government. In August 1946, Ukraine alleged that the policy of Greece was threatening peace in the Balkans. The allegation of Greece was that Yugoslavia, Albania and Bulgaria were provoking Communist guerillas against her. The Security Council appointed a Special Investigation Commission which reported that Yugoslavia, Albania and Bulgaria were actually aiding the pro-Communist revolutionaries of Greece. The General Assembly also appointed a Sub-Committee on the Balkans which reported that the Northern neighbours of Greece were giving large-scale aid to Greek guerillas. In December 1950, the General Assembly set up a Standing Committee to go into the matter.

Supported and incited by the Government of Pakistan, the tribal launched raids upon Kashmir in October 1947. On 1 January 1948, India lodged a complaint with the Security Council that the government of Pakistan was assisting the raiders who were attacking the State of Jammu and Kashmir. The Security Council established a United Nations Commission on India and Pakistan. The Commission asked the two Governments to stop fighting, withdraw their troops from the State of Jammu and Kashmir and a plebiscite be held to determine the future of the State. India and Pakistan agreed to those proposals and cease-fire became effective from 1 January 1949. The United Nations appointed Admiral Nimitz, Sir Owen Dixon and Dr. Frank Graham to mediate between the two countries. The Security Council also discussed the Kashmir issue on many occasions but nothing has come out of that. When there was a war between India and Pakistan in 1965, the Security Council issued several calls for an immediate cease-fire and withdrawal of armed forces. The efforts of the Security Council succeeded in bringing about a cease-fire between the two countries. When Pakistan attacked India in 1971, the Security Council asked both the parties to stop fighting. In spite of all the help given by the United Nations, the question of Kashmir remains unresolved.

When Britain announced her intention to terminate her mandate of Palestine, the General Assembly appointed a Sub-Committee on Palestine. The United Nations also appointed a mediator for Palestine. The United Nations also appointed a Truce Commission in April 1948. When Israel was attacked by the Arab States, a cease-fire was ordered by the Security Council and a truce was brought about. The United Nations appointed Count Bernadotte and Dr. Ralph Bunche to act as mediators. The General Assembly appointed a Conciliation Commission. It also established the United Nations Relief and Works Agency for Palestine refugees which has done a lot of useful work.

In 1946, India complained to the General Assembly against the discriminatory policies of the Government of South Africa which violated the principles enshrined in the United Nations Charter. The General Assembly took up the issue. Many resolutions have been passed by the United Nations against the Government of South Africa. It has also recommended mandatory sanctions against South Africa.

In June 1950, North Korea attacked South Korea. The matter was brought before the Security Council which directed North Korea to withdraw her troops. North Korea refused to withdraw. The Security Council branded North Korea as the aggressor. The United Nations appointed General MacArthur as the Supreme Commander of the forces sent to fight against North Korea. The offensive of North Korea was halted. The United Nations took keen interest in bringing about peace. In July 1953, a truce agreement was signed and hostilities ended.

In 1948, a complaint was made that a serious situation had arisen as a result of the unilateral imposition of restrictions by the Soviet Union on transport and communication between Western

Zones of occupation and Berlin. The President of the Security Council played an important part in the lifting of the Berlin blockade.

The United Nations played an important role in diffusing the situation created by the nationalisation of the Suez Canal in 1956. The General Assembly called upon France, Britain and Israel to withdraw their troops from the Egyptian territory. Ultimately, a cease-fire was arranged. Egypt agreed to the stationing of a United Nations force on her territory. The General Assembly authorised the Secretary-General of the United Nations to go ahead with the plan to clear the Canal area under the auspices of the United Nations and make the Canal ready for navigation. The United Nations played an effective role in the Suez crisis of 1956.

When the Soviet Union sent her troops to Hungary in 1956, there was criticism of her action. The Soviet Union continued in Hungary in spite of protests from many sources.

The General Assembly called upon the member states to recall their ambassadors and ministers from Franco's Spain. In spite of that, the United States entered into a treaty with Franco's Government on account of the strategic position of Spain in the world.

When there was trouble in the Congo after her independence in June 1960, the Secretary-General of the United Nations organised a United Nations operation in the Congo. The Congo question was referred to the General Assembly after its veto By the Soviet Union. The General Assembly directed the Secretary-General to continue his efforts "to assist the Central Government of the Congo" and created a Conciliation Commission of Asian and African representatives. A nominee of the Secretary-General of the United Nations visited the Congo. Dag Hammarskjoeld, Secretary-General was killed while bringing about peace in the Congo.

The General Assembly authorised the establishment of the United Nations temporary executive authority under the ultimate authority of the Secretary-General to take over West Iranian and hand over the same to Indonesia.

On the occasion of the Cuban crisis in 1962, U Thant, the Acting Secretary-General of the United Nations, took the initiative and ultimately succeeded in diffusing the situation.

Both the Security Council and the General Assembly took keen interest in maintaining peace in Cyprus after her independence.

In December 1966, the Security Council applied selective mandatory economic sanctions against Southern Rhodesia. In May 1968, the Security Council imposed comprehensive military sanctions and also set up a Sanctions Committee to enforce them. The Security Council condemned the Government of Southern Rhodesia when it declared herself a Republic in 1970. It also called upon its members to cut off all diplomatic, consular, trade, military and other relations with the Republic of Southern Rhodesia.

When Egypt closed the Straits of Tiran and the Gulf of Aqaba to Israel shipping, Israel asserted her right of free navigation in those waters. The Security Council held an urgent meeting to consider the situation and was in almost continuous session for many days. It unanimously adopted a resolution calling for an immediate cease-fire. Similar resolutions were passed again. The Security Council also adopted a resolution asking Israel to "ensure the safety, welfare and security of the inhabitants of the area where military hostilities have taken place and to facilitate the return of the Arab civilians in the areas occupied by her." The United Nations played its part in the crisis of 1967.

The Soviet Union intervened in Czechoslovakia first in 1948 and then in 1968. On 22 August 1968, the Security Council met to consider the situation arising out of Soviet intervention in Czechoslovakia. A resolution condemning the Soviet. Union was introduced in the Security Council but was vetoed by the Soviet Union.

When there was a war between Israel and the Arab countries in 1973, the Security Council called upon the parties to stop hostilities.

The Soviet Union sent her troops into Afghanistan in December 1979. She vetoed a resolution of the Security Council calling for an immediate and unconditional withdrawal of foreign troops from Afghanistan. In spite of its efforts, the Security Council failed to prevail upon the Soviet Union to withdraw from Afghanistan.

The Security Council adopted a resolution on 18 August 1982 for maintaining an international peace force in Lebanon.

In September 1980, a war started between Iraq and Iran and the same is continuing even now. The United Nations has not succeeded in stopping it.

The United Nations is concerned not only with the maintenance of peace but also with promoting the conditions under which genuine peace is possible. In the words of Philip E. Jacob, "In the long run, the United Nations leadership in the struggle for world welfare holds the chief promise of creating the underlying conditions of social stability and human satisfaction essential to a lasting peace." The Charter specifically provides that the United Nations shall promote "higher standards of living, full employment and conditions of economic and social progress and development." The responsibility for implementing those goals rests on the General Assembly and the Economic and Social Council. All functional and regional commissions and specialised agencies and committees are seeking in various ways to carry out the mandate of the Charter in economic and social fields.

The United Nations is supplying vital information to various countries. It publishes annual reports on world economic conditions. Many agencies and commissions of the United Nations have prepared important studies in the field of technical assistance and economic development. The United Nations also provides funds and loans through the International Bank and the International Development Association. These loans are of great help to developing countries. The Food and Agriculture Organisation has done a lot to meet the world food crisis. The International Labour Organisation has drafted scores of conventions and recommendations, collectively designated as the international labour code. The United Nations is concerned with the furtherance of human welfare, social justice and aspirations of men for a better lot in life. It provides advisory and social welfare services such as public welfare, child welfare, social insurance etc. The United Nations is giving help to physically handicapped. The World Health Organisation is the central directing and coordinating authority in international health work. It provides advisory and public health services to the member states. It administers health and sanitary regulations, maintains a medical library and an international centre for the compilation and analysis of medical and health statistics from all countries.

A large number of persons who have been uprooted in various parts of the world have benefitted from High Commissioner for Refugees. The UNESCO seeks to stimulate a world-wide attack on illiteracy and raise educational standards. It promotes international understanding. The Commission on Human Rights gives considerable attention to the right of self-determination. The United Nations has been successful in securing equality for women.

It is true that the United Nations has failed in tackling successfully the problem of collective security in the world, but that is a problem which is difficult to be tackled by any international organisation. Every state, whether big or small, seems to be determined to do all that it can to promote its own interests regardless of the interests of other states or mankind as a whole. In an atmosphere where there is violence all over the world and each state is spending recklessly to add to its armaments regardless of its costs and repercussions on its own economy or that of the world, peace in the world is a dream which no international organisation can achieve. All that can be done is to lessen the prevailing tension in the world and undoubtedly the United Nations has played its part. It is true that the United Nations is not a perfect organisation but its utility cannot be denied.

Donald J. Puchala writes, "Despite the paralysis of the Security Council and the often times vitriolic clamour of the General Assembly, the UNO has acted to diffuse international tensions surrounding a number of disputes. It has even played a modest part in Super-Power disputes. Moreover, it has acted to impose non-military sanctions pursuant to the enforcement of its decisions." (International Politics Today, p. 343).

Criticism of United Nations

There is a lot of hostile criticism of the United Nations. The very name "United Nations" has become a misnomer and a mockery for what could more appropriately be called "Disunited Nations." According to Bentwich and Martin, what was designed to be "an instrument of world peace has proved to be a forum of world conflict." Arthur Moore says that the United Nations "will go the way of the League, and that as the tempo of events is now faster than after the First World War, it will end much more quickly."

The United Nations is based on the principle of the sovereign equality of all the member-states. Whatever the size and resources of a state, it has the same position in the United Nations as any other insignificant state. This is hardly a happy state of affairs. Even if we refuse to recognize the differences, they are there all the same.

The United Nations is not a super-state. Every member-state retains its sovereignty and consequently is not bound by the decisions of the United Nations. The result is that the United Nations becomes merely an Internationals debating society in which each member-state participates.

The U.N. Charter gives the right of veto to the Big Five, *i.e.*, Great Britain, United State, Soviet Russia, France and China. The result is that no action can be taken without the unanimous consent of all the Big Powers. Very often, it has not been possible to secure unanimity among them. If any of the Five Powers is an aggressor or decides to favour of help an aggressor, no action can be taken by the United Nations. This weakens the United Nations. According to Lord Winster, "This organisation will be one for keeping small boys in order by prefects who are themselves exempt from the rules they administer." Dr. Murray says: "I strongly suspect that the first real strain on the new League will come when it attempts to give orders to some nation accustomed to freedom. It is a new provision that the Security Council should have the power to issue orders, while the fact that the Great Powers need not obey such orders will greatly weaken such moral authority as they might have had."

There is not much of harmony in the working of the United Nations. The Big Powers are divided into two blocs, *viz.*, the Soviet bloc and the Anglo-American bloc. The result is that the problems before the United Nations are not discussed on their merits. The object of each party is to humble the other. This creates a lot of bitterness and that is hardly desirable from the point of view of international cooperation. The ideologies of the two blocs differ and there is always a tug-of-war going on between the two. The cold war can develop into a shooting war at any time.

The views of the small states are not respected in the United Nations. The Big Power have their way on every point. In the matter of Tunisia, the Security Council rejected the unanimous demand of the representatives from Africa and Asia to include the question of Tunisia on its agenda. This was done because the United States and Great Britain did not want to put France in an awkward position.

The Security Council does not possess any coercive power to punish the offending states. It is true that provision has been made for the establishment of a Military Staff Committee but much cannot be expected from it under the circumstances. The United Nations has no force of its own to come to the help of any innocent state. According to Dr. Murray, "The security clause providing the new organization with teeth of enormous size and instantaneous action have been generally applauded as putting the new Charter on quite a different level of practical efficiency than the old covenant, and so it might well seem on first reading. But reflection raises doubts and even suspicions. The only Powers which are likely to possess enormous forces to put the peace of the world in peril have armed themselves to the full and insist that the great peace organization shall have no authority over them. They make certain general promises of good behaviour but remain free to do as they like. Meanwhile, we are expected to congratulate ourselves that the new League has teeth".

The Charter of the United Nations was the result of a series of compromises between the member-states. Hard bargaining behind the scene between the sovereign states represented secured agreements which are usually the next best. The Charter is an imperfect document and its machinery rather clumsy. Hasluck says: "Any defect in the text of a resolution was due to shortcomings in the agreement reached."

There is no universality of the membership of the United Nations. It has more a guiding than a determining principle. It is left to the Security Council to decide the fitness of applicants for membership, to define a "peace-loving" state, and to determine whether a state is "able and willing" to carry out its obligations or not. In practice, this has been determined almost solely by political considerations, to the detriment of the United Nation? Many states have been refused admission because of the exercise of the veto by one or the other member of the Security Council. It is desirable to maintain the largest possible degree of universality in the membership rather than confine it to "like-minded nations". That would destroy the very character of the United Nations and convert it into a very different kind of organisation. Extraneous considerations must be ignored by the Security Council while making recommendations regarding the admission of the new members "Package deals" which are the result of hard bargaining between the rival groups in the United Nations, must be encouraged. It is desirable to abolish the veto power of the Security Council in this connection and leave the matter entirely into hands of the General Assembly.

There is no proper representation of the various regions of the world on the Security Council although Article 23 (1) of the Charter contains the formula of "equitable geographical distribution" as a means of ensuring adequate representation of the various states. An analysis of representation during the last ten years shows that out of the six non-permanent seats, two have always been held by South American states, two more have been divided between the Eastern and Western Blocs, the Commonwealth of Nations has filled one seat by rotation among its members and the sixth seat has usually been held by a Middle-Eastern state. In practice, Asia and Africa as such have not really been represented at all. India and Pakistan have been represented simply because they happen to be members of the Commonwealth of Nations and not on account of regional or geographical considerations. Burma, Afghanistan, Thailand and Indonesia have not been represented at all on the Security Council. The prospects of additional representation for Asia are not bright. The only way out of the difficulty is that either the South American states give up one of the seats usually held by them or the number of the members of the Security Council should be increased by one and the additional seat should be given to representatives from Asia and Africa. Mr. Cassey has recognised the justness of Asia's case for representation in these words: "There are many new Asian nations and I feel that they are under-represented."

There has been a lot of criticism of Arttícle 2(7) which deals with the question of domestic jurisdiction. The construction of the phrase "essentially within the domestic jurisdiction" is not the work of laymen. Legal interpretation gives little indication of its meaning since the Security Council and the General Assembly have ignored the intentions of the framers of the San Francisco draft and have repeatedly defined domestic jurisdiction on purely political grounds. One view is that the guilty nations should not be allowed to take up the plea of domestic jurisdiction. However, there are others who feel that the extension of the functions of the United Nations is bound to result in trouble and might ultimately prove to be suicidal for the United Nations. According to Sir John Latham, "The United Nations should not be regarded as a means of conducting crusades against all the wrongs which exist in the world and in every country of the world. If every country in the world tries to introduce into other countries the institutions in which its people believe, there is no hope for the world. The idea that the United Nations Organization should attempt to deal in public wrongs everywhere represents a policy which it is impossible to carry into effect and which may destroy the United Nations Organization itself."

There has been criticism of the trusteeship system. The Trusteeship Council has often been reduced to little more than a political platform. The states in charge of the trust territories are condemned for their acts of omission arid commission. However, it is pointed out that much of the difficulty arises out of the lack of experience and expert knowledge of some members of the Trusteeship Council. Investigation of conditions in the colonial territory by visiting teams has produced a much clearer appreciation of the difficulties and has resulted in praise rather than criticism. In many cases, pinpricking criticism of the administering authority has created a feeling of irritation which leads to a tendency to do as little as possible to fulfil the letter of the Charter obligations. The solution of the problem lies in the widening of the experience of non-colonial powers by their close association with colonial experts. This may be a useful function of the Ad-hoc Committee on information. It may also be desirable to reconstitute the Trusteeship Council as a committee of experts.

Critics point out that some of the difficulties of the United Nations arise out of the atmosphere in which it is required to work. It is pointed out that its location in a small neutral state would have been conducive to a more rational discussion of issues by the United Nations. The cult of open diplomacy owed much to the moral convictions of President Wilson and the bitterness in the minds of the people against the secret treaties which preceded the First World War. It is pointed out that the pendulum has swung too far in the opposite direction. Diplomacy today tends to be by headlines. The debates in the General Assembly and the Security Council are pitched beyond the chamber to domestic or international audiences. Members of the committees can rarely serve in their private capacity as experts. Irreparable damage is done to international goodwill as well as to international peace and security by a debate over the microphone or by the teleprinter. Round-table discussion of disputes in camera, without the benefit of the press, would reduce tension. Only when agreement has been arrived at or a decision effected, should publicity be given to the terms. International accountability and responsibility would still be preserved and with them goodwill as well.

The provisions in the Charter with regard to the pacific settlement of disputes are unsatisfactory. It is regrettable that any state should be able to prevent the Security Council from embarking on efforts at conciliation and mediation. However, one of the consequences of the post-War power rivalry is the feeling, particularly on the Soviet side, that prestige is damaged by allowing an associate to be called upon to account for its conduct before the bar of world opinion. Such an attitude inflicts grave damage on the ability of the Security Council to discharge one of its major functions and on the confidence in the United Nations as a peace-preserving body.

Critics point out to the manner in which the provisions with regard to the exemption of procedural matter from veto have actually worked in practice. Their value has been seriously diminished by the failure to implement it in good Faith. The fact that the term is not defined in the Charter has left scope for the unscrupulous use of the "double veto". All efforts by the General Assembly to establish a more rational basis have failed on account of the resistance of the five Powers and efforts at formal change are likely to meet the same fate.

In the present age of international rivalries, the United Nations is a boon to humanity. It provides a forum at which the representatives of the various states of the world can meet together and give expression to their hopes and fears. It provides a meeting place for international understanding and co-operation. It is true that there are two camps in the United Nations and voting takes place usually on party lines, but still it cannot be denied that it is doing more good than harm to the world at large. Mankind would have been in a worse position if there had been no such organisation. However, it will be much better if the present grouping disappears and the nations start co-operating with one another in the larger and higher interests of humanity as a whole.

In his first report to the General Assembly, Trygve Lie. U.N. Secretary. General, wrote, "The United Nations is no stronger than the collective will of the nations that support it. Of itself it can do nothing. It is a machinery through which the nations can cooperate. It can be used and developed in the light of *its activities* and experience, to the untold benefit of humanity, or it can be discarded or broken. As in the control of the atomic power, the choice is between life and death, the failure of the United Nations would mean the failure of peace, the triumph of destruction."

SUGGESTED READINGS

Alien, C.K. : *Law in the Making.*

Alien, D. : *The Fight for Peace, 1930.*

Amos, S. : *Science of Politics.*

Asher, Robert E. : *The United Nations and Promotion of the General Welfare, Washington, 1957.*

Bailey, Sydney D. : *The United Nations, New York, 1963.*

Baker, P.J.N. : *The League of Nations at Work, 1926.*

Bartlett : *The League to Enforce Peace, 1944.*

Bassett, J.S. : *The League of Nations, London. 1928.*

Beer, M. : *The league on Trial, 1933.*

Bentwick and Martin : *Charter of the United Nations.*

Briefly, J.L. : *The League of Nations.*

Brown, W.J. : *The Austinian Theory of Law.*

Bryce : *Studies in History and Jurisprudence.*

Burton, M.E. : *The Assembly of the League of Nations*, 1941.

Cardozo : *The Growth of Law.*

Carter : *Law, Its Origin, Growth and Function.*

Chase, E.P. : *The United Nations in Action.*

Chowdhuri, R.N. : *International Mandates and Trusteeship System*, 1955.

Claude, Inis L. : *Changing United Nations*, New York, 1967.

Dealey, J.Q. : *The State and Government.*

Dickinson, B.G. : *The Equality of States in International Law.*

Duguit, L. : *Law in the Modern State.*

Eichelberger, C.M. : *U.N.: The First Twenty Years.*

Evatt, H.V. : *The United Nations.*

Feller, A.H. : *United Nations and the World Community*, Boston; 1952.

Fenwick : *International Law.*

Finer, H. : *Theory and Practice of Modern Government.*

Friedmann : *Legal Theory.*

Frye, William R. : *A United Nations Peace Force*, New York, 1957.

Garner, G.W. : *Political Science and Government.*

Gettell, R.G. : *Introduction to Political Science.*

Goodrich, Leland M. : *The United Nations*, London, 1960.

Gray : The Nature and Sources of Law.

Green, J.F. : The United Nations and Human Rights, Washington, 1956.

Holland, T.E. : *The Elements of Jurisprudence.*

Howard, Ellis C. : *The Origin, Structure and Working of the League of Nations*, 1928.

Jones, R. and Shermann, S.S. :*The League of Nations: From Idea to Reality*, 1929.

Krabbe, H. : *The Modern Idea of the State.*

Lippman, W. : *Public Opinion.*

MacIver, R.M. : *The Modern State.*

Maine, H.S. : *Ancient Law.*

Marriott, J.A.R. : *The Mechanism of the Modern Slate.*

Morrison, H.S. and others : *The League and the Future of the Collective System.*

Nicholas, H.G. : *The United Nations as a Political Institution*, New York, 1959.

Oppehheim : *International Law.*

Pollock, F. : *The League of Nations.*

Pound, R. : *Law and Morals.*

Ramaiyer : *Politics.*

Rappard, W. : *The Geneva Experiment*, 1932.

Shotwell : On The Rim of the Abyss, 1936.

Vandenboschand Hogan : The United-Nations, 1952.

Vinogradoff : *Commonsense in Law.*

Walters, F.P. : *A History of the League of Nations* 1952.

Wild, P.S. : *Sanctions and Treaty Enforcement* 1934.

Willpughby, W.W. : *The Fundamental Concepts of Public Law.*

Wilson, Woodrow : *The State.*

Wright, Q. : *Mandates under the League of Nations*, 1930.

CHAPTER

Forms of Government

Learning Objectives

- Monarchy
- Limited Monarchy
- Aristocracy
- The Autocratic State
- Myths of Autocracy
- Salient Features
- Dictatorship
- Characteristics
- Dictatorship and Democracy
- Merits of Dictatorship
- Demerits of Dictatorship
- Unitary Government
- Federal Government
- Federation and Confederation
- Federal and Unitary Government
- Conditions Necessary for Federation
- Essentials of a Federal State
- Merits of Federation
- Demerits
- Future of Federation
- Parliamentary Government
- Prerequisites of Parliamentary Government
- Merits of Parliamentary Government
- Demerits
- Presidential form of Government
- Merits
- Demerits
- Bureaucratic Government
- Suggested Readings

There is a difference of views among scholars whether it is appropriate to use the term classification of states or classification of governments. Professor Gilchrist prefers to use the term classification of governments. To quote him, "Strictly speaking, all states are the same. The student must bear this in mind – the form of state is really the form of governments." W.W. Willoughby also doubts the wisdom of classifying states. He says: "In essence, they are all alike – each and all being distinguished by the same sovereign attributes."

Attempts have been made from time to time to classify the various forms of government. Plato gave a threefold classification of governments, *viz.*, perfect state, imperfect state and state of ignorance. The perfect state was ruled selflessly by the philosopher king. In the imperfect state, people had great respect for law. In the state of ignorance, there was no law and the people had to live the life of the jungle. The following table illustrates the classification of Plato:

	State in which law is obeyed	*State in which law is not obeyed*
Rule by One	Monarchy	Tyranny
Rule by Few	Aristocracy	Oligarchy
Rule by Many	Moderate Democracy	Extreme Democracy

Aristotle classified the forms of government on the basis of two principles, *viz.*, the number of persons in whom the sovereign power was vested and the end or aim of the government. His view was that a government was normal when it was run in the interests of the people. It became perverted when it was not run in their interest. His classification is illustrated by the following table:

Rule	*Normal form*	*Perverted form*
One	Monarchy	Tyranny
The Few	Aristocracy	Oligarchy
The Many	Polity	Democracy

The view of Aristotle was that monarchy was the rule of one person for the good of the people and tyranny was the rule of one person for his selfish ends. Aristocracy was the rule of the few for the interests of the people and oligarchy was the rule of the few for their selfish interests. Polity was the rule of the many in the interests of the people and democracy was the rule of the many for their own interests.

Aristotle also referred to the cycle according to which the governments change. When monarchy became perverted, it degenerated into tyranny which was replaced by aristocracy. Aristocracy also degenerated into oligarchy which was replaced by polity. Polity degenerated into democracy which was set aside by monarchy. In this way, the cycle of governments continued.

The classification by Aristotle was more realistic than that of Plato. Gilchrist says: "The classification is not sufficient for modern forms of government but it has provided the historical basis of practically all classifications made hitherto". Professor Burgess also hold the same view. He considers Artistotle's classification both sound and logical.

However, critics point out that Aristotle's classification is not sound because it does not rest upon any scientific principle by which governments can be distinguished from one another in respect of their fundamental characteristics and form of organisation. The principle on which his classification rests is arithmetical rather than organic, quantitative rather than qualitative in character. Aristotle gave a wrong meaning to democracy which could have been better described as mobocracy. Sir John Seeley criticised the classification on the ground that it was not applicable to the modern governments. He pointed out that Aristotle knew only city-states and they were not like the "country states" of modern times. In Aristotle's classification, there is no place for a limited monarchy, a presidential form of government, a parliamentary form of government, unitary government and federal government. There is also no guarantee that governments change in the order indicated by Aristotle.

After Aristotle, many writers attempted classifications of forms of government. Polybius classified governments into monarchy, aristocracy and democracy. He believed that these governments along with their corrupt form followed one another in the form of a cycle and the order in which that happened was monarchy, tyranny, aristocracy, oligarchy, democracy and no rule. When mob rule became unbearable, it was superseded by monarchy and the cycle repeated itself as before.

Polybius was followed by Cicero. His great contribution was that he interpreted the three organs of governments as representing the three principles necessary for the stability of the state. His view was that monarchy represented the principle of force or authority. The Senate represented the principle of prestige and influence and popular assemblies represented the principle of liberty. When these three principles were combined in the right proportion in a state, there was order and forms of government, along with their corrupt forms, followed one another in the form of a cycle. Bodin based his classification solely on the number of men in whose hands the sovereign power resided. In the case of monarchy, the sovereign power was in the hands of one man. In the case of aristocracy, it was in the hands of less than a majority of citizens and in the case of democracy, it was in the hands of the majority. Bodin also classified monarchy into royal or pure, despotic and tyrannical.

About the forms of government, Hobbes wrote thus: "When the Representative is one man, then is the Commonwealth a Monarchy; when an assembly of all that will come together, then it is a Democracy or popular commonwealth; when an assembly of a part only, then it is called an Aristocracy." Locke also classified governments into monarchies, oligarchies and democracies. He subdivided monarchy into hereditary monarchy and elective monarchy. Rousseau divided Governments into monarchies, aristocracies and democracies. He further sub-divided aristocracies into natural, elective and hereditary aristocracies. His view was that elective aristocracy was the best and hereditary aristocracy was the worst. Rousseau was a champion of direct democracy. He also admitted the existence of mixed forms of Government. Montesquieu classified governments into republics, monarchies and despotisms. He subdivided republics into democratic republics and aristocratic republics. His view was that the various forms of government had a sustaining and driving power behind them. The spirit of public service was behind democracy, that of moderation behind aristocracy, that of honour behind monarchy and that of fear behind despotism. Bluntschli accepted the classification of Aristotle but added to it a fourth form called Theocracy, with its perverted form known as Idolocracy.

Waitz, a German scholar, classified states as republics, theocracies, kingdoms, unitary states, composite or compound states, federal states and confederations. Pradier-Federe, a French writer, classified states into two groups: single states and united states. In the first category, he put personal unions, real unions and incorporated unions. In the second category, he placed the confederated states and federal states. Robert Von Mohl, a German writer, classified states as follows: Patriarchal states, theocracies, patrimonial states, classic or antique states, legal states and despotic states. His classification was not based on any single logical or scientific principle. The terms used by him did not belong strictly to political science but to literature and history. Professor Jellinek divided states into two types: Monarchy and Republic. He defined monarchy as a state in which sovereignty rested in a single person. It was not necessary, that the power of the monarch should be original, underived and belonging to him in his own right. There could be a monarchy in which the monarch was regarded as God or His earthly representative. In the case of a republic, sovereignty resided not in one single person but in a group or college of persons more or less numerous. Republics could be democratic, aristocratic and oligarchic. Sir J.A.R. Marriot has classified constitutions as unitary and federal, rigid and flexible, monarchical and presidential. He also speaks of parliamentary and responsible or cabinet type of government.

The classification which is generally accepted is that given by Dr. Leacock and this is explained by the following diagram:

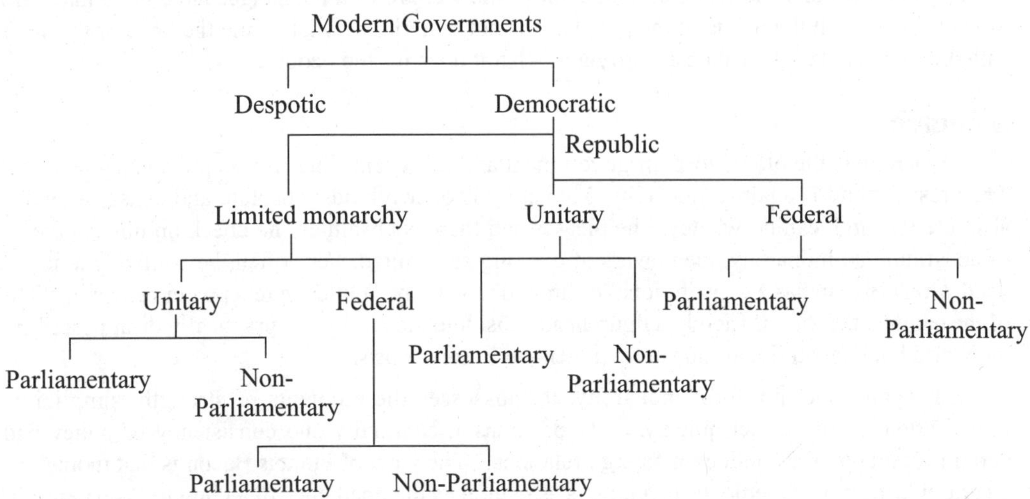

As regards the various forms of government mentioned by Leacock, a despotic government is one in which the will of one person prevails. He does whatever he pleases without caring for the consequences. A democratic government is that in which ultimately the will of the people prevails and the people are the sovereign. A limited monarchy is one in which the king is the nominal head and the real power vests in the hands of the popular ministers. A republican government is one in which the head of the state is elected for a few years. His office is not hereditary. A unitary form of government is that in which all the powers are concentrated in the hands of the Central Government and there is no division of powers. Great Britain has a unitary government. Before the coming into force of the Government of India Act 1935, India also had a unitary form of government. In a federal government, there is a division of powers between the federal government and the units and all of them are supreme in their own spheres. There is a federal system of government in the United States and India. In a parliamentary government, the executive is responsible to the legislature. However, in the case of a presidential form of government, the executive is not responsible to the legislature and both of them are independent of each other. The United States has a presidential from of government while Great Britain and India have a parliamentary form of government.

It is very difficult to have proper classification of modern governments. The form of government is the result of historical, geographical, social, economic and psychological factors. Some of these factors are permanent and others are not and they affect the institutions of the countries. It is true that both Britain and France have a cabinet system of Government but still they differ. Britain has a limited constitutional monarchy in theory but in actual practice, it is a democratic republic. In form, France is a Republic but it has the institutions of a monarchy and the spirit of an Empire. The French attach great importance to symbols. Siegfried says, "French politics are often both unrealistic and passionately ideological." Both the United State and Canada are federations but Lord Haldane was not prepared to designate Canada as a federation and Prof. Wheare calls it a "quasi-federal constitution." Unitary elements in Canada are being so worked as not to compromise with the federal principle. The United states has a federal constitution as well as federal Government, but there is a tendency towards more and more of centralisation. The Indian constitution is federal in form but there are unitary tendencies in it. Dr. Ambedkar was of the view that India was federation in times of peace but a unitary government in times of war. It follows that no two forms of government can be absolutely identical. No government remains the same and changes constantly go on taking place. The mechanism of the Governmert has to be changed to meet the demands of the atomic age. We should not confine ourselves to outward forms as they do not tell us the real purpose of the state. The primary purpose of every state is the same and that is to achieve the welfare of all. Changes have to be made from time to time to suit the needs of the people. It is not material by what name the head of the state is called. We must classify a state according to what it does for the people.

Monarchy

Monarchy is the oldest form of government and till recent times it was prevalent everywhere. The present trend is against monarchy. Monarchy is of two kinds: absolute and constitutional. An absolute monarch can do whatever he pleases and there is absolutely no check on him. In the case of constitutional monarchy, the powers of the king are limited. Very often, he is merely a nominal head. Great Britain has a constitutional or limited monarchy. While the real power rests in the hands of the cabinet, the king is merely a figurehead. Absolute monarchy has practically disappeared from the world but constitutional monarchy lingers on in some parts.

As regards the merits of monarchy, it "possesses the elements of strength, simplicity of organisation, ability to act quickly, unity of counsel, continuity and consistency of policy and a certain prestige in the conduct of foreign relations. "The view of Francis Bacon is that monarchy is a natural institution. Obedience to a king is as natural as the obedience of a child to his parents. The view of Filmer is that the state is an extension of the family. The king is the father and the people are his children.

The view of Rousseau is that the king embodies the principle of unity. To quote him, "The will of the people, the will of the prince, the public force of the State, and the particular force of the Government, all answer to a single motive power; all the springs of the machine are in the same hands; the whole moves towards the same end; there are no conflicting movements to cancel one another, and no kind of constitution can be imagined in which a less amount of effort produces a more considerable amount of action."

Burke supported monarchy for historical and practical reasons. Hereditary monarchy had been in existence for a long time and it was not desirable to abolish it. If necessary, the democratic elements could be grafted on to it. The view of Bodm was that monarchy was best adapted to deal with emergencies. It was not necessary for a monarch to consult others while deciding his course of action. Sir John Seeley says that the king could be the protector of the people from the tyranny of the few. To quote him, "A great population scattered over a large territory and struggling against the oppression of great magnates, being unable to organise concerted action over so large a space, may collect ail its power into the hands of an individual and arm him with a sort of iron mace strong enough to crush any or all of the enemies of the people".

Treitschke defended monarchy as superior to democracy. To quote him, "It is an ancient experience that monarchy presents more perfectly than any other form of government unity. Hence its marvellous appeal to the average understanding and to natural reason of which we Germans saw such a striking example in the early years of our new Empire." Again, "It is clear that a well-ordered monarchy can guarantee a much higher degree of freedom (than democracy) to its subjects." Again, "Furthermore, it is possible for a monarch from the height of his exalted station to see further than ordinary mortals, who survey only a narrow sphere of practical life and whose limitations are revealed by their well-nigh incredible prejudices. A monarch is competent to be judge of external relations in a manner far beyond the scope either of private individual or of republican administration. It fascinates the plain man to see a single figure at the helm on whose word all depends, and for such, the term 'father of his people' has genuine meaning – when the monarch is penetrated with a sense of lofty duty, it is glorious to behold the purifying influence of his exalted office."

J.S. Mill says that "Despotism is a legitimate mode of Government for dealing with barbarians, provided the end be their improvement and the means be justified by actually effecting that end." Absolute monarchy possesses the merits of strength, vigour, promptness of decision, unity of counsel, continuity and consistency of policy. The view of Lord Bryce is that the absolute monarchies of the 17th and 18th centuries "saw many reforms in European countries, which no force less than that of a strong monarchy would have carried through."

In his *The Monarchy in Politics*, Farrer says: "That an hereditary monarchy has advantage over an elective one is among the few things that historical experience can confidently claim to have proved. Lord Beaconsfield's dictum that our ancestors had done wisely in placing the prize of supreme power outside the sphere of human passions and ambitions hardly admits of serious challenge. But hereditary monarchy suffers from the drawback of placing that prize too much within the sphere of pure and uncontrollable chance; and the same system which made a Queen Victoria possible is also responsible for a George IV. Experience, therefore, though it has proved the superiority of an hereditary to an elective monarchy, cannot yet assert the superiority of an hereditary monarchy to a republican form of government." Dr. F.A. Woods has made a detailed study of a large number of European monarchs from the point of view of their intellectual and moral character. His conclusion is that dynastic families have "far exceeded the masses in the production of men of genius," that "royalty as a whole has been decidedly superior to all the average Europeans in capacity," and "that the royal breed, considered as a unit, is superior to any other one family, be it that of noble or commoner." Dr. Garner says that monarchy provides the most satisfactory government for those who cannot govern themselves and who "have not yet developed a high political consciousness and who therefore lack the capacity themselves for participating actively in the management of public affairs. Perhaps no better form could be devised for disciplining uncivilized people, leading them out of barbarism and inculcating in them habits of obedience."

Bagehot expressed his preference for monarchy in these words: "The mass of mankind understand it, and they hardly understand any other....The nature of a constitution, the action of an assembly, the play of parties, the unseen formation of a guiding opinion are complex facts, difficult to know and easy to mistake. But the action of a single will, the fiat of a single mind, are easy ideas: anybody can make them out and no one can ever forget them. Royalty is a government in which the attention of the nation is concentrated on one person doing interesting actions. A republic is a government in which that attention is divided between many, who are all doing uninteresting actions. Accordingly, so long as the human heart is strong and the human reason weak, royalty will be strong because it appeals to diffused feeling, and republics weak because they appeal to the understanding."

As regards the defects of monarchy, it is pointed out that ability, industry and good intentions are not hereditary and "history indicates that for a Louis XIV a country has to pay the price of a Louis XV and Louis XVI." If the king is bad, monarchy becomes the worst form of government. While a wise king realises the fact that the prosperity of the people will make him strong, a foolish king would try to keep them down so that they may never be able to resist him.

Lord Brougham says: "The tendency of all monarchy is towards despotism and its evils; and a constitutional monarchy which provides no checks, that is, a pure monarchy, has enormous defects, even if it should not degenerate into an Oriental despotisms. It leaves too great scope to the sovereign's interests or passions, benefits the people very little by the alliance he always forms with the nobles, gives facilities to humour his ambition by wars, allows reckless extravagance of every kind, encourages habits of costly ostentation and of pride towards inferiors, and begets a spirit of fawning and truckling towards those in authority." The view of Dr. Leacock is that "a hereditary ruler seems on the face of things as absurd as the hereditary mathematician or hereditary poet laureate."

Absolute monarchy may be a good form of Government but we do not believe in good Government unless it is self-government also. A good government is no substitute for self-government. "No government which does not rest upon the affections of the people, which does not stimulate among them an interest in public affairs and create an active, intelligent and alert citizenship, can be called ideal, and certainly no government from which the participation of the people in some form is excluded will ever be able to produce such a body of citizens."

Limited Monarchy

Absolute monarchy is becoming rare in modern times and what is more to be seen is some form of limited monarchy. It is true that the king is the head of the state but actually he is merely a constitutional ruler and the real power rests in the hands of the ministers who are the representatives of the people. An outstanding example of limited monarchy is Great Britain where the King or the Queen reigns but does not rule and all .power rests in the hands of the Council of Ministers. Woodrow Wilson points out that a limited monarchy "is one whose powers have been adapted to the interests of the people and to the maintenance of individual liberty.....Roughly speaking, constitutional government may be said to have had its rise at Runnymede when the barons of England exacted the Magna Carta from John."

The great merit of limited monarchy is that while the institution of monarchy is allowed to continue, actual power is in the hands of the people through their representatives. Moreover, as the king or the queen continues to reign for a long time without any intervals or any break, he or she comes to acquire great administrative experience. The view of Lowell is that the king of England exercises the "unifying, dignifying and stabilising influence." The King or Queen does not belong to any party and consequently he or she acts as an umpire in the midst of rival parties. He or she sees to it that the game of politics is played according to rules.

Aristocracy

Literally speaking, aristocracy is "government by the best citizens." The aristocracy may be of riches, nobility of birth or intellectual brilliance. In theory, there is much to be said in favour of aristocracy. It puts emphasis on quality and not quantity. The persons who are otherwise intelligent and wide-awake, are allowed to carry on the administration of the country. That is bound to result in efficiency of administration. Aristocracy avoids extremes of policy and favours moderation. Moderation is dictated by the need for their own security. They never forget that the masses are superior in number and physical force; and if a policy of moderation is not followed, there may be resistance to their authority.

The view of Rousseau was: "It is the best and most natural arrangement that the wisest should govern the many, when it is assured that they will govern for its profit and not for their own." Carlyle says: "It is the everlasting privilege of the foolish to be governed by the wise. Surely, of all 'rights of man', this right of the ignorant man to be guided by the wiser, to be, gently or forcibly, held in the true course by him, is the indisputablest. Nature herself ordains it from the first; society struggles towards perfection by enforcing and accomplishing it more and more..... In Rome and Athens, as elsewhere, if we look practically, we shall find that it was not by loud voting and debating of many, but by wise insight and ordering of a few that the work was done. So is it ever, so will it ever be."

J.S. Mill says that "the governments which have been remarkable in history for sustained mental ability and vigour in the conduct of affairs have generally been aristocracies." Lord Brougham points out that the qualities of an aristocratic form of government are its firmness of purpose, resistance to violent change, distrust of war-like policy and encouragement of genius. Bolingbroke says: "The Author of Nature has thought fit to mingle from time to time, among the societies of men, a few, but only a few, of those on whom He is graciously pleased to bestow a larger proportion of the ethereal spirit than is give in the ordinary course of His providence to the sons of men. These are those who engross almost the whole reason of the species, who are born to instruct, to guide, and to preserve; who are designed to be the tutors and the guardians of human kind".

Sir John Seeley defends aristocracy in these words: "A man who is the son of a statesman, who has grown up in the house of a statesman, may be presumed to have learnt something, if only some familiarity with public questions, some knowledge of forms of routine which others are likely to want; and there is a fair probability that he may have acquired more, and a certain possibility that, as the younger Pitt, he many have acquired very much and also inherited very much." Lecky says: "It is of no small importance that a nation should possess a class of men who have a large stake in the prosperity of the country, who possess a great position independent of politics, who represent very evidently the traditions and the continuity of political life, and who, whatever may be their faults, can at least be trusted to administer affairs with complete personal integrity and honour. In the fields of diplomacy and in those great administrative posts which are so numerous in an extended empire, high rank and the manners that commonly accompany it are especially valuable, and their weight is not the least powerfully felt in dealing with democracies." De Tocqueville says: "Almost all the nations which have exercised a powerful influence upon the destinies of the world by conceiving, following up and executing vast designs from Rome to England – have been governed by aristocratic institutions."

Aristocracies are conservative and an element of conservatism is necessary for the good of every government. Rash political experiments must be avoided at all costs. Every step must be taken continuously so that the country does not suffer.

There are certain defects in an aristocratic form of government. Very often aristocracies degenerate into oligarchies and that is always against the interests of the people. Bowman says: "The famous aristocracy of Venice is perhaps the best example of this. The almost unrestrained powers, which in the seventh century had been vested in the Doge were in 1172 limited by the institution of the Great Council, a body of 480 citizens. These, although originally elective, rapidly became a hereditary aristocracy. And out of this there developed a smaller executive council, the *pregadi* or Senate: and of this six were chosen as direct advisers of the Doge. But in the fourteenth century, owing to the attempts of the people to regain control over the Government, the aristocracy sacrificed their own power to the famous institution, the Council of Ten, a body whose criminal jurisdiction was so complete that the real government of the State fell into its hands."

An aristocratic government is very often reactionary and opposed to progressive ideas. Laveleye says: "There never was an aristocracy more devoted to liberty or more fitted to govern than that of England, yet it opposed every extension of the suffrage and often in legislation it sacrificed the interests of the people to its own privileges."

Very often, arrogance and pride are witnessed among the aristocrats. The ruling aristocrats "have often displayed towards the lower classes a harshness and cruelty which have been the most intolerable because accompanied by contempt." A reference in this connection may be made to the treatment of the Helots by the Spartans and the plebian debtors by the Roman patricians.

Bluntschli points out that aristocracy loses all vitality when the ruling class degenerates from the qualities which raised it to power, when its character decays and it becomes weak and vain.

It is not always possible to have brilliant persons at the helm of affairs. Very often, the people with money assert themselves and refuse to allow better people to carry on the administration. The result is that the administration is carried on in the interests of the rich and those of the poor are completely ignored.

Treitschke rightly points out that an aristocracy is "always difficult to manage because it is founded upon a conception of class distinctions which is undoubtedly at variance with the natural instincts of equality in the human race." There is something terribly inhuman and arrogant in a purely aristocratic temper of mind. Aristocracies look coldly upon the development of great and original personalities. They do not always allow great military glory to be won, on account of jealousy.

In spite of these defects, Lord Bryce rightly points out that all governments are aristocratic in a sense. "In all assemblies and groups and organised bodies of men, from a nation down to the committee of a club, directions and decisions rest in the hands of a small percentage, less and less in proportion to the larger size of the body, till in a great population it becomes an infinitesimally small proportion of the whole number. This is and always has been true of all forms of government, though in different degree."

Democracy. (This topic is discussed in a separate chapter).

The Autocratic State

An autocratic state is the opposite of a democratic state. It is a state in which there is the minimum popular influence and the leader or the party occupies an important place. An autocratic state does not tolerate opposition to the decisions taken by the leadership. Those decisions are promulgated with the full force of the state behind them. They often extend to every aspect of the lives of the people. There is practically no popular discussion of the merits of those decisions and almost no criticism.

An autocratic state is like a dictatorship but they are not the same. Dictatorship represents autocracy but all autocracies cannot be classified as dictatorships. Louis XIV of France was an autocrat but he was never called a dictator. Autocratic states have two broad aspects: authoritarianism and totalitarianism. Authoritarianism means that all authority and power are concentrated in the hands of a few. The people participate in few if any of their decisions but are subject to all of them. Totalitarianisms designates the all-pervading interest and the complete domination by the state. All aspects of the life of man including religion, marriage, love etc., are regulated by the totalitarian state. Examples of the authoritarian rulers are Louis XIV of France, Czar Nicholas II of Russia, Dr. Salazar of Portugal, etc.

The two terms authoritarian and totalitarian are not mutually exclusive. A state may be both authoritarian and totalitarian. A purely political dictatorship or kingship may not be totalitarian. The totalitarian state is a recent phenomenon and it represents the all-pervading interest of the state in all things of life. Nothing is so insignificant as to escape the attention of the totalitarian state. The Fascist state of Mussolini in Italy, Hitler's Nazi Germany, Mao's dictatorship in China and the Communist dictatorship in the Soviet Union are the best examples of the totalitarian states.

Myths of Autocracy

There are many myths connected with autocracy. (1) The advocates of autocracy declare that only the best should rule. Once they capture power, they are entitled to shut the door against others. Experience shows that the so-called "best" in an autocratic society capture power only through murder, deceit, violence and demagoguery.

(2) Another myth of autocracy is that the leader is omniscient and infallible. There can be no denying the fact that autocrats are not supermen. They differ from others primarily only in that they control a state. Their sycophants fawn upon and flatter them. As the leader controls all means of communication, his image is spread everywhere. The myth of the omniscient and infallible leader is as simple as this.

(3) Another myth of autocracy is that it is always more efficient than democracy because it can make decisions quickly without argument and discussion. However, efficiency cannot be measured by the mere speed with which decisions are reached. Mistakes are less likely when a decision is debated publicly than when the whim of an autocrat prevails.

(4) Another myth of autocracy is that it represents true democracy. Most autocrats denounce democracy as a disease and proudly proclaim the virtues of its opposites. Leaders of communist autocracy often contend that their state represents democracy in the fullest and truest sense of the term. It is contended that the so-called political democracy is not democracy at all. True democracy is economic democracy where all have the same economic power and strength. The fact is that they have neither political democracy nor economic democracy. They believe that a falsehood, if often repeated, will be believed by many. Sometimes, the Big Lie goes right on in the name of the state itself as is the case with "The People's Republic of China."

Salient Features

There are certain salient features of autocracy. (1) Most autocrats base their rule on demagoguery. They often rise to power on such a basis. Hitler was famous for his demagogic oratory. He was able to sway the mob with emotional and prejudiced appeals. His eloquence convinced many Germans that their salvation should rest in his hands. Even Neville Chamberlain, Prime Minister of Great Britain, said in 1938 that he considered Hitler as one of the greatest men he had ever met. Even Mussolini was impressed by Hitler. Even foreign diplomates in Berlin came under his spell. Mussolini himself was also a demagogue. Eva Peron of Argentina was a demagogue. Stalin was not an orator but he was a demagogue as he could appeal to the prejudices and emotions of the people to further his dictatorial ends. Lenin and Trotsky were orators as well as demagogues.

(2) Another salient feature of autocracy is that it has often been created through force and violence. Even in the few exceptions with apparently peaceful beginnings, there is usually a background of violence and intrigue. It is true that Hitler came to power through appointment as Chancellor in 1933 by Hindenburg, President of Germany. However, a critical study of the history of Germany before 1933 shows that even before that Hitler used the Storm Troops to break up the meetings of the rival parties, protect his own meetings and rallies, create disturbances, liquidate political enemies and molest Jews and other minorities. These troops were used by him in his actual march to power. Once he became Chancellor, he outlawed all political parties except his own. In the blood purge of 1934, his potential enemies and also some of his party members were eliminated. The same was the case in the Soviet Union. Trotsky was forced into exile and was finally killed in Mexico in 1940. Kamenev, Bukharin, Zinoviev and other old Bolsheviks were tried for treason and shot. In order to control the army, Stalin executed at least 75% of all officers of the rank of colonel and above. Beria,

head of the secret police, was liquidated by Malenkov and Khrushchev. Mussolini came to power by threat offered and maintained himself by force. King Victor Emmanuel of Italy invited Mussolini to become Prime Minister as a result of Mussolini's march on Rome in 1922. General Franco came to power as the victor in a bloody civil war and liquidated most of his opponents. The communists came to power in Czechoslovakia through *a coup d'etat.* General Naguib ousted King Farouk of Egypt. Peron, a high army officer in Argentina, used the army in his march to power and was driven out by similar tactics. Tito commended much of the resistance in Yugoslavia during World War II and rode into power when the Germans left a power vacuum in 1945. Kemal Ataturk of Turkey was a successful General and strong man.

(3) Another characteristic of autocracy is that it is retained by force. This requires the establishment of a police state. The leaders know that the critics must be silenced and hence they use the political police to stifle criticism before it begins. The political police can arrest a person on mere suspicion, without warrants from any court. It can try individuals before its own tribunals and in some cases sentence them to death. There are no guarantees of trial by jury, help of the counsel and confrontation by adverse witnesses. In most cases, the accused does not know who his accusers are. Everything depends upon the whim of the political police. Every one is encouraged to inform on others. It does not matter whether the accusations are correct or not. The authoritarian government must have victims for the altar of subversion and treason. People are often accused for trivial reasons and punished severely.

(4) Another feature of an autocratic state is its belief in the leadership principle. The cry is, "Give me a leader and I will follow." The leader pretends to be infallible and often comes to believe in his infallibility. It is not admitted that the dictator makes or has ever made an error. Underlings often must bear the cruel responsibility for the failure of their leader. The leader is considered to be an expert in everything. Stalin knew more about agronomy than the most highly educated agronomists. He was the final authority on the syntactical and grammatical structure of the Russian language. Higher mathematics was no mystery to him. He was the greatest military genius in history, being Alexander, Caesar and Napoleon rolled into one. He loved little children and understood all their problems. As a matter of fact, one can only conclude that Stalin was perfection itself if one believes only a fraction of Soviet propaganda concerning him. All autocratic leaders are like this. Once they admit the human frailties of uncertainty, lack of experience and error, they destroy the aura of leadership.

(5) All autocrats promise security and stability although in the long run they can produce neither. Mussolini promised that trains would run on time in Italy. Hitler promised that unemployment would be ended. Lenin promised that the World War I would be ended.

(6) Imperialism is frequently a characteristic of the authoritarian state. The autocrat often embarks on imperialist, expansionist programme. Hitler, Mussolini, Stalin, Mao Tse-tung, Nasser and other modern autocrats have embarked on such programmes. There is little doubt that both Hitler and Stalin wanted to rule the world. Mao Tse-tung and Chou En-lai have already shown their ambition to conquer vast areas of land. That was a part of the reason why India was attacked by China in 1962. With the same object, Nasser seized the Suez Canal. It is not always difficult to create a crisis to start a war. The Soviet Union declared in 1939 that she was "threatened" by Finland and on that plea attacked her: Likewise, Czechoslovakia and Poland were threatened by Germany and Albania, Greece and Ethiopia were threatened by Italy.

(7) The authoritarian state frequently attempts a fusion of the state and the church. The Catholic Church signed Concordats with both Mussolini and Hitler and at one time sent a delegation to the Soviet Union to secure a similar Concordat. In Germany, the Protestants attempted to settle with Hitler. General Franco of Spain maintained very close relations with the Catholic State Church. The dictator wants to use religion as a tool to maintain himself in power. It is often possible to use religion and the religious beliefs of the people to justify his own existence and position. The autocrat knows that religion is basic to most people and if he can transfer some of their devotion to himself, he will be in a more powerful position.

(8) In an autocratic state, the individual does not figure anywhere. All the emphasis is on the leader, the party or the state. They are everything. Hitler thought of himself as the personification of the German spirit. "Heil Hitler" was the military salute as well as a form of greeting. Stalin stood forth as the only apostle of Revolution. As an autocrat can never admit the value of the individual, he substitutes the state, leader or party and sometimes a confused blending of all three. In Germany, there was an idealised state, a party and a leader. The first loyalty was to the party.

(9) In an authoritarian state, there is fusion of powers. There is no separation of the legislative, executive and judicial powers. All of them are fused and concentrated so that the autocrat can control all of them. This is done for his convenience and is not an essential mark of autocracy. The essential factor of his autocratic status is the complete lack of responsibility to the people. Popular sovereignty can exist whether the executive, legislative and judicial powers are separated or fused.

Dictatorship

Dictatorship may be defined as that form of government in which the supreme power is exercised by one man in an autocratic manner. It is government by a single person as the head of the state. All the powers are concentrated in his hands and it is the duty of the people to obey his commands.

There is nothing new about dictatorships; there were dictators in the past also. However, dictatorships were established in many countries after World War I. The people were disgusted with the parliamentary institutions and it was felt that they could not help them to solve their difficulties. The problems were so great that the slow democratic process was considered to be unsuitable to tackle them. Every nation followed a policy of economic self-sufficiency. Economic depression hit the people-hard. The League of Nations failed to fulfil the hopes of the people. Many countries detested the provisions of the settlement of 1919-20. All these factors combined together to facilitate the establishment of dictatorships in Italy, Germany, Poland, Spain etc.

Characteristics

Reference may be made to some of the main characteristics of dictatorship in modern times. Dictatorship believes in one party, one leader and one programme. It is only the party of the dictator which is allowed to continue. All other parties are suppressed by fair or foul means. The Nazi Party alone was allowed to function in Germany. The Fascist Party did not tolerate any rival in Italy. The same can be said about the Communist Party of Soviet Russia. The people are expected to have complete faith in their leader who exercises dictatorial powers in the country. The dictator is considered to be the symbol of national prestige; he represents national unity. All powers are concentrated in his hands and his word is law in everything. The country has one programme and that is the programme of the party of the dictator.

There is no place for individual liberty. Liberty consists in obedience to the commands of the dictator. It is pointed out that there can be no liberty in a weak state. The people are not allowed to have any freedom of speech, press or association. All the means of propaganda are controlled by the dictator and no criticism of the governed is tolerated. The people are merely asked to believe and obey and not .raise any slogans. Instead of liberty, equality and fraternity, the people are expected to believe and act on the principle of duty, discipline and sacrifice. Mussolini said, "Liberty is a dead carcass, I kick it." Liberty is merely a concession by the state. Law and state are the supreme manifestations of liberty and the maximum of liberty coincides with the maximum of state force. The dictator is the sole judge of the nature and extent of liberty to be enjoyed by the people.

Dictatorship believes in an authoritarian, totalitarian and omnipotent state. It puts more emphasis on duties than on the rights of the citizens. The people should be prepared to make all kinds of sacrifices at the altar of the state. The state is an end and not a means. All is in the state and nothing human or spiritual exists and, much less, has any value outside the state. There is only one loyalty and that is to the dictator. The totalitarian state is not merely a night watchman. It controls the whole life of man. Dictatorship has no faith in democracy and liberalism. Democracy is described as stupid, corrupt, slow-moving, visionary, impracticable and inefficient. Parliaments are described as shops which cannot accomplish anything substantial. The masses are incompetent to govern themselves and it is only a few who have the capacity to rule. Power must be in the hands of the dictator.

Dictatorship puts emphasis on war. According to Mussolini, "Imperialism is the eternal and immutable law of life. Expansion is a matter of life and death. Either a country must expand or perish. War is to the man what maternity is to the woman. I do not believe in perpetual peace; not only do I not believe in it, but I find it depressing and a negation of all the fundamental virtues of man." Again, "War alone brings all human energies to their highest tension and imprints a seal of nobility on the people that have the virtue to face it." According to Hitler, "In eternal warfare mankind has become great; in eternal peace it will be ruined."

Dictators believe in the superiority of their nations. The view of Hitler was that the Germans were the best people on earth. A similar view was held by Mussolini about the Italians. The object was to create a sense of superiority among the people and thereby prepare them for wars of aggression.

Dictatorship and Democracy

There is a fundamental difference between dictatorship and democracy. Dictatorship is based on the principle of obedience and discipline. Democracy believes in the principle of mutual discussion and persuasion. In democracy there is equality for all; every man has one vote; the opinion of everybody counts. However, dictatorship glorifies in inequality. It believes in the principle of hierarchy. In democracy, there is emphasis on liberty, but that is not the case with dictatorship. The people are required to obey completely and unhesitatingly the orders of the state. In democracy, people are allowed to organise themselves into various parties and these are allowed to carry on propaganda and capture power by peaceful means. However, in the case of dictatorship, no party except that of the dictator is allowed to exist; the rest are suppressed. Democracy is based on reason while dictatorship is based on unquestioned obedience. Democracy believes in the worth of individuals who are considered to be ends in themselves. In the case of dictatorship, the state becomes the end and the individuals the means. In democracy, peaceful methods are adopted to change the government but violent methods are followed by dictators. They do not believe in arguments but in bullets. In democracy, emphasis is put on the rights of man, but in dictatorship emphasis is put on duties. Democracy acts upon the ideal of "live and let live", but dictatorship believes in wars of conquest. Democracy is slow in its working as all the people have to be persuaded to act. However, dictatorship is quick in its working.

Merits of Dictatorship

The great merit of dictatorship lies in the fact that it gives the people a strong government which is in a position to tackle the problems facing the country. Forces of lawlessness and disorder are suppressed. There is increased efficiency in administration. The dictator knows full well that he will not be able to continue his dictatorship if he does not give the people an efficient system of administration. There are no brakes on the dictator and he can do whatever he pleases. He can accomplish a great deal in a short period. Undoubtedly, Italy under Mussolini and Germany under Hitler made remarkable progress within a brief period. Dictators try to add to the strength and prestige of their countries. They put emphasis on the military preparations of the country. They conquer territories and raise the prestige of the nation. Dictatorship is found to be useful in times of national crisis. With their vigour and promptness, dictators succeed where democracy may not try to add to the strength and prestige of their countries. They conquer territories and raise the prestige of the nation. Dictatorship is found to be useful in times of national crisis. With their vigour and promptness, dictators succeed where democracy may not.

Demerits of Dictatorship

Dictatorship is opposed to democracy and liberalism. It does not believe in equality of men. It does not allow people to think for themselves. There is no place for the liberty of the individuals. They are required to be merely dumb-driven cattle. The individuals become the means and the state the end. They are required to be sacrificed at the altar of the state. Obviously, such a philosophy cannot be for the welfare of mankind.

Dictatorship glorifies war and describes peace as a coward's dream. Emphasis is put on violence and terrorism. However, experience shows that there can he no progress in society if it is dominated by fear and force. It is only justice and righteousness which can be the basis of a stable society. Might, without right, can at best be only temporary. It is might with right that can be a permanent basis of the state. Force crushes the might and spirit of individuals. Dictatorship is like an engine built for speed and aggressiveness and not for endurance.

Dictatorship results in too much centralisation and that is bound to result in the destruction of individual initiative. According to Einstein, "Dictatorship means muzzles all round and consequently stultification. Science can flourish only in an atmosphere of free speech."

According to Ferrero, "What force has created, force destroyed. The child of the armies, the Roman Empire, was destroyed by armies that had given it birth." Croce says: "Regimes of force can survive only among decadent peoples; they can figure only as temporary expedients in nations that are growing and in the ascendant; and repressions produce only more violent explosions of the forces they would restrain."

Dictatorship encourages the evils of narrow-mindedness and bigotry. The people are encouraged to love their own countries and condemn others. Aggressive nationalism advocated by dictators cannot give peace to humanity. Too much emphasis on war and bloodshed can result in turning human beings into savages.

Dictatorship can be a temporary expedient; it is not a substitute for democracy. People are not prepared to give up their right to govern themselves permanently. The state of emergency in a country may demand that power be entrusted to a particular individual for some period, but this cannot be done permanently. The power of the dictator is based on force and, as soon as that force weakens, dictatorship also evaporates.

Unitary Government

A unitary form of government is that in which all the powers are concentrated in the hands of the central government. The units are merely the creation of the central government and they exist as long as the central government allows them to exist. They are the "agents of the centre for the purpose of local rule and autonomy" and their powers "are more a matter of grace than right." Before the coming into force of the Government of India Act, 1935, India had a unitary form of government. It was in 1935 that provision was made for a federal form of government for the country. Even today, England and France have a unitary form of government.

The great merit of a unitary government is its strength. As all the powers are in the hands of the central government, it can do whatever it pleases. There is no hindrance from the units, whose duty is merely to carry out the instructions of the centre. It also leads to efficiency of administration. A uniform policy is laid down by the central government for the whole country and that is carried out faithfully by its agents. There is also no danger of the units seceding from the centre. The centrifugal tendencies are suppressed; as a matter of fact, there is no scope for them. The system of administration in a unitary government is simple and economical. There is no heavy expenditure on the administration of the units. There is no duplication of officials. A vigorous and uniform policy can be followed in a unitary government; there is no scope for differences National unity is emphasized and the people owe loyalty to the central government alone.

The great disadvantage of a unitary government is its centralization. Everything is done from the centre and consequently there is little scope for local initiative. Experience shows that a decentralized government is in the interests of the country as a whole. People can have more interest in such a government. According to Garner, a unitary government tends to repress local initiative, discourages rather than stimulates interest in the public affairs, impairs the vitality of the local governments, and facilitates the development of a centralised bureaucracy. Well enough adapted to a small country having a homogeneous population and especially a population among whom the habits and capacity of local self-government are not highly developed, it is unsuited to a country of vast extent, where there is a variety of local conditions and a diversity of standards and conceptions. Among a people who are animated by an attachment for local self-government and a love of local liberty, it is intolerable and impossible of long duration. "The evils of bureaucracy are increased in a unitary government. There is every possibility of the lessening of efficiency on account of centralization. It is possible that the central government may not understand and appreciate the problems and difficulties of the units. Under the circumstances, they may not be able to look after their interests adequately. If the country is a big one and the problems of the various parts are different, uniform legislation and administration in a unitary government are bound to fail in achieving the ideal of the good of the people. No wonder, there is a general preference for a federal form of government in modern times.

Federal Government

Professor Dicey defines federal government thus: "A federal state is a political contrivance intended to reconcile national unity and power with the maintenance of state rights." Hamilton defines a federal government as "an association of states to form a new state." According to Montesquieu, a federal government is "a convention by which several similar states agree to be members of a large one." Prof K.C. Wheare says that by the federal principle, "I mean the method of dividing powers so that the general and regional governments are each within a sphere, coordinate and independent."

A federation is a union of states and it is generally the result of two kinds of forces, *viz*, centripetal and centrifugal. A federation comes into being as a result of centripetal forces when independent states agree to join hands and thereby create a new state. That was the case in Australia and the United States. Sometimes, a unitary government is transformed into a federal government as a result of centrifugal forces. The units demand a large measure of autonomy which can be provided only in a federal structure. This is what was done in India by the Government of India Act, 1935, with a view to give greater autonomy to the provinces.

A Confederation is an association of sovereign states and they are brought together by means of a treaty in which are laid down the terms on which the states agree to join. According to Oppenheim, a confederacy consists of "a number of full sovereign states linked together for the maintenance of their external and internal independence by a recognised international treaty into a union with organs of its own which are vested with a certain power over the member states, but not over the citizens of these states." Hall says, "A confederation is a union strictly of independent states which consent to forego permanently a part of liberty of their action for certain specific objects and they are not so combined under a common government that the latter appears to their exclusion as the international entity." The examples of confederations are the German Confederation from 1815 to 1866, the Swiss Confederacy from 1815 to 1840 and the American Confederacy consisting of 13 American States from 1781 to 1789.

Federation and Confederation

Although the two words, federation and confederation, have been taken from a common root, their meanings are different. A confederation is a loose union and a federation is a stronger union. A confederation is a union of states or provinces for some particular purpose and when that is achieved, a confederation is liable to be dissolved. That is what happened in the case of the 13 colonies of America which revolted against England in the later half of the eighteenth century. They formed themselves into a confederation which, however, was transformed into a federation as a result of certain forces. The fact remains that the thirteen states could have separated from one another after winning the war. A federation, as distinguished from confederation, is a general union for common purposes and is intended to last for ever.

In a federation, a new state is created and a new sovereign comes into being. A confederation is a union of the existing states. The federating states do not give up their sovereignty. They merely combine for certain purposes.

In a federation, there is double citizenship for the individuals. They are the citizens of the state or the province in which they live. They are also the citizens of the federal government that comes into being. In a confederation, the individuals are the citizens of their own states. As no new state is created in the case of a confederation, no new citizenship comes into existence.

In the case of a federation, the federal government can deal directly with the people living in the units of the federation. In a confederation, the central government can deal with the states and not the individuals living therein.

A confederation is a temporary union and its members may leave it whenever they please or when the object of the combination has been realised. Separation is easy because each state keeps intact its separate individuality and sovereignty. However, separation is not possible in the case of a federation, which is a permanent union. There is a way into it but no way out of it. Having once joined a federation, no unit can leave it. The federal government can use force to bring back the rebellious unit or units to its fold. This happened in the United States when the southern states revolted on the question of slavery but were brought back by the federal government under the leadership of Abraham Lincoln.

Federal and Unitary Government

Professor Dicey says: "The essential difference between a federation and a unitary system of government is that while in a unitary system all the powers are vested in the hands of one authority, there is a division of powers in a federation." There is a concentration of powers in a unitary government; the central government can do whatever it pleases; there is absolutely no check on its authority. However, in federal government the powers are divided between the federal government and the units and each is independent in its own affairs. The federal government cannot interfere in those matters which are given to the units and *vice-versa.* The division of powers is not similar in all cases. The United States and Australia follow one pattern but Canada and India follow another. There may be exclusive spheres of jurisdiction for the federation and units and some concurrent powers for both. The residuary powers may be with the units, as in Australia and the United States, or with the federal government, as in Canada, or may be determined by a definite authority as in India.

In a federation, there is the supremacy of the constitution. A federation is a contractual union and its constitution embodies all the terms on which the units agree to join it and would like to continue in it. In such a case, the constitution becomes all important. Any law which violates any provision of the constitution in *ultra vires.* The constitution is supreme in the United States and whenever a new law is to be passed, the consideration is to see whether it is *ultra vires* or *intra vires* of the constitution. What matters is not whether it is for the good of the people or not. The paramount consideration is whether it is permissible under the constitution or not. In a unitary government, the centre can pass any law which it considers to be for the good of the people. There is absolutely no limitation or restriction on its powers.

In a federation, there is a strong desire on the part of the units to maintain their separate entity, although they would like to unite for certain purposes. The units are prepared to merge themselves. The federal sentiment of union without unity is essential for the successful working of the federation.

In a unitary government, the units merge themselves into the central government and lose their separate entity.

A unitary government works successfully where the people are relatively homogeneous. A federal government serves the needs of a country where the different parts have varying interests which demand satisfaction. In such a case, those parts can unite for certain common objects and manage their other affairs independently. A federal system alone helps the combination of territories which vary considerably from one another and in spite of that enjoy the fruits of union and autonomy.

Every federal government must have a written constitution and that must be a rigid one. The reason is that the units want to be sure of their autonomy in the future also. In a unitary government, no such thing is essential. The central government can do whatever it pleases. To all intents and purposes, it is omnipotent.

Conditions Necessary for Federation

Professor Dicey says that two things must be present for the formation of a federation. There must be strong desire to have a union; the will to have a union is the basis of federation. The component units of a federation must be inspired and bound together by common ties of national affinity and sentiment. There must be a community of political, economic and agricultural interests. At the same time, the units joining the federation must be determined to maintain their separate entity. There must be present what can be called the federal sentiment. To quote Dicey, "They must desire union and must not desire unity". It is the presence of this federal sentiment in the United States that has helped the working of the federal system and it was the lack of it under the Weimar Constitution of Germany that was responsible for its collapse.

Another necessary condition is that the units joining the federation must be comparatively equal as regards area and population. Union is possible only among equals. Otherwise, there is every possibility of the exploitation of the weaker by the stronger. The weaker units will not join because of the danger of their being swallowed up by the stronger ones. The federal system in Germany failed because the population of Prussia was three-fourths of the whole of Germany and its area was two-thirds of the total area of Germany. J.S. Mill says, "There should not be any one state so much more powerful than the rest as to be capable of vying in strength with many of them combined. If there be such a one, and only one, it will insist on being master of the joint deliberations; if there be two, they will be irresistible when they agree and whenever they differ everything will be decided by a struggle for ascendancy between the rivals". The view of K.C. Wheare is that "There must be some sort of reasonable balance which will ensure that all the units can maintain their independence within the sphere allotted to them and that no one can dominate the others. It must be the task of those who frame and work a federal government to see that no unit shall be too large, and, equally important, none too small."

The federating units must possess adequate economic resources. Both the federal government and the units must have sufficient independent economic resources so that they can perform their duties without dependence. It is rightly maintained that if sufficient independent economic resources are not given to the regional governments, "then no matter how much states desire a federal union and no" matter whether a federal constitution is drawn up, in practice federal government will not be possible. Soon the regional governments will be unable to perform their functions or they will be able to perform them only at the price of financial dependence upon the general government, that is, at the price of financial unification."

Another necessary factor for a federal system is geographical contiguity. The federating units should be situated near one another. This geographical nearness helps them to be together. It is the lack of this factor that makes impossible the establishment of a federation of the British Empire.

Common historical traditions, common language and literature and common relations also facilitate the establishment of a federal system. The existence of some earlier connections among the units is also helpful.

"Federal government requires a basis of political competence and general education among the people." A federal constitution can work successfully only when the people are educated and politically advanced. This is due to the fact that there is a dual polity in a federal system and the people are required to take care not only of their own states but also of the federal government.

Essentials of a Federal State

(1) There are certain things which every federal government must have and the most important of them is the supremacy of the constitution. This means that the constitution of a federation must be supreme. It should not be possible for the units or the federal government to change it whenever they please. Both of them must work within their allotted spheres. If they go beyond their spheres, they are bound to be checked by the judiciary. The laws passed by the units or the federal government can be declared *ultra vires*. Dicey says, "The law of the constitution must either be immutable or else capable of being changed only by some authority above and beyond the ordinary legislative bodies, whether federal or state legislatures, existing under the constitution." Professor Wheare says that "the terms of the agreement which establishes the general and the regional governments and which distributes power between them must be binding upon these general and regional governments. This is a logical necessity from the definition of federal government itself." A federal system requires not only a written constitution but also a rigid constitution. This is necessary in the interests of stability.

(2) In every federal system, there must be a division of powers between the federal government and the units. There is no uniformity of practice in the world with regard to the division of powers. In the case of the United States, when it was decided to have a federation in that country, the representatives of the states refused to join. They stood for the rights of the states and were prepared to give practically nothing to the federal government. The result was that not many powers were given to the federal government and hence the federal government set up at that time was a weak one. It is a different matter that the federal government has now become strong in that country as a result of the working of certain forces.

In the case of Canada, things were quite different at the time of the framing of the federal constitution. When the representatives of Canada met at Quebec in 1865 for that purpose, all powers at that time were in the hands of the federal government. There was a desire to keep a strong federal government. The patriots of Canada were not prepared to ignore the lesson which the civil war in the United States seemed to teach them. It was felt that if there had been a powerful central government in the United States, the Southern states would not have dared to raise the standard of revolt. No wonder, the fathers of the Canadian constitution gave very many powers to the federal government and made the provinces weak. The same applies to India. The present constitution of India was framed soon after the partition of the country. The result was that the federal government of India was made exceptionally strong in order to provide against the danger of a further, division of the country in the future.

(3) Another essential feature of a federal government is the authority of the courts to declare *ultra vires* and invalid the laws passed by the legislature. This is obviously due to the fact that both the units and the federal government must work within their allotted spheres and must not go beyond them. If they do so, the judiciary is there to check them. This work is done by the Supreme Court in India and the United States. J.S. Mill says: "It is evidently necessary not only that the constitutional limits of authority of each (central and regional governments alike) should be precisely and clearly defined, but the power to decide between them in any case of dispute should not reside in either of the governments, or in any functionary subject to it, but in an umpire independent of both. There must be a Supreme Court of Justice, and a system of coordinate courts in every State of the Union,

before whom such questions shall be carried, and whose judgement on them in the last stage on appeal, shall be final."

Merits of Federation

The great merit of a federal system is its strength. It is well known that union is strength and if many small states combine to form a federal government, they are bound to be stronger in their collective capacity. Their combined resources are bound to give them greater security and strength in the world. "In these days of land hunger and empire states, small states always live at the mercy of their stronger neighbours." It is the necessity of mere existence that brings them together.

A federal system is an admirable device by which national unity can be harmonised with local autonomy. While the unity of the country is maintained, the units are allowed to have autonomy in their own affairs. They are allowed to develop according to their circumstances and needs. The evils of a unitary government are avoided. A unitary government results in uniform legislation which is not proper in a country where the units have interests differing from one another. Obviously, an agricultural province does not require the same laws which are required by a highly industrialized province. In a federal system, it is possible for the federal government to confine its activities to only those objects which are common to the whole country and the units are given freedom of action in those matters which concern them alone and not the other units.

A federal system is based on the principle of decentralization and division of powers. There is every possibility of great efficiency in administration. The central government is not overburdened with work as it is shared by the units.

There are lesser chances of despotism in a federal system. The principle of checks and balances has its effect. The units will not allow the federal government to be despotic and *vice versa.* Each is a check on the other.

There is every likelihood of greater economy in a federal system. The units are prepared to tax themselves to manage their own affairs and thus the burden of the federal government is lessened. Moreover, when many states join together into a federation, there is bound to be more economy on account of the merging of those states for all important purposes like foreign affairs, defence, etc.

In a federation, there are greater chances of the people taking interest in their local affairs than is the case in a unitary government. The people of the units have certainly greater powers in federal government than in a unitary government.

"Federation provides a basis for a world state. It is maintained that if many states can join into a federation, there is nothing to stop all the states of the world from joining into a world federation. This raises high hopes for the future of mankind.

John Fiske says that the federal government is the only kind of government which is permanently applicable to a whole continent. Westerkamp says that the federal idea has spread until it embraces a portion of the globe equal to three times the territorial area of Europe. Montesquieu observes: "It is very probable that mankind would have been at length obliged to live continuously under the government of a single person had they not contrived a kind of constitution that has all the advantages of a republican together with the external forces of a monarchical government; I mean a confederate republic".

Demerits

Undoubtedly, a federal government is weaker than a unitary government. There cannot be promptness of action under a federal system as the views of the units have also to be taken into consideration. There is always the possibility of mutual conflicts between units and the federation and that is hardly conducive to the growth and prosperity of a country. In a unitary government, the central administration can do whatever it pleases without any let or hindrance from any quarter. Professor Dicey says: "The distribution of all the power of the state among co-ordinate authorities necessarily leads to the result that no one authority can wield the same amount of power as under a Unitarian constitution is possessed by the sovereign. A scheme of checks and balances in which the strength of the common government is, so to speak, pitted against that of the state governments leads, on the face of it, to certain waste of energy. A federation, therefore, will always be at a disadvantage in a contest with Unitarian states of equal resources."

In a federal system, there is always the danger of secession of units from the federal-government. As the units enjoy autonomy, there can develop a spirit of defiance and independence and that can ultimately result in a revolt against the federal government. Such a thing happened in the United States when the southern states seceded from the federation and were brought back with the help of force. In Canada, the Quebec legislature set up in May 1964 a committee to report on all the implications of a breakaway from the federation. The Frenchmen in Canada have their grievances and they feel that the development of the English-speaking provinces is at their expense. Unless they are reconciled, there is the possibility of trouble in the future. Gettell says: "The proper adjustment of central to local governments thus becomes a constant source of difficulty and the danger of rebellion or the formation of sectional factions is always present."

The view of Lord Bryce is that the foreign affairs of a federal government are not conducted properly. However, this view is not accepted by others. Professor Munro says: "America demonstrated to the world that federalism did not necessarily mean weak government but that it was quite reconcilable with a strong national administration. It has demonstrated the potential strength of a federal republic both in foreign and domestic policy."

A federal government is more expensive than unitary government. More money has to be spent not only on the maintenance of the federal government but also on the various units in the federation. There is the duplication of the administrative machinery and hence the expense.

Dr. Leacock says: "Federal government has very decided limitations, serious faults of structure, unheeded perhaps at the time of its inception, but likely to break down under the altering strain of a new environment. Politically and on its external side if has proved itself strong, but economically and in its internal aspect, it is proving itself weak." Dr. Garner says: "Among other weaknesses of the federal system may be mentioned its complexity, the danger of conflicts of jurisdiction between the national and state authorities, the duplication of government machinery and services which it involves and the consequent increased expense of operating it and the difficulties which are encountered in the administration of justice due to the network of state boundaries." According to Lord Bryce, the faults of a federal government are its weakness in the conduct of foreign affairs, its weakness in home government, that is to say, deficient authority over the component states and the individual citizens, liability to dissolution by the secession or rebellion of states and the liability to division into groups and factions by the formation of separate combinations of the component states.

Future of Federation

Writers hold conflicting views with regard to the future of federalism. One view is that a federal government is merely a transitory government. It is merely a half-way house to a unitary government. Dicey says: "Federalism, when successful, has generally been a stage towards a unitary government." Woodrow Wilson says: "It is plain from the history of modern federal states – a history as yet extremely brief – that the strong tendency of such organisations is towards the transmutation of the federal into a unitary state. After union is once firmly established, not in the interest only but in the affections of the people also, the drift would seem to be in all cases towards consolidation." Sait says: "States move forward from alliance to confederacy, from confederacy to federation, from federation to complete union, that is from lower to higher forms. These successive forms, therefore, may be regarded as a biological series." Lipson says: "Older patterns of decentralisation – whether in the form of local autonomy under a unitary system or of states' rights in a federal union – were doomed to dissolve in the corrosive acids of twentieth century politics, economics and technology. Virtually all the great driving forces in modern society combine in centralist direction." Professor W.F. Willoughby observes: "This step taken, there immediately develops a steady growth of the spirit of nationalism and, in response to needs actually felt, a progressive development, both absolutely and relatively, of the powers of the central government as opposed to those of the states. So marked is this that it may almost be said that from the moment the system of multiple government is adopted, the tendency is for efforts to be made to get away from the consequences of the decision that has been made."

There are other writers who hold the view that a federal government is more than merely a stage towards a unitary government. Professor Sidgwick says: "When we turn our gaze from the past to the future, an extension of federalism seems to me the most probable of the political prophecies relative to the form of government." A similar view is held by Wheare. He points out that the prophecy made by other writers with regard to the merging of a federal government into a unitary government is merely a prophecy and not a historical judgment. No federal government has become a unitary government. He admits that war and economic depression are the enemies of federal government and if they occur frequently, they "will almost certainly turn federal governments into unitary governments." While admitting all the difficulties facing a federation, Professor Wheare concludes: "The prospect of federal government is not so short as is suggested by those who concentrate entirely on the tendency of the general government to increase at the expense of the regions. Federal government is still desired by some regions in all the federations. There is no conclusive evidence that federal government is to be no more than a stage in the process towards unitary government."

On the whole, the future of federalism in the world is bright. The United States has set before the world a brilliant example of how a federal government can work successfully. Countries like India, though formerly unitary governments, have adopted federal constitutions. Professor Willoughby rightly says that we should not "close our eyes to the immense service which the development of the idea of multiple government has rendered in the past and may still .render in knitting together under a common government peoples whose political interests are largely identical but which for sentimental reasons are unwilling wholly to surrender their political autonomy." Professor Wheare is also of the view that the future of federalism is bright. To quote him, "Federalism marches towards triumph."

Parliamentary Government

A parliamentary form of government is that in which the executive is responsible to the legislature. It is also called the cabinet form of government. In India, Great Britain, Canada, Australia, etc., we have a parliamentary form of government.

There are certain characteristic features of a parliamentary form of government. There is always a dual executive. One executive is nominal and the other is real. In India, the nominal executive is the President of India and the real executive is the Prime Minister and his Cabinet. In England, the King is the nominal executive and the Prime Minister and the Cabinet are the real executive. The nominal executive does not exercise any powers. All the powers are enjoyed and exercised by the cabinet, which is responsible to the legislature and through it to the people. The ministers are chosen from the members of the legislature and are also responsible to it for all their acts of omission and commission. They can be asked questions and supplementary questions. A vote of no confidence can be passed against them. They remain in office so long as they enjoy the confidence of the House. They have no fixed term of office. If they are defeated in the legislature, they either have to resign and make room for others of appeal to the people against the verdict of the members of the legislature. In a parliamentary government, the Prime Minister is the leader and it is he who makes a choice of the members of his Cabinet. He presides over the meetings of the cabinet and has the power to reshuffle his cabinet. He can include or exclude any member he pleases. However, he would normally include in his cabinet all the important members of the party. That is the only way to make his cabinet strong. There is the principle of collective responsibility of the ministers. The defeat of one minister in the legislature results in the fall of the ministry as a whole. That is one of the reasons why the ministers help one another. The cabinet is the link between the legislature and the executive. Most of the legislation is initiated by the cabinet and the ministers are in charge of those bills in the legislature.

Prerequisites of Parliamentary Government

(1) There are certain prerequisites of a parliamentary government if it is intended to work successfully. The first prerequisite is the presence of a titular head of the government. It has already been pointed out that the King is the titular head in England and the President of India is the titular head in India, and the real power rests in the hands of the cabinet. Likewise the governors are the titular heads in the states in India and the real power rests in the hands of the chief ministers and their cabinets.

(2) Another prerequisite of a parliamentary government is that the party in power should have a clear and stable majority in the legislature. Such a situation existed in India for many years, as the Congress was able to win a majority of seats at the Centre and also in most of the states. A similar system prevails in England, Canada and Australia. The difficulty arises in a country like France where a multiple-party system exists and where there had to be coalition governments which collapsed in rapid succession. In such circumstances, the government is not stable. There is no one definite programme for the ministry in power to follow. There is no one leader to obey and no discipline to observe. The ministry is hesitant and is not able to take a long term view of policy. Under such circumstances, much cannot be expected in the form of results.

(3) Another prerequisite of a parliamentary government is the responsibility of the ministry to the legislature. Each minister is responsible to the legislature for the acts of omission and commission of his own department. Likewise, all the ministers are collectively responsible to the legislature for the collective policy of the ministry in power. If one minister is defeated, all must resign. Such system strengthens the hands of the ministry.

(4) Another prerequisite for the successful working of a parliamentary form of government is the existence of a spirit of moderation among the various political parties. It is absolutely essential that both the party in power and the opposition must understand and observe the rules of the game. They should never forget that their existence and continuance must depend upon the contribution they make towards the good of the people. Each party has to put forward its programme before the people and ask the electorate to vote for it so that they can accomplish what they have promised in their manifesto. It is up to the electorate to decide whether they want to be ruled by one party or other. Under such circumstances, there must be no scope for any bitterness between the parties. The defeated party must accept the verdict of the people and should do nothing to disrupt or in any way hamper the smooth working of the government. It should wait for another opportunity to oust the party in power through constitutional and peaceful means by putting before the electorate a more attractive programme and also creating among them the confidence that they can carry it out if they are returned to power. The party should never forget that a spirit of intolerance ultimately leads to the destruction of democracy itself. "Every trick, every method of obstruction and filibuster, is used to effect a certain political result and if everything else fails, force may eventually be applied.... When that occurs, orderly government often comes to an end and emergency decree takes the place of legislative act. From there it is only a step to dictatorship."

(5) Another prerequisite for the successful working of a parliamentary government is that the ministry in power must have the right of dissolution of the legislature. The necessity of this has been made clear by the working of the parliamentary institutions in France. The ministry in that

country had no such power and the result was that it was voted out of office by the members of the legislature whenever they pleased. If the ministry had possessed the power of dissolution, the mere threat of dissolution would have brought the members of the legislature to their senses. A dissolution means that the members must fight their elections once again. An election is a very costly affair and every member cannot afford to spend that much money very often. Even if money is spent, there is no surety that the election will be won. Hence the power of dissolution in the hands of ministry makes the members of the legislature reasonable and responsible. They must resist the temptation of frivolously voting against the ministry in power because the consequences are as suicidal to them as to the ministers.

(6) Another prerequisite for the successful working of a parliamentary government is the existence of secrecy among the members of the cabinet. They must deliberate in secret if mature, rational and independent discussion is to shape the policy of the government. These things cannot be done in public. Secrecy also helps the existence of harmony among the members of the Cabinet.

Merits of Parliamentary Government

(1) The most important merit of a parliamentary form of government is the harmony and co-operation between the legislature and the executive. This is due to the fact that only that party is allowed to form the ministry which has a majority in the legislature. As the ministry is always sure of its support in the legislature, it feels confident that whatever legislation it initiates in the legislature will be passed without any material alteration. The result is that there is coordination between the legislature and the executive. The ministry can draft all those measures which are considered to be necessary for the happiness and progress of the country and also see them through the legislature. So long as it is not turned out of office, it is bound to get them passed through the legislature. There is no such certainty in a presidential form of government. The executive may ask the legislature to pass certain measures but the latter may refuse to do so and the executive is absolutely helpless under the circumstances.

(2) In a parliamentary government, responsibility of the government is continuous and immediate. The acts of omission and commission of the government can be criticised and condemned without any loss of time. The legislature is sitting most of the time and the ministers also sit in the legislature. There is no difficulty in asking the ministers questions and supplementary questions. If the actions of the Government are wrong, the legislature can pass a vote of no confidence and turn the majority out of office without any loss of time. The legislature need not wait at all. If the legislature is not in session, a demand can be made for a special session and then the ministry can be voted out of office. There is no such elasticity in the presidential form of government. The President and his ministers do not sit in the legislature and consequently they cannot be asked to explain their conduct. The President is elected for a fixed period and he cannot be turned out from office before the end of that term except through the very difficult process of impeachment. Even if the President is incompetent to deal with the situation, he cannot be removed or replaced. He must be allowed to serve his full term of office regardless of the consequences. In a parliamentary government, if the ministry is found to be incompetent to deal with the situation, it can be voted out of office at once and a more competent ministry can take its place. This actually happened in England in 1940 when Churchill replaced Chamberlain. It is rightly stated that under a parliamentary government, "from first to last there is full and harmonious collaboration between the law-making and money-granting authorities, on the other.... With authority thus concentrated, the full power of government can be promptly brought to bear upon any great emergency." Lord Bryce says that a parliamentary system secures "swiftness in decision and vigour in action and enables the cabinet to pass through such legislation as it thinks needed, and to conduct both domestic and foreign policy with the confidence that its majority will support it against the attacks of the opposition."

(3) A parliamentary government helps the rise of men of outstanding ability. This is due to the fact that it is a difficult task to run the administration and at the same time satisfy the people. No wonder, men of extraordinary ability are required to manage both the executive and the legislature. The readiness of the opposition to expose the ministry on all occasions demands constant vigilance, ready wit and plenty of commonsense. No wonder, the qualities of leadership of a very high order are required from those who have to run the parliamentary machine.

(4) In a parliamentary system, the interest of the public in politics is maintained. A general election can come at any time and the parties are interested in keeping an intimate touch with the electorate at all times. The people can also get their grievances redressed at any time by putting questions and supplementary questions to the ministers through their representatives. This keeps the interest of the people alive.

(5) The cabinet system is highly educative. The problems of the country are thoroughly discussed in the legislature and the people take keen interest in those debates. The parliamentary debates are reported in the press at length; editorials are written on them and very often they are discussed from the platform also. The result is that the people get a lot of training in this manner. It is rightly stated that "the House is its platform, the newspapers are its microphones and the people is its audience."

(6) Another merit of parliamentary system of government is that it is flexible and elastic. In the words of Bagehot, under a parliamentary system, the people can "choose a ruler for the occasion" who is fit to meet the emergency. When the World War II started in 1939, Chamberlain was the Prime Minister of England. He was a weak man and he was not fit for the emergency facing the country. The result was that he was replaced by Churchill who was the Prime Minister of England during the rest of the World War II. Such a thing is not possible under a presidential form of government. To quote Bagehot, "The American Government calls itself a government of the supreme people; but at a quick crisis, the time when the sovereign power is most needed, you cannot find the supreme people... all the arrangements are for stated times. There is no elastic element; everything is rigid, specified and stated. Come what may, you quicken nothing and can retard nothing. You have bespoken your government in advance and whether it suits you or not, whether it works well or works ill, whether it is what you want or not, by law you must keep it." That shows the flexibility in the British system and the rigidity in the American system. It is contended that the British system enables the executive to meet any crisis in the social and political life of the people. It can explain to the legislature the situation facing the country and the means which it wants to adopt to meet the same. In 1931, the convention of collective responsibility of the ministers was given up for the time being when the ministers "agreed to differ." That was done to meet the economic crisis facing the country at that time.

(7) The parliamentary system has helped in democratizing the machinery of the government in all civilised countries. This is particularly so where there is hereditary monarchy. Britain is called the citadel of democracy. This is due to the fact that although Britain has a King, he reigns but does not govern. Lord Bryce has described the merit of this system in these words, "As the actual working Executive has necessarily a party character, it is a merit of this system that the National Executive, be he King or President, should be outside party, and represent that permanent machinery of administration which goes on steadily irrespective of party changes...when a cabinet fails, the transfer of power to another is a comparatively short and simple affair."

Lord Bryee says that a parliamentary government "concentrates the plenitude of power in one body, the legislature, giving to its majority that absolute control of the executive which enables the latter, when supported by the legislature, to carry out the wishes of the majority with the maximum of vigour and promptness. The essence of the scheme is that the executive and the majority in the legislature work together, each influencing the other. Being in constant contact with members of the opposition party as well as in still closer contact with those of their own, they have opportunities of feeling the pulse of the assembly and through it the pulse of public opinion. The system in therefore calculated to secure swiftness in decision and vigour in action and enables the cabinet to press through such legislation as it thinks is needed and to conduct both domestic administration and foreign policy with the confidence that its majority will support it against the attacks of the opposition. To these merits there is to be added the concentration of responsibility. For any faults committed, the legislature can blame the cabinet and the people can blame both the cabinet and the majority."

Demerits

If a parliamentary system has certain merits, it has its shortcomings also. Lord Bayce rightly says that the cabinet system "intensifies the spirit of party and keeps it always on the boil. Even if there are no important issues of policy before the nation, there are always the offices to be fought for. One party holds them, the other desires them, and the conflict is unending — it is like the incessant battle described as going on in the blood vessels between the red corpuscles and the invading microbes. In the legislature it involves an immense waste of time and force. Though in theory the duty of the opposition is to oppose only the bad measures and to expose only the misdoings of the administration, in practice it opposes most of their measures and criticizes most of their acts.... A system which makes the life of an administration depend upon the fate of the measures it introduces, disposes every cabinet to think too much of what support it can win by proposals framed to catch the fancy of the moment, and to think too little of what the real needs of the nation are, and may compel the retirement, when a bill is defeated, of men who can ill be spared from their administrative posts."

The parliamentary system violates the theory of separation of powers as it links up the executive and the legislature. However, this is merely a theoretical objection and it is recognized that the absolute separation of power is neither possible nor desirable.

The cabinet system has resulted in the dictatorship of the cabinet. All powers have come into the hands of the ministers who can do whatever they please. They can decide any policy, draft legislation to implement it and ultimately get it passed through the legislature. The legislature is reduced to the position of a mere agent of the cabinet. No wonder, we have "the dictatorship of one man or of a small group of men."

The view of Dicey is that a parliamentary government is weak in time of war or emergency. The ministry has not only to prosecute the war but has also to face hostile criticism day after day. That is hardly desirable under the circumstances. In a presidential system, the President can do whatever he likes and he is not bothered about criticism in the legislature. He knows that he cannot be turned out from office before the expiry of his term. In the case of a parliamentary government, the ministry can be outvoted by a hostile legislature. It is obvious that if the ministers are always worried about their existence, they cannot be expected to be enthusiastic about their work.

There is not much trouble about the working of a parliamentary government if there are two political parties in a country. The one party is in power and the other is in the opposition. The members of the party in power support the ministry. However, the problem becomes complicated if there are many parties in the country. Often no one party has an absolute majority in the legislature and many parties have to join hands to form a ministry. This is sometimes a difficult affair. Even if a coalition ministry is formed, it cannot be sure of a long life. The ministry may fall any day on account of the differences among the members belonging to the various parties. A ministry which is not sure of its future existence cannot be expected to be enthusiastic about its work. It is bothered more about its existence than about the service of the people.

In a parliamentary government, everything has to be placed before the legislature and discussed. The ministers are expected not to do anything at the back of the legislature. There can be no secrecy regarding the working of the government. This puts the government in an awkward position, particularly with regard to the conduct of foreign affairs. Some sort of secrecy has to be maintained during the negotiations and even when those are concluded, certain provisions of a treaty may have to be kept secret in the interest of the security of the state. Such a thing is difficult in a parliamentary government.

A lot of time of the ministers is wasted in the legislature and in attending various meetings and conferences. When the legislature is sitting, the ministers have to be in their seats to defend their policies and silence hostile criticism. The Prime Minister, Foreign Minister, and Finance Minister in particular and other ministers in general are required to participate in international conferences and that forces them to be away from their office for long intervals. There are other public engagements which keep the members away from their offices. The result is that the ministers are not left with enough time to look after the affairs of their departments.

Critics point out that a parliamentary government is inefficient because it is a government by amateurs. Very often, the ministers in charge of their departments know very little about their departments. Sometimes they are transferred from one department to another. The result is that they do not have enough experience of the working of the departments of which they are the heads. Hence, much cannot be expected from them in the form of efficiency of work. Sir Sydney Low says: "A youth must pass an examination in arithmetic before he can hold a second class clerkship in the Treasury; but a Chancellor of the Exchequer may be a middle-aged man of the world who has forgotten what little he ever learnt about figures at Eton or Oxford and is innocently anxious to know the meaning of those little dots when confronted with Treasury accounts worked out in decimals." It is rightly pointed out that an amateur is not always a gifted person. Weak persons, even incompetent persons, "are sometimes appointed to office or to inappropriate departments, out of such considerations of popularity, sometimes gained or faded a decade or more ago, or through the personal esteem or friendship of the Prime Minister." However, it is pointed out that this is not a defect at all. A parliamentary government cannot work without these amateur ministers. The system has its own merits which outweigh the defects. Ramsay MacDonald says: "The cabinet is the bridge linking up the people with the expert, joining principle to practice. Its function is to transform the message sent along sensory nerves. It does not keep the departments going; it keeps them going in certain directions."

Parliamentary government is unstable. It has no fixed life. Everything depends upon the whims of the members of the legislature. This is particularly so "if dominant majority in the representative chamber is either small or wanting in cohesion; and in the latter case it is also liable to be upset by a new combination of parties in the chamber — aided perhaps by personal intrigues — if the opportunity for the combination is skillfully chosen, so that the newly-formed majority is not reversed on an appeal to the country." The uncertainty facing the government does not allow it to follow a farsighted and consistent policy. The new ministry is likely to reverse the policy of the defeated ministry. This difficulty is particularly to be found in a country where there are many political parties.

Another defect of a parliamentary government is the tendency of the evergrowing size of the cabinet in every country. We can refer in this connection to the large number of ministers both in the central government of India and the various states. Even small states have more than 15 or 20 ministers. That not only results in a lot of expenditure but also makes it difficult for the machinery to work smoothly. Very often, the ministry becomes unmanageable, and much work cannot be done in such circumstances.

Dicey says that a cabinet government is government by a collegial or plural executive and for this reason is especially weak in time of war or grave national crises. Moreover, it is government of an extremely partisan character, that is, government of men who have risen to leadership, who are maintained in power by partisanship and whose policies are coloured by partisanship. Laski says that a cabinet government gives to the cabinet an opportunity for tyranny and under it the legislature may be reduced, as it was during the premiership of Lloyd George, to merely an organ for the registration of decisions which it is powerless either to criticise or to alter. Sidgwick points out that under a parliamentary government, ministers are likely to be distracted from their executive duties by their legislative tasks, while parliament is "tempted away from legislative problems by interesting questions of current administration, in which, especially in foreign affairs, it is liable to interfere to an excessive extent."

In spite of the above shortcomings, there is a general preference for a parliamentary form of government and the Constitution of India provides for such a system.

Presidential form of Government

The presidential form of government is that in which the executive is not responsible to the legislature. According to Garner, it "is a government in which the executive is independent of the legislature as regards its tenure and to a large extent as regards its policy and acts." Such a system exists in the United States. The American President is the executive and the Congress is the legislature. The President is elected for 4 years and cannot be removed earlier except through impeachment. The members of the House of Representatives are elected for two years and they cannot be sent home earlier. Likewise, the members of the Senate are elected for six years and they retire after the completion of their term. No hostile vote in the Congress can turn out the President and likewise no American President can dissolve the Congress. Both the President and the Congress look to the calendar and they are always sure of their future. The President and his ministers do not sit in the Congress and consequently they cannot be questioned on the floor of the Congress. The ministers of the President do not occupy the same position as the ministers in England do. The latter are the colleagues of the Prime Minister and they represent the people as much as the Prime Minister does. However, the ministers of the American President are merely his subordinates who are put in charge of various departments and they can be asked to get out any time by the President. They do not represent the people and their tenure of office depends upon the will of the President. In a presidential system, there is no titular executive like the King of England or the President of India. The American President is the real executive and all powers rest in his hands. He occupies a position similar to that of the Prime Minister of England. The presidential system is based on the theory of separation of powers, although it is difficult to achieve complete separation in actual practice.

According to Dr. Finer, the American presidency has six outstanding characteristics. It is not made executive but it has grown. It is a solitary not a collective executive. It is popularly elected, although the constitution provides for an indirect election. It is more than an executive. It is separated from the Congress. It may be tinkered with, but it cannot be reformed.

Merits

The great merit of a presidential system is its stability. The president is elected for four years and he cannot be turned out earlier except under very exceptional circumstances. The result is that the president can prepare his plans in such a way that he can execute them during the four years which are at his disposal. The president knows that he can carry out his programme without any let or hindrance from any quarter and that feeling must give him confidence and energy.

There is every possibility of greater efficiency in a presidential form of government as it is based on the principle of "division of labour." The president can attend to his work whole-heartedly without any interruption from any quarter and the same can be done by the Congress. There is no excessive work either for the legislature or for the executive. Work can be done satisfactorily. The president can take quick and prompt decisions and act firmly without any loss of time. Such a thing may not be possible under a parliamentary system. The unified control in administration in a presidential system makes for efficiency.

As the executive does not sit in the legislature, there can be no heckling of the ministers in a presidential government. There is no scope for destructive criticism and leg-pulling activities.

A presidential system is suitable for emergencies. This was amply proved by the manner in which the situation was handled by President Roosevelt during the 1930's and 1940's. All powers are concentrated in the hands of the president and he can afford to take prompt decisions to meet a crisis and also carry them out. He can direct the machinery of the state with energy, vigour and efficiency. All this is not possible under a parliamentary system. Even Prime Minister Churchill had not the personal powers of President Roosevelt. Dr. Jennings says, "The President pledged the United States in the realisation of the objectives of the Atlantic Charter while the War Cabinet, not the Prime Minister, pledged the United Kingdom". The President is the head of the nation. He is not merely a party leader. That gives him dignity, prestige and authority. In times of emergency, the nation looks up to him for guidance and action.

Under a Presidential system, experts can be appointed as heads of the Departments without consideration of their party affiliations. The President may appoint persons who belong to the opposite parties. President Cleveland appointed Walter G. Gresham as Secretary of State although he belonged to the opposite party. Theodore Roosevelt and Taft appointed a Democrat as Secretary of War. President Hoover appointed his Attorney-General a Democrat. President Roosevelt appointed Stimson as Secretary of War and Knox as Secretary of Navy although both of them were Republicans. Such a thing is not possible in a parliamentary system where the Prime Minister must appoint only those persons as ministers who belong to his party. If he does not do so, there is every possibility of the members of his party revolting against him and thereby bringing about his fall.

The Presidential system is best suited for countries which are inhabited by different communities with their diverse interests. In such a country, dual party system which is essential for the successful working of a parliamentary form of government, is not possible. A presidential system can serve the needs of such a country.

A presidential system is based on the theory of separation of powers which is considered to be essential for liberty by the Americans.

Demerits

The presidential system suffers from certain defects. The separation of the legislature from the executive is not always desirable. There is always the possibility of deadlocks between the legislature and the executive. The executive may ask the legislature to enact certain legislation which is necessary to meet the needs of the country but the legislature may refuse to do so. The legislature may pass certain laws and the executive may not enforce them in the spirit in which they are passed and thereby completely frustrate the object of the legislation. Such deadlocks are not in the interest of the country. Dr. Finer rightly says that the framers of the American constitution "separated the executive sources of knowledge from the legislative centre of their application: severed their connection between those who ask for supplies and those who have the power to grant them; introduced the continuous possibility of contest between two legislative branches; created in each the necessity for separate leadership in their separate businesses; and made this leadership independent of the existence and functions of the executive." Professor C.A. Beard says that although the checks and balances in the United States were designed to promote over-all equilibrium, they "often operate rather to aggravate than to ameliorate the ill effects of separation, as for example, in the case of the Presidential veto and Senatorial Assent to treaties."

Another defect of the system is that it leads to irresponsibility. The executive is not responsible to the legislature and consequently can do whatever it pleases. No immediate action can be taken against it. The general elections may be far off and the people might forget by that time the misdeeds of the executive. Thus, there is no immediate and continuous responsibility of the executive to the legislature. Under the circumstances, the executive can afford to rule arbitrarily.

There is no flexibility under the presidential system. Even if an emergency demands a change in the executive, that is not possible. The president can continue in office even if he is not competent to meet the situation successfully. The country has to suffer till such time as the new elections take place. It is rightly pointed out that, death and impeachment apart, nothing can remove the American President before the expiry of the term of his office. "There is no elastic element, everything is rigid, specified, stated." Bagehot says: "You have bespoken your government in advance and whether it suits you or not, whether it works well or ill, whether it is what you want or not, by law you must keep it."

A presidential system is not self-corrective. As the executive does not sit in the legislature, there is no criticism of the executive as in parliamentary government and consequently it becomes blind to its misgivings and shortcomings.

As the legislature and the executive are independent of each other in a Presidential system, there is no guarantee that the legislature will be doing what the executive needs. The executive cannot initiate the necessary legislation in the legislature and see it through. This is particularly so when the head of the executive belongs to a political party which does not command a majority in the legislature. The result is that there is no coordination of political energy or responsibility and each branch has its own derivation of authority and its morsel of responsibility.

It is contended that the presidential form is not equal to the task of conducting a vigorous foreign policy. As the President has to rely upon the cooperation of a Congress which may be hostile to him, the foreign policy of the United States is slow-moving and uncertain. It is difficult to say how far the commitments of the executive will be honoured or rejected by the Congress.

Lord Bryce Says, "The parliamentary system has many advantages for countries of moderate size; the presidential, constructed for safety rather than for promptitude in action and not staking large issues on sudden decisions, is to be preferred for states of vast area and population such as the United States and Germany."

Bureaucratic Government

Dr. Garner says: "Strictly speaking, a bureaucratic government is one which is carried on largely by ministerial bureaux and in which important policies are determined and decisions rendered by the administrative chiefs of such bureaux. In a wider sense, it means any government the administrative functionaries of which are professionally trained for the public service and who generally enjoy permanency of tenure, promotion within the service being partly by seniority and partly by merit. A bureaucratic government implies the rule of the bureaucracy. It means that it is the civil servants who are all powerful in the state in the last analysis, it is their opinion that counts and decides the matter. Even in a popular government, the ministers become merely tools in the hands of the civil servants. In a despotic government, the despot and the bureaucracy work hand in glove. There existed bureaucracy of the true type in Prussia from 1720 to 1808. The bureaucracy is very strong in France even today. It is also becoming all powerful in India on account of the network of planning in the country.

It goes without saying that bureaucracy can certainly give efficiency. As certain officials spend their whole lives in particular departments, they come to have expert knowledge and that can certainly bring about efficiency. J.S. Mill says: "It accumulates experience, acquires well-tried and well-considered traditional maxims and makes provision for appropriate practical knowledge in those who have the actual conduct of affairs." In a bureaucratic government, there is a lot of discipline. There is also team-work. A tradition of efficiency develops in the country. However, the considered view of J.S. Mill was that the defects of bureaucracy were more than its merits. To quote him, "The disease which afflicts bureaucratic governments and of which they die, is routine. They perish by the mutability of their maxims and still more by the universal law that whatever becomes a routine loses its vital principle." He also pointed out that there was a tendency on the part of bureaucracy to become pedantocracy. The view of Rohmer is that bureaucracy is the only form of government for which the philosophers have not been able to find any defence or justification.

It is also pointed out that "the trained officials hate the untrained and rude public." Bureaucracy is apt to become a government of men rather than of laws. It results in excessive formalism and red-tapism. There is a lot of delay in its decisions. "The machinery moves at a speed the slowness of which tries the patience of everybody concerned, and not infrequently, years pass before the most trifling matters are finally disposed of."

A bureaucratic government is highly conservative. It is always guided by precedents and traditions and it is always afraid of adopting a new course of action. It is not bothered about the wishes of the people and no wonder there is general hatred for a bureaucratic government in all democracies. However, bureaucracy becomes indispensable whenever the activities of the government multiply and the work of the government becomes more and more complicated. In such a situation, it is only the bureaucrats who can handle the situation, with all the evils that come in its wake.

SUGGESTED READINGS

Adams, H.	:	*The Degradation of Democratic Dogma.*
Aiyar, S.P. and Usha Mehta (Ed.)	:	*Essays an Indian Federalism.*
Alien C.K.	:	*Democracy and the Individual.*
Appleby, P.H.	:	*Big Democracy*, 1945.
Ashok Chanda	:	*Federalism in India.*
Babbit, L.	:	*Democracy and Leadership.*
Bagehot, W.	:	*The English Constitution.*
Barker, F.	:	*Reflections on Government.*
Beard, C.A.	:	*American Government and Politics.*
Beni, Prasad	:	*The Democratic Process.*
Birch, A.H.	:	*Representative and Responsible Government.*
Blaich, T.P.	:	*The Challenge to Democracy.*
Brogan, D.W.	:	*The American Political System.*
Bryce, J.	:	*The American Commonwealth.*
Burns, C.D.	:	*The Merits and Demerits of Democracy.*
Burns, C.D.	:	*Democracy: Its Defects and Advantages.*
Burns, C.D.	:	*The Challenge to Democracy.*
Cobban, Alfred	:	*Dictatorship.*
Dealey, J.Q.	:	*The Stales and Government.*
Dewey, J.	:	*The Public and its Problems.*
Dicey, A.V.	:	*Introduction to the Study of the Law of the Constitution.*
Flazar, D.J.	:	*The American Partnership: Inter-governmental Co-operation in the Nineteenth Century United States.*
Faguent, F.	:	*The Cult of Incompetence.*
Finer, H.	:	*The Theory and Practice of Modern Government.*
Finer, H.	:	*Mussolini's Italy.*

Ford, G.S. : *Dictatorship in the Modern World.*
Ford, H.J. : *Representative Government.*
Friedrich, Carl J. : *Constitutional Government and Democracy.*
Garner, J.W. : *Political Science and Government.*
Greaves, H.R.G. : *The Foundations of Political Theory.*
Hall : *Popular Government.*
Hearnshaw, F.J.C. : *Democracy and Labour.*
Hearnshaw, F.J.C. : *Democracy at the Cross-roads.*
Hoover, C.B. : *Dictatorship and Democracies.*
Jennings, W.I. : *Cabinet Government.*
Kennedy, W.P.M. : *The Constitution of Canada.*
Laski, H.J. : *Parliamentary Government in England.*
Laski, H.J. : *Democracy in Crisis.*
Lecky : *Democracy and Liberty.*
Lindsay, A.D. : *The Modern Democratic State.*
Lindsay, A.D. : *Essentials of Democracy.*
Lindsay, A.D. : *I Believe in Democracy.*
Lindsay, A.D. : *The Modern Democratic State.*
Lipson, L. : *The Great Issues of Politics.*
Lowell, A.L. : *Government of England, Vol. II, Part III.*
MacIver, R.M. : *The Modern State.*
MacMahon, A.W. : *Federalism: Mature and Emergent.*
Maine, H. : *Popular Government.*
Mallock, W.H. : *Limits of Pure Democracy.*
Maritian, Jacques : *Man and the State.*
Maxey : *Political Philosophies.*
Mayo, H.B. : *An Introduction to Democratic Theory.*
Merriam, C.E. : *What is Democracy?*
Mill, J.S. : *Representative Government.*
Mogi, S. : *The Problem of Federalism. 2 Vols.*
Parkinson, N.C. : *The Evolution of Political Thought.*
Pink, M.A. : *Realist Looks at Democracy.*
Rappard, W.E. : *The Crisis of Democracy, 1938.*
Rockefeller, N.A. : *The Future of Federalism.*
Sait, E.M. : *Political Institutions, A Preface.*

Sait, E.M.	:	*Democracy.*
Sharma, B.M.	:	*Federal Polity.*
Sidgwick, H.	:	*Elements of Politics.*
Smith, T.V.	:	*The Democratic Way of Life.*
Stamps, Norman L.	:	*Why Democracies Fail?*
Stephen Fitzjames	:	*Liberty, Equality and Fraternity.*
Suzanne, L.	:	*The Secret of Democracy.*
Treitschke	:	*Politics.*
Wallas, G.	:	*Human Nature in Politics.*
Watkins, F.	:	*The Political Tradition of the West.*
Wells, H.G.	:	*Democracy under Revision.*
Wheare, K.C.	:	*Federal Government.*
Willoughby	:	*The Government of Modern States.*
Wilson, Woodrow	:	*Congressional Government.*
Wright, H.W.	:	*Standards of Democracy.*

CHAPTER

The Constitution of the State

Definition

Learning Objectives

- Definition
- Necessity of a Constitution
- Written and Unwritten Constitutions
- Merits and Demerits
- Flexible and Rigid Constitution
- Characteristics of Good Constitution
- How does a Constitution Develop?
- Suggested Readings

Every state has a constitution and that may be written or unwritten, rigid or flexible. The question is what is a constitution. According to Woolsey, a constitution is "the collection of principles according to which the powers of the government, rights of the governed and the relations between the two are adjusted." Aristotle says: "Constitution is the way of life the state has chosen for itself." Bouvier defines a constitution as "the fundamental law of a state, directing the principles upon which the government is founded and regulating the exercise of the sovereign powers, directing to what bodies or persons these powers shall be confined and the manner of their exercise." George Cornewell Lewis describes the constitution as "the arrangement and distribution of the sovereign power in the community or the form of government." Charles Borgeaud says: "A constitution is the fundamental law according to which the relations of individuals or moral persons to the community are determined. It may be a written instrument, a precise text or series of texts enacted at a given time by a sovereign power; or it may be the more or less definite result of a series of legislative acts, ordinances, judicial decisions, precedents and customs of diverse origin and of unequal value and importance." Sir James Macintosh says: "By the constitution of a state, I mean the body of those written or unwritten fundamental laws which regulate the most important rights of the higher magistrates and the most essential privileges of the subjects." Cooley J. defines a constitution as "the fundamental law of the state, containing the principles upon which government is founded, regulating the division of the sovereign powers and directing to what persons each of these powers is to be confined and the manner in which it is to be exercised." Jellinek defines a constitution as the body of "juridical rules which determine the supreme organs of the state, which prescribes their mode of creation, their mutual relation, their sphere of action and finally the fundamental place of each of them in their relation to the state." Miller J. says: "A Constitution in the American sense of the word is a written instrument by which the fundamental powers of the government are established, limited and defined and by which those powers are distributed among several departments for their more safe and useful exercise for the benefit of the body politic." Dr. Finer says: "The state is a human grouping in which rules a certain power relationship between its individuals and associated constituents. This power relationship is embodied in political institutions. The system of fundamental political institutions is the constitution." Lord Bryce defines the constitution as "the aggregate of laws and customs under which the life of the state goes on," or "the complex totality of laws embodying the principles and rules whereby the community is organised, governed and held together." Dr. Wheare defines a constitution as "that body of rules which regulates the ends for which and the organs through which governmental power is exercised." According to Gilchrist, a constitution consists of "that body of rules or laws, written or unwritten, which determine the organisation of government, the distribution of powers to the various organs of government and the general principles on which these powers are to be exercised."

Necessity of a Constitution

A constitution is necessary for a variety of reasons, *viz.,* to curb the powers of government by a fundamental law, to restrain the government on behalf of the individuals and limit the vagaries of present and future generations. Schulze says: "Every community entitled to the name of state must have a constitution, *i.e.*, a collection of norms by which the legal relations between the government and its subjects are determined and in accordance with which the power of the state is exercised. A state without a constitution is unthinkable." A similar view is held by Jellinek. He says that a constitution is a necessity and every state must and does in fact possess one. A constitution is necessary even in the case of despotism. A state without a constitution is not a state but a regime of anarchy.

Written and Unwritten Constitutions

Constitutions have been classified as written constitutions, unwritten constitutions, flexible constitutions and rigid constitutions. A written constitution is one in which most of the provisions are put down in one written document. Jameson says: "It is a work of conscious art and the result of a deliberate effort to lay down a body of fundamental principles under which a government shall be organised and conducted." A written constitution may be one single document having one date. Such is the case in India, Burma and the United States. It may be in a series of documents; this is the case with France, Austria, etc. Whenever there is a written constitution in a country, a distinction is made between constitutional law and the ordinary laws. There is a special procedure laid down for the amendment of the written constitution. The ordinary law can be enacted, modified and repealed by a simple process which is different from the one laid down in connection with the constitution.

According to Jameson, "An unwritten constitution is made up largely of customs and judicial decisions, the former more or less evanescent and intangible, since in a written form they exist only in the unofficial collections or commentaries of publicists or lawyers." Again, "it is a record by, more or less, competent observers of fundamental changes which have occurred in the structure, principles or guarantees of the constitution considered as a fact. These changes are not made, but work themselves out under the operation of determinate social and political forces. They do not evolve themselves *per saltum* as in written constitutions, but gradually and continuously. They who transcribe such a constitution merely watch, pen in hand, the play of the producing forces and note results as they are achieved. These results become parts of the constitution as a fact, and the delineation of them, made by the observer, a part of the unwritten constitution considered as an instrument of evidence." The best example of an unwritten constitution is that of England. About that constitution, Dr. Jennings says: "If the constitution consists of institutions and not of the paper that describes them, the British constitution has not been made but has grown and there is no paper." To quote the same author, "Formed to meet immediate requirements, they were adapted to exercise more extensive and sometimes different functions. From time to time political and economic circumstances have called for reforms. There has been a constant process of invention, reform and amended distribution of powers. The building has been constantly added to, patched, and partially reconstructed so that it has been removed from century to century; but it has never been razed to the ground and rebuilt on new foundations." An unwritten constitution is the child of wisdom and chance; it is the product of history. As pointed out by Sir James Macintosh, constitutions grow, instead of being made.

It is rightly pointed out that the distinction between a written constitution and unwritten one is more a matter of degree than of kind. Experience shows that every written constitution begins to develop an unwritten part in the form of conventions. This fact can be illustrated by referring to a large number of conventions in the American constitution. In the case of unwritten constitution like that of England, many written elements came into existence in the course of time and they became as much a part and parcel of the constitution as the unwritten element. A reference may be made in this connection to the Magna Carta, Bill of Rights, Petition of Rights, Act of Settlement, Parliament Act of 1911, Statute of Westminster (1931), judicial decisions, etc. A large number of decisions have been given in England on constitutional points and are a part of the constitution of England. That is the reason why Dr. Garner observes thus: "The classification, therefore, of constitutions as written and unwritten is not only confusing and unscientific, but it results in placing in the category of written constitutions some which contain a large element of custom and convention, and in the category of unwritten constitutions others which to a large extent have been reduced to written form. Thus the constitutions of Hungary and Italy are usually classified as written, when in reality they are so overlaid with custom and possess such a high degree of flexibility that they contain more elements of true resemblance to the British constitution than they do to the constitution of the United States." Dr. Leacock says: "The distinction between states with written and those with unwritten constitutions is an illusory basis of state division."

Merits and Demerits

The great merit of a written constitution is that it is very definite. The people can refer to a document which contains all the fundamental principles with regard to the structure and working of the government. It is easy for the masses to understand a written document. Moreover, as the powers of the various organs are clearly defined in the constitution, there are less chances of confusion and disputes. Even if a dispute arises, it can be referred to the judiciary, whose duty it is to decide it. Authoritative pronouncements by the judiciary must settle all the disputes among the various organs. There is some sort of sanctity attached to a written constitution and the people know full well how they are going to be governed. Written constitutions are usually stable and that obviates the fear of uncertainty.

The major defect of a written constitution is that it is liable to be rigid. It may not be easy to amend the constitution to suit the changed circumstances. The atmosphere in the country may be such as to make it difficult for the conventions to grow. In such circumstances, a written constitution may fail to keep itself in touch with the changing needs of society. In a written constitution, the judges become all powerful. Chief Justice Hughes says: "We are under the constitution but the constitution is what judges say it is." Lord Macaulay says: "The great cause of revolutions is this: that while nations move onward, constitutions stand still."

The great merit of an unwritten constitution is its flexibility. There is no necessity of breaking the constitution because it can be bent and adjusted to suit the changed circumstances. This is particularly so in times of war or emergency. Moreover, society keeps on changing and along with that the constitution also must grow. This is very easy in the case of unwritten constitution which can go on changing along with the social changes. In an unwritten constitution, it is easy to adjust the relations between the various organs of the government. Cooley, J. says: "Of all the constitutions which may come into existence for the government of the people, the most excellent is obviously that which is the natural outgrowth of the national life and which, having grown and expanded as the nation has matured, is likely at any particular time to express the prevailing sentiment regarding government and the accepted principles of civil and political liberty." Lord Bryce says: "They can be stretched or bent so as to meet emergencies without breaking their framework; and when the emergency has passed, they slip back into their old form like a tree whose outer branches have been pulled aside to let a vehicle pass."

One serious defect of an unwritten constitution is that it is vague and indefinite. The man in the street does not understand the constitutional system of the country. He cannot refer to any document in which he can find all that he requires to understand the structure of the government of his country. An unwritten constitution requires a very high degree of political consciousness among the people to understand its spirit, and ordinarily that is not easy to find. Lord Bryce rightly points out that an unwritten constitution is unstable and there is no guarantee of solidity and permanence. Everything is in a state of perpetual flux like the liver of Heraclitus into which a man cannot step twice. The constitution becomes the "plaything of the judicial tribunals" because in the "vast storehouse of literary matter out of which their provisions are to be gathered, it is easy to find or not to find that which one will." It is also contended that an unwritten constitution is not suited to democracy. The masses like something which is plain, simple and direct and such a thing is not to be found in an unwritten constitution.

Jameson, J., describes the relative merits of written and unwritten constitutions in these words: "Considering the excellences and defects of the two varieties of constitutions, it is not easy to strike a balance between them. For a community whose political training has been carried to a high degree of perfection, in my view, an unwritten constitution would, on the whole, be preferable. In that training two elements would be of vital consequence to the safety of the system; first, an accurate understanding of their political rights and duties, generally among the citizens; second sleepless vigilance to detect violations of the constitution, and the utmost promptness and energy to resist and punish them. Without either of these elements, the usurpations of public functionaries must bring the system to speedy ruin. But for a community whose training has been imperfect or which is subject to fits of political apathy alternating with those of intense zeal for reform, a written constitution is, doubtless, the better one. While less flexible to the pressure of the national will, and, therefore, liable in many of its provisions to become obsolete and oppressive, it is a formidable barrier against usurpation. Its provisions are so plain that he who transgresses them must generally do so intentionally and the fact must be so apparent that usurpation would in most cases not be ventured upon, as likely, to arouse a dangerous opposition. The superiority of such a constitution in the circumstances supposed follows from the fact that immobility, with its train of possible evils, is leas dangerous than movement that is ill-judged or unconstitutional."

Flexible and Rigid Constitution

Lord Bryce classifies constitutions as flexible and rigid. A flexible constitution is one which can be amended easily. In a country like England, the organ which passes the ordinary laws has also the power to pass constitutional laws. There is absolutely no distinction with regard to the procedure of passing ordinary and constitutional laws. The English constitution is so flexible that anything can be changed at any time to meet any emergency. Such a thing was done in 1940 when by a law of the British Parliament, the Government was given complete control over everything in England. The passing of that law did not take more than three hours in all. There is absolutely no restriction or hindrance in the way of the British Parliament to pass or amend any law of the country.

In the case of a rigid constitution, it is not easy to amend it. Very often, the organ which passes the ordinary laws is not empowered to pass constitutional laws. Special majorities are required to pass or amend the constitutional laws. In the case of United States, while the Congress can pass the ordinary laws by a simple majority, a special procedure has to be adopted in the case of constitutional laws. A constitutional amendment has to be passed by a two-thirds majority of the Congress and three-fourths of the state legislatures. The American Constitution is considered to be so very rigid that it has not been possible to amend it except at the time of some serious national crisis such as the Civil War in the country in the time of President Lincoln.

The great merit of a flexible constitution is that it can be changed according to the circumstances. A flexible constitution is or wooden and static. As society grows, the constitution can be so amended as to meet the new requirements. There is no necessity of any revolution as the constitutional law of the country can be changed peacefully. However, in a constitution is very flexible, there is a danger of instability. The constitution becomes a plaything in the hands of unscrupulous politicians and statesmen. They keep on changing it to suit their whims and vested interests. Such a constitution can create an atmosphere of uncertainty which is absolutely undesirable from the point of view of the progress of the country. If once the people lose their faith in their constitution, there is every possibility of confusion and chaos. What is required is that the constitution should be flexible but not very flexible. What is good in moderation becomes a calamity if done in excess. Moreover, the public opinion should put a check on the activities of the unscrupulous politicians and demand that the constitution be treated as a sacred document, always to be worshipped and to be touched only when the higher interests of the nation demand it.

The great merit of a rigid constitution is that it is definite, stable and certain. The people know the constitutional law of the country and they have no uncertainty with regard to its future. No unscrupulous politician or political party can change it overnight. The various interests in the country are well protected. There is an atmosphere of confidence and growth. There is no fear regarding the future. Even if things change, they take a lot of time to do so. A rigid constitution is absolutely essential in the case of a federation. In a federal system, there is a division of powers between the centre and the units and the units are determined to maintain their autonomy in their own sphere. They are not prepared to allow the federal authority to encroach upon their sphere of action. Such a thing is possible only in the case of a rigid constitution. The constitution must be such as cannot be changed without much difficulty. It is only then that the units can feel safe regarding their future.

About a rigid constitution, Mr. Justice Jackson of Supreme Court of the United States says: "The very purpose of a Bill of Rights was to withdraw certain subjects from the vicissitudes of political controversy, to place them beyond the reach of majorities and officials and establish them as legal principles to be applied by the courts." About the Weimar constitution of Germany, Max Radin says: "The heaping up of constitutional changes by simple votes, the Reichstag destroyed what Professor Lowenstein of Yale aptly calls 'the constitutional conscience' of the nation, and rendered far-reaching and revolutionary changes by ordinance and coup d'etat less shocking." The main difficulty of a rigid constitution is that it cannot be changed to adjust itself to the changed circumstances; it can be broken and not bent. As a rigid constitution cannot be changed to meet an emergency, the only alternative is to break it. In many cases, people have revolted and set aside a rigid constitution. About a rigid constitution, Dr. Garner says: "It is like a attempt to fit a garment to an individual without taking into consideration his future growth and changes in size." Gilchrist observes: "Progress demands a adaptability and flexibility and such adaptability and flexibility can ably be secured in countries with rigid constitutions by a sufficiently easy method of amendment."

Characteristics of Good Constitution

A good constitution must have certain qualities. It must be definite. It must be put down in black and white in a document so that everybody can know what the constitutional law of the country is. The language of the document must not be too technical. It should be possible for the people to understand it. It must not be either too brief or too comprehensive. If it is voluminous, it will become difficult for the people to understand it. It will leave less scope for the future generations to add to it to suit their needs. However, it must not be very brief. The gaps in the constitution are bound to result in as much mischief as the volume of the constitution. It should be "neither so rigid as to prevent change nor so flexible as to encourage tampering with basic principles." While the constitution should be stable and durable, it must not be very rigid. It must go on changing with the changing times and circumstances. A constitution should suit the social, economic and political needs of the people. Lord Brougham says: "Constitutions must grow if they are of any value; they have roots, they ripen, they endure...Those that are fashioned, resemble painted sticks, planted in the ground, as I have seen in other countries what are called trees of liberty. They strike no root, bear no fruit, swiftly decay and ere long perish."

About the Indian constitution, Prime Minister Jawaharlal Nehru observed thus in the Constituent Assembly: "While we want this constitution to be as solid and permanent as we can make it, there is no permanence in constitutions. There should be a certain flexibility. If you make anything rigid and permanent, you stop the nation's growth of a living, vital, organic people. In any event, we could not make this constitution so rigid that it cannot be adapted to changing conditions."

How does a Constitution Develop?

No constitution can be static. It has to change with the passage of time in order to adjust itself to the changing needs of the people. A constitution is merely a means to an end and that end is the good of the people. Thus, many methods are adopted to develop a constitution.

Experience shows that in every country certain conventions grow up with the passage of time. These conventions are found to be necessary to give flexibility to the dry bones of law as embodied in the constitution. Although these conventions are not written, they are considered as a part of the constitution by all and every effort is made to avoid their violation.

The constitution can also be amended by the process of judicial interpretation. The constitution of a country is what it is interpreted to be by the courts of the country. The articles of the constitution come to have only that meaning which is put on them by the highest court of the country. It is well known that the scope of the Fundamental Rights In India is only that which is determined by the decisions of the Supreme Court of India. It is up to the Supreme Court to put a liberal interpretation or a strict one. It is possible that the decisions of the courts may completely change the spirit of the constitution. Chief Justice Hughes says about the American constitution: "We are under the constitution but the constitution is what the judges say it is." Mr. Justice Frankfurter goes to the extent of saying that the "Supreme Court is the Constitution."

Probably the most important method of developing the constitution is by amendment. No constitution can be permanent. It cannot provide for all times to come. It is too much to expect that the framers of a constitution will be like prophets who can foresee the future and embody in the constitution all that the future generations will require. It is rightly stated that a "living political constitution must be Darwinian in structure and in practice." That is the reason why the Americans have more than 20 amendments of the Constitution. Likewise, there have been both major and minor amendments of the Indian constitution during the course of the few years that it has remained in force.

SUGGESTED READINGS

Amos : *Science of Politics.*

Borgeaud : *Adoption and Amendment of Constitutions.*

Boutmy : *Studies in Constitutional Law.*

Bryce. J : *Studies in History and Jurisprudence.*

Cooley : *Constitutional Limitations.*

Dicey, A.V. : *The Law of the Constitution.*

Finer, H. : *The Theory and Practice of Modern Government.*

Garner, J.W. : *Political Science and Government.*

Gilchrist, R.N. : *Principles of Political Science.*

Goodnow : *Principles of Constitutional Government.*

Headlam-Morley : *The New Democratic Constitutions of Europe.*

Jameson : *The Constitutional Convention.*

Kelsen, H. : *General Theory of Law and State.*
Lowell, A.L. : *Government and Parties in Continental Europe.*
Lowell, A.L. : *Government of England, Vol. I, Chapter I.*
Lipson, L. : *The Great Issues of Politics (1954).*
Marriott, J.A.R. : *The Mechanism of the Modern State.*
Mcllwain. C.H. : *Constitutionalism and the Changing World.*
Newmann, R.G. : *European and Comparative Government.*
Roucek, Huzar and others. : *Introduction to Political Science.*
Sidgwick, H. : *Elements of Politics.*
Strong, C.F. : *Modern Political Constitution.*
Tiedman : *The Unwritten Constitution.*
Wheare, K.C. : *Modern Constitutions.*
Willougboy, W.F : *Governments of Modern State, Chaps. VI-VII.*
Wilson, Woodrow : *Congressional Government.*

24

CHAPTER

Theory of Separation of Powers

The Theory of Separation of Powers

Learning Objectives

- The Theory of Separation of Powers
- Criticism
- Suggested Readings

The theory of separation of powers occupies a very important place in the study of political science. It is not only famous but also ancient. Aristotle made a distinction between the deliberative, magisterial and judicial powers. Although Aristotle found it easy to separate those powers in theory, those were actually exercised by the same persons in ancient Greece. Polybius and Cicero put emphasis on the importance of a "balanced equilibrium of powers." They found the monarchic, aristocratic and democratic elements embodied in the Consuls, the Senate and the popular Assembly respectively. Each part of the government acted as a check upon the others. The view of Bodin was that the executive and judicial powers must be separated. The prince should not administer justice himself and he should give that work to an independent tribunal.

Cromwell separated the executive from the legislative powers but he did not establish an independent judiciary. John Locke divided the activities of the government into legislative, executive and federative, but he made only a passing reference to the theory of separation of powers. His main contribution was that he insisted that the functions of legislation and execution must be separated. It was not wise to invest the makers of law with the duty of enforcing them. There was always the possibility that the makers of law might exempt themselves from the application of those laws or suit the laws to serve their own ends.

The classic exposition of the theory of separation of powers occurs in Montesquieu's "The Spirit of Laws" which was published in 1748. He emphasized the fact that there must be a separation of powers if liberty is to be safeguarded. The separation of powers and liberty go hand in hand.

The famous statement of Montesquieu is in these words: "When the legislative and executive powers are united in the same person, or in the same body of magistrates there can be no liberty; because apprehensions may arise lest the same monarch or senate should enact tyrannical laws, and execute them in tyrannical manner. Again, there is no liberty if the judiciary power be not separate from the legislative and executive. Were it joined with the legislative, the life and liberty of the subject would be exposed to arbitrary control for the judge would then be legislator. Were it joined to the executive power, the judge might behave with violence and oppression. There would be an end of everything, were the same man or the same body...to exercise those three powers, that of enacting laws, that of executing the public relations, and of trying the cases of individuals."

The view of Montesquieu was that the stability of the English Constitution was due to the fact that there was a separation of powers in that country. This conclusion he arrived at after paying a visit to England. However, it is admitted on all hands that the view of Montesquieu was not correct. It is true that the cabinet system had still not developed fully in England when Montesquieu visited that country, but there was no separation of powers in England at that time.

A similar view was expressed by Blackstone in his *Commentaries on the Laws of England.* Blackstone said: "Whenever the right of making and enforcing the Law is vested in the same man or one and the same body of men, there can be no public liberty. The magistrate may enact tyrannical laws and execute them in a tyrannical manner since he is possessed with all the power which he as legislator thinks proper to give himself. Where it (the judicial power) joined with the legislature, the life, liberty, and property of the subject would be in the hands of arbitrary judges whose decisions would be regulated only by their opinions and not by any fundamental principles of law which though legislators may depart from yet judges are bound to observe. Where it joined with the executive this union might be an over-balance of the legislature."

There is a difference of opinion among scholars whether Montesquieu stood for an absolute separation of powers or a limited separation of powers. One school of thought holds the view that Montesquieu stood for an absolute separation of powers so that each department was independent and supreme in its own sphere. The view of the other school of thought is that Montesquieu stood for a limited separation of powers. Dr. Finer says: "Montesquieu was searching for means to limit the Crown; to make a constitution; to build canals through which, but not over which, power should stream; to create intermediary bodies, to check and balance probable despotism and yet he did not wish to fly to the extreme of democracy." G.H. Sabine has summed up Montesquieu's position in these words: "Montesquieu did not really contemplate an absolute separation of the three powers; the legislature ought to meet at the call of the executive; the executive retains a veto on legislation; the legislature ought to exercise extraordinary judicial powers."

The theory of separation of powers had profound influence not only on political thought but also on the practice of governments. The fathers of the American constitution were affected by this theory. It was probably because of their belief in this theory that they chose the presidential form of government in which the executive and legislature are separate and independent. They provided for an independent President, an independent Congress and an independent Supreme Court and the election of the judges and the governors in the states. Similarly, the constitutions of many American States laid down that "the accumulation of all powers, legislative, executive and judicial, in the same hands, whether of a few or many, whether hereditary, self-appointed or elective, may be justly pronounced the very definition of tyranny." Dr. Finer says: "We shall never know whether the Fathers of the American Constitution established the separation of powers from the influence of the theory, or to accomplish the immediately practical task of safeguarding liberty and property." Dr. Finer further says that the American Constitution "was consciously and elaborately made an essay in the separation of powers and is today the most important polity in the world which operates, upon that principle." Professor Zink says: "But while an emergency may bring temporary coordination and the use of patronage can usually be counted upon to pave the way to some action, the national government is still torn to parts by the provision which the framers made for separation of powers." About the influence of Montesquieu on the framers of the American Constitution, Madison says that Montesquieu was "the oracle who is always consulted and cited in the subject." Madison further says: "The legislative department is everywhere extending the sphere of its activity and drawing all power into its impetuous vortex...... They seem never to have recollected the danger from legislative usurpation which by assembling all power in same hands, must lead to the same tyranny as is threatened by executive usurpations." About the constitution of the State of Virginia, Jefferson observed thus: "All the powers of government, legislative, executive and judiciary, result to the legislative body. The concentration of these in the same hands, is precisely the definition of despotic government. It will be no alleviation that these powers will be exercised by a plurality of hands, and not by a single one. One hundred and seventy-three despots would surely be as oppressive as one." In the French Declaration of Rights of Man of 1789, it is specifically stated that "every society in which the separation of powers is not determined has no constitution." The French Constitution of 1791 made the executive and the legislature independent of each other, and the judges elective and independent.

The French scholars like Duguit preferred to give a two-fold division of powers. According to them, judicial function is merely another aspect of the executive action. In recent times, other divisions have been attempted. Professor Dealey has divided these functions into executive, administration, law-making department, legal sovereign, judicial system, the electorate, etc. However, it is the advocates of the trinity theory who hold the field.

Criticism

If this theory had profound influence in the past, it has been severely criticised by many scholars. It is contended that the theory of separation of powers cannot be accepted literally. It is true only in part. The state is an organic whole and just as the various parts of the body depend upon one another, so are the various parts of the state machinery inter-related. It is impossible to divide the departments of the government into three well defined watertight compartments, one having nothing to do with the other. Montesquieu himself did not intend to advocate the complete separation of powers or departments as he has been done by his followers. Madison says that Montesquieu's theory means that where all the powers of one department are exercised by the same hands which possess the whole powers of another department, the fundamental principles of a free government are endangered.

No rigid separation of powers is possible in any form of government. A rigid separation must lead to in articulation and deadlocks. Montesquieu himself says: "These three powers should bring about a state of repose or inaction. But since by the necessary movement of things, they are obliged to move, they will be forced to move in concert." Unfortunately, Montesquieu does not define the necessary movements. However, American experience shows that it has moved the machinery of the government towards articulation and concentration rather than separation. Laski says: "In practice, moreover, it is impossible to maintain any rigorous separation. Legislatures could not properly fulfil their task unless they were able both to interfere in the execution of law, and also on occasions to overrule by statute the decisions by judges the results of which are widely felt to be unsatisfactory. An executive is bound, in applying the law, to clothe general principle in the garment of detail, and, in the modern state, this function covers so wide an ambit that it is often difficult to distinguish it from the work of the legislature. The judiciary, finally, which settles either the competence of the executive (in which case it determines the substance of the legislative will) or dispute between two citizens (in which case it extends the legal imperatives of a state to cover new ground or denies that the ground involved comes within the ambit of these imperatives) is in fact performing a function which is legislative in character."

J.S. Mill also points out that complete independence would result in frequent deadlocks because "each department acting in defence of its own powers would never lend its aid to the other and the consequent loss in efficiency would outweigh all the possible advantages arising from independence." Blackstone himself, while defending the separation of the three departments, admitted that their "total disjunction" would ultimately produce the same tyrannical effects as their complete union in the same hands.

Montesquieu insisted on the intimate relation between liberty and separation of powers. He observed; "From the very nature of things, power should be a check to power, if liberty or law itself is to endure." However, experience shows that there exists no such relation between the two. Although the American constitution is based on the theory of separation of powers, the executive did in 1917 what it pleased. No separation of powers could save the liberty of the American people. Although the cabinet system of government is the very negation of the theory of separation of powers, Englishmen enjoyed comparatively greater liberty during the two World Wars. It can safely be maintained that liberty does not depend upon the mechanical separation of powers but upon factors other than that. The people enjoy liberty if they mean to do so and are prepared to pay the price for it.

If we insist on the application of the theory literally, we are bound to suffer. Experience shows that the election of judges in the states of the United States has not worked satisfactorily. The individuals have been made to suffer in order to test a theory. It has been seen that the practising lawyers know more of law than the presiding judges. It is difficult to get justice under those conditions. Moreover, when the judges have to look to the votes of the people for being elected, they cannot be expected to be impartial.

The theory of separation of powers should not be taken to mean the equality of the three powers. Professor MacIver rightly says that the legislative function is logically supreme. Bluntschli says: "As the whole is more than any of its parts, so the legislative power is superior to all the other particular powers." The view of Woodrow Wilson is that "Government is not a body of blind forces; it is a body of men, with highly differentiated functions. Their cooperation is indispensable; their warfare fatal."

The growth of administrative law is opposed to the theory of separation of powers. Under this system, judicial powers are given to the executive officials to try the servants of the government when they have committed any wrong in their official capacity.

The separation of powers results in jealousy, suspicion and internal friction. Experience shows that whenever anybody is given certain powers, he exercises them to the utmost limit and does not allow others to exercise their powers. Dr. Finer rightly says that the theory of separation of powers throws "government into alternating conditions of coma and convulsion." Another writer says: "Separation of powers means confusion of powers." According to Sabine, Montesquieu "was guilty of extreme over-simplification...he united his theory to a hasty and superficial analysis of the constitutional principles of liberty."

The concept of a welfare state has added to the powers and prestige of the executive. Moreover, planning requires fusion and not separation of functions. The result is that "moulds are broken in which the thoughts of law, Montesquieu and Madison were cast and their contents have spilled together."

The growth of the powers of political parties is making the separation of powers meaningless. The party in power controls both the legislature and the executive. Barker says: "If the growth of the legislative organ in consequence of the development of the cabinet system was the notable feature of the eighteenth century, it may be said that the growth of the executive organ in consequence of the extension of rights and the corresponding extension of service which mostly fall to the lot of the executive, is the notable feature of the twentieth."

The theory of separation of powers is not to be found in authoritarian states. A Nazi writer says: "The separation of powers belongs to a political era in which political unity was reduced to a minimum in the interest of an autonomous bourgeois society. However, national and ethnic unity and oneness demand that all political powers be gathered in the hands of one leader." Vyshinsky, a former Foreign Minister of the Soviet Union, says: "From top to bottom, the Soviet social order is penetrated by the single general spirit of the oneness of authority of the toilers. The programme of the All Union Communist Party rejects the bourgeois principle of separation of powers."

The separation of powers describes "the concert of leadership in the government." It separates the executive from the legislature and thus the legislature cannot utilise the executive experience and knowledge. Dr. Finer says: "There is no co-ordination of political energy or responsibility, but each branch has its own derivation and its own morsel of responsibility." Responsibility cannot be fixed at one place. There is a confusion of power.

About the theory of separation of powers, Geoffrey Marshall says that it is rarely clear whether and in what sense, there is a separation of powers. The argument that legislative, executive and judicial powers are constitutionally vested in particular persons or bodies is inconclusive. It is not clear what it is that is separated as the notions of legislation, adjudication and execution have not proved capable of precise definition. The theory has been used to cover ideas of physical separation of powers, legal incompatibilities between roles of officers, differentiation of functions, isolation or immunity of agencies and mutual checking, supervision or policing of one branch by another. In considering the mixing of Governmental functions, different treatment has been given to the division between legislative and executive functions from that accorded to the division between the judicial and other two functions. The doctrine provides no guidance as to whether voluntary transfers or partial delegations of functions between branches of Government are legitimate. The principle of separation of powers is infected with so much imprecision and inconsistency that it may be counted little more than a jumbled portmanteau of arguments for policies which ought to be supported or rejected on other grounds.

If we study some of the important constitutions of the world, we come to the conclusion that there is no separation of powers as suggested by Montesquieu. The presidential system of the United States seems to be based upon the theory of separation of powers. The President is elected by the people and the Congress is also elected by the people. Neither is the President responsible to the Congress nor vice versa. However, while the judges of the Supreme Court of America are nominated by the President, their appointments have to be ratified by the Senate. In certain circumstances, the Senate may refuse to ratify the choice made by the President. The Congress cannot be dissolved by the President and the President cannot be outvoted by the Congress. The President remains President for four years and the members of the Senate sit for six years and those of the House of Representatives for two years. However, the growth of a strong party system in the United States has linked up both the executive and the legislature. The President has been given the power of making appointments but those have to be ratified by the Senate. There is the convention of Senatorial Courtesy which forces the President to appoint persons according to the wishes of the Senators from the particular state concerned. The President can make treaties but those have to be ratified by the Senate. However, the President can avoid this check by not entering into formal treaties but making agreements with the states concerned. The President can declare war but he can do so only if he has got the approval of both houses of the Congress. It is true that the Congress has the power to make laws but the President has also the power of vetoing them. It is true that the Congress can pass the same bill a second time and thereby pass the law over the veto of the President. The President also has the power of sending messages to the Congress and thereby he can influence the course of legislation in the legislature. Moreover, if the President belongs to the same party which has a majority in the Congress, he can get anything done through the legislature. The President possesses judicial powers in the form of his right of pardon and reprieve.

England has a parliamentary form of government and that is the negation of the separation of powers. There is the combination of the executive and the legislature. The ministers sit in the legislature and are its members. They are responsible to the legislature. They can be outvoted by Parliament and the Prime Minister can also get the House of Commons dissolved by requesting the King to do so. The Lord Chancellor of England is the President of the House of Lords and as such belongs to the legislature. As the head of the judiciary, he is a part of judiciary. As a member of the cabinet, he belongs to the executive. Thus, he belongs to all the three departments and does not seem to care at all for the theory of separation of powers. In England, the judges are nominated on the recommendations of the executive. The House of Lords is the highest court of appeal for England. This means that the legislature possesses judicial powers. The growth of administrative justice in England is also against the theory of separation of powers.

There is no separation of powers in India. We have adopted the parliamentary system of government on the British model. At the centre, the ministers belong to the majority party in parliament and they are also responsible to the Lok Sabha. The Lok Sabha can pass a vote of no confidence against them and can turn them out, but the Prime Minister can also ask the President to dissolve the House.

A similar system prevails in the states. The Governors of states are constitutional heads. The same is the case with the President of India. The real power rests in the hands of the ministers both at the centre and in the states. The judges of the Supreme Court and the High Courts are appointed by the executive and they hold office during good behaviour till they reach the age of superannuation.

The chief value of the theory of separation of powers lies in the emphasis it put on the independence of the judiciary. However, such an end can be achieved easily by guaranteeing to the judges security of tenure, liberal salaries which cannot be changed against their interests and their freedom from party alignments or control. Another value of the theory is the emphasis it puts on the principle that government must act according to well-established rules or laws. An arbitrary government is the very negation of good government. The theory does not allow the executive to interfere with the administration of justice. The theory served as a safeguard against the despotism of the kings at one time and despotism of parliament later on. The defect in the theory is that it was taken to extremes.

SUGGESTED READINGS

Barker, F.	:	*Principles of Social and Political Theory.*
Black, H.C.	:	*The Relation of the Executive Power to Legislation.*
Fairlie, J.A.	:	*The Separation of Powers.*
Finer, H.	:	*Theory and Practice of Modern Government.*
Garner, J.W.	:	*Political Science and Government.*
Garner, J.W.	:	*Introduction to Political Science.*
Gilchrist, R.N.	:	*Principles of Political Science.*
Lipson, L.	:	*The Federalist, Everyman's Library, Dent.*
MacIver, R.M.	:	*The Modern State.*
Marriott, J.A.R.	:	*The Mechanism of the Modern State.*
Montesquieu, C.	:	*Spirit of the Laws.*
Sabine, G.H.	:	*A History of Political Theory.*
Webb, Sidney and Beatrice	:	*A Constitution of the Socialist Commonwealth of Great Britain.*

CHAPTER

The Legislature

Burke defines a government as "a contrivance of human wisdom to provide for human wants. Government is the agency, machinery or the magistracy through which the will of the state is formulated, expressed and realised." Government is an organisation which gives command to the community, governs in the interest of the community and punishes those who disobey its commands. It is thus a commanding and a punishing body.

Learning Objectives

- Functions of Legislature
- Organisation of the Legislature
- Bicameral System
- Criticism of Bicameral System
- Unicameral System
- Comparative Merits
- Composition of Upper Houses
- Composition of Lower Houses
- Powers of the two Houses
- Direct Legislation
- Merits of Direct Legislation
- Demerits
- Suggested Readings

In every modern government, there are three organs and those are the legislature, the executive and the judiciary. The legislature makes laws, the judiciary interprets them and the executive enforces them. It is difficult to think of a government without these three organs. Out of these three, the legislature is the most important. The executive and the judicial departments cannot function without the legislature. It is only when a law has been made by a legislature that the question of interpreting or enforcing it arises. Professor R.N. Gilchrist has compared the relation of the three departments to the major and minor premises and conclusion of a syllogism. He says: "The legislative authority forms the major premises: the judiciary the minor; and the executive, the conclusion."

Functions of Legislature

The basic function of the legislature is to make laws. It can not only make laws but also amend and repeal them. The will of the people is expressed through the laws of the country. The life of the people is bound to be affected by the nature of the laws passed by the legislature. Every bill has to go through many stages before it is finally passed by the legislature. Some of these stages are the first reading, second reading, committee stage, report stage and third reading. The greatest emphasis has to be put on the law-making powers of the legislature. Only those bills can be passed which enjoy the support of a majority of the members of the legislature, who represent the people. This is the guarantee that no bill will be passed which goes against the interests of the people.

A legislature performs financial functions. It has control over the budget. No money can be spent and no tax can be levied without the approval of the legislature. It is by means of its control over the purse that the legislature controls the executive. Ordinarily, the lower house has more control over money bills than the upper house.

The legislature exercises control over the executive in many ways. In a parliamentary form of government; only those persons can form the ministry who enjoy the confidence of the legislature;

they have to resign as soon as they lose that confidence. Members of the legislature can ask questions and supplementary questions and thereby expose the misdeeds of the executive. They can move adjournment motions and cut motions. A vote of no-confidence can be passed by the legislature against the executive. The government can be censured by the members. The legislature can set up commissions of inquiry to examine the working of certain departments of the government. This is particularly so in the case of presidential form of government.

So great emphasis is put on the function of controlling the executive that many statesmen put it in the first category of the functions of a legislature. In the list of functions to be performed by Parliament, legislation was put as the last by Bagehot. However, Taylor does not agree with Bagehot. To quote him, "Indeed much of the force of the criticising power of the House is derived from this fact; that it is a body which can, by means of passing laws, do anything it likes." Prof. Laski does not share the view of Taylor. Açcording to him, the function of legislation is not the only function of Parliament. "Its real function is to watch the process of administration, to safeguard the liberties of private citizens."

The legislature has also judicial functions. Cases of impeachment are tried by the legislature. One house starts the proceedings and the other decides whether the person concerned is guilty or not. The American Senate sits as a court of impeachment for the trial of the President and Vice President, while the charges of impeachment are preferred by the House of Representatives. In India, either of the two houses at the Centre can prefer a charge for the impeachment of the President. If the charge is preferred by the Lok Sabha, it is investigated by the Rajya Sabha and vice versa. The House of Lords is the highest court of appeal in England.

In some countries, the legislatures are given the power to change or amend the constitution of the country. The Indian Parliament has the power to amend certain provisions of the Constitution by following a particular procedure. In England, there is no distinction between ordinary laws and constitutional laws and the same Parliament can pass or amend both ordinary and constitutional laws.

In some countries, the legislature acts as an electoral board. In Switzerland, the members of the plural executive are elected by the members of legislature. In France, the President is elected by the members of legislature. In India, the President is elected by the members of Parliament and the state legislatures.

There are certain other miscellaneous functions which are performed by the legislature. In the United States, the Senate shares with the President the power of making all federal appointments. All treaties negotiated and concluded by the President require to be ratified by a two-thirds majority of the Senate. The President cannot declare war without the approval of the Congress. Parliament in India has the power to move for the removal of the Judges of the Supreme Court and High Courts on the ground of proved misbehaviour and incapacity. In England, Judges can be removed on the presentation of the joint address of both Houses of Parliament to the King.

American legislators devote a lot of their time to secure information. That provides a foundation for an informed legislature which can act more intelligently on its legislative problems. Criticism in recent years of investigating committees in the United States has been directed primarily at the methods employed and objectives allegedly sought. Less criticism has been raised concerning the basic function of legislature to secure information as a part of legislative process.

A prominent function of the legislators in America, and to some degree in other countries, is to provide governmental services for the members of their district. This is not always performed by the legislature as a body, except when in the form of a private bill which requires joint action. More frequently, the function required is to serve or perhaps to mollify a constituent who complains of actions of the Government. Most of the requests demand a considerable portion of the American legislator's time or that of his staff. It is an outgrowth of the emphasis of the local rather than more general representation.

Legislatures also work as organs of inquest or inquiries. They appoint commissions of inquiry to collect information, receive memoranda, hear evidence and make recommendations on problems facing the country. These have been found to be very useful.

Organisation of the Legislature

Ordinarily, there are two houses of a legislature. In England, the two houses are the House of Commons and the House of Lords. Their names in India are Lok Sabha and Rajya Sabha at the Centre and Legislative Council and Legislative Assembly in the States. In the United States, the two houses of the Congress are known as the Senate and the House of Representatives. It is true that the bicameral system came into existence by sheer chance in England, but it has been found to be so very useful that it has been adopted practically everywhere in the world.

Bicameral System

The advocates of the bicameral system point out certain advantages of the system. A second chamber is a safeguard against the despotism of a single chamber. The very fact that there is a second chamber, has a healthy effect on the members of the legislature. They know that whatever they pass will require the approval of another house and that fact forces them to pass the bill in such a form that it is acceptable to the other house as well. This puts a psychological check which is all for the good. Judge Story points out that there is a constant tendency on the part of legislative bodies to overstep their proper boundaries, from passion, from ambition, from inadvertence, from the prevalence of faction or from the overwhelming influence of private interests. Under these circumstances, the effective barrier against oppression, whether accidental or intentional, is to "separate its operations, to balance interest against interest, ambition against ambition, the combinations and spirit of dominion of one body against the like combinations and spirit of another." Jefferson says: "The executive power in our government is not the only, perhaps not even the principal object of my solicitude. The tyranny of the legislature is really the danger most to be feared and will continue to be so for many years to come." According to Lord Bryce, "The necessity of two Chambers is based on the belief that the innate tendency of an assembly to become hateful, tyrannical and corrupt, needs to be checked by the co-existence of another house of equal authority." Sidgwick says that the danger of encroachments by the legislature on the functions of the executive is diminished by the existence of two legislative chambers. J.S. Mill points out that a majority in a single assembly, with no check but their own will, "easily becomes despotic and overweening, if released from the necessity of considering whether its acts will be concurred in by another constituted authority."

A second chamber puts a check on hasty, rash and ill-considered legislation. If there is only one house, any bill can be passed in a hurry even if the nation has to repent later on. However, if there are two houses, the bill has to be sent to the other house. The other house will choose its own time to discuss the bill. In this way, the intervention of the second chamber does not allow a bill to be passed in a hurried manner. A second chamber is an appeal from "Philip drunk to Philip sober." The view of Aristotle was that law should be "reason without passion." There is every likelihood of the members of the popular house to be emotional. If the bill has to be approved of by the other house, the possibility of hurry or passion or emotion is avoided. Chancellor Kent says: "One great object of the separation of the legislature into two houses acting separately and with coordinate power is to destroy the evil effects of sudden and strong excitement and of precipitate measures springing from passion, caprice, prejudice, personal influence and party intrigue, which have been found by sad experience to exercise a potent and dangerous sway in single assemblies." Lecky says: "There is certainly no proposition in politics more indubitable than that the attempt to govern a great heterogeneous empire simply by such an assembly must ultimately prove disastrous, and the necessity of a second chamber to exercise a controlling, modifying, retarding and steadying influence has acquired almost the position of an axiom." Bluntschli rightly says that four eyes see better than two, especially when a subject may be considered from different standpoints.

The popular house is the house of the people. It is elected on the basis of one man, one vote. The second chamber can be used to give special representation to minorities, classes and vested interests. The view of Lord Acton was that a bicameral legislature could provide adequate protection to the minorities and vested interests. Bluntschli says, "We cannot ignore the distinction between the aristocratic and democratic elements in the population of the state and allow one of these elements alone representation in the legislature without doing the other an injustice."

The existence of a second chamber saves a lot of time of the popular house. If there is only one legislative chamber, all work, whether important or unimportant, has to be done there. If there are two houses, non-controversial and unimportant bills can be discussed in the second chamber, and thus the time of the lower chamber can be usefully employed in other important matters.

A finished Act of Parliament must be perfect so far as its drafting is concerned. The obvious reason is that if there are mistakes in drafting, that might lead to litigation and also administrative difficulties. If there is a second chamber, it can point out and correct the mistakes in drafting and also clear what is not clear.

A second chamber is necessary in a federal form of government. One house represents the people in general and the other house can be used to give representation to the units of the federation. In the United States, the House of Representatives is the house of the people and the Senate is the house of states. That is the reason why every state, whether big or small, is given the right to send two members to the American Senate.

A bicameral legislature represents a correct barometer of public opinion. If there is one house of the legislature and the members are elected for many years, they may become out of tune with the public opinion outside. This defect can be removed if there are two houses elected at different times or for different terms. Such a thing happens in the United States where the Senators are elected for 6 years, one-third of them retiring after every two years and the House of Representatives elected for only two years. A similar thing happens in India where the members of Rajya Sabha are elected for 6 years, one-third of them retiring after every two years and the Lok Sabha is elected for 5 years. As the elections for the two Houses take place at different times, the people get an opportunity to express their opinion and thus the legislature comes to be in harmony with popular opinion.

It is contended that a bicameral legislature protects individual freedom. If liberty is to be real and lasting, political direction of authority should not be concentrated at one place. To quote Madison "In framing a government which is to be administered by men over men, the great difficulty lies in this: it must first enable the government to control the governed and in the second place oblige it to control itself."

A second chamber affords protection against the tyranny of the majority party. J.S. Mill says: "A majority in a single chamber, when it has assumed a permanent character and always assured of its victory in their own house, easily becomes despotic." If there is a second chamber, that acts "as a saucer into which the steaming hot bills of the lower house come for cooling." The existence of two houses promotes the independence of the executive. The two houses, attack each other and consequently the executive comes to have "a greater degree of freedom of action and responsibility." A second chamber can be used for the purpose of bringing into the legislature, men and women who are not prepared to take the trouble of fighting election. Such persons can be safely nominated as members of the second chamber and advantage can be taken of their experience and brilliance. Such a thing is not possible if there is only one house, elected on the basis of adult franchise.

A second chamber helps the consideration of a question from various points of view. To quote Bluntschli, "It is clear that four eyes see better than two, especially when a subject may be considered from different standpoints."

Sir J.A.R. Marriott says that the verdict of history is in favour of the bicameral system. To quote him, "Experience has been in favour of two chambers; and it is not wise to disregard the lessons of history." Dr. Leacock says: "The unicameral system has been tried and found wanting."

Criticism of Bicameral System

Bentham says: "If a second chamber disagrees with the popular house, it is mischievous and if it agrees, it is superfluous." It is no use having a mischievous chamber or a chamber without which a country can afford to live.

Abbe Sieyes writes: "The law is the will of the people; the people cannot have at the same time different wills on the same subject; therefore, the legislature which represents the people is to be one. Where there are two cambers discord and division will be inevitable and the will of the people will be paralysed by inaction." Hence, there is no necessity of having a second chamber.

The bicameral system is expensive. The members of the second chamber have to be paid. They have also to be provided with residential accommodation. A separate building is also required for their discussions. A lot of money may be spent at the time of their elections. All that can be saved by adopting a unicameral system.

A second chamber is not a revising chamber. It merely duplicates the work of the lower house. There are hundreds of members of a legislature and they are bound to take into consideration the various aspects of the legislation before them. Thus, there is no danger of the members ignoring anything while discussing the bill. As a matter of fact, the lower house is likely to act irresponsibly if there is a second chamber as well. It can take it for granted that if certain mistakes are left in the bill passed by it, these will be Hiked into by the other chamber. If there is only one chamber, that is bound to act more responsibly cautiously.

There is no danger of hasty legislation in the case of a unicameral system. Experience shows that before a bill is formulated and discussed in the legislature, there is a lot of discussion on the subject in the press and among the various interests likely to be affected by the proposed legislation. Sometimes, it takes years before a bill is introduced in the legislature.

Ordinarily, the second chamber is the stronghold of the vested interests who are always reactionary. That is bound to block the passage of progressive legislation demanded by the people. The will of the people must be allowed to prevail and consequently the second chamber is undesirable.

A second chamber is not necessary for a federal state. The result of the growth of the party system is that the upper house does not represent the units of the federation. The same party which puts up candidates for the lower house, also puts up candidates for the upper house. The party programme is the same in both cases. Under the circumstances, the upper house is not likely to show any special consideration for the interests of the units.

Professor Laski says: "It is better to have a single chamber government and throw the burden of control upon the electorate which chooses the chamber and the executive which directs its activities."

Unicameral System

The view of Bagehot was that with an ideal lower chamber "perfectly representing the nation, always moderate, never passionate, abounding in men of leisure, never omitting the slow and steady forms necessary to good consideration," an upper chamber is not necessary. In the eighteenth century and the early part of the nineteenth century, unicameral legislatures were favoured. Benjamin Franklin was in favour of one house. He compared a bicameral legislature to a cart with a horse hitched to each end, both pulling in opposite directions. On account of his influence, the legislature of Pennsylyania was constituted on the unicameral principle. There were many supporters of unicameral legislature in France at the time of the French Revolution. This principle was incorporated in the Constitution of 1791. Lamartine advocated the unicameral principle in 1848. The unicameral system was used in England during the Commonwealth period, countries like Portugal, Naples, Mexico, Bolivia, Ecuador and Peru tried it for some time but later on gave it up. The Spanish Constitution of 1931 provided for a single chamber.

In a unicameral system, there are greater chances of unity. There is no occasion for deadlocks, rivalries and conflicts between the two houses. A single house can do whatever it pleases without any let or hindrance from any quarter. This facilitates the smooth working of the legislative machinery and work can be done with speed. The will of the people prevails; there is no brake from any reactionary quarter. The unicameral system ensures a liberal and progressive government. A unicameral legislature is the mirror of the national mind as its members are elected directly by the people. As there is only one house, there is less expense, less money spent on elections, the payment of members and their housing accommodation.

However, there is the possibility of a single chamber acting tyrannically. There are greater chances of hasty legislation. There is more scope for passion and emotion. There is no scope for giving special representation to minorities and other interests which require protection. It will not be possible to nominate brilliant persons to the legislature in the absence of a second chamber and they may not be willing to take all the trouble of fighting an election. There will be a special difficulty in the case of federations. There will be no house to represent and safeguard the interests of the units. In short, the country will be deprived of all the advantages which it can derive by having a bicameral system.

About the unicameral system, Lecky says: "Of all the forms of government that are possible among mankind, I do not know any which is likely to be worse than the government of a single omnipotent democratic chamber. It is at least as susceptible as an individual despot to the temptations that grow out of the possession of an uncontrolled power, and it is likely to act with much less sense of responsibility and much real deliberation." Kent says: "No portion of the political history of mankind is more full of instructive lessons on this object, or contains more striking proof of the faction, instability, and misery of state under the dominion of a single unchecked assembly, than that of the Italian republic of the Middle Ages which arose in great numbers and with dazzling but transient splendour, in the interval between the fall of the western and of the eastern empire of the Romans. They were all alike, ill constituted with a single unbalanced assembly. They were alike miserable and all in ended similar disgrace."

Comparative Merits

The question is whether we should have one or two houses of the legislature. There can be no single answer to this question on account of the varying conditions. Any list of arguments for one device may be altered slightly and provides a point for the opposite position. Some of the views for unicameralism are that a single house permits speedy action, avoids obstruction of the will of the people as found in its most representative body, permits clarity of responsibility in cabinet government's legislative relationships, reduces duplication and confusion of responsibility within the legislative process, improves quality of the legislator through the absence of conflict for prestige and is also less expensive. Some of the arguments in favour of bicameralism are that two houses provide a check on his hasty legislation, allow representation of different groups in the respective houses, allow time for careful revision of legislation, provide for a special group that may advise the executive, allow better representation because the more numerous legislators permit different groups of a complex society to appear and help divide the work-load. These opposing views do not reveal all the detailed arguments which can be presented when these general positions are applied to specific circumstances. There are always those who have specific reason, often economic, for retaining the existing arrangement. This fact has been sufficient in the majority of instances to retain or re-establish the bicameral legislature. Some admit the faults of bicameralism only to suggest that these could be remedied be specific limited reforms. They consider unicameralism as too drastic a remedy. Those who are sympathetic with the typical conservatism of upper houses are reluctant to take chances with a single chamber even though it might truly represent the majority opinion. There is almost unanimity that unicameralism at the local level is desirable for the large as well as the small city. The more limited scope of functions to be treated and the belief that limitations imposed by superior Governments serve as an adequate check provide support for this opinion.

Composition of Upper Houses

There is no one principle which governs the composition of the upper houses in various countries. Some of them are constituted wholly or predominantly upon the hereditary principle, some of them are appointed by the executive for life or a term of years, some of them are elected directly on the basis of the same suffrage as the lower house, some of them are elected indirectly on popular suffrage, some of them are elected by the local legislatures or councils and some combine two or more of these methods of selection. The House of Lords is predominantly hereditary. The members of the Canadian Senate are nominated for life. The members of the Senates of the United States and Australia are directly elected by the people. The Upper Chamber of Denmark is indirectly elected. Before 1913, the Senators of the United States were indirectly elected. About the hereditary second chamber. Thomas Paine says: "The idea of hereditary legislators is as inconsistent as that of hereditary judges or hereditary wise man, and as ridiculous as a hereditary poet laureate." About the Canadian Senate, Dawson says: "Senatorship has invariably been regarded as the choicest plums in the patronage basket and they have been used without compunction as rewards for faithful party service." Professor Goldwin describes the Canadian Senate "as nearly a cipher as it is possible for an assembly legally invested with large powers to be." Sir George Foster writes thus about the Canadian Senate: "Who on the street asks to know what is the opinion of the Senate upon this or that question? Who in the press really takes any trouble to know whether the Senate has any ideas and if so, what they are upon any branch of legislative concern, or upon conditions which require the best and most united work of all in order to arrive at successful conclusion."

The Rajya Sabha in India is indirectly elected by the State legislatures. The indirect system is not favoured. Laski says that "Of all methods of maximising corruption, indirect election is the worst." Again, "If such a chamber is, at the time of its selection, hostile to the government of the day, it is destructive of the quality of the work: while it is favourable, it is favourable, superfluous."

Composition of Lower Houses

Generally, the lower houses all over the world are elected directly by the people. The qualifications, of the voters and the candidates who stand for election may vary from country to country, but the principle of election is followed everywhere. The life of the lower house is not uniform in all the countries. In some countries it is two years. In some, it is five years. It may be four years in some others. The view of Laski is that "the best period of power for a legislature seems to be not less than four, nor more than five years." Dr. Finer fixes it at four years. To quote him: "My judgement that a four years' term is a modern necessity is reinforced by reflection on the obvious mounting trend to national planning. A longer term than four years is inadvisable because the broader the activity of government, especially when it is (as much must be) still of an experimental nature, the more opportunities ought there to be for reference back to the citizens. The way back must be kept open. The more massive and complicated the administrative appuratus, the more ought it to be subjected to the periodical lashing waves of popular opinion."

It is highly suggested that the two legislative chambers must be based on different principles. The constituencies must be different. The membership qualifications should differ their methods of election or nomination should be different. The electorate for both of them should be separate. If the two houses are elected on the same principle, it is useless to have a second chamber. Leiber writes: "If the two houses were elected for the same period by the same electors, they would amount in practice to little more than two committees of the same house; but we want two bona fide different houses representing the impulses as well as the continuity the progress and the conservation, the onward zeal and the retentive clement, innovation and adhesion, which must ever form internal elements of all civilisation. One house, therefore, ought to be large; the other comparatively small, and elected and appointed for a longer time."

Powers of the two Houses

A study of the legislatures of the various countries shows that generally the lower house is stronger than the upper house. The House of Commons in England and Canada are stronger than House of Lords and the Senate in the two countries. Likewise, the Lok Sabha in India is stronger than the Rajya Sabha. The simple reason is that the lower house is a house of the people and consequently it must have more powers than the upper house. In most cases, the lower house has complete control over money bills. If the ministry is defeated in the lower house, it must resign. In other words, the will of the lower house is the deciding factor. The case is different in the United States where the second chamber has been made deliberately stronger than the lower house. It is interesting to find that a seat in the Senate is considered to be a promotion for a member of the House of Representatives. On the whole, however, the upper house is a secondary house and the lower house occupies a dominant position.

The differences in the powers of the two houses of a legislature depend upon the mode and composition of the Upper House. If the Upper House is hereditary or nominated, its powers are limited. On the other hand, if it is an elected house, it stands on a footing of equality with the lower house because it is as much backed by the public as the other house. The general trend in the world is that the lower house has become the predominant partner and in the case of a conflict between the two, the verdict of the lower house prevails. The case of the American Senate is different as it is as much elected by the people as the lower house. Wherever the two houses possess equal powers, much of the utility of a bicameral system is lost. There is merely a duplication of powers. As a general rule, the upper house is a revising chamber. It is intended to exercise a moderating influence on the radicalism of the lower house. It is to act as a brake but not too tight a brake. If the public opinion supports the stand taken by the upper house, the lower house is bound to submit. It is rightly said that the true function of the upper house is to *resist* but not to *persist*.

Experience shows that certain special powers have been given to the upper chambers. The House of Lords is the highest Court of Appeal in Great Britain but that is not true of the House of Commons. Likewise, the American Senate acts as a court for the trial of impeachment cases. Under the French Constitution of 1875, the President of France was given the power to dissolve the Chamber of Deputies with the consent of the Senate. The American Senate possesses certain executive powers such as the ratification of treaties and the approval of certain appointments.

Direct Legislation

There are two types of democracies direct and indirect. In the case of direct democracy, all the people assemble together and carry on the administration of the country. In an indirect or representative democracy the people elect their representatives and allow them to carry on the administration on their behalf. In modern times, representative democracy is the general rule and direct democracy is the exception. However, there are some countries where the people have a direct hand in the making of laws and this they do by mcans of initiative, referendum and town meeting.

Direct legislation is a special contribution of Swiss democracy. It is as old as Swiss history itself. It is still to be found in some of the Cantons but in others it has been replaced by referendum and initiative. In the United States referendum was generally used for the ratification of new constitutions and their amendments later on. It was in 1898 that their use was extended for legislative purposes also. Many American states have some form of referendum. The use of both referendum and initiative prevails at the local level. More than half the American states provide for statutory and constitutional initiative. The system of direct legislation has been introduced in many European countries during the 20th century. The Constitution of the Soviet Union provides for referendum on legislative measures on the initiative of the Presidium or on the demand of the Union Republic.

Initiative enables the people to put on the statute book even those laws which legislators are not prepared to initiate and pass. In this way, the people can enact their own ideas into laws. It is a creative institution in the sense that a law can be passed even if the legislature is opposed to it. All that is required is that a specified number of persons must take the initiative and then the process starts. Initiative is like "a sword with which it cuts the way for the enactment of its own ideas into law." Initiative is of two kinds: formulative and in general terms. When the initiative is in general terms. When the initiative is in general terms, it is the duty of the legislature to draw, consider and pass the law. In the case of a formulative initiative, the bill comes in a complete form from the people and it is the duty of the legislature to consider it in the form in which it has come from the people.

In Switzerland, the institution of initiative exists both at the centre and in the Cantons. For constitutional amendment, the petition has to be made by 50,000 citizens. There is no federal initiative for ordinary laws. In the case of Cantons, the initiative applies both to constitutional and ordinary laws. In the United States, there is provision for initiative for constitutional amendments in 14 states and for ordinary laws in 19 states.

Literally, the term "referendum" means "must be referred". The institution of referendum arms the people with a veto on the acts of the legislature. Even when a law has been passed by the legislature, it can be set aside by the people when it is referred to them for their approval. It is a negative institution. It enables the people to protect themselves against the trickery of the legislators; it is like "a shield with which the people ward off undesirable legislation."

Referendum is of two kinds, compulsory and optional. In the case of compulsory referendum, the law passed by the legislature does not become law unless and until it has been referred to the people and approved by them. In the case of optional or facultative referendum, it is not necessary that every law passed by the legislature must be referred to the people for their approval. A reference may be made to the people or may not be made to them. The bill is submitted to the vote of the people, if a demand is made to that effect by a specified numbers of voters. In Switzerland, a petition for optional referendum is required to be made by 30,000 citizens or the legislatures of 8 Cantons for ordinary laws, unless the Assembly declares the matter urgent. In Switzerland and Australia, all constitutional amendments are subject to compulsory referendum. In some Cantons of Switzerland, there is compulsory referendum even for ordinary laws.

In some Cantons of Switzerland and in some states of America, there is a provision for a general meeting of people of the town to pass laws. The meeting is called a town meeting.

Merits of Direct Legislation

The institutions of referendum and initiative emphasize the sovereignty of the people. Ordinarily, the people count only after many years when general elections are held. Under the system of direct legislation, they are invited to give their opinions on the legislation of the country from time to time. In this way, the real wishes of the people can be found out and we have a barometer of public opinion on any particular point. The law of the country comes to have a greater force on account of its approval by the people who are the ultimate fountain of power. Lord Bryce says: "Direct legislation helps the legislature to keep in, touch with the people at other times than at general elections and in some respects a better touch, for it gives the voters an opportunity of declaring their views on serious issues apart from the destructive or distorting influence of party spirit."

Direct legislation reduces the importance of political parties and discourages party spirit. Much power is not left in the hands of the legislators and they cannot be sure of the ultimate passage of the law. The people may refuse to approve the actions of their legislators.

The educative value of direct legislation cannot be overemphasized. The people are provided not only with the text of the laws on which they are required to vote but also with explanatory notes. Every effort is made to help the people to understand the pros and cons of the proposed legislation. They can be expected to take more interest in public affairs on account of their knowledge.

Direct legislation is the most effective method of resolving deadlocks between the two houses of the legislature. In Switzerland, where the executive has not been given any power of veto and both houses of the National Assembly have equal powers, direct legislation comes to their rescue. Lord Bryce says: "There must somewhere in every government be a power which can say the last word, can deliver a decision from which there is no appeal. In a democracy, it is only the people who can thus put an end to controversy."

As referendum protects the people against the legislature's sins of commission, the initiative is a remedy for their omissions. In the case of direct legislation, the people have the power to put on the statute book a law even in the teeth of opposition from the legislature. The will of the people is allowed to prevail. "Why should a body of persons chosen by the people use the powers against the people themselves, allowing only such proposals as take their fancy to pass through so that the people can deal with them?"

The system of initiative lessens the chances of political trouble in the country as the people are in a position to initiate legislation which otherwise would not have been initiated by the legislature and would thereby have created bitterness and heart-burning.

Another advantage is that the people are in a position to separate a particular law from the general programme of the party in power. What Happens at the time of elections is that every party puts forward its own programme before the people and the people vote for that party whose programme appears to be the most attractive. Even if the people vote for a particular party, that does not mean that they have approved of all the items in the programme of that party. That only means that at the time of election, they approved of most of the points in the programme of the party. If there were to be no direct legislation, the people will have to put up with all the laws passed by the majority party in pursuance of the programme approved of by them. However, in the case of direct legislation, the people are in a position to veto those laws which relate to that part of the party programme which they did not approve of. That is a very valuable advantage.

The process of direct legislation is conservative. Experience has shown that the people on the whole are more conservative than the legislators. The result is, that they refrain from making sweeping changes.

The institution of initiative emphasizes the idea of popular sovereignty. It cannot be said that the people rule themselves if they have to act through their representatives. An individual can express himself only by his own voice and vote. Very often, the members of the legislatures do what they are asked to do by the political parties to which they belong. They do not represent the real will of the people. While initiative gives the people the positive right to frame laws which they desire, referendum gives them the negative right to reject what they do not approve of. While referendum protects the people against the sins of commission of the legislature, initiative is a remedy for their omissions.

It has been found by experience that the members of the legislatures are often apathetic to the needs of the people and they lag behind the public opinion. They are very much worried by the anxiety to push through the legislature their party programme. The question is asked, "Why should a body of persons chosen by the people close the door against the people themselves allowing only such proposals as take fancy to pass through so that the people can deal with them?" A bill which is initiated by the people has greater sanctity than the bill introduced by a political party in the legislature.

The institution of initiative minimises the possibilities of political upheavals because there is no indefinite postponement of legislation which is considered essential by the people for their welfare. They can take action whenever they consider the same to be essential.

Demerits

Direct legislation weakens the sense of responsibility of the legislators. This is due to the fact that the legislators never forget that they are not the ultimate authority to pass laws. They feel that if any mistake is left in a law passed by them, it can be rectified by the people. The legislators may be disposed to pass measures which their judgment disapproves, counting on the people to reject them, or may fear to pass laws lest they should be defeated by popular vote. If the people can put the blame on the legislature for having passed a foolish law, the legislators can also say in defence that it could have been rejected by the All-Wise People. Obviously such a state of affairs creates a division of responsibility which is suicidal for efficient working.

Modern legislation is becoming more and more complicated and technical and the result is that it is not possible for the people to understand all its implications. In spite of all their care and devotion to public duties, the people "have not and cannot have the knowledge needed to enable them to judge, nor can the pamphlets distributed and speeches made by the supporters and opponents of the measure convey to them the requisite knowledge. How can a peasant of Solouthurn in a lovely valley of the Jura form an opinion on the appropriations in a financial bill? Is the object a laudable one? Is it worth the money proposed to be allotted? Can the public treasury afford the expenditure?"

Experience shows that the people do not show much interest in direct legislation. It must be inconvenient for them to study all the literature on the proposed laws and then to take the trouble of going to the polling station on many occasions. It is bound to result in what is called "electoral fatigue."

The method adopted for discovering the will of the people is not a proper one. The voters are merely asked to say either "yes" or "no". This is a very unsatisfactory procedure. Every law is bound to have many provisions and it is impossible to think that all of its provisions will be approved of by the people. There is absolutely no scope for any discussion or amendment of any clause. Either the voters have to approve of the whole or reject the whole bill. This wholesale acceptance or rejection is the most unsatisfactory feature of direct legislation. Laski says: "The difficulty, in fact, which direct government invokes is the final difficulty that it is by its nature too crude an instrument to find room for the nice distinctions inherent in the art of government."

Many bills are delayed because they have to be referred to the people for their approval. Moreover, the people may not approve of them even if they are in the best interests of the country. The country may suffer on account of the conservative and reactionary attitude of the people in general towards certain problems.

The bills initiated by the people are very often "crude in conception, unskillful in form, marred by obscurities and omissions. "The language of the bills is defective and there is every possibility of litigation on account of conflicting interpretations. Lord Bryce says: "Sometimes, the prudence of the Cantonal Councils dissuading the people from the particular plan proposed and substituting a better one, averted unfortunate results while in the case of an ill-considered banking law, the federal authorities annulled the law as inconsistent with the Federal Constitution. Several times the people have shown their good sense in rejecting mischievous schemes proposed by this method."

Brilliant persons are not prepared to offer themselves as candidates for the legislature. They do not feel inspired to spend their time and money to become members of a body which has not the power to make laws which are considered to be necessary for the good of the people. If the laws passed by the legislature can be set aside by the people, brilliant persons would prefer to remain a part of the people rather than become legislators.

Droz says that direct legislation encourages demagogy and the growth of professional politicians who constantly try to spread discontent among the people.

Esmein points out that direct legislation is vicious, both in theory and practice. It is unsound in theory because it involves an appeal from knowledge to ignorance and from responsibility to irresponsibility. It is unsound in practice because it puts the final power in the hands of the illiterate people and thereby slows down the political, economic and social growth of the country. It is meaningless to ask a cowherd or a stable boy to give his opinion on a law concerning banking, about which he knows nothing. Neither does the man in the street understand the modern complicated legislation nor can he do so even if he tries; his capacity is limited.

A Swiss legislator says: "The referendum prevented what little good that we wish to do, but simply by standing as a warning before us, averted much evil. In spite of possible backward movements, it did not condemn democracy to a half, but has given steadiness to progress itself." The view of Dr. Finer is that direct legislation has done little good and its experience "would, perhaps, warn us not to accept direct legislation as a remedy for the defects of a parliamentary government. It improves nothing; neither the laws nor the people. It disturbs without providing solutions."

The institution of direct legislation is a difficult one and it requires certain qualities among the people concerned. It is true that political parties are necessary to run the democratic machinery but for the successful working of direct legislation, party sentiments must not dominate the minds of the citizens. Every proposal must be considered on its merits and voting must not be on party lines. Lord Bryce rightly points out that the Swiss voter, "always independent, is most independent when he has to review the action of his legislature." He attributes the success of the system in Switzerland to the historical antecedents of the Swiss people and also their long and continued practice of self-government. To quote him, "It is racy of the soil. There are institutions which like plants, flourish on their hillside and under their own sunshine." The people of Switzerland believe in tolerance and compromise. They are not extremists or believers in absolutes. There are no "talkers and fighters" in Switzerland. The Swiss consider politics as a game of veterans and they play the same in the spirit of a sportsman.

Even in Switzerland, there is no unanimity of opinion among scholars and statesmen regarding the value of direct legislation. There are some who praise it and there are others who condemn it. The critics point out that the institution of direct legislation requires the consultation of the people on matters which they do not understand and hence the consequences of such a system can well be imagined. They also refer to the delays involved in the working of referendum. It is contended that a lot of time of the people is wasted while participating in initiative and referendum. However, there are people who value the institution of direct legislation as a great privilege. They point out that fundamental changes shall have to be made in the whole Swiss administrative system if the institution of direct legislation is abolished. It appears that direct legislation has become a permanent institution is Switzerland.

The experience of countries other than Switzerland with regard to direct legislation is not very encouraging. It is maintained that direct legislation is not a remedy for the evils of parliamentary institutions. To quote Dr. Finer, "It improves nothing, neither the law nor the people. It disturbs without providing solution. It is an appeal from a court which has the makings and some of the equipment of a wise legislature, to all the crudities of a majority vote. Its operations leave stark naked the physical power of numbers, surely not a desirable thing."

SUGGESTED READINGS

Bryce, J. : Modern Democracies.

Finer, H. : Theory and Practice of Modern Government.

Garner, J.W. : Political Science and Government.

Gilchrist, R.N. : Principles of Political Science.

Harley : Second Chambers in Practice.

Laski, H.J. : A Grammar of Politics.

Lees–Smith, H.B. : Second Chamber in Theory and Practice.

Loewenstein, Karl : Political Power and the Government Process.

Lowell, A.L. : Government of England. Vol. I.

Luce, R. : Legislative Assemblies.

Macridis, Roy C, and Brown, Bernard E. : Comparative Politics : Notes and Readings.

Marriott, J.A.R. : Second Chambers, 1927.

Mill, J.S. : Representative Government.

Peaslee, Amos J. : Constitutions of the Nations.

Roche, John P., and Meerv S. Stedman, Jr. : The Dynamics of Democratic Government.

Sidgwick, H. : Elements of Politics.

Smith, T.V. : Legislative Way of Life.

Spender : One Chamber or two.

Temperley : Senates and Upper Chambers.

Willoughby, W.P. : Government of Modern State.

Wilson, Woodrow : Congressional Government.

26 CHAPTER

Problems Relating to Voting and Representation

Learning Objectives

- Theories of Franchise
- Optional or Compulsory Voting
- Plural and Weighted Voting
- Educational Qualification
- Property Qualification
- Excluded Classes
- Universal Suffrage
- Women Suffrage
- Joint Electorate and Communal Electorates
- Public Voting and Secret Ballot
- Bye-elections
- Single and Multiple Member Constituency
- Direct Elections
- Indirect Elections
- Annual Elections
- Types of Representatives
- Qualifications of Representative
- Territorial and Functional Representation
- Proportional Representation
- Merits of Proportional Representation
- Demerits
- Minority Representation
- Suggested Readings

The right to vote is a very precious right in a democratic set-up. It is this right which enables the people to have a government of their own choice. Without such a right, the people are bound to be helpless and democracy loses all its meaning.

Theories of Franchise

There are two schools of thought with regard to the nature of the right to vote. The view of one school is that it is a natural and inherent right to every citizen who is otherwise not disqualified on account of his conduct or physical unfitness. This right belongs to him by virtue of his membership of the state. Such a view dominated the political thought of the United States and France during the later, half of the eighteenth century. The view of Montesquieu was that all the inhabitants ought to have the right of voting at the election of representatives, except such as are in so mean a situation as to be deemed to have no will of their own. Rousseau stood for the sovereignty of the people and the right of voting followed as a logical corollary. The view of Robespierre was that sovereignty resided in the people and everybody must have the right to vote and the right to participate in the making of the laws.

The view of the other school is that the right to vote is rather a public office or function conferred upon the citizen for reasons of social expediency. It is not a natural right which belongs to all without distinction. The right to vote is a privilege but there is a difference of opinion whether it is a moral duty or a legal obligation. The view of Jameson is that suffrage "is not a right at all; it is a duty, a trust enjoined upon or committed to some citizens and not to others." In the case of Anderson *vs.* Baker, the Supreme Court of Maryland observed: "The right of suffrage is not an original, indefeasible right, even in the most free of republican governments; but every civilised society has uniformly fixed, modified or regulated it for itself, according to its own free will and pleasure."

The view of Duguit is that suffrage is at the same time a right and an office. The right is the right to be recognised as a citizen. That right carries with it the power to vote. The function implies the competence conferred upon a certain individual, invested with the quality of a citizen to exercise a certain public activity which calls him to vote. Malberg says that suffrage is both an individual right and a state office. "It is a right in so far as it belongs to the individual to exercise it. It is an office when it is viewed from the standpoint of the effects produced by it." The view of Esmein is also similar.

Professor Shepard refers to three theories of suffrage. According to him, the primitive tribal theory prevailed in the city states. It regarded the right to vote as a necessary attribute of membership in the state. The feudal theory regarded suffrage as a vested right usually accompanying the ownership of land. The ethical theory regards suffrage as a necessary and essential means for the development of individual personality.

Optional or Compulsory Voting

The question is whether voting should be optional or compulsory. In countries like India, Great Britain and the United States, the exercise of the right of voting is optional. If a voter does not go to the polling station to cast his vote, he is not fined or imprisoned. However, in countries like Belgium, voting is compulsory under the law. The Belgian Constitution of 1893 provided that every voter must vote. The penalties for failure to vote ranged from a reprimand or a fine of from one to three francs for a first offence to disfranchisement and disqualification from holding office for the fourth offence. Compulsory voting was introduced in Spain in 1907, in the Netherlands in 1917, in Rumania and Argentina in 1912 and in Czechoslovakia in 1920. There is also compulsory voting in some of the cantons in Switzerland. Professor Bartholemy made a careful study of the working of compulsory voting in Belgium and his conclusion was that it had proved an effective means of political education. Robson says that the wisdom of compulsory voting should be judged from its practical results and not from any theoretical consideration. What is to be seen is whether compulsory voting irritates the people and they regard it as a kind of tyranny or they obey it willingly, as is the case of Belgium.

Plural and Weighted Voting

The present view is that one man must have one vote and no man should be given more than one vote. However, there are some writers who advocate what is known as weighted voting. The view of Sidgwick was that if we want to lessen the evils of universal suffrage, we should give more weight to the votes of the more intelligent and more capable sections of the society. The view of Taine was that voices should be weighed and not counted. In the Belgian Constitution of 1893, a system was introduced by which every male citizen who was 25 years of age and who had resided for at least one year in the Commune, was given one vote. An additional vote was allowed to a citizen who had reached the age of 35 years, had a legitimate offspring and paid a tax of 5 francs to the state. This right was extended to every proprietor of 25 years of age owning land worth 2,000 francs. Two additional votes were allowed to every citizen of 25 years of age who possessed a diploma of higher learning or of secondary education or who held a public office or practised a private profession which required completion of secondary education. The only limitation was that no citizen was to have more than three votes in all.

J.S. Mill also supported weighted voting or plural voting as a "counterpoise to the numerical weight of the least educated." If universal suffrage was adopted in a country, it was desirable "to allow all graduates of universities, all persons who have passed creditably through the higher schools, all members of the liberal professions,, and perhaps some others who registered, specifically in, those characters, to give their votes as such in any constituency in which they choose to register; retaining in addition their votes as simple citizens in the localities in which they reside. All these suggestions are open to discussion as to details; but it is evident to me that in this direction lies the true ideal of representative government, and that to work toward it by the best practical contrivances which can be found is the path of real political improvement."

The chief difficulty in the way of weighted voting is how to find a just and practical standard or criterion by which the weight of different votes can be determined. In most cases, it is bound to be arbitrary. The possession of property is very often a matter of accident, and it is not just to base political rights on it. Weighted voting for the rich tends to establish a class government and government by the rich is the worst form of government. Esmein says that plural voting rests on a principle which is a logical contradiction. If its purpose is to counteract the evils incident to the incapacity of others, it would be logical to refuse entirely the right of voting to the latter. In admitting the latter to the suffrage, the law recognises in them a capacity. Maeterlinck says that plural voting is inconsistent with universal suffrage and has led to its logical annihilation.

Educational Qualification

The view of J.S. Mill was that a person who was not educated, had no right to vote. To quote him, "I regard it as wholly inadmissible that any person should participate in the suffrage without being able to read and write, and, I will add, perform the common operations of arithmetic... No one but those in *whom a priori* theory has silenced commonsense will maintain that power over others, and over the whole community, should be imparted to people who have not acquired the commonest and most essential requisites for taking care of themselves... It would be eminently desirable that other things besides reading, writing, and arithmetic should be made necessary to the suffrage; that some knowledge of the conformation of the earth, its natural and political divisions, the elements of general history and of the history and institutions of their own country, could be required of all electors." However, the view of Mill is not accepted today. It is found that even uneducated persons often exercise their right to vote in a more responsible manner than the educated voters. Education in itself has nothing which can make a person a better voter or a better citizen. Dr. Finer says: "It is a fundamental fallacy to argue that political behaviour has depended, depends now, or must depend upon instruction. It depends upon will, upon the passions...and men and women vote primarily for what they want and not from purely intellectual guidance."

Property Qualification

J.S. Mill was also a great supporter of property qualification of voters. His view was that the right of voting should be given only to those who possess property, because it is only those who have property can be said to have a stake in the country. To quote him, "It is important that the assembly which votes the taxes, either general or local, should be elected exclusively by those who pay something towards the taxes imposed. Those who pay no taxes, disposing by their votes of other people's money, have every motive to be lavish and none to economise as far as money matters are concerned, and any power of voting possessed by them is a violation of the fundamental principles, a severance of the powers of control from the interest in its beneficial exercise." This view is also not accepted in modern times. It is rightly pointed out that the right of voting is given to the individual and not to his property. Moreover, a person who pays taxes may be thoroughly selfish and he may act against the interests of the country. Even those who do not pay taxes have a right to protect themselves. Hence, everybody, whether he pays any tax or not and whether he has any property or not, has the right to vote.

Excluded Classes

Although the right of voting is to be given to all, there are certain persons living in a state who cannot be given that right. The right to vote is a political right which can be enjoyed only by citizens. Hence, aliens have no right to vote. There are certain age limits for the right to vote. It is only the adults who have the right to vote and not the minors. However, the age of voting varies. It is 21 years in India, the United States and England. It is 18 in Russia and 23 in Norway. Voters should also possess certain moral qualifications. The right of voting should not be given to those who are mentally unfit. It is on this ground that hardened criminals, bankrupts, lunatics, idiots and paupers are disfranchised.

Universal Suffrage

In all progressive countries, universal adult suffrage has been introduced. All men and women who have attained the age of majority are given the right to vote. The only limitation is that of age. The persons who are specifically excluded are the minors, lunatics, hardened criminals, idiots, bankrupts, paupers and aliens.

Many arguments are put forward in favour of universal adult franchise. It is contended that democracy is meaningless until all men and women are given the right to vote. Every individual must be able to decide who are going to be his rulers. Democracy cannot be government by the people unless all adults have the right to vote.

The right to vote is necessary for all sections of society as that alone can enable them to safeguard their special interests. Those interests may be communal or racial but there is no other way to protect them. Women can protect themselves only if they have the right to vote. The same applies to urban and rural interests. The labourers can get adequate protection only if they have the right to vote. A sound party system develops only if every man and woman has the right to vote. Adult franchise facilitates the development of parties with political and economic programmes.

The activities of the government directly affect the lives of the people and consequently every individual should be given a say in the affairs of the state. We must not ignore the principle: "What touches all should be decided by all."

Laski says: "To be free, a people must be able to choose its rulers at stated intervals simply because there is no other way in which their wants, as they experience those wants, will receive attention. Power that is unaccountable makes instruments of men who should be ends in themselves. Responsible government in a democracy lives always in the shadow of coming defeat; and this makes it eager to satisfy those with whose destinies it is charged." Another writer says: "Although the individuals who compose the association have the inalienable and sacred right to participate in the formation of the law, and if each could make his particular will known, the gathering of all these wills would invariably form the general will and this would be the final degree of political perfection. None can be deprived of this right upon any pretext or in any government." Critics of universal franchise point out that voting is not an inherent right which every individual must enjoy. As a matter of fact, it is a sort of special privilege which should be given to those who have a special aptitude to utilise it for the welfare of society. All individuals do not possess that aptitude and hence all need not be given the right to vote. On the whole, the masses are ignorant and illiterate. Even if they come to have some knowledge of reading, writing and arithmetic, that does not enable them to understand the political issues and express their considered views on them. The view of J.S. Mill was that only those persons should have the right to vote who possess some property, pay taxes and are educated. If that is not done, the rule of the ignorant masses must result in anarchy in the long run.

Women should be excluded from franchise as their interests are adequately safeguarded by their husbands, fathers and sons. According to some, only those persons should have the right to vote who possess property and pay taxes. Those who pay no taxes should have no right to vote. There should be no taxation without representation.

Lord Macaulay's view was that universal suffrage would lead to one "vast spoliation" and "a few half-naked fishermen would divide with the owls and foxes the ruins of the greatest of European cities." Lecky advocated restricted franchise based on education and property. He asked the question whether "the world should be governed by its ignorance or by its intelligence." The view of Sir James Stephen was that universal suffrage "tended to invert what I should have regarded as the true and natural relation between wisdom and folly." Sir Henry Maine says: "Universal suffrage which today excludes free trade from the United States would certainly have prohibited the spinning jenny and the powerloom. It would certainly have prohibited the threshing machine." The view of Emile Lavaleye is that the working of the parliamentary system of government would lead to "the loss of liberty, of order and of civilisation." Again, "Give the suffrage to the ignorant and they will fall into anarchy today and into despotism tomorrow."

Women Suffrage

For a long time, men alone were considered to be fit to enjoy the right of voting and this state of affairs continued up to the nineteenth century when writers like J.S. Mill advocated the cause of women and insisted that they also should be given the right to vote. To begin with, there was great opposition to this view, but later on the right to vote was given to women. This was done in England in 1918 and 1928. In India also, women enjoy the right of equal vote with men. Women are coming into limelight in every sphere of human activity and hence the right to vote cannot be refused to them.

It is rightly pointed out that there is absolutely no justification for refusing this all important right to women. The right to vote is given to individuals so that they may be able to develop their personalities and safeguard their interests. A woman has as good a personality as a man and consequently there is no ground for discrimination. Story says: "If it be said that all men have a natural, equal and inalienable right to vote because they are born free and equal; that they have common rights and interests entitled to protection and therefore an equal right to decide, either personally or by their chosen representatives, upon the laws and regulations which shall control, measure and sustain those rights and interests, what is there in those considerations which is not equally applicable to females as free, intelligent, moral beings entitled to equal rights and interests and protection and having a vital stake in all the regulations and laws of society?"

Men have no right to make laws for women. It is only the wearer who knows where the shoe pinches. It is women alone who can understand their difficulties. Men cannot put themselves into the place of women. Experience shows that in spite of their generosity, men have failed to pass all those laws which were in the interest of women. It is only after the enfranchisement of women and the sitting of their representatives in the legislatures that their interests have been adequately protected.

In a democracy, sovereignty must rest with all the people. It cannot be allowed to continue as the monopoly of men alone. Women are as much interested in good government as men and must have a share in the exercise of the sovereign powers.

Women are the cradle of civilisation. If they are given a share in politics, they are bound to become better citizens. As better citizens, they make their children also better citizens.

Women are physically weaker than men and consequently they stand in greater need of the protection of law than men. This they can get only if they have equal rights with men to fight for their interests.

The participation of women in politics will make domestic life richer and happier. Such women will be better companions of their husbands than is the case today. The importance of women will increase and men will gain much by mutual discussion. In modern times, women are playing an important part in society. They have proved their fitness to acquire the highest educational qualifications. They are occupying very high posts in government. They are doing their work excellently. Many of them are great educationists, scientists and politicians. Under the circumstances, there is no justification for excluding women from the right of voting.

Sidgwick says: "I see no adequate reason for refusing the franchise to any self-respecting adult, otherwise eligible, on the score of sex alone; and there is a danger of material injustice resulting from such refusal so long as the state leaves unmarried women and widows to struggle for a livelihood in the general industrial competition without any special privileges or protection." J.S. Mill says: "I consider it entirely irrelevant to political rights, as difference in the colour of the hair...If there be any difference, women require it more than men, since, being physically weaker, they are more dependent on law and society for protection." Again, "The worst that can be said is that they would vote as mere dependants at the bidding of their male relations. If it be so, let it be. If they think for themselves, great good will be done, and if they do not, no harm. It is a benefit to human beings to take off their fetters, even if they do not desire to walk. It would already be a great improvement in the moral position of women to be no longer declared by the law incapable of an opinion, and not entitled to a preference, respecting the most important concerns of humanity. There would be some benefit to them individually in having something to bestow which their male relatives cannot exact, and are yet desirous to have. It would also be no small thing that the husband would necessarily discuss the matter with his wife, and that the vote would not be his exclusive affair, but a joint concern."

The critics of women suffrage point out that the proper place for women is their home and it is not desirable to drag them into politics. "Woman was the ministering angel of home and maternity was her proper mission." Garner says: "The exactness of political life is inconsistent with the duties of child-bearing and the rearing of families."

If women are given the right to vote, there are bound to be differences in the family. A husband and wife may hold different views on political issues and that might embitter their mutual relations. The wife may belong to one party and her husband to another and that may destroy the harmony of family life.

Experience shows that women have usually been indifferent to politics. Even when they have been given the right to vote, they have shown no enthusiasm for it.

Women are already over-worked. Their duties and functions are innumerable. It is not desirable to add to their duties.

Dr. Finer says: "The wholesale entrance of women into politics must inevitably introduce complications, owing to the contact of different sexes. No one who has an experience of co-education and co-operation in industry can avoid the conclusion that the minds of men and women are often diverted from objective considerations and are seriously affected by considerations of courtesy and the personal beauty and desirability of one of the opposite sex whose fate or interest is involved. Boys and girls tell lies for each other, and turn in work in some one else's name, pugnacity is aroused in the presence of girls, and discipline is audaciously rejected because it is humiliating. Time is wasted in philandering and the mind loses itself in idle fancies. The business women are often shielded from responsibility because of their sex; they are appointed because they are pleasing; they are dismissed and passed over in promotion because they are ugly. Women become extraordinarily devoted to their work because they are devoted to a particular manager, and work badly for others in the firm. We all know such facts, and they should not escape us in public life. And although the vast majority of people in a representative assembly, its committees, and the ancillary organizations may be married, and therefore presumably (but only presumably) less susceptible to the charms and wiles of the opposite sex, everyday experience teaches us to expect certain results."

The question of women suffrage is merely an academic one. It is being realised all over the world that women should be given the right to vote on the same footing as men. In all progressive countries, women have equal political rights with men.

Joint Electorate and Communal Electorates

Under the system of joint electorates, all the voters belonging to a constituency vote together for a particular candidate. They are not given votes separately for communal representation. The person who is elected represents all the voters, irrespective of their religious differences. The system of joint electorates differs fundamentally from that of communal electorates which was introduced in India by British Government. To begin with, the British Government gave separate representation to the Muslims. After the lapse of some time, the Sikhs were given separate representation. Under the Government of India Act, 1935, provision was made for separate representation of Indian Christians, Anglo-Indians and Europeans also. Even the Scheduled Castes were put in a separate category. The net result of the introduction of communal representation in India was the establishment of Pakistan and the partition of India. It is for this reason that under the new Constitution of India, which came into force in 1950, joint electorates have been provided for. The object is to suppress the centrifugal tendencies in the country.

It cannot be denied that separate representation ultimately results in separate thinking and society is divided into hostile camps. Sectional interests dominate and the national interests are sacrificed. There can be no social harmony in such an atmosphere. The growth of the country is bound to be hindered.

Public Voting and Secret Ballot

Before the introduction of the secret ballot, a voter was required to go to the polling station and declare openly that he voted for a particular candidate. The voter could act according to his conscience but there was also the possibility of the opposite party giving him a good beating when he went back home. If certain interests were alienated on account of his public voting, they could harm him in many other ways even after elections. It was with a view to avoid the evils of public voting that the system of secret ballot was suggested and adopted. Under this system, a voter can vote for any candidate he pleases. While he can indicate his choice of a candidate, he is not required to write his name on the ballot paper. The secrecy of ballot is a great boon to democracy. There are greater chances of a voter voting independently and conscientiously. Nobody can say how a particular voter has voted and consequently the voter need not fear any evil consequences.

Bye-elections

At the time of general elections, all the seats in the legislature are filled up. However, there is a possibility that certain seats may fall vacant before the general elections are due on account of the death of certain members or their resignations. In such cases, bye-elections have to be ordered to fill the vacancies. Bye-elections serve a very useful purpose. They give an idea of the direction in which public opinion is moving and it is possible to surmise the results of the next general elections.

Single and Multiple Member Constituency

Ordinarily, the territory of a country is divided into as many constituencies as there are seats to be filled up and one member is returned from the constituency. Such a system exists in India, England and the United States and has obvious advantages. Each voter has one vote to give and he can be expected to do this intelligently and independently. Garner says that the single member constituency system "increases the responsibility of the voter in choosing his representative and at the same time, perhaps, intensifies the interest of the representative in and his responsibility to his constituency." The representative knows his constituency and he does all that he can to please the voters. As the constituency is small, less money is spent on elections. There is also less trouble as the number of voters is small.

One great disadvantage of single member constituency system is that it narrows the choice of elections and that can lead to the election of not only inferior but often corrupt representatives. Local interests dominate and the national interests are ignored. That is detrimental to national solidarity. Dr. Garner says: "The custom which regards the legislator as the representative of a particular locality is responsible for the election of men whose energies are likely to be engrossed with the pressure of petty local influences and, therefore, often deprives the state of the services of able statesmen who would be willing to serve in the legislature if could they be freed from such influences." Another defect is that in the hands of corrupt politicians, it can result in the evil of gerrymandering. The party in power cuts the constituencies in such a way that it secures the largest number of seats and loses the smallest number of votes.

In a multiple member constituency system, many members are elected from the same constituency and each voter has as many votes as there are seats to be filled. Such a system gives greater freedom in selecting candidates and thus superior type of men can be elected. The local interests do not dominate and the members can think in terms of the nation as a whole. Such a system also provides for the representation of minorities. Dr. Finer says: "The ideal system – that is to say, a system having exactness of representation as its only object – would be that in which the whole nation was taken as a single constituency, where lists of candidates for the whole number of members of the legislature could be presented and advocated by anybody. Such an arrangement, if it could be organised, would provide an exact reflection of majority and minority groups."

The defect of this system is that it leads to the multiplication of political parties and that confuses the electorate. That ultimately results in the instability of the government as no one political party has a majority in the legislature. Every ministry is bound to be a coalition ministry and such a ministry can fail at any time on any point. Moreover, as there are too many candidates from the same constituency, the voters cannot assess their qualifications and have to vote unintelligently. They vote not knowing for whom they are voting. There is no contact between the voters and the representatives. The representative does not know his voters and thus he is also not in a position to nurse his constituency. Moreover, there is no provision for bye-elections in such a system.

Experience shows that the people prefer the single member constituency system. However, the other system is also adopted in certain countries in order to provide for certain situations.

Direct Elections

There are two ways of electing representatives to the legislature. The voters may elect them directly or indirectly. In the case of direct elections, the voters elect the representatives themselves. In the case of indirect elections, the people elect the members of an electoral college and the latter elect a representative. However, it is to be noted that it is the system of direct elections which is becoming more and more popular in the world.

In the case of direct elections, the voters find greater interest in the politics of the country. A better sense of public spirit is created among them. They feel that they can effectively exercise their right to vote to send a representative to the legislature. That makes them active and alert.

The responsibility of the representative to the voters is direct. He knows that it is they who have elected him and it is they who can overthrow him next time if he fails to retain their goodwill. Direct responsibility has much to recommend itself. The voters can tell their representative that he must take into consideration their feelings. They can tell him plainly that if he does not act according to their wishes, there is every possibility of his being defeated next time. The representative can also understand the weight of contention of his constituents. It is obvious that the system of direct elections helps the people to have a real representative in the legislature.

The voters are directly approached by the various political parties at the time of elections. The various aspects of the national and local issues are put before the voters by the leaders to capture votes. An indirect result of all this campaigning is that the people acquire some knowledge of these issues. Their outlook is widened and this helps them to be better citizens.

There are less chances of corruption in a system of direct elections. That is partly due to the fact that the number of voters runs into millions and it is out of the question for any individual or any political party to bribe all the voters. The case is otherwise when the number of voters is very small, as in indirect elections.

However, there are certain defects of direct elections. As a rule, the masses do not have the intelligence to understand and appreciate the various aspects of the politics of the country. They cannot form their independent opinion and consequently their votes may not help to secure the election of the most competent persons. The masses may not understand their real interests and may be misguided by crooked politicians and cliques.

The leaders and the masses come into direct contact under a system of direct elections. That gives an opportunity to the demagogues to exploit the sentiments of the people. The people may be made to vote in the heat of the moment. Their actions may not be dictated by their better judgement.

The system of direct elections is very expensive. Millions of voters have to be approached by the political parties and their candidates. Sometimes the area is so large that it is difficult for the candidate to establish any direct contact with the voters. The ignorant masses may fail to appreciate the qualities of head and heart of intelligent and honest candidates. They may be deceived into voting in a particular way by clever and talkative politicians who may have no intention of fulfilling the promises made by them at the time of elections.

Indirect Elections

The great merit of indirect elections is that the dangers of the demagogues are avoided. The number of voters is very small and most of them are intelligent persons, and consequently it is difficult to appeal to their passions and sentiments. They can be expected to act intelligently and with a sense of responsibility. There are greater chances of their electing better representatives.

There is not much scope for election campaigns or party propaganda. There are only a few members of the electoral college and they are expected to vote according to their party affiliations. There is no scope for oratory. There is no scope for any election fights and lawlessness.

The system of indirect elections is useful for politically backward countries. As all the voters are not educated and intelligent, a few of them can be trusted to do the job which would otherwise have been done by the people at large.

Every indirect election implies two elections. One election is by the people themselves and the other election is by the representatives elected by them. That necessarily involves some delay which can serve a useful purpose. The members of the electoral college can act after cool consideration. The heat of the election is over and there is a better atmosphere for thinking dispassionately.

However, the system of indirect elections is absolutely undemocratic. The persons sitting in the legislature must be those who have been elected by the people themselves. If that is not done, there is no democracy in the real sense of the term. Even if the people have sent good persons to the college of electors, there is no guarantee that the ultimate choice of the electoral college will be an appropriate one. The people must not be forced to accept those persons in the legislatures in whom they have no confidence.

In the system of indirect elections, there is no direct responsibility of the representatives in the legislature to the people. They can with justice contend that they are not responsible to the people of any particular area. The voters of that area also cannot contend that the particular representative must act according to their wishes. They cannot say that they elected him as their representative in the legislature. Indirect responsibility is no responsibility. That responsibility alone is real which is direct and it is because of the realisation of this fact that provision is being made for direct elections everywhere in the world. The Senators in the United States were formerly indirectly elected but now the American Constitution has been amended to provide for their direct election.

The system of indirect elections damps the interest of the people in public affairs. They feel that their choice is not the final choice and consequently they do not feel any sense of responsibility. They feel more and more indifferent towards public affairs.

The chances of corruption and bribery are increased. As the number of voters is very small, there is a temptation to buy the votes. The funds of the political parties and the resources of the private individuals can manage this dirty game.

It is wrong to say that the evils of the party system are minimised under a system of indirect elections. The political parties are so highly organised in modern times that even in the case of indirect elections, the members vote according to the party affiliations.

The system of indirect elections is based on wrong assumptions. It is wrongly presumed that the primary voter is intelligent enough to select a good secondary voter but is not intelligent enough to elect a representative for the legislature directly. If he can do one thing intelligently, he can be trusted to do the other also equally intelligently.

Annual Elections

During the nineteenth century, there was a demand for annual elections of the members of the legislature. This was one of the demands of the Chartist Movement in England. It is true that if the representatives are elected for long periods, they lose touch with the people who elected them and they may be tempted even to go against the wishes of the voters. However, it is realised that annual elections will do more harm than good. Judge Story rightly says that the frequency of elections favours "rash innovations in domestic legislation and public policy and produces violent and sudden changes in the administration of public affairs founded upon temporary excitements and prejudices." Annual elections result in an "ever-recurring strain and excitement" and that is not a good thing at all. Elections are always expensive and no representative can be expected to spare money every year for his election. If there are elections every year, the people may get fed up with them and lose all interest in politics. They may leave everything in the hands of the political parties in disgust.

What is required is that the tenure of the representative should be neither too short nor too long. J.S. Mill says: "On the one hand, the member ought not to have so long a tenure of his seat as to make him forget his responsibility, take his duties easily, conduct them with a view to his own personal advantages, or neglect those full and public conferences with his constituents which whether he agrees or differs with them, are one of the benefits of the representative government. On the other hand, he should have such a term of office to look forward to as will enable him to be judged not by a single act, but by his course of action."

Types of Representatives

There are all kinds of representatives. They may be honest or dishonest, intelligent or stupid, learned or ignorant, patriots or subversive, energetic or lazy. Their jobs may be simple or complicated. They may be powerful or weak.

(1) There are a number of views regarding what a representative should be. One view is that he should be like a *mirror.* He should mirror or reflect the population he represents. He should be like the people. There should be rich and poor, lawyers and merchants, landlords and tenants, farmers and

urbanites in every legislature and they should be there in proportion to their ratio to the population of the state. If one-third of the population is agricultural, then approximately one-third of the members of the legislature should be farmers and the same applies to other professions of the people. Dr. W.I. Jennings says that there should be Tom, Dick and Harry in every Parliament. It is these people who will tell the government what it cannot do and what the people will not stand. When the representatives of this sort arrive at a consensus, they virtually do the same thing that the entire body politic would have done if it could have been brought together.

(2) The *chameleon type* is the representative who does what he asked to do by his constituents, nothing more, nothing less. He changes his colour as the chameleon to fit the place on which he stands. When he speaks, he merely phrasing the sentiments of his voters at home. When their sentiments change, he changes his course accordingly. He exercises little independent judgement except in the process of trying to find out what his constituents want. He never looks at any problem or piece of proposed legislation from any viewpoint other than those of his constituents. He is not only amenable to the wishes of his constituents, he has no wishes except their wishes. It is true that no legislator is completely like this, but there are some who approximate it and many people demand that their representatives must behave in this manner. Such a representative might more accurately be called a delegate. His duty is to all that lies in his power to further the interests of his voters He must try to secure all sort of concessions for them. The people have the right to send instructions to their representative and it is his duty to carry them out.

The critics of instructed representation point out that the representatives for the Central Legislature are not elected to represent the local interests which are better represented in the local bodies. The central legislature should represent the interests of the nation as a whole and not the local interests as such. Moreover, under the system of instructed representation, there is no place for able persons who cannot tolerate the idea of acting merely as the agents of the ignorant people. They will prefer to stay at home and direct the activities of the representatives rather than waste their time and energy in contesting elections. If we want intelligent persons to sit in the legislatures, we have to give them independence of action. It can be taken for granted that they will certainly take into consideration the interests of the people because their continuance in office depends upon their support.

Another practical difficulty is the manner in which instructions can be given to the representative. Will the representative get all the instructions at the beginning of a session, every month, every week or every day? Moreover, most of the voters are neither interested in the bills before the legislature nor competent to express their opinions on the subjects which are growing more and more technical and complicated every day. Ordinarily, a representative is more intelligent than most of his voters. It is as much his duty to give instructions as to receive them. A representative is not expected to be merely a cork on the ocean of public opinion.

Instructed representation will make the work of the legislature extremely difficult, every member seeking the mandate of the voters on every question that comes up for discussion. A lot of time will be wasted without much gain. The voters may be divided on a particular issue and may not be able to give any instruction.

Critics of instructed representation also point out that there are periodical elections for the legislature and there is no use in sending instructions to the representatives. The latter must be given the liberty to act. If the people do not approve of their actions, they can refuse to re-elect them at the time of the next elections.

(3) The *statesman-type* of representative is elected to represent the interests of the nation as a whole and it is his duty to see problems from national rather than from a provincial viewpoint. The views of Edmund Burke on this point are of great importance. Although he was returned to the British Parliament from Bristol, he maintained that he was not bound by the instructions of his electors. He admitted that he owed them his industry and judgement but he contended that he was not their

delegate. To quote him, "The representative should be a pillar of state, not a weather-cock on the top of the edifice exalted for his levity and versatility and of no use but to indicate the shiftings of every fashionable gate". He declared, "The Parliament is not a congress of ambassadors from different and hostile interests, which interests each must maintain, an agent and advocate against other agents and advocates. But Parliament is a deliberative assembly of one nation, with one interest, that of the whole, where not local purposes, not local prejudices ought to guide but the general good resulting from the general reason of the whole." He concluded by saying, "You choose a member indeed, but when you have chosen him, he is not a member of Bristol, but he is a member of Parliament." This does not mean that the representative does not care for his constituency. The fact is that it "ought to be the happiness and glory of a representative to live in the strictest union, the clearest correspondence and the most unreserved communication with his constituents. Their wishes ought to have great weight with him and their opinions high respect."

The view of Lord Brougham is that a member of Parliament "represents the people of the whole community, exercises his own judgement upon all measures, receives freely the communications of his constituents and is not bound by their instructions, though liable to be dismissed by not being re-elected in case the difference of opinion between him and them is irreconcilable and important." Bluntschli says that the representative is not bound to carry out the instructions of the voters and cannot be compelled to act in a particular way. St. Girons says that there is no place for instructions to the representative. Any candidate who promises to obey the orders or instructions of his constituency when those are contrary to his judgement and conscience, defeats his light to be a representative. The view of Esmein is that a representative is chosen to act freely and independently in the name of the people. The latter could neither recall him nor force him to act in a particular way. According to Malberg, there is no contract between the representative and the electorate by which the former is bound to carry out the instructions of the latter. Such a view is impossible because if he is merely an agent to represent the interests of a locality, he cannot represent the interests of the nation as a whole. Undoubtedly, some representatives today in most countries consider themselves (at least privately) to be of this type, although probably they would hesitate publicly to declare as such.

(4) Another type of representative is called the *party-member type* and most of the representatives are of this type today. This type of representative lives up to his party label in the legislature. He is asked to surrender some of his independence of judgement as well as his dependence upon the judgement of his constituents. He votes as his party leaders direct him to do. It is contended that the political party is the only real vehicle for the accomplishment of political programmes. Without party cohesiveness and cooperation, nothing could be accomplished in a legislature. Moreover, the average person votes for the party of his choice rather than for the individual. He votes for the Congress, Jan Sangh or the Communist Party. There is always some splitting of party tickets, but it is not the usual thing. It is contended that it is not right to be elected as a Congressman and then, once elected, to act independently and support a part or all of the programme of the other party. He must stay with his party as much as possible so that he can present a united front to the voters in his electoral appeal. Most political scientists agree that there is much to be said in support of the party-member type of representative.

Qualifications of Representative

The qualifications required for representatives are not the same in all countries. However, there are certain qualifications which are usually considered to be necessary.

It goes without saying that every representative must be a citizen of the state. He may be a citizen by birth or by naturalisation. No alien can be a representative. A person who does not belong to a country cannot be expected to keep in view the interests of that country while discharging his duties.

In some countries, it is required that the representatives must belong to the particular locality from which he is elected. The object of such a provision is that the representative will safeguard the interests of the locality which he represents. Moreover, as he himself belongs to that locality, he will be conversant with the needs of the people of that locality. However, such a provision does not exist in India or England. A person may belong to one state and may be returned to parliament or a state legislature from another state. Lord Bryce has criticised the system of residential qualification in these words: "The mischief is twofold. Inferior men are returned, because there are many parts of the country which do not produce statesmen, where nobody, or at any rate nobody desiring to enter Congress, is to be found above a moderate level of political capacity; and men of marked ability and zeal are prevented from forcing their way in. Such men are produced chiefly in the great cities of the older states. There is no room enough there for all of them, but no other doors to Congress are open. Boston, New York, Philadelphia, and Baltimore could furnish eight times as many good members as there are seats in these cities. As such men cannot enter from their place of residence, they do not enter at all, and the nation is deprived of the benefit of their services. Careers are moreover interrupted. A promising politician may lose his seat in his own district through some fluctuation of opinion or perhaps because he has offended the local wire-pullers by too much independence. Since he cannot find a seat elsewhere he is stranded; his political life is closed, while other youngmen inclined to independence take warning from his fate."

In practically all states, the representative is required to be of at least a certain age. Generally, the minimum age is between 21 and 25. Under the Government of India Act, 1935, the minimum age was 25 for the lower house and 30 for the upper house. Sometimes, a very high age is required for the second chamber. In the case of France, a Senator was required to be of at least 40 years of age.

In some countries, a representative is required to have property. The reason given for this requirement is that a person who has property is not worried about the problem of his livelihood. He can devote his time and attention to the work of the legislature. Moreover, such a person has a stake in the country and cannot be expected to be irresponsible or negligent in the performance of his duties. However, the general trend is towards the abolition of the requirement of property ownership. Such a demand is particularly made by the labour leaders who can offer only their services and nothing else. Moreover, the property qualification is the negation of a democratic ideal. It favours the rich against the poor and it is possible that the poor may be better than the rich in many cases.

Another requirement is that a representative must not hold an office of profit under the government. A representative is expected to be independent and he cannot be so if he is in the employment of the government. The result is that if a government employee wants to stand for election, he is required to resign before he is allowed to stand for election. If he fails to do so, his nomination papers are not considered to be proper and are rejected.

Every state requires that no candidate should resort to malpractices. If he is found to be guilty of a malpractice, his election is liable to be set aside. It is a very salutary provision. It goes without saying that the people who are the leaders of the country, and who profess to lay down the law of the country, must present themselves as an ideal before the people.

In some countries, certain religious qualifications may be prescribed for the members of the legislature. Sometimes, the requirement may be that a candidate professing a particular religion cannot be returned to the legislature. Sometimes, certain constituencies may be reserved for candidates belonging to a particular religion. However, the general trend is that no consideration should be given to the religion of a particular candidate or representative.

Certain writers demand that before a person is elected to a legislature, he should have served as a member of a local body for a specified number of years. Such a view is held by Professor Laski. The reason given in favour of his view is that before a person goes to the legislature, he must serve his period of apprenticeship in a local body. His character must be tested. If a person can prove his worth by serving a local body honestly and diligently, he can be expected to do the bigger job of serving a legislature with the same honesty and devotion. Such a requirement is to be found neither in India nor in England. However, it will be in the interest of all if such a provision is made in all countries.

Territorial and Functional Representation

The system of territorial representation prevails in most of the civilized parts of the world. According to this system, a country is divided into many territorial units and each such unit is allowed to send one or more representatives to the legislature. All those who reside in that locality or area, irrespective of their professions, vote together and elect someone who is expected to represent their interests.

However, in recent years, there has been a reaction against the system of territorial representation. It is contended that territorial representation is unreal and unsatisfactory and if representation is to serve any useful purpose, it must be on a functional basis. It is pointed out that the occupation which a person follows is much more important than the particular locality in which he may be living at any particular time. In one locality, there may be living together lawyers, professors, doctors, shop-keepers, carpenters, miners, drivers, coolies, etc. It is evident that there is not much in common in the interests of all these people. It is difficult to see how these diverse interests can be represented by any individual who follows one profession.

In order to remove the shortcomings of the present system, it is suggested that the only way out of the difficulty is that professional representation should be substituted for territorial representation. Doctors should vote for doctors, teachers for teachers, miners for miners and so on. Such a system was advocated by the Guild Socialists and also followed in the corporate state of Italy under Mussolini.

While nobody denies or minimises the importance of the economic factor in life, experience shows that professional representation will result in more troubles than it will be able to solve. There will be too many practical difficulties in the way of the enforcement of the system. The work of the preparation of the electoral lists will be extremely difficult and it will be impossible to conduct elections on a satisfactory basis. While one doctor may be working in a medical college, the second may work in a municipal hospital. One fails to understand how all these categories of doctors could be put in one electoral list. The interests of each of them are linked up with those working in the college, municipality, mine or those having private practice. Similarly, there is nothing in common between a teacher working in a municipality and a teacher working in a school run by the Arya Samaj. Their grades and standards are bound to be different. Thus, the practical problem will be whether a doctor working in a municipality should vote with the other employees of the municipality or with all the doctors in whatever line they are. If we follow the second course, the grouping will be absolutely arbitrary and the very object of professional or functional representation will be defeated.

As the number of hours of work of every labourer or worker is decreasing, it may be that he may take up another part-time job. Thus, a Professor of a medical college may have his independent practice at home. A private medical practitioner may be working as a medical officer in a college hostel. A lawyer may have his practice, be lecturing in a commercial college and also acting as a legal adviser to many companies dealing with diverse subjects. It is difficult to see how adequate and sufficient representation can be given to such a lawyer.

Another defect of the system is that it leads to class legislation. Functional representation puts unnecessary emphasis on the economic and professional aspects of life. It cannot be denied that man is not merely a carpenter, a doctor, a lawyer, a teacher or a miner. He is also a citizen, a father, a brother, etc. Representation has to be given to the whole of the personality of man and not merely to one aspect of his life. If an epidemic breaks out in one area, it makes no distinction between the people following different professions. The problems of sanitation, drainage, lighting, etc., are common problems. If a locality becomes unsafe because of bad characters, all the people belonging to that area are adversely affected. Problems of education of children are common to all the parents. It is difficult to see how professional representation can solve the various problems of the people.

Moreover, we want legislators to be men of liberal ideas and broad minds. It is difficult to see how that can be accomplished by a legislature consisting of miners, carpenters, drivers, hawkers, teachers, etc. There will be constant bickerings and faction-fights. The individuals sitting in the legislature will be bound to press the interests of their constituents only. The inevitable result would be that nobody will stand for the higher interests of the country as a whole. Such a legislature is not fit to formulate the foreign policy of the country or provide for its defence. It will not care to tackle the social and political problems of the country because the representatives may contend that they have no mandate for that purpose.

It is rightly pointed out that professional representation "would promote a struggle between different interests and forces, accentuate the feeling of antagonism between them and undermine the sound doctrine that a man's interest in the welfare of the group, class or profession to which he belongs, should be secondary to his interest in the welfare of the whole society."

Professor Esmein has described functional representation as "an illusion and false principle which would lead to struggles, confusion and even anarchy." Dr. Finer says that the principle of functional representation "does not proceed from the integration of the community, and then temper this with the representation of differences, but it proceeds at once from the postulate of disintegration into a large number of separate communities whose ultimate integration is thenceforward to be fabricated."

Professor Laski questions the very basis of functional representation in these words: "Why is a function, like that of medicine, for instance, properly relevant to the purpose of a legislative assembly? There is not a medical view of foreign policy, of the nationalisation of mines or of free trade." His conclusion is that "the territorial assembly built upon universal suffrage seems, therefore, the best method of making final decisions in the conflict of wills within the community." The interests of the various professions can be safeguarded if the legislature is made "to consult the organised wills of the community before it acted upon them."

The general view is against professional representation and in favour of territorial representation. "Weaver, miner, baker, teacher, each has his part to play in the commonwealth. But it would seem on the whole advisable that all these economic interests should combine to send to the Imperial Parliament a representative of the locality to which in common they belong, rather than by vocational representation to emphasize their class interests and exaggerate their economic antagonisms." It is also suggested that the purpose of vocational representation can be served by proportional representation in the form of single transferable vote. That proposal allows people to be represented according to their occupational interests if those are considered to be dominant over other interests. At the same time, that does not force the voters to be so represented if other interests are considered to be paramount.

Proportional Representation

The necessity for proportional representation has arisen on account of the defects in the majority-vote system. If there are 100 voters, the candidate getting 51 votes is elected and those who voted for the defeated candidate get no representation at all. If such a thing happens in all or most of the constituencies, the result is that while one party captures all the seats, the other party gets absolutely no representation. This is hardly fair but this is what actually happens in most of the countries where the system of majority vote prevails.

Things become much worse if there are three candidates standing from the same constituency. They may get 35, 33 and 32 votes respectively. Under the majority-vote-system, the candidate getting

35 votes will be declared elected although he represents merely a minority of the votes cast by the people and the defeated candidates together secured more votes than he has. In the general elections of November 1935, the pro-Baldwin group secured 430 seats in the House of Commons although their total voting strength in the country was 11,764,660. The parties opposed to the Baldwin ministry won 185 seats although they secured 10,071,993 votes. It is clear that the number of seats won by the Baldwin group was absolutely disproportionate to the number of votes secured by it as compared with opposition parties.

To remove this defect, the system of proportional representation has been put forward. Under this system, each party gets representation strictly in accordance with its voting strength. The legislature becomes the mirror of the public opinion outside. It can claim to give adequate representation to the different interests or shades of opinion among the public. J.S. Mill says: "In any really equal democracy, every or any section would be represented, not disproportionately, but proportionately. A majority of the electors would always have majority of the representatives; but a minority of the electors would always have a minority of the representatives. Man for man they would be as fully represented as the majority, and unless they are, there is not equal government, but a government of inequality and privilege – contrary to all just government, but above all, contrary to the principle of democracy which professes equality as its very roots and foundation."

Different methods of proportional representation have been advocated and adopted in certain countries. However, the most important of them are the Hare system and the List system. The Hare system is also known as the Andrae system, the preferential vote system or the single transferable vote system. Under this system each constituency returns a number of members to the legislature. The minimum is 3 and the maximum of 15 has been suggested by Lord Courtney. The quota required for the election of any candidate is fixed beforehand in accordance with the following formula:

Quota = Valid votes   Number of candidates +1   +1

Each voter is given as many votes as there are seats to be filled. However, he may exercise as many votes as he pleases. If there are nine seats to be filled, he may vote for all nine or only three or four. In every case, he is required to indicate his preference with numbers 1,2,3,4,5 and so on. The object of indicating the preference is that no vote of any elector is to be wasted. That must be utilised to return some candidate so that the voter feels that he is being represented by somebody in the legislature. At the first counting, only the first preferences are counted and if any candidate gets the required number of votes, he is declared elected. In case he secures votes in excess of the quota, the surplus votes are transferred to the second choices. In this way, the waste of votes is avoided. Votes are transferred not only from those candidates who have surplus votes but also from those candidates who have no chance of being elected at all on account of the very few first votes cast in their favour. Their ballot papers are also scrutinized to find out their second, third, fourth preference, etc., and the votes are transferred accordingly. This two-fold transference of votes is kept up among the contending candidates till all the seats are filled. The transferring of votes from the bottom takes place at a later stage, as that involves the exclusion of certain candidates.

According to the List system, each party is allowed to put up as many candidates as there are seats to be filled. The names of the candidates of each party are put down in a separate list. Each voter can cast his vote for any candidate he pleases. He can vote for three candidates from one list and two candidates from another list. There is absolutely no fetter on his discretion. Although he may vote for certain individuals whose names occur in the party list, those votes are to be counted as given not to those individuals but to the parties to which they belong. As in the case of the Hare system, the quota can be found by dividing the total number of votes cast by the number of seats to be filled. In order to find out how many seats are to be allotted to each party, the total number of votes secured by each party is divided by the quota. The votes are considered to be given to the party and the party alone is authorised to appoint the members of the legislature. The party enjoys absolute discretion in the matter. In case some person appointed by the party dies, the substitute is appointed by the party concerned. There are no bye-elections. The theory is that the party is entitled to a certain amount of representation in the legislature and hence it can appoint any person it pleases. The List system is a very simple one. The voter merely has to make a choice of the party he likes and can vote for all the candidates of the party.

Proportional representation has been adopted in many countries. In India, the members of Rajya Sabha are elected by the members of the State Legislative Assemblies in accordance with the system of proportional representation by means of single transferable vote. A similar system is used for the election of the President of India. The List system has been adopted with certain variations in France, Norway, Sweden, Denmark, Switzerland and Belgium.

There has been a persistent demand by the Opposition parties in India that the system of proportional representation be introduced for elections to Parliament and state legislatures. They maintain that in spite of their securing a majority of the votes polled in the general elections, they have not been able to come to power. The Congress Party which secured only about 45% of the total votes, has captured nearly two-thirds of the seats in Lok Sabha. The existing system suits the Congress Party which has turned down all demands for the formation of a National Government based on proportional representation. The Congress Party feels that the introduction of proportional representation is not in the interest of the country as a whole. That will result in the multiplication of political parties and that will not be conducive to a stable Government in the country.

Merits of Proportional Representation

Lord Acton says that the method of proportional representation "is profoundly democratic, for it increases the influence of thousands who would otherwise have no voice in the government; and it brings men more near an equality by so contriving that no vote shall be wasted and that every voter shall contribute to bring into Parliament a member of his own." According to J.S. Mill, proportional representation is "among the very greatest improvements yet made in the theory and practice of government." Its merit is that it secures representation even to the smallest minority. It gives every voter a real representative in whose choice he has a hand. It is "of all the modes in which a national representation can possibly be constituted" the one "which affords the best opportunity for the intellectual qualifications desirable in the representative. It tends to elevate the character of the legislative body by securing the election of more enlightened and distinguished representatives.

The List system has the merit of economy, simplicity, adaptability to large constituencies and its direct recognition of the party system. It secures the fairest and the most accurate distribution of seats among the various parties or groups within the state.

Proportional representation "recognises the nature of modern political parties as based not altogether on sectional divisions but on social and economic problems on national scope." There is no place for gerrymandering.

According to Keith, voters under proportional representation "will be able to vote for men of character and independence of judgement and they will not be forced to accept the policy of a particular party." Moreover, the "margin of unattached votes, the swing of which usually decides the fortune of elections, shall diminish to insignificance."

Demerits

Proportional representation is not an unmixed blessing. It involves the system of multiple-member constituencies. The number of candidates to be elected from one constituency is very large and that is bound to create confusion in the minds of the people, and under the circumstances they cannot be expected to vote intelligently.

Proportional representation inevitably leads to the multiplication of political parties. Even a small section of public opinion can manage to set up a new political party. Obviously, the multiplication of parties is not in the higher interests of the country. A few politicians may gain but the country as a whole is bound to suffer. Every government has to be a coalition government which is proverbially a weak government, and much cannot be expected from such a government. There is no security of tenure and there can be no continuity of policy. There is no vigour in administration; the ministers are worried more about their existence than about the completion of the work which can bring prosperity and strength to the country.

Proportional representation is expensive. Every constituency has to be a multiple-member constituency and hence the costs of elections are bound to mount up.

As a very large number of representatives are elected from the same constituency, no voter can say that he has voted for any particular representative. The representative who has been elected can also disown his direct responsibility to any particular section. The absence of direct responsibility is not a desirable thing.

There is no provision for bye-elections and consequently it is difficult to judge the trend of public opinion with the passage of time. There is every possibility of over-representation of small minorities in certain cases. The List system puts all the powers in the hands of the political parties and that can lead to a lot of corruption. In the case of multiple-member constituencies, there is always the possibility of jealousy among the various candidates belonging to the same political party.

According to Esmein, "To establish the system of proportional representation is to convert the remedy supplied by the bicameral system into a veritable poison; it is to organise disorder and emasculate the legislative power; it is to render cabinets unstable, destroy their homogeneity and make parliamentary government impossible." According to Sidgwick, "We want for legislatures men of some breadth of views and variety of ideas practised in comparing the different claims and endeavouring to find some compromise that will harmonize them as far as possible."

Dicey says that the mathematical representation of all sorts of opinion is highly objectionable. There may be an opinion which may be bad, foolish and even undesirable. Moreover, the more we make the system of elections complicated and difficult, the more we throw the voters into the clutches of the party agents and wirepullers.

The system of proportional representation "destroys any prospect of personal relation between the member and his constituents; he would simply become an item in a list, voted for almost entirely on party grounds." The election campaign becomes less intensive and more extensive. "It does not occupy itself with the cultivation of the individual voter by personal appeals, but in the institution of monster demonstrations like processions in which the mechanical apparatus for making a noise or creating a diversion is predominant.

We may conclude by saying that the system of proportional representation should be avoided as far as possible. However, if it has to be adopted, it must be done with a lot of caution and every effort should be made to avoid its shortcomings.

Minority Representation

According to Lecky, "The importance of providing some representation to minorities is extremely great. Where two-thirds of a constituency vote for one party and one-third for the other, it is obviously just that the majority should have two-thirds and the minority one-third of the representation. J.S. Mill says: "In any really equal democracy, every or any section would be represented not disproportionately but proportionately." It is obvious that if minorities are not given any representation, their interests are likely to suffer. In a perfect democracy, the legislature must be the mirror of public opinion outside but that is not possible if the minorities are given inadequate representation or no representation at all.

Minorities are of different kinds, *viz.*, racial, linguistic, national or religious. While in other countries, minorities are based on race, language or nationality, in India minorities are based on religion. It is the people professing different religions who have demanded and got the right of separate representation.

Many methods have been suggested for the representation of minorities. One method is proportional representation. Under this system, each party gets representation in the legislature in proportion to its voting strength among the people. Even the smallest section of the population gets its due representation in the legislature.

Another method is the limited vote system. Under this system, each constituency returns not one but many representatives and each voter is allowed only a limited number of votes. The result is that the minority can have the rest of the seats. For example, if from one constituency 5 members are to be returned, the voters may be allowed to vote for only 3 to 4 candidates. The result is that the minorities get two or one seat in the legislature. The defect of this system is that while the minority may get some representation, it may not get due representation according to its voting strength. Moreover, only the big minorities will be able to secure recognition and hence representation. This system has been tried in some American States and in Portugal.

Another method of minority representation is the cumulative vote system. Under this system, each voter is allowed to give all his votes to one candidate instead of distributing it among the different candidates. For example, there may be three seats to be filled and there may be two parties A and B having 3,000 and 2,000 votes respectively. Each voter has three votes. Under the majority vote system, A party will get all the seats because each of its three candidates will get 3,000 votes. However, if the cumulative vote system is adopted, B party can also get some representation. If each voter belonging to B party gives all the three votes to one candidate belonging to the party, the latter will get 6,000 votes and will thus be declared elected. The cumulative system is considered to be superior to the limited vote system because under this system even a small minority can have some representation by giving all the votes to one candidate. However, under this system, there can be much wastage of votes. The minority has to resort to a lot of guess work and arrange the accumulation of votes on certain candidates in such a way that there is less waste of votes and the party manages to capture more seats. Experience shows that in certain cases, a minority may get over-representation. However, whatever the defects, it enables the minority to get at least some representation and it is not completely at the mercy of the majority. The cumulative vote system prevails in the legislature of the state of Illinois in the United States.

Another method is the second ballot system. If there are more than two candidates from a constituency, the candidate elected may have secured only a minority of the total votes cast. The three candidates may have secured 4,000, 3000 and 2,000 votes respectively. It is true that under the majority vote system, the candidate who has secured 4,000 votes is declared elected, but he has not secured an absolute majority of all the votes cast. The other two candidates have collectively secured more votes than he has secured. Such a system is considered to be defective and hence the system of second ballot is suggested. What is done is that a second voting takes place between the two candidates securing the highest votes and the others are dropped. Whatsoever gets a majority of votes in the second ballot, is declared elected. Professor Gilchrist says: "The second ballot (there might be a third or further ballot where there are many seats) secures a more just reflection of the opinion of the electorate where three or more candidates seek election. The second ballot system demands a single member constituency and it does not secure proportional representation."

Another method is called the alternative or contingent vote system. Under this system, there is only one election and every voter is allowed to mark his preferences for the different candidates on the ballot paper. To begin with, the first preferences are counted and a candidate who gets an absolute majority is declared elected. The difficulty arises if no candidate gets an absolute majority.

In that case, the candidate who has got the least number of first preferences is dropped and his votes are distributed among the other candidates according to the second choices of the voters. Again, if a candidate secures an absolute majority, he is declared elected. If none gets absolute majority the process of dropping the candidate at the bottom is repeated and the votes are transferred according to the third choices of the voters. The process is continued till the candidate is elected with an absolute majority.

The British Government tried the experiment of communal representation in India with a view to give representation to different religious minorities. To begin with, the Muslims were given separate representation. After that, the Sikhs were given separate representation. Under the Government of India Act, 1935, separate representation was given to the Muslims, Sikhs, Scheduled Castes, Anglo-Indians and Indian Christians. It is only the followers of different religions who were required to vote in different constituencies reserved for the various religious minorities. One of the result of communal representation in India was the partitioning of the country in 1947.

It is admitted that the interests of the minorities must be safeguarded. A discontented minority is a source of danger to the country. However, minority representation has its own dangers. Experience shows that once a minority is always a minority. If separate representation is given to a minority, it loses its will to convert itself into a majority in the future and thus the problem of minorities becomes a permanent one. Minority representation leads to minority thinking. National interests are subordinated to sectional interests and that is hardly in the interests of the country as a whole.

SUGGESTED READINGS

Bonn : The Crises of European Democracy.
Bryce, J. : Modern Democracies.
Cole, G.D.H. : Guild Socialism Restated.
Commons, J.R. : Proportional Representation.
Dealey, J.Q. : Development of the State.
Dealey, J.Q. : The State Government.
Finer, H. : The Theory and Practice of Modern Government.
Garner, J.W. : Introduction to Political Science.
Garner, J.W. : Political Science and Government.
Gilchrist, R.N. : Principles of Political Science.
Hoag, C.G. and Hallet G.H. : Proportional Representation.
Humphreys, H. : Proportional Representation.
Lakemen, Enid, and James, D. : Voting in Democracies.
Laski, H.J. : A Grammar of Politics.
Lowell, A.L. : Public Opinion and Popular Government.
Marriott, J.A.R. : The Mechanism of the Modern State.
Mill, J.S. : Representative Government.
Ross, J.F.S. : Parliamentary Representation.
Seymour, C. and Fray, D.P. : How the World Votes.
Shepard, W.H. : Theory of the Nature of Suffrage.
Sidgwick, H. : Elements of Politics.
Smith, T.E. : Elections in Developing Countries.
Williams : The Reform of Political Representation.
Willoughby, W. : The Government of Modern States.

27

CHAPTER

The Executive

The term executive is derived from the word "execute". It "is the aggregate or totality of all the functionaries or agencies which are concerned with the execution of the will of the state as that will has been formulated and expressed in terms of law." Dr. Finer is of the opinion that "it is most useful to look upon the executive as the residuary legatee, for that explains the mixed nature of its functions and parts." It is well known that formerly all the powers in the state used to be in the hands of the executive. It was later on that the functions of the judiciary and the legislature were separated. The result is that the executive possesses today whatever has not been taken away by the other organs of the government.

Learning Objectives

- Kinds of Executive
- Requisites of a Properly Organised Executive
- Modes of Choice of Executive
- Term of Office
- Question of Re-eligibility
- Functions of the Executive
- Leadership of the Executive
- The Civil Service
- Duties of Civil Servants
- Functions of a Department
- Consultative and Advisory Bodies
- Economic Councils
- Suggested Readings

Kinds of Executive

(1) A distinction must be made between the various kinds of executives which are to be found in the world. The executive may be real or nominal. The American President is the real executive and he has actual control over the administration of the country. In the case of a country having a parliamentary form of government, there are two kinds of executive. While the Prime Minister and his colleagues are the real executive, the king or the President is the nominal and the Prime Minister and the members of his cabinet are the real executive. In India, the President is the nominal executive and the Prime Minister and his colleagues are the real executive. In the states in India, the Governor is the nominal executive and the Chief Ministers and their colleagues are the real executives.

(2) In the case of a single executive, the ultimate power in the state is in the hands of one person. In the case of a plural executive, the supreme executive authority lies in the hands of a group of persons. The American President is an example of the single executive and the Federal Council of Switzerland is an example of the plural executive. The President of the Federal Council is not the supreme authority and that vests in all the seven members of the Council. History also gives us certain examples of plural executive. In ancient Athens, the executive power was split up into fragments and divided among generals, archons, etc. The Roman constitution provided for two consuls such of whom was independent of the other. As a matter of fact, each could veto the action of the other. There were two kings in Sparta. The principle of plurality was extended to the organisation of subordinate offices. The French constitution of 1795 vested the executive authority in the Directory of five persons.

About the Directory, St. Girons says that it "was a sad government; it vacillated between feebleness and violence. The enfeeblement of the executive power led to the establishment of a turbulent and irresponsible assembly." In the Soviet Union, there is no formal presidency. The Presidium consists of 33 members and it is elected for four years by the Supreme Soviet. Stalin called the Presidium a collegiate President.

Many advantages have been claimed for the plural executive. It is contended that it furnishes greater guarantees against the dangers of executive abuse and oppression. It renders more difficult executive encroachment upon the sphere of the legislature and upon the liberties of the people in general. It is difficult to have a *coup d'etat* in a plural executive. It is likely to have a higher degree of ability and wisdom than is to be found in a single person. About the plural executive of Switzerland, Lord Brycesays that as it is a non-partisan body, it is able to influence the legislative assembly and adjust difficulties. It attracts and secures in the service of the nation the best talent of the country. It secures continuity of policy and permits traditions to be formed.

The great merit of a single executive is that it is based on the principle of unity which is very important in administration. According to Hamilton, "Energy in the executive is a leading characteristic in the definition of good government. It is essential to the protection of the community against attacks. It is not less essential to the study administration of the law ; to the protection of property against those irregular and high-minded combinations which sometimes interrupt the ordinary-course of justice; "to the security of liberty against the enterprises and assaults of ambition, of faction and of anarchy." Judge Story says: "The most distinguished statesmen have uniformly maintained the doctrine that there ought to be a single executive and a numerous legislature. They have considered energy as the most necessary qualification of the executive power and this is best attained by reposing it in a single hand.

(3) The cabinet form of government combines the single and plural executive. The Prime Minister follows the principle of single executive and his colleagues follow the principle of plural executive. The combination of the two is praised by the students of political science.

The Politburo or Presidium type of executive has developed in the Soviet Union and has been adopted by Yugoslavia, Poland, Czechoslovakia and China. It is a combination of formal governmental units and formal party structural units. The Politburo or Presidium is the top unit of the Communist Party and its members are the real policy-makers in Soviet Russia. The membership of the Politburo is composed of approximately 10 regular members with 4 or 5 alternates and is elected by the Central Committee of the party. The Soviet Constitution provides for a formal executive body comparable to the cabinet under the parliamentary system. The dominant role of the Communist Party in the Government has resulted in the development of absolute power for the Politburo. The supremacy of party over Government is guaranteed by the fact that the key personnel in the Council of Ministers are also members of the Politburo. The Council of Ministers is the executive agency of the Supreme Soviet, the highest legislative body in the Soviet Union. The Chairman of the Council of Ministers is also usually the Chairman of the Politburo. In addition to holding the principal positions in the party, the members of the Politburo hold many of the chief positions in the governmental structure as related to the chief legislative body, in industry, agriculture, trade unions and the armed forces. The result is that the Politburo has threads of control throughout this vast interlocking directorate which guide every aspect of Soviet lire. It is concerned with initiating policy, selecting key personnel, formulating legislative-executive decrees and supervising the execution of policy. The dominating force in the whole system is the will of Communist Party as expressed by its leader or leaders. As there are no opposition parties, this force is extremely significant. The Council of Ministers is actually not responsible to the legislature. Policies are formulated at the top and handed down to the lowest authority. As the Politburo represents the centre and actual location of power, the only check seems to be the failure of a major policy. The decision to change a policy is made by those who command the most power at the time.

The Fascist type of executive was established in Italy after Mussolini came to power in 1922. Under it, the forms of parliamentary government were maintained but all real power fell into the hands of Mussolini. Mussolini was the head of the Government and he was the Premier or President of the Fascist Grand Council, a body consisting of the leaders of the Fascist party, heads of the important departments of Government, the Presidents of the legislative bodies and other key leaders of state organised groups. All appointments to the Grand Council were made in secret on the recommendation of Mussolini. All substantive legislative power was in the hands of the executive. The power of the executive to issue decrees centralised all policy-formation in the hands of Mussolini. The decrees issued had the force of Jaw with or without the approval of parliament. As parliament was gradually replaced by the corporate organisation of society, the total control of the executive over all stages of policy-making became complete.

The Nazi executive was set up in Germany after Hitler came to power in 1933. The office of the President of the Reich was eliminated and all executive powerful in the hands of the Chancellor and Hitler himself was the Chancellor. Hitler was the Head of the Nazi Party and his ministers were chiefly high party officials. The Reichstag was a rubber stamp of the Nazi Party. It had no power to remove any minister or in any way put checks on his authority. An enabling law authorised Hitler and the members of his cabinet to make laws by executive decrees. All elements of society such as agriculture, industry, labour and the professions were tightly organised under state leadership. In order to consolidate control, important Nazi leaders were put in the chief positions in the Government organisation. Hitler was put forward as the embodiment of the German national spirit. He was regarded as the source of law. He was supreme in policy-making. The members of the Nazi Party who occupied all key positions in the Government, were under strict discipline and were responsible for supervising the execution of the policy handed down from the top. It was the duty of the party officials to act as special watchdogs and see to it that the policy of Hitler was strictly carried out. Those who failed to do so were promptly punished. The appointment and promotion of all officials had to be approved by the leader or his immediate subordinates. All party and governmental agencies of the executive were mobilized under Dr. Goebbels who was put incharge of the Propaganda Ministry. He effectively controlled the press and all other means of communication so that the Nazi policies and programmes could meet maximum support.

As regards the United Nations executive, it rests in the hands of the Secretary-General who is chosen for a term of 5 years by the Security Council and the General Assembly. As the chief executive of the United Nations, he acts in the most important area of international policy. He furnishes leadership on political issues. His action may mean the difference between peaceful negotiations and an outbreak of violence. His success depends on the timing, boldness, perseverance, initiative and ability to suggest satisfactory compromises. He is the liaison agent within the United Nations between the commissions and specialised agencies such as the International Labour Organisation, World Health Organization, United Nations Educational, Scientific and Cultural Organization, the General Assembly, the Security Council, the Economic and Social Council and the world public. He has his personal contacts with influential statesmen all over the world and that gives him a lot of prestige. His annual report to the General Assembly can be a constructive message in informing and influencing United Nations representatives and their governments. He also expresses his own views at the meeting of the General Assembly and the Security Council. In times of major crises, he can assume the role of a mediator. This was done by Trygve Lie on the occasion of the Berlin crisis between the Soviet Union and the United States. He has also the power to appoint the executive and administrative staff of the United Nations Secretariat. While making preparations for the meetings of the General Assembly and the Security Council he has the power to establish priority and to place items on the agenda. This authority is of very great importance. The forceful personalities of Trygve Lie and Dag Hammarskjold started a strong trend in the direction of a positive role for the, executive of the United Nations.

A distinction may be made between *political* and *permanent* executive. Political executive consists of those members of the executive who are the heads of the various departments but whose tenure of office is a temporary one. In a country like India, the political executive consists of the Prime Minister, the ministers and the parliamentary secretaries. They remain in office so long as their party has a majority in the legislature. They have to resign as soon as they are defeated. In the United States, the President is the political head. He is elected by the people for a period of four years. He has to go after that period unless he is re-elected. In Switzerland, the political executive is represented by the Federal Council. It is elected by the Federal Legislature. A political executive may be of the parliamentary type or presidential type. It may be a single executive or a plural executive. As regards the permanent executive, it consists of all those permanent and salaried officials and subordinates who carry on the day-to-day work of the administration. Their tenure of office is permanent and they are not affected by the ministerial changes. Most of them are recruited after a competitive examination. Their duty is to carry out the policy as laid down by the political executive even if they do not approve of the same.

Requisites of a Properly Organised Executive

(1) The first requisite which is accepted by all is the unity in the executive. Napoleon is said to have remarked that one bad general is better than two good ones. One of the causes of the failure of Aurangzeb was that he always put two persons in charge of an expedition. His object was that one would act as a check on the other. Actually what happened was that they hampered work and never succeeded in accomplishing what was given to them. There can never be any unity of purpose and promptness in action if there are many persons who have coordinate powers. The proper function of the executive is merely to carry out the will of the people as expressed by the legislature and for that work, unity is essential. Sometimes, certain matters of the executive have to be kept secret. That is not possible if there are many persons who have equal powers and they all have to share the secret. There is every possibility of its breaking out.

(2) Unity does not mean that the head of the executive cannot delegate his functions to his subordinates. He can appoint an executive council to help him in his work. However, if unity of action is to be maintained, he must have the final say in the matter. The working of the Regulating Act, 1773, showed that the position of the Governor-General became pitiable because he was bound to follow the majority decisions of his Council. It was because of that defect that later on the Governor-General was given the power to overrule his councillors and act according to his judgment. A similar power was given to the Secretary of State for India *vis-a-vis* his advisers or the members of the India Council.

(3) Another requisite for an efficient executive is that it should be sufficiently strong. It is obvious that a weak executive is not competent to perform its duties. It must possess all those powers which are necessary to meet any emergency. The constitution should be so flexible that the executive is in a position to assume all those powers which are necessary for its existence and its capacity to serve the people. Hamilton has rightly said that a weak government is another name for bad government. However, this does not mean that the government should be given too many powers. The reason is that if too many powers are given to the government, there is every possibility of a tyranny of the executive. Power must be relative to functions. Hence, only that much power should be given to the executive as is sufficient to enable it to perform its functions efficiently.

(4) Experience shows that the tenure of the executive should be neither too long nor too short. In case the executive power is kept in the hands of a person for a long time, there is every possibility of his abusing it. He may start thinking that he has a right to exercise those powers and forget altogether that his powers are merely a trust to be exercised for the good of the people. Similarly, if the tenure is very short, it may lead to many evils. This is clear from the experience of France where the ministries change very frequently. There is no continuity in the policy of the government. There is "an intolerable vacillation and imbecility." When there are too many elections at short intervals, the normal life of the people is unnecessarily disturbed. They are also burdened with a lot of expenditure on account of elections. Hence the duration should be moderate like that of the American President.

(5) Another requirement is that the relationship between the executive and the legislature should be such that there is co-operation between the two. It is only then that the will of the people can be carried out properly and efficiently. Such a system prevails in a parliamentary government like that of England. Where the executive and the legislature are separate, as in the United States, many difficulties have to be faced. The legislature may not give to the executive all those powers which are necessary for the performance of its duties and the executive may not enforce the laws passed by the legislature in the right spirit. The results are irresponsibility and inefficiency. There is no speed and no promptness.

(6) The executive must be responsible to the people. The latter should have the power to decide at regular intervals whether they want the continuation of the executive or not. Without this, the government will be a tyranny.

Hamilton has summed up the problem in the following words: "The ingredients which constitute energy in the executive are first, unity; secondly, duration; thirdly, an adequate provision for its support; fourthly competent powers. While those which constitute safety in the republican sense are first, a due dependence on the people; secondly, due responsibility."

Modes of Choice of Executive

(1) There are different methods of choosing the chief executive head of the state in different countries. In some, the *hereditary principle* prevails. This is so in countries like Great Britain where a monarchical form of government exists. The same is true about Japan, Iran, etc. Formerly, hereditary heads of states were to be found in many countries. However, since the end of the First World War, the trend is against this. Many monarchical governments have been superseded by republics, *e.g.* Germany, Austria-Hungary, Turkey, etc.

(2) Another method of choosing the chief executive is by *direct popular election.* Such a provision existed in the French Constitution of 1848 and that enabled Louis Napoleon to become the President in 1848. The Weimar Constitution of Germany provided for the direct election of the President of that country. The governors of the states in America are elected by the people. Likewise, the local executives of the Swiss Cantons are directly elected by the people. There was a proposal in the draft Constitution of India that governors of the states should be elected by the people but that was ultimately dropped. Some persons advocated the direct election of the President of the United States but ultimately provision was made for an indirect election.

The great merit of direct election is that the head of the state enjoys the confidence of the people. He who is unpopular with the people has no chance of being elected. Such a system of government can claim to be the government of the people. The will of the people is a deciding factor in such a system. However, the critics point out that the masses are ignorant and hence are very poor judges of the goodness or competence of a particular individual. They may be carried away by a popular name. Such a thing happened in France in 1848 when Louis Napoleon was able to carry the people with him on account of the attraction of the name of Napoleon. The system of direct elections by the people gives a lot of scope to demagogues who can play upon the sentiments and emotions of the people. Popular elections lead to rivalries, intrigues and wholesale corruption. Such a system does not fit in a parliamentary form of government where the head of the executive has to be a nominal one and he who is elected by the people cannot be nominal. Hamilton was right when he said that the system of direct election would "convulse the community with extraordinary and violent movements and lead to the heats and ferments." Professor Gilchrist says: "As soon as one candidate is elected, those who aspire to succeed him proceed to canvass the people. Party feeling is perpetuated and at election times it often becomes very bitter; it may even lead to foreign intrigues." It is well known that the head of the state of Poland before its partitions towards the end of the eighteenth century was elected by nobles and that lead to the intervention of neighbouring countries in the affairs of Poland.

(3) In some countries, the head of the state is *indirectly* elected by the people, as in the United States. The people elect the members of an electoral college and the latter elect the president. It is true that as a result of a convention, the election has practically become direct, but in the eye of law it is still indirect. The framers of the American Constitution were in favour of an indirect election on account of certain advantages. The view of Hamilton was: "It was desirable that the immediate election should be made by men most capable of analysing the qualities adapted to the station. A small number of persons selected by their fellow citizens from the general mass will be most likely to possess the information and discernment requisite to so complicated an investigation."

(4) In some countries, the head of the executive is *elected by the legislature.* The French Constitution of 1875 provided for the election of the President by the National Assembly consisting of the two houses of the legislature, *viz.*, the Senate and the Chamber of Deputies. Under the Fourth Republic of France, the President was chosen by a joint meeting of both the houses of legislature. In Switzerland the Federal Executive Council is also elected by the Federal legislature. The President of India is elected by an electoral college consisting of the members of both Houses of Parliament and the elected members of the legislatures of the states.

The merit of this system is that the members of the legislatures are undoubtedly more capable than the ordinary masses and hence can be expected to make an intelligent choice of the head of the executive. Moreover, as the head of the executive is elected by the members of the legislature, there are greater chances of harmony and co-operation between the legislature and the executive. However, the critics point out that such a system is against the theory of separation of powers which demands that the legislature, executive and judiciary must be independent of one another. Another defect is that it can lead to bargaining, intrigues and jobbery. Judge Story says: "It would be in the power of an ambitious candidate by holding rewards of office or other sources of patronage and honour silently but irresistibly to influence a majority of voters and thus by his own hold and unprincipled conduct to secure choice to the exclusion of the highest and purest and most enlightened men in the country."

(5) In some countries, the head of the executive is *nominated by the executive.* During the British Rule in India, the Governor-General and the Governors were nominated by the executive. The Governors-General of Canada and Australia are also nominated by the British Government with approval of the dominion government. The Governors of the states in India are nominated by the central government. The Lieutenant-Governors of Canada are nominated by the Federal government.

Term of Office

The term of office of the head of the executive varies from country to country. The governors of the states in America are elected for one year. The President of the United States is elected for four years. The President of India is elected for 5-years. The members of the Federal Council of Switzerland are elected for 4 years. The President of France is elected for 7 years. However, the feeling is that the term of office should be neither too long nor too short. The reason is that if it is too short, the executive becomes timid and weak; it is not in a position to accomplish anything it is all the time thinking of the next election which is never far off.

The only policy which a head can follow is one that will not do harm to anybody so that there is no opposition. However, he will be doing nothing positive for the good of the people. If the term of office is very long, that also is not good. The reason is that no immediate action can be taken against the executive if it becomes irresponsible or stupid. "A responsibility which cannot be enforced at shorter intervals than once in six or seven years manifestly loses much of its effectiveness." Chancellor Kent rightly says that the period should be reasonably long to make the executive "feel firm and independent in the discharge of his trust and to give stability and some degree of maturing to his system of administration."

Question of Re-eligibility

The question is whether or not the head of the executive should be allowed to be re-elected, and if so, how many times. It is well known that George Washington, the first President of the United States, refused to stand for the Presidency for the third term. That convention was scrupulously observes till President Roosevelt got himself elected for the third and fourth terms. The result was that the American Constitution was amended and a provision was made that no President would be allowed to stand for the third term. The Constitution of the Irish Free State provides for re-election for one term. There is a similar provision in the. Constitution of Burma. The law does not put any limit in India but Dr. Rajendra Prasad set up the convention by not standing for third time.

Many advantages are claimed for re-election. According to Hamilton, re-election is necessary "to enable the people when they see reason to approve of his conduct to continue him in the station in order to prolong the utility of his talents and virtues and to secure to the government the advantage of permanency in a wise system of government." Again, "The desire of reward and fame is one of the strongest incentives of human conduct: and the best security for the fidelity of mankind is to make their interest coincide with their duty." Judge Story says: "What could be more strange than to declare at the moment when wisdom was acquired that the possessor of it should no longer be enabled to use it for the very purpose for which it was acquired."

Functions of the Executive

According to Dr. Garner, the functions of the executive can be discussed under the following heads: diplomatic, administrative, military, judicial and legislative. As regards *diplomatic functions*, their necessity is increasing day by day as the whole world is becoming one unit. The result is that we require the appointment of ambassadors, ministers and personal representatives by the different governments. It is through them that their governments deal with other countries and enter into agreements and treaties. The procedure for treaty-making differs in different countries. In the United States, the President can make treaties but they must be ratified by the Senate. The check of the Senate is not nominal but real. It is well known that although the Treaty of Versailles was negotiated by President Wilson the American Senate refused to ratify it. In England, the power of making treaties rests with the executive and there is no necessity of its approval by Parliament. However, no government in England would enter into a treaty which is opposed by the people or Parliament. In France, the legislature cannot modify or amend treaties submitted for its consideration and must approve or reject them as a whole.

As regards *administrative functions*, they embrace "all those matters which have to deal more directly with the strict administration of the government such as the appointment, direction and removal of officers, the issue of instructions and ordinances and in general, all acts relating more directly to the execution of the laws." This sphere of executive is expanding every day as the modern governments are taking over more and more functions into their hands. The performance of those functions requires the employment of a large number of officials for running the show.

The duty of *defence* of a country rests with the executive. The executive has to maintain an efficient and sufficiently strong army, navy and air force to defend its frontiers against the attacks of outsiders. If the executive ignores this function, the very existence of the state is jeopardized. It is always in danger of being liquidated. It is well known that when India was attacked by China in 1962, Indian armies were defeated because the defence of the country had been neglected.

It is true that the judiciary must be independent and should also be kept separate from the executive, but that does not mean that the executive does not perform *any judicial functions*. In most countries, it is the executive that makes appointments of the judges and that system is preferred to other systems. The executive is concerned with the organisation of the judicial machinery and also grants pardon and reprieve. Regarding the power of pardon, Hamilton says: "One man appears to be more eligible dispenser of the mercy of government than a body of men". Moreover, the growth of administrative law and administrative justice is giving the executive a hand in the judicial field. Instead of allowing the regular courts to try cases, those are being disposed of by the administrative tribunals.

Although the executive is separate from the legislature, it exercises a lot of control in the *legislative field.* In a parliamentary form of government like that of England, it is the executive that is the leader of the legislature. The party having a majority in the legislature forms the government and continues in office so long as it enjoys the confidence of the legislature. The executive summons the legislature, draws up its time-table and also decides which bills are to be enacted into laws. Those bills are also drafted by the executive. The executive initiates the bills and also pilots them through. Under such a system, the power of veto of the executive is not used. In a country like the United States, the veto power of the President is real and puts a check on the independence of the legislature. The President can veto a bill passed by the Congress. In a country like India, the executive is given the power of making ordinances. Under the Government of India Act, 1935, the Government was given the power of making what were known as Acts of the Governor and Governor-General. In certain cases, the previous sanction of the Governor-General was also required even to introduce certain bills in the legislature.

The growth of *delegated legislation* is extending the sphere of the executive in the legislative field. There is a rush of work in the legislature. Laws are growing more and more complex every day. The result is that the system of passing what is known as skeleton bills is being resorted to. This enables the executive to supplement the law by issuing rules and regulations or orders-in-council.

The scope of the functions of the executive is bound to increase in the future. The old concept of a police state has been given up. We believe in the concept of a welfare state. If the functions of the state increase, the duties of the executive are bound to increase. Dr. Finer rightly points out that the scope of the state today "hardly fails to envisage any branch of the moral or material sides of human endeavour. The record is written on the roads, the gutters and the buildings and spells what the state has done in order that society may have a modicum of wisdom, protection of persons against criminals and mechanically propelled vehicles, and environmental and personal defence against deadly bacteria. The annual thousands of Rules and Orders, the detailed and present plan of activity of all modern States, reveal how the State concentrates upon each individual and weaves his very impulse into the myriad threaded warp of its existence...The State is everywhere, it leaves hardly a gap."

Leadership of the Executive

Barker says, "If the growth of the legislative organ, in consequence of the development of the cabinet system, was the notable feature of the eighteenth century, it may be said that the growth of the executive organ, in consequence of the extension of rights and the corresponding extension of services which mostly fall to the lot of the executive, is the notable feature of the twentieth." The executive today is not only the executive but also the legislature and the judiciary. Its functions have expanded in all directions.

The executive does the work of the legislature in many ways. Most of the legislation emanates from the executive. It is the executive which decides which policy is to be followed and what legislation is necessary to implement the same. With that object in view, legislation is introduced by the ministers concerned and they see to it that the same is passed. Dr. Ogg says that the cabinet "formulate policies, make decisions and draft bills on all significant matters which in their judgment require legislative attention, asking of Parliament only that it gives effect to such decisions and policies by considering them and taking the necessary votes." Dr. Jennings says, "In modern state, most legislation is directed towards the creation and modification of administrative powers."

This is true not only in a parliamentary system but also under a Presidential system. In the United States also, the President manages to get the required legislation passed from the Congress. The President can send messages to the Congress. He can recommend to the Congress certain measures to be passed by them. He can call for special sessions of the Congress. He can veto bills. He can influence the legislature in many other ways. "Jobs could be traded for votes. By effective appeals to the voters through the spoken word, press, radio and lately television, chief executives have been able to dramatize their programmes and compel consideration of their views."

The executive also issues decrees, ordinances, regulations and orders. As a result of various factors, skeleton legislation is resorted to by the legislature and a lot of discretion is given to the executive to fill in the blanks in order to meet the new situations which may arise in the future. The result is that delegated legislation has assumed alarming proportions and with that the field of the executive in legislation has expanded enormously. It is pointed out that in 1931 when Great Britain was facing a great economic crisis, the Gold Standard (Amendment) Act gave the Treasury the power to legislate for the control of the Exchange. The National Economy Act gave power to the King-in-Council to make reductions, including cuts in salaries. The National Recovery Act of 1933 gave authority to the American President to organise and regulate industries, to create new agencies, to delegate functions to subordinates and to do all other things which were considered necessary to meet the situation. The Trade Agreement of 1934 gave power to the American President to enter into trade agreements with foreign countries and lower the existing tariff rates by 50%. This phenomenon is not peculiar to the United States and Great Britain. The same applies to India. Here also there has been an enormous growth of delegated legislation. Reference to the Gazette of India and the State Gazettes will support this contention.

There has been not only the growth of delegated legislation, but also what is known as administrative justice. In many cases, the Departments concerned are given the authority to decide the disputes relating to those departments. Either the officials concerned or the minister who is the head of the Department is made the final authority to dispose of those disputes. The result is that the executive has come to exercise a lot of judicial powers. It is pointed out that when the legislature confers "a measure of legislative power upon the executive, it takes something away from itself; but when it confers upon the executive a measure of judicial power, it is diminishing not itself but an organ other than itself." Administrative adjudication is defined as "the process by which administrative agencies settle issues arising in the course of their work when legal rights are in question." Dr. White says, "Administrative adjudication means the investigation and settling of a dispute involving a private property on the basis of law and facts by an administrative agency.

The growth of political parties has added to the leadership of the executive. The result is that legislation is inspired by the executive. The budget is prepared by the executive. The foreign policy of a country is determined by the executive. The machinery of the state is also run by the executive.

The Civil Service

There was a time when the work of the government was carried on by ordinary citizens without any specialised qualifications. However, those days are gone. The old conception about the functions of the state has changed and that has led to the multiplication of the functions of the state. Moreover, the work of the government has become highly technical and that cannot be done by people without specialisation. It is these facts which have added to the importance of the role of the civil service in the working of the government.

Dr. Finer defines the "civil service" as "a professional body of officials, permanent, paid and skilled." Again, "It is different from business, from an art, from teaching, from other professions. Its objectives are individual, its spirit and methods are special." Willoughby defines the term civil service as "a system that offers equal opportunities to all citizens to enter the government service, equal pay to all employees doing work requiring the same degree of intelligence and capacity, equal opportunities for advancement, equally favourable conditions and equal participation in retirement allowances and makes equal demands upon the employees." Professor Milton Mandell defines the civil service as a system "predicated on recruiting young men and women with capacity to learning and growth, training them in order to develop and utilise their aptitudes and offering them opportunities for advancement in responsibility and remuneration." Sir William Beveridge says: "The civil service is a profession and I should like it to become and realise itself as a learned profession."

On the basis of experience, four principles have been evolved for the organization of the civil service. The first principle is that the political executive, which changes periodically, should not have a hand in the appointment of the members of the civil service. The experience of the spoils system of the United States supports this contention. Under that system, whenever a new President came, he dismissed all the civil servants who did not belong to his party and recruited new ones. The result was that the new entrants were expected to support the President in all that he did during the term of his office. Even at the time of election, they were expected to support the party to which the President belonged. They knew full well that if their party was defeated, they were likely to be dismissed from office. The evils of this system demanded a change and it was made later on. Under the old system, there were dangers of party patronage, favouritism and insecurity of service. If we stand for efficiency in administration, what is required is that a person should enter the civil service on the basis of certain qualifications or a test and he should not be liable to be removed unless he becomes physically or mentally unfit or corrupt in the performance of his duties. He should be able to continue in service till the age of superannuation. Formerly, the usual system of appointment used to be through nomination by the executive. Its evils pointed out the necessity of recruiting civil servants through a Public Service Commission whose impartiality and honesty are above reproach. The nature of the examinations held by the Public Service Commission varies. In England, the examinations aim at finding out the general intelligence of the candidates. Under such a system, the civil servants can be transferred from one department to another. In countries like France and the United States, the examinations aim at testing the particular or professional qualifications of the candidates for a particular line. In addition to the examinations, interviews of the candidates are held to judge their personality.

Another principle is that promotion should be given on the basis of seniority. The longer the service, the more increments a civil servant must have. That leaves less scope for personal favouritism. However, there is one exception. In certain cases, extra increments must be given on the ground of the efficiency of the individual. In the United States, a lot of progress has been made in the technique of rating the various civil servants according to their efficiency. They have correlated efficiency which rises and falls in salary, promotion, demotion and dismissal.

The third principle is that the members of the civil service should not take part in politics. While performing their duties, they should neither favour nor oppose any individual or any political party. What is expected of them is that they should faithfully carry out the instructions given to them by the heads of the departments concerned. It is this fact which enables them to continue in office despite the changes in the ministry. The civil servants are required to work faithfully and they must not allow their individual ideologies to influence their work. Heads of the departments must accept the responsibility for whatever is done by their subordinates. The civil servants should neither be praised nor condemned in the legislature or in public. The reason is obvious. They cannot defend themselves if they are criticised by the political leaders or otherwise. They are required to keep quiet and discipline demands that they must not come into the open to defend themselves.

The members of the civil service are required to maintain strict secrecy regarding the working of their departments. Experience shows that the interests of the government cannot be protected if the secrets of the government leak out. As a matter of fact, even the working of the government becomes impossible if everything that happens in a department leaks out to the public.

The members of the civil service must be given a decent salary. The obvious reason is that if they are poorly paid, there is always the temptation of accepting bribes and that is bound to affect adversely the efficiency of administration. Moreover, if the salaries of the government servants are low, there is every chance of their leaving the service and joining some private service. In that case, the government stands to lose, as all the experience which that person has acquired during the course of service under the government is lost, and the raw hand who takes his place cannot be expected to do his job efficiently. There is always the possibility of the government being put in difficulties on account of the ignorance or inefficiency of a government servant.

It is pointed out that the mere existence of a permanent bureaucracy is no guarantee of efficiency. The permanent bureaucracies of Western Europe give security for the most part to those who have secured positions, but they have not always been successful in securing the best qualified persons. In France, before World War II, the national service was practically divided into a number of bureaucracies operating as independent units for each major government agency. Top-rank positions were largely reserved for certain groups in French society which could secure what was considered appropriate education. Likewise, the old German bureaucracy had the characteristics of a closed corporation in which persons belonging to certain families alone could enter.

In the United States, the revolt against the spoils system began to be effective on a statewise and national basis in the 1880s. Progress was slow but the movement known as civil service reform was gradually extended. A lot has been achieved to put the civil service on merit basis. However, many supporters of civil service today are less extreme than their predecessors. They acknowledge that top positions and some of the immediate staff of these officials should be chosen with major concern for policy harmony with the chief executive. It is also admitted that the selection of the best qualified personnel for some kinds of jobs is not merely a matter of examiners' arithmetic. Merit system today is still concerned with the elimination of politics in the selection of government personnel, but a major emphasis has been placed upon techniques and procedures which would improve the government service. This is illustrated by in-service training, good promotion practices and various incentives. In the United States, the usual organisation to achieve these goals has been three-men commissions representing the two major parties, which develop a staff of trained personnel to perform many of the detailed jobs and conduct the general supervision required in a personnel system. At the national level, this agency is known as the United States Civil Service Commission but many states refer to their agencies as merit system councils.

Recruitment under a merit system is supposed not to be affected by political factors, but it is always possible for personal and political connections to have an effect on the selection of personnel in such a system. The best the merit system can do is to minimise these extraneous factors. In the United States, following the preparation of a list of qualified personnel rated by the evaluation of their examinations and qualifications, the appointing officer is given the opportunity of choice between the top three candidates. This gives him the discretion to choose the person whom he thinks will most adequately fill the vacancy. It also permits politics to affect his choice. In spite of the possible evil that this might encourage, many continue to recommend this element of choice. As a matter of fact, the first Hoover Commission which studied the reorganisation of the Federal Government recommended that it be increased to a choice among five rather than three. It is assumed that the top three or four applicants would have demonstrated their basic ability to perform the task and the remaining question would be merely which one would fit into the operating machine best.

An initial problem of recruitment is to secure the interest of well-qualified persons so that they may be considered for the post. Wherever the prestige of government service is high, there arises less difficulty in securing applicants. Compensation, security, working conditions, opportunities for advancement and other desirable features can be made effective inducement to a government career service. Frequently these features are not as attractive as in other employments and recruitment becomes a difficult matter.

In the early days of Prussian bureaucracy, the training of government servants tended to have a military flavour. European countries have often sought persons with legal training for government positions. This legal training is of a broader sociological nature than that common to American legal institutions. In the United States, there has been a tendency to emphasize specialised skills which are associated with particular positions rather than more general training. In Great Britain, emphasis has been put on a classical education in preparation for entry into high-ranking administrative posts. Each civil service system has positions which can be filled only by one with technical training and at the same time has jobs available for those with general administrative ability. It is primarily in the latter category that the question arises concerning the relative merits of generalist training or specialist training for one who is to fill a general administrative position.

Examinations to determine the relative capabilities of applicants under a merit system are a part of the recruitment process. These may be of many different types. A typist may be judged on the basis of a performance test demonstrating ability at typing. An applicant for a postal position might be required through written test to indicate his knowledge of postal rules and regulations as well as his general comprehension and adaptiveness. A lawyer may be examined purely on the basis of his training and experience records. Some tests may be oral and others may be combinations of written and oral. Oral tests are more subjective than written ones. Test may fail to determine the qualifications actually needed for a specific position. There is also the problem whether the examination or competition will be open to all or just to those within the service deemed to be eligible for advancement to a higher post. The decision on this point has to do a lot with the morale of lower echelons in the service.

For an efficient civil service, the question of compensation and tenure has to be taken into consideration. Compensation may be an inducement or a hindrance to the recruitment of competent persons. If direct compensation is low, other attractions may be added to make the civil service attractive. One of them could be the assurance of tenure except in cases of proved incompetence or when conditions required a reduction in the number of civil servants. There is always the danger that the security of tenure might turn the government employees into mediocres, but checks can be provided to avert this process. Assuring the applicant of a maximum degree of security in the maintenance of his position would prove to be attractive to many. If to this the service could add opportunities for advancement and adequate retirement compensation at the conclusion of active service, it will be considered a desirable career by many. As many governments now make provision for old age, the retirement-payment aspect of civil service is no longer attractive. In order to ensure an able bureaucracy, the total compensation and associated benefits and protection should by approximately equivalent to those of comparable employment by agencies other than government. If it is somewhat lower, the difference could be made up by the prestige of the service and the honour associated with public employment.

In a bureaucracy, formal disciplinary sanctions include reprimands, reduction in salary, transfer and dismissal. In actual practice, many employees are often shielded from dismissal by red tape and appeal procedures.

Every effort must be made to raise the morale of the civil servants. One of them is a promotion system that insures opportunities for advancement to those who enter the service. In most cases, compromise techniques are adopted to provide for promotion from within and entrance from without. The highest positions are normally closed to the career service and this may have some effect on the morale of the group. Political intervention and influence in the selection and the career of civil servants is discouraging to many able persons within the government service. If the highest efficiency is to be obtained, the factors which disturb the morale of the government employees must be attended to.

Regarding the position of the civil servants in England, Lord Balfour says: "They do not control policy; they are not responsible for it. Belonging to no party, they are for that very reason an invaluable element in Party Government. It is through them, especially through their higher branches, that the transference of responsibility from one party or one minister to another involves no destructive shock to the administrative machine. There may be a change of direction, but the curve is smooth."

About the British Civil Service, Dr. Ogg says : "Some are impelled by a sense of civic duty, some are drawn by the prospect of a career in a field in which the way is open for talent and industry irrespective of family connections; some no doubt are appealed to by a profession which promises a steady and assured income, without much risk."

Duties of Civil Servants

The civil servants are required to discharge their duties in accordance with the constitution and the laws. They have to carry out the orders of their superiors in so far as those are not inconsistent with the laws of the country. They are required to do their work with sincerity and impartiality. There must be a sense of devotion in their work. Experience has shown that when this quality is lacking, the administrative machinery slows down and ultimately the government loses. The civil servants must be punctual in their work. They must be prepared to undertake additional duties or other duties to which their training and capacity fit them. They must be truthful in their official work. They must not pass over in silence those matters which affect the interests of the state. They must not try to oblige any party and thereby injure the interests of the state. They must show respect to their superiors in their departments. They must be always courteous in their dealings with the public. They must not take employment outside without informing their department and must observe official secrecy.

Sir J.A.R. Marriot refers to the growing importance of the civil service in these words: "Partly owing to the increasing complexity of industrial and social conditions, partly under the subtle influence of Fabian Socialism, partly from the general abandonment of the principle of *laissez faire* and the growing demand for governmental guidance and control in all the affairs of life, partly from sheer despair of the possibility of coping with the insistent cry for legislation, Parliament has manifested a disposition to leave more and more discretion to administrative departments."

Functions of a Department

Generally, there are four functions of a Department. The Department is responsible to the people for its administration. As the administration is run by the Department, it must explain its conduct both to the people and the legislature. It has to supply the necessary information to the Minister so that he can defend the actions of his Department before the legislature and also in public. It is desirable that the work of the Department should be conducted in such a manner that it is capable of "articulate rational defence."

When the policy has been decided by the Cabinet, it becomes the duty of the Department concerned to find out ways and means to carry it out. The Department has either to depend upon its own experience or carry out the directions given by the Cabinet in that connection. Taking these facts into consideration, the Department concerned prepares a draft of the scheme and consults the various interests which are likely to be affected by it. If the scheme thus prepared cannot be carried out with the help of the existing law, the Department has to prepare a draft of the new legislation necessary for the purpose and it becomes the duty of the Minister concerned to see that the necessary legislation is passed by the legislature. The members of the civil service are always at the disposal of the Minister concerned to help him in his task of getting the bill through the legislature by supplying him all the information required by him in that connection.

On account of rush of work in the legislature and also on account of the growing complexity of legislation in modern times, most of the bills are passed by Parliament in a skeleton form and it is left to the Department concerned to fill in the blanks as and when the occasion arises. In this manner, the Department prepares the necessary rules and regulations and issues them in the Gazette. This work is very important and its volume is also growing day by day.

It is also the function of the Department concerned to implement the policy adopted by the Cabinet. It is the duty of the Department to issue the necessary directions and instructions and also to see that those are actually carried out. It has to keep watch over the various branches of the Department. It is to see that the policy has been carried out by the subordinate staff. It is the duty of the officials to carry out the instructions or directions given by the Department. However, they can make their suggestions to the Department and very often those suggestions are given great weight.

Consultative and Advisory Bodies

Professor Laski rightly says that "the first great need of the modern state is adequately to organise institutions of consultation." The reason is obvious. We in modern times believe, in the democratic process. We believe that the government must be carried on in the interests of the people. Experience shows that this is no possible without consultation. If law is to meet adequately the needs of the people, it is absolutely necessary that those who make the law must consult those who are going to be affected by it. It is rightly said that consultation to be effective must be representative and not selective. If the government appoints people of its own choice for consultation, that is no consultation at all. Every effort must be made to consult all shades of opinion. Partisans have no place in this field.

There are many advantages of consultation. The various parties which are interested in a particular decision to be taken by the Government, get an opportunity to represent their case before the government and also learn and appreciate the point of view of the Government. They can also appeal to public opinion to support their point of view. The representatives of the various interests supply the Government authentic and valuable information on which it can base its own policy or the necessary details of the case. The interested parties can also warn the Government of the probable results of the action intended to be taken. To quote Laski, "They form, in brief, a deposit of *expertise* upon the different aspects of policy which, effectively used, create an atmosphere of responsibility about governmental acts. If the Minister acts upon their opinion, he is at least building upon a foundation of experience; if he rejects them, the creation of an opposition and, as a consequence, of the discussion which is the lifeblood of the democratic governance, is adequately assured." If we want others who are not a part of the machinery of the government, to be responsible, they must be associated with it. To quote Laski, "The only way to do things for people is to make them do things for themselves." This makes the people feel that they are a part of the Government and the Government is theirs. Very often it happens that the decisions of the Cabinet or a Minister may not be in the interests of the people in general. Those decisions might have been taken with a view to strengthen the party in power and not to add to the welfare of the people. In such cases, the existence of consultative bodies is very useful. These bodies come to the forefront and expose the Government and thereby avoid the danger which might have adversely affected the people at large. Prof. Laski points out that "discussion is rooted in the principles of its subjects; personal considerations are, *a priori*, out of place. The minister is dealing directly with minds and only indirectly with votes. He is being driven to counter reason with reason. He is being trained in responsibility to those whose desires must shape his will."

The government may adopt various methods of consultation. It may interview the authorised representatives of various interests. It may ask them to submit their memoranda. Through the press, it may invite suggestions from ail quarters. Whatever the method adopted, the object is the same. It is an effort on the part of the government to ascertain certain facts regarding the proposed legislation. Laski says: "A government which embarks on a policy must offer the means of judging that policy. The opinion it has elicited by organised enquiry is fundamental to that end. The evidence it has collected, the facts at its disposal, can never be refused to its subjects if it is to build its opinion in the reasoned judgement of its citizens."

It is also suggested that certain advisory bodies should be set up on a permanent or a temporary basis to advise the government on different matters. These bodies should be neither too large nor too small. A body of 15 members is considered to be ideal. Laski says that the members of the advisory committees can be appointed for three years. They can also be re-appointed. They "should preferably be elected by the councils of these nominating bodies, miners by the executive of the Miners' Federation, teachers by the Council of the National Union of Teachers and so forth. They should also be paid for their services sufficiently to compensate for lost time but not enough to make their election sought after on ground of income."

Professor Wheare says that these advisory committees can be classified under six heads, *viz.*, committees to advise, committees to enquire, committees to negotiate, committees to legislate, committees to administer and committees to scrutinise and control. Whatever the committee, "the principle upon which arrangement has been made is that of the function or process which the committee carries out rather than of the institution of which it forms a part or with which it is connected."

It was in 1899 that provision was made in England for the appointment of Departmental Advisory Committees composed of non-governmental heads, *e.g.*, Board of Education, Board of Trade, etc. The Committee for Imperial Defence was set up in 1904. Later on, the Economic Advisory Council was set up in England. It is the duty of this Council to study and report to the Cabinet on commercial, industrial and other economic problems facing the country. During World War I, a large number of Committees attached to the various Departments were set up. Experience shows that these Departmental Advisory Committees perform very useful functions by bringing to the notice of the Department the necessary information and advice based on first hand knowledge. They also inspire greater public confidence in administrative authorities as they are guided by the information and advice of the Advisory bodies. These advisory bodies do not dictate any policy to the Department concerned but their duty is merely to advise and discuss matters brought before it.

A decision was taken by the Government of India in 1954 and as a result of it a large number of informal consultative committees of members of Parliament were set up. These Committees are intended to enable members of Parliament to have a glimpse into the working of the various Departments of the Government. Each Committee consists of about 30 members. These Committees do not have any statutory functions or responsibilities. Nothing is referred to them for their decision. It is for the Minister to decide what matter he will discuss with a particular Committee and what information he will give to the members. In 1962, there were about 500 such Advisory Committees in India. Some new Committees such as National Defence Council, Citizens' Central Council, Advisory Committee on Economic Policy and Board of Trade have been set up. The function of the Zonal Councils in India is also an advisory one.

The size of the Advisory Committees is very important. If a Committee is so large that its members have to stand up and address each other, it is unlikely to be effective. If the size of the Committee is small, there is more of give and take of discussion round the table and appreciation of the point of view of each other. The view of Prof. Wheare is that where an advisory body is large, it can be effective only if it breaks itself into sub-committees and meets as a full committee to discuss the reports of those sub-committees or to discuss certain questions of general principle. To quote Prof. Wheare, "In fact most advisory committees are small and where they are large, they break up into panels or sub-committees. If they do not do so, it is difficult to escape the conclusion either that they do not mean business or that they are intended to do business." The ideal number is 15 or nearabout. Prof. Wheare gives a warning that persons who are very big should not be appointed as members of these committees. The reason given by him is that these eminent and distinguished persons are found in practise so eminent and so busy and so remote from the day-to-day work of the organisation they represent, that they are in fact not of much use as advisers. They "circulate" from one advisory committee to another and seldom know much about the business of any committee. They have neither the time nor the initiative to master a subject and contribute to the discussion. Experience shows that better work is done by advisory committees consisting of less eminent people. To quote Prof. Wheare, "the best advice is often to be obtained from persons of less eminence, still so little in demand that they are able to master fully one branch of knowledge or activity."

Prof. Laski suggests the nomination of the consultative bodies for a period of 3 years subject to the renewal of the term depending upon the discretion of the appointing body.

The advisory committees perform very useful functions. They have the right to be consulted on all proposed bills before they are introduced in the legislature. The views of these committees are taken by the government before drafting the proposed legislation. These committees are also consulted upon general administrative policy. That does not mean that the minister concerned must adopt the advice given. He can reject it if he so pleases but while doing so, he must not forget the consequences of his acting against the expert advice. These committees are also given a lot of discretion in the matter of making suggestions and thereby making their contribution. Professor Laski says: "It is one of the few ways open to us to correct the danger of professional conservatism. A Committee of Ministry of Justice, for example, upon which the lay mind as well as the legal mind found place, could indicate a score of places in the law where the need for revision and experiment is essential."

About the usefulness of the advisory bodies, Lord Haldane's Committee on the Machinery of Government says: "We think that the more they are regarded as an integral part of the normal organisation of department, the more will ministers be enabled to command the confidence of Parliament and the public in their administration of the services which seem likely in an increasing degree to affect the lives of large sections of the community."

Economic Councils

In addition to the advisory committees mentioned above, Economic Councils have been appointed in many countries. The Weimar Constitution of Germany provided for the establishment of the National Economic Council of Germany and the same was actually set up in 1920. It had 326 persons as members, representing 10 occupational groups. Those groups were represented according to their economic and social importance. The Constitution provided that all important social and economic measures proposed by the Ministry should be submitted to the National Economic Council for its opinion before they were actually introduced in Parliament. The Council was also given the power to introduce those measures on its own initiative and have its proposals and views presented to the Reichstag whether the Ministry agreed or not. This Council furnished the legislature with expert advice and also kept it informed of the needs of the various interests represented by it. The view of Dr. Ogg is that during the first 10 years of its existence, the Council "rendered useful service in considering proposed economic and social legislation, initiating occupational measures for parliamentary consideration and giving the legislative authorities the benefit of its presumably expert advice." However, the view of Prof. Laski is that the Council's power of initiating measures in legislature "tends to lead it to multiply suggestions for legislation without having the responsibility to carry them into effect." Again, "The need to appear and speak before it, the knowledge that its activity is always encroaching upon the margin of the Reichstag's competence, the satisfaction of its immeasurable appetite for documents and information, are rather a hindrance than a help to the channels of administration proper."

Similar Councils were set up in Yugoslavia, Poland, Italy, Spain and Portugal. In 1925, a similar Council was set up in France. In 1936, it was enlarged and given a permanent statutory basis. Its General Assembly consists of more than 100 members representing the consumers, the labouring classes, agriculture, commerce, employers' associations, bankers, educationists, economists, etc. The President of the Council is the Prime Minister. The functions of the Council are the investigation of the national economic problems and giving of advice to the Government. All bills of an economic character have to be submitted by the Ministry to the Council. The same is true of the decrees having economic implications. The Ministry may also submit any economic question to it for study and the same may be done by any parliamentary committee. The Council may take up any economic problem and submit its recommendations on its own initiative. Any Plan, or any Bill dealing with a Plan, of an economic and social character is submitted to it for advice. The recommendations are made to the Prime Minister but its reports are placed before President.

There is a similar Council in Britain. The British Economic Council consists of 20 persons, with the Prime Minister as the ex-officio Chairman. Likewise, the Chancellor of the Exchequer and three other ministers are ex-officio members. It also includes such other ministers as the Prime Minister may desire. The view of Dr. Ogg is that "On the whole, the Council's usefulness has not yet been demonstrated convincingly."

In England, the Board of Trade set up what are called "working parties." Their function is to examine the organisation of the main consumer's goods industries and their methods of production and distribution and to make recommendations for increasing their efficiency. One-third members of each working party are appointed by the employers, one-third by the trade unions and one-third by the Board of Trade from the independent members. The President of the Board of Trade nominates an independent chairman.

About the working of the Economic Councils in general, the view of G.D.H. Cole is that "It has become plainer and plainer to those who have watched the operation of the Economic Councils in Germany and other countries that bodies which are based on the balancing of forces between the representatives of employers and workers are incapable of any real constructive achievement." There is always a conflict between the interests of the employers and the employees and there is not much hope to reconcile them. Moreover, the powers of these Councils are merely investigatory and advisory. Their authority is very much limited. To quote Cole again, "They have been constituted by too little of experts and too much of representatives of conflicting industrial interests, and their members have been, for the most part, far more intent on preserving the structure of capitalism and preventing the growth of socialist enterprise than on developing any coherent national industrial plan."

On the whole, it may be stated that these economic councils are regarded as a very valuable aid in the formulation of national policies in the economic field. Their functions are merely advisory and they provide "the regular political authorities with vocational representative bodies whose research work and counsel can be of considerable value."

SUGGESTED READINGS

Barker, E. : Reflections on Government.

Blunt, E. : The I.C.S.

Brown, B.E. : New Directions in Comparative Politics.

Bryce, J. : Modern Democracies.

Chapman, Brain : The Profession of Government : The Public Service in Europe.

Dealey, J.Q. : The State and Government.

Finer, H. : The British Civil Service.

Finer, H. : The Theory and Practice of Modern Government.

Garner, J.W. : Political Science and Government.

Gettell, R.G. : Introduction to Political Science.

Gilchrist, R.N. : Principles of Political Science.

Jennings, W. Ivor : Cabinet Government.

Lapalombara, Joseph : Bureaucracy and Political Development.

Laski, H.J. : Parliamentary Government in England.

Laski, H.J. : A Grammar of Politics.

Marriott, J.A.R. : The Mechanism of the Modern State.

Maheshwari, Shriram : Advisory Committees in the Central Government.

Ogg. F.A. : European Governments and Politics.

Riker, William H. : Democracy in the United States.

Sidgwick, H. : Elements of Politics.

Vernon, R.V., and Mansergh, N. : Advisory Bodies. A Study of their uses in relation to Central Government, 1919—1939.

Wheare, K.C. : Government by Committees.

White, L.D. : Introduction to the Study of Public Administration.

Willoughby, W.F. : Government of Modern States.

Willoughby, W.F and Rogers, L. : Introduction to Problems of Government.

28

CHAPTER

The Judiciary

Importance of the Judiciary

Learning Objectives

- Importance of the Judiciary
- Functions of the Judiciary
- Independence of the Judiciary
- Relation between Judiciary and Legislature
- Relation between Judiciary and Executive
- The Courts and Law
- Rule of Law
- Administrative Law
- Suggested Readings

Sidgwick says: "The importance of the Judiciary in political construction is rather profound than prominent. In determining a nation's rank in political civilization, no test is more decisive than the degree in which justice, as defined by the law, is actually realized in its judicial administration." Lord Bryce writes: "If the law be dishonestly administered, the salt has lost its flavour; if it be weakly and fitfully enforced, the guarantees of order fail, for it is more by the certainty than by the severity of punishment that offenders are repressed. If the lamp of justice goes out in darkness, how great is that darkness." Again, "There is no better test of the excellence of a Government than the efficiency of a judicial system; for nothing more clearly touches the welfare and security of the average citizen than the feeling that he can rely on the certain and prompt administration of justice." Laski says: "When we know how a nation-state dispenses justice, we know with exactness the moral character to which it can pretend." George Washington says: "Administration of justice is the firmest pillar of government. Law exists to bind together the community; it is sovereign and cannot be violated with impunity." According to Bentham, "The administration of justice by the state must be regarded as a permanent and essential element of civilization and as a device that admits of no substitute."

It is unfortunate that while the people attach too much importance to the legislature and the executive, the judiciary is usually ignored. The man in the street does not understand and appreciate the important part played by the judiciary in safeguarding the liberties of the individuals. Students of the Stuart period of the history of England know that in spite of the arbitrary rule of the kings, the people did not suffer much as the strong judiciary of England acted as a shield to protect the individuals. Wherever the judiciary is strong and not subservient, the executive dare not act arbitrarily in its relations with the people. It a person is unlawfully arrested, a writ *of habeas corpus* can bring that person to the court and he can be detained in jail only if the police or the executive can convince the judge concerned that his detention is according to law. The judiciary will see to it that the rights of the people are protected. Once the law has been made, it cannot be given any arbitrary interpretation by the executive. It is up to the courts to decide the meaning of the law.

Experience shows that the judgments given by the judges depend upon the individuality of the persons concerned. If a judge is a communalist, his judgments will be vitiated by his communalism. If he is corrupt, he cannot give justice to the parties concerned. If he is an upright man, he will not be afraid of calling a spade a spade. If the police has transgressed the limits of decency, the judge will not hesitate from passing strictures against it. The arbitrary action of the biggest official will be condemned by a court of law. That is the glory of the judiciary. Professor Laski says: "Men who are to make justice in the courts, the way in which they are to perform their functions, the methods by which they are to be chosen, the terms upon which they shall hold power, these and other related problems lie at the heart of political philosophy."

Although the importance of the judiciary cannot be doubted, the degree of importance varies. In a country like England where the laws are not codified, the judiciary not only interprets the law but also makes it. One has to dig deep into the precedents to find out the law of the country. Where the case law is held in respect, the importance of the judiciary becomes evident.

It is well-known that no legislator can make any law so comprehensive that can cover all possible cases. The result is that the judges are called upon to apply those laws in cases which are not exactly covered by the letter of the law. They are made to interpret the law according to what seems to them to be equitable. Experience shows that the interpretations given by the judges have changed the very spirit of law. The letter of the law may remain the same, but its substance may change. The subsequent judges usually follow the decisions and interpretations of their predecessors.

In the case of a rigid constitution, the judiciary becomes a coordinate department of the government along with the legislature and the executive. The judiciary is not only the final interpreter of the constitution, it is also its guardian. It is rightly pointed out that it is not the people who govern America but the 5 out of the 9 judges of the Supreme Court of America who decide what the law of the country is. The question is not whether a particular law is good or bad, what matters is whether the Supreme Court regards that law as *ultra vires* or *intra vires*. Lord Bryce says: "Where questions arise as to the limits of the powers of the executive or of the Legislature, or in a Federation as to the limits of the respective powers of the Central or national and those of the State Government, it is by a court of law that the true meaning of the constitution, as the fundamental and supreme law, ought to be determined, because it is the rightful and authorised interpreter of what the people intended to declare when they were enacting a fundamental instrument."

Functions of the Judiciary

The judiciary performs very important functions and the most important is that of the administration of just ice. Whenever a case comes before a judge, it is his duty to interpret the law of the country on that point in an impartial manner and give his decision accordingly. It is his duty to see that justice is dispensed according to the law. He must not give any arbitrary interpretation. He must not take upon himself the work of the legislature. However, while giving his decision, he is at liberty to discuss the law in detail and also give his honest opinion as to how he considers the law to be defective on that point. If he pleases, he can make his own suggestions. Whenever the various parties come to a court of law with their conflicting claims, it is the duty of the judge to decide which claim is according to the law of the country. It is also his duty to punish the culprit so that justice may prevail in the country.

Although a judge is not a legislator, he adds to the law of the country in his own way. A judge gives his own view of the meaning of a particular enactment and it is his interpretation that is considered to be the law of the country till it is set aside by a higher court or by a new law passed by a competent legislature. The judicial decisions play an important part in developing the legal system of a country.

The judiciary is the custodian of a written constitution. Judges are required to decide whether a particular law passed by the legislature is within its competence or not. If it is found to be not within its competence, it has to be declared *ultra vires.* The Supreme Court of India has declared *ultra vires* many laws passed by the Indian Parliament and the state legislatures.

The courts issue injunctions in certain cases and thereby help in checking the harm or mischief that might have resulted otherwise. An injunction of a court may order the government, a local body or a private individual, to desist from doing something. By issuing a writ of mandamus, the court may order the government to do a particular thing which the law of the country requires it to do. By a writ of *habeas corpus*, the court may order the release of a person who is illegally detained. By a writ of *certiorari*, the court may strike off an order passed by any official of the government, a local body or a statutory body. Other similar writs and directions can be issued by a competent court to give relief in certain matters.

In certain cases, receivers are appointed by the courts to take charge of the property in dispute. In cases of bankruptcy or insolvency, the courts play, an important part. The courts also appoint guardians of the person and property of the minors. Sometimes, the property of a minor may be taken over by a Court of Wards.

In certain cases, the advice of the court is sought by the government. The Government of India has the power to refer a particular point to the Supreme Court of India for its opinion. A similar function was performed by the Federal Court of India. The Judicial Committee of the Privy Council advises the government on many matters.

Chief Justice Taft observes thus about the functions of the judiciary: "But the judiciary are not representative in any such sense whether appointed or elected. The moment they assume their duties they must enforce the law as they find out. They must not only interpret or enforce valid enactments of the legislature according to its intention, but when the legislature in its enactments has transgressed the limitations set upon its powers in the constitution, the judicial branch of government must enforce the fundamental and higher law by annulling and declaring invalid the offending legislative enactment. Then, the judges are to decide between individuals on principles of right and justice. The great body of the law is unwritten, determined by precedent, and founded on eternal principles of right and morality. Thus, the courts have to declare and enforce. As between the individual and the State, as between the majority and the minority, as between the powerful and the weak, financially, socially, courts must hold an even hand and give judgment without fear or favour. In so doing they are performing a governmental function, but it is a complete misunderstanding of our form of government or any kind of government that exalts justice and righteousness to assume that judges are bound to follow the will of the majority of an electorate in respect of the issue of their decision."

Independence of the Judiciary

In every modern state, there has been a constant struggle to achieve the independence of the judiciary. This is due to the feeling that the protection of the rights of the individual citizens requires a government based on laws applied by judges who are independent in every way. The necessity of an independent judiciary has become all the more great on account of a change in the nature of the functions to be performed by the state. We no longer believe in a police state. We believe and act upon the principle of a welfare state. The result is that the functions of the state have multiplied and consequently the state has become the biggest litigant before the courts. The number of writ petitions in which the orders of the Government are challenged is multiplying every day and the judges are required to dispose of thousands of such applications. It is for this reason that it is contended that the appointment of the judges must not be in the hands of the Government. In a case between a Government and a citizen, the judge must be one who is not under the control of the Government and he must not be appointed by the Government. If that is not done and the executive is allowed to appoint the judges, it is likely to appoint those who will decide the cases in its favour and consequently the common man can have no faith that he will get justice from a judge nominated by the Government. Moreover, once a judge is appointed, it is necessary that the seniority rule must be applied because otherwise that judge who decides the cases in favour of the Government is likely to supersede those who do not. In

April 1973, the Government of India supersedes three senior-most judges of the Supreme Court and appointed a Chief Justice of India who was acceptable to it. The defence given by the Government was that the new Chief Justice appointed by it was the only judge who decided in favour of the Government in the Bank Nationalisation case while the other judges gave their decision against her. It was also contended by the Government that it had to take into consideration the "social philosophy" of the judges while appointing a Chief Justice. However, the theory of "committed judges" is foreign to democratic society and is the negation of the independence of the judiciary.

A similar thing was done by the Government of India in May 1974. While appointing a successor to Chief Justice O.K. Mahajan of the High Court of Punjab and Haryana, the Government of India superseded Mr. Justice P.C. Pandit who it that time was the senior-most judge of the High Court and appointed. Mr. Justice R.S. Narula who was very junior to him. No reason was given by the Government in support of its arbitrary action and the only conclusion is that the Government of India did not want Mr. Justice Pandit to occupy the position of the Chief Justice. That is going to have a very unfortunate effect on the independence of the judiciary. The Government is bent upon, having "pliable" judges who are willing to do whatever the Government wants them to do. In future the prospective judges or Chief Justice will have to find political backing for their appointment and their merits will be only a secondary consideration.

In England, the Court of Star Chamber operated specifically to carry out the orders of the King. Henry VIII used the Court of Star Chamber to dispose of his enemies and his discarded wives. Even today, high-handed or oppressive judicial action is referred to as Star Chamber proceedings. Such judicial proceedings have continued to the present day in autocratic regimes. One of the great reforms of the Glorious Revolution of 1688 was the Act of Settlement which was passed in 1701 and which provided that judges should hold office for life during good behaviour. So long as they performed their duties efficiently and honestly, they were to fear none. They could not be dismissed nor could their salaries be reduced. They could be removed only if a joint address was presented by both Houses of Parliament. The subordinate judges could be removed by Lord Chancellor, but the convention is that nobody has been turned out during the last two centuries.

In the United States, an attempt was made by President Franklin D. Roosevelt to pack the Supreme Court in order to get a court more favourable to New Deal Legislation.

There are many factors which help to ensure the independence of the judiciary. One of them is the method of their appointment. In some states of America, the judges are elected by the people. In some of the cantons of Switzerland, the judges are elected by the people. In the Soviet Union, the subordinate judges are elected by the people. Experience shows that this system is not at all desirable. The people are not competent to appreciate the qualities necessary for a good judge. While a judge is usually of a quiet temperament, the system of election demands that he must be talkative. A quiet man will not be able to carry the polls. Innumerable examples can be quoted from the United States to show that good candidates were defeated and worthless ones were successful. If a judge seeks to be re-elected, he must give those judgments which make him popular. He will not bother about the dictates of his conscience but he will act with an eye on his re-election. He will not give a judgment which is likely to alienate the voters. He has to say good-bye to all canons of justice. It is possible that such a judge may be quite ignorant of all the implications of the law of the country. As he is elected not because of his legal knowledge but because of his canvassing and influence, he may prove to be a buffoon in the court room. It must be a pitiable sight to see a judge who does not know the law but before whom eminent lawyers argue their cases. Much cannot be expected under such circumstances. Candidates for judicial office make poor judges. They cannot put before the electorate any programme which they will carry out if they are elected. The result is that politicians become judges and their entire outlook is partisan and hence there can be no independence of the judiciary in such a case. Prof. Laski says, "Of all the methods of appointment, that of election by the people at large is without exception the worst." About the system of election of judges by the people, Garner says, "It lowers the character of the judiciary, tends to make a politician of the judge and subjects the judicial mind to a strain which it is not always able to resist." Another writer observes, "The desire to court popularity is a temptation few will be able to resist when their reelection is dependent on their popularity."

In Switzerland the judges are elected for six years by the two federal chambers sitting together. The system has worked well in that country because of the small size of the legislature and also because judges are ordinarily re-elected again and again and that makes their tenure of office practically permanent. However, the system of election by the legislature is not satisfactory. Laski says, "If the choice is to be made on grounds of legal fitness the average member of a legislature has no special qualifications for judging and he is therefore likely to be swayed by political considerations irrelevant to the problem." Moreover, "Such party election encourages a type of judge far removed from the ideal of fairness and reasonableness which judicial decision demands." Such a system is also against the spirit of separation of powers. The persons who make the laws should not have a hand in the appointment of those who have to interpret them.

The view of Prof. Laski is that the system of appointment by the executive is "the best available method of choice." However, Laski does not consider simple nomination by the executive as an adequate system. His suggestion is that all judicial appointments should be made "on the recommendation of the Minister of Justice, with the consent of a standing committee of the judges which would represent all sides of their work." This method will ensure that only those persons are appointed who possess the requisite qualifications. In India, the higher judiciary is generally selected from the practising lawyers. The same is the case in England, Canada, Australia, etc.

In the United States, the federal judges are appointed by the President with the consent of the Senate and can be removed only by impeachment. In France, competitive examinations are held under the control of the Minister of Justice for recruitment purposes. The persons so selected are promoted on the basis of seniority and merit. Neither the legislature nor the executive can remove them. It is only the Court of Cessation acting through a Committee of seven judges, that can remove a judge in France. This provision is sufficient safeguard to protect them.

The system of appointment by the executive has one great defect. The executive may make appointments from its own party. It is said that Lord Halsbury made all appointments from his own party.

The tenure of judges is an important factor on which the independence of the judiciary depends. If the judges are appointed for short terms, much of their independence is gone because they are always thinking of their reappointment and naturally they would not like to do anything which is going to annoy those in whose hands their reappointment lies. That is the reason why the Act of Settlement provided that the judges were to hold office for life during good behaviour. So long as they continue to perform their duties efficiently and honestly, they were to fear none. They could neither be dismissed nor their salaries reduced. They could be removed only if a joint address was presented by both Houses of Parliament and that is rarely done. A similar system prevails in India. Judges of the Supreme Court, once appointed, continue to hold office till they reach the age of 65. In the case of judges of the High Courts, the age of retirement is 62, and the judges belonging to the subordinate judiciary retire at 58. However, this does not mean that judges cannot be removed at all. If a judge becomes thoroughly incompetent or unfit to perform his duties on account of the loss of mental faculties or physical unfitness, he can be removed from office. Such a thing was done in the case of Mr. Justice Imam of the Supreme Court of India, on account of his physical unfitness. Experience shows that such things are rare and judges continue to hold office during good behaviour. Hamilton says, "The standard of good behaviour for the continuance in office of the judicial magistracy is certainly one of the most valuable improvements in the practice of Government. In a monarchy, it is an excellent barrier to the despotism of the prince; in a Republic it is no less excellent barrier to the encroachments and oppressions of the representative body. And it is the best expedient which can be devised in any Government to secure a sturdy, upright and impartial administration of the laws."

In order to make the judges independent, they must be paid fixed and adequate salaries. The reason is that a judge, to be honest and upright, must be above want. If he cannot make his both ends meet, there is every possibility of his becoming corrupt. That is what actually happened in the case of Lord Bacon who was the Lord Chancellor of England. Judges must be paid handsomely so that the best brains are attracted to this line and while in office, they are able to discharge their duties in an upright manner. Moreover, we should not allow them to suffer from a sense of inferiority arising out of the fact that while they are getting so little, the lawyers practising before them are earning a lot. That is the reason why the judges in England are knighted as soon as they are appointed. In addition to salaries, their other conditions of service should be favourable so that they have enough to work in peace and without any worry. They should be paid adequate pension on retirement or retirement compensation. Hamilton says, "In the general course of human nature, a power over a man's subsistence amounts to a power over his will."

While appointing judges, we must see that only those persons are appointed as judges, who are highly qualified in the field of law. That is partly due to the fact that very often the lawyers practising before them are brilliant people arid if the judges are not so, they are likely to cut a sorry figure. They cannot be expected to command any respect.

Another essential thing for the independence of the judiciary is that there should be a separation of judicial functions from the executive functions. One of the Directive Principles of State Policy is the separation of judicial functions from the executive functions. In India, there has been an intermingling of the executive and the judicial functions. The Deputy Commissioner or the Collector who is the head of the District administration has also been the District Magistrate. Till recently, all the magistrates in the District were under him. That was not at all desirable from the point of view of the independence of the judiciary but the system was allowed to continue as it suited the English rulers in India. Sir Harvey Adamson, at one time Home Member in the Government of India, pointed out that "the exercise of executive control over the subordinate magistrates by whom the great bulk of criminal cases are tried is the point where the present system is defective. If the control is exercised by the officer who is responsible for the peace of the district, there is the constant danger that the subordinate magistrate may be unconsciously guided by other than purely judicial considerations." It is happy to find that the process of the separation of judicial functions from the executive has made progress in many states and judicial magistrates have been appointed who are directly under the control of the High Court.

About the independence of the judiciary Professor Willoughby observes thus: "Judges should be selected without regard to their political affiliations. Once selected, they shall hold office for a long term, for life or during good behaviour. They shall not be subject to dismissal by the executive, may be removed only for misconduct as established by a formal process of impeachment or address on the part of both Houses of Legislature. Their compensation shall not be withheld or diminished during their term of office."

Relation between Judiciary and Legislature

It goes without saying that the judiciary must be kept away from party politics. To the extent to which that is done, the independence of the judiciary is maintained. Consequently, it is contended that the legislature should not have the power to elect judges. Moreover, no member of a legislature should be eligible for a judicial office. However the legislature may be given the power of recommending the removal of judges either by the presentation of an address to the executive, as is the case in England, or by means of impeachment, as in the United States. This power is necessary to provide against those judges who may abuse their power and receive presents or bribes. Moreover, in a unitary government like that of Great Britain and France, the judiciary need not be given the power to question the validity of the laws passed by the legislature. However, such a power is necessary in the case of federal governments. The reason is that the law of the country is founded in a written constitution and it is necessary that the courts should be given the power to decide whether a particular law passed by the legislature is *intra vires* or *ultra vires* the constitution or otherwise unconstitutional or invalid.

In *McCulloch v. Maryland*, the Supreme Court of America upheld in 1819 the right of the Congress to establish the United States Bank even though the power to create banks is not specifically conferred by the Constitution. Instead, the Constitution provided the Congress with other powers from which it was reasonable to imply the power to establish the bank. Thus was born the doctrine of implied powers which has been useful to the Congress and the Supreme Court in making the Constitution applicable to the changing conditions.

In *Wickard v. Filburn* (1942), the Supreme Court was faced with the question whether wheat raised and consumed on Filburn's Farm was subject to controls based on the power of Congress over inter-state commerce. The Congress had enacted legislation to support farm prices through the establishment of marketing quotas tor farmers producing certain basic commodities. Filburn contended that the products raised and consumed on his own farm were not subject to the federal controls. The Supreme Court held that the regulation was applicable since the wheat was "available for marketing" even though it was not to be sold. The determination of policy in this way by the court makes more clear to Congress its power under the constitutional provision of inter-state commerce.

Judges not only interpret law, they also make law, although indirectly. Whenever a case before a court is not covered by law, it is the duty of the judge not to determine what the legislature meant but "to guess what it would have intended on a point not present, if the point had been present. In this way, judges legislate to till up the *casus ommissus* or the cases of omission. Judges also create law by trying to determine the exact meaning of law, expanding its details and applying the general principles of justice, equity and morality. In India, the United States and Great Britain, judicial decisions are cited as precedents which are considered binding in subsequent cases on the principle of *stare decisis* which means "stick with decisions once made." Precedents carry great weight and courts usually follow them. Decisions of major courts have a great influence on subsequent court-made law. Fred Rodell refers to law as a peculiar bird that attempts to fly forward while all the time looking backward. In justification of the practice, it can be said that through this method greater certainty is attained and the people feel more secure in their knowledge of how the law will be applied. Even so, mathematical certainty is not likely to evolve from complex human patterns of conflict which seldom are duplicated in their entirety. The result is that the doctrine of *stare decisis* is not always followed. In many cases, the Supreme Court of India has departed from its previous decisions.

The relation between the judiciary and the legislature must be one of the mutual respect. Each should mind its own business and not try to encroach upon the field of the other. Some time back, there was a very unhappy conflict between the judiciary and the legislature in Uttar Pradesh. The legislature of that state decided to take action against certain judges of the Allahabad High Court and that led to a very explosive situation. When the matter was referred to the Supreme Court by the President of India, Chief Justice Gajendragadkar observed that there was no conflict between the judiciary and the legislature and each must confine itself to its own sphere of action.

In the famous Golak Nath case decided by the Supreme Court of India in February 1967, it was held that the Parliament of India had not the power to take away the fundamental rights guaranteed by the Constitution. The challenge was accepted by the Indian Parliament and the 24th Amendment of the Constitution was passed. That Amendment expressly empowered the Parliament to amend any provision of the Constitution including those relating to fundamental rights. The validity of the 24th Amendment was challenged in the famous case of *Kesavananda v. State of Kerala* (AIR 1973 S.C.

1461). The Supreme Court held that the 24th Amendment of the Constitution was valid. In spite of this, the three senior-most judges of the Supreme Court who opposed the point of view of the Parliament were superseded. The relations between the judiciary and Parliament in India are not satisfactory.

Relation between Judiciary and Executive

The relation of the judiciary with the executive may be viewed from the standpoint of the judicial powers of the executive and its control over the judiciary and the administrative powers of the judiciary and its control over the executive. The former is a historical survival of the original unlimited powers of the executive. The latter depends upon the prevailing theory as to the proper separation of powers and the relative importance of government and individual liberty.

The executive exercises control over the judiciary because in the last resort judicial decisions are effective only if they are supported by the force of the state and that force is at the command of the executive. Moreover, the executive is usually given the power of making appointments to judicial offices. While the permanent tenure that follows appointment, prevents continued control, the complexion of the judiciary may be influenced by the political principles maintained by the executive at the time of appointment. For example, the appointment of John Marshall to the Supreme Court of America led to numerous decisions favourable to the federal government. The New Deal Legislation of President Roosevelt was opposed by the Supreme Court which did not see eye to eye with that legislation.

The courts depend upon the executive for carrying out their decisions and that is a great handicap to the judiciary. They do not possess the personnel or organisation to enforce their orders. They generally have personnel with authority to perform routine tasks such as serving papers, keeping records and preserving order in the court room. The lack of enforcement machinery has occasionally resulted in considerable embarrassment to the courts. During the Presidency of Andrew Jackson, Chief Justice Marshall of the American Supreme Court gave a decision which was not to the liking of President Jackson who is reported to have observed, "John Marshall has made his decision, now let him enforce it." Fortunately, such an attitude on the part of the executive is an exception and not the rule and ordinarily the decisions given by the courts are enforced by the executive. However, this illustrates the necessity and desirability of a high measure of respect and cooperation between the executive and judiciary.

A very difficult situation arose in the United States in the 1950s. The Supreme Court of America decreed the end of racial segregation in public schools. The executive officials in several states openly declared that they would not enforce any decree providing for integration. The result was that the Federal Government had to intervene to enforce the law as laid down by the Supreme Court.

In the famous case of *Virginia* v. *West Virginia,* the State of West Virginia refused to pay a share of the Virginia bonded debt after the Civil War. The matter was taken to the Supreme Court of America. On account of the reluctance or inability of the Supreme Court to devise methods to force West Virginiato pay the debt, no final decision was given by the Supreme Court for more than 50 years.

A reference may be made to the judicial powers exercised by the executive. These are concerned mainly with the maintenance of discipline in the army, navy and civil service and the application and enforcement of administrative law. Modern states create constitutional and statutory safeguards against the arbitrary use of those powers. The law of contempt of court is a survival of the time when a court was merely a division of administration and the disregard of its commands was an offence against the majesty of the king. The power of pardon is possessed by the executive and it is a direct survival of the original judicial functions of the executive.

The most important judicial powers of the executive are to be found in those countries where administrative law and administrative courts are to be found. Those courts try the servants of the government for illegal acts committed by them in the course of their official duties. In England, even the officers of the government are amenable to the jurisdiction of ordinary courts for things done by them in their official capacity. The legal immunity of the crown in England and the special procedure for the impeachment of the American President and other high officials in that country are exceptions. The members of the army and navy are responsible for their illegal acts even if those are done at the command of their superior officers. On the whole, the military administration is subordinate to civil administration.

The Courts and Law

The quality of justice depends upon the character of the judiciary. The general public in all parts of the world identifies law and justice with the judges. If the character of the judges is high and the laws are generally acceptable, the people are law-abiding. The few who break the law are punished and set apart if they are constant law-violators. When qualified judges give decisions which are generally regarded as just and fair, public opinion is a powerful psychological force in supporting the execution of those decisions.

In totalitarian states, the courts function according to the will of the executive. The decisions given by the courts are according to the needs of the executive and the judges are the creatures of the executive. The decrees of the courts are enforced by terror Public trials are held frequently for the purpose of frightening the people into conformance with the law. In some cases, public trials may be the instruments for preparing the public for some new programme. If that is so, their function is propaganda and not justice. The judges who perform these functions are not primarily interested in the law or justice. In fact, they are the tools of the political parties.

There are two views regarding the interpretation of law by the courts. Some courts apply the law strictly according to the letter of the law. There are others who interpret it according to the spirit of the law. Critics of strict interpretation of law contend that justice is not achieved by adhering too closely to the printed words. They believe that when laws are executed after taking into account the changed circumstances, they are more likely to be obeyed. A liberal interpretation of the law finds greater public favour than strict interpretation. Law enforcement in the courts nearest the people must be geared to the realities of the customs and attitudes of the community if it is to be obeyed by the people in general. The courts must be impartial and apply the law without special favour if their judgments are to be respected.

If the courts are to be effective, it is necessary that justice must be swift and inexpensive. Long delays in bringing cases to trial and long trials result in huge fees for lawyers and heavy court costs. After a long period has elapsed, it is frequently difficult, if not impossible, to locate all the witnesses. The person with an average income cannot finance a case which is on appeal for years. The record of the English courts in regard to speed and expense is much better than that of Indian courts and American courts. The English courts do not allow lawyers to dominate the court scene and carry on battles over technical details. Important trials are completed in England within a period of one week while it takes months or years in India. Long trials severely tax the court machinery and also help clog the channels of justice.

Rule of Law

The rule of law is one of the unique characteristics of the English Constitution. Bluntly put, it means that it is the law of England that rules the country and not the arbitrary will of any individual. The law is supreme over all; none can claim exemption or immunity from it. According to Dicey, the rule of law embraces three "distinct though kindred conceptions."

In the first place, it means that no man is punishable or can be lawfully made to suffer in body or goods except for a distinct breach of law established in the ordinary legal manner before the ordinary courts. This means that no person can be punished in England unless and until it is definitely proved that he has violated some definite law of the country. If a person cannot be held guilty of violating a particular law of the country, he must be set at liberty. There can be neither any illegal imprisonment nor illegal punishment. If a person has been imprisoned without any authority of law, an application can be made for a writ of *habe- as corpus* and if the detaining authority cannot put forward a legal plea in its defence, the person has to be discharged. The executive has no authority to put a person behind the bars arbitrarily.

Secondly, the rule of law means that, "no man is above law but that every man, whatever his rank or condition, is subject to the ordinary law of the realm and amenable to the jurisdiction of ordinary tribunal. What is law – legal rights and legal obligations—for one man must hold equally as such for all citizens." This means that Whatever the status of a person, he must submit to the ordinary law of the country and ordinary courts of the country. There are no separate courts and separate law for the trial of government servants in England, although there are in France. They have to be tried by the same law by which an ordinary citizen is tried. Moreover, no person can plead immunity from obedience to the law of the land.

In the third place, the rule of law means that "the general principles of the Constitution are the result of judicial decisions determining the rights of private persons in particular cases brought before the courts." This refers to the important parts played by the English judges in safeguarding the rights and liberties of Englishmen. Dicey was a Liberal of the 19th century and as such, paid a tribute to the Liberal judges who had played an important part in safeguarding the rights and liberties of Englishmen in the past.

Dicey put great emphasis on the rule of law in England. He glorified in the fact that the rule of law established the equality of all citizens before the courts of law. "Every official from the Prime Minister to a constable or collector of taxes is under the same responsibility for every act done without legal justification, as any other citizen." Moreover, there was no scope for any arbitrary detention or punishment. The law must have its own course.

Dicey pointed out that the rule of law had a healthy effect on the arbitrary tendencies of government servants. No government official could dare to put an Englishman behind bars without legal justification. He knew that if it was found that his action, was illegal, he was liable to be burdened with damages. Moreover, while carrying out the orders of their superiors, the government servants were always to keep in mind the fact that they must not go against the law of the country. If a soldier was ordered to disperse a mob, he was not to kill persons unnecessarily. He was merely to disperse the mob without causing injuries to the people. He was always to keep in mind the fact that if he killed any person, he was liable to be tried for murder and punished if found guilty. This fact was bound to have a healthy check on the actions of the government servants. Indirectly, it was conducive to the liberties of the Englishmen.

Critics point out that the rule of law which was so highly praised by Dicey is not to be found in England today. It is being violated in very many respects. The Public Authorities Protection Act, 1893 gives special protection to officials. Proceedings against them must be started within 6 months and if that is not done, they become time-barred. Moreover, if proceedings against a Government servant fail, the plaintiff has to pay very heavy costs. The object of this provision is to discourage private individuals from starting proceedings against Government servants.

The Home Secretary has an absolute discretion to grant certificates of naturalisation as British subject. He can cancel the certificate at any time he likes. He has full discretion in the matter of deporting any undesirable alien. For all these acts, he cannot be challenged in a court of law. The Crown has the power to grant or refuse passports to travel in any foreign country and the exercise of this power cannot be challenged in any court.

Foreign rulers and diplomats enjoy immunity before courts of law and they cannot be tried even if they violate any law of the country. No action lies against trading vessels belonging to a foreign state. No suit can be filed against a trade union for any act committed by its officers or members in furtherance of bonafide trade dispute. Lord Chamberlain has the power to censor the plays and if he imposes ban, the same cannot be challenged in any court of law. The power of the Home Secretary to open and detain letters is a violation of the rule of law. Judges cannot be held responsible for things done by them in the official course of their business. However, if a vacation judge unlawfully refuses a writ of *habeas corpus,* he can be sued and a penalty up to £ 500 can be imposed. The Crown can terminate any contract of service. It is not bound even by the express terms in a contract. The result is that the servants of the Crown hold their offices during the pleasure of the Crown.

Formerly, peers could be tried only by peers. However, this privilege was taken away by the Law Reform Act of 1947.

The Public Order Act of 1936 gives the police the power to regulate or prohibit public meetings and processions. It can also declare drilling and wearing of unauthorised uniforms as illegal. The Customs Consolidation Act, 1866 and Inland Revenue Act, 1890 give protection to customs and excise officials regarding anything done by them in the performance of their official duties.

Until 1947, the Crown was not liable for the tortuous acts of its servants and was liable only to a limited extent in contract, though the actual tortfeasor could be sued and the Crown often stood behind him and paid the damages awarded against him. Action in contract could only be started by a complicated procedure known as a Petition of Right, with the consent of the Crown given on the advice of the Attorney General. The Crown Proceedings Act, 1947 and the Rules of the Supreme Court (Crown Proceedings) Act, 1947 came into force on 1 January 1948. The effect of this legislation is to place the Crown as regards civil proceedings in the same position as a subject. Proceedings by Petitions of Rights were abolished and now all claims can be brought by ordinary action in accordance with the Act. The Crown is liable in contract and also in tort but there are certain exceptions. Regarding contractual claims, civil servants cannot sue the Crown for wrongful dismissal or arrears of pay. Action in tort lies against the Crown for the torts against civil servants or agents committed in the course of their employment, for breaches of duty owed at common law by an employer to his servants, for breach of duty attaching to the ownership, occupation, possession or control of property and for breach of statutory duties. No proceedings lie against the Crown in tort for acts done in private capacity. The law as to indemnity and contribution under the Law Reform (Married Women and Tortfeasors) Act, 1935 applies to Crown cases. If the Crown is a joint tortfeasor, it can claim a contribution from fellow wrong-doers and where the Crown is led to publishing a libel, it may claim indemnity against the party responsible. No action lies in torts against the Crown for anything done or omitted to be done in relation to any postal packet or telephone communication, except that an action will lie for damages for loss of a registered inland postal packet not being a telegram. Such action must be brought within 12 months of the date of the posting of the packet. Both the Crown and any member of the Armed Forces, are immune from liability in tort in respect of the death of or personal injury to another member of the Armed Forces on duty.

While a citizen is subject only to the ordinary law, he can be subject also to the special law affecting his particular profession. That special law may be enforced by special tribunals. The Armed Forces are subject to military law or naval law in addition to the ordinary law of the land and offences against that law are triable by court-martial. Likewise, the clergy are subject to ecclesiastical law enforced by the ecclesiastical courts. Solicitors are subject to the disciplinary powers of a statutory body composed of the members of the profession with a right of appeal in the High Court. The members of the medical profession are tried by the General Medical Council for professional misconduct. Similar powers are exercised by the General Dental Council over the dentists.

There are many special courts for the decision of issues which affect the proprietary right of citizens. Special tribunals appointed by ministers decide questions of insurability. They also decide the amount of compensation to be paid for the compulsory acquisition of the land. If a minister interested in carrying out a policy is allowed to give decision on a judicial issue, his action is against the rule of law.

According to Wade a Phillips, "The rule of law remains a principle of our constitution. It means the absence of arbitrary power; effective control of and people publicity for delegated legislation, particularly when it imposes penalties; that when discretionary power is granted the manner in which it is to be exercised should as far as is practicable be defined; that every man should be responsible to the ordinary law whether he be private citizen or public officer; that private rights should be determined by impartial and independent tribunals and that fundamental private rights are safeguarded by the ordinary law of the land. If this be accepted, it is only necessary to contrast the state of affairs in the totalitarian States, with their apparatus of secret police and people's courts administering not law, but the orders of those who can dictate what is the people's will, in order to answer affirmatively the question—does the rule of law today remain a principle of the Constitution? This does not mean that it is a fixed principle of law from which there can be no departure. Since Parliament is supreme, there is no legal sanction to prevent the enactment of a statute which violates the principle of the rule of law. The ultimate safeguard then is to be found in the acceptance of the principle as a guide to conduct by any political party which is in a position to influence the course of legislation."

Administrative Law

The term administrative law or *Droit Administratif* has been variously defined by different writers. Barthelemy says that it "consists of all the legal rules governing the relations of the public administrative bodies to one another and to individuals." Professor Rene David defines it "as the body of rules which determine the organisation and the duties of public administration and which regulate the relations of the administrative authorities towards the citizens of the state." According to Dr. Jennings, "Administrative law is the law relating to the administration. It determines the organisation, powers and duties of administrative authorities."

Dicey referred to two leading principles of the administrative law of France. The first principle was that the government and its servants possessed special rights, privileges or prerogatives as against private citizens. The extent of those rights, privileges or prerogatives was determined according to principles which were different from the considerations which fixed legal rights and duties of one citizen to the other. In his dealings with the state, an individual did not stand on the same footing as that on which he stood in his dealings with his neighbour. The second leading principle was the necessity of maintaining the separation of powers. The government, the legislature and the courts were to be prevented from encroaching upon the sphere of one another. While the ordinary judges were to be irremovable and independent of the executive, the government and its officials in their official capacity were to be independent and act to a great extent free from the jurisdiction of the ordinary courts.

Dicey also referred to what he considered to be the four distinguishing characteristics of administrative law in France. The first one was that the relations of the government and its officials with private citizens were regulated by a body of rules which were in reality laws but which differed considerably from the laws which governed the relations of one private individual to another. The second characteristic was that the ordinary courts had no concern whatsoever with matters at issue between private persons and the state. Those matters were to be determined by administrative courts which were connected with the government in one way or the other. There was a feeling in France that "the judges are the enemies of the servants of the state and that there is always reason to fear their attempts to compromise the public interests by their malevolent or at best rash interference in the usual course of government business." The third characteristic was the possibility of a conflict of jurisdiction between the administrative courts and the ordinary courts of justice. In such a case, the Court of Conflicts was to settle the question. The Council of State and the Court of Cessation were given equal representation on the Court of Conflicts which was presided over by the Minister of Justice. The fourth characteristic was the tendency to protect from the supervision or control of the ordinary law courts any servant of the state who was guilty of an illegal act, provided it was done in the discharge of his official duties and in bonafide obedience to the orders of his superiors. The servant of the state could not be made responsible before any court, whether judicial or administrative, for the performance of any act of the state. He was also protected from the penal consequences of any interference with the personal liberty of fellow citizens when the act complained of was under the orders of a superior. Moreover, without the permission of the Council of State, he could not be prosecuted or otherwise proceeded against for any act done by him in relation to his official duties.

Under the system of administrative law as it exists in France, the actions of the government servants are divided into two parts, *viz.,* those done by them in their official capacity and those done by them in their private capacity as ordinary citizens. So far as their private acts are concerned, they can be tried by the ordinary courts. However, there are separate courts to try those cases in which they act in their official capacity. Moreover, there are two different sets of courts. *viz.*, ordinary and administrative courts. While a codified law is administered by the ordinary courts, the administrative courts follow the precedents already established.

There used to be a lot of prejudice against administrative law. As a matter of fact. Dicey discussed the subject with a view to show that while the rule of law safeguarded the liberties of Englishmen, the system of administrative law which existed in France was its very negation. However, later on, he himself confessed that his information was not correct. It is now realised that the system of administrative law has certain advantages. While under the rule of law, a government servant is tried as an ordinary individual by an ordinary court, things are different under administrative law. An administrative court consists of the heads of the various departments and they can take into consideration the awkward position in which the government servant might have been placed at the time of the commission of the offence. It is pointed out that as the judges in the administrative courts belong to the different departments, they are likely to favour the government servants and the very object of law can be defeated. However, the unanimous view of all the writers is that in actual practice the judges of the administrative courts have acted in an impartial manner and have not shown any preference for those who belonged to their departments.

In one respect, the system of administrative law is superior to the rule of law. If an offence is committed by a government servant in England even in the performance of his official duties, his responsibility is only personal. The government does not accept any responsibility in that matter. The result is that the government servants are placed at great disadvantage. Knowing their responsibility, they may act in a timid fashion while performing their duties. Moreover, even if a decree has been secured against a public servant, it may not be possible to execute it against him as his salary may be too low for that purpose. However, in the case of France, the decretal amount can be realised from the State Treasury without any difficulty.

It is contended that as the government servants are not responsible for their official actions and the government has to pay the damages whenever required, they might act irresponsibly. Their zeal may increase unnecessarily and they might infringe on the liberties of the people. However, as departmental action is taken for every mistake made by a public servant, the danger is not real.

It is to be observed that the old prejudice against administrative law has practically disappeared.

SUGGESTED READINGS

Baldwin	: The American Judiciary.
Blachlay, F.F.	: Administrative Legislation and Administration.
Bryce, J.	: Modern Democracies, Vol. II.
Carpenter	: Judicial Tenure in the United States.
Carr. Robert K.	: The Supreme Court and Judicial Review. New York, 1942.
Corwin, E.S.	: The Doctrine of Judicial Review and the Constitution.
Dicev. A.V.	: The Law of the Constitution.
Finer, H.	: The Theory and Practice of Modern Government.
Frank, Jerome	: Courts on Trial.
Garner, J.W.	: Political Science and Government.
Goodnow. F.J.	: Principles of Constitutional Government.
Gray	: The Nature and Sources of Law.
Haines. Charles G.	: The American Doctrine of Judicial Supremacy. Berkeley, 1932.
Jennings. W.I.	: The Law and the Constitution.
Laski, H.J.	: A Grammar of Politics.
Lowell, A.L.	: Government of England. Vol. II.
Marriott, J.A.R.	: The Mechanism of the Modern State.
Rohson, W.A.	: Justice and Administrative Law.
Rochc, John P., and Steadman, Murrays	: The Dynamics of Democratic Government.
Sail, E.M.	: Government and Politics of France.
Sidgwick, H.	: Elements of Politics.
Warren, Charles	: The Congress, the Constitution and the Supreme Court.
Warren, Charles	: The Supreme Court in the United States History, 3 Vols, Boston, 1922.
Willoughby, W.F.	: Government of Modern States.

CHAPTER

Political Parties and Pressure Groups

Definition

Many definitions of political parties have been given by various writers. Gettell defines a political party as "a group of citizens, more or less organised, who act as a political unit and who by the use of their voting power aim to control the government and carry out their general policy." According to Gilchrist, a political party "is an organised group of citizens who profess to share the same political views and by acting as a political unit try to control the government." MacIver defines a political party as "an association organised in support of some principle of policy which by constitutional means it endeavours to make the determinant of government." Burke defines a political party as "a body of men united for the purpose of promoting by their joint endeavours the public interests upon some principle on which they are all agreed."

There is a fundamental distinction between a political party and a faction. While a political party is always guided by the national interests, a faction aims at the achievement of some sectional interest. A faction is like a clique or coterie and aims at some selfish private interests.

Essentials of a Political Party

The first essential of a political party is that its members must be organised. A parts must have its branches all over the country and it must enforce discipline among its members. It is impossible to think of political parties without organisation. The members of a political party must have practically the same views on important public matters. They must work for national interests and not sectional or private interests. They must aim at capturing power by peaceful and constitutional

Learning Objectives

- Definition
- Essentials of a Political Party
- Functions of Political Parties
- Basis of Political Parties
- Party System and Democracy
- Conditions Necessary for Successful Working of Parties
- Merits of Party System in General
- Demerits
- Merits of Two-Party System
- Demerits of Two-Party System
- Merits of Multiple Party System
- Demerits of Multiple Party System
- Single Party System
- Pressure Groups and Lobbies
- Pressure Groups and Political Parties
- Pressure Groups and Lobbies
- Pressure Groups and Elections
- Pressure Groups and Legislature
- Presure Groups and the Executive
- Pressure Groups and Judiciary
- Pressure Groups and Public Opinion
- Role of Pressure Groups
- Factors helping success of Pressure Groups
- Drawbacks
- Suggested Readings

means. If they are defeated, they must accept defeat with grace and start working for the next chance. They must not believe in using force to overthrow the government. They must have faith in the ballot-boxes and not in brute force to achieve their objective. Dr. Roucek rightly points out that a political party "is held together primarily by its ideology and organisation."

Functions of Political Parties

Many useful functions are performed by political parties. Experience shows that it is impossible to run the administrative machinery in a democratic government without the help of political parties. It is the political parties which prepare their election manifestoes and put before the people their separate programmes to be followed by them if they are returned to power. The masses do not think clearly and it is the political parties who clarify the atmosphere by putting before the people clear-cut programmes. The people know that the political parties will honour the promises made by them. Every effort is made by all the political parties to see that the people come to know their future programmes. For that purpose, they arrange public meetings, write in the press, distribute pamphlets and sometimes broadcast to the nation. Since the various parties present their respective points of view, the people have enough material before them to make their decisions.

Political parties play an important part in forming public opinion. Every party aims at popularity and if it manages to create public opinion in its favour, it is bound to win. Political parties have been described as the brokers of ideas. They influence the minds of the people in such a way that they are willing to vote for them.

Political parties make selections of candidates. It is true that there can be wrong choices in certain cases on account of the influence of some vested interests, but on the whole no party can afford to put forward worthless candidates. Only that person is selected as a candidate who enjoys a good reputation among the people. No party wants to be liquidated by putting forward unpopular candidates. If there were no political parties, any number of self-seekers could contest elections and confuse the public mind. Even if an independent person is elected there is no guarantee that he will honour the promises made by him at the time of election. He can Afford to repudiate himself completely soon after his election. He need not care lor the sentiments of the people during the tenure of his office. However, no political party can afford to do such a thing. It must honour the promises made at the time of election or lace liquidation at the next election. Even when elections are over, the organisation of a political party throughout the country helps to link up the voters with their representatives in the legislature. Through this channel, the people can pass on the grievances to their representatives and thus get them redressed.

In every democratic government, a large number of elections have to be fought. There are the national elections, the provincial or state elections and the local elections. Millions of voters have to be brought to the polling stations to cast their votes and this cannot be done by independent candidates. It is a costly affair and it is only the funds of the great political parties which can manage the whole show. Thousands of workers are required at the time of polling. Not only this, a lot of propaganda has to be carried on before the elections to win over the voters. The services of the great leaders are requisitioned to approach the people. Door to door canvassing can be done only by the organisations of the political parties. No wonder, it is rightly contended that an independent candidate, barring a few notable exceptions, has practically no chance of success in the elections.

The Opposition also serves a useful purpose. All that comes from the government is thoroughly scrutinised and every attempt is made by the Opposition to expose the acts of omission and commission of the government. This makes the government very cautious in its work. It knows full well that no action of the government will escape the vigilant eye of the Opposition. This feeling has a salutary effect on the government. It does not embark upon any foolhardy enterprises. It has rightly been stated that the Prime Minister of England knows more about the Leader of the Opposition than he knows about his wife.

Political parties help to maintain discipline in the legislature. The party whips see to it that the members of their party vote in a particular way and action is taken against those who defy the whip.

In a presidential form of government, political parties serve as a bridge between the legislature and the executive. The same party may have its own President and may also manage to have a majority in both houses of the legislature. In this way, the evils of the separation of powers are avoided.

A political party is a unifying agency between the executive and the legislature. "It is the work of the parties to bind the disconnected organs into a unity and secure the harmonious cooperation of the entire government." Dr. Finer says, "Without parties, an electorate would be either impotent or destructive by embarking on impossible policies that would only wreck the political machine."

The view of Professor Macpherson is that the main function of the party system is to moderate and contain a conflict of class interests in order to maintain a capitalist economy. Nothing except a party system can preserve the stability of a capitalist society where there is popular franchise or conversely the party system is essential to the maintenance of democracy in a capitalist society. Whether a two party or multi-party system will best serve the purpose of democracy depends upon the degree of class stratification and the degree of class consciousness. The more stratified the society, the more easily a multi-party system can be established. The greater the class consciousness, the more necessary is to have a multi-party system to preserve stability. Gunner Heckscher says that the view of Macpherson applies only to a democratic system of Government. Such thing is not possible in a totalitarian society which is based on the one-party system which is really a negation of the ideas of political parties (*The Study of Comparative Government and Politics,* p. 152).

Basis of Political Parties

Political parties come into existence owing to various circumstances. There may be political issues dividing the people and thus various political parties may be formed to further their respective viewpoints. It is well known that the Muslim League was founded to safeguard the interests of the Muslims and later on it was used by Mr. Jinnah to achieve his goal of Pakistan. There may be differences with regard to the form of government, the utility of any particular institution, the rights of the people, etc. Some people may stand for Dominion Status and others may stand for complete Swaraj. Some may stand for a strong central government and others may stand for a large measure of autonomy for the units. Some may stand for monarchy and others for a republican form of government.

There may be differences on economic issues. A particular party may stand for the perpetuation of landlordism in the country, while another may demand its abolition. One party may advocate the policy of wholesale nationalisation of all the resources of the country while the other may advocate private enterprise. One may stand for capitalism and the other for socialism or communism. Arthur Halcombe says: "National parties cannot be maintained by transitory impulses or temporary needs. They must be founded upon permanent sectional interests, above all, upon those of an economic character."

Sometimes, a political party may be formed to help the cause of social reform. The All India Depressed Classes League and the Scheduled Castes Federation aimed at the betterment of the lot of the Harijans or the untouchables.

Sometimes, political parties may be formed on the basis of religion or culture. In India, we have a large number of political parties which have only a religious appeal, *e.g.*, the Hindu Mahasabha, the Akali Party, the Muslim League, etc. Professor Beard says: "The wisest of leaders in all denominations have deplored the introduction of religious disputes into political discussions and campaigns."

There is a tendency towards combativeness in human nature. Fighting and quarreling form a part of the original nature of man. In civilised times, men "gang up" or choose sides, *i.e.*, create parties, in an attempt to give organised expression to this competitive instinct.

Another cause of the growth of political parties is the personality of a dynamic political leader. He inspires unthinking obedience in his followers who form a political party to support his struggle for power.

Political parties are also based on human nature. Some people are instinctively conservative and there are others who are instinctively progressive. Those who are conservative stand for the maintenance of *status quo* and those who are progressive want changes, sometimes radical changes. A King of Sweden is said to have observed thus: "A youngman, my dear Minister, who has not been a Socialist before he is five and twenty shows that he has no heart. But if he continues to be one after five and twenty, he shows that he has no head." This very view was put forward by W.S. Gilbert in the following lines:

"How nature does always contrive
That every boy and every gal
That's born into this world alive
Is either a little liberal
or else a little conservative."

In many cases, men inherit their politics and religion. It is not always that a man joins a particular party as a result of his convictions or long deliberation. He may join a political party because his parents belonged to that party. "Party allegiance, like property, is often transmitted from generation to generation." In many cases, settled political traditions have their effect. It used to be said of the United States that while the people of Irish descent always voted for the Democratic Party, those of German descent voted for the Republican Party. It was noticed in England that certain districts or regions voted for a particular party.

Lord Bryce says, "Though the professed reason for the existence of a party is the position of a particular set of doctrines, it has a concrete side as well as abstract doctrines. It is abstract in so far as it represents the adhesion of many minds to the same opinions. It is concrete as consisting of a number of men who act together in respect of their holding or professing to hold such opinions.

Party System and Democracy

There is an intimate connection between democracy and political parties. A critical examination of the problem shows that it is impossible to work the democratic machine without the help of political parties. It is the political parties which come forward with their programmes and thereby put before the people a clear picture of their future intentions. Every political party is honour bound to carry out the promises made by it at the time of elections. If it does not do so, the public is bound to react and turn out that party at the next election.

Political parties select candidates for the various constituencies. It is true that there can be bungling in some cases on account of the influence of the cliques and bosses, but on the whole the candidates put up by political parties are better than the independent candidates. The future of a party is at stake and whatever may be the case, it will not agree to put up worthless candidates. Thus, when the candidates have been put up by political parties, the people can be sure that they can vote safely for them.

Political parties employ all their resources to approach the voters even in anticipation of election. The leaders of the parties address meetings and they appeal to the people to vote for them. At the time of polling, the whole of the machinery of the party is employed to see that the people go to the polling stations and vote in their favour. Even when the elections are over, the party organisation in every locality helps the people to maintain their touch with their representatives in the legislature and thereby get their grievances redressed.

Even when the elections are over and the members take their seats in the legislature or a local body, parties maintain discipline in their ranks. This makes the work of the government smooth and it is easier to do more work in that way.

The party in power tries to fulfil the pledges made by it at the time of elections and brings forth legislation with that object in view. As it has got a majority and can count upon the support of the members, it can go on with its programme with confidence. The Opposition is also busy in its work of exposing the shortcomings of the government. It does not miss any opportunity to ventilate the grievances of the people. If the ministry is defeated, the Opposition gets a chance to form its own ministry. There is an automatic change of government without any bloodshed. Party government is just like a game of cricket and each party has its innings. There is no necessity for the use of force as the same objective can be achieved by merely appealing to the people. It is clear from above that the party system is a part and parcel of a democratic set-up. We cannot think of democracy without the party system. If there is no party system, we will have dictatorship.

MacIver says: "Without such party organisations, there can be no unified statement of principles, no orderly evolution of policies, no regular resort to the constitutional devices of parliamentary elections, nor of course any of the recognised institutions by means of which a party seeks to gain and maintain power." Again, "Without party system we may conclude, the *coup d'etat,* the Putsch or revolution, are the only methods of securing a change of government. Without it, the party in power is controlled only by the pressure of custom, which itself is weakest in times of crisis; by the desire for popularity which is easily overborne, by the ambitions of despotism, by the consideration, too insecure to allay the just fears of the subjects, of the advantage to itself of a contented prosperous people; beyond that by the fear of revolution. Without the party system, the State has no elasticity, no true self-determination. Without it, government is rigid and irresponsive, conceived in terms of mastery rather than of service." Lord Bryce says: "In popular governments, however, parties have a wider extension, if not a more strenuous life, for everywhere a citizen has a vote, with the duty to use it at elections, each of the parties which strive for mastery must try to bring the largest possible number of voters into the ranks, organise them locally, appeal to them by the spoken and printed words, bring them up to the polls. Ballots having replaced bullets in political life, every voter is supposed to belong to one of the partisan hosts to render more or less obedience to its leaders."

Political parties have been compared to the tides of the ocean. In the words of A.L. Lowell, "Their essential function and the true reason for their existence, is bringing public opinion to a focus and framing issues for a public verdict." They are the instruments through which popular government can be carried on. If there were no political parties, there will be utter chaos in politics. Political parties frame programmes and select candidates to carry out those programmes. They appeal to the people in the name of those programmes. When a political party comes to power, it can be presumed it will do its utmost to carry out its programme to the best of its ability. Without political parties, it will be impossible to run a democratic government.

Professor W.B. Munro writes: "Government by free political parties is merely another name for democratic government. Nowhere has there ever been a free government without political parties. Political parties existed even in ancient republics and mediaeval cities, although they were not known by that name. There were Lancastrians and Yorkists, Cavaliers and Roundheads in England long before the American Revolution. There were Whigs and Tories in the thirteen colonies. These rival factions sometimes settled issues by breaking heads rather than by counting them, but they were the ancestors of our political parties at the present day."

A well-organised political party is like a small state within a big state. It has its active and passive members. It has its local branches or constituencies. It has its branches for propaganda, fund-collecting and recruiting. It is responsible for the adoption of a party policy. It chooses its leaders. To quote Dr. Finer, " By degrees which to the ordinary citizen were imperceptible, these nation-wide fellowships have come into being and organised themselves with a gigantic and complex apparatus. They possess buildings and newspapers, printing presses and advertising experts, songs and slogans, heroes and martyrs, money and speakers, officials and prophets, feast days and fast days; like all religions they disrupt families and produce heretics, and among their agencies of discipline and subordination are the novitiate and penance." Dr. Soltau says, "The party branch is a local unit of the army, provides the recruits, and is also a centre of intelligence as to what is going on within the party and in the country in general."

It seems curious that although party system plays such a vital role in running the administrative machinery of a democracy, it is an extra-legal growth. It is not known to the Constitution. The American constitution does not presume the existence of political parties, but political parties actually appeared on the scene from the very beginning. In the Presidential election of 1796, there were two political parties, one supporting John Adams and the other Thomas Jefferson. By 1800, the party system had settled itself firmly in the government. Since then, political parties have played a vital role in the United States and they formed the hub of the political life of the nation, In the words of Prof. D.W. Brogan, "But for the appearance of a national party system, the election of a President really enough of a national figure to carry out his duties, might have been impossible. And it is certain that the greatest breakdown of the American constitutional system, the civil war, came only when the party system collapsed." The view of Prof. Gilchrist is that the "party system is really the method whereby the too great rigidity of the American Constitution has been broken down."

The same is true of Great Britain where the party system began first. If there were no political parties in Britain, it will not be possible to work the constitution in its' present form. Many of the conventions will become unworkable. His Majesty's Government is a party Government and the Prime Minister is the leader of the majority party. Likewise, the party in opposition is His Majesty's Opposition. Dr. Jennings rightly Says that "a realistic survey of the British Constitution today must begin and end with parties and discuss them at length in the middle."

Conditions Necessary for Successful Working of Parties

Experience shows that certain conditions are necessary for the successful working of parties. The people must be politically conscious. They must be educated and also interested in the politics of their country and the world. They must understand their rights and duties and must always be willing to play their part honestly and intelligently. They must have toleration. They must not condemn those who differ from them. They may have different views but once the electorate has given its verdict in favour of a party, the others should accept this without any hue and cry. There must not be too many parties in the country. They are bound to create more trouble for the people than help them in any way. Parties must not be organised on sectarian lines. They should frame their programmes in such a way that they aim at the betterment of the lot of the people. The officials of the government must remain away from the party organisation and must remain away from the party organisation and must not take active part in them. They should be willing to co-operate with any party which comes to power. There must be an alert public opinion in the country and a strong Opposition party. Too many political parties may not be allowed to come into existence. That can be done by legislation by prescribing certain conditions which must be satisfied by a political party before it can be recognised by the government. No political party should be allowed to maintain a private military force as was done by the Nazis in Germany and the Fascists in Italy. The only legitimate weapons which political parties can use are persuasion and conviction. All steps should be taken to break up the control of party bosses and time-servers. Men and women of outstanding ability and unimpeachable character must either place their services at the disposal of the parties or the political parties must persuade them to do so. An honest and well informed press is also necessary for the successful working of the party system.

Merits of Party System in General

There are both merits and demerits of the party system and no wonder we have its supporters and critics. As regards merits, the party system is absolutely essential for the successful working of democracy. It is impossible to think of democracy without an organised party system. "Without organisation, people can formulate no policy and carry through no project. Party system is necessary for advancement."

Political parties put forward their programmes before the public and therein try to win them over to their ranks. Since each party puts forward its election manifesto, the people can make their choice. They examine the contents of the manifestoes and base their judgement on reliable data.

Parties help the selection of good candidates for elections. They cannot afford to put forward foolish candidates as that may result in their liquidation. No political party can afford to think on those lines.

Some persons are very poor and cannot afford the election expenses, although they are otherwise very competent and ready and willing to serve the people. In such cases, political parties come to their rescue. They are ready to finance them and thereby enable them to serve the people.

A large number of elections have to be fought in every democratic country in the national provincial and local spheres. Millions of voters have to be taken to the polling stations. All that is not possible without party organisation.

The party system serves as a bridge between the executive and the legislature in a presidential form of government. The same party may be able to have its own candidate as the President and also have a majority in the legislature. Thus, the party system supplies a very necessary link between the legislature and the executive. A similar thing can happen in a parliamentary form of government. It is the majority party which forms the government and the government is always sure of the support from its members. There also party system links up the executive and the legislature.

In a two party system, one party is in power and the other in opposition. The opposition is always ready to criticise, condemn and ridicule the acts of omission and commission of the government. It is not prepared to spare it on any ground. It has a very healthy effect on the actions of the government, which is made to act cautiously.

Lord Bryce says: "Parties are inevitable. No free large country has been without them. No one has shown how representative government could be worked without them. They bring order out of the chaos of a multitude of voters. Of course, they cause some evils; they avert and mitigate others." President Lowell says: "The conception of government by the whole people in any large nation is, of course, a chimera; for wherever the suffrage is wide, parties are certain to exist and the control must really be in the hands of the party that comprises a majority or a rough approximation to a majority of the people." Dr. Finer rightly observes: "Without parties an electorate would be either impotent or destructive by embarking on impossible policies that would only wreck the political machine." Political parties lead in the sense of bringing to the individual citizen a vision of the whole nation, otherwise distant in history, territory and futurity. They broaden the horizon of voters and representatives by breaking sectional barriers and discounting local interest. They are nationalising agencies. They keep the mind of the nation active as the rise and fall of the sweeping tides freshens the water of long ocean inlets.

Demerits

The party system has certain shortcomings. It destroys the individuality of the members of political parties. They are required to vote and act in the way the party requires them to do. If a member dares to defy his party, he likely to be expelled and that may be tantamount to political suicide in many cases. Without the backing of his party, he may have no chance of being returned to the legislature. That is the reason why the members obey the verdict of their party even if it is a against their conscience.

The party system narrows the vision of the people. The members of a party put their party before the nation. They behave as partisans and not as citizens working for the good of the country as a whole. Goldsmith wrote the following lines on Burke:

> "Who born for the universe narrowed his mind
> And to party gave up what was meant for mankind."

The party system helps the rise of cliques and caucuses. Party organisation is a huge affair and people with money and influence manage to control it. Their control may not be for the good of the people, but in many cases it cannot be helped. It may result in the exclusion of good persons from service and that hardly desirable.

Political parties resort to all kinds of tactics to win popularity. Popular and uneconomic legislation may be initiated and passed by the legislature. The country may suffer but the political parties may care more to win votes than to realise the ideal of the welfare of society as a whole.

The party system may create artificial difficulties. The Opposition may challenge everything coming from the government, irrespective of its merits. An artificial atmosphere of a duel may be created by the opposing parties and the people may be confused thereby. They may not be able to know what to do. They may find the leaders of the opposite parties attacking one another vehemently. The party system disturbs the peaceful atmosphere of the country. A lot of stir is created in the country by the parties even when there is no occasion for it. Undignified speeches, are made by the leaders of various parties to please; their followers. Sometimes, there is a lot of hypocrisy about what the leaders state in their public speeches and writings.

The party system leads to favouritism. Jobs are given to those who belong to the party in power and even the most efficient hands from other parties are passed over. However, this evil is lessening on account of the civil service examination. There is less scope for the spoils system.

The party system turns the legislature into a battlefield. The debates in he legislature become a perpetual struggle between the ins and the outs. Party interests predominate and national interests are ignored. Lord Bryce says the same in these word: "The Parliament becomes a battlefield and its deliberations a perpetual struggle of the Ins and the Outs, in which the interests of the country are forgotten."

Critics point out that party system demoralises politics and makes it sordid. It encourages hollowness and insincerity. It crushes the individuality of the members of a party and reduces them to the position of camp followers. No scope is left for the exercise of their independent judgment. They have merely to do what their party orders them to do. There is no place for an independent citizen who is looked upon as a "crank" or a "goody-goody." Party system makes the political life of a country machine like. The members of the opposition oppose everything that comes from the party in power irrespective of the merits of the case. There is no place for compromise. There is no give and take. What is praised by one party must be denounced by the other. Party system gives an opportunity to self-seeking politician-adventurers to exploit the masses for their own personal interests. They create new parties to serve their own ends. As every cock likes to have his own dunghill to stand upon and crow, likewise, a political opportunist would like to have a party which he can use to capture power and exploit the masses for his own ends. The political problems of the country are complicated by the existence of a large number of political parties. Party government means excessive pandering to the people and that results in popular legislation to catch votes. There is no guarantee that legislation passed is in the interests of the people. There is a regular race in the job-hunting. Merit is not given to its,, due place. The tone of administration suffers. There is disaffection and dissatisfaction. The language used in the meetings of the political parties is often scandalous. Political parties try to impress upon the people. The truth of their views and the flashy of those of others. In this way parties are often guilty of the sins of *suppressio veri* and *sugestio falsi.* Party propaganda leaves no room for reason and independent thinking. Undesirable emotions are aroused among the people and the society as a whole suffers. The masses blindly follow their leaders. Very often, the political parties are controlled by caucuses or private cliques "which arrange matters to suit themselves." Political parties keep away from public life many good citizens who might otherwise have given a healthy political life to the country. Political parties adversely affect the local life of the people. The national parties enter the local elections and drag the national politics into the localities where they should not find any place. Issue are raised in local elections which are wholly irrelevant. Political parties create double governments. "The real governing power is without legal responsibility and is practically free from statutory and legal restrictions."

Lord Bryce says that on account of party, organisation and discipline, a party spirit comes into existence and that is wholly irrational. People are asked to vote from considerations which have little to do with love of truth or a sense of justice. Robert Michelo points out that political organisation becomes an end in itself. Organisation involves oligarchy and that is the negation of democracy.

Sidgwick has made certain suggestions for removing some of the defects of the party system. His view is that the influence of the party on the government will be greatly reduced if the President is elected by the legislature in a presidential form of Government. The subordinate executive officers should hold offices independently of party ties. In a parliamentary government, certain matters of legislation and administration are to be withdrawn from the control of the party in power. The work of preparing the legislation is to be given to a parliamentary committee other than the cabinet. A convention is to be evolved by which a minister is not to resign from office on account of the defeat of a legislative measure proposed by the Government. They should resign only when a formal vote of want of confidence is carried against them in legislature. The system of referendum can reduce some of the dangers of the party system.

Merits of Two-Party System

The chief merit of the two-party system is the stability of the government in power. When the elections are over, the party having a majority in the legislature is invited to form the ministry and the other party goes into the Opposition. The new ministry is homogeneous because all the ministers belong to the same party. They have a definite programme to execute which they put before the electorate at the time of elections. The party system in modern times has become rigid and consequently every member belonging to a party has to act according to the mandate of the party. Under the circumstances there is no possibility of the members voting against the party. The result is that the ministry does its work smoothly during the full term of the legislature. There is no danger of the fall of the ministry, as it can always rely upon the backing of its members who are in a majority.

Another advantage is that there is an automatic change of government. When the ministry is defeated, that means that it has lost its majority in the legislature and the Opposition has got a majority. If the ministry resigns, the Opposition automatically comes in and forms the ministry unless the ministry decides to challenge the legislature by demanding its dissolution. In the case of a multiple party system, there is no automatic change of government and ministry-making is a tedious affair on account of the many claimants in the form of various political parties. Laski says; "It is the only method by which the people can at the electoral period directly choose its government. It enables the government to drive its policy to the statute book. It makes known and intelligible the result of its failure. It brings an alternative government into mediate being."

The position of the Prime Minister in a two-party system is very strong. He can count upon the support and backing of the members of his party. He can even threaten the rebellious members with expulsion. However, the position of the Prime Minister in a multiple party system is pitiable. His greatest headache is to keep his flock together. He is always afraid of their desertion and the fall of his ministry. M. Briand observed on one occasion that the day on which a French Prime Minister takes office is the day on which one at least of his colleagues begins to prepare his downfall.

In a two-party system, the issues before the electorate are clear. They can vote for one political programme or the other. However, there is a lot of confusion in the case of, a multiple party system. Each party is bound to have its separate programme and it may not be possible for the masses to make a clear decision out of the lengthy manifestoes issued by a large number of political parties.

As the ministry is stable, it can afford to chalk out its policy with confidence and execute it with vigour. It has no fear of opposition from any quarter. It is on account of the useful work done by the leader of the Opposition in England that he is paid a decent salary out of the public funds.

In a two-party system, the people can easily guess the probable leaders in different parties. As a matter of fact, there are two shadow governments offering themselves for election by the electorate. When the voters vote for a particular party, that implies that they have voted for a particular set of ministers belonging to that party.

Dr. Finer says that the two parties "are better for the happiness and duty of nations than many parties and two parties contesting seats everywhere. For the lies and error may be in all places challenged, while destruction of will and disintegration of outlook are reduced." Professor Sail holds a similar view; The practical convenience of two parties must be preferred to the logical appropriateness of many.

Demerits of Two-Party System

The two party system has certain defects. It results in despotism of the party in power. The members of the majority party must approve of all the actions of their party and their government. They must learn to keep silent even if they find their government bungling. The party discipline is so rigid that any violation is bound to result in serious consequences. The dictatorship of the cabinet in England is partly due to the two-party system in that country.

The two-party system results in an intolerant party spirit. The members of a party feel that whatever is done by their party is right and they are bound to support it in a truly patriotic manner. Even the national interests may be sacrificed at the altar of the party interests. Devotion to party gains has more importance than devotion to the country.

Once the elections are over, the people become dumb-driven cattle. They are absolutely helpless even if the majority party bungles very badly. There is no provision for the recall of members and consequently the people cannot do anything effectively to stop the work of government. They can merely wait for the day when the new elections come and they are given an opportunity to have their revenge.

The late Professor Ramsay Muir was the greatest critic of the two-party system. He held the view that the two-party system was responsible for the gravest defects in the British system of government. It had destroyed the prestige of the legislature and made the British cabinet a dictator. It enabled the government not only to proposes but also to dispose whatever it wished to dispose. The government might even ignore the solemn pledges given at the time of elections. Under a two-party system, the choice of the voters was reduced to a simple acceptance or rejection of the whole political programme of one of the two parties. There is no other alternative.

The two-party system "substitutes blind devotion for intelligent appreciation and choice in both the followers and leaders." It creates strong vested interests and party prejudices.

Merits of Multiple Party System

The multiple party system is based on rational principles. Individuals have diverse interests and it is difficult to divide them into two watertight compartments. There is always scope for the formation of new parties to safeguard certain interests. If there are only two parties, those interests are likely to be ignored. A multiple party system gives scope for the greater elasticity and mobility.

"It does not divide the nation into irreconcilable groups. People can associate and organise without a serious compromise on principles."

The voters and the members of legislature have more independence of action. Even if a member of legislature defies his party on a particular issue, he can afford to join another party or start a new party of his own. The result is that there is a great scope for experimentation with new ideas. There is every chance of society benefiting by the richness of new experiments.

Demerits of Multiple Party System

The worst defect of the multiple party system is the instability of the ministry. As no party has a majority in the legislature, every ministry is bound to be a coalition ministry. Coaliation ministries are proverbially weak. They are merely a patch-work. The various parties joining a coalition ministry may quarrel at any time and thereby bring about the fall of that ministry.

There is no continuity in policy under a multiple party system. It is not sure of whether it is going to last tomorrow or not. It can collapse overnight or even within a few hours. This was the unhappy experience of France. Obviously, under such circumstances, no continuity of policy is possible.

There is no harmony in the government under a multiple party system. The various political parties which join a coalition ministry have separate programmes and ideologies. The programme of a coalition ministry is a mixture which pleases no party. The result is that they keep on pulling in different directions and under the circumstances much cannot be expected from them.

The position of the Prime Minister in a multiple party system is a difficult one. He is never sure of his followers. They can desert him at any time. No wonder, he is worried all the time to keep them together rather than look to the efficient administration of the country. The sense of self-preservation is found to be more important than the considerations of national good. A wise Prime Minister cares more to honour the leaders of the various parties and their wives than to think of the national policies which he may not be there to execute on account of his fall.

There is some sort of artificiality in the policies of the country. There is nothing concrete or definite in the manifestoes of the various parties. There is a lot of scope for political bungling. Sectional and party interests dominate. Cases of corruption are ignored. The supreme motto is self-preservation.

A comparison of the merits and demerits of the two-party system and the multiple party system shows that the two-party system is always to be preferred. The people should be prepared to make some sacrifices in order to have the advantages of a stable government in the country.

Single Party System

There are countries in the world where there are neither two parties nor many parties but only one party. Such was the case in Germany under Hitler, Italy under Mussolini and Soviet Russia. Even today there is only one party in the Soviet Union and Communist China.

The one party system was set up in Germany by Hitier after coming to power in January 1933. The strength and fury of the Nazi party led by Hitler was so great that all other political parties vanished from the political field. In July, 1933, Hitler declared: "The political parties have now been finally abolished. This is an historical event of which the importance and far-reaching effects have in many cases not yet been realised by all. We must not get rid of the last remains of democracy, especially of the method of voting and of the decision by majority. The party has now become the State." There were fresh elections in November 1933 and on that occasion, the Nazi list of candidates for the Reichstag was put before the country and all the candidates were duly elected. Dr. Ogg says that the climax was reached when one month later "the new all Nazi Reichstag held a seven-and-one-half minute session for the sole purpose of electing officers. 659 Brown Shirts rose and sat down in unison when the government's list was put to vote and went obediently about their own business.

The one party system was set up in Italy after Mussolini came to power in 1922. After that, only the Fascist party was allowed to function and the followers of other parties were assaulted and murdered. The result was that in the course of time all other parties ceased to exist. Mussolini wrote thus in 1932: "A party which entirely governs a nation is a fact entirely new to history; there are no possible references or parallels."

The dictatorship of the Communist Party was established in Russia after the overthrow of the Czarist regime in 1917. Out of the struggle for power, the Communist Party emerged victorious and in due course of time it completely wiped out all other parties. This state of affairs continued during the regime of Lenin and Stalin. When Khrushchev came to power, the rule of one man was finished but still the Communist Party continued to be supreme and unique in the country. The Communist Party of Russia is a united fighting organisation "bound by conscious iron proletarian discipline." It is strong through "its singleness of will and a singleness of action incompatible with deviation from the programme, with breach of party discipline or with the formation of faction inside the party. The Preamble of the party Charter says: "The Party is the leading nucleus of all organisations of toilers, both social and state, and ensures the successful construction of Communist Society." Article 126 of the Soviet Constitution provides: "The most active and politically conscious citizens in the rank of the working class and other sections of the working people unite in the Communist Party of the Soviet Union which is the vanguard of the working people in their struggle to strengthen and develop the socialist system and is the leading core of all organisations of the working people, both public and state."

The one-party system in China was set up after the overthrow of the Chiang Kai-shek regime in 1949 on the mainland. At present, the Communist Party of China is supreme in the country. No person has any prospect of gaining in political stature unless he occupies a high position in the party organisation. The extraordinary thing about that country is that the heads of the various departments of the government, whether civil or military, are those persons who have distinguished themselves in the service of the Communist Party. The Communist Party lays down the policy and this has to be carried out by all in the country.

On 25 January 1975, the Constitution of Bangladesh was amended and Sheikh Mujibur Rehman shed the office of Prime Minister and took over as President of Bangladesh. The new constitution provides for a President directly elected by the people. The powers of the President include the appointment of a Vice-President of the Republic, a Prime Minister as the head of a Council of Ministers and the formation of a national party which will be the only party in the state. No citizen will have the right to form a party other than the National Party. All matters relating to the nomenclature, programme, membership, organisation, discipline, finance and functions of the National Party are to be determined by an order of the President of Bangladesh.

The one party system can exist only in a totalitarian state. Its great virtue is that there is no waste of money or energy in fighting elections. The party puts up candidates and they are returned unopposed. As there is military discipline, they can all he expected to work with one will and devotion. They know full well that if they fail to do so, they are liable to be disposed of. A lot of work can be accomplished under such a system. It goes without saying that a lot was achieved by Germany under Hitler between 1933 and 1939. The achievements of the Communist Party of Russia are also known. The condition of the workers in that country has improved beyond imagination. The military build-up of that country is also remarkable. The same applies to Red China. The Communist Party of that country has forced the people to work day and night. In spite of the facts that the Chinese had very poor resources they have been able to accomplish a good deal in every field. Red China is a country which is feared and respected by many.

However, the defect of the one party system is that it destroys personality. There is no scope for individual thinking. The people cannot organise themselves into groups for the realisation of their individual interests. They are required to obey their leader. It is rightly pointed out that for Nazism, "the National Socialist Party is Hitler and Hitler is the Party." The oath of loyalty was to Hitler in these words: "I pledge allegiance to my Fuehrer, Adolph Hitler; I promise at all times to respect and obey him and the leaders whom he appoints over me." The motto which Mussolini put before his countrymen was: "Believe, obey and fight." When a person joined the Fascist Party, he had to take the following oath: "In the name of God and of Italy, I swear that I will obey the order of the leader without questioning." The same position was given to Lenin and Stalin. It is obvious that such an atmosphere is not congenial to the moral development of man. It is not correct to treat him as a slave and force him to carry out the orders of the party. It cannot be said that all dictators are infallible and hence it is not desirable to impose the will of one man on all the people.

Under one party rule, there is no place for toleration, discussion or compromise. One has merely to carry out the orders of the party or face the consequences. The people have no say in the choice of their rulers. They also have no peaceful method of changing their rulers. The rule of one party can be overthrown only by force.

Dr. Finer says : "Dictatorial parties are not parties, but doctrinal despotism; they do not spread and encourage leadership but monopolies it." Such a system can never be for the good of mankind. It may exist for some time but it can never be-a permanent solution for the problems of society.

Pressure Groups and Lobbies

A pressure group is an association of people having common interests who try to achieve that object by influencing the government. H. Zeigler defines pressure group as "an organised aggregate which seems to influence the context of governmental decision without attempting to its members informal governmental capacities." Pressure groups are a part of the political process and they attempt to reinforce or change the direction of government policy, but they do not wish, as pressure groups, to become the government. They range from powerful employer organisations and trade unions operating at the national level to small and relatively weak local civic groups trying to improve local amenities. According to Henry A. Twiner, "By definition, pressure groups are non-partisan organisations which attempt to influence some phase of public policy. They do not themselves draft party programmes or nominate candidates for public office. Pressure associations do, however, appear before the resolutions committees of the political parties to urge the endorsement of their programme as planks in the party's platform. They often attempt to secure the endorsement of both major parties and thus remove their programme from the arena of partisan controversy. Many groups are also active in the nomination and election of party members to public offices." V.O. Key has defined pressure groups as "private associations formed to influence public policy."

Sometimes in place of the term pressure groups, the term *interest group* is used but they mean the same thing. Prof. MacIver writes, "When a number of men united for the defence, maintenance or enhancement of any more or less enduring position or advantage which they possess alike in common, the term 'interest' is applied both to the group so united as to the cause which unites them. In the sense, the term is most frequently used in the plural, implying either that various similar groups or advantages combine to form a coherent complex, as in the term vested interests or that the uniting interest is maintained against an opposing one, as in the expressions conflict of interests or balance of interests. Interests so understood usually have an economic-political character." According to Almond and Powell, "By interest group we mean a group of individuals, who are linked by particular bonds of concern or advantage and who have some awareness of these bonds. The structure of interest group may be organised to include continuing role performance by all members of the group or it may reflect only occasional and intermittent awareness of the group interests on the part of individuals."

Pressure groups do not influence the electorate on the basis of certain programmes. They are concerned only with some special interests. They are neither political organisations nor they put up candidates for election. They simply influence the policies of the government to achieve some special purpose. A special interest is the root of the formation of a pressure group. There can be no group unless there is special interest which forces the individuals to resort to political means in order to improve or define their positions, one against another. Pressure groups play the role of hide and seek in politics. They are afraid of coming into politics to play their part *openly* and try to hide their political character by the logic of their being non-political entities.

Generally, no distinction is made between interest groups and pressure groups. However, there is some distinction between the two. An interest group is an association of people having a mutual concern. They become a pressure group as they seek government aid in accomplishing what is advantageous to them. An interest group is a formal organisation of people who share one or more common aim and when they start influencing the formation and administration of public policy by government, they become pressure groups.

Pressure Groups and Political Parties

There are similarities and dissimilarities between pressure groups and political parties. They resemble each other so far as they both seek to realise their objective by influencing the decision-making agency, V.O. Key writes, "political parties and pressure groups are informal and extra-constitutional agencies that provide a good deal of propulsion for the formal constitutional system."

As regards dissimilarities between the two, a political party is generally a much larger organisation than the pressure group. Parties seek to win the active support of millions of voters but pressure groups are very rarely supported by more than a small minority of the people who have some common interest. Political parties have policies on a wide range of issues. The programme of a pressure group is limited. It deals with a specific interest only. A political party submits its claims periodically to the electorate and is willing to assume responsibility for the operation of government but that is not done by an interest group. Apolitical party is a full-fledged political organisation and plays politics by profession. A pressure group becomes a political organisation only for a particular purpose to play politics on the ground of expediency. A party wants to assume direct responsibility for the implementation of policies by seeking to monopolise or share with other parties the position of a political power, but a pressure group is interested only in shaping public policy and not assuming responsibility for the government. A political party tries to have a nation-wide support from all citizens, but a pressure group is limited to a geographical area and has a membership restricted to a particular social group or economic group. The membership of a political party is exclusive. One citizen can be a member of one political party only. However, one individual can become a member of more than one pressure group. Political parties are active both within and outside the legislature, but pressure groups are active only outside the legislature. The main aim of a political party is to gain control of the government but the aim of a pressure group is to protect a particular interest. A political party aggregates interests in the desire to gather broad support, but that is not done by a pressure group. However, in spite of these differences, it is difficult to make a clear distinction between the two.

Pressure Groups and Lobbies

Pressure groups are not the same as lobbies and a distinction must be made between the two. Pressure groups are interested in influencing both the legislature and public opinion. Lobbies concentrate chiefly on the legislature while it is in : session and are concerned with the passage or defeat of particular bills. The activities of pressure groups are broader than those of lobbies. Most pressure groups also maintain lobbies in addition to their attempts to influence legislation indirectly through affecting public opinion. Among the usual lobbying tactics, special mention can be made of making representations before legislative committee and giving information to individual legislators. V.O. Key writes, "The political interests of agriculture, for example, may be advanced through lobbying and propaganda activities of pressure groups such as the American Farm Bureau Federation." The interest groups appoint their agents to establish personal contacts with the state and federal legislators to see that they are persuaded to vote for or against a bill.

According to H.A. Bone, techniques of lobbyists are stimulating grass-roots pressure on the various branches of government, meeting with legislators and administrators, making use of legislative committees, log-rolling and effecting alliances with and mutual assistance for other groups, influencing the election of friends and enemies and seeking the intervention of the courts, if possible. Bone and Ranney show how lobbyists try to influence the legislature. According to them, "Perhaps the most important point is that successful lobbying usually begins long before the opening session of the legislature. Members of the pressure organisation or hired lobbyists try to get acquainted with candidates during the campaign, and may as noted before assist them in their efforts to get elected. Lobbyists renew their personal friendship with the elected law-makers both before and during the session by means of cocktail parties, dinners, golf games and so on. Personal friendships are prime factors in the legislative and in all decision-making processes." (Politics and Voters, p. 80). Lobbyists also try to influence the members of the executive. In case they fail at the legislative and executive levels, they plan to appeal to the judiciary.

Pressure groups and lobbies carry on effective and widespread publicity and propaganda in favour of certain causes and try to pressurise the government for passing the necessary legislation. They may work against certain policies of the government and prevent the passage of certain types of bills. They conduct electioneering in favour of candidates who, in their opinion, would support their cause. They establish necessary contacts with government authorities to achieve their objectives. They also function within political parties. If necessary, they arrange for violent movements and strikes. They play an important part in creating and moulding public opinion. Dr. Herman Finer writes, "They have acquired the name the Third House, the Assistant Government. They have emerged into public and recognised position because of the appreciation that parties in a country so vast as the United States cannot possibly and certainly do not do the necessary work of representation of so many different purposes, and Congress itself has admitted the groups into its counsels through doors of its committees where the effective work of legislation is done." They influence the government in an informal way. Millions of people are able to express themselves through them. They represent and uphold various types of interests and causes. J.A. Corry writes, "The groups that exert pressure in Washington are organised to promote a bewildering variety of purposes. It would be difficult to classify them in a limited number of categories. Without attempting a classification it may be said that the more powerful groups are trade associations (representing industrial and commercial interests), labour unions, farm organisations, professional associations, national women's organisations, various reform leagues and a number of patriotic, ethnic and religious organisations." (Democratic Government and Politics, p. 308). They plan their work thoroughly with all the resources at their disposal. They spend millions to manipulate mass attitudes. They do much public relations work. An intensive short-term campaign may be designed to whip up public opposition to or in support of a particular legislative measure. To be differentiated from the whirlwind campaign is long-term effort to manage basic public attitudes towards the support of the broad point of view or to create a favourable sentiment towards a particular corporation or industry.

Pressure Groups and Elections

Elections are of great importance for pressure groups because it is through them that they can put their favoured men into the agencies of administration. Group politics play a vital role at different levels of an electoral process although they play a role of hide and seek and do not come on the scene. That is due to the fact that public identification of a candidate with a particular group may be of negative value and group endorsement may drive away more votes than it may attract.

At the stage of nomination, various groups are active to get the party ticket for the men favoured by them. A group may promote an aspirant through some party by securing its useful organisational support. It may contribute funds to the political party and secure the nomination of their favourite. A group may agree to the names of those candidates who are widely acceptable and utilise an opportunity of obliging them by withdrawing the names of their aspirants. A group may convince others of a sizeable cohesive bloc of voters in its pocket and thereby gain some name on the basis of adjustment. Some groups may increase their strength by joining hands with others and thereby force a political party to choose candidates in a way acceptable to them. For canvassing a campaign, the nominated candidates require money and that is given by the pressure groups to better the chances of success of their candidate. Such money is like a bribe given by a donor to a donee to have access to the government through them.

Pressure Groups and Legislature

After getting a candidate of their choice elected pressure groups can effectively participate in government decisions. The nature of the activity of pressure groups depends upon different conditions and different political systems. Members of the American Congress, particularly those in the House of Representatives, often find themselves virtually in the pockets of pressure groups and are compelled to do their biddings with far greater strength than the Congressmen feel themselves obliged to do at the biddings of the political party. The reason is that the legislators need money for election campaign which is provided by pressure groups and hence they must pay the price for the money received.

Lobbying is another important technique, used by pressure groups to protect their interests. Pressure groups and interest groups directly contact the legislature and make an attempt to influence them so that such laws are passed as protect and promote their interests. Pressure groups adopt all means to keep their control over the members of the legislature.

Pressure Groups and the Executive

Pressure groups also influence the executive which formulates the public policy. By putting questions and adjournment and call attention motions, legislators can force the ministers to implement policy decisions in their favour. Pressure groups also influence the executive through committees appoint for advice and consultation by the Department. Holtzman writes, "An executive unit that serves or regulates part of the general public needs the cooperation of those who are the recipients of its activities. As active organised units representing such recipients, interest groups have much to offer to an administrative bureaucracy. They may furnish special staff service for which the agency has neither the appropriations nor the skill. They can feedback to the administrator for the feeling and discontent of those most affected by this agency. Within the administrative frame of reference, therefore, they are valuable adjuncts of his leadership and useful allies for his agency."

Pressure Groups and Judiciary

The influence of pressure groups is also on the judiciary which is otherwise independent. An effective onslaught of public opinion is the very shrewd tactic in the hands of the interest groups to influence the judicial process from a distance. The creation of a healthy public opinion is a democratic way of lobbying the judges. The publication of articles and reviews in newspapers and magazines may go to the extent of shaping the minds of the judges. Chief Justice Warren of the Supreme Court of America admitted that the leading review articles were making available to the judges some of the best legal thinking in the country.

Pressure Groups and Public Opinion

Pressure groups employ various tactics to influence the public opinion. They use the device of argument to appeal to public mind by publishing various books, pamphlets etc. and by delivering speeches and calling press conferences. They use the strategy of persuasion to arouse hatred, love, fear or other emotions to serve their interests. They adopt the strategy of publicity to attract public opinion to their appeals. They make the most effective use of communication media, not only of mass media but also of personal contact of small groups, newspapers, bill boards, radio and television stations.

Role of Pressure Groups

In a modern political system, pressure groups occupy an important place and they exist in almost all democratic countries. No wonder, they have been called "the living public behind the parties." There was a time when pressure groups were considered immoral and were hated but that is not the position today. Now they are considered not only essential for democracy but are also regarded as the protectors of individual interests. Influence on legislation is increasing day by day and hence pressure groups are described as "legislature behind legislature." Dr. Finer describes them as "The Anonymous Empire".

The impact of pressure groups on policy formulation is very great. Ranney writes, "The many formal agencies of the government are more than mere collections of robots whose activities are entirely controlled by such extra-governmental forces as pressure groups and parties. The point to remember, however, is that pressure groups have a significant impact upon public policy in every modern democratic system." The importance of pressure groups has increased to such an extent that they have become king-makers in modern democratic republican societies. They help in forming a link between the people and the government of which administrators and legislators can make use in securing information on facts and attitudes. For example, any democratic government would like to consult farmers' association before formulating a new programme regarding farming. A free society welcomes groups because they represent the diverse and conflicting interests found among its citizens. Many groups can act as buffers against the growth of the power of the central government and serve as agencies by which public sentiment is affected. These organisations can be business, professional, racial, religious, fraternal or civic in character. An effective advocacy of both public and private points of view, particularly controversial ones, is enhanced by pressure groups.

Factors helping success of Pressure Groups

There are many factors which help the success of pressure groups. The size of a pressure group is one factor which helps it to obtain what it wants. The reason is that groups with many members are likely to be more successful than those with few members because the former represent many voters and the latter few voters. Another cause of success of a pressure group is its cohesion. Both in politics and in war, those who work unitedly and closely are more powerful than those who are loosely united or not united at all. Another secret of success is the leadership of a pressure group. Leadership is a prime factor. A good leader has to perform both internal and external functions for his group. The organisation, tactics and chances for success of any pressure group are affected by the political and governmental system in which it operates.

Drawbacks

However, the influence of pressure groups and lobbies is not all for the good. Some of them over-reach themselves and indulge in unwholesome and immoral activities. They bribe legislators. They give sumptuous free meals without number and great quantities of assorted intoxicating liquors to legislators. They procure for their entertainment lascivious women who are on the pay roll of the lobbyists. The unwholesome and vulgar tactics of pressure groups forced the American Government to pass the Federal Regulations of Lobbying Act, 1956 which requires individuals and groups to send quarterly reports of their activities, to mention the particular bills in connection with which they worked, to give a list of publications, to give names of persons who contributed 500 dollars or more and to present the expenditure including in it the names of persons who received ten dollars or more.

On the whole, it may be stated that pressure groups act as a powerful check upon the arbitrary exercise of power and as they themselves are prone to abuse their power, it is essential that various interest groups be allowed to act as a check upon one another in order to establish and sustain the system of checks and balances. Verney writes, "The use of the term pressure groups suggests that outside interests are obtaining special favours at the expense of the public, but it is also true that groups help to prevent Governments from imposing unfair burdens on the unorganised masses. Moreover, where party programmes tend of necessity to be general, group policies and proposals can be usefully specified." Ranney observes, "The right of citizens to organise and advance their ideals and interests by peaceful methods of discussion and negotiation is an essential principle of democracy. It is the basic justification not only for permitting the existence of pressure groups but for tolerating political parties as well. In any nation in which this right is guaranteed, pressure groups like political parties will continue to be organised and to play a significant role in the policy-making process of democracy."

SUGGESTED READINGS

Ball, A.R. : Modern Politics and Government, London, 1971.

Barker, E. : Reflections on Government.

Bentley, Arthur F. : The Process of Government:

Blondel, Jean : A Study of the Social Pressures, Chicago, 1952.

Bone, H.A. : An Introduction to Comparative Government, London, 1969.

Bone and Ranney : American Politics and the Party System, 1955.

Brown, Bernard E. : Politics and Voters, 1967.

Chandrasekharan, C.V. : New Directions in Comparative Politics, Bombay, 1962.

Corry, J.A. : Political Parties. Democratic Government and Politics, 1958.

Duverger, M. : Political Parties.

Eckstein, Harry : Pressure Group Politics, Stanford, 1960.

Field, G.E. : Political Theory.

Finer, H. : Theory and Practice of Modern Government.

Friedrich, Carl J. : Constitutional Government and Democracy, Oxford, 1966.

Gilchrist, R.N. : Principles, of Political Science.

Holcombe, A.N. : Political Parties of Today.

Holtzman, Abraham : Interest Groups and Lobbying, London, 1966.

Key, V.O. : Politics, Parties and Pressure Groups, 1959.

Latham : The Group Basis of Politics, New York, 1952.

Leacock, S. : Elements of Political Science.

Lowell, A.L. : Government and Parties in Continental Europe.

MacIver, R.M. : The Modern State.

Michels, Robert : Political Parties.

Miller : The Nature of Politics, London, 1962.

Munro, W.B. : Personality in Politics.

NeuMann, S. (Ed.) : Modern Political Parties: Approaches to Comparative Politics.

Ostrogorski, M. : Democracy and the Party System.

Penniman, H.R. : The American Political Process, 1962.

Ray, P.O. : Introduction to Political Parties and Practical Politics.

Rossiter, Clinton : Parties and Politics in America.

Sait. E.M. : American Parties and Elections.

Sail, E.M. : Political Institutions—A Preface.

Schapiro, Leonard : The Communist Party of Soviet Russia.

Schattschneider, E.E. : Party Government.

Sidgwick, H. : Elements of Politics.

Stewart, J.W. : British Pressure Groups: Their Role in Relation to the House of Commons, Oxford, 1958.

Truman, David : The Governmental Process, New York, 1964.

Verney, D.V. : An Analysis of Political System, London, 1959.

Wilson, F.G. : Elements of Modern Politics.

Zeigler, H. : Interest Groups in American Society, Prentice-Hall, 1964.

CHAPTER

Public Opinion

Learning Objectives

- Suggested Readings

The problem of public opinion has assumed great importance in modern times. Jose Y. Gassett, a Spanish writer, says, "Never has any one ruled on the earth by basing his rule essentially on any other thing than public opinion." Many definitions of public opinion have been given. L.W. Doob says, "Public opinion refers to people's attitudes on an issue when they are members of the same social group." To Roucek, "Public opinion is in the nature of a consensus arrived at on the basis of the predominating cross-currents of view that prevail in a given time or place. It is a relatively homogeneous expression of preference by members of a group concerning issues which, though debatable, concern the group as a whole." According to Wilhelm Bauer, public opinion "is a deeply pervasive organic force, intimately bound up with the ideological and emotional inter-play of the social groupings in which since the earliest times gregarious individuals have come together, it articulates and formulates not only the deliberative judgements of the rational elements within the collectivity but the evanescent common will, which somehow integrates and momentarily crystallizes the sporadic sentiments and loyalties of the masses of the population." Morris Ginsburg says, "Public opinion is a social product due to the interaction of many minds." Kimball Young writes, "Public opinion consists of the opinions held by a public at a certain time."

The view of Roucek is that public opinion implies four things. In the first place, there is a group of members or a public. Secondly, these members of the group have issues of common interest about which they communicate with each other, although at times they may differ from one another to some extent. In the third place, there is a leader or leaders of the group who take upon themselves the task of formulating opinion on certain important issues at a given time and of drawing the attention of the members of the group to that opinion. Fourthly, the members of the group adopt that opinion and acquiesce in the action necessitated by such opinion.

The concept of public opinion and its role in government is controversial. The Greeks and Romans employed somewhat comparable phrases but neither used the term in its present political context. During the Middle Ages, the proverb "Vox populi, vox dei" became popular in the writings of philosophers. Machiavelli compared the voice of the people with the voice of God. Alexander Pope wrote the following couplet: "The people's voice is odd. It is, and it is not, the voice of God." The phrase "public opinion" in the modern sense was noticed in the language of Western Europe through France where it was first used by Rousseau. Several circumstances combined to form a unique concept of public opinion during the early part of the 19th century. One was the prevailing view of the efficiency of public opinion in political life as indicated by the remark of Napoleon that "Opinion rules everywhere." The second was that several social science disciplines were still in the early stages of development. Governments gradually relaxed censorship control over publicly expressed political criticism.

It was maintained that the public was interested in public policy and it would deliberate and reach rational conclusions. Rationally conceived individual opinions would tend to be held uniformly throughout the social order. The public would make its will known at the polls and elsewhere. The will of the public or at least the views of majority would be enacted into law. Continued surveillance and constant criticism would ensure the maintenance of an enlightened public opinion and consequently a public policy based upon the principles of social morality and justice. These assumptions were critically examined by many scholars and there is a lot of literature on the subject. However, there is no unanimity among the writers. The generalization that a few thousand or million individuals can achieve a consensus and have a public opinion upon such diverse matters as race prejudice, free speech, agriculture, labour, taxation, foreign policy, etc., has been the subject of violent controversy. Several schools of thought have challenged the practicability of the traditional concepts. The pragmatic view is that at no time in history has absolute unanimity been achieved among the people of a state upon any weighty matter of public importance. The mechanistic attack denies the possibility of creating a political machinery which can measure and accurately record the opinions of the public. The socio-psychological attack examines the process by which opinions are formulated in the individual mind and expressed through the social dynamics and group action. The desirability of Government by mass opinion is seriously challenged. The challenge can be explained thus, "What opinion?" and "Whose opinion?" A political public may be all the citizens, the majority, the elite, the articulate minority, the group achieving a consensus, the electorate, the active voters, or an undisciplined mob. Opinions may be achieved through irrational as well as rational means. They may or may not be based upon facts. They may be believed intensely or entertained only for the sake of expediency. They may be expressed or unexpressed and be changed with ease or anchored in conviction. Walter Lippmann says in "*The Phantom Public*" that "All mankind was within hearing, that all mankind when it heard would respond homogeneously because it has a single soul. The appeal to this cosmopolitan, universal, disinterested intuition in everybody was equivalent to an appeal to nobody" (pp. 168-69).

The assumption that the public was a mass of people, possessing a common personality and expressing a collective will on matters of public policy, was debated. This image of the public was examined by Lord Bryce and his conclusion was that the issues of public policy were given a low rating among matters of importance in the daily life of the average citizen. When general interest was found in public questions, opinions were formulated by a small number of energetic people who were bent upon accomplishing a specific mission. These groups tried to gain wide acceptance of their views by the voting public. When any set of views was held by a majority of citizens, Lord Bryce believed that a public opinion had been achieved. A.L. Lowell attacked the concepts of an all-embracing public and a universal opinion. In order that an opinion might be public, it must be accepted by more than a majority of the citizens. It need not be unanimously held provided the minority accepted the majority decision voluntarily as a matter of conviction and, not coercion. Lippmann pointed to the relationship of man to his environment. His view was that man's political ideas are formulated to a great extent by information which he obtains from the world around him.

On account of the complexity of modern civilization, man is dependent upon many secondary sources of information such as newspapers, pictures, radio reports, and word-of-mouth accounts by others. The sources may be entirely unreliable. An intentional rumour may be started by a paid propagandist and repeated as fact by a trusted acquaintance. The opinions of the individuals are "the pictures in his head" based upon incomplete information of the real world outside. The combination of memory, imagination, prejudice, emotion and fragmentary information prevents rational judgements on matters of public policy. The individual goes through life observing the world imperfectly and accumulating imperfect judgements or fixed patterns of thought called stereotypes. The demands of earning a living in a competitive society left him with little leisure times for consideration of public affairs. For these reasons. Lippmann holds that the public, although lacking sufficient information to form a rational opinion, will align itself for or against a proposal when led by an individual or group capable of intellectually mastering the problem involved. Such a person or group is the master-creator of opinion.

It is now generally believed mat a public is essentially a segment of society and there are many different types of public. Publics may be identified by a specified geographic base, such as a township, city, country, State, or nation. A public may comprise of groups, sharing common interests such as a service club, a business organisation or a labour union. Some publics are relatively permanent while others are brought together temporarily by communication facilities such as a television or radio network. In the realm of politics, the important public is that which makes its influence felt in some phase of the formation and execution of public policy.

An opinion may be described as a belief which reflects the attitudes and personality of an individual. As a result of his contacts with the culture of his environment, an individual is said to develop tendencies to act positively or negatively towards another person, situation or idea. These are known as attitudes. When an attempt is made to express these attitudes in words, the individual is said to be expressing the opinion. An opinion is the manifestation of an attitude or belief. In the words of Albig, public opinion "is the expression of all those members of a group who are giving attention in any way to a given issue" (*Public Opinion,* p. 6).

Three institutions which influence the fundamental attitudes of the individuals towards society are home and family, the church and religion and the school and education. The child is influenced by a parent, brother or sister whom he loves. He imitates them even to the extent of reflecting the opinions of the older persons. One of the important legacies of the family environment is prejudice. He learns by observation and imitation that his family likes or dislikes certain things and he also comes to have the same prejudices unconsciously. Lacking other sources of information, he accepts many of them.

While the instruction afforded by the family is mostly informal, the school is well-equipped for indoctrination. Two primary influences to which the student is subjected are the curriculum and the teacher. Curriculums are constructed to impart skills, to provide facts, to offer value judgements for the interpretation of facts and to create an intellectual and physical environment wherein the growing child may mature. A difficult problem before those who are engaged in selecting materials for instruction is whether the individual be made to conform to society or the society be reordered to accommodate the individual. The school system is bound by shibboleths, rituals, superstitions, and taboos which reflect the prevailing culture of society. The school teacher also has his influence on the formation of public opinion and much depends upon the fact whether he is a progressive or reactionary or stands for the *status quo.*

The church also exercises its influence on public opinion. Churches have vested social, cultural and economic interests. They frequently act as pressure groups and often do not hesitate to wield political influence or to propagandise for or against issues in the realm of public politics. The church has played an important role in shaping many of our beliefs. An instance in point pertaining to Catholic countries is the practically uniform opinion held by the Catholics on the question of birth control. The Catholic church has issued many pronouncements and declarations on important economic and social issues. Many Muslim countries still adhere to mediaeval ideas concerning the State, property and inheritance, marriage and women and the treatment of "infidels". The ideology of capitalism and free enterprise is linked closely with the motive force of the Protestant Reformation. The family, the school and the church are merely representative institutions actively engaged in modifying and conditioning the attitude of the individuals and shaping their opinions.

Pressure groups also play an important role in moulding public opinion. They have lobbies of various kinds to influence the legislature at all levels. In the United States, there are lobbies representing chambers of commerce, the National Association of Manufacturers, farmers, organised labour, churches, minority groups of different kinds such as Jews and Negroes, etc. Even the government may become a pressure group. This is particularly so when a war is on or when the people have to be whipped up to accept a certain plan or programme sponsored by the Government. Every government has a well-organised department of information, publicity or public relations. Governments go to the extent of setting up information offices even in foreign countries. The propaganda done by the government is often highly coloured and is not always completely true to facts. A lot of cleverness is employed in the selection of news and views and these news and views are presented in the most plausible manner.

Well-organised political parties and communal groups also do a lot to mould public opinion. In the Soviet Union, the members of the Communist Party are only a small percentage of the total population and the rest are inert and may or may not support the opinions of the Communist Party. What passes as public opinion in that country is often the views of the inner clique within the party. It is true that the same does not apply to India but on many issues public opinion is synonymous with the views of the Congress Party. This does not mean that those views are necessarily selfish or anti-national. What is meant is that they are not truly representative. In China, public opinion is the result of careful "brain-washing". Many in that country applaud the achievements of their government without applauding the means of those achievements.

The main-springs of the origin, nature and behaviour of opinion are highly complex. The apparent inconsistencies of individual expressions of opinion are due to the extraordinary adjustments demanded of the individuals. The net product of approval or disapproval of an issue, candidate or programme depends upon the vagaries of "human nature". Much of the content of public opinion is derived from the culture in which it flourishes. It is also influenced by the past and present experiences of the individuals forming the public. Culture provides stereotypes, myths, legends and ideologies which the individual may accept or reject.

Stereotypes are developed by the individual to explain the reality of the surrounding environment. Some may be learnt in the school or through the home or church. The others are based upon the unique experiences of the individual concerned. Stereotypes are often accompanied by strong emotional bias. However, stereotypes have serious limitations as conveyors of ideas. They often are formed on little or no factual evidence. They may represent generalizations based upon too limited experience. They often result in pre-judgment, prejudice and fantasy.

Many of our beliefs are fanciful interpretations of events. Without any factual basis, myths are transmitted from one generation to another until they become generally acceptable. Legends are usually founded upon a factual fact but become embellished with fiction in retelling. Political Utopias such as Plato's *Republic* and Bacon's *New Atlantis* and the ideologies of Communism, Fascism and National Socialism are compounded of myth and legend. Much of the content of culturally derived public opinion is based upon the stereotypes, legends and mythology surrounding current political events, issues and personalities.

The proximate or primary causes of opinion consist in the things an individual sees, hears, and reads. The process of formulating public opinion usually involves several stages of development. The beginnings of public opinion may be found in the apparent discontent in some areas which may lead to group action. An alteration of the status of a religious, racial, labour, agricultural, business or political group might be the starting point of dissatisfaction. It may be a calculated move by individuals who wish to uproot the old social order and substitute a new one. Discussion is precipitated by the existence of a controversy. The second stage is reached when discussion becomes general as discontent spreads. Those who stand for existing order oppose the move. There is a lot of discussion. There are protests from both sides. Facts are mixed with fancy, truth with legend and myth and reason with emotion. Then the final stage is reached. Opinions may be registered in terms of an election, a policy decision or formal legislative action.

Many methods have been suggested for the measurement of the public opinion. One of them is public opinion poll and in this connection many newspapers and magazines can be mentioned, *e.g.*,

The Literary Digest, The Pathfinder, The Farm Journal, The New York Herald, etc. Much depends upon the size and nature of the sample taken for public opinion poll. It is impossible to cover the entire voting population. Sometimes a random sample is taken and sometimes a stratified sample is taken. There are area sampling and quota sampling. Sometimes interviews are held for purposes of public opinion poll and sometimes secret ballot and group interviews are held. It is pointed out that the system of public opinion poll is not perfect and there is always the possibility of mistakes. The person who is interviewed or asked to give his vote on a particular point is either to say "Yes" or "No" or "Don't know". In spite of the serious technical shortcomings and initial exaggerated claims the Pollsters are making constant progress in improving the polling instruments. Other techniques are being devised.

If public opinion is to have any meaning, it should be intelligent, intelligible and broad-based. It should be capable of careful exposition and lucid statement. It should be a synthesis of conflicting truths. In order to have sound public opinion, there must be free access to facts, to all facts and not only to one set of facts favourable to those setting them forth. There must be objectivity of outlook, calm reflection and mature judgment on the part of the leaders as well as the people. The people should be well-educated, reflective and free from prejudices. They must have a certain amount of leisure for the weighing of evidence and the reaching of well-reasoned conclusions. The people should be willing to stand up for their convictions even if that involves trouble. There must be relative freedom from the rigid control of political parties, trade unions, ecclesiastical or sectarian authorities and communal or linguistic groups.

As regards the implications of public opinion for democracy, opinions are expressions of attitudes which in turn have been formed by heredity, cultural environment and experience. Opinions exist in the minds of the individuals and are often highly irrational. Opinions are divided on most methods of public policy. There are as many different opinions as there are possible positions that can be taken on any issue. The motives for the expression of an opinion may be as diverse as the personalities holding that opinion. It is the clash of opinions which signalizes the struggle of ideas. Controversy reveals areas of agreement, disagreement and ignorance and these are of utmost importance in a democracy. The result of conflicting opinions upon the influence-weighing machinery of the political process is compromise. The agencies wielding political power respond to all politically oriented influences. Opinions expressed by a well-organised, competently led segment of the public will always be carefully weighed in the scales with other such opinions. The result of this compromise is reflected in public policy. Opinions may or may not be based upon facts. It is what the persons believe which is important in any analysis of political behaviour. The study of the science and art of communication and propaganda may help to distinguish between what it is and what the people believe it to be.

SUGGESTED READINGS

Albig, William : Modern Public Opinion. New York, 1956.

Berelson Bernard and Morris Janowitz (Eds.) : Reader in Public Opinion and Communication, Princeton, 1944.

Cantril, Hadley (Ed.) : Gauging Public Opinion, Princeton, 1944.

Dewey, J. : The Public and Its Problems.

Gallup, George : A Guide to Public Opinion Polls, Princeton, 1944.

Irion, F.C. : Public Opinion and Propaganda, New York, 1950.

Lippmann, Walter : The Phantom Public, New York, 1927.

Macdougal, C.D. : Understanding Public Opinion, New York, 1952.

Powell, Norman J. : Anatomy of Public Opinion, 1951.

Rogers, Lindsay : The Pollsters, New York, 1949.

31

CHAPTER

Local Government

Importance of Local Government

Learning Objectives

- Importance of Local Government
- Definition
- Functions of Local Bodies
- Advantages of Local Government
- Defects of Local Government
- Suggested Readings

The importance of local government cannot be overemphasized. According to Laski, "We cannot realise the full benefit of democratic government unless we begin by the admission that all problems are not central problems and that the results of problems not central in their incidence require decision at the place and by the persons where and by whom the incidence is most deeply felt." De Tocqueville says: "Local assemblies of citizens constitute the strength of free nations. Town meetings are to liberty what primary schools are to science; they bring it within the people's reach; they teach men how to use and how to enjoy it. A nation may establish a system of free government, but without the spirit of municipal institutions, it cannot have the spirit of liberty." Shri G.V. Mavalankar, a former Speaker of the Lok Sabha, says: "Our democracy can be truly and firmly led in the development of local self-government." Again, "It is these institutions which provide training ground for administrators and ministers. The government of states as also at the centre are only an apex of the pyramid which is broad-based on the various local self-governing bodies."

Definition

It is difficult to define local government. It is easier to say what local government is not than to say what local government is. It can be described and not defined. The position of local government is not the same as the position of a unit in a federal system. The reason is that while the existence and powers of local government depend upon the discretion of the central government, that is not the case with the units of a federation. The latter possess as much individuality as the federal government. They cannot be abolished at will by the federal government. Their existence and powers are guaranteed by the constitution. Likewise, it is not proper to say that local government is that whose area and population are less than those of the central government. It is possible that in a certain case the area and population of local government may be more than that of an independent state.

The real difference between a local government and the central government lies in the nature of functions performed by them. While the central government performs functions of a national character, the local government performs function of a local character. Thus, while the central government is concerned with functions like defence, foreign affairs, finance, etc, the local government is concerned with functions like water supply, lighting, construction and maintenance of roads, etc. However, it can be pointed out that there are functions which belong partly to one category and partly to another. For example, education and public health are of paramount importance to the nation, as a whole but their administration is in the hands of local bodies. What is actually done is that the central government gives a lot of money to the local bodies in the form of grants-in-aid so that they may be able to do their work efficiently.

It is difficult to draw a line of demarcation between the central government and the local government. The experiments of the various countries differ and there is no unanimity of opinion among the various writers. In countries like Great Britain, local bodies are given a lot of autonomy in their own affairs and the central government does not interfere in their day-to-day affairs. In countries like France, practically everything is regulated and directed by the central government. There is too much centralisation and uniformity. There is hardly any scope for local experimentation. It is rightly pointed out that if Paris sneezes, the whole of France catches cold. Such a system is destructive of all local initiative and strikes at the very root of democratic traditions.

Functions of Local Bodies

A large number of functions are performed by local bodies and the most important among them is that of public health. The three functions in this connection are the prevention of diseases, cure of diseases and promotion of health. It is the duty of the local bodies to look after the sewerage and drainage system so that sanitary conditions can be maintained within their jurisdiction. They must remove nuisances and regulate the offensive trades so that the people may not get suffocated on account of smoke, etc. They have to look after the water-supply both for drinking and other purposes. They have to collect all the refuse of the city and dispose of it in a proper manner. The bazars and streets have to be swept clean. Water is to be sprinkled with a view to lessen the nuisance of dust and dirt. The adulteration of food and drugs has to be stopped with a strong hand. Business must not be allowed to play with the health of the people by giving them adulterated food and drugs. Infectious diseases must be controlled. All kinds of preventive methods must be adopted. Emphasis should be put on disinfection and vaccination. Local bodies should also make provision for public baths and wash-houses. The problem of maternity and child welfare must be tackled satisfactorily by the local bodies. Mid-wives should be trained and a large number of them should be available to check infant mortality. There should be hospitals, dispensaries and clinics to cure people. The government should regulate the nursing homes. It should never be forgotten that the strength and prosperity of a country depend upon the good health of its people and there should be no hesitation in spending any amount to keep the people healthy and strong. All this work can be done adequately only by the local bodies.

The housing problem should also be given to the local bodies. It should always be remembered that people can never enjoy good health until they are given adequate living accommodation in healthy surroundings. People should not be allowed to build houses which are ill-ventilated and lack sanitary amenities. The local bodies should be given the work of slum-clearance. The slums which are inhabited by the poor people are the breeding places of all kinds of diseases and they must be cleaned at any cost. Local bodies can be given subsidies to do this work effectively. Every effort should be made by the local bodies to tackle the problem of over-crowding. New areas should be built and thus over-crowding should be lessened in the old ones. The old houses, which are unfit for human habitation, should be pulled down by the local bodies and the displaced families should be given accommodation outside the city. A lot of attention should be paid to the problem of planning. Without planning, towns are bound to grow up in a haphazard manner and thereby add to the headache of the well-wishers of society. Local bodies should take advantage of the services of the town-planners. Provision should be made for parks and open spaces so that the people may be able to enjoy fresh air and spend their leisure time in a useful manner.

It is also the duty of the local bodies to look after the elementary education of the people within their jurisdiction. Free and compulsory education must be enforced and the government should come forward with grants-in-aid to facilitate the work of local bodies in this connection. Provision should be made not only for general education but also for technical education.

Local bodies should also tackle the problem of poor relief. It should be realised that no poor person can be allowed to starve simply because he is a poor man. Institutions should be set up to give relief to the sick and the aged. Provision should also be made for outdoor relief. The children of the destitute, dead or imprisoned parents should be looked after by the local bodies. Destitution must not carry any stigma with it. Local bodies should come forward to put the unfortunate persons on their feet again.

The local bodies should construct and maintain roads. These roads may be purely local or of national importance but in these days of high speed roads cannot be allowed to remain in a bad condition. It must not be forgotten that good roads add to the progress and prosperity of a country by helping trade and commerce and national security. Road construction also involves the construction and maintenance of bridges.

It is the duty of the local authorities to maintain law and order within their area and for that purpose to make the necessary police arrangements. The local bodies have also to set up libraries, reading rooms, museums and art galleries. They should also look to the testing of gas, gas-meters, electricity meters and water meters. Provision has also to be made for fire-brigades to save the person and property of the people from fire. Premises for storing petroleum should be kept outside the city so that there may be no danger to the neighbouring area. Likewise, provision should be made for the grant of licences for entertainments. Weights and measures have also to be supervised to check the cheating of the people. Local bodies have to establish municipal markets, omnibuses and tramways. They have to provide for burial and cremation grounds. They have also to maintain records of births, deaths and marriages.

The functions of the local bodies are increasing every day. It is realised that the local bodies should perform more and more duties to make the people happier and prosperous. As compared with the local bodies of advanced countries, the functions of municipalities in India are less extensive in three directions, *viz.*, police, trading enterprises and social services such as health, housing, sickness and unemployment insurance. Some of these functions are not legally permitted to the municipality. Moreover, the actual standard of the services run by the local bodies in India is very low. It is pointed out that the Government of the local bodies in India is neither local nor it is Self-Government. Even if there were to the no legal restrictions, they have not the means to do much. They have to depend upon the Government for help and that is against the spirit of local Self-Government itself.

Advantages of Local Government

There are many advantages of local government. Since the local bodies are allowed to manage their own affairs in their own way, there is greater efficiency in administration. That is partly due to the self-interest of the people of the locality and partly to their local knowledge. It may be impossible for the central government to understand and appreciate all the problems of a locality and also provide for them adequately. According to Lord Bryce, "Local Government creates among the citizens a sense of their common interests in common affairs and their individual as well as common duty to see that these are efficiently and honestly administered." Again, "Popular or democratic governments rest on the principle that it is every citizen's business to see that the community is well-governed."

While inaugurating the first Local Self-Government Ministers' Conference in 1948, Prime Minister Nehru declared, "Local-Self-Government is and must be the basis of any true system of democracy. We have got rather into the habit of thinking of democracy at the top and not so much below. Democracy at the top may not be a success unless you build on this foundation from below." Local Government becomes real only if there is Self-Government. Lord Bryce says, "The best school of democracy and the best guarantee for its success is the practice of Self-Government."

Local government brings about a lot of economy in the cost of administration. If everything were to be done by the central government, the latter would have to spend a lot of money. However, if the work of administration is handed over to the local bodies and they are also allowed to tax themselves with a view to perform their duties efficiently and adequately, the financial burden is bound to be less on the central government.

Another advantage of local government is its educative value. In the local bodies, the people get their training in the art of self-government. These very persons, who have the experience of administration on a small scale, can be expected to do the same work on a larger scale in the central legislature and executive. It has rightly been stated that local bodies are nurseries of the future politicians of a country. It is sometimes suggested that the law of every country should lay down that no person can contest elections to the provincial or central legislature so long as he has not served in a local body for specified number of years. Burke has cogently said, "To be attached to the sub-division; to love the little platoon we belong to in society, is the first principle, the germ as it were of public affections. It is the first link in the series by which we proceed towards a love to our country and mankind."

Local bodies provide the soundest basis for the successful working of democracy. People who are accustomed to manage their local affairs without any interference from any quarter, will not allow the establishment of dictatorship. They are very particular about their autonomy and liberty. They will go to any extent to resist any encroachment on this. The foundations of democracy are very weak in a country in which the local bodies do not enjoy a large measure of autonomy and are not allowed to manage their affairs in their own way. According to Lord Bryce, "The best school of democracy and the best guarantee for its success is the practice of local self-government."

If everything is allowed to be administered by the central government, there is bound to be uniformity in everything. That is hardly desirable. The interests of various localities are bound to differ from one another and a uniform provision by the central government will be like a square peg in a round hole. Central administration is bound to involve a lot of red-tapism which unnecessarily delays matters and does not respond to local opinion.

Centralisation implies a bureaucratic system of government. A bureaucracy may be efficient but it is hardly a substitute for self-government. Local government is necessary for efficiency and responsibility.

Local bodies can serve as the deliberative organs of the central government. Whenever the central government has to do anything with any particular locality, it can ask for the advice of the local body concerned. The result is that the work of the central government becomes lighter and it acts on the basis of expert advice from the locality concerned.

Defects of Local Government

Critics of local government point out that it narrows the outlook of the people Instead of thinking in terms of the country as a whole, the people start thinking in terms of local interests. The parochial attitude is not good for the country as a whole. Regionalism, if taken in extremes, is bound to harm the national interests. Local patriotism is a thing to be condemned if it is not linked up with patriotism for the country.

It is also pointed out that the devolution of authority to local bodies multiples the staff to be employed and that is responsible for a lot of waste and extravagance. The officers of the local bodies are "locally selected and locally directed and locally controlled" and much cannot be expected from them. They do not possess the high standards of efficiency which their work demands. They manage to go on by influencing and humouring the local bosses or joining hands with the unscrupulous politicians. Very often, the local bodies are the centres of corruption and inefficiency. Group rivalries always stand in the way of efficient working of the local bodies. All this cannot change unless public spirited people make it a point to devote a part of their time to local affairs and thereby put everything in order.

A suggestion of Willoughby is that local officers should be appointed by the State Government and a local advisory council should be associated with them. This council should be given the responsibility and duty of advising local officers with local problems, to bring to the attention of their superior officers all cases of lapses on their part and to suggest proposals which they consider to be desirable. They should have the right to protest to the Government in case their areas do not receive fair treatment.

The degree of central control over local bodies varies from country to country and that is in proportion to the efficiency of a local body. If a local body is efficient, the necessity of central control is less. However, the Government control comes in if a local body has to ask for funds from the Government to perform its functions. Too much of control destroys democracy and the spirit of local government and hence it is necessary "to avoid reducing local authorities to the position of mere agents of the Central Government if they are to continue to make their indispensable contribution to the democratic way of life."

SUGGESTED READINGS

Clarke, J.J. : Outlines of Local Government.

Cole, G.O.H. : Local and Regional Government.

Finer, H. : Local Government.

Gilchrist, R.N. : Principles of Political Science.

Jackson, R.M. : The Machinery of Local Government.

Jenks, E. : English Local Government.

Laski, H.J. : A Grammar of Politics.

MacIver, R.M. : The Modern State.

Mahajan, V.D. : Essays in Municipal Administration.

Robson, A. : The Development of Local Government (1954).

Sidgwick. H. : Elements of Politics.

32

CHAPTER

The End and Functions of State

Learning Objectives

- End of the State
- Theories Regarding Functions of the State
- Functions of Modern Government
- Social Services
- Public Utility Services
- Public Health
- Social Security
- Social Reform
- Problem of Nationalisation
- Planning
- Limits of Political Control
- Suggested Readings

End of the State

There has been a lot of controversy on the point whether the state is a means or an end. One view is that the state is an end in itself and the individuals are only a means. The other view is that the state is a means and its duty is to do all that it can to secure the welfare of the people.

The view of the Greeks was that the state was an end in itself. The state was a moral organism and the individuals could find their perfection only by merging themselves in the state. It was only in a state that the individuals could become moral beings. Plato was prepared to go to the extent of asking the individuals to merge themselves into the state. They were required to do what the state wanted them to do. They were to sacrifice their property and families at the altar of the state. The individuals were merely a part of the state and consequently had no rights against the state. They were required to serve the state in the same way as the various organs of a human organism fulfil their respective functions. The welfare of the state was to be kept in the forefront and the welfare of the individuals had meaning only in the context of the welfare of the state itself. A similar view was given by Aristotle. The state was a moral organism and the individuals and associations were a part of it. The state was as natural as the individuals themselves. Man by nature was a political, animal and he could grow only in a state and not otherwise. The state was not created by men. It was the end of all individuals and associations and they could find their fruition and perfection only in the state.

The German Idealists also held the view that the state was an end and the individuals were a means. The view of Kant was that the state is omnipotent, infallible, divine in essence and its authority comes from God. It is the sacred duty of the individuals to obey the state even if the occupant of power at any time is a usurper. The individuals have no right to challenge the authority of the state. Hegel put forward an extreme view. According to him, the state is the reality of the ethical spirit, "the manifest self-conscious, substantial will of man, thinking and knowing itself and suiting its performance with knowledge or to the proportion of his knowledge." The state is perfected rationality and an absolute fixed end in itself. The state is the march of God on earth. The state is God itself. The state is the divine idea as it exists on earth. It is objective reason or spirit. It is only under a state that man raises his outward self to the level of his inward self of thought. The state is a separate entity and possesses a separate will and personality of its own, different from those of the individuals who live within it. Man is free only when he obeys the state. He has no right against the state. The state contains within itself and represents the morality of all its citizens. It can act irrespective of moral considerations. The view of Bradley was that the duty of man is to perform only those functions which are assigned to him by the state. The state fixes for him a station in iife and the duties to be performed by him in that capacity. Dr. Bosanquet identified the state with society. His view was: "The state is the guardian of the whole moral world and not a factor within an organised moral world."

The view of the Fascists is that the state is an end in itself and the individuals must be at the disposal of the state. They are bound to the state by duty, discipline and sacrifice. Liberty exists not for the individuals but for the state. The state has rights and the individuals have duties only. The life of the state extends beyond that of the individuals. The state is an end in itself and that end is apart from that of the individuals living within the state.

It is being realised in modern times that it is not proper to regard the state as an end in itself. The acceptance of such a view is detrimental to the welfare of society. The state must be considered as a means and its machinery must be used for the welfare of mankind. It must be considered merely a machinery whose justification exists in its usefulness for society. All the resources of the state must be used for the welfare of mankind.

The view of Bluntschli is that the state is both a means and an end. To quote him, "The form of the question itself, whether the state is a means or an end, leads to this one-sidedness and therefore to error. From one point of view, a thing may be regarded as a means for obtaining other ends, from another as an end in itself. A picture is often a means of obtaining a livelihood for an artist or a profit for the picture dealer. Yet a true work of art is to the artist the aim of his highest effort; he sees in the expression of his most vivid feelings, the embodiment of his ideal. In this way, it has an end in itself. So, too, marriage serves undoubtedly as a means for husband and wife to satisfy their individual needs, and to open to both a more happy existence. But marriage is also the union of two sexes separated by nature, and on this union is founded the family *i.e.* a higher collective unit.... Each member of the family is willing to sacrifice a part of his personal interests and will to the higher end which is involved in marriage and the family. The same is true of the state. On the one hand, it is a means for the welfare of the individuals who compose it. From another point of view, it is an end in itself and for its sake individuals are subordinate and bound to serve it."

Many views have been put forward regarding the end of the state. The view of the individualists is that the end of the state is the maintenance of law and order within the state. The state is merely to act as a policeman. Its duty is merely to remove hindrances in the way of the development of the individuals and it must not go beyond that limit. If it does so, the individuals are bound to suffer as they are not allowed to act according to their conscience. Critics point out that the Individualist view is a negative one and is not adequate to serve the needs of modern society.

According to the Utilitarians, the end of the state is the greatest happiness of the largest number. All legislation and state activity must be judged by this criterion. If that leads to the happiness of society, it is good. If it does not do so, it is bad or useless. Critics point out that the measuring rod provided by the Utilitarians is not a definite one and hence it is not possible to find out where the greatest good of the largest number lies.

In his *Introduction to Politics*, Laski says that "the power of the State can be justified only in terms of what it seeks to do. Its law must be capable of justification in terms of the demands it seeks to satisfy. The State presides over a vast welter of interests, personal and corporate, competing and cooperating. Its claim to allegiance must obviously be built upon its power to make the response to social demand maximal in character. It must strike such a balance of interest that what emerges as satisfied is greater than can be secured on any alternative programme."

In his *The State in Theory and Practice*, Laski says, "For its citizens, a State is what it does; it is not justified merely because it is a State." Again, "The philosopher may, like Burke, think of the State as a partnership in all virtue and all perfection; the common man thinks of it as a way of being ruled which satisfies his expectation of legitimate satisfactions."

Another view is that the end of the state is the maintenance of rights. It is only the guarantee of certain rights that can enable the individuals to develop their personalities. Hocking says: "It is right, absolute right, that individual shall develop the powers that are in him. He may be said to have natural rights to become what he is capable of becoming." Laski says: "It is clear, in such a view, that the citizens have a claim upon the state. It must give those conditions without which he cannot be that best self that he may."

According to another view, the end of the state is the development of the personalities of the individuals. Hocking says: "The state is a territorial body of people united under a sovereign power for the purpose of making a better breed of men and rendering more rational the inner play of social forces. "The state exists and should exist for the best realisation of the self. It is true that the very life in the state makes the individual more rational. By its very existence, the state performs a service. It is permanent and therefore it creates an atmosphere in which human purpose can be realised without undue interference. The individual is not required to devote his energies to preserving himself against the disorders of anarchy. However, the state can and should go further and try to provide the individual with those opportunities which can help him to realise the very best in him.

Another view is that the end of the state is the protection of interests: According to Pound, the end of law and the state is the definition and classification of interests and their protection. Law should formulate and protect the social interests which include general security, security of social institutions, use and conservation of natural resources, cultural, economic and political progress, the welfare of individuals and equitable adjustment of individual interests. According to Ihering, "The final end, then, of the state as of right and law, is the safeguarding and the conservation of the vital elements of society. Law exists because of society."

According to another view, the end of the state is social control for the satisfaction of wills. The ultimate purpose of the state is to satisfy as many individual wills as possible. It is the duty of the state to bring about a balance between the various wills. Catlin says: "The fact about the individuals which is relevant to discussion of politics is not their musical taste or the charm of their character, but that they have will and may be counted to endeavour to carry out what may happen to wills." It is pointed out that wills do not act in a vacuum. They must act in accordance with some purpose. The satisfaction of wills is merely a partial end of the state.

The view of Holtzendorff is that the state has a triple end.. The first end is power; the state must have sufficient power to preserve its existence. The second end is individual liberty; the individual must be protected from the interference of others. The third end is general welfare. While regarding this view as inadequate and incomplete, Professor Burgess points out that the end of the state should be threefold, *viz.,* the good of the individual, the good of association and the furthering of world progress or civilization.

There are writers who regard justice as the end of the state. Nobody will deny the desirability of giving justice to all. However, this alone is a narrow view of the end of the state. Interpretations of justice vary from person to person and from time to time. What is justice from the point of view of a rich man may be the very negation of it from that of a poor man. Complete justice involves complete knowledge which belongs to God alone. Hence, the difficulty of the realisation of this ideal in actual practice.

The view of Laski is that the Governments "are the trustees and governors and it is their business to glean the needs of society and to translate those needs into effective statutes. The purpose of the state finds its personification in them". The aim of the State is the promotion of individual welfare and the realisation of the collective ends of society. The State must create conditions for the freest possible development and creative self-expression of its members. It enables men to realise what is best in them. It helps the enrichment of their happiness and spiritual uplift.

Similarly, liberty, equality, fraternity, monarchy and democracy have been put forward as ends of the State. But they all seem to confuse the idea of the end of the state.

We may conclude with the following statement of Aristotle: "The state comes into being for the sake of mere life; it continues to exist for the sake of the good life."

Theories Regarding Functions of the State

There are many theories regarding the functions of the state. According to the Anarchists, the state is absolutely useless and unnecessary. It serves no purpose and results in greater evil than good. The laws of the state encourage selfishness, indolence, dishonesty and crimes. The state is a curse. All law-making is humbug. The state has failed to accomplish anything that is useful and noble. Experience shows that the state is incompetent and ineffective to do anything that is necessary. The state is superfluous in the field of art, science and business. All that work can be done by voluntary associations without the intervention of the state. The important advocates of the Anarchist view were Bakunin and Kropotkin. The Anarchist view is not accepted at all. It is realised that it is not possible for individuals even to exist without some sort of authority. Their lives and property will always be at the mercy of the stronger persons if there were no state. There will be no social, intellectual, material and moral progress of mankind. The assistance of the state cannot be dispensed with.

Another theory regarding the functions of the state is individualist theory. The greatest advocates of this theory were J.S. Mill and Herbert Sepencer. Their view was that the state was an evil but a necessary evil. Hence, the state was to be given as little scope for intervention as possible. The functions of the state were to be reduced to the minimum. According to Mill, the actions of the individuals were to be divided into two parts; self-regarding actions and others-regarding actions. The individual was to be left completely free in the field of self-regarding actions. The state was to interfere only in the field of others-regarding actions. Herbert Spencer went to the extent of saying that the state should try to make itself superfluous.

The Individualists justified their philosophy on many grounds. It was maintained by them that justice and morality demanded that the state should not interfere with the internal lives of the individuals. Every individual must be allowed to act according to his conscience. It is only then that he can be a moral person. According to Mill, "A people among whom there is no habit of spontaneous actions for collective interests, who look habitually to their government to command and prompt them in matters of joint concern, who expect to have everything done for them except that can be made an affair of mere habit and routine, have their faculties only half developed, their education is defective in one of its most important branches." Herbert Spencer pointed out that the control of the state resulted in monotony and uniformity.

The Individualists also put forward a biological argument in support of their view. The principle of the survival of the fittest worked everywhere and there was no reason why the same should not apply to individuals as well. That principle demanded that every individual must be left alone to struggle and thereby prove his fitness to live by surviving in the struggle. If the state helped the poor and the weaklings, society would be full of undesirable persons and that was not proper. Moreover, the poor were ordinarily ignorant persons and in a democratic government, they were bound to dominate as everyone had one vote. It was in the fitness of things that nature should be left alone to do its work in the interests of society.

Individualism was also supported on economic grounds. Human experience was that every individual did only that which was in his best interests. If the state did not interfere at all, the producers were bound to produce only that which brought them the highest profits and the consumers were bound to buy only from the person who charged them the lowest price. Under the circumstances, society was bound to gain the maximum. The interference of the state was likely to result in an unnatural setting of things.

Expediency also demanded that the policy of "let alone" should be followed. Experience showed that better work was done by private individuals than by the state. Most of the laws passed by the government in the past were stupid and consequently had to be set aside. They were a record of unhappy guesses. The servants of the government did not put in their very best and production could not be maximum.

The critics of individualism point out that it is wrong to say that the state exists because crime exists and a time will come when there wilt be absolutely no necessity of the state. Experience shows that as society has progressed, the necessity of the state has continued to increase. It is wrong to say that the state is an evil. It is more appropriate to say that it is a positive good. It is not true that the work done by the state is less efficient than the work done by the private individuals. If the work of the state seems to be less efficient, that is partly due to the fact that the achievements and failures of the state are given greater publicity than those of private individuals. Huxley says: "The state lives in a glass house; we see what it tries to do and all its failures, partial or total, are made the most of. But private enterprise is sheltered under wood, opaque bricks and mortar. The public rarely knows what it tries to do and comes to know its failures when they are gross and patent to all the world. "The policy of complete non-interference on the part of the state is not in the interest of the people in general. Experience of the nineteenth century shows that in the absence of state interference, the condition of the workers deteriorated and consequently the government had come in to protect them. Today it is realised more and more that if society is to progress, the state must come forward to play its part and give every individual his due. The poor, the orphans and the helpless cannot be left alone by society. Humanitarian considerations demand that something must be done for them. If their lives are saved, they are bound to add to the prosperity of the country. Thus, the old Individualist view regarding the functions of the state has rightly been given up.

The view of the state socialists is that all the factors of production must be in the hands of the state. There should be no private property. Everybody should be employed by the state and work for the state. There should be no competition in the field of production. Things should be produced according to the needs of the people and not with the motive of profit. There should be an equitable distribution of wealth. The ideal should be: "From each according to his capacity, to each according to his needs." This view is not accepted by many persons, who maintain that the workers should be paid according to their contribution to national production and such a system actually prevails in the Soviet Union.

The critics of the socialist view point out that there will be practically no scope for individual initiative and that will not be in the interest of human progress. There is the possibility of class war, violence and bloodshed and that is not conducive to human welfare. The total production is bound to fall as there is the likelihood of lethargy and indolence among those who work in state enterprises. This is exactly what has happened in India in the public sector.

In spite of the criticism of the socialist view, it is recognised that there is an important element of truth in it. Society is bound to gain as a result of co-operation. The state can alleviate a lot of human misery by intervention in certain fields.

The Idealist view is that the state is an end in itself and the individuals are merely tools in the hands of the state. The individuals should feel happy when they are asked to make sacrifices for the state. The latter represents the good of the whole society. The greater the activity of the state, the greater is going to be social good. Hence, the state should take over as many functions as possible.

The advocates of the welfare state maintain that the state should not act like a policeman. It should do all that lies in its power to achieve the welfare of the entire body of citizens in every sphere of activity. Every effort should be made by the state to add to the happiness and welfare of the people. Laski says: "State is an organisation to enable the aims of man to realise the social good on the largest possible scale." The state should maintain law and order in the country. It should protect the people from external dangers and internal troubles. It should give justice to the people. It should provide social security to its citizens. Social security implies that "man must feel secure through all the vicissitudes of unemployment, health, disability, youth and old age." The people must be given education and thereby made better citizens. Every effort should be made to remove poverty from the country. A vigorous campaign should be launched against diseases. All able-bodies persons should be given employment and during the period of unemployment, they should be given relief. Special attention should be given to the development programmes and the economic condition of the people should be improved. Every effort should be made to make the people cultured and civilised. The welfare of the individual and that of society should go together and should be adjusted with the welfare of human civilisation as well. Special attention should be paid to the nation-building activities. Emphasis should be put on co-operation among the people. No stone should be left unturned to develop the personalities of the individuals. The state must encourage and help the growth of arts, crafts, literature and science. In short, every effort should be made to produce intelligent, honest, hard working and patriotic citizens.

Functions of Modern Government

At every stage in the evolution of the state, there have been struggles and controversies over what the government should do and what it should not do. In the earliest stages of man when there was little organised activity, the power of an individual or a family determined what the government did. At that stage, the government was group activity to obtain food, wage war or settle disputes. As the state expanded and division of labour took place, more organised activity was necessary and the government performed more and broader functions. Other institutions such as the church also became powerful. The result was that there were clashes between the state, the church and other organisations. There is a reference to such a clash in the New Testament which gave rise to the saying of Jesus, "Render to Caesar the things that are Caesar's and to God the things that are God's." During the Middle Ages, there was strife and bloodshed over the proper sphere of state authority and activity and ultimately the church lost and the state won.

In the early stages of economic development in the modern state, mercantilism was the dominant pattern. It was a policy of controlling trade and colonial expansion in the interests of the national state. All trade and traffic was regulated in such a manner as gave a direct return to the state. The degree to which the state interfered depended upon its degree of interest. If the state expected to profit by having a complete monopoly for a given enterprise the same was done. In certain cases, states involved themselves intimately in the affairs of business enterprise.

Men like Adam Smith advocated a policy *of laissez-faire.* Their view was that the natural laws of economics were benevolent and should be permitted to operate without any interference from the state. The early prophets of capitalism maintained that the state should not interfere with industry on the ground that what was good for industry was also good for the state. Competition would see to it that the consumer got quality and quantity. It was presumed that, that government was the best which governed the least. The view of Herbert Spencer was hat the essential functions of the state were the enactment and enforcement of law, the administration of justice, the maintenance of order, the protection of life and property and the prevention of invasion by foreign powers. The assumption of any other function by the state was an invasion of private rights.

As a result of the Industrial Revolution in England, the United States and the other nations of the West, many abuses of the capitalist system worked on the basis of *laissez-faire* were noticed. Children were employed in factories and their condition was miserable. The same was true of women labourers. The people were paid very low wages and they were made to work for long hours in dangerous working conditions. There were mergers which stifled competition and established monopoly. Industrial and business concerns became bigger and more impersonal. It was found that economic laws were frequently not very beneficent. In an unregulated economy, large numbers of people were ill-housed, ill-fed and ill-clothes. It was felt that the government should control and regulate the business system both to prevent selfish excesses and to make the system work better in the interests of all. That involved direct regulation by the state to fix minimum wages, maximum wages, maximum hours of work, protection for labour unions, prohibition of child labour and unfair business practices.

All this is not considered enough. The government has also undertaken to shape the economic system in many other ways. It has taken over the role of the protector of the individual on the theory that the community is responsible for the misfortunes of the people. Social insurance covering the individual "from the cradle to the grave" has become a reality in Great Britain, the United States, Germany, the Scandinavian countries and the other industrial nations. The government provides, insurance for bank deposits, housing programmes and easy incorporation laws for credit unions. Legislation of the latter type is not so much regulation of the economic system as it is an adjustment of the system to extend its benefits to more and more people.

As society has grown more and more complex, the state at both the local and national levels has found it necessary to provide more and more services. Public education has become a regular function of the state in most advanced nations. Cities have built playgrounds, swimming pools, golf courses and other recreational facilities. Federal and state governments in the United States have provided highways. The cities provide streets for the use of all. The national governments of most of the modern states provide a wide variety of services to business, agriculture, labour and citizens in general.

The modern state has developed from the *laissez-faire* state into the one which undertakes a programme of regulation and service. This change has occurred because modern states, in turning their attention to the problems of society, have devised pragmatic answers to those problems.

The growth of socialism has also influenced the thinking of the people and the government with regard to the sphere of state activity. The view of the democratic socialists is that the capitalist system can be changed by legislation without violence. They are in favour of government ownership and operation of the principal manufacturing, mining and transportation services. They maintain that ownership and democratic control by the people is a proper function of collective or state activity. The socialists are willing to allow private enterprise in the retail trade services and some other sectors of the economy. State planning is regarded as a proper function for government and a dominant factor in determining the proper role of the state.

The view of the Communists is that the entire economic system should be owned and run by the government. The Communist states of the world are all socialistic in the sense that their governments own and operate the entire economic system. Even the official name of Russia is the Union of Soviet Socialist Republics. The Communists are not in favour of solving the problems with moderation and in a fashion most nearly acceptable to the majority. They prefer to cut the knot rather than untie it, regardless of the damage and the loose ends left dangling. The fallacy in this approach lies in the assumption that most of the social problems arise from the private ownership of the means of production. The truth is that social problems arise from many complex sources. They do not derive from a simple origin and hence cannot be solved simply. The assumption that public ownership and operation of the economic system will solve all problems is disproved by the Soviet experiment. Even after the lapse of many decades, the Soviet Union has not been able to solve her social and economic problems. One cannot say that all injustice and exploitation have disappeared from that country. And whatever has been achieved has been done at the cost of denying freedom to the people.

All those who believe in democracy do not want the government performing functions which are not essential. As to what is an essential and what is not an essential function of the modern state, is a question on which there is an honest difference of opinion. In the democracies, the people decide what the functions of the government should be. During the periods of war, economic crises or other emergencies, there is always a demand for giving more functions to the government and that adds to the activities of the state. During the World War II, the American Government built, owned and operated many plants manufacturing war materials. In Great Britain, the Labour Government which came to power after World War II, nationalised the basic industries. In the United States, many government-operated plants and emergency regulatory functions were discontinued as the war period ended. After the victory of the Conservatives in 1951 in Great Britain, the programme for nationalising additional industries was halted.

In view of the expansion of the functions of the government during the 20th century, the question is where the line is to be drawn between essential and non-essential functions. In the democratic states, the answer has been given in the growth of the welfare state. In the totalitarian states, the question is already answered by the very existence of total government. In the socialist state, the government owns and operates the economic system. In the non-Communist totalitarian dictatorship, the question of the functions of government is an idle one as the government control extends to every facet of society, regardless of title to productive property.

Woodraw Wilson divides the functions of a modern government into two parts, *viz.*, constituent or essential functions and ministrant or optional functions. The constituent functions must be performed by all the states, at all times, at all places and at all costs. The ministrant functions are optional in the sense that all progressive states perform them and the measure of the progress of a state is to be judged from the number of functions performed by it from the ministrant list.

The following are the constituent or essential functions of the state:

(1) Keeping of law and order and the provision for the protection of life and property from violence and robbery.

(2) The fixing of legal relations between man and his wife and between the parents and their children.

(3) The regulation of the holding, transmission and inter-change of property and the determination of its liability for debt or crime.

(4) The determination of contract rights between individuals.

(5) The definition and punishment of crime.

(6) The administration of justice in civil cases.

(7) The determination of political duties, privileges and relations of citizens.

(8) The dealings of the state with foreign powers and its protection from foreign aggression.

The state must maintain a strong army, navy and air force to protect its citizens from external attacks. The progress of society is impossible without security. If the people are always in danger of their lives, they cannot be good citizens. They are not likely to take interest in their work if they are always afraid of foreign attack. Moreover, law and order within the state itself is also essential for human progress. If there is always the danger of disorders, riots, revolution and attacks by the miscreants, there cannot be any progress in any field. People will be bothered more about their security than about their work. Human beings will be reduced to the status of brutes. Without the police and civil and criminal courts, there will be no safety of person and property. Anybody can be robbed, assaulted, insulted or murdered anywhere. The only place for a good man under those circumstances is jail itself. Without the sanctity of contracts, there can be no human progress. If there is no guarantee for the fulfilment of the promises made, all business activity is bound to come to a standstill.

Woodrow Wilson points out to the following ministrant or optional functions of the state:

(1) The regulation of trade and industry *e.g.*, coinage, weights and measures, tariffs, navigation laws, etc.

(2) The regulation of labour.

(3) The maintenance of thoroughfares.

(4) The maintenance of postal and telegraphic systems.

(5) The manufacture and distribution of gas, maintenance of waterworks, etc.

(6) Sanitation, including the regulation of industries and trades for sanitary purposes.

(7) Education.

(8) The care of the poor and the incapable.

(9) The care and cultivation of forests and stocking of rivers with fish.

(10) The sumptuary laws such as prohibition laws.

It is the duty of all progressive governments to regulate trade and industry in such a way as to realise the good of society as a whole. The importance of factory legislation cannot be over-emphasized. Labour must be given a fair deal. The workers must not be forced to work for very long hours. They must be given adequate wages so that they can not only keep their body and soul together but also live the lives of useful citizens. The state must look to the construction and maintenance of roads. It must set up libraries and reading-rooms for the people. Provision must be made for parks, gardens, museums and zoos for public enjoyment and information. These things cannot be done adequately by private agencies. The state must look to the health of the people. All kinds of preventive methods should be adopted to maintain their health. Hospitals and dispensaries should be established by the state to look after public health. The state should also set up a large number of schools and colleges to educate the people. Primary education should not only be compulsory but also free. The people cannot be expected to take interest in the affairs of the state unless they have been given the right type of education. The state must look after the poor, the aged and the weak. There must be work-houses to give employment to those who are able-bodied. For others, there must be institutions from where they can get help. They must not be forced to beg on the roads. Provision should be made for old age pensions and insurance against unemployment. The state should come forward with all kinds of facilities to help the people to raise their standard of living. It should also look to their moral and social welfare.

Social Services

Social services are those activities which are directed towards the material, mental and moral welfare of the citizens. Their object is to make the lives of the citizens full, happy and comfortable by removing such obstacles as poverty, ignorance and disease. Social services are "personal services and are distinct from environmental services."

The performance of the social services by the state is absolutely necessary if the ideal of welfare state or service-state is to be realised in actual practice. There are many types of social services. Some of them are performed by private individuals. They set up centres, hospitals, orphanages, etc., for the welfare of people. Some social services are performed by religious or semi-religious organisations. They also set up their schools, colleges, hospitals, orphanages, dispensaries, poor houses, etc. They do this work with a view to serve humanity and also to make their religion popular. There are some social services which are aided by the state but otherwise are managed by private individuals and organisations. For example, we have large number of schools which are run by individuals and societies but they receive monetary help from the state. There are certain social services which are run by corporations but are controlled by the state in many ways. The Reserve Bank of India has a lot of control over the banks operating in the country. The insurance companies are also controlled by the Government of India. The joint stock companies are under the control of the Government of India in certain respects. They are liable to be punished if they violate the laws governing them.

There are certain social services which are entirely financed and managed by the state. Thus, the state finances and manages the railways, posts and telegraphs, canals, roads, hospitals, technical institutions, etc. The modern view is that private individuals and religious organisations should be eliminated from the field of social services and the state should come forward and control them. It is realised that private individuals and organisations do not have enough funds to do the work adequately. Moreover, the problems are so great that they cannot cope with them. In some cases, a mercenary spirit is to be found in them. Some of the voluntary associations have commercialised education. They do not care for the physical, moral and intellectual growth of the students in their institutions. There is too much individualism, friction and mutual jealousy. The good of the individual is forgotten and personal interests become paramount. Such a state of affairs is not congenial to the progress of society. No wonder, there is a demand for the state to take the social services into its own hands.

Public Utility Services

It is the duty of the state to construct works of public utility for the prosperity of the people. Without them, it is difficult to improve the standard of living of the people. These services are run by the state not for private gain but for the happiness of the people. The important public utility services are the railways, roads, water and air transport, posts and telegraphs, telephones, water supply, electricity, gas, etc. In modern times, the greatest importance has to be attached to the means of communication and transport. Without pure water supply, it is difficult to maintain good health. The use of electricity has become practically indispensable in modern times. All this cannot be done by private individuals and organisations. They do not have enough funds for that purpose. Moreover, they are bound to run the services for private and not for public good.

There are many public utility services which are left in the hands of the local bodies. The municipalities look after the water supply. In many cases, they run buses and tram services and also provide electricity.

Public Health

It is the duty of the state to fight against poverty, disease, squalor and ignorance. The problem of public health cannot be left in the hands of private individuals and voluntary organisations. The state must take all those measures which can check diseases and also cure the diseased persons. The greatest amount of attention should be paid to the problem of sanitation. The drainage system must be properly maintained. The roads must be swept and kept clean. Filth should not be allowed to accumulate in any place. Whenever there is an outbreak of epidemic in any form the state must come forward to help the victims. It must issue the required instructions, provide for free vaccination, and set up infectious diseases hospitals. It must provide for hospitals and dispensaries for ordinary patients and set up medical schools and colleges to train a large number of doctors and nurses to fight the menace of diseases. Provision should be made for first aid centres. Laws should be passed to check the adulteration of food. Rules of sanitation and hygiene must be enforced.

Social Security

If the state is to be a welfare state, it must provide for social security. That means that every citizen must be offered protection in case he suffers from illness, old age, accident or unemployment. The people should be given security by means of insurance against sickness, old age, accident and unemployment. Provision should be made for pension and gratuities after retirement. Where there is no provision for pensions, gratuities must be given. There should be provision for a provident fund in all employments. Both the employees and the employers should be compelled to make their contributions towards the provident funds. Provision should also be made for the grant of pensions to the widows if their husbands die on duty.

Efforts are being made to achieve the ideal of social security. The Employees State Insurance Act was passed in 1948 to achieve that ideal. Provision has been made for sickness benefit, maternity benefit, disablement benefit, dependant's benefit and medical benefit. Employees are entitled to get certain benefits when they are unwell and cannot attend to their duty. Women are entitled to get wages for a certain period at the time of their confinement. If an employee meets with an accident, he is also entitled to certain benefits. If he dies in the course of employment, his dependants are entitled to certain benefits. The expenses for the above benefits are paid partly by the employees, partly by the employers and partly by the state. The scheme has been extended to certain states and in course of time it is expected to cover the whole of India.

Social Reform

It is realised in modern times that it is the duty of the state to remove the social evils from which society suffers. It is on this ground that a demand is made that the state must interfere to remove the evils from the present system of marriages, particularly the dowry system. That is also the reason why untouchability has been abolished in the country and *Suttee* was stopped and made a penal offence. A check was put on early marriages and slavery was abolished. The view of Mahatma Gandhi was that the habit of drinking was ruinous to society. He emphatically stated that the use of wine was "more damnable, than thieving and perhaps even prostitution." That was the reason why he insisted that a policy of prohibition must be enforced at all costs. The financial considerations must not be allowed to stand in the way. It is unfortunate that in spite of the policy of prohibition, the habit of drinking has increased tremendously in the country. While the states have lost crores of rupees in the farm of revenues, the common man, for whom this policy was meant, has not gained substantially.

Problem of Nationalisation

There is a demand that the government must follow a policy of nationalisation of all the resources of the country. It is pointed out that the capitalist system has failed to deliver the goods. While it has made a few persons very rich, it has rendered destitute millions of people. The condition of the poor has worsened. The measures adopted in various countries to help the working classes have not proved to be adequate or effective. Such a state of affairs cannot be allowed to continue for long as we believe in modern times in the welfare state. If the state exists for the welfare of all, the poor cannot be ignored. The only way out of the difficulty is that the resources of the country should be taken over by the state and worked in the interests of all the people. If there are profits, those must all go to the poor. The motive of profits must disappear from the field of production. Moreover, only those things must be produced which are useful and help to satisfy the needs of the people.

Nationalisation is also defended on the ground that private producers are selfish and they care only for their personal gains. They will not mind exploiting the mines in such a way that nothing is left for the future generations. If these resources are in the hands of the government, it will always keep in mind the future needs of the nation. Under a capitalist system, there is always a hunger for foreign markets and that ultimately leads to war. However, if all those resources are taken over by the state, the danger of wars becomes less.

A policy of wholesale nationalisation is not a safe one. Experience shows that the people who work in government offices are on the whole less energetic and less efficient than those working in private industries. The experience of India is a warning that the state enterprises may fail and a lot of national money may simply be squandered away. Instead of profits, there may be total or partial losses in public enterprises. Those who stand for nationalisation must see to it that the public servant becomes energetic, honest and faithful to his duties. So long as that is not possible, a policy of nationalisation will not succeed in achieving its objects.

Planning

Planning in modern times has become a necessity. Experience shows that non-planned economies have not been able to meet the needs of the modern world. While the capitalist countries with unplanned economies were facing a sort of crisis, the Communist countries, with their planned economies, were making progress. They were not facing any problems of unemployment, stagnation of economic life, falling prices, etc. As a matter of fact, all countries had to plan during the war and a similar situation had to be faced even after the war. Modern society has to deal with too many problems and as the resources are limited, things have to be planned so that the interests of all can be-safeguarded and all people, whether rich or poor, do well in life.

The first country to follow the policy of planning was the Soviet Union. After the overthrow of the Czarist regime in Russia, the Communist leaders hit upon the idea of planning. It was felt that if Communism was to hold its own against capitalism, it must show better results than capitalism. The resources of the country were very meagre and it was realised that the only way to fight successfully against capitalism was to follow a policy of planning. A haphazard policy could not be expected to yield excellent results. The experts must be employed to work out the details and find out how best the limited resources could be utilised by giving priorities to those things which were both essential and urgent. It was with this object in view that the Communist leaders in the Soviet Union prepared what are known as Five Year Plans and they have not one or two but many such Plans. When those plans were worked, it was found that they yielded excellent results. No wonder, one Five Year Plan was succeeded by another and the same policy is being followed even today in the Soviet Union.

When India became free in 1947, her great leaders like the late Prime Minister Jawaharlal Nehru borrowed the idea of planning from the Soviet Union and prepared the Five Year Plans. The object of these Five Year Plans has been to pool the resources of the country and try to get the maximum results by a system of priorities. The various Five Year Plans have done a lot of good. If the best results have not been achieved, that is partly owing to inefficiency and corruption prevailing in all spheres of life in the country. The Government of India has a separate department of planning under a separate minister. However, it is rightly pointed out that the expenditure incurred on planning is much more than the results achieved by planning.

The system of planning has also been followed in Communist China. That partly explains the reason why that country has made tremendous progress during a very short period since 1949. Some sort of planning is also being followed in Great Britain.

There is a fundamental difference between planning in a communist country and democratic planning. The former system is to be found in the Soviet Union and Communist China. India is an example of democratic planning. Democratic planning involves "the lay-out of all national resources in the national interest to a nationally desirable end, and the organisation of the necessary methods, by the use of all the means that the people in a democratic society are prepared to give to the government." The six elements in democratic planning are the choice of what is to be produced, the supply of the necessary labour, the supply of materials, the supply of capacity, the supply of the best location and the supply of finance.

The question has been raised as to whether planning is the enemy of liberty or not. The answer is that planning in a Communist state certainly stands in the way of liberty. There everything is regimented; the state exercises its control over the whole of the lives of the people and thus the people enjoy practically no freedom. However, that is not the case with democratic planning. It does not stand in the way of individual liberty. Herbert Morrison observed thus in October, 1946: "Britain is the first great nation to attempt to combine large-scale economic and social planning with a full measure of individual right and liberty." Professor Mannheim says: "While planlessness is anarchy and chaos, yet planning must not do violence to the spontaneous force in society." The great task of the political leaders in a democracy is that they "must learn to reconcile the essentials of his freedom with life in a planned society."

Limits of Political Control

Professor MacIver rightly says that the state is "a structure not coequal and coextensive with society, but built within it as a determinate order for the attainment of a specific end." There is a proper sphere in which the state must function. If it goes beyond that sphere, it is bound to bungle. The resources of every country are limited and they must be employed by the state to perform its essential functions. If the state fritters away its resources on non-essential things, the essential things are bound to be left out. Professor MacIver rightly says that omnicompetence is incompetence. It is desirable to discuss the limits of political control.

The state must not try to control public opinion. The people must be allowed to think and dream in their own way. If it tries to control public opinion, the results will be disastrous. Laski says: "Men who are prevented from thinking as their experience teaches them, will soon cease to think at all. Men who cease to think cease also to be in any genuine sense citizens. The instrument which makes them able to make effective their experience rusts into obsolescence by disuse." The very foundations of democracy will be sapped if public opinion is controlled by government. The government will find no support at the time of a crisis if the people have developed the habit of not thinking for themselves.

Every democratic government has to take into consideration the public opinion. It cannot afford to ignore it. But that does not mean that the government should be given the authority to choke public opinion by following certain methods. MacIver says: "To maintain the effectiveness of any authority, it is necessary under these conditions that government should utilise modern methods of feeling the pulse of the public, should sense the currents of opinion and adopt their presentation of policy accordingly, should acquire knowledge of the differential impact of new measures on the diverse groups of the community and of the influences and motivations that operate with them."

Religion also is a sphere in which the government must have no say. Religion is a matter of conscience and that is not the place where the authority of the state can operate. No wonder, the present trend in the world is to keep the state away from religion. It is no business of the state to tell the people what their religion should be. Experience shows that whenever the state has tried to interfere in that sphere, there has been opposition. Ultimately, that may result in a revolt or war. That is why the framers of the Indian Constitution embodied the principle of a secular state in the Indian Constitution. As regards the authority of the state over religion. Barker says: "The standards of religion can only be applied in the area of voluntary life which lies outside the State; and the quality of behaviour which they involve can only be achieved if it is sought freely and without any shadow of legal compulsion. If the State attempts to draw religious standard, and the quality of behaviours which they involve, into the area of the legal association, and to enforce them as the prescriptions and by the sanctions of law, it simply fails."

Morality is another sphere in which the state must not interfere. The moral code of every individual varies while the law of the state is uniform for all. This does not mean that .the state should not provide the conditions in which morality is possible. All that is demanded is that the state must not try to regulate morality or control it. MacIver says: "The major thesis is that law can no more be substitute for morality than the hand can be a substitute for the eye." The view of T.H. Green was that "the only acts which the,state ought to enjoin or forbid are those of which the doing or not doing, from whatever motive, is necessary to the moral end of society."

The state must also not try to control customs. What habit is to the individual, custom is to the community. Customs grow spontaneously and become a part and parcel of the lives of the individuals. The state can neither create customs nor destroy them. However, it can mould the customs by providing certain conditions in which the existing custom gets moulded on account of the changed environments. Experience shows that whenever an attempt has been made to change a custom there has been opposition and the government has become helpless. The wisest thing is not to touch customs unless those are found to be suicidal or in any way injurious to the growth of society. In that case, the state has to step in to undo the evil, but even then it has to exercise its authority with great restraints. About the state vis-a-vis custom, MacIver says: "Custom, when attacked, attacks law in turn, attacks not only the particular law which opposes it, but, what is more vital, the spirit of law-abidingness, the unity of the general will."

The state should also not try to control fashions. The people are prepared to follow a fashion by a private individual but not if it is imposed by the authority of law. Fashion is a matter of personal choice and preference and the state is helpless in this field. MacIver says: "A people will eagerly follow the dictates of fashion proclaimed by some unknown coterie in Paris or London or New York, but were the state to decree changes in themselves so insignificant, it would be regarded as monstrous tyranny—it might even lead to tyranny."

The state also must not try to impose one homogeneous culture on the people. Different groups in a state may have different cultures and all of them will be proud of their respective cultures. They would resist any attempt made by the state to obliterate the cultural differences and bring about uniformity in a field where there are bound to be differences. The real task before the state should be to create unity out of the diversity arising from different cultures.

SUGGESTED READINGS

Allen, C.K. : Democracy and the Individual.
Coker, F.W. : Recent Political Thought.
Dawson, Christopher : Religion and the Modern State.
Ehrmann, H.W. : Democracy in a Changing Society.
Garner, J.W. : Introduction to Political Science.
Gettell, R.G. : Introduction to Political Science.
Gilchrist, R.N. : Principles of Political Science.
Laski, H.J. : A Grammar of Politics.
Laski, H.J. : Liberty in the Modern State.
Leacock, S. : Elements of Political Science.
MacIver, R.M. : The Modern State.
Paul, W. : The State in Origin and Function.
Roche, John P., and Murray, S. Stedman, Jr. : The Dynamics of Democratic Government.
Sidgwich, H. : Elements of Politics.
Soltau, R.H. : An Introduction to Politics.
Titmuss, R.M. : The Economic Functions of the State.
Warbasse, J.P. : Co-operative Democracy.
Willoughby, W.W. : The Ethical Basis of Political Authority.
Willoughby, W.W. : The Government of Modern State.
Wilson, W. : The State.

CHAPTER

Liberal Theory of the Nature and Functions of the State

Classical Liberalism or laissez-faire individualism

Learning Objectives

- Classical Liberalism or laissez-faire individualism
- Adam Smith
- Bentham
- J.S. Mill
- Herbert Spencer
- William Senior
- Thomas Paine
- Nock
- Oakeshott
- Criticism of Laissez-faire Liberalism
- Modern or Positive Liberalism
- J.S. Mill
- T.H. Green
- Laski
- MacIver
- J.M. Keynes (1883-1946)
- John Galbraith
- Liberal View of Classification of State Functions
- Nature of the State
- Suggested Readings

The liberal theory of the nature and functions of the state can be discussed under two heads: classical liberalism and modern liberalism. According to the classical liberal view, the state comes into existence as a result of a contract for the sole purpose of preserving and protecting the natural rights of an individual to life, liberty and property. The relationship between the individual and the state is contractual. The state is the creation of man and it exists for the fulfilment of certain specific objectives.

The state is an evil but a necessary evil on account of the selfishness and egoism of man. It is a concession to human weakness. But for the restraining power of the state, there would be no social peace and order. The state should give its undivided attention to the protection of the individual but not promote his welfare. The guiding principle of the liberal individualist "is the maximum possible individual freedom and minimum possible state action." In the words of J.S. Mill, "Over himself, over his own body and mind, the individual is sovereign".

John Locke (1632-1704) is considered to be the father figure of the liberal tradition. According to him, the state exists for the people who form it and they do not exist for the state. The basis of the state is consent. The state exercises authority in terms of law. The state has limited power. It is limited not only by natural law but also by civil law which is a re-statement of natural law. Natural rights have the sanction of natural law and are inviolable. The state is tolerant and it tolerates the differences of opinion. The state has primarily negative functions. The only function of the state is to remove hindrances in the way of liberty.

Classical liberalism advocated the right of the individual to freedom of trade, freedom of contract, freedom to bargain and freedom of enterprise. It postulated private property as the condition of progress as property was considered to be a product of the individual's labour, ingenuity and enterprise. As all freedoms of the individual ensued from the element of reason, they were regarded valuable for society.

Classical liberalism advocated the policy of *Laissez-faire.* It signified nonintervention by the state in the economic activities of individuals. *Laissez-faire* individualism regards the property rights of individuals as a necessary condition of liberty and seeks to set definite and circumscribed limits on the regulatory powers vested in the Government over social and economic processes. This theory regards the state as a necessary evil because it imposes regulations and restricts the freedom of the individual. The exponents of *Laissez-faire* individualism include Adam Smith (1723-1790), Bentham (1748-1832), James Mill (1773-1836) and Herbert Spencer (1820-1903). J.S. Mill (1806-1973) also made an important contribution to the theory of *Laissez-faire* individualism.

Adam Smith

Adam Smith was influenced by the Physiocrats, a French school of economic thought which flourished during the eighteenth century. According to the Physiocrats, the aim of the Government should be to conform to nature. So long as men do not interfere with the liberty of each other and do not combine among themselves in order to encroach upon the liberty of others, the Government should leave them alone to find their own salvation. The state should not interfere in the activities of normal and law-abiding citizens. From this followed the doctrine of free trade between nations on grounds of justice and economy. Although Adam Smith learned much from the Physiocrats, yet he rejected the leading idea of the Physiocrats that agriculture was the sole source of the wealth produced. His own view was that commerce and industry, as well as agriculture, produced wealth. He wanted to find out which policy of the state would be conducive to increasing the wealth of the nation and promoting national prosperity.

In his *Wealth of Nations*, Adam Smith postulated a system of natural liberty in order to promote national prosperity. His argument was that the businessman knows his own interest better than any Government can tell him. The only wise policy for a Government to follow was *Laissez-faire.* He defined the system of natural liberty in these words: "Every man, as long as he does not violate the laws of justice, is left perfectly free to pursue his own interest in his own way, and to bring both his industry and capital into competition with those of any other man or order of men. The sovereign is completely discharged from the duty of superintending the industry of the private people and of directing it toward the employment most suitable to the interest of the society."

According to this system of natural liberty, the function of the Government is confined to three duties of great importance. The first duty of the state is to preserve the liberty of the people against foreign aggression and enslavement. The second duty of the state is to protect its citizens against injustice and oppression. The third duty is to provide basic amenities like roads, harbours and canals. The state should also provide education and public health. It should not allow any citizen to die of hunger. For this purpose, it can regulate the price of bread with a view to protecting the citizens against exploitation. Beyond that, the state had normally no role to play.

Bentham

Bentham made an important contribution to the theory of *Laissez-faire* individualism as the great exponent of utilitarianism. According to him, the business of the state is to promote the happiness of society by a system of punishments and rewards. It had no other justification for existence. A good Government is one which promotes the happiness of its subjects. Bentham treated the state as an instrument devised by man for the promotion of the happiness of the community, but he did not contemplate any wide scope of state activity. The view of Bentham was that the main function of the state is legislation and the chief objective of legislation is to remove all institutional restrictions on the free actions of individuals. The individual himself is to exercise his moral judgement and the state cannot promote character among the people. The only function of the state is to restrain individuals from indulging in activities which affect the general happiness adversely. It is the function of the state to punish offenders but the state should not interfere in the activities of law-abiding citizens as they are the best judges of what is right and what is wrong and what is moral and what is immoral.

Bentham dismisses the idea of natural rights as "rhetorical nonsense". The state is the sole source, of rights.

According to Bentham, the state "has not integral relation with the moral life of the citizen. It seeks to change his behaviour: it cannot change him. It cannot help him to develop his character, to bring out the best that is in him. For it is not the state that moulds the citizens, it is the citizens that mould the state."

According to Bentham, the state has originated because of its social utility and not because of any social contract. The basis, object and functions of the state could be ascertained on the basis of social utility. The functions of the state should also be based on this principle. Those functions should be the minimum as every individual is the best judge of his own interest. The state and society are for individuals and the state should not do those things which may cause pain to individuals. According to Bentham, "The business of Government is to promote the happiness of the society, by punishing and rewarding". The basis of government is not contract but human need and the satisfaction of human needs is its sole justification. The rulers should be granted the power to do good and deprived of the power to do evil. Bentham believed in the dogma of self-regulating and uncontrolled economy in which the state has virtually no role to play.

J.S. Mill

According to J.S. Mill, freedom of action is essential for the development of character. Without that freedom, the individual becomes a mere automaton. The highest development of the individual is possible only when there is an opportunity for self-reliance. The action of the Government is legitimate upto a certain point but beyond that, it cramps the individual. Excessive governmental interference kills individual initiative and creates a pauper mentality.

Herbert Spencer

The view of Herbert Spencer was that the functions of the state should be the minimum and society should be governed by the principle of "survival of the fittest". Only the fit persons have the right to survive. The health of society requires that week persons should not be given any assistance and be allowed to die. The state should not help the weak, the poor, and the handicapped. They should be allowed to die a natural death as the weak or the unfit should perish. The state should have the minimum role in the socio-economic sphere. It should not and cannot perform welfare functions and must not give assistance to weaker sections. According to Spencer, the state has only three functions and those are the protection of the individual against external enemies, the protection of the individual against internal enemies and the enforcement of the contracts lawfully made.

William Senior

The view of William Senior is that the functions of the state should be the minimum. According to him, "The essential business of Government is to afford defence, to protect the community against foreign or domestic fraud. Unfortunately, however, the Governments have generally supposed to be either their duty not merely to give security but wealth; not merely to enable their subjects to produce and enjoy safety, but to teach them what to produce and how to enjoy."

Thomas Paine

Thomas Paine supported the idea of natural rights of man. According to him, the state should have a limited scope and sphere of functions. To quote him, "While society in any state is a blessing, government, even in its best state, is but a necessary evil: in its worst state, an intolerable one".

Nock

According to Nock, the power of the state is not original but derived from the power of society. The state is turning every contingency into a resource for accelerating the conversion of social power into state power. This social power is used by the state to safeguard the interests of the capital class.

Oakeshott

According to M. Oakeshott, there is an essential unity and harmony in society. The functions of the state should be the minimum. Every individual should enjoy the maximum liberty. He considers collectivism as the enemy of a free society as collectivism stands for managed society and freedom is possible only in an unregulated competitive society. The task of the state is the establishment and maintenance of effective competition by means of an appropriate legal system. Oakeshott is opposed to any increase in the functions of the state as it is injurious to individual freedom. The only function of the state is to adjust the interests of the subjects. It has no social, political or economic function to perform.

F.A. Hayek, M. Friedmanand Nozickare opposed to social welfare-oriented planning and intervention of the state in economic affairs. They have strongly criticised the welfare or regulatory functions of the modern state. To quote Nozick, "Our main conclusions about the state are that a minimal state, limited to the narrow functions of protection against force, theft, fraud, enforcement of contracts and so on, is justified; that any more extensive state will violate a person's right not to be forced to do certain things and is unjustified; and that the minimal state is inspiring as well as right" (Anarchy, State and Utopia, p. ix)

Criticism of Laissez-faire Liberalism

Critics point out that though *Laissez-faire* liberalism contains an important truth, it exaggerates the same. It unduly emphasizes one aspect of man's social life at the expense of others. While reacting against petty laws and meddlesome legislation, it goes to the other extreme. The arguments in favour of *Laissez-faire* liberalism are one-sided and even false to some extent. The complex modern civilisation makes it difficult for the individual to develop all his powers all alone. There are many situations in the life of today which require the help of the state. State assistance becomes necessary. The view of *Laissez-faire* liberalism that man is fundamentally selfish is not correct. Man possesses both self-regarding and other-regarding instincts. Egoism and altruism are present in every individual. It is not desirable to build an entire theory of state action only on one aspect of human nature. Individual welfare and social welfare are not opposed to each other and are dependent upon one another. The view of *Laissez-faire* liberalism is that every man knows his interest the best. Critics point out that the individual may know his present interest and not his future interest. Even if he is the best judge of his interest, he may not be the best judge of the means to realise them. Even J.S. Mill admits that society should protect a man against himself when he tries to cross an unsafe bridge or contracts himself into slavery. The view of *Laissez-faire* liberalism is that if each man is allowed to pursue his own interests, everybody will be happy and society will become prosperous, but that will not be true if the interests of the individuals are at cross purposes with one another. There is the necessity of the state to act as the mediating power to settle the differences and conflicts.

The state is an organism and the interests of the individual are not entirely different from his fellowmen. The state is not an evil but a positive good. It is not an artificial creation hut a natural growth. Regulation by the Government does not necessarily imply the curtailment of individual freedom.

Critics point out that the law of demand and supply is not a scientific one. There is very little of free competition in practice. It leads to monopolies, trusts and cartels.

The views of Spencer are also criticised. The survival of the fittest does not necessarily mean the survival of the best. It only means that whatever survives deserves to survive. It is contended that "if the sole test of fitness to survive is found in the fact of survival, then the prosperous burglar becomes an object of commendation and the starving artisan a target of contempt". Hallowell is of the view that Spencer made the fatal mistake of transferring concepts that are appropriate to one science to another where the phenomena are quite different. Moreover, what is true of the lower animals is not necessarily true of man. Lower animals passively allow themselves to be adapted to nature but on account of his superior intelligence, man is able actively to change nature to his own benefit.

The view of the liberals is that as governments make mistake, the functions of the state should be reduced to the minimum. Critics point out that similar mistakes are also made by private agencies but those are not known to the public, while the mistakes made by the government are known to everybody.

Critics point out that if prevention is better than cure, the state should prevent injury to society as well as cure the injury. It is impossible for the state to follow a policy of non-intervention as its logical conclusion is anarchism. In the words of Prof. Laski, it means "poor health, undeveloped intelligence, miserable homes and work in which the majority can find no human interest. Undu advantage is taken of weakness. The bargaining capacity of the labourer not being the same as that of the capitalist, the labourer often loses out in the economic race. The haggling of the market is the apotheosis of inequality". (A Grammar of Politics, p. 191)

The conclusion is that a negatively regulative state has become out of date. No wonder, modern liberalism stands for the expansion of the functions of the state while conserving individual freedom and initiative.

Modern or Positive Liberalism

By the middle of the nineteenth century, classical liberalism lost its appeal. The concentration of the wealth on the one hand and mass poverty on the other posed a grave challenge to the assumptions of classical liberalism. The result was that Marx rejected this philosophy. On the liberal front, J.S. Mill took up the task of revising the liberal doctrine to present a positive view of the nature and functions of the state which were considered necessary to meet the new challenge. The view of H.M. Drucker is that the work of J.S. Mill marks the turning point between classical liberalism and contemporary liberalism. (The Political Uses of Ideology, p. 127)

J.S. Mill

J.S. Mill played an important role in drawing a distinction between the political and economic spheres and in working out the implications of liberal theory in those spheres. In the political sphere, he proved himself to be a strong supporter of constitutional and representative government. In the economic sphere, he showed socialist leanings and laid the foundations of the welfare state.

Although Mill was utilitarian, he revised the views of Bentham and others. The conclusion of Mill was that it is the business of the government actively to promote the happiness of the individuals. If it fails in this respect, it must give way to some other form of social organisation.

Mill disagreed with the view of Bentham that happiness could be measured by quantitative differences of pleasures, not by qualitative differences. The view of J.S. Mill was that some pleasures were qualitatively superior to others. Macpherson pointed out that Mill revolted against Bentham's material maximizing criterion of the social good. He did not agree that all pleasures were equal or the market distributed them fairly. Mill's view was that men were capable of something better than money grubbing, and starvation, avoiding existence to which they were condemned by Bentham.

Mill rejected the maximization of indifferent utilities as the criterion of social good. He put in its place the maximum development and use of human capacities, whether moral, intellectual, aesthetic or material.

J.S. Mill made a distinction between the self-regarding activities and others-regarding activities of the individuals and allowed the state to regulate and control the other-regarding activities. Mill defined a sphere where an individual's behaviour could be regulated in the interest of society. He was in favour of a positive role for the state to secure the welfare of the community even if it implied curbing the liberty of the individual to some extent.

To begin with, Mill made a strong plea for the security of property, but his later view was that the right to property was not absolute or sacrosanct. Mill went to the extent of advocating many restrictions on the rights of inheritance and bequest. The view of Mill was that the right to property in land was not sacrosanct because no man made the land. It was the original inheritance of all mankind. He pointed out that the incomes of landlords continued to increase without any effort, risk or sacrifice on their part. Hence, if the state appropriated the incomes of their wealth for diverting it to the use of the community, it was no violation of the principles on which the right to private property was founded or justified. On the general principle of social justice, the landlords had no claim to accession of such riches.

The view of Mill was that it was the duty of the state not only to remove obstacles in the way of individual progress but also to take positive steps for the well-being of the poor. The measures suggested by him include compulsory education, limiting the right of inheritance, factory legislation, control of monopolies by the state, lessening of the working hours and attaching of less sanctity to landed property. The state was required not only to watch every citizen's interest but also to work for his moral development.

J.S. Mill divided the functions of the state mainly into two categories—creative and prohibitive. The creative functions of the state include the creation of a free atmosphere in society in which each individual may search for truth and facilities for character formation, increase in experience, free play of opinions, peace and pleasure. As regards prohibitive functions, the state must interfere at the time of social disorders, anarchy and lawlessness. Mill had faith in the developmental capacity of the state which was missing in classical liberalism. He did not agree that free competition could create a free society in which each and every one could have free personal and social development.

According to Mill, the state had necessary and optional functions. The necessary functions included all those functions which were supported by classical liberalism. Among the optional functions, he included welfare functions of the state. He supported the concept of mixed economy in which public and private sectors were to operate side by side. To quote Mill, "There might be a national bank or a government manufactory, without any monopoly against private banks and manufactories. There might be a post office without penalties against the conveyance of letters by any other means. There may be a corps of government engineers for civil purposes, while the profession of a civil engineer is free to be adopted by every one. There may be public hospitals, without any restriction upon private medical or surgical practice".

The views of J.S. Mill on the subject may be summed up thus: The state is not the outcome of the selfish interests of individuals. It is the product of human will. It is not a necessary evil but an agency for social welfare. It creates an atmosphere in which individuals can develop their personality. There cannot be peaceful growth of society by the laws of free competition, free contract and free exchange. The state can perform economic functions like control of monopolies, working hours and working conditions of workers. Among the important functions of the state are public health, public security and public education. The state must encourage scientific research.

T.H. Green

T.H. Green revised the liberal theory of the state under the influence of the idealist theory. According to him, liberty is not the negative absence of restraint any more than beauty is the absence of ugliness. It is a positive power of doing or enjoying something worth doing or enjoying.

The exercise of true liberty postulates rights. Rights do not emanate from any transcendental law. They emanate from the moral character of man himself. Rights imply permission to pursue ideal objects. Rights exist within a social system. The recognising authority in the matter of rights is not the state but the moral consciousness of the community. Man can pursue his moral end and attain self-realisation only in a social community and not in isolation. Green is concerned not with legal rights but with ideal rights. Those rights can be realised in society when it is properly organised on the basis of goodwill.

The state is a product of moral consciousness. Human consciousness postulates liberty. Liberty involves rights and rights demand the state. The state is an instrument of perfection. It is not an embodiment of perfection. It owes its origin to the social nature of man. Genuine human personality is essentially a social phenomenon. An isolated natural man cannot be a moral agent. He exercises his moral system within the social organisation for which he needs rights. Rights are maintained by the state and hence the state serves as an essential base for human freedom.

Green is in favour of subordinating the individual to the community. He insists on the duty of the citizen to follow the general will for the common good. He does not treat the state and society as co-terminous. He remains in the liberal tradition by asserting the sovereignty of morals over politics. According to him, the state recognises and maintains rights, but it is not the source of rights. The real authority behind rights is the moral consciousness of the community. Green exalts society or the community as the primary eternal source of moral consciousness. The state is something secondary, a means or an instrument. It cannot serve the end of moral freedom directly but it can create favourable conditions for the exercise of moral freedom. The state and the law can regulate only the external order of society. The function of the state is to maintain conditions of life in which morality is possible and morality consists in the disinterested performance of self-imposed duties and not in obeying the commands of the state.

Although Green describes the function of the state as negative, yet he is not a champion of negative liberalism. He is definitely an exponent of positive liberalism. The state's function of removing obstacles in the way of man's pursuit of ideal objects is a positive function. His conception of the state as an agent for moral improvement led him to favour the intervention of the state to secure the welfare of the citizens. According to Green, the function of the state is to remove hindrances which come in the way of the development of human personality. The state is assigned moral functions. The state itself is not the highest morality. It is not an end in itself but merely a means to an end and that end is the social and personal development of man. The state is a moral institution. It has moral functions to perform. The state can merely establish the external conditions required for the inner development of man. Green regards the maintenance of the individual rights as the most important function of the state.

According to Green, ignorance, lack of education and poverty are the hindrances to moral development of human personality. It is the function of the state to remove all these hindrances and establish those external conditions which are necessary for the development of human personality.

Laski

As late as 1929, Laski believed in the pluralistic theory of the state "rooted in a denial that any association of man in the community is inherently entitled to primacy over any other association". However, there was a major shift from pluralistic view of the state to the state as "the keystone of social arch", "the coordinating factor in the community" and "the fundamental instrument of society". In his "The State in Theory and Practice" (1935), he defined the state as a national society which is integrated by possessing a coercive authority legally supreme over any individual or group which is a part of the society. It is by this coercive authority that the state is distinguished from all other forms of human associations. "The modern state is, a territorial society divided into government and subjects claiming, within the allotted physical area, a supremacy over all other institutions. It is, in fact, the final legal depository of the social will. It sets the perspective of all other organisations. It brings within its power all forms of human activity the control of which it deems desirable. It is, moreover, the implied logic of this supremacy that whatever remains free of its control, does so by its permission". The state is not an unchanging organisation. Its basis is neither fear, nor habit, nor utility. "The state as it was and is finds the roots of allegiance in all the complex facts of human nature; and a theory of obedience would have to weigh them differently for each epoch in the history of the state if it were to approximate to the truth".

Laski refused to accept the view of the Communists that the state is a class instrument. He firmly believed that the state can serve the general interest, bring unity and harmony in society and can reduce the gap between the rich and the poor. He believed that through the welfare functions of the state, the poor people are given the required assistance. To quote him, "There is hardly a function of social welfare undertaken by governments today which is not an effort to provide the poor with some, at least, of the amenities that the rich are able to provide for themselves. The state, that is, seeks to convince its citizens that its action is unbiased by organising for them the material conditions of an adequate life, and especially for those of its citizens who cannot afford those conditions for themselves". Illustrating the range of such services provided by the state since 1919, Laski writes, "Health, education, housing, social insurance, the regulation of hours and wages in industry, the control of factory conditions, the provision of meals for poor school children, are only outstanding examples of the range. We may say that it is outcome of a profounder social conscience". Again, "No modern state would subordinate human rights to the interests of property; this is shown by the whole character of modern legislation. When the state concerns itself with the quality of our food, the protection of child welfare, the safeguarding of the unemployed against industrial insecurity, the provision of educational opportunity—all of them services provided at the expense of that minority, the taxpayer—it is rhetorical exaggeration to regard it as a class instrument".

Laski did not accept the view that the state is the slave of capital or merely a class instrument. He had firm faith in the capacity of the state to check capitalism and profits of capitalists and help the workers.

Laski entrusted economic functions to the state and maintained that welfare functions of the state "is the price the rich have to pay for their security". He believed that in societies where the state is performing welfare functions and serving the common interests of society, a revolution will not occur.

Laski pleaded for state intervention in the production and distribution of essential commodities. He even went to the extent of advocating nationalisation of production and distribution of essential commodities. The major function of the state is to control production.

Enumerating the welfare functions of the state, Laski wrote: "Defence and police, the control of industry, social legislation including functions so far-reaching as education and insurance against sickness and unemployment, the encouragement of scientific research, the operation, with all the immense consequences, of a system of currency, the power of taxation, the definition of the terms upon which men may, for their various purposes, associate together; the maintenance of a system of courts in which the state's own legal principles will be given effect to, no matter what person or body of persons may be involved; merely, it is clear, to take a rapid view of its outstanding functions is to realise the degree to which it pervades and permeates the individual life".

According to Laski, the state must perform only general functions. It must coordinate the interests of various associations and institutions of society. It must bridge the gap between the rich and poor through its economic functions. It must perform the functions of social welfare such as education, health and residence. It must safeguard the interests of the working class and save them from exploitation. It must safeguard the rights and liberties of the people. It must control industries and the distribution of commodities.

Critics of Laski point out that a multiplication of state activities would result in the breakdown of the governmental machinery under its own weight. Laski is over-optimistic in the matter of management by the government. At the present stage of man's moral development, bureaucratic socialism would mean a tremendous increase of opportunities for corruption. Bureaucratic socialism is not conducive to human progress. The incentive to labour will probably be destroyed. The activities of the average man today are determined by the desire for social usefulness. The state of Laski is likely to check individual initiative. Life would become uniform and even stagnant. New wants would not be stimulated under a governmental regime. The working man is not as powerless as he is sometimes thought of. He is able to strike a bargain advantageous to himself with the help of trade unions and other forms of combinations. The view of Herbert Deane is that the collectivism of Laski would repress individuality. Genius would be sacrificed and citizens would become lazy. Individual spontaneity and responsibility would be sapped by bureaucracy and departmentalism would become strong. Production may suffer both in quantity and quality.

MacIver

According to Prof. R.M. MacIver, the state is an organ of the community. It is an association. "It commands only because it serves; it owns only because it owes. It creates rights not as the lordly dispenser of gifts, but as the agent of society for the creation of rights. The servant is not greater than his master". The state has power to guarantee rights but it cannot have unlimited powers. All civilised men are members of the state but they are also members of other associations. The state should know its limitations in controlling other associations.

The state is one among many other associations and we cannot concentrate in one agency all the activities of life. There are some tasks which the state alone can and should perform. There are also functions which the state cannot perform. Those functions should be left by the state for other associations. To quote MacIver, "we do not sharpen pencil with an axe".

According to MacIver, there are certain spheres of human activity which the state should not interfere. In the first place, the state should not try to control *opinion.* The reason given by MacIver is that when opinion is controlled by the state, the use of force becomes inevitable. "Force comes as a brutal alien into a sphere that is not its own, where it cannot regulate or convince, where it cannot stimulate or direct the healthy processes of thought, where its presence is destructive of good as well as of evil". Force is an ally of both truth and falsehood. If truth has to be revealed, opinion should be fought with opinion. When the law of the state is exercised over opinion, it becomes sheer coercion. However, the state may have to take cognizance of seditious utterances which are an assault on the principle of law-abidingness. The state can also check libellous or defamatory opinions or views.

The state should not interfere with *morality* and *religion.* The law can regulate only external conditions. It cannot control morality and religion. If moral obligations are turned into legal obligations, morality would be destroyed.

The state has little or no power to make or destroy *customs.* The attack on customs can prove dangerous for the state. Customs when attacked attack law in turn, not only law but also the spirit of law-abidingness.

The state cannot control and should not control *fashions and culture.* If the state is an association, it should not interfere with the working of other associations. However, the state has the right to declare war. "In declaring war the state puts a particular political object above the general ends of the family, of the cultural life, of the economic order. To secure this purpose, the state disrupts the family, breaks the fraternities of science and art, confounds the church, profoundly disturbs the economic system, ruins the commerce of nations, suppresses all cultural influences and inculcates a morality of violence, robbery, falsehood and murder, as between its members and those of its enemies, which is the direct contradiction of that on which society is founded".

According to MacIver, there are *three categories of functions of the state.* Those are order, protection and conservation and development. *The functions concerning order* include the establishment of areas and frontiers of political authority, establishment and control of the forms of communication, establishment of units and standards of computation, measurement, value etc., definition of political powers and spheres of authority, definition of general rights arid obligations of citizenship, persons and associations, collection and arrangement of statistics.

The second function of the state is *protection* of the weaker sections of society. "To protect the weak instead of the strong is on the whole a modern interpretation of the state's function". The functions concerning protection are the exercise of police function, securing life and property; maintenance and protection of authorities politically determined; maintenance and enforcement of rights and obligations politically determined; protection of the community against the encroachments of specific associations; assurance for the whole community of minimum standards of decent living, wage rates, employment and upbringing of children, care for and prevention of social wreckage.

The function of *conservation and development* includes promotion and regulation of the physical conditions of health; conservation and economic utilisation of natural resources, planning and general control of urban and rural development; establishment and development of facilities of education; promotion of the external conditions of opportunity, establishment of national museums, assistance in scientific research; promotion of industrial, agricultural, commercial and financial development in relation to general and not particular advantage; provision of the means of inquiry into social problems of general significance.

The view of MacIver is that in order to perform its essential functions efficiently, the state should not increase its functions unnecessarily. "What the state should do is what as an organ of the community, it can do. What service it should render is that of which it is in fact capable".

According to MacIver, the state is an instrument for the service of social man. It is an association like many other associations within the state. It performs limited functions and hence its powers should also be limited. The state cannot perform all functions efficiently. It can perform only general functions and the rest of the functions are left to other associations. The state should not perform certain functions such as control of opinion, morality etc. The state must establish law and order. The functions of the state change with changes in the needs of society.

J.M. Keynes (1883-1946)

The view of Kenyes is that in order to save the whole system, a part must be checked. Likewise, in order to save capitalism, the capitalists must be checked and controlled by the state.

John Galbraith

Prof. Galbraith has written about the role of the state in the changed circumstances after the World War II. He has analysed the outlook of the state on issues like production, demand, distribution, price-control, unemployment, poverty, scientific research, inflation, security of workers, banking, economic security, economic inequality, taxation, technological and industrial development, economic stability, education, wage control, planning and public services. He is a champion of mixed economy in which the public sector may play a dominant role but work in coordination with the private sector. He has recommended state intervention and control in many spheres.

According to Galbraith, the modern liberal democratic state has become an industrial state on account of its predominant role in the industrial system. To quote him, "The industrial system, in fact, is inextricably associated with the state. In notable respects, the mature corporation is an arm of the state. And the state, in important matters, is an instrument of the industrial system." Galbraith gives importance to the economic functions of the state. His view is that capitalism can be saved only by increasing the functions of the state.

Liberal View of Classification of State Functions

The functions of the modern liberal state can be divided into two parts: necessary or essential functions and non-essential or optional functions. As regards the *essential functions*, they include the maintenance of law and order, establishment of justice, defence and such other functions as the currency system, preservation of forests, minerals and public property, interpretation of rights, duties and mutual relationships of citizens.

As the state has assumed the duties of a nurse, a school master, trader and manufacturer, insurance agent, house-builder, town planner, railway controller etc., it has many *optional functions* to perform. Optional functions can be divided into economic functions, social functions, cultural functions and political functions.

Economic functions include the control of industries and nationalisation of essential and sick industries, the supply of essential commodities like wheat, rice, sugar, pulses, cement etc., checking of hoarding and black-marketing, trading and control of prices and measurements, improvements in agricultural production, checking of unemployment, control of banking, currency and inflation, provision of facilities for transport and communication, economic planning, protection of workers by regulating minimum wages, bonus, etc., and insurance and pension which may give security in old age and in case of accident. The *social functions* include family planning, checking of dowry, casteism and communalism, the removal of social exploitation and establishment of social unity, the provision of economic and other benefits to the weaker sections of society, social security to widows, orphans and the handicapped, the checking of food adulteration, the control of epidemics like plague, cholera and small-pox etc.

The *cultural functions* include the education of the masses, encouragement of music, art and literature, scientific and technological research and cultural exchanges to increase the spirit of cultural unity among the masses.

The *political functions* of the state include the safeguarding of the rights and liberties of citizens, the holding of free, fair and periodic elections, coordination of the interests of various parties, associations and groups of societies, checking of corruption in society and the provision of reasonable opportunities of participation in politics by the masses.

Woodrow Wilson has summed up the optional functions under the following heads: the regulation of trade and industry, regulation of labour, maintenance of thoroughfares, and postal and telegraph system, maintenance of water works etc., sanitation, education, care of the poor and incapable, care and cultivation of forests and such matters as the stocking of rivers with fish and sumptuary laws such as prohibition laws.

Nature of the State

The views of the classical and modern liberals regarding the nature of the state are almost similar. The classical liberals regard the state as a necessary evil and modern liberals regard the state as a necessary institution, but not an evil. The state is viewed as an instrument of social service and common welfare and not the enemy of liberty and rights of man. The old view "Man versus State" is no more accepted. In spite of these differences, the basic assumptions with regard to the nature of the state are similar.

The state is not a class instrument as contended by the Marxists. It is an instrument of the whole community. It serves the interests of the whole society by maintaining an equilibrium and balance in society. The state maintains unity in diversity and diversity in unity in society. What is required is not the finishing of the classes from society but their mutual adjustment. The basic principle of society is class harmony and not class struggle. In a pluralist society, the agency of the state is necessary to maintain law and order and justice in society.

The view of the liberals is that on account of democracy and periodic elections, the members of all classes can influence political power. Dahl writes, "All the active and legitimate groups in the population can make themselves heard at some crucial stage in the process of decision". Miliband points out that in Western democracies, power is competitive and diffused. Directly or indirectly, everybody has some power and nobody has or can have too much of it. Citizens enjoy universal suffrage, free and regular elections, representative institutions, effective citizen rights including the right of free speech, association and opposition. Both individuals and groups take ample advantage of these rights under the protection of law, an independent judiciary and a free political culture.

The state is an impartial institution to serve the common interests of society as a whole. Those interests may be social, economic, cultural, moral or political. The nature of capitalism has changed and the new states have become welfare states. Economic power is not in the hands of capitalists but in the hands of the managerial elite. The problem of politics now is not to modify or destroy capitalism and its institutions. The central issue is the social and political conditions of bureaucratic society. The state has become an Industrial State. It is penetrating into the economic system as a major partner. The public sector is growing in strength and many economic functions and even industries have been taken over by the state. The necessity of a socialist revolution is not considered desirable.

The present state is taxing the rich and helping the poor and thereby bringing about economic equality in society. The workers are also getting their proper share in the ownership and profits in the industries. They have become partners in industries. Peter Drucker writes, "If socialism is defined the way Marx did, as ownership of the means of production by the workers, the USA has become a truly socialist country". Daniel observes, "If we judge the measure outlined in Communist Manifesto, Great Britain and Scandinavia have almost completely realised the objective of proletarian revolution". (The Nature of Communism).

The above-mentioned views regarding the nature of the state have been criticised on many grounds. James Petras calls the liberal view as "the broker's view of the state". Prof. Randhir Singh writes, "By altering some of its forms, by mitigating some of its worst manifestations through a patch-work of welfare measures, the welfare state has only smoothed over the class antagonism, prevented the class struggle from assuming sharper revolutionary forms and thus ensured a better functioning of the existing economic and social system, a strengthening of the basic institutions of capitalism. It has acted as John Saville says, as a shock absorber and thereby contributing not to any transformation but only to the continued survival of the essentially unjust and irrational capitalist social order" (Reason, Revolution and Political Theory, p. 204).

SUGGESTED READINGS

Barker, Ernest	:	Political Thought in England, London, 1951.
Bullock, A. and M. Shock (Ed.)	:	The Liberal Tradition from Fox to Keynes, Oxford Clarendon Press, 1967.
Dahl. R.A.	:	A Preface to Democratic Theory, 1956.
Daniel, Randhir	:	The Nature of Communism, New York, 1862.
Dunham, Barrows	:	Thinkers and Treasurers.

Friedman, M.	:	Capitalism and Freedom, Chicago, 1962.
Galbraith, J.K.	:	The Affluent Society, 1958.
Galbraith, J.K.	:	The Industrial State, 1967.
Green, T.H.	:	Lectures on the Principles of Political Obligation, 1882.
Hacker, A.	:	Political Theory, 1961.
Hayek, F.A.	:	The Road to Serfdom, London, 1944.
Hobson, A.	:	Functions of the Modern State.
Keynes, J.M.	:	The General Theory of Employment, Interest and Money, 1936.
Laski, Harold J.	:	The State in Theory and Practice, 1935.
Laski, Harold J.	:	The Rise of European Liberalism, 1936.
Laski. Harold J.	:	A Grammar of Politics, 1925.
MacIver	:	The Modern State, 1926.
MacIver	:	The Web of Government, New York, The Free Press, 1947.
Macpherson, C.B.	:	Democratic Theory: Essays in Retrieval, Oxford University Press, London, 1973.
Maxey, C.C.	:	Political Philosophies, New York, 1950.
Miliband, R.	:	The State in Capitalist Society, London, 1973.
Mills, C. Wright	:	The Power Elite, 1956.
Nock, A.J.	:	Our Enemy The State, 1950.
Nozick, R.	:	Anarchy, State and Utopia, Oxford, 1974.
Oakeshott, M.	:	Rationalism in Politics and Other Essays, London, 1962.
Senior, N. William	:	Political Economy.
Singh, Randhir	:	Reason, Revolution and Political Theory, People's Publishing House, New Delhi, 1967.

34

CHAPTER

The Marxian Theory of the Nature and Functions of the State

Learning Objectives

- The Primitive-Communal System
- The Slave System
- The Feudal System
- The Capitalist System
- Repression
- Ideological-Cultural Function
- Economic Functions
- International Function
- The Capitalist State Today
- The Socialist System
- Functions of the State in a Socialist Society
- Criticism of the Socialist System
- Functions of state in a Developing Society
- Suggested Readings

According to the Marxian theory, the state is neither an expression of superior reason as contended by the idealists, nor a manifestation of superior will as maintained by the liberals but an instrument of class power designed to subserve the interests of the ruling class at the expense of its antagonistic class. The state has not existed from eternity. It owes its origin to the division of society into two classes— the haves and have-nots. It was created by the haves who were the owners of private property to oppress and exploit the have-nots who did not possess private property. In the words of Engels, the state is an organisation "for the purpose of forcibly keeping the exploited classes in the condition of oppression, corresponding with the given mode of production (slavery, serfdom, wage labour)".

The state is not a natural institution, but a man-made institution. It is an expression of human alienation. It is an instrument which has turned against its creators. Robert Tucker has mentioned that "Marx's early image of the state as alienated social power, a creature of society that comes to dominate its creator, persists in mature Marxism". The state is the product of class struggle. It is an instrument of class rule. The basis of state is force. To quote Marx, "The state is a parasite feeding upon and clogging free movement of society". The state forms a part of the super-structure that arises above the productive forces. The form of the government changes with a change in the mode of production. To quote Marx, "The specific economic form determines the relations of rulers and ruled". Again, "Legal relations such as forms of state are to be grasped neither from themselves nor from the general development of the human mind, but rather have their roots in the material conditions of life". The law of the bourgeois state is "subtle and poisoned instrument which defends the interests of the exploiters". The laws have been formulated by class enemies in the interests of the wealthy and propertied classes. The working classes who possess nothing, can only be bound by the law as long as they are not strong enough to change them. The political institutions of the state are a machine to crush and repress the toilers. Bukharin calls the state as "a league of robbers" and "a union of master class".

Marx made it clear in his early writings that the state is an organ of the economically dominant class and through the power of the state, this class, though in a minority, was able to have political dominance over the working class who were in a majority. Marx wrote, "The executive of the modern state is but a committee for managing the common affairs of the whole bourgeoisie". The state is an organised power of one class for oppressing another.

Marx never maintained that the state is a higher morality and can end all the conflicts in society and bring about unity and harmony. He criticised the Hegelian view that "the state is the march of God on earth". His contention was that the state is merely a servant of the property-owners. Political emancipation is not human emancipation. To quote him, "The limit of political emancipation is immediately apparent in the fact that the state may well free itself from some constraint, without man himself being really freed from it, and that the state may be a free state, without man being free".

According to Marx, the state is neither above society, nor it can organise the whole society and harmonise various interests. To quote him, "It is, therefore, not the state that holds the atoms of civil society together. Only political superstition today imagines that social life must be held together by the state, whereas in reality, the state is held together by civil life". Again, "Political conditions are only the official expression of civil society." The state is the product of social development. The modern democratic state is based on unhampered development of bourgeois society on the free movement of private interest". The state is not equal to society nor above it. It is merely its product at a certain stage of historical development.

The general Marxian view of the state is that it serves the interests of the dominant economic class, but in some circumstances, the state arises above classes and establishes itself as an absolute power above all classes. This happens when the classes in a society are in a balanced state. This position of the state is called Bonapartism by Marx. However, even in such a situation, the state remains a class instrument as it saves the socio-economic and political system of society as a whole. Sometimes, the state may take some steps against the ruling class, but in the final analysis, the state serves the interests of the dominant economic classes. For example, the state may curb hoarding, smuggling, profiteering and adulteration and take strong action against the traders involved in those activities, but ultimately all that is done by the state to save the capitalist system as a whole. This does not change the nature of the state. Sometimes, the state may accept some of the economic demands of the workers on account of their pressure and provide many welfare services for the them but that does not change the nature of the state. As long as there is private property and as long as there are classes in society, the state will remain a class instrument. The nature of the state can be ascertained only on the basis of the mode of production of the whole society.

The state maintains its exploitative class character right from its origin, through various phases of its development (Slave system, Feudal system, Capitalist system and Socialist system). A fundamental change occurs only at the time of transition from capitalism to socialism. The Marxian theory broadly divides the history of the state into five stages, viz., the Primitive-Communal system, the Slave system, the Feudal system, the Capitalist system and the Socialist system.

The Primitive-Communal System

This system denotes the earliest stage of social life. It is a pre-state stage. There is a social state and not a political state.

The Primitive-Communal system is also described as Primitive Communism. Under this system, the instruments of labour were of the most primitive kind. Those tools were held in common ownership by the members of the primitive community which engaged itself in common labour such as hunting, fishing etc. The fruits of the common labour were also shared in common. Society was not divided into haves and have-nots. There was no concept of private property and hence no exploitation of man by man. There was no need for special apparatus of coercion. The concept of a state was absent at that stage.

However, in course of time, there was the development of the productive forces. Metal instruments replaced stone and wooden instruments. New ways of production were discovered in the field of agriculture, animal husbandry and handicrafts. There was a division of labour and exchange of products. The tribe and the clan broke into families. Each family became an independent economic unit. Private property came into existence. There appeared the possibility of exploitation and that divided the society into masters and slaves.

The Slave System

Under this system, there came into existence private property not only in the form of means of production but also in the form of slaves who were treated as the property of their master. The entire earnings of the slaves became the property of their masters. They were merely given enough food to keep their body and soul together. Under this system, there was the domination of slaves by their masters. In order to crush any opposition from the slaves, the machinery of the state was created by the dominant class (masters). The chief function of the state was the protection of the private property of the slave-owners. The state was also to see that the slave owners got a constant supply of slaves from prisoners of war and bankrupt debtors who were turned into slaves. A system of law and juridical standards was evolved to suit the interests of the ruling class. The slave system existed in ancient Greek society. However, in due course of time, large-scale agriculture became the chief mode of production and the slave system was replaced by the feudal system.

The Feudal System

Under the Feudal system, the means of production consisted primarily in the form of land which was owned by feudal lords and labour was done by peasants. The serfs were bound to the soil and were bound to serve their lords. They were not treated as the private property of their feudal lords. The serfs had their personal belongings which were at their disposal. They tried their best to increase production. However, their obligations towards their lords were so many that they were subjected to a high degree of exploitation. During this stage, the feudal lords occupied the position of the dominant class and the serfs became dependants. The class struggle became more and more acute. There were peasant risings. There was mechanisation of production. The Feudal system was replaced by the Capitalist system.

The Capitalist System

The working of the capitalist system is the main focus of Marxist theory. As a matter of fact, Marxism arose as a protest against the defects of the capitalist system. The capitalist system denotes the stage of advanced industrial production under which the means of production are in the hands of a few capitalists and the majority of the workers are merely wage earners. Under this system, the workers are free to move from one industry to another. Likewise, the employers are free to employ and dismiss any worker.

According to Ralph Miliband, there are *four distinct functions of the state* in a capitalist society. Those are the repressive function, the ideological-cultural function, the economic function and the international function. These functions are common to all the capitalist states.

Repression

The chief function of the state in a capitalist society is repression of the working class movement. The quote Marx, "This executive power with its monstrous bureaucratic and military organisation, with its artificial state machinery embracing wide strata with a host of officials numbering half a million besides an army of another half million, this appalling parasitic growth, which enmeshes this body of French society like a net and chokes all its pores, sprang up in the days of absolute monarchy, with the decay of feudal system, which it helped to hasten". The first French Revolution developed centralisation of the bureaucratic power further. Napoleon also perfected that state machinery through a legal code. The parliamentary republic further strengthened the repressive state machinery of the French Government. All bourgeois revolutions in France perfected the coercive state apparatus.

According to Engels, "The modern state, no matter what its form, its essentially a capitalist machine, the state of the capitalists, the ideal personification of the total national capital. The more it proceeds to the taking over the productive forces, the more does it actually become the national capitalist, the more citizens does it exploit. The workers remain wage-workers—proletarians. The capitalist relation is not done away with" (Socialism—Utopian and Scientific, p. 123).

In his "State and Revolution", Lenin elaborated the repressive function of the capitalist state in its highest phase of imperialism. The quote Lenin, "Imperialism—the era of bank capital, the era of gigantic capitalist monopolies, of the development of monopoly capitalism into state monopoly capitalism—has clearly shown an extraordinary strengthening of the state machine and an unprecedented growth in its bureaucratic and military apparatus in connection with the intensification of repressive measures against the proletariat, both in the monarchical and freest republican countries". Again, "It is precisely the petty bourgeoisie that is attracted to the side of the big bourgeoisie and is subordinated to it to a large extent by means of this apparatus, which provides the upper strata of the peasantry, small artisans, tradesmen and the like with comfortable, quiet and respectable jobs which raise their holders above the people".

Through repression and gradual reform, the function of the state in capitalist society is to unite the small, medium and large property owners so that the entire bourgeois class benefits from the new techniques of production. Lenin writes, "The more the bureaucratic apparatus 'is redistributed' among the various bourgeois and petty-bourgeois parties the more clearly the oppressed classes, with the proletariat at its head, become conscious of their irreconcilable hostility to the whole of bourgeois society. That is why it is necessary for all bourgeois parties, even for the most democratic and revolutionary democratic parties, to increase their repressive measures against the revolutionary proletariat, to strengthen the apparatus of repression i.e. the state machine that we are discussing. This course of events compels the revolution 'to concentrate all its forces of destruction' against the state power, and to regard the problem,not as one of perfecting the state machine, but one of smashing and destroying it".

In spite of the long traditions of constitutionalism and provisions of civil liberties, the capitalist system benefits the well-to-do sections of society against the poor, the insecure and the migrant labour. Although trade unions, cooperatives, welfare associations, parties etc. are allowed to operate in a bourgeois democratic state, attempts are consistently made by business magnate's and industrial tycoons to curtail the rights and prerogatives of those organisations by adopting fair or foul means.

Ideological-Cultural Function

The welfare functions of the capitalist state are intended to project an image of rationality of the capitalist system. Their real purpose is to provide a widespread support to the capitalist system and save it from disintegration. This function is intended not only to generate consensus but also to discourage dissidence. To quote Miliband, "Such matters as law and order, health, education, housing, the environment and welfare in general, are, as all else, not only responsive to but determined, or at least powerfully affected, by the rationality of the system". (Marxism and Politics, p. 92).

John M. Maguire points out that the constitutional and representative character of the modern state creates only an illusion of common good on account of the dominance of the bourgeois ideology. The quote him, "This is a situation where everyone—that is, ...bourgeois and proletarians—accepts the legitimacy of the bourgeois relations of production and the roles which these impose. In this situation the state can be seen by everyone as a pure instrumentality which serves the 'common good', by settling questions which have to be settled at a general social level, and by preserving the condition for the market mechanism to reconcile individual and social benefit. In operating this way the state is in fact maintaining and servicing the bourgeois social order, and thus really servicing the bourgeoisie; but since everyone regards that order natural and proper, and thus accepts their place within it, everyone can see the state, in working this way, as 'representing' them, that is, as acting on their behalf" (Marx's Theory of Politics, pp. 19-20).

Economic Functions

Marxism recognises the increasing importance of state intervention in the system of capitalist production. Marx pointed out that centralisation and monopoly were a part of the laws of capitalist production. Lenin highlighted the economic functions of the state under imperialism which was the highest stage of capitalism. Miliband writes, "State intervention in economic life has always been a central, decisive feature in the history of capitalism so touch so that its history cannot begin to be understood without reference to the state action, in all capitalist countries and not only those, such as Japan, where the state was most visibly involved in the development of capitalism". (Marxism and Politics, p. 93).

International Function

The international function of capitalist state consists in the advancement of national interests in relation to external affairs. The capitalist state seeks to serve the interests of the ruling class not only within its own territory but also in relation to the ruling classes of other countries.

About the international function of a capitalist state, Hal Draper observes, "The state developed from the beginning on a national or imperial basis; it exists within territorial boundaries. As a national state, it manages the common affairs of the ruling class of that particular state as against the rival ruling classes of other national states. Entrenched behind the national boundaries, the separate states vie for trade, raw materials, investment, commercial advantage, and so on. Behind each boundary, one of the tasks of the state is to safeguard and advance the interests of its own ruling class against all rivals" (Karl Marx's Theory of Revolution, p. 258)

The Marxist view of the function of the state in a capitalist society has been restated by Gramsci and other European Communists. According to Gramsci, the ruling class in a capitalist society does not govern by repression alone. It also establishes its ideological hegemony over the proletariat through its control of the sources of knowledge, the mass media and educational institutions: The emancipation of the working class requires the establishment of proletarian hegemony in the ideological sphere. The political party of the working class should first make an attempt to break up the monopolistic control of the bourgeoisie in the sphere of art, literature, science and other forms of culture.

The Capitalist State Today

The capitalist state today is radically different from what was described by Marx, Engels and Lenin. The industrial scene has changed qualitatively. It no longer presents society divided into two distinct classes viz., the exploiters and the exploited. The individual ownership of industry has given way to corporate ownership. The day to day management of industry is in the hands of professionally qualified mangers. The motto of capitalist state is specialisation in Government and business. The economic condition of the workers has improved and they enjoy most of the luxuries of life, which are the exclusive privilege of the political and economic elites in the developing countries. The rising standards of living in the capitalist states have resulted in the migration of skilled manpower, technicians, scientists, intellectuals etc. with the result that there is brain-drain in the developing countries and increasing racial tensions in the developed countries.

The economic functions of a capitalist state have increased tremendously. Laws have been passed to check the growth of business monopolies, unhealthy trade practices and exploitation of consumers. Technological advances have resulted in efficiency in all directions, but they have also created the problem of pollution. In contemporary capitalist society, the media in the form of the press, radio and TV, has become very influential. It has its influence not on the election of important dignitaries, but it can also unmake them. It is well known that the Watergate incident which ultimately resulted in the disappearance of President Nixon from the political scene, was the work of the newspaper men. The media helps the big business. It is also influenced by it.

In the international field, the focus in a capitalist society has shifted from cold war to peaceful co-existence with the socialist states. A reference in this connection may be made to the political *rapprochement* between the United States and Communist China and the cooperation between the Soviet Union and the United States in the field of space exploration and scientific research.

The challenge to the capitalist state comes not only from the working class but from other sources also. The alienation of non-affluent racially discriminated sections of society within and poor nations always dependent on their mercies abroad resulting in perpetual tension. The chaos of competition in general and the mad race for the accumulation of economic and political power by the elite groups is another source of tension. There have been too many changes in the capitalist society in a very short time. Those changes have been given the name of "Future Shock." The people in capitalist societies suffer from what Toffler calls "the disease of change" and they do not know how to adjust themselves to the new change in a very brief period.

The capitalist state today enjoys a good deal of sympathy and support not only from the ideologically identical states but also from the socialist states. There is a consensus that the origin of the modern capitalist state lies in the nature of man who is an economic, social and political animal. The state and its machinery is considered to be a positive blessing. It exists for the common good of the whole community. The state is considered to be the protector of human liberties and fundamental rights. The state acts as an agency for resolving conflicts and promoting cooperation both within and outside its territory. State intervention in economic, moral, cultural and religious matters has increased tremendously. This is not considered to be an evil but a positive necessity. There is a strong commitment to the doctrine of political democracy. The sovereign character of the state is not questioned but it is also realised that a number of voluntary associations can ask for loyalty and obedience from citizens. The Government of the capitalist state is treated like a fire. "Under control, it is a useful servant, but out of control it is a ravaging tyrant".

The Socialist System

The socialist system comes into existence after the overthrow of the capitalist system through a proletarian revolution. The class struggle leads to the dictatorship of the proletariat and that itself constitutes only the transition to the abolition of all classes and a classless society. Between capitalist and communist society lies the period of the revolutionary transformation of the one into the other. There corresponds to this a political transition period in which the state can be nothing but the revolutionary dictatorship of the proletariat.

According to Martox, the Russian Menshevik leader, Marx and Engels originally conceived the idea of proletarian dictatorship in the late 1840s with its minority political dictatorship and the terror. Later on, when Marx and Engels were convinced that conscious support of the majority of the population was required for a socialist revolution, their conception of the proletarian dictatorship lost Jacobin content. Lenin made the dictatorship of the proletariat a crucial part of his doctrine. There was also a controversy between Lenin and Kautsky regarding the nature of the proletarian dictatorship. Kautsky put emphasis on true democratic character of the proletarian dictatorship as against rule by a single person.

According to Marx, the dictatorship of the proletariat is a transitional stage between the bourgeois state and the classless and stateless Communist society. As the state cannot exist without classes and class distinctions are abolished only after the proletarian revolution, the state assumes a temporary revolutionary form which is called the dictatorship of the proletariat. The dictatorship of the proletariat is considered necessary for crushing the resistance of the exploiters and for guiding the great mass of the population in the work of economic socialist reconstruction. One work is destructive and the other work is constructive. One work is political and the other work is economic. Stalin put emphasis on three aspects of the proletarian dictatorship viz., to crush the exploiters, defend the country and strengthen ties with proletarians in other countries, to enlist the masses for socialist reconstruction and to organise socialism, abolish classes and found a society without classes and without a state.

The two fundamental functions of the proletarian dictatorship are the suppression of the bourgeoisie and the establishment of socialism. The first function is comparatively easier but the second function involves great effort. After the abolition of the bourgeois state, the socialist state comes to have control over all means of production. In due course, the economic management of society and the proper utilisation of its, economic resources become an important function of the proletarian state. For that purpose,the proletarian state depends upon scientifically educated staff. The principle of distribution will be *to each according to his work.*

After the class are abolished, the state will have no suppressive function to perform. It will have only economic function. The state will gradually wither away as the people become accustomed to observing the rules of socialist life. The view of Lenin was that it will not take long for the state to wither away but even after decades, the state has not withered away in the Soviet Union. As a matter of fact, it is much more powerful today than it ever was at any time in history. However, the theory of the state withering away has not been officially given up. Stalin explained the position in these words in 1930: "We stand for the withering away of the state. At the same time we stand for the strengthening of the dictatorship of the proletariat which is the mightiest and strongest state power that has ever existed. Is this contradictory? Yes...But this contradiction is bound up with life and it fully reflects Marx's dialectics". In 1959, Khrushchev made the following statement, "We must advance step by step, creating the material and spiritual requisites for planned transition to Communism. It would be wrong, erroneous, to assume that Communism will somehow appear suddenly. The transition from socialism to communism is a continuous process. If we approach it dialectically, the question of withering away of the state is a question of evolution of the socialist state toward communist public self-government". The position indicated by Khruschev in 1959 is ideologically the same even today.

Functions of the State in a Socialist Society

Marx outlines the main features of a socialist state in these words: "The standing army should be replaced by a people at arms. Responsible councillors, mostly workers or recognised representatives of the working class, should form an assembly that would be essentially a labour body rather than having purely legislative or decorative functions; election would be by universal suffrage and could be revoked at any time. The police should be converted from being a component of the central government into a responsible agency of the assembly, deprived of any political assignments and liable to suspension at any time. Every branch of administration should be converted in a similar way. Public office should be made really democratic, ceasing to be the private preserve of the central government and its creatures and being discharged at all level by workers for a wage."

The function of socialist society is to consolidate the public power of the proletariat by smashing the bourgeoisie. Once that is done, the state loses its character as an instrument of class domination but it continues as an administrative agency for directing the process of production.

The establishment of an exploitation-free socialist economy based on social ownership of production is an important function of a socialist state. The socialist state has to abolish private property and establish social ownership of the means of production. This is done by the socialisation of industries. The socialist mode of production must have for its object the social welfare and the satisfaction of the material needs of society. Production has to be increased to enrich the material life of the whole population. The state has to establish cooperative and state farming. New scientific and technological means have to be applied for industrial and agricultural development. There is not to be haphazard economic development but planned economy. Production must be organised to meet the social requirements. There is to be proper distribution of consumer goods. The state has to regulate the working hours of the workers and also provide for rest, holidays and pension for them.

The socialist state has also to perform many socio-cultural functions. In a new socialist society, socialist culture and ethics are promoted and the capitalist moral, social and cultural structure are destroyed. A capitalist society is based on the personal interests of the individuals. There are selfish social, cultural and more norms. Those are replaced by new socialist social, cultural and moral norms. This is a difficult and long term function of the socialist state and cannot be done overnight. The change in the mode of production will not automatically lead to a change in the socio-cultural and moral super-structure. A socialist state has to adopt certain measures to bring about a change. Education should be scientific and should not be at the mercy of the economic capabilities of the parents. It should not be guided by job considerations. A socialist state has to establish not only economic equality but also social and cultural equality. In a socialist state, no consideration will be given to caste, religion, colour, region or language. Each group will be given equal opportunities. A socialist state has to establish a socialist morality in which selfish ideas and outlook will be replaced by a selfless and socialist outlook. Welfare of all will be the main consideration. In a socialist state, all the positive functions are performed in a simple way and the increase of specialised bureaucracy is generally discouraged. All the functions, whether economic, social, cultural or moral, are performed with due participation of the masses at all levels.

The socialist states believe in proletarian internationalism and they help the progressive movements of the masses and the working class throughout the world. The socialist states give asylum to the revolutionaries of the world. They work for the maintenance of peace, progress and justice.

Classical Marxism knew no national boundaries. Marx himself called upon the workers of the world to unite. Lenin sought to consolidate "socialism in one country" before it could be expanded in other countries. After the World War II, the idea of world communism was given up. The communist states like the Soviet Union, Communist China, Cuba and Yugoslavia exist as independent nations. The socialist states also follow a policy of "peaceful co-existence" which means that both capitalism and communism can exist side by side without fighting against each other all the time.

The Soviet state is materialistic. It recognises the primacy of the economic factor. All productive forces are either controlled or owned by the state. There is no exploiting class of the bourgeois capitalists.

The Communist Party of the Soviet Union is the proletarian party which represents the workers and peasants. It is the guardian of the socialist revolution. It is the vanguard of the proletariat. The Communist Party controls the state. It is the only party in the state. It is contended that there is no necessity of another party because "if it agrees with the official party, it is superfluous; if it does not, it is counter-revolutionary".

All the media in the Soviet Union are owned and controlled by the state. There is no freedom of expression except to support the accepted party line. Deviation in any form is considered to be an act of treason. It covers all philosophy, literature, art an science. Writers like Boris Pasternak, the author of Dr. Zhivago and Alexander Solzhenitsyn, the author of the First Circle and Gulag Archipelago, had to suffer terribly for their intellectual honesty.

In accordance with the views of Engels on the role of family and its description as an immature form of association, the Soviet state acts upon the principle that the children in the Soviet Union belong to society and it is the business of the state to look after them.

Strictly speaking, religion has no place or future in a communist state as it threatens to create a dual loyalty in a world in which all things have become the property of Caesar.

Criticism of the Socialist System

It cannot be denied that planned economy and the socialist mode of production in the Soviet Union and Communist China have led to rapid industrial and agricultural development. However, disparity of incomes still exists in the socialist countries and a scheme of incentives has been introduced in communist countries. There is no doubt that the performance of the communist states on the economic front has been commendable.

Marxism believes in the dictatorship of the proletariat. However, the working class has been refused due participation in the affairs of the state. A new revolutionary elite has emerged. The gap between the people and the Communist Party is increasing day by day. The Communist Party has the monopoly of all powers. Lenin and Stalin emphasized the unity, discipline and centralisation of the party. The leadership of the party has become a class in itself, different from the working class. There is no self-control and active participation of the working class at all the levels of the socio-economic system in the Soviet Union. There is relatively more participation of the workers. It is assumed that with the development in the level of consciousness of the workers, the working class will have more and more of the participation in the affairs of the state.

Lenin repeatedly warned against the increase of bureaucracy in communist states. In spite of that, bureaucracy and technocracy have virtually erased the achievements of the socialist revolution. Specialists are in control over the administration and industries. With the increase in bureaucracy, a new class with vested interests of its own has developed in socialist countries. It is hindering the self-management of industries by the workers. Instead of socialisation, what is emerging is bureacratisation.

The view of Umberto Melotti is that the proletariat is really an oppressed class in the Soviet Union, exploited and dominated by the bureaucracy. Pizzi writes, "We naively tell ourselves that property is 'nationalised'. For scientific Marxists that is not very much. We wonder what kind of 'nationalized' property this is, when it is exclusively controlled by a single class which then appropriates its fruits in just as blatant a fashion as did the former bourgeoisie. In practice there is in Russia an exploiting class that holds sway over the means of production and acts just if it owned them. Although it is not divided up into individual owners, its members as a class, *en masse*, are the real owners of all the 'nationalised' property".

The main features of bureaucratic collectivism in the Soviet Union are that property is owned by a class as a whole and not its individual owners. The economy is run in accordance with a central plan and is insulated from the market competition. The commanding position is occupied by the machinery for the extended reproduction of use-values. The exploitation of man by man is a direct process, operating by the appropriation and distribution of part of the total surplus product through the plan. Political and economic power is completely centralised.

Marx gave importance to the concept of alienation in a capitalist system, but the problem of alienation remains even in the socialist society. Private property has not been transformed into social property but into state property. The gap between the individual and society is still wide.

Critics point out that there has been no withering away of the state in the socialist countries. Prof. Stojanovic writes, "Although Marxism had developed as one of the most radical anti-statist conceptions, with suitable modifications it was transformed into a statist ideology" (Between Ideals and Reality, p. 8). The same author has strongly criticised those who are in favour of maintaining the state in a communist society. According to him, on account of the degeneration of the state in the Soviet Union, the state there can never wither away. The Russian socialist state is an alienated class power which will never wither away. Medvedev has also attacked the Soviet Union on this ground.

Critics also point out that there is nowhere a society where the haves and have-nots are sharply divided as held by the Marxists. From the economic point of view, between the upper and lower classes, there is a very large middle class. There is a constant vertical social mobility through various strata. The Marxist theory of the elimination of the middle class is not being realised anywhere. As a matter of fact, the size of the middle class is increasing with the advance of capitalism.

Critics also point out that the character of capitalism itself has undergone a fundamental change. The Marxian analysis of the functions of the state in capitalist society is no longer valid. There is an increasing replacement of individual ownership by corporate ownership dispersed over thousands of shareholders. There is the shift of power from the owners of industry to the professional managerial classes and technocrats. Most of the capitalist states have become welfare states and they are doing a lot to improve the lot of the working classes. The result is that economic disparities have lessened. Prof. Galbraith writes, "Few things are more evident in modern social history than the decline of interest in inequality as an economic issue. This has been particularly true in the United States. And it would appear, among western countries, to be least true of the United Kingdom. While it continues to have a large ritualistic role in the conventional wisdom of conservatives and liberals, inequality has ceased to preoccupy men's minds. And even the conventional wisdom has made some concessions to this new state of affairs" (Affluent Society, p. 79).

Critics also point out that even after the socialisation of the means of production, disparities in power continue to govern the behaviour of men in society. There are many subtle ways of subjugation and rule. When economic exploitation is not possible, oppression and exploitation can take other forms. The view of Ralph Miliband is that the state in the Soviet Union still remains an instrument of the power elite who "may be unable to derive vast material advantages from their position in the state system, yet who are able to use that, position to appropriate and enjoy far from negligible such advantages; and who are also able to enjoy power. On this view the notion of the state having as its function the advancement of the power and privileges of those who control it, and the repression of those who challenge it, remains fairly well intact" (Marxism and Politics, pp. 112-13).

The view of the Marxists is that religion, politics and morals prevailing in any society at any point of time, are essentially shaped by the prevailing mode of production. The mode of production is treated as the base or sub-structure and religion, politics etc. are treated as the super-structure. The critics of Marxism contend that this is not borne out by experience. The experience of the countries of Europe, Asia and Africa shows that wherever a similar mode of production prevailed, different ideas about religion, morals and politics were evolved. The objectives of socialism cannot be secured by changing the mode of production alone. Necessary changes have to be made in the super-structure also.

The view of Marx was that ideology is an attribute of the bourgeois state only, but the view of Lenin was that even a socialist state needed a socialist ideology to consolidate its position and to save the people from the dominance of counter ideology. Mao Tse-tung advocated the need for a permanent revolution for transforming the attitudes, beliefs and culture of the socialist society after accomplishing the economic revolution.

In spite of the criticism mentioned above, the merit of the Marxian view cannot be denied as Marxism has established its hold over about one-third of the world. It is not a small achievement. Prof. R.M. MacIver writes, "The transformation of a predominantly feudalist system into a collectivist one ruled by totally different principles was an extraordinary feat, whatever opinions we may hold regarding either the objective or the methods employed including the ruthless liquidation of the more prosperous farmers or kulaks in the process of establishing collective farms...Never has an industrial development been accomplished so rapidly on so grand a scale. The technological lag of Russia behind the major industrial countries was virtually eliminated within a generation. The illiteracy of the Russian peasant was overcome under a system of universal education which, though rigidly doctrinaire, at least provided for backward multitudes the first facilities of knowledge." (The Web of Government, p. 198).

Functions of state in a Developing Society

The term "developing society" is applied to those nations who got their independence after the World War II from their colonial rulers. They are also known as the Third World. They include a large number of countries of Asia, Africa and Latin America. These countries were exploited and impoverished by their colonial rulers and hence they remained under-developed in the economic, educational and political spheres. After their independence, they started the work of economic and political development and hence they are described as developing nations or developing societies.

In these developing countries, there are large disparities in wealth, influence and power between the people at large and an elite minority which controls the Government and economic structure of the society. Religion continues to be a dominant force in those countries. As the people won their freedom after a bitter struggle, they are very particular about their freedom. In view of the strong regional, tribal, communal and linguistic ties, the developing states are faced with perpetual problem of secession and civil strife. The state is controlled by the dominant ruling party where there is democratic set up in the country. Where there is no democratic tradition, the state is controlled by the dominant civil or military group in society. The state is neither capitalist nor socialist. There is a mixed economy.

In these countries the state is the symbol and instrument of economic and social progress. It is the best guarantee against internal strife and secession. It is the protector of national sovereignty and geographical boundaries.

In view of the fact that the state in developing societies has assumed immense political and economic power required for carrying out the tasks of development, there is hardly any area of activity which is not controlled by the state. However, the degree of control may vary from one developing society to another.

SUGGESTED READINGS

Chang, S.H.M. : The Marxian Theory of the State, New York, 1975.
Draper, Hal : Karl Marx's Theory of Revolution.
Engels : Socialism, Utopian and Scientific, Moscow, 1968.
Galbraith, J.K. : Affluent Society.
Hunt, Carew : The Theory and Practice of Communism.
Lenin, V.I. : The State and Revolution.
Lenin : Economics and Politics in the Era of Dictatorship.
MacIver, R.M. : The Web of Government.
Maguire, John M. : Marx's Theory of Politics.
Marx and Engels : The Holy Family.
Marx, Karl : Manifesto of the Communist Party.
Marx, Karl : The Poverty of Philosophy, London, 1936.
Marx, Karl : The Civil War in France.
Marx, Karl : The Class Struggle in France.
Merkl : Political Continuity and Change.
Miliband, Ralph : Marxism and Politics.
Serge, M. : Bureaucracy and Technocracy in the Socialist Countries, 1974.
Stalin, J.V. : The Foundations of Leninism, Peking, 1979.
Stojanovic, S. : Between Ideals and Reality, New York, 1973.
Toffler, Alvin : Future Shock, London, 1970.
Tucker, Robert : The Marxian Revolutionary Idea.
Williams, Roger : Politics and Technology.

CHAPTER

The Welfare State

Every state today would like to call itself a welfare state. Previously, our conception of a state was that of a police state whose primary function was to provide law and order. It was left to the individuals to do what they considered to be for their welfare. Prof. Laski did a lot to bring about a change in the thinking of the people with regard to the functions of the state. He emphasized the fact that it was the duty of the state to do all those things which were considered necessary for the welfare of the people.

Learning Objectives

- Definition of Welfare State
- Origin and Development of the Welfare State Ideal
- Features of the Welfare State
- Essentials of a Welfare State
- Hindrances in the Way of a Welfare State
- Welfare State and Social Justice
- Welfare State and Sarvodaya
- Suggested Readings

Definition of Welfare State

Many definitions of a welfare state have been attempted. Abraham defines a welfare state as "a community where state power is deliberately used to modify the normal play of economic forces so as to obtain a more equal distribution of income for every citizen, a basic minimum irrespective of the market value of his work and his property." T.W. Kent says that a welfare state is "a state that provides for its citizens a wide range of social services." Hobman describes the welfare state as a compromise between Communism on the one side and unbridled individualism on the other. The welfare state sets a pattern for any humane and progressive society. It guarantees a minimum standard of subsistence without removing incentives to provide enterprise and brings about a limited re-distribution of income by means of graduated high taxation. However, it does not pretend to establish economic equality among its citizens. All are assured of adequate help in case of need whether that is due to illness, old age, unemployment or any other cause.

According to G.D.H. Cole, "The welfare state is a society in which an assured minimum standard of living and opportunity becomes the possession of every citizen." In the opinion or Arthur Schlesinger, "The welfare state is a system wherein government agrees to under-write certain level of employment, income, education, medical, social security and housing for all its citizens." Herbert H. Lehman writes, "The welfare state is simply a state in which people are free to develop their individual capacities to receive just awards for their talents, and to engage in pursuit of happiness, unburdened by fear of actual hunger, actual homelessness or by oppression by reason of race, creed or colour."

According to Venkatagiri, "Welfare state is a state which does not confine itself to the discharging of mere police functions but takes a wider view of its obligation and undertakes all activities which are considered necessary and desirable to remove social evil and promote the welfare of population." MacIver writes, "The positive and negative tasks of the state are to establish order and respect personality." In the opinion of Hobson, "The state has assumed the duties of a doctor, a nurse, school master, trader and manufacturer, insurance agent, house-builder, town planner, railway controller and a hundred other things."

Asa Briggs says, "A welfare state is a state in which organised power is deliberately used (through politics and administration) in an effort to modify the play of market forces in at least three directions—first, by guaranteeing individuals and families a minimum income irrespective of the market value of their work or their property; second, by narrowing the extent of insecurity by enabling individuals and families to meet certain 'social contingencies' (for example, sickness, old age and unemployment) which lead otherwise to individual and family crisis; and third, by ensuring that all citizens without distinction of status or class are offered the best standards available in relation to a certain agreed range of social services." (Perspectives on the Welfare State, edited by S.P. Aiyar, p. 10).

Arnold J. Toynbee, the great historian, wrote in his book *Not The Age of Atoms but of Welfare of All* (1951) that three centuries from now the twentieth will be remembered not for its wars, horrors and crimes but for the fact that it is the first era in history in which people dared to think it practicable to make benefits of civilisation available for the whole human race. Almost every state, whether it is socialist, communist or capitalist, wishes to pursue the ideal of a welfare state.

In a welfare state, the help given by the state to individuals in need of it is not in the nature of charity, but as a matter of right. Welfare does not carry with it a stigma of poverty or begging. A welfare state demands a change in the outlook of the people. They must believe and act upon the principle: "Each for all and all for each." Every individual must feel that he is a part of society and it is his duty to do all that he can for the good of others and must not be contented with his good alone. He must feel convinced that the unhappiness of others is bound to make him unhappy in the long run as he cannot separate himself from the rest of society. If a welfare state is to be a blessing, a pauper mentality should not be created among the people. Those who receive help from the state must feel proud of the state and the society in which they live and should be happy to play their part to the best of their ability. They must not give up the qualities of initiative and self-help.

Origin and Development of the Welfare State Ideal

The idea of a welfare state can be traced back to the reign of Queen Elizabeth I when the first Poor Law Act was passed by British Parliament and provision was made for the establishment of work-houses for the able-bodied beggars and relief work for those who were disabled. The guardians of the Poor were appointed to see that the provisions of law were enforced. In the time of Napoleon III of France, certain measures were adopted for the welfare of the backward people. Their wages were increased. Provision was made for their housing accommodation and state-aided sickness insurance. Bismarck, Chancellor of Germany, provided for social insurance against sickness, accident, old age and disability.

The social conscience of the people in England was aroused by the writings of Dickens, Kingsley, Disraeli and others. Disraeli has been called the grand-father of the welfare state. Further encouragement was given to this idea by the members of the Fabian Society in England and the trade union leaders. Lloyd George introduced social insurance in England. The imposition of death duties and the introduction of the system of graduated high taxation were steps in the same direction. It was in the time of Prime Minister Attlee that the National Health Service Scheme was introduced in its full form. A series of measures were passed resulting in the nationalisation of railways, coal mines and steel, nationalisation of the Bank of England and transport. When the Conservative Party came to power, the only measure reversed by it was the nationalisation of steel and the rest were allowed to remain. Even the Labour Party today is cautious in the matter of nationalisation. Its slogan is "Socialisation without Nationalisation."

A vast social insurance scheme is in operation today in Britain. All persons of working age contribute to it except the housewife. Provision is made for old age retirement benefits, widow's benefit, unemployment benefits, family allowances for those with two or more children, milk for school children, milk and special food for expectant and nursing mothers, free medical service, free secondary education and liberal scholarships for higher education.

In the United States, the term welfare state is not popular as the people there stand for individual enterprise and do not like the control of the state in many fields. According to President Hoover, the welfare state is the "back road" to collectivism which is highly unpopular in the United States. The New Deal of President Roosevelt and the Fair Deal of President Truman have been described as "creeping socialism". The view of Senator Taft is that the welfare state will lead the United States to bankruptcy. W.J. Byrnes, a former Secretary of State of the United States, gave a warning against the big Government constantly growing bigger. The Americans are afraid of bureaucracy. They rely on self-help and oppose anything that destroys that quality. In spite of that, President Truman gave a Ten Point programme which included price support, a minimum wage of 75 cents per hour, development of natural resources, medicare, aid to education and insurance against sickness, old age, accident and unemployment. The Social Security Scheme is so comprehensive that it includes even white-collar workers, university teachers and self-employed persons.

Among the Continental countries, Sweden, Norway and Denmark have extensive welfare schemes supported by high taxation.

The socialist states also are welfare states, but their welfare is planned and executed from above. More attention is given to material welfare then to moral and spiritual welfare.

The ideal of a welfare state is embodied in the Indian Constitution, particularly in the Directive Principles of State Policy. Articles 38 provides that the state shall strive to promote the welfare of the people by securing and protecting as effectively as it may a social order in which justice, social, economic and political, shall inform all the institutions of national life. Article 39 refers to adequate means of livelihood, distribution of the natural resources of the country in a manner which subserve the common good, opposition to concentration of wealth in the hands of a few, equal pay for equal work for both men and women, conservation of health and strength of workers, particularly of women and children and the non-exploitation of children. Article 41 provides for the right to work, right to education and right to public assistance in cases of unemployment, old age, sickness and disablement. Provision has also been made for just and humane conditions of work and maternity relief, a aliving wage for workers, free and compulsory education up to the age of 14, promotion of the educational and economic interests of the Scheduled Castes, Scheduled Tribes and other weaker sections of society, duty of the state to raise the level of nutrition and standard of living and to improve public health. Legislation has been enacted by the Government of India to achieve the objectives embodied in the Indian Constitution. The Government has gone to the extent of laying down that any law which stands in the way of the implementation of the Directive Principles of State Policy, can be ignored even if that involves a violation of the fundamental rights guaranteed by the Constitution of India. Ambitious Five-Year-Plans have been implemented and the standard of living has been raised. Steps have been taken to increase the production of wealth by encouraging various types of industries. Concerted efforts have been made to step up agricultural production. Panchayati Raj has been organised almost everywhere in India and democracy taken to the grass-root level. Steps have been taken to increase opportunities of employment. The real income of the people of India today is more than the real income three decades ago.

Features of the Welfare State

There are certain basic features of a welfare state. The state is not contented merely with the collection of taxes and maintenance of law and order. It must also promote the interests of society.

It should undertake the responsibility of bringing about the material welfare of the people within the framework of democratic political institutions. It should take the initiative to protect the health of the people and to promote their economic security and welfare. It should adopt measures to abolish illiteracy, poverty and unemployment. It should establish schools, hospitals and other institutions to meet the needs of the people. It should provide unemployment relief, maternity benefits, old age pensions and other social benefits. It should uphold the rights of all without discrimination against any individual or group of people. It should respect human dignity and personality and give justice to all. It should help the poor by providing adequate opportunities for their growth. It should regulate the economic and other activities of the people in the larger interests of society. It should not allow any particular class to exploit the other classes. The welfare state is against the policy of maintaining a free economy. It stands for free society with a mixed economy of social and economic planning. It strikes a middle path avoiding totalitarian control and unbridled free enterprise.

Essentials of a Welfare State

The first essential for a welfare state is that the administrator must mix with the people. He must respond to the changing moods and requirements of the people. He must show due respect for the parliamentary and financial control over the administration. Public administration in the welfare state should be properly integrated and coordinated. The services rendered by the welfare state should be timely, ample, adequate and continuous. There should be people's participation at every level in the welfare state. There should not be any red-tapism in a welfare state. There should be careful determination of the goal to be realised and the means of realisation. There should be a periodic assessment of the success and failure of the administration.

Hindrances in the Way of a Welfare State

There are many hindrances in the way of the realisation of the ideal of a welfare state. Such a high ideal cannot be achieved unless and until the people of India not only try but actually achieve the target of high production. It is obvious that before anything can be distributed, that must be produced. Unless and until we produce more, there is nothing to distribute. All schemes for the welfare of the people are bound to fail if production does not go up and that requires a fundamental change in the outlook of the people towards work. Everybody in the country must realise that work is worship and hard work alone can prove to be salvation of India. We cannot banish hunger and poverty from the country and achieve the ideal of a welfare state, if its people refuse to work hard and produce more. A welfare state cannot be built by begging or borrowing from others. There is always a limit beyond which no self-respecting nation is willing to borrow. Begging involves so many ills that no good man would stand for it. A welfare state is an expensive state and it is impossible to achieve that ideal without working very hard and producing as much as any other great nation of the world is capable of producing.

The fear of high taxes is hindrance to the realisation of the welfare state. Some amount of self-sacrifice is necessary if a welfare state is to become a reality. No one pretends that he enjoys paying taxes. People are gradually changing their old attitude towards property.

Certain institutional changes are required to make the welfare state a success. There should be the nationalisation of key or heavy industries.

India is not socially or morally advanced enough to launch upon a nation-wide scheme of collective farming, but a limited amount of experimentation can be made with cooperative or joint farming. If that succeeds, there can be further extension of it. A network of small-scale and cottage industries can be established to expand production. The same applies to the expansion of transport and communication facilities.

The enormous increase in the population of India is a great hindrance to the establishment of a welfare state. Whatever economic improvement is made as a result of the policies of the government and the efforts, made by the people, is more than cancelled by the increase in population. It has rightly been said that if we fail to solve the population problem, all efforts to establish a welfare state will come to nothing.

Another hindrance to the establishment of a welfare state is the prevalence of narrow loyalties like that of the family, caste, tribe, religion or linguistic groups. These loyalties clash with national loyalties and unless these loyalties retrace before loyalty towards the nation, progress towards a welfare state is difficult, if not impossible.

Another hindrance is the prevailing climate in the country. One finds an atmosphere of corruption and bribery everywhere. Officers in all places accept bribes to show favours. What we require is a high degree of personal integrity. A big portion of the national expenditure goes waste on account of corruption in the country instead of being used for national development. We have in this country a top heavy administration. That leaves less to be spent on national development.

A lot of money is required for a welfare state and that is not forthcoming on account of the poverty of the people.

In a welfare state, the state assumes more responsibilities and the result is that the powers of the civil servants increase. They are likely to adopt an attitude which is not always consistent with the spirit of the welfare state.

A welfare state provides so many benefits to the people that they are likely to lose initiative and sense of responsibility. They may develop the habit of laziness. Such an eventuality has to be guarded against.

We have to create among the people an enthusiasm for the welfare state. Without that, hard work from the people will not be forthcoming. It is only when the people work for an ideal that they are willing to make sacrifices and are not bothered about inconveniences. There must be a spirit of self-discipline among the people. The virtues of hard work and discipline have to be cultivated.

The attitude of the people towards the payment of taxes must change. Those who have earned as citizens of India must be happy to pay their taxes. They should consider it as their duty. There can be no welfare state without high taxation. No scheme of the government can succeed without money and that must come from the people. There is also the necessity of a change in the attitude of the government in the matter of taxation. The tax structure must be radically changed to leave enough scope for the tax payers to save out of their earnings. It must be realised that too heavy taxation encourages corruption. If the tax structure takes away practically everything from the tax-payer and leaves very little behind, there is always the temptation to be dishonest in the payment of taxes. The government must not consider every tax-payer a criminal or suspect. He should be respected as a person who is making a solid contribution to the country by paying his taxes honestly and thereby helping in the achievement of the ideal of a welfare state.

There must be a coordination between the government and business interests in the country. They must not work at cross-purposes. The policies followed by the government must be stable and definite giving an opportunity to the people to plan in advance with confidence.

The old distinction between administrators and the people must go. The administrators who are the members of the bureaucracy must not consider themselves belonging to a superior social class. They must realise that they are not government servants but public servants and they will be judged by what they do for the good of the people who pay them their salaries. The people should be given an effective voice in the determination of the programme of the government. They should have a sense of participation at every stage. Neither the ruling party nor the administrators should consider the people as dumb-driven cattle but as their masters. It must be realised that governments are not run to provide salaries, for government servants. The latter are paid so that they may serve the people and not lord over them and treat them with contempt. The administrators must respond to the requirements of the people. They must not live in the ivory towers of their own without any touch with the people and their sentiments. The people should be encouraged to speak out their minds. It is the duty of the government to keep those views in mind while running the government. The administrators and politicians must care more for the spirit of law and not for the language. There should be a periodic assessment of the achievements and failures of the government. All schemes of the government must aim at the maximum benefit out of the minimum expenditure. There should be no temptation to help friends and favourites at the cost of the state. There should be coordination of efforts in various offices of the government. The officers-in-charge of those Departments must meet periodically to sort out their differences and evolve a policy which can give dividends. Efforts should be made to avoid regimentation of every kind because that is not conducive to progress. There should be decentralisation and voluntary organisation.

Every administrator must keep in mind the fact that a stitch in time saves nine and hence it is necessary that the service rendered must be timely. If the people are in trouble, help must come at once and no red-tapism should be allowed to stand in the way.

Welfare State and Social Justice

The term social justice includes both economic justice and social justice. The principle of social justice makes democracy significant, purposeful, meaningful and dynamic. Without social justice, democracy is poor in its content. Former Chief Justice P.B Gajehdragadkar wrote thus, "As soon as the ideal of a welfare state is accepted by democracy, it leads to one important consequence and that is that the claims of social justice must be treated as paramount and if the freedom of the individual and his individual rights need to be regulated in order to achieve social justice, that regulation is a part of the price which democratic citizens must cheerfully pay in order to sustain the democratic way of life" (Law, Liberty and Social Justice (1965). p. 80).

Welfare State and Sarvodaya

Critics maintain that the welfare state, as understood and practised at present, is essentially foreign to our culture. It is like a ripe fruit tied to a tree which has not produced it. The remedy is to prepare the minds and hearts of the masses and classes for it. The welfare state requires a lot of money, an army of public servants of various categories, a good amount of centralised government control, red-tapism and routine.

Sarvodaya stands for decentralisation in production and administration, simplification of life standards, reduction in the number of public servants and a self-regulating community operating through non-violence. However, Sarvodaya is still a dream which has not been accomplished even partially. As the needs of the people are stupendous, we cannot afford to throw away the tangible gains of the welfare state for the probable gains of Sarvodaya.

SUGGESTED READINGS

Aiyar, S.P. (Ed.) : Perspectives on the Welfare State, 1966.

Angell, Norman : From Chaos to Control.

Burns, C.D. : Political Ideals.

Ebenstein, W. : Modern Political Thought, 1960.

Ford, J. : Social Problems and Social Policy.

Gajendragadkar, P.B.	:	Law, Liberty and Social Justice, 1965.
Gandhi, M.K.	:	Towards Non-Violent Socialism.
Gandhi, M.K.	:	Sarvodaya.
Hobman, D.L.	:	The Welfare State.
Hobhouse, L.T.	:	Elements of Social Justice.
Hocking, W.E.	:	The Philosophy of Law and of Rights.
Hocking, W.E.	:	Lectures at Harvard.
Krabbe	:	Modern Idea of the State.
Laski, Harold J.	:	Plan or Perish.
MacIver, R.M.	:	The Modern State.
Marx, Herbert L.	:	The Welfare State, 1950.
Woolton, Barbara	:	Plan or No Plan.

CHAPTER

Utilitarianism

Learning Objectives

- Jeremy Bentham (1748-1832)
- James Mill (1773-1836)
- John Austin (1790-1859)
- John Stuart Mill (1806-1873)
- Criticism of Utilitarianism
- Estimate of Utilitarianism
- Suggested Readings

Utilitarianism was essentially an English doctrine which played an important part in the earlier half of the nineteenth century in effecting reforms of great importance. It was adopted by philosophical radicals who put forward a comprehensive programme of legal, economic and political reforms and connected it with the principle of the greatest happiness of the greatest number.

The utilitarian philosophy was based upon the English tradition in psychology as worked out by Locke and Hume. Its beginnings appeared in the seventeenth century in the writings of Richard Cumberland (1632-1719) who regarded general welfare as the highest good. The formula of "the greatest happiness of the greatest number" was first used by Francis Hutcheson (1694-1747).

The first proposition of utilitarianism is that "there is a science of the mind." The mind is at first composed of scattered sensations drawn from the environment in which it finds itself. The sensations are soon grouped by the law of attraction. Those grouped sensations can be characterised as agreeable or painful. Those which are agreeable become the objects of our desires and those which are painful are the objects of our aversions. All men seek pleasure and avoid pain. Truth and morality have no other meaning. A thing is true or good if it promotes happiness.

As regards the legal aspect of utilitarianism, all men want to be happy but the means employed by them to promote happiness are often contradictory. Two individuals who wish to live from the product of their labour, may dispute the ownership of the same piece of land. The lawful owner wishes to enjoy his land in peace. The other wishes to find happiness through usurping the property of another. The greatest happiness results from upholding the claim of the lawful owner by threatening the usurper with the infliction of a pain which will equal the intensity of the pleasure he hoped to get. This can best be done by the government through its legislators who determine that certain actions are harmful to public happiness and constitute those actions as crimes and providing appropriate punishments. Legislation is a science of intimidation. Human nature is about the same in all men and hence classes of crimes can be established and codified laws by the legislature. Through those codes of law, the legislator creates a moral order based on a balance of pleasures and pains.

In the legal part of their philosophy, the utilitarians adopted the principle of artificial identification of interests and wanted the government .to interfere in the lives of the people to artificially reconcile their, interests. The government was to take positive action to promote happiness. However, in its economic aspects, the utilitarians adopted a contradictory principle of natural harmony of interests.

Their contention was that happiness might be better promoted by allowing nature to take its course in the economic sphere. If the legislator did not interfere in economic matters, a natural order would arise spontaneously based on the division of labour and the automatic mechanism of exchange.

Politically, utilitarianism proved an invaluable aid to democracy. On the basis of its suppositions, democracy was found to be the best. The first supposition was that all individuals are perfectly egoistical. The second supposition was that the greatest happiness of the greatest number should be the goal of every government. It followed that an absolute ruler was the least safe of all masters and a democratic majority was the best of all masters. As each, individual is the best judge of his interests, the majority of the individuals will be able to estimate the interests of the greatest number.

Utilitarianism was closely associated with psychology, with law, with economics and with politics. It taught that each individual is largely determined by the social environment in which he lives. Men are moved mainly by the desire to obtain happiness and avoid pain. Legislation is necessary to limit the freedom of all but not so in the field of economics. It also taught that only through democracy, the greatest happiness of the greatest number could be achieved.

From the ethical point of view, utilitarianism is based on the assumption that man is a sentient being who seeks pleasure and avoids pain. All his actions are motivated by a desire to achieve happiness and avoid pain. To a utilitarian, actions are good or bad as they promote pleasure or pain. There is nothing inherently good or bad in them. Their ethical content is not intrinsic in them. It grows from their consequences of promoting pleasure or pain. There is no such thing as absolute justice. Tightness or wrongness. Pleasures and pains can be quantitatively measured and determined.

The utilitarians were individualistic. They advocated individual liberty as that promoted human happiness. The state was there for the sake of the individual and not individual for the state. The state maintains peace and order to enable the individual to achieve happiness. The utilitarians were individualists in the sense that they conceived the welfare of society in terms of individual welfare. Society is just a collection of individuals and social welfare is just a sum total of the welfare of individuals. It is for this reason that the utilitarians, particularly J.S. Mill, gave to individual liberty a large content.

The utilitarian philosophy was not based on abstract principles which were current in the eighteenth century, but on the hard realities of human life. Utilitarians believed that man is social by nature and is always moved to action by a desire to obtain happiness and avoid pain. Utilitarianism had a dose touch with practical politics and ethics. To the utilitarians, the state was a human necessity as it promoted general welfare.

Utilitarianism was experimental and experience was the ultimate criterion of the worth of any policy or measure.

Utilitarianism taught that actions must be judged by their results or their usefulness. In that sense, utilitarianism was revolutionary. It had no more respect for the old and traditional than it had for the theory of natural rights and social contract. It viewed the state neither as a mystical social organism nor as an association created to guard the natural rights of its citizens. Utilitarianism provided a useful measuring rod for the existing institutions. It made people think objectively in terms of human welfare and not theoretically in terms of unrealizable ideals.

Utilitarianism was hedonistic and pragmatic. It was a reaction against the idealism of the eighteenth century. It sought to replace it with empiricism. The utilitarians asserted that despite its hedonistic basis, utilitarianism was not egoistic but altruistic. The utilitarians held that all men possess self-regarding and others-regarding impulses in varying degrees. If the emotional satisfaction of impulses is a powerful factor in human conduct, the same is the case with reason which compels a man to be other-regarding. Reason compels a man to reconcile his self-regarding impulses with his other-regarding impulses.

According to Hallowell, utilitarianism "was an attempt to establish ethical and political theory upon a thorough-going scientific empiricism." (Main Currents in Modern Political Thought, p. 198).

It was closely associated with practical ethics and practical politics. It stood for the promotion of happiness of the people, both individual and social. It regarded the state neither as a mystical social organism nor as an artificial association created to protect the rights of its citizens. The state exists because it is necessary to promote general welfare. The duty of the legislators is to increase the happiness of the people and lessen their sorrows and sufferings. The happiness of an individual must not be separated from the happiness of other individuals. Every man is linked up with others by the bonds of altruism and human affection. The utilitarians were the champions of individual liberty and happiness and were opposed to tyranny and injustice of every kind.

There is a difference between Greek Hedonism and the utilitarian Hedonism. Greek Hedonism was egoistic and self-conceited in character but the utilitarian Hedonism was altruistic, regardful of others. For the Epicurians, happiness was the sole aim of life. They asked the people to judge everything from the standpoint of their happiness alone. However, the utilitarians sought the happiness of the individual by securing the greatest happiness of the greatest number.

On the basis of a theory of human nature, Bentham propounded his theory of utility which he defined as "that principle which approves or disapproves of every action whatsoever, according to the tendency which it appears to have to augment or diminish the happiness of the party whose interest is in question. This doctrine of utility is of great political significance and it made utilitarianism highly pragmatic in character. The utilitarian was not a Platonic type of philosopher who was divorced from the realities of life, but an active citizen". Davidson writes, "Utilitarianism is emphatically practical, and keeps in close touch with experience; and it is reformatory, having in view the constant elevation of human life and the furthering of human progress." (Political Thought in England—From Bentham to Mill, p. 3)

The utilitarians gave precedence to man more as a social being than as a solitary thinker. By temperament, training and conviction, the utilitarians-were pragmatic.

According to the utilitarians, the criterion of every action of the state was utility. That meant the greatest happiness of the greatest number. Utility was welfare and embraced all that determined and constituted man's happiness. It was the only standard of right and wrong. Maxey writes, "Political institutions and public policies were not to be rated as good or bad relative to some visionary, and always arbitrary, conjecture of human rights and obligations, but more or less beneficial according to some fixed standard of utility in human affairs. By their fruits, not by their ideality, should they be judged." The standard of utility was the happiness and satisfaction of the individual. Though the amalgamation of utilitarianism and individualism was never, complete, the utilitarians leaned towards individualism to a great extent. It was so because J.S. Mill was both a utilitarian and an individualist. In its early stage, utilitarianism leaned towards the view that society should be evaluated from the point of view of individual comfort. Like the individualists, the utilitarians were the supporters of private enterprise. Their view was that the maximum welfare of the individual is possible only when in the economic field the individual is left free and the state has minimum interference.

The utilitarians were opposed to abstract theory or speculation. They appealed to experience as the ultimate criterion. They dealt with actual men and women and not with abstractions alone. They stood for struggle in life and not for running away from it. It was a working creed and not a "cloistered virtue". It was essentially practical and judged everything from its practical utility. If a thing was not practical, it was useless. Practicability was the test of the goodness of a thing. Our sense of right or wrong is experimental in its origin and associated with the feeling of pleasure or pain. The value of a moral principle lies in its capacity to add to general happiness. For the theory of natural rights, Bentham substituted the principle of utility.

Utilitarianism was analytical, descriptive and inductive. It rested on ascertained facts. Its aim was to use facts in such a way as to advance the progress of society and improve the existing conditions of life.

Prof. Catlin says that the utilitarians struck four cardinal notes which were utility, pleasure or happiness, the greatest happiness of the greatest number and benevolence. The concept of utility was a familiar one. It was taken up by Godwin and David Hume. They borrowed the principle of pleasure or happiness from Hobbes.

Utilitarianism was popular in England in the nineteenth century. It reflected the aims and needs of the time. The rising middle class in England developed a social and political outlook and philosophy which had little sympathy with either the conservatism or traditionalism of Burke or the Utopian radicalism of Paine and Godwin. It wanted a political creed which was empirical and reformist. The Industrial Revolution had changed the structure of society in England which made political, social and legal reforms imperative. That could not be done during the Revolutionary and Napoleonic wars. However, from 1820 onwards, people clamoured for reform. Men engaged in industries believed in the policy of *Laissez faire* and free trade. On the political side, the free traders were individualists. The trade union movement created difficulties for the government. The industrial class demanded parliamentary reform and the reform of electoral law. Bentham and his disciples joined hands with the reformers. They produced a systematic body of political philosophy suited to the practical needs of the day and having a close touch with the practical welfare of human beings.

The utilitarians were not abstract philosophers who stood aloof from the world. They kept themselves in close touch with the concrete problems of the country. The leaders of the movement were active in public life. The reform of the legal and penal systems, the improvement of conditions in factories and mines, and the reforms of parliamentary suffrage and representation were largely due to their efforts. The reform of the Poor Law, the repeal of the Corn Laws and the gradual adoption of universal suffrage were based on the principles of utilitarianism.

The utilitarian philosophy has been compared with that of Hobbes. The utilitarians agreed with Hobbes that government is justified by its usefulness and the sanctions of religion and natural law are moonshine. However, while Hobbes advocated an adjustment of competing egotism, Bentham and his followers were more benevolent and constructive. They believed in the ameliorative function of the state and stood for improvement. They were concerned with the greatest happiness of the greatest number.

The political philosophy of utilitarianism was developed in the writings of Bentham and James Mill. It went through a decided transformation at the hands of J.S. Mill, Grote and Alexander Bain adopted its fundamental arguments. John Austin developed the utilitarian principles. Ricardo upheld them in political economy. The utilitarian principles were applied in practical politics by Romelly, Brougham, Hobhouse, Cobbett, Cobden and Bright.

Jeremy Bentham (1748-1832)

Bentham was the real founder of the utilitarian school of political philosophy. He represented a type of mind in England that had revolutionised industry through the application of steam to it. From Priestley's *Essay on Government*, he learnt that the true end of the state is to promote the happiness of the greatest number. In spite of the praise of the British Constitution and British laws by Blackstone, Bentham was convinced that the English laws were "a mass of obscurities, fictions and formalities", unsuited to England of his day.

In his first book "*Fragment on Government*", Bentham criticised Blackstone's commentaries on the British Constitution. That book was published for the first time in 1773. His second book, *Introduction to the Principles of Morals and Legislation*, was published in 1789. In that book, much light was thrown on the philosophy of utilitarianism. His slogan was: "Nature has placed mankind under the governance of two sovereign masters, pain and pleasure; it is for them to point out what we ought to do, as well as to determine what we shall do." According to Bentham, the only criterion to measure virtue and vice is pleasure and pain. If we derive pleasure from an action, that is a good action and if we get pain from it, it is a bad action. Good work is worth doing and bad action is to be discarded. Bentham gave a list of 14 pleasures and 12 pains. The task of the law-giver was simply to "sum up all the values of all pleasures on the one side and those of all the pains on the other. The value of a thing was more or less according to the number of persons taking part in a pleasure or pain. Bentham stood for the greatest happiness of the greatest number. The principle of utility was the criterion of every action. The primary concern of Bentham was the welfare of the community as a whole. He was convinced that his principle of utility could be applied to all social questions, particularly those concerning constitutional, legislative and law reform.

Bentham was not bothered about abstract principles. He was primarily concerned with the practical problems facing the society of his time. He mercilessly criticised the ideal of natural rights which were described by him as "simple nonsense", natural and imprescriptible rights, rhetorical nonsense, nonsense upon stilts."

Although Bentham had no faith in the goodness of human nature, he was as good as individualist as Paine, Rousseau or Locke.

Bentham was dissatisfied with the existing political institutions in England and he attacked them in right earnest. He challenged the utility of the House of Lords and monarchy on the ground that the interests of those institutions were not compatible with the interests of the people at large. He was in favour of a republican form of government because such a government was conducive to "both efficiency and economy and supremacy of the people."

Bentham was a great law reformer. He was eager "to see justice demonstrated and happiness secured to the deserving and oppressed". He criticised the machinery of justice in England. He would like to weed out the obsolete, discard the useless and classify and explain the rest. He stood for the codification of English law. He found that the system of punishments in England was rotten. It had no connection with the gravity of the offence. Bentham had no respect for judges and referred to them as "judge and company". He believed that "laws are made by judges for the benefit of judges." Bentham put emphasis on the deterrent aspect of punishment. According to him, punishment should fit the criminal and not vice versa. It should be graded according to the nature of the crime, previous behaviour of the offender, his parentage, the motive of the criminal, the kind of persons who have been injured and the circumstances in which the crime was committed.

Bentham was thoroughly dissatisfied with the existing prisons in the country. He made suggestions for removing the shortcomings. He put forward what is known as *Panopticon* which he described as "a mill grinding rogues honest and idle men industrious". It was in the form of a penitentiary for the reform of criminals.

Bentham was a forerunner in the field of educational reforms. He believed that mankind could be improved with the help of education. It was the duty of the state to look after the education of the poor children and for that purpose he suggested certain reforms in the administration of poor law.

Bentham attacked the Church of England for the sinecure offices, wealthy bishops and starved curates. He regarded the clergymen as the enemies of progress. They were "a class of persons who habitually exalt the part for the express purpose of depressing and discouraging the present generation."

Bentham praised the value of unrestricted competition and contended against monopolies and bounties. He had no sympathy with the imperial ideal. He believed that the possession of colonies was not essential to carry on trade with them and the capital invested in that trade could be applied equally elsewhere.

He criticised the existing laws and the machinery and methods of executing them and proposed detailed schemes of his own. He laid down principles of value regarding international law.

Bentham contributed, sometimes on request and sometimes as a volunteer, to the revision of the legal codes of many countries.

James Mill (1773-1836)

James Mill agreed with Bentham that the distinction between moral and immoral acts lies in their utility and it is the function of law to put the pressure of the community in order to secure the performance of acts conducive to general happiness and to prevent those that destroy happiness. He advocated a representative government and freedom of discussion. He held that the government was necessary to prevent encroachments. It was also desirable to prevent the government itself from unduly expanding its powers. He held that the House of Commons must be powerful enough to counter-balance both the King and the House of Lords. He shared Bentham's enthusiasm for law and legal reform. He urged the creation of a code of international law and the establishment of an international judicial tribunal.

John Austin (1790-1859)

Austin is best known for his definition of law and sovereignty. He gave clearness and precision to the confused mass of English law. He was logical and formal. He separated the theory of sovereignty from its ethical and historical background and gave us the science of positive law.

He rejected the theory of social contract and held that the state was the result of a slow process of growth. Men were bound together in political society not by formal consent, but by the habit of obedience. Sovereign was the person or persons who habitually received obedience from the bulk of the people in any society and who did not render similar obedience to any other superior. He rejected the idea of natural rights.

Austin defied law as a command given by a superior to an inferior. According to him, international law was not positive law as there was no sovereign power to enforce it. The sovereign was not bound by legal obligations as there was no higher authority to enforce them. Sovereignty must be unlimited and indivisible.

John Stuart Mill (1806-1873)

John Stuart Mill, the son of James Mill, was the last of the utilitarians and the foremost of the individualists. He was one of the greatest advocates of freedom of thought and expression and one of the foremost liberals of all times. His important writing were *On Liberty, Considerations on Representative Government* and *Utilitarianism.*

Though in his view J.S. Mill was a great supporter of Bentham's doctrine, in his later years, he modified the narrow and rigid principles of utilitarianism and in doing so he practically overthrew the whole utilitarian position and repudiated it altogether. (1) The first change made by him was that he admitted that pleasures differed not only in quantity but also in quality. There were higher and lower pleasures. To quote him, "It is better to be a human being dissatisfied than a pig satisfied; better to be Socrates dissatisfied than a fool satisfied." (2) The second change was that he narrowed the gulf between self-interest and general happiness. According to him, the utilitarian standard is not the agent's own greatest happiness but the greatest amount of happiness altogether. Maxey writes, "Bentham's principle of utility in a society of wolves would exalt wolfishness; in a society of saints it would exalt saintliness. Mill was determined that saintliness should be criterion in any society whatsoever." (3) While for Bentham all men are moved to action solely by the desire to obtain happiness and avoid pain, Mill placed some other end before men for their pursuit, other than their personal happiness. He introduced the concept of good life as something more than life devoted to pleasure. He placed moral ends above happiness. (4) While to Bentham the idea of a moral obligation was merely the product of past association of selfish desires and anticipation of man, Mill admitted that fear, memory, self-esteem, law, sympathy, religious emotion and even self-abasement play their part in its composition. According to Mill, the sense of moral obligation could not be explained in terms of the principle of utility. (5) While Bentham accepted only the external sanctions for constraining the individuals to promote general happiness, Mill admitted both internal and external sanctions. He held that every man possessed "a feeling for the happiness of mankind" and therefore he should desire and promote general happiness. Thus, Mill arrived at conclusions which cut at the very roots of the doctrine of utilitarianism. Mill was not a fanatic type of utilitarian. He was open-minded and intelligent and was ready to see the point of view of the opponent and accept the same if he found it agreeable. However, he did not abandon Bentham's principles in toto and tried to minimise the differences.

J.S. Mill was the advocate-in-chief of individuality and the necessity of developing the individual in all aspects. His book "On Liberty" became the greatest English classic containing the finest defence of liberty of thought and discussion. He emphasized the value of originality and the social benefits resulting from a variety of ideas and actions. To quote Mill, "The sole end for which mankind are warranted, individually or collectively, in interfering with the liberty of action of any of their number is self-protection. The only purpose for which power can be rightfully exercised over any member of a civilised community, against his will, is to prevent harm to others. His own good, either physical or moral, is not a sufficient warrant." Mill divided man's actions into two parts—self-regarding actions and others-regarding actions. An individual was allowed to do whatever he pleased as regards his self-regarding actions but if his actions in any way affected others, a check could be put on them by society or state. The view of Mill was that even the whole of mankind had no right to silence a dissenter. However, Mill was not in favour of giving that liberty to backward classes. Moreover, he allowed unfettered freedom only in thought and expression and not in the field of action.

According to Mill, political institutions are made by human voluntary agency. Political machinery does not act by itself. It requires active participation by the people. Mill's view was that state interference in some cases was necessary for the development of the individualities of the people. The state was to be so regulated that the best intellectual and moral qualities of the citizens were stimulated and utilised in the service of society.

The view of Mill was that a representative government was the best. However, his representative government was applicable only to advanced nations and not to backward or colonial people.

Regarding the role of Parliament, Mill's view was that the Parliament was to watch and control the government, to throw the light of publicity on its acts, to censure them if condemnable. It was not the business of Parliament to govern and administer. He wanted the work of legislation to be given to a "Small Commission of Legislation". Parliament was to function as "a Committee of Grievances" and a "Congress of Opinion."

According to Mill, property was a social institution necessary for the good and progress of mankind but he advocated the abolition of the law of primogeniture. The right of private property in land was not sacred.

It is worthy of notice that with the passage of time, Mill came to have more and more sympathy for the labouring classes and more and more appreciation of socialism. He had in view the ultimate goal of the working man to partnership in one of the two forms—association of labourers with the capitalists or association of labourers among themselves. He was averse to extreme socialism. However, he approved of trade unionism and the socialist idea of voluntary cooperation. He looked forward to the time when there might be "a common ownership in the raw materials of the globe and an equal participation of all in the benefits of combined labour." He tried to combine political liberalism with economic socialism.

Mill was not in favour of voting by secret ballot. He defended public voting on the ground that the duty of voting should be performed under the eye and criticism of the public. Secret voting was bound to encourage selfishness.

Mill advocated the plurality of votes to the highly educated citizens. He classified individuals into various groups for purposes of voting and advocated plural or weighted voting for educated people.

Mill wanted to give women the same position as men had. According to him, "Sex alone should not be a disqualification".

Mill was disturbed by the danger in a democracy that the majority will tyrannize over the minority. He believed that minorities were not sufficiently represented in the British Parliament. He supported the system of proportional representation so that the distribution of parliamentary seats might correspond closely to the votes cast by the party groups. Mill opposed payment to members of Parliament in the interest of purity of government.

Mill was the foremost liberal of his day. He was a champion of individual liberty. He made changes in Benthamism wherever he considered necessary. He was an intellectual with unbending moral standards. He was a man of conviction who did not follow any principles blindly. He was a real democrat who understood fully the value of human personality and development of the individual as a social being.

Criticism of Utilitarianism

Utilitarianism has been criticised on many grounds. It is contended that the ethical and psychological foundations of utilitarianism were not sound. The exponents of utilitarianism painted a very poor picture of human nature. It is not correct to say that human beings are merely selfish. They live not only for themselves but also for others. They are as much egoists as they are altruists. Pleasure is not the only motive force in their lives. Had that been so there would have been no place for moral obligations. Rational and emotional elements are as important in the life of an individual as the selfish element.

It is difficult to calculate the happiness of the people as pleasure and pain differ from one individual to another according to time and circumstances. The principle of the greatest happiness of the greatest number is ambiguous and vague and difficult to realise.

Pleasure in itself may not be highest end of life. Some people may hanker after happiness but that may not be true of others. There is no logical connection between the happiness of the greatest number and the greatest happiness. We should aim at moral perfection and not hanker after wordily pleasures.

Utilitarianism is based on the atomistic concept of society. It is not correct to say that society is merely a collection of individuals.

The view of Bluntschli is that the general happiness which the state is intended to promote cannot be secured because happiness depends upon the mental condition of human beings and is considerably independent of the activities of the state.

Utilitarianism lacks idealism. It fails to fire the imagination of the people. Man is moved by ideals and not by facts alone. However, it is pointed out that the utilitarians have their ideals. They have their vision of the future improvement of society and regeneration of mankind.

Utilitarianism has been condemned as materialistic. It degrades human beings. It stands for materialism in its worst ethical sense. It is suggested that the terms welfare and well-being may be substituted for utility and happiness.

Utilitarianism is criticised as the philosophy of expediency. However, the ideals of the utilitarians are praise-worthy.

Pleasures are individualistic in their nature. What gives pleasure to one individual may not give to another. Pleasure is a subjective experience. There is no such thing as general happiness or general pleasure. Pleasure is personal and not general. All that we can do is to sympathise with the pleasure and pain of another but we cannot feel the came. There is no logical connection between pleasure and general happiness.

The utilitarians gave a subordinate place to the maintenance of liberty as their chief pre-occupation was security.

Estimate of Utilitarianism

Whatever be the shortcomings of utilitarianism, it cannot be denied that it was responsible for a lot of good. It made the people think objectively and not just theoretically. It placed a definite ideal before politicians and statesmen. It gave a convenient criterion for judging the usefulness of legislation. It provided a measuring rod for the existing institutions.

Many of the important reforms of the nineteenth century in England can be traced to the effect of utilitarian philosophy. The whole of the English legal system was overhauled and its absurdities and cruelties were done away with. It was responsible for labour legislation which aimed at bettering the lot of the workers in factories and mines. It brought to the forefront the ideal that the well-being of society was to be kept in the forefront. The utilitarian philosophy awakened interest in psychological investigation and ethical discussion in the schools and in active politics, social reforms and beneficent legislation.

Utilitarianism was a British political philosophy. It represented the British reaction against the vague generalities about natural rights and social contract and the mystic idealism of the German political philosophers. It brought political theory back from the abstractions of the Age of Reason. The utilitarian philosophers gave simplicity and definiteness to political terminology. They have a new theory of government according to which government was based not on contract but on the habit of obedience born of utility. They put emphasis on individual liberty and checked the growing tendency to deify the state. The individual was saved from being absorbed by the state and became once again the prominent subject of political thinking.

SUGGESTED READINGS

Albee, E. : History or English Utilitarianism, 1902.
Alien : Social and Political Idea of the Revolutionary Era.
Atkinson, CM. : Jeremy Bentham.
Bentham, J. : An Introduction to the Study of Morals and Legislation.
Brinton, C. : English Political Thought in the Nineteenth Century, London, 1953.
Brown, Ivor : English Political Theory.
Burns, E.M. : Ideas in Conflict.
Davidson, W.L. : Political Thought in England from Bentham to J.S. Mill, 1916.
Doyle : A History of Political Thought.
Dunning, W.A. : Political Theories from Rousseau to Spencer.
Hallowell : Main Currents in Modern Political Thought.
Jones, W. : Masters of Political Thought, Vol. II.
Levi, A.W. : A Study in the Social Philosophy of John Stuart Mill, 1940.
MacCunn, John : Six Radical Thinkers, 1907.
Mill, J.S. : Utilitarianism.
Murray, R.H. : History of Political Science from Plato to the Present.
Packe, M.S.J. : Life of John Stuart Mill, 1954.
Plamenatz, John : Mill's Utilitarianism, 1949.
Rockow, J. : Contemporary Political Thought in England.
Sabine, G.H. : A History of Political Theory.
Stephen, Sir Leslie : The English Utilitarians.
Wayper, C.L. : Political Thought.

CHAPTER

Individualism

A distinction is made between traditional individualism and modern individualism. Individualism that prevailed till the end of the nineteenth century is known as traditional individualism and its main exponents were J.S. Mill, Herbert Spencer and F.A. Hayek. Modern individualism is a reaction against the absolutist collectivist theories of the state and its main exponents are Graham Wallas, Norman Angell, the Guild Socialists and the Syndicalists.

Learning Objectives

- Traditional Individualism
- Development of Individualism
- Exponents of Traditional Individualism : J.S. Mill (1806-1873)
- Herbert Spencer (1820-1903)
- Hayek
- Characteristic Features of Traditional Individualism
- Arguments in Favour of Individualism
- Case Against Individualism
- Modern Individualism
- Factors contributing to Growth of Modern Individualism
- Exponents of Modern Individualism
- Suggested Readings

Traditional Individualism

As a political philosophy, individualism implies a broad political system and it is difficult to give an exact definition of it. According to C.E.M. Joad, individualism as a social and political theory, was a product of the nineteenth century. It was first enunciated by Bentham and James Mill and it received its fullest expression in the works of J.S. Mill and Herbert Spencer. Dr. Leacock writes, "The individualist theory may be briefly stated in the proposition that the sole duty of government is to protect the individual from violence or fraud. According to this theory, the positive interference of the state with the individual even in his own interest, is not justified. Nor is the state justified in undertaking operations of an economic character or in imposing restriction (other than in prevention of violence or fraud) on the economic activities of its citizens."

Development of Individualism

The germs of individualism may be traced back to the ancient Greek philosophy, "Sophism". The social contract theory, particularly the ideas of Locke, laid stress on individualism. Individualism developed as an economic concept in the eighteenth century at the hands of the Physiocrats of France who raised the battle-cry of *Laissez faire. Laissez passer*, against the mercantilist measures of state control of industry and commerce. They opposed intervention in the sphere of industry. Their theory of non-intervention followed from their concept of the "natural order" whose basic ingredients were the right to enjoy the benefits of property and freedom of contract and the right to have such freedom as was consistent with the freedom of others to follow their self-interest.

The main object of the teachings of the Physiocrats was to assist in the removal of the obstacles that stood in the way of industrial capitalism. This creed of non-intervention spread from France to different parts of Europe. It received a comprehensive treatment in the writings of Adam Smith, particularly his book *Wealth of Nations* which was published in 1776. Adam Smith advocated the protection of self-interest of every individual in the field of industry, trade and commerce. He strongly supported private property and free competition. He opposed all sorts of state interference with the normal processes of industry and commerce. Individualism as a socio-political theory was developed by J.S. Mill and Herbert Spencer. Traditional individualism can also be found in the writings of contemporary thinkers like F.A. Hayek but it has almost completely broken down and its place taken over by modern individualism.

Exponents of Traditional Individualism: J.S. Mill (1806-1873)

J.S. Mill was the most ardent champion of individualism. He advocated complete individual freedom in the sphere which did not concern the community. The community was justified in restricting only that individual activity which had social consequences. Mill made a distinction between self-regarding and other-regarding activities of an individual and he allowed complete liberty in the sphere of self-regarding activities.

Mill insisted upon the value of human development and made an eloquent plea for the largest possible free initiative for the individual. Freedom from interference by political authority or from the tyranny of mob rule was an article of faith with him. According to him, the government was not competent to silence the opinions of those who held contrary views. To quote, "If all mankind minus one were of one opinion, mankind would be no more justified in silencing that one person than he, if he had the power, would be justified in silencing mankind."

It is the business of the government to promote happiness and hence it is not justified in infringing the happiness of minorities by suppressing their views even when it is backed by a compact majority of men holding contrary views. To quote Mill, "Mankind are greater gainers by suffering each other to live as seems good to themselves than by compelling each to live as seems good to the rest."

During his lifetime, under the influence of contemporary socio-economic situation in England, Mill recognised some utility of state intervention. The collectivist trend in England influenced his thinking in later life.

Herbert Spencer (1820-1903)

The individualism of Herbert Spencer was the outcome of his belief in natural rights, natural economic laws and non-conformist hostility to authority. He shared the view that human history is an orderly, continuous and beneficent change, naturally operating towards more enlightened ways of living and more perfect equilibrium of social forces. Hence natural laws demanded that the government should allow nature to function freely without any artificial hindrance.

Spencer applied the principle of organic evolution through natural selection to human society and came to the conclusion that the state should allow nature to do its work. The only function of the state is to assist nature which means to allow every individual to fight the struggle for existence. The state has only two sorts of duties. Its primary function is defence against external attack and secondary function is to prevent encroachments among the individuals within the state. The duty of the state in the domestic field is to secure justice which is described by him in these words: "Every man is free to do that which he wills, provided he infringes not the equal freedom of any other man. "Spencer was opposed to all organised charity, public or private, to all state help to education or industry and all government operation or regulation of industry. Compulsory education, poor relief and social legislation seemed to serve no useful purpose. Their only effect was to prolong the existence of those who ought to be eliminated. It was not the duty of the state to help the lame, dumb, poor, the old and the destitute. The state should not work the mint and post offices or erect light houses or life-saving stations because none of them fell under the category of justice which alone was the function of the state.

His view regarding the state is put in these words: "Be it or be it not true, that man is shapen in iniquity and conceived in sin, it is unquestionably true that government is begotten, of aggression and by aggression." In a perfect society, there is no *raison d'etre* for the state. He says: "Have we not shown that government is essentially immoral? Does it not exist because crime exists and must government not cease when crime ceases, for very lack of objects on which to perform its functions?" It was a mistake to regard the state as an eternal institution. Its existence was merely incidental. In *Social Statics* (1866), he maintained that the individual had the right to ignore the state, drop connection with it, refuse its protection, throw off its burdens and adopt a condition of voluntary outlawry. Past experience indicated that happiness came not from state action but by leaving the individual alone. The sphere of the state should be "negatively regulative". The only right of the individual is equal freedom with everybody else, and the only duty of the state is to protect that right against violence and fraud.

On the question of provision of educational facilities by the state, he observed that "taking away a man's property to educate his own or other people's children is not needful for the maintenance of his rights and hence is wrong." He went to the extent of maintaining that it is a "violation of the moral law for the state to interpose between quacks and those who patronise them."

In an essay entitled "The Sins of the Legislators", he condemned the legislation passed in the past. The laws of the state were a record of "unhappy guesses". Since most of the laws passed were repealed or amended later on, it follows that they should not have been passed.

Hayek

F.A. Hayek is a traditional thinker by logic and not by chronology. He advocates free enterprise and non-intervention by the state. His view is that state-sponsored economic planning is neither desirable nor practicable. The rule of law is the bedrock of democratic heritage and economic planning of the collectivist type is the very opposite of it. Governmental intervention through economic planning will reduce democracy to a shadow without substance. Governmental intervention is also dangerous to individuals and society. It may result in oppression and totalitarianism. According to Hayek, it leads to serfdom.

Critics point out that although total planning is neither desirable nor practicable, but partial planning is both desirable and practicable. Dr. Herman Finer writes, "As a result of several centuries of law-making or planning, legislative abilities have considerably increased. Consequently, planning can be delimited exclusively to the fields that the people, through their legislatures, desire." (The Theory and Practice of Modern Government, p. 27)

Characteristic Features of Traditional Individualism

Although the term individualism is a broad one, it has some distinct features. It believes in an atomistic concept of society which consists of isolated and ego-centric individuals. Like an atom, each individual is separated, solitary and isolated from others. His happiness is purely personal. There is no such thing as collective happiness. Every individual is concerned with himself and society is nothing but a collection of individuals.

Individualism regards individuals as the centre of all activities in society. Every individual is basically good. If he is given ample freedom, he can develop his personality fully. Every individual is endowed with reason and rationality. He can distinguish between what is good or bad for him and for society. He is far-sighted and knows what he wants. Every individual avoids pain and tries to secure happiness. That results in the greatest happiness of the greatest number.

Individualism puts emphasis on individual liberty. Individualism believes in open society of which liberty is the principal feature. Freedom is the heart of individualism.

According to individualism, the state is merely a means and the individual is an end. The goal of the state is the happiness of the individual. The state should leave the individual alone so long as he performs his functions well in society. The state is the servant and not master of the individual.

Individualism believes in minimum interference by the state in the lives of individuals. The work done by the individual is considered to be better than the work done by a state. The individual who works himself, educates his mind and strengthens his personality. The interference of the state should be as little as possible. The state is an evil but a necessary evil. The state should be regarded as a mere "night watchman". Individualism has a negative view of the state.

Individualism believes in free competition and free production in society. The state should not interfere in the economic field. Trade and industry flourish best if there is free competition and not any intervention by the state. Large-scale production will reduce the prices of commodities and thereby help the consumers.

Arguments in Favour of Individualism

Considerations of *justice and morality demand* that the state should not interfere with the free expression of the will of individuals. All individual can develop his faculties in the best manner only if there is no diversion of them by any external factor. Government action tends to destroy the sense of self-reliance and weakens the responsibility of an individual as a free agent. The view of J.S. Mill was that too much meddling by the government "starves the development of some portion of the bodily or mental faculties when it deprives one from doing what one is inclined to do or from acting according to one's judgement of what is desirable". The highest civilisation has developed under an individualistic society. J.S. Mill writes, "A people among whom there is no habit of spontaneous action for a collective interest, who look habitually to their government to command and prompt them in matters of joint concern, who expect to have everything done for them except that, that can be made an affair of mere habit and routine, have their faculties only half developed, their education is defective in one of its most important branches."

The *biological argument* is that nature should be given a free hand to work in its own way. According to the law of nature, the undesirable elements of society will be weeded out. It is only the efficient and fit who manage to survive unassisted and it is they who will live in the individualist society. Herbert Spencer maintains that the rich who are generally more educated and wise, multiply themselves less quickly than the poor who are, on the whole, less intelligent and more ignorant. In an individualist society, although more children will be born among the poor, as a result of the working of Malthus law of population, most of them will die on account of the lack of the necessities of life. All the children of the rich can afford to live. The result is that a balance is maintained between the rich and the poor and the rule of the wise-rich can be established. If the state comes to the assistance of the poor, there is the possibility of all of them surviving. The result will be that the poor will outnumber the rich who are intelligent and wise. In this way, the rule of the unwise, and ignorant people will be established and the intelligent rich will be tyrannised by the poor.

The *economic argument* is that every individual is actuated by his self-interest. He tries to get the maximum. As a result of the working of competing forces, society comes to have a reasonable price and maximum advantage. This will help internal and international trade and commerce. Inventions will multiply. Production will increase manifold. Competition will raise the standard of efficiency and things of a superior quality will be manufactured. Britain's lead in the industrial field was due to the lack of state intervention and free scope for individuals to experiment in their own way.

The *argument of experience* is that the historical examples of state regulation and control point to their futility and ineffectiveness. Most of the legislation is mischievous and ridiculous, *e.g.* prohibition of wearing of certain kinds of cloth and dress, export, import and manufacture of commodities of a particular pattern, the prescription of width and thickness of cloth and length of yarn, laws regulating wages of labour and fixing the prices of food, clothes and other necessities of life.

The individualists condemn the *incompetence and inefficiency of the state.* Mill said that the great majority of the things were worse done when done by a government than those done by individuals. The reason is that the people understand their own business and care for it more than any government could. Compare the promptitude observed in the disposal of orders from customers in a private shop and a government depot. The state is not a creative organ, but an organ which acts only by means of a complicated apparatus, composed of numerous wheels. It is an organ of criticism, generalisation and coordination and it cannot be the best agent.

The *scientific argument* of individualism is based on the Darwinian theory of evolution which says that free competition among species leads to the survival of the fittest. The weak and the unfit who cannot withstand competition with their fellow-beings, should be eliminated by natural process. Any assistance by the state to the weak and unfit will violate the scientific law of evolution.

Individualism has tremendous faith in the individual. Society is viewed as nothing but a mere collection of individuals. Individualism believes in liberty of an individual.

Individualism encourages self-reliance. It has put great emphasis on the dangers of state-interference. It underlines the importance of self-help for the good of the individuals and society.

Case Against Individualism

Individualism is not free from defects. The individualist view that the state is a necessary evil, is not correct. The state is the result of the social instinct of man. Huxley writes, "The higher the state of civilisation, the more completely do the actions of one member of the social body influence all the rest and the less it is possible for any one man to do wrong without interfering with the freedom of his fellow citizens. Even upon the narrowest view of the functions of the state, it must be admitted to have wider powers than the advocates of the *Laissez-faire* theory are disposed to admit." In a complex human society of today, state control has become necessary. Instead of being a necessary evil, the state has become a welfare institution which is essential for the development of human personality.

The view of J.S. Mill was that with the increase in the activities of the state, the number of laws will increase and the liberty of the individual will be curtailed. Moreover, laws do not control liberty.

The individualist view is that each and every individual is the best judge of his own interests. This is not true. All individuals are not so intelligent as to know what is good for them. Dr. Garner writes, "Not only is the individual not always a competent judge of his own interests as economic consumer, but in affairs of personal conduct, he is often not to be trusted, particularly in matters relating to health or safety or moral welfare. The fact is that society may be a better judge of the intellectual, moral and physical needs than he is himself."

The individualists stand for open competition but that has been found to be harmful to society. It has encouraged the exploitation of the workers. It is desirable that there should be state regulation and control over industries and trade.

The principle of the survival of the fittest is dangerous. It can create the conditions of a jungle where the stronger animals consider the weaker animals as their food. The principle is also cruel and inhuman. It can lead to the same anarchy which was described by Hobbes in the state of nature.

Contrary to what has been stated by Hayek in his book "Road to Serfdom", planning has done a lot of good to society and has not destroyed individual liberty at all. Total planning is neither possible nor desirable and the same is never attempted.

The individualists advocate free competition but experience shows that it has resulted in worsening the lot of the weaker sections. The rich have grown richer and the poor poorer. Some check has to be put on competition in the interest of society as a whole.

The view of the individualists is that state interference cripples human personality. Experience shows that state regulation in many cases has helped individuals to grow their personalities. We no longer believe in a negative state but in a welfare state which does a lot for the good of the people.

The atomistic concept of society has been criticised. An individual in society is not like an atom. The organic nature of society cannot be ignored.

There is no truth in the individualist contention that the work done by the state is less efficient than that done by individuals. There is nothing inherently wrong or good either in individual or state action. All depends upon the nature of the work. In certain cases, the machinery of the state can be employed with profit, but in certain other cases work can and should be left to private and individual enterprise.

It is not absolutely true that man is the best judge of his own interests and if he is left to himself, he will do only that which will be to his greatest advantage. Experience shows that in some cases society may guide him better and protect him better than he can do personally and individually. It may be that he may not understand his best interests on account of his ignorance of the complicated nature of the situation to be faced. Sidgwick writes, "As the appliances of life become more and more elaborate and complicated through the progress of inventions, it is only according to the general law of division of labour to suppose that an average man's ability to judge of the adaptation of means to end even as regards the satisfaction of his everyday needs, is likely to become continuously less. It is for this reason that in our times, the governments place restriction on the construction of building; use of water for drinking purposes may be prohibited from certain sources; the people may be forced to get themselves inoculated to check certain diseases; the construction of brick-kilns near the city may not be allowed".

In applying the biological analogy, the advocates of individualism fail to consider the essential difference between man and lower form of life. While the latter are at the mercy of their environment and are transformed by it, man transforms his environment and can remove the great waste which the process of natural selection necessitates. As the survival of the fittest means only the fittest under given circumstances and not necessarily the survival of the best, man, by improving those circumstances, can make the fittest the far more desirable product. Hence, collective activity instead of being an interference with a beneficent law, may remove the waste of competition, hasten progress and make possible a higher type of individual and society.

Critics point out that Herbert Spencer took the biological argument to extremes. It was contended that everybody should exert himself single-handed and thereby prove his fitness to live by his survival. It was not the duty of the state to help the poor, the needy, the orphans and the aged. However, the practical application of this principle resulted in great hardship. Kind-hearted people condemned individualist philosophy as cruel philosophy which preached selfishness in its nakedness and ignored all humanitarian principles. The people were prepared to abandon a philosophy which preached that the orphans, the poor and the aged be left to their fate. After all, man is not the economic man of the economists who is actuated purely by economic considerations.

The individualists maintained that the state was not justified in interfering between the employers and their employees and the capitalists and the factory hands. It was contended that both the employers and the employees were free to strike a bargain. The employers could offer any wage they please and the workers have the option to accept that wage or reject the same. Critics point out that the so-called freedom in the economic field does not actually exist. The worker as a rule lives from hand to mouth and has no reserves to fall back upon. Even if he is offered unreasonably low wages, he has to accept them because the alternative is the starvation of his family. Under the circumstances, the state has to intervene to bring the employer to his senses and ensure justice for the employees.

Individualism was a doctrine of production which left distribution entire out of account. The result was that in spite of the tremendous increase of national wealth, the misery of the underdog and the weaklings increased. Although the industrial magnates made fortunes, the people as a whole suffered because the distribution was wholly unsatisfactory.

Individualism was found to be inadequate to serve the needs of the times. The doctrine of liberty worked disastrously when applied in the economic field. It was based on three fallacies: (1) Each individual is equally far-sighted and has an equal capacity for knowing what he wants. (2) Each individual possesses an equal power of obtaining what he wants and an equal freedom of choice. (3) The satisfaction of the wants of all individuals is identical with the well-being of the community as a whole. The maxim, "Every man for himself and the Devil take the hindmost" is not an adequate basis for a contented society. It led to great distress. There was no point in telling a man that he will always choose what is for his own interest when he actually has no choice but to sell his labour for whatever is offered to him. A starving man has no alternative and he can find no satisfaction in the alleged freedom of contract. The miseries of long hours and low wages, of stunted lives and restricted development showed how injurious were the unchecked operations of the laws of demand and supply to the health and happiness of the people. It became evident that if the mass of the people were to rise above the level of mere wage slaves, they had to be protected against the evils of free and unrestricted competition, by a greater measure of interference with and regulation of industry by the state than had been done in the past.

Laski writes, "Individualism means poor health, undeveloped intelligence, miserable homes and work in which broadly speaking the majority can find no source of human interest." Gilchrist observes, "Individualism exaggerates the evils of state control when it forgets that there are more instances of good state action than of bad. It gives fundamentally false conceptions of individuality and finally it has proved unfit for the complexity of modern life."

In spite of many defects, there is substantial truth in individualism. It opposes maximum state interference in individual matters and puts special stress on self-reliance and self-help. As a political ideology, individualism will occupy a permanent place in political philosophy.

Modern Individualism

When individualism was taken to extremes, there was a reaction against it in favour of the State towards the close of the nineteenth century. It was found that individualism could not meet the challenge of the problems created by industrial capitalism. Unplanned production led to frequent fluctuations in income and employment, the exploitation of the people and mass poverty. Those problems required the intervention of the state. The advocacy of the principle of the survival of the fittest by Herbert Spencer discredited individualism and there was a wave in favour of the authority of the state. However, when the authority of the state was taken to extremes, there was again a reaction in favour of individualism. There was a protest against excessive state control and rebirth of the spirit of individualism. Prof. C.E.M. Joad writes, "The wheel has turned a full circle and the present dissatisfaction with the state has promoted a revival of individualist thinking akin in spirit, though not in form, to the individualism of the nineteenth century. Modern individualism condemns the omnipotence of the state. It protests against the despotism of the bureaucratic government. It criticises the tyranny exercised by the majority in parliamentary forms of government." The fundamental difference between traditional and modern individualism is that while the former put emphasis on the individual, the latter puts emphasis on groups and associations. It is realised that in the complicated society of today, the individual alone does not count. If he is to protect his interests, he must join some group or association for that purpose.

Factors contributing to Growth of Modern Individualism

Many factors have contributed to the growth of modern individualism. The first thing is the multiplication of voluntary associations in the economic, social, religious and moral fields. Each association looks after certain interests of the individual. There are occasions when the interests of an association clash with those of the state and the people are willing to defy the state and support the association. It is contended that associations are as important in the lives of man as the state itself. The state cannot claim any superior allegiance than claimed and exercised by associations. The state is merely one of the many associations which an individual joins for the protection of his interests. The only difference is that while the membership of the state is compulsory, that of other associations is voluntary, but that does not take away from the importance of associations or groups.

Another factor which has helped the growth of modern individualism is the sense of frustration crated by the World Wars. During the Wars, all kinds of demands were made on the people by the belligerent states. All kinds of sacrifices were demanded in the name of the state. At the beginning, the people responded willingly and enthusiastically but when the casualties of War began to mount, there was a reaction against the state. The people began to doubt the utility of the state which brought them wars and disaster. It was realised that their sufferings were due to the omnipotence of the state and hence there was the necessity to put a check on it. The enormous restrictions placed on the liberty of individuals during the Wars also created a reaction against the despotism of the state and in favour of modern individualism. Laski points out that modern individualism was born of reaction against the Moloch-like demands of the state in war times. Along with that, the inauguration of an era of economic planning encouraged increasing integration of social forces and the development of a powerful, centralised organisation. Wars and planning immensely expanded the province of state activity and the modern state has become a grand Leviathan reducing individual liberty almost to a marginal experience. Modern individualism is a protest against the rising tide of totalitarianism. It suggests a new institutional pattern woven by a multiplicity of autonomous groups and associations.

Another factor which helped the growth of modern individualism was the loss of faith in the parliamentary form of government by the people. The tyranny of the majority rule which is necessary in a parliamentary form of government, was condemned. It was felt that there was a serious threat to the liberty of the individual. The transfer of legal sovereignly to the majority in the legislature under the name of the state, was no guarantee of universal happiness. The only way out of the difficulty was to decentralise the powers and functions of the state which was possible only in an individualistic society and not under a collectivist regime.

The myth that parliamentary democracy is the sure condition of individual liberty, has been exploded now. The majority party in the legislature becomes more and more intolerant of political dissent. There is also the menace of mob psychology and the anonymous authority of public opinion enforcing conformity in human conduct. Parliamentary democracy has emancipated man from external restrictions, but the lack of spontaneous integration of individuals with society has created a sense of isolation and powerlessness which leads "to a compulsive conforming in the process of which the isolated individual becomes an automaton." These forces stifle the spontaneity of human action and there is no respect for the uniqueness of individual personality. To counteract these influences, modern individualism advocates devolution of power on a large scale.

According to the modern individualists, power should be decentralised and the state should not be more than a federation of groups or a community of communities. It is to be merely a piece of administrative machinery useful for coordinating activities and adjusting claims between conflicting groups and associations. The state has no superior moral position. It does not and cannot possess a real personality and real will over and above the personalities and wills of individuals and groups which compose the state. Loyalty of individuals to groups sometimes outweighs loyalty to the state. Laski writes, "The only state to which I owe allegiance is the state in which I discover moral adequacy." If the individual's church conflicts with the state, he chooses, and he alone can choose, where his allegiance should go."

According to modern individualism, groups and associations have their own personality and group interests should lie protected. State interference should not be excessive. Steps should be taken to stop the ever-increasing power of the state. Excessive state control defeats the very purpose for which the state was established. In states like the Soviet Union and Communist China, the state is all-powerful and the individual has no voice. Too much of state interference involves heavy and overburdened administrative set-up which is likely to be indifferent to public interest. Too much of state control destroys individual incentive and competition and result in inefficiency, red-tapism and corruption.

Modern individualism strikes a via-media between the absence of state control and excessive state control. It stands for the revival of groups and state intervention whenever necessary. It is a revolt against the despotism of the authoritarian and bureaucratic governments created after the World War I.

It is contended that the group is designed not only to protect but also to promote the interests of individuals. The integration of the individual on functional basis through the group is more real than the political integration of man through the state. The group is a small circle of persons suited to the development of individual personality. It can evoke better and more spontaneous loyalty of its members than the state.

Modern individualism embodies a distinct anti-intellectualist reaction. The intellectuals make no objective study of the world and human behaviour. Their ideas are not empirically verified. The use of the developed psychological tool helps the modern individualist to deny the possibility of *a priori* knowledge. They emphasize the role of observation and investigation. Graham Wallas reveals the irrational forces influencing human behaviour and the world of politics. He suggests the remodelling of political organisation with a view to offsetting the operation of irrational forces. The approach of modern individualists is empirical as opposed to the intellectualist strain evident in the Hegelian idealists.

Exponents of Modern Individualism

In his book "Great Society", *Graham Wallas condemns* the evils arising from over-developed states in which it is not possible for the people to express their true feelings. They can be hypnotized by the popular press and drugged by the demagogues. Graham Wallas advocates the adoption of both functional and territorial representation and the provision of certain safe against the tyranny of the majority. He suggests that the electorate should be divided into groups on vocational basis and each group should elect members of the second chamber which would be composed entirely of the representatives of different trades and professions. The lower chamber is to be elected on territorial basis. The object of Wallas is to safeguard the individual against the evils of unrestricted majority rule. He is afraid of the tyranny of mob mind.

In his book entitled "The Great Illusion", *Norman Agell* maintains that men are united by a community of feeling based on economic interests which frequently transcend national and geographical boundaries. At present, they often take wrong view of what is in their interest on account of the propaganda carried on by the competing states. Norman Angell writes, "It pays men better to think and feel as members of the universal economic society whose attribute is peace than to think and feel as members of limited political societies whose attribute is war." When people realise the evils of the present system, they will give up the present division of society into competing nationalist groups and adopt an economic stratification based on considerations of what is profitable. Norman Angell maintains that "a man will in politics, in a matter where patriotism is involved, act with irrationalism and an absence of any sense of responsibility which he would never display in the conduct of his private business." Norman Angell regards the state merely as a piece of administrative mechanism which can be superseded as soon as a better machinery is involved. He is in favour of the merger of the national state in the international order of society based on economic basis.

Like Graham Wallas, Angell protests against the overgrown state of today. He discovers the irrationalism of mob mind in politics. According to him, the modern state is a geographical and administrative unit. It is an artificial arrangement. It is a heterogeneous concept embodying cross-sections of economic interests. The diversity of economic interests leads to various concepts of life which are class oriented. The real bond of unity among men is the community of economic interests which transcends geographical and administrative divisions. Angell advocates the replacement of patriotic wars between nations by class conflicts between international parties espousing different class interests. Through such international conflicts, the real needs of man will become articulate and he will develop an international mind.

In his book entitled "The Service State", *Hilaire Belloc* advocates the establishment of guilds. The *Guild Socialists* regard society as a federation of two kinds of groups, representing the points of view of producers and consumers. The existing trade unions are taken as the germ from which the group organisations of society will be developed.

In his book entitled "The New State Group Organisation: The Solution of Popular Government", Miss Follett emphasizes "the group in relation" as the object of the study "if that study is to be fruitful for politics." We must not study the individual, the group or the state separately, but all in their relation to one another. The individual, the group and the state have all to be reckoned with and we cannot ignore or minimise the importance of any one. Neither is the individual to be sacrificed for the group nor the group for the state. To quote her, "No government will be successful, no government will endure, which does not rest on the individual, and no government has yet found the individual". Her individualism does not believe in the old and fallacious idea of "self-and-others" as the basis of society. She seeks "self-in-and-through-others" for the expression of personality. The potentialities of the individual remain merely potentialities until they are realised by group life. Man discovers his true nature and gains his true freedom only through the group. Group organisation must be the new method of politics because the modes by which the individual can be brought forth and made effective are the modes of practical politics. The state is not made by external acts but by the continuous thoughts and actions of the people who live its life. The life of the state is a moral ordering and the power of the state is a moral power. The state unifies the various interests of individuals. It is in "the ordering of its infinite series into their right relations that the greatest possible welfare of the total may be worked out." C.E.M. Joad points out that in modern individualism there is a disposition to anti-intellectualism directed against the state and in particular against the Hegelian and collectivist theories of the state. This expresses itself in hostility to concrete reasoned proposals, in the belief that the future will develop along its own line unaffected by the cerebrations of statesmen and of political theorists and in a faith in the ability of instinct or the sub-conscious to grapple successfully with each new situation as and when, it arises. There is also an affirmation of the real personality of groups in the same way as the State has a personality created by the consenting wills of its members. Groups are entitled to call upon the loyalty and service of their members. When that loyalty conflicts with the allegiance of a man to the state, there is no reason why the claims of the state should be regarded as necessarily paramount. The state tends to be regarded as little more than a federation of groups whose duty is to adjust the conflicting claims of the various groups.

SUGGESTED READINGS

Barker, E. : Principles of Social and Political Theory.

Barker, E. : Political Thought in England (1848-1914).

Burns, C.D. : Political Ideals.

Davidson, W.L. : Political Thought in England from Bentham to J.S. Mill.

Ebenstein : Modern Political Thought.

Finer, H. : The Theory and Practice of Modern Government.

Fromm, Erich : The Fear of Freedom.

Garner : Political Science and Government.

Hallowell : Main Currents in Modern Political Thought.

Joad, C.E.M. : Modern Political Theory.

Joad, C.E.M. : Guide to the Philosophy of Morals and Politics.

Laski, H.J. : An Introduction to Politics.

Laski. H.J. : Grammar of Politics.

Laski, H.J. : The State in Theory and Practice.

MacIver, R.M. : The Modern State.

Mackay, T. : A Plea for Liberty.

Maxey, C.C. : Political Philosophies.

Mill, J.S. : Utilitarianism.

Mill, J.S. : On Liberty.

Montague, F.G. : The Limits of Individual Liberty.

Ritchie, D.C. : Principles of State Interference.

Rockow, J. : Contemporary Political Thought in England.

Roll, Eric : A History of Economic Thought.

Sabine, G.H. : A History of Political Theory.

Wayper, C.L. : Political Thought.

Wilde, N. : The Ethical Basis of the State.

CHAPTER

Idealist Political Theory

In the words of L.W. Lancaster, "Idealist political theory is essentially an attempt to adapt to modern conditions the classic Greek view of the social nature of the individual. The modern additions were drawn principally from Hegel and Rousseau". Barker writes, "Idealism thus involves a revolution of ideas. Instead of starting from a central individual to whom the social system is supposed to be adjusted, the idealist starts from a central social system in which the individual must find his appointed orbit of duty."

The idealist theory of the state is also known as the absolute theory, philosophical theory or metaphysical theory. It is called an absolutist theory because it vests absolute power in the state. It is also known as metaphysical or philosophical theory as it advocates or regards the state as an ethical substance and explains its nature in philosophical terms.

Learning Objectives

- Origin of the Theory
- Kant (1724-1804)
- Fichte (1762-1814)
- Hegel (1770-1831)
- The English Idealists
- T.H. Green
- Bradley (1846-1924)
- Dr. Bosanquet (1848-1923)
- Basic Tenets of Idealist Theory
- Criticism of Idealist Theory
- Value of the Idealist Theory
- Suggested Readings

Origin of the Theory

The view of Dr. Bosanquet is that the German idealists owed much to the philosophy of Rousseau. The idea of the general will was evidently borrowed by Hegel from Rousseau and the same can be said about the absolute powers of the state. However, it is generally accepted that the origin of the idealist theory lies in the philosophy of Plato and Aristotle. Both of them regarded the state as natural and necessary self-sufficient entity identical to the whole of society. To them the state was all in all and apart from it man could not attain the highest possible perfection. According to Aristotle, "The state comes into being for the sake of mere life, it continues to exist for the good life." For both Plato and Aristotle, the state was primarily an ethical institution. It was a partnership in a life of virtue. This point of view of looking at the state from the moral point of view and approaching political theory through ethics tremendously influenced later idealist thinkers.

The second Greek influence to be found in the later Idealists was the complete identification of the state with society. That gives the state an absolute character. C.E.M. Joad writes, "Since the state is regarded as representing and containing within itself all the individual's social aspirations, and at the same time fulfilling all his social needs, whatever claims the state may make upon the individual are held to be based upon an absolute authority." So far as claims of other associations are concerned, the claims of the state override them. The Greek philosophers conceived of the state as an organic unity. For them, the state was a central social system in which the individual must find his proper place. He was an intrinsic part of the whole and had no meaning or significance by himself alone.

There was no distinction between an individual and the state. Both of them were one. Social life was to him a life of citizenship and the perfect life was the life of a citizen.

The third Greek influence was an entirely different view as to the nature both of man and society. The mere fact that man is social, it is natural for him to live in society. The life of the individual isolated from his fellows is a life against nature and the real nature of the individual can be developed only in society. C.E.M. Joad writes, "It is only by living in society that a man can realise all that he has to be, only by intercourse with his fellows, by the realisation of social duties and the fulfilment of social obligations that he can develop his full self. In addition, therefore, the obvious benefits against violence and redress against injustice that the individual receives from the state, he owes it a debt of gratitude for its bestowal upon him of his own individuality in all its richness and with all its potentialities."

These Greek truths were discovered by Rousseau who in turn influenced the German idealist thinkers. It was definitely with Rousseau that Greek political theory began to exercise a steady and continuous influence on modern political thought. It was with the help of Plato that Rousseau was successful in freeing himself from the individualist theory of Locke and expound a collectivist theory of state. In his book, *The Social Contract*, Rousseau advanced the concept of the state as a moral organism and the doctrine of the general will. He regarded the state essentially as a moral association through whose common life man reached his moral perfection and apart from which he was a stupid and limited animal. Rousseau influenced the thought of the German philosophers who in turn influenced the thought of the German idealists.

German philosophical idealism started as a reaction against the eighteenth century philosophy of Enlightenment and the Empirical tradition which the European Continent had inherited from Locke. It was Kant who laid the foundation of German Idealism, by virtually liquidating the whole philosophy of the Enlightenment. With the publication of Kant's work, the stage was set for the development of the most stimulating period of philosophic speculation.

Kant (1724-1804)

Kant is called the "father" of idealism in Germany. The free will of the individual was the core of his thought. The state was the result of a contract. Far from exalting the control of the state over the individual, he emphasized the necessary subordination of the state to the ideal of a permanent peace of Europe and advocated a federal league of nations, each subject to the adjudication of the general collective will.

The view of Kant was that men by nature are free and equal. The state represents in principle a contract by which the natural rights of each individual are placed under the guarantee of the whole people. According to him, the social contract was not a historical fact. Sovereignty resides in the people whose general will is the source of law. A just law is that to which the whole people can reasonably give assent. The adoption of a constitution represents the process by which the state is established and the general will is expressed. The functions of the state are legislative, executive and judicial. The authority of the people may be represented by elected deputies or may be represented by a king and a nobility. His ideal state is formed by voluntary agreement and its sovereignty, manifest in abstract law, was derived from the will of all. His practical state was based on force and reason and its sovereignty rested with those who had actual power. Kant denied the right of, revolution and maintained that changes in the constitution must be made in a legal way by the sovereign itself.

Kant had no idea of the corporate life of a national state. The free will of the individual was uppermost in his thought. He tried to discover the abstract principles which underlie morals, law and politics. Those he found in the right of each individual to will and to impose limitations upon himself. Kant tried to reconcile authority with perfect freedom which was essentially subjective. The individual was an end in himself. His attitude towards the state was individualistic.

The view of Kant was that the European system of a balance of power could never be the basis of lasting peace and states could never be entirely independent in their external dealings. He advocated the subordination of the state to a federal league of nations. His view was that it was the divine intention that mankind should ultimately be united in a world state. Kant believed that economic conditions would compel reasonable men to eliminate war.

Fichte (1762-1814)

Fichte agreed with Kant in his idealistic philosophy. However, he was more actively interested than Kant in the problems of practical politics. He was much influenced by the disasters of Prussia under Napoleon and the strong revival of national feeling that followed.

Fichte rejected the idea of a pre-political state of nature. His view was that the state is a natural condition of mankind. He sub-divided the social contract into three processes viz., the property contract, the protection contract and the union contract. By the property contract, men mutually agreed to limit their rights of free action in the external world of sense. By protection contract, they agreed to contribute their share of force necessary to maintain the former agreement. By the union contract,they united to form a sovereign state whose duty was to enforce the previous agreement. Beyond the protection of individual rights, the state should not interfere with the free actions of its citizens. Fichte was opposed to the idea of tree trade. The national state was an economic unit, enclosed within natural geographical boundaries. He considered ambitions and rivalries of world commerce as the chief cause of war.

Fichte believed that each nation has its peculiar contribution to make to the progress of civilisation. He did not find political consciousness among the people and he appealed to the patriotism of his countrymen and held up the ideal of German unity.

Hegel (1770-1831)

Hegel was the greatest idealist philosopher who exalted the state to the position of God. He regarded the state as "perfect rationality and an absolute fixed end in itself". The state is a moral organism. It is "the sole organiser of rights and guardian of moral values." It possesses a super personality representing the best individual wills. The state is the divine idea as it exists on earth.

Hegel rejected the idea of the origin of the state in a social contract. The state is a natural organisation. It is a whole of which the individuals and associations are parts. Those parts get their meaning and significance by their identification with and subordination to the state. Hegel viewed the state as a real person, its will as the manifestation of perfect rationality—the synthesis of universal and individual freedom. It is not a collection of individuals endowed with natural rights. "The state is not formed by a grant of certain arbitrarily selected powers from the individual but by taking unto itself the whole circle of his life. The individual, on the other hand, cannot be conceived apart from the community. He is what he is as a member of it, his whole life—physical, moral and intellectual—is drawn from it."

Hegel deified the state and called it the march of God on earth. The state was not subject to any restrictions, moral or legal. It itself was the creator of morality and law. As the embodiment of Reason, it alone determined what was good or bad, right or wrong. The law of nature was not superior to the state and was not a check on it.

The state is the realised ethical idea. It is the highest embodiment of reason, the guardian of liberty. It is the state which enables a man to enjoy his freedom by raising his outward self to his inward conception of freedom. This real freedom which is active and developing is a gift of the state and can exist only in the state. The state itself has a real personality and has a real will. It absorbs the will and personality of the individual. Individual rights emanate from the state and cannot conflict with those of the state. The state is a "self-knowing" and "self-actualising individual." The end of the state is liberty, but liberty cannot be realised without law. Hegel repudiated the notions of rights of man, popular sovereignty and Kantian internationalism. To him, liberalism represented a "simple disintegrative negation."

It is in the state that the individual, the family and civil society find their completion and security. The state represents the unity of objective and subjective freedom. The state is omnipotent, infallible and absolute. It is not a means but an end. It represents the rational ideal. It is the embodiment of reason and reflects the general will. The true freedom of the individual lies in obeying the laws of the state. The state represents the unity of individual and universal will. It represents the divine will and is divine.

Hegel denied any antagonism between the individual and the state, the latter covering the entire gamut of individual's life. The individual was an integral part of the state and found himself only through the medium of the state. The state can never act unrepresentatively. It contains within itself and represents the social morality of its citizens. The citizen must act as an integral part of the state.

According to Hegel, the sovereignty of the state resides not in the people representing an aggregate of individuals but in the state as a legal person. This personality must have an objective reality for practical purposes and the king bears the personality of the state with the sovereignty of the hereditary monarch.

Hegel believed that internationally each state was independent and had an individuality and integrity of its own. It was not subject to any external law. Neither international law nor morality could bind the state. The relationships between states were not permanent and no binding principles or regulations could govern them. There was no place for international law, international morality or international organisation (A World State).

Hegel's state is the "divine idea as it exists on earth." It has legitimate authority to completely control the lives of its citizens and that authority manifests itself in its full splendour in war-time. To quote Hegel, "The state of war shows the omnipotence of the state in its individuality: country and fatherland are then the power which convicts of nullity the independence of individuals. "Garner writes, "Thus, the state to Hegel is a God State, incapable of wrong, infallible, omnipotent and entitled to every sacrifice and devotion which it has a right to demand; it elevates and enables the individual whose tendency is to become selfish and self-centred and carries him into the life of universal substance."

The English Idealists

Political idealism in England grew up as a reaction to the prevailing doctrine of utilitarianism which rested on a set of assumptions about the nature of man, of society, of the state and its ends and functions, which the idealist thinkers systematically and severely repudiated, substituting for their static view of human nature and mechanistic conception of society, an outlook that was at once dynamic and organic. Important English Idealists were T.H. Green (1836-1882) Bradley (1846-1924) and Bosahquet (1848-1923).

T.H. Green

T.H. Green expressed the view that "will, not force, is the basis of the state." He made a distinction between real will and actual will. According to him, the state represents the real will which should prevail over the actual will. Green regarded the state as a moral entity and admitted state interference with reservation. To him, freedom does not mean "doing what one likes rather it is a positive power of doing and enjoying something worth doing or enjoying." He views liberty not only as a negative but also as a positive concept. To quote, "Just as beauty is not merely absence of ugliness but also the presence of virtues, so liberty is not only the absence of restraints but also the presence of opportunity."

Green departed from Hegel's view in many respects. He believed in international morality which was dismissed by Hegel. According to him, the power of the state was limited within and without the country and the life of a nation has no real existence except as the life of the individuals composing the state. War is the attribute of an imperfect state and can at the most be relatively right and never absolutely right. The state is the product of human reason. Human consciousness postulates liberty, liberty involves rights and rights demand the state. The state is meant to create those opportunities which are so necessary to the full moral development of individuals. The sovereign power which maintains rights, is not based on mere force. Green's General Will is very much different from Hegel's general will. He calls it "the common consciousness of common good", a sense of possessing common interest and a desire for common interest on the part of the people. The general will of Green is the will for the state, not the will of the state.

According to Green, rights are the outer conditions necessary for the inner development of man. The supreme right of every rational person is the right to become what a man should be. Natural rights help a man to become a moral and ideal human being dedicated to himself and the society of which he is a member.

Green believed that without the state man is not man at all. It is only in the state that he can fully express himself and his nature can develop to its fully capacity. He must look to the state not as a necessary evil which is the result of his viciousness, but as a natural and ethical necessity which is the result of his own inherent virtue. The political life of man "is a revelation of the Divine Idea". Green admitted the majesty and might of the state. According to him, rights exist because of society. Every right is derived from some social relation. Though the state does not create rights, it may still be true to say that the members of the state derive their rights from the state. Green concedes the right of resistance to the authority of the state but he makes the path of resistance so difficult that ultimately it may be considered a denial of the right. He emphasized the fact that resistance can never be justified merely because legislation runs against personal inclination. He warns the people that in resisting the authority of the state, they must not forget that they will probably be wrong and the state almost certainly right. The reason being that "the state will be speaking with wisdom of ages and man". He warns the resisters that they must not forget that resistance may lead to disastrous results. He commands them to put up with the undesired laws until they are repealed by constitutional means. Where the constitutional government does not exist, man should feel justified to resist the authority of the state when certain conditions obtain. It still requires serious thought and consideration before it is resorted to. Green says, "We must not sacrifice what is almost the whole for the sake of a part; we must not risk social chaos and the disturbance of the existing system of rights for the sake of adding a new element to the system."

Green was also concerned with the problem of freedom. According to him, freedom does not consist in being left alone to do what one likes. It all depends on what one likes to do. Man is free only when he is following his true good and his true good is also social good because individual good can only be achieved when the good of others is also realised. Freedom is a positive power or capacity of doing or enjoying something worth doing or enjoying. Freedom is positive and consists in doing something worth doing. Freedom of Green was not unlimited.

Green never regarded the state as an end in itself. It is a means to an end which is the full moral development of the individuals who compose the state.

Green does not make the state absolute and omnipotent. It is limited, both from within and without. The state and its laws deal only with the external actions of man. They have nothing to do with his intentions and motives. The state cannot make man moral. It can merely remove the obstacles which prevent man from becoming moral. According to Green, morality consists in "the disinterested performance of self-imposed duties." The functions of the state are negative and not positive. Green talks as an individualist but he is not completely an individualist. The reason is that in order to remove obstacles, the functions of the state become positive in content. Green asked the state to scc that mental and physical malnutrition are moved. It should make education compulsory, do away with the chances of intemperance by checking the growth of liquor shops and forbidding reckless beggary by providing certain pursuits which people may take up. To quote Green, "To uphold the sanctity of contract is doubtless a prime business of government, but it is no less its business to provide against contracts being made which from the helplessness of one of the parties to them, instead of being security for freedom, become an instrument of disguised oppression." Green justified the existence of capital, but he was against the continuance of the institution of landed property. He stood for the happiness of man so that every one could contribute something to the common good and to attain both, he justifies the intervention of the state. The view of Green is that punishment for those who violate laws should be proportionate and reformatory in order to create conditions which make moral life possible.

The state of Green is a community of communities and its supremacy over all is unquestioned. He resembled Hegel in that respect, but he also differs from him. The view of Green is that associations are important because they existed even prior to the state and they have their own system of rights. The state must be supreme over them because it must coordinate and adjust them. It must also preserve them. Wayper writes, "Thus, while for Hegel if associations do not result in the state, they arc not true associations; for Green if the state does not preserve associations, it is no true state. In both Hegel and Green, the fact of the state's supremacy is unquestioned. But in the one the exercise of the supremacy of the state is unlimited because of its own nature and the nature of associations. In the other, the exercise of the state's supremacy is limited by its own nature and the nature of associations."

Unlike Hegel, but like Kant, Green believes in the universal brotherhood of man. An international code is the obvious extension of the ethical system accepted within the state. Green condemned war as it violates the right of man to a free life. It may be justified only as "cruel necessity". Green is more near Kant than Hegel. In his views on individual freedom, war and international morality, Green is more Kantian than Hegelian. According to Green, the state is neither absolute nor omnipotent. Green emphasized the moral value of the majesty of the state.

Bradley (1846-1924)

According to Bradley, it is the duty of every individual to perform those duties which his station in life expects him to perform. If he does so, he obeys the law of his being. Man is an absolute being and he cannot live alone. As a man is a member of a community, the latter exerts its influence on him from every direction. The very atmosphere which he breathes is social. He is what he is by including in its essence the relations of the social state and if morality consists in the fulfilment of his relations, it consists in the fulfilment of those relations.

According to Bradley, the child is not merely the member of a family. He is born as a member of the English nation. The state is "a system of wholes". It includes all communities which have any bearing on man. It is a moral organism, a systematic whole, informed by a common purpose or function. Every part of the state organism has a spirit and consciousness of its own. However, state organism differs from an animal organism. State organism has life and continuity of its own. Individuals live their full lives only so far as they qualify in their special fields.

Bradley admitted that no state in actual practice was a perfect embodiment of his ideal. The morality of the state was always on a lower plane than the conscience of the people of ideal morality. Individuals may aspire to rise above their limitations and that may lead to the realisation of "all humanity as a divine organic whole."

Dr. Bosanquet (1848-1923)

Bonsanquet was a strong defender of the theory of the general will. He started with the concept of free moral will as expounded by Rousseau. He adopted the Hegelian view of the state as the sublimation of all virtue and authority. "State may legitimately do whatever is required for the preservation and improvement of the organised life of the community and is the sole judge of what is so required."

According to Bosanquet, "By the state, then, we mean society as a unit recognised as rightly exercising control over its members through absolute physical power." The state as a political organisation using force, is the narrow sense in which Bosanquet defines the state. His state is the supreme community, the guardian of morality and the supreme ethical institution. It is synonymous with society and represents the synthesis of life. To quote him, "The national state is the widest organisation which by common experience is necessary to found a common life." The state promotes common life which is a moral life and what it directs is always moral.

Bosanquet is near to Green regarding the nature and sphere of state action. Both believed that the state is an ethical institution. Both agreed that the state cannot be used directly to promote morality. To quote Bosanquet, "Art, philosophy and religion, though in a sense the very life-blood of society, are not and could not be directly fashioned to meet the needs and uses of the multitude and their aim is not in that sense social." Again, "It (the state) has no determinate function in a larger community, but is itself the supreme community; the guardian of a whole moral world, but not a factor within an organised moral world. Moral relations presuppose an organised life; but such a life is only within the state, not in relation between the state and other communities." The immoral acts of an agent of the state cannot be ascribed to the state. But the distinction between the acts of the state and the acts of its agents is unreal. Government is the agency of the state. The state is abstract while the government is concrete and a reality. The acts of the government are really the acts of the state. Barker writes, "If a citizen can treat his own state as legally responsible for damages, it is difficult to see why a state which can undergo legal responsibility should not also undergo moral responsibility, if there is any body of moral opinion to affix responsibility." Bosanquet does not permit the individual the right of rebellion against the authority of the state.

Basic Tenets of Idealist Theory

There are certain basic tenets of the idealist theory. The idealist political philosophers regard the state as a moral institution which represents social morality. Individuals should always obey the state. The state is the embodiment of the universal mind or world spirit. It is the sole organiser of rights and guardian of moral values.

According to Hegel, the state represents "perfected rationality". It is the embodiment of reason. To him rational is real. What is rational is actual and what is actual is rational. The state is a moral institution and is exalted to the position of God. It is the incarnation of universal reason.

The idealist state is absolute. It cannot be challenged. It is omnipotent and omnicompetent. It is the duty of the individuals to obey the state.

The idealists regard the state as an end in itself. It has a will of its own which is superior to the wills of the individuals. It has a personality and the development of the individual personality can take place only through the personality of the state. It is only through the state that the real personality of the individual can express itself. There can be no conflict of interests between the interests of the state and those of individuals.

The idealist philosophers believe in the organic nature of the state. They regard the state as an organism or an ethical whole. Individuals are parts of the state organism and they can realise their best selves only by merging themselves with the state. The state is a whole which is far greater than the parts which compose it.

The idealists regard the state as a vehicle of all individual development and progress. Apart from society, the individual has neither meaning nor significance. He has no natural rights. The state is the creator, maintainer and guarantor of the real personality of the individual. It guarantees rights by creating conditions for the full moral development of the personality of the individual. The freedom enjoyed by men as members of society is more real and positive than what they give up while entering society. Freedom is active and ever-developing. It manifests itself first in law, secondly in the rule of inward morality and thirdly in the whole system of social institutions and influences that make for the development of personality.

The individual and the state are not opposed to each other. The main objective of the state is the fullest and freest development of human personality. An individual can have no real rights which conflict with those of the state. His real rights are not those which he has brought with him from some hypothetical pre-social state of nature. The individual receives all his rights from the state. Therefore, he has only obligations towards the state. The individual depends upon the state or society for all his rights, including liberty. Barker writes, "Instead of starting from a central individual to whom the social system is supposed to be adjusted, the idealists start from a central social system in which the individual must find his appointed orbit of duty".

According to the idealists, the state has its own life, personality and will which is different from and transcends the lives, personalities and wills of its citizens. It represents the wills of all its citizens. It is in the General Will and in the personality of the state that the will and personality of each individual are made to transcend themselves. The general will is always for the good of all. It is always rational and right.

The basis of the state is will and not force. The state no doubt makes use of force but that is not its primary or essential quality. It is the embodiment of will. We obey the state because of the consciousness that it makes possible that system of rights and conditions of well-being which enable citizens to realise their true and rational selves. By obeying the state, we advance a common good of which individual good is an intrinsic part. Submission to law is not based on the fear of punishment or the blind following of customs. It is based on the consciousness of a common end.

According to idealists, law is the expression of passionless reason and not merely the command of a human sovereign. The idealists attempt to reconcile individual liberty with obedience to the laws of the state. There is complete identification between liberty and law. Real liberty can be attained only in and through obedience to law.

Bosanquet writes, "The state is the guardian of the whole moral world and not a factor within an organised moral world." The state is society recognised as a unit which exercises control over its members through absolute physical power.

According to Treitschke, the state is power and it is our duty to fall down and worship it. The state must be self-assertive, aggressive and militaristic. The progress of man is due to state. Man is helpless without the help of the state.

The idealist concept of liberty is not negative but positive. Just as beauty is not merely the absence of ugliness but also the presence of virtue, so liberty is not only the absence of restraint but also the presence of opportunities. Liberty is determinate. It involves the right to do those things which are for the good of the doer and society. Bradley says, "Human liberty consists in discharging the obligation of one's status in society and finding one's place in social life." As laws are the product of rational will, liberty of an individual lies in his obedience to the laws of the state.

The authority of the state is ultimately to be found in the common consciousness of a common end. We obey the state because there is a rational conviction that it makes possible that system of rights and conditions of well-being which enable citizens to realise their true and rational selves. Loyalty to the state is loyalty to our truer, higher and rational self. Submission to law is not based on the fear of punishment or the blind following of custom. It is based on the consciousness of a common end. Coercion may be essential for the existence of the state but it is not a creative sustaining factor. Force can vindicate rights, but cannot create them.

According to T.H. Green, "Human consciousness postulates liberty, liberty involves rights and rights demand the state." Real liberty is possible only through complete obedience to law. Obedience to the state is spiritual.

According to C.E.M. Joad,the three prominent characteristics of idealism are: (*a*) complete identification of law and liberty, (*b*) an organic conception of society and (*c*) the state as representation of social morality and social ethics.

Criticism of Idealist Theory

The idealist theory has been severely criticised by many writers on various grounds. Will, as the basis of the state, is criticised from the point of view of social psychology. However, it is contended that we have either individual wills or no wills at all. Hobson writes, "The concept of general will can also become the tactics of conservatism even in an undemocratic state. So long as there is no open rebellion, government can claim to be based on the implied consent of the people." MacIver observes, "General will is as much the will of the state as the will for the state, *i.e.*, will to maintain it."

The abstract and metaphysical nature of idealist philosophy is also criticised. It is not correct to say that "what is real is rational and what is rational is real." The fact is that what is real may not be rational and what is rational may not be real. The state of affairs in Russia before the Revolution of 1917 was real but not rational. Likewise, it may not be possible to realise in actual practice what is otherwise considered to be rational. The result is that the ideal state "may be laid up in heaven but is not established on earth".

The idealists refer to the omnipotence of the state. It is contended that there are no limits to the exercise of powers by the state. Such a view is neither practical nor desirable. The state acts through law which can regulate only the external actions of individuals and no state can exercise unlimited power in actual practice. Moreover, it is not desirable to give unlimited powers to the state. The exercise of unlimited power is bound to create unhappy conditions and make the executive tyrannical and arbitrary. That can hardly be in the interests of the people. In the long run, the exercise of unlimited power is bound to destroy those who exercise it.

The idealists contend that the state is infallible, but it is difficult to understand how the actions of a state can be infallible. Undoubtedly, the state acts through human-beings and to err is human. It is inconceivable that as soon as an individual enters government service, he becomes God and his actions can never be wrong.

The idealists make the state an end in itself and not a means to an end. If this view is accepted, individuals are likely to be sacrificed at the altar of the state. They will exist for the state and not vice versa. That is like putting the cart before the horse. The machinery of the state must exist for the good of the people and its worth should be judged from the way the machinery works. It is not correct that the state has a mind and will of its own which is different from that of the people who live within the state. The real will is the will of individuals. The state as such has no personality and cannot be an end in itself. It is merely a means to an end which is the happiness and welfare of individuals.

According to the idealists, the sphere of the state is identical with that of society and as much, the state has the same authority as society itself. This view is fallacious. "It is true that the state is at present necessary to society, but it is one of its conditions. The bony skeleton is necessary to the human body and in a sense holds it together, but it is hardly that which constitutes the life of the body, still less that which makes the life of the body desirable and beautiful." Again, "Much of the organisation of life is more extensive than any organised state, and many social divisions cut across state divisions, *e.g.*, the Church is a cosmopolitan and not a national organisation. Similarly, economic organisations may be world-wide, *e.g.*, the Socialists' International." While it is admitted that the authority of the state is necessary for the existence of society, it does not mean that the state is to be identified with society. Undoubtedly, the sphere of the state is circumscribed as compared with that of society. The state is concerned with our political actions, while society is concerned with the whole of the life of man. It is not only undesirable but also dangerous to equate society with state.

The idealist concept of liberty is erroneous. It is not correct to say that man is free when he obeys the state. As a matter of fact, man should be considered free only when he obeys his own conscience and not when he obeys an order of the state even when that is opposed to his own view. One fails to understand how the real will of an individual is actually merged into the will of the state. As a matter of fact, the state has no will of its own which is different from the wills of the people. It seems paradoxical that an individual can be made free even against his own will. It is ridiculous to maintain that even when a person is being taken to jail, he is being made free because his own real will is merged in the will of the state. Such a view is the very negation of liberty and no democrat will accept it.

The idealists do not make any distinction between political and moral obligations. According to Hobson, this is the central fallacy of idealist philosophy. It is not correct to say that what is legal is moral or what is moral is legal. To drive without light after sunset is illegal because it is against municipal law or traffic law, but it cannot be said that it is immoral. If we convert all legal obligations into moral obligations, life will not be worth living. The state will convert itself into a tyrant. There will be no place for the conscientious objector who believes that all war is a sin. Likewise, there will be no scope for differing from the authority of the state.

The idealists maintain that the actions of the state are not to be judged by the same standards of morality by which the actions of individuals are judged. If we accept such a view, there will be no place for individuals. There will always be a temptation for foresment servants to do something which is manifestly absurd and immoral. That would be tantamount to giving the state licence.

The idealist concept of the state hardly leaves any scope for an international order or international law. The idealist view is that it is the duty of individuals to obey their state alone. Beyond the state, there is a vacuum. Individuals cannot owe allegiance to any authority which is other than their own state. The state becomes absolutely self-sufficient. According to Bosanquet, "The state is the guardian of the whole moral world and not a factor within an organised moral world." Such a view is reactionary and retrograde. Instead of taking humanity a few steps forward, the idealists take it back by a few centuries. The world has become one or is becoming one and it is no use contending that beyond the frontiers of a state, there exists nothing. If we are idealists, we have to admit the existence of a world order and adjust the authority of the state against the background of world order.

The idealists refer to unity of the state, but that unity is a fiction. It does not exist in actual practice. Just as a groove of trees is not a tree, a flock of sheep is not a sheep, likewise an assemblage of individuals is not an individual. The unity of the state is merely imaginary and not based on facts. In every state, the number of groups or associations which clamour for recognition and which definitely render useful service to society is multiplying and consequently the unity of the state is also breaking up. We no longer believe in the monistic theory of the state. The pluralistic conception of the state is gaining ground and with that the unity of the state is also disappearing.

It is not possible to agree with Hegel that the state is the march of God on earth and to obey the state is to obey God and to disobey the state is to disobey God. It is too much to give to the state the status of God. Hobhouse writes, "The government, law and other political institutions are far from being the most successful of the experiments of mankind. They call aloud for criticism and to deify them is to establish fake Gods, Gods who at the present time figure as veritable Moloch before whom our sons are made to pass in millions through the fire." Again, "When we think of the actual inconsistencies of social morality, the blindness and rudity of law, the elements of class selfishness and oppression that have coloured it, mechanical dullness of state institutions given at their best, the massive misery that has lain at the foundation of all historical civilization, we deify the state."

Hobhouse has given his detailed criticism of the idealist theory of the state in his book "*Metaphysical Theory of the State*" published in 1918. According to him, the idealist theory is "a much more subtle and dangerous enemy to the ideal than any brute denial of absolutism emanating from a one-sided science." Hegel's "false and wicked doctrine of the God-state furnishes the basis of the most serious oppression to the rational democratic humanitarianism of the nineteenth century." "The Hegelian conception was designed to turn the edge of the principle of freedom by identifying freedom with law; of equality, by substituting the conception of discipline; of personality itself, by merging the individual in the state; of humanity, by erecting the state as the supreme and final form of human association. It set up the state as the greater being, a spirit, a super-personal entity in which individuals with their private conscience and claims of rights, the happiness or their misery, are merely subordinate elements." The doctrine that the individual has no freedom unless it is "in conformity with law and custom as interpreted by the ethical spirit of the particular society to which the individual belongs", is the negation of freedom. Hobhouse further adds, "When we are taught to think of the world which we know as a good world, to think of its justices, wrongs and miseries as necessary elements in a perfect ideal, then if we accept these arguments, power of revolt is atrophied, our reasoning is hypnotized, our efforts to improve life and remedy wrong fade away into a passive acquiescence in things as they are; or, still worse, into a slavish adulation of the Absolute in whose hands we are mere pawns." He concludes, "The state is a great organisation. Its well-being is something of larger and more permanent import than that of any single citizen. Its scope is vast. Its service calls for the extreme of loyalty and self-sacrifice. All this is true. Yet when the state is set up as an entity superior and indifferent to component individuals, it becomes a false God, and its worship the abomination of dissolution, as seen at Ypres or on the Somme."

The idealist theory is denounced as unsound in theory, untrue to facts and liable to extend a dangerous sanction to the more unscrupulous actions of the existing states in the sphere of foreign policy. Even if the claim of the state to complete omnipotence in respect of its own citizens be admitted, this claim can only be sustained on the assumption that the state represents and transcends in its own will the wills of all the individuals who compose it. There is no suggestion that the state represents the wills of citizens belonging to other states and hence it is omnipotent in respect of them. As the claim to omnipotence is used to justify the further claim to exemption from moral obligations, the exemption does not in any event extend to the relations between the state and other states. The state in its relationship with other states is assuredly not "the guardian of a whole world" and is "a factor within an organised moral world." The state has no justification for non-moral action in its dealings with other states.

C.E.M. Joad points out that the state exists for individuals and not vice versa. Liberty has meaning only for the individual and the welfare of society and the state has neither meaning nor value unless it carries with it the welfare of the individuals who compose the state. Any theory of the stale which admits the possibility that the welfare of the state may be achieved apart from oral the expense of the happiness of individuals and justifies its admission on the ground that the personality of the state contains and transcends that of the individual is like putting the cart before the horse. It is not correct to say that it is not possible for the state to promote its welfare at the expense of that of the individual or even to tyrannise over the individual since the welfare of the state is that of the individual and the will of the state is the will of individuals who are the victims of tyranny. A decision does not become my personal decision because it is carried against my will and vote by an association of which I am a member. By the mere fact of living together in a state, men do not cause a social miracle to take place by which their will is transformed into its direct opposite. There is no substance in a distinction between a real will and the so-called unreal will, the alleged real will being defined as a will to carry out every decision of the majority of an association to which I belong. The attribution of a real will to the individual which is necessarily and always in accord with the general will in which it is merged, is only a device for giving an appearance of justice and democracy to what must otherwise appear the purely arbitrary and tyrannical act of a sovereign state. The idealist theory of the state is in fact inimical to individual freedom because whenever a conflict occurs between the individual and the state, it takes the view that the latter must inevitably be right.

There has been an enormous growth of associations of individuals for economic and ethical purposes in recent times. The growth of economic associations has substituted economic bonds based on community of interest in money-making for the old national bonds based on the chances of birth. This change foreshadows the possibility of an organisation of society based on economic affinities as an alternative to the existing territorial division. On account of the growth of associations for ethical purposes, people are substituting a private morality of their own for the conventional morality prescribed by the state and to question on moral grounds any attempt on the part of the state to interfere with the pursuit of good life as they conceive it. Mere outward observance of state law does not demand a high degree of morality and a law-making citizen is frequently an immoral man.

Joad points out that the idealist theory ignores certain important facts when it asserts that the state will undoubtedly "when need arises of which it, through constitutional methods, is the sole judge, prohibit and prevent the expression in external acts of any loyalty but that to the community which it represents." In particular, it ignores the fact that economic and ethical associations now embrace all that is most intimate in the life of an individual, every activity that fills his pocket or enriches his soul is now carried out in associations not co-terminous with the state and those associations simply and in fact create a stratification of society different from and opposed to the state division based on geographical boundaries. A political philosophy which endeavours to embrace within its scope the existence of associations other than the state, to estimate the bearing of these associations upon the state, to strike a balance between their conflicting claims and to apportion their respective functions is more in accord with the facts of society then the idealist tendency to contemplate the state as an isolated and self-sufficient entity.

The idealist theory has done great harm to individuals. It has paved the way for the rise of dictatorship. The glorification of the state and the ascription of superior morality and super personality to the state, have proved to be "the most serious opposition to the rational democratic humanitarianism of the nineteenth century." When we are taught to think of the world which we know as a good world, to think of its injustices, wrongs and miseries as necessary elements in a perfect ideal, then, if we accept these arguments, our power of revolt is atrophied, our reason is hypnotised, our efforts to improve life and remedy wrong fade away into a passive acquiescence in things as they are; or still worse, into a slavish adulation of the Absolute in whose hands we are mere pawns."

The idealist characterization of the state as the final form of human organisation goes against the actual evolutionary process. The state is a product of evolution. The integration of families led to the emergence of the clan, further integration produced the tribes and still further integration led to the state. That process is continuing. The modern tendency is towards the establishment of a world state but the idealists consider the state as the final form of human organisation.

Hegelian idealism strengthened the hands of ruthless dictators like Hitler in the twentieth century. He could easily justify his acts of aggression in the name of the world spirit. Extreme idealism glorifies war and considers it as an act of virtue. Even Bosanquet says that the state cannot be criticised on moral grounds.

The idealist theory is an attempt to adapt the classical Greek view of the social nature of man to modern conditions. The Greek ideal was the city state where each individual knew others well. In such a society, the idea of the general will or common good might be materialised, but it is not possible in a vast modern state which is mostly governed by a large number of representatives.

Value of the Idealist Theory

It is true that the idealist theory suffers from many defects, but many of them have been exaggerated or are the result of misconception. Garner writes, "It may be said of much of the criticism which has been directed against the idealistic theory that it is unfair, exaggerated and based upon a misconception of the theory itself. In so far as the idealists exalted the state above all other human associations, regarded it as indispensable to the realisation of the good life and held that, as such, it is entitled to the loyalty of the citizen and may demand sacrifices of him to preserve its existence, that it is the sole source of law and of rights and that in it alone is the individual capable of realising fully the ends of his existence and that without it human progress and civilisation would be impossible, the theory is entirely sound and irreproachable."

By putting emphasis on the importance of the state, the idealists performed a very useful purpose. They subordinated the individual to the authority of the state and made it possible for the Germans to forge their unity. Without the philosophy of Hegel, the unification of Germany would have been a difficult, if not impossible, task. The idealist philosophy, particularly in Germany, was the philosophy of abnormal times and no wonder the individual was sacrificed at the altar of the state. However, it is not desirable to give too much authority to the state. Barker writes, "That philosophy could satisfy the new needs of social progress because it refused to worship a supposed individual liberty which was proving destructive of the real liberty of the vast majority and preferred to emphasize the moral well-being and betterment of the whole community, and to conceive of each of its members as attaining his own well-being and betterment in and through the community".

The idealists rendered a great service by establishing an intimate relationship between politics and ethics. They considered the state as an ethical entity. Man enjoys rights and freedom as a member of society. The state enables man to develop his personality provided it keeps itself within bounds and does not go on interfering with the lives of individuals.

The idealists fixed high ideals and even if they could not be reached, it is proper to have ideals towards which individuals and society can move. The idealists also gave a high place to mind and will. The doctrine of general will contains an element of truth. The idealist theory did great service to political thought by insisting on the organic unity of the state and showing how society is held together by the state. The idealist theory was a welcome reaction against the "pig-trough" philosophy of utilitarianism. The highest values are moral, cultural and spiritual and not material.

SUGGESTED READINGS

Barker, E. : Political Thought in England, 1848-1914.

Bosanquet : The Philosophical Theory of the State, London, 1920.

Brinton. C. : English Political Thought in the Nineteenth Century, London, 1933.

Brown, Ivor : English Political Theory.

Chin, Y.L. : The Political Theory of T.H. Green, 1920.

Coker, F.W. : Recent Political Thought.

Dewey, John : German Philosophy and Politics, 1915.

Dunning, W.A. : A History of Political Theories from Rousseau to Spencer.

Foster, M.B. : The Political Philosophy of Plato and Hegel, 1935.

Friedrich, K.J. ; Philosophy of Kant.

Garner, J.W. : Political Science and Government.

Gettell, R.G. : History of Political Thought, Delhi, 1981.

Green, T.H. : Principles of Political Obligation.

Hallowell, J.H. : Main Currents in Modern Political Thought.

Hobhouse, L.T. : Metaphysical Theory of the State, London, 1918.

Hoernle, R.F.A. : Idealism as a Philosophy, 1927.

Joad, C.E.M. : Modern Political Theory.

Joad, C.E.M. : Guide to the Philosophy of Morals and Politics.

Jones, Henry : Idealism as a Practical Creed.

Laski, H.J. : The State in Theory and Practice.

Lindsay, A.D. : Kant, London, 1934.

MacCunn, J. : Six Radical Thinkers, 1907.

McGovern, T.M. : From Luther to Hitler, Boston, 1941.

Sabine, G.H. : A History of Political Theory.

Vaughan : Studies in the History of Political Thought.

Wayper, C.L. : Political Thought.

Wilde, Norman : The Ethical Basis of the State, 1924.

CHAPTER

Socialism

Difficulties of defining Socialism

William Ebenstein rightly says that it is not easy to state when and where socialism first appeared. Some hold the view that socialism originated in the Republic of Plato as its ruling class had no property of its own and shared all things in common. Some trace its origin to the Bible, particularly the Old Testament. Some link socialism with the early Christians who rejected the concept of "Mine and Thine" and practised socialism in their everyday lives. During the Middle Ages, various sects and movements attacked wealth and commerce considering them to be wicked. During the Renaissance and the Reformation, there was a revival of protest against inequality based on wealth. The conclusion of Ebenstein is that "despite all such illustrations, socialism as a major political force can properly be said to have originated as a result of industrial capitalism."

It is difficult to define socialism and Prof. C.E.M. Joad in his Introduction to Modern Political Theory gives three reasons or three difficulties. The first difficulty is due to the fact that the word socialism is used to denote both a body of doctrines and a political movement. The second reason is that the body of doctrines which may roughly be called socialism, is by no means, wholly or even mainly, political. To a large extent, it is economic and economic and political theories are so closely interwoven that it is not practicable or desirable to confine our description solely to the political aspects of socialism. The third difficulty is that the Socialists are a divided house. They are divided into a number of opposing schools which are separated by acute differences both as regards their aims and methods. Due to such a wide range of disagreements with regard to the account of socialism, Joad observes, "More perhaps than other theory, socialism proves to be a different creed in the hands of each of its exponents, varying with the temperaments of its advocates and the nature of the abuses which have prompted their advocacy.

Learning Objectives

- Difficulties of defining Socialism
- Definition of Socialism
- Essentials of Socialism
- Criticism of Socialism
- Merits of Socialism
- Evolutionary and Revolutionary Socialism
- Evolutionary Socialism
- Criticism of Evolutionary Socialism
- Utopian Socialism
- Collectivism or State Socialism
- Criticism of State Socialism
- Democratic Socialism
- Its Origin
- Basic Principles of Democratic Socialism
- Methods of Democratic Socialism
- Merits of Democratic Socialism
- Defects
- Fabianism
- Its Essentials
- Methods of Fabian Socialists
- Assessment of Fabianism
- Syndicalism
- Origin and Growth of Syndicalism
- Exponents of Syndicalism
- Main Features of Syndicalism
- Criticism of Syndicalism

As the advocates of socialism are very numerous and many of them have been first-rate political pamphleteers, the literature of the subject is enormous, with the result that it is hard to say in what exactly it is that socialism consists. *Socialism, in short, is like a hat that has lost its shape because everybody wears it".*

Dr. Schadwell writes, "Socialism is the most complicated, many-sided and confused question that ever plagued the minds of men." Ramsay Muir says: "Socialism is a chameleon-like creed. It changes its colour according to its environment. For the street corner and the club room, it wears the flaming scarlet of class war; for the intellectuals it is red shot with tawny; for the sentimentalists, it becomes a delicate rose pink, and in clerical circles it assumes a virgin-white, just touched with a faint flush of generous aspiration."

Rappoport refers to the difficulty of defining socialism in these words: "If I am asked whether I am a socialist myself, I cannot but frankly reply: I do not know. It all depends upon what one understands by socialism.

"There are many mansions in the house of socialism. I have quoted about forty different definitions of socialism without being able to pretend that my list is exhaustive. Now, if socialism means justice, equality, real democracy, love of humanity, altruism, tolerance and individual liberty, high moral ideals, peace and goodwill, then I venture to say that I am a socialist. If, on the contrary, socialism stands for the crushing of individual liberty, for despotism, tyranny, oppression and destruction, then I am an opponent of socialism. If the real aim of socialism is 'to alter the too great inequality of wealth existing among men, to introduce an equilibrium by taking away from those who have too much without having worked for it, and giving it to those who have too little, in spite of hard work, then I must admit that I am a socialist at heart'. If, however, socialists are inspired by a spirit of plunder, intent upon picking the pockets of some who have worked hard and filling those of others who have done no work, then I am not a socialist. If socialism means the end of oppression and exploitation of man by man, 'the transformation of society in the sense of justice and equality', the abolition of regime of persecutions, massacres and fratricidal wars, in a word, if it is idealistic and means progress, then I am proud to be counted among the soldiers of the vast army of socialism. But if the aim of socialism is the introduction of class-war, the destruction of the possessing classes, and establishment of dictatorships, in any shape or form; if it is materialistic, atheistic and militant, ignoring the terms of right and justice, morality and ethics, then I am certainly not socialist. If the methods of socialism are persuasion and not force, if its ethics are the basis of peace, appealing to all that is best and noblest in man with a view to introducing an era of peace, justice and equality, then I am happy to be a socialist. If, however, the ethics of socialism are the ethics of war, if its methods consist in sending the bird of prey to hatch the egg of liberty with a view to producing the dove of peace, then I deprecate such methods. Justice, equality, a more equitable distribution of social wealth, abolition of inequalities, exploitation and misery, are ideals which I highly appreciate and cherish, but destruction, violence and dictatorships I abhor."

Definition of Socialism

In spite of the difficulties mentioned above, we give some important and popular definitions of socialism. According to the Encyclopaedia Britannica, "Socialism is that policy or theory which aims at securing by the action of democratic authority a better distribution and in due subordination thereto, a better production of wealth than now prevails". Socialism is defined in A Dictionary of Politics as "a political and economic theory according to which the means of production, distribution and exchange should be owned and controlled by the people. Everyone should be given an equal opportunity to develop his talents and the wealth of the community should be fairly distributed." Sellars defines socialism as "a democratic movement whose purpose is the securing of an economic organisation of society which will give the maximum at one time of justice and liberty."

According to Hughan, socialism is "the political movement of the working classes which aims to abolish exploitation by means of the collective ownership and democratic government of the basic instruments of production and distribution." Harold Laski writes, "Socialism implies such a control of the production and distribution of wealth as will enable the average citizen to have access to the resources, material and spiritual, which enable him, at least potentially to be himself at his best." According to Paul Janet, "We call socialism every doctrine which teaches that the state has a right to correct inequality of wealth which exists among men and legally establish the balance by taking from those who have too much in order to give to those who have not enough, and that in a permanent manner, and not in such and such in a particular case—a famine, for instance a public calamity etc."

Hubert Bland observes, "Socialism is the common holding of the means of production and exchange and the holding of them for the benefit of all." According to Bernard Shaw, "Socialism means equality of income and nothing else." G.D.H. Cole says, "Socialism means four closely connected things—a human fellowship which denies and expels distinctions of class social system in which no one is so much richer or poorer than his neighbours as to be unable to mix with him on equal terms, the common ownership and use of all the vital instruments of production and an obligation upon all citizens to serve one another according to their capacities." The view of Schaffle is that "the Alpha and Omega of socialism is the transformation of private and competing capitals into united collective capital." Prof. Ely says, "A socialist is one who looks to society organised in the state for aid in bringing about a more perfect distribution of economic goods and an elevation of humanity; the individualist regards each man, not as his brother's keeper, but as his own, and desires every man to work out his own salvation, material and spiritual."

According to Jayaprakash Narayan, socialism means "a classless society in which all are workers. It is a society in which human labour is not subject to exploitation with interest of private property, in which all wealth is truly national of commonwealth, in which there is no unearned income and no large income disparities, in which human life and progress are planned and where all live for all."

Essentials of Socialism

In spite of the numerous definitions of socialism and its various brands, there are certain essentials of socialism which are common to all forms, (*i*) *Socialism puts more emphasis on society than on individuals.* It subordinates individual interests to the higher interests of the society as a whole. According to Purcell, "Socialism is a state of society in which the administration of industry will be regarded solely from the point of view of the common good. Industrial development and the application of scientific processes will be encouraged to the advantage of the whole community." Adolf Held writes, "We may define as socialistic every tendency which demands the subordination of the individual's will to the community". Fred Bramley observes, "Socialism implies the subordination of the interests of the individual to the interests of the society." Roscher says, "Socialism stands for those tendencies which demand a greater regard for the common weal than agrees with human nature." "We are all socialists now." This statement emphasizes the fact that there is an increasing tendency to put emphasis on society and not individuals as was the case during the nineteenth century.

(2) Socialism aims at the *elimination of capitalism.* The capitalists and entrepreneurs are considered to be the natural enemies of the working class. As the state is the guardian of the masses and the repository of the interests of all, it must protect the people from the tyranny of capitalism and that can be done only by destroying it root and branch. Under the capitalist system of production, there is competition for the sake of profits alone. That is both unhealthy and anti-social. That also results in over-production. Sometimes the prices are fixed very low with a view to drive out small producers. A lot of money is spent on the advertisement of goods. Under socialism, this type of wastage resulting from competition would be ended. There will be no monopolies such as cartels, trusts and corporations which indulge in unhealthy competition.

(3) Socialism is *opposed to capitalism* which is based on the principle of profit-making and not increased production for the sake of common good. Capitalism leads to unequal distribution of wealth among the different classes. The rich grow richer and the poor become poorer. Socialism aims at the abolition of capitalism. It wants production to be carried on in accordance with the needs of the society and the distribution to be carried on in accordance with the principles of social justice.

(4) Socialism stands for the *elimination of competition* which involves too much of economic waste. Moreover, there is no fair competition between the rich and the poor on account of the existing economic inequality. The labourer must accept the wages offered because if he does not do so, he is bound to starve. It is the danger of starvation which forces him to accept whatever is offered to him by the capitalist. No wonder, the socialists stand for cooperation instead of competition. Dr. Haden Guest writes, "Socialism is, to my mind, the substitution of cooperation for competition in local, national and international affairs." Competition is antisocial. It encourages people to resort to unfair and dishonest means in order lo come out victorious in the race of competition. Competition also results in the formation of monopolies and the lowering of the standard of individual character. It also results in over-production for private gain.

(5) Socialism *stands for equality.* The socialists condemn the existing inequality created by the present capitalist system. Laveleye writes, "Every socialistic doctrine aims at introducing greater equality into social conditions. Socialism is an equaliser and leveller." Woolsey says, "If you go to the bottom of things, the strength of socialism which takes hold of the great mass of the party is not argument but the demand for equality." According to M. Tugan Baranowsky, "The ideal of equality of man must be recognised as the fundamental ethical tenet of modern socialism." G.D.H. Cole has given a good account of the socialistic style of equality. According to him, equality means that "society ought to afford to all its members, irrespective of their virtues or vices, their strength or weakness, a tolerable basic standard of living, high enough to keep them in health and reasonable comfort and to enable them to bring up their children after a fashion that will allow them, in their turn, as far as possible, an equal chance of making the best of their lives." There cannot be strict uniformity of either thought or treatment or conduct in a socialist society.

(6) Socialism stands for the *elimination of private property in land.* Land is a free gift of nature and it is no business of any individual to use it for his personal and selfish purpose. Robert Blatchford writes, "No man has right to call anything his own but that which he himself has made. No man makes land. The land is not created by labour, but it is the gift of God to all. It belongs to the people. Consequently, under socialism, no citizen should be allowed to call a single inch of land his own." The view of Davidson is that rent is brigandage reduced to a system. There is a difference of opinion among socialists regarding the method of abolition of landlordism. One view is that the property of all landlords should be confiscated and they should be paid nothing. Karl Marx and Engels were of the view that landlords must be destroyed and annihilated. Another view is that landlords should be given compensation. Ramsay MacDonald writes, "Socialism cannot come by confiscation." He does not approve of the idea of loot.

(7) Socialism stands for the *elimination of private enterprise.* With the abolition of capitalism, private enterprise is also to be abolished. All factors of production are to be put under the control of the state. There is to be nationalisation or socialisation of all the factors of production. Tom Johnston writes, "Private enterprise means private robbery." Blatchford observes that practical socialism is a "kind of national scheme of cooperation managed by the state. Its programme consists essentially of one demand, viz., that the land and other instruments of production shall be common property and shall be used and governed by the people for the people." Again, "Make the land and all instruments of production national property; put all farms, mines, ships and railways under national control and practical socialism is accomplished." Burns writes, "Socialism means abolition of private enterprise and the substitution of collective ownership and control for the benefit of the whole society, at least the principal instruments of production, distribution and exchange."

(8) Socialism emphasizes the *organic unity of society.* In pursuance of this ideal, it aims at organising socialism in the interests of individual freedom. This freedom does not mean complete absence of restraint, but means the provision of those opportunities which enable an individual to live a full and free life and to do that which is considered to be right by him. Asoka Mehta writes in his Democratic Socialism: "The inequality of the present situation demands of us an answer and we find that answer in socialism, wherein we feel human-beings will realise liberty and equality, wherein division of man between the oppressor and the oppressed, between the exploiters and the exploited will disappear and we shall have for the first time a society where man will act with man as a brother and as a fellow-being."

(9) The socialists consider the *state as an instrument of exploitation and compulsion* and hence they want to do away with the state. They believe that the state will wither away. Asoka Mehta writes, "All socialists, from the days of St. Simon to those of our times, have believed in and worked for, have cherished the vision of the time when the governance of man will yield place to administration of things; where there will be no police, no bureaucracy, no judiciary, no army, whereby spontaneous cooperation, by the flow of human goodwill, we shall be able to keep social life free from friction."

Criticism of Socialism

Socialism has been criticised on many grounds. It is contended that (1) the socialists distort and misrepresent facts. Their economic interpretation of history is a misrepresentation. While none will deny the importance of the economic factor, few will concede that economic motive is the only motive force behind all human activity. To the same category belongs the socialist contention that value is due to labour only, that capitalists are the enemies of labour, that the rich and the poor have irreconcilable interests and they must always be in opposite camps etc. The socialists can be accused of falsification of history and misrepresentation of facts.

(2) The socialist description of human nature is not correct. The socialists stand for the elimination of private enterprise and private property, but the acquisitive instinct of man requires them. Likewise, competition is in the blood of every individual. The demand for equality may be a good ideal but it is difficult to say how it can be realised and how far it is desirable.

(3) The economic theories propounded by the socialists are misleading. They twist the facts in the way that suits their interests. Their conclusions are based on half truths. They reproduce misleading quotations to create a fictitious air of authority and impartiality. For example, they do not attach any importance to the free gifts of nature and regard labour alone as productive of wealth and value. This is obviously wrong as nature also is a source of wealth.

(4) In a socialist regime, there is no incentive to work and produce. When the people cannot compete with one another and keep the private property created by their efforts to themselves, they will lose all incentive to work. A very important reason why we work is that we want to provide for

our families. As that is not so under socialism, few would put in their very best. It is difficult to believe that the people will work hard with the feeling of doing good to the whole society. The benefactors of society could be honoured and the inventions named after their inventors, but the mere recognition of their worth may not be enough to make them put in their best efforts. It is contended that socialism will result in a "slackening of energy, a cessation of enterprise, a fall in inventions, a stagnation of industry, fatal alike to progress and to productivity."

(5) The socialists fail to offer an equitable plan for the distribution of national wealth among the workers. Some stand for equality of payment but that would be unfair because the sluggard and the active cannot be paid the same wages. Justice demands that those who work hard must get their share proportionately. Another suggestion is: "From each according to his ability, to each according to his needs." The difficulty with this view is that it may not be possible to assess the working capacity of every worker. Even if that is found out, he may refuse to put in that much of work. Brailsford writes, "Socialised industry will succeed only if the public opinion of the workshop and trade union condemns and ostracises a man who does less than his best." Moreover, the system of giving everybody according to his needs will encourage idleness. Another method that is suggested is that the worker should be paid according to his merit. To quote Ramsay MacDonald, "Service is the only claim the socialist recognises to possession." His view is that the question of payment cannot be settled now as a speculative exercise, but should be left to experience.

(6) The socialist attitude is not conducive to the growth of trade and commerce. The socialists describe business as blackmail. They decry competition for new markets, expenditure on advertisement, window-dressing, commercial travelling etc. They condemn all modern methods of exchange.

(7) Liberty is likely to be restricted under a socialist regime. The individual will be too much under the control of the state. The state will have a say in every matter. There will be too much of uniformity and monotony. Socialism will bring about "the most sterilising despotism that the world has ever seen." Prof. Leacock writes, "Under socialism, freedom is gone, there is nothing but the rule of the elected boss. The worker is commanded to his task and obey he must. There is nothing like it among us at the present day except within melancholy precincts of the penitentiary. There and there only the socialist system is in operation."

(8) The socialists condemn religion on the ground that it is an ally of the capitalists and reactionary forces. Religion sanctifies the institution of private property. With the abolition of private property, religion also must go.

(9) Socialism has undesirable effects on society. It encourages class hatred and makes heroes out of the factory hands by designating them as "The Industrial Workers of the World". Antagonism between the rich and the poor and the employer and the employees can never be conducive to human progress and welfare. Socialism injects into the body-politic "a poison which inflames every wound and turns every trivial scratch into a malignant ulcer." All social progress will be hampered on account of too much control of the government.

(10) The effects of socialism in the political field will be unfortunate. The nationalisation of all the factors of production will bring all the power in the hands of the workers. They will be servants while they work for the state, but they will be also masters as voters. "They are both masters and servants; they clamour perpetually for an increase of their pay and in point of fact vote themselves an increase." The ignorant and illiterate workers are likely to become the victims of the propaganda of the demagogues and fiery orators from their own class.

(11) Socialist propaganda is the enemy of industrial peace and prosperity. The teaching of class war, sabotage, strike and revolution against the prevailing social system is bound to dislocate the economic system. A nation cannot think in terms of property when the workers regard the industrialists as blood-suckers and do not hesitate to injure them.

(12) Some of the ideas of the socialists are not only impracticable but also fantastic. It is not correct to say that private property in land and the instrument of production are opposed to morality and harmful from the economic point of view. Collective ownership will destroy one of the most powerful main-springs of human effort and industry. According to Laveleye, socialism rests on the principle that the able, industrious and prudent should share with the stupid, idle and the improvident whatever they obtain as reward of their energies and virtues. It is a system "which requires the state to do work and it is unfit to do in order to invest the working classes with privileges they have no right to get."

(13) The socialists over-estimate the capacity and efficiency of the state. Under a socialist regime, the functions of the state will multiply and it is too much to expect that all of them will be done in an efficient manner. Experience shows that the government is better fitted to restrain and regulate others than to do the work itself. The government will find it difficult to provide all the people with all the necessaries of life and at the same time manage labour and distribute production. Much will depend upon those who will run the machinery of the state. They may not be willing to do all those things which at present are being done by private enterprise. Production in the country will not be regulated by the law of demand and supply but by the whims of those in power. There is every possibility of a fall in the quality and quantity of the things produced. Red-tapism in government offices may destroy initiative.

Merits of Socialism

(1) The socialists depict, vividly and effectively, the evils of the existing system and thereby focus the attention of the people to remedy them. They arouse the conscience of the people to the sufferings and privations of the poor. Laveleye writes, "Socialism has rendered a real service by calling attention to the evils and iniquities of the existing social order and by awakening in the hearts of all good men the desire to apply a remedy."

(2) Socialism has emphasized the importance of environment in determining the character and destiny of individuals and nations. The socialists do not attribute the sufferings of the people to the doctrine of predestination or the will of God, but to the capitalist regime under which they live. They hold the existing circumstances in society responsible for the ills of society.

(3) The philosophy of socialism has given an impetus to the spirit of reform. The exposure of the evils of the capitalist system has created in the hearts of the reformers the desire to work for the eradication of those evils from the body politic. Socialism has helped the cause of reform by attacking privileges, monopolies, cruelty and tyranny.

(4) Socialism has emphasized the importance of the state and attributed to it a role in society that was denied under individualist philosophy. The old idea of the state as the rival of the individual has given place to that of the state as the great benefactor of mankind. Gronlund writes, "The state is not some power outside the people but the social organism itself, and as an organism it is destined to grow until it embraces all social activities."

(5) As a result of socialist philosophy and propaganda, the lot of the working classes has improved. "In uniting working men for the purpose of class-war, socialism has achieved something of permanent spirituel value. It has raised a mass of men whom it found in a state of brutalising servitude, to the human level of antagonists in a battle, has aroused in them a sense of their dignity and autonomy, and has advanced their differentiation as a class from within. The present position of the working man, as a man and not a mere machine or commodity, is largely due to socialism, which thus appears as the greatest movement of human emancipation since the French Revolution. If we remember the mean and inhuman harshness displayed by early nineteenth century liberals towards the urgent social problems of their time, we cannot deny that socialism, for all the defects of its ideology, has been an immense advance on the earlier individualism, and from the point of view of history, has been justified in attempting to submerge it beneath its own social flood."

(6) Socialism promotes social welfare. It aims at the welfare of all and not of a few. The functions of the state are not restricted in a socialist society. Most of the functions of the state are welfare functions such as education, health, sanitation etc. Socialism provides equal opportunity to all. The sufferings of the people are removed and they live in happiness and prosperity

(7) Socialism achieves rapid progress in the economic field. The evils of individualism like unemployment, over-production, wastage, slums and monopoly are not seen in socialism. Planning is a part of a socialism. The state diverts all its resources in a planned and systematic manner. It avoids wastage and extravagance which are the result of a competitive economy. It stands for cooperation and not competition.

(8) Socialism puts emphasis on society and not on the individual. Selfish interests of the individuals are not allowed to have their way. The whole society is organised in such a way that maximum benefit is achieved within the minimum possible time.

(9) In a capitalist society, the distribution of the ownership of the means of production is grossly unequal as distribution of income and wealth is also greatly unequal. Gross inequality is unjustified both ethically and economically. Through the establishment of social ownership of the means of production, the socialists seek to build up an egalitarian society. Unlike a capitalist society and economy there is no profit motive in socialist economy. The resources are directed into those channels only which are socially useful.

(10) Capitalist economy constantly oscillates between opposite swings of boom and slump. Periodical economic crises characterise capitalism with the result that social poise and stability are frequently disturbed. Comprehensive and integrated planning in a socialist state is designed to discipline and stabilise the operation of the blind forces of the economy. The result is that socialist society is comparatively stable.

(11) The democratic spirit of "give and take" does not grow in a capitalist society on account of gross social injustice and inequality. A country rent by sharp class divisions cannot develop a democratic mind. Socialism with its equalitarian ethos will help in creating a proper democratic milieu.

(12) The non-profit incentives to work under socialism will stimulate better and more productive work. Once the capitalist is expropriated and the workers are the state, men will feel that in working for society they are working for themselves They will do better work and do it more cheerfully."

(13) Socialism is acknowledged by the common people as a panacea for all their ills. It is held by them in reverence like a religious creed. It provides the hope for eradicating the evils of modern society. There will be complete transformation of society under this system. There will be more unity, cooperation and progress under socialism. The people see their salvation from age-old bondage and slavery and have maximum progress and happiness in socialism. Socialism bears a noble philosophy. It is a pilgrimage aiming at spontaneous integration of man with society. Erich Fronrm writes, "The aim of socialism is man's emancipation, his restoration to the unalienated, uncrippled individual who enters into a new, rich, spontaneous relationship with his fellowmen and with nature. Man should throw away the chains which bind him, the friction and unrealities and transform himself into a being who can make creative use of the powers of feeling and of thinking."

Evolutionary and Revolutionary Socialism

There is a distinction between evolutionary and revolutionary Socialism. Evolutionary socialism is achieved by an evolutionary process or by degrees and not by the wholesale transformation of society by a single stroke. Revolutionary socialism seeks to transform the social system thoroughly instead of accepting small concessions for the under-privileged sections. Evolutionary socialism admits an attitude of compromise between capitalism and socialism so that the capitalist system is allowed to continue with some changes here and there in the socialist direction. Revolutionary socialism makes a direct attack on the prevailing contradictions of the social order. It belongs to the Marxist tradition. Evolutionary socialism may be described as liberal socialism while revolutionary socialism may be called Marxian socialism. Evolutionary socialism relies on the democratic method, parliamentary reform and even economic planning so that the underprivileged sections, particularly the working classes, might be represented and taken care of by their representatives and leaders. Revolutionary socialism insists on organising the working class for fighting against capitalism in order to overthrow the capitalist order and establish complete socialisation of the instruments of production and distribution by revolution. Evolutionary socialism aims at securing the rights of the working classes, especially their economic rights, as a part of the supposed common interest of the community. It seeks to accommodate or reconcile the interests of the working classes with those of other classes. It subscribes to the theory of harmony or equilibrium as the governing principle of social relationship. Revolutionary socialism repudiates the theory of equilibrium or reconciliation between different interests in society. It seeks to reverse the position of the dominant and dependent classes in a capitalist society. It stands for the destruction of the capitalist society and the establishment of the dictatorship of the proletariat.

The evolutionary socialists accept Marx as the source of their inspiration but they have introduced certain new ideas and interpretations in the Marxian theory so that Marxism has lost its revolutionary character. The evolutionary socialists believe in the liberal ideas of justice, liberty and non-violent social change. The evolutionary socialists believe that although socialism is a superior doctrine to capitalism, the change-over to socialism should be gradual and non-violent. While the revolutionary socialists believe in the inevitability of a violent revolution as a pre-condition for setting up the dictatorship of the proletariat, evolutionary socialists put their faith in a peaceful, gradual and constitutional change aimed at the establishment of a socialist state. The differences in the approach of the revolutionary and evolutionary socialists is summed up by Ebenstein thus: "If the whole economic system be compared to a basket of eggs, communism (true Marxian socialism) burns the basket and scrambles all eggs at once—never to be unscrambled again. Democratic (or evolutionary) socialism keeps the basket and cooks only small orders of scrambled eggs at one time because it believes in Aristotle's wise counsel that the guest will judge better of a feast than the cook."

There are different brands of socialism such as Utopian Socialism, Fabianism, Democratic socialism. State socialism, Guild socialism. Syndicalism and Anarchism. All of them are known by the cover-term evolutionary socialism because the idea of evolutionary change is common to them all.

Evolutionary Socialism

The main contention of evolutionary socialism is that socialism can be established through evolutionary methods—through democratic reform, parliamentary institutions, progressive legislation, progressive taxation, nationalisation and capturing political power through elections. Evolutionary socialism does not believe in the Marxian theory of revolution for the overthrow of capitalism. It has faith in the capacity of the state to bring about socialism through gradual reform. It opposes the Marxian ideas of class struggle, dictatorship of the proletariat, withering away of the state and classless society. Evolutionary socialism proposes peaceful transition to socialism.

The basis of evolutionary socialism is the views of Bernstein (1850-1932). He criticised the Erfurt programme (1891) which was adopted by the German Marxists like Bebel, Liebknecht and Singer. That programme was based on the Marxian revolutionary theory. In a letter written in October 1898, Bernstein emphasized the following main features of evolutionary socialism: It is a mistake to believe that the collapse of capitalism is imminent. Its nature can be changed and it can be controlled. Private property can be gradually controlled and capitalism can be done away with through evolutionary changes. In capitalist democracies, change is possible through reforms. "The right to vote in a democracy makes its members virtually partners in the community and then virtual partnership must in the end lead to a real partnership." Through organised trade unions and their struggle for economic and other demands, the condition of the working class can be improved. The state is not a class instrument. It can also serve the interests of the working class through welfare measures. A democratic state can represent the whole nation, including the workers. Class struggle is not fundamental. Through the agency of the state, the interests of both the rich and the poor can be reconciled and both can cooperate with each other. There is no necessity of a revolution in a democratic state. "The more the political organisation of modern nations is democratised, the more the needs and opportunities of great political catastrophes are diminished." The dictatorship of the proletariat is not necessary. Socialism can come through parliamentary methods also. Neither the state can wither away not it should wither away because it is an instrument to bring about socialism. Evolutionary socialism becomes state socialism. It believes in nationalism and not internationalism.

If Marxism is the evolutionary philosophy of the working class, evolutionary socialism is the reformist and anti-revolutionary philosophy of the social democrats. Marxism attacks the exploitative mode of production of capitalism and puts emphasis on production. Evolutionary socialism puts emphasis on distribution and exchange. "Much more important to the socialists than production is the distribution of good produced in the society." Evolutionary socialism supports cooperatives of the producers, consumers and housing cooperatives. Evolutionary socialism is less critical of institutions and values associated with liberalism and does not aim to destroy the principles upon which liberalism is based. All the important features of evolutionary socialism are accepted by the liberal theory of welfare state and hence evolutionary socialism has been integrated into contemporary liberalism or liberal socialism or social liberalism. Sidney Olivier writes, "Socialism is merely individualism rationalised, organised, closed and in its right mind."

Criticism of Evolutionary Socialism

(1) Like Marxian socialism, evolutionary socialism has also been criticised on many grounds. If Marxian socialism has been mainly criticised by the Liberals, evolutionary socialism has been mainly criticised by the Marxists. Liberalism has adopted the programmes, policies, slogans and demands of evolutionary socialism and changed itself accordingly.

(2) The Marxists maintain that evolutionary socialism is "impotent socialism", "a broker's view of socialism", and revisionism. Evolutionary socialism is the greatest enemy of the working class as it gives legitimacy to the bourgeois state. It is basically a statist and anti-revolutionary theory. Lenin declared that evolutionary socialism is revisionist, opportunist and reformist. It is the greatest enemy of the working class because it does not stand for the complete overthrow of capitalism. As it stands for good relations and cooperation between the workers and the capitalists, it helps in the maintenance of the bourgeois socio-economic and political order. It lays the foundation of Fascism by establishing state monopoly capitalism. Evolutionary socialism is an unscientific vague and confusing theory. Its object is to misguide the working classes and not to emancipate them. It rejects the materialistic interpretation of history and theory of class struggle. It is a slave of parliamentary methods. It gives unlimited powers to the state. It can result in bureaucratisation and not socialisations It stands for giving more powers to big states which can put more restrictions on individual freedom.

(3) The orthodox liberals also criticise evolutionary socialism. According to them, it leads to collectivism which is a threat to individual liberties. The interference of the state in all the affairs of society gives birth to a closed society in which there is very little scope Tor the development of the individual. Evolutionary socialism also leads to the centralisation of economic and political power and hence there is no check on political power. Evolutionary socialism leads to nationalisation which is considered to be harmful to free industrial development and free competition. It decreases the production capacity of the economic system.

(4) Evolutionary theory is criticised on the ground that it has no coherent doctrine. There are very many varieties of evolutionary socialism and hence it is difficult to identify its essential contents. Evolutionary socialism is devoid of any general and consistent philosophy or programme. Different schools of evolutionary socialism seek to substitute class cooperation for class conflict, democracy for the dictatorship of the proletariat and an evolutionary method for the revolutionary method.

In spite of its shortcomings, evolutionary socialism has proved to be a tonic to the crisis-ridden capitalist economic system. It has improved the condition of the working class and thereby helped the survival of capitalist democracy. The fusion of evolutionary socialism and liberalism has given rise to the theory of liberal welfare state. It has saved the Western liberal democratic socio-economic and political systems based on capitalism. It has reduced the revolutionary temper of the working class. It is the bitter enemy of revolutionary socialism and a saviour of capitalism. It is definitely better than the crude form of capitalism.

Utopian Socialism

According to the dictionary meaning, Utopia is a place or a state of ideal perfection. The word Utopia denotes a stage of human and material perfection. It may be feasible in imagination. The notion of Utopia is suggestive of a system in which an ideal perfection could be achieved. The literal meaning of Utopia is an imaginary island described by Sir Thomas More in his famous book *Utopia* published in 1516. The word Utopianism means a body of ideas founded on ideal social perfectibility. Utopian socialism is an imaginary brand of socialism. It believes in criticising the existing institutions and sets forth an ideal social order which may not be attainable in reality. Utopian socialism means socialism unrelated to reality, aiming merely at condemning the existing institutions and societies without bothering about the remedial measures or spelling out the attainable. It implies a sincere belief in a degree of possible perfectibility of both human beings and institutions. It brings forth an ideal and not an attainable idea. The socialists before Karl Marx are normally called Utopian socialists and their socialism is called Utopian socialism. They gave only an ideal version of society and condemned private property. They did not say anything about the method through which the change was to be brought about. They relied upon persuasion and example and hoped that intelligent men would accept their ideal easily. They confined their philosophy either to the criticism of injustices in society and private property or laying down an ideal, unmindful of its attainability. In the words of Dr. Waper, "They conjured up visions of beautiful roses, but preparing no soil for the rose trees, left them to feed freely on beauty."

The Utopian socialists threw a crop of socialist ideas before Karl Marx. Saint Simon spread the idea of class war. Proudhon declared that property is theft. Fourier designated the middle classes as commercial despots. Owen believed that the new factory era would be one of cooperation and not competition. The Utopian socialists preached the doctrine of cooperation and developed schemes for ideal communities. They rejected the idea of revolution as a means to the end they sought and appealed to the spirit of benevolence in man.

It is difficult to say when the idea of Utopian socialism appeared. It may be found in Plato's Republic which is considered as socialist. The early Christians rejected the concept of mine and thine and practised socialism in their everyday lives. During the Renaissance and the Reformation, there was a revival of the protest against inequality based on wealth. All these events show the emergence of Utopian socialism. The main advocates of Utopian socialism were Saint Simon (1760-1825), Charles Fourier (1772-1837), Robert Owen (1771-1858) and Proudhon (1809-1865).

There were certain features of Utopian socialism. They expressed dissatisfaction with the existing institutions and societies of their times. Sir Thomas More attacked the institutions of his time in his book Utopia. Saint Simon spread the idea of class war. According to Proudhon, property is theft. Fourier held the view that the middle classes were commercial despots. The Utopian socialists were critical of the political and economic structure of society. They were shocked by the miserable conditions under which the workers lived and were induced to recommend a new social order free from the evils of the prevailing systems. The Utopian socialists insisted that changes in society to correct its evils should be on the lines suggested to them. The proposed new community should be based on the virtues of morality, honesty, justice and simplicity. According to Owen, the new factory era should be based on the principle of cooperation and not competition. Simon insisted that the renovation of society should be in accordance with human and divine justice so that the condition of the poor could be improved. The Utopian socialists were critical of the institution of private property. Proudhon regarded private property as theft. The view of Gray was that the wealth created by the working class was taken away by the greedy employers. According to Simon and Owen, private property was the cause of poverty. Coker writes, "These men regarded poverty as the principal source of ills of society and private property as the chief cause of poverty."

The Utopian socialists did not criticise man for his own moral and physical decay. However, they were critical of his pitiable condition which they attributed to corrupt institutions. The view of Owen was that the mill workers of New Lanark were surrounded by bad conditions which adversely affected their character and conduct. Men were not bad. It is the institutions which made them bad. Men were basically good.

Utopian socialism was mainly an economic doctrine. It was the outcome of the defective working of economic institutions, particularly the factory system. The view of Owen was that the new factory era based on competition led to various evils and it should be replaced by one of cooperation.

The Utopian socialists attacked the wrongs in the Capitalist system but not the system itself. They advocated means different those advocated by the Marxists. They did not look at all to revolutionary action or political action for bringing about the necessary change. They preached the doctrine of cooperation. They sought to set up "select communities" or "ideal communities", in which the principles of justice and benevolence were to rule and from the example of which the whole society was to be gradually converted to their ideals.

The Utopian socialists necessarily believed that in the capitalist economic system itself, the condition of the working class could be improved through social reform and evolutionary changes. Their appeal was based on humanism, morality and reason. According to Coker, the Utopian socialists "challenged the psychological and ethical assumptions upon which the current defences of private property rested and showed the inhuman and unnatural consequences of unrestrained competition. They looked for relief, however, not as the Marxists to the revolutionary or other aggressive action of oppressed groups organised to avail themselves of the benefits of a natural evolution of society, but to the deliberate and pacific efforts of men inspired by feelings of benevolence and justice."

Robert Owen (1771-1858) was not only the patron-saint of English socialism but also the father of the cooperative movement. He was a pioneer in advocating factory legislation and democratic education. As early as 1800, he started the experiment of creating a model factory at New Lanark. He attracted international attention by showing that workers could be treated well, even generously, without the employer incurring any loss. In 1825, he made an experiment of "New Harmony" in Indiana in the United States. It was designed as a voluntary and freely self-governing cooperative community. However, the experiment was a failure. Owen became a dreamer of dreams and his writings became more and more unrealistic and visionary. The core of his message was that the condition of men would improve if they replaced competition by cooperation as the mainspring of their economic activities and social life. If social conditions were bad, those could be changed. If the conditions were bad on account of bad human beings, those persons could be changed. The great need was for social and moral education. The minds of the people could be so changed that they came to appreciate the advantages of cooperation. Owen helped the growth of cooperative societies and the trade union movement.

Saint Simon (1760-1825) renounced his title during the French Revolution and made a fortune through speculation in church lands. His life was spent in the quest for a new source of authority and faith in an industrial age. He preached the gospel of work. He insisted that property rights must depend upon their social utility and not on any imprescriptible individual rights. He coined the slogan: "From each according to his capacity, to each according to his work." Saint Simon was not a systematic thinker but his speculations stimulated the minds of others. He criticised capitalism as wasteful and claimed that it pitted people against each other by imposing poverty on many and giving wealth to a few.

Charles Fourier (1772-1837) was a contemporary of Saint Simon and Robert Owen. He attacked all the ills of a commercial civilisation which made vice more profitable than virtue and set men in enmity with one another. The great sources of the evil were cut-throat competition, deceit, greed and inhumanity. In order to restore harmony to human life, there must be association and cooperation. In order to make work attractive, each worker must be given a share in the produce and guaranteed a sufficient minimum to free him from anxiety. His suggestion was that the dirty and unattractive work of the community should be done by children who at a certain age were providentially endowed with a love of being dirty. They would be "passionately attracted" to scavenging and would be always on foot or riding on their ponies at 3 A.M. even in the depths of winter, repairing roads, killing vermin, attending to animals and working in slaughter houses. Communities after the teachings of Fourier were set up during the 1840s in New Jersey, Wisconsin and Massachusetts.

Louis Blanc (1811-1882) was a journalist, author and politician. In 1840, he published his famous book "The Organisation of Labour". He denounced the existing competitive system. He advocated reforms which would establish the state on democratic basis. Then, the state was to provide social workshops—farms for agriculturists, factories for workmen and shops for tradesmen. The state was to provide for finances for starting the workshops. The workshops of the ideal of Louis Blanc were actually set up in France during the Revolution of 1848.

It is true that the Utopian socialists merely condemned the existing institutions and did practically little for the realisation of their ideals. However, this does not mean that their contribution was nil. The fact is that they prepared the ground for the later socialists upon which they erected their edifice. Dr. Wayper writes, "They voiced their irrational longings of the empty soul from which so much of the driving force of socialism comes. They provided him (Marx) with many a useful brick and tool. They popularised the idea of a socialist society. They elaborated the labour theory of value. But they failed where he (Marx) succeeded because they did not see that two requisites of socialism as a serious political factor were a doctrine which maintains that real social forces are making for socialism and a permanent contact with a source of power which can be harnessed for revolutionary socialist activity. They failed too, because they were unable to present their ideas with anything approaching Marx's religious fervour."

The chief contribution of the Utopian socialists was that they drew the attention of society to the inadequacies of the industrial system and gave a picture of society free from inequality, exploitation and injustice.

Collectivism or State Socialism

Collectivism as a form of socialism arose as a reaction against extreme individualism of the nineteenth century. It is a term for a trend in social development, a programme of economic reform and a theory of general welfare. Its principles can be found in the works of Eduard Bernstein in Germany, Jean Juares in France, Karl Branting in Sweden and Eduard Anseel in Belgium. It is not so radical as revolutionary socialism, communism, syndicalism or anarchism.

Collectivism wants to employ the state for the promotion of the common good. It does not want to abolish the state but stands for removing the evils of capitalism, private property and competition. It does not regard the state as an evil but a positive good which can be employed to serve the collective good. Unlike individualism, it gives a very wide scope to the activity of the state.

The state functioning according to collectivist principles can bring about the social, economic, moral and intellectual development of the community. Collectivism stands for the ideal of a welfare state. Unlike the anarchists and Marxists, the collectivists are pro-state. They firmly believe that state action alone can remove exploitation and promote general welfare.

Collectivism rejects the socialist doctrines of determinism, labour-created values and class war. It recognises that differences in wealth create divisions of the community into different and often opposing political groups, but discredits the doctrine of clear-cut distinction of classes and a continual antagonism between them. According to Prof. Ely, a collectivist is "a person who looks to society organised in the state for aid in bringing about a more perfect distribution of economic good and an elevation of humanity."

The main objectives of collectivism are to abolish private ownership of the means of production, to bring the main industries and services under public control and ownership, to press industry in serving the needs of the community as a whole and not the interests of a few, to eliminate the incentive of private profit in favour of the motive of social service and the possession and control of the chief factors of production under the central democratic authority and not under private capitalist. The means of production are to be nationalised and then put under democratic control. There is to be better production and better distribution of wealth. There should be a national minimum wage for workers and equal pay for equal work. There should be no unemployment. It is the task of the state to provide work. The state is to reduce drastically inequality in income by introducing a highly progressive system of income tax.

The state socialists have a well-planned programme and definite constructive proposals for the future set-up. They stand for the universal enforcement of the national minimum wages. Their object is to better the lot of the workers. The wages should be fixed at the lowest level and must facilitate the development of mind, body and character of the worker. The number of the working hours are to be reduced and workers have to be given equal pay for equal work. It is the function of the state, to prevent unemployment. All the factors of production are to be nationalised and put under democratic control so that the will of the people prevails. The workers are to possess liberty and equality both in political and economic spheres. The state socialists or collectivists aim at bringing about a revolution in the national finance. Their object is to lessen the burden of taxation on the poor. They stand for a highly progressive system of income tax. They advocate the levying of a capital levy for the payment of war debts and other debts of a like nature. Under the existing system, the unearned income goes into the pockets of private individuals but under state socialism, it will go to the national fund and spent in a manner most conducive to the betterment of society.

Many reasons are given in favour of collectivism or state socialism. It is contended that the nationalisation of industries is absolutely necessary to safeguard the interests of the public at large. That is the only way by which order can be brought about in a sphere in which there is otherwise all anarchy. The supporters of state socialism plead for "the state ownership of land and producers' capital as the means of absorbing for the public, both interest and the various forms of economic rent." There will be no wasteful or injurious competition. There will be no monopolies for any selfish worker. There will be neither duplication nor over-production.

Under state socialism, all the free gifts of nature will be conserved for the future happiness of man. Their stock will not be exhausted or destroyed by individuals for private gain. All the factors of production are to be employed or utilised in such a manner that they bring the maximum social advantage. A collectivist state is guided purely by considerations of service motive. There will be complete transformation of society under state socialism. There will be more unity and the principles of social service, social usefulness and love of society will be followed.

The state socialists advocate peaceful methods for the realisation of their goal. C.E.M. Joad writes, "True to the biological conception of society as a social organism, collectivist socialists have insisted that society is capable only of gradual change and that each change must be conditioned by the nature of the social structure that preceded it. From this point of view it is essential to start with what exists and allow the present to decide the direction as well as the rapidity of the steps which are taken into the future."

The collectivists are against the abolition of the state. The existing state is not to be overthrown. It is to utilised for making the proposed changes.

Those who believe in collectivism should disseminate their ideas and seek to capture power. They should employ all political, constitutional and educational methods to prepare the ground for a slow and evolutionary change.

The collectivists would like to organise a party of their own which must have a majority in the legislature. They can then form their government and introduce the necessary legislation for making collectivism a reality. The collectivists stand for the ballot box and not the bullet.

Criticism of State Socialism

There are many shortcomings in state socialism. (1) The state ownership, management and control of all the factors of production and distribution will result in an authoritarian and bureaucratic state. The number of officials and other employees will be very large. There is every likelihood of an increase in corruption, intrigue and personal spite. The evils of nepotism, red-tapism and favouritism will come in. The state socialists are over-optimistic regarding the part to be played by the state in the new set-up, but the difficulties of administration will be so many that there is every likelihood of the breakdown of state machinery. However, these defects can be avoided if people take interest in the affairs of the state and supervise the working of state machinery. There is nothing to stop them from directing the machinery of the state for their own good. The evils of bureaucracy can also be minimised. Instead of nationalisation of all the factors of production, very many services can be municipalised. This type of devolution of powers and functions can avoid many evils.

(2) Critics maintain that state ownership of all the factors of production is likely to destroy the chief incentive to individual effort and that is not desirable for the progress of society. Brilliant people will not be encouraged to put in their very best into their work. There will be no incentive to originality or motive for production. The most powerful spring of human activity is personal gain which will be lacking under state socialism. However, it is pointed out that non-material rewards are as much effective as material rewards to encourage human activity. Bertrand Russell writes. "Creative impulses in man are to be satisfied and the rendering of public service in any form by one who is fit to perform it according to his ability is in reality the greatest achievement of man." It is denied that people work only for material gain. Individuals have made greater sacrifices for society as a whole than for their families or themselves. Joad observes, "In all small communities, the desire to serve, to work for good, to stand well with the community is consistently operative and is one of the most powerful factors in life." The Russian and Chinese experiments have shown that when the nation as a whole works for the good of all, there can be no fear of a fall in production. Moreover, the problem which is more important than that of production, is the problem of distribution which can be tackled better under state socialism.

(3) The view of the critics is that state socialism may result in uniformity and make society static. It may worsen the lot of the workers instead of improving it. However, there is nothing to support such a view. There are more chances of things improving under state socialism than degenerating.

(4) Another criticism is that state socialism is another form of capitalism. Under state socialism, the capitalists will be able to capture the machinery of the state and use the same for their own interests. The monopoly of the state may not be for the good of all.

(5) As all the factors of production and distribution will come under the control of the state, struggle for power will become very bitter. The reason is that the party which captures power will have everything and the party which does not will have nothing. The result is that every party will do its best to capture the machinery of the state. That may result in violence also which may not be pleasing to the advocates of state socialism.

(6) State socialism may bring into existence cliques and bosses who will spend all their resources to capture the machinery of the state and use the same for their own selfish interests. State socialism is regarded as a half-way house to dictatorship. The object of state socialism is merely to pacify the workers by means of palliatives and thereby break the solidarity of the workers.

(7) State socialism may result in cast-iron centralisation which may not be desirable for the development of the personalities of individuals.

(8) State socialism may bring in its wake corruption and intrigues. The system may work well if those who run the administrative machinery are actuated by high ideals and they do not perform their duties merely to realise their own selfish ends. However, there is a possibility that those in power may abuse them and bring misery to the people in general.

In spite of its shortcomings, state socialism is making headway in the world and collectivist tendencies are seen everywhere.

Democratic Socialism

In the words of Ebenstein, "The link between democracy and socialism is the most important single element in socialist thought and policy." Democratic socialism means that brand of socialism in which socialist principles and policies are sought to be enforced gradually through democratic means and processes. According to the American Political Dictionary, democratic socialism is "an economic system established by a democratic nation in which the people through their government, take over ownership and direction of basic industries, banking, communication, transportation and other segments of the economy. The extent of government's role in the economy is determined by free elections rather than by ideological dogma. Although a private sector of the economy may continue to exist, much effort is expended by government in planning, directing and regulating and in providing welfare schemes for the needy." According to the Oxford Junior Encyclopaedia, democratic socialism implies a "peaceful transformation of the economic order from individualism to socialism by the methods of representative democracy achieved by common consent." The view of Coker is that democratic socialism "stands for an extensive control over the basic means of wealth and culture—a control to be exercised not by some class within the community but by the community itself and to be built up gradually and in orderly forms." Ebenstein defines democratic socialism as the "transition from a predominantly capitalist economy to a predominantly socialist economy, not as the result of a sudden revolutionary coup that makes the return to capitalism technically and administratively impossible (as in Russia) but as the result of gradual measures, none of which, by itself, irrevocably alters the nature of the whole economy."

Its Origin

Democratic socialism has grown up in those countries where the democratic tradition has been strong. Ebenstein writes, "Looking at the history of socialism, it can be quickly seen that successful socialist movements have grown up in nations with strong democratic traditions, such as Great Britain, the Scandinavian countries, Belgium, the Netherlands, Switzerland, Australia, New Zeland and more recently Israel. The reason for this parallelism is simple. Where democratic constitutional government is generally accepted, socialists can concentrate on their extensive economic and social reforms; to create more opportunity for the underprivileged classes; to end inequality based on birth rather than service, to open horizons of education to all the people; to eliminate practices based on sex, religion, race, or social class, to regulate and reorganize the benefits of the whole community; to maintain full employment; to provide adequate social security for the sick, unemployed, and aged; to replan the layout of towns and cities; to tear down the slums and build new houses; to provide medical facilities for everybody, regardless of the size of his purse, and finally, to rebuild society on the foundation of cooperation instead of competition, incentive and profit. All these goals of democratic socialism have one thing in common to make democracy more real by broadening the application of democratic principles from the political to the non-political areas of society."

Democratic socialists do not have any high priest to whose name a reference can be made. Ebenstein writes, "Socialist literature in England has no Marx or Lenin who lays down the law for all time. The most influential socialist thinkers in England have frequently been without any official position of party or government and their impact has been due primarily to their moral authority and felicitous literary style." Democratic socialists do not refer to great authorities or develop the cult of the individual. Likewise, one does not find in the ranks of democratic socialists the type of fanaticism commonly found among the Communists. Democratic socialism not only tolerates but also respects the opinions of others, unlike totalitarian Communism which seeks to wipe out any opposition in a violent manner.

The influence of R.H. Tanwney, the British democratic socialist in the first half of the twentieth century, has been great indeed. According to Ebenstein, "Many consider R.H. Tawney's 'The Acquisitive Society' (1921) one of the great classics of English literature as well as of socialist thought". Tawney strongly criticised functionless property as a danger not only to society but also to legitimate property itself. He was not against the right to property, but he was opposed to functionless property which was the instrument of exploitation. Capitalism enables individuals to develop property which they regard as a source of power and income and not an agent of social service. Such property is called functionless property. Functionless property puts power in the hands of a few persons who exercise it over other people who have no power and to whom they are responsible. That Jeads to tyranny. Tawney suggests three measures for removing the danger of functionless property. According to him, industry should be subordinated to the larger interests of the community as a whole. The people who render service should be honourably paid. They should not be ruled by an authority which they cannot control. The owners of industry should be responsible to those who are controlled by them.

Prof. Harold Laski was also a democratic socialist. He openly condemned the violent path to socialism. He asked the socialists to continue to operate by legal and constitutional means till their opponents adopted violent methods against them. Laski was not clear regarding the ownership of the means of production in socialist society. He wrote thus in A Grammar of Politics (1925): "Functionless property is the controlling factor in industrial production, the abolition of its right is the necessary path to justice." At another place in the same book, he observed that private ownership and private property should eliminated only from those industries "urgently affected by a public character which are monopolistic in their nature." Laski's commitment to democratic socialism did not deter him from conceding its limitations. In his Trade Unions in the New Society (1949), Laski wrote: "Democratic socialist government is always walking upon a razor's edge. Formally, the coercive power of the state is in its hands; actually, it knows perfectly well that it must not use it in such a way as to outrage the vested interests." Regarding the success of the democratic socialist regimes, Laski conceded in The Dilemma of Our Times (1952) that such regimes have hardly touched more than the outworks of the capitalist fortress." The reforms introduced "were always within the compass of a bourgeois democracy based upon universal suffrage."

Basic Principles of Democratic Socialism

(1) Democratic socialism puts great emphasis on the importance of the larger interests of society as a whole against the narrow and selfish interests of the individuals. It is against individualism

or *Laissez faire* which allows the individual full scope to do whatever he likes regardless of the welfare of the community. However, this does not mean that under democratic socialism, the interests of the individual are completely ignored. Democratic socialists believe in individual freedom and equality. What they want is that the principles of freedom and equality should be harmonised and properly balanced. The Oslo Declaration records, "To us both freedom and equality are precious and essential to human happiness. They are the twin pillars upon which the ideal of human brotherhood rests."

(2) The democratic socialists put emphasis on cooperation and not on competition. They believe that free competition is injurious and plays havoc in society. Hence, there should not be any type of free competition. Robert Owen built his entire programme on the basis of cooperation and not class war. His view was that there should be voluntary associations based on the principle of mutual help. The employers and the employees should cooperate with each other and consider themselves as partners in production.

(3) Democratic socialists put emphasis on the principle of equality. They believe in providing equal opportunities to all. They stand for passing legislation which gives equal opportunities to all for advancement in life. They do not stand for absolute equality because the same is impossible to achieve. However, they want to see that the fruits of labour are not taken away by the employer or anybody else.

(4) Democratic socialists do not approve of the concentration of wealth in the hands of a few persons. According to them, labour should be given a living wage and not exploited. Democratic socialism stands for progressive social and labour legislation. The rich should be taxed at a higher rate so that inequalities in the distribution of wealth become less. Democratic socialists stand for the nationalisation of the important means of production and not all the means of production. They are bothered about the main means of production to be brought under state control.

(5) Democratic socialism upholds the different kinds of rights. It believes in giving civil, political and economic rights to citizens. The citizens are free to lead their lives in any way they please. The individual is free to hold his views and practise his own religion without any interference from any quarter.

(6) The democratic socialists stand for broadening and widening the base of democracy. Democracy must be extended from political to social and economic fields. Their view is that democracy can be real and effective if its frontiers are extended to economic and social fields also. Democratic socialists want to apply the principle of democracy to production, exchange and distribution.

(7) Democratic socialists stand for the suppression of the anti-social activities of the state. The state must curb the anti-social activities of private producers who may bring about artificial scarcities to raise the prices of the commodities to the detriment of the whole society. State intervention is justified to provide justice to all the people.

(8) Democratic socialism stands for equality of opportunities. It sets its face against the ownership of land, factories and other means of production by a few at the cost of the community. Democratic socialism is not against all forms of private property but only against privately owned property which becomes the means of exploitation. Democratic socialism allows the ownership of small plots of land, houses and other limited property as they cannot be put to any anti-social use.

Methods of Democratic Socialism

Democratic socialists stand for democratic methods and processes. They advocate peaceful methods and the establishment of a new social order through the ballot box and not through the bullet. Their object is to capture power and implement their programme. Democratic socialists include various other activities in addition to the fighting of parliamentary elections. Those methods and activities include organisation, propaganda, agitation, struggle and constructive work. Durbin writes, "The problem of strategy facing the democratic socialists is to find a policy that makes an advance towards socialism and yet does not render the continuation of democracy impossible."

Merits of Democratic Socialism

Democratic socialism stands for the dignity of human personality. It stands for liberty and equality. It allows individuals to enjoy all kinds of rights. It puts society above the individual. It considers the good of all as something superior to the good of the individual. It eliminates the evils of capitalism like concentration of wealth in the hands of a few, destructive competition, over-production and wasteful advertisement. It eliminates the tyranny or misuse of private property. It strikes a balance between the rights of the individual and the rights of the community. It stands for ending the exploitation of the people and establishment of economic and social equality. It substitutes competition by cooperation. It considers property as an agency of service to the community and not an instrument of exploitation.

Defects

Critics of democratic socialism point out that democratic socialism may put too many powers in the hands of the government and that they may be a stepping stone towards totalitarianism. As the means of production are being taken over by the state, the incentive to produce more and more will be adversely affected. If the idle are treated on par with the diligent and industrious, the latter will be discouraged. With the absence of competition, there will be inefficiency in production. Quality also will fall. There is the danger of red-tape, bribery arid corruption. There is also the possibility of the degeneration of the characters of the individuals. Under democratic socialism, the consumer will suffer. He will have to adjust his needs to production which may involve hardship and privation. Democratic socialism is criticised on the ground that it is utilitarian and materialistic and does not care for ethical principles.

Fabianism

Fabianism is one of the form of socialism aiming at the promotion of the welfare of society through slow, evolutionary and democratic methods. Such a type of socialism could originate and grow only in a country like England where people were capable of evolving conventions and customs and were given to democratic methods of persuasion and constructive work. Fabianism could not originate in a backward country in which there was no middle class and the people were illiterate and ignorant.

The Fabian Society was formed in January 1884 and among its founders were luminaries like G.B. Shaw, Graham Wallas, Hubert Bland, Edward R. Pease, H.W. Massingham, Annie Besant, Sidney Webband Sidney Oliver. Ramsay MacDonald was also a Fabian. H.G. Wells was also a member of the Fabian Society for some time. Beatrice Webb, Keir Hardie. G.D.H. Cole, Pethic Lawrence, Emil Davis, Harold Laski, R.H. Tawney, Leonard Wolfe and Herman Finer also became Fabians. The Fabian Society was named after Fabius Cunciator, the dictator in ancient Rome, who followed the tactics of studied slowness against Hannibal of Carthage. When Hannibal invaded Italy, Fabius Cunctator went on following delayed tactics in order to strike against Hannibal at the right time. The motto of the Fabian Society was: "For the right moment you must wait as Fabius did, most patiently when warring against Hannibal though many censured his delay: but when time comes you must strike hard as Fabius did or your waiting will be in vain and fruitless."

The Fabians were primarily influenced by three philosophers viz., J.S. Mill, Henry George and Karl Marx. The influence of Marx is understandable as his philosophy was influencing the people of his time. Although J.S. Mill was an individualist, he developed socialist leanings in the later part of his life. He had written in his Autobiography: "The social problem of the future we consider to be, how to unite the greatest individual liberty of action with a common ownership hi the raw material of the globe and an equal participation of all in the benefits of combined labour". Henry George, the American philosopher, who was the author of *Progress and Poverty*, lectured in England in 1881 and greatly influenced the English socialist thinkers. The main point made by him was that poverty increased with progress as land, the basic natural resource, belonged to the few. The landlord had no right to profit from greater value of a piece of land over another which was attributable to its greater fertility or better location. His proposal was that society should confiscate that differential by a tax amounting to its entire value. Henry George influenced the Fabians in two ways. His glowing picture of a society without want fired their enthusiasm for getting rid of unearned wealth. His hint led them to find differential values other than economic rent—in profits, salaries and dividends, all of which were unearned to precisely the same degree as the rent appropriated by landlords.

Its Essentials

(1) The Fabian socialists sought to modify Marxian concepts in several ways. They based their economics on the Ricardian law of rent rather than on the labour theory of value. They did not rely exclusively on the working class for bringing about social change and set before themselves the task of "permeating" the middle class with the socialist message. They sought to introduce socialism, not in a single stroke, but by degrees through state and cooperative ownership of industry, increasing power of labour in legislative and executive offices, growth of trade unions and educational movements and development of social consciousness through gradual democratisation of society in the political, economic and intellectual fields.

(2) The Fabian socialists stood for the extinction of private property in land and of the consequent individual appropriation, in the form of rent, of the price paid for permission to use the earth, as well as for the advantages of superior soil and sites. They stood for the transfer of such industrial capital as can conveniently be managed socially to the community. The Fabians hoped that with the fulfilment of the above objectives, "rent and interest will be added to the reward of labour, the idle class now living on the labour of others will necessarily disappear and practical equality of opportunity will be maintained by the spontaneous action of economic forces with much less interference with personal liberty than the present system entails." In addition to the extinction" of private property in land and community ownership and management of the wage system in which the worker received a wage without any regard to his contribution towards production and the amount required to maintain him and his family. The Fabians stood for the enrolment of every able-bodied person in the service of the community. They also believed that for the successful establishment of socialism, there must be strict subordination, discipline and obedience to orders.

(3) The Fabians aimed at emancipating land and industrial capital from individual and class ownership and its vesting in the community as a whole. The administration of industrial capital, as far as possible, was to be transferred to the community. That was necessary because industrial capital had become a monopoly in the hands of a class of proprietors on whom the majority depended for their livelihood.

(4) The Fabian Society desired to conduct on a large scale the spread of socialist views with a view to bring about great social and economic changes and provide equality of opportunity to all. Propaganda was expected to change the minds of the people in favour of the required changes.

(5) The Fabian socialists rejected the materialistic conception of history and the doctrine of economic determinism. They did not believe in the inevitable, automatic and scientific process by which a social revolution would come of its own accord. They did not believe in the theory of class war and forcible revolution. They stood for the progressive, transformation of society into such channels as would remove the glaring inequalities resulting from capitalism. They did not condemn

outright capitalism. They did not identify it with exploitation. They did not believe in the theory of surplus value of Marx. They did not take "abstract labour" as the basis of value. However, they emphasized the fact that labourers were perpetually exploited by landlords and capitalists and placed the elimination of capitalists and expropriation of landlords in the forefront of their programme. Unlike the Communists who maintained that the state will "wither away" and disappear altogether, the Fabian socialists proposed to make the state the main organ for the permanent administration of the cooperative commonwealth.

(6) The Fabians believed in evolution and not revolution, in constitutional and not violent methods. They advocated reforms as opposed to destruction. Moderation was the keynote of their technique. Theirs was a policy of persuasion and permeation. They avoided giving shocks to society. They suggested that they were not socialists at all but merely social reformers. They endeavoured to win over the sympathy of all persons and impressed upon them the fact that socialism was nothing more than applied Christianity. Their method of attack on capitalism was one of sapping rather than assault, craft rather than force, of subtlety rather than violence. "Permeation" was their watch-word. They tried to create the impression that socialism and collectivism were synonymous terms and what they were aiming at was a harmless and beneficent extension of the state and municipal enterprise.

(7) *The Fabian socialists justified their type of socialism on various grounds.* They justified it on *historical grounds.* According to Sidney Webb, the nineteenth century witnessed the almost complete failure of individualism and continuous record of the progress of socialism. History was a witness to social dynamism and failure of individualism. Society was dynamic and not static. Every thinker looked forward to the gradual evolution of a new social order. England provided a historical basis to socialism by accepting changes which were peaceful, gradual, ethical and democratic.

William Clarke justified socialism *on industrial grounds.* His view was that in the beginning the capitalist worked hard and got the wages of his superintendence. However, he gradually handed over his work to others who were paid by him for their work. The result was that the capitalist ceased to be useful to the community but still continued as a mere receiver of rent and interest. At that stage, society had no need of the capitalist who could be got rid of in the same way in which a slave driver or feudal baron was eliminated. Clarke made out a strong case for bringing all joint stock companies and combines under public ownership.

G.B. Shaw justified socialism *on economic grounds.* He criticised rent and private property. He contended that in modern times, great fortunes were being made not by hard work but by appreciation in the value of land and the stocks of corporations. The increase in value was the contribution of the entire society and not of any owner of property. "For all practical purposes, the owners have been able to sit with folded hands, or to devote their lives to golf and fox-hunting and the rise in values has occurred just the same". Shaw referred to the helplessness of workers who had no control over their labour. Their condition was miserable and their poverty existed in the midst of plenty.

Sidney Oliver justified socialism *on moral grounds.* According to him, socialism was not the enemy but the child of individualism. It was nothing but individualism which is "rationalised, organised, clothed and in its right mind." Private property in its existing form had no moral basis and the capitalists did not work for what they got.

Annie Besant justified socialism *on the ground of incentive.* She maintained that the existing social and economic system in which the rich alone had the incentive to work should be changed and the ordinary people should be given a strong incentive to work. "The desire to excel, the joy in creative work, the longing to improve, the eagerness to win social approval, the instinct of benevolence: all these will start into full life and will serve at once as the stimulus to labour and the reward of excellence".

Methods of Fabian Socialists

The Fabian Socialists were against revolutionary and bloody methods. Their methods were sober and dignified. They were free from class bias, hatred and fanaticism and were thus able to exercise much influence in Britain. They did not believe in class war or the theory of surplus value. They did not want the state to be overthrown. As a matter of fact, they would like to use the machinery of the state for the good of the community. They were for the continuation of the state. Their methods were evolutionary and extremely moderate. They called themselves social reformers and not socialists in the strict sense of the term. They criticised capitalism in a mild fashion but their attack was subtle. They spread their ideas through their literature. They did not appeal to the masses. They did not have a political party of their own. They believed that in all groups and parties, there were people who would be responsive to their views. They did not have dogmas or principles to swear. Though they addressed themselves to a small circle of influential and reasonable people, their ideas spread rapidly in Britain. A large number of members of the British Parliament subscribed to the Fabian views. Fabianism as a separate school of political thought has ceased to exist.

Assessment of Fabianism

As very eminent men with international reputation were the members of the Fabian Society, the people were influenced by their views. By their sober and dignified methods, the Fabians were able to push forward socialist ideas and that was done without bitterness and fanaticism. Unlike Marxism which advocated violence fanaticism and hatred, the Fabians possessed reasonableness, dignity and sobriety. Their approach was non-partisan. It cannot be denied that the Fabians did a lot to improve the lot of labour. The labour movement in Britain owed a lot to the help given by the Fabians.

However, the Fabians were also attacked on many grounds. It was contended that the Fabians overlooked the fact that the machinery of the state represented by its army of civil servants might be as great an exploiter as private businessmen. They identified the state with the people through the medium of civil servant. There was no guarantee that the civil servants who were entrusted with the task of managing socialism would remain unassuming and would not constitute a superior ruling elite apart from the ruled masses. Fabian philosophy was "quite thin". The Fabian Socialists contributed more to practice than to theory. The Fabian view appeared to be consistent with the requirements of political democracy. To quote Lancester, "Surely there is something incompatible with democracy in a plan under which men are enrolled in the service of the community under strict subordination and paid by bureaucratically determined allowances".

The Fabian methods have been severely criticised. According to Mallock, the Fabian writers have been playing fast and loose with their language and their thought. They define socialism as being in essence one thing but actually they mean quite another. They stand for the elimination of capitalism, expropriation of the landlord, the extinction of private enterprise and eradication of competition but actually they bring in more of state and municipal enterprise, the setting up of gas works, water works, baths, laundries etc. Ernest Barker writes, "The Fabian Society is the least open and least straightforward socialist organisation. It habitually and on principle sails under a false flag, wishing not to arouse suspicion as to its objects. Fabians rely for their success chiefly on their artfulness". Arnold Forster says that the Fabians "do not come into the controversy with clean hands." Skelton designates the Fabians as "the typical opportunists of socialists. They laboured ingeniously to show that an unconscious socialism is already in full swing in Britain, in post office and public schools, in hawkers' licences and factory inspection and income taxation, drawing the deduction that the nation as well be hanged for a sheep as for a lamb, and go consciously to the end of the socialist road." Dr. Engels wrote thus, "Their (Fabian) tactics are to fight the liberals not as decided opponents, but to drive them on to socialistic consequences; therefore to trick them, to permeate liberalism with socialism and not to oppose socialist candidates to liberal ones, but to palm them off to thrust upon them under some pretext. All is rotten". The Fabians have been called "the Jesuits of Socialism".

Syndicalism

In the words of Sorel, syndicalism is "revisionism of the left." It is an attempt to revise Marxism in the light of new experience which was not available to Marx. Syndicalism is the vision of a new stateless and classless society with the trade union as its base.

According to C.E.M. Joad, "Syndicalism is the name given both to a body of social doctrine or theory of social organisation and to a plan of action." The view of Ernest Barker is that "Syndicalism like Marxism, is a doctrine inimical to the bourgeois or capitalistic state; but while Marxism erects a whole class, called the proletariat, as the enemy of the bourgeois state, and proposes to build on that class, a new state representing the dictatorship of the proletariat. Syndicalism has evolved a different system of tactics. It erects as the enemy of the bourgeois state the various and separate syndicates or unions of the workers, each acting on the basis of its own industry or occupations, each proceeding by its own method of the industrial or occupational strike, but all conceivably and even ideally, combining their separate strike by a sort of spontaneous parallelism into one simultaneous or general strike." J.S. Roucek defines syndicalism as "a revolutionary labour movement making trade unions as the basis of social revolution as well as of the future society. It combines the political theory that distrusts the state as a tool of the capitalists with direct non-political methods of trade unionism." According to F.W. Coker, "Syndicalism, loosely defined, holds that the workers alone must control the conditions under which they work and live, the social changes they need can be achieved only by their own efforts by direct action in their own associations and through means suited to their peculiar needs."

Syndicalism is derived from the word "Syndicate" which is the French name for a trade union. Sometimes the word Syndicalism is used to denote ordinary trade unionism in France. Syndicalism can best be described as revolutionary trade unionism. It draws its inspiration from the words of Proudhon and not of Karl Marx. On account of its close association with anarchism, it is often called "Anarcho Syndicalism." It has also been called an "organised anarchy." From the very beginning, it had an anti-authoritarian and revolutionary tendency. It is frankly socialistic in the sense that it adopts the general socialist view of capital as theft, endorses or rather extends the notion of class war as fundamental in a capitalist society and proposes to abolish private ownership of the means of production and substitutes ownership by the community. Syndicalism insists on the importance of the producer. Pelloutier writes, "The task of the revolution is to free mankind not only from all authority but also from every institution which has not for its essential purpose the development of production."

Origin and Growth of Syndicalism

Syndicalism originated in France in the second half of the nineteenth century when the French Government removed the hurdles in the way of workers by legislation. Originally, the workers in France were prohibited from forming trade unions or associations but the laws of 1864, 1868 and 1884 conceded to the workers the right of forming associations. The attitude of Waldeck Rousseau, the Minister of the Interior in the cabinet of Jules Ferry, was favourable to the formation of trade unions. In 1887, an organisation was set up in Paris and others were founded in the provincial towns. Six years later, a national federation of the Bourses known as "Federation de Bourses du Travail de France" was formed. Very soon, it became the centre of the labour movement in France. Two years after, a new organisation known as "Confederation Generale du Travail" or CGT (Central Federation of Labour) was created. It became the chief national organisation in France.

When the World War I broke out, the majority of the Syndicalists belonging to the General Confederation of Labour gave up their anti-war and anti-government policy and made a compromise with the government and the socialists in order to promote war efforts. The majority of the Syndicalists who were moderates, gave up violence altogether. However, there were a few Syndicalists who were not prepared to give up their old methods. After the War, the moderate Syndicalists separated themselves from the militants in 1922. The militants formed the General Confederation of United Labour and followed the principles and aims of the Communist International. The differences between the two groups of the Syndicalists led to the emergence of New Syndicalism whose principles were elucidated by Syndicalist thinkers like Jouhaux, Perrot and Leroy. New Syndicalism did not stand for class war and violence. It desired "to supplant the negative, destructive tactics- of the older syndicalism by a positive and comprehensive policy." Emphasis was put on collaboration and coordination among the various kinds of manual workers.

Syndicalism went beyond the frontiers of France and spread to England, Spain, the United States and Italy. Tom Mann, a militant trade union leader, tried to spread syndicalist ideas in England. He established the Industrial Syndicalist Educational League and propagated his ideas through his monthly journal and pamphlets. The spread of syndicalism led to many strikes in England. Syndicalism did not progress in England on account of opposition from the people to militant trade unionism. In Spain, syndicalism was suppressed during 1936-39. In Italy, it was put down by Mussolini. Unlike French syndicalism, American syndicalism was not militant. It organised peaceful strikes. However, the government suppressed the strikes during the World War I. After the War, the syndicalist movement in the United States became impotent.

Exponents of Syndicalism

The exponents of syndicalism were the active leaders of trade union movement and a galaxy of brilliant intellectuals. Fernand Pelloutier (1867-1901), Emile Pouget and others were helped by their own experience to formulate the main tenets of syndicalism. George Sorel (1847-1922) and Hubert Lagardelle provided its philosophical foundation. Pelloutier called upon the workers to remain aloof from politics and exert themselves through labour exchanges and better their own condition through cooperation. Sorel was a brilliant intellectual. He was the philosopher-saint of syndicalism. He, "having started out with Marx, ends up with Bergson." From Marx, he took the idea of class struggle as the key to social change. At the same time, his desire was to purge Marxism of its non-essential features. His view was that the new society would come not as a result of technological and social changes as advocated by Marx, but as a result of a general strike. Bergson provided Sorel his theory of intuition according to which the aims of man's actions are governed not by intelligent evaluation or reason but by intuition. Sabine writes, "The myth in Sorel's syndicalism is the creation of this type of intuition. It is a body of images capable of evoking sentiment instinctively." For the working class people, Sorel held out the myth of the general strike. The view of Sorel was that action must be instinctive and spontaneous and not the outcome of a logical process of thinking. Sorel rejected totally the democratic method of peaceful persuasion and accepted the path of "proletarian violence." His view was that "social struggle must assume the character of pure struggle similar to those of armies in a campaign. Continuous recourse to violence will show the impossibility of social peace and harmony. It will strengthen the moral fibre of the proletariat by stimulating to prepare themselves for the final assault on capitalism." Sorel refused to assign reason the pride of place in human action. Instead, he endowed intuition with sovereign importance. He rejected the rule of opinion and accepted the rule of force. Sorel was in favour of establishing an industrial self-government of the working class. His views were antidemocratic, anti-middle class and pro-Marxist. The workers were to organise a general strike and paralyse the government. That would put an end to capitalism and give rise to syndicalism.

Main Features of Syndicalism

(1) It is not possible to give a clear picture of syndicalist society because the Syndicalists themselves tried to avoid creating a clear image. The view of Sorel was that the giving of a clear picture of the future state of affairs would be detrimental to the interests of the workers. However,

the Syndicalists were anti-democratic. According to them, democracy is a farce. In the name of democracy, a few seize and exercise political power. The syndicalists have no faith in the institution of political parties or the party system on which modern democracy rests. They consider political parties as artificial groups.

(2) The syndicalists are opposed to the state which they call a bourgeois and middle class institution. The state is not only an instrument of capitalist exploitation of society but from its very nature it must remain a middle class institution in the society of tomorrow. The services of the state make man bureaucratic and unsympathetic to the needs and aspirations of those who are engaged in the actual work of production. The state has been designed to suit the convenience of the capitalists. It is not helpful and sympathetic to the cause of the workers. It protects the interests of the consumers and not producers. The authority of the state has always been used on behalf of the rich and against the workers. There has been a lot of bloodshed at the hands of the state. The existence of the state perpetuates injustice. It is only with the help of the state that the capitalists manage to save themselves and their privileges. "The central organisation tends to uniformity, to routine, to lack of imagination and initiative and to distrust of local development and enterprise." The state embodies the impossible ideal of social unity. The society is essentially pluralistic and no political philosophy can make it otherwise. The various groups have separate divergent interests and it is out of the question to reconcile them. The state stands in the way of the realisation of their ideal by the workers.

(3) The syndicalists are anti-militants. Their contention is that the workers have absolutely no interest in wars which are the outcome of the conflicting interests of the capitalists and hence the workers should keep aloof. They should not take part in war either on one side or the other. All the workers of the world have common interests and consequently they should not shed their blood aimlessly.

(4) The Syndicalists distrust middle class socialism. According to them, syndicalism is the only socialistic doctrine which is the product of the workers themselves. All other forms of socialism have emanated from the brains of clever middle class theorists. They show a tendency to regiment the workers in conformity with some pre-arranged system of society which has seemed good to a clique of intellectuals. They are out of touch with the needs of the workers which can be adequately expressed only by a system which is devised by the workers themselves.

(5) The Syndicalists insist on the control of the workers on society. Their view is that the workers create all value and hence they should be the controllers of society. They should exercise control not only in the economic or industrial sphere but also in the political field. They want the functions of the state to be taken over by the bodies of producers organised on occupational basis. The control of production by the workers would increase both the freedom of the workers and efficiency in industry. The workers will take personal interest in the management of industry. That will give them a sense of pride in their work and ultimately that would lead to improvement in the quantity and quality of the things produced.

(6) The Syndicalists are not in favour of joining conciliations for solving political problems. According to them, social classes and their conditions vary from place to place. Each society lays down its own standard of judging things. Each trade union has a right to decide its own policy and line of action. In the existing state and society, the property-owning class is ruling and society can be reformed only through workers' associations. Those associations should protect the material interests of the workers and also educate them. The Syndicalists preach the ideal of free work in a free society. The present society can be changed by the proper organisation of unions, labour exchanges, confederations and federations.

(7) The Syndicalists have no faith in parliamentary methods and they would like to boycott all parliamentary institutions because they are the product of the bourgeoisie and as such cannot be helpful to the workers. The association of the workers with parliamentary institutions is likely to lessen class

consciousness among them which alone can help them to overthrow the present capitalist society. The Syndicalists point out that whenever the workers entered legislatures and became ministers, they lost their enthusiasm for the cause of the workers. Millerand was a socialist but after joining the ministry, he ceased to be a socialist.

(8) The Syndicalists do not believe in constitutional and peaceful methods. They stand for violent and revolutionary methods of direct action. The methods advocated by them are *strikes*, sabotage, boycott and the label. Out of these, they put the greatest emphasis on strike. According to them, the workers working in various industries should resort to strikes very often. Those strikes are to be taken as rehearsals for the general strike which was to be resorted to in the long run for the purpose of ousting the capitalists and capturing the machinery of the state. The Syndicalists believe that strikes have an educative purpose. At the time of a strike, workers learn the lesson of obedience and discipline which are great virtues. Strikes have to be encouraged wherever and whenever possible. There can be strikes tor better wages or shorter hours of work. There is nothing objectionable about strikes. They give a feeling of solidarity to the workers.

The idea of a general strike as a political weapon was derived from Blanqui, the French Socialist writer. A general strike is not bound to be a strike of all the workers. It is possible that an adequate number of workers may not be guided by a vigorous class-conscious spirit. All that is wanted is a strike by a sufficiently large number of persons employed in key industries. That should be enough to paralyse capitalism. Such a result is possible on account of the increasing interdependence of modern industries. A general strike is to be declared as soon as an adequate number of class-conscious workers are prepared to go on sterile.

According to Sorel, the general strike is to be a "myth" to the workers, a myth being an idea which fills man with ardour, as the expectation of Christ's second Coming inspired the early Christians. Any attempt to rationalise the myth is bound to be misleading. For the purpose of estimating the worth or purpose of the general strike, "all the methods of discussion which are current among politicians, sociologists or people who pretend to political science, must be abandoned." The merit of this view is that it makes the concept unassailable. It is difficult to find a better weapon for the purposes of political controversy. As strikes are undertaken from motives which lie deep down in the institutional part of our nature, they "have engendered in the proletariat the noblest, deepest and most loving sentiments they possess; the general strike groups them all in a coordinated picture, and by bringing them together, gives to each one of them its maximum intensity. We thus obtain that intuition of socialism which language cannot give us with perfect clearness—and we obtain it as a whole, perceived instantaneously."

Another kind of action is *sabotage* which is of two kinds: peaceful and violent. The object of sabotage is to injure as much as possible the capitalists. The worker can injure his master without resorting to violent means. A shop assistant can sabotage the interests of his master by telling the customer that a particular article is old and not fresh. He can do the same by telling the customer the real quality of the article although it is concealed through the devices of his master. A worker can injure the interests of his master by working slowly and not as fast as he can. He can obey the letter of the order of his master and not the spirit. He can do the work so minutely that there is a fall in the output. Violent methods of sabotage are well-known. Workers may deliberately destroy the machinery with a view to injure the owner. While manufacturing a particular machine, workers may leave some loophole in it and when millions have been spent on it, it may collapse in no time. Undoubtedly, sabotage is destructive and for this reason some Syndicalists do not subscribe to it and put more emphasis on the weapon of general strike.

The policy of *boycott and label* shows that the work has been done under the trade union conditions. Ca canny methods can also result in loss to the employer.

(9) The Syndicalists are not in favour of piece-meal reforms as they deceived the workers. They believe in catastrophic revolutionary upsurge as a matter of social change. Reforms when gained through pressure inside the legislature, become an essay in class collaboration, but the Syndicalists believe in the theory of class war and not collaboration.

(10) The Syndicalists do not pin their faith in the revolution led by the whole mass of the proletariat. They depend upon a conscious and militant minority to inspire and lead the otherwise passive proletariat. "Every strike, every great demonstration, is generally started by a small and daring group with a vision." Again, "The effect of political majorities when they do make themselves felt, is to hinder advance and to suppress the progressive, active and more developed minorities. "The Syndicalists emphasise the permanent hegemony of an informed, determined minority over the inert proletariat. The Syndicalist accent on elitism reminds one of similar emphasis in Leninism.

(11) The Syndicate or the trade union is the base of Syndicalist society. It consists of workers engaged in one trade. They have to use social wealth for social benefit with the consent of society. The connecting link between the Syndicate and the rest of society is provided by the Bourse Du Travail or City Trade Union Council and the General Confederation of Labour. The relations of the local Syndicate with the General Confederation "will be indirect and mainly by mediation of the Bourse du Travail. Relations with the latter will be of permanent importance as Bourse du Travail will be the centres of economic activity."

(12) In a Syndicalist Society, there is no place for the state. Like the Marxists, the Syndicalists find the state to be "arbitrary and oppressive in its very nature." Modern state, through its legislative institutions, decides on subjects with which it has no intimate and genuine relation. However, when a syndicate decides, that would be in the light of an intimate knowledge of the concrete problem. Moreover, the state is the instrument of despotic class rule. The place of the state will be occupied by the local and national organisations in the new society.

Criticism of Syndicalism

(1) Syndicalism has been criticised on many grounds. Its philosophy represents only one side of the picture. It cares only for the interests of the producers and completely ignores the interests of consumers. Such a philosophy can positively harm the interests of the consumers and hence there can be no peace in society.

(2) The violent methods of the Syndicalists are condemned by critics. Those methods are bound to result in loss of life and property. Critics maintain that the same results could be achieved by constitutional and peaceful methods. "A general strike is unnecessary because a general election is never far off."

(3) There is no guarantee that the general strike will certainly succeed. The workers may not be able to carry their point on account of their weak position. They may not have enough resources to fall back upon during the period of the general strike. The armed forces of the state may be so strong that they may crush any attempt at a general strike. The failure of the general strike is bound to demoralise the workers. Sabotage is also destructive and harmful to society. If there is unnecessary waste, society as a whole suffers. Sabotage in production is bound to affect adversely the interests of the workers also.

(4) It is contended that the Syndicalists have deliberately kept their picture of the future vague and indefinite. That vagueness may turn out to be a weakness. The workers may not feel enthusiastic for a cause about whose future they are absolutely in the dark. Only the certainty regarding the future is likely to inspire the workers and prepare them for sacrifices.

(5) The Syndicalist picture of the future social order is also criticised. It is pointed out that too much attention has been given to the rights and responsibilities of producers and too little of the consumers. Too much emphasis has been put on control by local bourses and tool little on control by national units.

(6) The Socialists question the moral value of violence praised by Sorel and the desirability of laying so much emphasis on the negative side of the class struggle.

(7) Syndicalism is unrealistic. It wants to degrade the state. The aim of the Syndicalists is to break the backbone of the state but that would lead to anarchy. Syndicalism is wedded to violence which is the mother of several individual and social evils. Syndicalism gives a free hand to those who want to lessen production through sabotage and go slow tactics. These activities are harmful to society as a whole. Syndicalism is unpatriotic and anti-national.

(8) The Syndicalist assumption that the trade union is the most fundamental and permanent grouping and is most effective in inspiring man's active loyalty is open to objection. The same can be said about other social groupings like the family and the church.

(9) The perpetuation of conditions of naked violence and insurrection which the Syndicalist plan of action entails amounts to surrender of reason and abiding values of human civilisation to unreason and forces of barbarism. Gasset writes, "Under the species of syndicalism, there appears for the first time in Europe a type of man who does not want to give reason or be right but simply shows himself resolved to impose his opinions. This is the new thing: The right not be reasonable, the reason of unreason" (The Revolt of the Masses, p. 80).

(10) The Syndicalist picture of new society is subjected to criticism. Laidler writes, "Too much attention has been given to the rights and responsibilities of producers; too little to those of consumers. Too much emphasis has been put on control by the local bourses; too little on control by national units." (Social-Economic Movements, pp. 306-7).

(11) The anti-state sentiment in syndicalism and its impatience with every form of state control reveal the lack of awareness of living political realities. Pragmatic thinking demands recognition of the utility of the state as an integrating focus of the great society. The existing state structure may be defective, but the same can be modified and remodelled. The Syndicalist attempt to abandon it totally indicates a sense of unreality among the advocates of syndicalism.

(12) Ramsay MacDonald writes about syndicalism, "Society is in process of change, and the workers who are toiling for greater justice are only retarding progress by following the wrong-doing of which they are victims, rather than strengthening the social tendencies which make for their emancipation. The creative vitality of society is neither expressed nor strengthened by sabotage, riots, destruction of industrial capital, or any one of other minor violences of the Syndicalist programme."

The Syndicalist movement in France profoundly influenced socialist thinking in other parts of the world. It exposed the inadequacies of parliamentary democracy and emphasized the danger of bureaucratic distortion of socialism in state-socialist society. The guild socialist movement drew its inspiration from syndicalism in France. The stress on the leadership of an enlightened militant minority in early Bolshevik movement could be traced to syndicalism.

As a school of thought, syndicalism rendered great service to the world of workers by making them conscious of their position and galvanising and vitalising them to action. It stimulated socialist thinking and commanded the attention of democracy, parliamentarianism and state socialism. Syndicalism is right so far as it exposed the selfishness of the capitalists. According to Prof. Joad, "One of the merits of this doctrine is that by enabling Sorel to convict of irrelevance not only criticism but even discussion of the general strike, it makes the conception unassailable. It could be difficult to find a better weapon for the purpose of political controversy." While commending syndicalism, Bertrand Russell writes, "Whatever may be thought of the practicability of syndicalism, there is no doubt that ideas which it has put into the world have done a great deal to revive the labour movement and to recall it to certain things of fundamental importance which it had been in danger of forgetting."

Guild Socialism

Guild socialism is a mid-way house between the extremes of syndicalism and collectivism or state socialism. It is described as the intellectual child of English Fabianism and French Syndicalism. Fabianism proved too weak to eradicate the evils of capitalism and syndicalism was too revolutionary to suit the British temperament. According to F.W. Coker, "Guild socialism is like the earlier French Syndicalism in its aversion to all doctrines that make productive activity dependent upon political authority. It would protect the worker not only against exploitation by capitalists but also against any bureaucratic suppression of craftsmanship. Its object is to make work more interesting and the whole economic structure of society more democratic." Florence Elliot calls guild socialism "a British variant of syndicalism." According to G.D.H. Cole, "Guild socialism is based on the idea of partnership between the producers and the state in the control of industry. Guild socialism recognises that the state is necessary and that a purified parliament is necessary. At the same time. Guild Socialists hold that the first need of socialism is the placing of industrial power in the hands of the workers and that without such industrial freedom every change in the structure of society must be a bureaucratic sham." C.E.M. Joad writes, "The Guild Socialists may best be described as a small body of intellectual theorists working within the Labour movement with the object of converting the influential men of the movement of their views but not as a general rule making any direct appeal for the support of the masses."

The Guild Socialists are opposed to the cast-iron centralisation and regimentation of state socialism which they describe as "bureaucracy masquesading as democracy." The Guild Socialists advocate that "the real and effective power ought to be in the hands of the workers." Guild socialism aims at placing power in the hands of democracies of producers and democracies of consumers within the frame-work of the state. The Guild Socialist movement advocated the restoration of Medieval guild system along modern lines. The Guild Socialists believed that value was created corporately by society and not by individuals singly. The capitalist economists defended the acquisition of wealth without reference to the responsibilities and opportunities for rendering service to the community. The trade unions were to be organised as guilds to take over and run their respective industries after nationalisation.

Origin and Growth of Guild Socialism

Guild socialism originated in the second decade of the twentieth century, though its basic ideas were given by A.J. Penty (1875-1935) as early as 1906 in his book "The Restoration of the Guild System." In 1915, the Guild Socialists established the National Guilds League in Britain. This organisation could boast of having eminent thinkers like Hobson, Penty, Orage and G.D.H. Cole as its members.

The view of Penty was that on account of the large-scale industry under state socialism, no scope was left in actual practice for beauty and craftsmanship. The individual worker became merely a cog in the machine and his individuality completely disappeared. A worker was merely one of the very many who contributed towards the making of the things which appeared in the final form. Penty advocated the creation of guilds on the lines which existed in Medieval times.

George Hobson (1864-1904) and A.R. Orage (1873-1934) studied the guild socialist principles of Penty. They tried to modify the ideas of Penty to suit modern conditions. Orage powerfully expressed his views through the columns of the weekly *New Age* which he was editing. Those articles were in course of time published in a book form called "National Guilds, An Enquiry into the Wage System and the Way Out." This book gave a systematic exposition of the views of Hobson and Orage.

G.D.H. Cole was the "infant prodigy of guild socialism." He joined the Fabian Society when he was merely an under-graduate. In 1912, he organised the Fabian Research Department for the purpose of studying labour problems. In 1913, he became a Guild Socialist. He was the most prolific and active propagandist of the movement. His important works were. "The World of Labour" 1913, "Self-Government in Industry" (1917), "Social Theory" (1920), Guild Socialism Restated (1920), British Trade and Industry (1931), Economic Tracts for The Times (1932) and "The Intelligent Man's Guide Through World Chaos" (1932).

The goal of the Guild Socialists as described by the National Guilds League was the "abolition of the wage system and the establishment by the workers of self-government in industry through a democratic system of national guilds working in conjunction with other democratic functional organisations in the community." According to the Guild Socialists, "The real and effective power ought to be in the hands of the workers."

Favourable Factors for Growth of Guild Socialism

There were certain factors which were favourable for tae growth of guild socialism in England. The works of great writers like Thomas Carlyle, William Morris and John Ruskin who criticised the evils of industrial capitalism and praised the advantages of medieval guilds, supported the cause of guild socialism. They criticised the ugliness and monotony of machine production and looked back to the times when independent Guildsmen of the Medieval Ages took pride in their creative work and created the greatest art of which the world could boast of. The French Syndicalist movement and theories of American industrial political action and their slogan "*All power to the workers or producers*" helped the rise of guild socialism. The writings of G.K. Chesterton and Hilaire Belloc who criticised the policy of the British Government as one leading to the establishment of a "servile state" and pleading in favour of a "distributive state" also strengthened the cause of guild socialism. During the twentieth century, the Socialists condemned the wage system of capitalism and suggested production on non-profit basis. That led to the idea that the determination of wages, mode of production etc. should be left to the producers or workers. That also gave support to guild socialism. The evils of individualism also helped the growth of guild socialism. The shortcomings of individualism were highlighted and that helped guild socialism.

Essentials of Guild Socialism

(1) The Guild Socialists attacked the capitalist system of production under which the workers did not get their due share and the capitalists got more than their proportionate share. They also protested against the dehumanising effects of the machine system under which the processes of production were so minutely distributed that the working life of each labourer consisted merely of routine refixations of automatic responses. The individuality of the worker was lost and he became merely a cog in the machine.

(2) The Guild Socialists were opposed to the democratic system of government as it worked in actual practice. They attacked the system of territorial representation on the ground that a person who represented his locality could not be expected to decide questions relating to the relationship between producers and consumers. They advocated the reorganisation of society on a functional basis. According to them, there were to be as many separately elected groups of representatives as there were distinct and essential groups of functions to be performed. Each man was to be given as many votes as his separate interest demanded. Each industry was to be administered by a cooperative organisation of all those who worked in that industry. This work was to be put into the hands of a guild which was defined as "a self-governing association of mutually dependent people organised for the responsible discharge of a particular function of society." Each guild was to include all the workers who took any part in a particular service for which that guild existed. It was immaterial whether the work was manual or technical, skilled or unskilled, clerical or managerial, but all those workers were to belong to the same guild. Each guild was to be given complete autonomy in its work but not absolute freedom.

(3) There was a difference of opinion among the Guild Socialists regarding the organisation of guilds. Some were opposed to the organisation of guilds on a national basis on the ground that in that case the very object of guild socialism would be frustrated. They advocated the organisation of guilds on local basis only. However, a majority of the Guild Socialists were in favour of the organisation of guilds on national basis. Their view was that the system could not work properly unless the activities of the various guilds in different parts of the country were coordinated and that was not possible if every guild of a locality was given complete autonomy and had nothing to do with the guilds in other localities. However, they were in favour of a lot of local autonomy for the individual guilds. The amount of centralisation or local autonomy was to depend upon the nature of the industry or the service concerned.

(4) It is true that every local guild was given a lot of autonomy, but provision was also made for taking appeals to the national guilds. According to Cole, a National Industrial Guild Congress was to represent all the national guilds. It was to be the final representative of the guild system as a whole. It was to perform the important function of laying down and interpreting the essential principles of guild organisation in practice. It was to act as the guild legislature and the final court of appeal in matters relating to guilds. It was to dispose of all disputes among the various guilds, act as their representative in their common external relations and lay down general principles for the guidance of the guilds. It was to levy taxes on various guilds and raise the necessary revenue for its work. It was to act as a representative of producers in their negotiations with the representatives of consumers. Every guild was to be so organised as to coordinate its productive activity with that of other guilds on a national scale. Every allowance was to be made for differences in localities and industries. No effort was to be spared to encourage individual initiative and self-expression.

(5) As guilds were put incharge of the whole of the production system of the country, there was always the possibility of a danger to society. The guilds may ignore altogether the interests of the consumers. They may not produce the type of goods required by the consumers. They may demand unreasonably high prices for the goods manufactured by them. With a view to provide against those and other dangers, the Guild Socialists advocated joint consultation between the Producers Guilds and Consumers Councils. It was in those meetings that the question of costs and prices and other relevant matters concerning both the parties were to be discussed and settled.

(6) The Guild Socialists stood for functional democracy. Their view was that political democracy was meaningless without democracy in the industrial field. Economic power precedes political power. If capitalists were to continue to exercise their control in the industrial field, political democracy was meaningless. The machinery of the state was bound to be worked in the interests of the capitalists. That explains why the Guild Socialists wanted to put the workers incharge of the whole of the production system. There was no other way to emancipate the workers from the tyranny of capitalists.

(7) The Guild Socialists were not opposed to the institution of the state as such. However, the various exponents of guild socialism were not agreed with regard to the part to be played by the state. According to Hobson, the state was to continue as the representative of the community as a whole. It was to continue to occupy a place of authority and supremacy but was to delegate some of its functions and powers to other associations. The authority of the state was to be lessened but not eliminated altogether. The state was to own all the plants and tools and was to lease them out to the various guilds. It was to act as a court of final appeal in cases of disputes between the guilds. It was to have authority to levy taxes on various guilds. It was to finance those guilds which rendered useful service to society in the form of education, public health etc. It was to lay down the outlines of policy to be followed by those guilds. It was to give protection to the people, both from within and without. For that purpose, it was to maintain an army, a navy and a police force. It was to set up civil and criminal courts and enforce the law of the country. It was to regulate international relations in economic and political fields.

However, the view of Cole was different. He did not give the state the same authority which was given by Hobson. He tried to put the state on the same footing as the other guilds. The state was to be an association like other associations and its functions were to be proportionate to the duties performed by it. The guilds were to control and manage the whole of production. The state was to look after the interests of the consumers and for that purpose was to regulate prices and distribution of income. It was to perform such functions as the regulation of marriage and divorce, education of children, prevention and punishment of crimes, defence of the country etc. In the case of a conflict between the guilds and the state the institution known as the Supreme Court of Functional Equity was to have the final word. It was also to possess the supreme power of coercion.

Cole did not content himself with this role of the state. He went a step further by minimising the importance of the state. His view was that the state could be allowed to wither away and ultimately disappear altogether "either after a frontal attack or by atrophy following upon dispossession of its vital power." The various guilds were to be organised into communes and given separate powers and functions. They were to control prices and also fix the amount of money to be spent in various industries and services. They were to have the power of revising and ratifying the objects of the various guilds. They were to settle disputes between various guilds and distribute powers among the various guilds. They were to have power of declaring war and making peace, conducting foreign relations, fixing territorial boundaries and regulating and controlling the relations of the people in matters of property etc.

(8) The Guild Socialists advocated the use of constitutional and peaceful methods for the establishment of a Guild Socialist society. They were against the violent methods advocated by the Syndicalists. They were prepared to use the machinery of the state for passing legislation which aimed at the amelioration of the working classes and elimination of evils in the capitalist society. They were prepared to cooperate will all those parties which aimed at the good of the workers. Cole explained the method of guild socialism in these words: "The thing to be aimed at is not evolutionary development with a view to making the revolution which in a sense must come, as little as possible a civil war and as much as possible registration of accomplished facts and a culmination of tendencies already in operation."

(9) The Guild Socialists advocated the policy of "encroaching control." They aimed at snatching, bit by bit, from the hands of capitalists as many functions of control as possible and exercising them. Workers were to have the right to elect their foremen and overseers. They were to regulate the environments in which they were to work. There was to be no interference from outside. They were to follow a policy of collective contracts. Guilds were to take over the whole of the work and distribute the various functions among themselves. It was felt that a sense of responsibility would grow among workers and help the growth of personalities.

Criticism of Guild Socialism

(1) Guild socialist philosophy has been criticised on many grounds. It is contended that it is not possible to divide economic and political questions into watertight compartments. In actual practice, it is difficult to see how economic questions can be given completely to guilds and political questions to the state.

(2) Guild socialism was bound to fail on account of the inter-dependence of all the activities of "the great societies of today. To assign international relations to the state and economic production to the guilds is futile. International relations involve the question of economic production and vice versa. Guild socialism is illogical".

(3) Guild Socialists stood for two parliaments. The political parliament was to be organised on territorial basis and economic parliament on functional basis. The question was if there was a conflict between the two, how the same was to be resolved. A joint committee of two parliaments having equal

powers may not be helpful in solving the difficulty. There was always the necessity of a supreme power which could not be any other than the state. Hobson writes, "The notion of two states—one a federation of trades and guilds running through the whole body of economic arrangement for the nation by representative committees based upon the, common interests of the industry and the other of political state running the services relating to internal and external order and only concerned to intervene in economic affairs at a few reserved points of contact, will not bear criticism."

(4) Critics maintain that the control of production by guilds will bring about stagnation in industry. There will be indiscipline and slackness in work and hence no efficiency. The total production of the country will fall which will not be desirable from the point of view of workers and consumers. The mere motive of social service will not be strong enough to give the necessary incentive to hard work. There may be no encouragement for inventions or new methods of production. In other words, guild socialism "discourages and damps down all the instincts of hard and creative toil and its genius its purely predatory."

(5) The despotic nature of the monopoly to be exercised by guilds was liable to lead to bankruptcy of the country. The guilds may start quarrelling with one another and that might create an intolerable situation. The interests of the country as a whole may be subordinated to those of the various guilds.

(6) Critics point out the difficulty, if not the impossibility, of a super-imposing guild structure of the Middle Ages on modern industry. They particularly criticise Penty's advocacy of the revival of old guilds with handicraftmanship, as opposed to machine production and their local units of organisation. In the light of international trade, capitalist enterprises and division of labour, such an attempt at restoration is chimerical. The guilds of the Middle Ages should not be over-idealised. Before their dissolution, guilds had fallen into the hands of cliques. Their journeymen were considered inferior to the associates in industry. The regulations imposed by them were often arbitrary and monopolistic. They were destroyed through their own failures as much as through anti-social institutions emerging at that time.

(7) Cole differed from Penty in striving to establish the spirit of the guilds and not their structure. He did not believe in local industry. He was in favour of accelerating present day economic concentration. The view of Carpenter is that the guild system and modern industrialism "are cast of entirely different metal. The one was built around highly skilled, small skilled handicrafts, rigidly restricted, strongly traditional, fiercely local. The other takes for granted the unskilled, minutely divided labour; large-scale machine production; remorseless change and innovation; national and even international organisation."

(8) Many writers have questioned the desirability of destroying the state as proposed by Cole and then building up the commune with its potentially great industrial and economic power. Others maintain that with the checks and balances proposed for the commune, it will not be able to reach decisions on many questions placed before it for consideration. Carpenter writes that the guild commune "would organise people upon the basis of their different and divergent interests; would give them an opportunity to thwart each other and would give nobody—not even the population as whole—a chance to make them compose their differences. The omni-competent state admittedly works badly at times; but it does work which is more than the important commune would be likely to do." MacIver observes, "The danger is not that particular interests will not be focussed and asserted, but rather that the general interest may suffer domination through their urgency. Against this danger the general bulwark is the state, because its organisation presupposes and in some degree realizes the activity of the general will."

(9) Under guild socialism, each group may not be able to speak with authority on all questions and on all problems. A producers' association may be able to speak with authority on particular issues but has no moral authority to speak for the whole of the vocational world. The vocational associations can speak with authority on particular problems but they cannot do the same with

general questions. When the general questions come up before them, their judgement is not valid. If they approach the general questions from the larger standpoint, they no longer speak as members of the craft. Vocational bodies may be valuable to deal with functional problems but they are not competent to deal with general issues. Some vocations within a given unit may not be adequately represented. A medical guild may be dominated by the general practitioners and they cannot speak with authority on issues concerning dentists, nurses, etc. Even if a satisfactory system for functional representation can be devised, it is difficult to settle its relations with the state. It is also difficult to allocate the subjects with which the state is to concern itself. Any system of functional representation must take into consideration the vital fact of the division of society into two groups, the capitalists and the proletariat. A government built upon such functional representation will be a complicated one, not within the grasp of the ordinary citizens. There is every likelihood of the functional groups falling in the hands of party bosses and they would control the policy of the state also. Such a state of affairs is not congenial to a democratic system. While introducing functional representation, it will be difficult to decide the ratio in which labour and capital are to be represented. There is also the problem of representation of women. If they are to be represented as a functional group in proportion to their numbers, a distinction will have to be made between married house-wives and the unmarried women, as unmarried women have problems different from those of married women. There can be no justice unless both the married and unmarried women are given representation in proportionate to their numbers. Moreover, functional representation is not relevant to the purpose of a legislative assembly. There cannot be a medical view of foreign policy.

(10) The doctrine of guild socialism is unrealistic and bound to fail in practice. It looks nice on paper to divide powers between the state and the various guilds, without giving the state the necessary powers to function. In view of such division, even with the best of intentions and intelligence, it may fail in practice. The theory of guild socialism is illogical because economic and political functions cannot be strictly divided into weatertight compartments.

(11) The approach of Guild Socialists is doctrinaire. It is not possible to get rid of sovereignty as Guild Socialists imagine. While Guild Socialists like Cole may succeed in destroying sovereignty, they will create another organisation which will, have to take the place of the state and exercise sovereignty. One type of sovereignty will have to make way for another type of sovereignty. Hearnshaw writes, "The constitution of the state contemplated by Cole is a complicated nightmare of committees and joint committees which reminds one of the machinery made by boy out to Meccano."

Merits of Guild Socialism

Guild socialism is in line with the modern trend which encourages pluralist thinking among the producers and gives a blow to the absolute sovereignty of the state. Guild socialism preaches the idea of participation of the workers in the management of industries. This idea of joint management by employers and employees appeals to man and has paved the way for the modern concept of workers' participation in management. After the World War I, the Guild Socialists raised the question of housing in England and enthusiastically undertook the task of constructing buildings and different guilds were integrated into the National Building League. However, the experiment failed and the National Guilds League was abolished in 1925.

Anarchism

The word anarchism is taken from the Greek word *Anarchia* which means no rule. Florence Elliott defines anarchism as "a political doctrine advocating the abolition of organised authority. Anarchists hold that every form of government is evil and tyranny. They want a free association of individuals, without armed forces, courts, prisons or written law." According to Kropotkin, anarchism is "a principle or theory of life and conduct under which society is conceived without government—harmony in such a society being obtained not by submission to law or by obedience to any authority, but by free agreements concluded between the various groups, territorial and professional, freely constituted for the sake of production and consumption, as also for the satisfaction of the infinite variety of needs—aspirations of a civilised being." F.W. Coker defines anarchism as "the doctrine that political authority in any of its forms, is unnecessary and undesirable. In recent anarchism, theoretical opposition to the state has usually been associated with opposition to the institution of private property and also with hostility to organise religious authority." E.M. Burns writes, "Correctly defined, anarchism means opposition to government based upon force. No Anarchist with pretensions to philosophical understanding has ever proposed to dispense entirely with government. He condemns the state conceived as an agency of coercion with armies, jails and police, but he regards government as at least potentially a beneficent institution." Bertrand Russell observes, "Anarchism, as its derivation indicates, is the theory which is opposed to every kind of forcible government. It is opposed to the state as the embodiment of the force employed in the government of the community. Such government as anarchism can tolerate, must be free government, not merely in the sense that it is that of majority, but in the sense that it is that assented to by all. Anarchists object to such institutions as the police and the criminal law by means of which the will of one part ot the community is forced upon another part. Liberty is the supreme goal to the Anarchist creed and Liberty is sought by the direct road of abolishing all forcible control over the individual by the community." C.E.M. Joad writes, "The sources of authority from which anarchism would emancipate the individual may be reduced to three: (1) It would free man as a producer from the yoke of the capitalists. (2) It would free man as a citizen from the yoke of the state. (3) It would free man as an individual from the authority of religious morality derived from hypothetical, metaphysical entities such as an omnipotent God."

Exponents of Anarchism

The chief exponents of anarchism were Godwin (1756-1836) Hodgskin, Proudhon (1809-1865), Warren, Tucker, Schmidt, Thoreau (1817-62), Count Tolstoy (1828-1910), Bakunin (1814-76) and Kropotkin (1842-1921). Modern anarchism seems to have been first suggested by Godwin who was opposed both to political authority and private property. Proudhon was possibly the first writer to declare himself openly an Anarchist. In his book "What is Property?", Proudhon wrote, "I am, in the full sense of the word, an Anarchist." He called property as theft and found the origin of the state in the institution of private property which was the purpose of the state to maintain. According to him, political authority was the enemy of justice, reason and fair deal.

There are two groups of Anarchist writers: Individualistic Anarchists and Communistic Anarchists. *The Individualistic Anarchists* were content with philosophical and literary expositions of their doctrine. They had sublime faith in the individual and invested him with property rights. The view of Max Stirner was that the individual was the only reality and his right to freedom entitled him to overthrow any authority whatsoever. His ideas reappeared in the philosophy of Nietzsche which was characterised by the exaltation of the rights of the Superman. The theory of individualistic anarchism was popularised in the United States by Warren and Tucker. However, it did not make much headway there.

The *Communistic Anarchists* formulated distinct political and social doctrines. They liked to replace the state by voluntary associations and believed in revolutionary rather than evolutionary methods for bringing about the necessary changes. Bakunin belonged to this group. According to him, the eventual disappearance of political authority, private property and religion was written in the logic of human evolution. Those institutions were symptomatic of man's primitive nature and would be superseded by higher and nobler developments. He criticised political authority because it perpetuated inequitable economic conditions and debased human morality. In his opinion, both evolutionary and revolutionary techniques would be necessary to achieve the anarchist goal. After the liquidation of state and private property, a free society based on mutuality would be established. The principle of individual allegiance will not be legal and compulsive but spontaneous and voluntary.

The ideas of Bakunin were adopted by Kropotkin. He was also inspired by Darwin's biological principle of mutual aid. The view of Kropotkin was that the state is unnatural and artificial because it imposes restraints and compulsions on the naturally cooperative instincts and impulses of man. It sustains some laws for the benefit of a group or property-owners. The state did not make any positive contribution to civilisation. Its activities were superfluous and those could be taken over by voluntary associations. The state was not competent to discharge the functions already taken over by it. Tolstoy blended the theory of anarchism with Christian Socialism. The ideas of Proudhon, Bakunin and Kropotkin were popularised in France by Elisee Reclus and Jean Grave.

Main Characteristics of Anarchism

(1) The Anarchists stand for a social system organised on a voluntary basis. They do not like authority in any shape or form. They would like to destroy all kinds of authorities. Particularly, they attack the state, the Church and private property or capitalists. They point out the evils involved in allowing the authority of the Church. The Church has always been an ally of the rich. It has preached to the poor the philosophy of contentment and submission to the iniquities existing in the present social system. Religion is the opium of the people. It is static and opposed to progress. Social progress is impossible so long as the authority of the Church or religion is not eliminated altogether. Religion makes the people superstitious and tolerant of the injustices of the political authorities and capitalists. The Church is the friend of the state and capitalists. It has been misleading and befooling the poor and the needy by reconciling their lot with the existing system. Religion is a force of evil. Religious institutions are the centres of corruption.

(2) The Anarchists are opposed to private property. Proudhon called private property as theft. Private property leads to the misery of the people. It gives rise to the questions of mine and thine. It is the source of disputes and quarrels among the people. It results in the exploitation of the vast majority of the people. It is the root cause of capitalism. Capitalism flourishes under private property. In turn, capitalism leads to various evils like the degradation of those who work, the enjoyment by the few who do not work, poverty and suffering to the millions, extravagance and vulgar ostentation of the rich, the enormous waste in society, immorality and unemployment. Capitalism results in injustice. In enables a few to enjoy the fruits of the labour of many. It encourages wars. It results in the economic dependence of the poor. It is responsible for spiritual and social immobility.

(3) Anarchism is anti-state with a vengeance. It condemns the state as not only undesirable but also unnecessary. The state has only one function and that is "to sign its own death warrant and then to die". The state is not only superfluous but also injurious to society. The police, jails, courts etc. which have been established by the state, tend rather to increase than to check evils and vices in society. The state has been responsible for perpetuating inequalities and injustice in society. The state makes the innocent persons criminals and then punishes them because they are criminals. It has miserably failed to protect the interests of those who really stand in need of protection. It acts through force and the use of force by the state corrupts those who exercise it and debases and dehumanises those on whom it is exercised. It makes them selfish, cruel and arrogant. It destroys all moral values. Lowes Dickinson writes in Modern Symposium, "Modern Government means compulsion, exclusion, distribution, separation; while anarchy is freedom, union and love. Government is based on egotism and fear, anarchy on fraternity. It is because we divide ourselves into nations that we endure the oppression of armaments; because we isolate ourselves as individuals that we invoke the protection of laws." Kropotkin says: "This or that despicable minister might have been an excellent man, if power had not been given to him."

(4) The state is superfluous. There is nothing which the state does and which cannot be done without its existence. The state performs the duty of the defence of the country against foreign

invaders. It maintains armed forces for that purpose. The view of the Anarchists is that the same work can be done more effectively if the state ceases to exist. Kropotkin writes, "Standing armies are always beaten by invaders who have historically been repulsed only by spontaneous uprising." A citizen army is a much better effective weapon for defence than mercenary soldiers employed by the state. Hence, the state is not necessary for defence.

(5) Likewise, state is not necessary for maintaining law and order. The necessity of boundaries arises in a state on account of the existence of the social order based on injustice and inequality. The authority of the police and magistracy is required for the purpose of maintaining the status quo. In the anarchist society based on justice, freedom and voluntary cooperation of the people, there will be no necessity for the state. Man by nature is not bad, but he is made bad by his environments. There will be no necessity of any authority to maintain law and order because there will be no temptation for the individual to wrong another individual. The state disturbs the Law of evolution which, in the words of Bakunin is "a progressive negation of man's original bestiality and progressive evolution of his humanity." The state is not required for educational purposes. Even in the present society based on injustice, a lot of educational work is done by voluntary associations. The state does only a past of the work. The Anarchists maintain that in anarchist society, the state will not be required for the education of the people. All that is required is an increase in the number of societies, clubs and academies engaged in the work of education.

C.E.M. Joad writes, "The state as it exists today is used by the few as an instrument to protect their unjust monopolies of those things which rightly belong to all. For this very reason, therefore, the state cannot be used to accomplish the abolition of the monopolies it protects. It follows that, until the state is replaced by some organisation other than the State, Capitalism and private property can never pass away. The state, in short, can never be seized and used, as some socialists suggest, for the purpose of inaugurating a new era of society. For this reason, the Anarchists are opposed to any extension of the present function of government, even when they appear to be in the interests of the masses, nor do they encourage working men to join political parties or to obtain election to the national parliament."

(6) The Anarchists are opposed to representative government which they consider as a sort of fraud. Joad writes, "Representative government is a government by men who know just enough about everything to enable them to do everything badly, and not enough about everything to enable them to do anything well." Representative government is a government by amateurs and cannot be expected to be efficient. The whole of the representative system is unreal. It is difficult to say that any person can represent the people adequately. The representative may express his opinion on a particular matter but not on every matter that comes before the legislature. It is possible that a general view may not agree with the views of the people.

(7) The Anarchists would like to set up a *stateless and classless society.* People with common tastes will join together for particular purposes. They will cooperate with one another to produce things required for society. There will be no compulsion for grouping. The people will group themselves in a way which is most advantageous to their growth and development. There will be no competition but free cooperation. There will be no conflict but mutual aid. There will be no coercion but voluntary grouping. Each will help the other to do that which is in the highest interest of society as a whole. Such a thing is possible because human nature grows when there are no unnecessary restrictions or interruptions from without. According to Bakunin, man's liberty is only the mirroring of his humanity, *i.e.*, all his human rights are the consciousness of his brother. In anarchist society, there is bound to be a lot of decentralisation. A beginning is to be made with small groups on a local basis. Then the local groups will be consolidated and integrated into bigger groups covering the whole country. Grouping is to be from below upwards and not vice versa. If there are disputes among the groups, those are to be adjusted. It is hoped that there will be practically no dispute as society is organised on a voluntary basis. The spirit of natural friendliness and cooperation will

prevail in society and hence there will be very little possibility of any conflict. The grouping will be natural and harmonious. Fourier writes, "Take pebbles, put them into a box and shake them and they will arrange themselves into a mosaic that you could never get by entrusting to any one the work of arranging them harmoniously." Joad observes, "Anarchism is first and foremost a plea for decentralisation, both territorial and functional."

Methods of Anarchists

There are two schools of thought among the Anarchists regarding the method by which anarchist society is to be established. One school advocates the use of violence and the other stands for an evolutionary and peaceful process. The advocates of the revolutionary school believe in the wholesale destruction of the existing society. Their view is that anarchist society can be established only by violent methods because the institutions of the state, capitalism and religion cannot be eliminated without force. The vested interests are bound to resist with force and the only way to deal with force is to employ force. The Anarchists believe even in murders. They murdered Tsar Alexander of Russia, King Humbert of Italy, President Carnot of France, Empress Elizabeth of Austria and President McKinley of the United States.

However, Anarchists like Tolstoy stand for the employment of peaceful methods. They aim at weakening the state step by step and finally destroying it through love and persuasion. They believe that human society is developing in such a manner that the state will become unnecessary. It will disappear when it is not needed. Anarchist society can be established by the methods of education, example and persuasion.

Criticism of Anarchism

(1) Critics point out that anarchism is a philosophy of destruction. It relies upon brute force for the realisation of its goals. By resorting to violence, destruction and murder, the Anarchists want to establish a society based on love, persuasion and cooperation. That is a human impossibility. Love cannot come out of murder, destruction or violence. The remedy suggested is worse than the disease. The Anarchists stand for the complete destruction of the state which is neither practical, feasible or desirable. The voluntary associations advocated by the Anarchists will not be able to discharge some of the functions of the state and authority in one form or the other will be necessary. Otherwise, there will be chaos and the law of the jungle will prevail. Bertrand Russell writes. "The state in spite of what anarchists urge seems a necessary institution for certain purposes. Peace and war, Tariffs, regulation of sanitary conditions and of the sale of noxious drugs, the preservation of a just system of distribution; these, among others, are functions which could hardly by performed in a community in which there was no central government. The state, though at present a source of much evil, is also a means to certain good things, and will be needed so long as violent and destructive impulses remain."

(2) Critics point out that the Anarchists are wrong in presuming that there is fundamental contradiction between authority and liberty. The fact is that there is no antagonism between authority and liberty. Experience shows that in the absence of the state and government, there is no freedom for any one except the strong, the crooked and the dare-devils. Might will be right. It is the authority of the state which regulates and guarantees liberty.

(3) The spontaneous development of individuals is not possible without a state. It is true that morality is self-developed but the state also can help its development by creating the circumstances under which morality can grow.

(4) Experience shows that the growth of civilisation and the existence of the state have gone hand in hand. Without the state, there is neither peace nor progress. The state creates the surroundings in which civilisation can grow. There must be some sort of government among civilised men without which civilisation cannot progress. Even if the present state is destroyed and its place is taken over

by the other associations, there will come into existence some institutions like that of the state which will mean merely a change of government.

(5) The problems of the modern world and society have become so complex and complicated that they cannot be solved without the authority of the state. Human beings are selfish and it may be difficult to control them without the authority of the state. The members of voluntary associations may not be intelligent enough to tackle successfully the problems of modern society.

(6) The assumptions of anarchism are not warranted by facts. F.W. Coker writes, "Most anarchist doctrines rest upon assumptions of the predominance of the social and cooperative, not the self-seeking and competitive instincts of man" However, the competitive instincts of man are as powerful as his cooperative instinct. Anarchism is based on faith in innate human rationality. The exploration of the world of human psychology suggests the preponderance of irrational forces determining human behaviour.

(7) Another criticism is that the Anarchist description of the nature of the state as a coercive authority is grossly exaggerated. The state functions both through compulsion and cooperation. Many areas of state activity such as those involving social services, are free from force and coercion.

(8) The picture of anarchist society is the picture of a millennium which is an unrealisable ideal. The assumptions on which anarchist society is to be built are not based on realities of life. Without a state, liberty degenerates into tyranny of the strong. A condition of unlimited liberty aimed at by the Anarchists is a vision which cannot be realised. The Anarchist belief in automatic harmony in society in which there are very many groups, smacks of Utopianism. The existence of many groups must result in clashes and only an authority can control them.

Merits

Although there are many shortcomings in anarchist philosophy, it has certain merits also. There has been an all-round expansion of the functions and powers of the state in modern times with the result that a servile state has emerged which is administered by a powerful bureaucracy regimenting and controlling the life of man. The Anarchists have done well by highlighting the dangers of the over-growth of political power. By weakening the state and the creation of voluntary associations and groups, the Anarchists emphasize the importance of cooperation among the people and individual initiative which is conducive to social progress. The Anarchists condemn the institution of private property and capitalism. By doing so, they highlight the evils of private property and capitalism in modern society. Their plea for eliminating exploitation, oppression, misery and injustice is laudable. The Anarchists have done great service by exposing the exploitation of man in the name of religion and superstition. Another thing emphasized by the Anarchists is that, no person or association has any right to rule over any individual without his consent and justice and freedom are possible only when there is no coercion.

Lancaster writes about anarchism, "Essentially it is a protest against the speedy centralization of political power and the increasing mechanization of life generally. It is on the side of federalism, regionalism, and the small social unit and is a defence of cultural variety and the virtues of voluntary associations. Against the tendency to standardize and level out, it sets the creativeness of the free individual and the spontaneous group. It emphasizes the good qualities of liberty and justice as contrasted with what its abhorents regard as inhuman and sterile efficiency."

SUGGESTED READINGS

Baradat, L.P.	:	Political Ideologies, Their Origin and Impact, Englewood Cliffs, 1979.
Barker, Ernest	:	Political Thought in England (1848-1914).
Beer, M.	:	History of British Socialism, New York, 1921.
Bernstein, E.	:	Evolutionary Socialism, New York, 1909.
Burns, E.M.	:	Ideas in Conflict, 1960.
Coker, F.W.	:	Recent Political Thought, 1957.
Cole, G.D.H.	:	Fabian Socialism, London, 1943.
Cole, G.D.H.	:	Guild Socialism Re-stated.
Cole G.D.H.	:	Socialist Thought, Marxism and Anarchism, 1850-90.
Davis, J.	:	Contemporary Social Movements.
Durbin, F.F.M.	:	The Politics of Democratic Socialism.
Ebenstein	:	Modern Political Thought, 1960.
Ebenstein	:	Great Political Thinkers.
Ebenstein, W.	:	Today's Isms.
Ensor, R.	:	Modern Socialism.
Field, G.C.	:	Guild Socialism.
Gettell	:	History of Political Thought.
Graham Wallas	:	Human Nature in Politics.
Hallowell, J.H.	:	Main Currents in Modern Political Thought.
Harley, J.H.	:	Syndicalism.
Joad, C.E.M.	:	Introduction to Modern Political Theory, London, 1954.
Jaures, J.	:	Studies in Socialism, 1906.
Kirkup, T.	:	A History of Socialism.
Kropotkin, P.	:	Anarchism, its Philosophy and Ideal.
Laidler, H.W.	:	History of Socialism, London, 1908.
Laidler, H.W.	:	Social-Economic Movements.
Lancaster	:	Masters of Political Thought.
Levine, L.	:	Syndicalism in France.
Macdonald, J.R.	:	Syndicalism.
MacIver, R.M.	:	The Modern State.
Mahajan, V.D.	:	Recent Political Thought.
Maxey, C.C.	:	Political Philosophies.
Miliband, R.	:	Parliamentary Socialism, London, 1961.
Pease, E.R.	:	History of the Fabian Society, New York, 1925.
Pigou, A.C.	:	Socialism versus Capitalism, 1937.
Popper, K.	:	The Open Society and Its Enemies, London, 1945.

Rappoport	:	Dictionary of Socialism.
Roucek (Ed.)	:	Twentieth Century Political Thought.
Roucek, J.S. and Others	:	Introduction to Political Science, 1954.
Sabine, G.H.	:	A History of Political Theory.
Shaw, G.B. and Others	:	Fabian Essays, Boston, 1908.
Sorel	:	Reflections on Violence.
Spargo and Arer	:	Elements of Socialism.
Tawney, R.H.	:	The Acquisitive Society.
Taylor, G.R.	:	The Guild State.
Ulam, Adam B.	:	Philosophical Foundations of English Socialism.
Vizetelly, E.A.	:	The Anarchists.
Wayper, C.L.	:	Political Thought.
Wilson, C.	:	Anarchism.

40

CHAPTER

Marxism and Bolshevism

Learning Objectives

- Its Importance
- Karl Marx (1818-1883)
- Dialectical Materialism
- Historical Materialism
- Economic Interpretation of History or Economic Determinism
- Theory of Class Struggle
- Labour Theory of Value
- Theory of Surplus Value
- Marx on Capitalism
- Theory of Revolution
- Withering Away of the State
- Concept of Freedom
- Marx on State
- Concept of Alienation
- Marx as a Child of His Times
- Criticism of Marxism
- Merits of Marxism
- Bolshevism
- Lenin's Attitude towards Religion
- Lenin's Theory of Imperialism
- Lenin on Democracy
- Lenin on State
- Lenin on Revolution
- Solidarity of the Party
- Lenin on War
- Lenin and Marx
- Stalin (1879-1953)
- Khrushchev
- Brezhnev
- Suggested Readings

Its Importance

There are many reasons why the study of Marxism is necessary today. Marxism is the official philosophy of one-third of human race and the area of influence of Marxism is increasing every day. In order to have a complete picture of modern society, a study of Marxism is very essential as it is playing an important part in the lives of millions of human-beings all over the world. Even if there are shortcomings in the philosophy of Marx, it has to be studied. The thoroughness with which Marx came to his conclusions creates respect for him. Marxism contains many truths about human society in which we live and we are asked to give up many of our illusions. Marxism provides the intellectual drama of our time. The writings of Marx contain comprehensive statements about the elements and structure of society. More than a hundred years have passed when Karl Marx published his Communist Manifesto in 1848 and during this period, both politicians and intellectuals have been studying his ideas. Among his followers are scholars, intellectuals, politicians, fanatics and opportunists. It is true that some profess Marxism with a view to come to power but there are others who have taken to his ideas so seriously that their inner and outer lives are identical.

The reason why the philosophy of Marx appeals to people all over the world is that most of the people live unsatisfactory lives. They suffer from different kinds of disabilities. Marxism is basically a politics of hunger and no wonder it appeals to the poor and down-trodden. The ideological message of Marxism is in these terms:

"You do not have to be poor any longer. Everywhere men have always lived as exploiters and exploited. As long as the means of producing goods were not sufficient to provide for all, perhaps this evil condition was inevitable.

"It is no longer inevitable.

"You do not have to be poor.

"You are poor, not because of anything you have done or anything you have failed to do, not because of original sin or the will of God or because of bad luck. You are poor because of the economic and political conditions. These conditions are called capitalism. At first capitalism was a progressive force in man's history; under it men built enormous facilities for the production of all things they need.

"You are poor and you are exploited and you are going to be exploited as long as capitalism prevails. For capitalism has ceased to be a progressive force; it has become an obstacle to your progress. It enters into every feature of human life private and public, and all of them it corrupts. Capitalism is the system that exploits you.

"You do not have to be poor. The conditions that make you poor can be changed. They are going to be changed. Inside capitalism itself are the seeds of its own destruction. What will happen, whether you are yet aware of it or not, is that you are going to make a revolution. Those who rule over you and keep you poor will be overthrown. This is the next step forward in human progress. You are going to take that step. By the revolution you can eliminate once and for all the exploitation of man by man; you can enter into a socialistic society in which mankind conquers nature. And no man any longer will know poverty and exploitation".

The style of Marx is bound to create an impression on the minds of the people who are otherwise suffering day after day and have little hope of any improvement in their lives. A specimen of his style is the following passage with which Communist Manifesto begins:

"A spectre haunts Europe—the spectre of Communism. All the powers of old Europe have entered into a holy alliance in order to lay this spectre: Pope and Tzar, Metternich and Guizot: French Radicals and German Police spies.

"The Communists disdain to conceal their views and their aims. They openly declare that their ends can be attained only by the forcible overthrow of all existing social conditions. Let the ruling classes tremble at a communist revolution. The proletarians have nothing to lose, but their chains. They have a world to win. Working men of all countries, unite".

Karl Marx (1818-1883)

Karl Marx was born in 1818 in the Rhineland. He was the son of Herschel Marx, a German Jew. He got an excellent University education in which he specialised in jurisprudence and philosophy. He was a precocious child and the view of his teachers was that "he will fulfil the favourable expectations that are justified by his abilities". In 1841, he submitted a doctorate thesis at the Jena University. He hoped to become a Professor in that University but he lost the chance on account of the dismissal of his friend Bauer. The result was that he became a journalist. He undertook the editorship of a liberal newspaper, The Rhinische Zeitung. He wrote with confidence in a vigorous style. In 1844, he left Germany. He met Proudhon in Paris. In 1848, he drafted the famous Communist Manifesto, that monumental work was written by him at the age of 30. It is the most widely read of all the socialist documents and has been translated into almost every language of the world. "It contains the clearest and most compact statement of Marx's conceptions of the past struggle between economic classes, the modern bourgecisie-proletarian conflict, the inevitable movement of present day capitalism towards division and destruction and the programme of action working classes must adopt in order to fit in their efforts with the actual march of events." In 1849, Karl Marx, ran away to England where he spent the rest of his life. He acted as the correspondent of the New York Tribune. He was instrumental in the formation of the First International in 1864. He died in England in 1883.

Marx was a calm thinker and passionate fighter. Throughout his life, he suffered due to poverty and repression. His friendship with Engels lasted for forty years and both of them are regarded the fathers of Marxism. Their important writings are the Poverty of Philosophy (1844), The Economic and

Philosophic Manuscripts of 1844, thesis on Feuerbach (1845), Poverty of Philosophy, The German Ideology, The Communist Manifesto (1848), Class Struggle in France (1848-50), The Eighteenth Brumaire of Loius Bonaparte (1852), The Critique of Political Economy (1859), Value, Price and Profit (1865), Das Kapital, The Civil War in France (1871), The Gotha Programme (1875), Anti Duhring (1878), The Origin of the Family, Private Property and the State (1884) etc. Marx was a sociologist, he analysed the capitalist economic system. He scientifically analysed the socio-economic, political, moral and cultural aspects of capitalism and tried to prove its exploitative character. He pointed out the revolutionary way of changing that system and replacing it with a Communist society.

Marx was influenced by the French materialists (Helvetius and Holbach) and contemporary German idealist philosophy (particularly Hegel), but in course of time he rejected their systems. While he appreciated materialist attack on religion, he did not support their belief in a Supreme Being and qualitatively non-changing character of the materialist doctrine. German philosophy influenced Marx first through Hegel and then through Feuerbach who broke away from Hegel's idealism. Marx was profoundly influenced by Feuerbach's thesis that God Himself is but a beautiful projection of human hopes and aspirations. God, therefore, is the creation of man. Marx wrote, "Man makes religion; religion does not make man. Religion is the sigh of the oppressed creature, the feelings of a heartless world, just as it is the spirit of unspiritual conditions. It is the opium of masses".

Although Marx criticised Hegel for identifying the Idea or the Absolute with reality, his dialectic provided Marx a basis for his theory of social and political change. Marx was basically a revolutionary. To quote him, "*The philosophers have only interpreted the world in various ways; the point however is to change it*".

Dialectical Materialism

One of the outstanding achievements of Hegel's thought was to create a philosophy of history and he became the chief exponent of the dialectical method. The word dialectical originally referred to the process whereby ideas are formed and clarified in the course of intellectual debate. A proposition or thesis is first advanced, and then challenged by a counter-proposition, or antithesis. Since both are apt to be partly true, the normal outcome of the ensuing discussion is a revised proposition or synthesis that combines the valid elements of each.

The original idea or proposition or thesis does not represent the truth. The counter-proposition or antithesis which is just the opposite or a negation of the thesis also does not represent the truth. When the thesis and antithesis clash with each other, they tend to destroy each other's untrue elements (because true elements cannot be destroyed). The resultant proposition or the synthesis which embodies the true elements of both the thesis and antithesis and is free from the untrue elements of the two, is nearer truth or perfection as compared to those two. However, the synthesis so evolved may not be the whole truth. It therefore takes the form of a new thesis and undergoes the same process of clash with its antithesis and thus emerges a new synthesis. This process of negation of negation continues till it reaches the absolute truth, the perfect stage. According to Hegel, the universe is a coherent whole. In this organic unity, the idea of spirit or reason or divine mind is the only reality. It is only through the nature of spirit or reason that we can know all things. The idea or reason develops through the history of the world. It leans more and more until it reaches its final goal Since reality is dynamic and evolutionary in nature, it cannot be understood by means of the static concepts of formal logic. Hegel formulated the new logic called dialectics.

Hegel propounded the belief through his dialectics that all development or evolution proceeds not in a straight line but in a zig-zag manner following the formula of thesis, antithesis and synthesis. Action is followed by reaction, From the opposition thus engendered a harmony or synthesis results. Human history shows that men go from despotism (thesis) to democracy (antithesis) and finally reaction from unlicensed democracy leads them not back to democracy but to constitutional monarchy (synthesis). This new way of looking at historical and social changes led Hegel to the view that history is not a bare succession of events but a process of unfolding or development. Hegel saw the nation state as the highest stage of social evolution, as the embodiment of truth, "the march of God on earth", the perfect form of social institutions.

Though Marx was greatly impressed by the Hegelian logic, he rejected Hegelian idealism which regarded ideas as the principle cause of the historical process and absolute ideas fully conscious of themselves as the goal of the evolutionary process. The view of Marx was that matter and not spirit or idea, was the ultimate reality and society organised for production in which there was to be no exploitation of one class by another, was the goal of the evolutionary process. The world by its nature develops in accordance with the laws of the movement of matter. Marx believed that different social ideas and theories which appeared at different periods of history, were merely reflection of the material laws of society. Matter is active and not passive and moves by an inner necessity of its nature. To quote Engels, "The dialectical materialism grasps things and images, ideas essentially in their sequence, their movement, their birth and death".

The dialectical materialism of Marx differs from Hegel's dialectics. Whereas for Hegel, the ultimate reality is reason or spirit, for Marx it is matter in motion. According to Hegel, historical development takes place under the stress of conflict between rations and its moving force is ideas. The view of Marx is that the cause. A of historical development are economic causes and not nations. The goal towards which the dialectical materialism is moving is the society perfectly organised for production in which there shall be no class distinctions or exploitation. To quote Marx, "My own dialectical method is not only different from Hegel but is its direct opposite". Though Marx differed from Hegel in dialectics, he adopted this attitude in order to turn Hegelian dialectics right side up, otherwise he took from Hegel the apparatus of the dialectics. Like Hegel's thesis and antithesis and synthesis, Marx also based his dialectical materialism on the following three laws:

(1) The first law is the transformation of quantity into quality and vice-versa. This law professes that change takes place by quantitative transformation until there arises a point which Hegel calls the node beyond which a thing cannot vary while remaining the same. The classical illustration is the change of a state of a substance as when water turns to steam at 100°C and into ice at 0°C. Just as the change occurs abruptly so that water is at one moment water, at the next moment steam or ice, likewise the progress of humanity is not affected by the gradual process, of growth but by sudden jumps. Marx calls the jumps revolution and shows its inevitability. Monopoly capitalism represents the last stage beyond which it cannot develop. Having come into existence, it will develop quantitatively until the point is reached when the dialectical leap occurs and it passes into socialism.

(2) The second law is the unity of opposites. This asserts not only the contradictory nature of reality but also that contradictions thus revealed exist in unity. So far from being opposites, positive and negative express no absolute difference, just as a road to the East is also a road to the West. Just as science has proved that every unity contains within itself polar opposites, such as the positive and negative poles of the electron, Likewise these opposites are independent. In a capitalist society, the bourgeoisie and the proletariat are thus connected. Though both are opposite to each other, neither of them can develop without the other. Marxists use contradictions to explain the evolution of society and so important a part it plays in their thought that Lenin calls it "the salt of dialectics".

(3) The third law is the negation of the negation. Thesis, antithesis and synthesis are forms or stages of development. The thesis breaks down by reason of its internal contradictions and gives way to the antithesis which attempts to remove those contradictions. That also breaks down for the same reason and synthesis is developed. The synthesis negates the antithesis which is first negation and it is the negation of the negation.

The above can be illustrated by the trio, feudalism, capitalism and socialism. The internal contradictions of feudalism lead to its negation by capitalism which represents an advance over the earlier state. The internal contradictions of capitalism lead to socialism which is the negation of the negation.

Marx drew certain conclusions from the theory of dialectical materialism. He held that phenomena are not disconnected and unrelated, but are dependent upon other phenomena. Hence they must be studied in the light of this interaction. Phenomena must also be studied as changing and developing. No one can get a true perspective of capitalism unless it is viewed as a transitional stage in the process of historical development from feudalism to socialism. The Communists take it as truth that capitalism is destined to pass into socialism. Moreover, whenever we find opposites, we must look for their positive inter-connections. As opposites are always united, for example attraction and repulsion in nature, it is only by recognising this that the problem of a socialist society can be solved. We must also look for contradictions in the process of nature and society as contradiction is the motive force behind all development. The fundamental contradiction of capitalism is that it is based on the one hand on cooperative production and on the other on private ownership as the means of production. Hence, socialism arises out of the conflict between the two opposing elements within material process.

Critics find fault with the dialectical materialism of Marx. According to Sabine and Wayper, the difficulty that confronts the students of dialectical materialism is that Marx and Engels never worked out their ideas in detail. The reason may be that Marx was more interested in law, politics and economics rather than philosophy. The view of Hallowell is that Marx himself was not a profound philosopher. Whatever profundity his system has, was borrowed from Hegelian philosophy. Plamenatz is of the view that "dialectical materialism is not a theory at all. It means very little. It is a kind of preliminary model to prepare the mind for historical materialism which no more rests on it than a ship does on its own reflection in the water". Prof. Hunt says that dialectical materialism might give us valuable insight into the history of human development, but the claim of Marx that it constitutes the scientific approach to reality cannot be accepted. It is not in tact scientific at all because we are never sure what constitutes a thesis, antithesis and synthesis. Dialectical theories thrive on verbal, terminological ambiguities. Marx himself was interested in it only as a suggestive work in hypothesis.

We may conclude by saying that though Marx had claimed that by his dialectical materialism he had turned Hegelian dialectics right side up, his claim is not completely true though it may be partially accepted because dialectical materialism has its internal defects and fallacies.

Historical Materialism

In the words of Plamenatz, "Historical materialism is the heart of Marxism" G.D.H. Cole calls it "the realistic interpretation of history". Historical materialism is the extension of the principles of dialectical materialism to the study of social life, an application of the principles of dialectical materialism to the phenomena of the study of society and its history. It provides both the philosophy of revolutionary change as well as the scientific method of bringing about revolution. It explains the laws of evolution of human society. It is a method of interpreting the past understanding the present and projecting the future. It analyses the historical process, describes the laws of social development and suggests ways of changing the present day society. It presents the dynamics of change. Hegelian dialectics had given a method of understanding past history. It did not pretend to gaze into the future. It also did not aspire to shape the course of human affairs. Marxism presents a theory of revolutionary change and the laws of social change are derived from the materialistic interpretation of the historical process.

According to Marx, production and the exchange of things produced is the basis of every social order. In every society which has appeared in history, the distribution of wealth and the division of society into classes is dependent upon what is produced, how it is produced and how the products are exchanged. The ultimate causes of all social changes and political revolutions are to be sought not in man's brains, not in their growing insight into eternal truth and justice, but in changes in the modes of production and exchange. They are to be sought not in the philosophy but in the economics of each particular epoch. History is the history of man's productive activity. Production is a process which creates definite relations between man and man. The economic structure (the sum total of production relations) is the base and political, philosophical, religious, cultural, ethical and other structures are determined by the economic foundation. "Whatever is the mode of production of a society, such in the man is the society itself, ideas and theories, its political views and institutions". Every society is characterised by its mode of production. While interpreting the development of Western society, Marx pointed out five specific modes of production and five different kinds of societies viz., primitive Communist society, slave-owning society, feudal society, capitalist society and socialist society.

According to Marx, any meaningful change means change in the mode of production. Without changing the production relations, **no** meaningful change can be brought about. No piecemeal engineering, no gradual reforms, no incremental change will bring about any fundamental change in society because they do not affect the basic structure (mode of production) of society.

According to Marx, classes are determined by the mode of production and struggle between the classes with opposite interests is fundamental. To quote Marx, "The history of all hitherto existing society is the history of class struggle." Change cannot be brought about by reconciling class interests. The interests of antagonistic classes cannot be reconciled through cooperation and harmony of interests. The classes which are dominant are interested in maintaining the status quo and classes which are oppressed work for change. Change is always sought by the oppressed and exploited class. It is always opposed by the class whose interest is served by the maintenance of the social system. Class struggle is an inevitable product of the contradiction between the productive forces and production relations. Struggle between the two classes is fundamental. It is the driving force for social and historical change. Class struggle is the vehicle of change. When the dominant class is defeated and a new class takes over, it is revolutionary change. It is a qualitative change and one mode of production is replaced by another mode of production. When the contradiction between the relations of production and forces of production reaches a climax, revolution occurs and there is the transformation of one mode of production into another. Revolutionary change means fundamental change. It is not a change within the existing system. It is a change of one system by another. The old system must go lock stock and barrel. Class struggle is a driving force of change and revolution is the midwife which helps the delivery of a new society out of the womb of the old one.

According to Marx, the essence of dialectics is process and change through contradictions and development to higher and complex stages through struggles of the opposites. Social change and social movements occur because of conflict and contradictions within the society. There is always a conflict between the present state of affairs and what is coming. Society contains within itself the seeds of its own destruction and transformation to a higher stage. Causes of change are internal contradictions of a system. The basis of change is internal contradictions and the subjective factors constitute the conditions of change. Historical process is not mechanical process. Many other factors influence the process of change.

Marxism is not historical fatalism. It does not believe that changes will come automatically. Revolutionary action is fundamental to the Marxian theory of change. Marx believed that the future depends on ourselves. He criticised the mechanical materialists and maintained that "the materialist doctrine concerning the changing of circumstances and upbringing forgets that circumstances are changed by man". Circumstances make man just as much as man makes circumstances. However, men do not act out of historical context. They are not free to make change as they please. They act not as individuals but as members or representatives of classes. To quote Marx, "Men make their own history, but they do not make it just as they please; they do not make it under circumstances chosen by themselves, but under circumstances directly encountered, given arid transmitted from the past. The traditions of all the dead generations weigh like a nightmare on the brain of the living". Men produce society and are produced by it. Marxism presents a systematic theory of social and political change through the revolutionary method.

Sabine writes, "Thus economics becomes for Marx a combination of history and analysis, analysis of the relations prevailing in any given system of production, supplemented by the history of the rise and development of that system".

Economic Interpretation of History or Economic Determinism

Before Marx, history was interpreted in several typical ways. Some writers sought the key to history in the working of Divine Providence and contended that the form of human development had been but a part of the unfolding of the Divine Will. Another approach to the understanding of human history was political according to which great Emperors, kings, legislators and soldiers were the decisive forces in history. Such a view was held by Carlyle. According to the Hegelian view prevalent in the time of Marx, history was supposed to be the result of the impact of ideas which were conceived as the living forces behind historical development and material conditions of society were thought of as essentially derived from and caused by great motivating ideas. The emphasis on ideas also implied that history was progressively evolving.

Karl Marx took this dynamic view of history as a continuous and logical solution and gave it a different interpretation. He rejected what he considered to be a serious defect in Hegel's philosophy of history. He was mainly concerned with the idealistic view of history that men were what they were by virtue of ideal influence and they were fashioned by their religion, traditions, literature and art. According to Marx, ideas are not the basic reality. They were only the creatures of experience. Marx regarded all creeds as consequences rather than causes in the major movements of history. He contrasted his materialism with the idealistic interpretation of Hegel. According to him, economic factors alone are responsible for changes in history. They constitute the dynamic factors in history in the light of which every other structure of society, religion, law etc. must find its implementation. Marx starts by asking what is the principle which governs all human relationship and his answer is the common end which all men pursue, to secure the means of production to support life and next to production, the exchange of things produced. The theory begins with the simple truth that "man must eat to live". Hence, the ultimate determinant of social change is not to be found in the ideas of eternal truth and social justice but in the changes of the mode of production and exchange. Men enter into definite relations that are independent of their will and those relations of production correspond to a definite state of development of their material force of production. The sum total of these relations of production makes the economic structure of society the real foundation on which arise legal and political super-structure to which correspond definite form of social consciousness. The mode of production in material life determines the general and spiritual process of life. It is not the consciousness of men that determines their existence. It is their social existence that determines their consciousness.

According to Marx, everything is ultimately determined by economic factors which means the method of production used at a particular time in history. The hand-mill gives your society a feudal lord. The steam mill gives society an industrial capitalist. The structure of society changes creeds, attitudes and civilisation. It is only on the substratum of modes of production that the super-structure of religion, morality and political and intellectual institution is raised. The substratum is never stable. It is in continuous flux. It is always developing in consonance with necessities inherent in it so as to produce their successors merely by their own working. No stage in history will endure. It has become a halter rather than a spur in the forces of production. Take for an example an agricultural country. The productive forces primarily will be those implements and tools which are required for its development. They will bring into existence a type of production appropriate to them and their production relation will be reflected in the laws and institutions of the community. If it is found that a country possesses a certain quantity of coal and oil and if it is decided to explore and exploit those resources, a new concept of productive forces will come into being with corresponding changes in the production relations. The land-owners will give place to manufacturers and cultivators to industrial workers. With this, there would be a corresponding change in the laws and institutions. However, this change will not take place without a struggle. As a new and more productive economy will be restricted by all those who have an interest in maintaining the old and less productive, order, there would emerge a class struggle between the two sides and only a revolution will finally decide the issue.

To understand social revolution, we have to distinguish between changes in productive forces and various ideological forms in which man becomes conscious of the conflict and finds it out. Man as an individual is insignificant. What he is, is due to the economic position of his growth. Marx found the most important manifestation of economic determinism in the constant presence of economic classes. The Communist Manifesto opens with the sentence, "A history of all hitherto existing societies is the history of class struggle". Every system of production has given rise to two principal mutually hostile classes, for example, freemen and slaves, feudal lords and serfs and capitalists and labourers. The contribution of Marx lies in the fact that class antagonism centres around the prevailing mode of production with its economic system.

According to Marx, "All the social, political and industrial relations, all religious and legal system, all theoretical outlooks which merge in the course of history are derived from the material conditions of life". Again, "Since the mode of production constitutes the material basis of the society, the history of be society is primarily the history of the development of production,the history of the various modes of the production that succeed one another with the growth of productive forces". Revolution takes place when the social order becomes incompatible with the changes in the productive system. When changes become more marked and pronounced, a stage comes where the pressure on the old institutions becomes too strong and a violent and radical change takes place which is called revolution by Marx. Economic forces determine the course of history and are responsible for bringing about changes.

The above-mentioned economic interpretation of history given by Marx has been challenged and rejected by eminent sociologists like Giddings and Hobhouse. Their view is that human history has been determined not by one single factor, whether economic, political or racial, but by a large number of factors such as geographical, economic, racial, religious, psychological, sexual etc. The economic factor is only one of them. The view of Marx is hopelessly one-sided.

Critics also point out that Marx ignores the fact that human passions, sentiments, emotions, religion etc. also influence human activities. To quote Russell, "Larger events in our political life are determined by the interaction of material conditions and human passions". The material factor itself is influenced by other factors.

As a philosophical doctrine, the materialistic conception of history is incapable of universal application. Prof. Laski writes, "The insistence upon an economic background as the whole explanation is radically false." Laski point outs that the Balkan nationalism could not be explained in the light of economic background only. Christopher Lloyd observes, "The materialistic interpretation of history does not explain the decline of Rome or the outbreak of our recent wars. It is too rational to account for psychological movements like the advance of nationalism, too materialistic to explain the power of ideals over the mind." It follows that the Marxist view is of limited application.

The view of Marx was that historical changes take place on the basis of materialism according to the principle of dialectic and that process is bound to lead to the establishment of socialism. According to Marx, feudalism gave place to capitalism, capitalism to advanced capitalism or imperialism and that inevitably will give place to socialism. However, history has not vindicated the view of Marx. Although Russia was primarily an agricultural country in 1917, the revolution took place and socialism came in that country but not in England, Germany and the United States although they were highly industrialised countries.

The conclusion is that Marx over-emphasized the extent to which material causes could be found for legal and political institutions. He also admitted that political power could close some parts of economic development and open others, but could not alter the course of history. However, in spite of certain defects, the materialistic conception of history given by Marx is a great contribution which cannot be lightly overlooked. His theory brought Marx more lasting fame than any other. Joad writes, "It would be difficult to over-estimate the influence of this theory on working class thought; it has played much larger part than Marx's theory of surplus value in making his name venerated as the father of socialism. The secret of its attraction lies in the fact that it gives the working classes the assurance of being on the winning side." The view of Sabine is that "by his development of suggestive hypothesis, Marx was the most important social philosopher in the whole of the nineteenth century".

Theory of Class Struggle

According to Marx, classes are the fundamental categories of a social organisation and class struggle is the driving force of social and political change. Classes are determined on the basis of the economic structure of the society and their relations with the means of production. In every class-divided society, there are mainly two classes—one that possesses the ownership of private property and the other the property-less class. The objective basis of class can be determined on the basis of the mode of production of a given society. Another important requirement of class is class-consciousness.

In the Communist Manifesto, Marx presented a simple two-class model of the capitalist society. According to it, there are mainly two classes in the capitalist society—the bourgeoisie and the proletariat. Marx and Engels wrote, "Our epoch, the epoch of the bourgeoisie, possesses, however, this distinctive feature: it has simplified the class antagonisms. Society as a whole is more and more splitting up into two great hostile camps, into two great classes directly facing each other— bourgeoisie and proletariat."

The view of Marx was that in a class-divided society, the interests of the owners of the means of production and non-owners are contradictory to each other. Because of this antagonistic nature of their class interests, class struggle is fundamental and class interests are irreconcilable. The basis of development and change is not the honeymoon of different classes, but class struggle. There exists an antagonistic contraction between the owners and non-owners. Marx denied social unity in a class-divided society and rejected the theories of social stratification or conflicts on the basis of caste, religion, sex, colour and nationality. Marx maintained that class struggle is the vehicle of historical development and social and political change.

According to Marx, all the revolutions and struggles in history can be understood on the basis of class struggle. The struggle of the Roman slaves under the leadership of the Spartacus was the struggle of the slave class against their owners. The Glorious Revolution of 1689 in England and the French Revolution of 1789 were the revolution of the bourgeoisie against the feudal classes. The Marxist view is that the Russian Revolution of 1917 and the Chinese Revolution of 1949 were the revolutions of the working class against the bourgeoisie for the establishment of a socialist state. Likewise, the freedom struggle in India was led by the bourgeoisie in India and after the independence of India in 1947, the power of the state came in the hands of the bourgeoisie.

The Marxist view is that class struggle in the modern capitalist societies is straight, sharp and simple. The interests of the capitalists and workers are clearly antagonistic to each other. The interests of these two classes can never be reconciled. The struggle of these classes will give birth to socialist revolution, the dictatorship of the proletariat and a classless society. The class struggle will inevitably lead to revolution.

The development of modern industry cuts under its feet the very foundation on which the bourgeoisie produces and appropriates produce. What the bourgeoisie produces, above all, are its own grave-diggers. Its fall and the victory of the proletariat are equally inevitable. Marx shows that capitalism sows the seeds of its own destruction. Society as a whole is more and more splitting up into two great hostile camps, into two great classes directly facing each other, the bourgeoisie and the proletariat.

This theory of class struggle has been criticised by many writers on various grounds. The view of Lancaster is that for purposes of propaganda, this theory is excellent. It puts the worker on the winning side and gives him the assurance of victory in the struggle. However, the vagueness in the definition of the term "class" has been responsible for many errors. Sabine writes, "Though Marxists have always believed the class struggle to be the only reliable guide to political strategy, the vagueness of Marx's concept of a social class was responsible for some of his worst errors in prediction".

Critics also point out that class struggle cannot come into existence unless the social classes possess the solidarity and unity of purpose. The view of Popper is that the divergence of interests within the ruling and the ruled classes go so far that Marx's theory of classes must be considered as a dangerous over-simplification, even if we admit that the issue between the rich and the poor is always of fundamental importance. The fight between the Popes and Emperors in medieval Europe could not be interpreted as a quarrel between the exploiter and the exploited.

The view of Prof. Carew Hunt is that Marx's theory of class struggle as an explanation of history, is untenable. To quote him, "Marx's thesis that all conflict among men arises from the class struggle, albeit of undoubted tactical value as calculated to convince the masses that their misfortunes are attributed to the capitalist system and will disappear with the victory of the proletariat, is nonetheless fallacious. For the supreme source of conflict in life is the inevitable opposition between the claims of the individual and those of society, a conflict which is not reducible to class struggle and cannot be dialectically resolved because it is part of the unchanging human situation."

The view of Marx was that with the division of society into the bourgeoisie and the proletariat, all other classes would disappear in future. However, that prophecy has not come out to be true and against the expectations of Marx, a new middle class is now emerging which is taking the place of the old middle class. The conclusion is that Marx's prophecy regarding the division of society into two classes, the bourgeoisie and the proletariat, seems to be incorrect.

The view of Ramsay McDonald is that class war has found its way into the general body of the earliest dogmas quite simply. Marx saw that no proletarian movement could be created in Europe without some passion. The wage-earners had to feel enmity. They had to be marshalled as a class. The idea of class war does not represent the motive forces organising socialism and forming the earliest movement.

Another criticism is that the Marxian prophecy of the ultimate victory of the proletariat is not based upon scientific grounds. The view of Marx was that capitalism was doomed to perish and communism was bound to be triumphant. Laski writes, "The breakdown of capitalism might result not in Communism but in anarchy from which there might emerge some dictatorship unrelated in principle to Communist ideals."

The view of Marx was that capitalism would slowly weaken itself but that prophecy has been proved to be false. The fact is that capitalism has considerably strengthened itself. It has changed its character according to the changing circumstances.

The view of Plamenatz is that the theory of class struggle is contradictory in itself. On the one hand it is asserted that the division of society into a number of social classes is determined by the relations of production prevailing in it and on the other it is asserted that the number of classes under capitalism is eventually reduced to two as a result of conflict.

The theory of class war is extremely pernicious in the sense that according to it, all workers ought to regard themselves as proletarians and feel convinced with the hopelessness of their situation and hate their employer. The theory creates feelings of hostile antagonism between the two classes and tells the proletariat that it is now war to the death with victory assured to them. The theory thoroughly ignores the forces of law, cooperation and sacrifice. The comment of Murray is that Marx "was a Mahdi preaching a holy war, a Peter the Hermit preaching a crusade for the recovery of the holy city from the infidels who had impiously taken possession of it. Only the name of the holy city is Wealth, the infidels are the Capitalists and the motives appealed to are somewhat different." Marxism seems to identify every social force with a class having an economic condition and that equates its struggle between the classes of the exploiters and then equates its struggle, between the classes of the exploiters and the exploited. On so many occasions, there have been a series of fights even among the ruling classes.

The prophecy of Marx has been disproved by the actual conditions of the twentieth century. The combinations of the petty bourgeoisie in the shape of cartels and joint stock companies have saved the middle class from extinction and assimilation either with the bourgeoisie or the proletariat.

In developing the doctrine of class war, Marx had before him the labour conditions of England which "had all the symptoms of a hunger revolt based on acute misery". Carew Hunt says that "nowhere Marx seeks to prove that the worker is, in fact, fitted for the role assigned to him, nor does it occur to him that the negation of capitalism may lead to the emergence of a wholly new class which is, strictly speaking, neither capitalist nor proletariat. The belief in human perfectibility that he had inherited from the eighteenth century led him to believe that a classless society inherently desirable on ethical grounds, must be the next stage in evolution, which as a revolutionary and an agitator he saw in the working class movement the only available instrument for the achievement of this aim in the immediate future and was thus induced to regard it as the final negation".

On the theory of class war, Lancaster observes, "If Marx and Engels mean by this no more than that every society consists of conflicting groups each striving for ends which it cannot realize except at the expense of others with whom it must compromise or whom it must destroy, they say no more than the obvious. For every society exhibits such clashes with the defeats, victories and compromises implicit in them. But they are really saying very much more for they are asserting that at last the lines are rigidly drawn between the two classes—bourgeoisie and proletariat — between whom it is now war to death with victory assured to workers. Moreover, belief in the dialectic requires them to hold that the bourgeoisie, by an iron law of development, should provide its own enemies. It can win its wholly temporary victories only by creating and training a class that will inexorably drive it from the field."

Labour Theory of Value

Marx took from the earlier economists like Adam Smith and Ricardo and Lassalle the idea of labour power as creating value in the commodities. On that basis, he propounded his own theory of value. That theory has two aspects known as the labour theory of value and the theory of surplus value. The labour theory of value regards labour as the single creator of value in a commodity and insists that the value of a commodity is determined by the amount of labour power spent over the production of that commodity. Marx uses the term "exchange value" to denote the worth of an article in terms of its relation to other articles. This exchange which is commonly represented by price, may fluctuate according to the market conditions, but those fluctuations are accidental and do not eliminate or even obscure the real influence which determines both the value and exchange value of a commodity. Thus, the labour time which is socially necessary for the production of commodities asserts itself like an over-riding law of nature in spite of superficial variations in exchange values, as the real standard or measure of exchange value.

According to Spargo, "The value of commodities is determined by the amount of social labour necessary, on the average, for their production". The sum and substance of the labour theory of value is that all real economic value is created by human labour alone. Value is a quality inherent in a thing or commodity. That value is entirely due to labour. All factors, other than labour, are unimportant and not essential.

Critics point out that the labour theory of value does not take into consideration the factor of demand. Value is a psychological phenomenon. It is not to be found in the commodity but in the desire of the mind. It is also wrong to say that the only active essential element in production is labour or that the wage of the labourer is the only "justifiable element in determining cost of production". However, the actual fact is that in addition to labour, there are other factors which determine the value of a thing and those are land, capital and organisation.

Theory of Surplus Value

The theory of surplus value is one of the significant contributions of Karl Marx to political theory. This theory is based on Marx's labour theory of value. Sabine rightly says that the theory of surplus value is an extension of the labour theory of value. The theory was first propounded by Sir William Penty in England and was developed by Adam Smith and Ricardo.

According to this theory, the wealth of capitalist societies in the last resort is an enormous collection of commodities which have value proportionate to their capacity for supplying human wants or their usefulness. We assess the amount of usefulness which an object possesses by finding out what it can be exchanged for and Marx uses the words "exchange value" to denote the worth of an article in terms of its relation to other articles. The exchange value, commonly known as price, may fluctuate according to market conditions, but those fluctuations are accidental and do not eliminate or even obscure the real influence which determines both the value and the exchange value of commodities. This influence is the average amount of labour time spent in the production of the commodity. The labour time necessary for the production of commodities asserts itself like an overriding law of nature. Human labour cannot by itself create value. It must use instruments without which it cannot work. Those instruments are machinery, factories, steam power, electric power etc.

As a result of the inventions of the late eighteenth and early nineteenth centuries, the instruments of the creation of value have increased enormously in number and efficiency. Those are owned by a relatively small class known as the capitalist class. The capitalist buys the labour power of the workman, applies it to the machinery and raw material which he owns and produces a commodity having exchange value. The difference between the exchange value of the manufactured commodity and the price paid to the workman for his labour is called surplus value. It is brought into being by the labour of the workman and appropriated by the capitalist who employs him. In fact, it is the product of unpaid labour.

This appropriation of surplus value by the capitalist constitutes the fundamental injustice of the modern industrial system. The capitalist industrial system is different only in form from a slave society. The slaves worked and created surplus value under compulsion and the modern workman creates surplus value under a free contract which he voluntarily joins. The workman has no alternative but to sell the only commodity which he possesses—labour. According to Spargo, "The value of commodities is determined by the amount of social labour necessary on the average, for their production".

The theory of surplus value is that the real economic value is inherent in a commodity and that is created by labour alone. All factors other than labour are unimportant.

The theory of surplus value is full of truths and half-truths. It is not correct to say that every capitalist is a member of the idle rich. The persons who manage the factories are paid handsomely and they work day and night. It cannot be said that they are me members of the idle rich. It is true that in large scale industries, some capitalists are idle. That applies to the case of shareholders who do nothing to run the factories but pocket a share of the profits. The same applies to the directors of companies who very rarely do anything and the day to day work is done by the salaried staff. The same is the case with some other classes. It is not correct to say that every capitalist is an idle person. Marx glorified the manual workers and did not give due importance to the salaried experts who actually run the public undertakings. The result is that those experts are not sympathetically inclined towards Marxism. Marx did not give due place to the brain workers.

The criticism which applies to the labour theory of value also applies to the theory of surplus value. Labour alone does not create value and hence the labourer alone is not entitled to the whole of the price fetched by a commodity produced by him. In modern times, a labourer cannot work without the help of machinery, steam, power etc. He also gets the help of the free gifts of nature such as coal and other minerals. Both capital and labour are required for the creation of value or wealth. Even Engels had to admit that "the perfecting of machinery is making human labour superfluous". In modern times, skill in industry, enterprise, knowledge and the organisational capacity of the entrepreneurs are more important for the creation of wealth than the mere employment of proletarian labour.

Critics also point out that the capitalist has not only to pay the labourer but also to make other payments. He has to pay taxes, provide for depreciation charges and improvements. He has to make provision for all those things which go to the betterment of the lives of the labourers. It is too much to say that labour alone creates value or wealth. The view of Russell is that the theory of surplus value is rather to be viewed as a translation into abstract terms of the hatred with which Marx regarded the prevalent system than as a contribution to pure theory. The theory of surplus value required a lot of abstract discussion of pure economic theory without "having much bearing upon the practical truth or falsehood of socialism".

The view of Prof. Simckhovitch is that there are few theories which have been so carefully examined, thoroughly sifted and completely condemned upon their own documentary evidence as the theory of surplus value by Marx.

Beer says that "it is impossible to set aside the view that Marx's theory of value has rather the significance of a political and social slogan than an economic truth". Again, "Unique as an investigator of the laws of the proletarian movement, eminent and even a great pioneer as a sociologist, Marx is in respect of economic theory predominantly an agitator."

Prof. Cole says that the theory of surplus value is "to a great extent a polemic which continues to thrive as a result of persistent understanding of it by Marx's own discipline."

James Bonar says that "the charm of the writings of Marx lies, perhaps, chiefly in the tenacity and confidence with which he applies his key to lock after lock. He never doubts his key will open all locks."

Marx says that "the cost of labour is the socially necessary cost" but he does not take into account the pressure of the trade unions and social consciousness.

As the aim of the theory of surplus value is to show the exploitation character of the capitalists and to remove the exploitation of workers by socialism, its name should be the theory of exploitation and not the theory of surplus value.

According to Wayper, if the theory of surplus value is an attempt to explain prices, it soon succumbs into difficulty. If surplus value is produced by the consumption of labour power, an industry in which capital is invested in labour would be more profitable than one in which capital is invested in machinery. That is an absurd proposition. The fact is that Marx's theory of surplus value is not the theory of price. It has an appeal to value only. It is a protest against the treatment of labour as commodity.

However, the theory of surplus value cannot be rejected as a whole. Popper writes, "I think that even if Marx's analysis was defective, his effort to explain the phenomenon of exploitation deserves the greatest respect."

Marx on Capitalism

Marx attacked capitalism from various angles. As regards its social aspect, he condemned capitalism because it exalted the fortunate few at the expense of the oppressed many and cheated millions of people of the just fruit of their labour. On the one hand, it resulted in concentration of capital in the hands of a few and on the other there was misery, agony, toil, slavery, brutality and degradation for others. That led to crimes. Capitalism resulted in a hell for the common man.

From the ethical point of view, capitalism is exploitative, oppressive and dehumanizing. It is unfair and results in inequality. It deprives the poor of a good part of their earnings. The appropriation of surplus value is nothing less than highway robbery.

Marx attacked capitalism also on aesthetic ground. Production under capitalism is hostile to art. It is responsible for ugliness and vulgarity. It fills the landscape with factories which give out stench and filth. It raises mansions for the rich and hovels for the poor. All creative activity depends upon the whims of the capitalists. Capitalism is dirty and vulgar. It is the sinister way of life under which men who value beauty, good manners and noble thoughts cannot hope to create or even live.

Marx condemned capitalism also on economic grounds. According to him, capitalism had run its course and outlived its historic mission. It did not enable the common man to realise his material well-being. It was wasteful of natural resources and not capable of making quick use of innovations. It was unstable. Although goods were produced on a large scale, they did not satisfy the needs of the common man. The situation created under capitalism was like water everywhere but not a drop to drink.

Marx attacked capitalism also on psychological grounds. According to him, capitalism injured the spirit of man. The workers were worse off psychologically than materially. The modern man had forgotten that the machine built by him and the goods produced were intended to serve his needs and he was not to become a slave of the machine.

Marx attacked capitalism on political grounds because it distributed both power and freedom in unequal amounts. It reduced the representative government to a mockery and led to imperialism, colonialism and war.

Marx believed that the inner contradictions in capitalism would ultimately lead to its destruction. The lot of the masses was bound to worsen. The class struggle was bound to increase and nothing could save capitalism from self-immolation. Marx predicted the destruction of capitalism in these words: "Along with constantly diminishing number of the magnates of capitalism.... grows the mass of misery, oppression, slavery, degradation and exploitation. But with this too grows the revolt of the working class, a class always increasing in number, discipline, united, organised by the very mechanism of the process of capitalistic production itself. The monopoly of capitalism becomes a fetter upon the mode of production. Centralisation of the means of production and socialisation of labour at last reach a point where they become incompatible with their capitalist integument. This integument is burst asunder. The knell of capitalist private property sounds. The expropriators are expropriated. This is the end of capitalism."

The view of Karl Marx that capitalism is its own grave-digger has been criticised on many grounds. Marxian prophecy has been proved to be wrong. Capitalism has come to stay in the modern times. Marxian assertion that there would be a continued deterioration in the condition of workers has come to be untrue. From the time of Marx, there has been an improvement in the condition of the workers. The view of Marx was that capitalism would first flourish and then it will be overthrown by the proletariat through a revolution. Proletarian revolution has occurred in the backward states of Russia and china and not in the highly industrialised states of Britain, the United States and Germany. Marxian view of international class consciousness has been rejected by posterity. During the two World Wars, the workers of one state fought against the workers of another state. Marx took a superficial view of society when he wrote that there were only two classes in society. He completely ignored the existence of the middle class. His belief in the progressive destruction of capitalism was based upon the wrong principles of the dialectical, theory of surplus value and class struggle. His belief that the dictatorship of the proletariat would result in a classless and stateless society has been proved to be wrong by the happenings in the Soviet Union and Communist China. We may conclude that the theory of increasing misery of workers and faith in the inevitable breakdown of capitalism and the emergence of a Communist society as put forth in the Communist Manifesto are not in accord with facts. The developments, in capitalism after Marx show that his teachings need revision and modification.

Theory of Revolution

Revolution for Marx is a social, economic, technological, political, legal and ideological phenomenon. The whole of his theory of revolution is set in the frame of materialist conception of history. The view of Marx was that class struggle and revolution were the driving forces of history. Class struggle in society would move ahead in the direction, of revolution. The economically dominant class would not give up its economic and political power of its own free will or through evolutionary methods. It was to be removed forcibly through a revolution by the oppressed class. Revolution was to act as a midwife in the process of change. Out of the womb of old society, the new society was to emerge through a revolution. Without a revolution, one mode of production could not change into another mode of production and without such a change, the class basis of power could not change.

The Marxian theory of revolution fits all the revolutions. Particularly, it is a theory of social revolution to be brought about by the working class to overthrow the socio-economic and political system of capitalism. The value, worth and radicalism of a revolution depend on the class that carries it out. The bourgeois revolution was carried out by the minority class of the bourgeoisie, but the socialist revolution will be a revolution by the working class which is always in a majority. To quote Marx, "All previous historical movements were movements of minorities or in the interests of minorities. The proletarian movement is the self-conscious, independent movement of the immense majority, in the interests of the immense majority. The proletariat, the lowest stratum of our present society, cannot stir, cannot raise itself up without the whole superincumbent strata of official society being sprung into the air". The proletarian revolution will be social revolution as the proletariat can represent the interests of society as a whole.

According to Marx, revolution will not come on its own, without the revolutionary activity of human beings. There must be the revolutionary consciousness to bring about a revolution. Marxism is not historical fatalism. It does not believe that history will take its own course and human-beings have nothing to do. There has to be revolutionary activity of the oppressed class. A theory becomes revolutionary when it travels from the head to the hands and comes into action.

Marx was a revolutionary and his theories were for a revolution to change the world in a meaningful way. For Marx, revolution was not merely a way to capture political power. It was also the means of transforming the society as a whole.

Marx not only gave a theory of revolution but also suggested ways and means to bring about a revolution. A revolution was not a conspiracy or a forceful struggle of the progressive class. Revolution could come through an intensification of the class struggle and class struggle could be intensified through class consciousness and militant political organisation of the class. Regarding the proletarian revolution, Marx wrote, "The proletariat during its contest with the bourgeoisie, is compelled by the force of circumstances to organise itself as a class by means of a revolution; it makes itself the ruling class and as such sweeps away by force the old conditions of production". The immediate aim of any revolution is to capture political power. Marx was against the use of terror, but he was also in favour of peaceful means. He believed that physical force must be used wherever necessary. After the failure of the Paris Commune in 1871, Marx declared, "We must make clear to the governments. We know that you are the armed power that is directed against the proletariat. We will proceed against you by peaceful means where that is possible and with arms when it is necessary". Revolution did not rule out the use of physical force if that was considered necessary. When the ruling classes resist with arms, they must be met with arms and hence an armed revolution cannot be ruled out. The use of arms cannot be one way traffic. If the bourgeoisie use arms against the working class, the working class must retaliate with bullets and bombs.

Marx emphasized the inevitability of revolution for social and political change. In one of his lectures in 1872, Marx expressed the view that in the developed liberal democracies of Britain and the United States, peaceful transition to socialism was possible on account of the increasing strength of the working class. However, Lenin ruled out in 1917 that possibility and maintained that on account of the tremendous increase in bureaucracy, army and police, the possibility of peaceful transition did not exist.

Marxism is a theory of revolutionary change. The capture of political power by the working class through a socialist revolution is the beginning. After that, the dictatorship of the proletariat should be established and the massive task of social and economic transformation should be carried out.

Both Marx and Engels have left many issues regarding revolution unresolved. The most important among them are the means by which the revolution is to be accomplished and the nature of the political organisation between the capture of power and the future society. As regards the means by which the revolution is to be brought about, many alternative solutions such as violence, peaceful transition, unilateral action of the proletariat, alliance with the progressive bourgeoisie, creation of bourgeois democracy and immediate passage to a proletarian regime have been offered. As regards the nature of the political organisation between the capture of power and the future society, there is to be the dictatorship of the proletariat. It is a dictatorship of the working class over the capitalist class. The work of levelling down the rich is to be carried out and ultimately a classless society is to be established.

Withering Away of the State

When the work of the dictatorship of the proletariat is over, a stateless and classless society will be established. There will be no exploitation of man by man and no distinction between one class and another. When that happens, the state will cease to exist. It will gradually wither away. It is not abolished and disbanded. It just fades away and its place is taken by an administrative apparatus which will control and manage the instruments of production.

When the state withers away, a classless society will emerge. The new society will be based on classlessness. In that class-less society, family and religion as institutions will disappear or die away. Religion is considered as the opiate of the people and it will die a natural death in a socialist society. The Marxists considered family as a bourgeois institution for perpetuating property rights. Under the new regime, the principle would be "From each according to his capacity, to each according to his needs". This principle has been modified in the Soviet Union into "From each according to his capacity, to each according to his work." Marx advocated the establishment of socialism in the world but Stalin gave a new idea and a new dimension to Marxism by giving the idea of socialism in one country.

Concept of Freedom

Marxism is primarily a philosophy of human freedom. In its essence, it aims at the liquidation of the conditions of domination and subjection in society. Freedom consists not only in securing material satisfaction of human needs, but also in removing the conditions of dehumanization, estrangement and alienation. Engels has stated that the capitalist system is characterised by necessity as opposed to freedom. Necessity denotes the condition under which the life of man is governed by the inevitable laws of nature which exist independent of the will of man. Man can acquire scientific knowledge of those laws for his own benefit, but he cannot change them at his will. Freedom does not consist in the escape from necessity to a dreamland, but in the knowledge of those laws and the capacity to make those laws work towards definite ends. A sound knowledge of the productive forces operating behind the capitalist system and a programme to make those forces work towards human ends—towards the emancipation of human society—were essential instruments of human freedom. That knowledge revealed that only a programme of socialist revolution could accomplish humanity's "leap from the kingdom of necessity to the kingdom of freedom."

Marx on State

According to Marx, the state is nothing more than a machine for the exploitation and oppression of one class by another. The edifice of state is rooted in class war. The state is not a natural institution. It comes into being when the society is divided into irreconcilable and antagonistic groups. According to the Communist Manifesto, the state is the "executive committee of the bourgeoisie". As the capitalist class is in power, it uses the state, as an instrument to exploit and oppress the proletariat. The whole paraphernalia of the state is so devised as to consolidate the hold of the bourgeoisie over the proletariat.

The state is an institution of violence. It stands not on the will of the people but on violence. It uses violence. The dominant class employs every instrument to exploit and suppress the dependent class. The military, police, courts, law, bureaucracy etc. are all employed to use violence and force for the good of the dominant class. While these things are in the hands of the bourgeoisie in a capitalist society and are being used against the proletariat, the position will be reversed in a socialist society, where the working class will take hold of them and use them against the bourgeoisie. Every society undergoes a change by means of a revolution.

Marx considered the state a temporary institution. After the overthrow of the bourgeoisie, the state will have a quasi character. It will be an instrument in the hands of the proletariat to be used against the bourgeoisie and other reactionary and counter-revolutionary forces. The party which "has triumphed in the revolution is necessarily compelled to maintain its rule by means of that fear with which its arms inspire the reactionaries". The proletariat will set up its own centralised apparatus of forces in order to complete the defeat of the capitalist class and defend the new order against attack from enemies both from and without. This period is called the dictatorship of the proletariat. Ultimately, the state will wither away and a stateless and classless society will come into existence.

During the transitional period, the state has to take certain steps. Property in land should be abolished and rents used for public purposes. A progressive income tax should be levied. The right of inheritance should be abolished. The property of emigrants and rebels should be confiscated. There should be state control, centralisation and monopoly of credit. The state must control and centralise transportation and communication. There should be expansion of state control of production and state improvement of agriculture. There should be reinforcement of the obligation of all persons to work. Agricultural and manufacturing industries should be combined to eliminate urban-rural division. Child labour should be abolished and a system of free public education established.

During the dictatorship of the proletariat, the primary object of the state is to destroy the capitalist system, transfer the control of the means of production from private to public hands and set up a centralised planned economy. The establishment of a classless society will prepare the ground for a stateless society in which regular military and police will be substituted by people's militia. The assemblies and councils will be substituted by voluntary groups or associations of the people. That will be the stage of Communism and the state will wither away to find its place in the museum with bronze axe and spinning wheel. The proletariat needs the state not for freedom but to suppress its opponents. When it becomes possible to speak of freedom, the state as such ceases to exist.

The Marxian theory of state has been criticised on many grounds. It is contended that Marx had studied the origin of state from a wrong point of view. To call the state an institution of violence or class coercion is not justified. The state is the first condition of a civilised life and its termination is bound to call back the horrible state of nature as described by Hobbes. It is true that at times the state has done exploitation of and oppression over the people, but that does not destroy the real nature and significance of the state. Right from the days of Plato and Aristotle, it has been believed that the state is an ideal institution, a moralising agency and an instrument of public welfare. The state strives by its policy to effect such an adjustment of the relationship between citizens as will enable each of them to realise the fullest implications of human personality. Ebenstein writes, "If Marx had accorded the political factor its due weight, if he had fully grasped the importance of Reform Act in England and of the Jacksonian revolution in the United States, he might have realised that socialism too might be accomplished without violence in countries that possessed the democratic traditions strong enough to absorb far-reaching social and economic changes without resorting to civil war".

Critics point out that the existing dictatorship of the proletariat frustrates the purpose of Marx. It is found that the dictatorship of the proletariat is really dictatorship over the proletariat and the ruling class is so ambitious that it does not look like relinquishing political authority in a form eventually leading to the withering away of the state.

The Marxian theory of state denounces the democratic character of authority and wants to substitute it with a new type of democracy called "people's democracy". However, that is no democracy at all. It is also contended that the state is not a class institution based on violence. It is based on the will of the people and not on force. The state is a moral institution whose aim is to develop human personality. Marx ignored the fact that the machinery of a democratic state can be used for the betterment of the lives of the workers.

Concept of Alienation

Alienation constitutes one of the little known aspects of the political theory of Marx because it was without any significance as far as Marx's theory was concerned. The idea of alienation is mainly drawn from Marx's Economic and Political Manuscripts (1843) which is known for its humanist content and written by Marx when he was in his mid-twenties. The credit for re-discovery goes to George Lukacs, a Hungarian philosopher and his teacher George Simmel.

In simple words, alienation is powerlessness, meaninglessness, normalessness, isolation and self-estrangement. The concept involves a view of human relationship not based on the principle of equality but of one man being superior to another, one man a master and another man a slave.

According to Hegel, the goal of man is the realisation of self or freedom. That condition is not achieved due to two factors viz., necessity and alienation. While necessity refers to natural and physical constraints, alienation is dissociation of subject from the object. Man wants to be a master of himself but he becomes a plaything in the hands of others. The failure to realise oneself is the chief reason for human alienation.

Marx gave a new meaning to the idea of alienation. It was not the result of man's failure to realise himself or the outcome of religious superstition. It has to do with man's work. "In locating man's alienation in work, Marx had taken the revolutionary step of grounding philosophy in concrete human activity". As a result of division of labour, man has lost control of process of work and also over product of his labour. That has led to dehumanisation and depersonalisation respectively. The manufacturing process or the technology is mainly responsible for changing the relationship between the craftsman and his product. A worker cannot buy what he produces and those who can afford possession of product do not work. They are idlers. The object of socialism is to overcome alienation.

Marx has identified four levels of alienation. In the first place, man is alienated from his own product and from his work process because of worker plays no part in deciding what to produce and how to produce it. Secondly, man is alienated from nature. His work does not give him a sense of satisfaction as a creative worker. Under mechanisation, the work tends to become increasingly routinised and monotonous. Thirdly, man is alienated from other men through the competitive character of the economic system, which forces everyone to live at the expense of someone else and divide society into irreconcilable class interests. Finally, man is alienated from himself because the realm of necessity dominates his life and reduces him to the level of an animal existence, leaving no room for a taste of literature, art and cultural heritage. The introduction of the theory of alienation to Marxist theory initiated some new trends in Marxist social analysis.

Marx as a Child of His Times

Karl Marx was successful because he caught the temper of his times. He knew that he must speak the language of the country if he wanted to be successful. If he wanted to be heard, he must use the magic words of science, he must be realistic and must consider struggle and violence as inevitable. He must be a thorough materialist. He must be the Darwin of social sciences if he wanted to command the respect of Europe. Marx was in swing with the age when he used Hegelian philosophy and Darwin's science to explain all human history and all social arrangements. He adopted a dynamic and evolutionary explanation of the phenomena he dealt with in contrast to the static views. It was a materialistic age and Marx gave his dogmatic and thorough-going materialism. Realism was in the air and Marx explained it as a class struggle. From Hegel, Marx got the dialectic but he rejected Hegelian idealism.

The contribution of English economists to Marxism was the analytical approach. England made Marx an analytical critic of the capitalist system. Marx accepted the laws propounded by Adam Smith, Ricardo and Mill but modified them later on. From Malthus, he got the notion of struggle for survival which he converted from a struggle among individuals to a struggle among classes. From Ricardo, he got the labour theory of value from which he deduced his surplus theory of value. Marx's proletariat is nothing more than Ricardo's economic man with dirty hands.

Marx lived in a world where the word socialism was already known. There were Robert Owen, St. Simon and Fourier. They had their Utopian schemes. Their failure seems to be due chiefly to the method adopted by them. Marx was influenced by them.

From Germany, Marx got Hegel's doctrine which he placed upon its feet to serve his revolutionary ends. From the English, he got the abstract science of economics. From the socialists and the Revolution of 1848, he got the notion of a class war. By 1848, Marx was qualified to be the prophet of a revolution which ignored nationalities and concentrated on classes.

Criticism of Marxism

(1) The philosophy of Marx has been criticised on many grounds. While interpreting history in terms of the economic factor, Marx ignored the role played by the non-economic factors. Human history is not determined by a single factor but by a large number of factors and the economic factor is only one of the them. The other factors are religious, geographical, cultural, psychological etc. Even the economic factor is influenced by other factors. Bertrand Russell points out that larger events in our political life are determined by the interaction of material, conditions and human passions. The Marxists do not take into account either the human factor or human passions. The most glaring difficulty of the materialistic conception of history lies in its helplessness when confronted with the problem of mind and the influence of mind on mind. There are instances where great men have been influenced by the environment and the minds of others.

(2) Critics find fault with the concept of class war as advocated by the Marxists. Even an examination of the Western civilisation does not support the view that economic position always determines social existence. The static conception of classes is not correct. Classes are not fixed and rigidly maintained blocks. There is a constant movement from class to class. Sorel writes, "The English are distinguished by an extraordinary lack of understanding of the class war. Marx refers to the existence of only two classes but there was has emerged a new class of mangers and skilled technical advisers labour and capital are not regarded as contradictory forces but partners in industrial production. The working classes have shares and are sharing more and more the gains of more production.

(3) The Marxian concept of surplus value is fallacious. Labour power alone does not create value and hence labour alone is not entitled to the whole of the value fetched by a commodity. The industrialists have not only to pay for labour but also for machinery, rent of building, interest on borrowed money, cost of raw material etc. They have also to make provision for depreciation. Hence, labour alone cannot claim to be the sole creator of value of the commodity. As a theory of price, the theory of surplus value is rubbish because if surplus value is created by the consumption of labour power, an industry in which capital is invested in labour would be more profitable than the one in which capital is invested in machinery. The conclusion is that the theory of surplus value is more in the nature of a political slogan than an economic truth.

(4) The economic analysis given by Marx, particularly that relating to capitalist development, is not supported by facts. The prediction of Marx was that in capitalist society, the rich will get richer and the poor will become poorer. However, this has not come out to be true. In the industrialised societies of the West, there is a marked improvement in the economic conditions and standard of living of the working class. In industrialised countries like England, France, Germany, the United States, Canada etc. even the workers are the owners of houses and cars. Moreover, the economic disparities predicted by Marx with the development of capitalism are not greater today than what they were in the time of condition of the working class. The new concept of the welfare state has revolutionised the condition of the workers. Marx had also predicted that in the development of industrial capitalism, the bigger capitalists will swallow the smaller ones. Experience shows that side by side with the big capitalists, there are small industrialists also. As a matter of fact, the number of smaller capitalists is on the increase.

(5) Critics find fault with the methods advocated by Marx to bring about the change from the capitalist order to a socialist society. Marx advocated the method of class war and the use of violence. It is contended that the method of revolution and violence will create chaos in society. Even the makers of revolution may not survive to guide it successfully and consolidate its gains. Marx anticipated that the new social order will be permeated by the spirit of love, fellowship and regard for the common good. There is no foundation for such an expectation. The reason is that if violence is used to overthrow those who are in power, it is impossible to expect peace. The point is illustrated by the example of a surgeon. If he uses infected tools in performing an operation, that would certainly lead to complications and infection which may delay the healing of the patient.

(6) Marx had predicted the inevitability of socialism but that has not been proved by historical developments since his time. The view of Marx was that in the process of capitalist development, a stage will come when capitalism will dig its own graveyard and destroy itself. Experience shows that although Russia was a very backward country in 1917 in which agriculture and not industry was predominant, socialism came in that country and not in Germany although that country was highly industrialised.

(7) The Marxist concept of the withering away of the state is misleading. The view of Marx was that after the proletarian revolution and the establishment of socialist society, the state will wither away. Although the socialist state was established in Russia in 1917, the state has not withered away. As a matter of fact, it has become all—powerful.

(8) Marxism is criticised as the enemy of individual's individuality, initiative and freedom. It destroys man's individuality by making him a prisoner of society and the whole of social development. It subordinates man to the march of history. By enthroning a collectivity, it creates individuals—tyrants—who embody and interpret the will of that collectivity according to their preferences. It is regarded as an enemy of the rights and liberties of the individual.

(9) On philosophical basis, Marxism is criticised as dogmatism, historicism, utopianism, historical fatalism, essentialism and holism. Karl Popper has given a philosophical criticism of Marxism. His view is that Marxism is not a scientific philosophy. Dialectical and historical materialism are concepts which are very complex and unclear. Marx never gave a full interpretation of those concepts. While over-emphasizing materialistic elements, Marxism ignores spiritual and other elements which play an important part in the historical development of society. Dialectics is self-contradictory. Marxism regards economic substructure—the mode of production—as the basis of socio-political, cultural, ethical and ideological super-structure, but the dichotomy between sub-structure and super-structure is invalid and both influence each other. The view of Marx is that the basis of historical development of society is changes in the mode of production, but critics maintain that historical developments do not take place on the basis of economic changes alone. There are ideological, demographic, geographic, psychological and other factors which are equally important. The Marxists divide human societies into five different kinds of societies viz., primitive, communist, slave-owning, capitalist and socialist. Critics point out that contemporary anthropological studies have proved this division to be baseless.

(10) Marxian theory of classes and class struggle has been severely criticised on the ground that classes are not the chief factors in social stratification. There are many other bases on which society is divided. The theory of class struggle is criticised on the ground that society develops through class harmony and cooperation and not through class struggle. Conflicts reflect the disease of the system and cooperation and harmony reflect the health of the system.

(11) The view of Dahrendorf, Raymond Aron and S.M. Lipset is that Marx's analysis was accurate for the nineteenth century society but not now. The present industrial societies have become far more complex than those described by Marx in which there was a conflict between two classes. Moreover, class antagonisms have abated in intensity largely through the extension of welfare services of the state to all social strata, redistribution of income and wealth through progressive taxation and increased rate of social mobility. Social stratification in the multi-dimensional industrial society is "diamond shaped". The working classes have been integrated into the society and they have adopted the bourgeois norms, values and life-styles. The rise of the middle class in the industrial societies has made the theory of class struggle impracticable. Classes can never vanish from society as there are inequalities among the people on the basis of ability. Various theories of social conflict have been built up by liberal sociologists to show that class conflict is one among various forms of social conflict. The view of Marx was that on account of class struggle in the Western societies, there was bound to be a polarisation of classes. However, on account of the regulation of capitalism by the state, polarisation has not taken place. The modern welfare state can regulate class struggle and represent the interests of the whole community.

(12) The supporters of evolutionary socialism maintain that social and political changes can be brought about through evolutionary methods and revolutionary methods are not essential for bringing about socialism. Instead of revolutionary change, incremental changes can maintain social equilibrium, social harmony and social unity. Revolution is destructive and hence should be avoided. The dictatorship of the proletariat destroys the liberties available in an open society and gives birth to a closed society. Classes are not abolished by revolution and class struggle continues even after the revolution. During the revolution, one generation has to pay a very heavy price. It is illogical that one generation should sacrifice itself for the sake of coming generations.

(13) Marxism fails to take into account the forces of nationalism and even racialism. The two World Wars have proved conclusively that the workingmen of the world do not at all unite together in putting down wars which are capitalistic in character. Instead, they support the governments of their own countries and bring about untold hardships to the working classes everywhere. Although Marxism attacks religion mercilessly, it has become a rival religion of man. Hallowell writes, "In theory Marxism rejects religion but in practice the passion which informs it is religious in character."

(14) Marxism is mistaken in denying the eternal and universal principles of moral conduct. Moral judgements are relative, but moral principles are absolute. Marxism is too abstract and doctrinaire. It is a rapid generalisation on the basis of slender evidence. Several of the predictions of Marx have not come true. Marxism is apocalyptic in nature in that it builds a beautiful vision of the future without taking into account some of the baser elements of human nature.

(15) Marx considered production as the prime mover of history but he did not make it clear whether by production he meant productive forces or modes of production or productive relations. They do not have the same meaning. Marx arid Engels are ambiguous in their statements. Moreover, the mode of production is not determined only by technology but also by other factors including "the state of science generally". Once we agree to bring in "other factors", the relationship of sub-structure and super-structure cannot remain the same. Hence, Marxism is "methodologically deficient".

(16) Advancements in the field of science and technology cannot be determined by the requirements of productive forces. Hallowell writes, "To say that scientific investigation is conditioned by the environment in which it takes place is one thing; to say, as Marx and Engels do, that it is determined by the economic environment is nonsense."

(17) The view of Marx and Engels is that there are no absolute, universal and eternal principles of right and wrong. It is true that these principles are relative and differ with each social development but it is not correct that there are no absolute standards.

(18) Marx divides history into four main periods but that is arbitrary. Whatever does not fit well in the dialectical process has been ignored by Marx. History proceeds from an unending stream of which no one knows the beginning or the end. It is difficult to determine the stages of history which correspond to thesis, antithesis or synthesis.

(19) If every movement of history is a movement towards progress in terms of the dialectical process, the question arises how we can account for "dissolution and decay" in society. Can we say that this part of history cannot be subjected to dialectic?

(20) Marxism is silent about the role great men have played in changing the course of history. The reason is that the view that history is shaped by great men, is inconsistent with the dialectical principle and its economic interpretation. The poetry of Homer, the philosophy of Plato, the science of Newton and the spirituality of St. Paul is not reducible to economic forces.

(21) The analysis of history given by Marx does not make any allowance for chance happenings which have great historical significance. It is well-known that the course of history would have been different if Lenin had not been allowed to return to Russia through Germany in 1917 or if Hitler had not attacked Russia during the second World War.

(22) According to Louis Halle, Marx was primarily a dramatist like Aeschylus. He composed his drama of the revolution on the mythic frame-work of Hegel's philosophy as Aeschylus had composed the drama of Prometheus on the framework of Greek myth. He was a revolutionary merely in trying to achieve its production. Marx was always absolute in his conviction that whatever conception he was expounding represented the absolute truth. In doing so, he was more like an Old Testament prophet than like any of the social philosophers from Plato to De Tocqueville.

(23) Marxism is a religion to its followers. A true Marxist accepts the dogma of Marx as a gospel of salvation. Hallowell writes, "The doctrines of Marx are never held with the scientific detachment with which scientific hypotheses are held by a natural scientist but as an act of religious faith, as a doctrine without which life would have neither meaning nor direction". The inadequacy of Marxism as a religion is due to its effort to solve the total human problem in political terms and its limitations as a political philosophy and strategy are derived from its religio-dogmatic over-simplifications. Marxism attributes practically all ills from which humanity suffers to the capitalistic social order and promises every type of redemption in a new society in which the productive process is owned by the while society. Both of them are untrue.

Merits of Marxism

Although a number of points have been made against the Marxist doctrine, it can neither be dismissed nor ignored. It is the revolutionary philosophy of the working class. It has inspired and guided the working class in the world. Marxism is a scientific philosophy which helps in understanding the laws of social development and suggests the revolutionary ways of changing the present society. It aims at the end of exploitation of man by man. It is not a mere theory. Equal emphasis has been put on practice also. Marxism is neither historicism nor historical fatalism. It emphasised both revolutionary and conscious activity of man (praxis). Marxism does not present merely the social, political, cultural and ethical interpretation of society, but has also a revolutionary message. Marxism brings to the forefront the question of the inadequacy of the present social organisation. It presents an admirable diagnosis of capitalism. It is a coherent socialist system with a definite purpose and a dear programme of action. It treats socialism as a historical product and gives to the proletariat its historical mission. It is exclusively proletarian socialism. It lays special emphasis on the importance of production. The previous socialists had centred their attention upon the question of just distribution. Marx rightly said that the distribution of the means of consumption depends upon the mode of production.

It has rightly been said that the magnitude of the achievements of Marxism cannot be denied even by its most unsympathetic critics. His ideas struck the world like a flaming religion. As a result, conversion to his creed appeared like conversion to a religion and to the acceptance of an entirely working class philosophy utterly uncompromising in its hostility to capitalism. The ideas of Marx inculcated a sense of class-consciousness among the labour class. In 1883 Engels said about Marx, "We are what we are because of him; without him we should be still sunk in slough of confusion". The view of Liebnecht is that Marx "has raised social democracy from a sect, from a school, to a party which now already fights unconquered, and in the end will win the victory". Alexander Gray observes, "Yet despite his prosy and interminable dullness, the confusions and inherent contradictions of his theories, despite his manifold defects in temperament and disposition rendering him the least fitted of men to be a hereof the people, the indubitable fact remains that Marx has proved to be the most influential figure of the nineteenth century".

The view of Wayper is that Marx was one of the most important and most influential political philosophers who ever lived. To the Communists all over the world, he was a great thinker and a great prophet who lived and worked for the working class. Marx succeeded because he was such an explosive compound of Hebrew prophet and scientific propounder of political and economic theory. Wayper concludes. "For the power of his message, for the inspiration of his teachings and for his effect upon future developments, Marx can be sure of his place in any collection of the world's great masters of political thought".

According to Catlin, "What Marx did was to provide a movement with a creed, a movement which hitherto had no adequate theory. Owen, St. Simon and Proudhon may have expressed truths of the first order, neglected by Marx. Bur their theories had been intellectual patch-work. Marx gave the movement whole cloth Hegel. He did more. The workers had leaders who dreamed beautiful dreams of brotherly love. Marx did for the socialist movement what Machiavelli did for the state theory. As Marx spat on the beautiful comforting maxims of the schooiman, unrelated to actual human conduct, so Marx expanded his contemptuous wit on those who hesitated to tell the capitalists just where armed revolt would place a limit to their power. Marx's concern was to build up in effect a military machine. He returned to the study of politics as the science of power. The drawbacks were that his policy of action was primarily—and this agreed with his whole temperament—negative, destructive, bellicose; and that Marxism turned away from the peaceful, constructive schemes of Owenites and Co-operators and of the Quakers, the Monks and the Early Christian communities before them."

Christopher Lloyd says, "Marx was correct in prophesying the increasing importance of economics in politics: he was correct In showing that the economic elements have been overlooked by historians; he was the first to expose the fallacy of commercialism, to show that the volume of trade is no true test of national well-being; he foresaw the increasing severity of the trade cycle and advance of trustification; he foretold communism, though he thought it would occur first in a highly industrialised country like Germany and not in an agricultural country like Russia. On the other hand, he never saw the possibilities of the trade union movement, or the Social Service State; he said that 'Capitalism produces its own grave-diggers' whereas in reality it produces a host of petty capitalists, shareholders, etc., who are far from wishing to destroy the state. He never considered the psychological aspect of politics. He did not realise that most men hate violence and love their country. The century which came after him produced a great War, race hatred, economic nationalism, even a measure of planned 'capitalism, not the international solidarity of the working-class or a world revolution".

C.C. Maxey observes, "It is doubtless true, as often asserted, that every stone of the Marxian edifice was prefigured in the works of political and economic thinkers antedating Marx, but that does not stamp Marx as a second hand philosopher or lessen the significance of what he did. The important thing about the work of Marx was not its originality, but its synthetic power. He seized upon philosophic materials which had been lying about loose and largely unused for many years and fused them into a systematic whole that supplied the proletarian movement with a dynamic theory and a tremendous impulse to action. Proletarianism before Marx was mainly protest and aspiration; Proletarianism after Marx confidently put forth the claim that science was on its side, knew what objectives it wished to attain, had a definite technique of organisation and attack, and thus became militantly aggressive. It was the avowed purpose of Marx to make socialism scientific. It has been said that he succeeded only to the extent of making it pseudo-scientific, but there is no denying that he made it a tremendous force".

According to Isaiah Berlin, "The nineteenth century contains many remarkable social critics and revolutionaries no less original, no less violent, no less dogmatic than Marx, but not one so rigorously single-minded, so absorbed in making every word and every act of his life a means towards a single, immediate, practical end, to which nothing was too sacred to sacrifice".

About the influence of Marx, Prof. William Ebenstein says, "The doctrines of Marx and Engels made a profound impression on social thinkers, reformers and revolutionaries everywhere. In Western Europe and the United States, Marxism was not too successful because the liberal tradition in these countries kept the way open for social reform and progress by peaceful, constitutional means. However, many critics of the injustices and abuses of capitalism accepted a large measure of the Marxian economic analysis and indictment of capitalism without embracing Marx's remedy of despair—the revolutionary dictatorship of the proletariat. In Western Europe and the United States, the political rights of the people were constantly enlarged through the widening of the franchise at the very time when Marx claimed that a ruling class would never abdicate peacefully. Forward-looking democrats and social reformers felt that, if the political position of the people could be radically improved by constitutional means, social and economic issues would ultimately be solved in the same manner. In France, the ideals of the French Revolution, Liberty, Equality, Fraternity and not the Marxian doctrine of class war and hatred, provided the abiding inspiration for the socialist movement.

"In England the firm foundations of parliamentary government, accepted as supreme by all social classes since 1688, made it possible for the working-class to use the existing machinery of government for purposes of social reform, just as the middle class had used it earlier for political reform. Whereas the working-classes in many countries of continental Europe and elsewhere had to agitate simultaneously for political democracy and social democracy, the English workers had the immense benefit of operating within the premises of parliamentary government from the start.

"In the United States, Marxian doctrines have found little resonance because the vast opportunities of a new world have generated hope, prosperity, and optimism, which belies the Marxian prognosis of the progressive impoverishment of the masses. Also, Marxism had made little headway in the United States because it has attacked the political foundations of American democracy as well as the economic foundations of American capitalism".

BOLSHEVISM

Bolshevism represents the Russian form of Communism and it is necessary to discuss in this connection the contribution made by Lenin, Stalin and Khrushchev.

As regards Lenin (1870-1924), he was himself not a workman but a member of the middle-class intelligentsia who had become interested in the revolutionary movement and Marxism in his youth. There were many ups and downs in his life. He was imprisoned and exiled to Siberia. He escaped and carried on agitation against the Russian Government from abroad and also from within Russia. He favoured immediate preparation for a revolution in Russia. He managed to become the majority or Boisnevik of the Social Democrats. The moderates who believed in peaceful and constitutional methods became the minority of the Mensheviki. In March 1917, when the Czar was overthrown, the Mensheviks came to power and they were prepared to work the bourgeois democratic institutions. However, they were overthrown in November 1917 by the Bolsheviks headed by Lenin.

From 1900 to 1914, Lenin was busy in propagating his views and organising the people of Russia. That work continued upto the outbreak of the World War I in 1914. Lenin was happy that Russia was participating in the war. He believed that Russian participation in the war would be in the interests of the workers. From 1914 to 1917, be continued his ruthless campaign against the Czar and his government. He dènounced even those persons who in any way helped the Russian Government, in the prosecution of war. He believed that an opportunity for the workers could arise only in the event of the defeat of Russia in the war. Such an opportunity came in 1917 when the Czar was overthrown. The German General Staff imported Lenin into Russia. However, he reached late and power fell into the hands of the Mensheviks. In November 1917, Lenin and his followers were able to oust the Mensheviks. It was in this way that the Bolshevik Government was established in Russia.

After capturing power, Lenin had to fight against heavy odds. Russia was attacked on many sides. It was a heroic job to beat back the foreign invaders. War was taken to the Polish soil. It was in this way that the foreign danger was met.

Lenin was confronted with a formidable economic problem and he met the situation boldly and the people were saved from starvation. His economic policy started the country on the road to material prosperity. He put emphasis on the electrification of the country. It was felt that through electrification, the prosperity of the country could be increased.

Leinin died in January 1924. He possessed a grim and humorous face. He loved the workers and hated the Czar. He hated the bourgeoisie most. Probably, he was the most influential man in the history from the time of Julius Caesar. He was the hammerer of world revolution.

Lenin's Attitude towards Religion

As with other Communists, religion had no place in the philosophy of Lenin. He condemned the philosophy of Tolstoy whom he called the "exhausted, hysterical, misery-mongering Russian intellectual". The view of Lenin was that religion helped the exploiters to exploit the poor. Fear created the Gods. Fear of the blind forces of capital threatened the workers and the small businessman with sudden, unexpected accidental destruction and ruin, bringing in their train beggary, pauperism, prostitution and deaths from starvation. The Party of the Proletariat demands that the Government shall declare religion as a private matter but it does not for a moment regard the question of the fight against religion as a private matter. Religion was not to be regarded as a private matter in the Communist Party.

Lenin's Theory of Imperialism

In his book entitled "Imperialism: The Highest State of Capitalism", Lenin expounded his theory of his view was that the lower middle classes and the skilled workmen of advanced industrial countries were saved from the increasing misery which was predicted for them by Karl Marx on account of the creation of empires by those countries. If those countries had no empires to dominate and exploit, the condition of their workers and middle classes would have deteriorated. It was the exploitation of the people of the colonial territories that helped them to improve their position. However the result of that was that the condition of the people of the colonial territories became miserable and they became the genuine proletariat. The people of the dominating country became the capitalists. Lenin maintained that the state of imperialism was not a contradiction of the teachings of Marx but merely a fulfilment of it. As capitalism developed, units of industrial production grew bigger and combined in trusts and cartels to produce monopoly capitalism. The same was the case in the financial world. Banks combined and became masters of capital which was used by the industrialists to create monopoly capitalism. Monopoly-financed capitalism was aggressively expansionist. Its characteristic export was capital and it had three consequences. It resulted in the exploitation of the colonial peoples. It produced wars between nations. It brought about the end of capitalism and the emergence of a new order. With the arming and military training of the workers, the wars which began as national wars ended as class wars. The view of Lenin was that Marx was not wrong and he had merely paid less attention to one stage.

It is contended that Lenin's theory of imperialism was a good answer to the criticism against Marx but such a view would not have been maintained by Marx himself. Lenin used an early or a late date for the beginning of the period of Imperialism to suit the changing needs of his argument. The dominance of industrial combinations did not take place earlier than the first decade of the 20th century. While discussing the political consequences of industrial and financial trustification, Lenin had to choose an early opening date for the period of imperialism. The partitioning of the New World was complete before the end of the 19th century. Although Great Britain had the largest empire in the world, she was never dominated by finance capitalism as defined by Lenin.

The view of Lenin was that the investing capitalists pushed their government into dangerous diplomatic adventures and the rich were the cause of wars in the age of imperialism. However, in practice, the very opposite has happened. It were the Governments of Italy and Russia who pushed their financiers into situations which made war against Turkey and Japan extremely probable. When they did so, they were importers of capital and not exporters as maintained by Lenin. The financiers may have pushed Great Britain towards the Boer War in South Africa but other factors also played their part in precipitating the war.

The view of Lenin was that the export of capital did not "develop formidable proportions until the beginning of the twentieth century" and the greater part of British capital was invested in the British colonies. Critics point out that Lenin was wrong in both cases. There was no inseparable connection between the export of capital and empire. Although the people of Switzerland had no empire, there was a lot of export of Swiss capital to foreign countries. Lenin maintained that the possession of empire led a labour aristocracy in the Mother country to enjoy a high standard of living by exploiting the people of the colonial territories. However, it is pointed out that although Sweden and Denmark do not have empires, the standard of living of their people is much higher than that of the people of France and Belgium who possessed empires. The view of Lenin was that impoverishment and servitude accompanied capital when the same was sent abroad. The answer is that although it is sometimes the case, there is no general rule as such. For a long time, the United States, Canada, Australia and New Zealand imported a lot of capital from other countries but in spite of that, they did not suffer from poverty or subjection. Experience shows that poverty was to be found in those countries where capital exports were low. The view of Prof. Staley is that the relationship between the movement of capital and poverty seems to be the direct opposite of what Lenin declared it to be. Critics point out that Lenin's theory of imperialism is not true as a defence of Marxism.

Lenin on Democracy

According to Lenin, pure democracy was the phrase of the Liberals who wanted to dupe the working classes. He condemned the writings of Kautsky for their attitude towards the so-called bourgeois democracy. He stood for the dictatorship of the Proletariat. He had no faith in the democratic traditions as they existed in the world in modern times.

Lenin was not in favour of peaceful means for bringing about the transition from capitalism to communism. He openly stood for the employment of violent means for the achievement of this purpose. According to him, revolution is undoubtedly the most authoritarian thing in the world. It is an act in which one section of the population imposes its will upon the other by rifles, bayonets, guns and other authoritarian means. The revolutionary dictatorship of the Proletariat is violence in respect of the bourgeoisie and the need of such violence is caused by the fact that there exist an army and bureaucracy. As long as classes exist, the liberty and equality of classes is a bourgeois deception. The Proletariat takes over power, becomes the ruling class, smashes the bourgeois parliamentarianism and suppresses the bourgeoisie, suppresses all attempts of all other classes to return to capitalism, gives real liberty and equality to the toilers, gives them not only the right to, but the real use of that which had been taken away from the bourgeoisie. The view of Lenin was that democracy of the Proletariat was the democracy of the poor and not of the rich. There was no place for the rich in such a democracy. They were to be scrupulously excluded from participation in such a democracy. Such a democracy was a million times more democratic than the bourgeois democracy. The violent method was necessary because the capitalists were not expected to abdicate their power without a bitter struggle. Any other method was bound to fail.

Lenin on State

Like other Communists, the view of Lenin was that the state was not a permanent organisation. It was merely a class organisation for exploitation. To quote Lenin. "The state is nothing but the machine for the suppression of the one class by another. To suppose that in any serious revolution the issue is decided by the simple relation between majority and minority is the acme of stupidity". Lenin , quoted with approval the following statement of Dr. Engels with regard to the state: "As the state is only a temporary institution which is to be made use of in the revolution, in order forcibly to suppress the opponents, it is a perfect absurdity to speak about the free popular state. So long as the Proletariat still needs the state, it needs it not in the interests of freedom, but in order to suppress the opponents and when it becomes possible to speak of freedom, the state as such ceases to exist".

The view of Lenin was that the Bolsheviks had as their final aim, the destruction of the state, or every organised and systematic violence against man in general. Striving for socialism, they were convinced that it would extend further into communism. Side by side with this, there will vanish all need for force for the subjection of one man to another, of one section of society to another, as people grow accustomed to observe the elementary conditions of social existence without force and without subjection. "When all, or be it even only the greater part of society, have learnt how to govern the state, have taken this business into their own hands, have established a control over the insignificant minority of capitalists, over the gentry with capitalist leanings, and workers thoroughly demoralised by capitalism from this moment the need for any government begins to vanish. The more complete the democracy, the nearer the movement it ceases to be necessary. The more democratic the state consisting of armed workers which is no longer a state in the ordinary sense of the term, the more rapidly does every form of the state begin to decay..." Regarding the role of the state Lenin wrote, "By ourselves, we workers relying on our experience as workers, must create unshakable and iron discipline supported by the power of the armed workers; we must reduce the role of the state officials to that of simply carrying out our instructions; they must be responsible, revocable, moderately paid managers and clerks".

Lenin on Revolution

Lenin put too much emphasis on a violent revolution for the establishment of communism. It is not sufficient for revolution that the exploited and oppressed should understand that they cannot go on living in the old way and that they should demand a change. Likewise, it is not necessary for revolution that the exploiters should not be able to govern in the old way. Only when the lower classes do not want the old and when the upper classes cannot continue in the old way, only then the revolution will be victorious. Revolution is impossible without a national crisis affecting both the exploited and the exploiters. For revolution, it is necessary that the majority of the workers should fully understand the necessity for and be prepared to sacrifice their lives for it. The ruling class should experience a government crisis which draws into politics even the most backward masses and makes it possible for the revolutionaries quickly to overthrow it.

According to Lenin, the process of revolution in Great Britain was slow because the British bourgeoisie were in a position to create better conditions for the aristocracy of labour.

According to Lenin, under the ideal Communist Commonwealth, the principle of "from each according to his ability, to each according to his need"should prevail. Until that state was reached, the principle of equal work and equal pay would have to be made effective. The need principle could be made operative when men "have become accustomed to observe the fundamental principles of social life" and their labour will have become "so productive that they will voluntarily work according to their abilities. The narrow horizon of bourgeois law which compels one to calculate, with the pitilessness of Shylock where one has not worked half an hour more than another—this narrow horizon will then be left behind. Then will there be no need for any exact calculation by society of the quantity of products to be distributed to each of its members. Each will take freely according to his needs."

Solidarity of the Party

While Marx put too much emphasis on the development of class-consciousness among the workers, Lenin put too much emphasis on the party organisation. His view was that without a strong and vigorous party organisation, it was not possible to bring about a revolution. To quote him, "The proletariat has no weapon in the struggle for Power except organisation; Constantly pushed out of depths of complete poverty, the Proletariat can and will inevitably become an unconquerable force only as result of this: that its ideological union by means of the principles of Marxism is strengthened by the material union of an organisation holding together millions of toilers in the army of the working class."

The resolution of 1920 emphasized the role of the party in these words: "The Communist Party is part of the working class: it is the most progressive, most class conscious and, therefore most revolutionary part. The Communist Party is created by means of selection of the best most class-conscious, most self-sacrificing and far-sighted workers. The Communist Party is the level of political organisation, with the help of which more progressive part of the working class directs on the right path of the whole mass of the proletariat and the semi-Proletariat."

Lenin did not believe that the members of a party were to be allowed the right of criticising the party. He pointed out the danger of doing so in these words: "We are marching in a compact group along a precipitous and difficult path, firmly holding each other by the hand, we are surrounded on all sides by enemies, and are under their almost constant fire. We have combined voluntarily especially for the purpose of fighting the enemy and not to retreat into the adjacent marsh. And now several in our crowd begin to cry out—let us go into this Marsh". Again, "Opportunity for open fighting. Opinions expressed. Tendencies revealed. Groups defined. Hands raised. A decision taken. A stage passed through. Forward. 'That's what I like' 'That's life.' It is something different from the endless, wearing intellectual discussions, which finish not because people have solved the problem, but simply because they have got tired of talking."

By the principle of democratic centralism. Lenin tried to combine a measure of democracy with one of discipline. Under that system, party members were to elect their own officials at all levels and they were to be accountable to those who elected them. However once decisions were taken, there was to be no dissent. The decisions of the higher bodies were binding on the lower ones. There was to be a combination of the principle of mass participation at the bottom and the concentration of leadership at the top.

The great achievement of Lenin was the reconstruction of the Communist Party which became the vanguard of the Soviet people in their struggle to strengthen and develop the socialist system. Outwardly, the Communist Party and the Soviet state were separate, but actually there was no difference between the two. It was the Communist Party which ran the State machinery. To quote Lenin, "The workers themselves do not know as yet how to rule and would have first to go through years of schooling. Hence in order to rule, an army of revolutionary Communists hardened in battle is necessary. We have such, it is party."

While Lenin stood for the solidarity of the Communist party, he was in favour of entering into a compromise tor bringing about a national crisis in the long run. He wanted the Communist Party in England to enter into a compromise election agreement with the members of the Labour Party in England, viz., to march together against the' alliance of Lloyd George and Churchill while the Communist Party was to retain complete liberty to carry on agitation, propaganda and political activity.

The view of Marx was that the growing class-consciousness of the Proletariat would weaken and break the nationalist sentiment which tied the workers to their country. Patriotism was a fetish of the bourgeoisie to control the exploited arid the oppressed classes. In the long run, the Proletariat would come to realise the strategy of the bourgeoisie and defeat his effort by giving their loyalty to their fellow workers in the world irrespective of their national boundaries. Marxism was an international movement. However, it was found during the World War I that the members of the working classes of the different countries showed their enthusiasm to support their own Governments and did not bother about the solidarity of the working classes of the world. This was not liked by Lenin who openly worked hard for the defeat of his own country in the war.

Lenin stood for retaining the elective representative institutions in the Soviet Union, but those institutions were to be different from bourgeois institutions which were condemned by him as "talking shops". Lenin was not in favour of giving immunities to the deputies in their work. He was in favour of the complete demolition of the bourgeois state apparatus. The new Soviet State was to be based upon the Soviets of the workers and was to be directed by the Communist Party.

Lenin on War

Lenin put special emphasis on war in bringing about a Proletarian revolution. His view as that war severs the last chain that binds the workers to the masters, from slavish submission through imperialist state.

About Bolshevism as promised to the people of Russia by Lenin, Bertrand Russell wrote, "Bolshevism has supplied the new religion. It promises glorious things: an end of the injustice of rich and poor, an end of economic slavery, an end of war. It promises an end of the disunion of classes which poisons political life and threatens our industrial system with destruction. It promises an end to commercialism, that subtle falsehood that leads men to appraise everything by its money value, and to determine money value often merely by the caprices of idle plutocrats. It promises a world where all men and women shall be kept sane by work, and where all work shall be of value to the community, not only to a few wealthy vampires. It is to sweep away listlessness and pessimism and weariness and all the complicated miseries of those whose circumstances allow idleness and whose energies are not sufficient to force activity. In place of palaces and hovels, futile vice and misery, there is to be wholesome work, enough but not too much, all of it useful, performed by men and women who have no time for pessimism and occasion for despair."

The view of William Ebenstein is that the most important single contribution of Lenin to the theory of Marxism was his concept of the professional revolutionary. Marx had assumed that working classes would spontaneously develop its class consciousness in the daily struggle for economic existence and its leadership would largely come from its own ranks. Lenin did not agree with this view. According to him. Communist activity was to be carried on along two lines. Workers were to form labour organisations with primarily economic objectives, operating openly, legally and as publicly as conditions allowed. Side by side with those organisations, there were to be small groups of professional revolutionaries, patterned after the army and the police, highly select, entirely secret. Lenin did not care whether the professional revolutionary was of proletarian origin or not as long as he did his job well. The organisations of the professional revolutionaries were to be highly centralised and constantly guide and supervise the open Communist led economic associations—the trade unions, the cooperatives etc. Lenin particularly advised the professional revolutionaries to infiltrate and form cells in all existing social, political, educational and economic bodies in society, whether they were schools, churches, labour unions or political parties. Above all, Lenin advised professional 'revolutionaries to' infiltrate the armed forces, the police and the government.

Lenin made it perfectly clear that the Communists should engage in illegal work even where legal Communist Parties were permitted. Legal opportunities should be utilised to the fullest extent. He specifically advised Communist activists to work through front organisations, constantly changing names and officers of organisations, but always keeping the ultimate objectives in mind which was the seizure of power by revolutionary means.

One of the greatest contributions of Lenin was that he adapted Marxism to Russia. Lenin was a Russian and he had an instinctive understanding of the Russian situation. As a revolutionary, he realised that revolution was possible in Russia only under certain circumstances. The Czar must be defeated in the war and there must be a group of highly disciplined and professional revolutionaries who must be in a position to take over the government of the country. Lenin believed that there was going to be a war and Russia was bound to be defeated in that war, but the question was how to train revolutionaries who could take over the Government when Russia was defeated. The view of Marx was that a revolution could take place only in a country where there was full-fledged capitalism. There were no short-cuts to revolution. Revolutionary movements could arise spontaneously and could not outrun the underlying industrial and economic conditions which gave rise to them. The philosophy of Marx could not be applied to Russia which was an agriculturist country. In spite of that difficulty, the view of Lenin was that a successful revolution could be led by the creation of a disciplined and undemocratic party.

Lenin and Marx

Lenin was a follower of Karl Marx but he was the disciple who brought about changes in Marxian philosophy. Lenin put emphasis on the revolutionary aspect of Communism and not the evolutionary one. He had faith only in revolutionary methods. He believed that the transition from capitalism to Communism could not be brought about by peaceful means. That is why he criticized Kautsky and others like him. He believed in revolution and not in waiting for the events to shape themselves.

Lenin adapted the Marxian philosophy to the needs of Russia. The view of Karl Marx was that capitalism had in itself the seeds of destruction. The growth of capitalism was to result in intensified class-consciousness among the workers. However, Lenin had to deal with a country which was industrially backward. He was pledged to overthrow the Czar and his regime. Under the circumstances prevailing in Russia, the desired change was not possible. That is the reason why Lenin put more emphasis on the solidarity of the Communist Party to bring about the revolution by violent means. He was not prepared to wait for the growth of class-consciousness among the workers of Russia to bring about a revolution.

Lenin brought the Marxian philosophy uptodate. From the time of writings of Karl Marx, certain events had occurred which Marx evidently could not have taken into consideration. Lenin took into account the latest factors in his philosophy. Lenin's philosophy is considered to be Marxism in the imperialist stage of the capitalist system.

Stalin (1879-1953)

After the death of Lenin in 1924, there was a struggle for power and ultimately Stalin came out successful. He was able to dispose of all his rivals. For a long time, he was both the Secretary of the Communist Party and the Prime Minister of the Soviet Union. In his time, Stalin was the most-feared man in the world. Every move of his was watched with keen interest by millions of people all over the world. He was described as "the greatest genius on earth", "greatest architect of Communism", "Wise teacher and leader", "Inspirer of our glorious victories" and "Foremost authority on science, literature, linguistics, music, etc."

During the 1930's. Stalin followed the policy of joining the League of Nations and entering into international alignments with a view to check the rising power of Hitler in Germany and Mussolini in Italy. When Stalin did not get a good response from the Western democratic states for a mutual defensive pact, he entered into a non-aggression pact with Germany on the eve of the World War II in 1939. However, when Hitler attacked Russia, it was under the leadership of Stalin that the Russians were able to beat back the invaders. After the overthrow of Hitler in 1945, the whole world was threatened by the fear of Russian penetration.

Regarding the question of wages to be paid to the labourers, every one was to be paid in accordance with the work done by him. Everybody could not be paid the same wages irrespective of the work done by him. "Whoever draws up wage-scales on the principle of equality and ignores the difference between skilled and unskilled labour is at logger-heads with Marxism and Leninism."

Stalin was the champion of the principle of "Socialism in a single country" provided the country concerned had a large territory, a large population and abundant natural resources. The idea of world revolution was not given up but it was not an active factor in Soviet policies, whether national or international. In his international relations, Stalin sought the co-operation of the capitalist states. So far as Russia was concerned, he embarked upon vast schemes of economic reconstruction embodied in the Five-Year Plans. In 1937, Stalin declared that his policy of "socialism in a single country" was successful. The principle of "socialism in a single country" was a departure from the Marxian theory of international Communism. According to Marx, state was to exist only so long as there were classes and with the elimination of private ownership of the means of production, class distinctions disappeared and the state should also begin to "wither away". The view of Stalin was that withering of the state could be accomplished not through the weakening of the state power but through the maximum increase of its strength. The contradiction between the Communist Commonwealth of Marx and Lenin and the Soviet Union as it existed was due to the capitalist environment. That was particularly due to the activities of "foreign spies, assassins and wreckers" sent to the Soviet Union by foreign intelligence services. The view of Stalin was that Dr. Engels never discussed the position of a single socialist state encircled by hostile capitalist nations. "Engel's general formula about the destiny of the socialist state in general cannot be extended to the partial and specific case of the victory of socialism in one country alone. A country which is surrounded by capitalist world and subject to the menace of the foreign military attack, cannot, therefore, abstract itself from the international situation and must have at its disposal a well-trained army, well-organised punitive organs and a strong intelligence service—consequently must have its own state strong enough to defend the conquests of socialism from foreign attacks."

Stalin divided the history of Soviet Russia into two stages. During the first stage, the exploiting classes were to be eliminated. The state was to suppress the exploiters at home and defend itself against foreign aggression. In the second stage, there was the construction of Socialism in the country after the liquidation of capitalist elements. The Soviet state was to move towards. Communism. The question was raised whether the state was still to be maintained under Communism and the reply of Stalin was that "it will be maintained unless the capitalist environment has been liquidated, unless the danger of military aggression from outside is removed." Stalin further maintained that the State will wither away if the capitalist environment was removed and its place was taken over by a socialist environment.

The Stalin Constitution of 1936 was a reflection of the changed economic and social conditions which had resulted from the industrialisation under the Five-Year Plans and the collectivisation of agriculture. The year 1936 was accepted as a date for which many had been waiting. It marked the end of the controls established by the resolution to make certain that no combination of forces would arise which could threaten seriously the continued existence of the Soviet Government and the political and economic systems for which it had previously been discriminated against in legislation relating to education, military service and even the obtaining of employment. The Soviet Constitution of 1936 changed all this by eliminating discrimination on the ground of social origin or occupation. To quote Stalin, "The most important thing is that capitalism has been banished entirely from the sphere of our industry, while the socialist form of production now holds undivided sway in the sphere of our industry. In the sphere of agriculture, instead of the ocean of small individual peasant-farms, with their poor technical equipment and a strong Kulak influence, we now have mechanised production conducted on a scale larger than anywhere else in the world with up-to-date technical equipment, in the form of all-embracing system of collective farms and state farms. As for the country's trade, the merchants and profiteers have been banished entirely from this sphere. All trade is now under the influence of the State, the co-operative societies and collective farms. The landlord class has already been eliminated. The capitalist class in the sphere of industry has ceased to exist. The Kulak class in the sphere of agriculture has ceased to exist. And the merchants and profiteers in the sphere of trade have ceased to exist. Thus all the exploiting classes have now been eliminated. There remains the working class. There remains the peasant class. There remains the intelligentsia."

Khrushchev

After the death of Stalin in 1953, there was a struggle for power and ultimately Khrushchev was able to consolidate his position by 1957. In 1964, he was ousted from power.

In 1956, Khrushchev openly condemned the methods of Stalin, particularly his atrocities. He declared that in future there would be no repetition of the crimes committed during the regime of Stalin and everybody in the Soviet Union would have freedom of action. Every official in the Soviet Union will be able to take the initiative in his work without any fear. He emphasized the fact that law will be supreme in the country and the government will do its utmost to promote the welfare of the people.

The view of Stalin was that a war between the Soviet Union and the capitalist countries was inevitable. The view of Khrushchev was that war between the two was not inevitable. To quote Khrushchev, "As long as imperialism exists, the economic base that gives rise to wars will also remain. That is why we must display the greatest vigilance. As long as capitalism survives in the world, reactionary forces that represent the interests of the capitalist monopolies will also continue their drive towards military gambles and try to unleash war. But war is not a fatalistic inevitability. Today, there are mighty social and political forces possessing formidable means to prevent the imperialists from unleashing war, and if they try to start it to give a smashing rebuff to the aggressor and frustrate their adventurist plans. For this it is necessary for all anti-war forces to be vigilant and mobilised. They must act as united front and not relax their efforts in the struggle for peace. The more actively the people defend peace, the greater the guarantee that there will be no war."

Khrushchev believed in a policy of peaceful co-existence. This does not mean that he believed in accepting the existing relations between capitalism and communism. To quote him, "Society develops in accordance with its laws and now the era has come where capitalism must make way for socialism as a higher social system than capitalism." He did not believe that the change from capitalism to socialism will come in peaceful manner in all countries. To quote him again, "In those countries where capitalism is still strong, where it possesses a tremendous military and police force, serious resistance by reactionary forces is inevitable. The transition in these countries will take place amid sharp class-struggle."

Khrushchev pledged himself to help all those countries which were fighting against colonialism. His view was; "The struggle against imperialism can be successful only if the aggressive actions of imperialism are firmly resisted. Verbal denunciations will not restrain the imperialist adventures. There is only one way to curb imperialism—by tirelessly strengthening the economic, political and military might of the socialist states, by rallying and strengthening the world revolutionary movement in every way and by mobilising the broad masses for the struggle to ward off the danger of war."

Khrushchev believed that the standard of living of the Soviet people could be raised only if the Soviet Union came to some understanding with the West. It was only then that the colossal amounts which were spent on armaments could be diverted to peaceful purposes and then alone the people could have more for themselves. That partly explains why Khrushchev did not precipitate war on the question of West Berlin. Likewise, he did not go to war against the United States in 1962 on the question of Cuba.

Khrushchev believed that Marxism was not a static but a dynamic concept. Communist philosophy must take into consideration the peculiar circumstances prevailing in various countries. He was willing to adopt parliamentary methods for the establishment of communism provided the leadership was in the hands of the Communists. Khrushchev was accused of revisionism. There was a division of world communism into two blocs, one led by the Soviet Union and the other by Communist China.

It is true that Khrushchev stood for certain measure of individual freedom which was certainly much more than what had ever existed in the Soviet Union since 1917 but he subordinated the individual to the Communist Party. He insisted that the Communist must continue to play a leading role in the country and the individuals must not do anything against what was prescribed by the Party. The Party was the guardian of the interests of the people and devoted to their welfare.

The view of Khrushchev was that while the State might "wither away" the Party would not. It would continue to guide the stateless society. It would become stronger than ever before by performing the various functions. He believed that it was the duty of the Party to create discipline among the people. He tried to create initiative among the people for achieving the goal set by the Party. He widened the opportunities for popular participation in public activities.

Khrushchev was undoubtedly one of the master-builders of the Soviet Union. The eleven years of his rule (1953-64) were years of radical and hopeful changes. Stalin had transformed the Soviet Union economically and made her a military power second only to the United States. Khrushchev demolished the Stalin cult and presented a new thesis for achieving Communism. His policy of co-existence was sincere. His policy was one of liberalisation on all fronts.

Brezhnev

After the exit of Khrushchev in 1964, Brezhnev was able to consolidate his position in the Soviet Union and he became not only the Secretary of the Communist Party but also the President of the Soviet Union. It was under his leadership that the new Soviet Constitution of 1977 was adopted on 7 October, 1977. The Preamble to that Constitution says that the Great October Revolution made by the workers and peasants of Russia under the leadership of the Communist Party headed by Lenin, overthrew capitalist and land-owner rule, broke the fetters of oppression, established the dictatorship of the proletariat and created the Soviet State. After achieving victory in the Civil War and repulsing imperialist intervention, the Soviet Government carried through far-reaching social and economic transformations and put an end to exploitation of man by man, antagonisms between classes and strife between nationalities. The unification of the Soviet Republics in the Union of Soviet Socialist Republics multiplied the forces and opportunities of the people of the country in the building of socialism. Social ownership of the means of production and genuine democracy for the working masses were established. For the first time in the history of mankind, the socialist society was created. The strength of socialism was demonstrated by the immortal feat of the Soviet people and their armed forces in achieving their historic victory in the Great Patriotic War. This victory consolidated the influence and international standing of the Soviet Union and created new opportunities for the growth of the forces of socialism, national liberation, democracy and peace throughout the world. The working people of the Soviet Union have ensured rapid, all-round development of the country and steady improvement of the socialist system. They have consolidated the alliance of the working class collective-farm peasantry and people's intelligentsia and friendship of the nations and nationalities of the USSR. Socio-political and ideological unity of Soviet society, in which the working class is the leading force, has been fulfilled, *the Soviet State has become a state of the whole people.* In the USSR a developed socialist society has been built. At this stage, when socialism is developing on its own foundations, the creative forces of the new system and the advantages of the socialist way of life are becoming increasingly evident and the working people are more and more widely enjoying the fruits of their great revolutionary gains.

SUGGESTED READINGS

Afanasyev, V.G. : Marxist Philosophy.

Anderson, P. : Consideration on Western Marxism, London, 1976.

Burns, Emile : What is Marxism?

Catlin, G : Story of the Political Philosophers.

Chang, S.H. : The Marxian Theory of the State.

Dahrendorf, R. : Class and Class Conflict in Industrial Society, 1959.

Durbin, E.F.M. : The Politics of Democratic Socialism.

Ebenstein : Today's Isms.

Engels : Anti-Duhring, 1878.

Fishcher, Ernst : Marx in His Own Words.

Giddens, A.	:	The Class structure of the Advanced Societies, 1973.
Gray, Alexander	:	The Socialist Tradition.
Halle, Louis J.	:	The Ideological Imagination.
Hallowell	:	Main Currents in Modern Political Thought.
Hearnshaw (Ed.)	:	The Social and Political Ideas of Some Representative Thinkers of the Victorian Age.
Hunt, R.N. Carew	:	The Theory and Practice of Communism, 1950.
Joad, C.E.M.	:	Modern Political Theory.
Kolakwoski, L.	:	Main Currents of Marxism, Oxford, 1978.
Laidler, Harry W.	:	Social-Economic Movements.
Lancaster, L.W.	:	Masters of Political Thought, Vol. III.
Laski	:	Karl Marx.
Laski	:	Communism.
Lewis, John	:	The Marxism of Marx, London, 1972.
Lichtheim, George,	:	Marxism, London, 1961.
Marx and Engels	:	The Communist Manifesto.
Marx	:	A Contribution to the Critique of Political Economy, 1859.
Marx	:	The Poverty of Philosophy, 1844.
Maxey	:	Political Philosophies.
McLeaan, David	:	The Thought of Karl Marx.
Murray	:	History of Political Science from Plato to the Present.
Popper Karl	:	The Open Society and Its Enemies, 1945.
Popper Karl	:	The Poverty of Historicism, London, 1961.
Seligman	:	The Economic Interpretation of History.
Swingewood	:	Marx and the Modern Social Theory, London, 1975.
Tucker, R.C.	:	The Marxian Revolutionary Idea, London.
Wayper, C.L.	:	Political Thought.

Fascism

Definition of Fascism

Learning Objectives

- Definition of Fascism
- Rise of Fascism
- Sources of Fascism
- Salient Features of Fascism
- Socio-Economic Basis of Fascism : Liberal view
- Marxist View
- Fascism as a Theory of Reaction and Counter-Revolution
- Achievements of Fascism
- Fascism and Communism
- Points of Distinction
- Nazism in Germany
- The Nazi Ideology
- The State
- The Nazi Party
- Propaganda
- Force
- Imperialism
- Anti-Jewish Policy
- Religion
- Women
- Guns or Butter
- Internationalism
- Economic Control
- Suggested Readings

Fascism is considered as one of the two great authoritarian mass movements launched during the twentieth century in conscious opposition to the middle class capitalist civilisation of the nineteenth century. Communism was the first major revolutionary totalitarian revolt against the liberal way of life and Fascism was the second.

According to J.S. Barnes, "Fascism may be defined generally as a political and social order based upon the current of traditions that have formed our European civilisation, traditions created by Rome, first by the Empire and subsequently by the Catholic Church. Conversely, Fascism may be described as the repudiation of that individualist mentality that found expression first in the pagan Renaissance, then in the Reformation, and later in the French Revolution." It was essentially a reaction against the inefficiency and failure of democratic liberalism.

The view of Sabine is that "the philosophy of Fascism has been largely *ad hoc* and has been patched together from the existing fund of ideas, either to justify what has already been done or to meet situations that were immediately in prospect." Ebenstein holds that "Fascism is a revolutionary totalitarian revolt against the liberal way of life. Stripped to its essentials, Fascism is the totalitarian organisation of government and society by a single party dictatorship, intensely nationalist, militarist and imperialist." Coker writes, "Fascism is described and widely applauded as empirical and pragmatic, acting first, theorising, when it does theorize, afterwards, deriving its creed from experience, not from reasoning." Mussolini himself observed, "Fascism is based on reality, Bolshevism is based on theory. We do not want to be definite and real. We want to come out of the cloud of discussion and theory." Again, "My programme is action, not talk." "Fascism was an ideology compounded of the teachings of Machiavelli's doctrine of oppression, Hegel's political absolutism, Sorel's doctrine of violence and William James' pragmatism. Fascism did not have a dogmatic ideology and adapted its doctrine as the exigencies of the movement required."

Rajni Palme Dutt Writes, "Fascism is, in fact, no peculiar independent doctrine and system arising in opposition to existing capitalist society. Fascism, on the contrary, is the most complete and consistent working out in certain conditions of extreme decay of the typical tendencies and policies of modern capitalism." J.S. Roucek and others write, "Fascism in its most accomplished form is a one party system controlled by a personal dictator operating in a totalitarian state which has combined nineteenth century nationalism in politics with twentieth century collectivism in economics. The Fascists hate Communism, liberalism and internationalism. Secondly, Fascism is rampant nationalism. Thirdly, Fascism is anti-intellectual, grossly emotional, chauvinistic, always aggressive, full of sound, fury and force." A Political Science Dictionary defines Fascism as "a political system of extreme right, which incorporates the principles of the leader, a one-party state, totalitarian regimentation of economic and social activity and the arbitrary exercise of absolute power by the regime." Florence Elliot describes Fascism as "a nationalist, anti-Communist and authoritarian political creed followed by Benito Mussolini in Italy in 1919." According to Mario Einaud, Fascism is used primarily to identify the political system by which Italy was ruled from 1922 to 1945. It was also used to identify a proto-type of totalitarianism and it applied to variations of political systems thought to parallel the Italian one. As compared to the coherent and carefully developed philosophy of Marxism, Fascism was a "mushroom growth" and the driving force was quest for absolute power, whatever served the purpose of gaining and consolidating power was ideologically justified.

Fascism is described as the most anti-democratic, oppressive, anti-humanitarian, reactionary and counter-revolutionary form of dictatorship. It was a curious amalgam of deception, orthodoxy, hero-worship, power-worship, aggressive nationalism, racism, absolution, irrationalism and spiritualism. Fascist dictators came to power through mass action. Though the World War I was fought for the defence of democracy. Fascist dictatorships emerged in Italy, Germany and Spain after the War. Kitchen writes, "After the First World War there were" movements in almost all European states which showed distinct Fascist tendencies. They rejected the idea of parliamentary democracy. They opposed the organised working mass and the philosophy of socialism. They were violently nationalistic. They subscribed to a vague anti-capitalism. They preached submission to authority, discipline and irrational sense of the community." The Fascists were even worse than reactionaries. Barrows Dunhary writes, "Reactionaries are men who maintain their privileged economic position within a context of political democracy; Fascists are men who propose to overthrow political democracy on behalf of their privileged economic position."

Fascism emerged as a result of the failure of the uneasy marriage between capitalism and democracy. To quote Prof. Laski, "The liberal phase of capitalism when it made its marriage with democracy a universal ideal, corresponded with its phase of expansion. But as soon as capitalism ran into difficult weather. Fascism came to rescue capitalism. By the abrogation of democracy, it has entrusted unlimited political power to those who own and control the means of production." Again, "The use of the state power by capitalists assumes a Fascist complexion whenever their security is seriously in question. Capitalism in difficulties uses the predominant position of capitalists in any society to devote the state power to suppressing its opponents. To secure the conditions under which it may restore profit-making, it embarks upon those experiments which it believes will assist that restoration."

Rise of Fascism

The term Fascism was derived from the Latin word "Fasces" which means "bundles" denoting in ancient Rome a bundle of rods with an axe. Those were used as a symbol of authority. This term was adopted by the followers of Mussolini in Italy.

Fascism arose in Italy immediately after the World War I because although Italy was one of the victors of the War, she was deprived of the gains of victory by the Treaty of Versailles of 1919. Mussolini exhorted the masses and formed a party in March 1919. In 1921, the Fascists organised themselves into a political party. In October 1922, the Fascists marched to Rome. The democratic government of Italy was not able to meet the situation and the King of Italy invited Mussolini to form the government. In due course of time, Mussolini set up a Fascist state in Italy.

Likewise, a Fascist state was set up in Germany under Hitler who took advantage of the grievances of the Germans arising out of the Treaty of Versailles and the events that followed in Germany after 1919. In the United Kingdom, a Fascist movement was active between 1931 and 1939. It was proscribed in 1940 but revived again in 1948 under the leadership of Sir Oswald Mosley. Likewise, a Fascist government was set up in Spain under General Franco after the overthrow of Republican government in Spain.

Sources of Fascism

Fascist ideas have been taken from various sources. Mussolini borrowed the idea of constant struggle from the social Darwinists who believed that all life and progress are based on the principle of struggle for existence, elimination of the unfit and survival of the fittest. Mussolini advocated the use of violence, glorified war and denounced peace. In one of his speeches, he said, "Strife is the origin of all things. Strife will always remain at the root of human nature like a supreme fatality and on the whole, it is well that it is so. Today strife is possible in war, in economics, in ideas, but the day in which there would be no more strife would be a day of melancholy, of the end of things of ruin."

Fascism also borrowed from irrationalism and anti-intellectualism. The philosophy of Mussolini was a sort of reaction against the philosophy of rationalism which dominated the European thought. The Fascists held that man is essentially an irrational animal and all his social and political activity should be founded on this basic rule. Man is not all reason. He is governed more by his instincts than by reason. The Fascists borrowed these ideas from anti-intellectualism.

The Fascist philosophy of irrationalism was borrowed from the writings of Schopenhauer (1788-1860) and Nietzsche (1844-1900). The view of Schopenhauer was that reason could comprehend only the phenomenal, the temporal and the outward appearance of the universe. It does not tell us about the real nature of the world. The reality is the will, the will to live. Nietzsche was a disciple of Schopenhauer. He agreed with the view that will was the primary force of universe. However, he added that its manifestation was will to power (the desire to dominate) and not the will to live. He also gave the idea of the Superman who was independent of the conventional rules of moral conduct but was himself the standard of value. Henri Bergson (1859-1941) made a distinction between intellect and intuition. According to him, the faculty of intellect is not sufficient to give us complete picture of the reality. It requires to be supplemented by intuition, a mystical experience. Intuition is the super-rational creative force. It is only with intuition that we can understand the reality. The irrational philosophy based on will, power, insight and intuition was the philosophy of the man who believed in action. Fascism absorbed a good deal of irrationalism as a result of which their slogans roused emotions and sentiments.

Fascism was also affected by the elitist writers including Vilfredo Pareto. They focussed their attention on the fact that real political power was concentrated in a small minority of the ruling class which kept itself in power partly by force and partly by the consent of the governed.

Fascism was also influenced by the philosophy of Sorel (1847-1922). According to him, the General Strike was understood partly as an actual uprising of the workers and partly as a myth. The myth part of his social philosophy influenced Mussolini who declared in 1922, "We have created our myth...Our myth is the nation, our myth is the greatness of the nation." The myth made Fascist Italy a spiritual heir of the Roman Empire.

Hegel's theory of the state also fascinated the Fascist philosophers. Mussolini wrote, "It is not the nation which generates the state...Rather it is the state which creates the nation."

Another source of Fascism was traditionalism. Mussolini's admiration of tradition was due to his being a staunch nationalist. Nationalism and traditionalism go together. The view of Mussolini was that a nation is what it has been because of the experiences it has undergone. Mussolini adopted traditionalism because he found in it a valuable ally from the pragmatic point of view.

Fascism also borrowed from idealism. Mussolini himself was not a believer in Hegelian philosophy but he and his followers used idealism to give support to the principle of social Darwinism and irrationalism. They used idealistic weapons to defend Fascism and attack liberalism. They borrowed the concept of liberty from the idealists. After coming to power, Mussolini declared, "The Fascist state has curtailed useless or harmful liberties while preserving those which are essential. In such matters the individual cannot be the judge, but the state only." The Fascists also borrowed from the idealists the idea of spirit and spiritual. The view of Mussolini was that the Fascist idea of life was a spiritual one while that of liberalism was materialistic. The spirit unfolded itself, as pointed out by the Idealists, through human institutions like family, society and ultimately the state. According to the Idealists, the state is the march of God on earth. The state is the Divine Will. The Idealists' doctrines advocated by the Fascists were simply a paraphrase of the doctrines of Hegel.

Salient Features of Fascism

Fascism was not a doctrine and had no elaborate programme. It was a technique of gaining and retaining power by violence. To quote Mussolini, "Our programme is simple; we wish to govern Italy. They ask us for programmes, but there are already too many. It is not programmes that are wanting for the salvation of Italy but men and will power. Formal principles are iron and tin fetters. The Fascists are the gypsies of Italian politics; not being tied down to any fixed principles, they proceed unceasingly towards one goal, the future well-being of the Italian people."

(1) The Fascists glorified the nation. According to them, the nation had a personality, a will and an end of its own apart from those of the individuals. They did not believe in an atomistic conception of, society. They believed in the organic nature of the state and society. According to them, a nation was a harmonious group of persons who were united together by a common language, customs, traditions and religion. The individuals had a meaning only in the context of national life and were merely abstractions when separated from it. The nation was a self-sufficient entity and its life was continuous and ever-lasting. The nation "recapitulates within its unity not only the living members alone but an indefinite series of generations." The nation was the supreme arbiter of the people whose duty was to serve the nation. Only those actions, thoughts and sentiments of the people were to be considered good which were conducive to the growth of the power of the nation. The Fascists put the greatest emphasis on devotion to the nation. The daily press and periodicals, the radio and films were used to imprint on the minds of the people the glory of the nation. The thoughts and sentiments of the people were controlled in such a way that the idea of the nation became paramount in their minds.

(2) The Fascists glorified the state which was regarded as an end in itself. The state was glorified even at the cost of the individuals. The quote Mussolini, "Everything within the state, nothing against the state, nothing outside the state." The Fascists view was that the state was an independent entity with a real will of its own. They regarded the state as a spiritual being. Mussolini once declared, "For us, the Fascists, the state is not merely a guardian, pre-occupied solely with the duty of assuring the personal safety of the citizens, nor is it an organisation with purely material aims such as to guarantee a certain level of well-being and peaceful conditions of life, for a mere council of administration would be sufficient to realise such objects, nor is it a purely political creation—the state as conceived of and as created by Fascism, is a spiritual and a moral fact in itself." On another occasion Mussolini said, "The Fascist state is not a night watchman solicitous only of personal safety and object for guaranteeing

a certain degree of material prosperity. But it is a spiritual entity for securing political, judicial and economic organisation of the nation which in its origin and growth is a manifestation of the spirit."

(3) The Fascists did not believe in reason. Reason did not appeal to them. Distrust of reason was perhaps the most important trait of Fascism. The Fascists regarded man as an irrational animal and his social and political activities were based on that principle. Fascism was a revolt against reason. It stood in favour of the superiority of the instinct over reason, action over talk. Ebenstein writes, "Psychologically, Fascism is fanatical rather than reflective, dogmatic rather than open-minded; as a result each Fascist regime has its taboo issues such as race, or the empire, or the leader, the nature of which demands that it be accepted on faith alone and never critically discussed." The picture of Mussolini was shown in every class room in Italy under the caption, "Mussolini is always right." The Fascists acted instinctively and not rationally. They put emphasis on such irrational concepts as authority, obedience, honour, duty, discipline, fatherland, purity of race, faith in leadership, instincts and hero-worship. They believed in blind obedience and the leadership principle. Reason was discouraged and emotions and sentiments which were blind and faith which was orthodox in nature, were encouraged.

(4) Fascism believed in myths. Instead of scientific education, emphasis was put on propaganda. Lies were spoken again and again. It was assumed that if a lie was spoken hundreds of times, it became a truth. In Italy, the myth of "Fatherland" was used. In Germany, the myth of "superiority and purity of race" was accepted.

(5) The Fascists did not believe in basic human equality. Ebenstein writes, "The denial of basic human equality is a common denominator of all Fascist movements and states. True enough, democratic societies do not always live up to the ideal of human equality, but they at least accept equality as the long-term goal of public policy. By contrast. Fascist societies not only accept the fact of human inequality, but go further and affirm inequality as the ideal." In Fascist code, men are superior to women, soldiers to civilians, party members to non-party members, one's own nation to others, the strong to the weak and the victors in the war to the vanquished. Hallowell writes that Fascism repudiates the concept of both individual liberty and equality.

(6) Fascism put emphasis on violence and lies and glorified war and violence. Fascism defended violence as a means of achieving political end. Violence played a major part in the movement through which Mussolini captured power in Italy. Violence was considered morally necessary. The Fascists knew only enemies and not opponents and their view was that the enemies must be annihilated. Fascism justified mass murders in concentration and slave camps. War was considered not only necessary but even inevitable. Mussolini used to say, "War is to man, what maternity is to woman." Again, "Three cheers for the war. Three cheers for Italy's war and three cheers for war in general. Peace is hence absurd or rather a pause in war." Peace is the slogan of the weak and impotent nations. War increases discipline, self-confidence and love for one's nation. To quote Hitler, "War is eternal, war is universal. There is no beginning and there is no peace. War is life. Any struggle is war. War is the origin of all things."

(7) There was not much scope for liberty under the Fascist state because the Fascists put more emphasis on the might of the state than on the liberty of the individuals. The liberty of the state depended upon the strength of the nation. The greater the might of the state, the greater is the scope for liberty. "There is no liberty but the liberty which is inherent in state". The state is "an authorised body for the repression of arbitrary will and a guarantee to society in general and to the individual citizen in particular, that the safety is guarded by the mailed first of the law." Liberty was not a natural endowment of nature. It was merely a concession by the state. Liberty consisted in "subjection to law." An individual was free only if he identified himself with the will of the people. Freedom was another name for slavery of the state. According to Gentile, the chief theorist of fascism, "Law and state are the supreme manifestation of liberty" and "The maximum of liberty coincides with

maximum of human force," the state was the sole judge of the nature and extent of the liberty to be enjoyed by the people.

(8) The Fascists believed in an authoritarian, totalitarian and omnipotent state. They put emphasis on the duties of the citizens and not on their rights. They were always prepared to sacrifice the individual at the altar of the state. "Fascism proclaims the rights of the state, the pre-eminence of its authority and the superiority of its ends. No aspect of social life escapes the wise discipline of Fascism."

(9) The Fascists were the enemies of democracy and liberalism. They had no faith in a parliamentary form of government which they described as stupid, corrupt, slow-moving, visionary, impracticable and inefficient. They called it a decaying corpse. They referred to parliaments as talking shops which could not accomplish anything substantial. They considered democracy as something unnatural. They denied the very basis of democracy. They did not believe in the inherent worth of man and held the view that the greatest virtue of man was to obey the state and ultimately merge himself into it.

(10) The Fascists believed that the masses were not competent to govern themselves. It is only a few who have the capacity to rule. It is in the fitness of things that power in the state must be in the hands of a few persons. The people had no right to criticise the government. Their only function was to perform those duties which were assigned to them by the state. According to the Fascists, society was to be built upon an hierarchical order. The leaders were not to be elected by the people. They were not to be responsible to the people. On the other hand, the people were to be responsible to the leaders. There was to be military discipline and blind obedience in every walk of life. The Fascists did not believe in the theory of class war or the materialistic conception of history. They rejected the view that everything if life is controlled by economic factors. They believed that religion and patriotism play a vital part in the life of the people. They believed in "holiness and heroism." They rejected the idea that human happiness lies only in economic well-being. To quote Mussolini, "Economic well-being would reduce man to the level of animals caring for one thing only, to be fed and well fed and would thus degrade humanity to a purely physical existence."

(11) The Fascists did not believe in the *Laissez faire* principles of individualism. They did not accept the idea of public ownership as advocated by state Socialists. They believed in the institution of private property which was to be worked in the interest of the nation. There were to be no strikes or lock-outs. Complete harmony was to be secured in industry in order to achieve the goal of highest production.

(12) Fascism was opposed to internationalism. "International peace is a coward's dream." In the words of Mussolini. "Imperialism is the eternal and immutable law of life." Again, "Italian expansion is a matter of life and death. Italy must expand or perish."

(13) Fascism believed in the existence of one party in the state and the entire administration was to be run by that party. The basic slogan of fascism was: "One Party, One Leader." According to Gentile, the Fascist Party was "the conscience of the state."

(14) Fascism gave utmost regard to leaders who were worshipped as heroes or supermen. Hitler in Germany and Mussolini in Italy were virtually worshipped and wide publicity was given to their photographs and greatness. It was maintained that Hitler was Germany and Germany was Hitler. Fascism was anti-revolutionary and anti-democratic. It resisted all changes and crushed all movements which stood for a change. It used naked force to resist change and maintain the *status quo.* Fascism did not find any merit in democracy.

(15) The Fascists set up a corporate state in Italy. They rejected the principle of territorial representation and substituted in its place the principle of functional representation. Each functional group was given a separate corporation. The relations between the various corporations were regulated by the state. There was a network of corporations covering agriculture, commerce, industry, credit, insurance and fine arts. There were also corporations of state employees, disabled soldiers and of

universities and primary schools. Those corporations were arranged on a hierarchical basis. They submitted lists of names for appointment to the Chamber of Deputies. Each list was usually twice as big as the number of seats allotted. The names were examined by the Fascist Grand Council and a list was ultimately returned to be chosen or rejected by the corporations concerned. If the approved list was not chosen, a re-election was necessary. All laws were initiated by the Fascist Party. The Chamber of Deputies could only discuss them but could not reject them.

(16) Up to 1921, Mussolini and the Fascists were opposed to the Church. However, their attitude changed afterwards. That was partly due to the fact that many of those Italians who joined the Fascist Party were favourably inclined towards the catholic Church. The Fascists also realised that the Church was a potential rival and could be silenced through conciliation and not by frontal attack. The result was that in February 1929, the "Vatican-Italian Accord" was arrived at. As a result of that, the animosity which had continued between the Italian state and Pope ended. The Pope recognised the authority of the Kingdom of Italy under the Fascists and the Italian State recognised the temporal authority of the Pope in the "city of the Vatican."

(17) Fascism was opposed to all human values and feelings. It took a stand against intellectualism. The Fascists wanted absolute obedience from all. All were to behave like faithful dogs to the Duce who had no use of the intellectual power of the people. The people could not understand national problems and their only work was "to have faith, to obey and to fight". According to the fascists, educated people talked unnecessarily and played with knowledge without understanding their own responsibilities. The only force which Fascism recognised was brute force which was used on all occasions.

(18) Mussolini spoke in terms of racial superiority. In this respect, he was like Hitler though he did not reach the heights of Hitler. As the ruling class could dominate over all in a nation, a superior nation could dictate terms to the inferior and weak nations in the world.

Socio-Economic Basis of Fascism : Liberal view

There is a difference of opinion among the Marxist and non-Marxist writers regarding the socio-economic basis of fascism. The Marxist writers associate Fascism with capitalism and maintain that in a crisis-ridden capitalist society which is on the verge of disintegration, the possessive classes resort to Fascism to save the class-divided capitalist society. Non-Marxist writers do not see any class relationship between Fascisms and capitalism. They emphasize the political, organisational, ideological, psychological and cultural structures of Fascism and undermine the socio-economic basis. Prof. Gregory denied that Fascism is identified with capitalism in decay. The essence of capitalistic system is freedom of enterprise and the right of the individual to economic self-expression, whereas Fascism is authoritarian and believes in the principle of corporate state. The programme of the Fascists is socialistic and Fascisms has not merged in the most developed capitalist states like the United States and Britain. It has emerged in Italy and Germany where full-fledged capitalist system never existed. Many liberal writers maintain that Fascism is expressive of a post-War situation in certain countries in which non-economic factors were as important as economic ones. Fascism has nothing to do with the inherent defects of capitalism.

Some liberal writers maintain that the socio-economic basis of Fascism is the middle class. Talcott has examined the social structure of Western capitalist societies to find the roots of Fascism and has come to the conclusion that Fascism nothing to do with the crisis of capitalism. The view of S.M. Lipset is that Fascism is an extremist movement of the middle class. The root cause of fascism lies in the desperate middle class which was threatened from above by the monopoly capitalists and from below by the working class. Fascism promised a third way between monopoly capitalism and socialism which attracted the middle class. To the middle class educated youngmen, Fascism promised jobs in bureaucracy and military, to the small shop-keepers protection from the big capitalists, to the small landlords protection from big landlords etc.

The view of William Ebenstein is that conditions of capitalism do not by themselves give rise to Fascism. It arises only where democracy is particularly weak. To quote him, "Industrialists are not, as a class, any more fascist-minded than other social groups; in countries with strong liberal and democratic traditions, for example, industrialists have neither more nor less faith than other people in the democratic process. But where democracy has been weak, as it was in Germany, Italy and Japan, it took only a few wealthy industrialists and landowners to supply fascist movements with ample funds" (Today's Isms, p. 112).

Ebenstein further says that even the conditions of economic depression need not necessarily lead to the rise of Fascism, but the fear and frustration arising out of economic depression can lead to it. To quote him, "In times of depression, fear and frustration undermine faith in the democratic process, and where the faith in rational methods weakens, fascism is the potential gainer. The small businessman blames big business for his troubles; big business puts the blame on the unreasonableness of the labor unions; labour feels that the only way out is to soak the rich; the farmers feel that they are not getting enough for farm products and that the prices they pay for manufactured goods are too high; and—worst of all—there is the large mass of unemployed people" (Ibid., p. 114).

Ebenstein further observes that even the economic suffering caused by unemployment can be mitigated by adequate relief, but the feeling of being useless, unwanted and outside the productive ranks of society paves the way for the rise of Fascism. To quote him again, "It is among these spiritually homeless that Fascism makes serious inroads during a depression; by putting an unemployed person into a uniform, a Fascist movement makes him feel that he 'belongs', and by telling him that he is a member of a superior race or nation, such a movement restores some of his self-respect" (Ibid.).

Marxist View

Marxist scholars identify Fascism with capitalism. According, to them, "Fascism was a defensive action by monopoly capitalism in response to growing proletariat militancy," Fascism was an offensive by the bourgeoisie against the working class. Marxists maintain that Fascism is a different form of bourgeois state in which labour movements and revolutionary parties are mercilessly crushed in the name of industrial peace, stability, law and order, discipline and unity. Wage reductions, ban on strikes and destruction of the trade union movements are the universal features of Fascism.

According to the Marxists, Fascism emerged due to the inbuilt crisis of the liberal bourgeois society. Faced with threats from the labour movements, the capitalists rejected their belief in democracy and hence Fascism is a theory of liberal capitalist society in crisis. According to Herbert Marcuse and F. Neumann, the roots of Fascism lie within liberal socio-economic order and it is the inevitable result of monopoly capitalism. In a situation of extreme socio-economic and political instability, Fascism restored political stability by smashing the democratic opposition. Economic stability was restored by the destruction of the labour movement which threatened the economic base of capitalist society. Fascism developed as a reactionary theory of right radicalism within the frame-work of monopoly capitalism. The big capitalists hoped to use Fascism to destroy the labour movement and neutralise the dis-satisfaction and aggression of the middle classes within the frame-work of monopoly capitalism. The army and bureaucracy supported the Fascist regime.

According to the Marxist writers, Fascism was the open, terrorist dictatorship of the most reactionary, chauvinist and imperialist elements of finance capital. Hitler offered the industrialists the destruction of labour movement, lower wages to workers, decisive action to stimulate the economy, re-armaments and the creation of a strong and forceful national government. The socio-economic programme of the Fascists for economic and military reconstruction profited industries, the corporate state and state monopoly capitalism helped big business. It reduced the element of competition within the economy. It tried to establish "class peace" by forbidding strikes, crushing the working classes and ban on trade unions. The re-armament policy and war helped the big industries. Fascism resulted from the fears of the bourgeoisie that the liberal democratic system was no longer in a position to guarantee their interests. The crisis-ridden economic conditions and rising working class movements made them uncertain and fearful. Fascism emerged as the naked rule of the big capitalists, designed to preserve the economic and social position of the capitalist class.

Fascism as a Theory of Reaction and Counter-Revolution

It is contended that the doctrine of Fascism arose as a theory of reaction to democracy. Socialism and communism. While democracy and Communism represented progressive forces of modern society. Fascism was a movement towards a reverse direction, in support of the former outmoded, repressive social and political conditions. Fascism rejected equality and substituted the principle of hierarchy culminating in a supreme leader or dictator whose will was law. It repudiated individualism and asserted that all values derived from the state against which the individual had no rights. True liberty was found only in subjection to state authority. The Fascist state required complete conformity, rigid discipline and unquestioning obedience. The use of force to achieve the above objectives was justified. Unlike the cult of reason advocated by liberalism and democracy. Fascism relied upon faith and emotion as the motive force of human actions. Instead of regarding the individual as an end and the state as a means. Fascism exalted the state as an end and reduced the individual to the position of means. It established the monopoly of the nation-state in all internal and external matters. It did not tolerate any human association or organisation within the state which could compete with the state for the loyalty of the citizens. It repudiated the pluralistic position of liberal democracy. It did not support the international organisation for the settlement of disputes and relied upon military solution. It repudiated the progressive idea of human equality as the basis of their rational organisation into a nation or other associations. It sought unity through homogeneity. It followed the policy of concentrating all political power in the hands of the dictator and a single political party.

Fascism created a peculiar authoritarian system which tried to create mass enthusiasm for the Fascist regime and policies. Mussolini emerged as an extremely popular leader enjoying immense authority in the state. He had his personal army. The Blackshirt Militia, bound exclusively to his service. The new political structure of the Fascist dictatorship in Italy was built inside the pre-existing system until all that remained of the old order was a hollow facade. The King of Italy still reigned and the Senate still met, but Mussolini, backed by his disciplined supporters, commanded Italy.

The proletariat and the intelligentsia in Italy and Germany were suppressed on account of their radical outlook. Educational institutions were used for conducting Fascist and racialist propaganda. State centralisation replaced the autonomy of social life. The civil service, judiciary, army and universities were purged of anti-Fascist elements. No criticism of the reactionary policies of the Fascist regime was permitted in the press. Leading anti-Fascist intellectuals and political activists were killed, imprisoned or exiled. The mysterious disappearance of Matteotti in Italy in 1924, the slow killing of Gramsci, the Italian Marxist leader, through torture and the execution of Roehm and his group in Germany in 1934 are merely examples of what was done on a large scale in the country. Fascism used all kinds of psychological methods to appeal to the irrational sentiments of the mob. It made use of colourful processions, military uniforms, and speeches full of the rhetoric to rouse the crowd. The Fascist state maintained prisons and concentration camps for the political adversaries. It is said that during the first few months of their coming to power, the Nazis put 50,000 to 80,000 political prisoners in the concentration camps and they died in millions. The mass media in the Fascist countries was required to support solidly the policies of the government. According to Goebbels, the press was to be converted into a piano upon which the Propaganda Ministry of the Fascist state could play any tune it liked. There was to be only one public opinion and the nation was to speak with one voice. The speeches of the Fascist leaders were a series of war-like harangues. Preparation for war was the one constant theme of all Fascist propaganda. Listening to a foreign radio station was a crime punishable with death. In a Fascist state, the official chief of the press decided what news were to be published and what was to be suppressed. The individual in the Fascist state was completely subordinated to the authority of the state and Fascist hierarchy. The Fascist oath was in these words: "In the name of God and Italy, I swear to execute without discussion the orders of the Duce and to serve with all my strength and if necessary with my blood the cause of the Fascist revolution."

Fascism started as a, movement demanding revolutionary changes in the social and political structure of Italy. However, it soon developed into a force against revolution itself, particularly against the revolutionary force of Communism. Fascism can be regarded as counter-revolutionary because it sought to promote concentration of economic control in a few hands in order to stop the diffusion of political power. It stripped capitalism of its democratic character. Under Fascism, the masses were left with no rights or safeguards against their oppression by the Fascist ruling party. Under capitalism, the capitalists were somewhat prepared to pay the price of people's support in the form of some concession, but under the Fascist regime they were not required to pay that price. The profit-making motive of the capitalists was no longer restrained by the demands or expectations of the people. The result was lower wages for workers, inferior general conditions of industry, lowering of taxation upon capital and contraction of social services.

The view of Prof. Laski is that so long as the marriage of capitalism and democracy continued, capitalism made concessions to the masses which gave them a sense of satisfaction. When it sought to withdraw those concessions, it resorted to Fascism. To quote Laski, "Fascism came to rescue capitalism from this dilemma. By the abrogation of democracy, in one form or another, it has entrusted unlimited political power to those who own and control the means of production...All political parties which deny its purposes have been suppressed. The free trade unions have gone, and, with them, the right to strike. Wages have been reduced either unilaterally by the employers, or with the approval of the state. The right to free criticism has been suppressed; and the power of the electorate to change its government has been withdrawn."

The Fascists curbed individual liberty by obstructing the supply of the true news. They brought the press, the wireless, the cinema, the theatre and the publishing trade directly under the control of the government. The neutrality of the civil service was given up. The judiciary was subordinated to the service of the state. The Fascists built their authority on the loyalty of the armed forces. They also armed the forces of their own partisans. Fascism tried to avert the transformation of capitalist system into a democratic welfare state. It tried to maintain the exploitative character of the capitalist patterns of production in the name of national interest, national unity, discipline, industrial peace and higher introduction.

Fascism tried to dilute the revolutionary content of Communism by an improvised anti-Marxist theory. It tried to replace materialism by a mystical political idealism. It rejected the theory of class war in favour of the organic unity of the nation state. It repudiated the economic motive behind human actions which could give rise to class struggle. Mussolini himself said that Fascism believed in holiness and heroism. It believed in actions influenced by no economic motive, direct or indirect. Fascism tried to project an image of a unified nation with an indiversible interest to repudiate the theory of class conflict. It refused to rely on reason for arriving at the truth. It praised the creative power of the myth to muster the support of all classes in society. Mussolini said in 1922, "We have created our myth. The myth is a faith, it is passion. It is not necessary that it shall be a reality. It is a reality by the fact that it is goad, a hope, a faith, that it is courage, Our myth is the nation, our myth is the greatness of the nation."

Authority, discipline and anti-Communism were the watch-words of the Fascist Party in Italy. The motto given to the youth of Italy by Mussolini was: "To believe, To obey, To fight". That clearly showed the reactionary and counterrevolutionary character of Fascist theory. Fascism glorified the nation and emphasized the idea of the state as a power system. Narrow nationalism, chauvinism, aggressive warfare and imperialist expansion were some of the essentials of the Fascist movement in Europe. The view of the Fascists was that international peace was a coward's dream and pacifism was an act of cowardice. The Fascists exploited the nationalist sentiments. They exaggerated and misinterpreted the internationalism of the Socialists and Communists. Ebenstein writes, "Totalitarian, imperialist Fascists look on war as the highest form of national life; Communists—while rejecting, in theory, war between nations—accept the inevitability of war between classes and the liquidation of the bourgeoisie by violent means."

Mussolini and Hitler openly advocated the necessity of conquering other inferior nations through war against them. War was necessary for the development of many qualities in the citizens of the country. Fascism chose an internal policy which involved war as its external consequence. The Fascists believed in the power of the victorious armed forces to realise all important national goals. Without a strong army, navy or air force, it was not possible to protect the national interests. The Fascist counter-revolution met its death during the Second World War.

Achievements of Fascism

It cannot be denied that to begin with. Fascism did a lot for the people of Italy. The Fascists brought order out of chaos and restored the old prestige and glory of Italy. They united the nation in an unprecedented manner. They put new life into a dying nation. As a matter of fact, the Italians were reborn under the guidance of Mussolini. "Mussolini made the rail-roads run on time." The Fascists improved the public finances, secured a more efficient operation of the public services, usefully exploited the natural resources of Italy, carried out vast projects of land reclamation and other public works and greatly enlarged the facilities of popular education. They stimulated private industrial activity and put loan end to violent labour disputes. The Fascists established better working relations with the Church of Rome, strengthened the international position of Italy, satisfied national pride and made the government acceptable to the masses.

The view of Prof. C.C. Maxey is that Fascism sugar-coated raw power with a mystical idealism. It supplied a moral justification for violence. It exploited patriotism to the utmost limit. It rationalised the minority rule. It capitalised on the widespread fear of Communism. It offered the masses a new religion with a new God to worship. Mussolini once boasted, "Fascism is bound to become, the standard type of civilisation of our country for Europe, the forerunners of European Renaissance."

If Fascism had certain achievements, it had many shortcomings also. It was against socialism. The Fascists supported private property and private enterprise and denounced Socialism. The propertied classes found general support in Fascism and hence Fascism was the opposite of Socialism.

Fascism was inimical to the development of art, literature and culture. It led to dictatorship and totalitarianism. "Dictatorship means muzzles all-round and consequently stultification. Science can flourish only in an atmosphere of free speech." Coker writes, "A highly centralised and coercive direction of public cultural life of a nation destroys the possibility of great learning, literature and art."

Another defect of Fascism was that it glorified war and violence to such an extent that it became unbearable for society. A society based on fear and violence cannot last long and is bound to collapse one day or lead to a revolution. Fascism actually collapsed during World War II.

The Fascists had a false notion and belief in national unity. Regimes of force could survive only among the decadent people. They could only be temporary expedients in nations that were growing and in the ascendant. Repression produced more violent explosions of the forces restrained by it. Fascism was opposed to intellectualism. The Fascists criticised the educated people on the ground that they talked unnecessarily and played with knowledge without knowing their own responsibility. The Fascist doctrine was alien to human understanding and reason. Fascism believed in propaganda for indoctrinating the minds of the people. It believed in brain-washing which was not warranted.

The Fascist movement was vague in many ways. It was a jumbling of ideas borrowed from various sources. Sabine writes about Fascism, "It is a body of ideas taken from various sources and put together according to the exigencies of the situation. It was difficult to combine Hegelian nationalism, Plato's government by aristocracy, Bergosonian anti-intellectualism etc. and to work them successfully in active practice."

Fascism was the negation of democratic philosophy and principles. Although Fascism regimes were established with popular support, they did not care for continuous majority support. They believed that the masses should blindly follow the leader.

Fascism had no faith in liberal concepts like liberty of thought and expression and equality of human beings. Hence, it was authoritarian.

Fascism had all the essential features of dictatorships—an official ideology, a single mass party, terroristic police control, monopoly control—of mass communication, monopoly of all means of effective armed combat and the central bureaucratic control of entire economy.

Although Mussolini contended that the Fascist state was not a police state, it was nothing else in reality. Chapman maintains that police states "occur independently of the political philosophy of the state. They grow up when authoritarian philosophies meet resistance. They are created in reaction to a special kind of dissidence in society." (Police State, p. 135).

According to Louis J. Halle, "What the Fascist movements lacked in philosophy, they made up in theatre. It is surely no accident that the extreme of Fascism was realised in two countries most notable for their contributions to grand opera."

Laski writes, "Fascism, when closely examined, proves to be nothing more than an ill-assorted rag-bag in which all kinds of remnants from the most diverse philosophies seek, as best they may, to find a place." (The State in Theory and Practice, p. 193).

Fascism was criticised by the Liberals because it did not accept the principle of responsible government. Fascism was opposed to democratic principles and institutions. It opposed freedom of opinion and disallowed dissent. Fascism was the enemy of international law, order and peace. It advocated the open use of force in the settlement of international disputes. Liberal writers attacked Fascism on the ground that it had anti-humanitarian ideas and was based on deception and fraud. It denied cherished human values and did not accept any ideology or system or values. It was naked Machiavellianism which disregarded human values.

The view of the Marxists is that Fascism was the bulwark of capitalism. It was a conspiracy on the part of the capitalists to protect, preserve and perpetuate the capitalistic property system. Although Hitler criticised Communism in very strong term, he never repudiated the concept of liberty. Hence, Fascism was capitalism in decay. The view of Hallowell is that there are elements of truth, but it is not the whole truth, nor the principal truth.

The view of Laski is that Fascism cannot be identified with capitalism in decay for three reasons. Fascism is authoritarian but capitalism stands for freedom. Fascism and Communism have much more in common than Fascism and Capitalism. If capitalism is breaking down, evidence for that should come from the United States and Britain and not from the Balkan States and South America.

Fascism and Communism

A comparison of Fascism with Communism points out certain points of agreement and distinction between the two systems. As regards the main points of agreement, both Fascism and Communism are the result of post-War conditions. The leaders in both countries took advantage of the chaotic conditions prevailing in those countries and set up their authority. However, Fascism collapsed in Italy during World War II, but Communism is still continuing in Russia and in the neighbouring countries.

Both Communism and Fascism believe in a totalitarian form of government. They have no faith in democratic methods. They condemn parliamentary democracy as inefficient and unnatural. They rely on force and not on the voluntary cooperation of the people.

Both Fascism and Communism put emphasis on state and give the individuals a subordinate position. They stand for an authoritarian political system. They believe in the dictatorship of one party and do not allow other parties to exist.

Communism believes in class-conflict, the conflict between the rich and poor, and the Fascists believe in a national conflict.

Points of Distinction

Fascism and Communism differ from each other in many respects. The Fascists put too much emphasis on the state. According to Mussolini, "State is the embodiment of the Fascist ideal". According to the Communists, the state was to exist only in the transitional stage. When the resistance of the bourgeoisie was crushed, the state was to wither away. To quote Lenin, "The state is simply the weapon with which the proletariat wages its class war, a special sort of bludgeon, nothing more."

The Communists aim at the establishment of a classless society in which there will be no exploitation of one part by the other. The Fascists intended to maintain the *status quo* with regard to the social strata. They believed in the perpetuation of human inequality and the leadership of many by a few.

The Communists are the enemies of capitalism and imperialism. The Fascists were prepared to retain both. Capitalist democracies had more in common with Fascism than with Communism.

The Communists stand for the elimination of exploitation of man by man, class by class and nation by nation. On the other hand, Fascism wanted "to tie down the common man to the chariot-wheel of a mystical, imaginary and God-like state which in practice would mean the ruling caste or the Fascist Party." Communism is a philosophy of creative action but Fascism stood for the perpetuation of exploitation, injustice, autocracy and oppression.

The Communists put too much emphasis on class-war and believe that there can be no cooperation between the rich and the poor, the haves and the have-nots. According to the Fascists, there was no inherent hostility among the different classes and they could all be made to work in harmonious cooperation for the glory and prosperity of the nation.

Communism is atheistic. It stands for the abolition of the Church and religion. According to Marx, religion is the opium of the people. However, the Fascists made peace with the Church and tried to get as much of its cooperation as possible.

The Communists welcome racial diversities and stand for the equality of both sexes. On the other hand, the Fascists stood for the purity of race and also believed in the subordination of women to men.

Nazism in Germany

Hitler captured power in Germany in 1933. He disposed of all his rivals and set up a sort of dictatorship in the country which lasted till his death in 1945. During the regime of Hitler, the Nazi Party was all-powerful. It had its own ideology.

The Nazi Ideology

The Nazi ideology was not a well-worked-out theory of the state or government. It kept on changing or adjusting itself according to the exigencies of the situation. In many ways, it can be compared to thc Fascist ideology. Not only did the personality of Hitler contribute a great deal towards its development, but also the writings of persons like Kant, Fichte, Hegel, Rosenberg, and H.S. Chamberlain.

The State

Nazism gave too much importance to the state. This was in keeping with the Hegelian tradition which had deified the state. According to the Nazis, the state was a super human entity, the "Volk" or the community was the raw material out of which the state was built. "The individual is nothing—Das Volk is everything."

The Nazi Party

The Nazi Party was the connecting link between the "Volk" or the community and the state. It was with the help of that party that the Germans were united under a common leadership. The state gave its weight of authority to the programme and activities of the Nazi Party. It is no exaggeration to say that the state was the Nazi Party, and the Nazi Party was the state. No other party was tolerated within the country.

The Nazis were true to the German traditions of leadership and obedience to authority. The hierarchy advocated by them did not work from bottom upwards, but in the opposite direction. They had no faith in the democratic leadership. They believed in the leadership of one man. According to them, some were born to lead and the others were born to obey and follow. According to the Nazi ideology. Hitler was the head of the state, the government and the army. His word was law. He was a god. "He does not talk—he orates; he does not discuss—he pronounces judgement; he does not walk—he strides." According to Goering, "We Nazis believe that, in political affairs, Adolf Hitler is infallible, just as the Roman Catholics believe that, in religious matters, the Pope is infallible... His will is my law. The laws of nature demand that authority should be exercised from above downwards and responsibility from the low upwards—the leader at the top is responsible to the people as a whole and to their future."

The place occupied by Hitler in the minds of the people can be found from the following extract from a Nazi school text-book which every German child had to use:

"Our Leader, Adolf Hitler.
We love you
We pray for you
We like to hear you
We work for you. Heil."

The Nazi Party dominated every aspect of the life of the people. Only the leading members of the party were appointed to the high and low posts in the country. The Nazis controlled the Labour Unions. The labour front was completely a Nazi organisation. The Storm Troopers and the Blackguards were always ready to carry out the orders of the leaders. There was no place for a person or an organisation which dared to challenge the Nazi leaders or the government. So great was the hold of the Nazi Party that even children were prepared to give evidence against their parents and vice versa. The Hitler Youth Organisation played a very important part.

Propaganda

The Nazis were past-masters in the art of propaganda. The Nazi machine was able to control the Germans in every walk of life. Children, youngmen and women, industrialists and labourers were pressed into service to do the Nazi propaganda. The pulpit, the stage, the cinema, the radio, the press, art, science, literature and schools were used to carry out Nazi propaganda. Dr. Goebbels was put in charge of the work of propaganda. Both Goering and Hitler were themselves masters of the art of propaganda.

Force

The Nazis believed in the well-known saying that might is right. While propounding this thesis, they seem to have judged the German mind correctly. It was only a militant programme that could attract the Germans. The Nazis also preached and practised the philosophy of the sword. According to Hitler. "He who would live must fight. He who does not wish to fight in this world has not the right to exist. Such a saying may sound harsh, but that is how the matter stands."

Imperialism

If the Germans were taught to be militant and warlike, they were bound to follow a policy of expansion and conquest. The activities of the Nazis from 1933 to 1945 support the truth of this statement. In spite of his professions of peace. Hitler embarked upon a career of conquest. The result was that the whole of Europe was brought under the hegemony of Germany.

Anti-Jewish Policy

Soon after his accession to power. Hitler followed a policy of ruthless persecution of the Jews in Germany. They were made the scapegoats for the miseries of the German nation. They were held responsible for all the sins of omission and commission of the German statesmen. So great was the fury against the Jews that thousands of them were put in concentration camps. Millions of them ran away from the country. The Nazis did not bother about the consequences of losing brilliant men among the Jews. A Nazi saying ran thus: "The Jew is our misfortune. Hitler is our Saviour."

The Nazis believed in the purity of the Aryan blood. According to them, the Aryans were the master-builders of civilization. The other stocks were of an inferior quality.

Religion

The Nazis condemned both the Protestant and the Catholic Church on account of their slave mentality and internationalism. According to Professor Bergmann. "We of the German religion today turn to this ancient Nordic. Indo-Germanic Light-Hero figure and get rid of false and deceased Christ picture, created by the Christian Pope and Church to the heart of humanity. The high priest of the new German paganism is Hitler himself. He is real Holy Ghost". Again, "Hitler is lonely, so is God. Hitler is like God. Hitler is a new, a greater, and a more powerful Jesus Christ." No wonder, the Churches in Germany were kept under the control of the state and any criticism resulted in putting the critics in the concentration camps.

Women

According to the Nazis, the only function for women was to breed more pure Nordic children and preserve the Nordic race. According to Von Papen, "Mothers must exhaust themselves in order to give life "to children. Fathers must fight on the battle-field in order to secure the future of their sons." According to a declaration, "There is no higher or finer privilege for a woman than that of sending her children to war." Hitler expressed himself on this point in these words: "In the education of women, emphasis must be paid primarily on physical development. Only afterwards must consideration be given to spiritual values and lastly to mental development. Motherhood is undeniably the aim of feminine education." No wonder, birth control was prohibited in Germany. The function of women to add to the population of the country is pointed out in these words by Dr. Willibald Hentschel: "Round up a thousand German girls of the purest stock. Isolate them in a camp. Then let them be joined by a hundred German men equally of purest stock. If a hundred such camps were set up, you would have a hundred thousand thorough-bred children at one stroke."

Guns or Butter

The Nazis were faced with big problems and one of them was whether they would buy butter or guns with their money. They could not have both. The Germans decided to have guns because the latter could give them butter also. According to Goering, "We had to make up our minds whether we would use our foreign exchange for metals or for other things. We could either buy butter and surrender our freedom or we could seek to win our freedom and give up our butter. We have decided in favour of force. The German people have demonstrated that it is ready to make great sacrifices for a great purpose."

Internationalism

The Nazis were patriots *par excellence.* They loved their country and hated all others. They were the enemies of internationalism. They believed merely in the supremacy of their own country. The international ties were bound to lessen the burning patriotism and zeal of the Germans and hence opposition to internationalism. No wonder, the Nazis under Hitler gave up the membership of the League of Nations. According to Herr Buch, "Whoever wishes to play a leading part in Germany can no longer belong to any group which in any way has international ties."

Economic Control

The Nazis believed in the policy of autarchy of economic self-sufficiency of the state. According to them, the industries of the country were to be controlled by the state. Similarly, the state was to control both imports and exports. No money could be taken out of the Reich. Even fresh capital could not be secured without the permission of the government. Strikes and lock-outs were forbidden. Labour Courts were set up. The state took into its hands the duty of fixing the prices of the goods and the wages of the labourers. In other words, the whole of the economic life of the country was controlled by the state.

SUGGESTED READINGS

Brandy, R.A. : The Spirit and Structure of German Fascism, 1937.
Chapman : The Police State.
Dimitrov, G. : On United Front, New Delhi. 1971.
Dunham, B. : Man Against Myth, New York, 1962.
Dutt, R.P. : Fascism and Social Revolution, 1934.
Ebenstein : Great Political Thinkers.
Ghosh, Shibdas : Fascism, Calcutta, 1975.
Halle, Louis J. : The Ideological Imagination.
Hallowell : Main Currents in Modern Political Thought.
Hayes, P. : Fascism, 1973.
Kitchen, M. : Fascism, London, 1976.
Laski, H.J. : The State in Theory and Practice, London.
Laski, H.J. : The Rise of European Liberalism, London, 1936.
Lindsay, A.D. : I Believe in Democracy.
Maxey, C.C. : Political Philosophies, 1959.
Merkl : Political Continuity and Change.
Mowrer, E.A. : Immortal Italy.
Mussolini, Benito : The Political and Social Doctrine of Fascism, 1933.
Notle, E. : Three Faces of Fascism, 1965.
Osborn, R. : The Psychology of Reaction, 1938.
Poulantzas, N. : Fascism and Dictatorship, London, 1974.
Rocco, A. : The Political Doctrines of Fascism, 1926.
Sabine : History of Political Theory.
Salvemini, G. : Under the Axe of Fascism, 1928.

CHAPTER 42

Democracy

Meaning of Democracy

In the words of George Orwell, "In the case of a word like democracy not only is there no agreed definition but the attempt to make one is resisted from all sides...The defenders of any kind of regime claim that it is a democracy and fear that they might have to stop using the word if it were tied down to any one meaning." Likewise, G. Sartori writes, "Democracy could be defined as a high-flown name for something which does not exist." J.R. Lucas says, "Democracy is a noun but should be an adjective". B. De Jouvenal observes, "Discussions about democracy, arguments for against it, are intellectually worthless because we do not know what we are thinking about". Cranston writes, "Democracy is nothing but different doctrines in different people's minds". Bernard Crick says that democracy is perhaps the most promiscuous word in the world of public affairs. "She is everybody's mistress and yet somehow retains her magic even when a lover sees that her favours are being, in his light, illicitly shared by many another. Indeed even amid our pain at being denied her exclusive fidelity, we are proud of her adaptability to all sorts of company". Mussolini claimed his Fascist dictatorship to be "the realisation of true democracy". Joseph Goebbles hailed Hitler's Third Reich as the "most ennobled form of modern democratic state". Dorothy Pickles ascribes the difficulty in defining democracy to the fact that political systems are in a continual state of evolution. "Ideas regarding what ought to be the scope of governmental intervention in the lives of individuals have also changed and are continually changing. As ideas change, so the content of the word democracy changes in peoples' minds".

C.D. Burns writes in his *Democracy* (1935): "Democracy is a word with many meanings and some emotional colour. It is not an algebraical symbol, but a flag or the call of a trumpet for some; and for others an obsolete mythology which has undesirable connections

Learning Objectives

with capitalism and imperialism". Dr. Finer observes, "Democracy has come to mean different things, some very hostile to each other, that it needs careful analysis if misunderstanding and idle controversies are to be avoided and if the possible and quite legitimate differences of connotation and its very varied institutional arrangements are to be revealed". E.M. Burns says in his "*Ideas in Conflict*" (1960): "Few words have been more loosely and variously defined than democracy. It has almost literally meant all things to all men."

Definitions of Democracy

Definitions of democracy have been attempted by various persons from time to time. The Greek philosopher Cleon defined in 422 B.C. democracy thus: "That shall be democratic which shall be of the people, by the people, for the people." Likewise, President Lincoln defined democracy as the government of the people, by the people and for the people. According to Juarez, democracy is the government of the cattle, by the cattle and for the cattle. Lord Bryce defined democracy in these words, "The word democracy has been used ever since the time of Herodotus to denote that form of government in which the ruling power of a state is legally vested, not in any particular class or classes, but in the members of the community as a whole. This means, in communities which act by voting, that rule belongs to the majority as no other method has been found for determining peaceably and legally what is to be deemed the will of a community which is not unanimous. Usage has made this the accepted sense of the term and usage is the safest guide in the employment of the word". Bassett writes, "Democracy is essentially a matter of political method. Democracy is not a particular kind of civilisation; it is rather a civilised way of taking political action. Democracy constitutes an attempt to reconcile freedom with the need for law and its enforcement. It may be defined as a political method by which every citizen has the opportunity of participating through discussion in an attempt to reach voluntary agreement as to what shall be done for the good of the community as a whole. It resolves itself, in practice, into a continuous search for agreement, through discussion and compromise, and action on the basis of the maximum measure of agreement obtainable."

J.S. Mill defines democracy as that form of government in which "the whole people or some numerous portion of them, exercise the governing power through deputies periodically elected by themselves". Sir John Seeley defines democracy as "a government in which everyone has a share". O.K. Chesterton says that democracy is, in its essence, a government which is in accord with the general will of the governed. Sir Stafford Cripps observes, "Democracy is a system of government in which every adult citizen is equally free to express his views and desires upon all subjects in whatever way he wishes and to influence the majority of his fellow citizens to decide according to those views and to influence those desires." Dewey says, "To say that democracy is only a form of government is like saying that home is more or less geometrical arrangement of bricks and mortar, or that church is a building with pews, pulpit and spire". According to Barker, democracy is a mode of spirit, an attitude of mind of those who profess it and those who profess it alone can practise it.

According to Hall, "Democracy is that form of political organisation in which public opinion has control". H.B. Mayo writes, "A democratic political system is one in which public policies are made on a majority basis by representatives subject to effective popular control at periodic elections which are conducted on the principle of political equality and under conditions of political freedom". Sartori observes, "A democratic political system is one which makes government responsive and accountable and its effectiveness depends first and foremost on the efficiency and skill of its leadership". S.M. Lipset says, "Democracy may be defined as a political system which supplies regular constitutional opportunities for changing the governing officials and a social mechanism which permits the largest possible part of the population to influence major decisions by choosing among contenders for political office". According to C.B. Macpherson, "Democracy is merely a mechanism for choosing and authorising government or in some other way getting laws and political decisions made".

According to Prof. Dicey, "Democracy is a form of government in which the governing body is a comparatively large fraction of the entire nation". Gettell writes, "Democracy is that form of government in which the mass of the population possesses the right to share in the exercise of sovereign power." Hearnshaw observes, "A democratic state, in short, is simply one in which the community as a whole possesses sovereign authority, maintains ultimate control over affairs and determines what sort of government machinery shall be set up. Democracy, as a form of state, is not merely a mode of government, but is also mainly a mode of appointing, controlling and dismissing a government."

According to President F.D. Roosevelt, "Democracy was not a mere matter of universal suffrage and unhampered expression of the popular will. It must be a positive and constructive force in the daily lives of the people and provide not merely for political but economic needs also. If men were forced to choose between liberty and bread, they would choose bread". C.C. Maxey writes, "Democracy as re-interpreted in the twentieth century is thus seen to be more than a political formula, more than a system of government, more than asocial order. It is a search for a way of life in which the voluntary free intelligence and activity of man can be harmonised and coordinated with the least possible coercion, and it is the belief that such a way of life is the best way for all mankind, the way most in keeping with the nature of man and the nature of the universe". Prof. R.M. MacIver observes, "Democracy is not a way of governing whether by way of majority or otherwise but primarily a way of determining who shall govern and broadly, to what ends".

Whatever the differences in the definitions, there are certain features of a democratic political system. There is the supremacy of the will of the people. The government is run by those people who are duly elected by the people at the time of elections which are held at periodic intervals. The government is responsible to the people and it aims at social welfare. Political power is a trust of the people in the hands of the government. It is the primary duty of the government to safeguard the rights of the people. There must be responsible and limited government. There must be an independent judiciary and at least two political parties and pressure groups.

Democracy means a form of government, a form of the state and also a way of life. As a form of government, it means that the legal power in the community is vested in the people as a whole and the rule belongs to the majority in the electorate in communities which act by voting. Democracy also signifies a way of life. Barker writes, "Democracy is two things. It is principle of the action of the human spirit, the principle that free spirits in the area of social and political actions of individual life should freely guide themselves to freely determined ends. It is also a system of institutions, operative in a political community which enables the principle to be realised and serves as the means of its realisation. Both these things are essentially inter-connected and both of them must be present in order to constitute democracy in the full and general sense of the word". As a social philosophy, democracy has possessed from the very outset in natural law a libertarian and egalitarian aspect. It relies upon the American Declaration of Independence of 1776 and the French Declaration of the Rights of Man and Citizen of 1789. The doctrines of popular sovereignty and natural rights of man, "to liberty, property, security and resistance to oppression" have been its core. The emphasis has been on the affirmation of the personality of man, his inviolability, his dignity, the recognition of the fact that every individual has the right to life and the right freely to achieve the purposes he freely determines. This fact gives to democracy its humaneness, its finality and its eternal usefulness.

Basic Principles of Democracy

There are certain basic principles of democracy. Democracy allows every individual to speak, criticise and disagree with others. Democracy is based on the principle of tolerance. Individuals can have their separate ideas and ideologies and democracy does not believe in crushing them. Democracy believes in the method of persuasion and peace both in internal and international spheres. A democratic government does not use illegitimate coercion in the name of social welfare. Democracy upholds the dignity of human personality and various kinds of rights are given to every individual. Liberty and equality are the foundations of democracy. In a democratic government, the people are the sovereign. Democracy is based on the principle of majority rule, but this does not mean that the rights of the minorities can be ignored. The rights of all have to be protected. A democratic Government is a government by the representatives of the people. The voters are free to vote according to their choice without coercion or pressure from any quarter. A democratic government is carried on according to the principles laid down in the Constitution. Adequate opportunities are given to all for the development of their personalities. Democracy aims at the welfare of all. It believes in a change in government through constitutional methods and not through violence. In a democracy, the power of taking basic decisions relating to the government are vested in all the members of the community and not in any particular class of persons. The people alone possess the supreme power. Rousseau rightly said, "Voice of the people is voice of God". The policy of the government should be determined by the public opinion. Legislature provides an important institutional machinery to ascertain the wishes of the people but alternative methods can also be adopted. Democracy is based on the principle of consent and not coercion. The bullet is replaced by ballot. The use of force is the minimum. Force can be used as a medicine and not as daily diet. Democracy is identified with open society. In a democracy, every individual has the right to speak and criticise the government. The change of a government takes place through constitutional means.

Presumptions in a Democratic State

There are certain presumptions in a democratic state. One presumption is that the individual is rational and he has the capacity to think and discuss the general problems of the community and also take decisions. Human beings are egoistic. Their happiness is purely personal. The individual is sovereign over his body and mind. There is no scope for the use of physical force or violence in solving problems. Every human being is fallible and can make mistakes. There is no conflict between the good of the individual and the good of the community. Individuals do not resort to violence to get their grievances redressed.

Forms of Democracy

According to Sartori, there are four major forms or types of democracy. (1) *Social democracy* is neither capitalist nor socialist. It is partly liberal and partly socialist. It aims at social equality and welfare of the people. (2) Karl Marx replaced political democracy with *economic democracy* as the determining factor of politics. It is the economic democracy which determines political democracy and not the vice-versa. True democracy is one where in addition to political democracy, there is economic democracy which in other words is economic equality. There cannot be absolute equality but there should not be too much of economic inequality in society.

(3) *Industrial democracy* is basically a guild socialist idea and Cole was its exponent. Its aim is the management of industry by workers on self-governing lines.

(4) The term *Peoples' democracy* is commonly used by Communist states. It is intended to put emphasis on the politico-economic, macro-micro and supra-infra nature of their democracy.

Size of Democracy

Robert A. Dahl and Edward R. Tufte have examined the relationship between the size of a country and the effective working of democracy. They point out that in small democracies, there is an effective participation of the people in decision-making. There is also voluntary compliance of rules by the people with less coercion. The people are homogeneous with respect to beliefs, values and goals. There is better understanding of public interests. There is loyalty to a single integrated community. The leaders are responsive to the views of the citizens. There is better communication between the people and their representatives. There are personal civic relations in a small democracy.

As regards the larger democracies, there is participation of the people at the time of elections. The people are better prepared to meet external threats. There is diversity in beliefs, values and goals of the people. In a large country, there are multiple loyalties to various communities. The people have more alternatives before them on account of the size of the country.

According to Robert A. Dahl and Edward R. Tufte, whether a country is small or large, an ideal democracy is that where the polity has the capacity to respond fully to the collective preferences of its citizens and the citizens fully control the decisions of the polity.

KINDS OF DEMOCRACY

Democracy is of two kinds: direct and indirect. In a direct democracy, all the people assemble at one place and decide the matters which concern them. In the small city-states of ancient Greece, the adult male citizens were expected to meet together in the Assembly and decide the important issues of the day. Direct democracy is found today in Switzerland. The people of the Cantons meet in the Landsgemeinde and elect Cantonal Officers and adopt legislation. The main features of direct democracy in Switzerland are the *referendum*, initiative and recall. There is special procedure of referring a particular bill or constitutional amendment for popular vote. If a majority of people vote in his favour, the bill becomes law. It is a negative power of the people to put a check on undesirable legislation by the government. *Initiative* is a device which enables a specified number of people to draft a bill and send it to the legislature for its consideration. It is a positive power in the hands of the people to initiate a law which they desire to be passed. The system of *recall* enables the majority of a constituency to recall their representative from his office if they are not satisfied with his work.

There are certain merits and demerits of direct democracy. As regards *merits*, citizens are highly devoted to the state and they take pride in participating in the affairs of the state. Every citizen gets an opportunity to serve the state in some capacity, on account of the small size of the state. Direct democracy enabled the citizens of Athens to have a partnership in a life of virtue and happiness and enjoy the fruits of a higher life. Direct democracy promotes a sense of patriotism among the people. As regards the *demerits* of direct democracy, it is unsuitable for big states. All people cannot have experience and knowledge of administrative work and they have to depend on the bureaucracy for work. Direct democracy demands a high sense of responsibility and training which the people ordinarily do not possess. The fruits of direct democracy in Greece were enjoyed only by a few. Aliens, women and slaves were not considered as citizens and were deprived of the right to participate in the affairs of the state. Liberty and equality which are essential for democracy, were missing in ancient Greece.

Indirect Democracy

Indirect democracy or representative democracy is that form of government in which the people elect their representatives to carry on the administration of the country. Representative democracy is the prevailing form of democracy in the world.

According to W.F. Willoughby, a representative government is that form of government which results where a legally sovereign electorate, instead of itself attempting to act as the directing head of the machinery of the government, brings into existence an organ or organs to represent and act for it in this capacity. There are certain characteristics of indirect democracy. It is a representative form of government in which sovereignty is vested in the people. The government is run on behalf of the people who do not have a direct share in it They only control the government through periodic elections. Indirect democracy is the only kind of democracy which is possible in modern states on account of their large size.

Conditions Necessary for Successful Working of Democracy

Experience shows that democratic institutions work successfully only in a particular atmosphere and when that is lacking, they do not work satisfactorily. Democracy demands that there should be a *high standard of honest and honour* among the people. There should be honesty not only among the leaders but also in the rank and file. A corrupt democracy is the vilest and most helpless of political organisations. The people should stand for justice not only for themselves but also for others. There should be equality of opportunity and equality before law.

The people should have a high level of intelligence and a sound system of *education.* If the people do not possess the spirit of "normal reasonableness", democracy degenerates into mob rule which is set aside by dictatorship. Well-intentioned fools are worse than intelligent villains in a democracy. The people are the masters and it is necessary that they should be educated. That is the reason why a great emphasis is put on the right to education in modern times. It is only then that the following view of President Lincoln can be true. "You can fool part of the people all the time and all the people part of the time, but you cannot fool all the people all the time". It must not be forgotten that ignorance and illiteracy are the worst enemies of democracy.

Another necessary condition is that the people should be conscious of the community as a whole. They must possess "a strong sense of solidarity, an intense conviction of unity, a pervasive feeling of communal life". They should not absorb themselves in petty conflicts and sacrifice the interests of the community in order to secure their private ends. They should always remember the famous saying that as the strength of the wolf is the pack, the strength of the pack is the wolf.

Another necessary condition is that there should be a *strong and vigorous public opinion.* When that is lacking, democracy has the foundations of sand and cannot be expected to last long. Hence, utmost emphasis has to be put on creating a strong and sound public opinion which puts the nation first and everything else second.

The people must take *interest in public affairs.* That is possible only if they are given an opportunity for effective participation in politics. This does not mean that every single individual must take an active part in politics. It is enough if a considerable majority does so. It is also enough if only a minority takes interest in politics provided that minority is distributed throughout the different sections of the community and is not confined exclusively to one class or group.

There must *be free expression of opinion and free discussion.* The connection between freedom of discussion and democracy is essential for the fulfilment of the aims of democracy. The twin virtues of independence and tolerance necessarily express themselves in the habit of free discussion and can be developed only in such an atmosphere. What we call public opinion cannot develop if all the information and expression of opinion come from only one source. There can be no question of the opinion of the people having effective influence on the decisions of the government because that opinion may be just what the government in power chooses to make it.

Another condition for successful working of democracy is that the minds of the people must be in some degree open to influence by free discussion. However, we must not look for any immediate effect in that direction. It is not necessary that in a short space of time by a single train of reasoning or even in a single election campaign, it is possible to convert the people from one opinion to another. That may happen occasionally but it is rare and also not necessarily desirable. Those who expect immediate results are certain to be disappointed and are bound to end up by saying that other people, or at any rate their political opponents, are quite impervious to argument. Prime Minister Attlee wrote thus to Prof. Harold Laski, "In my time, I have seen a lot of useful legislation, but I count our progress much more by the extent to which what we cried in the wilderness five and thirty years ago has now become part of the assumptions of the ordinary men and women". If the habit of free discussion is developed and generally accepted, it must have some effect on the opinions of the people, sooner or later. That may vary in degree and some conditions may be more favourable to democracy than others.

Democracy can succeed only in that country where the vast majority of the people have a *genuine thirst for democracy* as a form of government and a way of life and they are willing to pay any price to preserve the same. The people in England and the United States have an intense urge to participate in the affairs of the government and they refuse to be led by the nose. They want to have a say in the affairs of the government. The desire for democracy rises from the "mental habit and temperament of the people".

If *eternal vigilance* is the price of the liberty, eternal vigilance is necessary for protecting democracy. The people who are indolent and are not interested in what is happening in the country cannot be the guardians of democracy. The people must cherish the principles of democracy and have a determination to keep alive the flame of democracy.

Democracy can thrive only in an atmosphere of peace. If there are conflicts going on in the country, democracy is not the form of government for them. People can have a conflict of ideas but *no violent conflicts.* The people must have sympathy for one another and must try to understand sympathetically the point of view of the other. A sympathetic understanding and mutual tolerance is necessary for the smooth working of democracy. H.B. Mayo writes, "A democracy is unique in recognising the political expression of such conflicts as legitimate and in providing for their peaceful adjustment through the negotiations of politics, as an alternative to their settlement by force of fiat". There is *no place for coercion in democracy.* Y.R. Simon observes, "Democracy implies, then, that every government has a duty to seek the maximum of voluntary cooperation, to explain its purposes and methods, to educate the governed, to appeal indefatigably to whatever element of goodwill can be found in them, and never to resort to coercion unless persuasion proves impossible".

Another condition for the smooth working of democracy is the existence of *good leadership.* The leaders in a democracy must be far-sighted, enlightened and effective. They should have the personality to lead the country. Great leaders like Winston Churchill, Attlee, Jawaharlal Nehru, Abraham Lincoln and Washington helped democracy to work successfully. Poor leadership in backward countries stands in the way of the successful working of democracy. Confucius says, "The example of those in high place is like the breeze and the behaviour of ordinary people is like grass. When the breeze blows upon the grass, the grass assuredly bends in the desired direction".

Another important condition is the existence of a *free, fearless and independent press* which is ready to criticise the government when it is going wrong and is not afraid of it. Such a press also creates a healthy public opinion. It informs and enlightens the people and enables them to understand the problems of democracy and discharge their duties and responsibilities successfully.

Another necessary condition for the success of democracy is that the people must not be suffering from too much of poverty which is considered to be the worst obstacle. Poverty keeps the people uneducated, backward and timid. The result is that a few rich people in such a country capture power and use the same to their own advantage. Abba Eban writes, "Hungry people are not likely for ever to remain peaceful people or to cherish democratic forms of life".

According to Barker, two conditions are necessary for the successful working of democracy. Those are *material or external conditions* and *mental or internal conditions.* National homogeneity and social homogeneity constitute the material base of democracy. The concept of national homogeneity is fostered by the prevalence of a common medium of expression and a common heritage. J.S. Mill insists on the *mono-national state* as a condition of successful democracy. Social homogeneity is another important material condition because a country which is rent by class division, cannot develop a democratic mind. Some form of economic equality is also necessary. Freedom from fear of unemployment, reasonable wages, state-aided compulsory education upto a certain standard for all and the lessening of disparities in income and wealth also help in creating a social climate in which the people can actively participate in public affairs.

According to Barker, the spiritual base of democracy is "a *mental habit of agreement upon* a number of axioms". One of those axioms is the "agreement to differ". This means agreement on a fundamental issue confronting the country and difference on the choice of policy to be followed. The second axiom is the majority principle which implies an agreement or obligation of all to accept the decision of the greater number as the decision of all. If the majority and the minority sit together and discuss the problems facing the country in an ideal spirit of mutual give and take, the result is that the majority decision has some of the ideas of the minority which give it an abiding value. It is in this way that the will of the majority becomes the will of all. Another axiom is the principle of compromise which requires mutual tolerance and respect for the viewpoint of each other. The spiritual conditions are closely associated with material conditions. The attitude of give and take is not possible where the people are separated by class or caste discriminations.

According to Mannheim. "*Balance in the structure of society* is a pre-requisite to the maintenance of democracy". This means that no power-group should be allowed to exert undue pressure on the functioning of the government. An alert and vigilant public opinion can serve as a necessary check.

Another necessary condition for the successful of democracy is the *combination of popular rule with skilled administration.* This means that the administrative machinery in a democracy must be prompt and smooth working. The future of democracy is dependent on the development of an efficient state apparatus which can harmonise popular control with expert government. The people will not care for a government which is inefficient and corrupt and will be willing to vote for another form of government which can give them efficient administration.

Another necessary condition is the *democratic organisation of political parties.* It cannot be denied that democracy can work only if there are political parties but the parties must be organised in such a manner that the people have full say in the policy-making decisions of the government.

According to J.S. Mill, a democratic government depends for permanence on three fundamental conditions. The people should be willing to receive it. They should be willing and able to do what is necessary for its preservation. They should be willing and able to fulfil the duties and discharge the functions which it imposes on them.

Democracy succeeds only in a *democratic society.* In a state where non-political associations do not allow liberty, equality discussion, opposition and tolerance, democracy cannot function. Robert A. Dahl says that a democratic society is a "social system that not only has democratic political system but also a number of other sub-systems that operate so as to contribute directly or indirectly to the strength of the democratic political processes".

The existence of a *written constitution* also helps the successful working of democracy. All authorities in the state have to function within the four corners of the constitution and there is no scope for the exercise of arbitrary power. A democratic constitution provides for freedom of speech, assembly, association and safeguards against arbitrary imprisonment. It provides for the popular control of the key officials. It provides for a fearless, impartial and learned judiciary which upholds the rule of law against arbitrary government. All individuals in the state are bound by the law.

The existence of an *effective opposition* also helps the successful working of democracy. An effective opposition can emerge when there are two political parties as in Britain. If the ruling party abuses power and acts contrary to democratic principles, the opposition is ready to put a check on it or overthrow it and form its own government in a democratic manner. The two political parties must strictly follow the rules of the political game and must always keep in mind the interests of the nation and those of democracy as a form of government and way of life.

Another factor that helps the successful working of democracy is the existence of local self-governing bodies functioning on democratic lines. By working in those local bodies, the people acquire democratic habits and a passion for democracy. When they go to the centre, they behave in a similar manner. Democracy is safe in their hands and not in the hands of those who start their political career straight in the central legislature.

Democracy works well if there is *no concentration of power.* Authority should be decentralised so that there can be scope for appeal. The officials should act as servants and not masters.

Democracy is compared with "a game which can be played only when the players respect the rules of the game." Hence, democracy will be successful if the citizens are democratic-minded and have the desire to respect the principles of democracy. The best defence of democracy lies in the character of the people. According to Henry Mayo, a true democrat values political freedom. He loves to be self-governing. He possesses an inquiring, independent and rational attitude. He considers himself to be a part of the democratic system. He sympathises with others and has no desire to dominate them. He is willing to express his own opinion and also possesses an ability to compromise and accept compromises. He values peace and order and is neither extremely pessimistic nor optimistic. According to Harold D. Laswell, a good citizen in a democracy must maintain an open mind as against a closed ego. He should have a tendency to share rather than to hoard or monopolise. He should have confidence in the benevolent capabilities of man.

Prof. Garner has laid down certain conditions which are essential for the working of democracy. According to him, there should be a relatively high degree of political intelligence and abiding interest in public affairs, a keen sense of public responsibility and a readiness to accept and abide by the decision of the majority, coupled with respect for the rights of minorities. There should be facilities for elementary education and an education in political matters and training in the habits of government. There should also be a high moral level of the people.

W.E. Hocking lays down the conditions essential for the success of democracy. According to him, democracy cannot be any better than the education, training and efficiency of the people. Success in democracy calls for ability to think behind superficial contiguity. Democracy cannot succeed without truth and true data. Democracy depends upon the goodwill of the masses. Democracy requires a spirit of humility or teachableness on the part of the people and that requires a religious spirit. Democracy requires the faith of the leaders in the masses. Every man and leader of men tends to become cynical as he grows old. There are many things to disillusion him. If democracy is to succeed, it must base itself not on men as they are, but on men as they can be. That means faith. Democracy can thrive on an inner current of religion and faith.

Lowell sums up the conditions for successful democracy in these words: "The duration of any form of government depends upon how far it develops a people qualified to carry it on and how successfully it brings to front those most fit to lead...Does democracy tend to produce a people disposed to place the general welfare above partial interest, a people with keen sympathy and absence of jealousy between classes, with the will to bear present ills for future good, with foresight and fortitude, and does it select for its respresentatives and magistrates men who possess these qualities in a high degree? If it does these things, the squalls that arise will not disturb its foundations and it will stand unshaken though storms may rage in other lands. So far as it does not do this, the iron of its feet is mixed with miry clay."

Durbin points out that the first essential condition for the successful working of democracy is the ability of the people to choose a government. The right to choose government implies the negative power of destroying a government and putting anew one its place. The government must be responsible to the people and the people should be the judges of its goodness or badness. The second essential condition is that the people should have the freedom to oppose the government of the day. The party in power must learn to tolerate the opposition. To the extent to which opposition is persecuted and rendered illegal or stamped out of existence, democracy is not present. There must be an implicit undertaking among the various parties contending for power in the state not to persecute one another. Mutual toleration is the keystone of the arch and the corner-stone of the building.

Sir Stafford Cripps says that in a democracy, the people must have a free and unfettered choice of their representatives with a right of recall at stated periods. They must signify their choice of the policy they like to be followed and the representatives must act according to the wishes of the people.

The view of Barthelemy is that democracy can work successfully only if it is "directed by the wisest, the most intelligent and the best, in a word, although it excites prejudice, by the elite of the population".

Evaluation of Democracy

Democracy as a form of government has been the subject of great controversy. Extreme views have been expressed both for and against the democratic form of government. There are some with whom democracy is almost a religion. They worship it blindly and deliberately close their eyes to its obvious defects. They are convinced that the principle of democratic rule has now become a permanent and essential factor in political institutions and it alone can form the basis of the states of the future. There are others who are the uncompromising critics of democracy. Carlyle refers to democracy as the combination of millions mostly fools who are incapable of governing themselves or choosing governors to rule them. The view of H.G. Wells is that all arguments in favour of democracy can be knocked to pieces in five minutes. The truth lies between the two extremes. Democracy has both its merits and demerits.

Merits

The great merit of democracy lies not in its efficiency but in the fact that it gives the people an opportunity to rule themselves. A good government is not that under which the people get a lot to eat. In the words of Lowell, it lies in the character a polity tends to create among the citizens. "The best government in the long run is one that nurtures a people strong in moral fibre, in integrity, industry, self-reliance and courage". Democracy develops the political intelligence of the people. It demands from all the citizens a certain degree of intelligence, honesty, public spirit and discipline. In the words of Woodrow Wilson, these virtues give the people "self-possession, self-mastery, the habit of order and peace and common counsel and reverence for law which will not fail when they themselves become the makers of law; the steadiness and self-control of political maturity".

In a democratic system, there is no danger of a revolution. The reason is that a democratic system gives enough opportunity for a change in the government through peaceful means. There is enough of freedom of action and expression of opinion. There is no feeling of suffocation by any section of society which can force it to resort to revolution. Dr. Finer writes, "Since the law will be made and the administration be given momentum and controlled by us voters, and since our power can be successfully exerted by association and persuasion, the impulse of the system is to foster fellowship and a common conscience among all men".

Democracy is based on the principle of equality of all men and women. It does not believe in the foolish principle that "some are born to rule and others to be ruled". Even the humblest person has a chance of rising in life. His humble parentage is not a permanent hindrance in his way. If he works hard, there is every likelihood of his beating others who may have started their careers in better circumstances. No discrimination is practised against any particular individual or class. All are equal before the law and the same punishment is meted out to all if law is broken.

Democracy protects the interests of all the people. It is not expected to serve the interests of a particular individual or class but to serve the larger interests of all. That is not the case with monarchy or aristocracy or dictatorship. The people in power in a democracy are the representatives of the people and they know where the shoe pinches.

Democracy ennobles the people. It puts emphasis on self-help, initiative and individual responsibility. J.S. Mill says that the great merit of democracy lies in the fact that "It promotes a better and higher form of national character than any other polity whatever". Lord Bryce is of the view that the right to vote gives dignity to individuals. A man feels that he also counts in society and is not merely a plaything. Under no other form of government self-realisation is as easily possible as under democracy.

It is the glory of democracy that it elevates the masses, develops their faculties and stimulates their patriotism by allowing them a share in administration. J.S. Mill says that the man who has no vote in the government to which he is subject and who has no prospect of obtaining, will either be a malcontent or will feel as one whom the general affairs of society do not concern. There is no willingness on the part of the people to make sacrifices for a government in which they have no hand. Democracy strengthens love for the country. The people feel that the government is their own creation.

Democracy upholds liberty. Every individual is free to think, speak and act and develop his own personality in his own way. He has the freedom to live in his own way, speak the language he likes, read the books of his choice, express his opinion in his own way, have his own culture or way of living, choose the vocation he likes and hold his own religious beliefs. He cannot be coerced to do anything against his will. He enjoys certain fundamental rights which are guaranteed by an independent judiciary. A.D. Lindsay writes, "Democracy is a revolutionary form of government. For its aim is to find a place for continual change within government. Its law exists to foster freedom; its force exists to protect law. It is an organisation to preserve, leave room for these precious things of the spirit, which in their nature cannot be organised". (The Modern Democratic State (1959), p. 266).

A democratic government is responsible to the people. It cannot act arbitrarily or ride roughshod over the wishes of the people. It must respect their wishes. If the rulers in a democratic state misbehave and act contrary to the wishes and interests of the people, they can be pulled up by the people. If they want to continue to be in power, they must act as servants of the people and serve the interests of the people. No minister can get away with impunity after having acted arbitrarily. Public opinion is very strong in this matter. In 1963, Profumo, the War Minister of England, had to resign because he told a lie to Parliament to which he was responsible.

Democracy trains the people in the art of government. People can participate in political and other activities and thus learn how to run their own institutions. A democratic government functions in the open and sovereignty rests with the people. An authoritarian government teaches the people to obey its laws blindly even if they are bad. It does not encourage them or give them any training in self-government. Democracy is a government of the people and all are associated with it. No individual, whatever his status, is debarred from participation in the political affairs of the country. F.W. Coker writes, "Participation in the control of public affairs removes the individual from narrow egotism and enlarges the range of self-interest and imagination". He is encouraged to come forward and make his own contribution to the state. According to Garner, "The greatest glory of democracy in the opinion of its votaries does not flow so much from its own inherent excellence as a form of government, as from its influence in elevating the masses of the people, developing their faculties, stimulating interest among them in public affairs and strengthening their patriotism by allowing them a share in its administration".

Democracy is built upon the rational premise that no man is infallible and he is liable to make mistakes. As none is infallible, democracy adopts a process of discussion and criticism in which every individual can take part. According to Popper, the rational attitude "is bound up with the idea that everybody is liable to make mistakes which may be found out by himself with the assistance or criticism of others. It therefore suggests the idea that nobody should be his own judge". The continuous process of discussion and scrutiny in democracy acts as a necessary corrective to abuse power or error in judgement and testifies to the rational character of democratic government. Democracy pins its faith in pooling individual knowledge with a view to perfecting its scale of operation. All the sane adults are allowed an active share in the process of government so that the common fund of knowledge and judgement may be enriched. Democracy challenges the claim of the dictatorial doctrine to infallibility or omniscience of the governing class. The democratic approach "assumes politics to be a matter of trial and error and regards political systems as pragmatic contrivances of human ingenuity and spontaneity".

Because of its inter-locking system operating through its multiple checks, democracy cannot create in the governing class a consciousness of superiority. In democracy, the government is a trust and hence the governing class does not feel tempted to glorify or abuse power.

The view of J.S. Mill is that democracy is superior to other forms of government in two ways. Under a democratic system, the rights and interests of the individual can be safeguarded only when he is able to "stand up" for them. There is a greater degree of general prosperity which is more widely diffused as the energies and interests of all the people are stimulated. Indirect democracy does not mean actual rule by the people themselves. They merely "determine the ends towards which their government shall aim and watch over those into whose hands they have placed the actual power of administration".

Democracy is an ideal. It is a doctrine of human optimism. According to Dr. Finer, democracies "admit the pragmatic nature of their search for perfection and recognise that of perfection there is no single exclusive principle. Yet they surmise that if such there should be, it is one yet to be discovered in a process of evolution, and if the unfolding is to arrive at unsoundness, it must be founded on the unfettered expression and interplay of all opinion".

Dr. Finer says that the political, social and economic advantages of democracy are very important. Under a democratic government, "we have the assurance that the sphere of our private life—our family, our diversions, our worship, our work—will not be invaded except by due process of law in which we have an equal say with any. We rest tranquil that officials and judges will not abuse us and that they themselves will have to answer for discrimination and bias and unauthorised invasions of our private and public life to a public tribunal in which we, as of right, sit as judge and jury".

One of the merits of democracy is the spirit of compromise and agreement. "The democratic method involves the determination of political principles as a result of discussion. A compromise, of course, is only a settlement by mutual concession and in practice, any agreement involves a measure of compromise. Compromise, therefore, far from being the source of political immaturity, is, from the democratic standpoint, one of the cardinal virtues."

H.B. Mayo refers to certain values of a democratic system. Those are the peaceful voluntary adjustment of disputes, orderly succession of rulers, the minimum of coercion, attainment of justice and freedom, promotion of science, guarantee of diversity and peaceful change in a changing society. (An Introduction to Democratic Theory). According to E.B. Schulz, "An asserted view of democracy is that each individual is regarded as an end in himself and not merely as a pawn to be manipulated for the benefit of privileged few. The dignity of the individual is enhanced, a high value is attached to personal freedom and every person, knowing that he and his fellow citizens wield ultimate control over government, normally develops a state of mind that is dominated by hope rather than despair concerning present and future opportunities for development". Again, "Democracy is also favoured on the ground that it is the only system that permits the people to bring about a change in government in a peaceful and orderly manner as soon as, or at least shortly after, dissatisfactory policies are put into effect". C.D. Burns says. "The whole movement towards democracy implied a repudiation of the older traditional institution on government—war and preparation for war".

A democratic government is always liberal. It changes according to the changes in time. Reforms are more possible in democracy. Democracy is a liberal government as it enables the people to introduce reforms according to their needs.

Demerits of Democracy

If democracy has merits, it has also its demerits. It is contended that the working of democracy brings in its wake all the evils of party politics. While party system is absolutely indispensable for democracy, it encourages hollowness and insincerity, carries the national divisions into local elections, leads to the spoils system and debases normal standards. The rigidity of party system is responsible for the destruction of the liberty of the people. Votes have to cast on party lines. The people have to choose between candidates who may be either knaves or fools and they may not want any of them. They have to decide between two or more ideas while actually they do not approve of any one of them.

In a democracy, government is in the hands of the party which has a majority and that party can afford to tyrannise over the people. The party which can command vast resources is able to seize power and then can use the government as its tools. Though technically the majority party runs the democratic show, actually it violates the true spirit of democracy. F.W. Coker writes, "What standard of judgement can make us believe the opinion of any 55% of the people to be wiser or fairer than that of the other 45%? What quality has the majority in greater amount of highest value except the one quality of superior force?" The government by majority may lead to the oppression of the minorities whose political, social and cultural interests may be completely neglected or trampled under foot. In a democratic country, the people can do practically nothing against the majority party in power which can pass legislation to further their selfish interests. Good laws are not passed and the welfare of the people is neglected. Y.R. Simon writes, "The danger of oppression by the majority is so obvious that the history of modern democracy is haunted by the ambition of including the minority in the controlling electoral body. The method calculated to achieve such inclusion is known as proportional representation".

Democracy is a very expensive form of government. In a democracy, everyone has to be cared for and consequently it requires a lot of money to satisfy the needs of all. Moreover, a lot of money has to be spent on the organisation of public opinion, propaganda and frequent elections. Nursing a constituency involves great expense. Democracy has been described as an "exaggerated committee" and a committee has been defined as seven men doing in seven days what one man can do in one day.

The paraphernalia of democracy is very costly. Compared to monarchy or dictatorship, democracy is expensive because the government machinery is complex and complicated. There are legislatures, consultative and advisory bodies, committees and commissions which involve a heavy burden on the public treasury.

Democracies are proverbially slow and sluggish in their movement. They take a lot of time to execute their plans. Democracy is government by consultation and criticism and hence it takes a lot of time to arrive at decisions. Even intelligent and able men in high seats of power cannot act with energy and promptitude on account of the procedural delays. Many times, procedures kill the spirit of government and real progress becomes difficult. Sluggishness and reluctance to take quick decisions bring democracies into disrepute.

Democracy is the cult of incompetence. It means an irresponsible government. It is a government by amateurs or by those who are hopelessly amateur. It rests upon a broken reed because it is based on the common multitude which is ungrateful, emotional and passionate. Robert Browning has beautifully expressed this idea in his poem "The Patriot". He has shown how people applaud the leader at one time and how the same people send him to the gallows. The masses are inconsistent and fickle-minded.

The people are short-sighted and do not see far enough into the future. In certain democratic countries, there is a strong tendency among the people to excessive interference in the work of government by means of mandates, petitions and protests. In some other countries, there is a tendency to insubordination and anarchy. The leaders of the people are like school masters who are elected by their pupils and are liable to be punished and dismissed by them.

Democracy puts emphasis on quantity and not quality. It make the decision of the majority the law even if the majority is a small one. It is immaterial even if the opinion of the minority is better on account of the superior wisdom of those who constitute the minority. Democracy puts emphasis on the principle of equality and makes every individual the equal of the other. It either underestimates the value of special training and expert knowledge in administration or makes it difficult to get experts into public service.

Democracy is the rule of the people but the masses do not appreciate the significance of liberty and individuality. There is the intolerance of the crowd. Even the most gifted persons become victims of the tyranny of the masses. They are liable to be persecuted for holding views in advance of their times. Democracy is the most meddlesome of all politics.

In democratic states, there is a large and increasing mass of hasty and ill-digested legislation The average representative is not bothered about any consideration other than that of making himself popular with the people. There is a craze for legislation which can impress the people. That legislation may be uneconomic but that is no concern of the politician who is more concerned with his personal popularity and not the ultimate good of society.

Bribery and corruption are the common abuses of democracy. Not only the votes are bought, even the members of the legislatures are bribed. Money plays an important part in politics and that lowers the moral standards.

There is no moral value in democracy. In democracy, there is always a temptation for falsification and lies. X calls Y a liar and Y condemns X as a bigger liar. In order to appeal to the people, issues are vulgarised and popularised. Questions are discussed more with a view to catch votes than to secure the good of the society as a whole. There is no love for truth and justice. The foremost thought is merely to capture votes.

In a democracy, local interests tend "to obscure and to defeat the interests of the state at large". In a general scramble for power and patronage, the idea of public good is set aside and respresentatives compete with one another in obtaining whatever they can, irrespective of its effect on the welfare of the country at large.

Democracy is an inefficient form of government in which ignorant and worthless men wield power. Men of calibre, competence and integrity are hardly rewarded. There is no fear of dismissal for inefficient and dishonest men if they are backed by the party in power. Democracies "distrust natural leaders and are a prolific breeding ground for agitators, flatterers, bosses and demagogues". Again, "they are said to be wasteful and extravagant; they tend to level society down rather than up; and they are indifferent to, if not actually hostile to, the advancement of education, science, literature and art".

Critics maintain that the view that power in a democracy resides in the hands of the people, is a myth. The people are controlled and blindly led by a few people who rise to the top by fair or foul means. The people are deceived and made to feel that power is in their hands. F.W. Coker observes, "All the institutional and ideological paraphernalia of modern democracy facilitate rather than obstruct the operation of despotic rule. Unorganised masses are always controlled by some alert, resolute, organised minority—military despots, big businessmen, party managers or social reformers—who are skillful in adjusting popular ideas and emotions to the limited interests or beliefs of some small group".

There is a wide gap between democracy in theory and democracy in practice. Most of the democratic governments do not act strictly according to democratic principles. There is talk of the sovereignty of the people, welfare of the people and the principle of consent and criticism. However, in actual practice, many democratic governments violate the spirit of the true principles of democracy. C.D. Burns says that democracy "rests upon certain pretences, not to say frauds. Political parties are supposed to be free associations. But in fact most members of a party belong to it because of their parent's politics or because of some irrelevant connection between the party and some locality or economic interest or religion".

Democracy postulates rule by average man and woman. Such a rule reflects the traits of their character. The ordinary people have a deep involvement in traditional ways of living and thinking. They are bound by habits and customs. The conservatism of the people hinders the artistic and scientific progress of society. The result is that democracy becomes a synonym for conservatism. The view of Sir Henry Maine is that there is no belief less warranted by actual experience than that a democratic republic is given to reforming legislation.

Democracy is considered to be hostile to the spirit of liberty. An ordinary man neither desires freedom for himself nor tolerates it in others. To place supreme power in the hands of the common people is like placing it in the hands of those who have no understanding of the spiritual value of liberty and lack the necessary character for vindicating liberty.

The view of some critics is that pronounced tendencies are found in modern democratic states. According to Robert Michels, the operation and organisation of parties violate closely the "iron law of oligarchy". The ordinary people do not possess the ability to make any political decisions. In a political party, the leaders decide and the rank and file obey the same. This submission of the masses to the domination of political leaders makes a mockery of democracy.

Lord Bryce refers to the baneful effect of "money power in politics" and comments on "the power of money to pervert administration or legislation" in democracies. The temptation of money disturbs the natural character of the state mechanism which tilts in favour of those who are in a position to bribe.

Some critics maintain that democracy is an unscientific dogma. Their arguments are based on psychological and biological evidence. The psychological criticism is based on a study of mass-psychology. Graham Wallas writes, "Politics is only in a slight degree the product of conscious reason; is largely a matter of subconscious processes of habit and instinct, suggestion and imitation". The man in the crowd misses his personality—consciousness and awareness of self-action. He immediately succumbs to the influence of suggestion. "Modern elections are an exercise in spell-binding".

Le Bon writes that legislatures frame laws which a legislator in his individual capacity may consider as improper. Actually men who behave quite reasonably in their individual dealings with others become abruptly irrational as members of a group. Crowd-psychology is manifest in every political system. The biological school discovers the unscientific character of the democratic system. The democratic system with its principle of political equality does not accord with the pattern of natural biological classification revealed generally in the prevalent social and economic classification.

The present system of democracy based on geographical representation is faulty because it works under the illusion that a representative can represent a voter's various interests. No person can represent another in relation to every conceivable question and interest. One can represent only some specific function. According to Cole, all true and democratic representation is functional representation.

The Fascists condemn democracy as "decrepit, decaying, stale and out of date". According to them, democracy is a false ideal. A democratic government is inefficient. Parties are selfish and corrupt. While they put emphasis on principles, in actual practice they do not act upon them. A democratic government is an impossibility.

The Communists condemn the so-called capitalist democracy which is called empty, hollow and unreal for most of the people. Democracy in capitalist economy is in fact the dictatorship of the capitalists over the proletariat,, the working class people. The logic of democracy stands in contradiction to the logic of capitalism. Political equality under capitalist democracy is merely the protective shell of capitalism. Such a democracy is only for the rich and real power rests only in their hands. The machinery of the state is used by the capitalists in their own interest and against the workers. Although everybody is given the right of vote, the majority of the people do not benefit on account of their economic condition.

The Socialists also criticise the democratic form of government. Prof. Laski writes, "In the marriage between capitalism and democracy which has given us our system of parliamentary democracy, capitalism is more important than democracy because the relations of property that it imposes give to democracy its constitutive principle. Democracy denies that principle without, as it were, dissolving the marriage that gave it birth. It may survive but that will be on the condition only that, it is a divorce by consent".

Talleyrand describes democracy as "an aristocracy of black guards". Sir Henry Maine writes, "Popular governments have been repeatedly overturned by mobs and armies in combination; of all governments they seem least likely to cope successfully with a breaking up of political power into morsels and the giving to each person an infinitesimally small portion; they rest upon universal suffrage which is the natural basis of tyranny; they are unfavourable to intellectual progress and the advance of scientific truth; they lack stability and they are governments by the ignorant and unintelligent". Lecky describes democracy as government by the poorest, the most ignorant, the most incapable who are necessarily the most numerous". According to Sidgwick, "Democracy lacks the means of securing an enforceable responsibility". Responsibility cannot be achieved by popular election of officials, short tenures and rotation of office. It can be more easily achieved by the security of tenure.

According to Lord Bryce, the defects of democracy are the power of money to prevent administration or legislation, the tendency to make politics a gainful profession, extravagance in administration, the abuse of the doctrine of equality and failure to appreciate the value of administrative skill, the undue power of party organisation and the tendency of legislators and political officials to play for votes in the passing of laws and in tolerating breaches of order. There is fickleness and instability in a democracy. There is insubordination, internal dissension, disregard of authority, with a frequent resort to violence, bringing in anarchy which ends in military tyranny. It is incapable of acting with promptitude at the time of an emergency.

Faguet writes, "Government is .an art and it presupposes knowledge but the people are governed by men who have neither knowledge nor art and were chosen because they have them not". Incompetence permeates all branches of the government in France, particularly the judiciary and Faguet attributes that to the democratic form of government.

Prof. Barthelemy writes that the great weakness of democracy is the incompetence of those who govern, the prevalence of amateurism in public service and the general belief that everyone is fit to govern. His view is that democratic government requires a great deal of technical skill which is lacking. Democracy insists upon certain formal qualifications for appointments to interior posts, but none for the higher ones. The higher the office, the less is the evidence of capacity required.

According to Hearnshaw, democracy has failed to secure good government because it has failed to attract the best brains of the community. That is why Hartmann describes it as the paradise of the shrieker, babbler, word-spinner, flatterer and tuft-hunter. In a democracy, there is the delegation of sovereignty to the demagogue, the grafter and the boss. It has failed to lay down sound lines of policy. It suffers chronically from indifference of apathy. It is carried on by amateur politicians who have no special qualification for their work. It is led by idealism and abstract theory. It is a victim to catch-words. It worships the demagogue who becomes the idol of the masses. It is shifting and therefore unstable and incalculable. The people who are acclaimed and honoured today are shunned, despised and forgotten tomorrow. Democracy can desecrate sanctities, flout traditions, abolish venerable customs, break the continuity of national life and destroy the organic development of body politics. Democracy perpetrates intolerance and immoderation. The tyranny of the majority knows no bounds. The people are short-sighted because they are moved more by selfish and momentary interests than by general and permanent good of the nation. There is a tendency to insubordination and anarchy in democracy because ministers cannot afford to be unpopular. They keep their eyes fixed on the next election. They cannot work with vigour and strength. Democracy perishes by disintegration.

It is true that there are many shortcomings of democracy but those can be lessened through efforts. On the whole, a democratic government has been found to be more stable than others. Hence preference for democracy. C.D. Burns writes, "No one denies that the existing representative assemblies are defective; but even if an automobile does not work well, it is foolish to go back into a farm cart, however romantic".

Development of Concept of Democracy

In the words of W.F. Willoughby, "The origin of this doctrine (of popular sovereignty) is to be found in the early Greek and Roman Republics. In a very true sense, their government may be said to have rested on this principle." The term democracy was coined by the Greeks. It appeared in Herodotus' History in connection with the notion of isonomia, equality before the law. From that time, the term has remained a part of the political vocabulary. The Greek city-states experimented with direct democracy. Liberty was the principle of public life. The life of the Athenian citizen had a quality of intimacy. The city was a life in common. Its constitution was the mode of life rather than a legal structure.

There were certain features of the Greek city-states. Those states were known as city states because the total area of each state was not more than the area of a modern city. Athens had a population of about three lacs. Government was both local and national in character. The citizens normally spent their entire life in the city state. The city was both urban and rural. Plato called the urban city the city of the rich and the rural city the city of the poor. The state was divided into three main classes viz., the slaves, resident foreigners and citizens. Not only slaves and foreign residents were excluded from the right of citizenship, that right was also denied even to women and children. Citizenship at that time was more than the periodical right to vote. It meant a share in the running of the administration of the state itself. Greek democracy was based on the principle that the well-being of the state and individual was inseparable.

The government of the city state was divided into three main organs viz., the Assembly of the citizens, the Council and the Juries. The Assembly was the sovereign body which represented the will of the people. It consisted of all the male citizens above the age of 30. Its total actual membership varied between 3000 to 6000. The Council was the Executive or Steering Committee. It had 500 members who were chosen annually from a panel of citizens elected by the electoral districts. The Council met every day. The Juries were the guardians of the constitution and law and order. The Juries consisted of 6000 citizens chosen annually by lot. In addition, there were ten Generals who were elected by the people and their main function was the defence of the state.

The democratic system of the Greek city-states was criticised by Socrates, Plato and Aristotle. Plato went to the extent of branding democracy as the third corruption of the ideal state. According to him, in its life democracy is not lovely and in its death, it prepares the way for tyranny which was the lowest and most degraded type of state.

Although the Greek system stood for political equality, it is not workable in a modern state on account of its large population and area. Moreover, the system of choosing representatives by lot is objectionable. The modern government requires specialization and expertise which was not known before.

With the fall of Rome and the coming of the Dark Age in Europe, democracy had no scope at all. In the feudal system of medieval Europe, the barons were very powerful and the people had no power. The result was that there was no scope for democracy.

There was a strong reaction against the tyrannical arid oppressive rulers of Europe who ruled by the theory of divine right. The new ideas given by Voltaire and Rousseau weakened the hold of the monarchs over their subjects. In England, there was a struggle for supremacy between the Stuart kings and British Parliament and ultimately the Parliament won and thus parliamentary democracy was established in England.

Small reformist groups like the Diggers and Levellers raised their voice against the political rights bestowed on a minority class. The Levellers were the early advocates of radical middle class democracy. At that time, the social contract theories became popular. John Locke was of the view that the legislature was the supreme power in the government. He suggested that representation to Parliament should be fair and equal. The American Declaration of Independence in 1776 and the French Declaration of the Rights of Man were important developments. They resulted in the framing of the first written constitution based on the principles of representative government and the principles of equality of man and popular sovereignty. The growth of the party system helped the growth of representative democracy. Democratic governments were set up both in the United States and France.

In the twentieth century, democracy seems to have entered its golden age. Among European peoples, democracy became almost a passion. The World War I was fought by the United States and Britain to make the world safe for democracy. After the World War I, new states were carved out and everywhere it became a fashion to establish a democratic form of government. F.W. Coker writes, "Many of the transformations that arose from the upheavals of the World War seemed to strengthen the traditional faith in some sort of heroic law of democracy. Popular revolutions, peaceful or bloody, swept away—by assassination, deposition or forced abdication—a Tsar, a Sultan, three emperors and nearly a score of minor kings, grand dukes, dukes and princes". However, the golden age of democracy came to an end very soon with the rise of dictators like Mussolini in Italy and Hitler in Germany. The dictators plunged the world into the Second World War. After the War, many countries in Asia and Africa became independent and set up democratic governments.

Theories of Democracy

Liberalism gave support to democratic ideas and ideals from the very beginning. It had faith in the worth of man and his natural rights. Liberal democratic ideas emerged during the seventeenth century and were prominent till the beginning of the present century. Among the liberals there were three theories of democracy and those were classical liberal theory of democracy, the Elitist theory of democracy and the Pluralist theory of democracy. Their basic philosophical assumptions were the same. In addition to these theories of democracy, there is also the Marxist theory of democracy.

(1) THE CLASSICAL LIBERAL THEORY OF DEMOCRACY

The classical liberal theory of democracy is also known as popular, Modisonian and populist theory. The view of Robert Dahl is that this type of theory never existed. Plamenatz maintains that the classical theory of democracy "is an idea or set of ideas that belonged much more to political rhetoric than to systematic political theory". The view of Pateman is that "the notion of a classical theory of democracy is a myth". However, Macpherson is of the view that the classical theory of democracy emerged during the nineteenth century and was especially designed to suit the class-divided society. Classical liberal democratic ideas emerged mainly during the modern period when the importance of the dignity of man came to be recognised. It was maintained that all the social institutions were for the betterment of man as an individual. The development of personality of man became the central point of human thinking. Hobbes put forward the proposition that the state was created by the people through a social contract. John Locke also made his contribution to the theory of classical democracy. He regarded the consent of the people as the basis of political power. His contention was that political power is the trust of the people in the hands of the government. Locke was also of the view that people in the state of nature had three natural rights viz., right to life, liberty and property. Locke also gave the theory of limited and constitutional government. Although he could not elaborate clearly the principles of majority rule, representative government, theory of separation of powers and parliamentary form of government, all those were implied in his political theory.

The ideas of Locke were clarified and given practical shape by the thinkers and politicians of the succeeding centuries. During the eighteenth century, philosophers of rationalism and enlightenment elaborated many classical liberal democratic views. Montesquieu gave the theory of separation of powers, Rousseau gave the theory of the general will. He is known as the prophet of direct democracy. Philosophers like Mably, Diderot, Helvetius and Holback raised their voice in support of democracy. The American revolutionaries and constitutionalists like Jefferson and Madison laid down the institutional basis of classical liberal democratic theory. During the nineteenth century, systematic ideas regarding the classical theory of democracy developed. Bentham and Mill advocated the right to vote and representative government. They laid down the theoretical foundations of adult franchise. It is said of J.S. Mill that he lifted participatory democracy "out of the context of a city state of peasant proprietors" and placed it in a modern political system. He believed that participatory institutions can force an individual to widen his horizon and to take the public interest into account. Participation works best at the local level. To quote J.S. Mill, "We do not learn to read or write, to ride or swim, by being merely told how to do it, but by doing it, so it is only by practising popular government on a limited scale that the people will ever learn how to exercise it on a larger scale". J.S. Mill desired that the wisest and best men should be elected to hold public office. His view was that responsible political participation requires education and experience. He recommended extra votes for the better educated persons. Mill extended the concept of participatory democracy to industry. He had the highest regard for the viewpoint of the minority, howsoever insignificant it was. To quote him, "If all mankind minus one were of one opinion and only one person was of the contrary opinion, mankind would be no more justified in silencing that one person than he, if he had the power, would be justified in silencing mankind."

The idea of democracy found support in the writings of T.H. Green and many other supporters of the classical liberal theory during the twentieth century like Hobhouse, Dr. Lindsay, Ernest Barker, Prof. Laski, MacIver, John Dewey, Woodrow Wilson and G.D.H. Cole. In the twentieth century, the classical Theory of democracy was strengthened on account of the extension of franchise to women and lowering of the age of voting to 18 years. Liberal democracy became more egalitarian. After the World War II, the classical theory of democracy was challenged by the Elitist theory of democracy. There is a trend to remoralise democracy under the banner of "participatory democracy".

Four Principles. In his *Political Continuity and Change*, Peter H. Merkl has enumerated four principles of classical liberal theory of democracy. (1) One principle is that democracy is a government by consent. Rational consent can be obtained by persuasion for which an atmosphere of free discussion is necessary. On account of the highly technical nature of modern administration and the great volume and urgency of government decisions, it is not possible to consult the people on every detail of every policy. However, there can be discussion of the broad issues before the country. Discussion is usually held at two levels. There is discussion among the representatives of the people in the legislatures of the country. At the public level also, there is direct communication between the leadership and the people. Leadership in a democracy is expected to keep itself in touch with public opinion on the major issues of the day. The ruling party is required to seek a fresh mandate of the people at regular intervals.

(2) Another principle of liberal democracy is the majority rule which means that the decisions in the legislatures, committees, cabinets and the executive or regulative bodies are taken by the majority vote on the principle of one man, one vote. There is no privileged position for any section of society. There is no special weightage for any one. There is no discrimination on the ground of religion, race, caste, sex, place of birth, ownership of property or even education. Any restriction of suffrage is based on a rational ground such as the person excluded is a convicted criminal, or a mental patient

or a minor. The principle of majority rule relies on the wisdom of the majority. The minority can try to convert itself into majority by persuasion.

(3) Another principle is the recognition of minority rights. The minorities may be racial, religious, linguistic or cultural, but there is not to be any persecution or harassment of those minorities. Legal safeguards can be provided to protect the interests of the minorities. That can create a favourable climate for the successful working of democracy.

(4) Another principle of liberal democracy is constitutional government which means a government by laws and not by men. There must be definite processes and procedures to carry on the government. A well-established tradition of law and constitution is necessary for the stability of a democratic government. If that is not done, the flood-gates of corruption may be thrown wide open which is not desirable for democracy.

In his book *Modern Politics and Government*, Alan Ball has identified some *characteristics of liberal democracy*. There is more than one political party competing for political power. That competition is open and not secretive. It is based on established and accepted forms of procedure. Entry and recruitment to positions of political power are relatively open. There are periodic elections based on universal suffrage. There are also pressure groups to influence the decisions of the government. Civil liberties are recognised and protected. There is substantial amount of independence and freedom from government control. There is also the separation of powers in some form. The legislature has control over the executive and the judiciary is independent of both the legislature and the executive. There can be some flexibility in these conditions during the period of emergency.

The advocates of liberal democracy maintain that the supreme merit of democracy lies in the fact that "it promotes a better and higher form of national character than in any other polity". The view of Barker is that the dignity of individuals is enhanced by political enfranchisement. Democracy is conducive to the development of man every way. Under no other political system there is so much self-realisation as it is under democracy. The best political system is not one which is most efficient but one which makes the best possible human beings. In dictatorship or bureaucracy, individuals and groups can suffer without affecting the rest of the community, but in a democracy, there is not a single man who suffers without the rest of the community sharing in his suffering. A democracy is sensitive to the wishes and sufferings of the people. It ties a nerve to every individual. It creates a link between him and the centre.

Democracy is an experiment in public education on a large scale. It stimulates public interest in the government. It tends to create a higher type of mind and character among the people. Every rational opinion is given a chance to express itself at the time of a general election. Public issues are discussed at length. What was private becomes public. Speeches are delivered. Articles are written. Policies are propounded and programmes are put before the public for their consideration and decision. The result is a popular understanding of the problems of the government. C.D. Burns writes, "All government is a method of education, but the best education is self-education; therefore, the best government is self-government which is democracy".

The advocates of liberal democracy maintain that mere efficiency of government is not enough. They point out that soulless efficiency destroyed the Roman Empire. The government by experts is not enough as they do not know the mind of the people. Specialisation may warp the intellect. The expert knows his own side of the case but he does not know the effect of his policies on the people. The wearer knows where the shoe pinches and hence there should be cooperation or a working alliance between the expert and the layman. That is possible only in a democracy. The rule by the highly educated alone is catastrophic. It is likely to be abstract and doctrinaire which is removed from the actualities of life.

The advocates of liberal democracy also maintain that democracy promotes patriotism. According to Laveleye, the French people never really loved France until after the French Revolution when they got a share in the government. After that, they became passionate lovers of their country. Democracy also reduces the danger of a revolution. The reason is that democracy is government by persuasion and there can be change of government by peaceful methods. Every other form of government rests on force to a greater or lesser degree. Democracy is the only political system where both order and progress can go together and there is no necessity of a revolution. Dictatorship can give order but not much progress. Democracy acts as a check on revolution by emphasizing the principle of legal and political equality. Democracy provides an open road to talent. The view of some liberal writers is that democracy makes for greater efficiency than under any other form of government. The reason given is that popular election, popular control and popular responsibility insure a greater degree of efficiency than under any other system of government. Democracy combines efficiency with liberty.

It is the basic assumption of the classical liberal theory of democracy that election is a process by which the general masses are given an opportunity to participate in the political system and election results reflect the public opinion. The will of the people is expressed through the vote and the right to vote makes the people responsible and saves them from frustrations. The right to vote is not merely a mechanical device to elect the government. It is also a condition for the all-round development of human personality. It is necessary for the security of all the members against irresponsible government. Elections are there to know the pulse of the people and they reflect the dynamic spirit of public opinion. The right to vote coordinates the interests of the governors and the governed. The government can be made responsible to the people through elections. The natural corrupting tendency of political power can be tamed through periodic elections. This theory emphasizes the active participation of the people and their association in the political process. Vigilance of the general public and political alertness of the common man is a precondition for a responsible and welfare democracy. The people not only honour their representatives but also have the power to punish undemocratic, opportunist and anti-people politicians.

Democracy gives the people an opportunity to participate in the political process and thereby helps the development of the personality of man. Davis writes, "Participation in the management of public affairs would serve as a vital means of intellectual, emotional and moral education leading towards the full development of the capacities of individual human beings. The key to the realisation of human potentialities and creation of genuine community becomes the pursuit of the common good through political activity". Democracy provides a safe device for bringing about a political change. It also provides scope for mutli-dimensional development of human personality. This aspect has been emphasized by Mill. Green, Lindsay. Barker and Laski. Democracy is not merely a political system. It is a way of life. Together with liberty, equality, and rights, democracy provides the necessary conditions for a moral life.

The voting process is regarded as the best method for the expression of the general will of the people. The rationality of the voter and the worth of the voting process was emphasized by J.S. Mill in these words: "The voter is under an absolute moral obligation to consider the interests of the public, not his private advantage, and to give his vote, the best of his judgement, exactly as he would be bound to do if he were the sole voter and the election depended upon him alone". According to Davis, this theory posits "the existence of rational and active citizens who seek to realise a generally recognised common good through collective initiation, discussion and decision of policy questions concerning public affairs and who delegate authority to agents (elected government officials) to carry through the broad decisions reached by the people through majority vote". Schumpeter also writes, "The democratic method is that institutional arrangement for arriving at political decisions which realise common good by making the people itself decide issues through the election of individuals who are to assemble in order to carry out its will".

Criticism of the Classical Liberal Theory of Democracy

This theory has been attacked by various writers on various grounds. The Elitists feel that democracy is rule by an irresponsible elite. Pareto considers it as a degenerated and perverted form of government. Democracy in practice leads to oligarchy of the worst kind. In a democracy, power falls into the hands of the demagogue, the grafter and the boss. Leaders of first-rate ability are not chosen. People are jealous of excellence and choose popular men rather than able men to lead them. Democracy is biological monstrosity which means that democracy is not in line with the process of social evolution. The higher we ascend in the scale of evolution, the greater is the degree of centralisation. Pareto interprets democracy to mean extreme decentralisation and therefore incompetence. Democracy is not friendly to liberty and individuality as it is meddlesome. In a democracy, a large number of hasty and ill-digested laws are passed with unfortunate consequences. The average representative feels that the only way in which he can justify his existence in the legislature is to get some new law passed, irrespective of its utility or rationality.

The view of Mosca is that democracy results in the tyranny of the majority. It easily falls a prey to demagogy, bossism and vicious pressure politics. The average voter is not interested, in national affairs and on many subjects which are discussed, there is no common opinion. The apathy of the voter in many democratic countries has been demonstrated in several election surveys.

The view of Pareto and Michels is that democracy in practice means party politics and political parties constitute an invisible oligarchy. Michels refers to the iron law of oligarchy which is inherent in the organisation and functioning of every political party. While the party system is indispensable to a democracy, it carries the national divisions into local elections and debases moral standards. The working of the party machine gives no opportunity or freedom to the individual to exercise his judgement. He has to choose between two or more candidates who may be either knaves or fools and for none of whom he cares and decide between two or three issues, none of which meets with his approval.

The Elitists describe democracy as the cult of incompetence. It is a government by amateurs. It rests upon a broken reed because it rests upon the common multitude which is irrational, emotional and passionate. The common people do not reason much. They are fickle in their loyalty to persons and principles. One day they praise a man to the skies and the next day they cast him down in the mire. They are not motivated by any consistent and unifying ideals. At times, they are given to idealism and hero-worship. They are easily swept off their feet by popular slogans. At times, they become obscurantists and obstruct all progress. They are like school masters who are elected by their pupils and are liable to be punished and dismissed by them.

The Elitists attack democracy also from the psychological standpoint. According to them, the people are sheep-minded, ape-minded and wolf-minded. "They are credulous, impulsive, panicky, intolerant, unconscionable, cruel, unjust, stupid and everything but rational". Democratic government is "prone to indecision, feebleness, instability and stupidity because of the volatility, irrationality and ineptitude of the masses".

Democracy is a very expensive form of government. It involves the organisation of opinion, propaganda and frequent elections and all that involves a lot of expenditure. The money which should have been spent for productive purposes is spent on electioneering and nursing the constituency. There is waste not only of money but also of time and opportunity. According to Pareto, democracy is the most inefficient, extravagant, factional, intolerant and stagnant political system.

The Elitist view is that democracy is a process of dis-education, rather than of education. It flatters people. It produces a pretentious proletariat. It hides from the people their deficiency. It creates in them a false sense of equality. Every man comes to believe that he is as good as anybody else for the governance of his country and it requires no special effort or training. In a democracy, an appeal is made to mob psychology. Every effort is made to pamper the people who as a whole are indifferent, if not hostile, to the advancement of education, science, literature and art. The civilisation produced by democracy is based on the celebration of mediocrity.

The ethical value of democracy has also been attacked by some Elitist writers. Their view is that in a democracy, there is always a temptation to falsify. Issues are vulgarized and popularised before an appeal is made to the people. Questions are not discussed dispassionately but in the spirit of vote-catching. Bribery and corruption are the common abuses of democracy. There are several instances in which voters, members of legislatures, administrative officials and even judicial officials were caught while taking bribes. There are greater opportunities of illicit gain under democracy than under any other form of government. Local interests are emphasized and they not only obscure but also defeat the national interests. In the scramble for power and patronage, the general well-being of the nation is ignored.

The classical theory is based on the assumption that there is a specified common good of the society which every person knows and which can be served by a democratic government. The fact is that the concept of common good differs from person to person and cannot be defined. To quote Schumpeter, "There is no such thing as an uniquely determined common good that all people could agree on or be made to agree on by the force of rational argument...To different individuals and groups, the common good is bound to mean different things".

The classical theory believes in political equality of the people in general, but this is not true in the class-divided Western democracies. In every society, there is an elite which enjoys political power. Democracy is not a system in which everyone has an equal share in political power.

The classical theory is based on the assumption that the elected government reflects the will of the people, but that is not so in actual practice. The truth is that the government itself manufactures the will of the people through vast ideological apparatuses at its command. Public opinion as the basis of government is also a myth. Actually, public opinion does not make the government, rather the government makes the public opinion. The classical view regarding the rationality of man and his political behaviour is attacked. It is pointed out that open participation of the people in politics converts democracy into mobocracy. The people fall a prey to demagogues and unscrupulous politicians who establish their dictatorship by misusing The mandate of the people. According to Pateman, the classical picture of democratic man is hopelessly unrealistic.

The classical theory does not give proper consideration to the need of stability or equilibrium of the political system. It puts all the emphasis on consent, discussion, debate and consultation. However, consensus is more important than consent. Mass democracy, unable to satisfy the demands of all the individuals, needs general consensus. The people have the right to overthrow the government but that is not enough.

The classical theory of democracy is unrealistic. Its assumptions about man and society are unrealistic because democracy employs conceptions of the nature of man and the operation of society which are Utopian and it does not provide adequate operational definitions of its key concepts.

The classical theory of democracy puts more emphasis on democratic values than on democratic mechanism. It is concerned with *ought* and not with what actually is. It ignores the realities of political life. The behavioural political scientists point out that facts are more important for political scientists than values.

The highly technical and complex process of policy-making is over-simplified and misunderstood by the exponents of the classical theory. The complex political processes in modern democracies are beyond the mental approach of a layman.

The classical theory of democracy does not see any contradiction between the democratic political system and the capitalist economic system. The assumption chat liberal democracy and the welfare and regulatory state will moderate and smooth over the conflicts of class interests is not correct. Reliance on the goodwill of the democratic state or cooperative intelligence is a misnomer.

The classical theory of democracy is based on the principle of participation but some contemporary writers point out the dangers of such participation. Herbert McClosky advocates political apathy or non-participation and gives reasons in support of his view. According to him, little is gained and something may be lost, by encouraging the involvement of men and women who are politically misinformed and un-interested. Little is gained merely by increasing the number of voters. A vote may be used to elect a Hitler as well as a Roosevelt or Churchill. Hence, apathy is better than heedless participation. The business of politics might better be turned over to those active minorities who are capable of governing in a democracy. A too active electorate may impede those who rule from making the decisions they are best qualified to make.

Doughlas Verney has also criticised the classical participatory theory of democracy. According to him, participation primarily deals with political participation "leaving untouched the economic and social influence of the bourgeoisie". It leads to the tyranny of the masses over the minority and mediocrity over talent. It is more of an ideal than actual politics. It is unworkable in a modern complex political system. It assumes a dichotomy between the state and the individual. It is deficient in its assumptions of equality and its treatment of the problem of leadership.

It is true that there are certain shortcomings in democracy but all the criticism is not justified. Some of the arguments of the critics contradict each other. According to some, democracy means hero-worship and idolatry, while according to others it means insubordination and anarchy. Some contend that democracy is given to idealism and worship of abstract theory, while others maintain that there is no place for sentiments and principles in democracy.

Some critics blame democracy for many of the evils which the two World Wars have brought about. They hold it responsible for world-wide depression and unemployment of the 1930's. The fact is that democracy is not responsible for all that. J.H. Hallow ell writes, "It is not fair to rate the soundness of a man's judgement by his behaviour when fighting, when drunk or when scared. Nor can we measure democracy by events that occur under highly abnormal conditions." It is also pointed out that there is no other political system which is as good as democracy. The world has tried aristocracy, monarchy and dictatorship and all of them have been found to be wanting. Their demerits are more than their merits.

Modern democracies realise that government is an art and it can be safely entrusted to those who specialise in it. Democracy does not exclude government by experts.

It is not correct to say that democracy is an incompetent form of government. Even in a democratic system, the government is actually carried on by experts who are selected by means of competition. In an aristocracy, the expert may keep himself aloof from the people but in a democracy the expert has to take into consideration the sentiments and interests of the people. He cannot ignore them.

It is also not correct to say that democracy is a speciality of the white races only. Democracy has been tried among the non-whites and has worked successfully. Maxey writes. "There is no credible scientific proof that white races are innately superior in political genius or any other mental quality to the black, brown or yellow races" (Political Philosophies, p. 687).

The critics of classical democracy criticise the principle of representation but whatever the shortcomings in the systems of representation, there is no alternative to it. Dictatorships have been tried and have not worked for long. Democracy can work properly if the people care to choose their leaders with care.

The critics criticise the party system, but there is no alternative. The party system can be reformed but it cannot be dispensed with. Parties bring order out of chaos. They mould and educate public opinion. Lord Bryce writes. "Parties keep a nation's mind alive, as the rise and fall of the sweeping tide freshens the water of long ocean inlets. Party discipline puts a check on self-seeking and corruption."

The elite theory proclaims the death of democracy. However, it is wrong to say that democracy has no future. There seem to be no signs of the abandonment of democracy in favour of dictatorship or any other form of government. Democracy can adjust itself to all kinds of situations. Leaders like Churchill in England and Roosevelt in the United States were given enormous powers during the World War II and those powers disappeared after the war. The people had confidence that the powers given to them would not be abused and were actually not abused. Dr. Lindsay writes "A democratic society sure of itself can be indefinitely elastic in its methods. It can, as in a time of crisis, give enormous powers into the hands of its government in cheerful confidence that the crisis past, it can take them back". (I Believe in Democracy, p. 17).

Critics say that democracy means diseducation but that defect can be removed by educating the people. With the spread of education, that defect will be lessened.

Democracy is a rational organisation and is based on a rational principle. The defects in its working can be eliminated by the people themselves by proper education, reflection and experience. It is not correct that the only way to cure the evils of democracy is to abolish democracy itself. Democracy is based on humanism. Dewey writes. "The foundation of democracy is faith in the capacities of human nature, faith in human intelligence and in the power of pooled and cooperative experience" (German Philosophy of Politics, p. 49).

(2) ELITIST THEORY OF DEMOCRACY

The Elitist theory of democracy has developed mainly during the present century. It is mainly concerned with the institutions of democracy and realities of the Western liberal democratic political system. It provides a description, an explanation and justification of the existing political systems in Western democracies. This theory arose due to the need for the maintenance of stability and equilibrium in the capitalist liberal societies. It does not aim at change in the existing socio-economic situation. Its object is to suggest a political system best suited to the existing order.

The dictionary meaning of elite is the chosen element in the population. According to Suzanne Keller, "Elites are those minorities which are set apart from the rest of society by their pre-eminence in one or more of these various distributions". In order to be really effective, an elite group should possess three qualities viz., group consciousness, coherence and conspiracy. Elites are divided into two categories—strategic elites and segmental elites. The strategic elites are those who claim or exercise wide influence over the entire spectrum of social set-up. The segmental elites are those who have influence or responsibilities only in a sub-domain of society. However, both of them draw their elite status from either or a combination of the following factors: heredity, excellence in arts and literature, position in the ruling class or party or bureaucratic hierarchy, material affluence and physical prowess. Out of the two, the strategic elites are more important.

The essential theme of this theory is that there is in every society a minority of the population which takes the major decisions in the society. As those decisions have political implications, the elite exercise considerable political influence. The important advocates of this theory are Vilfredo Pareto (1848-1923), Gaetano Mosca (1858-1941), Robert Michels, James Burnham, Joseph A. Schumpeter, Raymond Aron, Giovanni Sartori and Karl Mannheim.

Gaetano Mosca propounded the elitist theory of democracy in his famous work "The Ruling Class" (1939). *Vilfredò Pareto* discussed the elite theory of democracy in his book "The Mind and Society" (1915-1919). Robert Michels gave his views in his book "Political Parties". The views of Pareto and Mosca are generally identical with each other. They emphasize the application of the sociological method to the study of politics and democracy. Pareto was interested in general social analysis and the study of social problems as a whole, but Mosca displayed great interest in political analysis. However, both of them rejected the classical theory of democracy as a government of the people and argued that society is invariably divided between a minority which rules and the majority which is ruled. Both of them emphasize the irrational basis of politics and express the view that talent and intelligence is a monopoly of the few who constitute the elite. According to both of them, war and revolution are inevitable in every age. There was a continuous change of ruling classes from time to time. They propounded the law of the *circulation of elites* in history. No political system or regime could be regarded as stable or permanent. The view of Mosca was that the classification of the governments into monarchy, oligarchy or democracy was not meaningful at all. There has been essentially one type of government in history and that is oligarchy. There has always been a distinction between those who govern and those who are governed. It is the elite which governs. The elite is in a minority but it enjoys all the privileges and comforts available to those who control society. The masses obey the commands of the elite. Those commands may be enforced legally or illegally. The masses work to satisfy the wants of the ruling class. The common people do influence the political behaviour of the elite through peaceful elections and the formation of interest groups. The elite can be pressurised through agitation and violent rebellion. However, no elite can go on ruling permanently. Heredity, ideology and force are used by the elite to maintain their power but ultimately all elites are dethroned. Perpetual exercise of authority makes the ruling elite lazy, weak and luxury-loving. When that happens, a group of talented and industrious individuals revolt and capture power from the enfeebled elite. Every ruling elite uses a political formula to stabilise its position. The political elite do not want to justify their right to rule in terms of naked force. They prefer to legitimize their authority in terms of legal and moral principles and popularly accepted traditions and beliefs.

The elite who continue to change their environments, may retain their authority. The elite who fail to transform themselves in accordance with the changing circumstances, fall from power. The French aristocracy lost power because it could not adjust itself to new democratic surroundings. The view of Mosca is that a clever elite would allow gradual expansion of its membership by recruiting new members from the subject classes on the basis of talent and merit. The elite should include all important elements representing wealth, military power, religion, education, science etc. Mosca admired the anti-democratic ideas of Bismarck, Cavour and Hegel.

The view of Pareto was that democracy was unrealizable. He regarded socialism and humanism as hypocrisy and delusion. He regarded man as weak and depraved being. The view of Pareto was that man is guided by his sentiments and passions. He is basically a creature of impulses and instincts.

Every society has two types of individuals — foxes and lions. Foxes are bold and courageous but they are not cautious and they use their cunningness to survive. Lions are strong, conservative, tradition-loving, orthodox and loyal to the ideals of family, religion and country. They prefer to use force and not cleverness. They like stable income from rent or interest. People get their rulers from these two categories of lions and foxes.

According to Pareto, society can be divided into the elite and non-elite. The elite can be further divided into governing elite and counter-elite. The view of Pareto is that the elites are formed in all professions including prostitutes and thieves. There is an uninterrupted cycle of the rise and decline of elite in history. In every society, the talented and meritorious members of the lower classes become new claimants for elitist status and privileges. In this way, the elite rise and fall from power. History is a graveyard of the numerous fallen elites. In capitalist society, private enterprise helps the transformation of the existing elites but democracy prevents progress.

The main interest of Pareto was in the nature of the governing elite. According to him, top leaders of political parties constitute the governing elite. Their power is based partly on force and partly on consent. However, the element of force is more important. The governing elite uses bribery, deceit and cunningness to secure the consent of the subject classes. The rulers can secure obedience by the use of money, but they must use force to keep the masses under their control. A weak elite is easily overthrown.

According to *Mosca,* society is divided into two classes: the class which rules and the class which is ruled. The key to the elite power is one's ability for organisation. A small group is more easily organised than an unorganised purposeless majority. Its channels of communication and information are better and quicker. The result is that any minority is able to formulate policies speedily. The principle of minority control works best in political parties which are controlled by bosses.

The view of *Robert Michels* is that a democratic system is in practice a party system. Thus, democracy becomes a "party-cracy". Party organisation is controlled by a group of leaders who cannot be checked or held accountable by persons who elect them. That is due to organisational factors such as party funds, control over the press and control over the mass media by the party in power and psychological factors such as the apathy of the majority,technical incompetence etc. This principle applies to all organisations.

Michels propounded his "Iron law of oligarchy". His view was that whatever form of government is adopted, in practice it is inevitably reduced to oligarchy or the rule of the chosen few.

In his book "The Managerial Revolution" (1941), *James Burnham* tried to combine eliticism with Marxism. His view was that the capitalist system would be replaced by a society controlled economically and politically by a managerial elite as the capitalist had passed on the control of business to his professional managers. The basis of elite power (political power and social prestige) was the control over production. The managerial revolution ultimately leads to a consolidation of the managerial power as the state takes over the industry and the manager and the bureaucrat become interchangeable.

In his book "The Power Elites" (1959), *C. Wright Mills* maintains that the basis of elite power is economic and social. Power in the modern society belongs to certain institutions which occupy pivotal positions in society. Those who occupy top positions in those institutions are the power elite. They move on to positions of power in the government.

In his book "Capitalism, Spcialism and Democracy" (1942), *Joseph A. Schumpeter* writes that the forms of government should be distinguished by their institutions, particularly by their methods of appointing and dismissing the supreme makers of law and policy. The democratic method is the institutional arrangement for arriving at political decisions in which individuals acquire the power to decide by means of a competitive struggle for the votes of the people. This implies that in a democracy, political decisions are taken by the leadership and not by the people themselves and there is free competition among the leaders for winning the votes of the people. This shows that democracy is not a government of the people or a means to give effect to the will of the people. Rulers comprise a different set of individuals from the common people. The role of the people is merely to choose their rulers from the competing elites. The one great merit of democracy is that it does not allow political leadership to wield absolute power. Leadership must draw up Policies to win over the electorate. The initiative remains in the hands of the leaders and the people have merely to decide which leader they want to represent them. Leaders trade in votes and better the policies they put forward,the more votes they win.

Raymond Aron has given his views on democracy in his book "Social Structure and the Ruling Class" (1950). According to him, liberal democracy is characterised by a general system of checks and balances and plurality of elites. The Soviet type of society has a unified elite belonging to the Communist Party. The Western type of society has a divided elite which makes it a pluralistic society. With the plurality of the elite, government becomes a business of compromise. Those in power are aware of their precarious position. However, the initiative still remains in the hands of the elite and the only role which the people can play is to choose the ruling elite and put pressure on them in their work.

Giovanni Sartori has given his views in his book "Democratic Theory". He regards democracy as a procedure in which leaders compete for authority to govern at the time of elections. The role of the elite does not suggest any imperfection of democracy. Any notion of self-governing people is a delusion. The people exercise their right to govern only at the time of elections. The real danger to democracy is not from leadership but from the absence of leadership. Leadership plays an important part in educating public opinion.

In his book "Ideology and Utopia: An Introduction to the Sociology of Knowledge", *Karl Mannheim* writes that society does not cease to be democratic by entrusting the actual shaping of policy to the elite. The people cannot participate directly in the government. They can express their views only at certain intervals at the time of elections and that is sufficient for democracy. To quote him, "In a democracy, the governed can always act to remove their leaders or force them to take decisions in the interests of the many". Mannheim insists that selection must be by merit and the distance between the elite and the people must be very little.

The elitist theory is more a theory of democratic machinery and less of democratic humanism. It is opposed to mass participation and hot politics on the ground that it leads to increase of cleavages and conflicts. It supports elections as a way of peaceful resolution of conflicts. The responsibility of maintaining the democratic system cannot be entrusted to the masses. It can only be entrusted to the competing elites. The elites are the angels who maintain the necessary democratic balance and equilibrium in society. The equilibrium can be achieved by small participation of the people and by reducing the ideological gap between parties. Political parties should not differ very much on fundamental issues and the people should not expect that the change of rule from one elite to another elite will make much difference. To quote Lipset, "A stable democracy must rest on the general belief that the outcome of an election will not make too great a difference in society". The political parties must represent all the strata of society. In order to be a good democracy, there must be a balance between involvement and indifference, stability and flexibility, progress and conservatism, consensus and cleavage and individualism and collectivism. In order to maintain equilibrium and stability, ideological differences should not be given too much importance. The elitist theory of democracy does not give importance to ideologies and puts all the emphasis on stability and equilibrium.

According to the elitist theory, the elite must have faith in democratic values and processes. They should represent all sections of society. They should be experienced and able. They should not remain aloof from the general masses. They must have the best possible accord with the masses and often exchange views with them. They must be plural and compete for the votes of the people. They must believe in the politics of consensus and not of confrontation. There must not be too great ideological differences between the elites. The elite must be an open one. People with higher ability must have full opportunity to enter the elite. The circulation of elites must be possible. The people should not interfere in the working of the elite.

Comparison of Elitist and Classical Theories of Democracy

There are certain differences between elitist and classical theories of democracy. The elitist theory is based on the realities of contemporary Western liberal democracies, particularly that of the United States. The classical theory is based on democratic ideals and values like rights, liberty, equality and development of human personality. The classical theory puts emphasis on basic equality among people. The elitist theory justifies inequality on the basis of ability, character, capability, experience and wealth. The classical theory holds the view that the people are capable of rational behaviour. The elitist view is that the people are ignorant and hence they should not be allowed to take part in the politics of the country because their participation is injurious to the stability and peace and order of the political system. The elitist theory regards democracy as a mechanism to maintain stability and equilibrium in society. According to the classical view, democracy is a moral system which aims at the all-round development of man. The (elitist view is that the so-called will of the people is a myth which is manufactured by the elites themselves. This view is not accepted by the classical theory which believes in and gives great importance to the will of the people and demands that the government must work in accordance with that will. The elitist view is that elections are held merely to elect the ruling elite. The classical view is that the will of the people expresses itself through elections which enable the establishment of a representative and responsible government. The elitist view is that the responsibility of the governing elite to the public is a myth because the elite who are experts cannot be responsible to the people who are ignorant. This view is opposed by the classical theory. It considers the responsibility of the governing elite to the public an important feature of democracy. The elitist theory does not believe in the concept of common good as the term is understood differently by different people. The classical view is that the government must be carried on with the object of serving the common good. The elitist theory does not believe in majority rule. It believes in the rule of an oligarchy which is a minority. The classical theory of democracy believes in majority rule. Whichever party secures a majority at the time of elections,is entitled to form the government. While the classical theory puts great emphasis on public opinion, the elitist theory ignores it on the ground that public opinion itself is moulded by the elite. The elitist theory gives importance to consensus among the people. The classical theory gives importance to the consent of the people. The elitist theory has faith in the capacity of the leaders to maintain democracy, but the classical theory has faith in the people and not in the leaders. The elitist theory is conservative because it justifies the existing social, economic and political system of liberal democracy.

Criticism of Elitist Theory

The elitist theory has been criticised by Duncan and Lukes, Bottomore, Goldschmidt, Walker, Bachrach Pateman, Plamenatz, Bay and Machpherson or various grounds. They point out that this theory has no faith in the people. It has faith only in the elite who discourage the participation of the people in politics. They consider political apathy as a virtue. They believe that the participation of the people will destroy the equilibrium and stability of the political system and enable the unscrupulous politicians to run the government for their own selfish end. This view is not accepted because the people are the soul of a democracy and they must be given a share to run the government. Democracy cannot be a rule over the "sleeping beauties". By denying the right to the people to participate in the running of the government, the elitist theory empties the democratic theory of its moral and developmental contents. The full development of the personalities of the people is the target of democracy. Democracy does not flow out of ballot boxes. It is based on the active developmental participation of the people. The advocates of the elitist theory deprive the workers and other exploited classes of their due share in public affairs. That is not proper.

The elitist theory is a conservative theory. It is based on conservative values. Instead of suggesting measures to improve the working of the existing system, the elite justify the existing defective system. The theory is based on certain conservative values like stability, equilibrium, harmony, consensus, coordination, changelessness, political apathy and support of the existing socio-economic system. However, these values are inferior to those of classical liberal democracy. The supporters of the elitist theory proceed on the assumption that the functioning of American democracy is perfect and democratic theory must be moulded accordingly. However, that is not true. This theory destroys the progressive nature of democratic theory.

The elitist theory puts too much emphasis on equilibrium in society. The issue of maintaining equilibrium in a conflict-ridden society is an important one, but the high ideals of democracy cannot be compromised for the sake of equilibrium. In order to maintain equilibrium, the causes of social conflict must be traced and remedies found for them. Too much emphasis is put on equilibrium which is not proper.

A democratic society is one in which there is a free play of opinions and the people freely participate in all the social activities. However, the elitist theory considers that to be dangerous for the stability of the democratic political system.

The elitist theory does not give due importance to ideologies. It is based on the institutional aspect of democracy. It believes in the theory of "end of ideology". That is not a correct view. The elitist theory regards man as the means and the democratic political system as the end. However, that is not correct. According to this theory, the object of democracy is not the upliftment and development of human beings. They are to be kept in ignorance. The classical theory justifies democracy on the ground that it is the most suitable for the all-round development of human personality. The elitist theory regards man as the means and the democratic system as the end and gives very little importance to the development of human beings.

The elitist theory gives too much importance to leaders. The theory does not .give importance to politics but gives importance to politicians. There is always the danger of the misuse of powers by the political elite.

The classical theory gives great importance to public opinion and the will of the people in a democratic set-up. However, the elitist theory considers public opinion as the basis of government to be meaningless. In reality, public opinion is manufactured by those who rule the country.

The elitist theory rejects the principle of social and political equality. It is based on the right of the elite to rule on the basis of their intelligence and ability. The elitist theory does not accept the view that the government is responsible to the people. Actually, in a democratic set-up, the government has to be responsible to the people.

The elitist theory strengthens the forces supporting the creation of a centralised bureaucratic power. It under-estimates the power of the electorate. It is an attempt by the privileged classes to rationalise the retention of economic and political power by them. Michels, iron law of oligarchy is also criticised on the ground that he confuses an iron law of bureaucracy with an iron law of oligarchy. He is not clear about the distinction between oligarchy and organisation. Moreover, Michels generalised what he found in the German Democratic Party. It is also pointed out that it is one thing to say that parties are not democratic and another thing to conclude that democracy is not democratic.

Conclusion

In spite of criticism, the elitist theory contains truth regarding the working of Western democracies. It cannot be denied that there is political apathy among the people. All democracies are controlled by elites of one type or another. Verney writes, "General and equal participation seems indeed almost like a temporary aberration". (The Analysis of Political Systems, p. 160). Inequality preached by the elitist theory is a universally accepted fact. Elite control has a history to support it. Even liberal democracies are in effect elite democracies. Modern governments require expertise in various spheres for effective functioning and that is provided by the elite minority. The role of elite may differ from country to country but it is there. Elite control in a liberal democracy and in a Communist state do not mean the same thing. To quote Verney, "Elite rule appears to be the more tolerable when elites are open and not closed, that is to say when there is comparative freedom of access to the elite for those who merit or demand it". In spite of its criticism, the concept of Michels holds good. Whether it is a law of bureaucracy or organisation, it has not been invalidated. What Was true of the German Social Democratic Party in 1914 was also true of all other European parties at that time. Hence, the generalisation of Michels was not off the mark. If political parties are not democratic, democracy also cannot be democratic. We may conclude by saying that the elitist theory is an interesting theory so long as it is understood as a description of contemporary liberal democracies, but it is a bad theory if we look at its justification of Western democracies. Its value lies in the fact that it exposes the undemocratic nature of contemporary Western democracies.

(3) PLURALIST THEORY OF DEMOCRACY

The pluralist theory of democracy has been expounded during the present century by American political scientists mainly to support the contention that the socialist political systems which have one political party and the centralisation of all political power, are undemocratic. The main object of this theory is to show that the Western liberal political systems, particularly that of the United States, are pluralist and therefore democratic. As the political systems of the Soviet Union and China are not pluralist, they are undemocratic. The pluralist theory of democracy emphasizes the role of multi-party system and pressure groups in a political system. Democracy maintains unity in diversity. The destruction of diversity for the sake of unity is undemocratic. H. Sherman writes, "The pluralists assert that the United States government is not a class dictatorship but a democracy reflecting many interest groups, that power is not held by one group but plurally by many groups" (Radical Political Economy).

The pluralists maintain that power in society is shared by many groups and it is not enjoyed by any elite. They stand tor the decentralisation of political power. Political power should be shared between the government and different interest groups which operate in a society. Democracy means the decentralisation of power or the plurality of the centres of decision. Centralised power is always unlimited. It is against the principle of democracy.

The main contention of pluralist democracy is that power should be shared by all the groups of society and all organised groups must have a share in policy-making. All important decisions in social, economic and political matters should be taken after due consultation with the groups whose interests are going to be affected by such decisions. Important problems of society should be faced by all the organisations. Each social organisation must have a share in the decision-making process and thereby decentralise the political structure. Presthus writes that pluralist democracy is "a socio-political system in which the power of the state is shared with a large number of private groups, interest organisations and individuals represented by such organisations. Pluralism is a system in which political power is fragmented among the branches of government; it is moreover shared between the state and a multitude of private groups and individuals". Whenever the state makes a policy, the groups interested in it must be consulted. In this way, better policies can be framed and power is decentralised. Any single political elite, even if elected by the people, must not enjoy all the political power. The pluralists do not agree that citizens are incapable of rational behaviour. "A belief of pluralism is that most citizens are wise enough to make judgements about public affairs and to help manage them. Pluralism has meant more than the control of public affairs by organisational leaders".

The pluralist theory of democracy does not accept the view that modern industrial societies are mass societies. People of every society form associations with like-minded people having a common interest to pursue. Every individual has a fundamental right to form an association and become a member of any association. The basis of the pluralist theory of democracy is not an alienated individual. Its bases are the various organisations, pressure groups, trade unions, political parties and other social and economic associations.

The exponents of the pluralist theory of democracy plead for limitations on the authority of the state. The powers of the state should be organised in such a way that one organ of the Government may be able to control another organ. The Pluralist theory of democracy is a vague concept. Different writers have supported this theory with different objectives during this century.

The view of *A.F. Bentley* is that democracy is a political game played by a great variety of groups. The government is the focal point for public pressure and its task is to make policies which reflect the highest common group demand. Democracy is a pluralist society where the management of public affairs is shared by a number of groups having different values, sources and methods of influence.

The policy-making process, however centralised it may appear in form, is in reality a highly decentralised process of bargaining among relatively autonomous groups. Public policy is not the result of the will of the elite or the chosen few. It is the outcome of the interaction of all groups who make claims upon or express interest in that particular issue.

According to this theory, the power of the state is shared between the government and the maximum number of leaders, groups and associations. To quote Geraint Parry, "Whereas the classical elitists see the social structure as analogous in shape to a single pyramid, the pluralist theory sees it as a range of pyramids". There are as many elites as there are activities and each one of them forms itself into an interest group.

Alien Potter has divided the interest groups into two main groups—spokesman groups and promotional groups. Spokesman groups represent and defend established sectional interests while promotional groups champion particular causes and organise people who share a particular attitude.

According to R.A. Dahl, democracy is a political method with electoral process as its centre. It is through the electoral process that leaders are chosen by the non-leaders. It is the small minority which takes all important decisions. The people at large do not exercise any power due to non-participation and apathy.

Berelson has indicated the following conditions which are necessary for the survival of democracy; intensity of the conflict must be limited. The rate of change must be restrained. The social and economic stability should be maintained. There should be a pluralist social organisation along with basic consensus on the values of the system. Berelson further says that heterogeneity is better for democracy than hemogencity. He favours limited participation and apathy at high levels of participation and interests are required for a minority of citizens only and the apathy and dis-interest of the majority play a valuable part in maintaining the stability of the system as a whole. The greatest danger to democracy comes from mediocrity and undemocratic counter-elites. Greater participation leads to totalitarianism. The best situation is when people only react to the initiative and policies of the competing elites.

The pluralist theory of democracy is based on sociological investigation and presents the truth about present day political life. Elections are an important part of the system. It is through elections that decision-makers are elected and with this the participation should normally end. Equality is equality to vote at the time of elections. Excessive participation is dangerous to political stability. There are as many elites as there are human activities. Different sets of persons are involved in each particular area of policy-making. Elite leaders are generally specialists in "one issue" area. A consensus with regard to the values of a political system is important for its survival.

The pluralist theory of democracy is a mixture of the theories of classical democracy and elitist democracy. This theory does not agree that through popular participation, people can develop their personality. However, it emphasizes the need for participation by the people through their organisations only for better policies, democratic loyalty and obedience.

(4) MARXIST THEORY OF DEMOCRACY

Each class has a social philosophy of its own which is the basis of its social, economic, cultural, moral and political values. Liberalism is the philosophy of the capitalist class and liberal democracy serves the interests of that class. In the same way, Marxism is the philosophy of the proletariat and the dictatorship of the proletariat is the democratic political system of the working class. The Marxist philosophy was a reaction against the liberal philosophy and its political system in the nineteenth century. The liberal theory of democracy was established against the special privileges of feudalism, the Pope and monarchy. In the same way, the Marxian theory of democracy is against the special privileges of the capitalist class and its social, economic and political systems. Marxism does not regard democracy merely as a political system. It is accepted more as a process. According to H. Lefebyre, Marx considered democracy "not as a system but as a process which comes down essentially to a struggle for democracy. The latter is never completed because democracy can always be carried forward or forced back. The purpose of struggle is to go beyond democracy and beyond the democratic state, to build a society without state power". (The Sociology of Marx, p. 138). In order to understand the Marxist theory of democracy, we have to discuss the criticism of bourgeois democracy by the Marxists, the dictatorship of the proletariat and the Communist society as envisaged by the Marxists.

Marxist Criticism of Bourgeois Democracy

The Marxists condemn bourgeois democracy in very strong terms. According to them. Western liberal democracies are sham democracies or bourgeois democracies. They are the dictatorships of the bourgeoisie over the working class. Political power is in the hands of the capitalist class and hence liberal democracy serves the interests of the capitalist class. The interests of the working class are completely ignored and they are exploited. According to Lenin, in capitalist society, democracy is always hemmed in by the narrow limits set by capitalist exploitation and consequently always remains a democracy only for the propertied classes and the workers are crushed by want and poverty. The majority of the population is debarred from participation in public and political life. Capitalist democracy is democracy only for the rich who form an insignificant minority. It is a democracy of capitalist society. The essence of capitalist democracy is that "the oppressed are allowed once every few years to decide which particular representatives of the oppressing class shall represent and repress them in Parliament." Capitalist democracies are confined to the political sphere only and the working class has a very limited role to play which is confined merely to voting at the time of elections held after certain intervals.

The basis of bourgeois democracy is the capitalist economic system in which the means of production are owned by the capitalist class. The society is divided into two classes, the capitalists and the workers, the exploiters and the exploited. The capitalist system is based on profit motive in which the workers are exploited and oppressed. They have to sell themselves to avoid starvation.

The important features of bourgeois democracy are elections, multi-party system, liberty and rights, independent judiciary and the constitution. On a critical examination, it can be said that they are merely shams so far as the working class is concerned. The workers have a right to vote but they have no option but to vote for one bourgeois party out of the two or many different bourgeois parties. They have no real choice. Money plays a very important part in elections and the working class which consists of poor people cannot capture political power through elections. Political parties win by taking currency notes from the rich and collecting votes from the poor. After winning elections, the policies of the government serve the interests of the rich and the poor are appeased merely with slogans and speeches, The Marxists also point out that elections are held only for members of Parliament while real power vests in army, bureaucracy, police and courts which are not elected by the people. To quote Lenin, "Parliament is given up to talk for special purpose of fooling the common people."

It is true that there are many political parties in a liberal democracy but there is no fundamental difference between them. The two political parties in a democracy are compared to two bottles of the same wine with different labels. The result is that the existence of many political parties does not help the-working class. They all represent the interests of the capitalist class.

It is true that in a liberal democracy there exists the liberty of thought, expression, belief, faith and worship, of forming associations, engaging in any trade or profession and having property etc. But in actual practice, the workers are not able to take advantage of them. Moreover, the press, radio, TV and cinema are controlled by property-owners. The talk of rights and equality in a society divided into owners and non-owners is hollow.

It is true that in a liberal democracy, there is provision for an independent judiciary, but the Marxists contend that the judicial system is a part of the whole political system which has a class character of its own. The judiciary is there to maintain the political system and safeguard the constitution from internal and external attacks. In actual practice, the workers who are poor cannot expect to get justice as they have neither the time nor the money to engage lawyers to fight their cases in the courts. The workers consider it cheaper to suffer injustice than to try to get justice from the courts which demand a lot of expenditure.

It is true that liberal democracies have their constitution. Although they are framed in the name of the people, they have a class character. Their object is to provide a political system which serves the interests of the capitalist class. There are special provisions to protect the political system at the time of crisis.

It is true that the Marxists condemn the bourgeois democracies for their shortcomings, but they also maintain that bourgeois democracies can be used by the working class to organise themselves and to increase the level of their political consciousness. Democratic institutions can be used by the working class to strengthen themselves and to further the cause of the socialist revolution. The working class can weaken the capitalist system by properly using those institutions. Marx and Engels did not dismiss democratic political institutions as useless. To quote Robert Tucker, "Rather they saw in them a school of political training for the working class in bourgeois society, a stimulus to the growth of revolutionary class-consciousness in the proletariat." (The Marxian Revolutionary Idea, p. 68). Lenin wrote in *State and Revolution*, "Democracy is of great importance for the working class and its struggle for freedom against the capitalists. But democracy is by no means a limit one may not overstep; it is only one of the stages in the course of development from feudalism to capitalism and from capitalism to Communism".

The Marxists prefer bourgeois democracy to the open, naked Fascist regimes of the bourgeoisie. They also recognise the progressive role played by liberal democracies against feudalism and monarchies. It is admitted that liberal democracies provide the best conditions for the working class parties to strengthen themselves and they can make use of the bourgeois political institutions for furthering the cause of socialist revolution. However, their objection is that bourgeois democracies provide only political democracy and deny social and economic democracy.

John Plamenatz has enumerated four outstanding reasons advanced by the Marxists for calling bourgeois democracy a sham. (1) Where there are great inequalities of wealth, then whatever the form of government, power and influence always belong mostly to the wealthy because they alone can afford to provide their children with the expensive schooling needed to fit them for positions carrying power and influence. (2) Where the political system, to work effectively, calls for large organisations, power and influence belong to their leaders rather than to the rank and file. (3) Where there are great social inequalities, leaders, no matter how modest their social origins, soon acquire the attitudes and ambitions of the privileged and lose touch with their followers. (4) Power and influence depend greatly on information and the wealthy are better placed than the poor both to get information and to control the distribution of it.

"According to the Marxists, the state and other political institutions represent the super-structure of society raised on its system of material production which constitutes their base. As the capitalist system of production is designed to serve the economic interests of the bourgeoisie, its political super-structure cannot be made to serve the interests of the common people. Society is divided into the "haves" and "have-nots," the "dominant" and "dependent" classes and the bourgeoisie and the proletariat. Their interests are diametrically opposed to each other. Political power is only hand-maid of economic power. Political institutions of a capitalist society are bound to serve the interests of the bourgeoisie and not of the worker. Liberal democracy represents the political institutions of the capitalist economic system. It pays lip-service to the sovereignty of the people to make itself legitimate. John M. Maguire points out that such a state is in fact "maintaining and servicing the bourgeois social order and is thus really serving the bourgeoisie; but since everyone regards such order as natural and proper, and thus accepts their place within it, everyone can see the state, in working this way, as "representing" them, that is acting on their behalf" (Marx's Theory of Politics, pp. 19-20).

Liberal democracy creates ideological misconceptions by setting up representative institutions which pretend to work for all but actually work only for the dominant class which means the bourgeoisie. Despite formal equality of political rights, anti-capitalist programmes reach the electorate only in the distorted versions through the bourgeois press. The poorly educated masses are susceptible to capitalist propaganda. Liberal democracy, is a formal facade obscuring domination by an economic class. Legal forms of elections, freedoms of speech, publication and association are not enough in themselves to warrant calling a state a democracy. The idea behind these forms is frustrated by the economic power and the state is a disguised oligarchy.

Liberal democracy does not provide an effective mechanism for transforming the economic relations of society to serve the common interest. As a matter of fact, it perpetuates the economic division of society into haves and have-nots and the values of bourgeois society which support and legitimize that division. Lenin writes, "Democracy for an insignificant minority, democracy for the rich—that is the democracy of capitalist society. Marx grasped this essence of capitalist splendidly when he said that the oppressed are allowed every few years to decide which particular representatives of the oppressing classes shall represent and repress them in Parliament."

Dictatorship of the Proletariat

The working class democracy is known as socialist democracy or the dictatorship of the proletariat. It means a political system in which the proletariat is organised as a ruling class. It is the naked rule of the working class over the property owners. It is the dictatorship of the working class over the capitalist class. It is directed against the exploiters for their oppression of the peoples and nations and is aimed at abolishing all exploitation of man by man. It expresses the interests of the working class and the working people. It aims at building up a new socialist society. It is a new kind of democracy whose basis is the working class which is the majority class. To quote Lenin, "The revolutionary dictatorship of the proletariat is rule by one and maintained by the use of violence by the proletariat against the bourgeoisie, rule that is unrestricted by any law."

The dictatorship of the proletariat can be established only through a socialist revolution under the leadership of organised working class party. For its establishment, the machinery of the bourgeois state must be destroyed and a new state machinery of the working class has to be set up. The proletarian revolution is not possible without the forcible destruction of the bourgeois state machine and its substitution by the state of the working people. This cannot be done without a violent revolution. Dictatorship of the proletariat can arise only as a result of the smashing of the bourgeois state machine, the bourgeois bureaucratic apparatus and the bourgeois police. It is the state of a new class. The capitalist class state is replaced by a working class state. As the bourgeois state machine was designed to serve the interests of the capitalist class, it could not serve the interests of the working class.

Dictatorship of the proletariat is a democracy of and for the working class. It is a dictatorship over the property-owning class. Its object is to finish exploitation for ever by finishing the class division of society and establishing social ownership of the means of production. The power of the state is used to build up a socialist production system. The dictatorship of the proletariat is the most determined and ruthless war waged by the working class against the bourgeoisie whose resistance is increased on account of its overthrow. Dictatorship of the proletariat is a stubborn struggle against the forces and traditions of capitalist society. It is a bloody, military and economic struggle. It aims at unity in society not by mutual cooperation and harmony of different classes but by the abolition of classes. The dictatorship of the proletariat is not pure democracy. It is a working class democracy. In comparison to bourgeois democracy, it is more democratic as it is the democracy of the working class which is always in majority. To quote Lenin, "Proletarian democracy is a million times more democratic than any bourgeois democracy; Soviet power is a million times more democratic than the most democratic bourgeois republic."

The dictatorship of the proletariat is not to last for ever. It is required only for the transitional period during which the change is to take place from capitalism to communism. Once a classless communist society is established, the state will become redundant and it will "wither away."

The main objectives of the dictatorship of the proletariat are to abolish private property, to destroy remnants of bourgeois culture and ideology, to crush the resistance of the overthrown exploiting classes, to abolish classes and to create necessary conditions for the establishment of a Communist society. Its object is to build a socialist economy through social ownership of the means of production.

The functioning of socialist democracy is different from liberal democracy. The workers are given the maximum share in the social, economic and cultural spheres. The people are encouraged to take part not only in political affairs but also in all the spheres of social life. Through the process of education, the working class is made sufficiently capable of participating in the social affairs. The function of the state and economic management are simplified so that the workers can take part in them.

The dictatorship of the proletariat is different from the popular notion of dictatorship which is considered as the selfish, immoral, irresponsible and unconstitutional political rule of one man or small political clique characterised by the oppression of the masses. The dictatorship of the proletariat implies a stage where there is complete socialisation of the major means of production, *de novo* planning of material production to serve social needs and to provide for an effective right to work, education, health and housing for the masses and the development of science and technology to multiply material production to achieve greater social satisfaction.

The dictatorship of the proletariat is only for the transitional period during which the working class must destroy the machinery of the existing bourgeois state and set-up its own machinery. The state will wither away when a truly rational organisation of production becomes possible. To quote Marx, "As soon as the goal of the proletarian movement, the abolition of classes, shall have been reached, the bower of the state whose function is to keep the great majority of producers beneath the yoke of a small minority of exploiters, will be transformed into simple administrative functions."

The dictatorship of the proletariat is a dictatorship of a special kind. While bourgeois democracy is a dictatorship of the bourgeois minority against the proletarian majority, the dictatorship of the proletariat is a socialist democracy of the proletarian majority against the bourgeois minority. It is a dictatorship only in the sense of the domination of minority by the majority. This dictatorship is democratic. S.H. Change writes, "There is no contradiction between proletarian dictatorship and proletarian democracy. It is with reference to the bourgeoisie that the proletarian state is a proletarian dictatorship and it is with reference to the proletariat that the proletarian state is a proletarian democracy." (The Marxian Theory of the State, p. 105). Under the dictatorship of the proletariat, the state starts withering away as there are no classes to be suppressed. The process of withering away is completed as we reach the stage of complete communism. In the view of Lenin, democracy becomes superfluous when under communism, the state has completely disappeared. Sartori writes, "In the context of bourgeois democracy, democracy does not exist by definition; in the context of the dictatorship of the proletariat, there is more democracy than before (which is not a large concession, since before there was none at all), but all the same real democracy still cannot exist; and in the context of communism, democracy should not exist because it is superfluous." (Democratic Theory, p. 424).

Difference between Socialist and Bourgeois Democracy

There are certain differences between socialist and bourgeois democracies. The socialist democracies emerged through socialist revolutions under the leadership of the working class.

Bourgeois democracies emerged through the revolutionary struggle of the bourgeoisie against the Papacy, feudalism and monarchy. The economic basis of socialist democracies is the socialist mode of production which is passed on social ownership of the means of production. In bourgeois democracy, there is private ownership of the means of production. Socialist democracy is the rule of the majority over the minority because the working class is always in majority and the rich are always in minority. In a bourgeois democracy, the rich who are in a minority rule over, the working class who are in a majority. Socialist democracy stands for the abolition of exploitation for ever by abolishing private property and classes from society, but bourgeois democracies continue with that exploitation. Socialist democracies want unity in society by abolishing the classes. Bourgeois democracy is not opposed to the existence of different classes. It believes in the coordination of the different interests of the different classes. In a socialist democracy, the right to personal property is recognised but not the right to private property. In a bourgeois democracy, the right to private property is considered sacred. In a socialist democracy, the working class is given a share in social, economic, political and administrative affairs, but in a bourgeois democracy, popular participation is confined to periodic elections only. In a socialist democracy, there is only one political party of the working class. The contention is that as there is only one class, there can be only one party to represent that class. In a bourgeois democracy, there can be many political parties. In a socialist democracy, the right to work, education, leisure, health and old age security are guaranteed. However, that is not the case in a bourgeois democracy. In a socialist democracy, the development of bureaucracy is restricted but in a bourgeois democracy, bureaucracy goes on increasing day by day and a new despotism is emerging now. A socialist democracy follows the principle of democratic centralism, but bourgeois democracy is based on the principle of bureaucratic centralism.

Socialist democracy is a transitional state. It will wither away as soon as a classless society is established. Bourgeois democracy is not transitional. Socialist democracies have faith in proletarian internationalism. Their slogan is: "Workers of the world, unite." They strongly oppose colonialism and imperialism. However, bourgeois democracies are nationalist in nature and generally imperialistic tendencies develop there. Socialist democracies have faith in social, economic, cultural and political equalities. Bourgeois democracies allow inequalities on the basis of private property.

Difference between Marxist Theory and Elitist Theory

The Elitist theory of democracy shares some of its tenets with the Marxian theory of democracy. In some respects it differs from it. Both the Marxists and Elitists agree that so long as society is divided into classes, real political equality cannot be secured merely through a democratic form of government. However, they differ regarding the nature of the social division and the scope of social change etc.

The Marxian view is that so long as the institution of state exists, society remains divided into two economic classes and the economically dominant class is invariably the ruling class. The political and legal super-structure is always raised on the economic sub-structure. The class having economic power also has political power concurrently. The Elitist view is that society is broadly divided into the elite and the masses on account of natural differences in the capability and aptitudes of different individuals. The elites manage to secure and maintain political power on account of their qualities and cleverness.

The Marxist view is that the ruling class is a cohesive group which maintains its stronghold on political power. The elitist view is that there are many elites and a competition among them results in the circulation of elites. The Marxist view is that the masses take an active part in the revolution. The elitists assign a passive role to the masses.

The Marxist view is that the society is divided into dominant and dependent classes and their interests are mutually antagonistic. That results in class conflict. The goal is the establishment of a classless society. The elitist view is that the division of society into the rulers and the ruled is instinctive and voluntary. There is no fundamental conflict of interests. Both the elites and the masses compensate each other to evolve a social organisation.

The Marxist view is that the division of society into dominant and dependent classes is not according to reason. There is oppression and exploitation of the masses. That results in injustice. There can be justice only if the divisions in society are removed. The elitist view is that no injustice is involved in the division of society. The division is natural, rational and functional.

The Marxist view is that political domination is based on economic domination. As the economic structure of society is alterable, political domination is also alterable. The elitist view is that the domination of the elite is inherent in social organisation and is not alterable. The scope of social change is limited to the circulation of elites by which one elite is replaced by a new energetic elite.

The Marxist view is that true democracy cannot be achieved so long as society remains divided into dominant and subordinate classes on account of the division of society into haves and have-nots. Periodical elections based on universal suffrage are an eyewash as they cannot bring about an effective change in social relations until the mode of production is fundamentally changed. The Elitist view is that democracy can be realised in a liberal society if there is an open elite system and the ordinary people are given an opportunity to choose the ruling elites at regular intervals.

Criticism of Marxist Theory of Democracy

The Marxian theory of democracy has been criticised by many writers. It is contended that the dictatorship of the proletariat is a dictatorship, pure and simple. Western democracies are true democracies because they are based on pluralism and limited constitutional government. Sartori considers the dictatorship of the proletariat as "phantom alternative." The view of Karl Popper is that the Marxist theory of democracy gives birth to a closed society in which there is neither freedom nor democracy. The dictatorship of the proletariat is the dictatorship of one particular class. Even the dictatorship of the majority cannot be called democracy. Democracy needs a plurality of political parties but in socialist countries only one party is allowed. That leads to totalitarianism. The opponents are deprived of their right to oppose the rulers. If the opposition has no freedom to criticise the government, that is no democracy. Socialist democracy aims at destroying the other classes, but it cannot be done in a democracy. Democracy aims at unity in diversity and diversity in unity. Political liberties are essential for a healthy democracy but those are not there in a Marxist system. Decentralisation of power is essential for democracy, but there is too much of centralisation in a Communist system. An independent and impartial judiciary is necessary for the success of democracy, but that is missing in a socialist society. The use of the term Dictatorship of the proletariat is not correct. In fact, it is the dictatorship over the proletariat. In a Marxist system, the economic and political powers are concentrated in the hands of the government but democracy and freedom require their separation. In a socialist democracy, elections are not real because the people have no choice. There are no political parties with their manifestos. The people have merely to choose only between the different candidates of one party. In a democracy, there can be a conflict of different views and ideologies but in a socialist democracy, only one ideology is recognised and the other views are suppressed. Bureaucracy is increasing in socialist democracies and it is highly irresponsible and authoritative. Democracy requires a limited government but in a socialist democracy, the powers of the government are unlimited.

The view of the revisionists is that for the establishment of socialism in Western democracies, neither revolution not dictatorship of the proletariat is necessary. They believe that the conditions of working class will improve through strikes, economic struggles, elections and participation in the bourgeois parliamentary system. A socialist revolution is not necessary as change can easily be made through peaceful and constitutional methods. Socialism can be established by cooperating with political parties, by pressurising the state and through struggles wherever those are essential.

The welfare democratic state can play an important part in bringing about socialism. The democratic state can control capitalism and transform in into socialism through peaceful means. The revisionists believe that change can be brought about without uprooting the existing socio-economic and political system. The welfare state can regulate capital, control the economic system and production and distribution system and nationalise the basic industries in the interests of the whole community.

The view of the anarchists is that the dictatorship of the proletariat is not required during the transition period from capitalism to socialism. They oppose the centralisation of authority and support liberty, equality, fraternity and justice. The anarchists do not accept the class basis of the state and want to abolish the state without the abolition of classes.

Critics maintain socialism can be brought about without revolution, through peaceful means and by using bourgeois democratic institutions. The working class can form a united front with other democratic forces of the society. Peace, progress and socialism can be established through the medium of liberal democracy.

Benn and Peters point out that the Marxists equate the dictatorship of the proletariat with democracy because they exclude any but the workers from 'the people'. But that is not what is meant by the people. A system is undemocratic if it denies people the right to vote because they are rich in the same way if it denies them the right to vote because they are poor. The cause of democracy is served if people of all sections are given equal weightage as regards their share in government. But the Marxists believe in the dictatorship of the proletariat in which the rights are only with the working class and not with others.

The Marxists insist that a government must always be committed to one particular set of interests so long as economic conflicts remain. However, the dictatorship of the proletariat ushers in a society without conflicts and in such a society sensitivity to competing claims would be meaningless.

Critics maintain that the dictatorship of the proletariat holds no promise of a classless society. The Marxist view was that the root cause of conflict was the capitalist system of production and when that was overthrown and replaced by a socialist system of production, a classless society was to come into existence. Although proletarian revolutions took place in Russia in 1917 and in China in 1949, no classless society has been established. In those countries, there is competition for power, sharp political rivalries and the suppression of those who sincerely believe themselves to be true Marxists. The dictatorship of the proletariat was intended to be a temporary phase but in actual practice, it has perpetuated itself and there are no signs of its disappearance. Prof. R.M. MacIver writes, "The doctrine of the temporary dictatorship is contradicted by the intensive centralization of economic and cultural activities, and the 'stateless' society is relegated to the Greek Kalends. The doctrine of the people's rule is flatly rejected by the rigorous insistence on the party line... There is an impressive framework of electoral systems stretching all the way from the local Soviets to the Supreme Soviet of the U.S.S.R. There are everywhere People's Courts and People's Commissars. But the voting at elections is practically unanimous, and the one party retains complete control. The doctrine of the abolition of class has been negated by the occupational gradings, but far more thoroughly by the pyramid of power, which rises as steeply as, and perhaps more rigidly than, it did under the Czarist regime." (Web of Government, p. 194).

Critics point out that the Communists do not argue logically. They make use of jargon which can confuse the electorate. Their opponents are reactionaries, imperialists, colonialists, anti-democratists, monopolists, rightists, C.I.A. agents, class enemies, anti-people, anti-working class and peasants. Any move or measure not liked by them is anti-people. Once power is seized, democratically or otherwise, the media becomes an instrument of party propaganda. The Opposition dies or the machinery of the state is used to exterminate the enemies of the socialist state.

The proletarian revolution is not brought about by the majority. It is a dictatorship of the revolutionary people and not of the whole people. It is after the proletarian revolution that the majority is won over. If that is so, there is no guarantee that the majority is not won over by force or coercion. Any person opposing the revolution becomes a class enemy and is exterminated.

Marx and Lenin wanted the proletariat as the dictator but in reality we have in the Communist countries state dictatorship or party dictatorship. Even worse than that, it is a dictatorship over the proletariat.

The doctrine of class struggle leads to the survival of only one class. There is no compromise. That approach is hardly democratic.

The liberals fight elections and also lose them, but the Communists believe in crushing the opposition on the ground that it works against the interests of the people. The election won by the Communist Party is ordinarily the last open and free election because at the next election, either the system of holding election or the opposition would not be there.

In a liberal democracy, elections offer a choice of candidates but that is not so in a Communist state as there is only one party which puts up candidates for election.

In a liberal democracy, there is a change of government without violence. However, that is not so under the dictatorship of.the proletariat.

According to K.R. Popper, "Democracy cannot be fully characterised as the rule of the majority, although the institution of general elections is most important. For majority might rule in a tyrannical way. In a democracy, the powers of the rulers must be limited; and the criterion of a democracy is this: In a democracy, rulers can be dismissed by the ruled without bloodshed. Thus if the men in power do not safeguard those institutions which secure to the minority the possibility of peaceful change, then their rule is tyranny." (The Open Society and Its Enemies, Vol. II, p. 160).

The Marxist theory had anticipated the collapse of the capitalist system on account of its inner contradictions. However, that has not happened in actual practice. Communist states have been set up only in Russia and China. Liberal democracies have been able to face the Communist challenge.

It has rightly been said that democracy as an ideal can be achieved neither only through political institutions, nor only through a transformation of the mode of production. It has to be achieved in all the spheres. In the cultural sphere, it has to be achieved through the inculcation of new values of human equality. In the economic sphere, it has to be achieved through the socialist mode of material production. In the political sphere, it has to be achieved through constitutional structures.

DEMOCRACY IN INDIA

The Constitution of India which came into force on 26 January 1950 provides for a Sovereign, Democratic, Secular and Socialist Republic, The Constitution provides for a democratic form of government with parliamentary institutions.

Although a lot has been borrowed from the British Constitution, there are certain differences between the Constitutions of India and Britain. Britain has more experience in democracy than India which has become a democracy only recently. In England, the widening of the franchise was done in many stages and each concession/extension was the result of agitation. Although the people of India are mostly poor, the new Constitution of India provides for adult franchise. There is a vast difference between the people of India and those of Britain from the political and constitutional point of view. India has just started an experiment in democracy. The democratic traditions and institutions of England are very old. The standard of living in Britain is high, but it is still very low in India. The poverty of India is the mother of several evils which are obstacles in the way of the working of democracy. In Britain, there is almost cent percent literacy, but that is not so in India. The democratic experiment in India is going on for about forty years and it has worked satisfactorily. There are many reasons for that.

The Indians have more experience in the political and constitutional field than the people in most of the other under-developed countries. India has been fortunate in having eminent leaders whose keen intellect, commonsense, sobriety, patience and tolerance could stand the test of the most trying years. India had the advantage of the wisdom and experience of dynamic leaders like Mahatma Gandhi, Pandit Jawaharlal Nehru, Sardar Vallabhbhai Patel, C. Rajagopalachari, Dr. Rajendra Prasad and many others. N. Weiner writes, "India, however, has been fortunate in that its nationalist leaders have served throughout the Constitution-making, the initial task of state integration, the first and perhaps most crucial phase of national economic planning and more recently a period in which regional agitation has increased. When Pandit Jawaharlal Nehru died in 1964, he was succeeded by Lal Bahadur Shastri who proved himself to be competent for the job. When Lal Bahadur Shastri died in January 1966, there was a peaceful change of government and Mrs. Indira Gandhi became the Prime Minister of India. Her election was set aside by Mr. Justice J.M.L. Sinha of the Allahabad High Court but she continued to be Prime Minister after imposing internal emergency. She was defeated in March 1977 when fresh elections were held. The Janata Party ruled from 1977 to 1979 and Morarji Desai was the Prime Minister. He was followed by Chaudhri Charan Singh as Prime Minister. Mrs. Indira Gandhi became Prime Minister once again in January 1980 after winning the general elections. She was still Prime Minister when she was assassinated on 31 October 1984. She was succeeded by Rajiv Gandhi as Prime Minister. The changes in government have taken place smoothly.

It is worthy of notice that the people of India have cooperated with their leaders and have shown tolerance and patience. When India was attacked by China in 1962 and by Pakistan in 1965 and 1971, the people of India rallied around the banner of their country.

Many advanced countries have been friendly with India and they took genuine interest in the success of the democratic institutions in India. The United States was very generous to India and she extended her helping hand whenever India needed it. At present, the Soviet Union is helping India.

By and large, the people of India have shown a democratic spirit. There have been many general elections and the people have shown keen interest in the affairs of the government.

However, there are many obstacles in the way of working of democracy in India. One great obstacle is widespread illiteracy in the country. Education is the foundation of democracy and illiteracy is a great hurdle. It is the duty of the government to take all possible steps to spread literacy in the country. The people of India are also backward. That does not allow them to achieve political maturity. The poverty of the people is also a great hurdle. It is rightly said that some sort of prosperity of the people is essential for the successful working of democracy, but that is lacking in India. The people who are living from hand to mouth cannot spare time and energy to take part in the politics of the country. The people of India suffer from linguistic, regional, caste, communal and religious prejudices and hence they are incapable of understanding and appreciating democratic principles, ideals and values. A person with strong caste prejudice cannot understand the value of liberty and equality and he cannot be democratic-minded. Even after the lapse of about forty years when India became independent, casteism, linguism and regionalism have not been diluted. To many people, the caste comes first and the country afterwards. To many people the regional language is more important than the national language. Narrow-mindedness and parochial prejudices are doing havoc to national solidarity. Another defect in Indian democracy is that more emphasis has been put on personalities and less on principles and the political parties. At different times, the personalities of Jawaharlal Nehru, Indira Gandhi and Rajiv Gandhi have been put forward and the Indian National Congress has been thrown into the background. That is not correct. In order to strengthen democratic forces, it is necessary that more emphasis should be put on political parties and principles and not on individuals.

Another difficulty in India has been the absence of a strong Opposition party both in Parliament and the State Assemblies. There have been too many political parties in the country. For various reasons, the Indian National Congress is the only party which has commanded a majority both at the Centre and in the States. The other parties are very small. Whenever a non-Congress ministry has been formed, it is a coalition ministry which has not lasted very long in many cases. The constituent units quarrel and hence the ministry falls. So long as there are too many political parties, it is difficult to have a strong Opposition.

There is widespread bribery and corruption in the country. That also stands in the way of the successful working of democracy.

On the whole, the press in India has played an important part. It has not hesitated to criticise the government, whenever an occasion has arisen. However, many newspapers are in the hands of industrial barons and hence their independence is likely to be affected.

Linguistic animosities in India are also disturbing the working of democratic institutions in the country. Although the regional languages have been given all encouragement, there exists a strong sentiment in the South against the so-called imposition of Hindi on them. Language is acting as a divisive force in Indian politics.

Contrary to the expectations of the founding fathers of the Indian Constitution, the federal pattern in India has encouraged regionalism in the country. In order to please the people of their respective regions, the leaders of the states are acting against the democratic spirit of the Constitution.

Communalism is another enemy of democracy in India. Communalism resulted in the partition of India. Although the Constitution does not provide for communal electorates, fundamentalism is growing in this country and leaders belonging to different religions are appealing to their co-religionists to vote for them. Everything is being looked from the communal point of view. This may prove suicidal in the long run.

It is rightly said that the narrow loyalties will not allow the people of India to think and act in the interests of the nation as a whole.

Pakistan

In 1947, democratic institutions were set up both in India and Pakistan. However, the working of democracy has been interrupted in Pakistan from time to time. For ten years from 1958 to 1969, Pakistan was under the military dictatorship of Field Marshal Ayub Khan who claimed that Pakistan also had democracy, but it was of a special type known as Controlled Democracy. The hand of President Ayub Khan could be seen in everything. Yahya Khan was also an army chief and it could not be expected that he would restore democracy. In December 1971, Yahya Khan had to resign and he was succeeded by Bhutto. In 1978, Zia-ul-Haq removed Bhutto from power by a coup and his dictatorship is going on in Pakistan. A measure of democracy has now been introduced in Pakistan.

Indonesia

If Pakistan had Controlled Democracy, Indonesia had *Guided Democracy*, Sukarno was the first President of Indonesia. There was a lot of instability in the country and guided democracy was introduced to solve its problems. Although the name was democracy, the real power was in the hands of President Sukarno. He was not responsible to the Parliament or people. President Sukarno wielded dictatorial power in the name of guided democracy. The cabinet and parliament were weak and important discussions took place not in the cabinet or parliament but at the conferences of military officers and the National Council. The political set-up was such that political parties were of little significance.

Critics point out that the guided democracy of Sukarno was a farce. Naked dictatorship was given the name of guided democracy. The instability of the politics of Indonesia and the frequent changes in the government necessitated the abandonment of democracy as understood in Western countries. Under the charismatic leadership of Sukarno, his word was law and parliamentary institutions were treated with scant respect. Sukarno could introduce new institutions and .modify or abolish the existing institutions as he liked. Under guided democracy, the political parties in Indonesia were at the mercy of the government. They could not function freely as their activities were subject to several restrictions and army control. There were no civil liberties and freedom of the press. In March 1966 Sukarno surrendered authority to Army Commander Suharto who even now is the President of Indonesia. The Times of India wrote on 23 June 1970 about guided democracy on the occasion of the death of Sukarno: "Despite his charisma, he could neither organise a mass party with a pragmatic programme nor build a democratic political structure. The so-called guided democracy which he evolved was no more than a cover for erratic personal rule."

SUGGESTED READINGS

Agger, R.E. and Others : The Rulers and the Ruled, New York, 1964.

Appleby, P.H. : Big Democracy, New York, 1945.

Apthekar, H. : Marxism and Democracy, New York, 1965.

Aron, Raymond : Social Structure and the Ruling Class, 1950.

Babbit, Irving : Democracy and Leadership, 1924.

Ball, Alan : Modern Politics and Government.

Benn, S.I. and Peters, R.S. : Social Principles and Democratic State.

Bentley, A.F. : The Process of Government.

Burns, C.D. : Democracy.

Burns, E.M. : Ideas in Conflict.

Chang, S.H. : The Marxian Theory of the State.

Chapman, J.W. (Ed.) : Participation in Politics, New York, 1973.

Cohen, R.S. : Marxism and Democracy, New York, 1965.

Dahl, R.A. : Preface to Democratic Theory.

Dahl, R.A. : Who Governs? Democracy and Power in American City, New Haven, 1961.

Dahl, Robert : Modern Political Analysis.

Dewey, John : German Philosophy of Politics.

Dewey, John : Liberalism and Social Action, 1935.

Durkheim, E. : Division of Labour, Glencoe, 1947.

Eulau and others (Ed.) : Political Behaviour: A Reader in Theory and Research, Glencoe, 1956.

Fischer, Ernst : Marx in his Own Words.

Friedrich, C.J. : The New Image of the Common Man, Boston, 1950.

Hallowell, J.H. : Main Currents in Political Thought.

Hallowell, J.H. : The Moral Foundation of Democracy, University of Chicago Press, 1954.

Hunt, R.N. : The Political Ideas of Marx and Engels.

Hunt, R.N. : Marxism and Totalitarian Democracy.

Kariel, H.S. (Ed.) : Frontiers of Democratic Theory, New York, 1970.

Latham, B. : The Group Basis of Politics, New York, 1952.

Lefebvre, H. : The Sociology of Marx, Penguin, 1968.

Lenin, V.I. : The State and Revolution, 1917.

Lindsay, A.D. : The Modern Democratic State, 1951.

Lindsay, A.D. : I Believe in Democracy.

Lipset, S.M. : Political Man, London, 1959.

Lucas, J.R. : Democracy and Participation, Penguin, 1976.

MacIver, R.M. : Web of Government.

Macpherson, C.B. : The Life and Times of Liberal Democracy, Oxford, 1977.

Macpherson, C.B. : Democratic Theory: Essays in Retrieval, Oxford, 1973.

Maguire, John M. : Marx's Theory of Politics.

Mannheim, Karl : Essays on the Sociology of Culture, London, 1956.

Mannheim, Karl : Ideology and Utopia: An Introduction to the Sociology of Knowledge.

Marx and Engels : The Communist Manifesto.

Maxey, C.C. : Political Philosophies.

Mayo, H.B. : An Introduction to Democratic Theory, New York, 1970.

Medvedev, R.A. : On Socialist Democracy, London, 1975.

Meisel, J.H. : The Myth of the Ruling Class: Gaetano Mosca and the Elite, 1958.

Merkl, Peter H. : Political Continuity and Change.

Michels, R. : Political Parties, London, 1915.

Micklem, N. : The Idea of Liberal Democracy, London, 1957.

Mill, J.S. : Representative Government, Everyman Library.

Mills, C. Wright : The Power Elite, New York, 1956.

Mosca, G. : The Ruling Class, New York, 1939.

Pareto, Vilfredo : The Mind and Society, London, 1935.

Parry, Geraint : Political Elites.

Pateman, C. : Participation and Democratic Theory, Cambridge, 1970.

Patridge, P.H. : Consent and Consensus, London, 1971.

Pickles, Dorothy : Democracy.

Plamenatz, John : Democracy and Illusion: An Examination of Certain Aspects of Modern Democracy, London, 1973.

Popper, K.	:	The Open Society and Its Enemies, London, 1945.
Ranney, Austin	:	Governing: A Brief Introduction to Political Science.
Ross, A.	:	Why Democracy? Massachusetts, 1952.
Rostow, W.W.	:	Politics and the Stages of Growth.
Sartori, G.	:	Democratic Theory, New Delhi, 1965.
Schumpeter, Joseph A.	:	Capitalism, Socialism and Democracy, 1942.
Sherman, H.	:	Radical Political Economy. New York, 1972.
Shroff, P.J.	:	Democracy in India, A Symposium, 1960.
Stojanovic, S.	:	Between Ideals and Reality, New York, 1973.
Swingewood, A.	:	Marx and Modern Social Theory, London. 1975.
Truman, David	:	The Governmental Process.
Tucker, Robert	:	The Marxian Revolutionary Idea.
Tucker, R.C.	:	The Soviet Political Mind.
Verney, Doughlas V.	:	The Analysis of Political Systems.
Wolfe, R.P.	:	A Critique of Tolerance.

CHAPTER

Nationalism and Internationalism

Nationalism is the most significant force in modern times. For students of political theory, "an understanding of nationalism is as indispensable as a possession of a master key to a person seeking to enter all the rooms in a building. Indeed, the total behaviour of the state system in our day may largely be explained in terms of national hopes, national fears, national ambitions and national conflicts." Carlton J.H. Hayes writes, "So much is nationalism a commonplace in the modes of thoughts and action of the civilised populations of the contemporary world that most men take nationalism for granted. Without serious reflection they imagine it to be the most natural thing in the universe and assume that it must always have existed."

Learning Objectives

- Meaning of Nationalism
- Historical Development of Nationalism
- Factors Responsible for Growth of Nationalism
- Features of Nationalism
- Merits of Nationalism
- Demerits of Nationalism
- Internationalism
- Meaning of Internationalism
- Evolution of Concept of Internationalism
- Factors Helping Growth of Internationalism
- Factors Hindering Internationalism
- World Federation or World Government
- Nationalism and Internationalism
- Suggested Readings

Meaning of Nationalism

Nationalism is a spiritual concept which originates in the people having the same race, language, traditions and culture, religion, politics, inhabiting a territory of a geographic unity. It is a historically constituted stable community of people, formed into political body. Gross writes, "It is sentimental political concept directly related to struggle for power, which respects the individuality of states, recognises variations in law and government and segregates group from group on the basis of common core of ideals and beliefs." The view of G.P. Gooch is that "nationalism is an organism, a spiritual entity and all attempts to penetrate its secrets by the light of mechanical interpretation break down before the test of experience." Arnold J. Toynbee observes that nationalism is "nothing material or mechanical, but a subjective, psychological feeling in a living people." Alfred D. Grazia says, "Nationalism combines love of country and suspiciousness of foreigners. Love of country comes from shared values and suspiciousness of foreigners comes from the belief that foreigners do not share such values in the same strength. The first shared value is the love of familiar places—the neighbourhood, the land, the homes, the valleys and the mountains, all of the surroundings that one loves because they have been part of oneself from infancy." (The Elements of Political Science, Political Behaviour (1962), p. 290). According to John H. Randall, "Nationalism is almost the one idea for which masses of men will still die".

Hans Kohn writes, "Nationalism is a state of mind, permeating the large majority of people and claiming to permeate all its members. It recognises the nation state as the ideal form of political organisation and the nationality as the source of all creative energy and of economic well-being. The supreme loyalty is therefore due to his nationality, as his own life is supposedly rooted in and made possible by its welfare." (The Idea of Nationalism, p. 16). Again, "Nationalism is first and foremost a state of mind, an act of consciousness."

In the words of Louis L. Snyder, "Nationalism as a product of political, economic, social and intellectual factors at a certain stage in history, is a condition of mind, feeling or sentiment of a group of people living in a well-defined geographical area, speaking a common language, possessing a literature in which the aspirations of the nation have been expressed, attached to common traditions and common customs, venerating its own heroes and in some cases, having a common religion." Hertz defines nationalism as a "community formed by the will to be a nation."

According to Thorsten V. Kilijasje, "Nationalism is instinctive with man; it does grow out of the emotional and instinctive characteristics of modern society and as such in many instances it is not a product of reason but of feeling aroused by the effect of current affairs upon several of man's primary instincts or characteristics". In the view of K. Roberts, "Nationalism is an ideology, based on the premise that it should be organised on the basis of nationality." C.D. Burns observes, "It is a sentimental political concept directly related to the struggle for power which respects the individuality of states, recongnises the variations in law and government and separates from group on the basis of ideals and beliefs. "According to Dr. Garner, "It is one of the characteristic features of modern nationalism that most peoples who constitute a nationality aspire either to be independent and to be under a state organisation of their own choice and creation or at least to be accorded a large political autonomy where they are united with another nationality or nationalities in the same state."

Aurobindo Ghose gave a new meaning to the term nationalism. He wrote, "Nationalism is a religion that has come from God; nationalism is a creed in which you shall have to live. It is an attitude of the heart, of the soul. What the intellect could not do, this mighty force of passionate conviction born out of the very faith of national consciousness, will be able to accomplish."

Historical Development of Nationalism

In ancient and medieval times, human loyalties did not go beyond the frontiers of locality or village or city state or feudal manor. The Jews and the Greeks were fully conscious of their separate nationality, but their concept of nationalism was narrow. In the medieval period, the Holy Roman Empire acted as the stumbling block to the rise of the nation state. Feudalism and other factors also were detrimental to the growth of nationalism. England and France evolved national feelings during the Hundred Years, War. The Renaissance and the Reformation made the English conscious that they were a distinct national unity. In France, the French, Revolution played an important part in building up national sentiment. The Napoleonic Wars aroused the minds of the people whose national aspirations were unjustly suppressed. The nationalities ignored and wronged by the Congress of Vienna (1815) rebelled against the unjust decisions which wanted to seal their fate. Germany and Italy were kept divided and nationalism was suppressed. The Belgians under Holland and the Greeks under Turkey fought to assert their national rights. Several social philosophers like J.S. Mill in the nineteenth century believed that free institutions and nationalism should go hand in hand. Fichte spoke very highly of devotion to the nation state. Mazzini wrote with mystical fervour. He defined a nation in these words, "By nation we understand the totality of Italians bound together by a common past and governed by the same laws." His view was that every nation has a mystic soul which is specially created by God. The nation is to be worshipped and served as an emanation of the deity. God had set geographical boundaries to separate nations.

Upto about 1880, nationalism was closely identified with the crusade for tree and democratic government. Both nationalism and liberalism marched shoulder to shoulder. The leaders of nationalism were also the leaders of democracy and liberalism. The nationalism of that period produced an epidemic of bloody wars whose object was political consolidation, self-determination and liberalisation and not economic aggrandizement and expansion. However, after 1880, the motivation and the philosophy of nationalism underwent a great change. After the establishment of independent and liberal governments, the national aspirations began to centre round economic considerations. That tendency was encouraged by the Industrial and Commercial Revolutions which pitted nation against nation in a struggle for materials and markets. A new form of nationalism emerged which proclaimed the right of a nation not only to be but also to grow, to gain a place in the sun, to fulfil its manifest destiny, to take up the Whiteman's burden and to carry on its mission of civilisation. Nationalism grew into economic nationalism which ultimately flowered into economic imperialism. The new nationalism brought in more wars in its wake. There were trade wars, tariff wars, currency wars, shipping wars, concession wars and wars of shot and shell. It turned peace into war. When the World War I started in 1914, it was the old nationalism which furnished most of the shibboleths, but it was the new nationalism that fought the war and made the peace. President Woodrow Wilson enunciated the principle of self-determination. Small nation states like Czechoslovakia, Poland, Lithuania, Latvia, Esthonia, Hungary, Rumania and Yugoslavia fell a prey to power hungry dictators like Hitler and Stalin. Nationalism was also responsible for the creation of independent states of India, Pakistan, Burma and Sri Lanka in Asia and a large number of nation states in Africa.

Nationalism arose in democratic countries like Britain, France and the United States spontaneously. It was based on democratic principles like liberty and equality. The personality of the individual was fully recognised and he felt the national urge in an atmosphere of complete freedom of thought and action.

In totalitarian countries like Germany, Italy, Soviet Russia, Japan and Communist China, nationalism arose on the basis of a militant and aggressive spirit. It divorced itself completely from the methods of peace and persuasion. These totalitarian states provoked the individual to develop an extremely aggressive type of nationalism which was opposed to peaceful co-existence. In Italy, under Mussolini, Fascist nationalism rejected parliamentarianism and democracy. It repudiated peace and harmony and prepared the nation for war. Nationalism in its extreme form was built on Nazism in Hitler's Germany. It was based on the false facial theory of Nordic superiority and on militarism and aggressive imperialism. Imperial Japan tried to fulfil its own mission in the Eastern hemisphere. Communist China whipped up aggressive nationalism under Mao Tse-tung.

Factors Responsible for Growth of Nationalism

Various factors promote the feelings of nationalism. (1) *Common territory or* geographical unity is an important factor which helps the growth of nationalism in the hearts of the people. The people who reside on a fixed territory naturally develop feelings of cooperation, love and protection. They develop distinct habits, traditions, customs, cultural interests etc. which help in promoting nationalism. A common land creates a clear image in the minds of the people and a strong feeling of attachment is created. In India, the Himalayas, the great rivers like the Ganga and the beautiful plains have created strong patriotic feelings. Mazzini wrote, "Our country is our home, the house that God has given us, placing therein a numerous family that loves us and whom we love: a family with whom we sympathise more readily and whom we understand more quickly than we do others and which from its being centred around a given spot and from the homogeneous nature of its elements, is adapted to a special branch of activity." Geographic unity is also helpful in promoting and maintaining nationalism. Natural boundaries are helpful in this matter. They create common physical, mental and psychological traits and help cooperation and mutual understanding among the people. Ruthnaswamy writes. "Politics divides us, religion divides us, culture divides us. But the land and the love of the land of India may unite us."

Sometimes, groups of people living in different states develop the spirit of oneness and common consciousness, but they remain a nationality only and do not become a nation till they acquire a common land of their own. Before the World War I, the Poles and Yugoslavs were nationalities and not nations. The Jews could not claim full nationhood till the creation of the independent state of Israel in 1948.

(2) Another factor which promotes nationalism is *common historical background.* A historical background presenting great triumphs and achievements, common joys and sorrows, common sufferings and political bondage also serves as a good basis for nationalism.

Common history of the people helps in the formation and continuation of nationality. It develops a spirit of oneness among the people. J.S. Mill writes, "Sometimes it is the effect of identity of race and descent, community of language and community of religion greatly contribute to it. Geographical limits are one of its causes. But the strongest of all is its identity of political antecedents, the possession of national history and consequent community of recollections, collective pride and humiliation, pleasure and regret connected with the same incidents in the past." Ramsay Muir observes. "Heroic achievements, agonies heroically endured, these are the sublime food by which the spirit of nationhood is nourished."

(3) *Common interests* of the people, whether economic, political, social or cultural, help in uniting them together. If the interests of the people are identical, it is natural that they will form association to work together. The workers unite themselves and work for their economic cause, though they may differ in other respects. Common interest can help in the formation of a union or association but not a nation. Gilchrist writes that common interests are aids towards strengthening union than fundamental agents of union. Common interests are not an essential condition for the growth of nationalism.

(4) *Common race* also helps in the formation and strengthening of nationalism. Generally, the people belonging to the same race have the same culture, language, religion, history, customs, traditions, problems etc. and these factors help the formation of national feelings among them. This view is not accepted by some scholars. Their contention is that racial unity is not necessary for nationalism. Haves writes, "Purity, if it exists at all, exists now-a-days only among uncivilised tribesmen." Pillsbury says, "In the determination of national lines, in general, race is no more important. There is no pure race in any nation. Man is everywhere a mongrel." Mussolini writes, "Race is a feeling, not a reality. Nothing will ever make me believe that biologically pure races can be shown to exist today." We have the example of Canada which is inhabited by two races. English and French. In Switzerland, we have the Germans, the French and the Italians. Dr. Garner writes, "Race is a physical phenomenon, whereas nationality is a complex phenomenon into which spiritual elements enter. Nationality is concerned with the psychic oneness of the people and not with the colour and creed of the people whereas the race is concerned with colour and creed of the people."

Chauvinists like Hitler spoke in terms of racial purity which was made the bedrock of militant and aggressive nationalism in Germany. He repeated the myth of Nordic superiority and asserted that the Germans who belonged to a superior race had the right to dominate over the inferior races.

(5) Another factor which promotes nationalism is *Common language* through which we can express our ideas to others we can understand others only through (Tie common language. According to Joseph, common language enables the people to express the same ideas and same sentiments, creates common standards regarding morals, manners and justice. Ramsay Muir writes, "There is nothing that will give unity to divergent races as the use of common tongue and in very many cases unity of language and community of ideas which it brings have proved the main binding force in a nation. Garner says, "Community of language is the most important factor in moulding a people into a nationality." Mazzini, Fichte and Ramsay Muir regard language as the most important factor in the growth of nationalism. A common language welds the people into a nation. Language is the expression of culture and ideals. A common medium of expression creates sympathy, understanding and a sense of belonging among the people. The rise of vernaculars in different countries facilitated

the growth of nationalism. The Congress leaders in India made use of the English language as the medium of expression. The Indians coming out of educational institutions and universities could understand one another through the English language. The people from different European countries made the United States their permanent home and became one American nation through the common bond of the English language.

Language can also become a dividing force. The different languages in India have created problems for the country as each language group cares only for itself and not others. However, linguistic differences may not stand in the way of national unification in every state if the people are open-minded, rational and friendly in their approach.

(6) *Common religion* of the people promotes feelings of nationalism. Religion, along with other factors, immensely strengthened nationalism in the past. When the Spanish Armada attacked England in 1588, both the Protestants and Catholics fought against the common enemy. In the time of Henry VIII, an independent Anglican Protestant Church was set up in England after overthrowing Papal authority. The Scots were unified by their Presbyterian leader, John Knox. In Japan, Shintoism was an important factor which provided a strong base for nationalism. Religion has played an important part in the growth of Muslim nationalism in India. Religion played an important part in the establishment of the state of Israel in 1948. Religion held the Jews together although they were scattered all over the world for centuries. Religious awakening among the Hindus in India led to national consciousness. In Pakistan, Bangladesh and other Muslim states, religion is an important factor. However, religion can also become a source of trouble if there are two irreconcilable religious groups. In 1947, the Muslims of India got Pakistan which is a state based on religion.

(7) *Common culture* is another factor which promotes nationalism. Unity of ideas and ideals helps the people to be close with one another. They develop a strong sense of unity. Zananiecki writes, "We find that at a certain stage in the evolution of every national culture, society includes only a relatively small number of intellectuals who are united by the belief that they belong to a community with a common culture different from other cultures and who cooperate in perpetuating and developing that culture."

It cannot denied that common culture does not always help in promoting or maintaining nationalism. Sometimes, the people have a common culture but they do not have the same nationality. There is common culture in India and Burma, but they have separate nationalities.

(8) Another factor which helps the growth of nationalism is *common subjection and common suffering*. Zimmern says, "In Europe, nationality is an instinct which has been stung into morbid and acute self-consciousness by political oppression." However, this factor is not very essential for the growth of nationalism. Joseph writes, "Oppression of a group does not itself transform it into a nationality."

(9) Another factor which helps the growth of nationalism is the *existence of common political aspirations*. This factor is more important than common race, language, religion and history. So many nations were established in Asia and Africa. When a clear common political goal is fixed, a nationality can work to become a full-fledged nation. The Indian National Congress expressed the common political aspirations of the people of India during the British rule in India.

(10) A *common government* also helps in the promotion of nationalism. The Germans under Austria-Hungary during the nineteenth century felt a kind of unity in their subjection. Alien control acted as a cementing force in Germany. Likewise, the British rule in India brought about unity among the Indians.

(11) *Common symbols* have helped the growth of nationalism in the world. Heroes like George Washington, Napoleon Bonaparte, Mahatma Gandhi, Lenin and Mao Tse-tung, tombs like Lenin's

tomb and Mahatma Gandhi's Samadhi, songs like *Jan Gan Man* and flags like the Union Jack of England and the Tricolour in India enable the people to remember their separate national identity. Organski writes, "Flags make excellent national symbols, for they can be carried into battle and thus share in the glory of victory or the ignobility of defeat, and they are all just alike so that any single flag can be made to stand for all other flags of the same pattern that have been associated with the glorious events in the nation's past. One knows after all, that the young recruit marching by has not yet participated in any action more glorious than basic training, and even the veteran has fought in only one or two wars, but the flag has shared in all the wars and all the glories."

(12) Another important factor promoting nationalism is the *actual feeling of nationalism* among the people. Such a feeling must rise spontaneously in the minds of the people and cannot be manufactured outside and thrust inside the minds in an artificial manner. Nationalism is essentially psychological, emotional, spiritual and subjective. No one factor or a group of factors can make a people a nation unless they actually feel the spirit of national oneness. Like human love and affection, nationalism is subjective. It is created by nature and not by artificial means. It can never be super-imposed from outside. It has to be born within. Popular will can create the actual feeling of national consciousness. The view of Toynbee is that the will to be a nation is the major element of nationality. According to Renan, nationality is based on a keen desire to live together.

Buck observes thus regarding the factors which promote nationalism: "Nationality is essentially subjective, an active sentiment of unity within a "fairly extensive group, a sentiment based upon real but diverse factors, political, geographical, physical and social, any or all of which may be present in this or that cause, but no one of which must be present in all cases." Schleicher comments, "Nationalism is neither a biological nor a psychological necessity, but there are certain human characteristics which, under proper conditions, are conducive to or at least do not prevent its development. Thus, human nature is the root of nationalism."

Features of Nationalism

There are certain features of nationalism. It puts emphasis on the fact that every national group has an individuality of its own and if it is given an opportunity, it can make a distinctive contribution to humanity at large. Every nation demands the right of self-determination. It must be given the right to govern itself according to its own lights If a nation is under foreign rule, it demands liberation and also prepares to make sacrifices to achieve the goal. National independence is considered to be the birthright of every nation and every opposition is resented and resisted. Indian nationalism took the form of a movement whose main object was to drive out the Englishmen from India. Chinese nationalism demanded that all foreigners must leave China. The same can be said about Egyptian nationalism. Jewish nationalism aimed at the establishment of a Jewish state. Arab nationalism brings all the Arabs together for unified action. Once a national state has been established, it strives for greatness and glory. That is possible only if a policy of expansion is followed. That involves a struggle for markets. A national group is prepared to go to the extent of war to realise its objective. War is justified on the ground that it is a biological phenomenon and nations which do not grow begin to degenerate in the long run. Nationalism has become a religious faith. People love and worship their nations in the same way as they do in the religious field. The state is referred to as the Motherland or the Fatherland. It is described as the march of God on earth. A true nationalist loves his own country and he is also prepared to hate all those who are the enemies of his country or stand in the way of her progress.

Merits of Nationalism

(1) A great merit of nationalism is that it creates love for the country. When people begin to love their country, the latter can expect to make progress in every direction. No sacrifice is considered to

be too high if national interests demand. Nationalism has inspired deeds of heroism and sacrifices among the people. Nationalism creates a spirit of fellow-feeling and a determination to improve the lot of all those who live in the same country and are not otherwise happily placed in society.

(2) Nationalism preserves national culture. Every national group has a culture of its own and the feeling of nationalism creates a feeling of pride among those people.

(3) Nationalism creates a healthy spirit of national rivalry. Every nation tries to go ahead of others and humanity as a whole gains on account of healthy competition.

(4) Many poets, orators and painters have been inspired by the spirit of nationalism and they have given to the world their immortal works. The result is that art and culture have gained a lot from nationalism.

(5) Nationalism demands the liberation of every country and when that is done, there is bound to be less tension, struggle and bitterness in the world. When every state becomes independent and begins to grow in its won way, there are lesser chances of war and greater chances of world peace.

(6) The tide of imperialism can be checked by the forces of nationalism. The people are prepared to make any sacrifices to maintain their independence. It is the growth of nationalism in Asia which demands the ending of imperialism on the Continent.

(7) Nationalism offers dynamic forces for cultural and economic creativity. It has proved useful in giving birth to democratic ideas. It increases the loyalty of the people towards their government. It provides stability to the state.

(8) Nationalism infuses the spirit of patriotism in the minds of the people and helps them to become independent. Through nationalism, feelings of high and low and caste are banished from the minds of the people and social unity is achieved. It creates the spirit of heroism and self-sacrifice. It leads to economic prosperity. Nationalism enables the country to face the economic and political crises effectively. It leads to political unity and stability. It helps in curbing mutual conflicts and quarrels and the attention of the people is drawn towards big problems. Man gives up his selfish interest and works for national interest.

(9) Nationalism breeds legitimate pride and self-respect in a country. It creates a healthy spirit of competition among the nations of the world. The feeling of nationalism unites the people and they work hard for the economic prosperity of their country. They bear the burden of extra taxes for national interest. The history of freedom movement in every country is full of examples of men and women who sacrificed their lives at the altar of the motherland.

(10) Nationalism offers dynamic forces for cultural and economic creativity. The nationalists find nationality as the source of all creative energy and economic well-being. The opinion of Ramsay Muir is that nationalism promotes civilisation and culture. It has proved useful for the birth of democratic ideas. It represents ideals like freedom, equality and fraternity. It promotes mutual cooperation, sympathy and goodwill among the people of a country. It inspires them to work for the progress of their country. It increases the loyalty of the people towards their government and provides stability to the state. It promotes internationalism. Only nationalism can lead to internationalism.

(11) Nationalism can mobilise and unity people as nothing else can. It is one of the most important forces working for unity. It breeds legitimate pride and self-respect in a country. It makes no compromise with slavery and foreign domination. It has an ennobling effect on human mind. It is based on the ideas of liberalism and humanism. The history of freedom movement in every country is full of instances of men and women who sacrificed their lives for the sake of their country.

(12) Nationalism helps in promoting internationalism. The view of Gandhiji is that only nationalism can lead to internationalism. It is the first step towards internationalism.

Demerits of Nationalism

If there is praise for nationalism, there is criticism also. (1) It is contended that nationalism is the greatest enemy to internationalism. According to Hayes, nationalism has been "a curse and nothing but a curse." Rabindranath Tagore describes nationalism as the organised self-interest of a whole people. Nationalism is a great menace because it calls for a "strenuous effort after strength and efficiency and thereby drains man's energy from his higher nature, where he is self-sacrificing and creative."

(2) Victor Gollancz writes, "Of all the evils I hate, I think I hate nationalism most." Arnold Toynbee refers to crimes committed in the name of nationalism during the last three or four hundred years. About nationalism, Vladimir Solovyer writes, "In its extreme form, it destroys a nation, for it makes it the enemy of mankind." According to Joseph, "It is dangerous in principle and constitutes a chief obstacle to world progress. The view of Lord Acton is that nationalism overrules the rights and wishes of the inhabitants. It absorbs their divergent interests in a fictitious unity. It sacrifices their several inclinations and duties to the higher claims of nationality. It crushes all natural rights and all established liberties. Hayes observes, "Modern nationalism has indeed been a peculiar bloody religion. Vastly more persons have been slain in the nationalist wars of the first half of the present century than in the four centuries of medieval crusading".

(3) Ebenstein writes, "Since the French Revolution at least, nationalism has been one of the driving forces of domestic, imperial and international politics. Complex in its origins, it has developed along many and often contradictory lines. In its name, some of the greatest acts of heroism and liberty have been committed, but also crimes of cruelty and fanaticism. In the first half of its existence-from the late eighteenth to the middle of the nineteenth century—nationalism was essentially inspired by humanitarian, democratic ideas, this was the story of early French, American, Czech, Italian, Irish and the Polish nationalism. In the last eighty years on the other hand, nationalism has tended totally itself with parochialism, intolerance, bigotry, persecution of minorities, racialism and finally imperialism and aggression—the recoil of Pan-Germanism, Hungarian imperialism, Japanese militarism and finally Fascism."

(4) The love of one's country can never be bad but it must not be directed into a narrow channel to affect adversely the interests of other countries. If love of one's country implies hatred for another country, such nationalism is bound to stand in the way of human development. It was the prevalence of feelings of bitterness and hatred among the French and Germans which was partly responsible for the two World Wars. Every child in France was taught after 1871 that he or she was to take revenge against Germany who had humiliated France in 1871. If every national group follows the imperialist policy, there is bound to be conflict and bitterness.

(5) Extreme nationalism creates a spirit of intolerance. Every country considers itself to be the best and the others worthless. Such an atmosphere is hardly conducive to human welfare. Humanity progresses only when there is a spirit of cooperation and not when there is too much inequality.

(6) Nationalism results in imperialism which creates the problem of national minorities. When territories are conquered by a dominant nation, there cannot be homogeneity among the people. There are bound to be sections of the people who do not see eye to eye with the ruling group. The imperialist power is bound to adopt all the methods to impose its culture and civilisation among the cultured people. However, such an attempt is bound to be resisted by the minority.

(7) Nationalism can also act as a disintegrating force. Big states may have many nationalities within their borders. The minorities are bound to agitate for their independence. Austria-Hungary was a great empire during the nineteenth century but it broke up because all the nationalities continued their agitation for independence. Such a danger exists for all countries which have many nationalities.

(8) Aggressive nationalism ignores altogether the welfare of other countries. It does not bother about their sufferings. When Japan was busy conquering China during the 1930s, she did not care for the sufferings of her victims.

(9) According to Shillito, nationalism has become "man's other religion." It is "sentimental, emotional and inspirational." It has more fanatical followers than any other living religion. It claims to have a mission for the world. In the name of national rights, national honour and national policy, millions of lives have been lost and billions of dollars have been wasted. Nationalism leads to hatred towards outsiders. This aggressive kind of nationalism has been called "wolf pack" nationalism. It breeds war. Its examples are to be found in pre-1945 Japan, Fascist Italy and Nazi Germany.

(10) The consequences of nationalism have been bad in the economic and political field. Economic nationalism known as autarchy aims at complete economic self-sufficiency which ultimately leads to war. It is like a boomerang which brings great harm upon its own head. Autarchy is a folly. It has resulted in the burning of wheat in Canada, the dumping of apples and milk into the rivers in the United States and the throwing of coffee into the sea in Brazil.

One may conclude by saying that when nationalism becomes synonymous with purest patriotism, it is a unique blessing to humanity and the world but it results in wars and destruction if it becomes exclusive and selfish. For all its faults, nationalism remains a powerful force in the world of today. Every country acts upon the principle: "My nation is always right and other nations are always wrong."

INTERNATIONALISM

Meaning of Internationalism

In the words of Goldsmith, "Internationalism is the feeling that the individual is not only a member of his state but also a citizen of the world". Another writer says that internationalism is "a system of thought and action designed to promote peaceful cooperation among the states of the world." Internationalism implies an international society composed of national societies existing together in close harmony, goodwill and cooperation. It involves the acceptance of such limitations on their sovereignty as are necessary in the interest of peace and preservation. The idea of nationalism is based on the idea of cooperation of the states in common interest without encroaching upon the domestic jurisdiction of each other. Internationalism stands for peaceful cooperation among the nations of the world who are united to each other by ties of equality and peaceful co-existence. It implies a feeling of brotherhood nourished by all the people of the world.

It is not correct to say that internationalism stands for the abolition of all national states. The fact is that the ideal of internationalism is compatible with the existence of national states which continue to exist as a part of the international order. It is rightly said that internationalism cannot be expected to grow in the graveyard of nationalism. The creation of a super-national society envisaged by internationalism must reckon national states as units. Internationalism implies international cooperation and coordination in political, economic and cultural spheres. It is an ideology which anticipates international organisation of sovereign states to foster international cooperation for the solution of political, social and economic issues confronting the international society. Internationalism envisages a peaceful world order. This does not mean that there will be no conflicts in the world. What it means is that if conflicts arise those will be settled amicably. The goal of internationalism as a political ideology is an international order where there is no war. Internationalism requires the establishment of some sort of organisation with authority over the national governments. Some advocate existence of an organisation of sovereign states whose representatives meet and discuss issues confronting the world. Internationalism also implies the existence of a body of rules which regulate the behaviour of national states. These rules prescribe the manner in which the nation states are expected to behave in a particular situation.

Internationalism is the most important concept of today on account of the destructive potential of the lethal weapons invented by man as a result of scientific and technological advancement. The Atom Bomb, the Hydrogen Bomb, the Cobalt Bomb and the ballistic missiles can destroy the entire world. It is contended that if there is a third World War, the fourth was of the world would be fought with stones because no body can calculate the extent and magnitude of the destruction to be brought about by the third World War.

Internationalism is not an automatic, transplantable political creed. It is a spiritual and moral habit which every nation should cultivate and sincerely follow it in thought, speech and action. The holocaust of the third World War can be avoided only if all nations agree to accept whole-heartedly the cult of peaceful coexistence. Hugh Gaitskell writes, "The challenge of co-existence is not merely how to avoid a third World War, not merely how to settle international disputes peacefully, to live and let live, not merely how to conduct ideological totalitarian Communism, but how to do these things and also to bring them to those people who do not now enjoy the benefits of liberty and true self-government." Prof. Laski observes, "There are no longer lotus fields where men may linger careless of the life about them. The world is one and indivisible in a sense so compelling that the only question before us is the method by which we represent its unity."

Evolution of Concept of Internationalism

Perhaps the earliest known idea on internationalism begins with Dante's "De Monarchia" in which he made a plea for a world empire. Sully, the famous statesman of France in the reign of King Henery IV, drafted a scheme known as the Grand Design in which he recognised the autonomy of different states. Europe was to be constituted into a Christian Republic from which Russia and the Ottoman Empire were to he excluded. A provision was made for a Council or perpetual Senate of 64 Commissioners to assist the Emperor in deciding questions of common interest and the preservation of peace by settling disputes among nations. The Council was to have at its disposal an international army and navy.

Another scheme was put forward by Abbe de St. Pierre by which the whole of Europe was to be a single society and no single state was to be allowed to have mastery over another. All European powers were to maintain the territorial integrity of one another. They were to suppress revolutions and keep monarchs on their thrones The City of Utrecht was to be the city of peace where delegates of different states were to meet in an assembly to discuss common problems and pass laws by a majority vote. The scheme failed because it aimed at the maintenance of the status quo. It ignored altogether the people.

The view of Rousseau was that international strife was the result of the relationship among sovereign independent nations. His scheme provided for a federated Europe in which the member states were to enter into an irrevocable contract. Disputes among states were to be decided by arbitration. The federal government was to guarantee the territorial integrity and the existing form of government in different states.

Bentham suggested disarmament, defensive alliances and the abandonment of colonial imperialism for averting wars. He pleaded that secret diplomacy, tariffs bounties and colonies must be abolished because they posed a threat to international peace.

In his essay "Towards Eternal Peace," Kant advocated the maintenance of the independence of all states, acceptance of the principle of non-intervention and the gradual abolition of standing armies. He advocated republican constitutions for all states and world citizenship.

Saint Simon proposed the establishment of a general Parliament for Europe. Lord Bryce proposed a scheme for uniting great and small powers.

Clarence Streit gave his proposal for a Federal Union of American and Western European democracies. Provision was made for a Federal Legislature, a Federal President, a Federal Prime Minister and Cabinet. The Federal Government was to exercise complete control over questions such as war and peace, defence and foreign relations, postage and currency. Within the Union, there was to be "one citizenship, one defence force, one free trade area, one money and one stamp. The colonial possessions of the member states were to be conjointly administered by the Federal Union with a view to make them fit to become the members of the Federation as soon as possible."

Madariaga advocated the idea of a world community which did not limit its membership to European states. He urged the necessity of a World Bank, a World Trade Commission, a World Trust for Colonies, an International Police Force and an International Civil Service.

In his book "World Federation" published in 1939, Oscar Newfang maintained that the machinery of the League of Nations could be easily transformed into a world federation. He advocated the removal of trade barriers and the introduction of a single monetary system. The World Court was to have compulsory jurisdiction. The member states were required to transfer their armed forces to the central authority of the Federation.

Sir William Beveridge confined his federation to Britain, France, Germany, Switzerland and the five British dominions. Defence and foreign policy were to be transferred immediately to the federal authority. Subjects like the management of dependencies, currency, trade and migration were to be transferred gradually. Dr. W.R. Inge proposed a federation of the English speaking countries of the world including the United States, Great Britain and her dominions. Dr. Ivor Jennings gave a scheme for a federation of the countries of Western Europe. The main object of the federation was to "render war among the nations of Western Europe absolutely and literally impossible." The view of D.N. Pritt, a great lawyer and jurist, was that a partial federation was worse than no federation at all and was even worse than an empire as there would be constant friction between the federation and the excluded powers. He also maintained that as long as imperialism and capitalism existed, a federation of the world was merely an illusion.

The failure of the different schemes shows that mere insistence on the organisational form is not adequate to promote internationalism which requires that doctrine of absolute state sovereignty must be surrendered voluntarily. A strong international machinery should be established for the maintenance of constructive peace. Economic equality among the different countries of the world must be achieved. Individuals must be guaranteed social security.

Factors Helping Growth of Internationalism

Many factors have helped the growth of internationalism and the most important among them is scientific inventions which have linked up the whole world. Distance and time have been annihilated. No country can be isolated front the rest of the world. We have the fastest aeroplanes which can take the people to different parts of the world within a few hours. We have big steamers visiting every part of the world. Radio, television, wireless etc. have linked up the world. International news agencies act as a great unifying force. The whole world becomes acquainted with the happenings in any remote corner of any country. All this creates an international feeling. A movement in one part of the world has its repercussions in other parts of the world. If there is slump in one country, that affects other countries also. There is too much of economic inter-dependence. The whole world has become one economic unit. There is always going on an exchange of commodities among the various nations. No country can continue to export if it is not prepared to import. It must import if it has to export.

Emphasis is being put on internationalism by those who want the welfare of mankind. There is a realisation that war is becoming more and more destructive and if we are going to use the atom bomb and the hydrogen bomb in the next World War, there is every possibility of humanity being completely destroyed. It is this danger which makes intelligent people all over the world to advocate a policy of internationalism. They would prefer one country to lose a little rather than allow the whole world to be involved in a suicidal war.

Capitalism has created an international market supplanting all national barriers and breaking the iron bars of isolation in one country after another. If it led to competitive wars between capitalist nations, it compelled the generous minds in every nation to pause and think and find out the means of outlawing war as such. Moreover, the growth of an international labour movement may be regarded as an inevitable by-product of the rise of capitalism. Prof. Laski says that the above factors have produced a greater consciousness of international solidarity. The creation of the League of the Nations and the United Nations is a proof of that consciousness.

The development of trade and commerce has united the entire world into a single economic unit. Nations have become dependent upon each other for material goods. The concept of economic nationalism has been substituted by economic internationalism.

Internationalism is emerging as a powerful force in the world. The unity of the world in the realm of culture and economy has made people internationally-minded. There is evolving the spirit of internationalism in the world. The threat of nuclear war has led the people to cling to international organisation to protect them. People find solace in internationalism.

Factors Hindering Internationalism

There are many factors which hinder the growth of internationalism. Nationalism is a great challenge to internationalism. Nations have flouted international law on the pretext of safeguarding national interest. International peace has been broken and wars have been fought to justify national interest. The Union of South Africa and Southern Rhodesia disregarded international public opinion and continued to follow policies dictated by their national interest.

Another hindrance in the way of internationalism is the concept of sovereignty. The traditional concept of sovereignty implies freedom of external action on the part of a sovereign state. Any imposition made by an International Organisation or International law is considered derogatory to national sovereignty. This attitude of the sovereign states hinders the growth of internationalism.

Imperialism also hinders the growth of internationalism. Under it, the national states cling to their colonies and empires. An air of disbelief and distrust has been created in inter-state relations and that checks the growth of healthy internationalism.

Another hindrance to the growth of internationalism is ideological diversity among the nations of the world. Ideological bi-polarization of the world has divided the entire world into irreconcilable parts. Totalitarian and militant ideologies have proclaimed the inevitability of war and leave no scope for coexistence.

Regionalism is another hindrance in the way of internationalism. Nations have formed regional organisations for political, economic and military purposes. Those organisations have tackled those problems but their attitude towards international order and peace is lukewarm.

Tendencies such as racialism, colonialism and Fascism act as powerful deterrents to international unity and cooperation.

It is contended that world peace depends upon the abolition of capitalism as it is a pre-condition for the abolition of national sovereignty which alone can guarantee peaceful relations among the different communities of the world. The view of Laski is that all attempts at international organisation which ignore this fundamental principle, are predestined to failure. International government is impossible in view of the serious antagonisms that have historically divided the capitalist world. With the emergence of the Soviet Union and other Communist states on the world scene, there has emerged another source of antagonism between the capitalist and Communist blocs of states.

The contemporary history of the major capitalist countries shows that capitalism, sovereignty and war are intimately connected with one another. By its unequal distribution of income in the community, every capitalist society creates a contradiction between its production and consumption. The capitalist class does not meet the crisis by a change in the relations of production but by a policy of economic imperialism. That brings one capitalist government in conflict with another for the possession of colonies, protectorates, spheres of influence or zones of legitimate aspiration which can serve as sources of raw materials and markets for the finished goods or as areas where the surplus capital may be exported and reinvested.

The view of Laski is that the imperialist phase of capitalist development necessarily involves war and an effective international order is incompatible with it. The sovereign capitalist state must be sent to the dust-bin of history before any serious attempt to define the nature of an effective world organisation can be made. It is impossible to build an international system based on mutual cooperation of the national communities so long as a class formulates the foreign policies of the nation states. An international order, to be effective, must control things like currency, tariffs, labour standards, migration, access to raw materials, the penetration of backward areas etc. To control these things, it must be able to override the existing vested interests which use the sovereignty of the state for their protection It cannot override them as the world at present organised. They arise inherently from the close relations of a capitalist society. The forces which protect them are exactly the same as the forces which protect the power of the capitalist inside the national society to which he belongs. Exactly as the sovereign state protects in the internal sphere a system of legal rights intended to safeguard his supremacy, likewise externally its external authority must be used to impose that supremacy upon others. It is only as these close relations are transformed that state antagonisms become capable of any fundamental reconciliation. Upon the existing basis, the utmost goodwill in international relations can only postpone the ultimately inevitable conflict. The seeds of the present international unrest are rooted in the inner drive of capitalism towards imperialist expansion. The conclusion of Laski is that capitalist imperialism is incompatible with the foundation of a peaceful world order. Only an international Commonwealth of socialist nations can bring about those conditions which are considered as the foundation of a genuinely peaceful world society. A new society of nations must be built on the basis of the liquidation of imperialism in its political and economic aspects. It must encourage and bring about a rapid industrialisation and modernisation of the colonial and semi-Colonial areas of the world. It must ensure an equitable distribution of wealth in every national community. If these conditions are fulfilled, an international government can be successful and prevent the possibility of a future war.

World Federation or World Government

There is a strong movement in favour of a world government or world federation. The supporters of this movement demand that the nation states should give up a part of their sovereignty and thereby allow the establishment of a world government or world federation. All the nations of the world are to be united in that international organisation. While the units are to be given autonomy in their own affairs, a common policy is to be followed with regard to matters which affect not one nation but many nations. The chances of international conflict can be lessened in that manner. The representatives of various states can put forward their own point of view and a remedy can be found without much difficulty. There will be international peace and cooperation these will be no mutual hatred or unhealthy competition among the various countries. The World Government will be able to tackle international disputes and raise the standard of living of the people.

The critics of world government point out that it is not possible to set up such an international authority as states are not prepared to give up their sovereignty. Those who control the machinery of the state and thereby manage to do whatever they please, are not prepared to surrender the sovereignty of the state. All the big powers, whether Communist or capitalist, are bound to oppose the idea of a world federation.

Another hindrance in the way of world government is nationalism. It is not possible to decide whether the world government is to be a federal state or a unitary state, whether it is to have a parliamentary or presidential form of government, or which international language is to be used for the work of the world government.

It is also maintained that a world government will not be in the interests of humanity as a whole. There will be an absence of struggle and struggle has always been the basis of human progress. The elimination of struggle and competition will slow down the progress of the world. Life will become dull. There will be too much of uniformity and less variety.

Nationalism and Internationalism

Nationalism has expressed itself through national sovereignty which claims freedom from international law. Ideological fanaticism of national states has made them irreconcilable with world peace. Economic, military and political interests of nations have brought them together in regional organisations. It appears that nationalism stands in the way of internationalism. Nationalism and internationalism seem to be so much inconsistent with each other that there is a demand for the abolition of nationalism in these words, "Nationalism has had its day. It was the political principle appropriate to the post-feudal and pre-atomic age. For the technology of the steam engine, it was indeed a good measure, a force for progress. In the atomic age, it must give way for a political principle of larger dimensions in the world-wide configurations of interest and power of the age." However, it is difficult to destroy nationalism as it is so consonant with fundamental human nature and so integral to the modern state that to speak of its abolition is hardly short of quixotic.

The question is whether nationalism and internationalism can be reconciled with each other or not. The answer is in the affirmative. There is nothing inconsistent if a person who loves his own country, also loves his neighbouring state. The love of one's country must not demand the destruction of others. We can aim at the greatness of our country and at the same time feel happy if other nations also prosper. The love of one's country does not demand the hatred of others. Experience shows that whenever narrow nationalism was preached in any country, that resulted in war. Narrow nationalism is bound to result in international conflicts and in such an atmosphere there can be no peace and progress of the world. The Whole world has become one. Whatever happens in one part of the world affects the other part of the world. The whole world has become inter-dependent. The only way for the world to exist and progress is through cooperation. Hence, nationalism and internationalism have to be reconciled. If nationalism is allowed to defy internationalism, there is bound to be misery for the world. Hence, all sane persons in the world demand that some curb must be put on extreme nationalism so that the good of humanity as a whole may be secured.

SUGGESTED READINGS

Barker, Ernest	:	National Character and the Factors in Its Formation, 1927.
Burns	:	Political Ideals, 1932.
Demishkevich, Michael	:	The National Mind—English, French and German, 1938.
Ebenstein, William	:	Modern Political Thought.
Garner, J.W.	:	Political Science and Government.

Gilchrist, R.N.	:	Indian Nationality.
Gooch, G.P.	:	Nationalism.
Hayes, C.J.H.	:	Essays on Nationalism, 1926.
Jenks, Edward	:	The State and the Nation.
Jennings, Sir ivor	:	A Federation for Western Europe.
Joseph, Bernard	:	Nationality.
Kohn, Hans	:	The Idea of Nationalism, 1946.
Kohn, Hans	:	Nationalism in the East.
Laski, H.J.	:	A Grammar of Politics.
Madariaga, Salvador De	:	The World's Design.
Muir, Ramsay	:	Nationalism and Internationalism.
Palmer and Perkins	:	International Relations.
Pillsbury, W.B.	:	The Psychology of Nationality and Internationalism.
Pritt, D.N.	:	Federal Illusion.
Rose, J. Holland	:	Nationality in Modern History, 1916.
Tagore, Rabindranath	:	Nationalism.
Toynbee, Arnold	:	Nationality and the War.
Watson, John	:	The State in Peace and War, 1919.
Woolf, L.S.	:	International Government.
Zimmern, A.E.	:	Nationality and Government.

CHAPTER

Imperialism

Learning Objectives

- Causes for Rise of Imperialism
- Development of Imperialism
- Modern Imperialism
- Lease-holds
- Protectorates and Semi-Protectorates
- Sphere of Influence
- Condominium
- Financial Control
- Tariff Control
- Extra-territoriality
- Informal Control
- Military Alliances
- Mandate System
- Trust Territories
- Ideological Influence
- Merits of Imperialism
- Defects of Imperialism
- Suggested Readings

It is difficult to give a definition of imperialism which will apply to both ancient and modern empires. Even in modern times, imperialism has assumed many forms. Today, the colonialisation is not as important a factor as the economic and political control of the backward regions of the world. Modern empires are largely for economic and trade purposes. Formerly, it used to be said: "Trade follows the flag" or "Flage follows the trade". Some empires came into existence by mere accident and some were the outcome of deliberate planning. Some regard imperialism as a foster child of aggressive nationalism. It is defined as "a phase of competitive struggle for power among sovereignties." Imperialism is often identified with colonialism. Joseph Chamberlain once said, "The Empire is commerce."

According to Prof. Schuman, "Imperialism is the imposition by force and violence of alien rule upon subject people, despite all moralizing and pretensions to the contrary." Parker T. Moon defines imperialism as "the domination of non-European native races by totally dissimilar European nations." Schumpeter defines imperialism as an "atomistic force, ancient in inception, decadent and self-conscious in an age of nationalism, yet still powerful enough to lord it over its rival, the up start capitalism." According to the Encyclopaedia of Social Sciences, imperialism is "a policy which aims at creating, organising and maintaining an empire: that it is a state of vast size composed of various more or less distinct national units and subject to a single, centralised will."

According to H.G. Wells, "All our modern imperialisms are, thus the more or less conscious efforts of one nation state to become world-wide." M.J. Bonn writes, "Imperialism is a policy which aims at creating, organising and maintaining an empire, that is a state of vast size composed of various more or less distinct national units and subject to a single centralised will." Beard says, "Imperialism is employment of the engines of government and diplomacy to acquire territories, protectorates and /or spheres of influence occupies totally by other races or peoples and to promote industrial, trade and investment opportunities." According to C.D. Burns, imperialism is "a name given to a single system of law and government in many different lands and races."

According to Ebenstein, imperialism is a chief distortion of nationalism. To quote him, "Love of oneself becomes hatred of others and enslavement of others is clothed in such masks as the 'Whiteman's burden' or the need for 'living space'. Even highly democratic nations have at one time or another fallen victims to the disease of imperialism." To some, imperialism is synonymous with economic exploitation and political domination of weaker races and for gross materialism. To others, it is a sacred duty which must not be shirked by the advanced countries of the world in their relation to backward countries. Both of these views are extremes. A well-planned and carefully worked out programme of ruthless exploitation of backward regions is as foreign to the general history of imperialism as a conscious civilising mission typified in the much abused phrase "The Whileman's burden."

Causes for Rise of Imperialism

Many causes are responsible for the growth of imperialism from time to time. (1) In its earlier and more primitive form, imperialism was a manifestation of The predatory instinct of man. Different tribes and races moved from one part of the world to another in search of new pastures, food etc. and conquered all those who came in their way or after driving them away occupied their territories. There were bloody wars and a lot of destruction. Later on, it was the thirst for conquest and struggle for power which brought empires into existence. Cecil Rhodes boasted that he thought in terms of continents. Mussolini declared in 1932 "The Fascist State is a will to power and an empire. The Roman tradition is the idea of force. In the Fascist doctrine, the imperial idea is not only a territorial, military and mercantile expression but also one of spiritual and moral expansion. For Fascism, the tendency to imperial idea means expansion of the nation and is a manifestation of vitality."

(2) The advocates of imperialism maintain that a nation has a *civilising mission*.. Its people belongs to a superior race whose duty is to protect and control incompetent savages. Rhodes wrote in 1877, "I contend that we are the first race in the world and that the more of the world we inhabit, the better it is for the human race. The Christian missionaries and humanitarians also believed in the mission of Great Britain to protect and civilise the primitive races of the world. They were responsible for the emancipation of the slaves. The view of Lord Lugard is that Great Britain should hold her colonies as a "dual mandate". She must act "as trustee on the one hand for the advancement of the subject races and on the other hand for the development of material resources for the benefit of mankind."

We find references to what is known as "Whiteman's burden" in connection with imperialism. There is also a talk of "imperialism of responsibility." The imperialists maintains that by conquering the backward people, they are bestowing great favours on them. Their object is to bring enlightenment to the conquered people. They aim at abolishing cannibalism, slavery, serfdom and usury. The view of the critics is that the original cause of imperialism was never humanitarian. It was merely an after-thought or a lip-service. If there is no substance in the theory of "Whiteman's burden", there is more reality in "Blackman's burden". The imperialist powers have not done much to improve the lot of the conquered people. The money spent on their education, sanitation and the general improvement of the people is very small. The people are left to their fate and they continue to suffer. Julian Huxley tells us that in spite of the rule of imperialist powers, infant mortality ranged from one in four to one in two. Probably every adult Negro was infected with one or more kinds of worms, including hook-worms and often with malaria. In most cases, about 90% of the people suffered from venereal diseases which were imported by the Whitemen. The people continued to suffer from gross malnutrition and vitamin deficiency. Very few children went to schools. Schuman writes, "It is no more the purpose of imperialism to confer benefit upon its victims than to confer benefits upon the home country."

(3) *Religious and humanitarian considerations* are put forward in support of imperialism. The annexation of Siam by France was generally the work of Jesuit millionaires. David Livingstone

was a great missionary and his name is the most outstanding in the history of empire-builders. The London Missionary Society was closely linked up with the spread of British imperialism in Africa. President Coolidge of the United State is said to have obtained, "The legions which (America) sends forth are armed not with the sword but with the cross." General MacArthur advocated a similar policy with regard to Japan after her military defeat in 1945. Imperialism today is generally indifferent to the conversion of the backward classes to Christianity and sometimes even opposes the work of missionaries because that might give the subject people a new dignify and new freedom. However, Christian missionaries in the past were the open or secret allies of the imperialists and they received a warm welcome from empire-builders. In many cases, the missionary was the fore-runner of the trader and the ruler. Christian missionaries in India were given all possible help by the British administrators in India.

(4) Colonial possessions are also desired for *surplus population.* During the nineteenth century the populations of various European states increased by leaps and bounds and there was not enough space for them. Under the circumstances, emigration became a necessity. Great Britain sent her surplus population to Australia, Canada and South Africa. Italy claimed for years that her "narrow but adorable Peninsula" was unable to accommodate her teeming millions and hence she required fresh colonies for her surplus population. A similar plea was put forward by Japan. It was maintained that if the surplus population of a country moved to another country like the United States, those people were completely lost to the mother country. However, if a colony was acquired by the mother country and surplus population was settled there, that added to her prestige and strength and there was no loss to the mother country. However, it is pointed out that in actual practice imperialism has not proved to be an effective remedy for surplus population. The number of the Japanese who migrated to Korea, Formosa and Manchuria and settled there after conquest was very small. Likewise, the number of Italians who left the shores of Italy for settlement in Libya and Italian Somaliland was negligible.

(5) Another cause of imperialism was the *search for raw materials* from the backward countries. Highly industrialised countries required raw materials for their factories and it was easy to get them if they had their own colonies. Not only the source of raw material was secured, those could be got even cheaper from a conquered territory. Dr. Schacht writes, "The fight for raw materials plays the most important part in world politics, and even greater role than before the war (1914)." However, critics point out that no imperial country has been able to depend upon its colonial possessions alone for the supply of all the raw materials required by her barker T. Moon writes that there is no truth in the view generally held that an imperial country gets most of its raw materials from its colonies. To quote him, "Raw materials, in general, are colour blind. They recognise no national flag. They follow the supply and demand and of distance and transportation costs. They obey economic rather than political control."

(6) Colonies are valued even more as *markets for finished* products than as producers of raw materials. It is generally found that whenever a state is industrialised, a stage comes after some time when the home market reaches the saturation point. Then it becomes necessary to export the surplus product. During the nineteenth century. Britain was to workshop of the world and when other countries were also industrialised, competition started and there arose the necessity of having territories to which the surplus goods could be exported. To quote Joseph Chamberlain. "The Empire is commerce." Preferences are given to the goods imported from the mother country. The view of Andrew Carnegie is that trade always does not follow the flag but follows the lowest current price. The conclusion of R.L. Buell is that only one-fifth of the world trade is from countries which come under imperial control and the remaining four-fifths with independent states. However, it cannot be denied that "imperialism affords an additional margin of marketing facilities for an industrial nation's goods."

(7) Empires are also valued for *the export of surplus capital.* It is well known that the United States exerts great influence in Central and South America on account of her vast investment. This is known as "Dollar diplomacy", it is as effective as a foreign army of occupation. It is rightly said that if money talks. American dollars snouts. Lenin writes. "Imperialism is capitalism in that stage of development in which the domination of monopolies and finance capital has taken shape, in which the export of capital has acquired preponderant importance, in which the division of the world by international trusts has begun and in which the partition of the territory of the earth by the greatest capitalist countries have been completed." Capital may be lent not only by imperialist countries but also by their individual citizens and private companies. This tendency is to be seen where labour is cheap and abundant and is not able to defend itself. If a country is not able to exploit its own natural resources to the full, some advanced country has a right to do so On the ground that the resources of the world belong to those who can best use them.

(8) Another cause of imperialism in modern times is *diplomatic.* Imperialism breeds imperialism. The vital interests of Britain in the Suez Canal, her efforts to establish some form of authority and friendly relations in West Asia and her partial occupation of Iran are to explained in relation to her control over India. The British naval base at Singapore was & reminder to Japan that she could not attack Australia or any part of the British Empire in the East, with impunity. For the same reason, France controlled Djibuti.

(9) The *necessity of acquiring strategic bases* is also responsible for a policy of imperialism. It was with that idea that Great Britain acquired Girbraltar, Malta, Aden and Singapore. The same can be said about the American search for strategic bases all over the world in modern times. It was with a view to defend her possessions in India that Britain established her control over Egypt and the Suez canal.

(10) The *desire to have prestige in the world* has also been responsible for the annexation of other territories. Experience shows that the possession of colonies became a hall-mark of respectability in the international world. Although it brought no material gain to her. Italy was proud of her possession of Libya. The same could be said of the possession of territories by many other imperialist powers. It is said that every Englishman had a feeling of pride that he was a part owner of the mighty British Empire. Hans Kohn writes. "Besides the economic urge, psychological motive played a great role in imperialism—the lust for ad venture and for power, the added prestige and glory which seemed to accrue from a vast colonial empire not only to the governing classes but even to the masses of the colonising nations, the new sentiment of pride and superiority which animated even the lowest members of the White races in their dealings with the backward races."

(11) Imperialism provides *employment facilities for the people of the mother country* in the colonies. The citizens of the imperial state work as consuls, proconsuls and diplomats. They are given high posts in the civil service, in the army and in other Departments of the government. Merchants, traders, planters and joint stock companies belonging to the mother country control the trade and commerce in the colony. Manufacturers of arms and armaments, military uniforms and shipowners also benefit by imperialism.

(12) Imperialism may also be based *on political ideology.* Communist states have decided to acquire ideological influence in other countries. That ultimately leads to complete control over those areas. For example, Tibet has come under the complete control of China.

The Soviet Union started as an anti-imperialist country, but even she has now become an imperialist power. A reference may be made in this connection to the conquest of Finland by the Soviet Union. She has also established her control over East Germany, Poland, Czechoslovakia, Hungary and Rumania. She interfered militarily in Hungary and Czechoslovakia when those countries started following liberal policies. She has occupied Afghanistan.

To begin with, the United States was an opponent of colonialism and imperialism but even she is following indirectly an imperialist policy. She has secured strategic naval, aerial and military bases in different parts of the world with a view to check the advance of the Soviet Union and Communist China. She has entered into military alliances such as the NATO and the SEATO. She has special military commitments with Japan and Pakistan. She has alliance with Australia and New Zealand. England has become the latest "colonial possession" of the United States.

Communist China has also emerged as a great imperialist power. She has virtually Annexed Tibet. As a result of her invasion of India in 1962, she is in virtual occupation of more than 12500 Sq. miles of Indian territory. She is determined to get back from the Soviet Union all those territories which were taken away by her from China during the nineteenth century. She is equally determined to get back all those territories which were once occupied by Japan. Her designs to conquer the neighbouring territories are very ambitious.

Development of Imperialism

The concept of empire was there in ancient times. Alexander, the Great was a great empire-builder. To begin with, the Romans had no imperial pretensions, but the war with Cartage and the growing necessity of controlling the trade routes in the Mediterranean led them gradually to the road to empire. The Roman Empire was tolerant towards the local customs.

After the decline of the Roman empire, many big and small feudal states came into existence. An imperialist tendency could be seen in them. Charlemagne tried to re-establish a vast empire in Europe. The Arabs established a vast empire from Spain to Sind. During the tenth century, the Turks established a vast empire over Central Asia and Afghanistan. During the twelfth century, the Mongols rose into power and established their vast empires in China. Central Asia and Russia. The Afghans established their empire in India. The same was done by the Mughals in India.

The Spanish, Portuguese and Dutch empires were essentially of a commercial nature although there was a certain amount of missionary zeal in them. The native civilisations of Central and Southern America were exterminated by the Spaniards in their lust for gold. Their exploitation of the people was of the most brutal type. Religious intolerance and economic laziness brought about the fall of the Spanish empire.

The beginnings of the British Empire were made with the colonization of Virginia. The Pilgrim Fathers went to North America for the sake of religious freedom. The English East India Company was founded in 1600 for trade with India. Similar companies were started by the French and the Dutch. The British had to fight against the French and the Dutch to establish their empire in India and North America. The struggle was practically over by the end of the Seven Years War.

Before the American War of Independence, the British colonial system was based on mercantilist principle. Colonies were meant for exploitation by the mother country. They were not given any freedom to manage their affairs in their own way. However, after the loss of the thirteen colonies in North America. Britain learnt a lesson. Particularly after the Durham Report in 1839, a liberal policy was followed towards the colonies. Interference in their internal affairs was lessened by slow degrees and colonies were allowed to managed their own affairs. The Imperial Conference of 1926 defined the position of the dominions as "equal in status, in no way subordinate to one another in any respect of their domestic or external affairs though united by a common allegiance to the Crown and freely associated as members of the British Commonwealth of Nations." This position was legalised by the Statute of Westminster in 1931. A lot of progress was made after that.

Modern imperialism, so far as most of the European nations are concerned, began in 1884 with the scramble for Africa. All European nations became empire-conscious and they competed with one another to acquire as much of territory as they could on the Dark Continent. Between 1884 and

1914, Germany acquired one million square miles of new territory with a population of 15 millions. France acquired four million square miles with 50 million inhabitants. Great Britain acquired more than three million square miles of territory with a population of 57 millions. In 1892, the White people controlled 9% of the surface of the world, but in 1935, they controlled 85%. In 1850, Disraeli referred to the "wretched colonies" as "dead weights", but later on he himself became a great imperialist. He was responsible for the purchase of the shares of the Suez Canal which led to the domination of Egypt by Grate Britain. It was during his regime that Queen Victoria became the Queen Empress of India. Sir John Seeley popularised the imperialist idea by writing his famous book. "The Expansion of England". Rudyard Kipling put forward the creed of the Whiteman's burden. Ruskin expressed the same sentiment in these words: "This is what England must either do or perish: she must found colonies as fast and as far as she is able, formed of her most energetic and worthiest men; seizing every piece of fruitful waste ground she can set her foot on, and then teaching these her colonists that their chief virtue is the fidelity to their country, and that their first aim is to be to advance the power of England by land and sea." Bernard Shaw gave his description of British imperialism in "The Man of Destiny" (1896) in these words: "Every Englishman is born with a certain miraculous power that makes him the master of the world. When he wants a thing, he never tells himself that he wants it. He waits patiently until there comes into his mind, no one knows how a burning conviction that it is his moral and religious duty to conquer those who possess the thing he wants. Then he becomes irresistible. He is never at a loss for an effective moral attitude. As the great champion of freedom and national independence, he conquers and annexes half the world and calls it colonisation. When he wants a new market for his adulterated Manchester goods, he sends a missionary to teach the natives the Gospel of Peace. The natives kill the missionary; he flies to arms in defence of Christianity; fights for it, conquers for it and takes the market as a reward from heaven.

During the nineteenth century, Russia established her empire as far as Central Asia. Japan extended her empire in certain parts of China and Korea. Italy conquered Ethiopia.

During the twentieth century, two World Wars took place among the imperialist powers as their interests clashed. As a result of the two World Wars and the spread of nationalism in the world, the colonies in Asia, Africa and South America were successful in becoming independent. After the second World War, India, Pakistan, Burma, Indonesia, Israel, Ghana, Egypt, Syria, Algeria, Morocco. Zimbabwe and other African countries became independent. At present, there is a great reaction against imperialism. Old imperialism is vanishing but imperialism is appearing in new forms.

MODERN IMPERIALISM

Modern imperialism is indirect and relies more on diplomacy and international agreements than on the sword. A modern imperialist state is more interested in the control of the commerce, industry, rail roads, ports and strategic bases than physical control of a colony. It takes the form of lease-holds, protectorates and semi-protectorates, sphere of influence, condominium, financial control, tariff control, extra-territoriality, informal control, intervention, military alliances, mandates and trusteeship system.

Lease-holds

Weak and backward countries are persuaded or compelled to give up portions of their territories for a number of years, usually 99 years for commercial or strategic reasons. The nominal sovereignty still remain with the country granting the lease but actual control is in the hands of the lessee. For all practical purposes, the lease-hold is a colony until the lease expires. In 1898. Russia got from China a lease of the Manchurian port for a period of 25 years. Likewise, Japan held Port Arthur and Darien from China. Great Britain got from China a lease of Wei-hai-wai. The United States has a sort of protectorate over the Republic of Panama. The US authorities have full sovereignty over the Canal zone. It is a sort of imperialism under a different garb.

Protectorates and Semi-Protectorates

Protectorates are of different kinds. In almost all cases, foreign relations and defence are in the hands of the imperialist power. In many cases, financial control is also exercised by the imperialist power over the country under her protection. The best example of a protectorate in recent times was that of Egypt. Great Britain occupied Egypt in 1882. Egypt was declared independent on 28 February 1922, but many restrictions was put on her. From 1922 to 1936. Egypt was to all intents and purposes, the disguised protectorate. Great Britain reserved to herself the right of the security of the communications of the British Empire in Egypt. She was also responsible for the defence of Egypt against all foreign aggression or interference, whether direct or indirect. She was also responsible for the protection of foreign interests in Egypt and the protection of minorities. Cuba and Haiti were examples of semi-protectorates. Abyssinia was an example of an international protectorate. According to the Convention of 1906, Great Britain, France and Italy agreed to protect the integrity of Abyssinia and not to compete with one another for concessions.

Sphere of Influence

In the case of sphere of influence, the state holding the territory is given "preferential or exclusive rights to make loans, construct railways, operate mines or develop public works." Very often, the establishment of a sphere of influence ultimately results in a protectorate or annexation. By the Anglo-Russian Convention of 1907, Great Britain and Russia carved out their respective spheres of influence in Persia (Iran). Northern Persia was to be under the sphere of influence of Russia and South Persia under the sphere of influence of Great Britain. There were similar spheres of influence of England and France in Siam. Sometimes a distinction is made between a sphere of influence and a sphere of interest. The former implies vague political privileges short of a protectorate, but the latter is strictly economic. About the sphere of influence, Buell writes, "This form of control has probably led to more disputes than it has settled."

Condominium

Condominium implies joint government or control by two or more powers over a disputed territory with a view to avoid colonial rivalry. Great Britain, France and Spain exercised such control over the City of Tangier in Morocco. A similar control was exercised by Great Britain and France over the New Hebrides. Similar control was exercised by Great Britain and Egypt over the waters of the Nile in the Sudan. Experience shows that this kind of control is always unsatisfactory and does not work for long. That is partly due to the divided responsibility of the powers concerned.

Financial Control

In a number of cases, capitalist countries either through government officials or representatives of banks, control the revenues and expenditures of the governments of the backward countries which are otherwise independent. Such control may be exercised by one state or by several states. Such control is exercised by the United States over certain Caribbean and Central American countries.

Tariff Control

Western countries, in order to dump their goods upon backward regions, compel the under-developed countries not to raise the tariff duties on foreign goods. This system brings profits to the Western countries at the cost of indigenous industry. China, Turkey, Morocco, Siam and Persia were victims of this kind of control.

Extra-territoriality

In some countries, foreign governments have claimed to exercise the right to establish their own courts for the trial of their own nationals. The justification given is that the standard of justice in the backward countries is not high and consequently the nationals of foreign governments are likely to utter if they are forced to be tried by native courts according to their own procedures. Such a right was claimed and established in all Muslim countries. China, Japan, Korea and Siam. However, those claims were given up after the lapse of some time when things improved in the backward countries and the standard of justice was raised. The Unites States gave up her such claim over Japan in 1894. In 1924, the Soviet Union gave up similar claims in China. After the World War II, Great Britain and the United States gave up their similar claims in China. Experience shows that these claims were frequently abused.

Informal Control

In some cases, a sort of informal control is exercised by one country over another. The method of such control is described by Buell as "extra-legal" or "backstairs method". Various devices are adopted to exercise this type of control. The United States used her marines in Nicaragua. Santo Domingo and the Caribbean. A similar thing was done by Great Britain in Persis, Iraq and Egypt in matters of finance. The United States intervened in Latin American countries in the name of the Monroe doctrine. Many wars have been fought to impose the policy of "open door" on a weak country. Under such a system, no discrimination is exercised against the nationals of any foreign country. What is required is an equality of opportunity for both the imperial and other foreign countries. The United States stood tor a policy of open door in China as she did not like to be excluded from that country while others powers were enjoying their privileges and concessions. The "closed door" policy is the opposite of the open door policy. That involves preferences, discriminations and monopolies in trade, commerce, shipping, investment etc. The object of such a policy is to strengthen the economic ties between the mother country and the colony and to exclude foreigners. The United States followed such a policy towards the Philippine Islands. The closed door policy has usually three forms viz., tariffs, shipping and concessions. Buell writes. "From the standpoint of the consumer, the closed door means high prices; from the standpoint of a native, it is but one more phase of the polity of exploitation: from the standpoint of the world at large, it means the perpetuation of the worst forms of nationalistic imperialism."

Military Alliances

The members countries of a military alliance are independent and sovereign but they agree to pursue a common military policy. Generally, they are all united under the hegemony of a strong and powerful nation. The NATO, SEATO AND CENTO are examples of military alliances. When aggression is committed against a member of a military alliance, the other countries are pledged to give whole-hearted support.

Mandate System

After the World War I, a new policy was followed with regard to the colonial possessions of the defeated Powers. It was maintained at the Peace Conference of 1919 that the rights of the backward people should be the first concern of the Allies and no single Allied Power should be allowed to become the sole possessor of any of the colonial territories of the former enemy countries. That led to be establishment of the mandate system whose object was to safeguard the interests of the native population and to avoid friction and rivalry among the Imperial powers. Three kinds of mandates were provided depending upon the stage of development of the country concerned. The work of administering the mandates was given to the advanced nations which were required to submit their annual reports regarding the work done by them. It is true that the mandate system was started in good faith but it did not work well. Instead of regarding the mandates as trusts of civilisation, the mandatory powers considered the territories entrusted to them as annexation. Schuman writes, "For all practical purposes , the C mandates were treated as annexations and the B Mandate administration was scarcely distinguishable from that which would have been provided for outright conquest. The A Mandates were also under effective control of the mandatories." It was found that with the exception for Iraq, the mandatory states ruthlessly crushed the legitimate aspirations of the people for independence and self-government. Even in the matter of the choice of the mandatory state, the wishes of the people concerned were not respected. The people of Syria wanted the United State to be appointed as the mandatory power but actually France was given the mandate. The League of Nations failed to have an effective control over the mandatory states. The view of Schuman is that the Mandates Commission "has not acted vigorously as a bold and independent agency." The recommendations of the Commission were merely of an advisory nature and did not bind anybody. The people of the mandated territories were not allowed to approach the League of Nations for the redress of their grievances. The Mandates Commission did not visit the mandated territories to see the lot of the people.

Trust Territories

These were those territories whose people were not considered to be fit for self-government. Those territories were taken over by the United Nations from the defeated powers after World War II. Those states were distributed among the Allied Powers who were to administer them on behalf of the United Nations with a view to prepare them for self-government. IT is also considered to be a form of imperialism.

Ideological Influence

Although the Communist countries criticise imperialism, they themselves practise ideological imperialism. Bulgaria, Rumania etc. are supposed to be Republics. They all have facades of a sovereign state. However, the strong ideological influence under which they function, has virtually reduced their independence to nil. Likewise, North Korea and Vietnam are under the strong ideological influence of Moscow or Peking. Their domestic and foreign policies are directed from Moscow or Peking. These are cases of ideological imperialism.

Merits of Imperialism

The view of C.D. Burns is that imperialism breaks down the narrowness of village politics and leads to internationalism and world brotherhood. From the ideological point of view, it is in the real interest of the vigorous races to be "kept up to a high pitch of external efficiency by contest, chiefly by way of war with inferior races and with equal races by the struggle for the trade routes and for the sources of raw material and of food supply." It is in the interest of humanity that there should continue a struggle between races with different traits of character and different types of civilisation. "It is desirable that the earth should be peopled, governed and developed as far as possible by the races which can do this work best *i.e.* by the races of highest social efficiency." A race of higher social efficiency can conquer, subjugate and extinguish races of lower social efficiency. From the biological point of view, in the history of man, stronger races have, form time to time, trampled down, enslaved and exterminated the other races. From the ethical point of view, the conquest of the weaker by the stronger has been the prime condition and mode of progress in the past and it is desirable that the same should continue in the future. From the religious point of view, European imperialism gave the backward races of the world the blessings of European civilisation and teachings of Christianity. Imperialism has abolished cannibalism, slavery and crude forms of justice and government. Roads have been built and railways have been constructed. Hospitals have been set up. Education has been started and encouraged. Trade has been developed. All this has been done by the imperial powers.

The argument of the imperialists is that the dependent countries are benefited because the different cultures, races and nationalities are united under one banner and they become politically conscious. Political unity in India was the result of British imperialism. In a vast empire, different races get opportunities of mutual contacts and their outlook is broadened. When many countries become a part and parcel of a big empire, they get trading facilities, not available otherwise. When backward races come into touch with the developed nations, they make tremendous progress. The aggressiveness of the dependent countries is destroyed by the imperialist power and a new awakening and strength is infused into them.

To the imperial Powers themselves, imperialism gives a sense of prestige and ensures them a steady market and raw materials. "National empires may becomes instruments of enlightened rule, just as Government at home may be expanded in purpose and functions to save the welfare of many nations than few. No one can deny the devotion to duty of colonial administration, none fails to appreciate the willing sacrifice of medical, educational and religious missions."

Defects of Imperialism

The critics of imperialism point out the defects of imperialism. The view of J.A. Hobson is that imperialism is rapacious and immoral. It results in racial arrogance, brutality, ruthlessness, exploitation, misery and poverty. A reference is made to the atrocities committed by the Belgians in the Cango, indentured labour and virtual slavery which prevailed in many parts of the tropical empire. Enormous tracts of land were usurped by a handful of Whites in Kenya and South Africa. It has been calculated that in South Africa, 15 lacs of Whites owned about 28 crores of acres of land while 55 lacs of Negroes possessed only 2.7 crores of acres of land. As a result of the policy of Apartheid or racial segregation, the Negores, the Indians and other non-Whites in South Africa were driven to the ghettoes. In 1958, 67 Negores were shot dead ad many more were seriously injured when the Negroes protested against the law which compelled them to carry pass cards. The view of Barnes is that in the mining districts of Africa, conditions analogous to slavery prevailed. Native labourers were recruited by deception. The compound system under which many of them lived, was detrimental to their health, morals and economic uplift. In a Transvaal and Natal, "No male native may be employed outside the farm on which he resides unless he carries a document from the farmer permitting him to seek employment."

Lenonard Woolf points out that in the year 1924, out of an estimated revenue of about two million pounds, the government of Kenya spent £ 44,000 on prisons and £ 37,000 on education. The policy of the government was to favour about 10,000 European at the expense of 36,000 Asian and 25,000 Africans. All the best land was reserved for Europeans and the "native is on the road which leads to economic slavery." Things were very bad in Southern Rhodesia (now Zimbabwe) where a handful of the Whites ruled over the vast majority of natives.

What is true of other countries was equally true of India under the British rule. It is true that Englishmen gave law and order to the people of India. It is also true that they gave us roads, canals, hospitals, schools etc. They also established in India a uniform system of law and law courts. However, India had to pay a very heavy price. There was the great economic drain from the country. India was ruled not in the interests of the people of India but in the interests of England. Englishmen had a monopoly of all the big jobs in the government and in the army. There was no outlet for any brilliant Indian and that had a demoralising effect on the people of the country. The health of the people was very poor. The rate of infant mortality was very high. The revenues of India were meant for the enjoyment of the Britishers in India. Parker Moon writes, "The reason why the British first entered India and the primary reason why they have remained there was not to benefit India but to benefit Great Britain. Mahatma Gandhi wrote, "The government established by law in British. India is carried on for the exploitation of the masses. No sophistry, no jugglery in figures can explain away the evidence the skeletons in many villages present to the naked eye." It is no wonder that there was a demand n the country that the foreigners must leave and ultimately India won her independent in 1947.

Schuman tells us that the imperial powers adopt various methods to maintain their stranglehold over the backward territories. They crush native resistance by force and devise various means to enfeeble their victims. They use persuasion, education and coercion to make the people loyal to the empire. They replace the language and culture of the people by their own language and culture. They make "a pretence of colonial participation in the national government", but keep the real power in their own hands. They use the native princes and the vested interests as their agents to keep the people divided so that they cannot unite against the foreign government. They do not allow the executive to be controlled by the legislature. To quote Schuman, "So long as those who resist alien rule are weaker than the foreign conquerors, resistance merely intensifies foreign oppression and prolongs the dictatorial regime imposed from without." Public disorders are created. Inter communal rivalries are encouraged. The people are not give a chance to grow and they are told that they will be put incharge of their government when they prove their fitness to rule themselves.

The imperialist powers introduce their own religion, morals and social institutions in the territories under their control and thereby they destroy the indigenous culture and create social chaos and demoralisation. The people lose their arts, morals and folkways and become "grotesque and debased caricatures of Western Whitemen." Modern imperialism is through-going in its application to the people. It destroys the best in their culture and civilisation. It calls them people of "lesser breeds without the law".

The imperial power kills the incentive of the colonial people and provides them with that much of education which makes them clerks. It crushes native resistance by force. It follows different tactics to make the colonial people the loyal subjects of the empire.

Imperialism is responsible for racial hatred and friction. The Western imperial powers have a superiority complex. They try to impose their customs, culture, civilisation, language and religion. That results in the destruction of indigenous culture which leads to social chaos and demoralisation.

Imperialism also leads to war. Even after subjugation, the imperial power maintains a huge army to protect its interests and prestige. There is always the danger of a revolt by the native people and the possibility of rival imperial power grabbing the colony. The occupation of a colony always leads to bloodshed. It is rightly said that the path of empire is red with the blood of its victims. "Diplomacy, coercion and military force are the necessary accompaniments of imperialism."

Imperialism does not help the masses in the imperial country. It brings advantages only to a favoured few. Likewise, particular industries may get some benefit but not industries in general. Imperialism may confer some indirect benefit upon the ordinary people belonging to the imperial country, but that is not true in all cases. If at all they get any benefit, they pay it back in the form of taxes to maintain a huge army which is necessary to protect a far flung empire. Imperialism results in the lowering of wages and standard of living in the imperial country because the capitalists invest more money in the backward countries to get quick returns for their money. Imperialism destroys the moral standard of the people of the imperial country and debases their conscience. Despotism, repression and brutality perpetrated upon the colonial people are also practised over their own countrymen in the long run. The military excesses of the imperial power required for protecting the empire pose a big problem for the rights and liberties of the people belonging to me imperial power. Imperialism destroys any possibility of cordial relationship between the people of the colony and the imperial power. They look upon each other with suspicion and hatred.

A direct legacy of imperialism is constant friction among the races inhabiting the territory under imperialist control. When India was still not free, the Dean of Worcester referred to her in these words, "Let us turn to the root of the troubles in India. Our rule in that country has undoubtedly conferred great benefits upon it. We have kept the peace during a long period between warring factions. We have made rail roads. We have fought famine. We have improved health. We have increased fertility... We have done much for the material needs of India, but we have not won the love of her people. Why Not? Because we have hurt their souls."

Norman Thomas says, "Many a man without six feet of earth in which to be buried is swollen with pride because his country 'owns' an empire." In the German colonies before the World War I, "Whitemen carried around ships as naturally as they did handkerchiefs." H.G. Wells says that imperialism means "arrogant swagger, the opposite of cosmopolitanism." Hocking's view is that imperialism "destroys even without knowing that it destroys."

Imperialism breeds imperialism and that ultimately leads to war. It is rightly said that the path of an empire is red with the blood of its victims. It is also maintained that "diplomacy, coercion and military posts are the necessary accompaniments of imperialism."

It is contended that imperialism does not bring any great material advantage to the people of the mother country. It is true that imperialism is a great tonic for a people suffering from a feeling of inferiority, but it does not help the masses materially. To quote Schuman. "Libya constitutes one of the most perfect examples of colonial possession acquired and held at a great cost to the tax-payers of the home country for reasons of diplomatic powers and prestige, with only moderate profits accusing to privileged investors and concessionaires and no economic gains whatever occurring to the nation as a whole." The gains go only to a favoured few but the nation as a whole pays the piper without calling the tune. It is pointed out that even the policy of imperial preference did not bring much relief to the British empire. The Times of London wrote, "In the seven years between Ottawa and the outbreak of War. Great Britain and the dominions simultaneously learned that their most pressing economic problems and the hopes of solving them turned on their trade relations not with one another but with the rest of the world."

In order to protect a big empire, the imperial power is forced to maintain a large army, navy and air force. That means extra burden on the tax-payers of the imperial country. A stage comes when it becomes too much to put up with that burden and the country is forced to cut her military expenditure. That can be done only by giving up the empire. It is well-known that it was partly on account of this factor that Great Britain gave independence to India. Burma, Ceylon, Singapore and other countries under her control.

Critics point out to the moral effects of imperialism upon the victors themselves. Hocking says, "It is especially dangerous for any people to live long among a population which it holds in contempt." The standard of morality of the victors is lowered and their conscience is debased. If injustice is tolerated in a colony, it has its effect on the mother country. Referring to the administrators, soldiers and businessmen who come back to their mother country after a long stay in a colony. J.A. Hobson says, "Everywhere they stand for coercion and for resistance to reform... It is indeed a nemesis of imperialism that the arts and crafts of tyranny, acquired and exercised in our unfree Empire, should be turned against our liberties at home." It is pointed out that the freedom-loving Englishmen have lost some of their original zeal for freedom partly on account of the mentality imbibed by them on account of the military excesses of their countrymen abroad and the restrictions placed by them on freedom in various parts of their empire.

Critics point out that imperialism in practice is not conducive to peace. At best, it means armed neutrality. Imperialism means international rivalry and competition. It means a struggle for markets, raw materials and places for capital investment. There is going to be struggle between the imperial powers for colonies and markets. To quote Leonard Barnes, "It is true and fair to say that

Britain's possession, on the present privileged terms, of a vast dependent Empire is incompatible with peace."

A question has been asked whether there is any alternative to imperialism. The answer give is that if imperialism is to justify itself, imperialism of responsibility should replace imperialism of exploitation. A new mentality should replace the old mentality. Instead of keeping its eye on the exploitation of the people, the imperial power should aim at the happiness and welfare of the people under his control. The selfish and grabbing policy must be given up. The alienation of native land and the exploitation of native labour should be forbidden by law. Restrictions should be put on the free flow of private capital into the backward areas. It is suggested that an International Board of Colonial Investment should be set up to help the backward areas so far as their financial needs are concerned so that the chances of their exploitation at the hands of the unscrupulous foreign investors are eliminated altogether or lessened to a very great extent. Every effort must be made to give facilities to the people of the backward areas so that they can develop their faculties as quickly as possible and are in a position to rule themselves in as short a period as possible. L. Woolf says, "Unless Europe does its best to help Asia to pass from imperialist subjection to complete independence without resistance and friction, the world may find itself faced with a conflict and outburst of nationalism compared with which the Great War was the mildest of evils."

Ismail of Egypt has laid down the following duties for the imperialist powers:

"To accept government only if by so doing you benefit the race you rule;"

"To lead, not drive, the people to a higher civilization;

"To abandon relations with your native land;

"To resist other governments, and keep intact the sovereignty of the state whose bread you eat;

"To represent the native when advising...on any question which your own or any foreign government may wish solved; and in this

"To have for prop and guide that which is universally right throughout the world, that which is best for the people of the state you serve."

SUGGESTED READINGS

Barker, E.	:	Nietzsche and Treitschke, 1914.
Barnes, Leonard	:	The Duty of Empire.
Brewer, Anthony	:	Marxist Theories of Imperialism: A Critical Survey, London, 1980.
Burns, CD.	:	Political Ideals, World Press, Calcutta, 1965.
Darmole, Mashood B.O.	:	The Heritage of Imperialism.
Davis, H.C.W.	:	The Political Thought of Heinrich von Treitschke, 1915.
Frank, A.G.	:	Capitalism and Underdevelopment in Latin America, London, 1967.
Hausrath, A.	:	Treitschke: His Life and Works, 1914.
Hobson, J.A.	:	Imperialism, A Study.
Lichtheim, George	:	Imperialism, the Penguin Press, London, 1971.
Moon. P.T.	:	Imperialism and World Politics.

Moussa	:	Under-Privileged Nations.
Owen, Roger and Bob Sutcliffe (Eds.)	:	Studies in the Theory of Imperialism, Longmans, London, 1972.
Peruam	:	Colonial Reckoning.
Schumpeter, Joseph A.	:	Capitalism, Socialism and Democracy, New York, 1962.
Slade	:	Belgian Cango.
Treitschke	:	Politics (2 Vols.)
Wallerstein, I.	:	The Capitalist World Economy, Cambridge University Press, 1979.
Winslow, E.M.	:	The Pattern of Imperialism, 1948.
Woolf, L.	:	Imperialism and Civilisation.
Zimmern, A.E.	:	The Third British Empire.

CHAPTER

Political Thought of Harold J. Laski (1893–1950)

Learning Objectives

- State Sovereignty
- Authority as Federal
- Rights
- Safeguards for Rights
- Particular Rights
- Capitalism and War
- Capitalism and Democracy
- Importance of Economic Factor in Politics
- Liberty
- Equality
- Property
- Suggested Readings

Professor Harold J. Laski was on the greatest political scientists of our times. He was born in 1893 at Manchester in a Jewish family. From the very beginning, he was a genius and he struck every body with his wonderful memory and studious habits. He studied at the New College, Oxford, from 1911 to 1914. His teachers at Oxford were H.A.L. Fisher, F.W. Maitland and Ernest Barker. For about one year, he worked as a lecturer at the Mac Gill University, Montreal in Canada and in January 1916 shifted to the Harvard University where he stayed up to 1920. From 1920 to 1950, he worked at the London School of Economics. He was appointed as Professor of Political Science in place of Graham Wallas. While in London, he came into contact with the greatest personalities of his day. He impressed everyone by his ability and knowledge. He had a passion for teaching and loved his students from the very core of his heart. He worked day and night for their welfare. In addition to teaching and writing on political science, he indulged in a lot of free-lance journalism. He wrote for the daily press and periodicals. At the same time he took keen interest in the politics of his country. He was a member of the Fabian Society and later on became the Chairman of the Labour Party and played a leading role in labour politics during the 1930's and 1940's.

Laski was a great writer. He wrote innumerable articles which can fill many volumes. However, his important books are *A Grammar of Politics, Authority in the Modern State, Liberty in the Modern State, The State in Theory and Practice: Parliamentary Government in England, The American Presidency, The American Democracy and Political Thought in England From Locke to Bentham.*

State Sovereignty

As regards his political philosophy, he was a great critic of the theory of sovereignty as given by Austin. To quote him, "No sovereign has anywhere possessed unlimited power and the attempt to exert it has always resulted in the establishment of safeguards. Even the Sultan of Turkey in the height of its power was himself bound down to a code of traditional observance obedience of which was practically compulsory upon him. In law, there was no part of the social fact he could not alter;

in practice he survived only by willing not to will those changes which might have proved him the sovereign of Austinian jurisprudence". Laski pointed out that it was difficult to find an unlimited sovereign in the United States. Neither the President not the Congress possessed unlimited power. To quote Laski again, "In the theoretical sense, therefore, the U.S.A. has no sovereign organ, for the judges of the Supreme Court, being over-ridden by the constitutional amendments, are a court of reference." Laski pointed out that the difficulty of discovering a sovereign was not confined only to a federal system. It was doubtful whether in the Austinian sense, Belgium could be called a sovereign state at all. The Constitution guaranteed certain rights to every citizen regarding his religion, property, right of assembly etc. If the Austinian view of sovereignty was to be accepted, either Belgium was not a sovereign state in its internal affairs or its sovereignty resided in the electorate. Laski quoted with approval the view of Henry Maine that from the historical point of view, "the Austinian theory is artificial to the point of absurdity."

According to Austin, law is essentially a command. However, Laski points out that "to think of law as simply a command is, even for the jurist, to strain definition to the verge of decency." While law is the same for both the legislators and the subjects, the same is not true of command. A command separates the giver from the person who obeys the command. The man who gives the command does not obey it. The characteristic of law is that it is obeyed not only by the people for whom it is made, but also by the legislators who make it. Thus, law is universal and uniform for all, while command is not. Laski points out that the element of command does not enter into enabling statutes. When a Franchise Act gives the right of vote to women, it cannot be interpreted as a command. No obligation is imposed unless we regard the duty of the Legislative officer to accept women as voters as an obligation. It is difficult to see how the exercise of delegated authority can be interpreted as a command.

The view of Laski is that from whatever point of view the theory of legal sovereignty is examined, it suffers from serious drawbacks. There is a lot of convincing evidence against it. It is difficult to accept the theory either in toto or in part. One might conclude with the following words of Laski in *A Grammar of Politics:* "It would be of lasting benefit to political science if the whole concept of sovereignty were surrendered."

Authority as Federal

According to Laski, all authority is federal. There is no authority which can claim absolute control over individuals. At the most, the state can exercise a partial control over the lives of individuals. Man is a bundle of wants to fulfil which he joins many associations, each one of which makes its contribution to he development of his personality. Each of these associations makes only a partial contribution to his life. A trade union can safeguard the economic interests of a labourer and the church caters to his spiritual needs. The state as constituted can satisfy the political needs of the people and not their spiritual and moral requirements. The contribution made by the state to our lives is partial and consequently the obedience that we owe to the state is also proportionately partial. It is an elementary principle of politics that rights and powers are relative to functions. No wonder, the allegiance demanded by the state must be partial. Laski maintains that whatever aspect of life we might take, authority is found to be federal everywhere. Even in the matter of legislation on any topic, the work cannot be given to any single individual. As a law has to serve the interests of all, all must be consulted in the making of it so that their points of view may be taken into consideration at the time of the enactment of the bill into law.

Rights

According to Laski, every state is known by the rights it maintains. We judge the state according to its contribution to the happiness of men. This does not mean that the state creates rights. The fact is that it merely recognises them. Rights do not mean the grant of some historic conditions possessed in the childhood of mankind but lost in course of time. There is no golden age to which we can return. The position of the modern state is not what it was ever before. Rights also do no imply the establishment of any natural order which does not change, There can be no permanency with regard to the rights which must be guaranteed to individuals. Rights also do not imply the power to satisfy desires. There are desires like those of murder or homicide which cannot be recognised by any decent society. No society will survive if it accepts such a proposition.

According to Laski, rights are those conditions of social life without which no man can seek, in general, to be himself at his best. Rights are prior to the state in the sense that whether they are recognised or not, they are there. Rights are not historical in the sense that they have at some time won their recognition. They are not natural in the sense that a permanent and unchanging catalogue of them can be prepared. They are historical in the sense that at some given period and place, they are demanded by the character of its civilisation. They are natural in the sense that under certain limitations, the facts demand their recognition. Rights have a content which changes with time and place. Rights are rights because they are useful to the citizens of the state. They may be opposed to the social, economic and political order in a country, but their validity cannot be challenged because those are necessary for the progress of the people concerned.

The question has been raised whether an individual can have any right against the state or not. The reply of Laski is in the affirmative. According to him, it is the duty of the state to provide individuals with those outward environments which are essential for the development of their character. The citizen has claims upon the same and the latter must protect them. The state must grant those conditions without which an individual cannot attain his best self.

Rights also imply duties. If I have a right, the enjoyment of that right implies a corresponding duty on the part of others. Rights are real only to the extent to which they have been accepted by others as an obligation. The larger the number of rights enjoyed by me, the greater must be the duty to be discharged by others.

Rights are co-relative with functions. The number of rights possessed by an individual must correspond to the contribution which he makes in person to society. The rights which I can claim must correspond to my contribution. The contribution must be personal or it is no contribution at all. I do not contribute by being the child of my parents. I must do something personally which is useful to society.

Rights at a minimum basis are identical. It is the duty of the state to guarantee a certain minimum of rights without which it is impossible for individuals to live a creative life. When those minimum needs have been satisfied, then alone arises the question of differentiation.

Safeguards for Rights

According to Laski, there are three general conditions which facilitate the task of guaranteeing rights to the people. The first condition is that the state must be decentralised one. In such a state, the people are bound to take more interest in those problems which affect them intimately. As the authority functions before their very eyes, any infringement of any law is noticed by the people and they start taking more interest in the affairs of the state. A sense of responsibility can be inculcated among the people through the exercise of power. Concentration of all power at one place is bound to create a sense of irresponsibility.

The second general condition is that the central government should be surrounded by consultative bodies. To every department should be attached a group of experts of the line whose duty is to advise the department regarding the problems facing it. The object is to enable the consultative bodies to put forward their own point of view for consideration.

The third general condition is that the state should refrain from interfering with the internal life of other associations. Associations must be allowed full opportunity to chalk out their own programmes and act accordingly. The state should not intervene so long as an association does not openly advocate the use of force for its overthrow

Particular Rights

Prof. Laski has specifically referred to those rights which he considers to be absolutely essential for the development of the personalities of individuals.

(1) According to him, every citizen has a right to work. That does not mean that he has a right to any particular kind of work. The right to work merely means the right to be occupied in producing a share of those goods and commodities which are useful for society. If a citizen is not given the right to work he is virtually denied the right to express his personality.

(2) A citizen has also the right to adequate wages. This right does not mean that every individual has the right to equal wages. Such a proposition is impracticable. What this right means is that all those work be given sufficient wages to maintain themselves. Nobody would like the idea of dying from starvation when he is giving his very best to society.

(3) Every citizen has the right to reasonable hours of work. What is contended is that every individual must put in that amount of work which does not exhaust him completely and thereby makes him unfit to fulfil his duties as a citizen. It is only the leisure which helps the individual to discover the land of the mind which is "the key to the intellectual heritage of the race."

(4) Every citizen has the right to education. It is education which makes a man a good citizen. The right to education does not mean the right to an identical intellectual training for all citizens. Every individual must be given that minimum of education which is essential for the performance of his duties. Every citizen is authorised to demand elementary education and it is only when this has been guaranteed to all that provision should be made for higher education for a few individuals.

(5) Every individual-has the right to political power. This right implies that every individual should have the right to vote, right to be elected as a representative and also the right to assume office and run the administrative machinery. The basis of franchise may be occupational or geographical and citizens may be grouped by their voluntary choice, but neither sex not property, race or creed ought to prevent the citizen from aiding in the choice of his rulers. Even if the choice is wrong, the people should be allowed to profit by the method of trial and error.

(6) Every individual must be guaranteed his freedom of speech. Its necessity arises from the fact that man must give expression to his inner self. If that right is denied, man will stop growing. The exercise of this right will enable him to ventilate his grievances and organise public opinion in its support.

(7) Every individual must be guaranteed freedom of association and public meeting. Experience shows that the denial of these rights leads to the creation of secret societies aiming at the destruction of the state.

(8) Every citizen has the right to be provided with those judicial safeguards which can guarantee liberty to him. This means that justice should be administered without fear or favour. It must not be harsher upon the poor than upon the rich. The officers of the Government should not be given any privileged position.

(9) Every individual has the right to property. His right to property is limited only to that extent which is necessary for the growth of his personality. He is not entitled to possess more property than the minimum mentioned above.

According to Laski, any system of rights has three aspects and those are the interests of the individual, group and the community. Rights must aim at the enrichment of all the three.

Capitalism and War

The view of Laski is that capitalism means war. War is inevitable in a capitalist society on account of the class relationship. This view is challenged by others who maintain that there is no evidence to show that capitalism necessarily leads to war. The reply of Laski is that capitalism may be so in theory but it has not proved itself to be so in practice. The capitalism to which the other writers refer, has never existed outside the economic literature. It is the creation of their imagination. Capitalism in actual practice has secured the protection and help of states and thereby penetrated into countries for economic exploitation. States step in to protect the interests of the capitalists and thereby bring about wars.

According to Laski, imperialism requires militarism to defend it. To end militarism, we must end imperialism. It is absurd to talk of disarmament when each nation knows that it can get more by resorting to war. The League of Nations failed because capitalism created irreconcilable interests which did not admit of settlement by peaceful means. The vested interests controlled the government and whenever their interests were endangered, they invoked the aid of the state. The League could succeed only if the states gave up their sovereignty. That was possible only if capitalism was abolished was abolished because capitalism defended the sovereignty of the state with a view to use it for its own personal ends. Without capitalism, state sovereignty will disappear and when that happens there will be no war because each state, being not a sovereign, will not have the right to go to war.

Capitalism and Democracy

The view of Laski is that democracy and capitalism can never go together. The problem of capitalist democracy can only be solved either by the supersession of capitalism or by the suppression of democracy. The first means an economic revolution and the second a political revolution. The first means the communal ownership of the means of production. That involves a revolution in our way of living. The suppression of democracy does not involve any such fundamental change in class relationship. The view of Laski is that capitalism and democracy worked side by side only in a period of economic expansion. In such case, the capitalists make enormous profits and out of them they can well afford to give a lot of money to the masses in the form of concessions. A democratic state is bound to work in the interests of the whole society. Consequently, the party in power is bound to pass legislation aiming at the betterment of the people. The result is that the rich are taxed at a very high rate. They can afford to pay those taxes during the period of expansion and prosperity. In case of depression, they cannot afford to pay the heavy demands made on their earnings. The result is that the capitalists prefer to destroy democracy rather than allow themselves to be ruined. The view of Laski was that the capitalists had no special fondness for democracy. It is true that capitalism and democracy were the product of the nineteenth century but that was merely accidental. Capitalism allowed democracy to exist side by side because its existence did not in any way harm the foundations of capitalist society. Capitalism was in a constant stage of expansion during the nineteenth century and hence it did not find any danger from democracy. However, capitalist economy could not expand indefinitely. A point was reached beyond which capitalist economy could not expand. It was at that stage that the capitalists began to feel the pinch of the ever-growing demands of democracy on the rich. It was felt that it was impossiblc to submit to those demands. Only two ways were open : one was to abolish capitalism and the other to set aside democracy and the latter course was actually followed. Laski refers to the rise of Hitler in Germany and Mussolini in Italy in support of his contention. The view of Laski was that the evils inherent in the capitalist regime were such as could not be remedied in any way except by the evolution of the system itself. Capitalism leads to over-production and that cannot be avoided without the control of the means of production by society and that implies the destruction of capitalism.

Laski points out that as the state always works on the side of those who possess economic power, capitalism puts the industrial classes in a position of vantage. As the masses do not like their privileged position, they would like to pull them down by capturing the political power and working the democratic machine in their own interests. As the industrialists or capitalists do not want to be deprived of their political and economic power, they do not find any hesitation in setting aside democracy.

According to Laski, if democracy is to work without being in constant danger of being destroyed, the only way is that capitalism should be destroyed. When this has been done, there will be no class of vested interests which would like to destroy democracy to save itself. In such an atmosphere, democratic institutions will work because it will not pay any section of society to destroy them. Advocates of democracy must stand for the abolition of capitalism.

Importance of Economic Factor in Politics

According to Laski, the economic factor plays an important part both in society and Government. A change in the economic system produces a change both in society and state. They are linked up with each other. Changes in the methods of economic production are the most vital factor in the making of changes in all other social patterns. Experience shows that economic relations cannot be changed in any fundamental way except through a change in the Government. It is only a change in the Government itself which bring about fundamental changes in the economic field. This fact is amply proved by the Russian Revolution of 1917.

According to Laski, the basic struggles are always between economic classes to secure control of the sovereign power. Those who already possess the control, try to retain it and those who are out of power, try to capture the same. The reason for the struggle to capture the state is that whosoever captures it, can use its machinery to get all that is in his favour. It is through the use of the machinery of the state that fundamental changes can be made in the social and economic fields. The state is never impartial. It always works in the interests of those who have captured it.

According to Laski, although the non-economic factors also play their part, the economic factor is the most important.. Laski does not deny the influence of personality, tradition and logic but still maintains that the economic factor occupies the first place. It is the bedrock upon which the social superstructure is built.

According to Laski, there is a fundamental clash of interests between the workers and the employers. The reason is that as the total social product is limited, the more goes in the form of wages to the masses, the less is left in the form of profits, rent and interest for the capitalist. The level of wages is always set by the level of profits which are considered sufficient to induce the capitalist to invest the money in any particular undertaking. If the capitalist cannot make profits, he will not invest and that means either unemployment or reduction in wages. There is implicit in the private ownership of the means of production the basic antagonism between interests of capital and labour.

Liberty

According to Laski, liberty means the eager maintenance of that atmosphere in which men have the opportunity to be their best selves and liberty is the product of rights. Without rights there can be no liberty because in that case men are the subjects of law unrelated to needs of personality. Freedoms are opportunities which history has show n to be essential for the development of personality and freedoms are inseparable from rights. If the rights are not guaranteed, liberty becomes uncertain.

Laski refers to certain conditions which must be provided if liberty is to be maintained. The first necessary safeguard is that there should be no special privilege in society. All persons must be equal before law and should enjoy equal opportunities. No person should inherit any special privilege merely because he happens to be born in a rich family. The existence of a privileged class is suicidal. That does not allow the growth of the atmosphere in which alone people enjoy their freedom. The people who are privileged come to believe that their privileges are natural. The second safeguard for liberty is that the rights of some should not depend upon the pleasure of others. The employer should not have the right to remove a worker arbitrarily. The livelihood of a person should not depend upon the whim of another. If such a danger can be created at any time by the management, he cannot be said to have enjoyed liberty. Another safeguard is that the incident of state action should be unbiased. This is a very difficult ideal to achieve but every effort should be made to reach it as far as possible. In the last resort, the liberty of the people depends upon their determination to fight for it. In the words of Pericles, "The secret of liberty is courage".

Equality

According to Laski, there can be no equality if there are special privileges in society. Every person must be equal before law. There can be no moral justification for the existence of any privileges based upon birth or property. Every individual must have equal opportunity for progress and growth. Equality means that adequate opportunities are laid open to all. Adequate opportunities do not imply equal opportunities. It merely means that all those opportunities should be given to individuals which are considered to be essential for their growth and without which there is all frustration. Equality is largely a problem in proportions. Every individual must eat, drink and obtain shelter. Even these needs depend upon the particular function performed by an individual in society. There can be no equality of wages as there is no equality of capacity to work. Equality involves identity of responsibility to primary needs. There must be economic equality if there is going to be political equality.

According to Laski, the so-called equality of states in the international field is meaningless. Petty states cannot be put on the same footing as the great powers. What is practical is that each state can be allowed to have complete freedom in all those matters which concern her alone. As regards other matters which affect other states also, she cannot be allowed that freedom.

Property

Laski held definite views on the subject of property. He criticised the present-day system of property and considered the same to be wholly inadequate. According to him, it is psychologically inadequate because, by appealing mainly to the emotion of fear, it inhibits the exercise of those qualities which enable them to live a full life. It is morally inadequate because it confers rights upon those who have done nothing to earn them. It makes a part of the community parasitic upon the rest. It deprives the rest of the opportunity to live simple lives. It is economically inadequate because it fails so to distribute the wealth it creates as to offer the necessary conditions of health and security to those who live by its processes. The result is that it has lost the allegiance of the majority of the people. Some regard it with hate and the majority regard it with indifference.

Laski was in favour of confiscation of property and giving compensation to the owners. They were to be given guarantees of living according to the same standard to which they were accustomed before the acquisition of their property by the state. The state was to guarantee them the same income which they were getting before the acquisition of their property. When the owner died, there was to be a reduction in the amount of money to be given to the family. The widow was to be given so much of money as was adequate to enable her to live in the same way as she did in the lifetime of her husband. When she died, her allowance was to be stopped. The children of the owner were to be given the same education as they would have got from their father if he had not been deprived of his property. When they completed their education, the contribution of the state towards them was also to stop. In this way, Laski proposed the tackling of the problem of property.

Laski says, "There is nothing inherently wrong in the notion of private property. There is a sense in which it may be so held as genuinely to express personality and to contribute to its enrichment. But, so to be held, it must be derived from personal effort organised in such a way as to involve an addition to the common welfare. It must never be so large in amount that its owner exercises power by reason of its sheer magnitude; it must never be so small that its possessor cannot be himself at his best. The more equal its distribution, the more likely is the contribution of the citizen to be judged in terms of its social value, to become implicit with purpose as the way to recognition. Regarded as the result of function, it falls naturally into its proper place in society. It ceases to dominate our minds. The excess of it no longer produces idleness and waste ; the failure to win a living wage will no longer breathe in man that sense of outlawry, as in some, or that feverish envy, as with others. Men are no longer set over against society, either snatching from some chance opportunity of advantage, or seeking to exploit it to some end which their conscience tells them to be mean and dishonourable".

SUGGESTED READINGS

Deane, H.	:	The Political Ideas of Harold J. Laski.
Fadiman, Chaiffton (Ed.)	:	I Believe : The Personal Philosophies of Certain Eminent Men and Women of Our Time.
Howe, M. De Wolfe (Ed.)	:	Holmes-Laski Letters (1953).
Martin, Kingsley	:	Harold Laski, A Biographical Memoir.
Roucek, J. C. (Ed.)	:	Twentieth Century Political Thought.

46

CHAPTER

Political Thought of Mahatma Gandhi

Introductory

The political philosophy of Gandhiji is "not a set of doctrines or dogmas, rules or regulations, injunctions or inhibitions, but it is a way of life. It indicates a new attitude or restates an old one towards life's issues and offers ancient solutions for modern problems". Gandhiji himself never claimed that he had any cut and dried views. There was no rigidity about them. His whole life was an unending experiment. He named his autobiography as *My Experiments with Truth.* About his own philosophy, Gandhiji observed thus in 1936: "There is no such thing as Gandhism and I do not want to leave any sect after me. I do not claim to have originated any new principle or doctrine. I have simply tried in my own way to apply the central truths to our daily life and problems. The opinions I have formed and conclusions I have arrived at are not final. I may change them tomorrow. I have nothing to teach to the world. Truth and non-violence are as old as the hills. All I have done is to try experiments in both on as vast a scale as I could do. In doing so, I have sometimes erred and learnt by my error. Well, all my philosophy, if it may be called by that pretentious name, is contained in what I have said. You will not call it Gandhism; there is no 'ism' about it".

Learning Objectives

- Introductory
- Various Influences on Gandhiji
- Gandhiji and Tolstoy
- Religion and Politics
- Technique of Gandhiji
- Means and Ends
- Non-violence
- Satyagraha
- Satyagraha must not be confused with passive resistance
- Private Property and Trusteeship
- Patriotism
- On Human Nature
- Attitude towards State
- Representation
- Rule by Majority
- Sphere of State
- Reform of Criminals
- Police
- Justice
- Taxes
- Rights and Duties
- Internationalism
- Gandhiji and Marx
- Sarvodaya
- Suggested Readings

Various Influences on Gandhiji

Reference may be made to the various influences which moulded the political thought of Gandhiji. The most important influence was that of the *Gita* which he read in 1889, and which remained his constant companion for the rest of his life. He himself wrote thus: "When doubts surround me, when disappointments stare me in the face and I see not one ray of light on the horizon. I turn to the *Bhagavad Gita and find a verse to comfort me, and I immediately begin to smile in the midst of overwhelming sorrow. My life has been full of external tragedies and if they have not left any visible effect on me. I owe it to the teachings of Bhagavad Gita.*" Mahatma Gandhi became a great *Karmayogi as a result of the teachings of the Gita.* He wrote thus in 1929: "Let it be granted that according to the letter of *Gita* it is possible to say that warfare is consistent with renunciation of fruit but after 40 years' unremitting endeavour fully to enforce the teaching of *Gita* in my own life, I have, in all humility, felt that perfect renunciation is impossible without perfect observance of Ahimsa in every shade and form".

Mahatmaji was also influenced by the Jain monk Beacharji Swami, who helped him to go to England for his studies. Before Gandhiji left for London, the Swami administered to him an oath and he took three vows: not to touch wine, women or meat. Buddhism also had its influence on Gandhiji.

John Rukin's book *Unto This Last* had an enormous influence on the life of Gandhiji. This book was given to him by S.L. Polak. After the study of that book, Gandhiji decided to change his own life in accordance with the ideals of that book. To quote Gandhiji, "That book marked a turning point in my life". Gandhiji learnt three lessons from that book. That economy was good which was conducive to the good of all. The work of a lawyer had the same value as that of a barber. The life of labour was the life worth living.

Gandhiji was in prison in 1908, and then he read Thoreau's *Essay on Civil Disobedience.* It is pointed out that Gandhiji got his idea of *Satyagraha* from Thoreau, but he himself denied that in 1935 in these words: "The statement that I had derived my idea of civil disobedience from the writings of Thoreau is wrong. The resistance to authority in South Africa was well advanced before I got the essay of Thoreau on Cilil Disobedience". However, Gandhiji admitted that the study of the writings of Thoreau left a deep impression on him.

Gandhiji was also influenced by Tolstoy, particularly his book entitled *The Kingdom of God is Within You.* Gandhiji himself admitted that "its reading cured me of my scepticism and made me a firm believer in Ahimsa". In a letter to Tolstoy written in April 1910, Gandhiji described himself as a humble follower of Tolstoy. In a letter addressed to Gandhiji, Tolstoy observed thus: "I just received your letter and your book, *Indian Home Rule.* I read your book with great interest because of the things and questions you treat in it; passive resistance is a question of the greatest importance, not only for India, but for the whole of humanity". Gandhiji is stated to have remarked that "Tolstoy is one of the three moderners who have exerted the greatest spiritual influence on my life".

Raychandra, a distinguished reformer of Bombay, also exercised a lot of influence on the life of Mahatma Gandhi. After his return from England. Gandhiji came into intimate contact with him. He created in Gandhiji keenness for the study of Hindu scriptures.

The political philosophy of Mahatma Gandhi is to be found in the large number of books written by him, in the articles contributed by him to various journals like *Young India* and *Harijan* and the reported speeches delivered by him from time to time. Mahatma Gandhi put too much emphasis on non-violence and Satyagraha. His philosophy of Satyagraha was essentially practical and not theoretical. He was a *Karmayogi*, a practical idealist and his philosophy grew, out of his own experience and experiments with truth and non-violence. He taught only what he himself practised and what he considered to be practicable for everybody making the necessary effort. Gandhiji laid stress on the individual as the starting point of social progress. The problem of the group was essentially the problem of the individual. Man is above all the soul and the progress of society depends on the soul force of the average individual. Unlike Marxists, Gandhiji started from the soul within and worked his way out to the environment. But this does not mean that Gandhiji sacrificed society for the sake of the individual.

Gandhiji and Tolstoy

There is a striking similarity between the philosophies of Tolstoy and Mahatma Gandhi. Both of them denounced modern civilization as based on force and exploitation. Both of them were opposed to violent methods of fighting evil. Both laid stress on the reform of the individual. Both concerned themselves with the purity of means. Both advocated an ascetic morality and preached extreme simplicity of life, bread-labour and virtual celibacy.

However, there were differences between the two. Gandhiji was far more practical than Tolstoy. He was essentially a man of compromise in the case of non-essentials. He was always ready to adapt his actions to the demands of the changing world. Moreover, his conception of non-violence was slightly different from that of Tolstoy. Avoiding to Tolstoy, non-violence implied the avoidance of force in all its forms. Gandhiji put emphasis on motive and defined non-violence as the avoidance of injury or pain to any creature out of anger or from a selfish motive. Tolstoy turned away from life because it involved some form of violence. On the other hand. Gandhiji followed the ideal of the *Gila* which stands for action without attachment.

Religion and Politics

Gandhiji was not prepared to separate religion from politics. To quote him, "Those who say that religion has nothing to do with politics, do not know what religion means". Again, "He does not know what patriotism or feeling for one's country is who does not know true duty or religion". Again, "If I take part in politics, it is only because politics today encircles us like the coils of the snake from which one cannot get out, no matter how one tries. I wish to wrestle with the snake.... I am trying to introduce religion into politics. There are no politics devoid of religion. Politics bereft of religion are a death-trap because they kill the soul. At the back of every word that I have uttered since I have known what public life is, and of every act that I have done, there was a religious consciousness and a downright religious motive. My motive has been purely religious. I could not be leading a religious life unless I identify myself with the whole of mankind; and this I could not do unless I took part in politics. The full gamut of man's activities today constitutes an indivisible whole. You cannot divide social, political and religious work into watertight compartments. I do not know any religion apart from human activity. It provides a moral basis to all other activities which if they would otherwise lack reduce life to a thing of sound and fury signifying nothing". Religion was the very breath of Gandhiji's life. He was a seeker of truth and his God manifested Himself in Truth and Love. Love and Ahimsa had the same meaning for him. Without Ahimsa, Truth could not be found. Gandhiji wanted to moralize man and society and he found it difficult to separate politics from religion. His contention was that there could not be two consciences of man, one individual and social and the other political. The same code of morality had to be observed in all spheres of human activity. To quote him, "We have to make truth and non-violence matters not merely for individual practice, but for practice by groups, communities and nations. That at any rate is my dream". Again, "I do not believe that the spiritual law works in a field of its own. On the contrary, it expresses itself from the ordinary activities of life. It does affect the economic, social and political fields".

Technique of Gandhiji

With the object of moralizing the individuals and society, Gandhiji laid down certain principles for adoption by the people and those were truth, non-violence and scrupulous regard for means. As regards truth, there was no God higher than truth and every individual must be a seeker after truth. Truth and non-violence were inseparable. Wherever there was violence, there could be no truth. He who believed in truth would not injure even an opponent. People should follow the path of service.

Means and Ends

According to Gandhiji, means and ends were convertible terms. The two were inseparable and must be equally pure. Not only should the end be high and laudable, but the means should also be moral. "As the means, so the end. The means may be likened to a seed, the end to a tree; and there is just the same inviolable connection between the means and the end as there is between the seed and the tree".

As Gandhiji put emphasis on the importance of means, it is not to be taken for granted that he did not attach importance to the end. He believed that the means and ends were inseparably connected. He insisted that our means must be as pure as our end. With regard to the means, we must take our stand on the firm and solid ground of unadulterated good. Gandhiji's effort to give concrete expression in the form of Satyagraha to this principle of moral approximation of the end to the means is the most unique contribution of our times to the philosophy and technique of revolution.

Non-violence

According to Gandhiji, non-violence or Ahimsa is the heart of all religions. Ahimsa is truth itself, its very soul, and its maturest fruit. Truth and Ahimsa are two sides of a smooth unstamped metallic disc and are so interwined that it is difficult to disentangle and separate them. Gandhiji put more emphasis on truth than on Ahimsa because he believed that truth existed beyond and unconditioned by space and time, but Ahimsa existed only on the part of all finite beings. Ahimsa divorced from truth would be demoralising. Gandhiji was prepared to sacrifice Ahimsa for the sake of truth and not *vice versa.* To quote him, "The jewel of non-violence was discovered during the search for and contemplation of truth".

Gandhiji referred to three levels of non-violence. The highest form was what he called the enlightened non-violence of resourcefulness or the non-violence of the brave. It was the non-violence of one who adopted it not by painful necessity but by inner conviction based on moral considerations. This non-violence was not merely political but pervaded in every sphere of life. It was the non-violence without any mental reservation. It was such non-violence that moved mountains and transformed life.

The second kind of non-violence was adopted as a measure of expediency and sound policy in some spheres of life. That was the non-violence of the weak or the passive non-violence of the helpless. It is weakness rather than moral conviction which rules out the use of violence. If pursued honestly and scrupulously with real courage so long as it is accepted as a policy, it is capable of achieving results to a certain extent. However, it is not as effective as the non-violence of the brave. It is not based on any conviction but on expediency and consequently permits the use of violence, where necessary.

According to Gandhiji, non-violence presupposes the ability, though not the willingness to strike. To quote him, "Man for man, the strength of non-violence is in exact proportion to the ability, not the will, of the non-violent person to inflict violence". Non-violence is the quality of the brave and strong and is not possible without fearlessness.

The third kind of non-violence is the passive violence of the coward and the effeminate. According to Gandhiji, "Cowardice and Ahimsa do not go together any more than water and fire". A coward runs away from danger instead of facing it? It is unmanly, unnatural and dishonourable. The non-violence of the coward is really violence in suspension or inactive violence. If a choice is to be made between violence and cowardice, Gandhiji would have preferred violence. To him, vengeance was superior to passive and helpless submission. "It is better to be violent if there is violence in our breast than to put on the cloak of non-violence to cover impotence". Again, "There is hope for a violent man to be some day non-violent but there is none for a coward. I have, therefore, said more than once that if we do not know how to defend ourselves, our women and our places of worship by force of suffering, *i.e.*, by non-violence, we must if we are men, be at least able to defend all these by fighting".

There is nothing like failure in non-violence as there in nothing like success in violence. Non-violence is not a cloistered virtue, confined only to the hermit and the cave-dweller. Being soul-force, it is capable of being practised equally by all. Even the masses can practise non-violence, "not with full knowledge of its implications but because it is the law of our species."

Satyagraha

Gandhiji evolved a way of resisting evil through the instrumentality of Satyagraha. The technique of Satyagraha was the unique and distinctive contribution of Gandhiji. It was the technique of resisting all that was evil and unjust, impure or untrue and removing all difficulties in human relations by love, voluntary suffering and self-purification by appealing to the divine spark in the soul of the opponent. Satyagraha "is a vindication of Truth by bearing witness to it through self-suffering or love. It is the opposite of coercion. It is the weapon of the strongest and the bravest. The Satyagrahi establishes spiritual identity with the opponent and awakens in him a feeling that he cannot hurt him without hurting himself." All conflicts "are sought to be resolved by the mighty weapon of Satyagraha by lifting these from the gross physical plane to the elevated spiritual and moral plane where they can be adjusted by the union of souls, by the deep calling unto the deep."

Satyagraha must not be confused with passive resistance

It is true that both are methods of meeting aggression, settling conflicts and bringing about social and political changes. However, the two differ from each other fundamentally. Passive resistance as practised is a political weapon of expediency but Satyagraha is a moral weapon based on the superiority of soul force over physical force. Passive resistance is the weapon of the weak but Satyagraha can be practised only by the bravest who have the courage of dying without killing. A passive resister aims at embarrassing the opponent into submission. A Satyagrahi aims at weaning the opponent from error by love and patient suffering. There is hardly any place for love for the opponent in the case of passive resistance. In Satyagraha: there is no room for hatred or ill will. To quote Mahadeo Desai, "Satyagraha is dynamic, passive resistance is static. Passive resistance acts negatively and suffers reluctantly. Satyagraha acts positively and suffers with cheerfulness and makes the sufferings fruitful. Passive resistance is not by its very nature universal in its application. It cannot be directed against one's nearest relations as Satyagraha can be. Passive resistance offered in a spirit of weakness and despair weakens the resister psychologically and morally. Satyagraha emphasises all the time internal strength and actually develops the same. Satyagraha can offer more effective determined opposition to injustice and tyranny than passive resistance".

The technique of Satyagraha may take the form of non-co-operation, civil disobedience, Hijrat, fasting and strike. As regards non-co-operation, Gandhiji pointed out that oppression and exploitation were possible only on account of the co-operation of the people. If the people refused to co-operate with the government, the latter could not function. To quote him, "Even the most despotic government cannot stand except with the consent of the governed, which consent is often forcibly procured by the despot. Immediately the subject ceases, to fear the despotic force, his power is gone". Non-co-operation may manifest itself in the form of *hartals*, social ostracism or picketing. Hartal involved the stopping of work as a measure of protest and its object was to strike the imagination of the people and the Government. Hartals to be effective were to be voluntary and no violence was to be used". Those were not to be frequent as those were likely to lose all their effect. The persons who refused to co-operate with the public in their programme of non-cooperation with the government, were to be boycotted. In the case of picketing also, no force was to be used. Only the persuasive methods were to be employed. To quote Gandhiji, the "object of peaceful picketing is not to block the path of a person wanting to do a particular thing, but to rely on the force of public opprobrium and to warn and even shame the blacklegs. Picketing should avoid coercion, intimidation, discourtesy, burning or burning of effigies and hunger-strikes".

Another form of Satyagraha recommended by Gandhiji was civil disobedience. This was regarded by him as "a complete, effective and bloodless substitute of armed revolt." Statutory enactments were to be challenged and violated. Civil disobedience signified "the resister's outlawry in a civil, *i.e.* non-violent manner." Gandhiji was so afraid of the civil disobedience movement becoming violent that he put the greatest emphasis on the word "civil". To quote him, "Disobedience to be civil, must be sincere, respectful, restrained, never defiant, must be based upon some well-understood principle, must not be capricious and must have no ill-will or hatred behind it." Again, "Its use must be guarded by all conceivable restrictions. Every possible provision should be made against outbreak of violence or general lawlessness. The area as well as scope should also be limited to the barest necessity of the case." Gandhiji's view was that civil disobedience was to be practised only by a selected few and not by the rank and file of the people. The leader, and not the Satyagrahis, were to decide as to which laws were to be violated. Another form of Satyagraha recommended by Gandhiji was Hijrat which implied voluntary exile from the permanent place of residence. This was tote done by those "who feel oppressed, cannot live without loss of self-respect in a particular place and lack the strength that comes from true non-violence of the capacity to defend themselves violently." Hijrat was recommended by Gandhiji in 1928 to the people of Bardoli and in 1939 to those of Junagarh, Vithalagad and Limbdi. The Harijans of Kaith were advised in 1935 to migrate as the Hindus "were regularly terrorising them and this had caused extreme despondency among the Harijans."

Another form of Satyagraha recommended by Gandhiji was fasting. This was considered by him as a fiery weapon and no doubt Gandhiji recommended the greatest caution in resorting to it. Fasting was not meant for all occasions but only for rare occasions. It could be undertaken for penance and self-purification or for the purpose of resisting injustice and converting the evil-doer. Fasting was to be undertaken only by those who possessed spiritual fitness.. It required purity of mind, discipline, humility and faith. Gandhiji's view was that fasting stirred the sluggish conscience and fired the loving hearts to action. "Those who bring about radical changes in human conditions and surroundings cannot do it except by raising ferment in society. There were only two methods of doing this—violence and non-violence. Non-violent pressure exerted through self-suffering by fasting touches and strengthens the moral fibre of those against whom it is directed.

Another method of Satyagraha was in the form of strike. However, Gandhiji's view of strike was different from that advocated by the socialists and communists. According to him, strike was a voluntary, purificatory suffering undertaken to convert the erring opponent. Gandhiji did not believe in the theory of class-war. He did not subscribe to the proposition that labour and capital must remain in opposite camps. His view was that industry was a joint enterprise of labour and capital, and both of them were trustees. The strikers were required to put forward their demands in very clear terms. Those were not to be unjust and must be within the reach of the capitalist to concede. The strikers were required to learn some manual craft so that during so that during the strike period they may not have to depend upon the strike fund.

Gandhiji recommended Satyagraha even in the case of foreign invasion. He explained his technique thus: "A non-violent man or society does not anticipate, or provide for attacks from without. On the contrary, such a person or society firmly believes that nobody is going to disturb them. If the worst happens, there are two ways open to non-violence. To yield possession but non-co-operate with the aggressor. Thus supposing that a modern edition of Nero descended upon India, the representatives of the state will let him in but tell him that he will get no assistance from the people. They will prefer death to submission. The second way will be non-violent way. They would offer themselves unarmed as fodder for the aggressors cannon. The underlying belief in either case is that even a Nero is not devoid of a heart. The unexpected spectacle of endless rows upon rows of men and women simply dying rather than surrender to the will of an aggressor must ultimately melt him and his soldiery". Such advice was given by Gandhiji to the people of Abyssinia when their country was attacked by Italy. The same advice was given to the people of Czechoslovakia and Poland when those countries were attacked by Hitler. When there was the danger of an attack of England by Germany in 1940, Gandhiji gave similar advice to the people of England. When China was being conquered by Japan, Gandhiji observed thus: "If the Chinese had non-violence of my conception, there would be no use left for the latest machinery of destruction which Japan possesses. The Chinese would say to Japan, 'Bring all your machinery. We present half of our population to you But the remaining two hundred millions won't bend their knees to you'. If the Chinese did that,. Japan would become China's slave".

Private Property and Trusteeship

Gandhiji was in favour of dispossessing every person of all his private property if that could be achieved by truthful and non-violent methods. So long as people were not prepared to give up possessions beyond their immediate needs, they should change their attitude towards property. They should act not as proprietors of property but as trustees of property. They should utilise their property for the benefit of the community. If non-possession, trusteeship and bread-labour were universally practised, they would lead to economic equality and equitable distribution. To quote Gandhiji, "My ideal is equal distribution, but so long as I can see it is not to be realised. I therefore work for equitable distribution".

Gandhiji was an egalitarian. He believed that the ideal of non-violence could be achieved only if the gulf dividing the rich and the poor was made as small as possible. He realised that absolute equality was impossible. To quote him, "Economic equality must never be supposed to mean possession of an equal amount of worldly goods by everyone. It does mean, however, that everyone will have a proper house to live in, sufficient and balanced food to eat, and sufficient Khadi with which to cover himself. It also means that cruel inequality that obtains today will be removed by purely non-violent means".

To achieve his ideals, Gandhiji did not suggest any wholesale confiscation of property of the landlords and capitalists. He was in favour of trying to change their mentality by peaceful means. They were to be persuaded to act as the trustees of peasants and workers, "supply grain to them and remove the present terrible inequality between them and peasant and workers". There was to be no class-antagonism but "class-collaboration and class-co-ordination as the first step towards the classless democracy in which everyone will perform some form of productive physical labour and there will be no exploiters". The landlords and capitalists were to use their talents and riches for the good of society. They were to be entitled to adequate compensation according to their contribution. If the capitalists and landlords refused to act as trustees, the policy of non-cooperation was to be followed against them. The peasants were to work in such a way that it became impossible for the landlords to exploit them.

The concept of trusteeship was explained in these words by Gandhiji: "(1) Trusteeship provides a means of transforming the present capitalist order of society into an egalitarian one; it gives no quarter to capitalism, but gives the present owning class a chance of reforming itself. It is based on the faith that human nature is never beyond redemption. (2) It does not recognise any right of private ownership of property except inasmuch as it may be permitted by socicty for its own welfare. (3) It does not exclude legislative regulation of the ownership. (4) Thus, under state-regulated trusteeship, an individual will not be free to hold or use his wealth for selfish satisfaction or in disregard of the interests of society. (5) Just as it is proposed to fix a living minimum wage, even so a limit should be fixed for the maximum income that could be allowed to any person in society. The difference between such minimum and maximum incomes should be reasonable and equitable and variable and from time to time so much so that the tendency would be towards obliteration of itself. (6) Under the Gandhian economic order the character of production will be determined by social necessity and not by personal whim or greed".

Gandhiji's view was that if the capitalists failed to act as trustees, their industries were to be takenover by the government. Those industries were to be worked not for profit but for the benefit of humanity. The workers were to be given a share in management of those industries along with the government. As far as possible, there was to be decentralisation, as centralisation and large-scale production were considered to be enemies of democracy. Centralised industries and non-violence could not exist together. If a choice was to be made between individual violence and state violence, Gandhiji was in favour of the former. To quote him, "If the state suppresses capitalism by violence, it would be caught in the coils by violence itself....and fail to develop non-violence at any time. The state represents violence in a concentrated and organised form. The individual has soul, but the state is a soulless machine...hence I prefer the doctrine of trusteeship".

Patriotism

Gandhiji put emphasis on his duty towards his own country. But this does not mean that he stood for any narrow or aggressive form of nationalism or patriotism. He never ignored the higher interests of humanity but felt at the same time that his first duty was serve the people of India. To quote him, "My patriotism is both exclusive and inclusive. It is exclusive in the sense that in all humility, I confine my attention to the land of my birth, but it is inclusive in the sense that my service is not of a competitive or antagonistic nature". Again, "I want India's rise so that the whole world may benefit. I do not want India to rise on the ruin of other nations".

On Human Nature

Gandhiji was not a visionary but a practical idealist. He an accurate student of human nature, having studied it in all its shades. His intensive tours of India and intimate contact with the people helped him to understand human nature in its right perspective. He was concerned with human nature not only as it was but also as it could be trained and moulded. He did not believe that man was all good or an angel. He admitted that every one of us was a mixture of good and evil. The difference was only one of degree. He admitted the animal ancestry of man. To quote him, "We were, perhaps, all originally brutes. I am prepared to believe that we have become men by a slow process of evolution from the brute". Even the greatest men of the world had their shortcomings. To quote him, "There is no one without faults, not even men of God. They are men of God not because they are faultless but because they know their own faults and are ever ready to correct themselves".

This does not mean that Gandhiji believed that human beings were merely brutes and depraved. Sins and errors were not the true self of man. Man was able to mould himself and consequently Gandhiji had unshakable faith in human nature. Even the worst of the people could be transformed. There was a self-conscious will in man which could be used to revolutionise his life. To quote Gandhiji, "We were born with brute strength, but we were born in order to realise God who dwells in us. That indeed is the privilege of man and it distinguishes him from the brute creation".

Gandhiji believed in the inherent goodness of human nature. He was convinced that man was by nature going higher. Human nature was in its essence one and every man had the capacity for the highest possible development. To quote him, "The soul is one in all. Its possibilities are, therefore, the same for everyone".

Attitude towards State

Gandhiji was a philosophical anarchist. He repudiated the state on ethical, historical and economic grounds. The compulsive nature of state authority took away the moral value of the individual's action. A man is moral when he acts voluntarily. To quote Gandhiji, "The state represents violence in a concentrated and organised form. The individual has a soul, but as the state is a soulless machine, it can never be weaned from violence to which it owes its very existence". Again, "I look upon an increase in the power of the state with the greatest fear, because although while apparently doing good by minimising exploitation, it does the greatest harm to mankind by destroying individuality, which lies at the root of all progress. We know of so many cases where men have adopted trusteeship, but none where the state has really lived for the poor."

The ideal of Mahatma Gandhi was stateless democracy where social life was self-regulated. To quote him, "In such a state, everyone is his own ruler. He rules himself in such a manner that he is never a hindrance to his neighbour. In the ideal state, therefore, there is no political power because there is no state". The ideal democracy was to be a federation of Satyagrahi village communities. "Society based on non-violence can only be of groups settled in villages in which voluntary co-operation is the condition of dignified and peaceful existence." The federation and the groups were to be organised on a voluntary basis. Society was to be decentralised and equality was to prevail in every sphere of life. In the social sphere, it was to be expressed through the law of Varna combined with the ideals of non-possession and bread-labour. Every individual was to be given fullest freedom to devoid himself to social service according to his capacity.

The ideals of non-possession and bread-labour implied an agricultural and rural civilization based on handicrafts. There was no room in such a society for exploitation. Everybody was to be his master and no one a hired labourer. Although Gandhiji was not against machinery as such, he was opposed to centralised mass-production and the profit motive. Centralised production led to concentration of power, needed control of big markets and vast quantities of raw material and that led to exploitation. Consequently, a non-violent civilization could not grow upon a factory system.

Gandhiji was opposed to heavy transport, courts, lawyers, the modern system of medicine and big cities. He was confident that the people will not be worse off if all the doctors and lawyers disappeared.

Gandhiji confessed that his ideal of society was not likely to be realised in its entirety. To quote him, "A government cannot succeed in becoming entirely non-violent because it represents all the people. I do not today conceive of such a golden age, but I do believe in the possibility of a predominantly non-violent society and I am working for it". The ideal non-violent society of Gandhiji indicated the direction rather than the destination, the process rather than the consummation. The structure of the state was to emerge as a result of non-violent revolution, was to be a compromise between ideal non-violent society and the facts of human nature. Gandhiji admitted to Lord Lothian that "democratic government was a distant an inviolable creed, not a mere policy". The state was to continue to exist on account of the anti-social tendencies of certain individuals and groups. There was also the danger of anarchy to be guarded against.

According to Gandhiji, the state was not an end in itself but "one of the means of enabling people to better their condition in every department of life". The state was only one of the means to secure the greatest good of all. There was nothing sacred about the actions of the state. The institution of the state was due to human weakness. Gandhiji distrusted the state and sought to develop in the people, through Satyagraha, the capacity to resist the state authority when it was abused. To quote him, "Real Swaraj will come not by the acquisition of authority by a few but the acquisition of the capacity by all to resist authority when abused".

Gandhiji was opposed to the theory of the absolute sovereignty of the state. He believed in the sovereignty of the people based on pure moral authority. According to him, a man owed only a limited and relative loyalty to the state as to other associations. That loyalty was conditional on the state appealing to the conscience of the people. That might involve a perpetual danger of anarchy, but that was the only adequate safeguard against the abuse of political power. Gandhiji made the disobedience of laws a right and a duty of the citizen if those offended his moral sense but he provided ample safeguards against anarchy by making that disobedience non-violent.

Representation

Gandhiji was not opposed to the institutions of representation and elections. According to him, "By Swaraj I mean the Government of India by the consent of the people as ascertained by the largest number of adult population, male or female, native born or domiciled who have contributed by manual labour to the service of the state and who have taken the trouble of having their names registered as voters". Again, "If independence is born non-violently all the component parts will be voluntarily interdependent working in perfect harmony under representative central authority which will derive its sanction from the confidence reposed in it by the component parts".

In 1931 and 1942, Gandhiji advocated the system of direct elections to the village Panchayats. According to him, the seven hundred thousand villages of India were to be organised according to the wills of their citizens. All of them were to have the right of voting. All those villages were to elect their district administrations, but each village was to exercise one vote. The district administrations were to elect the provincial administration. The provincial administrations were to elect the president. In this way, power was to be decentralised among all the villages. There was to be voluntary co-operation in all the villages.

Gandhiji fixed certain qualifications for the candidates for election. They were to be selfless, able and incorruptible. They were to be free from the craze for office, self-advertisement, running down of opponents and exploitation of voters. Votes were not to be got by means of canvassing but by means of serving the people. The spirit of service was to dominate their lives.

As regards the qualifications of voters Mahatma Gandhi stated that "the qualifications for franchise should be neither property not position but manual work. Literary or property test has proved to be elusive. Manual work gives an opportunity to all who wish to take part in the Government and the well-being of the State". Labour-franchise was the application to politics of the ideal of bread-labour which aimed at making life self-sufficient and people self-reliant and fearless.

Rule by Majority

Democracy involves rule by the majority. But this does not mean that the view of the minority was always to be disregarded by majority. Mahatmaji's view was that in matter of conscience, the law of the majority had no place. To quote him, "The rule of majority has a narrow application, *i.e.*, one should yield to the majority in matters of detail. But it is slavery to be amenable to the majority, no matter what its decisions are. Democracy is not a state in which people act like sheep." Again, "The rule of majority does not mean it should suppress the opinion of even an individual if it is sound. An individual's opinion should have greater weight than the opinion of many, if that opinion is sound. That is my view of real democracy".

Gandhiji advocated the spirit of magnanimity on the part of the majority towards the minority. There was to be no tyranny of the majority. However, he wanted the minority to submit ordinarily to the majority because otherwise it was not possible to carry on a democratic government. It was both the right and duty of the minority to convert the majority to its own point of view. Likewise, the majority was also not to ignore completely the views of the minority.

Sphere of State

Gandhiji was not in favour of multiplying the functions of the state. He wanted them to be reduced to the minimum. Most of the functions of the state were to be transferred to the voluntary associations.

According to him, "Self-government means continuous effort to be independent of government control, whether it is foreign or whether it is national. Swaraj Government will be sorry affair if people look up to it for the regulation of every detail of life". Again, "I admit that there are, certain things which cannot be done without political power, but there are numerous other things which do not at all depend upon political power. That is why a thinker like Thoreau said that, that government is best which governs the least. This means that if people come into possession of political power, the interference with the freedom of the people is reduced to a minimum. In other words a nation that runs its affairs smoothly and effectively without much state interference is truly democratic. Where such condition is absent, the form of government is democratic in name only."

According to Gandhiji, the state was to perform its functions with the minimum use of coercion. It was to rule "though its moral authority based upon the greatest goodwill of the people". Both crime and coercion were to decrease in a non-violent state. This does not mean that crime was to disappear altogether. Gandhiji admitted that there were to remain some anti-social, parasitic individuals who might, due to lack of self-control, resort to violence and disobey laws. When a non-violent state was set up, there was the possibility of certain violent organisations trying to upset a non-violent government. Under such circumstance, it was the duty of the government to crush them. To quote him, "No Government can allow private military organisations to function without endangering public peace." A non-violent state could not tolerate crimes and the degeneration of civil liberty to licence. No government worth its name could allow anarchy to prevail in the country.

Reform of Criminals

According to Gandhiji, prisons were to be regarded not as an agency created by society for revenge, but as reformatories, hospitals and schools combined into one. The prisons were to be maintained for the purpose of converting the defectives to the non-violent way of life. Criminals were to be educated for better lives. That was to be done by their examination and treatment by expert psychologists, proper education, the system of probation and parole, adequate opportunities for self-government and by setting right their grievances.

In 1922, Gandhiji prepared a plan for the reform of prisons. All the jails were to be turned into hand-spinning and hand-weaving institutions. Prisoners were to be treated as defectives and not criminals who were to be looked down upon. The wardens were not to be a terror to the prisoners, but their friends and instructors.

Police

Gandhiji recognised the necessity of police force. However, great changes were to be made in the present police system. To quote him, "The police of my conception will, however, be of a wholly different pattern from the present-day force. Its ranks will be composed of believers in non-violence. They will be servants, not masters of the people. The people will instinctively render them every help, and through mutual co-operation they will easily deal with the ever-decreasing disturbances. The police force will have same kind of arms but they will be rarely used if at all. In fact, the policemen will be reformers. The police work will be confined to robbers and dacoits."

He was in favour of allowing the police to have arms, but they were to use them sparingly. However, the police could use physical force to restrain lunatics run amuck bent upon murder. He also allowed use of tear-gas by the police to prevent crimes.

Justice

According to Gandhiji, the administration of justice was to be made cheaper for the man in the street. Parties in civil suits were to be encouraged to refer their disputes to arbitration. The decision of the Panchayat was to be final except in cases of corruption or misapplication of law. Multiplicity of intermediate courts waste be avoided. Case law was to be abolished and the general procedure was to be simplified. Lawyers may remain but their fees were to be regulated. They were to keep before themselves the ideal of service and not their enrichment. The judicial work of the state was to be lessened.

Taxes

As regards taxes, Gandhiji was in favour of their payment in the form of labour and not in the form of coins. To quote him, "Payment in labour invigorates the nation. Where people perform labour voluntarily for the service of society, exchange of money becomes necessary. The labour of collecting the taxes and keeping accounts is saved and the results are equally good." If taxes were paid in the form of labour, these were liable to be used for the benefit of the area from which those were collected.

Rights and Duties

Gandhiji advocated both rights and duties. He approved of the rights as given in the Resolution of the Karachi Session of the Congress. Many of those rights have been included in the Fundamental Rights as given in the new Constitution of India which came into force in 1950. Those rights guarantee to every citizen of India the right of free expression of opinion, rights of free association and combination and the right to assemble peacefully and without arms. Every citizen was to have freedom of conscience and also the right to profess and practise his religion. The culture, language and script of the minorities were to be protected. All citizens were to be equal before law, irrespective of caste, creed or sex. No citizen was to be penalised on account of his religion. The state was not to give any titles, etc. However, Gandhiji was always prepared to make changes in the contents of these rights in the light of new experience and circumstances.

Gandhiji attached more importance to duties than to rights. According to him, the right to perform one's duties was the only right that was worth living for and dying for. It covered all legitimate rights. If a right was demanded or recognized without the claimant possessing the capacity to perform the corresponding duty, the purpose of the right was not attained and the right could not be sustained. There was no right without a corresponding duty and *vice versa.* Rights accrued only to that person who served the state to which he belonged. To quote Gandhiji, "The true source of right is duty. If we all discharge our duties, right will not be far to seek. If leaving duties unperformed, we run after right, they will escape us like a will of the wisp. The more we pursue them, the further they will fly."

Internationalism

Gandhiji was not only a nationalist, but also an internationalist. His nationalism was not exclusive, aggressive or destructive. It was constructive and humanitarian. The methods of conversion and not coercion were to be employed. According to Gandhiji, "It is impossible for one to be internationalist without being a nationalist. It is not nationalism that is an evil; it is the narrowness, selfishness, exclusiveness which is the bane of modern nations which is an evil. Indian nationalism wants to organise itself or to find full self-expression for the benefit and service of humanity at large." Again, "We want freedom for our country but not at the expense or exploitation of others....I want freedom of my country, so that the resources of my country might be utilised for the benefit of mankind...A country has to be free in order that it may die, if necessary, for the benefit of the world...My idea of nationalism is that my country may die so that the human race my live. There is no room for race-hatred there."

Gandhiji did not believe in the isolation of one country from the rest of the world. There was no isolated independence but healthy and dignified interdependence of the various states. To quote him: "The better mind of the world desires today not absolutely independent states warring one against another but a federation of friendly interdependent states." The non-violent would try to live on the friendliest terms with his neighbours and not desire their territory.

Gandhiji and Marx

Mashruwala says : "It has been often said that Gandhiji was a communist minus violence. Indeed, it is possible to quote Gandhiji himself in support of this proposition. Gandhiji was not in the habit of rejecting descriptions of him or his principles, if they were meant as compliments, and if they helped his main mission. But in a careful examination of principles, such description should not be regarded as very accurate and must not be used as handy definition. The error of such descriptions lies in its capacity to conceal the full implications of the differential factor. When it is said that Gandhism is Communism minus violence, the impression created is that the minus violence' factor in Communism is some small impurity the removal of which will make it the same as Gandhism. As a matter of fact, even if it were possible to so equate Gandhism in terms of Communism, the 'minus violence' factor is a major factor of considerable value. The implications of 'minus violence' are so great as to make the equation so illusory as to say that red is green minus yellow and blue, or a worm is a snake minus poison".

The fundamental difference between Gandhiji and Marx lies in their different approaches towards life and universe. All other differences, whether of ends and means or ideas about political, social, economic or religious order, arise from this basic difference. Both Gandhiji and Marx wanted to establish an order which would make the masses co-sharers in the gifts of nature and fruits of human labour and genius. But while Gandhiji insisted upon adherence to truth and non-violence for achieving this object, Marx did not care for the means provided they could achieve the end as quickly as possible. Marx put forward the theories of class-war, the dictatorship of the proletariat, nationalisation of industries and regimentation of life and labour. On the other hand, Gandhiji propounded the theories of Varna Dharma or performance of class duties, Satyagraha, arbitration, decentralisation, trusteeship and as much of individual liberty and democratisation as possible in social life.

Gandhiji was not a systematic thinker. He was an inspired teacher and prophet who had no intention to work out a logical and theoretical construction. He poured forth the results of his deepest feelings and the most sincere realisations of truth. However, in all his writings one finds a unity of them. On the other hand, Marx was trained in the traditions of German Hegelian metaphysics. He believed in the efficacy of logical reason and for over 30 years he laboured persistently to give finishing touches to his system.

Gandhiji possessed an attractive personality of a prophet and he was shown the greatest reverence even by his enemies. Marx was engaged in a bitter and furious controversy with Proudhon, Bakunin and Lassalle. He possessed an aggressive personality and he complained that his towering intellectual strength was not recognised by others.

Gandhiji represented metaphysical idealism and Marx dialectical materialism. Gandhiji started with the conception of an omnipresent fundamental spiritual reality. He inherited a strong faith in the existence of a deeper spiritual power. His view was that spiritual truth could not be realised by dialectical skill but by spiritual experience, pure and disciplined life and an effort to live up to the ideal of Ahimsa. Gandhiji claimed to be a true scientist in the sense that he constantly experimented with truth and tried to make his propositions sounder by repeated observations. On the other hand, Marx was a rationalist. He condemned mysticism and faith. He criticised idealistic philosophy.

Gandhiji believed in ethical absolutism and Marx in ethical relativism. Gandhiji accepted idealism and hence he believed in the superiority of ethical absolutism and the philosophy of Sarvodaya. He considered truth and nonviolence to be absolutely binding. On the other hand, Marx accepted the relativism of the moral criterion. His view was that our ethical codes were the products of our social growth. There were no eternal moral principles and the ethical system was related to the relations of production.

Both Gandhiji and Marx differed on the question of religion as a factor in history. As Gandhiji believed in truth and non-violence, he accepted the force of religion in human history. On the other hand, Marx was an advocate of dialectical materialism and he considered religion to be a reactionary force. Religion was irrational. The ghosts and gods of different kinds were advocated by religion instead of scientific knowledge and light. Religion substituted the empty future consolation of an immortal destiny for the present subjection to misery, exploitation and oppression. At times, religion is hypocritical. Bishops and priests preach vague and fantastic gospels of eternity and the kingdom of God because they are in the service of the worldly powers. Religion contains the remants of antiquated conceptions of old. Religion is an ideology fitted to the production, organisations and relations of the time. With the dawn of the society of freedom, abundance and equality, man would not require the consolation of religion.

Gandhiji and Marx provided divergent solutions for mankind. The central evils against which Gandhiji fought were racialism, imperialism, communalism and untouchability. The problems of labour versus capital were not important for him. Marx fought against the reactionary policies of the Prussian Government. For some time, he was engaged in the Revolution of 1848. He organised and led the First International and concentrated on bringing about proletarian solidarity. Gandhiji considered imperialism as the enemy. According to Marx, bourgeois capitalism was the enemy.

Gandhiji challenged the foundations of modern civilisation. He considered it as equivalent to darkness and disease and preached a return to nature. He advocated simplicity in everything. His slogan was: "Back to the Village." On the other hand, Marxism grew as the creed of the Western industrial world. The workers suffering under the injustices of the early years of industrial capitalism found in it the gospel of emancipation. Many worked out a philosophy of history. According to him, the forces of production were the ultimate determining factors. History moves through the struggles of different classes. It is moving towards the destruction of the present capitalist society. Capitalism has in itself contradictions which lead to its destruction.

Both Gandhiji and Marx succeeded because they tried to find a solution to the eternal problem of man which is to provide him with bread. Marx called the capitalists as robbers. The view of Gandhiji was that anybody who had more than what he barely needed was a thief. Marx challenged the theory and practice of capitalist accumulation. Gandhiji challenged accumulation in all its shapes.

Although both Gandhiji and Marx were opposed to the capitalistic process of social and economic exploitation, their emphases were on different points. Gandhiji was a moral and spiritual individualist. The view of Marx was that not an appeal to the sentiment of justice by individual self-sacrifice but organised expropriation by the armed proletariat of the expropriators would destroy the evils of society.

In a sense, both Gandhiji and Marx were anarchists. Gandhiji considered the state as an organisation of violence and force. His view was that in the ideal state of Ram Rajya, there will be the sovereignty of the moral authority of the people and the state as a machine of violence will disappear. Gandhiji did not stand for the immediate ending of the state power. The view of Marx was that the capitalist state was to be replaced by the proletarian dictatorship. The dictatorship of the proletariat was to be highest concentration of state power! It was to build the foundations of the ultimate classless society.

Gandhiji was not a philosopher of history but he accepted theological determinism. He literally believed that nothing could happen without the sanction of God. However, his determinism never degenerated into fatalism. He was a strong advocate of action on the lines of the *Gita.* He combined a faith in God with insistence on constant action. Gandhiji was not prepared to compromise with evil, lust or slavery. He was opposed to large scale industrialism and mechanisation. On the other hand, Marx believed in the power of reason to create a better society and happier future for men. He was a product of the Renaissance spirit. He believed that by harnessing the powers and capacities of mind, more and more could be achieved. Nature was not to be worshipped as God but was to conquered. Large-scale planning was to create conditions for increased production with less work. Marx was a child of the scientific bourgeois civilisation of the capitalistic West. He advocated not the limitation of needs and wants but the use of mechanised power to satisfy the needs of the people. Marx believed in the powers of man, society and science to satisfy all human wants.

Gandhiji took into consideration not only the ends but also the means. He insisted that noble ends must be achieved through noble means. He did not believe that end justifies the means. On the other hand, Marx did not care for the means provided those could achieve the end as quickly as possible.

Gandhiji preached the philosophy of love while Marx advocated that of hatred. Gandhiji stood for democratic guidance and Marx for the dictatorship of the proletariat. Gandhiji was essentially a democrat and believed that democracy was essential for the well-being of man but that was not true of Marx. Gandhiji stood for decentralised democracy but Marx did not believe in it.

Ramaswarup says, "Gandhism and Communism do not represent arithmetical quantities, with more of the one quantity and less of the other. They represent two different tempers of mind, two ways of life, two incompatible world views and life views. The one is based on and founded in God; the other denies God. The difference is most fundamental. Other differences regarding centralisation of politics and production, violent and non-violent revolution are important so far as they go, but as compared to the former difference they belong to the second order of smalls. Even the similarity in their humanism is more apparent than real. The humanism of the one leads to democracy, to tolerance, to faith, to hope; while the humanism of the other leads of violence, wholesale massacre, thought-control, purges, dictatorship, over-centralisation, secret police, forced concession and mutual spying. In short, though both the creds stress man, the one tries to serve him by nourishing his charity, love, faith and patience, the other by nourishing his suspicion, his hatred, his fears, greed and possessive instinct."

It is difficult to give an estimate of the greatness of Mahatma Gandhi and the depth of his ideas. It has rightly been said that the was "the spokesman of the conscience of all mankind." Sir Stafford Cripps says: "I know of no other man of any time or indeed recent history, who so forcefully and convincingly demonstrated the power of spirit over material things." Rabindra Nath Tagore says that Gandhiji was great as a politician, as an organiser, as a leader of men, as a moral reformer and, above all, as a man.

Sarvodaya

The term Sarvodaya is made up of two words, "Sarva" and "Udaya" and their literal meaning is "Uplift of all". However, it has been variously translated as "Good of all", "Service to all", "Welfare of all", "Gandhian Socialism" and "Co-operative Commonwealth". Mahatma Gandhi coined this term in 1904 in his attempt to paraphrase Ruskin's *Unto This Last.* It embraces within its fold all the three teachings of *Unto This Last* as Gandhiji understood them. Those are: (1) the good of the individual is contained in the good of all, (2) a lawyer's work has the same value as that of the barber in as much as both have the right of earning their livelihood from their work; and (3) a life of labour, *i.e.*, the life of the tiller of the soil and the handicraftsman, is the life worth living.

Sarvodaya is the Gandhian panacea for modern socio-economic ills from which the world is suffering at present. Its central problem is to reconcile the demands of egoism and altruism. It is based on Advaita Vedanta philosophy. It demands a transformation of the ego-centric outlook into altruistic outlook. The change is to be brought about from within and not from without and this can be done by means of persuasion.

Sarvodaya aims at creating a high moral atmosphere in the country. That is to be achieved by following the Gandhian principles of truth, non-violence and purity of means. The power of the people, called "Lok Shakti," is to be developed.

Self-sacrifice is the essence of Sarvodaya. Every individual is to be ready and willing to sacrifice his happiness for the sake of others. Everyone is to follow the policy of giving and not taking. He should feel happy when he is giving and not when he is taking. He should work for others and not expect anything in return for this.

Sarvodaya puts emphasis on villagers and stands for their rehabilitation. The village is the bulwark of Indian life. We must direct our attention from cities to villages. The villages have to be given more than what they have got today. They have been exploited for long and that must end now.

The people are to elect the members of the village Panchayats on a non-party basis and the village Panchayats are to elect the members of the Thana Panchayats. Likewise, other elections are to be held indirectly.

Political parties, professional politicians, elections, majority rule, hasty legislation and centralisation of power are all condemned by the exponents of Sarvodaya. Parties are "conspiracies against the people". They make the people crazy for power. There is a rush for party-tickets which usually go to the rich people who use their position in the legislatures for their selfish ends. Elections are compared to tuberculosis and leaders to "bidders at the auction of, popularity". The situation in India is much worse on account of the existence of casteism, linguism, provincialism, sectionalism, ignorance and illiteracy among the people. Democracy in India becomes the cult of incompetence and the majority rule is described as the rule of fifty-one over forty-nine.

Sarvodaya emphasizes the necessity of improving the human material first before anything else can be achieved. Unless every person is motivated by truth, honesty, non-violence and fellow-feeling for others, no progress is possible. Everyone must feel for others. He must have the following thought: "I am in everybody and everybody is in me".

Satya and Ahimsa are the foundations of Sarvodaya Raj. Its citizens are to be persons of lofty character. There is to be no exploitation of man by man, Everyone is to live a life of virtue. There is to be no gambling, immorality or class-hatred. Every member of the Raj is to contribute his or her quota for the welfare of all. Everyone is to receive education. There are to be no rich or poor, high or low, privileged or unprivileged persons in Sarvodaya Raj. The Governor of the state is to live in a cottage and he is to set an example for all. His motto is to be one of plain living and high thinking. Being a citizen of India, a Sarvodayite is to be a citizen of the world. The people have to be given more and more individual freedom to develop their personality and righteousness. The minority is not to be exploited by the majority. In matters of conscience, the law of majority is to have no place. There is to be adult franchise.

Sarvodaya is more of socio-religious creed than a political one. It stands for the self-limitation of human wants. It distrusts the state and advocates the decentralisation for power and direct democracy.

Bhoodan has been made the main plank of the Sarvodaya movement of Vinoba Bhave because land is the most universal and intimate property of the individual in India. He has combined the Bhoodan movement with the health, labour and brain-gift movement. What is wanted is that everybody must make his contribution to the good of society as a whole.

Sarvodaya stands for national unity and solidarity and condemns provincialism and religious fanaticism. To quote Gandhiji, "The bane of our life is our exclusive provincialism, whereas my province must be co-extensive with the Indian boundary so that ultimately it extends to the boundary of the earth. Else it perishes. The State should undoubtedly be secular."

The critics of Sarvodaya point out that while its theoretical perfection cannot be denied, it is impossible to realise in actual practice its ideal. Sarvodaya is bound to flounder on the rock of human nature. We are expecting too much from human beings as they are. Most of them are selfish and it is too much to expect that they will change overnight or change at all. The whole basis of Sarvodaya is the transformation of the present man and if that does not happen, the rest of the superstructure cannot be raised at all.

The advocates of Sarvodaya stand for the abolition of political parties as they do not work properly. However, that is not the right way of doing things. According to Burns, "No one denies that existing representative assemblies are defective, but even if an automobile does not work well, it is foolish to go back into a farmcart, however romantic." The political parties are bound to stay so long as there is freedom of thought and human nature is what it is. Our attempt must not be at the abolition of political parties but at their reformation and reorganisation.

The advocates of Sarvodaya attack majority rule. However, it is pointed out that the majority does not always and necessarily reduce the minority to a cipher. Moreover, unanimity in the field of legislation is an impossibility. It is true that legislation cannot be successful without public co-operation but legislation also helps a lot in creating conditions for better living.

While decentralisation is a welcome suggestion, it should not be based on the self-sufficiency of the villages. Geographical decentralisation may not prove a panacea for all problems. It might add to the evils of localism and provincialism.

Sarvodaya seems to go wrong not in its diagnosis of the evils of modern society but in the remedies suggested for the same. What is needed is not the renunciation of politics but raising it to a higher level of understanding and action. What is needed is not less of democracy but more.

Sarvodaya stands for direct democracy but it cannot be denied that direct democracy is not suited to modern conditions of society.

Sarvodaya does not recognise the necessity of analysing social development from a scientific point of view. It ignores the reality of class divisions in society and consequently it is unrealistic.

We might conclude by saying that Sarvodaya is a powerful intellectual attempt to build a plan of political and social reconstruction on the basis of metaphysical idealism. It is an attempt to develop the ideas of Gandhiji in the framework of independent India. It is a dynamic philosophy which can make possible the advent of a radically transformed humanity. It is not a complete philosophy but it gives an integrated thought-structure. We may not agree with all the detailed techniques and formulas of Savodaya, but its vision is definitely majestic and inspiring. Its great contribution lies in the assertion of a moral approach to the problems of man. It gives us a better and higher value of life. It gives us the message of love for all. It can help humanity to solve many of its problems.

SUGGESTED READINGS

Agarwala, A.N. : Gandhism, A Socialist Approach.

Andrews, C.F. : Mahatma Gandhiji's Ideas, 1930.

Bandyopadhyaya, J. : Social and Political Thought of Gandhi, Bombay, 1969.

Bari, S.A. : Gandhi's Doctrine of Civil Resistance, New Delhi, 1971.

Bhattacharya, Buddhadeva : Evolution of the Political Philosophy of Gandhi.

Bihari, Bipin : Gandhian Economic Philosophy, Bombay, 1963.

Datta, D.M. : The Philosophy of Mahatma Gandhi.

Dhawan, G.N. : The Political Philosophy of Mahatma Gandhi, 1946.

Doctor, A.H. : Sarvodaya, Calcutta, 1962.
Gadre, Kamala : The Coming Struggle for Trusteeship, New Delhi, 1971.
Gupta, Nagendra Nath : Gandhi and Gandhism, 1945.
Horace, Alexander : Social and Political Ideas of Mahatma Gandhi.
Horace, Alexander : Gandhi Through Western Eyes, 1969.
Iyer, Raghvan : The Moral and Political Thought of Mahatma Gandhi.
Kriplani, J.B. : The Gandhian Way, 1938.
Kriplani, J.B. : Gandhi, His Life and Thought, Government of India, New Delhi, 1970.
Kumarappa, J.C. : Gandhian Economic Thought, Varanasi, 1962.
Lohia, Rammanohar : Marx, Gandhi and Socialism, Hyderabad, 1963.
Mashruwala, K.G. : Gandhi and Marx, 1954.
Mathur, J.S. (Ed.) : Gandhian Thought and Contemporary Society.
Majumdar, B.B. : The Gandhian Concept of the State.
Menon, V.L. : Ruskin and Gandhi, Varanasi, 1965.
Munshi, M.K. : Reconstruction of Society Through Trusteeship, Bombay.
Nag, Kalidas : Tolstoy and Gandhi, Patna, 1950.
Namboodiripad, E.M.S. : The Mahatma and the Ism, 1958.
Narayan, Shriman : Gandhi—The Man and His Thought, Publications Division, Government of India, 1969.
Prabhu, R.K. and Rao U.K. : The Mind of Mahatma Gandhi, 1945.
Pradhan, Benudhar : The Socialist Thought of Mahatma Gandhi, Vol. II, Delhi, 1950.
Prasad, Mahadeo : Social Philosophy of Mahatma Gandhi, Gorakhpur, 1958.
Raghuvan, Iyer : Moral and Political Thought of Mahatma Gandhi.
Rajendra Prasad : Legacy of Gandhi, Agra, 1962.
Ram Rattan : Gandhi's Concept of Political Obligation.
Rao, S.K. Ramchandra : The Idea of Sarvodaya, Bangalore, 1957.
Sarkar, Dandana (Ed.) : Towards Trusteeship, Tamilnad Sarvodaya, Sangh, Coimbatore, 1974.
Sharma, B.S. : Gandhi as a Political Thinker, Allahabad, 1956.
Sitaramayya, B.P. : Gandhi and Gandhism, 1942.
Sitaramayya, B.P. : Socialism and Gandhism, 1938.
Swarup, Ram : Gandhism and Communism, New Delhi, 1955.
Tandon, V. : The Social and Political Philosophy of Sarvodaya After Gandhi, Varanasi, 1965.
Varma, V.P. : The Political Philosophy of Mahatma Gandhi and Sarvodaya, Agra, 1965.
Verma, S. : Metaphysical Foundation of Mahatma Gandhi's Thought, Orient Longmans, 1970.
Wellock, Wilfred : Gandhi as a Social Revolutionary, 1953.

INDEX

A

B

C

G

H

I

J

K

L

M

N

O

P

R

S

T

U

V

W